SIGHT REDUCTION TABLES
FOR SMALL BOAT NAVIGATION

ALSO BY HEWITT SCHLERETH:

Commonsense Celestial Navigation
Commonsense Sailboat Buying
Commonsense Coastal Navigation

The Cruising Navigator Series

The Cruising Navigator—No. 00

SIGHT REDUCTION TABLES FOR SMALL BOAT NAVIGATION

Latitudes 0°–58° | **Declinations 0°–29°**

ADAPTED FROM HO 229

by Hewitt Schlereth

SEVEN SEAS PRESS, INC.
NEWPORT, RHODE ISLAND

PUBLISHED BY Seven Seas Press, Inc.
Newport, Rhode Island 02840

Introduction Copyright © 1983 by Hewitt Schlereth

1 3 5 7 9 KP/KP 0 8 6 4 2

ISBN: 0-915160-54-4

Designed by Irving Perkins Associates

Printed in the United States of America

DEDICATED TO:
A. H. LOVELL

The Origin of This Book

AS ANYONE who has learned or practiced celestial navigation knows, there are three basic ways to solve the so-called "navigational triangle":

1. Compute the solution directly from fundamental formulas by means of a calculator.
2. Compute the solution directly by means of a general table of logarithms or a specifically-tailored table of logarithms such as HO 208 or HO 211.
3. Use a table in which solutions of the navigational triangle are precomputed and, thus, need only to be looked up. Two existing tables of this type are HO 229 and HO 249.

While it is obvious that the third method is the easiest, it does suffer from one drawback: bulk. The least of these tables —HO 249—requires nearly 700 8½" x 11" pages; the largest —HO 229—over 2000. The logarithmic methods are typically contained in 45 to 60 pages of standard book size (6" x 9"), but typically require 40 to 50 steps to compute.

It is possible, however, to thin the precomputed tomes and

produce a table that has a large measure of the virtues of both: the portability of a logarithmic method, the speed of the precomputed method.

Using HO 229 as a base, this table was constructed by first abridging the latitudes covered. Since most yachting is done between the latitudes of 58°N and 58°S, discarding coverage of the rest immediately reduced the size of the table by 700 pages.

Limiting the declination coverage to the range of 30°N to 30°S allowed reduction of the page size from 8½" x 11" to 6" x 9". This range of declinations gives complete coverage for sun, moon and planets. Thirty of the 57 navigational stars have declinations in this range and are judged sufficient for yacht navigation that relies almost exclusively on sun sights.

The final reduction in bulk was achieved by giving solutions only for triangles whose local hour angles (LHA) and latitudes are in *even* instead of merely *whole* degrees. This means that the assumed position (AP) can fall as much as 1° away from the dead reckoning (DR) position. But, in the context of small boat navigation, the loss of accuracy is slight and not of consequence.

In any case, speaking as a long-time small-boat navigator and delivery skipper, I would much rather have a handy little book like this that I can pack easily in a duffle and that covers every contingency I'm likely to meet in practice, than to lug the elephantine alternatives on the off-chance that Miaplacidus will be the only star in sight.

For most yachtsmen and many professionals, therefore, this book can be the sole sight reduction table. At the very least, it can be the back-up to a calculator or a traditional table. It is small enough to be stowed along with an inexpensive plastic sextant and long-term almanac as part of a liferaft kit.

How to Use This Book

Basically, the table is organized by local hour angle (LHA), beginning with 0° and going upwards in 2° steps, 0°, 2°, 4°, 6° . . . etc. Six pages cover each LHA and, on any opening, the left-hand page covers 20° of latitude (also in 2° steps) with solutions for triangles in which declination and latitude have the *same* name, while the right-hand page lists solutions for triangles in which latitude and declination are of *contrary* name.

Declinations from 0° to 29° are listed for every whole degree, as in all of the standard precomputed tables; and, so, the one interpolation required (for the actual declination at the time of the sight) is exactly the same with this method as any other. Since the simplest form of the *"60th times"* table needed for this interpolation is the one in HO 249, it is reprinted at the back of this book.

The only thing different about this table from other precomputed tables, therefore, is that this table requires that the assumed position be placed on an *even* degree of latitude; and its longitude on that even degree of latitude must be selected such that the LHA will be a *whole* and *even* number of degrees. For example:

I. LHA less than 90° or greater than 270°, latitude SAME name as declination. These LHA's are in the upper left corners of the left-hand pages.

DR: 36°50'N
                71°05'W

Ho: 60°02'
Dec: 21°23'N
GHA: 100°45'
aλ: 70°45'W   aL: 36°N
LHA: 30°00'

Solution for this is found on page 94, reproduced here as Figure 1:

Hc = 59°51′2   d = +34′9   Z = 111°7

Searching in the interpolation table (Figure 2) for the amount (23') by which the actual declination exceeds the tabulated declination (21° exactly) and finding the point at which the 23' column crosses the 35' (34′9 rounded) now gives a correction of +13'. The computed altitude (Hc) for the assumed position of 36°00'N, 70°45'W, is, therefore, 59°64′2, or 60°04'.

True bearing (Zn) is found from the tabulated azimuth angle (Z) by the usual rules:

Assumed position (AP) in N. Lat:

LHA greater than 180° .... Zn = Z
LHA less than 180° .... Zn = 360° − Z

AP in S. Lat:

LHA greater than 180° .... Zn = 180° − Z
LHA less than 180° .... Zn = 180° + Z

In this case, the assumed position has a north latitude and LHA is less than 180°, so the true bearing is 360° − 112° (111.7 rounded), or 248°.

Dec.	20° Hc	d	Z	22° Hc	d	Z	24° Hc	d	Z	26° Hc	d	Z	28° Hc	d	Z
0	54 28.1	+34.8	120.6	53 24.8	+37.3	123.0	52 17.6	+39.5	125.2	51 06.7	+41.6	127.2	49 52.6	+43.4	129.1
1	55 02.9	33.9	119.2	54 02.1	36.4	121.7	52 57.1	38.7	123.9	51 48.3	40.9	126.1	50 36.0	42.8	128.0
2	55 36.8	32.7	117.8	54 38.5	35.4	120.3	53 35.8	37.9	122.6	52 29.2	40.1	124.9	51 18.8	42.1	126.9
3	56 09.5	31.7	116.3	55 13.9	34.5	118.9	54 13.7	37.0	121.3	53 09.3	39.3	123.6	52 00.9	41.5	125.8
4	56 41.2	30.4	114.7	55 48.4	33.3	117.4	54 50.7	36.1	120.0	53 48.6	38.5	122.4	52 42.4	40.7	124.6
5	57 11.6	+29.3	113.2	56 21.7	+32.3	115.9	55 26.8	+35.0	118.6	54 27.1	+37.6	121.0	53 23.1	+40.0	123.4
6	57 40.9	28.0	111.5	56 54.0	31.2	114.4	56 01.8	34.1	117.1	55 04.7	36.7	119.7	54 03.1	39.1	122.1
7	58 08.9	26.6	109.9	57 25.2	29.9	112.8	56 35.9	32.9	115.6	55 41.4	35.7	118.3	54 42.2	38.3	120.8
8	58 35.5	25.3	108.2	57 55.1	28.6	111.2	57 08.8	31.8	114.1	56 17.1	34.7	116.9	55 20.5	37.3	119.5
9	59 00.8	23.8	106.4	58 23.7	27.3	109.6	57 40.6	30.6	112.5	56 51.8	33.6	115.4	55 57.8	36.4	118.1
10	59 24.6	+22.2	104.6	58 51.0	+25.9	107.8	58 11.2	+29.3	110.9	57 25.4	+32.5	113.9	56 34.2	+35.4	116.6
11	59 46.8	20.8	102.8	59 16.9	24.5	106.1	58 40.5	27.9	109.3	57 57.9	31.3	112.3	57 09.6	34.3	115.2
12	60 07.6	19.1	100.9	59 41.4	22.9	104.3	59 08.4	26.6	107.5	58 29.2	30.0	110.7	57 43.9	33.1	113.6
13	60 26.7	17.4	99.0	60 04.3	21.4	102.4	59 35.0	25.2	105.8	58 59.2	28.6	109.0	58 17.0	32.0	112.1
14	60 44.1	15.7	97.1	60 25.7	19.7	100.6	60 00.2	23.6	104.0	59 27.8	27.3	107.3	58 49.0	30.7	110.4
15	60 59.8	+13.9	95.1	60 45.4	+18.1	98.6	60 23.8	+22.1	102.1	59 55.1	+25.9	105.5	59 19.7	+29.4	108.8
16	61 13.7	12.1	93.1	61 03.5	16.3	96.7	60 45.9	20.4	100.2	60 21.0	24.3	103.7	59 49.1	28.0	107.1
17	61 25.8	10.3	91.0	61 19.8	14.6	94.7	61 06.3	18.7	98.3	60 45.3	22.7	101.8	60 17.1	26.6	105.3
18	61 36.1	8.3	89.0	61 34.4	12.7	92.7	61 25.0	17.0	96.3	61 08.0	21.1	99.9	60 43.7	25.0	103.5
19	61 44.4	6.5	86.9	61 47.1	10.8	90.6	61 42.0	15.1	94.3	61 29.1	19.4	98.0	61 08.7	23.4	101.6
20	61 50.9	+4.5*	84.8	61 57.9	+8.9	88.5	61 57.1	+13.3	92.3	61 48.5	+17.6	96.0	61 32.1	+21.8	99.7
21	61 55.4	2.5	82.6	62 06.8	7.0	86.4	62 10.4	11.4	90.2	62 06.1	15.8	94.0	61 53.9	20.0	97.7
22	61 57.9	+ 0.6	80.5	62 13.8	5.0*	84.3	62 21.8	9.5	88.1	62 21.9	13.9	91.9	62 13.9	18.3	95.7
23	61 58.5	- 1.4	78.4	62 18.8	3.0	82.1	62 31.3	7.5*	85.9	62 35.8	12.0	89.8	62 32.2	16.4	93.6
24	61 57.1	3.3	76.3	62 21.8	+ 1.1*	80.0	62 38.8	5.5*	83.8	62 47.8	10.0*	87.6	62 48.6	14.5	91.5
25	61 53.8	- 5.3*	74.1	62 22.9	- 1.0*	77.8	62 44.3	+ 3.5*	81.6	62 57.8	+ 8.0*	85.5	63 03.1	+12.6	89.4
26	61 48.5	7.3	72.0	62 21.9	3.0*	75.7	62 47.8	+ 1.4*	79.4	63 05.8	6.0*	83.3	63 15.7	10.6*	87.2
27	61 41.2	9.1	69.9	62 18.9	5.0	73.5	62 49.2	- 0.6*	77.2	63 11.8	3.9*	81.1	63 26.3	8.5*	85.0
28	61 32.1	11.0	67.9	62 13.9	6.9	71.4	62 48.6	2.6*	75.1	63 15.7	+ 1.8*	78.9	63 34.8	6.4*	82.8
29	61 21.1	12.9	65.8	62 07.0	8.9	69.2	62 46.0	4.7*	72.9	63 17.5	- 0.2*	76.7	63 41.2	4.4*	80.6

Dec.	30° Hc	d	Z	32° Hc	d	Z	34° Hc	d	Z	36° Hc	d	Z	38° Hc	d	Z
0	48 35.4	+45.1	130.9	47 15.6	+46.6	132.5	45 53.2	+48.0	134.1	44 28.7	+49.2	135.5	43 02.1	+50.4	136.8
1	49 20.5	44.6	129.9	48 02.2	46.1	131.6	46 41.2	47.6	133.2	45 17.9	48.9	134.7	43 52.5	50.0	136.1
2	50 05.1	44.0	128.9	48 48.3	45.7	130.6	47 28.8	47.2	132.3	46 06.8	48.6	133.9	44 42.5	49.8	135.3
3	50 49.1	43.3	127.8	49 34.0	45.1	129.7	48 16.0	46.7	131.4	46 55.4	48.1	133.0	45 32.3	49.5	134.5
4	51 32.4	42.8	126.7	50 19.1	44.6	128.6	49 02.7	46.1	130.3	47 43.5	47.7	132.1	46 21.8	49.0	133.7
5	52 15.2	+42.1	125.5	51 03.7	+44.0	127.6	49 48.9	+45.8	129.5	48 31.2	+47.3	131.2	47 10.8	+48.7	132.9
6	52 57.3	41.3	124.4	51 47.7	43.3	126.5	50 34.7	45.1	128.5	49 18.5	46.8	130.3	47 59.5	48.3	132.0
7	53 38.6	40.6	123.2	52 31.0	42.7	125.4	51 19.8	44.6	127.4	50 05.3	46.3	129.3	48 47.8	47.9	131.1
8	54 19.2	39.8	121.9	53 13.7	42.0	124.2	52 04.4	44.0	126.3	50 51.6	45.8	128.3	49 35.7	47.4	130.2
9	54 59.0	38.9	120.6	53 55.7	41.3	123.0	52 48.4	43.4	125.2	51 37.4	45.3	127.3	50 23.1	46.9	129.2
10	55 37.9	+38.1	119.3	54 37.0	+40.4	121.7	53 31.8	+42.6	124.1	52 22.7	+44.6	126.2	51 10.0	+46.4	128.3
11	56 16.0	37.0	117.9	55 17.4	39.7	120.5	54 14.4	41.9	122.9	53 07.3	44.0	125.1	51 56.4	45.9	127.2
12	56 53.0	36.1	116.5	55 57.1	38.7	119.1	54 56.3	41.2	121.6	53 51.3	43.3	124.0	52 42.3	45.3	126.2
13	57 29.1	35.0	115.0	56 35.8	37.8	117.8	55 37.5	40.3	120.4	54 34.6	42.6	122.8	53 27.6	44.7	125.1
14	58 04.1	33.9	113.5	57 13.6	36.8	116.3	56 17.8	39.4	119.0	55 17.2	41.9	121.6	54 12.3	44.0	124.0
15	58 38.0	+32.7	111.9	57 50.4	+35.7	114.9	56 57.2	+38.6	117.7	55 59.1	+41.0	120.3	54 56.3	+43.3	122.8
16	59 10.7	31.4	110.3	58 26.1	34.6	113.3	57 35.8	37.5	116.2	56 40.1	40.2	119.0	55 39.6	42.5	121.6
17	59 42.1	30.1	108.6	59 00.7	33.4	111.8	58 13.3	36.5	114.8	57 20.3	39.2	117.6	56 22.1	41.8	120.3
18	60 12.2	28.8	106.9	59 34.1	32.2	110.1	58 49.8	35.3	113.3	57 59.5	38.3	116.2	57 03.9	40.9	119.0
19	60 41.0	27.2	105.1	60 06.3	30.9	108.5	59 25.1	34.2	111.7	58 37.8	37.2	114.7	57 44.8	40.0	117.6
20	61 08.2	+25.8	103.3	60 37.2	+29.5	106.7	59 59.3	+32.9	110.1	59 15.0	+36.2	113.2	58 24.8	+39.0	116.2
21	61 34.0	24.1	101.4	61 06.7	28.0	104.9	60 32.2	31.7	108.4	59 51.2	34.9	111.7	59 03.8	38.1	114.8
22	61 58.1	22.5	99.4	61 34.7	26.4	103.1	61 03.9	30.2	106.6	60 26.1	33.8	110.0	59 41.9	36.9	113.2
23	62 20.6	20.7	97.5	62 01.1	24.9	101.2	61 34.1	28.8	104.8	60 59.9	32.4	108.3	60 18.8	35.7	111.7
24	62 41.3	19.0	95.4	62 26.0	23.2	99.2	62 02.9	27.2	103.0	61 32.3	31.0	106.6	60 54.5	34.6	110.0
25	63 00.3	+17.0	93.3	62 49.2	+21.4	97.2	62 30.1	+25.6	101.1	62 03.3	+29.5	104.8	61 29.1	+33.2	108.3
26	63 17.3	15.1	91.2	63 10.6	19.6	95.2	62 55.7	23.9	99.1	62 32.8	28.0	102.9	62 02.3	31.8	106.6
27	63 32.4	13.2*	89.1	63 30.2	17.7	93.1	63 19.6	22.1	97.1	63 00.8	26.4	101.0	62 34.1	30.3	104.8
28	63 45.6	11.1*	86.9	63 47.9	15.7	90.9	63 41.7	20.3	95.0	63 27.2	24.6	99.0	63 04.4	28.8	102.9
29	63 56.7	9.0*	84.6	64 03.6	13.8*	88.7	64 02.0	18.4*	92.8	63 51.8	22.9	96.9	63 33.2	27.2	100.9

Figure 1.

d / ′	1	2	3	4	5	6	7	8	9	10	11	12	13	14	15	16	17	18	19	20	21	22	23	24	25	26	27	28	29	30
0	0	0	0	0	0	0	0	0	0	0	0	0	0	0	0	0	0	0	0	0	0	0	0	0	0	0	0	0	0	0
1	0	0	0	0	0	0	0	0	0	0	0	0	0	0	0	0	0	0	0	0	0	0	0	0	0	0	0	0	0	0
2	0	0	0	0	0	0	0	0	0	0	0	0	0	0	0	1	1	1	1	1	1	1	1	1	1	1	1	1	1	1
3	0	0	0	0	0	0	0	0	0	0	1	1	1	1	1	1	1	1	1	1	1	1	1	1	1	1	1	1	1	2
4	0	0	0	0	0	0	0	1	1	1	1	1	1	1	1	1	1	1	1	1	1	1	2	2	2	2	2	2	2	2
5	0	0	0	0	0	0	1	1	1	1	1	1	1	1	1	1	1	1	2	2	2	2	2	2	2	2	2	2	2	2
6	0	0	0	0	0	1	1	1	1	1	1	1	1	1	2	2	2	2	2	2	2	2	2	2	2	3	3	3	3	3
7	0	0	0	0	1	1	1	1	1	1	1	1	2	2	2	2	2	2	2	2	2	3	3	3	3	3	3	3	3	4
8	0	0	0	1	1	1	1	1	1	1	1	2	2	2	2	2	2	2	3	3	3	3	3	3	3	3	4	4	4	4
9	0	0	0	1	1	1	1	1	1	2	2	2	2	2	2	2	3	3	3	3	3	3	3	4	4	4	4	4	4	4
10	0	0	0	1	1	1	1	1	2	2	2	2	2	2	2	3	3	3	3	3	4	4	4	4	4	4	4	5	5	5
11	0	0	1	1	1	1	1	1	2	2	2	2	2	3	3	3	3	3	3	4	4	4	4	4	5	5	5	5	5	6
12	0	0	1	1	1	1	1	2	2	2	2	2	3	3	3	3	3	4	4	4	4	4	5	5	5	5	5	6	6	6
13	0	0	1	1	1	1	2	2	2	2	2	3	3	3	3	3	4	4	4	4	5	5	5	5	5	6	6	6	6	6
14	0	0	1	1	1	1	2	2	2	2	3	3	3	3	4	4	4	4	4	5	5	5	5	6	6	6	6	7	7	7
15	0	0	1	1	1	2	2	2	2	2	3	3	3	4	4	4	4	4	5	5	5	6	6	6	6	6	7	7	7	8
16	0	1	1	1	1	2	2	2	2	3	3	3	3	4	4	4	5	5	5	5	6	6	6	6	7	7	7	7	8	8
17	0	1	1	1	1	2	2	2	3	3	3	3	4	4	4	5	5	5	5	6	6	6	7	7	7	7	8	8	8	8
18	0	1	1	1	2	2	2	2	3	3	3	4	4	4	4	5	5	5	6	6	6	7	7	7	8	8	8	8	9	9
19	0	1	1	1	2	2	2	3	3	3	3	4	4	4	5	5	5	6	6	6	7	7	7	8	8	8	9	9	9	10
20	0	1	1	1	2	2	2	3	3	3	4	4	4	5	5	5	6	6	6	7	7	7	8	8	8	9	9	9	10	10
21	0	1	1	1	2	2	2	3	3	4	4	4	5	5	5	6	6	6	7	7	7	8	8	8	9	9	9	10	10	10
22	0	1	1	1	2	2	3	3	3	4	4	4	5	5	6	6	6	7	7	7	8	8	8	9	9	10	10	10	11	11
23	0	1	1	2	2	2	3	3	3	4	4	5	5	5	6	6	7	7	7	8	8	8	9	9	10	10	10	11	11	12
24	0	1	1	2	2	2	3	3	4	4	4	5	5	6	6	6	7	7	8	8	8	9	9	10	10	10	11	11	12	12
25	0	1	1	2	2	2	3	3	4	4	5	5	5	6	6	7	7	8	8	8	9	9	10	10	10	11	11	12	12	12
26	0	1	1	2	2	3	3	3	4	4	5	5	6	6	6	7	7	8	8	9	9	10	10	10	11	11	12	12	13	13
27	0	1	1	2	2	3	3	4	4	4	5	5	6	6	7	7	8	8	9	9	9	10	10	11	11	12	12	13	13	14
28	0	1	1	2	2	3	3	4	4	5	5	6	6	7	7	7	8	8	9	9	10	10	11	11	12	12	13	13	14	14
29	0	1	1	2	2	3	3	4	4	5	5	6	6	7	7	8	8	9	9	10	10	11	11	12	12	13	13	14	14	14
30	0	1	2	2	2	3	4	4	4	5	6	6	6	7	8	8	8	9	10	10	10	11	12	12	12	13	14	14	14	15
31	1	1	2	2	3	3	4	4	5	5	6	6	7	7	8	8	9	9	10	10	11	11	12	12	13	13	14	14	15	16
32	1	1	2	2	3	3	4	4	5	5	6	6	7	7	8	9	9	10	10	11	11	12	12	13	13	14	14	15	15	16
33	1	1	2	2	3	3	4	4	5	6	6	7	7	8	8	9	9	10	10	11	12	12	13	13	14	14	15	15	16	16
34	1	1	2	2	3	3	4	5	5	6	6	7	7	8	8	9	10	10	11	11	12	12	13	14	14	15	15	16	16	17
35	1	1	2	2	3	4	4	5	5	6	6	7	8	8	9	9	10	10	11	12	12	13	13	14	15	15	16	16	17	18
36	1	1	2	2	3	4	4	5	5	6	7	7	8	8	9	10	10	11	11	12	13	13	14	14	15	16	16	17	17	18
37	1	1	2	2	3	4	4	5	6	6	7	7	8	9	9	10	10	11	12	12	13	14	14	15	15	16	17	17	18	18
38	1	1	2	3	3	4	4	5	6	6	7	8	8	9	10	10	11	11	12	13	13	14	15	15	16	16	17	18	18	19
39	1	1	2	3	3	4	5	5	6	6	7	8	8	9	10	10	11	12	12	13	14	14	15	16	16	17	18	18	19	20
40	1	1	2	3	3	4	5	5	6	7	7	8	9	9	10	11	11	12	13	13	14	15	15	16	17	17	18	19	19	20
41	1	1	2	3	3	4	5	5	6	7	8	8	9	10	10	11	12	12	13	14	14	15	16	16	17	18	18	19	20	20
42	1	1	2	3	4	4	5	6	6	7	8	8	9	10	10	11	12	13	13	14	15	15	16	17	18	18	19	20	20	21
43	1	1	2	3	4	4	5	6	6	7	8	9	9	10	11	11	12	13	14	14	15	16	16	17	18	19	19	20	21	22
44	1	1	2	3	4	4	5	6	7	7	8	9	10	10	11	12	12	13	14	15	15	16	17	18	18	19	20	21	21	22
45	1	2	2	3	4	4	5	6	7	8	8	9	10	10	11	12	13	14	14	15	16	16	17	18	19	20	20	21	22	22
46	1	2	2	3	4	5	5	6	7	8	8	9	10	11	12	12	13	14	15	15	16	17	18	18	19	20	21	21	22	23
47	1	2	2	3	4	5	5	6	7	8	9	9	10	11	12	13	13	14	15	16	16	17	18	19	20	20	21	22	23	24
48	1	2	2	3	4	5	6	6	7	8	9	10	10	11	12	13	14	14	15	16	17	18	18	19	20	21	22	22	23	24
49	1	2	2	3	4	5	6	7	7	8	9	10	11	11	12	13	14	15	16	16	17	18	19	20	20	21	22	23	24	24
50	1	2	2	3	4	5	6	7	8	8	9	10	11	12	12	13	14	15	16	17	18	18	19	20	21	22	22	23	24	25
51	1	2	3	3	4	5	6	7	8	8	9	10	11	12	13	14	14	15	16	17	18	19	20	20	21	22	23	24	25	26
52	1	2	3	3	4	5	6	7	8	9	10	10	11	12	13	14	15	16	16	17	18	19	20	21	22	23	23	24	25	26
53	1	2	3	4	4	5	6	7	8	9	10	11	11	12	13	14	15	16	17	18	19	19	20	21	22	23	24	25	26	26
54	1	2	3	4	4	5	6	7	8	9	10	11	12	13	14	14	15	16	17	18	19	20	21	22	22	23	24	25	26	27
55	1	2	3	4	5	6	6	7	8	9	10	11	12	13	14	15	16	16	17	18	19	20	21	22	23	24	25	26	27	28
56	1	2	3	4	5	6	7	7	8	9	10	11	12	13	14	15	16	17	18	19	20	21	21	22	23	24	25	26	27	28
57	1	2	3	4	5	6	7	8	9	10	10	11	12	13	14	15	16	17	18	19	20	21	22	23	24	25	26	27	28	28
58	1	2	3	4	5	6	7	8	9	10	11	12	13	14	14	15	16	17	18	19	20	21	22	23	24	25	26	27	28	29
59	1	2	3	4	5	6	7	8	9	10	11	12	13	14	15	16	17	18	19	20	21	22	23	24	25	26	27	28	29	30

Figure 2.

31	32	33	34	35	36	37	38	39	40	41	42	43	44	45	46	47	48	49	50	51	52	53	54	55	56	57	58	59	60	d/′
0	0	0	0	0	0	0	0	0	0	0	0	0	0	0	0	0	0	0	0	0	0	0	0	0	0	0	0	0	0	0
1	1	1	1	1	1	1	1	1	1	1	1	1	1	1	1	1	1	1	1	1	1	1	1	1	1	1	1	1	1	1
1	1	1	1	1	1	1	1	1	1	1	1	1	1	2	2	2	2	2	2	2	2	2	2	2	2	2	2	2	2	2
2	2	2	2	2	2	2	2	2	2	2	2	2	2	2	2	2	2	2	2	3	3	3	3	3	3	3	3	3	3	3
2	2	2	2	2	2	2	3	3	3	3	3	3	3	3	3	3	3	3	3	3	3	4	4	4	4	4	4	4	4	4
3	3	3	3	3	3	3	3	3	3	3	4	4	4	4	4	4	4	4	4	4	4	4	4	5	5	5	5	5	5	5
3	3	3	3	4	4	4	4	4	4	4	4	4	4	4	5	5	5	5	5	5	5	5	5	6	6	6	6	6	6	6
4	4	4	4	4	4	4	4	5	5	5	5	5	5	5	5	5	6	6	6	6	6	6	6	6	7	7	7	7	7	7
4	4	4	5	5	5	5	5	5	5	5	6	6	6	6	6	6	6	7	7	7	7	7	7	7	7	8	8	8	8	8
5	5	5	5	5	5	6	6	6	6	6	6	6	7	7	7	7	7	7	8	8	8	8	8	8	8	9	9	9	9	9
5	5	6	6	6	6	6	6	6	7	7	7	7	7	8	8	8	8	8	8	8	9	9	9	9	9	10	10	10	10	10
6	6	6	6	6	7	7	7	7	7	8	8	8	8	8	8	9	9	9	9	9	10	10	10	10	10	10	11	11	11	11
6	6	7	7	7	7	7	8	8	8	8	8	9	9	9	9	9	10	10	10	10	10	11	11	11	11	11	12	12	12	12
7	7	7	7	8	8	8	8	8	9	9	9	9	10	10	10	10	10	11	11	11	11	11	12	12	12	12	13	13	13	13
7	7	8	8	8	8	9	9	9	9	10	10	10	10	10	11	11	11	11	12	12	12	12	13	13	13	13	14	14	14	14
8	8	8	8	9	9	9	10	10	10	10	10	11	11	11	12	12	12	12	12	13	13	13	14	14	14	14	14	15	15	15
8	9	9	9	9	10	10	10	10	11	11	11	11	12	12	12	13	13	13	13	14	14	14	14	15	15	15	15	16	16	16
9	9	9	10	10	10	10	11	11	11	12	12	12	12	13	13	13	14	14	14	14	15	15	15	16	16	16	16	17	17	17
9	10	10	10	10	11	11	11	12	12	12	13	13	13	14	14	14	14	15	15	15	16	16	16	16	17	17	17	18	18	18
10	10	10	11	11	11	12	12	12	13	13	13	14	14	14	15	15	15	16	16	16	16	17	17	17	18	18	18	19	19	19
10	11	11	11	12	12	12	13	13	13	14	14	14	15	15	15	16	16	16	17	17	17	18	18	18	19	19	19	20	20	20
11	11	12	12	12	13	13	13	14	14	14	15	15	15	16	16	16	17	17	18	18	18	19	19	19	20	20	20	21	21	21
11	12	12	12	13	13	14	14	14	15	15	15	16	16	16	17	17	18	18	18	19	19	19	20	20	21	21	21	22	22	22
12	12	13	13	13	14	14	15	15	15	16	16	16	17	17	18	18	18	19	19	20	20	20	21	21	21	22	22	23	23	23
12	13	13	14	14	14	15	15	16	16	16	17	17	18	18	18	19	19	20	20	20	21	21	22	22	22	23	23	24	24	24
13	13	14	14	15	15	15	16	16	17	17	18	18	18	19	19	20	20	20	21	21	22	22	22	23	23	24	24	25	25	25
13	14	14	15	15	16	16	16	17	17	18	18	19	19	20	20	20	21	21	22	22	23	23	23	24	24	25	25	26	26	26
14	14	15	15	16	16	17	17	18	18	18	19	19	20	20	21	21	22	22	22	23	23	24	24	25	25	26	26	27	27	27
14	15	15	16	16	17	17	18	18	19	19	20	20	21	21	21	22	22	23	23	24	24	25	25	26	26	27	27	28	28	28
15	15	16	16	17	17	18	18	19	19	20	20	21	21	22	22	23	23	24	24	25	25	26	26	27	27	28	28	29	29	29
16	16	16	17	18	18	18	19	20	20	20	21	22	22	22	23	24	24	24	25	26	26	26	27	28	28	28	29	30	30	30
16	17	17	18	18	19	19	20	20	21	21	22	22	23	23	24	24	25	25	26	26	27	27	28	28	29	29	30	30	31	31
17	17	18	18	19	19	20	20	21	21	22	22	23	23	24	25	25	26	26	27	27	28	28	29	29	30	30	31	31	32	32
17	18	18	19	19	20	20	21	21	22	23	23	24	24	25	25	26	26	27	28	28	29	29	30	30	31	31	32	32	33	33
18	18	19	19	20	20	21	22	22	23	23	24	24	25	26	26	27	27	28	28	29	29	30	31	31	32	32	33	33	34	34
18	19	19	20	20	21	22	22	23	23	24	24	25	26	26	27	27	28	29	29	30	30	31	32	32	33	33	34	34	35	35
19	19	20	20	21	22	22	23	23	24	25	25	26	26	27	28	28	29	29	30	31	31	32	32	33	34	34	35	35	36	36
19	20	20	21	22	22	23	23	24	25	25	26	27	27	28	28	29	30	30	31	31	32	33	33	34	35	35	36	36	37	37
20	20	21	22	22	23	23	24	25	25	26	27	27	28	28	29	30	30	31	32	32	33	34	34	35	35	36	37	37	38	38
20	21	21	22	23	23	24	25	25	26	27	27	28	29	29	30	31	31	32	32	33	34	34	35	36	36	37	38	38	39	39
21	21	22	23	23	24	25	25	26	27	27	28	29	29	30	31	31	32	33	33	34	35	35	36	37	37	38	39	39	40	40
21	22	23	23	24	25	25	26	27	27	28	29	29	30	31	31	32	33	33	34	35	36	36	37	38	38	39	40	40	41	41
22	22	23	24	24	25	26	27	27	28	29	29	30	31	32	32	33	34	34	35	36	36	37	38	38	39	40	41	41	42	42
22	23	24	24	25	26	27	27	28	29	29	30	31	32	32	33	34	34	35	36	37	37	38	39	39	40	41	42	42	43	43
23	23	24	25	26	26	27	28	29	29	30	31	32	32	33	34	34	35	36	37	37	38	39	40	40	41	42	43	43	44	44
23	24	25	26	26	27	28	28	29	30	31	32	32	33	34	34	35	36	37	38	38	39	40	40	41	42	43	44	44	45	45
24	25	25	26	27	28	28	29	30	31	31	32	33	34	34	35	36	37	38	38	39	40	41	41	42	43	44	44	45	46	46
24	25	26	27	27	28	29	30	31	31	32	33	34	34	35	36	37	38	38	39	40	41	42	42	43	44	45	45	46	47	47
25	26	26	27	28	29	30	30	31	32	33	34	34	35	36	37	38	38	39	40	41	42	42	43	44	45	46	46	47	48	48
25	26	27	28	29	29	30	31	32	33	33	34	35	36	37	38	38	39	40	41	42	42	43	44	45	46	47	47	48	49	49
26	27	28	28	29	30	31	32	32	33	34	35	36	37	38	38	39	40	41	42	42	43	44	45	46	47	48	48	49	50	50
26	27	28	29	30	31	31	32	33	34	35	36	37	37	38	39	40	41	42	42	43	44	45	46	47	48	48	49	50	51	51
27	28	29	29	30	31	32	33	34	35	36	36	37	38	39	40	41	42	42	43	44	45	46	47	48	49	49	50	51	52	52
27	28	29	30	31	32	33	34	34	35	36	37	38	39	40	41	42	42	43	44	45	46	47	48	49	49	50	51	52	53	53
28	29	30	31	32	32	33	34	35	36	37	38	39	40	40	41	42	43	44	45	46	47	48	49	50	50	51	52	53	54	54
28	29	30	31	32	33	34	35	36	37	38	38	39	40	41	42	43	44	45	46	47	48	49	50	50	51	52	53	54	55	55
29	30	31	32	33	34	35	35	36	37	38	39	40	41	42	43	44	45	46	47	48	49	49	50	51	52	53	54	55	56	56
29	30	31	32	33	34	35	36	37	38	39	40	41	42	43	44	45	46	47	48	48	49	50	51	52	53	54	55	56	57	57
30	31	32	33	34	35	36	37	38	39	40	41	42	43	44	44	45	46	47	48	49	50	51	52	53	54	55	56	57	58	58
30	31	32	33	34	35	36	37	38	39	40	41	42	43	44	45	46	47	48	49	50	51	52	53	54	55	56	57	58	59	59

II. LHA less than 90° or greater than 270°, latitude CON-
TRARY name to declination. These LHA's are in the
upper right corners of the right-hand pages.

DR: 36°50′N
71°05′W

Ho: 25°22′
Dec: 21°23′S
GHA: 100°45′
aλ: 70°45′W   aL: 36°N
LHA: 30°00′

Solution for this triangle is found on page 95, reproduced
here as Figure 3:

Hc = 26°19′5   d = −53′6   Z = 148°6

In the interpolation table (Figure 4) correction for the actual declination which is 23′ greater than that tabluated
gives a computed altitude (Hc) of 25°59′ (26°19′5 *minus*
21′, then rounded).

By the rules for finding Zn, Zn = 360° − 149° (148°6
rounded), or 211°.

III. LHA between 90° and 180°; or between 180° and 270°.
These LHA's are in the lower right corner of the right-
hand pages. Latitude is always SAME name as declination,
since, at these LHA's, bodies of contrary declination are
below the horizon (represented by the horizontal line in
the latitude blocks).

DR: 36°50′N
71°05′W

Ho: 6°31′
Dec: 21°23′N
GHA: 168°45′
aλ: 70°45′W   aL: 36°N
LHA: 98°00′

LATITUDE **CONTRARY** NAME   L.H.A. 30°, 330°

20°			22°			24°			26°			28°			
Hc	d	Z	Hc	d	Z	Hc	d	Z	Hc	d	Z	Hc	d	Z	Dec.
° ′	′	°	° ′	′	°	° ′	′	°	° ′	′	°	° ′	′	°	
54 28.1	− 35.8	120.6	53 24.8	− 38.1	123.0	52 17.6	− 40.3	125.2	51 06.7	− 42.2	127.2	49 52.6	− 44.0	129.1	0
53 52.3	36.7	122.0	52 46.7	38.9	124.3	51 37.3	41.0	126.4	50 24.5	42.8	128.3	49 08.6	44.6	130.2	1
53 15.6	37.5	123.3	52 07.8	39.7	125.5	50 56.3	41.6	127.5	49 41.7	43.5	129.4	48 24.0	45.0	131.2	2
52 38.1	38.4	124.6	51 28.1	40.5	126.7	50 14.7	42.3	128.7	48 58.2	44.0	130.5	47 39.0	45.6	132.2	3
51 59.7	39.2	125.9	50 47.6	41.1	127.9	49 32.4	42.9	129.8	48 14.2	44.5	131.5	46 53.4	46.0	133.1	4
51 20.5	− 39.9	127.1	50 06.5	− 41.8	129.0	48 49.5	− 43.5	130.8	47 29.7	− 45.1	132.5	46 07.4	− 46.5	134.1	5
50 40.6	40.6	128.3	49 24.7	42.4	130.2	48 06.0	44.1	131.9	46 44.6	45.5	133.5	45 20.9	46.9	135.0	6
50 00.0	41.2	129.5	48 42.3	43.0	131.2	47 21.9	44.5	132.9	45 59.1	46.0	134.4	44 34.0	47.3	135.8	7
49 18.8	41.9	130.6	47 59.3	43.5	132.3	46 37.4	45.1	133.9	45 13.1	46.4	135.3	43 46.7	47.6	136.7	8
48 36.9	42.6	131.7	47 15.8	44.1	133.3	45 52.3	45.5	134.8	44 26.7	46.8	136.2	42 59.1	48.1	137.5	9
47 54.3	− 43.0	132.7	46 31.7	− 44.6	134.3	45 06.8	− 45.9	135.8	43 39.9	− 47.3	137.1	42 11.0	− 48.3	138.4	10
47 11.3	43.6	133.8	45 47.1	45.0	135.3	44 20.9	46.4	136.7	42 52.6	47.5	138.0	41 22.7	48.7	139.1	11
46 27.7	44.2	134.8	45 02.1	45.5	136.2	43 34.5	46.8	137.5	42 05.1	47.9	138.8	40 34.0	49.0	139.9	12
45 43.5	44.6	135.7	44 16.6	46.0	137.1	42 47.7	47.1	138.4	41 17.2	48.3	139.6	39 45.0	49.2	140.7	13
44 58.9	45.1	136.7	43 30.6	46.3	138.0	42 00.6	47.5	139.2	40 28.9	48.6	140.4	38 55.8	49.6	141.4	14
44 13.8	− 45.5	137.6	42 44.3	− 46.7	138.9	41 13.1	− 47.9	140.1	39 40.3	− 48.8	141.1	38 06.2	− 49.7	142.1	15
43 28.3	45.9	138.5	41 57.6	47.1	139.7	40 25.2	48.1	140.9	38 51.5	49.2	141.9	37 16.5	50.1	142.8	16
42 42.4	46.3	139.4	41 10.5	47.5	140.6	39 37.1	48.5	141.6	38 02.3	49.4	142.6	36 26.4	50.3	143.5	17
41 56.1	46.7	140.3	40 23.0	47.7	141.4	38 48.6	48.7	142.4	37 12.9	49.6	143.3	35 36.1	50.5	144.2	18
41 09.4	47.1	141.1	39 35.3	48.1	142.2	37 59.9	49.1	143.1	36 23.3	49.9	144.0	34 45.6	50.7	144.9	19
40 22.3	− 47.4	141.9	38 47.2	− 48.4	142.9	37 10.8	− 49.3	143.9	35 33.4	− 50.1	144.7	33 54.9	− 50.9	145.5	20
39 34.9	47.7	142.7	37 58.8	48.7	143.7	36 21.5	49.5	144.6	34 43.3	50.4	145.4	33 04.0	51.1	146.2	21
38 47.2	48.0	143.5	37 10.1	48.9	144.4	35 32.0	49.8	145.3	33 52.9	50.5	146.1	32 12.9	51.2	146.8	22
37 59.2	48.4	144.3	36 21.2	49.2	145.1	34 42.2	50.0	146.0	33 02.4	50.8	146.7	31 21.7	51.5	147.4	23
37 10.8	48.6	145.0	35 32.0	49.4	145.9	33 52.2	50.2	146.6	32 11.6	50.9	147.3	30 30.2	51.6	148.0	24
36 22.2	− 48.8	145.8	34 42.6	− 49.7	146.5	33 02.0	− 50.4	147.3	31 20.7	− 51.1	148.0	29 38.6	− 51.7	148.6	25
35 33.4	49.1	146.5	33 52.9	49.9	147.2	32 11.6	50.6	147.9	30 29.6	51.3	148.6	28 46.9	51.9	149.2	26
34 44.3	49.4	147.2	33 03.0	50.1	147.9	31 21.0	50.8	148.6	29 38.3	51.4	149.2	27 55.0	52.1	149.7	27
33 54.9	49.5	147.9	32 12.9	50.2	148.5	30 30.2	50.9	149.2	28 46.9	51.6	149.8	27 02.9	52.2	150.3	28
33 05.4	49.8	148.5	31 22.7	50.5	149.2	29 39.3	51.2	149.8	27 55.3	51.8	150.3	26 10.7	52.3	150.8	29

30°			32°			34°			36°			38°			
Hc	d	Z	Hc	d	Z	Hc	d	Z	Hc	d	Z	Hc	d	Z	Dec.
° ′	′	°	° ′	′	°	° ′	′	°	° ′	′	°	° ′	′	°	
48 35.4	− 45.6	130.9	47 15.6	− 47.1	132.5	45 53.2	− 48.4	134.1	44 28.7	− 49.6	135.5	43 02.1	− 50.7	136.8	0
47 49.8	46.1	131.9	46 28.5	47.5	133.5	45 04.8	48.7	134.9	43 39.1	49.9	136.3	42 11.4	51.0	137.6	1
47 03.7	46.5	132.8	45 41.0	47.9	134.3	44 16.1	49.1	135.7	42 49.2	52.0	137.1	41 20.4	51.2	138.3	2
46 17.2	47.0	133.7	44 53.1	48.2	135.2	43 27.0	49.4	136.5	41 59.0	50.5	137.8	40 29.2	51.4	139.0	3
45 30.2	47.4	134.6	44 04.9	48.6	136.0	42 37.6	49.8	137.3	41 08.5	50.8	138.5	39 37.8	51.7	139.6	4
44 42.8	− 47.7	135.5	43 16.3	− 49.0	136.8	41 47.8	− 50.0	138.1	40 17.7	− 50.9	139.2	38 46.1	− 51.8	140.3	5
43 55.1	48.2	136.3	42 27.3	49.2	137.6	40 57.8	50.3	138.8	39 26.8	51.3	139.9	37 54.3	52.1	140.9	6
43 06.9	48.4	137.2	41 38.1	49.6	138.4	40 07.5	50.5	139.5	38 35.5	51.4	140.6	37 02.2	52.3	141.6	7
42 18.5	48.8	138.0	40 48.5	49.8	139.1	39 17.0	50.8	140.2	37 44.1	51.7	141.2	36 09.9	52.5	142.2	8
41 29.7	49.1	138.8	39 58.7	50.1	139.9	38 26.2	51.0	140.9	36 52.4	51.8	141.9	35 17.4	52.6	142.8	9
40 40.6	− 49.4	139.5	39 08.6	− 50.4	140.6	37 35.2	− 51.3	141.6	36 00.6	− 52.1	142.5	34 24.8	− 52.8	143.4	10
39 51.2	49.7	140.3	38 18.2	50.6	141.3	36 43.9	51.4	142.2	35 08.5	52.2	143.1	33 32.0	52.9	143.9	11
39 01.5	50.0	141.0	37 27.6	50.8	142.0	35 52.5	51.7	142.9	34 16.3	52.4	143.7	32 39.1	53.1	144.5	12
38 11.5	50.2	141.7	36 36.8	51.1	142.6	35 00.8	51.8	143.5	33 23.9	52.6	144.3	31 46.0	53.3	145.0	13
37 21.3	50.4	142.4	35 45.7	51.3	143.3	34 09.0	52.0	144.1	32 31.3	52.7	144.9	30 52.7	53.3	145.6	14
36 30.9	− 50.7	143.1	34 54.4	− 51.4	143.9	33 17.0	− 52.2	144.7	31 38.6	− 52.9	145.4	29 59.4	− 53.5	146.1	15
35 40.2	50.8	143.7	34 03.0	51.6	144.5	32 24.8	52.4	145.3	30 45.7	53.0	146.0	29 05.9	53.6	146.6	16
34 49.4	51.1	144.4	33 11.4	51.9	145.2	31 32.4	52.5	145.9	29 52.7	53.1	146.5	28 12.3	53.8	147.1	17
33 58.3	51.3	145.0	32 19.5	51.9	145.8	30 39.9	52.6	146.4	28 59.6	53.3	147.1	27 18.5	53.8	147.6	18
33 07.0	51.4	145.6	31 27.6	52.2	146.3	29 47.3	52.8	147.0	28 06.3	53.4	147.6	26 24.7	53.9	148.1	19
32 15.6	− 51.6	146.2	30 35.4	− 52.3	146.9	28 54.5	− 52.9	147.5	27 12.9	− 53.4	148.1	25 30.8	− 54.1	148.6	20
31 24.0	51.8	146.8	29 43.1	52.4	147.5	28 01.6	53.0	148.1	26 19.5	53.6	148.6	24 36.7	54.1	149.1	21
30 32.2	52.0	147.4	28 50.7	52.6	148.0	27 08.6	53.2	148.6	25 25.9	53.7	149.1	23 42.6	54.2	149.6	22
29 40.2	52.1	148.0	27 58.1	52.7	148.6	26 15.4	53.2	149.1	24 32.2	53.8	149.6	22 48.4	54.3	150.0	23
28 48.1	52.2	148.6	27 05.4	52.8	149.1	25 22.2	53.4	149.6	23 38.4	53.9	150.1	21 54.1	54.3	150.5	24
27 55.9	− 52.4	149.1	26 12.6	− 52.9	149.7	24 28.8	− 53.5	150.1	22 44.5	− 54.0	150.6	20 59.8	− 54.4	151.0	25
27 03.5	52.4	149.7	25 19.7	53.1	150.2	23 35.3	53.5	150.7	21 50.5	54.0	151.0	20 05.4	54.5	151.4	26
26 11.1	52.7	150.2	24 26.6	53.1	150.7	22 41.8	53.7	151.1	20 56.5	54.1	151.5	19 10.9	54.6	151.9	27
25 18.4	52.7	150.8	23 33.5	53.2	151.2	21 48.1	53.7	151.6	20 02.4	54.2	152.0	18 16.3	54.6	152.3	28
24 25.7	52.8	151.3	22 40.3	53.4	151.7	20 54.4	53.8	152.1	19 08.2	54.3	152.4	17 21.7	54.7	152.7	29

Figure 3.

$\frac{d}{\prime}$	1	2	3	4	5	6	7	8	9	10	11	12	13	14	15	16	17	18	19	20	21	22	23	24	25	26	27	28	29	30
0	0	0	0	0	0	0	0	0	0	0	0	0	0	0	0	0	0	0	0	0	0	0	0	0	0	0	0	0	0	0
1	0	0	0	0	0	0	0	0	0	0	0	0	0	0	0	0	0	0	0	0	0	0	0	0	0	0	0	0	0	0
2	0	0	0	0	0	0	0	0	0	0	0	0	0	0	0	1	1	1	1	1	1	1	1	1	1	1	1	1	1	1
3	0	0	0	0	0	0	0	0	0	0	1	1	1	1	1	1	1	1	1	1	1	1	1	1	1	1	1	1	1	2
4	0	0	0	0	0	0	0	1	1	1	1	1	1	1	1	1	1	1	1	1	1	1	2	2	2	2	2	2	2	2
5	0	0	0	0	0	0	1	1	1	1	1	1	1	1	1	1	1	2	2	2	2	2	2	2	2	2	2	2	2	2
6	0	0	0	0	0	1	1	1	1	1	1	1	1	1	2	2	2	2	2	2	2	2	2	2	3	3	3	3	3	3
7	0	0	0	0	1	1	1	1	1	1	1	1	2	2	2	2	2	2	2	2	2	3	3	3	3	3	3	3	3	4
8	0	0	0	1	1	1	1	1	1	1	1	2	2	2	2	2	2	2	3	3	3	3	3	3	3	3	4	4	4	4
9	0	0	0	1	1	1	1	1	1	2	2	2	2	2	2	2	3	3	3	3	3	3	3	4	4	4	4	4	4	4
10	0	0	0	1	1	1	1	1	2	2	2	2	2	2	2	3	3	3	3	3	4	4	4	4	4	4	4	5	5	5
11	0	0	1	1	1	1	1	1	2	2	2	2	2	3	3	3	3	3	3	4	4	4	4	4	5	5	5	5	5	6
12	0	0	1	1	1	1	1	2	2	2	2	2	3	3	3	3	3	4	4	4	4	4	5	5	5	5	5	6	6	6
13	0	0	1	1	1	1	2	2	2	2	2	3	3	3	3	3	4	4	4	4	5	5	5	5	5	6	6	6	6	6
14	0	0	1	1	1	1	2	2	2	2	3	3	3	3	4	4	4	4	4	5	5	5	5	6	6	6	6	7	7	7
15	0	0	1	1	1	2	2	2	2	2	3	3	3	4	4	4	4	4	5	5	5	6	6	6	6	6	7	7	7	8
16	0	1	1	1	1	2	2	2	2	3	3	3	3	4	4	4	5	5	5	5	6	6	6	6	7	7	7	7	8	8
17	0	1	1	1	1	2	2	2	3	3	3	3	4	4	4	5	5	5	5	6	6	6	7	7	7	7	8	8	8	8
18	0	1	1	1	2	2	2	2	3	3	3	4	4	4	4	5	5	5	6	6	6	7	7	7	8	8	8	8	9	9
19	0	1	1	1	2	2	2	3	3	3	3	4	4	4	5	5	5	6	6	6	7	7	7	8	8	8	9	9	9	10
20	0	1	1	1	2	2	2	3	3	3	4	4	4	5	5	5	6	6	6	7	7	7	8	8	8	9	9	9	10	10
21	0	1	1	1	2	2	2	3	3	4	4	4	5	5	5	6	6	6	7	7	7	8	8	8	9	9	9	10	10	10
22	0	1	1	1	2	2	3	3	3	4	4	4	5	5	6	6	6	7	7	7	8	8	8	9	9	10	10	10	11	11
23	0	1	1	2	2	2	3	3	3	4	4	5	5	5	6	6	6	7	7	8	8	8	9	9	9	10	10	11	11	11
24	0	1	1	2	2	2	3	3	4	4	4	5	5	6	6	6	7	7	8	8	8	9	9	10	10	10	11	11	12	12
25	0	1	1	2	2	2	3	3	4	4	5	5	5	6	6	7	7	8	8	8	9	9	10	10	10	11	11	12	12	12
26	0	1	1	2	2	3	3	3	4	4	5	5	6	6	6	7	7	8	8	9	9	10	10	10	11	11	12	12	13	13
27	0	1	1	2	2	3	3	4	4	4	5	5	6	6	7	7	8	8	9	9	9	10	10	11	11	12	12	13	13	13
28	0	1	1	2	2	3	3	4	4	5	5	6	6	7	7	7	8	8	9	9	10	10	11	11	12	12	13	13	14	14
29	0	1	1	2	2	3	3	4	4	5	5	6	6	7	7	8	8	9	9	10	10	11	11	12	12	13	13	14	14	14
30	0	1	2	2	2	3	4	4	4	5	6	6	6	7	8	8	8	9	10	10	10	11	12	12	12	13	14	14	14	15
31	1	1	2	2	3	3	4	4	4	5	6	6	7	7	8	8	9	9	10	10	11	11	12	12	13	14	14	15	15	16
32	1	1	2	2	3	3	4	4	5	5	6	6	7	7	8	9	9	10	10	11	11	12	12	13	13	14	14	15	15	16
33	1	1	2	2	3	3	4	4	5	6	6	7	7	8	8	9	9	10	10	11	12	12	13	13	14	14	15	15	16	16
34	1	1	2	2	3	3	4	5	5	6	6	7	7	8	8	9	10	10	11	11	12	12	13	14	14	15	15	16	16	17
35	1	1	2	2	3	4	4	5	5	6	6	7	8	8	9	9	10	10	11	12	12	13	13	14	15	15	16	17	17	18
36	1	1	2	2	3	4	4	5	5	6	7	7	8	8	9	10	10	11	11	12	13	13	14	14	15	16	16	17	18	18
37	1	1	2	2	3	4	4	5	6	6	7	7	8	9	9	10	10	11	12	12	13	14	14	15	15	16	17	17	18	18
38	1	1	2	3	3	4	4	5	6	6	7	8	8	9	10	10	11	11	12	13	13	14	15	15	16	16	17	18	18	19
39	1	1	2	3	3	4	5	5	6	6	7	8	8	9	10	10	11	12	12	13	14	14	15	16	16	17	18	18	19	20
40	1	1	2	3	3	4	5	5	6	7	7	8	9	9	10	11	11	12	13	13	14	15	15	16	17	17	18	19	19	20
41	1	1	2	3	3	4	5	5	6	7	8	8	9	10	10	11	12	12	13	14	14	15	16	16	17	18	18	19	20	20
42	1	1	2	3	4	4	5	6	6	7	8	8	9	10	10	11	12	13	14	14	15	15	16	17	18	18	19	20	20	21
43	1	1	2	3	4	4	5	6	6	7	8	9	9	10	11	11	12	13	14	15	15	16	17	18	18	19	19	20	21	22
44	1	1	2	3	4	4	5	6	7	7	8	9	10	10	11	12	12	13	14	15	15	16	17	18	18	19	20	21	21	22
45	1	2	2	3	4	4	5	6	7	8	8	9	10	10	11	12	13	14	14	15	16	16	17	18	19	20	20	21	22	22
46	1	2	2	3	4	5	5	6	7	8	8	9	10	11	12	12	13	14	15	15	16	17	18	18	19	20	21	21	22	23
47	1	2	2	3	4	5	6	6	7	8	9	9	10	11	12	13	13	14	15	16	16	17	18	19	20	20	21	22	23	24
48	1	2	2	3	4	5	6	6	7	8	9	10	10	11	12	13	14	14	15	16	17	18	18	19	20	21	22	22	23	24
49	1	2	2	3	4	5	6	7	7	8	9	10	11	11	12	13	14	15	16	16	17	18	19	20	20	21	22	23	24	24
50	1	2	2	3	4	5	6	7	8	8	9	10	11	12	12	13	14	15	16	17	18	18	19	20	21	22	22	24	25	25
51	1	2	3	3	4	5	6	7	8	8	9	10	11	12	13	14	14	15	16	17	18	19	20	20	21	22	23	24	25	26
52	1	2	3	3	4	5	6	7	8	9	10	10	11	12	13	14	15	16	16	17	18	19	20	21	22	23	23	24	25	26
53	1	2	3	4	4	5	6	7	8	9	10	11	11	12	13	14	15	16	17	18	19	19	20	21	22	23	24	25	26	26
54	1	2	3	4	4	5	6	7	8	9	10	11	12	13	14	14	15	16	17	18	19	20	21	22	22	23	24	25	26	27
55	1	2	3	4	5	6	6	7	8	9	10	11	12	13	14	15	16	16	17	18	19	20	21	22	23	24	25	26	27	28
56	1	2	3	4	5	6	7	7	8	9	10	11	12	13	14	15	16	17	18	19	20	21	21	22	23	24	25	26	27	28
57	1	2	3	4	5	6	7	8	9	10	10	11	12	13	14	15	16	17	18	19	20	21	22	23	24	25	26	27	28	28
58	1	2	3	4	5	6	7	8	9	10	11	12	13	14	14	15	16	17	18	19	20	21	22	23	24	25	26	27	28	29
59	1	2	3	4	5	6	7	8	9	10	11	12	13	14	15	16	17	18	19	20	21	22	23	24	25	26	27	28	29	30

Figure 4.

31 32 33	34 35 36	37 38 39	40 41 42	43 44 45	46 47 48	49 50 51	52 53 54	55 56 57	58 59 60	$\frac{d}{i}$
0 0 0	0 0 0	0 0 0	0 0 0	0 0 0	0 0 0	0 0 0	0 0 0	0 0 0	0 0 0	0
1 1 1	1 1 1	1 1 1	1 1 1	1 1 1	1 1 1	1 1 1	1 1 1	1 1 1	1 1 1	1
1 1 1	1 1 1	1 1 1	1 1 1	1 1 2	2 2 2	2 2 2	2 2 2	2 2 2	2 2 2	2
2 2 2	2 2 2	2 2 2	2 2 2	2 2 2	2 2 2	2 2 3	3 3 3	3 3 3	3 3 3	3
2 2 2	2 2 2	2 3 3	3 3 3	3 3 3	3 3 3	3 3 3	3 4 4	4 4 4	4 4 4	4
3 3 3	3 3 3	3 3 3	3 3 4	4 4 4	4 4 4	4 4 4	4 4 4	5 5 5	5 5 5	5
3 3 3	3 4 4	4 4 4	4 4 4	4 4 4	5 5 5	5 5 5	5 5 5	6 6 6	6 6 6	6
4 4 4	4 4 4	4 4 5	5 5 5	5 5 5	5 5 6	6 6 6	6 6 6	6 7 7	7 7 7	7
4 4 4	5 5 5	5 5 5	5 5 6	6 6 6	6 6 6	7 7 7	7 7 7	7 7 8	8 8 8	8
5 5 5	5 5 5	6 6 6	6 6 6	6 7 7	7 7 7	7 8 8	8 8 8	8 8 9	9 9 9	9
5 5 6	6 6 6	6 6 6	7 7 7	7 7 8	8 8 8	8 8 8	9 9 9	9 9 10	10 10 10	10
6 6 6	6 6 7	7 7 7	7 8 8	8 8 8	8 9 9	9 9 9	10 10 10	10 10 10	11 11 11	11
6 6 7	7 7 7	7 8 8	8 8 8	9 9 9	9 9 10	10 10 10	10 11 11	11 11 11	12 12 12	12
7 7 7	7 8 8	8 8 8	9 9 9	9 10 10	10 10 10	11 11 11	11 11 12	12 12 12	13 13 13	13
7 7 8	8 8 8	9 9 9	9 10 10	10 10 10	11 11 11	11 12 12	12 12 13	13 13 13	14 14 14	14
8 8 8	8 9 9	9 10 10	10 10 10	11 11 11	12 12 12	12 12 13	13 13 14	14 14 14	14 15 15	15
8 9 9	9 9 10	10 10 10	11 11 11	11 12 12	12 13 13	13 13 14	14 14 14	15 15 15	15 16 16	16
9 9 9	10 10 10	10 11 11	11 12 12	12 12 13	13 13 14	14 14 14	15 15 15	16 16 16	16 17 17	17
9 10 10	10 10 11	11 11 12	12 12 13	13 13 14	14 14 14	15 15 15	16 16 16	16 17 17	17 18 18	18
10 10 10	11 11 11	12 12 12	13 13 13	14 14 14	15 15 15	16 16 16	16 17 17	17 18 18	18 19 19	19
10 11 11	11 12 12	12 13 13	13 14 14	14 15 15	15 16 16	16 17 17	17 18 18	18 19 19	19 20 20	20
11 11 12	12 12 13	13 13 14	14 14 15	15 15 16	16 16 17	17 18 18	18 19 19	19 20 20	20 21 21	21
11 12 12	12 13 13	14 14 14	15 15 15	16 16 16	17 17 18	18 18 19	19 19 20	20 21 21	21 22 22	22
12 12 13	13 13 14	14 15 15	15 16 16	16 17 17	18 18 18	19 19 20	20 20 21	21 21 22	22 23 23	23
12 13 13	14 14 14	15 15 16	16 16 17	17 18 18	18 19 19	20 20 20	21 21 22	22 22 23	23 24 24	24
13 13 14	14 15 15	15 16 16	17 17 18	18 18 19	19 20 20	20 21 21	22 22 22	23 23 24	24 25 25	25
13 14 14	15 15 16	16 16 17	17 18 18	19 19 20	20 20 21	21 22 22	23 23 23	24 24 25	25 26 26	26
14 14 15	15 16 16	17 17 18	18 18 19	19 20 20	21 21 22	22 22 23	23 24 24	25 25 26	26 27 27	27
14 15 15	16 16 17	17 18 18	19 19 20	20 21 21	21 22 22	23 23 24	24 25 25	26 26 27	27 28 28	28
15 15 16	16 17 17	18 18 19	19 20 20	21 21 22	22 23 23	24 24 25	25 26 26	27 27 28	28 29 29	29
16 16 16	17 18 18	18 19 20	20 20 21	22 22 22	23 24 24	24 25 26	26 26 27	28 28 28	29 30 30	30
16 17 17	18 18 19	19 20 20	21 21 22	22 23 23	24 24 25	25 26 26	27 27 28	28 29 29	30 30 31	31
17 17 18	18 19 19	20 20 21	21 22 22	23 23 24	25 25 26	26 27 27	28 28 29	29 30 30	31 31 32	32
17 18 18	19 19 20	20 21 21	22 23 23	24 24 25	25 26 26	27 28 28	29 29 30	30 31 31	32 32 33	33
18 18 19	19 20 20	21 22 22	23 23 24	24 25 26	26 27 27	28 28 29	29 30 31	31 32 32	33 33 34	34
18 19 19	20 20 21	22 22 23	23 24 24	25 26 26	27 27 28	29 29 30	30 31 32	32 33 33	34 34 35	35
19 19 20	20 21 22	22 23 23	24 25 25	26 26 27	28 28 29	29 30 31	31 32 32	33 34 34	35 35 36	36
19 20 20	21 22 22	23 23 24	25 25 26	27 27 28	28 29 30	30 31 31	32 33 33	34 35 35	36 36 37	37
20 20 21	22 22 23	23 24 25	25 26 27	27 28 28	29 30 30	31 32 32	33 34 34	35 35 36	37 37 38	38
20 21 21	22 23 23	24 25 25	26 27 27	28 29 29	30 31 31	32 32 33	34 34 35	36 36 37	38 38 39	39
21 21 22	23 23 24	25 25 26	27 27 28	29 29 30	31 31 32	33 33 34	35 35 36	37 37 38	39 39 40	40
21 22 23	23 24 25	25 26 27	27 28 29	29 30 31	31 32 33	33 34 35	36 36 37	38 38 39	40 40 41	41
22 22 23	24 24 25	26 27 27	28 29 29	30 31 32	32 33 34	34 35 36	36 37 38	38 39 40	41 41 42	42
22 23 24	24 25 26	27 27 28	29 29 30	31 32 32	33 34 34	35 36 37	37 38 39	39 40 41	42 42 43	43
23 23 24	25 26 26	27 28 29	29 30 31	32 32 33	34 34 35	36 37 37	38 39 40	40 41 42	43 43 44	44
23 24 25	26 26 27	28 28 29	30 31 32	32 33 34	34 35 36	37 38 38	39 40 40	41 42 43	44 44 45	45
24 25 25	26 27 28	28 29 30	31 31 32	33 34 34	35 36 37	38 38 39	40 41 41	42 43 44	44 45 46	46
24 25 26	27 27 28	29 30 31	31 32 33	34 34 35	36 37 38	38 39 40	41 42 42	43 44 45	45 46 47	47
25 26 26	27 28 29	30 30 31	32 33 34	34 35 36	37 38 38	39 40 41	42 42 43	44 45 46	46 47 48	48
25 26 27	28 29 29	30 31 32	33 33 34	35 36 37	38 38 39	40 41 42	42 43 44	45 46 47	47 48 49	49
26 27 28	28 29 30	31 32 32	33 34 35	36 37 38	38 39 40	41 42 42	43 44 45	46 47 48	48 49 50	50
26 27 28	29 30 31	31 32 33	34 35 36	37 37 38	39 40 41	42 42 43	44 45 46	47 48 48	49 50 51	51
27 28 29	29 30 31	32 33 34	35 36 36	37 38 39	40 41 42	42 43 44	45 46 47	48 49 49	50 51 52	52
27 28 29	30 31 32	33 34 34	35 36 37	38 39 40	41 42 42	43 44 45	46 47 48	49 49 50	51 52 53	53
28 29 30	31 32 32	33 34 35	36 37 38	39 40 40	41 42 43	44 45 46	47 48 49	50 50 51	52 53 54	54
28 29 30	31 32 33	34 35 36	37 38 38	39 40 41	42 43 44	45 46 47	48 49 50	50 51 52	53 54 55	55
29 30 31	32 33 34	35 35 36	37 38 39	40 41 42	43 44 45	46 47 48	49 49 50	51 52 53	54 55 56	56
29 30 31	32 33 34	35 36 37	38 39 40	41 42 43	44 45 46	47 48 48	49 50 51	52 53 54	55 56 57	57
30 31 32	33 34 35	36 37 38	39 40 41	42 43 44	44 45 46	47 48 49	50 51 52	53 54 55	56 57 58	58
30 31 32	33 34 35	36 37 38	39 40 41	42 43 44	45 46 47	48 49 50	51 52 53	54 55 56	57 58 59	59

Solution of this triangle is found on page 251, reproduced here as Figure 5:

Hc = 6°03.5   d = +35.5   Z = 68.4

Using the interpolation table (Figure 6) for the declination increment of 23' and d of 36' (35.5 rounded) gives +14' to be added to 6°04' (6°03.5 rounded) to get a computed altitude at the assumed position of 6°18'.

By the rules for finding true bearing, 360° − 68° is 292°.

STARS

The stars whose declinations lie within those covered by this sight reduction table—i.e. those having declinations between 30°S and 30°N—are:

Alpheratz	REGULUS
Diphda	Denebola
Hamal	Gienah
Menkar	SPICA
ALDEBARAN	ARCTURUS
RIGEL	Zubenelgenubi
Bellatrix	Alphecca
Elnath	ANTARES
Alnilam	Sabik
BETELGEUSE	Rasalhague
SIRIUS	Nunki
Adhara	ALTAIR
PROCYON	Enif
POLLUX	FOMALHAUT
Alphard	Markab

20° Hc	d	Z	22° Hc	d	Z	24° Hc	d	Z	26° Hc	d	Z	28° Hc	d	Z	Dec.
7 30.9	−20.8	92.8	7 24.8	−22.7	93.0	7 18.3	−24.7	93.3	7 11.2	−26.6	93.5	7 03.5	−28.4	93.8	0
7 10.1	20.9	93.7	7 02.1	22.8	93.9	6 53.6	24.8	94.2	6 44.6	26.7	94.4	6 35.1	28.5	94.7	1
6 49.2	20.9	94.6	6 39.3	23.0	94.9	6 28.8	24.8	95.1	6 17.9	26.7	95.3	6 06.6	28.7	95.5	2
6 28.3	21.1	95.6	6 16.3	23.0	95.8	6 04.0	25.0	96.0	5 51.2	26.9	96.2	5 37.9	28.7	96.4	3
6 07.2	21.2	96.5	5 53.3	23.1	96.7	5 39.0	25.0	96.9	5 24.3	26.9	97.1	5 09.2	28.7	97.3	4
5 46.0	−21.3	97.5	5 30.2	−23.2	97.7	5 14.0	−25.1	97.9	4 57.4	−27.0	98.0	4 40.5	−28.9	98.2	5
5 24.7	21.4	98.4	5 07.0	23.3	98.6	4 48.9	25.2	98.8	4 30.4	27.0	98.9	4 11.6	28.8	99.1	6
5 03.3	21.4	99.3	4 43.7	23.4	99.5	4 23.7	25.3	99.7	4 03.4	27.2	99.8	3 42.8	29.0	100.0	7
4 41.9	−21.5	100.3	4 20.3	23.4	100.4	3 58.4	25.3	100.6	3 36.2	27.1	100.7	3 13.8	29.0	100.8	8
4 20.4	21.6	101.2	3 56.9	23.5	101.4	3 33.1	25.4	101.5	3 09.1	27.2	101.6	2 44.8	29.0	101.7	9
3 58.8	−21.7	102.2	3 33.4	−23.6	102.3	3 07.7	−25.4	102.4	2 41.9	−27.3	102.5	2 15.8	−29.1	102.6	10
3 37.1	21.7	103.1	3 09.8	23.6	103.2	2 42.3	25.5	103.3	2 14.6	27.3	103.4	1 46.7	29.0	103.5	11
3 15.4	21.8	104.0	2 46.2	23.6	104.1	2 16.8	25.4	104.2	1 47.3	27.3	104.3	1 17.7	29.1	104.3	12
2 53.6	21.8	105.0	2 22.6	23.7	105.0	1 51.4	25.6	105.1	1 20.0	27.3	105.2	0 48.6	29.2	105.2	13
2 31.8	21.8	105.9	1 58.9	23.7	106.0	1 25.8	25.5	106.0	0 52.7	27.4	106.1	0 19.4	−29.1	106.1	14
2 10.0	−21.9	106.8	1 35.2	−23.7	106.9	1 00.3	−25.6	106.9	0 25.3	−27.3	107.0	0 09.7	+29.1	73.0	15
1 48.1	21.9	107.8	1 11.5	23.8	107.8	0 34.7	25.5	107.8	0 02.0	+27.4	72.2	0 38.8	29.1	72.2	16
1 26.2	21.9	108.7	0 47.7	23.8	108.7	0 09.2	−25.6	108.7	0 29.4	27.3	71.3	1 07.9	29.1	71.3	17
1 04.3	22.0	109.6	0 23.9	23.7	109.6	0 16.4	+25.6	70.4	0 56.7	27.3	70.4	1 37.0	29.0	70.4	18
0 42.3	22.0	110.5	0 00.2	−23.8	110.6	0 42.0	25.5	69.5	1 24.0	27.4	69.5	2 06.0	29.1	69.5	19
0 20.3	−21.9	111.5	0 23.6	+23.8	68.5	1 07.5	+25.6	68.5	1 51.4	+27.2	68.6	2 35.1	+29.0	68.7	20
0 01.6	+22.0	67.6	0 47.4	23.7	67.6	1 33.1	25.5	67.6	2 18.6	27.3	67.7	3 04.1	28.9	67.8	21
0 23.6	22.0	66.7	1 11.1	23.8	66.7	1 58.6	25.5	66.7	2 45.9	27.2	66.8	3 33.0	29.0	66.9	22
0 45.6	21.9	65.7	1 34.9	23.7	65.8	2 24.1	25.4	65.8	3 13.1	27.2	65.9	4 02.0	28.8	66.0	23
1 07.5	22.0	64.8	1 58.6	23.6	64.8	2 49.5	25.4	64.9	3 40.3	27.1	65.0	4 30.8	28.8	65.2	24
1 29.5	+21.9	63.9	2 22.2	+23.7	63.9	3 14.9	+25.4	64.0	4 07.4	+27.0	64.1	4 59.6	+28.7	64.3	25
1 51.4	21.8	62.9	2 45.9	23.6	63.0	3 40.3	25.3	63.1	4 34.4	27.0	63.2	5 28.3	28.7	63.4	26
2 13.2	21.9	62.0	3 09.5	23.5	62.1	4 05.6	25.2	62.2	5 01.4	26.9	62.3	5 57.0	28.5	62.5	27
2 35.1	21.8	61.1	3 33.0	23.5	61.2	4 30.8	25.2	61.3	5 28.3	26.8	61.4	6 25.5	28.5	61.6	28
2 56.9	21.7	60.1	3 56.5	23.5	60.2	4 56.0	25.1	60.4	5 55.1	26.8	60.5	6 54.0	28.3	60.7	29

30° Hc	d	Z	32° Hc	d	Z	34° Hc	d	Z	36° Hc	d	Z	38° Hc	d	Z	Dec.
6 55.4	30.3	94.0	6 46.7	32.1	94.3	6 37.5	33.8	94.5	6 27.9	35.5	94.7	6 17.8	37.2	94.9	0
6 25.1	30.4	94.9	6 14.6	32.1	95.1	6 03.7	33.9	95.3	5 52.4	35.6	95.5	5 40.6	37.3	95.7	1
5 54.7	30.4	95.8	5 42.5	32.2	96.0	5 29.8	33.9	96.2	5 16.8	35.7	96.3	5 03.3	37.3	96.5	2
5 24.3	30.5	96.6	5 10.3	32.3	96.8	4 55.9	34.1	97.0	4 41.1	35.7	97.1	4 26.0	37.4	97.3	3
4 53.8	30.6	97.5	4 38.0	32.4	97.7	4 21.8	34.0	97.8	4 05.4	35.8	98.0	3 48.6	37.4	98.1	4
4 23.2	30.6	98.4	4 05.6	32.4	98.5	3 47.8	34.2	98.6	3 29.6	35.8	98.8	3 11.2	−37.4	98.9	5
3 52.6	30.7	99.2	3 33.2	32.4	99.3	3 13.6	34.1	99.5	2 53.8	35.8	99.6	2 33.8	37.5	99.7	6
3 21.9	30.7	100.1	3 00.8	32.5	100.2	2 39.5	34.2	100.3	2 18.0	35.9	100.4	1 56.3	37.5	100.5	7
2 51.2	30.8	100.9	2 28.3	32.5	101.0	2 05.3	34.3	101.1	1 42.1	35.9	101.2	1 18.8	37.5	101.2	8
2 20.4	30.8	101.8	1 55.8	32.6	101.9	1 31.0	34.2	101.9	1 06.2	35.9	102.0	0 41.3	37.5	102.0	9
1 49.6	30.8	102.7	1 23.2	32.5	102.7	0 56.8	34.2	102.7	0 30.3	35.9	102.8	0 03.8	−37.6	102.8	10
1 18.8	30.9	103.5	0 50.7	32.6	103.5	0 22.6	34.3	103.6	0 05.6	+35.9	76.4	0 33.8	+37.5	76.4	11
0 47.9	30.8	104.4	0 18.1	32.6	104.4	0 11.7	−34.3	75.6	0 41.5	35.9	75.6	1 11.3	37.5	75.7	12
0 17.1	30.9	105.2	0 14.5	+32.5	74.8	0 46.0	34.2	74.8	1 17.4	35.9	74.8	1 48.8	37.5	74.9	13
0 13.8	−30.9	73.9	0 47.0	32.6	73.9	1 20.2	34.2	74.0	1 53.3	35.9	74.0	2 26.3	37.4	74.1	14
0 44.7	+30.8	73.1	1 19.6	+32.5	73.1	1 54.4	−34.2	73.1	2 29.2	−35.8	73.2	3 03.7	−37.4	73.3	15
1 15.5	30.8	72.2	1 52.1	32.4	72.3	2 28.6	34.2	72.3	3 05.0	35.8	72.4	3 41.1	37.4	72.5	16
1 46.3	30.8	71.3	2 24.7	32.4	71.4	3 02.8	34.2	71.5	3 40.8	35.7	71.6	4 18.5	37.3	71.7	17
2 17.1	30.8	70.5	2 57.1	32.5	70.6	3 37.0	34.0	70.7	4 16.5	35.7	70.8	4 55.8	37.3	71.0	18
2 47.9	30.7	69.6	3 29.6	32.4	69.7	4 11.0	34.1	69.9	4 52.2	35.7	70.0	5 33.1	37.2	70.2	19
3 18.6	+30.7	68.8	4 02.0	−32.3	68.9	4 45.1	−34.0	69.0	5 27.9	−35.6	69.2	6 10.3	+37.2	69.4	20
3 49.3	30.7	68.0	4 34.3	32.3	68.0	5 19.1	33.9	68.2	6 03.5	35.5	68.4	6 47.5	37.0	68.6	21
4 20.0	30.6	67.0	5 06.6	32.3	67.2	5 53.0	33.8	67.4	6 39.0	35.4	67.6	7 24.5	37.0	67.8	22
4 50.6	30.5	66.2	5 38.9	32.1	66.3	6 26.8	33.8	66.5	7 14.4	35.3	66.8	8 01.5	36.9	67.0	23
5 21.1	30.4	65.3	6 11.0	32.1	65.5	7 00.6	33.7	65.7	7 49.7	35.3	65.9	8 38.4	36.8	66.2	24
5 51.5	+30.4	64.4	6 43.1	+32.0	64.6	7 34.3	−33.5	64.9	8 25.0	−35.1	65.1	9 15.2	+36.7	65.4	25
6 21.9	30.3	63.6	7 15.1	31.9	63.6	8 07.8	33.5	64.0	9 00.1	35.1	64.3	9 51.9	36.5	64.6	26
6 52.2	30.1	62.7	7 47.0	31.7	62.9	8 41.3	33.4	63.2	9 35.2	34.9	63.5	10 28.4	36.5	63.8	27
7 22.3	30.1	61.8	8 18.7	31.7	62.1	9 14.7	33.2	62.4	10 10.1	34.8	62.7	11 04.9	36.3	63.0	28
7 52.4	30.0	61.0	8 50.4	31.6	61.2	9 47.9	33.1	61.5	10 44.9	34.6	61.8	11 41.2	36.2	62.2	29

Figure 5.

d/′	1	2	3	4	5	6	7	8	9	10	11	12	13	14	15	16	17	18	19	20	21	22	23	24	25	26	27	28	29	30
0	0	0	0	0	0	0	0	0	0	0	0	0	0	0	0	0	0	0	0	0	0	0	0	0	0	0	0	0	0	0
1	0	0	0	0	0	0	0	0	0	0	0	0	0	0	0	0	0	0	0	0	0	0	0	0	0	0	0	0	0	0
2	0	0	0	0	0	0	0	0	0	0	0	0	1	1	1	1	1	1	1	1	1	1	1	1	1	1	1	1	1	1
3	0	0	0	0	0	0	0	0	0	0	1	1	1	1	1	1	1	1	1	1	1	1	1	1	1	1	1	1	1	2
4	0	0	0	0	0	0	0	1	1	1	1	1	1	1	1	1	1	1	1	1	1	1	2	2	2	2	2	2	2	2
5	0	0	0	0	0	0	1	1	1	1	1	1	1	1	1	1	1	2	2	2	2	2	2	2	2	2	2	2	2	2
6	0	0	0	0	0	1	1	1	1	1	1	1	1	1	2	2	2	2	2	2	2	2	2	2	2	3	3	3	3	3
7	0	0	0	0	1	1	1	1	1	1	1	1	2	2	2	2	2	2	2	2	2	3	3	3	3	3	3	3	3	4
8	0	0	0	1	1	1	1	1	1	1	1	2	2	2	2	2	2	2	3	3	3	3	3	3	3	3	4	4	4	4
9	0	0	0	1	1	1	1	1	1	2	2	2	2	2	2	3	3	3	3	3	3	3	4	4	4	4	4	4	4	4
10	0	0	0	1	1	1	1	1	2	2	2	2	2	2	2	3	3	3	3	3	4	4	4	4	4	4	4	5	5	5
11	0	0	1	1	1	1	1	1	2	2	2	2	2	3	3	3	3	3	3	4	4	4	4	4	5	5	5	5	5	6
12	0	0	1	1	1	1	1	2	2	2	2	2	3	3	3	3	3	4	4	4	4	5	5	5	5	5	5	6	6	6
13	0	0	1	1	1	1	2	2	2	2	2	3	3	3	3	4	4	4	4	4	5	5	5	5	6	6	6	6	6	6
14	0	0	1	1	1	1	2	2	2	2	3	3	3	3	4	4	4	4	5	5	5	5	5	6	6	6	6	7	7	7
15	0	0	1	1	1	2	2	2	2	2	3	3	3	4	4	4	4	4	5	5	5	6	6	6	6	6	7	7	7	8
16	0	1	1	1	1	2	2	2	2	3	3	3	3	4	4	4	5	5	5	5	6	6	6	7	7	7	7	7	8	8
17	0	1	1	1	1	2	2	2	3	3	3	3	4	4	4	5	5	5	5	6	6	6	7	7	7	7	8	8	8	8
18	0	1	1	1	2	2	2	2	3	3	3	4	4	4	4	5	5	5	6	6	6	7	7	7	8	8	8	8	9	9
19	0	1	1	1	2	2	2	3	3	3	3	4	4	4	5	5	5	6	6	6	7	7	7	8	8	8	9	9	9	10
20	0	1	1	1	2	2	2	3	3	3	4	4	4	5	5	5	6	6	6	7	7	7	8	8	8	9	9	9	10	10
21	0	1	1	1	2	2	2	3	3	4	4	4	5	5	5	6	6	6	7	7	7	8	8	9	9	9	9	10	10	10
22	0	1	1	1	2	2	3	3	3	4	4	4	5	5	6	6	6	7	7	7	8	8	8	9	9	10	10	10	11	11
23	0	1	1	2	2	2	3	3	3	4	4	5	5	5	6	6	7	7	7	8	8	8	9	9	10	10	10	11	11	12
24	0	1	1	2	2	2	3	3	4	4	4	5	5	6	6	6	7	7	8	8	8	9	9	10	10	10	11	11	12	12
25	0	1	1	2	2	2	3	3	4	4	5	5	5	6	6	7	7	8	8	8	9	9	10	10	10	11	11	12	12	12
26	0	1	1	2	2	3	3	3	4	4	5	5	6	6	6	7	7	8	8	9	9	10	10	10	11	11	12	12	13	13
27	0	1	1	2	2	3	3	4	4	4	5	5	6	6	7	7	8	8	9	9	10	10	10	11	11	12	12	13	13	14
28	0	1	1	2	2	3	3	4	4	5	5	5	6	6	7	7	8	8	9	9	10	10	11	11	12	12	13	13	14	14
29	0	1	1	2	2	3	3	4	4	5	5	6	6	7	7	8	8	9	9	10	10	11	11	12	12	13	13	14	14	14
30	0	1	2	2	2	3	4	4	4	5	6	6	6	7	8	8	8	9	10	10	10	11	12	12	12	13	14	14	14	15
31	1	1	2	2	3	3	4	4	5	5	6	6	7	7	8	8	9	9	10	11	11	12	12	13	13	14	14	15	16	16
32	1	1	2	2	3	3	4	4	5	5	6	6	7	7	8	9	9	10	10	11	11	12	12	13	13	14	14	15	15	16
33	1	1	2	2	3	3	4	4	5	6	6	7	7	8	8	9	9	10	10	11	12	12	13	13	14	14	15	15	16	16
34	1	1	2	2	3	3	4	5	5	6	6	7	7	8	8	9	10	10	11	11	12	12	13	14	14	15	15	16	16	17
35	1	1	2	2	3	4	4	5	5	6	6	7	8	8	9	9	10	10	11	12	13	13	14	14	15	16	16	17	17	18
36	1	1	2	2	3	4	4	5	5	6	7	7	8	8	9	10	10	11	11	12	13	13	14	14	15	16	16	17	17	18
37	1	1	2	2	3	4	4	5	6	6	7	7	8	9	9	10	10	11	12	12	13	14	14	15	15	16	17	17	18	18
38	1	1	2	3	3	4	4	5	6	6	7	8	8	9	10	10	11	11	12	13	13	14	15	15	16	16	17	18	18	19
39	1	1	2	3	3	4	5	5	6	6	7	8	8	9	10	10	11	12	12	13	14	14	15	16	16	17	18	18	19	20
40	1	1	2	3	3	4	5	5	6	7	7	8	9	9	10	11	11	12	13	13	14	15	15	16	17	17	18	19	19	20
41	1	1	2	3	3	4	5	5	6	7	8	8	9	10	10	11	12	12	13	14	14	15	16	16	17	18	18	19	20	20
42	1	1	2	3	4	4	5	6	6	7	8	8	9	10	10	11	12	13	13	14	15	15	16	17	18	18	19	20	20	21
43	1	1	2	3	4	4	5	6	6	7	8	9	9	10	11	11	12	13	14	14	15	16	16	17	18	19	19	20	21	22
44	1	1	2	3	4	4	5	6	7	7	8	9	10	10	11	12	12	13	14	15	15	16	17	18	18	19	20	21	21	22
45	1	2	2	3	4	4	5	6	7	8	8	9	10	10	11	12	13	14	14	15	16	16	17	18	19	20	20	21	22	22
46	1	2	2	3	4	5	5	6	7	8	8	9	10	11	12	12	13	14	15	15	16	17	18	19	20	20	21	22	22	23
47	1	2	2	3	4	5	6	7	7	8	9	9	10	11	12	13	13	14	15	16	16	17	18	19	20	20	21	22	23	24
48	1	2	2	3	4	5	6	6	7	8	9	10	10	11	12	13	14	14	15	16	17	18	18	19	20	21	22	22	23	24
49	1	2	2	3	4	5	6	7	7	8	9	10	11	11	12	13	14	15	16	16	17	18	19	20	20	21	22	23	24	24
50	1	2	2	3	4	5	6	7	8	8	9	10	11	12	12	13	14	15	16	17	18	18	19	20	21	22	22	23	24	25
51	1	2	3	3	4	5	6	7	8	9	9	10	11	12	13	14	14	15	16	17	18	19	20	20	21	22	23	24	25	26
52	1	2	3	3	4	5	6	7	8	9	10	10	11	12	13	14	15	16	16	17	18	19	20	21	22	23	23	24	25	26
53	1	2	3	4	4	5	6	7	8	9	10	11	11	12	13	14	15	16	17	18	18	19	20	21	22	23	24	25	26	26
54	1	2	3	4	4	5	6	7	8	9	10	11	12	13	14	14	15	16	17	18	19	20	21	22	22	23	24	25	26	27
55	1	2	3	4	5	6	6	7	8	9	10	11	12	13	14	15	16	16	17	18	19	20	21	22	23	24	25	26	27	28
56	1	2	3	4	5	6	7	7	8	9	10	11	12	13	14	15	16	17	18	19	20	21	21	22	23	24	25	26	27	28
57	1	2	3	4	5	6	7	8	9	10	11	12	12	13	14	15	16	17	18	19	20	21	22	23	24	25	26	27	28	29
58	1	2	3	4	5	6	7	8	9	10	11	12	13	14	14	15	16	17	18	19	20	21	22	23	24	25	26	27	28	28
59	1	2	3	4	5	6	7	8	9	10	11	12	13	14	15	16	17	18	19	20	21	22	23	24	25	26	27	28	29	30

Figure 6.

Proportional parts table — value = nearest whole of (column × d) / 60.

31	32	33	34	35	36	37	38	39	40	41	42	43	44	45	46	47	48	49	50	51	52	53	54	55	56	57	58	59	60	$\dfrac{d}{'}$
0	0	0	0	0	0	0	0	0	0	0	0	0	0	0	0	0	0	0	0	0	0	0	0	0	0	0	0	0	0	0
1	1	1	1	1	1	1	1	1	1	1	1	1	1	1	1	1	1	1	1	1	1	1	1	1	1	1	1	1	1	1
1	1	1	1	1	1	1	1	1	1	1	1	1	1	2	2	2	2	2	2	2	2	2	2	2	2	2	2	2	2	2
2	2	2	2	2	2	2	2	2	2	2	2	2	2	2	2	2	2	2	2	3	3	3	3	3	3	3	3	3	3	3
2	2	2	2	2	2	2	3	3	3	3	3	3	3	3	3	3	3	3	3	3	3	4	4	4	4	4	4	4	4	4
3	3	3	3	3	3	3	3	3	3	3	4	4	4	4	4	4	4	4	4	4	4	4	4	5	5	5	5	5	5	5
3	3	3	3	4	4	4	4	4	4	4	4	4	4	4	5	5	5	5	5	5	5	5	5	6	6	6	6	6	6	6
4	4	4	4	4	4	4	4	5	5	5	5	5	5	5	5	6	6	6	6	6	6	6	6	6	7	7	7	7	7	7
4	4	4	5	5	5	5	5	5	5	5	6	6	6	6	6	6	6	7	7	7	7	7	7	7	7	8	8	8	8	8
5	5	5	5	5	5	6	6	6	6	6	6	6	7	7	7	7	7	7	8	8	8	8	8	8	8	9	9	9	9	9
5	5	6	6	6	6	6	6	6	7	7	7	7	7	8	8	8	8	8	8	8	9	9	9	9	9	10	10	10	10	10
6	6	6	6	6	7	7	7	7	7	8	8	8	8	8	8	9	9	9	9	9	10	10	10	10	10	10	11	11	11	11
6	6	7	7	7	7	7	8	8	8	8	8	9	9	9	9	9	10	10	10	10	10	11	11	11	11	11	12	12	12	12
7	7	7	7	8	8	8	8	8	9	9	9	9	10	10	10	10	10	11	11	11	11	11	12	12	12	12	13	13	13	13
7	7	8	8	8	8	9	9	9	9	10	10	10	10	10	11	11	11	11	12	12	12	12	13	13	13	13	14	14	14	14
8	8	8	8	9	9	9	10	10	10	10	10	11	11	11	12	12	12	12	12	13	13	13	14	14	14	14	14	15	15	15
8	9	9	9	9	10	10	10	10	11	11	11	11	12	12	12	13	13	13	13	14	14	14	14	15	15	15	15	16	16	16
9	9	9	10	10	10	10	11	11	11	12	12	12	12	13	13	13	14	14	14	14	15	15	15	16	16	16	16	17	17	17
9	10	10	10	10	11	11	11	12	12	12	13	13	13	14	14	14	14	15	15	15	16	16	16	16	17	17	17	18	18	18
10	10	10	11	11	11	12	12	12	13	13	13	14	14	14	15	15	15	16	16	16	16	17	17	17	18	18	18	19	19	19
10	11	11	11	12	12	12	13	13	13	14	14	14	15	15	15	16	16	16	17	17	17	18	18	18	19	19	19	20	20	20
11	11	12	12	12	13	13	13	14	14	14	15	15	15	16	16	16	17	17	18	18	18	19	19	19	20	20	20	21	21	21
11	12	12	12	13	13	14	14	14	15	15	15	16	16	16	17	17	18	18	18	19	19	19	20	20	21	21	21	22	22	22
12	12	13	13	13	14	14	15	15	15	16	16	16	17	17	18	18	18	19	19	20	20	20	21	21	21	22	22	23	23	23
12	13	13	14	14	14	15	15	16	16	16	17	17	18	18	18	19	19	20	20	20	21	21	22	22	22	23	23	24	24	24
13	13	14	14	15	15	15	16	16	17	17	18	18	18	19	19	20	20	20	21	21	22	22	22	23	23	24	24	25	25	25
13	14	14	15	15	16	16	16	17	17	18	18	19	19	20	20	20	21	21	22	22	23	23	23	24	24	25	25	26	26	26
14	14	15	15	16	16	17	17	18	18	18	19	19	20	20	21	21	22	22	22	23	23	24	24	25	25	26	26	27	27	27
14	15	15	16	16	17	17	18	18	19	19	20	20	21	21	21	22	22	23	23	24	24	25	25	26	26	27	27	28	28	28
15	15	16	16	17	17	18	18	19	19	20	20	21	21	22	22	23	23	24	24	25	25	26	26	27	27	28	28	29	29	29
16	16	16	17	18	18	18	19	20	20	20	21	22	22	22	23	24	24	24	25	26	26	26	27	28	28	28	29	30	30	30
16	17	17	18	18	19	19	20	20	21	21	22	22	23	23	24	24	25	25	26	26	27	27	28	28	29	29	30	30	31	31
17	17	18	18	19	19	20	20	21	21	22	22	23	23	24	25	25	26	26	27	27	28	28	29	29	30	30	31	31	32	32
17	18	18	19	19	20	20	21	21	22	23	23	24	24	25	25	26	26	27	28	28	29	29	30	30	31	31	32	32	33	33
18	18	19	19	20	20	21	22	22	23	23	24	24	25	26	26	27	27	28	28	29	29	30	31	31	32	32	33	33	34	34
18	19	19	20	20	21	22	22	23	23	24	24	25	26	26	27	27	28	29	29	30	30	31	32	32	33	33	34	34	35	35
19	19	20	20	21	22	22	23	23	24	25	25	26	26	27	28	28	29	29	30	31	31	32	32	33	34	34	35	35	36	36
19	20	20	21	22	22	23	23	24	25	25	26	27	27	28	28	29	30	30	31	31	32	33	33	34	35	35	36	36	37	37
20	20	21	22	22	23	23	24	25	25	26	27	27	28	28	29	30	30	31	32	32	33	34	34	35	35	36	37	37	38	38
20	21	21	22	23	23	24	25	25	26	27	27	28	29	29	30	31	31	32	32	33	34	34	35	36	36	37	38	38	39	39
21	21	22	23	23	24	25	25	26	27	27	28	29	29	30	31	31	32	33	33	34	35	35	36	37	37	38	39	39	40	40
21	22	23	23	24	25	25	26	27	27	28	29	29	30	31	31	32	33	33	34	35	36	36	37	38	38	39	40	40	41	41
22	22	23	24	24	25	26	27	27	28	29	29	30	31	32	32	33	34	34	35	36	36	37	38	38	39	40	41	41	42	42
22	23	24	24	25	26	27	27	28	29	29	30	31	32	32	33	34	34	35	36	37	37	38	39	39	40	41	42	42	43	43
23	23	24	25	26	26	27	28	29	29	30	31	32	32	33	34	34	35	36	37	37	38	39	40	40	41	42	43	43	44	44
23	24	25	26	26	27	28	28	29	30	31	32	32	33	34	34	35	36	37	38	38	39	40	40	41	42	43	44	44	45	45
24	25	25	26	27	28	28	29	30	31	31	32	33	34	34	35	36	37	38	38	39	40	41	41	42	43	44	44	45	46	46
24	25	26	27	27	28	29	30	31	31	32	33	34	34	35	36	37	38	38	39	40	41	42	42	43	44	45	45	46	47	47
25	26	26	27	28	29	30	30	31	32	33	34	34	35	36	37	38	38	39	40	41	42	42	43	44	45	46	46	47	48	48
25	26	27	28	29	29	30	31	32	33	33	34	35	36	37	38	38	39	40	41	42	42	43	44	45	46	47	47	48	49	49
26	27	28	28	29	30	31	32	32	33	34	35	36	37	38	38	39	40	41	42	42	43	44	45	46	47	48	48	49	50	50
26	27	28	29	30	31	31	32	33	34	35	36	37	37	38	39	40	41	42	42	43	44	45	46	47	48	48	49	50	51	51
27	28	29	29	30	31	32	33	34	35	36	36	37	38	39	40	41	42	42	43	44	45	46	47	48	49	49	50	51	52	52
27	28	29	30	31	32	33	34	34	35	36	37	38	39	40	41	42	42	43	44	45	46	47	48	49	49	50	51	52	53	53
28	29	30	31	32	32	33	34	35	36	37	38	39	40	40	41	42	43	44	45	46	47	48	49	50	50	51	52	53	54	54
28	29	30	31	32	33	34	35	36	37	38	38	39	40	41	42	43	44	45	46	47	48	49	50	50	51	52	53	54	55	55
29	30	31	32	33	34	35	35	36	37	38	39	40	41	42	43	44	45	46	47	48	49	49	50	51	52	53	54	55	56	56
29	30	31	32	33	34	35	36	37	38	39	40	41	42	43	44	45	46	47	48	48	49	50	51	52	53	54	55	56	57	57
30	31	32	33	34	35	36	37	38	39	40	41	42	43	44	44	45	46	47	48	49	50	51	52	53	54	55	56	57	58	58
30	31	32	33	34	35	36	37	38	39	40	41	42	43	44	45	46	47	48	49	50	51	52	53	54	55	56	57	58	59	59

These are 30 of the 57 stars commonly called the "navigational stars." The list contains 12 of the 18 first magnitude stars (capitalized), including the brightest of all, Sirius. As can be seen from Figures 7 and 8, which show the north and south

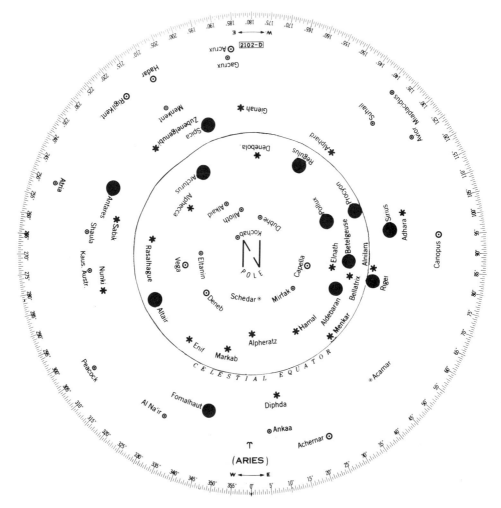

Figure 7.

faces of a Weems & Plath 2102-D Starfinder, coverage is quite good. The first magnitude stars in the above list are the large circles, the asterisks are the dimmer ones.

Figure 8.

OFFSETS

Due to the fact, with this table, that the AP can be as much as 1° away from the DR, the distance along the LOP from the intercept can approach 90 nautical miles (90′ of arc). Since the LOP is a straight line substituting for the actual curved edge of the circle of equal altitude, at high altitudes the difference (offset) between the LOP line and perimeter of the altitude circle can be significant. Using the following table, a correction can be made by drawing another LOP from the intercept to a point offset *toward* the GP by the amount given in the table.

As you can see by inspecting the table, however, if you keep your sights within the comfortable range of 10° to 70°, there is little to be gained from this table for the purposes of practical navigation in small boats.

Distance Along LOP from Intercept

	10′	20′	30′	40′	50′	60′	70′	80′	90′
Ho	—Difference between LOP and Altitude Circle—								
20°	0′	0′	0′	0′	0′	0′	1′	1′	1′
30°	0′	0′	0′	0′	0′	1′	1′	1′	1′
40°	0′	0′	0′	0′	0′	1′	1′	1′	1′
50°	0′	0′	0′	0′	1′	1′	1′	1′	2′
60°	0′	0′	0′	0′	1′	1′	1′	2′	2′
70°	0′	0′	0′	1′	1′	2′	2′	3′	3′
72°	0′	0′	0′	1′	1′	2′	2′	3′	4′
74°	0′	0′	0′	1′	1′	2′	3′	3′	4′
76°	0′	0′	1′	1′	1′	2′	3′	4′	5′
78°	0′	0′	1′	1′	2′	3′	3′	4′	6′
80°	0′	0′	1′	1′	2′	3′	4′	5′	7′
82°	0′	0′	1′	2′	3′	4′	5′	7′	9′
84°	0′	1′	1′	2′	3′	5′	7′	9′	11′
86°	0′	1′	2′	3′	5′	8′	10′	14′	18′
88°	0′	2′	4′	7′	11′	16′	23′	31′	41′

SIGHT REDUCTION TABLES
FOR SMALL BOAT NAVIGATION

	0°			2°			4°			6°			8°		
Dec.	Hc	d	Z	Hc	d	Z	Hc	d	Z	Hc	d	Z	Hc	d	Z
°	° ′	′	°	° ′	′	°	° ′	′	°	° ′	′	°	° ′	′	°
0	90 00.0	−60.0	90.0	88 00.0	+60.0	180.0	86 00.0	+60.0	180.0	84 00.0	+60.0	180.0	82 00.0	+60.0	180.0
1	89 00.0	60.0	0.0	89 00.0	+60.0	180.0	87 00.0	60.0	180.0	85 00.0	60.0	180.0	83 00.0	60.0	180.0
2	88 00.0	60.0	0.0	90 00.0	−60.0	90.0	88 00.0	60.0	180.0	86 00.0	60.0	180.0	84 00.0	60.0	180.0
3	87 00.0	60.0	0.0	89 00.0	60.0	0.0	89 00.0	+60.0	180.0	87 00.0	60.0	180.0	85 00.0	60.0	180.0
4	86 00.0	60.0	0.0	88 00.0	60.0	0.0	90 00.0	−60.0	90.0	88 00.0	60.0	180.0	86 00.0	60.0	180.0
5	85 00.0	−60.0	0.0	87 00.0	−60.0	0.0	89 00.0	−60.0	0.0	89 00.0	+60.0	180.0	87 00.0	+60.0	180.0
6	84 00.0	60.0	0.0	86 00.0	60.0	0.0	88 00.0	60.0	0.0	90 00.0	−60.0	90.0	88 00.0	60.0	180.0
7	83 00.0	60.0	0.0	85 00.0	60.0	0.0	87 00.0	60.0	0.0	89 00.0	60.0	0.0	89 00.0	+60.0	180.0
8	82 00.0	60.0	0.0	84 00.0	60.0	0.0	86 00.0	60.0	0.0	88 00.0	60.0	0.0	90 00.0	−60.0	90.0
9	81 00.0	60.0	0.0	83 00.0	60.0	0.0	85 00.0	60.0	0.0	87 00.0	60.0	0.0	89 00.0	60.0	0.0
10	80 00.0	−60.0	0.0	82 00.0	−60.0	0.0	84 00.0	−60.0	0.0	86 00.0	−60.0	0.0	88 00.0	−60.0	0.0
11	79 00.0	60.0	0.0	81 00.0	60.0	0.0	83 00.0	60.0	0.0	85 00.0	60.0	0.0	87 00.0	60.0	0.0
12	78 00.0	60.0	0.0	80 00.0	60.0	0.0	82 00.0	60.0	0.0	84 00.0	60.0	0.0	86 00.0	60.0	0.0
13	77 00.0	60.0	0.0	79 00.0	60.0	0.0	81 00.0	60.0	0.0	83 00.0	60.0	0.0	85 00.0	60.0	0.0
14	76 00.0	60.0	0.0	78 00.0	60.0	0.0	80 00.0	60.0	0.0	82 00.0	60.0	0.0	84 00.0	60.0	0.0
15	75 00.0	−60.0	0.0	77 00.0	−60.0	0.0	79 00.0	−60.0	0.0	81 00.0	−60.0	0.0	83 00.0	−60.0	0.0
16	74 00.0	60.0	0.0	76 00.0	60.0	0.0	78 00.0	60.0	0.0	80 00.0	60.0	0.0	82 00.0	60.0	0.0
17	73 00.0	60.0	0.0	75 00.0	60.0	0.0	77 00.0	60.0	0.0	79 00.0	60.0	0.0	81 00.0	60.0	0.0
18	72 00.0	60.0	0.0	74 00.0	60.0	0.0	76 00.0	60.0	0.0	78 00.0	60.0	0.0	80 00.0	60.0	0.0
19	71 00.0	60.0	0.0	73 00.0	60.0	0.0	75 00.0	60.0	0.0	77 00.0	60.0	0.0	79 00.0	60.0	0.0
20	70 00.0	−60.0	0.0	72 00.0	−60.0	0.0	74 00.0	−60.0	0.0	76 00.0	−60.0	0.0	78 00.0	−60.0	0.0
21	69 00.0	60.0	0.0	71 00.0	60.0	0.0	73 00.0	60.0	0.0	75 00.0	60.0	0.0	77 00.0	60.0	0.0
22	68 00.0	60.0	0.0	70 00.0	60.0	0.0	72 00.0	60.0	0.0	74 00.0	60.0	0.0	76 00.0	60.0	0.0
23	67 00.0	60.0	0.0	69 00.0	60.0	0.0	71 00.0	60.0	0.0	73 00.0	60.0	0.0	75 00.0	60.0	0.0
24	66 00.0	60.0	0.0	68 00.0	60.0	0.0	70 00.0	60.0	0.0	72 00.0	60.0	0.0	74 00.0	60.0	0.0
25	65 00.0	−60.0	0.0	67 00.0	−60.0	0.0	69 00.0	−60.0	0.0	71 00.0	−60.0	0.0	73 00.0	−60.0	0.0
26	64 00.0	60.0	0.0	66 00.0	60.0	0.0	68 00.0	60.0	0.0	70 00.0	60.0	0.0	72 00.0	60.0	0.0
27	63 00.0	60.0	0.0	65 00.0	60.0	0.0	67 00.0	60.0	0.0	69 00.0	60.0	0.0	71 00.0	60.0	0.0
28	62 00.0	60.0	0.0	64 00.0	60.0	0.0	66 00.0	60.0	0.0	68 00.0	60.0	0.0	70 00.0	60.0	0.0
29	61 00.0	60.0	0.0	63 00.0	60.0	0.0	65 00.0	60.0	0.0	67 00.0	60.0	0.0	69 00.0	60.0	0.0

	10°			12°			14°			16°			18°		
Dec.	Hc	d	Z	Hc	d	Z	Hc	d	Z	Hc	d	Z	Hc	d	Z
°	° ′	′	°	° ′	′	°	° ′	′	°	° ′	′	°	° ′	′	°
0	80 00.0	+60.0	180.0	78 00.0	+60.0	180.0	76 00.0	+60.0	180.0	74 00.0	+60.0	180.0	72 00.0	+60.0	180.0
1	81 00.0	60.0	180.0	79 00.0	60.0	180.0	77 00.0	60.0	180.0	75 00.0	60.0	180.0	73 00.0	60.0	180.0
2	82 00.0	60.0	180.0	80 00.0	60.0	180.0	78 00.0	60.0	180.0	76 00.0	60.0	180.0	74 00.0	60.0	180.0
3	83 00.0	60.0	180.0	81 00.0	60.0	180.0	79 00.0	60.0	180.0	77 00.0	60.0	180.0	75 00.0	60.0	180.0
4	84 00.0	60.0	180.0	82 00.0	60.0	180.0	80 00.0	60.0	180.0	78 00.0	60.0	180.0	76 00.0	60.0	180.0
5	85 00.0	+60.0	180.0	83 00.0	+60.0	180.0	81 00.0	+60.0	180.0	79 00.0	+60.0	180.0	77 00.0	+60.0	180.0
6	86 00.0	60.0	180.0	84 00.0	60.0	180.0	82 00.0	60.0	180.0	80 00.0	60.0	180.0	78 00.0	60.0	180.0
7	87 00.0	60.0	180.0	85 00.0	60.0	180.0	83 00.0	60.0	180.0	81 00.0	60.0	180.0	79 00.0	60.0	180.0
8	88 00.0	60.0	180.0	86 00.0	60.0	180.0	84 00.0	60.0	180.0	82 00.0	60.0	180.0	80 00.0	60.0	180.0
9	89 00.0	+60.0	180.0	87 00.0	60.0	180.0	85 00.0	60.0	180.0	83 00.0	60.0	180.0	81 00.0	60.0	180.0
10	90 00.0	−60.0	90.0	88 00.0	+60.0	180.0	86 00.0	+60.0	180.0	84 00.0	+60.0	180.0	82 00.0	+60.0	180.0
11	89 00.0	60.0	0.0	89 00.0	+60.0	180.0	87 00.0	60.0	180.0	85 00.0	60.0	180.0	83 00.0	60.0	180.0
12	88 00.0	60.0	0.0	90 00.0	−60.0	90.0	88 00.0	60.0	180.0	86 00.0	60.0	180.0	84 00.0	60.0	180.0
13	87 00.0	60.0	0.0	89 00.0	60.0	0.0	89 00.0	+60.0	180.0	87 00.0	60.0	180.0	85 00.0	60.0	180.0
14	86 00.0	60.0	0.0	88 00.0	60.0	0.0	90 00.0	−60.0	90.0	88 00.0	60.0	180.0	86 00.0	60.0	180.0
15	85 00.0	−60.0	0.0	87 00.0	−60.0	0.0	89 00.0	−60.0	0.0	89 00.0	+60.0	180.0	87 00.0	+60.0	180.0
16	84 00.0	60.0	0.0	86 00.0	60.0	0.0	88 00.0	60.0	0.0	90 00.0	−60.0	90.0	88 00.0	60.0	180.0
17	83 00.0	60.0	0.0	85 00.0	60.0	0.0	87 00.0	60.0	0.0	89 00.0	60.0	0.0	89 00.0	+60.0	180.0
18	82 00.0	60.0	0.0	84 00.0	60.0	0.0	86 00.0	60.0	0.0	88 00.0	60.0	0.0	90 00.0	−60.0	90.0
19	81 00.0	60.0	0.0	83 00.0	60.0	0.0	85 00.0	60.0	0.0	87 00.0	60.0	0.0	89 00.0	60.0	0.0
20	80 00.0	−60.0	0.0	82 00.0	−60.0	0.0	84 00.0	−60.0	0.0	86 00.0	−60.0	0.0	88 00.0	−60.0	0.0
21	79 00.0	60.0	0.0	81 00.0	60.0	0.0	83 00.0	60.0	0.0	85 00.0	60.0	0.0	87 00.0	60.0	0.0
22	78 00.0	60.0	0.0	80 00.0	60.0	0.0	82 00.0	60.0	0.0	84 00.0	60.0	0.0	86 00.0	60.0	0.0
23	77 00.0	60.0	0.0	79 00.0	60.0	0.0	81 00.0	60.0	0.0	83 00.0	60.0	0.0	85 00.0	60.0	0.0
24	76 00.0	60.0	0.0	78 00.0	60.0	0.0	80 00.0	60.0	0.0	82 00.0	60.0	0.0	84 00.0	60.0	0.0
25	75 00.0	−60.0	0.0	77 00.0	−60.0	0.0	79 00.0	−60.0	0.0	81 00.0	−60.0	0.0	83 00.0	−60.0	0.0
26	74 00.0	60.0	0.0	76 00.0	60.0	0.0	78 00.0	60.0	0.0	80 00.0	60.0	0.0	82 00.0	60.0	0.0
27	73 00.0	60.0	0.0	75 00.0	60.0	0.0	77 00.0	60.0	0.0	79 00.0	60.0	0.0	81 00.0	60.0	0.0
28	72 00.0	60.0	0.0	74 00.0	60.0	0.0	76 00.0	60.0	0.0	78 00.0	60.0	0.0	80 00.0	60.0	0.0
29	71 00.0	60.0	0.0	73 00.0	60.0	0.0	75 00.0	60.0	0.0	77 00.0	60.0	0.0	79 00.0	60.0	0.0

0° Hc	d	Z	2° Hc	d	Z	4° Hc	d	Z	6° Hc	d	Z	8° Hc	d	Z	Dec.
90 00.0	-60.0	90.0	88 00.0	-60.0	180.0	86 00.0	-60.0	180.0	84 00.0	-60.0	180.0	82 00.0	-60.0	180.0	0
89 00.0	60.0	180.0	87 00.0	60.0	180.0	85 00.0	60.0	180.0	83 00.0	60.0	180.0	81 00.0	60.0	180.0	1
88 00.0	60.0	180.0	86 00.0	60.0	180.0	84 00.0	60.0	180.0	82 00.0	60.0	180.0	80 00.0	60.0	180.0	2
87 00.0	60.0	180.0	85 00.0	60.0	180.0	83 00.0	60.0	180.0	81 00.0	60.0	180.0	79 00.0	60.0	180.0	3
86 00.0	60.0	180.0	84 00.0	60.0	180.0	82 00.0	60.0	180.0	80 00.0	60.0	180.0	78 00.0	60.0	180.0	4
85 00.0	-60.0	180.0	83 00.0	-60.0	180.0	81 00.0	-60.0	180.0	79 00.0	-60.0	180.0	77 00.0	-60.0	180.0	5
84 00.0	60.0	180.0	82 00.0	60.0	180.0	80 00.0	60.0	180.0	78 00.0	60.0	180.0	76 00.0	60.0	180.0	6
83 00.0	60.0	180.0	81 00.0	60.0	180.0	79 00.0	60.0	180.0	77 00.0	60.0	180.0	75 00.0	60.0	180.0	7
82 00.0	60.0	180.0	80 00.0	60.0	180.0	78 00.0	60.0	180.0	76 00.0	60.0	180.0	74 00.0	60.0	180.0	8
81 00.0	60.0	180.0	79 00.0	60.0	180.0	77 00.0	60.0	180.0	75 00.0	60.0	180.0	73 00.0	60.0	180.0	9
80 00.0	-60.0	180.0	78 00.0	-60.0	180.0	76 00.0	-60.0	180.0	74 00.0	-60.0	180.0	72 00.0	-60.0	180.0	10
79 00.0	60.0	180.0	77 00.0	60.0	180.0	75 00.0	60.0	180.0	73 00.0	60.0	180.0	71 00.0	60.0	180.0	11
78 00.0	60.0	180.0	76 00.0	60.0	180.0	74 00.0	60.0	180.0	72 00.0	60.0	180.0	70 00.0	60.0	180.0	12
77 00.0	60.0	180.0	75 00.0	60.0	180.0	73 00.0	60.0	180.0	71 00.0	60.0	180.0	69 00.0	60.0	180.0	13
76 00.0	60.0	180.0	74 00.0	60.0	180.0	72 00.0	60.0	180.0	70 00.0	60.0	180.0	68 00.0	60.0	180.0	14
75 00.0	-60.0	180.0	73 00.0	-60.0	180.0	71 00.0	-60.0	180.0	69 00.0	-60.0	180.0	67 00.0	-60.0	180.0	15
74 00.0	60.0	180.0	72 00.0	60.0	180.0	70 00.0	60.0	180.0	68 00.0	60.0	180.0	66 00.0	60.0	180.0	16
73 00.0	60.0	180.0	71 00.0	60.0	180.0	69 00.0	60.0	180.0	67 00.0	60.0	180.0	65 00.0	60.0	180.0	17
72 00.0	60.0	180.0	70 00.0	60.0	180.0	68 00.0	60.0	180.0	66 00.0	60.0	180.0	64 00.0	60.0	180.0	18
71 00.0	60.0	180.0	69 00.0	60.0	180.0	67 00.0	60.0	180.0	65 00.0	60.0	180.0	63 00.0	60.0	180.0	19
70 00.0	-60.0	180.0	68 00.0	-60.0	180.0	66 00.0	-60.0	180.0	64 00.0	-60.0	180.0	62 00.0	-60.0	180.0	20
69 00.0	60.0	180.0	67 00.0	60.0	180.0	65 00.0	60.0	180.0	63 00.0	60.0	180.0	61 00.0	60.0	180.0	21
68 00.0	60.0	180.0	66 00.0	60.0	180.0	64 00.0	60.0	180.0	62 00.0	60.0	180.0	60 00.0	60.0	180.0	22
67 00.0	60.0	180.0	65 00.0	60.0	180.0	63 00.0	60.0	180.0	61 00.0	60.0	180.0	59 00.0	60.0	180.0	23
66 00.0	60.0	180.0	64 00.0	60.0	180.0	62 00.0	60.0	180.0	60 00.0	60.0	180.0	58 00.0	60.0	180.0	24
65 00.0	-60.0	180.0	63 00.0	-60.0	180.0	61 00.0	-60.0	180.0	59 00.0	-60.0	180.0	57 00.0	-60.0	180.0	25
64 00.0	60.0	180.0	62 00.0	60.0	180.0	60 00.0	60.0	180.0	58 00.0	60.0	180.0	56 00.0	60.0	180.0	26
63 00.0	60.0	180.0	61 00.0	60.0	180.0	59 00.0	60.0	180.0	57 00.0	60.0	180.0	55 00.0	60.0	180.0	27
62 00.0	60.0	180.0	60 00.0	60.0	180.0	58 00.0	60.0	180.0	56 00.0	60.0	180.0	54 00.0	60.0	180.0	28
61 00.0	60.0	180.0	59 00.0	60.0	180.0	57 00.0	60.0	180.0	55 00.0	60.0	180.0	53 00.0	60.0	180.0	29

10° Hc	d	Z	12° Hc	d	Z	14° Hc	d	Z	16° Hc	d	Z	18° Hc	d	Z	Dec.
80 00.0	-60.0	180.0	78 00.0	-60.0	180.0	76 00.0	-60.0	180.0	74 00.0	-60.0	180.0	72 00.0	-60.0	180.0	0
79 00.0	60.0	180.0	77 00.0	60.0	180.0	75 00.0	60.0	180.0	73 00.0	60.0	180.0	71 00.0	60.0	180.0	1
78 00.0	60.0	180.0	76 00.0	60.0	180.0	74 00.0	60.0	180.0	72 00.0	60.0	180.0	70 00.0	60.0	180.0	2
77 00.0	60.0	180.0	75 00.0	60.0	180.0	73 00.0	60.0	180.0	71 00.0	60.0	180.0	69 00.0	60.0	180.0	3
76 00.0	60.0	180.0	74 00.0	60.0	180.0	72 00.0	60.0	180.0	70 00.0	60.0	180.0	68 00.0	60.0	180.0	4
75 00.0	-60.0	180.0	73 00.0	-60.0	180.0	71 00.0	-60.0	180.0	69 00.0	-60.0	180.0	67 00.0	-60.0	180.0	5
74 00.0	60.0	180.0	72 00.0	60.0	180.0	70 00.0	60.0	180.0	68 00.0	60.0	180.0	66 00.0	60.0	180.0	6
73 00.0	60.0	180.0	71 00.0	60.0	180.0	69 00.0	60.0	180.0	67 00.0	60.0	180.0	65 00.0	60.0	180.0	7
72 00.0	60.0	180.0	70 00.0	60.0	180.0	68 00.0	60.0	180.0	66 00.0	60.0	180.0	64 00.0	60.0	180.0	8
71 00.0	60.0	180.0	69 00.0	60.0	180.0	67 00.0	60.0	180.0	65 00.0	60.0	180.0	63 00.0	60.0	180.0	9
70 00.0	-60.0	180.0	68 00.0	-60.0	180.0	66 00.0	-60.0	180.0	64 00.0	-60.0	180.0	62 00.0	-60.0	180.0	10
69 00.0	60.0	180.0	67 00.0	60.0	180.0	65 00.0	60.0	180.0	63 00.0	60.0	180.G	61 00.0	60.0	180.0	11
68 00.0	60.0	180.0	66 00.0	60.0	180.0	64 00.0	60.0	180.0	62 00.0	60.0	180.0	60 00.0	60.0	180.0	12
67 00.0	60.0	180.0	65 00.0	60.0	180.0	63 00.0	60.0	180.0	61 00.0	60.0	180.0	59 00.0	60.0	180.0	13
66 00.0	60.0	180.0	64 00.0	60.0	180.0	62 00.0	60.0	180.0	60 00.0	60.0	180.0	58 00.0	60.0	180.0	14
65 00.0	-60.0	180.0	63 00.0	-60.0	180.0	61 00.0	-60.0	180.0	59 00.0	-60.0	180.0	57 00.0	-60.0	180.0	15
64 00.0	60.0	180.0	62 00.0	60.0	180.0	60 00.0	60.0	180.0	58 00.0	60.0	180.0	56 00.0	60.0	180.0	16
63 00.0	60.0	180.0	61 00.0	60.0	180.0	59 00.0	60.0	180.0	57 00.0	60.0	180.0	55 00.0	60.0	180.0	17
62 00.0	60.0	180.0	60 00.0	60.0	180.0	58 00.0	60.0	180.0	56 00.0	60.0	180.0	54 00.0	60.0	180.0	18
61 00.0	60.0	180.0	59 00.0	60.0	180.0	57 00.0	60.0	180.0	55 00.0	60.0	180.0	53 00.0	60.0	180.0	19
60 00.0	-60.0	180.0	58 00.0	-60.0	180.0	56 00.0	-60.0	180.0	54 00.0	-60.0	180.0	52 00.0	-60.0	180.0	20
59 00.0	60.0	180.0	57 00.0	60.0	180.0	55 00.0	60.0	180.0	53 00.0	60.0	180.0	51 00.0	60.0	180.0	21
58 00.0	60.0	180.0	56 00.0	60.0	180.0	54 00.0	60.0	180.0	52 00.0	60.0	180.0	50 00.0	60.0	180.0	22
57 00.0	60.0	180.0	55 00.0	60.0	180.0	53 00.0	60.0	180.0	51 00.0	60.0	180.0	49 00.0	60.0	180.0	23
56 00.0	60.0	180.0	54 00.0	60.0	180.0	52 00.0	60.0	180.0	50 00.0	60.0	180.0	48 00.0	60.0	180.0	24
55 00.0	-60.0	180.0	53 00.0	-60.0	180.0	51 00.0	-60.0	180.0	49 00.0	-60.0	180.0	47 00.0	-60.0	180.0	25
54 00.0	60.0	180.0	52 00.0	60.0	180.0	50 00.0	60.0	180.0	48 00.0	60.0	180.0	46 00.0	60.0	180.0	26
53 00.0	60.0	180.0	51 00.0	60.0	180.0	49 00.0	60.0	180.0	47 00.0	60.0	180.0	45 00.0	60.0	180.0	27
52 00.0	60.0	180.0	50 00.0	60.0	180.0	48 00.0	60.0	180.0	46 00.0	60.0	180.0	44 00.0	60.0	180.0	28
51 00.0	60.0	180.0	49 00.0	60.0	180.0	47 00.0	60.0	180.0	45 00.0	60.0	180.0	43 00.0	60.0	180.0	29

Dec.	20° Hc	d	Z	22° Hc	d	Z	24° Hc	d	Z	26° Hc	d	Z	28° Hc	d	Z
0	70 00.0	+60.0	180.0	68 00.0	+60.0	180.0	66 00.0	+60.0	180.0	64 00.0	+60.0	180.0	62 00.0	+60.0	180.0
1	71 00.0	60.0	180.0	69 00.0	60.0	180.0	67 00.0	60.0	180.0	65 00.0	60.0	180.0	63 00.0	60.0	180.0
2	72 00.0	60.0	180.0	70 00.0	60.0	180.0	68 00.0	60.0	180.0	66 00.0	60.0	180.0	64 00.0	60.0	180.0
3	73 00.0	60.0	180.0	71 00.0	60.0	180.0	69 00.0	60.0	180.0	67 00.0	60.0	180.0	65 00.0	60.0	180.0
4	74 00.0	60.0	180.0	72 00.0	60.0	180.0	70 00.0	60.0	180.0	68 00.0	60.0	180.0	66 00.0	60.0	180.0
5	75 00.0	+60.0	180.0	73 00.0	+60.0	180.0	71 00.0	+60.0	180.0	69 00.0	+60.0	180.0	67 00.0	+60.0	180.0
6	76 00.0	60.0	180.0	74 00.0	60.0	180.0	72 00.0	60.0	180.0	70 00.0	60.0	180.0	68 00.0	60.0	180.0
7	77 00.0	60.0	180.0	75 00.0	60.0	180.0	73 00.0	60.0	180.0	71 00.0	60.0	180.0	69 00.0	60.0	180.0
8	78 00.0	60.0	180.0	76 00.0	60.0	180.0	74 00.0	60.0	180.0	72 00.0	60.0	180.0	70 00.0	60.0	180.0
9	79 00.0	60.0	180.0	77 00.0	60.0	180.0	75 00.0	60.0	180.0	73 00.0	60.0	180.0	71 00.0	60.0	180.0
10	80 00.0	+60.0	180.0	78 00.0	+60.0	180.0	76 00.0	+60.0	180.0	74 00.0	+60.0	180.0	72 00.0	60.0	180.0
11	81 00.0	60.0	180.0	79 00.0	60.0	180.0	77 00.0	60.0	180.0	75 00.0	60.0	180.0	73 00.0	60.0	180.0
12	82 00.0	60.0	180.0	80 00.0	60.0	180.0	78 00.0	60.0	180.0	76 00.0	60.0	180.0	74 00.0	60.0	180.0
13	83 00.0	60.0	180.0	81 00.0	60.0	180.0	79 00.0	60.0	180.0	77 00.0	60.0	180.0	75 00.0	60.0	180.0
14	84 00.0	60.0	180.0	82 00.0	60.0	180.0	80 00.0	60.0	180.0	78 00.0	60.0	180.0	76 00.0	60.0	180.0
15	85 00.0	+60.0	180.0	83 00.0	+60.0	180.0	81 00.0	+60.0	180.0	79 00.0	+60.0	180.0	77 00.0	+60.0	180.0
16	86 00.0	60.0	180.0	84 00.0	60.0	180.0	82 00.0	60.0	180.0	80 00.0	60.0	180.0	78 00.0	60.0	180.0
17	87 00.0	60.0	180.0	85 00.0	60.0	180.0	83 00.0	60.0	180.0	81 00.0	60.0	180.0	79 00.0	60.0	180.0
18	88 00.0	60.0	180.0	86 00.0	60.0	180.0	84 00.0	60.0	180.0	82 00.0	60.0	180.0	80 00.0	60.0	180.0
19	89 00.0	+60.0	180.0	87 00.0	60.0	180.0	85 00.0	60.0	180.0	83 00.0	60.0	180.0	81 00.0	60.0	180.0
20	90 00.0	-60.0	90.0	88 00.0	+60.0	180.0	86 00.0	+60.0	180.0	84 00.0	+60.0	180.0	82 00.0	+60.0	180.0
21	89 00.0	60.0	0.0	89 00.0	+60.0	180.0	87 00.0	60.0	180.0	85 00.0	60.0	180.0	83 00.0	60.0	180.0
22	88 00.0	60.0	0.0	90 00.0	-60.0	90.0	88 00.0	60.0	180.0	86 00.0	60.0	180.0	84 00.0	60.0	180.0
23	87 00.0	60.0	0.0	89 00.0	60.0	0.0	89 00.0	60.0	180.0	87 00.0	60.0	180.0	85 00.0	60.0	180.0
24	86 00.0	60.0	0.0	88 00.0	60.0	0.0	90 00.0	-60.0	90.0	88 00.0	60.0	180.0	86 00.0	60.0	180.0
25	85 00.0	-60.0	0.0	87 00.0	-60.0	0.0	89 00.0	-60.0	0.0	89 00.0	+60.0	180.0	87 00.0	+60.0	180.0
26	84 00.0	60.0	0.0	86 00.0	60.0	0.0	88 00.0	60.0	0.0	90 00.0	-60.0	90.0	88 00.0	60.0	180.0
27	83 00.0	60.0	0.0	85 00.0	60.0	0.0	87 00.0	60.0	0.0	89 00.0	60.0	0.0	89 00.0	+60.0	180.0
28	82 00.0	60.0	0.0	84 00.0	60.0	0.0	86 00.0	60.0	0.0	88 00.0	60.0	0.0	90 00.0	-60.0	90.0
29	81 00.0	60.0	0.0	83 00.0	60.0	0.0	85 00.0	60.0	0.0	87 00.0	60.0	0.0	89 00.0	60.0	0.0

Dec.	30° Hc	d	Z	32° Hc	d	Z	34° Hc	d	Z	36° Hc	d	Z	38° Hc	d	Z
0	60 00.0	+60.0	180.0	58 00.0	+60.0	180.0	56 00.0	+60.0	180.0	54 00.0	+60.0	180.0	52 00.0	+60.0	180.0
1	61 00.0	60.0	180.0	59 00.0	60.0	180.0	57 00.0	60.0	180.0	55 00.0	60.0	180.0	53 00.0	60.0	180.0
2	62 00.0	60.0	180.0	60 00.0	60.0	180.0	58 00.0	60.0	180.0	56 00.0	60.0	180.0	54 00.0	60.0	180.0
3	63 00.0	60.0	180.0	61 00.0	60.0	180.0	59 00.0	60.0	180.0	57 00.0	60.0	180.0	55 00.0	60.0	180.0
4	64 00.0	60.0	180.0	62 00.0	60.0	180.0	60 00.0	60.0	180.0	58 00.0	60.0	180.0	56 00.0	60.0	180.0
5	65 00.0	+60.0	180.0	63 00.0	+60.0	180.0	61 00.0	+60.0	180.0	59 00.0	+60.0	180.0	57 00.0	+60.0	180.0
6	66 00.0	60.0	180.0	64 00.0	60.0	180.0	62 00.0	60.0	180.0	60 00.0	60.0	180.0	58 00.0	60.0	180.0
7	67 00.0	60.0	180.0	65 00.0	60.0	180.0	63 00.0	60.0	180.0	61 00.0	60.0	180.0	59 00.0	60.0	180.0
8	68 00.0	60.0	180.0	66 00.0	60.0	180.0	64 00.0	60.0	180.0	62 00.0	60.0	180.0	60 00.0	60.0	180.0
9	69 00.0	60.0	180.0	67 00.0	60.0	180.0	65 00.0	60.0	180.0	63 00.0	60.0	180.0	61 00.0	60.0	180.0
10	70 00.0	+60.0	180.0	68 00.0	+60.0	180.0	66 00.0	+60.0	180.0	64 00.0	+60.0	180.0	62 00.0	+60.0	180.0
11	71 00.0	60.0	180.0	69 00.0	60.0	180.0	67 00.0	60.0	180.0	65 00.0	60.0	180.0	63 00.0	60.0	180.0
12	72 00.0	60.0	180.0	70 00.0	60.0	180.0	68 00.0	60.0	180.0	66 00.0	60.0	180.0	64 00.0	60.0	180.0
13	73 00.0	60.0	180.0	71 00.0	60.0	180.0	69 00.0	60.0	180.0	67 00.0	60.0	180.0	65 00.0	60.0	180.0
14	74 00.0	60.0	180.0	72 00.0	60.0	180.0	70 00.0	60.0	180.0	68 00.0	60.0	180.0	66 00.0	60.0	180.0
15	75 00.0	+60.0	180.0	73 00.0	+60.0	180.0	71 00.0	+60.0	180.0	69 00.0	+60.0	180.0	67 00.0	+60.0	180.0
16	76 00.0	60.0	180.0	74 00.0	60.0	180.0	72 00.0	60.0	180.0	70 00.0	60.0	180.0	68 00.0	60.0	180.0
17	77 00.0	60.0	180.0	75 00.0	60.0	180.0	73 00.0	60.0	180.0	71 00.0	60.0	180.0	69 00.0	60.0	180.0
18	78 00.0	60.0	180.0	76 00.0	60.0	180.0	74 00.0	60.0	180.0	72 00.0	60.0	180.0	70 00.0	60.0	180.0
19	79 00.0	60.0	180.0	77 00.0	60.0	180.0	75 00.0	60.0	180.0	73 00.0	60.0	180.0	71 00.0	60.0	180.0
20	80 00.0	+60.0	180.0	78 00.0	+60.0	180.0	76 00.0	+60.0	180.0	74 00.0	+60.0	180.0	72 00.0	+60.0	180.0
21	81 00.0	60.0	180.0	79 00.0	60.0	180.0	77 00.0	60.0	180.0	75 00.0	60.0	180.0	73 00.0	60.0	180.0
22	82 00.0	60.0	180.0	80 00.0	60.0	180.0	78 00.0	60.0	180.0	76 00.0	60.0	180.0	74 00.0	60.0	180.0
23	83 00.0	60.0	180.0	81 00.0	60.0	180.0	79 00.0	60.0	180.0	77 00.0	60.0	180.0	75 00.0	60.0	180.0
24	84 00.0	60.0	180.0	82 00.0	60.0	180.0	80 00.0	60.0	180.0	78 00.0	60.0	180.0	76 00.0	60.0	180.0
25	85 00.0	+60.0	180.0	83 00.0	+60.0	180.0	81 00.0	+60.0	180.0	79 00.0	+60.0	180.0	77 00.0	+60.0	180.0
26	86 00.0	60.0	180.0	84 00.0	60.0	180.0	82 00.0	60.0	180.0	80 00.0	60.0	180.0	78 00.0	60.0	180.0
27	87 00.0	60.0	180.0	85 00.0	60.0	180.0	83 00.0	60.0	180.0	81 00.0	60.0	180.0	79 00.0	60.0	180.0
28	88 00.0	60.0	180.0	86 00.0	60.0	180.0	84 00.0	60.0	180.0	82 00.0	60.0	180.0	80 00.0	60.0	180.0
29	89 00.0	+60.0	180.0	87 00.0	60.0	180.0	85 00.0	60.0	180.0	83 00.0	60.0	180.0	81 00.0	60.0	180.0

20°			22°			24°			26°			28°			
Hc	d	Z	Hc	d	Z	Hc	d	Z	Hc	d	Z	Hc	d	Z	**Dec.**
° ′	′	°	° ′	′	°	° ′	′	°	° ′	′	°	° ′	′	°	°
70 00.0	−60.0	180.0	68 00.0	−60.0	180.0	66 00.0	−60.0	180.0	64 00.0	−60.0	180.0	62 00.0	−60.0	180.0	0
69 00.0	60.0	180.0	67 00.0	60.0	180.0	65 00.0	60.0	180.0	63 00.0	60.0	180.0	61 00.0	60.0	180.0	1
68 00.0	60.0	180.0	66 00.0	60.0	180.0	64 00.0	60.0	180.0	62 00.0	60.0	180.0	60 00.0	60.0	180.0	2
67 00.0	60.0	180.0	65 00.0	60.0	180.0	63 00.0	60.0	180.0	61 00.0	60.0	180.0	59 00.0	60.0	180.0	3
66 00.0	60.0	180.0	64 00.0	60.0	180.0	62 00.0	60.0	180.0	60 00.0	60.0	180.0	58 00.0	60.0	180.0	4
65 00.0	−60.0	180.0	63 00.0	−60.0	180.0	61 00.0	−60.0	180.0	59 00.0	−60.0	180.0	57 00.0	−60.0	180.0	5
64 00.0	60.0	180.0	62 00.0	60.0	180.0	60 00.0	60.0	180.0	58 00.0	60.0	180.0	56 00.0	60.0	180.0	6
63 00.0	60.0	180.0	61 00.0	60.0	180.0	59 00.0	60.0	180.0	57 00.0	60.0	180.0	55 00.0	60.0	180.0	7
62 00.0	60.0	180.0	60 00.0	60.0	180.0	58 00.0	60.0	180.0	56 00.0	60.0	180.0	54 00.0	60.0	180.0	8
61 00.0	60.0	180.0	59 00.0	60.0	180.0	57 00.0	60.0	180.0	55 00.0	60.0	180.0	53 00.0	60.0	180.0	9
60 00.0	−60.0	180.0	58 00.0	−60.0	180.0	56 00.0	−60.0	180.0	54 00.0	−60.0	180.0	52 00.0	−60.0	180.0	10
59 00.0	60.0	180.0	57 00.0	60.0	180.0	55 00.0	60.0	180.0	53 00.0	60.0	180.0	51 00.0	60.0	180.0	11
58 00.0	60.0	180.0	56 00.0	60.0	180.0	54 00.0	60.0	180.0	52 00.0	60.0	180.0	50 00.0	60.0	180.0	12
57 00.0	60.0	180.0	55 00.0	60.0	180.0	53 00.0	60.0	180.0	51 00.0	60.0	180.0	49 00.0	60.0	180.0	13
56 00.0	60.0	180.0	54 00.0	60.0	180.0	52 00.0	60.0	180.0	50 00.0	60.0	180.0	48 00.0	60.0	180.0	14
55 00.0	−60.0	180.0	53 00.0	−60.0	180.0	51 00.0	−60.0	180.0	49 00.0	−60.0	180.0	47 00.0	−60.0	180.0	15
54 00.0	60.0	180.0	52 00.0	60.0	180.0	50 00.0	60.0	180.0	48 00.0	60.0	180.0	46 00.0	60.0	180.0	16
53 00.0	60.0	180.0	51 00.0	60.0	180.0	49 00.0	60.0	180.0	47 00.0	60.0	180.0	45 00.0	60.0	180.0	17
52 00.0	60.0	180.0	50 00.0	60.0	180.0	48 00.0	60.0	180.0	46 00.0	60.0	180.0	44 00.0	60.0	180.0	18
51 00.0	60.0	180.0	49 00.0	60.0	180.0	47 00.0	60.0	180.0	45 00.0	60.0	180.0	43 00.0	60.0	180.0	19
50 00.0	−60.0	180.0	48 00.0	−60.0	180.0	46 00.0	−60.0	180.0	44 00.0	−60.0	180.0	42 00.0	−60.0	180.0	20
49 00.0	60.0	180.0	47 00.0	60.0	180.0	45 00.0	60.0	180.0	43 00.0	60.0	180.0	41 00.0	60.0	180.0	21
48 00.0	60.0	180.0	46 00.0	60.0	180.0	44 00.0	60.0	180.0	42 00.0	60.0	180.0	40 00.0	60.0	180.0	22
47 00.0	60.0	180.0	45 00.0	60.0	180.0	43 00.0	60.0	180.0	41 00.0	60.0	180.0	39 00.0	60.0	180.0	23
46 00.0	60.0	180.0	44 00.0	60.0	180.0	42 00.0	60.0	180.0	40 00.0	60.0	180.0	38 00.0	60.0	180.0	24
45 00.0	−60.0	180.0	43 00.0	−60.0	180.0	41 00.0	−60.0	180.0	39 00.0	−60.0	180.0	37 00.0	−60.0	180.0	25
44 00.0	60.0	180.0	42 00.0	60.0	180.0	40 00.0	60.0	180.0	38 00.0	60.0	180.0	36 00.0	60.0	180.0	26
43 00.0	60.0	180.0	41 00.0	60.0	180.0	39 00.0	60.0	180.0	37 00.0	60.0	180.0	35 00.0	60.0	180.0	27
42 00.0	60.0	180.0	40 00.0	60.0	180.0	38 00.0	60.0	180.0	36 00.0	60.0	180.0	34 00.0	60.0	180.0	28
41 00.0	60.0	180.0	39 00.0	60.0	180.0	37 00.0	60.0	180.0	35 00.0	60.0	180.0	33 00.0	60.0	180.0	29

30°			32°			34°			36°			38°			
Hc	d	Z	Hc	d	Z	Hc	d	Z	Hc	d	Z	Hc	d	Z	**Dec.**
° ′	′	°	° ′	′	°	° ′	′	°	° ′	′	°	° ′	′	°	°
60 00.0	−60.0	180.0	58 00.0	−60.0	180.0	56 00.0	−60.0	180.0	54 00.0	−60.0	180.0	52 00.0	−60.0	180.0	0
59 00.0	60.0	180.0	57 00.0	60.0	180.0	55 00.0	60.0	180.0	53 00.0	60.0	180.0	51 00.0	60.0	180.0	1
58 00.0	60.0	180.0	56 00.0	60.0	180.0	54 00.0	60.0	180.0	52 00.0	60.0	180.0	50 00.0	60.0	180.0	2
57 00.0	60.0	180.0	55 00.0	60.0	180.0	53 00.0	60.0	180.0	51 00.0	60.0	180.0	49 00.0	60.0	180.0	3
56 00.0	60.0	180.0	54 00.0	60.0	180.0	52 00.0	60.0	180.0	50 00.0	60.0	180.0	48 00.0	60.0	180.0	4
55 00.0	−60.0	180.0	53 00.0	−60.0	180.0	51 00.0	−60.0	180.0	49 00.0	−60.0	180.0	47 00.0	−60.0	180.0	5
54 00.0	60.0	180.0	52 00.0	60.0	180.0	50 00.0	60.0	180.0	48 00.0	60.0	180.0	46 00.0	60.0	180.0	6
53 00.0	60.0	180.0	51 00.0	60.0	180.0	49 00.0	60.0	180.0	47 00.0	60.0	180.0	45 00.0	60.0	180.0	7
52 00.0	60.0	180.0	50 00.0	60.0	180.0	48 00.0	60.0	180.0	46 00.0	60.0	180.0	44 00.0	60.0	180.0	8
51 00.0	60.0	180.0	49 00.0	60.0	180.0	47 00.0	60.0	180.0	45 00.0	60.0	180.0	43 00.0	60.0	180.0	9
50 00.0	−60.0	180.0	48 00.0	−60.0	180.0	46 00.0	−60.0	180.0	44 00.0	−60.0	180.0	42 00.0	−60.0	180.0	10
49 00.0	60.0	180.0	47 00.0	60.0	180.0	45 00.0	60.0	180.0	43 00.0	60.0	180.0	41 00.0	60.0	180.0	11
48 00.0	60.0	180.0	46 00.0	60.0	180.0	44 00.0	60.0	180.0	42 00.0	60.0	180.0	40 00.0	60.0	180.0	12
47 00.0	60.0	180.0	45 00.0	60.0	180.0	43 00.0	60.0	180.0	41 00.0	60.0	180.0	39 00.0	60.0	180.0	13
46 00.0	60.0	180.0	44 00.0	60.0	180.0	42 00.0	60.0	180.0	40 00.0	60.0	180.0	38 00.0	60.0	180.0	14
45 00.0	−60.0	180.0	43 00.0	−60.0	180.0	41 00.0	−60.0	180.0	39 00.0	−60.0	180.0	37 00.0	−60.0	180.0	15
44 00.0	60.0	180.0	42 00.0	60.0	180.0	40 00.0	60.0	180.0	38 00.0	60.0	180.0	36 00.0	60.0	180.0	16
43 00.0	60.0	180.0	41 00.0	60.0	180.0	39 00.0	60.0	180.0	37 00.0	60.0	180.0	35 00.0	60.0	180.0	17
42 00.0	60.0	180.0	40 00.0	60.0	180.0	38 00.0	60.0	180.0	36 00.0	60.0	180.0	34 00.0	60.0	180.0	18
41 00.0	60.0	180.0	39 00.0	60.0	180.0	37 00.0	60.0	180.0	35 00.0	60.0	180.0	33 00.0	60.0	180.0	19
40 00.0	−60.0	180.0	38 00.0	−60.0	180.0	36 00.0	−60.0	180.0	34 00.0	−60.0	180.0	32 00.0	−60.0	180.0	20
39 00.0	60.0	180.0	37 00.0	60.0	180.0	35 00.0	60.0	180.0	33 00.0	60.0	180.0	31 00.0	60.0	180.0	21
38 00.0	60.0	180.0	36 00.0	60.0	180.0	34 00.0	60.0	180.0	32 00.0	60.0	180.0	30 00.0	60.0	180.0	22
37 00.0	60.0	180.0	35 00.0	60.0	180.0	33 00.0	60.0	180.0	31 00.0	60.0	180.0	29 00.0	60.0	180.0	23
36 00.0	60.0	180.0	34 00.0	60.0	180.0	32 00.0	60.0	180.0	30 00.0	60.0	180.0	28 00.0	60.0	180.0	24
35 00.0	−60.0	180.0	33 00.0	−60.0	180.0	31 00.0	−60.0	180.0	29 00.0	−60.0	180.0	27 00.0	−60.0	180.0	25
34 00.0	60.0	180.0	32 00.0	60.0	180.0	30 00.0	60.0	180.0	28 00.0	60.0	180.0	26 00.0	60.0	180.0	26
33 00.0	60.0	180.0	31 00.0	60.0	180.0	29 00.0	60.0	180.0	27 00.0	60.0	180.0	25 00.0	60.0	180.0	27
32 00.0	60.0	180.0	30 00.0	60.0	180.0	28 00.0	60.0	180.0	26 00.0	60.0	180.0	24 00.0	60.0	180.0	28
31 00.0	60.0	180.0	29 00.0	60.0	180.0	27 00.0	60.0	180.0	25 00.0	60.0	180.0	23 00.0	60.0	180.0	29

	40°			42°			44°			46°			48°		
Dec.	Hc	d	Z	Hc	d	Z	Hc	d	Z	Hc	d	Z	Hc	d	Z
°	° ′	′	°	° ′	′	°	° ′	′	°	° ′	′	°	° ′	′	°
0	50 00.0	+ 60.0	180.0	48 00.0	+ 60.0	180.0	46 00.0	+ 60.0	180.0	44 00.0	+ 60.0	180.0	42 00.0	+ 60.0	180.0
1	51 00.0	60.0	180.0	49 00.0	60.0	180.0	47 00.0	60.0	180.0	45 00.0	60.0	180.0	43 00.0	60.0	180.0
2	52 00.0	60.0	180.0	50 00.0	60.0	180.0	48 00.0	50.0	180.0	46 00.0	60.0	180.0	44 00.0	60.0	180.0
3	53 00.0	60.0	180.0	51 00.0	60.0	180.0	49 00.0	60.0	180.0	47 00.0	60.0	180.0	45 00.0	60.0	180.0
4	54 00.0	60.0	180.0	52 00.0	60.0	180.0	50 00.0	60.0	180.0	48 00.0	60.0	180.0	46 00.0	60.0	180.0
5	55 00.0	+ 60.0	180.0	53 00.0	+ 60.0	180.0	51 00.0	+ 60.0	180.0	49 00.0	+ 60.0	180.0	47 00.0	+ 60.0	180.0
6	56 00.0	60.0	180.0	54 00.0	60.0	180.0	52 00.0	60.0	180.0	50 00.0	60.0	180.0	48 00.0	60.0	180.0
7	57 00.0	60.0	180.0	55 00.0	60.0	180.0	53 00.0	60.0	180.0	51 00.0	60.0	180.0	49 00.0	60.0	180.0
8	58 00.0	60.0	180.0	56 00.0	60.0	180.0	54 00.0	60.0	180.0	52 00.0	60.0	180.0	50 00.0	60.0	180.0
9	59 00.0	60.0	180.0	57 00.0	60.0	180.0	55 00.0	60.0	180.0	53 00.0˙	60.0	180.0	51 00.0	60.0	180.0
10	60 00.0	+ 60.0	180.0	58 00.0	+ 60.0	180.0	56 00.0	+ 60.0	180.0	54 00.0	+ 60.0	180.0	52 00.0	+ 60.0	180.0
11	61 00.0	60.0	180.0	59 00.0	60.0	180.0	57 00.0	60.0	180.0	55 00.0	60.0	180.0	53 00.0	60.0	180.0
12	62 00.0	60.0	180.0	60 00.0	60.0	180.0	58 00.0	60.0	180.0	56 00.0	60.0	180.0	54 00.0	60.0	180.0
13	63 00.0	60.0	180.0	61 00.0	60.0	180.0	59 00.0	60.0	180.0	57 00.0	60.0	180.0	55 00.0	60.0	180.0
14	64 00.0	60.0	180.0	62 00.0	60.0	180.0	60 00.0	60.0	180.0	58 00.0	60.0	180.0	56 00.0	60.0	180.0
15	65 00.0	+ 60.0	180.0	63 00.0	+ 60.0	180.0	61 00.0	+ 60.0	180.0	59 00.0	+ 60.0	180.0	57 00.0	+ 60.0	180.0
16	66 00.0	60.0	180.0	64 00.0	60.0	180.0	62 00.0	60.0	180.0	60 00.0	60.0	180.0	58 00.0	60.0	180.0
17	67 00.0	60.0	180.0	65 00.0	60.0	180.0	63 00.0	60.0	180.0	61 00.0	60.0	180.0	59 00.0	60.0	180.0
18	68 00.0	60.0	180.0	66 00.0	60.0	180.0	64 00.0	60.0	180.0	62 00.0	60.0	180.0	60 00.0	60.0	180.0
19	69 00.0	60.0	180.0	67 00.0	60.0	180.0	65 00.0	60.0	180.0	63 00.0	60.0	180.0	61 00.0	60.0	180.0
20	70 00.0	+ 60.0	180.0	68 00.0	+ 60.0	180.0	66 00.0	+ 60.0	180.0	64 00.0	+ 60.0	180.0	62 00.0	+ 60.0	180.0
21	71 00.0	60.0	180.0	69 00.0	60.0	180.0	67 00.0	60.0	180.0	65 00.0	60˙.0	180.0	63 00.0	60.0	180.0
22	72 00.0	60.0	180.0	70 00.0	60.0	180.0	68 00.0	60.0	180.0	66 00.0	60.0	180.0	64 00.0	60.0	180.0
23	73 00.0	60.0	180.0	71 00.0	60.0	180.0	69 00.0	60.0	180.0	67 00.0	60.0	180.0	65 00.0	60.0	180.0
24	74 00.0	60.0	180.0	72 00.0	60.0	180.0	70 00.0	60.0	180.0	68 00.0	60.0	180.0	66 00.0	60.0	180.0
25	75 00.0	+ 60.0	180.0	73 00.0	+ 60.0	180.0	71 00.0	+ 60.0	180.0	69 00.0	+ 60.0	180.0	67 00.0	+ 60.0	180.0
26	76 00.0	60.0	180.0	74 00.0	60.0	180.0	72 00.0	60.0	180.0	70 00.0	60.0	180.0	68 00.0	60.0	180.0
27	77 00.0	60.0	180.0	75 00.0	60.0	180.0	73 00.0	60.0	180.0	71 00.0	60.0	180.0	69 00.0	60.0	180.0
28	78 00.0	60.0	180.0	76 00.0	60.0	180.0	74 00.0	60.0	180.0	72 00.0	60.0	180.0	70 00.0	60.0	180.0
29	79 00.0	60.0	180.0	77 00.0	60.0	180.0	75 00.0	60.0	180.0	73 00.0	60.0	180.0	71 00.0	60.0	180.0

	50°			52°			54°			56°			58°		
Dec.	Hc	d	Z	Hc	d	Z	Hc	d	Z	Hc	d	Z	Hc	d	Z
°	° ′	′	°	° ′	′	°	° ′	′	°	° ′	′	°	° ′	′	°
0	40 00.0	+ 60.0	180.0	38 00.0	+ 60.0	180.0	36 00.0	+ 60.0	180.0	34 00.0	+ 60.0	180.0	32 00.0	+ 60.0	180.0
1	41 00.0	60.0	180.0	39 00.0	60.0	180.0	37 00.0	60.0	180.0	35 00.0	60.0	180.0	33 00.0	60.0	180.0
2	42 00.0	60.0	180.0	40 00.0	60.0	180.0	38 00.0	60.0	180.0	36 00.0	60.0	180.0	34 00.0	60.0	180.0
3	43 00.0	60.0	180.0	41 00.0	60.0	180.0	39 00.0	60.0	180.0	37 00.0	60.0	180.0	35 00.0	60.0	180.0
4	44 00.0	60.0	180.0	42 00.0	60.0	180.0	40 00.0	60.0	180.0	38 00.0	60.0	180.0	36 00.0	60.0	180.0
5	45 00.0	+ 60.0	180.0	43 00.0	+ 60.0	180.0	41 00.0	+ 60.0	180.0	39 00.0	+ 60.0	180.0	37 00.0	+ 60.0	180.0
6	46 00.0	60.0	180.0	44 00.0	60.0	180.0	42 00.0	60.0	180.0	40 00.0	60.0	180.0	38 00.0	60.0	180.0
7	47 00.0	60.0	180.0	45 00.0	60.0	180.0	43 00.0	60.0	180.0	41 00.0	60.0	180.0	39 00.0	60.0	180.0
8	48 00.0	60.0	180.0	46 00.0	60.0	180.0	44 00.0	60.0	180.0	42 00.0	60.0	180.0	40 00.0	60.0	180.0
9	49 00.0	60.0	180.0	47 00.0	60.0	180.0	45 00.0	60.0	180.0	43 00.0	60.0	180.0	41 00.0	60.0	180.0
10	50 00.0	+ 60.0	180.0	48 00.0	+ 60.0	180.0	46 00.0	+ 60.0	180.0	44 00.0	+ 60.0	180.0	42 00.0	+ 60.0	180.0
11	51 00.0	60.0	180.0	49 00.0	60.0	180.0	47 00.0	60.0	180.0	45 00.0	60.0	180.0	43 00.0	60.0	180.0
12	52 00.0	60.0	180.0	50 00.0	60.0	180.0	48 00.0	60.0	180.0	46 00.0	60.0	180.0	44 00.0	60.0	180.0
13	53 00.0	60.0	180.0	51 00.0	60.0	180.0	49 00.0	60.0	180.0	47 00.0	60.0	180.0	45 00.0	60.0	180.0
14	54 00.0	60.0	180.0	52 00.0	60.0	180.0	50 00.0	60.0	180.0	48 00.0	60.0	180.0	46 00.0	60.0	180.0
15	55 00.0	+ 60.0	180.0	53 00.0	+ 60.0	180.0	51 00.0	+ 60.0	180.0	49 00.0	+ 60.0	180.0	47 00.0	+ 60.0	180.0
16	56 00.0	60.0	180.0	54 00.0	60.0	180.0	52 00.0	60.0	180.0	50 00.0	60.0	180.0	48 00.0	60.0	180.0
17	57 00.0	60.0	180.0	55 00.0	60.0	180.0	53 00.0	60.0	180.0	51 00.0	60.0	180.0	49 00.0	60.0	180.0
18	58 00.0	60.0	180.0	56 00.0	60.0	180.0	54 00.0	60.0	180.0	52 00.0	60.0	180.0	50 00.0	60.0	180.0
19	59 00.0	60.0	180.0	57 00.0	60.0	180.0	55 00.0	60.0	180.0	53 00.0	60.0	180.0	51 00.0	60.0	180.0
20	60 00.0	+ 60.0	180.0	58 00.0	+ 60.0	180.0	56 00.0	+ 60.0	180.0	54 00.0	+ 60.0	180.0	52 00.0	+ 60.0	180.0
21	61 00.0	60.0	180.0	59 00.0	60.0	180.0	57 00.0	60.0	180.0	55 00.0	60.0	180.0	53 00.0	60.0	180.0
22	62 00.0	60.0	180.0	60 00.0	60.0	180.0	58 00.0	60.0	180.0	56 00.0	60.0	180.0	54 00.0	60.0	180.0
23	63 00.0	60.0	180.0	61 00.0	60.0	180.0	59 00.0	60.0	180.0	57 00.0	60.0	180.0	55 00.0	60.0	180.0
24	64 00.0	60.0	180.0	62 00.0	60.0	180.0	60 00.0	60.0	180.0	58 00.0	60.0	180.0	56 00.0	60.0	180.0
25	65 00.0	+ 60.0	180.0	63 00.0	+ 60.0	180.0	61 00.0	+ 60.0	180.0	59 00.0	+ 60.0	180.0	57 00.0	+ 60.0	180.0
26	66 00.0	60.0	180.0	64 00.0	60.0	180.0	62 00.0	60.0	180.0	60 00.0	60.0	180.0	58 00.0	60.0	180.0
27	67 00.0	60.0	180.0	65 00.0	60.0	180.0	63 00.0	60.0	180.0	61 00.0	60.0	180.0	59 00.0	60.0	180.0
28	68 00.0	60.0	180.0	66 00.0	60.0	180.0	64 00.0	60.0	180.0	62 00.0	60.0	180.0	60 00.0	60.0	180.0
29	69 00.0	60.0	180.0	67 00.0	60.0	180.0	65 00.0	60.0	180.0	63 00.0	60.0	180.0	61 00.0	60.0	180.0

LATITUDE **CONTRARY** NAME L.H.A. 0°, 360°

40°			42°			44°			46°			48°			Dec.
Hc	d	Z	Hc	d	Z	Hc	d	Z	Hc	d	Z	Hc	d	Z	
° ′	′	°	° ′	′	°	° ′	′	°	° ′	′	°	° ′	′	°	°
50 00.0	– 60.0	180.0	48 00.0	– 60.0	180.0	46 00.0	– 60.0	180.0	44 00.0	– 60.0	180.0	42 00.0	– 60.0	180.0	0
49 00.0	60.0	180.0	47 00.0	60.0	180.0	45 00.0	60.0	180.0	43 00.0	60.0	180.0	41 00.0	60.0	180.0	1
48 00.0	60.0	180.0	46 00.0	60.0	180.0	44 00.0	60.0	180.0	42 00.0	60.0	180.0	40 00.0	60.0	180.0	2
47 00.0	60.0	180.0	45 00.0	60.0	180.0	43 00.0	60.0	180.0	41 00.0	60.0	180.0	39 00.0	60.0	180.0	3
46 00.0	60.0	180.0	44 00.0	60.0	180.0	42 00.0	60.0	180.0	40 00.0	60.0	180.0	38 00.0	60.0	180.0	4
45 00.0	– 60.0	180.0	43 00.0	– 60.0	180.0	41 00.0	– 60.0	180.0	39 00.0	– 60.0	180.0	37 00.0	– 60.0	180.0	5
44 00.0	60.0	180.0	42 00.0	60.0	180.0	40 00.0	60.0	180.0	38 00.0	60.0	180.0	36 00.0	60.0	180.0	6
43 00.0	60.0	180.0	41 00.0	60.0	180.0	39 00.0	60.0	180.0	37 00.0	60.0	180.0	35 00.0	60.0	180.0	7
42 00.0	60.0	180.0	40 00.0	60.0	180.0	38 00.0	60.0	180.0	36 00.0	60.0	180.0	34 00.0	60.0	180.0	8
41 00.0	60.0	180.0	39 00.0	60.0	180.0	37 00.0	60.0	180.0	35 00.0	60.0	180.0	33 00.0	60.0	180.0	9
40 00.0	– 60.0	180.0	38 00.0	– 60.0	180.0	36 00.0	– 60.0	180.0	34 00.0	– 60.0	180.0	32 00.0	– 60.0	180.0	10
39 00.0	60.0	180.0	37 00.0	60.0	180.0	35 00.0	60.0	180.0	33 00.0	60.0	180.0	31 00.0	60.0	180.0	11
38 00.0	60.0	180.0	36 00.0	60.0	180.0	34 00.0	60.0	180.0	32 00.0	60.0	180.0	30 00.0	60.0	180.0	12
37 00.0	60.0	180.0	35 00.0	60.0	180.0	33 00.0	60.0	180.0	31 00.0	60.0	180.0	29 00.0	60.0	180.0	13
36 00.0	60.0	180.0	34 00.0	60.0	180.0	32 00.0	60.0	180.0	30 00.0	60.0	180.0	28 00.0	60.0	180.0	14
35 00.0	– 60.0	180.0	33 00.0	– 60.0	180.0	31 00.0	– 60.0	180.0	29 00.0	– 60.0	180.0	27 00.0	– 60.0	180.0	15
34 00.0	60.0	180.0	32 00.0	60.0	180.0	30 00.0	60.0	180.0	28 00.0	60.0	180.0	26 00.0	60.0	180.0	16
33 00.0	60.0	180.0	31 00.0	60.0	180.0	29 00.0	60.0	180.0	27 00.0	60.0	180.0	25 00.0	60.0	180.0	17
32 00.0	60.0	180.0	30 00.0	60.0	180.0	28 00.0	60.0	180.0	26 00.0	60.0	180.0	24 00.0	60.0	180.0	18
31 00.0	60.0	180.0	29 00.0	60.0	180.0	27 00.0	60.0	180.0	25 00.0	60.0	180.0	23 00.0	60.0	180.0	19
30 00.0	– 60.0	180.0	28 00.0	– 60.0	180.0	26 00.0	– 60.0	180.0	24 00.0	– 60.0	180.0	22 00.0	– 60.0	180.0	20
29 00.0	60.0	180.0	27 00.0	60.0	180.0	25 00.0	60.0	180.0	23 00.0	60.0	180.0	21 00.0	60.0	180.0	21
28 00.0	60.0	180.0	26 00.0	60.0	180.0	24 00.0	60.0	180.0	22 00.0	60.0	180.0	20 00.0	60.0	180.0	22
27 00.0	60.0	180.0	25 00.0	60.0	180.0	23 00.0	60.0	180.0	21 00.0	60.0	180.0	19 00.0	60.0	180.0	23
26 00.0	60.0	180.0	24 00.0	60.0	180.0	22 00.0	60.0	180.0	20 00.0	60.0	180.0	18 00.0	60.0	180.0	24
25 00.0	– 60.0	180.0	23 00.0	– 60.0	180.0	21 00.0	– 60.0	180.0	19 00.0	– 60.0	180.0	17 00.0	– 60.0	180.0	25
24 00.0	60.0	180.0	22 00.0	60.0	180.0	20 00.0	60.0	180.0	18 00.0	60.0	180.0	16 00.0	60.0	180.0	26
23 00.0	60.0	180.0	21 00.0	60.0	180.0	19 00.0	60.0	180.0	17 00.0	60.0	180.0	15 00.0	60.0	180.0	27
22 00.0	60.0	180.0	20 00.0	60.0	180.0	18 00.0	60.0	180.0	16 00.0	60.0	180.0	14 00.0	60.0	180.0	28
21 00.0	60.0	180.0	19 00.0	60.0	180.0	17 00.0	60.0	180.0	15 00.0	60.0	180.0	13 00.0	60.0	180.0	29

50°			52°			54°			56°			58°			Dec.
Hc	d	Z	Hc	d	Z	Hc	d	Z	Hc	d	Z	Hc	d	Z	
° ′	′	°	° ′	′	°	° ′	′	°	° ′	′	°	° ′	′	°	°
40 00.0	– 60.0	180.0	38 00.0	– 60.0	180.0	36 00.0	– 60.0	180.0	34 00.0	– 60.0	180.0	32 00.0	– 60.0	180.0	0
39 00.0	60.0	180.0	37 00.0	60.0	180.0	35 00.0	60.0	180.0	33 00.0	60.0	180.0	31 00.0	60.0	180.0	1
38 00.0	60.0	180.0	36 00.0	60.0	180.0	34 00.0	60.0	180.0	32 00.0	60.0	180.0	30 00.0	60.0	180.0	2
37 00.0	60.0	180.0	35 00.0	60.0	180.0	33 00.0	60.0	180.0	31 00.0	60.0	180.0	29 00.0	60.0	180.0	3
36 00.0	60.0	180.0	34 00.0	60.0	180.0	32 00.0	60.0	180.0	30 00.0	60.0	180.0	28 00.0	60.0	180.0	4
35 00.0	– 60.0	180.0	33 00.0	– 60.0	180.0	31 00.0	– 60.0	180.0	29 00.0	– 60.0	180.0	27 00.0	– 60.0	180.0	5
34 00.0	60.0	180.0	32 00.0	60.0	180.0	30 00.0	60.0	180.0	28 00.0	60.0	180.0	26 00.0	60.0	180.0	6
33 00.0	60.0	180.0	31 00.0	60.0	180.0	29 00.0	60.0	180.0	27 00.0	60.0	180.0	25 00.0	60.0	180.0	7
32 00.0	60.0	180.0	30 00.0	60.0	180.0	28 00.0	60.0	180.0	26 00.0	60.0	180.0	24 00.0	60.0	180.0	8
31 00.0	60.0	180.0	29 00.0	60.0	180.0	27 00.0	60.0	180.0	25 00.0	60.0	180.0	23 00.0	60.0	180.0	9
30 00.0	– 60.0	180.0	28 00.0	– 60.0	180.0	26 00.0	– 60.0	180.0	24 00.0	– 60.0	180.0	22 00.0	– 60.0	180.0	10
29 00.0	60.0	180.0	27 00.0	60.0	180.0	25 00.0	60.0	180.0	23 00.0	60.0	180.0	21 00.0	60.0	180.0	11
28 00.0	60.0	180.0	26 00.0	60.0	180.0	24 00.0	60.0	180.0	22 00.0	60.0	180.0	20 00.0	60.0	180.0	12
27 00.0	60.0	180.0	25 00.0	60.0	180.0	23 00.0	60.0	180.0	21 00.0	60.0	180.0	19 00.0	60.0	180.0	13
26 00.0	60.0	180.0	24 00.0	60.0	180.0	22 00.0	60.0	180.0	20 00.0	60.0	180.0	18 00.0	60.0	180.0	14
25 00.0	– 60.0	180.0	23 00.0	– 60.0	180.0	21 00.0	– 60.0	180.0	19 00.0	– 60.0	180.0	17 00.0	– 60.0	180.0	15
24 00.0	60.0	180.0	22 00.0	60.0	180.0	20 00.0	60.0	180.0	18 00.0	60.0	180.0	16 00.0	60.0	180.0	16
23 00.0	60.0	180.0	21 00.0	60.0	180.0	19 00.0	60.0	180.0	17 00.0	60.0	180.0	15 00.0	60.0	180.0	17
22 00.0	60.0	180.0	20 00.0	60.0	180.0	18 00.0	60.0	180.0	16 00.0	60.0	180.0	14 00.0	60.0	180.0	18
21 00.0	60.0	180.0	19 00.0	60.0	180.0	17 00.0	60.0	180.0	15 00.0	60.0	180.0	13 00.0	60.0	180.0	19
20 00.0	– 60.0	180.0	18 00.0	– 60.0	180.0	16 00.0	– 60.0	180.0	14 00.0	– 60.0	180.0	12 00.0	– 60.0	180.0	20
19 00.0	60.0	180.0	17 00.0	60.0	180.0	15 00.0	60.0	180.0	13 00.0	60.0	180.0	11 00.0	60.0	180.0	21
18 00.0	60.0	180.0	16 00.0	60.0	180.0	14 00.0	60.0	180.0	12 00.0	60.0	180.0	10 00.0	60.0	180.0	22
17 00.0	60.0	180.0	15 00.0	60.0	180.0	13 00.0	60.0	180.0	11 00.0	60.0	180.0	9 00.0	60.0	180.0	23
16 00.0	60.0	180.0	14 00.0	60.0	180.0	12 00.0	60.0	180.0	10 00.0	60.0	180.0	8 00.0	60.0	180.0	24
15 00.0	– 60.0	180.0	13 00.0	– 60.0	180.0	11 00.0	– 60.0	180.0	9 00.0	– 60.0	180.0	7 00.0	– 60.0	180.0	25
14 00.0	60.0	180.0	12 00.0	60.0	180.0	10 00.0	60.0	180.0	8 00.0	60.0	180.0	6 00.0	60.0	180.0	26
13 00.0	60.0	180.0	11 00.0	60.0	180.0	9 00.0	60.0	180.0	7 00.0	60.0	180.0	5 00.0	60.0	180.0	27
12 00.0	60.0	180.0	10 00.0	60.0	180.0	8 00.0	60.0	180.0	6 00.0	60.0	180.0	4 00.0	60.0	180.0	28
11 00.0	60.0	180.0	9 00.0	60.0	180.0	7 00.0	60.0	180.0	5 00.0	60.0	180.0	3 00.0	60.0	180.0	29

2°, 358° L.H.A. LATITUDE **SAME** NAME

Dec.	0° Hc	d	Z	2° Hc	d	Z	4° Hc	d	Z	6° Hc	d	Z	8° Hc	d	Z
0	88 00.0	−14.2·	90.0	87 10.3	+35.6·	135.0	85 31.7	+52.0·	153.4	83 40.6	+56.4	161.5	81 45.3	+58.0	165.9
1	87 45.8	35.5·	63.4	87 45.9	+14.2·	116.5	86 23.7	+46.7·	146.3	84 37.0	+54.8·	158.2	82 43.3	+57.4	164.0
2	87 10.3	46.6·	45.0	88 00.1	−14.2·	90.0	87 10.4	+35.6·	135.0	85 31.8	+52.1·	153.4	83 40.7	+56.4	161.5
3	86 23.7	52.0·	33.7	87 45.9	35.5·	63.4	87 46.0	+14.3·	116.5	86 23.9	+46.7·	146.3	84 37.1	+54.9·	158.2
4	85 31.7	54.8·	26.5	87 10.4	46.6·	44.9	88 00.3	−14.1·	89.9	87 10.6	+35.7·	135.0	85 32.0	+52.1·	153.4
5	84 36.9	−56.3	21.7	86 23.8	−52.0·	33.6	87 46.2	−35.6·	63.3	87 46.3	+14.4·	116.6	86 24.1	+46.8·	146.4
6	83 40.6	57.3	18.4	85 31.8	54.8·	26.4	87 10.6	46.6·	44.8	88 00.7	−14.2·	89.9	87 10.9	+35.9·	135.1
7	82 43.3	58.0	15.9	84 37.0	56.3	21.7	86 24.0	52.0·	33.5	87 46.5	35.6·	63.2	87 46.8	+14.4·	116.6
8	81 45.3	58.4	13.9	83 40.7	57.3	18.3	85 32.0	54.8·	26.3	87 10.9	46.7·	44.7	88 01.2	−14.2·	89.9
9	80 46.9	58.7	12.4	82 43.4	58.0	15.8	84 37.2	56.4	21.6	86 24.2	52.0·	33.3	87 47.0	35.7·	63.0
10	79 48.2	−58.9	11.2	81 45.4	−58.4	13.9	83 40.8	−57.3	18.2	85 32.2	−54.8·	26.2	87 11.3	−46.7·	44.5
11	78 49.3	59.1	10.2	80 47.0	58.7	12.4	82 43.5	58.0	15.7	84 37.4	56.4	21.4	86 24.6	52.1·	33.2
12	77 50.2	59.2	9.3	79 48.3	58.9	11.1	81 45.5	58.4	13.8	83 41.0	57.3	18.1	85 32.5	54.9·	26.0
13	76 51.0	59.4	8.6	78 49.4	59.1	10.1	80 47.1	58.7	12.3	82 43.7	58.0	15.6	84 37.6	56.4	21.3
14	75 51.6	59.4	8.0	77 50.3	59.2	9.2	79 48.4	58.9	11.0	81 45.7	58.4	13.7	83 41.2	57.3	17.9
15	74 52.2	−59.5	7.4	76 51.1	−59.4	8.5	78 49.5	−59.1	10.0	80 47.3	−58.7	12.2	82 43.9	−58.0	15.5
16	73 52.7	59.5	6.9	75 51.7	59.4	7.9	77 50.4	59.2	9.2	79 48.6	59.0	10.9	81 45.9	58.4	13.5
17	72 53.2	59.6	6.5	74 52.3	59.5	7.3	76 51.2	59.4	8.4	78 49.6	59.1	9.9	80 47.5	58.8	12.0
18	71 53.6	59.6	6.1	73 52.8	59.5	6.9	75 51.8	59.4	7.8	77 50.5	59.2	9.1	79 48.7	58.9	10.8
19	70 53.9	59.6	5.8	72 53.3	59.6	6.4	74 52.4	59.5	7.3	76 51.3	59.4	8.3	78 49.8	59.1	9.8
20	69 54.3	−59.7	5.5	71 53.7	−59.7	6.1	73 52.9	−59.5	6.8	75 51.9	−59.4	7.7	77 50.7	−59.3	9.0
21	68 54.6	59.8	5.2	70 54.0	59.7	5.7	72 53.4	59.7	6.4	74 52.5	59.5	7.2	76 51.4	59.3	8.2
22	67 54.8	59.7	4.9	69 54.3	59.7	5.4	71 53.7	59.6	6.0	73 53.0	59.5	6.7	75 52.1	59.4	7.6
23	66 55.1	59.8	4.7	68 54.6	59.7	5.1	70 54.1	59.7	5.6	72 53.5	59.6	6.3	74 52.7	59.5	7.1
24	65 55.3	59.8	4.5	67 54.9	59.7	4.9	69 54.4	59.7	5.3	71 53.9	59.7	5.9	73 53.2	59.6	6.6
25	64 55.5	−59.8	4.3	66 55.2	−59.8	4.6	68 54.7	−59.7	5.0	70 54.2	−59.7	5.5	72 53.6	−59.6	6.2
26	63 55.7	59.8	4.1	65 55.4	59.8	4.4	67 55.0	59.8	4.8	69 54.5	59.7	5.2	71 54.0	59.7	5.8
27	62 55.9	59.8	3.9	64 55.6	59.8	4.2	66 55.2	59.7	4.5	68 54.8	59.7	5.0	70 54.3	59.6	5.5
28	61 56.1	59.9	3.8	63 55.8	59.8	4.0	65 55.5	59.8	4.3	67 55.1	59.8	4.7	69 54.7	59.8	5.1
29	60 56.2	59.4	3.6	62 56.0	59.9	3.8	64 55.7	59.8	4.1	66 55.3	59.7	4.5	68 54.9	59.7	4.9

Dec.	10° Hc	d	Z	12° Hc	d	Z	14° Hc	d	Z	16° Hc	d	Z	18° Hc	d	Z
0	79 48.2	+58.8	168.6	77 50.2	+59.2	170.5	75 51.6	+59.4	171.8	73 52.7	+59.6	172.8	71 53.6	+59.6	173.6
1	80 47.0	58.4	167.4	78 49.4	58.9	169.6	76 51.0	59.3	171.2	74 52.3	59.4	172.3	72 53.2	59.6	173.2
2	81 45.4	58.0	165.9	79 48.3	58.8	168.6	77 50.3	59.1	170.5	75 51.7	59.4	171.8	73 52.8	59.5	172.8
3	82 43.4	57.4	164.0	80 47.1	58.4	167.0	78 49.4	59.0	169.6	76 51.1	59.3	171.2	74 52.3	59.5	172.3
4	83 40.8	56.5	161.6	81 45.5	58.1	165.9	79 48.4	58.8	168.7	77 50.4	59.1	170.5	75 51.8	59.4	171.8
5	84 37.3	+54.9·	158.2	82 43.6	+57.4	164.1	80 47.2	+58.5	167.5	78 49.6	+59.0	169.7	76 51.2	+59.3	171.2
6	85 32.2	52.2·	153.5	83 41.0	56.5	161.6	81 45.7	58.1	166.0	79 48.6	58.8	168.7	77 50.5	59.2	170.5
7	86 24.4	46.9·	146.4	84 37.5	55.0·	158.3	82 43.8	57.4	164.1	80 47.4	58.5	167.5	78 49.7	59.0	169.7
8	87 11.3	36.0·	135.2	85 32.5	52.3·	153.6	83 41.2	56.6	161.7	81 45.9	58.1	166.0	79 48.7	58.9	168.7
9	87 47.3	+14.5·	116.7	86 24.8	47.1·	146.6	84 37.8	55.0·	158.4	82 44.0	57.5	164.2	80 47.6	58.5	167.6
10	88 01.8	−14.2·	89.8	87 11.9	+36.1·	135.3	85 32.8	+52.4·	153.7	83 41.5	+56.6	161.8	81 46.1	+58.2	166.1
11	87 47.6	35.7·	62.9	87 48.0	+14.6·	116.6	86 25.2	47.3·	146.7	84 38.1	55.1·	158.5	82 44.3	57.5	164.3
12	87 11.9	46.9·	44.3	88 02.6	−14.2·	89.8	87 12.5	36.3·	135.5	85 33.3	52.5·	153.9	83 41.8	56.7	161.9
13	86 25.0	52.2·	33.0	87 48.4	35.9·	62.7	87 48.8	+14.8·	117.0	86 25.8	47.4·	146.9	84 38.5	55.2·	158.7
14	85 32.8	54.8·	25.9	87 12.5	47.0·	44.0	88 03.6	−14.2·	89.8	87 13.2	36.5·	135.7	85 33.7	52.7·	154.0
15	84 38.0	−56.5	21.1	86 25.5	−52.2·	32.7	87 49.0	−35.8·	62.4	87 49.7	+14.9·	117.2	86 26.4	+47.6·	147.1
16	83 41.5	57.4	17.8	85 33.3	55.0·	25.6	87 13.2	47.1·	43.8	88 04.6	−14.4·	89.7	87 14.0	36.8·	136.0
17	82 44.1	58.0	15.3	84 38.3	56.5	20.9	86 26.1	52.4·	32.5	87 50.2	36.2·	62.2	87 50.8	+15.1·	117.0
18	81 46.1	58.4	13.4	83 41.8	57.4	17.6	85 33.7	55.0·	25.4	87 14.0	47.3·	43.4	88 05.9	−14.5·	89.7
19	80 47.7	58.8	11.9	82 44.4	58.0	15.1	84 38.7	56.5	20.7	86 26.7	52.4·	32.2	87 51.4	36.5·	61.9
20	79 48.9	−58.9	10.7	81 46.4	−58.5	13.2	83 42.2	−57.5	17.4	85 34.3	−55.1·	25.1	87 14.9	−47.5·	43.1
21	78 50.0	59.1	9.7	80 47.9	58.7	11.8	82 44.7	58.1	15.0	84 39.2	56.6	20.5	86 27.4	52.6·	31.9
22	77 50.9	59.3	8.8	79 49.2	59.0	10.5	81 46.6	58.3	13.1	83 42.6	57.5	17.2	85 34.8	55.1·	24.8
23	76 51.6	59.4	8.1	78 50.2	59.1	9.6	80 48.2	58.8	11.6	82 45.1	58.1	14.7	84 39.7	56.7	20.2
24	75 52.2	59.4	7.5	77 51.1	59.3	8.7	79 49.4	59.0	10.4	81 47.0	58.5	12.7	83 43.0	57.6	16.9
25	74 52.8	−59.5	7.0	76 51.8	−59.4	8.0	78 50.4	−59.1	9.4	80 48.5	−58.8	11.4	82 45.4	−58.1	14.5
26	73 53.3	59.6	6.5	75 52.4	59.4	7.4	77 51.3	59.3	8.6	79 49.7	59.0	10.2	81 47.3	58.5	12.7
27	72 53.7	59.6	6.1	74 53.0	59.5	6.8	76 52.0	59.4	7.9	78 50.7	59.2	9.2	80 48.8	58.8	11.2
28	71 54.1	59.6	5.7	73 53.5	59.6	6.4	75 52.6	59.4	7.3	77 51.5	59.3	8.4	79 50.0	59.1	10.1
29	70 54.5	59.7	5.4	72 53.9	59.6	6.0	74 53.2	59.6	6.7	76 52.2	59.4	7.7	78 50.9	59.1	9.1

0°			2°			4°			6°			8°			Dec.
Hc	d	Z	Hc	d	Z	Hc	d	Z	Hc	d	Z	Hc	d	Z	
88 00.0	-14.2'	90.0	87 10.3	-46.6'	135.0	85 31.7	-54.8'	153.4	83 40.6	-57.4	161.5	81 45.3	-58.4	165.9	0
87 45.8	35.5'	116.6	86 23.7	52.0'	146.3	84 36.9	56.4	158.2	82 43.2	57.9	164.0	80 46.9	58.7	167.4	1
87 10.3	46.6'	135.0	85 31.7	54.8'	153.4	83 40.5	57.3	161.5	81 45.3	58.4	165.9	79 48.2	59.0	168.6	2
86 23.7	52.0'	146.3	84 36.9	56.4	158.2	82 43.2	57.9	164.0	80 46.9	58.7	167.4	78 49.2	59.1	169.6	3
85 31.7	54.8'	153.5	83 40.5	57.3	161.6	81 45.3	58.4	166.0	79 48.2	59.0	168.7	77 50.1	59.2	170.5	4
84 36.9	-56.3	158.3	82 43.2	-57.9	164.1	80 46.9	-58.7	167.5	78 49.2	-59.1	169.7	76 50.9	-59.2	171.2	5
83 40.6	57.3	161.6	81 45.3	58.4	166.0	79 48.2	59.0	168.7	77 50.1	59.2	170.5	75 51.5	59.4	171.8	6
82 43.3	58.0	164.1	80 46.9	58.7	167.5	78 49.2	59.1	169.7	76 50.9	59.4	171.2	74 52.1	59.5	172.4	7
81 45.3	58.4	166.1	79 48.2	58.9	168.7	77 50.1	59.2	170.6	75 51.5	59.4	171.9	73 52.6	59.6	172.9	8
80 46.9	58.7	167.6	78 49.3	59.1	169.8	76 50.9	59.4	171.3	74 52.1	59.5	172.4	72 53.0	59.6	173.3	9
79 48.2	-58.9	168.8	77 50.2	-59.3	170.6	75 51.5	-59.4	171.9	73 52.6	-59.6	172.9	71 53.4	-59.6	173.7	10
78 49.3	59.1	169.8	76 50.9	59.3	171.3	74 52.1	59.5	172.5	72 53.0	59.6	173.3	70 53.8	59.7	174.0	11
77 50.2	59.2	170.7	75 51.6	59.4	172.0	73 52.6	59.6	172.9	71 53.4	59.6	173.7	69 54.1	59.7	174.3	12
76 51.0	59.4	171.4	74 52.2	59.5	172.5	72 53.1	59.6	173.4	70 53.8	59.7	174.0	68 54.4	59.8	174.6	13
75 51.6	59.4	172.0	73 52.7	59.6	173.0	71 53.5	59.7	173.7	69 54.1	59.7	174.3	67 54.6	59.8	174.8	14
74 52.2	-59.5	172.6	72 53.1	-59.6	173.4	70 53.8	-59.7	174.1	68 54.4	-59.7	174.6	66 54.9	-59.8	175.1	15
73 52.7	59.5	173.1	71 53.5	59.6	173.8	69 54.1	59.7	174.4	67 54.7	59.8	174.9	65 55.1	59.8	175.3	16
72 53.2	59.6	173.5	70 53.9	59.7	174.1	68 54.4	59.7	174.7	66 54.9	59.8	175.1	64 55.3	59.8	175.5	17
71 53.6	59.7	173.9	69 54.2	59.7	174.5	67 54.7	59.8	174.9	65 55.1	59.8	175.3	63 55.5	59.8	175.7	18
70 53.9	59.6	174.2	68 54.5	59.7	174.7	66 55.0	59.8	175.2	64 55.3	59.8	175.5	62 55.7	59.8	175.8	19
69 54.3	-59.7	174.5	67 54.8	-59.8	175.0	65 55.2	-59.8	175.4	63 55.5	-59.8	175.7	61 55.9	-59.9	176.0	20
68 54.6	59.8	174.8	66 55.0	59.8	175.2	64 55.4	59.8	175.6	62 55.7	59.8	175.9	60 56.0	59.8	176.2	21
67 54.8	59.7	175.1	65 55.2	59.8	175.5	63 55.6	59.8	175.8	61 55.9	59.9	176.1	59 56.2	59.8	176.3	22
66 55.1	59.8	175.3	64 55.4	59.8	175.7	62 55.8	59.9	176.0	60 56.0	59.8	176.2	58 56.3	59.8	176.4	23
65 55.3	59.8	175.6	63 55.6	59.8	175.8	61 55.9	59.8	176.1	59 56.2	59.9	176.4	57 56.4	59.8	176.5	24
64 55.5	-59.8	175.7	62 55.8	-59.8	176.0	60 56.1	-59.9	176.3	58 56.3	-59.8	176.5	56 56.6	-59.9	176.7	25
63 55.7	59.8	175.9	61 56.0	59.8	176.2	59 56.2	59.9	176.4	57 56.5	59.9	176.6	55 56.7	59.9	176.8	26
62 55.9	59.8	176.1	60 56.2	59.9	176.3	58 56.4	59.9	176.5	56 56.6	59.9	176.7	54 56.8	59.9	176.9	27
61 56.1	59.9	176.2	59 56.3	59.9	176.5	57 56.5	59.9	176.7	55 56.7	59.9	176.8	53 56.9	59.9	177.0	28
60 56.2	59.8	176.4	58 56.4	59.8	176.6	56 56.6	59.8	176.8	54 56.8	59.9	177.0	52 57.0	59.9	177.1	29

10°			12°			14°			16°			18°			Dec.
Hc	d	Z	Hc	d	Z	Hc	d	Z	Hc	d	Z	Hc	d	Z	
79 48.2	-58.9	168.6	77 50.2	-59.3	170.5	75 51.6	-59.4	171.8	73 52.7	-59.6	172.8	71 53.6	-59.7	173.6	0
78 49.3	59.1	169.6	76 50.9	59.3	171.2	74 52.2	59.5	172.3	72 53.1	59.6	173.2	70 53.9	59.7	173.9	1
77 50.2	59.3	170.5	75 51.6	59.5	171.8	73 52.7	59.6	172.8	71 53.5	59.7	173.6	69 54.2	59.7	174.2	2
76 50.9	59.4	171.2	74 52.1	59.5	172.3	72 53.1	59.6	173.2	70 53.8	59.7	173.9	68 54.5	59.8	174.4	3
75 51.5	59.4	171.8	73 52.6	59.6	172.8	71 53.5	59.7	173.6	69 54.1	59.7	174.2	67 54.7	59.8	174.7	4
74 52.1	-59.5	172.3	72 53.0	-59.6	173.2	70 53.8	-59.7	173.9	68 54.4	-59.7	174.5	66 54.9	-59.8	174.9	5
73 52.6	59.6	172.8	71 53.4	59.6	173.6	69 54.1	59.7	174.2	67 54.7	59.8	174.7	65 55.1	59.8	175.1	6
72 53.0	59.6	173.2	70 53.8	59.7	173.9	68 54.4	59.7	174.5	66 54.9	59.8	174.9	64 55.3	59.8	175.3	7
71 53.4	59.6	173.6	69 54.1	59.7	174.2	67 54.6	59.7	174.7	65 55.1	59.8	175.1	63 55.5	59.8	175.5	8
70 53.8	59.7	174.0	68 54.4	59.7	174.5	66 54.9	59.8	175.0	64 55.3	59.8	175.3	62 55.7	59.8	175.7	9
69 54.1	-59.7	174.3	67 54.6	-59.7	174.8	65 55.1	-59.8	175.2	63 55.5	-59.8	175.5	61 55.8	-59.8	175.8	10
68 54.4	59.7	174.5	66 54.9	59.8	175.0	64 55.3	59.8	175.4	62 55.7	59.9	175.7	60 56.0	59.9	176.0	11
67 54.6	59.7	174.8	65 55.1	59.8	175.2	63 55.5	59.9	175.5	61 55.8	59.8	175.8	59 56.1	59.9	176.1	12
66 54.9	59.8	175.0	64 55.3	59.8	175.4	62 55.6	59.8	175.7	60 56.0	59.9	176.0	58 56.2	59.9	176.2	13
65 55.1	59.8	175.2	63 55.5	59.9	175.6	61 55.8	59.8	175.9	59 56.1	59.9	176.1	57 56.4	59.9	176.3	14
64 55.3	-59.8	175.4	62 55.6	-59.8	175.8	60 56.0	-59.9	176.0	58 56.2	-59.8	176.3	56 56.5	-59.9	176.5	15
63 55.5	59.8	175.6	61 55.8	59.8	175.9	59 56.1	59.9	176.2	57 56.4	59.9	176.4	55 56.6	59.9	176.6	16
62 55.7	59.9	175.8	60 56.0	59.9	176.1	58 56.2	59.8	176.3	56 56.5	59.9	176.5	54 56.7	59.9	176.7	17
61 55.8	59.8	176.0	59 56.1	59.9	176.2	57 56.4	59.9	176.4	55 56.6	59.9	176.6	53 56.8	59.9	176.8	18
60 56.0	59.9	176.1	58 56.2	59.8	176.3	56 56.5	59.9	176.5	54 56.7	59.9	176.7	52 56.9	59.9	176.9	19
59 56.1	-59.9	176.2	57 56.4	-59.9	176.5	55 56.6	-59.9	176.6	53 56.8	-59.9	176.8	51 57.0	-60.0	176.9	20
58 56.3	59.9	176.4	56 56.5	59.9	176.6	54 56.7	59.9	176.7	52 56.9	59.9	176.9	50 57.0	59.9	177.0	21
57 56.4	59.9	176.5	55 56.6	59.9	176.7	53 56.8	59.9	176.8	51 57.0	59.9	177.0	49 57.1	59.9	177.1	22
56 56.5	59.9	176.6	54 56.7	59.9	176.8	52 56.9	59.9	176.9	50 57.1	60.0	177.1	48 57.2	59.9	177.2	23
55 56.6	59.9	176.7	53 56.8	59.9	176.9	51 57.0	59.9	177.0	49 57.1	59.9	177.2	47 57.3	59.9	177.3	24
54 56.7	-59.9	176.8	52 56.9	-59.9	177.0	50 57.1	-59.9	177.1	48 57.2	-59.9	177.2	46 57.4	-60.0	177.3	25
53 56.8	59.9	176.9	51 57.0	59.9	177.1	49 57.2	60.0	177.2	47 57.3	59.9	177.3	45 57.4	59.9	177.4	26
52 56.9	59.9	177.0	50 57.1	59.9	177.2	48 57.2	59.9	177.3	46 57.4	60.0	177.4	44 57.5	59.9	177.5	27
51 57.0	59.9	177.1	49 57.2	60.0	177.3	47 57.3	59.9	177.4	45 57.4	59.9	177.5	43 57.6	60.0	177.5	28
50 57.1	59.9	177.2	48 57.3	60.0	177.3	46 57.4	59.9	177.4	44 57.5	59.9	177.5	42 57.6	59.9	177.6	29

| | **20°** | | | **22°** | | | **24°** | | | **26°** | | | **28°** | | |
Dec.	Hc	d	Z	Hc	d	Z	Hc	d	Z	Hc	d	Z	Hc	d	Z
0	69 54.3	+59.7	174.2	67 54.8	+59.8	174.7	65 55.3	+59.8	175.1	63 55.7	+59.9	175.4	61 56.1	+59.8	175.7
1	70 54.0	59.7	173.9	68 54.6	59.7	174.4	66 55.1	59.8	174.9	64 55.6	59.8	175.3	62 55.9	59.9	175.6
2	71 53.7	59.6	173.6	69 54.3	59.8	174.2	67 54.9	59.8	174.7	65 55.4	59.8	175.1	63 55.8	59.8	175.4
3	72 53.3	59.6	173.2	70 54.1	59.6	173.9	68 54.7	59.7	174.4	66 55.2	59.8	174.9	64 55.6	59.8	175.1
4	73 52.9	59.6	172.8	71 53.7	59.7	173.6	69 54.4	59.8	174.2	67 55.0	59.8	174.7	65 55.5	59.8	175.1
5	74 52.5	+59.4	172.3	72 53.4	+59.6	173.2	70 54.2	+59.7	173.9	68 54.8	+59.7	174.5	66 55.3	+59.8	174.9
6	75 51.9	59.5	171.8	73 53.0	59.6	172.8	71 53.9	59.6	173.6	69 54.5	59.8	174.2	67 55.1	59.8	174.7
7	76 51.4	59.3	171.2	74 52.6	59.5	172.4	72 53.5	59.7	173.2	70 54.3	59.7	173.9	68 54.9	59.8	174.5
8	77 50.7	59.2	170.6	75 52.1	59.4	171.9	73 53.2	59.5	172.8	71 54.0	59.7	173.6	69 54.7	59.7	174.2
9	78 49.9	59.0	169.7	76 51.5	59.4	171.3	74 52.7	59.5	172.4	72 53.7	59.6	173.3	70 54.4	59.7	174.0
10	79 48.9	+58.9	168.8	77 50.9	+59.2	170.6	75 52.2	+59.5	171.9	73 53.3	+59.6	172.9	71 54.1	+59.7	173.6
11	80 47.8	58.6	167.6	78 50.1	59.1	169.8	76 51.7	59.4	171.3	74 52.9	59.5	172.5	72 53.8	59.7	173.3
12	81 46.4	58.1	166.2	79 49.2	58.8	168.9	77 51.1	59.2	170.7	75 52.4	59.5	172.0	73 53.5	59.6	172.9
13	82 44.5	57.7	164.4	80 48.0	58.6	167.7	78 50.3	59.1	169.9	76 51.9	59.4	171.4	74 53.1	59.5	172.5
14	83 42.2	56.7	162.0	81 46.6	58.3	166.3	79 49.4	58.9	169.0	77 51.3	59.2	170.7	75 52.6	59.5	172.0
15	84 38.9	+55.4	158.8	82 44.9	+57.7	164.5	80 48.3	+58.7	167.8	78 50.5	+59.2	170.0	76 52.1	+59.4	171.5
16	85 34.3	52.8*	154.3	83 42.6	56.8	162.2	81 47.0	58.2	166.4	79 49.7	58.9	169.0	77 51.5	59.3	170.8
17	86 27.1	47.8*	147.4	84 39.4	55.4	159.0	82 45.2	57.8	164.7	80 48.6	58.7	167.9	78 50.8	59.2	170.1
18	87 14.9	37.1*	136.3	85 34.8	53.0*	154.5	83 43.0	56.9	162.3	81 47.3	58.3	166.6	79 50.0	58.9	169.2
19	87 52.0	+15.2*	117.6	86 27.8	48.0*	147.7	84 39.9	55.6	159.2	82 45.6	57.9	164.8	80 48.9	58.8	168.1
20	88 07.2	−14.6*	89.7	87 15.8	+37.5*	136.6	85 35.5	+53.1*	154.7	83 43.5	+57.0	162.5	81 47.7	+58.4	166.7
21	87 52.6	36.8*	61.6	87 53.3	+15.4*	117.9	86 28.6	48.3*	148.0	84 40.5	55.7	159.4	82 46.1	57.9	165.0
22	87 15.8	47.6*	42.7	88 08.7	−14.8*	89.6	87 16.9	37.8*	137.0	85 36.2	53.3*	155.0	83 44.0	57.1	162.8
23	86 28.2	52.7*	31.4	87 53.9	37.0*	61.2	87 54.7	+15.7*	118.2	86 29.5	48.6*	148.3	84 41.1	55.8	159.7
24	85 35.5	55.3*	24.5	87 16.9	47.9*	42.2	88 10.4	−15.0*	89.6	87 18.1	38.1*	137.4	85 36.9	53.5*	155.4
25	84 40.2	−56.7	19.9	86 29.0	−52.8*	31.0	87 55.4	−37.3*	60.8	87 56.2	+15.9*	118.6	86 30.4	+48.9*	148.7
26	83 43.5	57.7	16.7	85 36.2	55.4*	24.1	87 18.1	48.2*	41.8	88 12.1	−15.1*	89.6	87 19.3	38.5*	137.8
27	82 45.8	58.1	14.3	84 40.8	56.8	19.6	86 29.9	53.0*	30.6	87 57.0	37.7*	60.4	87 57.8	+16.2*	118.9
28	81 47.7	58.6	12.5	83 44.0	57.7	16.4	85 36.9	55.5	23.8	87 19.3	48.4*	41.3	88 14.0	−15.3*	89.5
29	80 49.1	58.8	11.0	82 46.3	58.2	14.0	84 41.4	56.9	19.3	86 30.9	53.2*	30.1	87 58.7	38.1*	59.9

| | **30°** | | | **32°** | | | **34°** | | | **36°** | | | **38°** | | |
Dec.	Hc	d	Z	Hc	d	Z	Hc	d	Z	Hc	d	Z	Hc	d	Z
0	59 56.4	+59.9	176.0	57 56.7	+59.9	176.2	55 56.9	+59.9	176.4	53 57.1	+59.9	176.6	51 57.3	+60.0	176.8
1	60 56.3	59.8	175.9	58 56.6	59.9	176.1	56 56.8	59.9	176.3	54 57.0	60.0	176.5	52 57.3	59.9	176.7
2	61 56.1	59.9	175.7	59 56.5	59.8	176.0	57 56.7	59.9	176.2	55 57.0	59.9	176.4	53 57.2	59.9	176.6
3	62 56.0	59.9	175.6	60 56.3	59.9	175.9	58 56.6	59.9	176.1	56 56.9	59.9	176.3	54 57.1	60.0	176.6
4	63 55.9	59.8	175.5	61 56.2	59.9	175.8	59 56.5	59.9	176.0	57 56.8	59.9	176.2	55 57.1	59.9	176.4
5	64 55.7	+59.9	175.3	62 56.1	+59.9	175.6	60 56.4	+59.9	175.9	58 56.7	+59.9	176.1	56 57.0	+59.9	176.3
6	65 55.6	59.8	175.1	63 56.0	59.8	175.5	61 56.3	59.9	175.8	59 56.6	59.9	176.0	57 56.9	59.9	176.2
7	66 55.4	59.8	174.9	64 55.8	59.9	175.3	62 56.2	59.9	175.6	60 56.5	59.9	175.9	58 56.8	59.9	176.1
8	67 55.2	59.8	174.7	65 55.7	59.8	175.1	63 56.1	59.8	175.5	61 56.4	59.9	175.8	59 56.7	5 9.9	176.0
9	68 55.0	59.8	174.5	66 55.5	59.8	175.0	64 55.9	59.9	175.3	62 56.3	59.9	175.7	60 56.6	59.9	175.9
10	69 54.8	+59.7	174.3	67 55.3	+59.8	174.8	65 55.8	+59.9	175.2	63 56.2	+59.9	175.5	61 56.5	+59.9	175.8
11	70 54.5	59.8	174.0	68 55.1	59.8	174.5	66 55.6	59.9	175.0	64 56.1	59.8	175.4	62 56.4	59.9	175.7
12	71 54.3	59.7	173.7	69 54.9	59.8	174.2	67 55.5	59.8	174.8	65 55.9	59.9	175.2	63 56.3	59.9	175.5
13	72 54.0	59.6	173.4	70 54.7	59.7	174.0	68 55.3	59.8	174.6	66 55.8	59.8	175.0	64 56.2	59.9	175.4
14	73 53.6	59.7	173.0	71 54.4	59.7	173.7	69 55.1	59.8	174.3	67 55.6	59.8	174.8	65 56.1	59.8	175.2
15	74 53.3	+59.5	172.6	72 54.1	+59.7	173.4	70 54.9	+59.7	174.1	68 55.4	+59.8	174.6	66 55.9	+59.9	175.1
16	75 52.8	59.5	172.1	73 53.8	59.7	173.1	71 54.6	59.7	173.8	69 55.2	59.8	174.4	67 55.8	59.8	174.9
17	76 52.3	59.5	171.6	74 53.5	59.5	172.6	72 54.3	59.7	173.5	70 55.0	59.8	174.1	68 55.6	59.8	174.7
18	77 51.8	59.3	170.9	75 53.0	59.6	172.2	73 54.0	59.7	173.1	71 54.8	59.7	173.9	69 55.4	59.8	174.5
19	78 51.1	59.2	170.1	76 52.6	59.4	171.6	74 53.7	59.6	172.7	72 54.5	59.7	173.6	70 55.2	59.8	174.2
20	79 50.3	+59.0	169.3	77 52.0	+59.4	171.0	75 53.3	+59.5	172.3	73 54.2	+59.7	173.2	71 55.0	+59.7	173.9
21	80 49.3	58.8	168.2	78 51.4	59.2	170.3	76 52.8	59.5	171.7	74 53.9	59.6	172.8	72 54.7	59.8	173.6
22	81 48.1	58.4	166.9	79 50.6	59.0	169.4	77 52.3	59.4	171.1	75 53.5	59.6	172.4	73 54.5	59.6	173.3
23	82 46.5	58.0	165.2	80 49.6	58.9	168.4	78 51.7	59.2	170.4	76 53.1	59.5	171.9	74 54.1	59.7	172.9
24	83 44.5	57.2	163.0	81 48.5	58.5	167.1	79 50.9	59.1	169.6	77 52.6	59.4	171.3	75 53.8	59.6	172.5
25	84 41.7	+56.0	160.0	82 47.0	+58.0	165.4	80 50.0	+58.9	168.5	78 52.0	+59.3	170.6	76 53.4	+59.5	172.0
26	85 37.7	53.7*	155.7	83 45.0	57.4	163.3	81 48.9	58.6	167.3	79 51.3	59.1	169.7	77 52.9	59.4	171.4
27	86 31.4	49.2*	149.2	84 42.4	56.1	160.3	82 47.5	58.1	165.7	80 50.4	59.0	168.7	78 52.3	59.3	170.7
28	87 20.6	39.0*	138.3	85 38.5	53.9*	156.1	83 45.6	57.5	163.5	81 49.4	58.6	167.5	79 51.7	59.2	169.9
29	87 59.6	+16.5*	119.4	86 32.4	49.6*	149.6	84 43.1	56.2	160.6	82 48.0	58.2	165.9	80 50.9	58.9	168.9

20° Hc	d	Z	22° Hc	d	Z	24° Hc	d	Z	26° Hc	d	Z	28° Hc	d	Z	Dec.
69 54.3	− 59.8	174.2	67 54.8	− 59.8	174.7	65 55.3	− 59.8	175.1	63 55.7	− 59.8	175.4	61 56.1	− 59.9	175.7	0
68 54.5	59.7	174.4	66 55.0	59.8	174.9	64 55.5	59.9	175.3	62 55.9	59.9	175.6	60 56.2	59.9	175.9	1
67 54.8	59.8	174.7	65 55.2	59.8	175.1	63 55.6	59.8	175.4	61 56.0	59.9	175.7	59 56.3	59.9	176.0	2
66 55.0	59.8	174.9	64 55.4	59.9	175.3	62 55.8	59.9	175.6	60 56.1	59.9	175.9	58 56.4	59.9	176.1	3
65 55.2	59.8	175.1	63 55.6	59.9	175.5	61 55.9	59.8	175.8	59 56.2	59.9	176.0	57 56.5	59.9	176.2	4
64 55.4	− 59.9	175.3	62 55.7	− 59.8	175.6	60 56.1	− 59.9	175.9	58 56.4	− 59.9	176.1	56 56.6	− 59.9	176.3	5
63 55.5	59.8	175.5	61 55.9	59.9	175.8	59 56.2	59.9	176.0	57 56.5	59.9	176.3	55 56.7	59.9	176.4	6
62 55.7	59.9	175.6	60 56.0	59.9	175.9	58 56.3	59.9	176.2	56 56.6	59.9	176.4	54 56.8	59.9	176.6	7
61 55.9	59.9	175.8	59 56.2	59.9	176.0	57 56.4	59.9	176.3	55 56.7	59.9	176.5	53 56.9	59.9	176.6	8
60 56.0	59.9	175.9	58 56.3	59.9	176.2	56 56.5	59.9	176.4	54 56.8	60.0	176.6	52 57.0	60.0	176.7	9
59 56.1	− 59.8	176.1	57 56.4	− 59.9	176.3	55 56.6	− 59.9	176.5	53 56.8	− 59.9	176.7	51 57.0	− 59.9	176.8	10
58 56.3	59.9	176.2	56 56.5	59.9	176.4	54 56.7	59.9	176.6	52 56.9	59.9	176.7	50 57.1	59.9	176.9	11
57 56.4	59.9	176.3	55 56.6	59.9	176.5	53 56.8	59.9	176.7	51 57.0	59.9	176.8	49 57.2	59.9	177.0	12
56 56.5	59.9	176.5	54 56.7	59.9	176.6	52 56.9	59.9	176.8	50 57.1	59.9	176.9	48 57.3	60.0	177.0	13
55 56.6	59.9	176.5	53 56.8	59.9	176.7	51 57.0	59.9	176.9	49 57.2	60.0	177.0	47 57.3	59.9	177.1	14
54 56.7	− 59.9	176.6	52 56.9	− 59.9	176.8	50 57.1	− 60.0	176.9	48 57.2	− 59.9	177.1	46 57.4	− 60.0	177.2	15
53 56.8	59.9	176.7	51 57.0	59.9	176.9	49 57.1	59.9	177.0	47 57.3	59.9	177.1	45 57.4	59.9	177.2	16
52 56.9	59.9	176.8	50 57.1	60.0	177.0	48 57.2	59.9	177.1	46 57.4	60.0	177.2	44 57.5	59.9	177.3	17
51 57.0	60.0	176.9	49 57.1	59.9	177.0	47 57.3	60.0	177.2	45 57.4	59.9	177.3	43 57.6	60.0	177.4	18
50 57.0	59.9	177.0	48 57.2	59.9	177.1	46 57.3	59.9	177.2	44 57.5	60.0	177.3	42 57.6	59.9	177.4	19
49 57.1	− 59.9	177.1	47 57.3	− 60.0	177.2	45 57.4	− 59.9	177.3	43 57.5	− 59.9	177.4	41 57.7	− 60.0	177.5	20
48 57.2	59.9	177.2	46 57.3	59.9	177.2	44 57.5	60.0	177.4	42 57.6	59.9	177.4	40 57.7	59.9	177.6	21
47 57.3	60.0	177.2	45 57.4	59.9	177.3	43 57.5	59.9	177.4	41 57.7	60.0	177.5	39 57.8	60.0	177.6	22
46 57.3	59.9	177.3	44 57.5	60.0	177.4	42 57.6	60.0	177.5	40 57.7	59.9	177.6	38 57.8	59.9	177.6	23
45 57.4	59.9	177.4	43 57.5	59.9	177.5	41 57.6	59.9	177.5	39 57.8	60.0	177.7	37 57.9	60.0	177.7	24
44 57.5	− 60.0	177.4	42 57.6	− 59.9	177.6	40 57.7	− 59.9	177.6	38 57.8	− 59.9	177.7	36 57.9	− 60.0	177.8	25
43 57.5	59.9	177.5	41 57.7	60.0	177.6	39 57.8	60.0	177.7	37 57.9	59.9	177.7	35 57.9	59.9	177.8	26
42 57.6	59.9	177.6	40 57.7	59.9	177.6	38 57.8	59.9	177.7	36 57.9	60.0	177.8	34 58.0	60.0	177.8	27
41 57.7	60.0	177.6	39 57.8	60.0	177.7	37 57.9	60.0	177.8	35 57.9	59.9	177.8	33 58.0	59.9	177.9	28
40 57.7	59.9	177.7	38 57.8	59.9	177.8	36 57.9	59.9	177.8	34 58.0	60.0	177.9	32 58.1	60.0	177.9	29

30° Hc	d	Z	32° Hc	d	Z	34° Hc	d	Z	36° Hc	d	Z	38° Hc	d	Z	Dec.
59 56.4	− 59.9	176.0	57 56.7	− 60.0	176.2	55 56.9	− 59.9	176.4	53 57.1	− 59.9	176.6	51 57.3	− 59.9	176.8	0
58 56.5	59.9	176.1	56 56.7	59.9	176.3	54 57.0	60.0	176.5	52 57.2	59.9	176.7	50 57.4	60.0	176.8	1
57 56.6	59.9	176.2	55 56.8	59.9	176.4	53 57.0	59.9	176.6	51 57.3	60.0	176.8	49 57.4	59.9	176.9	2
56 56.7	59.9	176.3	54 56.9	59.9	176.5	52 57.1	59.9	176.7	50 57.3	59.9	176.8	48 57.5	60.0	177.0	3
55 56.8	59.9	176.4	53 57.0	59.9	176.6	51 57.2	59.9	176.8	49 57.4	60.0	176.9	47 57.5	59.9	177.0	4
54 56.9	− 60.0	176.5	52 57.1	− 60.0	176.7	50 57.3	− 60.0	176.8	48 57.4	− 59.9	177.0	46 57.6	− 60.0	177.1	5
53 56.9	59.9	176.6	51 57.1	59.9	176.8	49 57.3	59.9	176.9	47 57.5	60.0	177.0	45 57.6	59.9	177.1	6
52 57.0	59.9	176.7	50 57.2	60.0	176.9	48 57.4	60.0	177.0	46 57.5	59.9	177.1	44 57.7	60.0	177.2	7
51 57.1	59.9	176.8	49 57.3	60.0	176.9	47 57.4	59.9	177.0	45 57.6	60.0	177.2	43 57.7	59.9	177.2	8
50 57.2	60.0	176.9	48 57.3	59.9	177.0	46 57.5	60.0	177.1	44 57.6	59.9	177.2	42 57.8	60.0	177.3	9
49 57.2	− 60.0	177.0	47 57.4	− 60.0	177.1	45 57.5	− 59.9	177.2	43 57.7	− 60.0	177.3	41 57.8	− 59.9	177.4	10
48 57.3	60.0	177.0	46 57.4	59.9	177.1	44 57.6	60.0	177.3	42 57.7	59.9	177.3	40 57.9	60.0	177.4	11
47 57.3	59.9	177.1	45 57.5	59.9	177.2	43 57.6	59.9	177.3	41 57.8	60.0	177.4	39 57.9	59.9	177.4	12
46 57.4	59.9	177.1	44 57.6	60.0	177.2	42 57.7	60.0	177.3	40 57.8	59.9	177.5	38 57.9	59.9	177.5	13
45 57.5	60.0	177.2	43 57.6	59.9	177.3	41 57.7	59.9	177.4	39 57.9	60.0	177.5	37 58.0	60.0	177.6	14
44 57.5	− 59.9	177.3	42 57.7	− 60.0	177.4	40 57.8	− 60.0	177.4	38 57.9	− 60.0	177.5	36 58.0	− 60.0	177.6	15
43 57.6	60.0	177.3	41 57.7	59.9	177.4	39 57.8	59.9	177.5	37 57.9	59.9	177.6	35 58.0	59.9	177.6	16
42 57.6	59.9	177.4	40 57.8	60.0	177.5	38 57.9	60.0	177.5	36 58.0	60.0	177.6	34 58.1	60.0	177.7	17
41 57.7	60.0	177.4	39 57.8	59.9	177.5	37 57.9	59.9	177.6	35 58.0	59.9	177.6	33 58.1	59.9	177.7	18
40 57.7	59.9	177.5	38 57.8	59.9	177.6	36 57.9	59.9	177.6	34 58.0	59.9	177.7	32 58.1	59.9	177.7	19
39 57.8	− 60.0	177.5	37 57.9	− 60.0	177.6	35 58.0	− 60.0	177.7	33 58.1	− 60.0	177.7	31 58.2	− 60.0	177.8	20
38 57.8	59.9	177.6	36 57.9	59.9	177.7	34 58.0	59.9	177.7	32 58.1	60.0	177.8	30 58.2	60.0	177.8	21
37 57.9	60.0	177.6	35 58.0	60.0	177.7	33 58.1	60.0	177.8	31 58.1	59.9	177.8	29 58.2	59.9	177.9	22
36 57.9	59.9	177.7	34 58.0	59.9	177.8	32 58.1	60.0	177.8	30 58.2	60.0	177.9	28 58.3	60.0	177.9	23
35 58.0	60.0	177.7	33 58.0	59.9	177.8	31 58.1	59.9	177.8	29 58.2	59.9	177.9	27 58.3	59.9	177.9	24
34 58.0	− 60.0	177.8	32 58.1	− 60.0	177.8	30 58.2	− 60.0	177.9	28 58.2	− 59.9	177.9	26 58.3	− 59.9	178.0	25
33 58.0	59.9	177.8	31 58.1	59.9	177.9	29 58.2	60.0	177.9	27 58.3	60.0	178.0	25 58.4	60.0	178.0	26
32 58.1	60.0	177.9	30 58.2	60.0	177.9	28 58.2	59.9	178.0	26 58.3	60.0	178.0	24 58.4	60.0	178.0	27
31 58.1	60.0	177.9	29 58.2	60.0	178.0	27 58.3	60.0	178.0	25 58.3	59.9	178.0	23 58.4	60.0	178.1	28
30 58.1	59.9	178.0	28 58.2	59.9	178.0	26 58.3	60.0	178.0	24 58.4	60.0	178.1	22 58.4	59.9	178.1	29

Dec.	40° Hc	d	Z	42° Hc	d	Z	44° Hc	d	Z	46° Hc	d	Z	48° Hc	d	Z
°	° ′	′	°	° ′	′	°	° ′	′	°	° ′	′	°	° ′	′	°
0	49 57.5	+60.0	176.9	47 57.7	+59.9	177.0	45 57.8	+60.0	177.1	43 58.0	+59.9	177.2	41 58.1	+60.0	177.3
1	50 57.5	59.9	176.8	48 57.6	60.0	177.0	46 57.8	60.0	177.1	44 57.9	60.0	177.2	42 58.1	60.0	177.3
2	51 57.4	59.9	176.8	49 57.6	59.9	176.9	47 57.8	59.9	177.0	45 57.9	60.0	177.1	43 58.1	59.9	177.2
3	52 57.3	60.0	176.7	50 57.5	60.0	176.8	48 57.7	60.0	177.0	46 57.9	59.9	177.1	44 58.0	60.0	177.2
4	53 57.3	59.9	176.6	51 57.5	59.9	176.8	49 57.7	59.9	176.9	47 57.8	60.0	177.0	45 58.0	60.0	177.1
5	54 57.2	+59.9	176.5	52 57.4	+60.0	176.7	50 57.6	+60.0	176.8	48 57.8	+60.0	177.0	46 58.0	+59.9	177.1
6	55 57.1	60.0	176.4	53 57.4	59.9	176.6	51 57.6	59.9	176.8	49 57.8	59.9	176.9	47 57.9	60.0	177.0
7	56 57.1	59.9	176.4	54 57.3	59.9	176.5	52 57.5	60.0	176.6	50 57.7	60.0	176.8	48 57.9	59.9	177.0
8	57 57.0	59.9	176.3	55 57.2	60.0	176.5	53 57.5	59.9	176.6	51 57.7	59.9	176.8	49 57.8	60.0	176.9
9	58 56.9	59.9	176.2	56 57.2	59.9	176.4	54 57.4	59.9	176.6	52 57.6	60.0	176.7	50 57.8	59.9	176.9
10	59 56.8	+60.0	176.1	57 57.1	+59.9	176.3	55 57.3	+60.0	176.5	53 57.6	+59.9	176.7	51 57.8	+59.9	176.8
11	60 56.8	59.9	176.0	58 57.0	60.0	176.2	56 57.3	59.9	176.4	54 57.5	60.0	176.6	52 57.7	60.0	176.7
12	61 56.7	59.9	175.8	59 57.0	59.9	176.1	57 57.2	60.0	176.3	55 57.5	59.9	176.5	53 57.7	59.9	176.7
13	62 56.6	59.9	175.7	60 56.9	59.9	176.0	58 57.2	59.9	176.2	56 57.4	59.9	176.4	54 57.6	60.0	176.6
14	63 56.5	59.8	175.6	61 56.8	59.9	175.9	59 57.1	59.9	176.1	57 57.3	60.0	176.3	55 57.6	59.9	176.5
15	64 56.3	+59.9	175.4	62 56.7	+59.9	175.7	60 57.0	+59.9	176.0	58 57.3	+59.9	176.2	56 57.5	+60.0	176.5
16	65 56.2	59.9	175.3	63 56.6	59.9	175.6	61 56.9	59.9	175.9	59 57.2	59.9	176.2	57 57.5	59.9	176.4
17	66 56.1	59.8	175.1	64 56.5	59.9	175.5	62 56.8	59.9	175.8	60 57.1	60.0	176.1	58 57.4	59.9	176.3
18	67 55.9	59.9	174.9	65 56.4	59.8	175.3	63 56.7	59.9	175.6	61 57.1	59.9	175.9	59 57.3	60.0	176.2
19	68 55.8	59.8	174.7	66 56.2	59.9	175.2	64 56.6	59.9	175.5	62 57.0	59.9	175.8	60 57.3	59.9	176.1
20	69 55.6	+59.8	174.5	67 56.1	+59.9	175.0	65 56.5	+59.9	175.4	63 56.9	+59.9	175.7	61 57.2	+59.9	176.0
21	70 55.4	59.8	174.3	68 56.0	59.8	174.8	66 56.4	59.9	175.2	64 56.8	59.9	175.6	62 57.1	59.9	175.9
22	71 55.2	59.8	174.0	69 55.8	59.8	174.6	67 56.3	59.8	175.1	65 56.7	59.9	175.4	63 57.0	60.0	175.8
23	72 55.0	59.7	173.7	70 55.6	59.8	174.4	68 56.1	59.9	174.9	66 56.6	59.9	175.3	64 57.0	59.9	175.6
24	73 54.7	59.7	173.4	71 55.4	59.8	174.1	69 56.0	59.8	174.7	67 56.5	59.8	175.1	65 56.9	59.9	175.5
25	74 54.4	+59.7	173.0	72 55.2	+59.7	173.8	70 55.8	+59.8	174.4	68 56.3	+59.9	175.0	66 56.8	+59.8	175.4
26	75 54.1	59.6	172.6	73 54.9	59.8	173.5	71 55.6	59.8	174.2	69 56.2	59.8	174.8	67 56.6	59.9	175.2
27	76 53.7	59.5	172.1	74 54.7	59.6	173.1	72 55.4	59.8	173.9	70 56.0	59.9	174.5	68 56.5	59.9	175.0
28	77 53.2	59.5	171.6	75 54.3	59.7	172.7	73 55.2	59.7	173.6	71 55.9	59.8	174.3	69 56.4	59.8	174.8
29	78 52.7	59.4	170.9	76 54.0	59.5	172.3	74 54.9	59.7	173.3	72 55.7	59.7	174.0	70 56.2	59.9	174.6

Dec.	50° Hc	d	Z	52° Hc	d	Z	54° Hc	d	Z	56° Hc	d	Z	58° Hc	d	Z
°	° ′	′	°	° ′	′	°	° ′	′	°	° ′	′	°	° ′	′	°
0	39 58.2	+60.0	177.4	37 58.4	+59.9	177.5	35 58.5	+60.0	177.5	33 58.6	+60.0	177.6	31 58.7	+60.0	177.6
1	40 58.2	60.0	177.4	38 58.3	60.0	177.4	36 58.5	59.9	177.5	34 58.6	60.0	177.6	32 58.7	60.0	177.6
2	41 58.2	60.0	177.3	39 58.3	60.0	177.4	37 58.4	60.0	177.5	35 58.6	59.9	177.5	33 58.7	59.9	177.6
3	42 58.2	60.0	177.3	40 58.3	60.0	177.4	38 58.4	60.0	177.4	36 58.5	60.0	177.5	34 58.6	60.0	177.6
4	43 58.1	60.0	177.2	41 58.3	59.9	177.3	39 58.4	60.0	177.4	37 58.5	60.0	177.5	35 58.6	60.0	177.5
5	44 58.1	+60.0	177.2	42 58.2	+60.0	177.3	40 58.4	+60.0	177.4	38 58.5	+60.0	177.4	36 58.6	+60.0	177.5
6	45 58.1	59.9	177.1	43 58.2	60.0	177.2	41 58.4	59.9	177.3	39 58.5	60.0	177.4	37 58.6	60.0	177.5
7	46 58.0	60.0	177.1	44 58.2	60.0	177.2	42 58.3	60.0	177.3	40 58.5	59.9	177.4	38 58.6	60.0	177.4
8	47 58.0	60.0	177.0	45 58.2	59.9	177.1	43 58.3	60.0	177.2	41 58.4	60.0	177.3	39 58.6	59.9	177.4
9	48 58.0	59.9	177.0	46 58.1	60.0	177.1	44 58.3	60.0	177.2	42 58.4	60.0	177.3	40 58.5	60.0	177.4
10	49 57.9	+60.0	176.9	47 58.1	+60.0	177.1	45 58.3	+59.9	177.2	43 58.4	+60.0	177.2	41 58.5	+60.0	177.3
11	50 57.9	60.0	176.9	48 58.1	59.9	177.0	46 58.2	60.0	177.1	44 58.4	60.0	177.2	42 58.5	60.0	177.3
12	51 57.9	59.9	176.8	49 58.0	60.0	177.0	47 58.2	60.0	177.1	45 58.4	59.9	177.2	43 58.5	60.0	177.3
13	52 57.8	60.0	176.7	50 58.0	60.0	176.9	48 58.2	59.9	177.0	46 58.3	60.0	177.1	44 58.5	60.0	177.2
14	53 57.8	59.9	176.7	51 58.0	59.9	176.8	49 58.1	60.0	177.0	47 58.3	60.0	177.1	45 58.5	59.9	177.2
15	54 57.7	+60.0	176.6	52 57.9	+60.0	176.8	50 58.1	+60.0	176.9	48 58.3	+59.9	177.1	46 58.4	+60.0	177.2
16	55 57.7	59.9	176.6	53 57.9	60.0	176.7	51 58.1	59.9	176.9	49 58.2	60.0	177.0	47 58.4	60.0	177.1
17	56 57.6	59.9	176.5	54 57.9	59.9	176.7	52 58.0	60.0	176.8	50 58.2	60.0	177.0	48 58.4	60.0	177.1
18	57 57.6	59.9	176.4	55 57.8	60.0	176.6	53 58.0	59.9	176.8	51 58.2	59.9	176.9	49 58.4	59.9	177.0
19	58 57.5	60.0	176.3	56 57.8	59.9	176.5	54 58.0	59.9	176.7	52 58.2	59.9	176.9	50 58.3	60.0	177.0
20	59 57.5	+59.9	176.2	57 57.7	+60.0	176.5	55 57.9	+60.0	176.6	53 58.1	+60.0	176.8	51 58.3	+60.0	176.9
21	60 57.4	59.9	176.2	58 57.7	59.9	176.4	56 57.9	59.9	176.6	54 58.1	59.9	176.7	52 58.3	60.0	176.9
22	61 57.3	60.0	176.1	59 57.6	60.0	176.3	57 57.8	60.0	176.5	55 58.1	59.9	176.7	53 58.3	59.9	176.8
23	62 57.3	59.9	175.9	60 57.6	59.9	176.2	58 57.8	59.9	176.4	56 58.0	60.0	176.6	54 58.2	60.0	176.8
24	63 57.2	59.9	175.8	61 57.5	59.9	176.1	59 57.8	59.9	176.3	57 58.0	59.9	176.5	55 58.2	60.0	176.7
25	64 57.1	+59.9	175.7	62 57.4	+60.0	176.0	60 57.7	+59.9	176.3	58 57.9	+60.0	176.5	56 58.2	+59.9	176.7
26	65 57.0	59.9	175.6	63 57.4	59.9	175.9	61 57.6	60.0	176.2	59 57.9	59.9	176.4	57 58.1	60.0	176.6
27	66 56.9	59.9	175.3	64 57.3	59.9	175.8	62 57.6	59.9	176.1	60 57.8	60.0	176.3	58 58.1	59.9	176.5
28	67 56.8	59.9	175.3	65 57.2	59.9	175.7	63 57.5	60.0	176.0	61 57.8	59.9	176.2	59 58.0	60.0	176.4
29	68 56.7	59.9	175.1	66 57.1	59.9	175.5	64 57.5	59.9	175.9	62 57.7	60.0	176.1	60 58.0	60.0	176.4

40°			42°			44°			46°			48°			Dec.
Hc	d	Z	Hc	d	Z	Hc	d	Z	Hc	d	Z	Hc	d	Z	
° ′	′	°	° ′	′	°	° ′	′	°	° ′	′	°	° ′	′	°	°
49 57.5	-59.9	176.9	47 57.7	-60.0	177.0	45 57.8	-59.9	177.1	43 58.0	-60.0	177.2	41 58.1	-60.0	177.3	0
48 57.6	60.0	177.0	46 57.7	59.9	177.1	44 57.9	60.0	177.2	42 58.0	60.0	177.3	40 58.1	59.9	177.4	1
47 57.6	59.9	177.0	45 57.8	60.0	177.1	43 57.9	60.0	177.2	41 58.0	59.9	177.3	39 58.2	60.0	177.4	2
46 57.7	60.0	177.1	44 57.8	60.0	177.2	42 57.9	59.9	177.3	40 58.1	60.0	177.4	38 58.2	60.0	177.4	3
45 57.7	60.0	177.1	43 57.8	59.9	177.2	41 58.0	60.0	177.3	39 58.1	60.0	177.4	37 58.2	59.9	177.5	4
44 57.7	-59.9	177.2	42 57.9	-60.0	177.3	40 58.0	-60.0	177.4	38 58.1	-59.9	177.4	36 58.3	-60.0	177.5	5
43 57.8	60.0	177.2	41 57.9	59.9	177.3	39 58.0	59.9	177.4	37 58.2	60.0	177.5	35 58.3	60.0	177.5	6
42 57.8	59.9	177.3	40 58.0	60.0	177.4	38 58.1	60.0	177.4	36 58.2	60.0	177.5	34 58.3	60.0	177.6	7
41 57.9	60.0	177.3	39 58.0	60.0	177.4	37 58.1	60.0	177.5	35 58.2	60.0	177.6	33 58.3	59.9	177.6	8
40 57.9	60.0	177.4	38 58.0	59.9	177.5	36 58.1	59.9	177.5	34 58.2	59.9	177.6	32 58.4	60.0	177.6	9
39 57.9	-59.9	177.4	37 58.1	-60.0	177.5	35 58.2	-60.0	177.6	33 58.3	-60.0	177.6	31 58.4	-60.0	177.7	10
38 58.0	60.0	177.5	36 58.1	60.0	177.6	34 58.2	60.0	177.6	32 58.3	60.0	177.7	30 58.4	60.0	177.7	11
37 58.0	60.0	177.5	35 58.1	60.0	177.6	33 58.2	59.9	177.6	31 58.3	59.9	177.7	29 58.4	60.0	177.7	12
36 58.0	59.9	177.6	34 58.1	59.9	177.6	32 58.3	60.0	177.7	30 58.3	59.9	177.7	28 58.4	59.9	177.8	13
35 58.1	60.0	177.6	33 58.2	60.0	177.7	31 58.3	60.0	177.7	29 58.4	60.0	177.8	27 58.5	60.0	177.8	14
34 58.1	-60.0	177.6	32 58.2	-60.0	177.7	30 58.3	-60.0	177.7	28 58.4	-60.0	177.8	26 58.5	-60.0	177.8	15
33 58.1	59.9	177.7	31 58.2	59.9	177.7	29 58.3	59.9	177.8	27 58.4	60.0	177.8	25 58.5	60.0	177.9	16
32 58.2	60.0	177.7	30 58.3	60.0	177.8	28 58.4	60.0	177.8	26 58.4	59.9	177.9	24 58.5	60.0	177.9	17
31 58.2	60.0	177.8	29 58.3	60.0	177.8	27 58.4	60.0	177.8	25 58.5	60.0	177.9	23 58.5	59.9	177.9	18
30 58.2	59.9	177.8	28 58.3	60.0	177.8	26 58.4	60.0	177.9	24 58.5	60.0	177.9	22 58.6	60.0	177.9	19
29 58.3	-60.0	177.8	27 58.3	-59.9	177.9	25 58.4	-60.0	177.9	23 58.5	-60.0	177.9	21 58.6	-60.0	178.0	20
28 58.3	60.0	177.9	26 58.4	60.0	177.9	24 58.4	59.9	177.9	22 58.5	60.0	178.0	20 58.6	60.0	178.0	21
27 58.3	60.0	177.9	25 58.4	60.0	177.9	23 58.5	60.0	178.0	21 58.5	59.9	178.0	19 58.6	59.9	178.0	22
26 58.3	59.9	177.9	24 58.4	60.0	178.0	22 58.5	60.0	178.0	20 58.6	60.0	178.0	18 58.6	60.0	178.1	23
25 58.4	60.0	178.0	23 58.4	59.9	178.0	21 58.5	60.0	178.0	19 58.6	60.0	178.1	17 58.7	60.0	178.1	24
24 58.4	-60.0	178.0	22 58.5	-60.0	178.1	20 58.5	-59.9	178.1	18 58.6	-60.0	178.1	16 58.7	-60.0	178.1	25
23 58.4	60.0	178.0	21 58.5	60.0	178.1	19 58.6	60.0	178.1	17 58.6	60.0	178.1	15 58.7	60.0	178.1	26
22 58.4	59.9	178.1	20 58.5	60.0	178.1	18 58.6	60.0	178.1	16 58.6	59.9	178.1	14 58.7	60.0	178.2	27
21 58.5	60.0	178.1	19 58.5	59.9	178.1	17 58.6	60.0	178.1	15 58.7	60.0	178.2	13 58.7	60.0	178.2	28
20 58.5	60.0	178.1	18 58.6	60.0	178.2	16 58.6	60.0	178.2	14 58.7	60.0	178.2	12 58.7	59.9	178.2	29

50°			52°			54°			56°			58°			Dec.
Hc	d	Z	Hc	d	Z	Hc	d	Z	Hc	d	Z	Hc	d	Z	
° ′	′	°	° ′	′	°	° ′	′	°	° ′	′	°	° ′	′	°	°
39 58.2	-59.9	177.4	37 58.4	-60.0	177.5	35 58.5	-60.0	177.5	33 58.6	-60.0	177.6	31 58.7	-60.0	177.6	0
38 58.3	60.0	177.4	36 58.4	60.0	177.5	34 58.5	60.0	177.6	32 58.6	60.0	177.6	30 58.7	60.0	177.7	1
37 58.3	60.0	177.5	35 58.4	60.0	177.5	33 58.5	60.0	177.6	31 58.6	60.0	177.6	29 58.7	60.0	177.7	2
36 58.3	60.0	177.5	34 58.4	60.0	177.6	32 58.5	59.9	177.6	30 58.6	59.9	177.7	28 58.7	60.0	177.7	3
35 58.3	59.9	177.5	33 58.4	59.9	177.6	31 58.6	60.0	177.6	29 58.7	60.0	177.7	27 58.7	59.9	177.7	4
34 58.4	-60.0	177.6	32 58.5	-60.0	177.6	30 58.6	-60.0	177.7	28 58.7	-60.0	177.7	26 58.8	-60.0	177.8	5
33 58.4	60.0	177.6	31 58.5	60.0	177.7	29 58.6	60.0	177.7	27 58.7	60.0	177.7	25 58.8	60.0	177.8	6
32 58.4	60.0	177.6	30 58.5	60.0	177.7	28 58.6	60.0	177.7	26 58.7	60.0	177.8	24 58.8	60.0	177.8	7
31 58.4	60.0	177.7	29 58.5	60.0	177.7	27 58.6	60.0	177.8	25 58.7	60.0	177.8	23 58.8	60.0	177.8	8
30 58.4	59.9	177.7	28 58.5	59.9	177.7	26 58.6	59.9	177.8	24 58.7	60.0	177.8	22 58.8	60.0	177.9	9
29 58.5	-60.0	177.7	27 58.6	-60.0	177.8	25 58.7	-60.0	177.8	23 58.7	-59.9	177.8	21 58.8	-60.0	177.9	10
28 58.5	60.0	177.8	26 58.6	60.0	177.8	24 58.7	60.0	177.8	22 58.8	60.0	177.9	20 58.8	60.0	177.9	11
27 58.5	60.0	177.8	25 58.6	60.0	177.8	23 58.7	60.0	177.9	21 58.8	60.0	177.9	19 58.8	59.9	177.9	12
26 58.5	60.0	177.8	24 58.6	60.0	177.9	22 58.7	60.0	177.9	20 58.8	60.0	177.9	18 58.9	60.0	177.9	13
25 58.5	59.9	177.8	23 58.6	60.0	177.9	21 58.7	60.0	177.9	19 58.8	60.0	177.9	17 58.9	60.0	178.0	14
24 58.6	-60.0	177.9	22 58.6	-59.9	177.9	20 58.7	-60.0	177.9	18 58.8	-60.0	178.0	16 58.9	-60.0	178.0	15
23 58.6	60.0	177.9	21 58.7	60.0	177.9	19 58.7	59.9	178.0	17 58.8	60.0	178.0	15 58.9	60.0	178.0	16
22 58.6	60.0	177.9	20 58.7	60.0	178.0	18 58.8	60.0	178.0	16 58.8	60.0	178.0	14 58.9	60.0	178.0	17
21 58.6	60.0	177.9	19 58.7	60.0	178.0	17 58.8	60.0	178.0	15 58.8	59.9	178.0	13 58.9	60.0	178.0	18
20 58.6	59.9	178.0	18 58.7	60.0	178.0	16 58.8	60.0	178.0	14 58.9	60.0	178.0	12 58.9	60.0	178.1	19
19 58.7	-60.0	178.0	17 58.7	-60.0	178.0	15 58.8	-60.0	178.1	13 58.9	-60.0	178.1	11 58.9	-60.0	178.1	20
18 58.7	60.0	178.0	16 58.7	59.9	178.1	14 58.8	60.0	178.1	12 58.9	60.0	178.1	10 58.9	59.9	178.1	21
17 58.7	60.0	178.1	15 58.8	60.0	178.1	13 58.8	60.0	178.1	11 58.9	60.0	178.1	9 59.0	60.0	178.1	22
16 58.7	60.0	178.1	14 58.8	60.0	178.1	12 58.8	59.9	178.1	10 58.9	60.0	178.1	8 59.0	60.0	178.1	23
15 58.7	60.0	178.1	13 58.8	60.0	178.1	11 58.8	60.0	178.1	9 58.9	60.0	178.1	7 59.0	60.0	178.2	24
14 58.7	-59.9	178.1	12 58.8	-60.0	178.1	10 58.9	-60.0	178.2	8 58.9	-60.0	178.2	6 59.0	-60.0	178.2	25
13 58.8	60.0	178.1	11 58.8	60.0	178.2	9 58.9	60.0	178.2	7 58.9	60.0	178.2	5 59.0	60.0	178.2	26
12 58.8	60.0	178.2	10 58.8	60.0	178.2	8 58.9	60.0	178.2	6 58.9	59.9	178.2	4 59.0	59.9	178.2	27
11 58.8	60.0	178.2	9 58.8	59.9	178.2	7 58.9	60.0	178.2	5 59.0	60.0	178.2	3 59.0	60.0	178.2	28
10 58.8	60.0	178.2	8 58.9	60.0	178.2	6 58.9	60.0	178.2	4 59.0	60.0	178.2	2 59.0	60.0	178.2	29

Dec.	0° Hc	d	Z	2° Hc	d	Z	4° Hc	d	Z	6° Hc	d	Z	8° Hc	d	Z
°	° ′	′	°	° ′	′	°	° ′	′	°	° ′	′	°	° ′	′	°
0	86 00.0	− 7.4°	90.0	85 31.7	+21.0°	116.5	84 20.7	+39.5°	134.9	82 47.6	+48.5°	146.2	81 03.7	+53.0	153.3
1	85 52.6	20.9°	76.0	85 52.7	+ 7.4°	104.0	85 00.2	31.8°	126.8	83 36.1	44.9°	141.2	81 56.7	51.2°	150.1
2	85 31.7	31.6°	63.4	86 00.1	− 7.3°	89.9	85 32.0	21.1°	116.5	84 21.0	39.6°	134.9	82 47.9	48.7°	146.2
3	85 00.1	39.4°	53.1	85 52.8	20.8°	75.9	85 53.1	+ 7.5°	103.9	85 00.6	31.9°	126.8	83 36.6	45.0°	141.3
4	84 20.7	44.7°	44.9	85 32.0	31.6°	63.3	86 00.6	− 7.3°	89.9	85 32.5	21.2°	116.5	84 21.6	39.7°	134.9
5	83 36.0	−48.4°	38.6	85 00.4	−39.4°	53.0	85 53.3	−20.8°	75.8	85 53.7	+ 7.6°	103.9	85 01.3	+32.0°	126.8
6	82 47.6	51.0°	33.6	84 21.0	44.7°	44.8	85 32.5	31.6°	63.2	86 01.3	− 7.2°	89.8	85 33.3	21.3°	116.5
7	81 56.6	52.9	29.6	83 36.3	48.4°	38.4	85 00.9	39.3°	52.8	85 54.1	20.8°	75.7	85 54.6	+ 7.7°	103.9
8	81 03.7	54.2	26.4	82 47.9	51.0°	33.4	84 21.6	44.8°	44.7	85 33.3	31.6°	62.0	86 02.3	− 7.1°	89.7
9	80 09.5	55.3	23.8	81 56.9	52.9	29.5	83 36.8	48.4°	38.3	85 01.7	39.4°	52.6	85 55.2	20.9°	75.5
10	79 14.2	−56.0	21.6	81 04.0	−54.2	26.3	82 48.4	−51.0°	33.3	84 22.3	−44.8°	44.5	85 34.3	−31.6°	62.8
11	78 18.2	56.6	19.7	80 09.8	55.2	23.6	81 57.4	52.9	29.3	83 37.5	48.5°	38.1	85 27.7	39.5°	52.4
12	77 21.6	57.1	18.2	79 14.6	56.1	21.4	81 04.5	54.3	26.1	82 49.0	51.0°	33.1	84 23.2	44.8°	44.2
13	76 24.5	57.5	16.8	78 18.5	56.6	19.6	80 10.2	55.2	23.5	81 58.0	52.9	29.1	83 38.4	48.6°	37.8
14	75 27.0	57.7	15.6	77 21.9	57.1	18.0	79 15.0	56.0	21.3	81 05.1	54.3	25.9	82 49.8	51.1°	32.8
15	74 29.3	−58.1	14.6	76 24.8	−57.4	16.7	78 19.0	−56.7	19.4	80 10.8	−55.3	23.3	81 58.7	−52.9	28.9
16	73 31.2	58.2	13.7	75 27.4	57.8	15.5	77 22.3	57.1	17.9	79 15.5	56.0	21.1	81 05.8	54.3	25.7
17	72 33.0	58.5	12.9	74 29.6	58.1	14.4	76 25.2	57.4	16.5	78 19.5	56.7	19.2	80 11.5	55.3	23.1
18	71 34.5	58.6	12.1	73 31.5	58.2	13.5	75 27.8	57.8	15.3	77 22.8	57.1	17.7	79 16.2	56.1	20.9
19	70 35.9	58.7	11.5	72 33.3	58.5	12.7	74 30.0	58.1	14.3	76 25.7	57.5	16.3	78 20.1	56.7	19.0
20	69 37.2	−58.8	10.8	71 34.8	−58.6	12.0	73 31.9	−58.2	13.4	75 28.2	−57.8	15.1	77 23.4	−57.1	17.5
21	68 38.4	59.0	10.3	70 36.2	58.7	11.3	72 33.7	58.5	12.6	74 30.4	58.0	14.1	76 23.6	57.5	16.1
22	67 39.4	59.0	9.8	69 37.5	58.8	10.7	71 35.2	58.6	11.8	73 32.4	58.3	13.2	75 28.8	57.8	14.9
23	66 40.4	59.1	9.3	68 38.7	59.0	10.2	70 36.6	58.7	11.2	72 34.1	58.5	12.4	74 31.0	58.1	13.9
24	65 41.3	59.2	8.9	67 39.7	59.0	9.7	69 37.9	58.9	10.5	71 35.6	58.6	11.6	73 32.9	58.3	13.0
25	64 42.1	−59.2	8.5	66 40.7	−59.1	9.2	68 39.0	−58.9	10.0	70 37.0	−58.7	11.0	72 34.6	−58.5	12.2
26	63 42.9	59.3	8.1	65 41.6	59.3	8.8	67 40.1	59.0	9.5	69 38.3	58.8	10.4	71 36.1	58.6	11.5
27	62 43.6	59.3	7.8	64 42.5	59.3	8.4	66 41.1	59.1	9.0	68 39.5	59.0	9.8	70 37.5	58.7	10.8
28	61 44.3	59.3	7.5	63 43.2	59.2	8.0	65 42.0	59.2	8.6	67 40.5	59.0	9.3	69 38.8	58.9	10.2
29	60 45.0	59.5	7.2	62 44.0	59.4	7.7	64 42.8	59.2	8.2	66 41.5	59.1	8.9	68 39.9	58.9	9.7

Dec.	10° Hc	d	Z	12° Hc	d	Z	14° Hc	d	Z	16° Hc	d	Z	18° Hc	d	Z
°	° ′	′	°	° ′	′	°	° ′	′	°	° ′	′	°	° ′	′	°
0	79 14.2	+55.4	158.1	77 21.6	+56.8	161.4	75 27.0	+57.7	163.9	73 31.2	+58.2	165.8	71 34.5	+58.6	167.2
1	80 09.6	54.4	155.9	78 18.4	56.2	159.9	76 24.7	57.2	162.7	74 29.4	58.0	164.9	72 33.1	58.4	166.5
2	81 04.0	53.1	153.3	79 14.6	55.4	158.1	77 21.9	56.8	161.4	75 27.4	57.6	162.7	73 31.5	58.3	165.8
3	81 57.1	51.3°	150.2	80 10.0	54.5	155.9	78 18.7	56.3	159.9	76 25.0	57.3	162.7	74 29.8	58.0	164.9
4	82 48.4	48.7°	146.2	81 04.5	53.1	153.4	79 15.0	55.5	158.1	77 22.3	56.9	161.4	75 27.8	57.7	163.9
5	83 37.1	+45.2°	141.3	81 57.6	+51.4°	150.2	80 10.5	+54.6	156.0	78 19.2	+56.3	159.9	76 25.5	+57.3	162.8
6	84 22.3	39.8°	135.0	82 49.0	48.9°	146.3	81 05.1	53.2	153.4	79 15.5	55.6	158.1	77 22.8	57.0	161.5
7	85 02.1	32.2°	126.9	83 37.9	45.3°	141.4	81 58.3	51.5°	150.3	80 11.1	54.7	156.0	78 19.8	56.4	160.0
8	85 34.3	21.5°	116.5	84 23.2	40.0°	135.1	82 49.8	49.1°	146.4	81 05.8	53.3	153.5	79 16.2	55.6	158.2
9	85 55.8	+ 7.8°	103.9	85 03.2	32.4°	127.0	83 38.7	45.4°	141.5	81 59.1	51.7°	150.4	80 11.8	54.8	156.1
10	86 03.6	− 7.1°	89.7	85 35.6	+21.7°	116.6	84 24.3	+40.3°	135.2	82 50.8	+49.2°	146.5	81 06.6	+53.5	153.6
11	85 56.5	20.9°	75.4	85 57.3	+ 7.9°	103.9	85 04.6	32.6°	127.1	83 40.0	45.6°	141.5	82 00.1	51.8°	150.5
12	85 35.6	31.7°	62.6	86 05.2	− 7.1°	89.6	85 37.2	21.8°	116.7	84 25.6	40.5°	135.4	82 51.9	49.4°	146.7
13	85 03.9	39.6°	52.2	85 58.1	20.9°	75.2	85 59.0	+ 8.1°	103.9	85 06.1	32.9°	127.2	83 41.3	45.8°	141.8
14	84 24.3	44.9°	44.0	85 37.2	31.9°	62.4	86 07.1	− 7.1°	89.5	85 39.0	22.1°	116.8	84 27.1	40.8°	135.6
15	83 39.4	−48.6°	37.6	85 05.3	−39.7°	51.9	86 00.0	−21.0°	75.0	86 01.1	+ 8.2°	104.0	85 07.9	+33.1°	127.5
16	82 50.8	51.2°	32.6	84 25.6	45.0°	43.7	85 39.0	32.0°	62.1	86 09.3	− 7.1°	89.4	85 41.0	22.4°	117.0
17	81 59.6	53.0	28.6	83 40.6	48.7°	37.3	85 07.0	39.9°	51.6	86 02.2	21.2°	74.8	86 03.4	+ 8.4°	104.1
18	81 06.6	54.4	25.4	82 51.9	51.3°	32.3	84 27.1	45.1°	43.3	85 41.0	32.2°	61.8	86 11.8	− 7.2°	89.4
19	80 12.2	55.3	22.8	82 00.6	53.1	28.3	83 42.0	48.9°	36.9	85 08.8	40.0°	51.2	86 04.6	21.3°	74.6
20	79 16.9	−56.1	20.6	81 07.5	−54.4	25.1	82 53.1	−51.3°	30.0	84 28.8	−45.3°	43.0	85 43.3	−32.4°	61.5
21	78 20.8	56.7	18.8	80 13.1	55.4	22.5	82 01.8	53.2	28.0	83 43.5	49.0°	36.6	85 10.9	40.2°	50.8
22	77 24.1	57.2	17.2	79 17.7	56.1	20.4	81 08.6	54.5	24.8	82 54.5	51.5°	31.6	84 30.7	45.5°	42.6
23	76 26.9	57.5	15.9	78 21.6	56.7	18.6	80 14.1	55.4	22.2	82 03.0	53.2	27.7	83 45.2	49.2°	36.2
24	75 29.4	57.8	14.7	77 24.9	57.2	17.0	79 18.7	56.2	20.1	81 09.8	54.6	24.5	82 56.0	51.6°	31.2
25	74 31.6	−58.1	13.7	76 27.7	−57.6	15.7	78 22.5	−56.8	18.3	80 15.2	−55.5	21.9	82 04.4	−53.4	27.3
26	73 33.5	58.3	12.8	75 30.1	57.9	14.5	77 25.7	57.3	16.7	79 19.7	56.3	19.8	81 11.0	54.6	24.1
27	72 35.2	58.5	12.0	74 32.2	58.1	13.5	76 28.4	57.6	15.4	78 23.4	56.8	18.0	80 16.4	55.6	21.6
28	71 36.7	58.7	11.3	73 34.1	58.3	12.6	75 30.8	57.9	14.3	77 26.6	57.3	16.5	79 20.8	56.4	19.5
29	70 38.0	58.7	10.6	72 35.8	58.5	11.8	74 32.9	58.1	13.2	76 29.3	57.6	15.1	78 24.4	56.9	17.7

LATITUDE **CONTRARY** NAME L.H.A. 4°, 356°

0° Hc	d	Z	2° Hc	d	Z	4° Hc	d	Z	6° Hc	d	Z	8° Hc	d	Z	Dec.
86 00.0	− 7.4•	90.0	85 31.7	− 31.7•	116.5	84 20.7	− 44.8•	134.9	82 47.6	− 51.1•	146.2	81 03.7	− 54.3	153.3	0
85 52.6	20.9•	104.0	85 00.0	39.4•	126.8	83 35.9	48.5•	141.3	81 56.5	53.0	150.2	80 09.4	55.4	155.9	1
85 31.7	31.6•	116.6	84 20.6	44.7•	135.0	82 47.4	51.1•	146.3	81 03.5	54.3	153.4	79 14.0	56.1	158.1	2
85 00.1	39.4•	126.9	83 35.9	48.5•	141.3	81 56.3	52.9	150.2	80 09.2	55.3	156.0	78 17.9	56.7	159.9	3
84 20.7	44.7•	135.1	82 47.4	51.0•	146.3	81 03.4	54.2	153.4	79 13.9	56.1	158.1	77 21.2	57.1	161.5	4
83 36.0	− 48.4•	141.4	81 56.4	− 52.9	150.3	80 09.2	− 55.3	156.0	78 17.8	− 56.6	160.0	76 24.1	− 57.5	162.8	5
82 47.6	51.0•	146.4	81 03.5	54.2	153.5	79 13.9	56.0	158.2	77 21.2	57.1	161.5	75 26.6	57.9	164.0	6
81 56.6	52.9	150.4	80 09.3	55.3	156.1	78 17.9	56.7	160.0	76 24.1	57.5	162.9	74 28.7	58.1	165.0	7
81 03.7	54.2	153.6	79 14.0	56.0	158.3	77 21.2	57.1	161.6	75 26.6	57.9	164.0	73 30.6	58.3	165.9	8
80 09.5	55.3	156.2	78 18.0	56.6	160.1	76 24.1	57.5	163.0	74 28.7	58.0	165.1	72 32.3	58.4	166.7	9
79 14.2	− 56.0	158.4	77 21.4	− 57.1	161.7	75 26.6	− 57.8	164.1	73 30.7	− 58.3	166.0	71 33.9	− 58.6	167.5	10
78 18.2	56.6	160.3	76 24.3	57.5	163.1	74 28.8	58.0	165.2	72 32.4	58.5	166.8	70 35.3	58.8	168.1	11
77 21.6	57.1	161.8	75 26.8	57.8	164.2	73 30.8	58.3	166.1	71 33.9	58.6	167.5	69 36.5	58.9	168.7	12
76 24.5	57.5	163.2	74 29.0	58.0	165.3	72 32.5	58.4	166.9	70 35.3	58.7	168.2	68 37.6	58.9	169.3	13
75 27.0	57.7	164.4	73 31.0	58.3	166.2	71 34.1	58.6	167.6	69 36.6	58.8	168.8	67 38.7	59.1	169.7	14
74 29.3	− 58.1	165.4	72 32.7	− 58.4	167.0	70 35.5	− 58.8	168.3	68 37.7	− 58.9	169.3	66 39.6	− 59.1	170.2	15
73 31.2	58.2	166.3	71 34.3	58.6	167.8	69 36.7	58.8	168.9	67 38.8	59.0	169.8	65 40.5	59.2	170.6	16
72 33.0	58.5	167.1	70 35.7	58.8	168.4	68 37.9	58.9	169.5	66 39.8	59.2	170.3	64 41.3	59.2	171.0	17
71 34.5	58.6	167.9	69 36.9	58.8	169.0	67 39.0	59.1	170.0	65 40.6	59.1	170.7	63 42.1	59.3	171.4	18
70 35.9	58.7	168.5	68 38.1	58.9	169.6	66 39.9	59.1	170.4	64 41.5	59.3	171.1	62 42.8	59.3	171.7	19
69 37.2	− 58.8	169.2	67 39.2	− 59.1	170.1	65 40.8	− 59.1	170.8	63 42.2	− 59.2	171.5	61 43.5	− 59.4	172.0	20
68 38.4	59.0	169.7	66 40.1	59.1	170.5	64 41.7	59.3	171.2	62 43.0	59.4	171.8	60 44.1	59.4	172.3	21
67 39.4	59.0	170.2	65 41.0	59.1	171.0	63 42.4	59.3	171.6	61 43.6	59.3	172.2	59 44.7	59.5	172.6	22
66 40.4	59.1	170.7	64 41.9	59.3	171.4	62 43.1	59.3	171.9	60 44.3	59.5	172.5	58 45.2	59.4	172.9	23
65 41.3	59.2	171.1	63 42.6	59.2	171.7	61 43.8	59.4	172.3	59 44.8	59.4	172.7	57 45.8	59.6	173.1	24
64 42.1	− 59.2	171.5	62 43.4	− 59.4	172.1	60 44.4	− 59.4	172.6	58 45.4	− 59.5	173.0	56 46.2	− 59.5	173.4	25
63 42.9	59.3	171.9	61 44.0	59.3	172.4	59 45.0	59.4	172.9	57 45.9	59.5	173.2	55 46.7	59.5	173.6	26
62 43.6	59.3	172.2	60 44.7	59.4	172.7	58 45.6	59.5	173.1	56 46.4	59.5	173.5	54 47.2	59.6	173.8	27
61 44.3	59.3	172.5	59 45.3	59.5	173.0	57 46.1	59.5	173.4	55 46.9	59.6	173.7	53 47.6	59.6	174.0	28
60 45.0	59.5	172.8	58 45.8	59.4	173.2	56 46.6	59.5	173.6	54 47.3	59.5	173.9	52 48.0	59.6	174.2	29

10° Hc	d	Z	12° Hc	d	Z	14° Hc	d	Z	16° Hc	d	Z	18° Hc	d	Z	Dec.
79 14.2	− 56.1	158.1	77 21.6	− 57.2	161.4	75 27.0	− 57.9	163.9	73 31.2	− 58.4	165.8	71 34.5	− 58.7	167.2	0
78 18.1	56.7	159.9	76 24.4	57.6	162.7	74 29.1	58.1	164.9	72 32.8	58.5	166.6	70 35.8	58.9	167.9	1
77 21.4	57.2	161.4	75 26.8	57.9	163.9	73 31.0	58.4	165.8	71 34.3	58.7	167.3	69 36.9	58.9	168.5	2
76 24.2	57.6	162.8	74 28.9	58.1	164.9	72 32.6	58.5	166.6	70 35.6	58.9	167.9	68 38.0	59.0	169.0	3
75 26.6	57.8	163.9	73 30.8	58.3	165.8	71 34.1	58.7	167.3	69 36.7	58.9	168.5	67 39.0	59.2	169.5	4
74 28.8	− 58.1	164.9	72 32.5	− 58.6	166.6	70 35.4	− 58.8	167.9	68 37.8	− 59.0	169.0	66 39.8	− 59.2	169.9	5
73 30.7	58.3	165.9	71 33.9	58.5	167.3	69 36.6	58.9	168.5	67 38.8	59.1	169.5	65 40.6	59.2	170.3	6
72 32.4	58.5	166.7	70 35.3	58.8	168.0	68 37.7	59.0	169.0	66 39.7	59.2	169.9	64 41.4	59.3	170.7	7
71 33.9	58.7	167.4	69 36.5	58.9	168.6	67 38.7	59.1	169.5	65 40.5	59.2	170.3	63 42.1	59.3	171.0	8
70 35.2	58.7	168.0	68 37.6	59.0	169.1	66 39.6	59.1	170.0	64 41.3	59.3	170.7	62 42.8	59.4	171.4	9
69 36.5	− 58.9	168.6	67 38.6	− 59.0	169.6	65 40.5	− 59.3	170.4	63 42.0	− 59.3	171.1	61 43.4	− 59.5	171.7	10
68 37.6	59.0	169.2	66 39.6	59.2	170.0	64 41.2	59.2	170.8	62 42.7	59.4	171.4	60 43.9	59.4	171.9	11
67 38.6	59.0	169.7	65 40.4	59.2	170.5	63 42.0	59.4	171.1	61 43.3	59.4	171.7	59 44.5	59.5	172.2	12
66 39.6	59.1	170.1	64 41.2	59.2	170.9	62 42.6	59.3	171.5	60 43.9	59.4	172.0	58 45.0	59.5	172.5	13
65 40.5	59.2	170.5	63 42.0	59.3	171.2	61 43.3	59.4	171.8	59 44.4	59.4	172.3	57 45.5	59.6	172.7	14
64 41.3	− 59.3	170.9	62 42.7	− 59.4	171.5	60 43.9	− 59.5	172.1	58 45.0	− 59.6	172.5	56 45.9	− 59.6	172.9	15
63 42.0	59.3	171.3	61 43.3	59.4	171.9	59 44.4	59.4	172.4	57 45.4	59.5	172.8	55 46.3	59.5	173.1	16
62 42.7	59.3	171.6	60 43.9	59.4	172.2	58 45.0	59.5	172.6	56 45.9	59.5	173.0	54 46.8	59.7	173.4	17
61 43.4	59.4	171.9	59 44.5	59.5	172.4	57 45.5	59.6	172.9	55 46.3	59.5	173.2	53 47.1	59.6	173.6	18
60 44.0	59.4	172.2	58 45.0	59.5	172.7	56 45.9	59.5	173.1	54 46.8	59.6	173.4	52 47.5	59.6	173.7	19
59 44.6	− 59.5	172.5	57 45.5	− 59.5	172.9	55 46.4	− 59.5	173.3	53 47.2	− 59.7	173.6	51 47.9	− 59.7	173.9	20
58 45.1	59.5	172.8	56 46.0	59.5	173.2	54 46.8	59.6	173.5	52 47.5	59.6	173.8	50 48.2	59.7	174.1	21
57 45.6	59.5	173.0	55 46.5	59.6	173.4	53 47.2	59.6	173.7	51 47.9	59.6	174.0	49 48.5	59.7	174.2	22
56 46.1	59.5	173.3	54 47.1	59.6	173.6	52 47.6	59.6	173.9	50 48.3	59.7	174.2	48 48.8	59.7	174.4	23
55 46.6	59.6	173.5	53 47.3	59.6	173.8	51 48.0	59.7	174.1	49 48.6	59.7	174.3	47 49.1	59.7	174.6	24
54 47.0	− 59.6	173.7	52 47.7	− 59.6	174.0	50 48.3	− 59.6	174.3	48 48.9	− 59.7	174.5	46 49.4	− 59.7	174.7	25
53 47.4	59.6	173.9	51 48.1	59.7	174.2	49 48.7	59.7	174.4	47 49.2	59.7	174.6	45 49.7	59.7	174.8	26
52 47.8	59.6	174.1	50 48.4	59.6	174.4	48 49.0	59.7	174.6	46 49.5	59.7	174.8	44 50.0	59.8	175.0	27
51 48.2	59.6	174.3	49 48.8	59.7	174.5	47 49.3	59.7	174.7	45 49.8	59.7	174.9	43 50.2	59.7	175.1	28
50 48.6	59.7	174.5	48 49.1	59.7	174.7	46 49.6	59.7	174.9	44 50.1	59.8	175.1	42 50.5	59.8	175.2	29

Dec.	20° Hc	d	Z	22° Hc	d	Z	24° Hc	d	Z	26° Hc	d	Z	28° Hc	d	Z
0	69 37.2	+58.9	168.4	67 39.4	+59.1	169.4	65 41.3	+59.3	170.2	63 42.9	+59.4	170.9	61 44.3	+59.5	171.5
1	70 36.1	58.7	167.9	68 38.5	59.0	169.0	66 40.6	59.1	169.9	64 42.3	59.3	170.6	62 43.8	59.4	171.2
2	71 34.8	58.7	167.3	69 37.5	58.9	168.4	67 39.7	59.2	169.4	65 41.6	59.3	170.2	63 43.2	59.4	170.9
3	72 33.5	58.4	166.6	70 36.4	58.8	167.9	68 38.9	59.0	169.0	66 40.9	59.2	169.9	64 42.6	59.4	170.6
4	73 31.9	58.3	165.8	71 35.2	58.7	167.3	69 37.9	58.9	168.5	67 40.1	59.1	169.4	65 42.0	59.3	170.3
5	74 30.2	+58.0	164.9	72 33.9	+58.5	166.6	70 36.8	+58.8	167.9	68 39.2	+59.1	169.0	66 41.3	+59.2	169.9
6	75 28.2	57.8	163.9	73 32.4	58.3	165.8	71 35.6	58.7	167.3	69 38.3	59.0	168.5	67 40.5	59.2	169.5
7	76 26.0	57.4	162.8	74 30.7	58.1	165.0	72 34.3	58.6	166.5	70 37.3	58.8	167.4	68 39.7	59.1	169.0
8	77 23.4	57.0	161.6	75 28.8	57.8	164.0	73 32.9	58.4	165.9	71 36.1	58.8	167.4	69 38.8	59.0	168.5
9	78 20.4	56.5	160.1	76 26.6	57.5	162.9	74 31.3	58.1	165.0	72 34.9	58.6	166.7	70 37.8	58.9	168.0
10	79 16.9	+55.8	158.3	77 24.1	+57.1	161.6	75 29.4	+57.9	164.1	73 33.5	+58.4	166.0	71 36.7	+58.8	167.4
11	80 12.7	54.8	156.2	78 21.2	56.5	160.2	76 27.3	57.6	163.0	74 31.9	58.2	165.1	72 35.5	58.6	166.8
12	81 07.5	53.7	153.7	79 17.7	55.9	158.4	77 24.9	57.1	161.8	75 30.1	57.9	164.2	73 34.1	58.5	166.0
13	82 01.2	51.9*	150.7	80 13.6	55.0	156.4	78 22.0	56.7	160.3	76 28.0	57.7	163.1	74 32.6	58.2	165.2
14	82 53.1	49.6*	146.9	81 08.6	53.8	153.9	79 18.7	56.0	158.6	77 25.7	57.2	161.9	75 30.8	58.1	164.3
15	83 42.7	+46.1*	142.0	82 02.4	+52.1*	150.9	80 14.7	+55.1	156.6	78 22.9	+56.8	160.5	76 28.9	+57.7	163.2
16	84 28.8	41.1*	135.8	82 54.5	49.8*	147.1	81 09.8	53.9	154.1	79 19.7	56.1	158.8	77 26.6	57.3	162.0
17	85 09.9	33.4*	127.7	83 44.3	46.4*	142.3	82 03.7	52.3	151.1	80 15.8	55.2	156.8	78 23.9	56.9	160.6
18	85 43.3	22.7*	117.2	84 30.7	41.3*	136.1	82 56.0	50.1*	147.4	81 11.0	54.2	154.3	79 20.8	56.2	159.0
19	86 06.0+	8.5*	104.2	85 12.0	33.8*	128.0	83 46.1	46.7*	142.6	82 05.2	52.5	151.4	80 17.0	55.4	157.0
20	86 14.5-	7.2*	89.3	85 45.8	+23.0*	117.4	84 32.8	+41.6*	136.4	82 57.7	+50.3*	147.7	81 12.4	+54.3	154.6
21	86 07.3	21.5*	74.4	86 08.8	+ 8.7*	104.3	85 14.4	34.2*	128.3	83 48.0	47.0*	142.3	82 06.7	52.8	151.7
22	85 45.8	32.6*	61.1	86 17.5	- 7.2*	89.3	85 48.6	23.3*	117.7	84 35.0	42.0*	136.8	82 59.5	50.5*	148.0
23	85 13.2	40.4*	50.4	86 10.3	21.7*	74.1	86 11.9	+ 8.9*	104.4	85 17.0	34.6*	128.7	83 50.0	47.4*	143.3
24	84 32.8	45.8*	42.1	85 48.6	32.9*	60.7	86 20.8	- 7.3*	89.2	85 51.6	23.6*	118.0	84 37.4	42.4*	137.2
25	83 47.0	-49.3*	35.7	85 15.7	-40.7*	49.9	86 13.5	-21.9*	73.8	86 15.2	+ 9.1*	104.6	85 19.8	+35.0*	129.1
26	82 57.7	51.8*	30.8	84 35.0	46.0*	41.6	85 51.6	33.2*	60.3	86 24.3	- 7.3*	89.1	85 54.8	24.0*	118.4
27	82 05.9	53.5	26.9	83 49.0	49.5*	35.2	85 18.4	41.0*	49.4	86 17.0	22.2*	73.5	86 18.8	+ 9.3*	104.8
28	81 12.4	54.8	23.8	82 59.5	52.0*	30.3	84 37.4	46.3*	41.1	85 54.8	33.5*	59.8	86 28.1	- 7.4*	89.1
29	80 17.6	55.7	21.2	82 07.5	53.6	26.4	83 51.1	49.7*	34.7	85 21.3	41.4*	48.9	86 20.7	22.5*	73.2

Dec.	30° Hc	d	Z	32° Hc	d	Z	34° Hc	d	Z	36° Hc	d	Z	38° Hc	d	Z
0	59 45.5	+59.6	172.0	57 46.6	+59.7	172.5	55 47.6	+59.7	172.9	53 48.5	+59.7	173.2	51 49.3	+59.8	173.5
1	60 45.1	59.5	171.8	58 46.3	59.6	172.3	56 47.3	59.6	172.7	54 48.2	59.7	173.0	52 49.1	59.7	173.4
2	61 44.6	59.5	171.5	59 45.9	59.5	172.0	57 46.9	59.7	172.5	55 47.9	59.7	172.9	53 48.8	59.7	173.2
3	62 44.1	59.5	171.3	60 45.4	59.5	171.8	58 46.6	59.6	172.3	56 47.6	59.7	172.7	54 48.5	59.8	173.1
4	63 43.6	59.4	171.0	61 45.0	59.5	171.5	59 46.2	59.6	172.1	57 47.3	59.6	172.5	55 48.3	59.7	172.9
5	64 43.0	+59.4	170.6	62 44.5	+59.5	171.3	60 45.8	+59.6	171.8	58 46.9	+59.7	172.3	56 48.0	+59.7	172.7
6	65 42.4	59.3	170.3	63 44.0	59.4	171.0	61 45.4	59.5	171.6	59 46.6	59.6	172.1	57 47.7	59.6	172.5
7	66 41.7	59.3	169.9	64 43.4	59.4	170.7	62 44.9	59.5	171.3	60 46.2	59.6	171.8	58 47.3	59.7	172.3
8	67 41.0	59.2	169.5	65 42.8	59.4	170.3	63 44.4	59.5	171.0	61 45.8	59.5	171.6	59 47.0	59.6	172.1
9	68 40.2	59.1	169.1	66 42.2	59.3	170.0	64 43.9	59.4	170.7	62 45.3	59.5	171.3	60 46.6	59.6	171.9
10	69 39.3	+59.0	168.6	67 41.5	+59.2	169.6	65 43.3	+59.4	170.4	63 44.8	+59.5	171.1	61 46.2	+59.6	171.6
11	70 38.3	59.0	168.1	68 40.7	59.2	169.1	66 42.7	59.3	170.0	64 44.3	59.5	170.8	62 45.8	59.5	171.3
12	71 37.3	58.8	167.5	69 39.9	59.0	168.7	67 42.0	59.3	169.6	65 43.8	59.4	170.4	63 45.3	59.4	171.1
13	72 36.1	58.7	166.9	70 38.9	59.0	168.2	68 41.3	59.2	169.2	66 43.2	59.4	170.1	64 44.9	59.4	170.8
14	73 34.8	58.5	166.1	71 37.9	58.9	167.6	69 40.5	59.1	168.8	67 42.6	59.3	169.7	65 44.3	59.3	170.5
15	74 33.3	+58.4	165.3	72 36.8	+58.7	167.0	70 39.6	+59.0	168.3	68 41.9	+59.2	169.3	66 43.8	+59.4	170.2
16	75 31.7	58.0	164.4	73 35.5	58.6	166.3	71 38.6	58.9	167.7	69 41.1	59.2	168.9	67 43.2	59.3	169.8
17	76 29.7	57.8	163.4	74 34.1	58.4	165.5	72 37.5	58.8	167.1	70 40.3	59.0	168.4	68 42.5	59.2	169.4
18	77 27.5	57.5	162.2	75 32.5	58.2	164.6	73 36.3	58.7	166.4	71 39.3	59.0	167.8	69 41.8	59.2	169.0
19	78 25.0	56.9	160.8	76 30.7	57.9	163.6	74 35.0	58.4	165.6	72 38.3	58.9	167.2	70 41.0	59.1	168.5
20	79 21.9	+56.4	159.2	77 28.6	+57.5	162.4	75 33.4	+58.3	164.8	73 37.2	+58.7	166.6	71 40.1	+59.0	168.0
21	80 18.3	55.6	157.2	78 26.1	57.1	161.0	76 31.7	58.0	163.8	74 35.9	58.5	165.8	72 39.1	58.9	167.4
22	81 13.9	54.5	154.9	79 23.2	56.5	159.4	77 29.7	57.6	162.6	75 34.4	58.3	165.0	73 38.0	58.8	166.7
23	82 08.4	53.0	152.0	80 19.7	55.7	157.5	78 27.3	57.2	161.3	76 32.7	58.1	164.0	74 36.8	58.6	166.0
24	83 01.4	50.8*	148.4	81 15.4	54.7	155.2	79 24.5	56.7	159.7	77 30.8	57.8	162.9	75 35.4	58.4	165.2
25	83 52.2	+47.7*	143.7	82 10.1	+53.3	152.4	80 21.2	+55.9	157.8	78 28.6	+57.3	161.6	76 33.8	+58.2	164.2
26	84 39.9	42.9*	137.6	83 03.4	51.1*	148.8	81 17.1	54.9	155.6	79 25.9	56.8	160.0	77 32.0	57.9	163.1
27	85 22.8	35.4*	129.5	83 54.5	48.1*	144.1	82 12.0	53.5	153.1	80 22.7	56.1	158.2	78 29.9	57.4	161.8
28	85 58.2	24.5*	118.8	84 42.6	43.3*	138.1	83 05.5	51.4*	149.2	81 18.8	55.1	155.9	79 27.3	57.0	160.3
29	86 22.7	+ 9.5*	105.0	85 25.9	36.0*	130.0	83 56.9	48.5*	144.6	82 13.9	53.8	153.2	80 24.3	56.2	158.5

20°			22°			24°			26°			28°			Dec.
Hc	d	Z	Hc	d	Z	Hc	d	Z	Hc	d	Z	Hc	d	Z	°
69 37.2	−59.0	168.4	67 39.4	−59.1	169.4	65 41.3	−59.3	170.2	63 42.9	−59.4	170.9	61 44.3	−59.5	171.5	0
68 38.2	59.0	169.0	66 40.3	59.3	169.9	64 42.0	59.4	170.6	62 43.5	59.5	171.2	60 44.8	59.5	171.8	1
67 39.2	59.2	169.4	65 41.0	59.2	170.3	63 42.6	59.3	170.9	61 44.0	59.5	171.5	59 45.3	59.6	172.0	2
66 40.0	59.2	169.9	64 41.8	59.4	170.6	62 43.3	59.5	171.3	60 44.6	59.6	171.8	58 45.7	59.6	172.3	3
65 40.8	59.2	170.3	63 42.4	59.4	171.0	61 43.8	59.5	171.6	59 45.0	59.5	172.1	57 46.1	59.6	172.5	4
64 41.6	−59.4	170.6	62 43.0	−59.4	171.3	60 44.3	−59.5	171.8	58 45.5	−59.6	172.3	56 46.5	−59.6	172.7	5
63 42.2	59.3	171.0	61 43.6	59.4	171.6	59 44.8	59.5	172.1	57 45.9	59.6	172.5	55 46.9	59.7	172.9	6
62 42.9	59.4	171.3	60 44.2	59.5	171.9	58 45.3	59.5	172.3	56 46.3	59.6	172.7	54 47.2	59.7	173.1	7
61 43.5	59.5	171.6	59 44.7	59.5	172.1	57 45.8	59.6	172.6	55 46.7	59.6	172.9	53 47.6	59.7	173.3	8
60 44.0	59.4	171.9	58 45.2	59.6	172.4	56 46.2	59.6	172.8	54 47.1	59.7	173.1	52 47.9	59.7	173.5	9
59 44.6	−59.5	172.2	57 45.6	−59.6	172.6	55 46.6	−59.7	173.0	53 47.4	−59.6	173.3	51 48.2	−59.7	173.6	10
58 45.1	59.6	172.4	56 46.0	59.5	172.8	54 46.9	59.6	173.2	52 47.8	59.7	173.5	50 48.5	59.7	173.8	11
57 45.5	59.5	172.7	55 46.5	59.7	173.0	53 47.3	59.7	173.4	51 48.1	59.7	173.7	49 48.8	59.8	173.9	12
56 46.0	59.6	172.9	54 46.8	59.6	173.2	52 47.6	59.6	173.5	50 48.4	59.7	173.8	48 49.0	59.7	174.1	13
55 46.4	59.6	173.1	53 47.2	59.6	173.4	51 48.0	59.7	173.7	49 48.7	59.8	174.0	47 49.3	59.8	174.2	14
54 46.8	−59.6	173.3	52 47.6	−59.7	173.6	50 48.3	−59.7	173.9	48 48.9	−59.7	174.1	46 49.5	−59.7	174.3	15
53 47.2	59.7	173.5	51 47.9	59.7	173.8	49 48.6	59.7	174.0	47 49.2	59.7	174.3	45 49.8	59.8	174.5	16
52 47.5	59.6	173.7	50 48.2	59.7	173.9	48 48.9	59.8	174.2	46 49.5	59.8	174.4	44 50.0	59.8	174.6	17
51 47.9	59.7	173.8	49 48.5	59.7	174.1	47 49.1	59.7	174.3	45 49.7	59.8	174.5	43 50.2	59.7	174.7	18
50 48.2	59.7	174.0	48 48.8	59.7	174.2	46 49.4	59.7	174.5	44 50.0	59.8	174.7	42 50.5	59.8	174.8	19
49 48.5	−59.7	174.2	47 49.1	−59.7	174.4	45 49.7	−59.8	174.6	43 50.2	−59.8	174.8	41 50.7	−59.8	175.0	20
48 48.8	59.7	174.3	46 49.4	59.7	174.5	44 49.9	59.7	174.7	42 50.4	59.8	174.9	40 50.9	59.8	175.1	21
47 49.1	59.7	174.5	45 49.7	59.8	174.7	43 50.2	59.8	174.9	41 50.6	59.8	175.0	39 51.1	59.8	175.2	22
46 49.4	59.4	174.6	44 49.9	59.7	174.8	42 50.4	59.8	175.0	40 50.8	59.8	175.1	38 51.3	59.9	175.3	23
45 49.7	59.8	174.8	43 50.2	59.8	174.9	41 50.6	59.8	175.1	39 51.0	59.8	175.2	37 51.4	59.8	175.4	24
44 49.9	−59.7	174.9	42 50.4	−59.8	175.1	40 50.8	−59.8	175.2	38 51.2	−59.8	175.3	36 51.6	−59.8	175.5	25
43 50.2	59.8	175.0	41 50.6	59.7	175.2	39 51.0	59.8	175.3	37 51.4	59.8	175.4	35 51.8	59.9	175.6	26
42 50.4	59.7	175.1	40 50.8	59.7	175.3	38 51.2	59.8	175.4	36 51.6	59.8	175.5	34 52.0	59.9	175.7	27
41 50.7	59.8	175.3	39 51.1	59.8	175.4	37 51.4	59.8	175.5	35 51.8	59.8	175.6	33 52.1	59.8	175.7	28
40 50.9	59.8	175.4	38 51.3	59.8	175.5	36 51.6	59.8	175.6	34 52.0	59.9	175.7	32 52.3	59.8	175.8	29

30°			32°			34°			36°			38°			Dec.
Hc	d	Z	Hc	d	Z	Hc	d	Z	Hc	d	Z	Hc	d	Z	°
59 45.5	−59.5	172.0	57 46.6	−59.6	172.5	55 47.6	−59.7	172.9	53 48.5	−59.7	173.2	51 49.3	−59.8	173.5	0
58 46.0	59.6	172.3	56 47.0	59.6	172.7	54 47.9	59.7	173.1	52 48.8	59.8	173.4	50 49.5	59.7	173.7	1
57 46.4	59.7	172.5	55 47.3	59.6	172.9	53 48.2	59.7	173.2	51 49.0	59.8	173.5	49 49.8	59.8	173.8	2
56 46.7	59.6	172.7	54 47.7	59.7	173.1	52 48.5	59.7	173.4	50 49.3	59.8	173.7	48 50.0	59.8	173.9	3
55 47.1	59.7	172.9	53 48.0	59.7	173.2	51 48.8	59.8	173.5	49 49.5	59.8	173.8	47 50.2	59.8	174.0	4
54 47.4	−59.6	173.1	52 48.3	−59.7	173.4	50 49.0	−59.7	173.7	48 49.7	−59.8	173.9	46 50.4	−59.8	174.2	5
53 47.8	59.7	173.3	51 48.6	59.8	173.6	49 49.3	59.8	173.8	47 49.9	59.7	174.1	45 50.6	59.9	174.3	6
52 48.1	59.7	173.4	50 48.8	59.7	173.7	48 49.5	59.8	174.0	46 50.2	59.8	174.2	44 50.7	59.8	174.4	7
51 48.4	59.7	173.6	49 49.1	59.8	173.9	47 49.7	59.7	174.1	45 50.4	59.9	174.3	43 50.9	59.8	174.5	8
50 48.6	59.7	173.7	48 49.3	59.7	174.0	46 50.0	59.8	174.2	44 50.5	59.8	174.4	42 51.1	59.8	174.6	9
49 48.9	−59.7	173.9	47 49.6	−59.8	174.1	45 50.2	−59.8	174.3	43 50.7	−59.8	174.5	41 51.3	−59.9	174.7	10
48 49.2	59.8	174.0	46 49.8	59.8	174.3	44 50.4	59.8	174.5	42 50.9	59.9	174.6	40 51.4	59.8	174.8	11
47 49.4	59.7	174.2	45 50.0	59.8	174.4	43 50.6	59.8	174.6	41 51.1	59.8	174.7	39 51.6	59.9	174.9	12
46 49.7	59.8	174.3	44 50.3	59.8	174.5	42 50.8	59.9	174.7	40 51.3	59.9	174.8	38 51.7	59.8	175.0	13
45 49.9	59.8	174.4	43 50.4	59.8	174.6	41 50.9	59.8	174.8	39 51.4	59.8	175.0	37 51.9	59.9	175.1	14
44 50.1	−59.8	174.5	42 50.6	−59.8	174.7	40 51.1	−59.8	174.9	38 51.6	−59.9	175.0	36 52.0	−59.8	175.2	15
43 50.3	59.8	174.7	41 50.8	59.8	174.8	39 51.3	59.8	175.0	37 51.7	59.8	175.1	35 52.2	59.9	175.3	16
42 50.5	59.8	174.8	40 51.0	59.8	174.9	38 51.5	59.9	175.1	36 51.9	59.9	175.2	34 52.3	59.9	175.4	17
41 50.7	59.8	174.9	39 51.2	59.8	175.0	37 51.6	59.8	175.2	35 52.0	59.8	175.3	33 52.4	59.8	175.4	18
40 50.9	59.8	175.0	38 51.4	59.9	175.1	36 51.8	59.9	175.3	34 52.2	59.9	175.4	32 52.6	59.9	175.5	19
39 51.1	−59.8	175.1	37 51.5	−59.8	175.2	35 51.9	−59.8	175.4	33 52.3	−59.8	175.5	31 52.7	−59.9	175.6	20
38 51.3	59.8	175.2	36 51.7	59.8	175.3	34 52.1	59.9	175.4	32 52.5	59.9	175.6	30 52.8	59.9	175.6	21
37 51.5	59.8	175.3	35 51.9	59.9	175.4	33 52.2	59.8	175.5	31 52.6	59.9	175.6	29 52.9	59.8	175.7	22
36 51.6	59.8	175.4	34 52.0	59.8	175.5	32 52.4	59.9	175.6	30 52.7	59.7	175.7	28 53.1	59.9	175.8	23
35 51.8	59.8	175.5	33 52.2	59.9	175.6	31 52.5	59.8	175.7	29 52.9	59.8	175.8	27 53.2	59.9	175.9	24
34 52.0	−59.8	175.6	32 52.3	−59.8	175.7	30 52.7	−59.9	175.8	28 53.0	−59.9	175.9	25 53.3	−59.8	175.9	25
33 52.1	59.7	175.7	31 52.5	59.9	175.7	29 52.8	59.8	175.9	27 53.1	59.9	175.9	25 53.4	59.9	176.0	26
32 52.3	59.8	175.8	30 52.6	59.8	175.8	28 52.9	59.8	175.9	26 53.2	59.9	176.0	24 53.5	59.9	176.1	27
31 52.5	59.9	175.8	29 52.8	59.9	175.9	27 53.1	59.9	176.0	25 53.3	59.8	176.1	23 53.6	59.9	176.1	28
30 52.6	59.8	175.9	28 52.9	59.9	176.0	26 53.2	59.9	176.1	24 53.5	59.9	176.1	22 53.7	59.9	176.2	29

Dec.	40° Hc	d	Z	42° Hc	d	Z	44° Hc	d	Z	46° Hc	d	Z	48° Hc	d	Z
0	49 50.0	+59.8	173.8	47 50.7	+59.8	174.0	45 51.3	+59.9	174.3	43 51.9	+59.9	174.4	41 52.5	+59.8	174.6
1	50 49.8	59.8	173.7	48 50.5	59.8	173.9	46 51.2	59.7	174.1	44 51.8	59.8	174.4	42 52.3	59.9	174.5
2	51 49.6	59.7	173.5	49 50.3	59.8	173.8	47 51.0	59.8	173.9	45 51.6	59.9	174.3	43 52.2	59.9	174.5
3	52 49.4	59.7	173.4	50 50.1	59.8	173.7	48 50.8	59.9	173.9	46 51.5	59.8	174.2	44 52.1	59.9	174.4
4	53 49.1	59.8	173.2	51 49.9	59.8	173.5	49 50.7	59.8	173.8	47 51.3	59.9	174.0	45 52.0	59.8	174.3
5	54 48.9	+59.7	173.1	52 49.7	+59.8	173.4	50 50.5	+59.8	173.6	48 51.2	+59.8	173.9	46 51.8	+59.9	174.2
6	55 48.6	59.7	172.9	53 49.5	59.7	173.3	51 50.3	59.8	173.6	49 51.0	59.8	173.8	47 51.7	59.8	174.1
7	56 48.3	59.7	172.7	54 49.3	59.7	173.1	52 50.1	59.8	173.4	50 50.8	59.9	173.7	48 51.5	59.9	174.0
8	57 48.0	59.7	172.6	55 49.0	59.7	172.9	53 49.9	59.7	173.3	51 50.7	59.8	173.5	49 51.4	59.8	173.8
9	58 47.7	59.7	172.4	56 48.7	59.7	172.8	54 49.6	59.8	173.1	52 50.5	59.8	173.4	50 51.2	59.9	173.7
10	59 47.4	+59.7	172.2	57 48.5	+59.7	172.6	55 49.4	+59.8	173.0	53 50.3	+59.8	173.3	51 51.1	+59.8	173.6
11	60 47.1	59.6	171.9	58 48.2	59.7	172.4	56 49.2	59.7	172.8	54 50.1	59.7	173.2	52 50.9	59.8	173.5
12	61 46.7	59.6	171.7	59 47.9	59.6	172.2	57 48.9	59.7	172.6	55 49.8	59.8	173.0	53 50.7	59.8	173.4
13	62 46.3	59.6	171.5	60 47.5	59.6	172.0	58 48.6	59.7	172.5	56 49.6	59.8	172.9	54 50.5	59.8	173.2
14	63 45.9	59.5	171.2	61 47.2	59.6	171.8	59 48.3	59.7	172.3	57 49.4	59.7	172.7	55 50.3	59.8	173.1
15	64 45.4	+59.5	170.9	62 46.8	+59.6	171.5	60 48.0	+59.7	172.1	58 49.1	+59.7	172.5	56 50.1	+59.8	172.9
16	65 44.9	59.5	170.6	63 46.4	59.6	171.3	61 47.7	59.7	171.8	59 48.8	59.8	172.3	57 49.9	59.8	172.8
17	66 44.4	59.4	170.3	64 46.0	59.5	171.0	62 47.4	59.6	171.6	60 48.6	59.7	172.1	58 49.6	59.8	172.6
18	67 43.8	59.5	169.9	65 45.5	59.5	170.7	63 47.0	59.6	171.4	61 48.3	59.6	171.9	59 49.4	59.7	172.4
19	68 43.2	59.3	169.5	66 45.0	59.4	170.4	64 46.6	59.5	171.1	62 47.9	59.7	171.7	60 49.1	59.7	172.2
20	69 42.5	+59.2	169.1	67 44.5	+59.4	170.0	65 46.1	+59.6	170.8	63 47.6	+59.6	171.5	61 48.8	+59.7	172.0
21	70 41.7	59.2	168.6	68 43.9	59.3	169.7	66 45.7	59.5	170.5	64 47.2	59.6	171.2	62 48.5	59.7	171.8
22	71 40.9	59.1	168.1	69 43.2	59.3	169.2	67 45.2	59.4	170.2	65 46.8	59.6	170.9	63 48.2	59.6	171.5
23	72 40.0	59.0	167.6	70 42.5	59.2	168.8	68 44.6	59.4	169.8	66 46.4	59.5	170.6	64 47.8	59.7	171.3
24	73 39.0	58.8	166.9	71 41.8	59.1	168.3	69 44.0	59.3	169.4	67 45.9	59.5	170.3	65 47.5	59.6	171.1
25	74 37.8	+58.7	166.2	72 40.9	+59.0	167.7	70 43.3	+59.3	169.0	68 45.4	+59.4	170.0	66 47.1	+59.5	170.8
26	75 36.5	58.5	165.4	73 39.9	59.1	167.1	71 42.6	59.2	168.5	69 44.8	59.4	169.6	67 46.6	59.5	170.5
27	76 35.0	58.2	164.5	74 38.8	58.8	166.4	72 41.8	59.1	167.9	70 44.2	59.3	169.1	68 46.1	59.5	170.1
28	77 33.2	58.0	163.4	75 37.6	58.6	165.6	73 40.9	59.0	167.3	71 43.5	59.2	168.7	69 45.6	59.4	169.7
29	78 31.2	57.6	162.1	76 36.2	58.3	164.7	74 39.9	58.8	166.7	72 42.7	59.2	168.2	70 45.0	59.4	169.3

Dec.	50° Hc	d	Z	52° Hc	d	Z	54° Hc	d	Z	56° Hc	d	Z	58° Hc	d	Z
0	39 53.0	+59.9	174.8	37 53.5	+59.9	174.9	35 53.9	+59.9	175.1	33 54.4	+59.9	175.2	31 54.8	+59.9	175.3
1	40 52.9	59.9	174.7	38 53.4	59.9	174.9	36 53.8	60.0	175.0	34 54.3	59.9	175.1	32 54.7	60.0	175.2
2	41 52.8	59.9	174.6	39 53.3	59.9	174.8	37 53.8	59.9	174.9	35 54.2	59.9	175.1	33 54.7	59.9	175.2
3	42 52.7	59.8	174.5	40 53.2	59.9	174.7	38 53.7	59.9	174.9	36 54.1	60.0	175.0	34 54.6	59.9	175.1
4	43 52.5	59.9	174.5	41 53.1	59.9	174.6	39 53.6	59.9	174.8	37 54.1	59.9	174.9	35 54.5	60.0	175.1
5	44 52.4	+59.9	174.4	42 53.0	+59.9	174.6	40 53.5	+59.9	174.7	38 54.0	+59.9	174.9	36 54.5	+59.9	175.0
6	45 52.3	59.9	174.3	43 52.9	59.9	174.5	41 53.4	59.9	174.7	39 53.9	59.9	174.8	37 54.4	59.9	175.0
7	46 52.2	59.8	174.2	44 52.8	59.9	174.4	42 53.3	59.9	174.6	40 53.8	60.0	174.7	38 54.3	60.0	174.9
8	47 52.0	59.9	174.1	45 52.7	59.8	174.3	43 53.2	59.9	174.5	41 53.8	59.9	174.7	39 54.3	59.9	174.8
9	48 51.9	59.9	174.0	46 52.5	59.9	174.2	44 53.1	59.9	174.4	42 53.7	59.9	174.6	40 54.2	59.9	174.8
10	49 51.8	+59.8	173.9	47 52.4	+59.9	174.1	45 53.0	+59.9	174.3	43 53.6	+59.9	174.5	41 54.1	+59.9	174.7
11	50 51.6	59.9	173.8	48 52.3	59.8	173.9	46 52.9	59.9	174.3	44 53.5	59.9	174.4	42 54.0	60.0	174.6
12	51 51.5	59.8	173.7	49 52.2	59.8	173.9	47 52.8	59.9	174.2	45 53.4	59.9	174.4	43 54.0	59.9	174.6
13	52 51.3	59.8	173.5	50 52.0	59.8	173.8	48 52.7	59.9	174.1	46 53.3	59.9	174.3	44 53.9	59.9	174.5
14	53 51.1	59.9	173.4	51 51.9	59.8	173.7	49 52.6	59.9	174.0	47 53.2	59.9	174.2	45 53.8	59.9	174.4
15	54 51.0	+59.8	173.3	52 51.7	+59.9	173.6	50 52.5	+59.8	173.9	48 53.1	+59.9	174.1	46 53.7	+59.9	174.3
16	55 50.8	59.8	173.1	53 51.6	59.8	173.5	51 52.3	59.9	173.8	49 53.0	59.9	174.0	47 53.6	59.9	174.3
17	56 50.6	59.8	173.0	54 51.4	59.9	173.3	52 52.2	59.8	173.7	50 52.9	59.9	173.9	48 53.5	59.9	174.2
18	57 50.4	59.7	172.8	55 51.2	59.9	173.2	53 52.0	59.9	173.5	51 52.8	59.9	173.8	49 53.4	59.9	174.1
19	58 50.1	59.8	172.7	56 51.1	59.8	173.1	54 51.9	59.8	173.4	52 52.7	59.9	173.7	50 53.3	59.9	174.0
20	59 49.9	+59.8	172.5	57 50.9	+59.8	172.9	55 51.7	+59.9	173.3	53 52.5	+59.9	173.6	51 53.2	+59.9	173.9
21	60 49.7	59.7	172.3	58 50.7	59.8	172.8	56 51.6	59.8	173.2	54 52.4	59.8	173.5	52 53.1	59.9	173.8
22	61 49.4	59.7	172.1	59 50.5	59.7	172.6	57 51.4	59.8	173.0	55 52.2	59.9	173.4	53 53.0	59.9	173.7
23	62 49.1	59.7	171.9	60 50.2	59.8	172.4	58 51.2	59.8	172.9	56 52.1	59.9	173.3	54 52.9	59.8	173.6
24	63 48.8	59.7	171.7	61 50.0	59.7	172.2	59 51.0	59.8	172.7	57 51.9	59.9	173.1	55 52.8	59.8	173.5
25	64 48.5	+59.7	171.5	62 49.7	+59.8	172.0	60 50.8	+59.8	172.5	58 51.8	+59.9	173.0	56 52.6	+59.9	173.4
26	65 48.2	59.6	171.2	63 49.5	59.7	171.8	61 50.6	59.8	172.4	59 51.6	59.8	172.8	57 52.5	59.9	173.3
27	66 47.8	59.6	171.0	64 49.2	59.6	171.6	62 50.4	59.7	172.2	60 51.4	59.8	172.7	58 52.3	59.9	173.1
28	67 47.4	59.5	170.6	65 48.8	59.7	171.4	63 50.1	59.7	172.0	61 51.2	59.8	172.5	59 52.2	59.8	173.0
29	68 46.9	59.5	170.3	66 48.5	59.6	171.1	64 49.8	59.8	171.8	62 51.0	59.8	172.3	60 52.0	59.8	172.8

40°			42°			44°			46°			48°			Dec.
Hc	d	Z	Hc	d	Z	Hc	d	Z	Hc	d	Z	Hc	d	Z	
49 50.0	-59.8	173.8	47 50.7	-59.8	174.0	45 51.3	-59.8	174.3	43 51.9	-59.8	174.4	41 52.5	-59.9	174.6	0
48 50.2	59.8	173.9	46 50.9	59.8	174.1	44 51.5	59.9	174.4	42 52.1	59.9	174.5	40 52.6	59.9	174.7	1
47 50.4	59.8	174.0	45 51.1	59.9	174.3	43 51.6	59.8	174.5	41 52.2	59.9	174.6	39 52.7	59.9	174.8	2
46 50.6	59.8	174.2	44 51.2	59.8	174.4	42 51.8	59.9	174.5	40 52.3	59.9	174.7	38 52.8	59.9	174.9	3
45 50.8	59.8	174.3	43 51.4	59.9	174.5	41 51.9	59.9	174.6	39 52.4	59.9	174.8	37 52.9	59.9	174.9	4
44 51.0	-59.8	174.4	42 51.5	-59.8	174.6	40 52.1	-59.9	174.7	38 52.5	-59.8	174.9	36 53.0	-59.9	175.0	5
43 51.1	59.8	174.5	41 51.7	59.9	174.7	39 52.2	59.9	174.8	37 52.7	59.9	175.0	35 53.1	59.9	175.1	6
42 51.3	59.8	174.6	40 51.8	59.8	174.7	38 52.3	59.9	174.9	36 52.8	59.9	175.0	34 53.2	59.9	175.2	7
41 51.5	59.8	174.7	39 52.0	59.9	174.8	37 52.4	59.9	175.0	35 52.9	59.9	175.1	33 53.3	59.9	175.2	8
40 51.6	59.8	174.8	38 52.1	59.9	174.9	36 52.6	59.9	175.1	34 53.0	59.9	175.2	32 53.4	59.9	175.3	9
39 51.8	-59.9	174.9	37 52.2	-59.8	175.0	35 52.7	-59.9	175.1	33 53.1	-59.9	175.3	31 53.5	-59.9	175.4	10
38 51.9	59.9	175.0	36 52.4	59.9	175.1	34 52.8	59.9	175.2	32 53.2	59.9	175.3	30 53.6	59.9	175.4	11
37 52.0	59.9	175.0	35 52.5	59.9	175.2	33 52.9	59.9	175.3	31 53.3	59.9	175.4	29 53.7	59.9	175.5	12
36 52.2	59.9	175.1	34 52.6	59.9	175.2	32 53.0	59.9	175.4	30 53.4	59.9	175.5	28 53.8	60.0	175.5	13
35 52.3	59.9	175.2	33 52.7	59.9	175.3	31 53.1	59.9	175.4	29 53.5	59.9	175.5	27 53.8	59.9	175.6	14
34 52.4	-59.8	175.3	32 52.8	-59.8	175.4	30 53.2	-59.9	175.5	28 53.6	-59.9	175.6	26 53.9	-59.9	175.7	15
33 52.6	59.9	175.4	31 53.0	59.9	175.5	29 53.3	59.9	175.6	27 53.7	59.9	175.6	25 54.0	59.9	175.7	16
32 52.7	59.9	175.4	30 53.1	59.9	175.5	28 53.4	59.9	175.6	26 53.8	60.0	175.7	24 54.1	59.9	175.8	17
31 52.8	59.9	175.5	29 53.2	59.9	175.6	27 53.5	59.9	175.7	25 53.8	59.9	175.8	23 54.2	60.0	175.8	18
30 52.9	59.9	175.6	28 53.3	59.9	175.7	26 53.6	59.9	175.8	24 53.9	59.9	175.8	22 54.2	59.9	175.9	19
29 53.0	-59.8	175.7	27 53.4	-59.9	175.7	25 53.7	-59.9	175.8	23 54.0	-59.9	175.9	21 54.3	-59.9	175.9	20
28 53.2	59.9	175.7	26 53.5	59.9	175.8	24 53.8	59.9	175.9	22 54.1	59.9	175.9	20 54.4	59.9	176.0	21
27 53.3	59.9	175.8	25 53.6	59.9	175.9	23 53.9	59.9	175.9	21 54.2	59.9	176.0	19 54.5	60.0	176.1	22
26 53.4	59.9	175.9	24 53.7	59.9	175.9	22 54.0	59.9	176.0	20 54.3	60.0	176.1	18 54.5	59.9	176.1	23
25 53.5	59.9	175.9	23 53.8	59.9	176.0	21 54.1	59.9	176.1	19 54.3	59.9	176.1	17 54.6	59.9	176.2	24
24 53.6	-59.9	176.0	22 53.9	-59.9	176.1	20 54.2	-60.0	176.1	18 54.4	-59.9	176.2	16 54.7	-59.9	176.2	25
23 53.7	59.9	176.1	21 54.0	59.9	176.1	19 54.2	59.9	176.2	17 54.5	59.9	176.2	15 54.8	60.0	176.3	26
22 53.8	59.9	176.1	20 54.1	59.9	176.2	18 54.3	59.9	176.2	16 54.6	59.9	176.3	14 54.8	59.9	176.3	27
21 53.9	59.9	176.2	19 54.2	60.0	176.2	17 54.4	59.9	176.3	15 54.7	60.0	176.3	13 54.9	59.9	176.4	28
20 54.0	59.9	176.3	18 54.2	59.9	176.3	16 54.5	59.9	176.3	14 54.7	59.9	176.4	12 55.0	59.9	176.4	29

50°			52°			54°			56°			58°			Dec.
Hc	d	Z	Hc	d	Z	Hc	d	Z	Hc	d	Z	Hc	d	Z	
39 53.0	-59.9	174.8	37 53.5	-60.0	174.9	35 53.9	-59.9	175.1	33 54.4	-60.0	175.2	31 54.8	-60.0	175.3	0
38 53.1	59.9	174.9	36 53.5	59.9	175.0	34 54.0	59.9	175.1	32 54.4	59.9	175.2	30 54.8	59.9	175.3	1
37 53.2	59.9	174.9	35 53.6	59.9	175.1	33 54.1	60.0	175.2	31 54.5	60.0	175.3	29 54.9	60.0	175.4	2
36 53.3	59.9	175.0	34 53.7	59.9	175.1	32 54.1	59.9	175.2	30 54.5	59.9	175.3	28 54.9	59.9	175.4	3
35 53.4	59.9	175.1	33 53.8	59.9	175.2	31 54.2	59.9	175.3	29 54.6	59.9	175.4	27 55.0	60.0	175.5	4
34 53.5	-60.0	175.1	32 53.9	-59.9	175.3	30 54.3	-59.9	175.4	28 54.7	-60.0	175.4	26 55.0	-59.9	175.5	5
33 53.5	59.9	175.2	31 54.0	60.0	175.3	29 54.4	60.0	175.4	27 54.7	59.9	175.5	25 55.1	60.0	175.6	6
32 53.6	59.9	175.3	30 54.0	59.9	175.4	28 54.4	59.9	175.5	26 54.8	59.9	175.5	24 55.1	59.9	175.6	7
31 53.7	59.9	175.3	29 54.1	59.9	175.4	27 54.5	59.9	175.5	25 54.8	59.9	175.6	23 55.2	60.0	175.7	8
30 53.8	59.9	175.4	28 54.2	59.9	175.5	26 54.5	59.9	175.6	24 54.9	59.9	175.6	22 55.2	59.9	175.7	9
29 53.9	-59.9	175.5	27 54.3	-60.0	175.5	25 54.6	-59.9	175.6	23 55.0	-60.0	175.7	21 55.3	-60.0	175.8	10
28 54.0	59.9	175.5	26 54.3	59.9	175.6	24 54.7	60.0	175.7	22 55.0	59.9	175.7	20 55.3	59.9	175.8	11
27 54.0	59.9	175.6	25 54.4	59.9	175.6	23 54.7	59.9	175.7	21 55.1	60.0	175.8	19 55.4	60.0	175.8	12
26 54.1	59.9	175.6	24 54.5	60.0	175.7	22 54.8	59.9	175.8	20 55.1	59.9	175.8	18 55.4	59.9	175.9	13
25 54.2	59.9	175.7	23 54.5	59.9	175.8	21 54.9	60.0	175.8	19 55.2	60.0	175.9	17 55.5	60.0	175.9	14
24 54.3	-60.0	175.7	22 54.6	-59.9	175.8	20 54.9	-59.9	175.9	18 55.2	-59.9	175.9	16 55.5	-59.9	176.0	15
23 54.3	59.9	175.8	21 54.7	60.0	175.9	19 55.0	60.0	175.9	17 55.3	60.0	176.0	15 55.6	60.0	176.0	16
22 54.4	59.9	175.8	20 54.7	59.9	175.9	18 55.0	59.9	176.0	16 55.3	59.9	176.0	14 55.6	59.9	176.0	17
21 54.5	60.0	175.9	19 54.8	60.0	176.0	17 55.1	60.0	176.0	15 55.4	60.0	176.0	13 55.7	60.0	176.1	18
20 54.5	59.9	176.0	18 54.8	59.9	176.0	16 55.1	59.9	176.0	14 55.4	59.9	176.1	12 55.7	60.0	176.1	19
19 54.6	-59.9	176.0	17 54.9	-59.9	176.0	15 55.2	-60.0	176.1	13 55.5	-60.0	176.1	11 55.7	-59.9	176.2	20
18 54.7	59.9	176.1	16 55.0	60.0	176.1	14 55.2	59.9	176.1	12 55.5	59.9	176.2	10 55.8	60.0	176.2	21
17 54.7	60.0	176.1	15 55.0	59.9	176.1	13 55.3	59.9	176.2	11 55.6	60.0	176.2	9 55.8	59.9	176.2	22
16 54.8	59.9	176.2	14 55.1	60.0	176.2	12 55.4	60.0	176.2	10 55.6	59.9	176.3	8 55.9	60.0	176.3	23
15 54.9	59.9	176.2	13 55.1	59.9	176.2	11 55.4	59.9	176.3	9 55.7	60.0	176.3	7 55.9	60.0	176.3	24
14 55.0	-60.0	176.2	12 55.2	-60.0	176.3	10 55.5	-60.0	176.3	8 55.7	-59.9	176.4	6 55.9	-59.9	176.3	25
13 55.0	59.9	176.3	11 55.3	60.0	176.3	9 55.5	59.9	176.4	7 55.8	60.0	176.4	5 56.0	60.0	176.4	26
12 55.1	60.0	176.3	10 55.3	59.9	176.4	8 55.6	60.0	176.4	6 55.8	60.0	176.4	4 56.0	60.0	176.4	27
11 55.1	59.9	176.4	9 55.4	60.0	176.4	7 55.6	59.9	176.5	5 55.8	59.9	176.5	3 56.1	60.0	176.5	28
10 55.2	59.9	176.4	8 55.4	59.9	176.5	6 55.7	60.0	176.5	4 55.9	60.0	176.5	2 56.1	59.9	176.5	29

Dec.	0° Hc	d	Z	2° Hc	d	Z	4° Hc	d	Z	6° Hc	d	Z	8° Hc	d	Z
°	° ′	′	°	° ′	′	°	° ′	′	°	° ′	′	°	° ′	′	°
0	84 00.0	− 4.9	90.0	83 40.6	+14.6	108.4	82 47.6	+30.3	123.6	81 31.3	+40.7	134.8	80 00.7	+47.0	142.9
1	83 55.1	14.5	80.5	83 55.2	+ 5.0	99.4	83 17.9	23.1	116.4	82 12.0	36.1	129.6	80 47.7	44.3	139.2
2	83 40.6	22.9	71.5	84 00.2	− 4.8	89.9	83 41.0	14.7	108.3	82 48.1	40.7	134.8	81 32.0	40.7	134.8
3	83 17.7	30.1	63.4	83 55.4	14.4	80.4	83 55.7	+ 5.2	99.3	82 18.5	23.3	116.4	82 12.7	36.3	129.6
4	82 47.6	35.9	56.2	83 41.0	22.9	71.4	84 00.9	− 4.8	89.8	83 41.8	14.9	108.2	82 49.0	30.6	123.5
5	82 11.7	−40.4	50.1	83 18.1	−30.0	63.2	83 56.1	−14.3	80.3	83 56.7	+ 5.3	99.2	83 19.6	+23.5	116.3
6	81 31.3	43.9	44.8	82 48.1	35.8	56.1	83 41.8	22.8	71.3	84 02.0	− 4.7	89.7	83 43.1	15.0	108.2
7	80 47.4	46.7	40.4	82 12.1	40.3	49.9	83 19.0	30.0	63.1	83 57.3	14.2	80.1	83 58.1	+ 5.4	99.1
8	80 00.7	48.9	36.6	81 32.0	43.9	44.7	82 49.0	35.7	55.9	83 43.1	22.8	71.1	84 03.5	− 4.6	89.6
9	79 11.8	50.6	33.4	80 48.1	46.7	40.2	82 13.3	40.4	49.7	83 20.3	30.0	62.9	83 58.9	14.1	80.0
10	78 21.2	−51.9	30.7	80 01.4	−48.9	36.5	81 32.9	−43.9	44.5	82 50.3	−35.8	55.7	83 44.8	−22.8	70.9
11	77 29.3	53.1	28.3	79 12.5	50.6	33.2	80 49.0	46.7	40.0	82 14.5	40.4	49.5	83 22.0	30.1	62.6
12	76 36.2	54.0	26.2	78 21.9	52.0	30.5	80 02.3	48.9	36.2	81 34.1	43.9	44.2	82 51.9	35.8	55.4
13	75 42.2	54.7	24.4	77 29.9	53.0	28.1	79 13.4	50.6	33.0	80 50.2	46.7	39.8	82 16.1	40.4	49.2
14	74 47.5	55.3	22.7	76 36.9	54.0	26.0	78 22.8	52.0	30.2	80 03.5	49.0	36.0	81 35.7	44.0	43.9
15	73 52.2	−55.8	21.3	75 42.9	−54.7	24.2	77 30.8	−53.0	27.8	79 14.5	−50.6	32.7	80 51.7	−46.8	39.5
16	72 56.4	56.3	20.0	74 48.2	55.3	22.5	76 37.8	54.0	25.8	78 23.9	52.0	30.0	80 04.9	49.0	35.7
17	72 00.1	56.6	18.9	73 52.9	55.8	21.1	75 43.8	54.7	23.9	77 31.9	53.1	27.6	79 15.9	50.6	32.5
18	71 03.5	57.0	17.8	72 57.1	56.3	19.8	74 49.1	55.4	22.3	76 38.8	54.0	25.5	78 25.3	52.1	29.7
19	70 06.5	57.2	16.9	72 00.8	56.6	18.7	73 53.7	55.8	20.9	75 44.8	54.7	23.7	77 33.2	53.1	27.3
20	69 09.3	−57.5	16.0	71 04.2	−57.0	17.6	72 57.9	−56.3	19.6	74 50.1	−55.4	22.1	76 40.1	−54.1	25.2
21	68 11.8	57.7	15.2	70 07.2	57.2	16.7	72 01.6	56.6	18.4	73 54.7	55.8	20.6	75 46.0	54.7	23.4
22	67 14.1	57.8	14.5	69 10.0	57.5	15.8	71 05.0	57.2	17.4	72 58.9	56.3	19.3	74 51.3	55.4	21.8
23	66 16.3	58.0	13.8	68 12.5	57.7	15.0	70 08.0	57.2	16.4	72 02.6	56.7	18.2	73 55.9	55.9	20.3
24	65 18.3	58.2	13.2	67 14.8	57.8	14.3	69 10.8	57.5	15.6	71 05.9	56.9	17.1	73 00.0	56.3	19.1
25	64 20.1	−58.3	12.6	66 17.0	−58.0	13.6	68 13.3	−57.7	14.8	70 09.0	−57.3	16.2	72 03.7	−56.7	17.9
26	63 21.8	58.4	12.1	65 19.0	58.2	13.0	67 15.6	57.8	14.1	69 11.7	57.5	15.3	71 07.0	57.0	16.9
27	62 23.4	58.5	11.6	64 20.8	58.3	12.4	66 17.8	58.1	13.4	68 14.2	57.7	14.5	70 10.0	57.3	15.9
28	61 24.9	58.6	11.1	63 22.5	58.4	11.9	65 19.7	58.1	12.8	67 16.5	57.8	13.8	69 12.7	57.5	15.1
29	60 26.3	58.7	10.7	62 24.1	58.5	11.4	64 21.6	58.3	12.2	66 18.7	58.1	13.2	68 15.2	57.7	14.3

Dec.	10° Hc	d	Z	12° Hc	d	Z	14° Hc	d	Z	16° Hc	d	Z	18° Hc	d	Z
°	° ′	′	°	° ′	′	°	° ′	′	°	° ′	′	°	° ′	′	°
0	78 21.2	+50.9	148.8	76 36.2	+53.4	153.2	74 47.5	+55.1	156.5	72 56.4	+56.1	159.1	71 03.5	+56.9	161.2
1	79 12.1	49.3	146.1	77 29.6	52.3	151.1	75 42.6	54.3	155.0	73 52.5	55.7	157.9	72 00.4	56.7	160.2
2	80 01.4	47.1	142.9	78 21.9	51.0	148.8	76 36.9	53.5	153.2	74 48.2	55.1	156.5	72 57.1	56.2	159.1
3	80 48.5	44.4	139.2	79 12.9	49.4	146.1	77 30.4	52.4	151.2	75 43.3	54.5	155.0	73 53.3	55.8	157.9
4	81 32.9	40.9	134.8	80 02.3	47.2	142.9	78 22.8	51.1	148.8	76 37.8	53.6	153.2	74 49.1	55.2	156.5
5	82 13.8	+36.5	129.6	80 49.5	+44.6	139.2	79 13.9	+49.6	146.1	77 31.4	+52.5	151.2	75 44.3	+54.5	155.0
6	82 50.3	30.8	123.5	81 34.1	41.2	134.8	80 03.5	47.4	143.0	78 23.9	51.3	148.9	76 38.8	53.7	153.2
7	83 21.1	23.7	116.4	82 15.3	36.6	129.7	80 50.9	44.8	139.3	79 15.2	49.7	146.2	77 32.5	52.8	151.3
8	83 44.8	15.1	108.2	82 51.9	31.0	123.5	81 35.7	41.3	134.9	80 04.9	47.6	143.1	78 25.3	51.4	149.0
9	83 59.9	+ 5.6	99.1	83 22.9	23.9	116.4	82 17.0	36.9	129.7	80 52.5	45.0	139.4	79 16.7	49.9	146.3
10	84 05.5	− 4.5	89.5	83 46.8	+15.4	108.2	82 53.9	+31.3	123.6	81 37.5	+41.6	135.0	80 06.6	+47.8	143.2
11	84 01.0	14.2	79.8	84 02.2	+ 5.7	99.0	83 25.2	24.1	116.4	82 19.1	37.2	129.9	80 54.4	45.2	139.5
12	83 46.8	22.8	70.7	84 07.9	− 4.4	89.4	83 49.3	15.6	108.2	82 56.3	31.5	123.7	81 39.6	41.9	135.2
13	83 24.0	30.1	62.4	84 03.5	14.2	79.7	84 04.9	+ 5.4	99.0	83 27.8	24.4	116.5	82 21.5	37.4	130.0
14	82 53.9	35.9	55.1	83 49.3	22.9	70.5	84 10.7	− 4.3	89.3	83 52.2	15.8	108.2	82 58.9	31.7	123.9
15	82 18.0	−40.5	48.9	83 26.4	−30.1	62.1	84 06.4	−14.2	79.5	84 08.0	+ 6.0	99.0	83 30.8	+24.6	116.7
16	81 37.5	44.1	43.6	82 56.3	36.1	54.8	83 52.2	23.0	70.2	84 14.0	− 4.3	89.2	83 55.4	16.1	108.3
17	80 53.4	46.8	39.2	82 20.2	40.6	48.6	83 29.2	30.3	61.8	84 09.7	14.3	79.3	84 11.5	+ 6.1	99.0
18	80 06.6	49.1	35.4	81 39.6	44.2	43.3	82 58.9	36.1	54.5	83 55.4	23.0	69.9	84 17.6	− 4.2	89.1
19	79 17.5	50.7	32.1	80 55.4	46.9	38.8	82 22.8	40.8	48.2	83 32.4	30.4	61.5	84 13.4	14.3	79.1
20	78 26.8	−52.1	29.4	80 08.5	−49.1	35.0	81 42.0	−44.3	42.9	83 02.0	−36.4	54.1	83 59.1	−23.2	69.6
21	77 34.7	53.2	27.0	79 19.4	50.9	31.8	80 57.7	47.1	38.4	82 25.6	40.9	47.8	83 35.9	30.6	61.1
22	76 41.5	54.1	24.9	78 28.5	52.1	29.0	80 10.6	49.2	34.6	81 44.7	44.5	42.5	83 05.3	36.5	53.6
23	75 47.4	54.8	23.1	77 36.3	53.3	26.6	79 21.4	50.9	31.4	81 00.2	47.2	38.0	82 28.8	41.1	47.3
24	74 52.6	55.4	21.5	76 43.1	54.1	24.6	78 30.5	52.3	28.6	80 13.0	49.4	34.2	81 47.7	44.7	42.0
25	73 57.2	−55.9	20.0	75 49.0	−54.9	22.7	77 38.2	−53.3	26.3	79 23.6	−51.0	31.0	81 03.0	−47.4	37.5
26	73 01.3	56.4	18.8	74 54.1	55.5	21.1	76 44.9	54.3	24.2	78 32.6	52.4	28.2	80 15.6	49.5	33.7
27	72 04.9	56.7	17.6	73 58.6	55.9	19.7	75 50.6	54.9	22.4	77 40.2	53.4	25.9	79 26.1	51.2	30.5
28	71 08.2	57.0	16.6	73 02.7	56.4	18.4	74 55.7	55.5	20.8	76 46.8	54.3	23.8	78 34.9	52.5	27.8
29	70 11.2	57.3	15.6	72 06.3	56.8	17.3	74 00.2	56.0	19.4	75 52.5	55.0	22.0	77 42.4	53.5	25.4

	0°			2°			4°			6°			8°			Dec.
	Hc	d	Z	Hc	d	Z	Hc	d	Z	Hc	d	Z	Hc	d	Z	
	84 00.0	− 4.9·	90.0	83 40.6	−23.0·	108.4	82 47.6	−36.0·	123.6	81 31.3	−44.1·	134.8	80 00.7	−49.1	142.9	0
	83 55.1	14.5·	99.5	83 17.6	30.2·	116.5	82 11.6	40.6·	129.7	80 47.2	46.9·	139.3	79 11.6	50.8	146.1	1
	83 40.6	22.9·	108.5	82 47.4	35.9·	123.7	81 31.0	44.0·	134.9	80 00.3	49.0	143.0	78 20.8	52.2	148.9	2
	83 17.7	30.1·	116.6	82 11.5	40.5·	129.8	80 47.0	46.8·	139.3	79 11.3	50.8	146.2	77 28.6	53.2	151.2	3
	82 47.6	35.9·	123.8	81 31.0	43.9·	135.0	80 00.2	49.0	143.1	78 20.5	52.0	148.9	76 35.4	54.1	153.3	4
	82 11.7	−40.4·	129.9	80 47.4	−46.7·	139.6	79 11.2	−50.7	146.3	77 28.5	−53.2	151.3	75 41.3	−54.8	155.1	5
	81 31.3	43.9·	135.2	80 00.3	48.8	143.4	78 20.5	52.0	149.0	76 35.3	54.0	153.4	74 46.5	55.4	156.7	6
	80 47.4	46.7·	139.6	79 11.4	50.6	146.4	77 28.5	53.1	151.4	75 41.3	54.8	155.2	73 51.1	56.0	158.1	7
	80 00.7	48.9	143.4	78 20.8	52.0	149.2	76 35.4	54.0	153.5	74 46.5	55.4	156.8	72 55.1	56.3	159.4	8
	79 11.8	50.6	146.6	77 28.8	53.1	151.6	75 41.4	54.7	155.3	73 51.1	55.9	158.2	71 58.8	56.7	160.5	9
	78 21.2	−51.9	149.3	76 35.7	−54.0	153.6	74 46.7	−55.4	156.9	72 55.2	−56.3	159.5	71 02.1	−57.1	161.5	10
	77 29.3	53.1	151.7	75 41.7	54.7	155.5	73 51.3	55.9	158.3	71 58.9	56.7	160.6	70 05.0	57.2	162.5	11
	76 36.2	54.0	153.8	74 47.0	55.3	157.1	72 55.4	56.3	159.6	71 02.2	57.0	161.7	69 07.8	57.6	163.3	12
	75 42.2	54.7	155.6	73 51.7	55.9	158.5	71 59.1	56.6	160.8	70 05.2	57.3	162.6	68 10.2	57.7	164.1	13
	74 47.5	55.3	157.3	72 55.8	56.2	159.8	71 02.5	57.0	161.8	69 07.9	57.5	163.5	67 12.5	57.9	164.8	14
	73 52.2	−55.8	158.7	71 59.6	−56.7	160.9	70 05.5	−57.2	162.8	68 10.4	−57.7	164.2	66 14.6	−58.1	165.5	15
	72 56.4	56.3	160.0	71 02.9	57.0	162.0	69 08.3	57.5	163.6	67 12.7	57.8	165.0	65 16.5	58.2	166.1	16
	72 00.1	56.6	161.1	70 05.9	57.2	162.9	68 10.8	57.7	164.4	66 14.9	58.1	165.6	64 18.3	58.3	166.7	17
	71 03.5	57.0	162.2	69 08.7	57.5	163.8	67 13.1	57.9	165.1	65 16.8	58.2	166.2	63 20.0	58.6	167.2	18
	70 06.5	57.2	163.1	68 11.2	57.6	164.6	66 15.2	58.0	165.8	64 18.6	58.3	166.8	62 21.6	58.6	167.7	19
	69 09.3	−57.5	164.0	67 13.6	−57.9	165.3	65 17.2	−58.2	166.4	63 20.3	−58.4	167.4	61 23.0	−58.6	168.2	20
	68 11.8	57.7	164.8	66 15.7	58.0	166.0	64 19.0	58.3	167.0	62 21.9	58.5	167.9	60 24.4	58.7	168.6	21
	67 14.1	57.8	165.5	65 17.7	58.2	166.6	63 20.7	58.4	167.5	61 23.4	58.6	168.3	59 25.7	58.8	169.0	22
	66 16.3	58.0	166.2	64 19.5	58.3	167.2	62 22.3	58.6	168.0	60 24.8	58.7	168.8	58 26.9	58.9	169.4	23
	65 18.3	58.2	166.8	63 21.2	58.4	167.7	61 23.8	58.6	168.5	59 26.1	58.8	169.2	57 28.1	58.9	169.8	24
	64 20.1	−58.3	167.4	62 22.8	−58.5	168.2	60 25.2	−58.7	168.9	58 27.3	−58.8	169.6	56 29.2	−59.0	170.1	25
	63 21.8	58.4	167.9	61 24.3	58.6	168.7	59 26.5	58.7	169.4	57 28.5	58.9	169.9	55 30.2	59.0	170.5	26
	62 23.4	58.5	168.4	60 25.7	58.7	169.1	58 27.8	58.9	169.7	56 29.6	59.0	170.3	54 31.2	59.1	170.8	27
	61 24.9	58.6	168.9	59 27.0	58.7	169.5	57 28.9	58.9	170.1	55 30.6	59.0	170.6	53 32.1	59.1	171.1	28
	60 26.3	58.7	169.3	58 28.3	58.8	169.9	56 30.0	58.9	170.5	54 31.6	59.0	170.9	52 33.0	59.1	171.4	29

	10°			12°			14°			16°			18°			Dec.
	Hc	d	Z	Hc	d	Z	Hc	d	Z	Hc	d	Z	Hc	d	Z	
	78 21.2	−52.2	148.8	76 36.2	−54.2	153.2	74 47.5	−55.6	156.5	72 56.4	−56.6	159.1	71 03.5	−57.3	161.2	0
	77 29.0	53.3	151.2	75 42.0	55.0	155.0	73 51.9	56.1	157.9	71 59.8	56.9	160.2	70 06.2	57.5	162.1	1
	76 35.7	54.2	153.2	74 47.0	55.5	156.5	72 55.8	56.5	159.2	71 02.9	57.2	161.2	69 08.7	57.7	162.9	2
	75 41.5	54.8	155.0	73 51.5	56.1	157.9	71 59.3	56.8	160.3	70 05.7	57.4	162.1	68 11.0	57.9	163.7	3
	74 46.7	55.5	156.6	72 55.4	56.4	159.2	71 02.5	57.2	161.3	69 08.3	57.7	163.0	67 13.1	58.1	164.4	4
	73 51.2	−56.0	158.0	71 59.0	−56.8	160.3	70 05.3	−57.4	162.2	68 10.6	−57.9	163.7	66 15.0	−58.2	165.0	5
	72 55.2	56.4	159.3	71 02.2	57.1	161.3	69 07.9	57.6	163.0	67 12.7	58.0	164.4	65 16.8	58.3	165.6	6
	71 58.8	56.7	160.4	70 05.1	57.3	162.3	68 10.3	57.8	163.8	66 14.7	58.2	165.1	64 18.5	58.5	166.2	7
	71 02.1	57.1	161.4	69 07.8	57.6	163.1	67 12.5	58.0	164.5	65 16.5	58.3	165.7	63 20.0	58.5	166.7	8
	70 05.0	57.3	162.4	68 10.2	57.8	163.9	66 14.5	58.1	165.2	64 18.2	58.4	166.2	62 21.5	58.7	167.1	9
	69 07.7	−57.6	163.2	67 12.4	−58.0	164.6	65 16.4	−58.3	165.8	63 19.8	−58.5	166.8	61 22.8	−58.7	167.6	10
	68 10.1	57.9	164.0	66 14.4	58.1	165.2	64 18.1	58.4	166.3	62 21.3	58.6	167.2	60 24.1	58.8	168.0	11
	67 12.4	57.9	164.7	65 16.3	58.2	165.9	63 19.7	58.5	166.8	61 22.7	58.7	167.7	59 25.3	58.9	168.4	12
	66 14.5	58.1	165.4	64 18.1	58.4	166.4	62 21.2	58.6	167.3	60 24.0	58.8	168.1	58 26.4	58.8	168.8	13
	65 16.4	58.2	166.0	63 19.7	58.5	166.9	61 22.6	58.7	167.8	59 25.2	58.8	168.5	57 27.5	59.0	169.1	14
	64 18.2	−58.4	166.5	62 21.2	−58.5	167.4	60 23.9	−58.7	168.2	58 26.3	−58.9	168.9	56 28.5	−59.1	169.5	15
	63 19.8	58.4	167.1	61 22.7	58.7	167.9	59 25.2	58.9	168.6	57 27.4	59.0	169.2	55 29.4	59.1	169.8	16
	62 21.4	58.6	167.6	60 24.0	58.7	168.3	58 26.3	58.8	169.0	56 28.4	59.0	169.6	54 30.3	59.1	170.1	17
	61 22.8	58.8	168.0	59 25.3	58.8	168.7	57 27.5	59.0	169.4	55 29.4	59.1	169.9	53 31.2	59.2	170.4	18
	60 24.2	58.8	168.5	58 26.5	58.9	169.1	56 28.5	59.0	169.7	54 30.3	59.1	170.2	52 32.0	59.2	170.6	19
	59 25.4	−58.7	168.9	57 27.6	−59.0	169.5	55 29.5	−59.1	170.0	53 31.2	−59.1	170.5	51 32.8	−59.2	170.9	20
	58 26.7	58.9	169.3	56 28.6	58.9	169.8	54 30.4	59.1	170.4	52 32.1	59.2	170.8	50 33.6	59.3	171.2	21
	57 27.8	58.9	169.6	55 29.7	59.1	170.1	53 31.3	59.1	170.6	51 32.9	59.3	171.0	49 34.3	59.3	171.4	22
	56 28.9	59.0	170.0	54 30.6	59.1	170.5	52 32.2	59.2	170.9	50 33.6	59.2	171.3	48 35.0	59.4	171.6	23
	55 29.9	59.0	170.3	53 31.5	59.1	170.8	51 33.0	59.2	171.2	49 34.4	59.3	171.5	47 35.6	59.4	171.8	24
	54 30.9	−59.1	170.6	52 32.4	−59.2	171.0	50 33.8	−59.2	171.4	48 35.1	−59.3	171.8	46 36.3	−59.4	172.1	25
	53 31.8	59.1	170.9	51 33.2	59.2	171.3	49 34.6	59.3	171.7	47 35.8	59.4	172.0	45 36.9	59.4	172.3	26
	52 32.7	59.2	171.2	50 34.0	59.2	171.6	48 35.3	59.3	171.9	46 36.4	59.3	172.2	44 37.5	59.4	172.5	27
	51 33.5	59.2	171.5	49 34.8	59.3	171.8	47 36.0	59.3	172.1	45 37.1	59.4	172.4	43 38.1	59.5	172.7	28
	50 34.3	59.2	171.7	48 35.5	59.3	172.1	46 36.7	59.4	172.4	44 37.7	59.4	172.6	42 38.6	59.4	172.9	29

Dec.	20° Hc	d	Z	22° Hc	d	Z	24° Hc	d	Z	26° Hc	d	Z	28° Hc	d	Z
°	° ′	′	°	° ′	′	°	° ′	′	°	° ′	′	°	° ′	′	°
0	69 09.3	+57.5	162.9	67 14.1	+58.0	164.3	65 18.3	+58.3	165.5	63 21.8	+58.6	166.5	61 24.9	+58.9	167.4
1	70 06.8	57.4	162.1	68 12.1	57.9	163.7	66 16.6	58.2	164.9	64 20.4	58.6	166.0	62 23.8	58.7	167.0
2	71 04.2	57.0	161.2	69 10.0	57.6	162.9	67 14.8	58.1	164.3	65 19.0	58.4	165.5	63 22.5	58.7	166.5
3	72 01.2	56.7	160.2	70 07.6	57.4	162.1	68 12.9	57.9	163.7	66 17.4	58.2	165.0	64 21.2	58.5	166.0
4	72 57.9	56.3	159.1	71 05.0	57.1	161.2	69 10.8	57.7	162.9	67 15.6	58.2	164.3	65 19.7	58.5	165.5
5	73 54.2	+55.9	157.9	72 02.1	+56.8	160.3	70 08.5	+57.4	162.1	68 13.8	+57.9	163.7	66 18.2	+58.3	165.0
6	74 50.1	55.3	156.6	72 58.9	56.4	159.2	71 05.9	57.2	161.3	69 11.7	57.8	163.0	67 16.5	58.2	164.4
7	75 45.4	54.7	155.1	73 55.3	56.0	158.0	72 03.1	56.9	160.3	70 09.5	57.5	162.2	68 14.7	58.0	163.7
8	76 40.1	53.8	153.3	74 51.3	54.8	156.7	73 00.0	56.5	159.3	71 07.0	57.3	161.3	69 12.7	57.9	163.0
9	77 33.9	52.9	151.3	75 46.7	54.8	155.2	73 56.5	56.1	158.1	72 04.3	57.0	160.4	70 10.6	57.6	162.3
10	78 26.8	+51.6	149.1	76 41.5	+54.0	153.4	74 52.6	+55.6	156.8	73 01.3	+56.6	159.4	71 08.2	+57.4	161.4
11	79 18.4	50.1	146.4	77 35.5	53.0	151.5	75 48.2	54.9	155.3	73 57.9	56.2	158.2	72 05.6	57.1	160.5
12	80 08.5	48.0*	143.3	78 28.5	51.8	149.2	76 43.1	54.2	153.6	74 54.1	55.7	156.9	73 02.7	56.7	159.5
13	80 56.5	45.5*	139.7	79 20.3	50.3	146.6	77 37.3	53.2	151.6	75 49.8	55.1	155.4	73 59.4	56.3	158.3
14	81 42.0	42.2*	135.4	80 10.6	48.3*	143.5	78 30.5	52.0	149.4	76 44.9	54.3	153.7	74 55.7	55.8	157.0
15	82 24.2	+37.8*	130.2	80 58.9	+45.8*	139.9	79 22.5	+50.6	146.8	77 39.2	+53.4	151.8	75 51.5	+55.3	155.6
16	83 02.0	32.1*	124.1	81 44.7	42.5*	135.6	80 13.0	48.6*	143.7	78 32.6	52.2	149.6	76 46.8	54.5	153.9
17	83 34.1	25.0*	116.8	82 27.2	38.1*	130.4	81 01.6	46.1*	140.1	79 24.8	50.8	147.0	77 41.3	53.6	152.0
18	83 59.1	16.3*	108.4	83 05.3	32.5*	124.3	81 47.7	42.8*	135.9	80 15.6	48.9*	144.0	78 34.9	52.5	149.9
19	84 15.4	+ 6.3*	99.0	83 37.8	25.4*	117.0	82 30.5	38.5*	130.7	81 04.5	46.4*	140.4	79 27.4	51.0	147.3
20	84 21.7	- 4.2*	89.0	84 03.2	+16.5*	108.6	83 09.0	+32.9*	124.6	81 50.9	+43.2*	136.2	80 18.4	+49.2*	144.3
21	84 17.5	14.3*	78.9	84 19.7	+ 6.5*	99.0	83 41.9	25.7*	117.2	82 34.1	38.9*	131.0	81 07.6	46.7*	140.8
22	84 03.2	23.4*	69.3	84 26.2	- 4.1*	88.9	84 07.6	16.9*	108.7	83 13.0	33.3*	124.9	81 54.3	43.6*	136.5
23	83 39.8	30.8*	60.7	84 22.1	14.5*	78.6	84 24.5	+ 6.6*	99.1	83 46.3	26.1*	117.5	82 37.9	39.4*	131.4
24	83 09.0	36.8*	53.2	84 07.6	23.6*	68.9	84 31.1	- 4.1*	88.8	84 12.4	17.2*	108.9	83 17.3	33.7*	125.2
25	82 32.2	-41.3*	46.8	83 44.0	-31.0*	60.2	84 27.0	-14.6*	78.4	84 29.6	+ 6.9*	99.2	83 51.0	+26.6*	117.8
26	81 50.9	44.9*	41.5	83 13.0	37.1*	52.7	84 12.4	23.8*	68.6	84 36.5	- 4.2*	88.7	84 17.6	17.5*	109.1
27	81 06.0	47.6*	37.0	82 35.9	41.6*	46.3	83 48.6	31.3*	59.7	84 32.3	14.7*	78.1	84 35.1	+ 7.1*	99.2
28	80 18.4	49.7	33.2	81 54.3	45.1*	41.0	83 17.3	37.4*	52.1	84 17.6	24.1*	68.1	84 42.2	- 4.2*	88.6
29	79 28.7	51.3	30.0	81 09.2	47.8*	36.5	82 39.9	41.9*	45.7	83 53.5	31.7*	59.2	84 38.0	14.9*	77.8

Dec.	30° Hc	d	Z	32° Hc	d	Z	34° Hc	d	Z	36° Hc	d	Z	38° Hc	d	Z
°	° ′	′	°	° ′	′	°	° ′	′	°	° ′	′	°	° ′	′	°
0	59 27.6	+59.1	168.1	57 30.1	+59.1	168.8	55 32.2	+59.3	169.4	53 34.2	+59.4	169.9	51 36.0	+59.5	170.3
1	60 26.7	58.9	167.8	58 29.2	59.1	168.5	56 31.5	59.3	169.1	54 33.6	59.3	169.6	52 35.5	59.4	170.1
2	61 25.6	58.9	167.4	59 28.3	59.1	168.1	57 30.8	59.1	168.8	55 32.9	59.3	169.4	53 34.9	59.4	169.9
3	62 24.5	58.8	167.0	60 27.4	59.0	167.8	58 29.9	59.2	168.5	56 32.2	59.3	169.1	54 34.3	59.4	169.6
4	63 23.3	58.7	166.5	61 26.4	58.9	167.4	59 29.1	59.1	168.1	57 31.5	59.2	168.8	55 33.7	59.3	169.4
5	64 22.0	+58.6	166.1	62 25.3	+58.9	167.0	60 28.2	+59.0	167.8	58 30.7	+59.2	168.5	56 33.0	+59.3	169.1
6	65 20.6	58.5	165.6	63 24.2	58.7	166.6	61 27.2	59.0	167.4	59 29.9	59.2	168.2	57 32.3	59.3	168.8
7	66 19.1	58.4	165.0	64 22.9	58.7	166.1	62 26.2	58.9	167.0	60 29.1	59.0	167.8	58 31.6	59.2	168.5
8	67 17.5	58.3	164.4	65 21.6	58.6	165.6	63 25.1	58.8	166.6	61 28.1	59.1	167.5	59 30.8	59.2	168.2
9	68 15.8	58.1	163.8	66 20.2	58.4	165.1	64 23.9	58.8	166.2	62 27.2	58.9	167.1	60 30.0	59.1	167.9
10	69 13.9	+57.9	163.1	67 18.6	+58.4	164.5	65 22.7	+58.6	165.7	63 26.1	+58.9	166.7	61 29.1	+59.1	167.5
11	70 11.8	57.7	162.4	68 17.0	58.1	163.9	66 21.3	58.5	165.2	64 25.0	58.8	166.3	62 28.2	59.0	167.2
12	71 09.5	57.5	161.5	69 15.1	58.0	163.2	67 19.8	58.4	164.6	65 23.8	58.7	165.8	63 27.2	58.9	166.8
13	72 07.0	57.2	160.6	70 13.1	57.8	162.5	68 18.2	58.3	164.0	66 22.5	58.6	165.3	64 26.1	58.9	166.3
14	73 04.2	56.8	159.6	71 10.9	57.6	161.7	69 16.5	58.0	163.3	67 21.1	58.5	164.7	65 25.0	58.5	165.8
15	74 01.0	+56.5	158.5	72 08.5	+57.3	160.8	70 14.5	+57.9	162.6	68 19.6	+58.3	164.1	66 23.8	+58.6	165.4
16	74 57.5	56.0	157.2	73 05.8	57.0	159.8	71 12.4	57.7	161.8	69 17.9	58.2	163.5	67 22.4	58.6	164.9
17	75 53.5	55.4	155.8	74 02.8	56.6	158.7	72 10.1	57.4	160.9	70 16.1	58.0	162.8	68 21.0	58.4	164.3
18	76 48.9	54.6	154.2	74 59.4	56.1	157.4	73 07.5	57.1	160.0	71 14.1	57.7	162.0	69 19.4	58.3	163.6
19	77 43.5	53.9	152.3	75 55.5	55.6	156.0	74 04.6	56.8	158.9	72 11.8	57.6	161.1	70 17.7	58.0	163.0
20	78 37.4	+52.7	150.1	76 51.1	+54.9	154.4	75 01.4	+56.3	157.7	73 09.4	+57.2	160.2	71 15.7	+57.9	162.2
21	79 30.1	51.3	147.6	77 46.0	54.0	152.6	75 57.7	55.7	156.3	74 06.6	56.9	159.1	72 13.6	57.7	161.4
22	80 21.4	49.5*	144.7	78 40.0	53.0	150.5	76 53.4	55.1	154.7	75 03.5	56.4	157.9	73 11.3	57.3	160.4
23	81 10.9	47.1*	141.1	79 33.0	51.6	148.0	77 48.5	54.3	152.9	75 59.9	56.0	156.6	74 08.6	57.1	159.4
24	81 58.0	44.0*	136.9	80 24.6	49.8*	145.0	78 42.8	53.2	150.8	76 55.9	55.3	155.0	75 05.7	56.6	158.2
25	82 42.0	+39.8*	131.8	81 14.4	+47.5*	141.5	79 36.0	+51.9	148.3	77 51.2	+54.5	153.2	76 02.3	+56.1	156.9
26	83 21.8	34.3*	125.6	82 01.9	44.5*	137.3	80 27.9	50.2	145.4	78 45.7	53.5	151.2	76 58.4	55.6	155.4
27	83 56.1	27.0*	118.2	82 46.4	40.3*	132.2	81 18.1	48.0*	142.0	79 39.2	52.2	148.8	77 54.0	54.7	153.6
28	84 23.1	17.9*	109.4	83 26.7	34.8*	126.1	82 06.1	44.9*	137.8	80 31.4	50.6	145.9	78 48.7	53.8	151.6
29	84 41.0	+ 7.3*	99.4	84 01.5	27.5*	118.6	82 51.0	40.8*	132.7	81 22.0	48.4*	142.5	79 42.5	52.6	149.2

LATITUDE **CONTRARY** NAME L.H.A. 6°, 354°

20° Hc	d	Z	22° Hc	d	Z	24° Hc	d	Z	26° Hc	d	Z	28° Hc	d	Z	Dec.
69 09.3	–57.8	162.9	67 14.1	–58.1	164.3	65 18.3	–58.5	165.5	63 21.8	–58.7	166.5	61 24.9	–58.9	167.4	0
68 11.5	57.9	163.7	66 16.0	58.3	164.9	64 19.8	58.6	166.0	62 23.1	58.8	167.0	60 26.0	59.0	167.8	1
67 13.6	58.2	164.3	65 17.7	58.4	165.5	63 21.2	58.6	166.5	61 24.3	58.9	167.4	59 27.0	59.0	168.1	2
66 15.4	58.2	165.0	64 19.3	58.6	166.1	62 22.6	58.8	167.0	60 25.4	58.9	167.8	58 28.0	59.1	168.5	3
65 17.2	58.4	165.6	63 20.7	58.6	166.6	61 23.8	58.8	167.4	59 26.5	59.0	168.2	57 28.9	59.1	168.8	4
64 18.8	–58.5	166.1	62 22.1	–58.7	167.0	60 25.0	–58.9	167.8	58 27.5	–59.0	168.5	56 29.8	–59.2	169.1	5
63 20.3	58.6	166.6	61 23.4	58.8	167.5	59 26.1	59.0	168.2	57 28.5	59.1	168.9	55 30.6	59.2	169.4	6
62 21.7	58.7	167.1	60 24.6	58.9	167.9	58 27.1	59.0	168.6	56 29.4	59.2	169.2	54 31.4	59.3	169.7	7
61 23.0	58.7	167.5	59 25.7	58.9	168.3	57 28.1	59.1	168.9	55 30.2	59.2	169.5	53 32.1	59.2	170.0	8
60 24.3	58.9	167.9	58 26.8	59.0	168.6	56 29.0	59.1	169.2	54 31.0	59.2	169.8	52 32.9	59.4	170.2	9
59 25.4	–58.9	168.3	57 27.8	–59.1	169.0	55 29.9	–59.2	169.5	53 31.8	–59.3	170.0	51 33.5	–59.3	170.5	10
58 26.5	58.9	168.7	56 28.7	59.0	169.3	54 30.7	59.2	169.8	52 32.5	59.3	170.3	50 34.2	59.4	170.7	11
57 27.6	59.0	169.0	55 29.7	59.2	169.6	53 31.5	59.2	170.1	51 33.2	59.3	170.5	49 34.8	59.4	170.9	12
56 28.6	59.1	169.4	54 30.5	59.2	169.9	52 32.3	59.3	170.4	50 33.9	59.3	170.8	48 35.4	59.4	171.1	13
55 29.5	59.1	169.7	53 31.3	59.2	170.2	51 33.0	59.3	170.6	49 34.6	59.4	171.0	47 36.0	59.5	171.3	14
54 30.4	–59.2	170.0	52 32.1	–59.2	170.4	50 33.7	–59.3	170.9	48 35.2	–59.4	171.2	46 36.5	–59.4	171.5	15
53 31.2	59.2	170.3	51 32.9	59.3	170.7	49 34.4	59.4	171.1	47 35.8	59.4	171.4	45 37.1	59.5	171.7	16
52 32.0	59.2	170.5	50 33.6	59.3	170.9	48 35.0	59.4	171.3	46 36.4	59.5	171.6	44 37.6	59.5	171.9	17
51 32.8	59.3	170.8	49 34.3	59.4	171.2	47 35.6	59.4	171.5	45 36.9	59.5	171.8	43 38.1	59.5	172.1	18
50 33.5	59.3	171.0	48 34.9	59.4	171.4	46 36.2	59.4	171.7	44 37.4	59.4	172.0	42 38.6	59.6	172.3	19
49 34.2	–59.3	171.3	47 35.6	–59.4	171.6	45 36.8	–59.4	171.9	43 38.0	–59.5	172.2	41 39.0	–59.5	172.4	20
48 34.9	59.3	171.5	46 36.2	59.4	171.8	44 37.4	59.5	172.1	42 38.5	59.6	172.4	40 39.5	59.6	172.6	21
47 35.6	59.4	171.7	45 36.8	59.5	172.0	43 37.9	59.5	172.3	41 38.9	59.5	172.5	39 39.9	59.5	172.7	22
46 36.2	59.4	171.9	44 37.3	59.4	172.2	42 38.4	59.5	172.5	40 39.4	59.5	172.7	38 40.4	59.6	172.9	23
45 36.8	59.4	172.2	43 37.9	59.5	172.4	41 38.9	59.5	172.7	39 39.9	59.6	172.9	37 40.8	59.6	173.1	24
44 37.4	–59.4	172.4	42 38.4	–59.5	172.6	40 39.4	–59.5	172.8	38 40.3	–59.6	173.0	36 41.2	–59.6	173.2	25
43 38.0	59.5	172.5	41 38.9	59.5	172.8	39 39.9	59.6	173.0	37 40.7	59.5	173.2	35 41.6	59.7	173.4	26
42 38.5	59.5	172.7	40 39.4	59.5	172.9	38 40.3	59.5	173.1	36 41.2	59.6	173.3	34 41.9	59.6	173.5	27
41 39.0	59.5	172.9	39 39.9	59.5	173.1	37 40.8	59.6	173.3	35 41.6	59.6	173.5	33 42.3	59.6	173.6	28
40 39.5	59.5	173.1	38 40.4	59.5	173.3	36 41.2	59.6	173.5	34 42.0	59.7	173.6	32 42.7	59.7	173.8	29

30° Hc	d	Z	32° Hc	d	Z	34° Hc	d	Z	36° Hc	d	Z	38° Hc	d	Z	Dec.
59 27.6	–59.0	168.1	57 30.1	–59.2	168.8	55 32.2	–59.3	169.4	53 34.2	–59.4	169.9	51 36.0	–59.5	170.3	0
58 28.6	59.1	168.5	56 30.9	59.3	169.1	54 32.9	59.3	169.6	52 34.8	59.4	170.1	50 36.5	59.5	170.5	1
57 29.5	59.2	168.8	55 31.6	59.2	169.4	53 33.6	59.4	169.9	51 35.4	59.5	170.3	49 37.0	59.5	170.7	2
56 30.3	59.2	169.1	54 32.4	59.4	169.6	52 34.2	59.4	170.1	50 35.9	59.4	170.5	48 37.5	59.5	170.9	3
55 31.1	59.3	169.4	53 33.0	59.3	169.9	51 34.8	59.4	170.3	49 36.5	59.6	170.7	47 38.0	59.6	171.1	4
54 31.8	–59.3	169.7	52 33.7	–59.3	170.1	50 35.4	–59.5	170.6	48 37.0	–59.6	170.9	46 38.4	–59.6	171.3	5
53 32.6	59.4	169.9	51 34.3	59.4	170.4	49 35.9	59.4	170.8	47 37.4	59.5	171.1	45 38.8	59.6	171.4	6
52 33.2	59.3	170.2	50 34.9	59.4	170.6	48 36.5	59.5	171.0	46 37.9	59.6	171.3	44 39.2	59.6	171.6	7
51 33.9	59.4	170.4	49 35.5	59.4	170.8	47 37.0	59.6	171.2	45 38.4	59.6	171.5	43 39.6	59.6	171.8	8
50 34.5	59.4	170.6	48 36.1	59.5	171.0	46 37.5	59.6	171.4	44 38.8	59.6	171.7	42 40.0	59.6	171.9	9
49 35.1	–59.4	170.9	47 36.6	–59.5	171.2	45 37.9	–59.5	171.5	43 39.2	–59.6	171.8	41 40.4	–59.7	172.1	10
48 35.7	59.5	171.1	46 37.1	59.5	171.4	44 38.4	59.6	171.7	42 39.6	59.6	172.0	40 40.7	59.7	172.2	11
47 36.2	59.4	171.3	45 37.6	59.5	171.6	43 38.8	59.5	171.9	41 40.0	59.6	172.1	39 41.1	59.7	172.4	12
46 36.8	59.5	171.5	44 38.1	59.5	171.8	42 39.3	59.6	172.0	40 40.4	59.7	172.3	38 41.4	59.6	172.5	13
45 37.3	59.5	171.7	43 38.5	59.5	171.9	41 39.7	59.6	172.2	39 40.7	59.6	172.4	37 41.8	59.7	172.6	14
44 37.8	–59.5	171.8	42 39.0	–59.6	172.1	40 40.1	–59.6	172.4	38 41.1	–59.6	172.6	36 42.1	–59.7	172.8	15
43 38.3	59.6	172.0	41 39.4	59.6	172.3	39 40.5	59.7	172.5	37 41.5	59.7	172.7	35 42.4	59.7	172.9	16
42 38.7	59.5	172.2	40 39.8	59.6	172.4	38 40.8	59.6	172.6	36 41.8	59.7	172.8	34 42.7	59.7	173.0	17
41 39.2	59.6	172.4	39 40.2	59.6	172.6	37 41.2	59.6	172.8	35 42.1	59.7	172.9	33 43.0	59.7	173.1	18
40 39.6	59.6	172.5	38 40.6	59.6	172.7	36 41.6	59.7	172.9	34 42.4	59.6	173.1	32 43.3	59.7	173.3	19
39 40.0	–59.5	172.7	37 41.0	–59.6	172.9	35 41.9	–59.7	173.1	33 42.8	–59.7	173.2	31 43.6	–59.7	173.4	20
38 40.5	59.6	172.8	36 41.4	59.7	173.0	34 42.2	59.6	173.2	32 43.1	59.7	173.3	30 43.9	59.8	173.5	21
37 40.9	59.7	173.0	35 41.7	59.6	173.1	33 42.6	59.7	173.3	31 43.4	59.7	173.5	29 44.1	59.7	173.6	22
36 41.2	59.6	173.1	34 42.1	59.7	173.3	32 42.9	59.7	173.4	30 43.7	59.8	173.6	28 44.4	59.7	173.7	23
35 41.6	59.6	173.2	33 42.4	59.6	173.4	31 43.2	59.7	173.6	29 43.9	59.7	173.7	27 44.7	59.8	173.8	24
34 42.0	–59.7	173.4	32 42.8	–59.7	173.5	30 43.5	–59.7	173.7	28 44.2	–59.7	173.9	26 44.9	–59.7	173.9	25
33 42.3	59.6	173.5	31 43.1	59.7	173.7	29 43.8	59.7	173.8	27 44.5	59.7	173.9	25 45.2	59.8	174.0	26
32 42.7	59.7	173.6	30 43.4	59.7	173.8	28 44.1	59.7	173.9	26 44.8	59.8	174.0	24 45.4	59.7	174.1	27
31 43.0	59.6	173.8	29 43.7	59.7	173.9	27 44.4	59.7	174.0	25 45.0	59.7	174.1	23 45.7	59.8	174.2	28
30 43.4	59.7	173.9	28 44.0	59.6	174.0	26 44.7	59.7	174.1	24 45.3	59.7	174.2	22 45.9	59.7	174.3	29

Dec.	40° Hc	d	Z	42° Hc	d	Z	44° Hc	d	Z	46° Hc	d	Z	48° Hc	d	Z
0	49 37.6	+59.6	170.7	47 39.2	+59.5	171.1	45 40.6	+59.6	171.4	43 41.9	+59.7	171.7	41 43.1	+59.7	171.9
1	50 37.2	59.5	170.5	48 38.7	59.6	170.9	46 40.2	59.6	171.2	44 41.6	59.6	171.5	42 42.8	59.7	171.8
2	51 36.7	59.5	170.3	49 38.3	59.6	170.7	47 39.8	59.7	171.1	45 41.2	59.7	171.4	43 42.5	59.7	171.7
3	52 36.2	59.4	170.1	50 37.9	59.5	170.5	48 39.5	59.6	170.9	46 40.9	59.7	171.2	44 42.2	59.8	171.6
4	53 35.6	59.5	169.9	51 37.4	59.5	170.3	49 39.1	59.5	170.7	47 40.6	59.6	171.1	45 42.0	59.6	171.4
5	54 35.1	+59.4	169.6	52 36.9	+59.5	170.1	50 38.6	+59.6	170.5	48 40.2	+59.6	170.9	46 41.6	+59.7	171.3
6	55 34.5	59.4	169.4	53 36.4	59.5	169.9	51 38.2	59.6	170.4	49 39.8	59.6	170.8	47 41.3	59.7	171.1
7	56 33.9	59.3	169.1	54 35.9	59.4	169.7	52 37.8	59.5	170.2	50 39.4	59.6	170.6	48 41.0	59.7	171.0
8	57 33.2	59.3	168.9	55 35.3	59.4	169.4	53 37.3	59.5	169.9	51 39.0	59.6	170.2	49 40.7	59.6	170.8
9	58 32.5	59.3	168.6	56 34.8	59.3	169.2	54 36.8	59.5	169.7	52 38.6	59.6	170.2	50 40.3	59.6	170.6
10	59 31.8	+59.2	168.3	57 34.1	+59.4	168.9	55 36.3	+59.4	169.5	53 38.2	+59.5	170.0	51 39.9	+59.6	170.4
11	60 31.0	59.2	168.0	58 33.5	59.3	168.7	56 35.7	59.4	169.3	54 37.7	59.5	169.8	52 39.5	59.6	170.3
12	61 30.2	59.1	167.6	59 32.8	59.3	168.4	57 35.1	59.4	169.0	55 37.2	59.5	169.6	53 39.1	59.6	170.1
13	62 29.3	59.1	167.3	60 32.1	59.2	168.1	58 34.5	59.4	168.7	56 36.7	59.5	169.3	54 38.7	59.5	169.9
14	63 28.4	59.0	166.9	61 31.3	59.2	167.7	59 33.9	59.3	168.5	57 36.2	59.4	169.1	55 38.2	59.6	169.6
15	64 27.4	+58.9	166.5	62 30.5	+59.1	167.4	60 33.2	+59.3	168.1	58 35.6	+59.4	168.8	56 37.8	+59.5	169.4
16	65 26.3	58.8	166.0	63 29.6	59.0	167.0	61 32.5	59.2	167.8	59 35.0	59.4	168.6	57 37.3	59.4	169.2
17	66 25.1	58.7	165.5	64 28.6	59.0	166.6	62 31.7	59.2	167.5	60 34.4	59.3	168.3	58 36.7	59.5	168.9
18	67 23.8	58.7	165.0	65 27.6	58.9	166.2	63 30.9	59.1	167.1	61 33.7	59.3	168.0	59 36.2	59.4	168.7
19	68 22.5	58.5	164.4	66 26.5	58.8	165.7	64 30.0	59.0	166.7	62 33.0	59.2	167.6	60 35.6	59.3	168.4
20	69 21.0	+58.3	163.8	67 25.3	+58.7	165.2	65 29.0	+59.0	166.3	63 32.2	+59.2	167.3	61 34.9	+59.4	168.1
21	70 19.3	58.2	163.2	68 24.0	58.6	164.6	66 28.0	58.9	165.9	64 31.4	59.1	166.9	62 34.3	59.3	167.8
22	71 17.5	58.0	162.4	69 22.6	58.5	164.0	67 26.9	58.8	165.4	65 30.5	59.0	166.5	63 33.6	59.2	167.4
23	72 15.5	57.8	161.6	70 21.1	58.3	163.4	68 25.7	58.6	164.8	66 29.5	59.0	166.0	64 32.8	59.2	167.1
24	73 13.3	57.5	160.7	71 19.4	58.1	162.7	69 24.3	58.6	164.2	67 28.5	58.8	165.6	65 32.0	59.1	166.7
25	74 10.8	+57.2	159.7	72 17.5	+57.9	161.9	70 22.9	+58.4	163.6	68 27.3	+58.8	165.1	66 31.1	+59.0	166.2
26	75 08.0	56.8	158.5	73 15.4	57.6	161.0	71 21.3	58.2	162.9	69 26.1	58.6	164.5	67 30.1	58.9	165.8
27	76 04.8	56.3	157.2	74 13.0	57.4	160.0	72 19.5	58.0	162.1	70 24.7	58.5	163.9	68 29.0	58.9	165.3
28	77 01.1	55.8	155.7	75 10.4	56.9	158.9	73 17.5	57.8	161.3	71 23.2	58.4	163.2	69 27.9	58.7	164.7
29	77 56.9	55.0	154.0	76 07.3	56.6	157.6	74 15.3	57.5	160.3	72 21.6	58.1	162.4	70 26.6	58.6	164.1

Dec.	50° Hc	d	Z	52° Hc	d	Z	54° Hc	d	Z	56° Hc	d	Z	58° Hc	d	Z
0	39 44.2	+59.8	172.2	37 45.3	+59.8	172.4	35 46.3	+59.9	172.6	33 47.3	+59.9	172.8	31 48.2	+59.9	172.9
1	40 44.0	59.8	172.1	38 45.1	59.8	172.3	36 46.2	59.8	172.5	34 47.2	59.8	172.7	32 48.1	59.9	172.9
2	41 43.8	59.7	172.0	39 44.9	59.8	172.2	37 46.0	59.8	172.4	35 47.0	59.9	172.6	33 48.0	59.8	172.8
3	42 43.5	59.8	171.8	40 44.7	59.8	172.1	38 45.8	59.8	172.3	36 46.9	59.8	172.5	34 47.8	59.9	172.7
4	43 43.3	59.7	171.7	41 44.5	59.7	172.0	39 45.6	59.8	172.2	37 46.7	59.8	172.4	35 47.7	59.9	172.7
5	44 43.0	+59.7	171.6	42 44.2	+59.8	171.8	40 45.4	+59.8	172.1	38 46.5	+59.9	172.3	36 47.6	+59.8	172.5
6	45 42.7	59.7	171.4	43 44.0	59.8	171.7	41 45.2	59.8	172.0	39 46.4	59.8	172.2	37 47.4	59.9	172.4
7	46 42.4	59.7	171.3	44 43.8	59.7	171.6	42 45.0	59.8	171.9	40 46.2	59.8	172.1	38 47.3	59.9	172.4
8	47 42.1	59.7	171.1	45 43.5	59.8	171.5	43 44.8	59.8	171.8	41 46.0	59.8	172.0	39 47.1	59.9	172.3
9	48 41.8	59.7	171.0	46 43.3	59.7	171.3	44 44.6	59.7	171.6	42 45.8	59.8	171.9	40 47.0	59.8	172.2
10	49 41.5	+59.7	170.8	47 43.0	+59.7	171.2	45 44.3	+59.8	171.5	43 45.6	+59.8	171.8	41 46.8	+59.8	172.1
11	50 41.2	59.6	170.7	48 42.7	59.7	171.0	46 44.1	59.8	171.4	44 45.4	59.8	171.7	42 46.6	59.9	172.0
12	51 40.8	59.7	170.5	49 42.4	59.7	170.9	47 43.9	59.7	171.3	45 45.2	59.8	171.6	43 46.5	59.8	171.9
13	52 40.5	59.6	170.3	50 42.1	59.7	170.7	48 43.6	59.7	171.1	46 45.0	59.8	171.5	44 46.3	59.8	171.8
14	53 40.1	59.6	170.1	51 41.8	59.7	170.6	49 43.3	59.8	171.0	47 44.8	59.7	171.3	45 46.1	59.8	171.6
15	54 39.7	+59.6	169.9	52 41.5	+59.6	170.4	50 43.1	+59.7	170.8	48 44.5	+59.8	171.2	46 45.9	+59.8	171.5
16	55 39.3	59.5	169.7	53 41.1	59.6	170.2	51 42.8	59.7	170.7	49 44.3	59.7	171.1	47 45.7	59.8	171.4
17	56 38.8	59.6	169.4	54 40.7	59.7	170.0	52 42.5	59.7	170.5	50 44.0	59.8	170.9	48 45.5	59.8	171.3
18	57 38.4	59.5	169.3	55 40.4	59.6	169.8	53 42.2	59.6	170.3	51 43.8	59.7	170.8	49 45.3	59.7	171.1
19	58 37.9	59.5	169.1	56 40.0	59.5	169.6	54 41.8	59.7	170.2	52 43.5	59.7	170.6	50 45.0	59.8	171.0
20	59 37.4	+59.4	168.8	57 39.5	+59.6	169.4	55 41.5	+59.6	170.0	53 43.2	+59.7	170.4	51 44.8	+59.8	170.9
21	60 36.8	59.4	168.6	58 39.1	59.5	169.1	56 41.1	59.6	169.8	54 42.9	59.7	170.3	52 44.6	59.7	170.7
22	61 36.2	59.4	168.2	59 38.6	59.5	168.9	57 40.7	59.6	169.6	55 42.6	59.7	170.1	53 44.3	59.8	170.6
23	62 35.6	59.4	167.9	60 38.1	59.5	168.7	58 40.3	59.6	169.3	56 42.3	59.6	169.9	54 44.0	59.8	170.4
24	63 35.0	59.2	167.5	61 37.6	59.4	168.4	59 39.9	59.5	169.1	57 41.9	59.7	169.7	55 43.8	59.7	170.2
25	64 34.2	+59.3	167.3	62 37.0	+59.4	168.1	60 39.4	+59.5	168.9	58 41.6	+59.6	169.5	56 43.5	+59.7	170.1
26	65 33.5	59.2	166.9	63 36.4	59.3	167.8	61 38.9	59.5	168.6	59 41.2	59.5	169.3	57 43.1	59.7	169.9
27	66 32.7	59.1	166.5	64 35.7	59.3	167.5	62 38.4	59.5	168.3	60 40.7	59.6	169.0	58 42.8	59.7	169.7
28	67 31.8	59.0	166.0	65 35.0	59.3	167.1	63 37.9	59.4	168.0	61 40.3	59.5	168.8	59 42.5	59.6	169.5
29	68 30.8	58.9	165.5	66 34.3	59.1	166.7	64 37.3	59.3	167.7	62 39.8	59.5	168.5	60 42.1	59.6	169.2

40°			42°			44°			46°			48°			Dec.
Hc	d	Z	Hc	d	Z	Hc	d	Z	Hc	d	Z	Hc	d	Z	
° ′	′	°	° ′	′	°	° ′	′	°	° ′	′	°	° ′	′	°	°
49 37.6	− 59.5	170.7	47 39.2	− 59.7	171.1	45 40.6	− 59.7	171.4	43 41.9	− 59.7	171.7	41 43.1	− 59.8	171.9	0
48 38.1	59.6	170.9	46 39.5	59.6	171.2	44 40.9	59.6	171.5	42 42.2	59.8	171.8	40 43.3	59.7	172.1	1
47 38.5	59.6	171.1	45 39.9	59.6	171.4	43 41.2	59.7	171.7	41 42.4	59.7	172.0	39 43.6	59.8	172.2	2
46 38.9	59.6	171.3	44 40.3	59.7	171.6	42 41.5	59.6	171.8	40 42.7	59.7	172.1	38 43.8	59.7	172.3	3
45 39.3	59.6	171.4	43 40.6	59.6	171.7	41 41.9	59.7	172.0	39 43.0	59.7	172.2	37 44.1	59.8	172.4	4
44 39.7	− 59.6	171.6	42 41.0	− 59.7	171.9	40 42.2	− 59.7	172.1	38 43.3	− 59.8	172.3	36 44.3	− 59.8	172.5	5
43 40.1	59.6	171.7	41 41.3	59.7	172.0	39 42.5	59.8	172.2	37 43.5	59.7	172.4	35 44.5	59.7	172.6	6
42 40.5	59.7	171.9	40 41.6	59.7	172.1	38 42.7	59.7	172.4	36 43.8	59.8	172.6	34 44.8	59.8	172.7	7
41 40.8	59.6	172.0	39 41.9	59.6	172.3	37 43.0	59.7	172.5	35 44.0	59.7	172.7	33 45.0	59.8	172.8	8
40 41.2	59.7	172.2	38 42.3	59.8	172.4	36 43.3	59.7	172.6	34 44.3	59.8	172.8	32 45.2	59.8	172.9	9
39 41.5	− 59.7	172.3	37 42.5	− 59.7	172.5	35 43.5	− 59.7	172.7	33 44.5	− 59.8	172.9	31 45.4	− 59.8	173.0	10
38 41.8	59.7	172.4	36 42.8	59.7	172.6	34 43.8	59.8	172.8	32 44.7	59.8	173.0	30 45.6	59.8	173.1	11
37 42.1	59.7	172.6	35 43.1	59.7	172.8	33 44.0	59.7	172.9	31 44.9	59.8	173.1	29 45.8	59.8	173.2	12
36 42.4	59.7	172.7	34 43.4	59.8	172.9	32 44.3	59.8	173.0	30 45.1	59.7	173.2	28 46.0	59.8	173.3	13
35 42.7	59.7	172.8	33 43.6	59.7	173.0	31 44.5	59.7	173.2	29 45.4	59.8	173.3	27 46.2	59.8	173.4	14
34 43.0	− 59.7	172.9	32 43.9	− 59.7	173.1	30 44.8	− 59.8	173.3	28 45.6	− 59.8	173.4	26 46.4	− 59.9	173.5	15
33 43.3	59.7	173.1	31 44.2	59.8	173.2	29 45.0	59.8	173.4	27 45.8	59.8	173.5	25 46.5	59.8	173.6	16
32 43.6	59.8	173.2	30 44.4	59.7	173.3	28 45.2	59.8	173.5	26 46.0	59.8	173.6	24 46.7	59.8	173.7	17
31 43.8	59.7	173.3	29 44.7	59.8	173.4	27 45.4	59.8	173.5	25 46.2	59.8	173.7	23 46.9	59.8	173.8	18
30 44.1	59.7	173.4	28 44.9	59.8	173.5	26 45.6	59.7	173.6	24 46.4	59.8	173.8	22 47.1	59.9	173.9	19
29 44.4	− 59.8	173.5	27 45.1	− 59.7	173.6	25 45.9	− 59.8	173.7	23 46.6	− 59.9	173.8	21 47.2	− 59.8	173.9	20
28 44.6	59.7	173.6	26 45.4	59.8	173.7	24 46.1	59.8	173.8	22 46.7	59.8	173.9	20 47.4	59.8	174.0	21
27 44.9	59.8	173.7	25 45.6	59.8	173.8	23 46.3	59.8	173.9	21 46.9	59.8	174.0	19 47.6	59.9	174.1	22
26 45.1	59.7	173.8	24 45.8	59.8	173.9	22 46.5	59.8	174.0	20 47.1	59.8	174.1	18 47.7	59.8	174.2	23
25 45.4	59.8	173.9	23 46.0	59.8	174.0	21 46.7	59.8	174.1	19 47.3	59.8	174.2	17 47.9	59.8	174.2	24
24 45.6	− 59.8	174.0	22 46.2	− 59.8	174.1	20 46.9	− 59.8	174.2	18 47.5	− 59.9	174.3	16 48.1	− 59.9	174.3	25
23 45.8	59.7	174.1	21 46.4	59.7	174.2	19 47.1	59.9	174.3	17 47.6	59.8	174.4	15 48.2	59.8	174.4	26
22 46.0	59.7	174.2	20 46.7	59.8	174.3	18 47.2	59.8	174.4	16 47.8	59.8	174.4	14 48.4	59.8	174.5	27
21 46.3	59.8	174.3	19 46.9	59.8	174.4	17 47.4	59.8	174.4	15 48.0	59.8	174.5	13 48.5	59.8	174.5	28
20 46.5	59.8	174.4	18 47.1	59.8	174.5	16 47.6	59.8	174.5	14 48.2	59.9	174.6	12 48.7	59.9	174.6	29

50°			52°			54°			56°			58°			Dec.
Hc	d	Z	Hc	d	Z	Hc	d	Z	Hc	d	Z	Hc	d	Z	
° ′	′	°	° ′	′	°	° ′	′	°	° ′	′	°	° ′	′	°	°
39 44.2	− 59.7	172.2	37 45.3	− 59.8	172.4	35 46.3	− 59.8	172.6	33 47.3	− 59.8	172.8	31 48.2	− 59.8	172.9	0
38 44.5	59.8	172.3	36 45.5	59.8	172.5	34 46.5	59.8	172.7	32 47.5	59.9	172.9	30 48.4	59.9	173.1	1
37 44.7	59.8	172.4	35 45.7	59.8	172.6	33 46.7	59.9	172.8	31 47.6	59.8	172.9	29 48.5	59.9	173.1	2
36 44.9	59.8	172.5	34 45.9	59.8	172.7	32 46.8	59.8	172.9	30 47.7	59.8	173.0	28 48.6	59.9	173.2	3
35 45.1	59.8	172.6	33 46.1	59.9	172.8	31 47.0	59.9	173.0	29 47.9	59.9	173.1	27 48.7	59.8	173.2	4
34 45.3	− 59.8	172.7	32 46.2	− 59.8	172.9	30 47.1	− 59.8	173.0	28 48.0	− 59.9	173.2	26 48.9	− 59.9	173.3	5
33 45.5	59.8	172.8	31 46.4	59.8	173.0	29 47.3	59.9	173.1	27 48.1	59.8	173.3	25 49.0	59.9	173.4	6
32 45.7	59.8	172.9	30 46.6	59.8	173.1	28 47.5	59.9	173.2	26 48.3	59.9	173.4	24 49.1	59.9	173.5	7
31 45.9	59.8	173.0	29 46.8	59.9	173.2	27 47.6	59.8	173.3	25 48.4	59.9	173.4	23 49.2	59.9	173.5	8
30 46.1	59.8	173.1	28 46.9	59.8	173.2	26 47.7	59.8	173.4	24 48.5	59.8	173.5	22 49.3	59.9	173.6	9
29 46.3	− 59.9	173.2	27 47.1	− 59.8	173.3	25 47.9	− 59.9	173.4	23 48.7	− 59.9	173.5	21 49.4	− 59.9	173.6	10
28 46.4	59.8	173.3	26 47.2	59.8	173.4	24 48.0	59.8	173.5	22 48.8	59.9	173.6	20 49.5	59.9	173.7	11
27 46.6	59.8	173.4	25 47.4	59.9	173.5	23 48.2	59.9	173.6	21 48.9	59.8	173.7	19 49.6	59.8	173.8	12
26 46.8	59.8	173.4	24 47.5	59.8	173.6	22 48.3	59.9	173.7	20 49.0	59.8	173.7	18 49.7	59.8	173.8	13
25 46.9	59.8	173.5	23 47.7	59.9	173.6	21 48.4	59.8	173.8	19 49.1	59.9	173.8	17 49.8	59.9	173.9	14
24 47.1	− 59.8	173.6	22 47.8	− 59.8	173.7	20 48.6	− 59.9	173.8	18 49.2	− 59.8	173.9	16 49.9	− 59.9	173.9	15
23 47.3	59.9	173.7	21 48.0	59.9	173.8	19 48.7	59.9	173.9	17 49.4	59.9	173.9	15 50.0	59.9	174.0	16
22 47.4	59.8	173.8	20 48.1	59.8	173.9	18 48.8	59.9	173.9	16 49.5	59.9	174.0	14 50.1	59.9	174.1	17
21 47.6	59.8	173.8	19 48.3	59.9	173.9	17 48.9	59.8	174.0	15 49.6	59.9	174.1	13 50.2	59.9	174.1	18
20 47.7	59.8	173.9	18 48.4	59.8	174.0	16 49.1	59.9	174.1	14 49.7	59.9	174.1	12 50.3	59.9	174.2	19
19 47.9	− 59.8	174.0	17 48.6	− 59.9	174.1	15 49.2	− 59.9	174.1	13 49.8	− 59.9	174.2	11 50.4	− 59.9	174.2	20
18 48.1	59.9	174.1	16 48.7	59.9	174.1	14 49.3	59.9	174.2	12 49.9	59.9	174.3	10 50.5	59.9	174.3	21
17 48.2	59.8	174.2	15 48.8	59.8	174.2	13 49.4	59.9	174.3	11 50.0	59.9	174.3	9 50.6	59.9	174.4	22
16 48.4	59.9	174.2	14 49.0	59.9	174.3	12 49.5	59.8	174.3	10 50.1	59.9	174.4	8 50.7	59.9	174.4	23
15 48.5	59.9	174.3	13 49.1	59.9	174.4	11 49.7	59.9	174.4	9 50.2	59.9	174.4	7 50.8	59.9	174.5	24
14 48.6	− 59.8	174.4	12 49.2	− 59.9	174.4	10 49.8	− 59.9	174.5	8 50.3	− 59.9	174.5	6 50.9	− 59.9	174.5	25
13 48.8	59.9	174.4	11 49.3	59.8	174.5	9 49.9	59.9	174.5	7 50.4	59.9	174.6	5 51.0	59.9	174.6	26
12 48.9	59.8	174.5	10 49.5	59.9	174.6	8 50.0	59.9	174.6	6 50.5	59.8	174.6	4 51.1	59.9	174.6	27
11 49.1	59.9	174.6	9 49.6	59.9	174.6	7 50.1	59.9	174.7	5 50.7	59.9	174.7	3 51.2	59.9	174.7	28
10 49.2	59.8	174.7	8 49.7	59.8	174.7	6 50.2	59.8	174.7	4 50.8	59.9	174.7	2 51.3	59.9	174.7	29

LATITUDE **SAME** NAME

Dec.	0° Hc	d	Z	2° Hc	d	Z	4° Hc	d	Z	6° Hc	d	Z	8° Hc	d	Z
°	° ′	′	°	° ′	′	°	° ′	′	°	° ′	′	°	° ′	′	°
0	82 00.0	- 3.7•	90.0	81 45.3	+11.1•	103.9	81 03.7	+24.1•	116.4	80 00.7	+34.2•	126.6	78 42.3	+41.2•	134.7
1	81 56.3	11.0•	82.9	81 56.4	+ 3.9•	97.0	81 27.8	18.1•	110.4	80 34.9	29.6•	121.8	79 23.5	38.1•	130.9
2	81 45.3	17.7•	75.9	82 00.3	- 3.6•	89.9	81 45.9	11.3•	103.8	81 04.5	24.3•	116.3	80 01.6	34.4•	126.6
3	81 27.6	23.9•	69.4	81 56.7	10.8•	82.7	81 57.2	+ 4.0•	96.9	81 28.8	18.2•	110.3	80 36.0	29.8•	121.7
4	81 03.7	29.2•	63.3	81 45.9	17.6•	75.8	82 01.2	- 3.5•	89.7	81 47.0	11.5•	103.7	81 05.8	24.5•	116.2
5	80 34.5	-33.8•	57.8	81 28.3	-23.8•	69.2	81 57.7	-10.7•	82.6	81 58.5	+ 4.1•	96.8	81 30.3	+18.4•	110.2
6	80 00.7	37.6•	52.9	81 04.5	29.2•	63.1	81 47.0	17.5•	75.6	82 02.6	- 3.3•	89.6	81 48.7	11.7•	103.6
7	79 23.1	40.8•	48.6	80 35.3	33.7•	57.7	81 29.5	23.7•	69.0	81 59.3	10.6•	82.4	82 00.4	+ 4.3•	96.7
8	78 42.3	43.5•	44.7	80 01.6	37.5•	52.7	81 05.8	29.1•	62.9	81 48.7	17.4•	75.4	82 04.7	- 3.2•	89.4
9	77 58.8	45.6•	41.3	79 24.1	40.8•	48.4	80 36.7	33.7•	57.4	81 31.3	23.6•	69.2	82 01.5	10.5•	82.2
10	77 13.2	-47.5	38.3	78 43.3	-43.4•	44.5	80 03.0	-37.5•	52.5	81 07.6	-29.0•	62.7	81 51.0	-17.5•	75.2
11	76 25.7	49.1	35.6	77 59.9	45.6•	41.1	79 25.5	40.7•	48.1	80 38.6	33.7•	57.2	81 33.6	23.6•	68.6
12	75 36.6	50.3	33.2	77 14.3	47.5	38.0	78 44.8	43.5•	44.2	80 04.9	37.5•	52.2	81 10.0	29.1•	62.4
13	74 46.3	51.4	31.1	76 26.8	49.0	35.4	78 01.3	45.6•	40.8	79 27.4	40.8•	47.8	80 40.9	33.7•	56.9
14	73 54.9	52.3	29.2	75 37.8	50.3	33.0	77 15.7	47.5	37.8	78 46.6	43.4•	43.9	80 07.2	37.5•	51.9
15	73 02.6	-53.1	27.4	74 47.5	-51.4	30.8	76 28.2	-49.0	35.1	78 03.2	-45.7•	40.5	79 29.7	-40.8•	47.5
16	72 09.5	53.8	25.9	73 56.1	52.3	28.9	75 39.2	50.3	32.7	77 17.5	47.5	37.5	78 48.9	43.5•	43.6
17	71 15.7	54.3	24.5	73 03.8	53.1	27.2	74 48.9	51.4	30.5	76 30.0	49.0	34.8	78 05.4	45.7•	40.2
18	70 21.4	54.9	23.2	72 10.7	53.8	25.6	73 57.5	52.3	28.6	75 41.0	50.3	32.4	77 19.7	47.6	37.1
19	69 26.5	55.3	22.0	71 16.9	54.3	24.2	73 05.2	53.1	26.9	74 50.7	51.5	30.2	76 32.1	49.0	34.4
20	68 31.2	-55.7	20.9	70 22.6	-54.9	22.9	72 12.1	-53.8	25.3	73 59.2	-52.3	28.3	75 43.1	-50.4	32.0
21	67 35.5	56.0	19.9	69 27.7	55.3	21.7	71 18.3	54.3	23.9	73 06.9	53.1	26.6	74 52.7	51.5	29.9
22	66 39.5	56.3	19.0	68 32.4	55.7	20.7	70 24.0	54.9	22.6	72 13.8	53.8	25.0	74 01.2	52.3	28.0
23	65 43.2	56.6	18.2	67 36.7	56.0	19.7	69 29.1	55.3	21.4	71 20.0	54.4	23.6	73 08.9	53.2	26.2
24	64 46.6	56.8	17.4	66 40.7	56.3	18.7	68 33.8	55.7	20.4	70 25.6	54.9	22.3	72 15.7	53.8	24.7
25	63 49.8	-57.1	16.6	65 44.4	-56.6	17.9	67 38.1	-56.0	19.4	69 30.7	-55.3	21.1	71 21.9	-54.4	23.2
26	62 52.7	57.2	15.9	64 47.8	56.8	17.1	66 42.1	56.3	18.4	68 35.4	55.7	20.0	70 27.5	54.9	22.0
27	61 55.5	57.4	15.3	63 51.0	57.0	16.3	65 45.8	56.6	17.6	67 39.7	56.0	19.0	69 32.6	55.3	20.8
28	60 58.1	57.5	14.7	62 54.0	57.3	15.6	64 49.2	56.8	16.8	66 43.7	56.4	18.1	68 37.2	55.7	19.7
29	60 00.6	57.7	14.1	61 56.7	57.4	15.0	63 52.4	57.1	16.0	65 47.3	56.6	17.3	67 41.5	56.1	18.7

Dec.	10° Hc	d	Z	12° Hc	d	Z	14° Hc	d	Z	16° Hc	d	Z	18° Hc	d	Z
°	° ′	′	°	° ′	′	°	° ′	′	°	° ′	′	°	° ′	′	°
0	77 13.2	+46.1•	141.0	75 36.6	+49.6	145.9	73 54.9	+51.9	149.8	72 09.5	+53.7	153.0	70 21.4	+54.9	155.5
1	77 59.3	44.0•	138.0	76 26.2	48.1	143.6	74 46.8	51.0	148.0	73 03.2	52.9	151.5	71 16.3	54.4	154.3
2	78 43.3	41.4•	134.7	77 14.3	46.3	141.0	75 37.8	49.7	145.9	73 56.1	52.1	149.8	72 10.7	53.8	153.0
3	79 24.7	38.3•	130.9	78 00.6	44.2•	138.0	76 27.5	48.2	143.6	74 48.2	51.0	148.0	73 04.5	53.0	151.5
4	80 03.0	34.6•	126.5	78 44.8	41.6•	134.7	77 15.7	46.5	141.0	75 39.2	49.9	145.9	73 57.5	52.2	149.8
5	80 37.6	+30.0•	121.7	79 26.4	+38.5•	130.8	78 02.2	+44.4•	138.0	76 29.1	+48.4	143.6	74 49.7	+51.3	148.0
6	81 07.6	24.8•	116.2	80 04.9	34.8•	126.5	78 46.6	41.9•	134.7	77 17.5	46.7	141.0	75 41.0	50.0	146.0
7	81 32.4	18.6•	110.1	80 39.7	30.3•	121.6	79 28.5	38.7•	130.9	78 04.2	44.7•	138.1	76 31.0	48.7	143.7
8	81 51.0	11.8•	103.6	81 10.0	24.9•	116.2	80 07.2	35.1•	126.6	78 48.9	42.1•	134.7	77 19.7	46.9	141.1
9	82 02.8	+ 4.5•	96.6	81 34.9	18.9•	110.1	80 42.3	30.5•	121.7	79 31.0	39.0•	130.9	78 06.6	44.9•	138.1
10	82 07.3	- 3.0•	89.3	81 53.8	+12.0•	103.5	81 12.8	+25.3•	116.2	80 10.0	+35.3•	126.6	78 51.5	+42.4•	134.8
11	82 04.3	10.5•	82.0	82 05.8	+ 4.7•	96.5	81 38.1	19.1•	110.1	80 45.3	30.9•	121.7	79 33.9	39.3•	131.0
12	81 53.8	17.4•	75.0	82 10.5	- 2.9•	89.2	81 57.2	12.2•	103.5	81 16.2	25.5•	116.2	80 13.2	35.7•	126.7
13	81 36.4	23.6•	68.3	82 07.6	10.4•	81.8	82 09.4	+ 4.9•	96.4	81 41.7	19.4•	110.1	80 48.9	31.1•	121.8
14	81 12.8	29.1•	62.1	81 57.2	17.4•	74.7	82 14.3	- 2.8•	89.0	82 01.1	12.5•	103.5	81 20.0	25.9•	116.2
15	80 43.7	-33.7•	56.6	81 39.8	-23.6•	68.0	82 11.5	-10.4•	81.7	82 13.6	+ 5.0•	96.3	81 45.9	+19.7•	110.2
16	80 10.0	37.6•	51.6	81 16.2	29.2•	61.8	82 01.1	17.3•	74.5	82 18.6	- 2.7•	88.9	82 05.6	12.7•	103.6
17	79 32.4	40.9•	47.1	80 47.0	33.8•	56.2	81 43.8	23.8•	67.7	82 15.9	10.3•	81.4	82 18.3	+ 5.2•	96.3
18	78 51.5	43.5•	43.2	80 13.2	37.7•	51.2	81 20.0	29.2•	61.5	82 05.6	17.4•	74.2	82 23.5	- 2.6•	88.8
19	78 08.0	45.8•	39.8	79 35.5	41.0•	46.8	80 50.8	33.9•	55.8	81 48.2	23.8•	67.4	82 20.9	10.3•	81.2
20	77 22.2	-47.6	36.7	78 54.5	-43.6•	42.8	80 16.9	-37.9•	50.8	81 24.4	-29.4•	61.1	82 10.6	-17.5•	73.9
21	76 34.6	49.2	34.0	78 10.9	45.9•	39.4	79 39.0	41.1•	46.3	80 55.0	34.0•	55.4	81 53.1	23.9•	67.0
22	75 45.4	50.4	31.6	77 25.0	47.7	36.3	78 57.9	43.7•	42.4	80 21.0	38.0•	50.3	81 29.2	29.5•	60.7
23	74 55.0	51.5	29.5	76 37.3	49.2	33.6	78 14.2	46.0•	38.9	79 43.0	41.3•	45.9	80 59.7	34.2•	54.9
24	74 03.5	52.4	27.6	75 48.1	50.5	31.2	77 28.2	47.8	35.9	79 01.7	43.9•	41.9	80 25.5	38.2•	49.8
25	73 11.1	-53.3	25.9	74 57.6	-51.6	29.1	76 40.4	-49.4	33.2	78 17.8	-46.2•	38.4	79 47.3	-41.5•	45.0
26	72 17.8	53.8	24.3	74 06.0	52.5	27.2	75 51.0	50.6	30.8	77 31.6	47.9	35.4	79 05.8	44.1•	41.4
27	71 24.0	54.5	22.9	73 13.5	53.3	25.4	75 00.4	51.7	28.6	76 43.7	49.5	32.7	78 21.7	46.3•	37.9
28	70 29.5	54.9	21.6	72 20.2	53.9	23.9	74 08.7	52.6	26.7	75 54.2	50.7	30.3	77 35.4	48.1	34.9
29	69 34.6	55.4	20.4	71 26.3	54.5	22.5	73 16.1	53.3	25.0	75 03.5	51.8	28.2	76 47.3	49.6	32.2

0°			2°			4°			6°			8°			Dec.
Hc	d	Z	Hc	d	Z	Hc	d	Z	Hc	d	Z	Hc	d	Z	
° ′	′	°	° ′	′	°	° ′	′	°	° ′	′	°	° ′	′	°	°
82 00.0	– 3.7°	90.0	81 45.3	– 17.9°	103.9	81 03.7	– 29.5°	116.4	80 00.7	– 37.9°	126.6	78 42.3	– 43.9°	134.7	0
81 56.3	11.0°	97.1	81 27.4	24.0°	110.5	80 34.2	34.0°	121.9	79 22.8	41.1°	131.0	77 58.4	46.0	138.1	1
81 45.3	17.7°	104.1	81 03.4	29.3°	116.5	80 00.2	37.8°	126.7	78 41.7	43.8°	134.8	77 12.4	47.8	141.1	2
81 27.6	23.9°	110.6	80 34.1	33.9°	122.0	79 22.4	40.9°	131.1	77 57.9	45.8	138.2	76 24.6	49.3	143.7	3
81 03.7	29.2°	116.7	80 00.2	37.7°	126.9	78 41.5	43.7°	134.9	77 12.1	47.7	141.2	75 35.3	50.5	146.1	4
80 34.5	– 33.8°	122.2	79 22.5	– 40.8°	131.2	77 57.8	– 45.7°	138.3	76 24.4	– 49.2	143.9	74 44.8	– 51.6	148.2	5
80 00.7	37.6°	127.1	78 41.7	43.6°	135.1	77 12.1	47.7	141.3	75 35.2	50.5	146.2	73 53.2	52.5	150.1	6
79 23.1	40.8°	131.4	77 58.1	45.7	138.5	76 24.4	49.1	144.0	74 44.7	51.5	148.3	73 00.7	53.3	151.8	7
78 42.3	43.5°	135.3	77 12.4	47.5	141.5	75 35.3	50.4	146.4	73 53.2	52.5	150.2	72 07.4	53.9	153.3	8
77 58.8	45.6°	138.7	76 24.9	49.1	144.2	74 44.9	51.4	148.5	73 00.7	53.2	151.9	71 13.5	54.5	154.7	9
77 13.2	– 47.5	141.7	75 35.8	– 50.3	146.6	73 53.5	– 52.4	150.4	72 07.5	– 53.8	153.5	70 19.0	– 55.0	156.0	10
76 25.7	49.1	144.4	74 45.5	51.5	148.7	73 01.1	53.2	152.1	71 13.7	54.5	154.9	69 24.0	55.4	157.2	11
75 36.6	50.3	146.8	73 54.0	52.3	150.6	72 07.9	53.8	153.7	70 19.2	54.9	156.2	68 28.6	55.8	158.2	12
74 46.3	51.4	148.9	73 01.7	53.1	152.3	71 14.1	54.4	155.1	69 24.3	55.4	157.3	67 32.8	56.1	159.2	13
73 54.9	52.3	150.8	72 08.6	53.8	153.9	70 19.7	54.9	156.3	68 28.9	55.7	158.4	66 36.7	56.4	160.1	14
73 02.6	– 53.1	152.6	71 14.8	– 54.4	155.3	69 24.8	– 55.3	157.5	67 33.2	– 56.1	159.4	65 40.3	– 56.7	161.0	15
72 09.5	53.8	154.1	70 20.4	54.9	156.6	68 29.5	55.8	158.6	66 37.1	56.4	160.3	64 43.6	56.9	161.7	16
71 15.7	54.3	155.5	69 25.5	55.3	157.7	67 33.7	56.0	159.6	65 40.7	56.6	161.1	63 46.7	57.1	162.5	17
70 21.4	54.9	156.8	68 30.2	55.7	158.8	66 37.7	56.3	160.5	64 44.1	56.9	161.9	62 49.6	57.3	163.2	18
69 26.5	55.3	158.0	67 34.5	56.0	159.8	65 41.4	56.7	161.4	63 47.2	57.1	162.7	61 52.3	57.5	163.8	19
68 31.2	– 55.7	159.1	66 38.5	– 56.1	160.7	64 44.7	– 56.8	162.1	62 50.1	– 57.2	163.4	60 54.8	– 57.6	164.4	20
67 35.5	56.0	160.1	65 42.2	56.6	161.6	63 47.9	57.1	162.9	61 52.9	57.5	164.0	59 57.2	57.7	165.0	21
66 39.5	56.3	161.0	64 45.6	56.8	162.4	62 50.8	57.2	163.6	60 55.4	57.6	164.6	58 59.5	57.9	165.5	22
65 43.2	56.6	161.8	63 48.8	57.1	163.1	61 53.6	57.4	164.2	59 57.8	57.7	165.2	58 01.6	58.0	166.0	23
64 46.6	56.8	162.6	62 51.7	57.2	163.8	60 56.2	57.6	164.8	59 00.1	57.8	165.7	57 03.6	58.1	166.5	24
63 49.8	– 57.1	163.4	61 54.5	– 57.4	164.5	59 58.6	– 57.7	165.4	58 02.3	– 58.0	166.2	56 05.5	– 58.2	166.9	25
62 52.7	57.2	164.1	60 57.1	57.6	165.1	59 00.9	57.9	165.9	57 04.3	58.1	166.7	55 07.3	58.2	167.4	26
61 55.5	57.4	164.7	59 59.5	57.7	165.6	58 03.0	57.9	166.4	56 06.2	58.2	167.2	54 09.1	58.4	167.8	27
60 58.1	57.5	165.3	59 01.8	57.8	166.2	57 05.1	58.1	166.9	55 08.0	58.2	167.6	53 10.7	58.4	168.2	28
60 00.6	57.7	165.9	58 04.0	58.0	166.7	56 07.0	58.1	167.4	54 09.8	58.4	168.0	52 12.3	58.5	168.5	29

10°			12°			14°			16°			18°			Dec.
Hc	d	Z	Hc	d	Z	Hc	d	Z	Hc	d	Z	Hc	d	Z	
° ′	′	°	° ′	′	°	° ′	′	°	° ′	′	°	° ′	′	°	°
77 13.2	– 48.0	141.0	75 36.6	– 50.8	145.9	73 54.9	– 52.8	149.8	72 09.5	– 54.3	153.0	70 21.4	– 55.4	155.5	0
76 25.2	49.4	143.7	74 45.8	51.8	148.0	73 02.1	53.5	151.5	71 15.2	54.8	154.3	69 26.0	55.8	156.7	1
75 35.8	50.6	146.0	73 54.0	52.6	149.9	72 08.6	54.2	153.0	70 20.4	55.3	155.6	68 30.2	56.1	157.7	2
74 45.2	51.7	148.1	73 01.4	53.5	151.6	71 14.4	54.7	154.4	69 25.1	55.6	156.8	67 34.1	56.4	158.6	3
73 53.5	52.6	150.0	72 07.9	54.1	153.1	70 19.7	55.2	155.6	68 29.5	56.1	157.7	66 37.7	56.7	159.5	4
73 00.9	– 53.4	151.7	71 13.8	– 54.6	154.5	69 24.5	– 55.6	156.8	67 33.4	– 56.3	158.7	65 41.0	– 56.9	160.3	5
72 07.5	54.0	153.2	70 19.2	55.1	155.7	68 28.9	55.9	157.8	66 37.1	56.6	159.6	64 44.1	57.2	161.1	6
71 13.5	54.5	154.6	69 24.1	55.5	156.9	67 33.0	56.3	158.8	65 40.5	56.9	160.4	63 46.9	57.3	161.8	7
70 19.0	55.1	155.8	68 28.6	55.9	157.9	66 36.7	56.6	159.7	64 43.6	57.1	161.2	62 49.6	57.5	162.4	8
69 23.9	55.4	157.0	67 32.7	56.2	158.9	65 40.1	56.8	160.5	63 46.5	57.3	161.9	61 52.1	57.7	163.1	9
68 28.5	– 55.9	158.1	66 36.5	– 56.5	159.8	64 43.3	– 57.0	161.3	62 49.2	– 57.4	162.5	60 54.4	– 57.8	163.6	10
67 32.6	56.1	159.0	65 40.0	56.8	160.6	63 46.3	57.2	162.0	61 51.8	57.5	163.2	59 56.6	57.9	164.2	11
66 36.5	56.5	159.9	64 43.2	57.0	161.4	62 49.1	57.4	162.7	60 54.2	57.8	163.7	58 58.7	58.0	164.7	12
65 40.0	56.7	160.8	63 46.2	57.1	162.1	61 51.7	57.6	163.3	59 56.4	57.9	164.3	58 00.7	58.2	165.2	13
64 43.3	56.9	161.6	62 49.1	57.4	162.8	60 54.1	57.7	163.9	58 58.5	58.0	164.8	57 02.5	58.2	165.6	14
63 46.4	– 57.2	162.3	61 51.7	– 57.5	163.4	59 56.4	– 57.9	164.4	58 00.5	– 58.1	165.3	56 04.3	– 58.4	166.1	15
62 49.2	57.3	163.0	60 54.2	57.7	164.0	58 58.5	57.9	165.0	57 02.4	58.2	165.8	55 05.9	58.4	166.5	16
61 51.9	57.5	163.6	59 56.5	57.8	164.6	58 00.6	58.1	165.5	56 04.2	58.3	166.2	54 07.5	58.5	166.9	17
60 54.4	57.6	164.2	58 58.7	57.9	165.1	57 02.5	58.2	165.9	55 05.9	58.3	166.6	53 09.0	58.5	167.2	18
59 56.8	57.8	164.8	58 00.8	58.1	165.6	56 04.3	58.2	166.4	54 07.6	58.5	167.0	52 10.5	58.6	167.6	19
58 59.0	– 57.9	165.3	57 02.7	– 58.1	166.1	55 06.1	– 58.4	166.8	53 09.1	– 58.5	167.4	51 11.9	– 58.7	168.0	20
58 01.1	58.0	165.8	56 04.6	58.2	166.5	54 07.7	58.4	167.2	52 10.6	58.6	167.8	50 13.2	58.7	168.3	21
57 03.1	58.1	166.3	55 06.4	58.4	167.0	53 09.3	58.5	167.6	51 12.0	58.7	168.1	49 14.5	58.8	168.6	22
56 05.0	58.2	166.7	54 08.0	58.4	167.4	52 10.8	58.5	167.9	50 13.3	58.7	168.4	48 15.7	58.8	168.9	23
55 06.8	58.3	167.2	53 09.6	58.4	167.8	51 12.3	58.7	168.3	49 14.6	58.7	168.8	47 16.9	58.9	169.2	24
54 08.5	– 58.4	167.6	52 11.2	– 58.6	168.1	50 13.6	– 58.6	168.6	48 15.9	– 58.8	169.1	46 18.0	– 58.9	169.5	25
53 10.1	58.4	168.0	51 12.6	58.6	168.5	49 15.0	58.8	169.0	47 17.1	58.8	169.4	45 19.1	59.0	169.8	26
52 11.7	58.5	168.3	50 14.0	58.6	168.8	48 16.2	58.7	169.3	46 18.3	58.9	169.7	44 20.1	58.9	170.0	27
51 13.2	58.6	168.7	49 15.4	58.7	169.1	47 17.5	58.9	169.6	45 19.4	59.0	169.9	43 21.2	59.1	170.3	28
50 14.6	58.7	169.0	48 16.7	58.8	169.5	46 18.6	58.8	169.9	44 20.4	58.9	170.2	42 22.1	59.0	170.5	29

Dec.	20° Hc	d	Z	22° Hc	d	Z	24° Hc	d	Z	26° Hc	d	Z	28° Hc	d	Z
°	° ′	′	°	° ′	′	°	° ′	′	°	° ′	′	°	° ′	′	°
0	68 31.2	+55.9	157.7	66 39.5	+56.6	159.4	64 46.6	+57.2	160.9	62 52.7	+57.7	162.2	60 58.1	+58.0	163.3
1	69 27.1	55.5	156.6	67 36.1	56.3	158.6	65 43.8	56.9	160.2	63 50.4	57.4	161.6	61 56.1	57.9	162.8
2	70 22.6	55.0	155.5	68 32.4	56.0	157.7	66 40.7	56.7	159.4	64 47.8	57.3	160.9	62 54.0	57.7	162.2
3	71 17.6	54.5	154.3	69 28.4	55.6	156.6	67 37.4	56.4	158.6	65 45.1	57.0	160.2	63 51.7	57.5	161.6
4	72 12.1	53.9	153.0	70 24.0	55.1	155.6	68 33.8	56.1	157.7	66 42.1	56.8	159.5	64 49.2	57.3	161.0
5	73 06.0	+53.2	151.5	71 19.1	+54.7	154.4	69 29.9	+55.7	156.7	67 38.9	+56.5	158.6	65 46.5	+57.2	160.3
6	73 59.2	52.4	149.9	72 13.8	54.0	153.0	70 25.6	55.3	155.6	68 35.4	56.2	157.7	66 43.7	56.9	159.5
7	74 51.6	51.5	148.1	73 07.8	53.4	151.6	71 20.9	54.8	154.4	69 31.6	55.9	156.7	67 40.6	56.6	158.7
8	75 43.1	50.2	146.0	74 01.2	52.6	150.0	72 15.7	54.2	153.1	70 27.5	55.4	155.7	68 37.2	56.3	157.8
9	76 33.3	48.9	143.8	74 53.8	51.6	148.2	73 09.9	53.6	151.7	71 22.9	54.9	154.5	69 33.5	56.0	156.8
10	77 22.2	+47.2	141.2	75 45.4	+50.5	146.1	74 03.5	+52.7	150.1	72 17.8	+54.4	153.2	70 29.5	+55.6	155.8
11	78 09.4	45.1*	138.3	76 35.9	49.1	143.9	74 56.2	51.9	148.3	73 12.2	53.8	151.8	71 25.1	55.1	154.6
12	78 54.5	42.7*	135.0	77 25.0	47.5	141.3	75 48.1	50.7	146.3	74 06.0	53.0	150.2	72 20.2	54.6	153.3
13	79 37.2	39.7*	131.2	78 12.5	45.4*	138.4	76 38.8	49.4	144.0	74 59.0	52.0	148.4	73 14.8	53.9	151.9
14	80 16.9	36.0*	126.9	78 57.9	43.0*	135.1	77 28.2	47.7	141.5	75 51.0	51.0	146.5	74 08.7	53.2	150.4
15	80 52.9	+31.5*	122.0	79 40.9	+40.1*	131.4	78 15.9	+45.8*	138.4	76 42.0	+49.6	144.2	75 01.9	+52.3	148.6
16	81 24.4	26.2*	116.5	80 21.0	36.3*	127.1	79 01.7	43.4*	135.3	77 31.6	48.1	141.7	75 54.2	51.3	146.7
17	81 50.6	20.0*	110.3	80 57.3	31.9*	122.2	79 45.1	40.4*	131.6	78 19.7	46.1*	138.9	76 45.5	49.9	144.5
18	82 10.6	13.0*	103.5	81 29.2	26.6*	116.6	80 25.5	36.7*	127.3	79 05.8	43.8*	135.6	77 35.4	48.4	142.0
19	82 23.6	5.4*	96.2	81 55.8	20.4*	110.4	81 02.2	32.3*	122.4	79 49.6	40.8*	131.8	78 23.8	46.5*	139.1
20	82 29.0	– 2.5*	88.6	82 16.2	+13.2*	103.5	81 34.5	+27.0*	116.8	80 30.4	+37.1*	127.5	79 10.3	+44.1*	135.9
21	82 26.5	10.3*	81.0	82 29.4	+ 5.6*	96.2	82 01.5	20.7*	110.5	81 07.5	32.8*	122.6	79 54.4	41.2*	132.1
22	82 16.2	17.6*	73.6	82 35.0	– 2.4*	88.5	82 22.2	13.6*	103.6	81 40.3	27.4*	117.5	80 35.6	37.7*	127.9
23	81 58.6	24.1*	66.6	82 32.6	10.4*	80.8	82 35.8	+ 5.8*	96.2	82 07.7	21.1*	110.7	81 13.3	33.2*	122.9
24	81 34.5	29.7*	60.2	82 22.2	17.6*	73.3	82 41.6	– 2.4*	88.4	82 28.8	13.9*	103.7	81 46.5	27.9*	117.3
25	81 04.8	–34.4*	54.4	82 04.6	–24.3*	66.2	82 39.2	–10.4*	80.5	82 42.7	+ 5.9*	96.1	82 14.4	+21.5*	110.9
26	80 30.4	38.5*	49.3	81 40.3	29.9*	59.7	82 28.8	17.8*	72.9	82 48.6	– 2.3*	88.2	82 35.9	14.2*	103.8
27	79 51.9	41.6*	44.8	81 10.4	34.8*	53.9	82 11.0	24.5*	65.7	82 46.3	10.4*	80.3	82 50.1	+ 6.2*	96.2
28	79 10.3	44.3*	40.8	80 35.6	38.6*	48.8	81 46.5	30.2*	59.2	82 35.9	18.0*	72.5	82 56.3	– 2.3*	88.1
29	78 26.0	46.5*	37.4	79 57.0	41.9*	44.2	81 16.3	35.0*	53.3	82 17.9	24.7*	65.3	82 54.0	10.5*	80.0

Dec.	30° Hc	d	Z	32° Hc	d	Z	34° Hc	d	Z	36° Hc	d	Z	38° Hc	d	Z
°	° ′	′	°	° ′	′	°	° ′	′	°	° ′	′	°	° ′	′	°
0	59 02.9	+58.3	164.3	57 07.1	+58.5	165.1	55 10.9	+58.7	165.9	53 14.4	+58.9	166.6	51 17.5	+59.1	167.1
1	60 01.2	58.1	163.8	58 05.6	58.5	164.7	56 09.6	58.7	165.5	54 13.3	58.8	166.2	52 16.6	59.0	166.9
2	60 59.3	58.1	163.3	59 04.1	58.3	164.3	57 08.3	58.6	165.1	55 12.1	58.8	165.9	53 15.6	58.9	166.6
3	61 57.4	57.9	162.8	60 02.4	58.3	163.8	58 06.9	58.5	164.7	56 10.9	58.7	165.5	54 14.5	58.9	166.2
4	62 55.3	57.8	162.2	61 00.7	58.1	163.4	59 05.4	58.4	164.3	57 09.6	58.7	165.2	55 13.4	58.9	165.9
5	63 53.1	+57.6	161.6	61 58.8	+58.0	162.8	60 03.8	+58.4	163.9	58 08.3	+58.6	164.8	56 12.3	+58.8	165.6
6	64 50.7	57.5	161.0	62 56.8	57.9	162.3	61 02.2	58.2	163.4	59 06.9	58.5	164.4	57 11.1	58.7	165.2
7	65 48.2	57.2	160.3	63 54.7	57.7	161.7	62 00.4	58.1	162.9	60 05.4	58.4	163.9	58 09.8	58.7	164.8
8	66 45.4	57.0	159.6	64 52.4	57.6	161.1	62 58.5	57.9	162.3	61 03.8	58.3	163.5	59 08.5	58.5	164.4
9	67 42.4	56.8	158.8	65 50.0	57.3	160.4	63 56.4	57.9	161.8	62 02.1	58.2	163.0	60 07.0	58.5	164.0
10	68 39.2	+56.4	157.9	66 47.3	+57.1	159.7	64 54.3	+57.6	161.1	63 00.3	+58.0	162.4	61 05.5	+58.4	163.5
11	69 35.6	56.2	156.9	67 44.4	56.9	158.9	65 51.9	57.5	160.5	63 58.3	57.9	161.9	62 03.9	58.3	163.0
12	70 31.8	55.7	155.9	68 41.3	56.6	158.0	66 49.4	57.2	159.8	64 56.2	57.8	161.3	63 02.2	58.1	162.5
13	71 27.5	55.3	154.8	69 37.9	56.3	157.1	67 46.6	57.0	159.0	65 54.0	57.6	160.6	64 00.3	58.0	162.0
14	72 22.8	54.8	153.5	70 34.2	55.9	156.0	68 43.6	56.8	158.1	66 51.6	57.4	159.8	64 58.3	57.9	161.4
15	73 17.6	+54.1	152.1	71 30.1	+55.5	154.9	69 40.4	+56.4	157.2	67 49.0	+57.1	159.1	65 56.2	+57.7	160.7
16	74 11.7	53.4	150.6	72 25.6	54.9	153.7	70 36.8	56.1	156.2	68 46.1	56.9	158.3	66 53.9	57.5	160.1
17	75 05.1	52.6	148.9	73 20.5	54.4	152.3	71 32.9	55.6	155.1	69 43.0	56.6	157.4	67 51.4	57.3	159.3
18	75 57.7	51.5	146.9	74 14.9	53.7	150.8	72 28.5	55.2	153.9	70 39.6	56.2	156.4	68 48.7	57.1	158.5
19	76 49.2	50.3	144.8	75 08.6	52.8	149.1	73 23.7	54.6	152.6	71 35.8	55.9	155.4	69 45.8	56.7	157.6
20	77 39.5	+48.7	142.3	76 01.4	+51.8	147.2	74 18.3	+53.9	151.1	72 31.7	+55.3	154.2	70 42.5	+56.4	156.7
21	78 28.2	46.9*	139.5	76 53.2	50.6	145.1	75 12.2	53.1	149.4	73 27.0	54.6	152.9	71 38.9	56.1	155.6
22	79 15.1	44.5*	136.2	77 43.8	49.1	142.6	76 05.3	52.1	147.5	74 21.9	54.1	151.4	72 35.0	55.6	154.5
23	79 59.6	41.7*	132.5	78 32.9	47.2*	139.8	76 57.4	50.9	145.4	75 16.0	53.4	149.8	73 30.6	55.0	153.2
24	80 41.3	38.1*	128.2	79 20.1	45.0*	136.6	77 48.3	49.5	143.0	76 09.4	52.5	147.9	74 25.6	54.5	151.7
25	81 19.4	+33.8*	123.3	80 05.1	+42.2*	132.9	78 37.8	+47.7*	140.2	77 01.9	+51.2	145.8	75 20.1	+53.6	150.1
26	81 53.2	28.3*	117.6	80 47.3	38.7*	128.6	79 25.5	45.5*	137.0	77 53.1	49.9	143.4	76 13.7	52.8	148.3
27	82 21.5	22.0*	111.2	81 26.0	34.2*	123.7	80 11.0	42.7*	133.3	78 43.0	48.2*	140.7	77 06.5	51.7	146.2
28	82 43.5	14.5*	104.0	82 00.2	28.9*	118.0	80 53.7	39.2*	129.1	79 31.2	45.9*	137.5	77 58.2	50.3	143.9
29	82 58.0	+ 6.4*	96.2	82 29.1	22.4*	111.4	81 32.9	34.8*	124.1	80 17.1	43.2*	133.8	78 48.5	48.6	141.2

20°			22°			24°			26°			28°			Dec.
Hc	d	Z	Hc	d	Z	Hc	d	Z	Hc	d	Z	Hc	d	Z	
° ′	′	°	° ′	′	°	° ′	′	°	° ′	′	°	° ′	′	°	°
68 31.2	−56.2	157.7	66 39.5	−56.8	159.4	64 46.6	−57.4	160.9	62 52.7	−57.7	162.2	60 58.1	−58.1	163.3	0
67 35.0	56.5	158.6	65 42.7	57.1	160.2	63 49.2	57.5	161.6	61 55.0	57.9	162.8	60 00.0	58.2	163.8	1
66 38.5	56.8	159.5	64 45.6	57.3	161.0	62 51.7	57.7	162.2	60 57.1	58.1	163.4	59 01.8	58.3	164.3	2
65 41.7	57.0	160.3	63 48.3	57.5	161.6	61 54.0	57.8	162.8	59 59.0	58.1	163.9	58 03.5	58.4	164.8	3
64 44.7	57.2	161.0	62 50.8	57.6	162.3	60 56.2	58.0	163.4	59 00.9	58.3	164.4	57 05.1	58.5	165.2	4
63 47.5	−57.4	161.7	61 53.2	−57.8	162.9	59 58.2	−58.1	163.9	58 02.6	−58.3	164.8	56 06.6	−58.6	165.6	5
62 50.1	57.5	162.4	60 55.4	57.9	163.5	59 00.1	58.2	164.4	57 04.3	58.4	165.2	55 08.0	58.6	166.0	6
61 52.6	57.8	163.0	59 57.5	58.0	164.0	58 01.9	58.3	164.9	56 05.9	58.6	165.7	54 09.4	58.7	166.4	7
60 54.8	57.8	163.5	58 59.5	58.2	164.5	57 03.6	58.4	165.3	55 07.3	58.5	166.1	53 10.7	58.8	166.7	8
59 57.0	58.0	164.1	58 01.3	58.2	165.0	56 05.2	58.4	165.7	54 08.8	58.7	166.4	52 12.0	58.8	167.0	9
58 59.0	−58.1	164.6	57 03.1	−58.3	165.4	55 06.8	−58.6	166.1	53 10.1	−58.7	166.8	51 13.2	−58.9	167.4	10
58 00.9	58.2	165.1	56 04.8	58.4	165.8	54 08.2	58.6	166.5	52 11.4	58.8	167.1	50 14.3	58.9	167.7	11
57 02.7	58.3	165.5	55 06.4	58.5	166.2	53 09.6	58.6	166.9	51 12.6	58.8	167.4	49 15.4	59.0	168.0	12
56 04.4	58.3	165.9	54 07.9	58.6	166.6	52 11.0	58.7	167.2	50 13.8	58.8	167.8	48 16.4	58.9	168.2	13
55 06.1	58.5	166.3	53 09.3	58.6	167.0	51 12.3	58.8	167.6	49 15.0	59.0	168.1	47 17.5	59.1	168.5	14
54 07.6	−58.5	166.7	52 10.7	−58.7	167.3	50 13.5	−58.9	167.9	48 16.0	−59.0	168.3	46 18.4	−59.0	168.8	15
53 09.1	58.6	167.1	51 12.0	58.7	167.7	49 14.6	58.8	168.2	47 17.1	59.0	168.6	45 19.4	59.1	169.0	16
52 10.5	58.6	167.5	50 13.3	58.8	168.0	48 15.8	58.9	168.5	46 18.1	59.0	168.9	44 20.3	59.1	169.3	17
51 11.9	58.7	167.8	49 14.5	58.9	168.3	47 16.9	59.0	168.7	45 19.1	59.1	169.2	43 21.2	59.2	169.5	18
50 13.2	58.8	168.1	48 15.6	58.9	168.6	46 17.9	59.0	169.0	44 20.0	59.1	169.4	42 22.0	59.2	169.7	19
49 14.4	−58.8	168.4	47 16.7	−58.9	168.9	45 18.9	−59.0	169.3	43 20.9	−59.1	169.6	41 22.8	−59.2	170.0	20
48 15.6	58.9	168.7	46 17.8	58.9	169.2	44 19.9	59.1	169.5	42 21.8	59.1	169.9	40 23.6	59.2	170.2	21
47 16.7	58.9	169.0	45 18.9	59.0	169.4	43 20.8	59.1	169.8	41 22.7	59.2	170.1	39 24.4	59.2	170.4	22
46 17.8	58.9	169.3	44 19.9	59.0	169.7	42 21.7	59.1	170.0	40 23.5	59.2	170.3	38 25.2	59.3	170.6	23
45 18.9	59.0	169.6	43 20.8	59.0	169.9	41 22.6	59.1	170.2	39 24.3	59.2	170.5	37 25.9	59.3	170.8	24
44 19.9	−59.0	169.8	42 21.8	−59.1	170.2	40 23.5	−59.2	170.5	38 25.1	−59.3	170.7	36 26.6	−59.3	171.0	25
43 20.9	59.0	170.1	41 22.7	59.1	170.4	39 24.3	59.2	170.7	37 25.8	59.2	170.9	35 27.3	59.3	171.2	26
42 21.9	59.1	170.3	40 23.5	59.1	170.6	38 25.1	59.2	170.9	36 26.6	59.3	171.1	34 28.0	59.4	171.3	27
41 22.8	59.1	170.6	39 24.4	59.2	170.8	37 25.9	59.3	171.1	35 27.3	59.3	171.3	33 28.6	59.3	171.5	28
40 23.7	59.1	170.8	38 25.2	59.2	171.1	36 26.6	59.2	171.3	34 28.0	59.3	171.5	32 29.3	59.4	171.7	29

30°			32°			34°			36°			38°			Dec.
Hc	d	Z	Hc	d	Z	Hc	d	Z	Hc	d	Z	Hc	d	Z	
° ′	′	°	° ′	′	°	° ′	′	°	° ′	′	°	° ′	′	°	°
59 02.9	−58.4	164.3	57 07.1	−58.6	165.1	55 10.9	−58.8	165.9	53 14.4	−59.0	166.6	51 17.5	−59.1	167.1	0
58 04.5	58.5	164.7	56 08.5	58.7	165.5	54 12.1	58.8	166.2	52 15.4	59.0	166.9	50 18.4	59.1	167.4	1
57 06.0	58.5	165.2	55 09.8	58.7	165.9	53 13.3	58.9	166.6	51 16.4	59.0	167.2	49 19.3	59.2	167.7	2
56 07.5	58.6	165.6	54 11.1	58.8	166.3	52 14.4	59.0	166.9	50 17.4	59.1	167.4	48 20.1	59.2	167.9	3
55 08.9	58.7	165.9	53 12.3	58.8	166.6	51 15.4	59.0	167.2	49 18.3	59.1	167.7	47 20.9	59.2	168.2	4
54 10.2	−58.8	166.3	52 13.5	−58.9	166.9	50 16.4	−59.0	167.5	48 19.2	−59.2	168.0	46 21.7	−59.2	168.4	5
53 11.4	58.8	166.6	51 14.6	59.0	167.2	49 17.4	59.1	167.7	47 20.0	59.2	168.2	45 22.5	59.3	168.6	6
52 12.6	58.8	167.0	50 15.6	59.0	167.5	48 18.3	59.1	168.0	46 20.8	59.2	168.5	44 23.2	59.3	168.9	7
51 13.8	58.9	167.3	49 16.6	59.0	167.8	47 19.2	59.1	168.3	45 21.6	59.2	168.7	43 23.9	59.3	169.1	8
50 14.9	59.0	167.6	48 17.6	59.1	168.1	46 20.1	59.2	168.5	44 22.4	59.3	168.9	42 24.6	59.4	169.3	9
49 15.9	−58.9	167.9	47 18.5	−59.1	168.3	45 20.9	−59.2	168.8	43 23.1	−59.3	169.1	41 25.2	−59.3	169.5	10
48 17.0	59.1	168.2	46 19.4	59.1	168.6	44 21.7	59.2	169.0	42 23.8	59.3	169.3	40 25.9	59.4	169.7	11
47 17.9	59.0	168.4	45 20.3	59.2	168.8	43 22.5	59.3	169.2	41 24.5	59.3	169.5	39 26.5	59.4	169.8	12
46 18.9	59.1	168.7	44 21.1	59.2	169.1	42 23.2	59.2	169.4	40 25.2	59.3	169.7	38 27.1	59.4	170.0	13
45 19.8	59.2	168.9	43 21.9	59.2	169.3	41 24.0	59.3	169.6	39 25.9	59.4	169.9	37 27.7	59.5	170.2	14
44 20.6	−59.1	169.2	42 22.7	−59.2	169.5	40 24.7	−59.4	169.8	38 26.5	−59.4	170.1	36 28.2	−59.4	170.4	15
43 21.5	59.2	169.4	41 23.5	59.3	169.7	39 25.3	59.3	170.0	37 27.1	59.4	170.3	35 28.8	59.5	170.5	16
42 22.3	59.2	169.6	40 24.2	59.3	169.9	38 26.0	59.3	170.2	36 27.7	59.4	170.4	34 29.3	59.5	170.7	17
41 23.1	59.2	169.8	39 24.9	59.2	170.1	37 26.7	59.4	170.4	35 28.3	59.4	170.6	33 29.8	59.5	170.9	18
40 23.9	59.3	170.0	38 25.6	59.3	170.3	36 27.3	59.4	170.6	34 28.9	59.5	170.8	32 30.4	59.5	171.0	19
39 24.6	−59.3	170.3	37 26.3	−59.3	170.5	35 27.9	−59.4	170.8	33 29.4	−59.4	171.0	31 30.9	−59.5	171.2	20
38 25.3	59.3	170.5	36 27.0	59.4	170.7	34 28.5	59.4	170.9	32 30.0	59.5	171.1	30 31.4	59.6	171.3	21
37 26.0	59.3	170.6	35 27.6	59.4	170.9	33 29.1	59.5	171.1	31 30.5	59.5	171.3	29 31.8	59.5	171.5	22
36 26.7	59.3	170.8	34 28.2	59.4	171.1	32 29.6	59.4	171.3	30 31.0	59.5	171.4	28 32.3	59.5	171.6	23
35 27.4	59.3	171.0	33 28.8	59.4	171.2	31 30.2	59.5	171.4	29 31.5	59.5	171.6	27 32.8	59.6	171.8	24
34 28 0	−59.3	171.2	32 29.4	−59.4	171.4	30 30.7	−59.4	171.6	28 32.0	−59.5	171.7	26 33.2	−59.5	171.9	25
33 28.7	59.4	171.4	31 30.0	59.4	171.6	29 31.3	59.5	171.7	27 32.5	59.5	171.9	25 33.7	59.6	172.0	26
32 29.3	59.4	171.5	30 30.6	59.5	171.7	28 31.8	59.5	171.9	26 33.0	59.5	172.0	24 34.1	59.5	172.2	27
31 29.9	59.4	171.7	29 31.1	59.4	171.9	27 32.3	59.5	172.0	25 33.5	59.6	172.2	23 34.6	59.6	172.3	28
30 30.5	59.4	171.9	28 31.7	59.5	172.0	26 32.8	59.5	172.2	24 33.9	59.5	172.3	22 35.0	59.6	172.4	29

Dec.	40° Hc	d	Z	42° Hc	d	Z	44° Hc	d	Z	46° Hc	d	Z	48° Hc	d	Z
0	49 20.4	+59.2	167.7	47 23.1	+59.2	168.1	45 25.5	+59.4	168.6	43 27.8	+59.5	168.9	41 30.0	+59.5	169.3
1	50 19.6	59.1	167.4	48 22.3	59.3	167.9	46 24.9	59.4	168.4	44 27.3	59.4	168.8	42 29.5	59.5	169.1
2	51 18.7	59.1	167.1	49 21.6	59.2	167.7	47 24.3	59.3	168.1	45 26.7	59.4	168.6	43 29.0	59.5	168.9
3	52 17.8	59.1	166.9	50 20.8	59.2	167.4	48 23.6	59.3	167.9	46 26.1	59.4	168.4	44 28.5	59.5	168.8
4	53 16.9	59.0	166.6	51 20.0	59.2	167.2	49 22.9	59.3	167.7	47 25.5	59.4	168.2	45 28.0	59.5	168.6
5	54 15.9	+59.0	166.3	52 19.2	+59.1	166.9	50 22.2	+59.2	167.4	48 24.9	+59.4	167.9	46 27.5	+59.4	168.4
6	55 14.9	58.9	165.9	53 18.3	59.1	166.6	51 21.4	59.2	167.2	49 24.3	59.3	167.7	47 26.9	59.4	168.2
7	56 13.8	58.8	165.6	54 17.4	59.0	166.3	52 20.6	59.2	166.9	50 23.6	59.3	167.5	48 26.3	59.4	168.0
8	57 12.6	58.8	165.3	55 16.4	59.0	166.0	53 19.8	59.1	166.7	51 22.9	59.2	167.2	49 25.7	59.4	167.8
9	58 11.4	58.7	164.9	56 15.4	58.9	165.7	54 18.9	59.1	166.4	52 22.1	59.3	167.0	50 25.1	59.3	167.5
10	59 10.1	+58.7	164.5	57 14.3	+58.8	165.3	55 18.0	+59.0	166.1	53 21.4	+59.1	166.7	51 24.4	+59.3	167.3
11	60 08.8	58.6	164.1	58 13.1	58.8	165.0	56 17.0	59.0	165.8	54 20.5	59.2	166.4	52 23.7	59.3	167.1
12	61 07.4	58.4	163.6	59 11.9	58.8	164.6	57 16.0	59.0	165.4	55 19.7	59.1	166.2	53 23.0	59.3	166.8
13	62 05.8	58.4	163.2	60 10.7	58.6	164.2	58 15.0	58.8	165.1	56 18.8	59.1	165.8	54 22.3	59.2	166.5
14	63 04.2	58.3	162.7	61 09.3	58.6	163.7	59 13.8	58.8	164.7	57 17.9	59.0	165.5	55 21.5	59.1	166.3
15	64 02.5	+58.1	162.1	62 07.9	+58.4	163.3	60 12.6	+58.8	164.3	58 16.9	+58.9	165.2	56 20.6	+59.2	166.0
16	65 00.6	58.0	161.5	63 06.3	58.4	162.8	61 11.4	58.6	163.9	59 15.8	58.9	164.8	57 19.8	59.0	165.7
17	65 58.6	57.8	160.9	64 04.7	58.2	162.3	62 10.0	58.6	163.4	60 14.7	58.8	164.4	58 18.8	59.1	165.3
18	66 56.4	57.6	160.2	65 02.9	58.1	161.7	63 08.6	58.4	163.0	61 13.5	58.7	164.0	59 17.9	58.9	165.0
19	67 54.0	57.5	159.5	66 01.0	58.0	161.1	64 07.0	58.2	162.5	62 12.2	58.7	163.6	60 16.8	58.9	164.6
20	68 51.5	+57.2	158.7	66 59.0	+57.7	160.5	65 05.4	+58.2	161.9	63 10.9	+58.6	163.1	61 15.7	+58.9	164.2
21	69 48.7	56.9	157.9	67 56.7	57.6	159.8	66 03.6	58.1	161.3	64 09.5	58.4	162.7	62 14.6	58.7	163.8
22	70 45.6	56.6	156.9	68 54.3	57.4	159.0	67 01.7	57.9	160.7	65 07.9	58.3	162.1	63 13.3	58.7	163.4
23	71 42.2	56.2	155.9	69 51.7	57.1	158.2	67 59.6	57.7	160.0	66 06.2	58.2	161.6	64 12.0	58.5	162.9
24	72 38.4	55.8	154.8	70 48.8	56.8	157.2	68 57.3	57.5	159.3	67 04.4	58.1	161.0	65 10.5	58.5	162.4
25	73 34.2	+55.3	153.5	71 45.6	+56.4	156.2	69 54.8	+57.3	158.5	68 02.5	+57.8	160.3	66 09.0	+58.3	161.8
26	74 29.5	54.8	152.1	72 42.0	56.0	155.1	70 52.1	56.9	157.6	69 00.3	57.7	159.6	67 07.3	58.2	161.2
27	75 24.3	53.9	150.5	73 38.0	55.6	153.9	71 49.0	56.7	156.6	69 58.0	57.5	158.8	68 05.5	58.0	160.6
28	76 18.2	53.1	148.7	74 33.6	55.0	152.5	72 45.7	56.3	155.5	70 55.5	57.1	157.9	69 03.5	57.8	159.9
29	77 11.3	52.1	146.7	75 28.6	54.3	151.0	73 42.0	55.8	154.3	71 52.6	56.9	157.0	70 01.3	57.6	159.1

Dec.	50° Hc	d	Z	52° Hc	d	Z	54° Hc	d	Z	56° Hc	d	Z	58° Hc	d	Z
0	39 32.0	+59.6	169.6	37 33.9	+59.7	169.9	35 35.8	+59.6	170.1	33 37.5	+59.7	170.4	31 39.1	+59.8	170.6
1	40 31.6	59.6	169.5	38 33.6	59.6	169.7	36 35.4	59.7	170.0	34 37.2	59.7	170.3	32 38.9	59.8	170.5
2	41 31.2	59.6	169.3	39 33.2	59.6	169.6	37 35.1	59.7	169.9	35 36.9	59.8	170.1	33 38.7	59.7	170.4
3	42 30.8	59.5	169.1	40 32.8	59.6	169.5	38 34.8	59.7	169.8	36 36.7	59.7	170.0	34 38.4	59.7	170.3
4	43 30.3	59.5	169.0	41 32.4	59.6	169.3	39 34.5	59.6	169.6	37 36.4	59.7	169.9	35 38.2	59.7	170.2
5	44 29.8	+59.6	168.8	42 32.0	+59.6	169.2	40 34.1	+59.7	169.5	38 36.1	+59.7	169.8	36 37.9	+59.8	170.1
6	45 29.4	59.5	168.6	43 31.6	59.6	169.0	41 33.8	59.6	169.3	39 35.8	59.7	169.7	37 37.7	59.7	169.9
7	46 28.9	59.4	168.4	44 31.2	59.6	168.8	42 33.4	59.6	169.2	40 35.5	59.7	169.5	38 37.4	59.7	169.8
8	47 28.3	59.5	168.2	45 30.8	59.5	168.7	43 33.0	59.6	169.0	41 35.2	59.6	169.4	39 37.1	59.8	169.7
9	48 27.8	59.4	168.0	46 30.3	59.5	168.5	44 32.6	59.6	168.9	42 34.8	59.7	169.2	40 36.9	59.7	169.6
10	49 27.2	+59.5	167.8	47 29.8	+59.5	168.3	45 32.2	+59.6	168.7	43 34.5	+59.6	169.1	41 36.6	+59.7	169.4
11	50 26.7	59.3	167.6	48 29.3	59.5	168.1	46 31.8	59.5	168.5	44 34.1	59.7	168.9	42 36.3	59.7	169.3
12	51 26.0	59.4	167.4	49 28.8	59.5	167.9	47 31.4	59.5	168.4	45 33.8	59.6	168.8	43 36.0	59.7	169.2
13	52 25.4	59.3	167.2	50 28.3	59.4	167.7	48 30.9	59.6	168.2	46 33.4	59.6	168.6	44 35.7	59.6	169.0
14	53 24.7	59.4	166.9	51 27.7	59.4	167.5	49 30.5	59.5	168.0	47 33.0	59.6	168.5	45 35.3	59.7	168.9
15	54 24.1	+59.2	166.6	52 27.1	+59.4	167.3	50 30.0	+59.5	167.8	48 32.6	+59.6	168.3	46 35.0	+59.6	168.7
16	55 23.3	59.3	166.4	53 26.5	59.4	167.0	51 29.5	59.4	167.6	49 32.2	59.5	168.1	47 34.6	59.7	168.6
17	56 22.6	59.1	166.1	54 25.9	59.3	166.8	52 28.9	59.5	167.4	50 31.7	59.6	167.9	48 34.3	59.6	168.4
18	57 21.7	59.2	165.8	55 25.2	59.3	166.5	53 28.4	59.4	167.2	51 31.3	59.5	167.7	49 33.9	59.6	168.2
19	58 20.9	59.1	165.5	56 24.5	59.3	166.2	54 27.8	59.4	166.9	52 30.8	59.4	167.5	50 33.5	59.6	168.0
20	59 20.0	+59.0	165.1	57 23.8	+59.2	166.0	55 27.2	+59.3	166.7	53 30.3	+59.4	167.3	51 33.1	+59.5	167.9
21	60 19.0	59.0	164.8	58 23.0	59.2	165.6	56 26.5	59.4	166.4	54 29.7	59.5	167.1	52 32.6	59.6	167.7
22	61 18.0	58.9	164.4	59 22.2	59.1	165.3	57 25.9	59.2	166.1	55 29.2	59.4	166.8	53 32.2	59.5	167.5
23	62 16.9	58.9	164.0	60 21.3	59.0	165.0	58 25.1	59.3	165.8	56 28.6	59.4	166.6	54 31.7	59.5	167.2
24	63 15.8	58.7	163.6	61 20.3	59.0	164.6	59 24.4	59.2	165.5	57 28.0	59.3	166.3	55 31.2	59.5	167.0
25	64 14.5	+58.7	163.1	62 19.4	+58.9	164.2	60 23.6	+59.1	165.2	58 27.3	+59.3	166.0	56 30.7	+59.4	166.8
26	65 13.2	58.6	162.6	63 18.3	58.8	163.8	61 22.7	59.1	164.9	59 26.6	59.2	165.8	57 30.1	59.5	166.5
27	66 11.8	58.4	162.1	64 17.1	58.8	163.4	62 21.8	59.0	164.5	60 25.9	59.2	165.4	58 29.6	59.3	166.3
28	67 10.2	58.3	161.5	65 15.9	58.7	162.9	63 20.8	59.0	164.1	61 25.1	59.2	165.1	59 28.9	59.4	166.0
29	68 08.5	58.2	160.9	66 14.6	58.6	162.4	64 19.8	58.9	163.7	62 24.3	59.1	164.8	60 28.3	59.3	165.7

40° – 48°

40° Hc	d	Z	42° Hc	d	Z	44° Hc	d	Z	46° Hc	d	Z	48° Hc	d	Z	Dec.
49 20.4	−59.2	167.7	47 23.1	−59.3	168.1	45 25.5	−59.4	168.6	43 27.8	−59.4	168.9	41 30.0	−59.5	169.3	0
48 21.2	59.2	167.9	46 23.8	59.4	168.4	44 26.1	59.4	168.8	42 28.4	59.5	169.1	40 30.5	59.6	169.5	1
47 22.0	59.3	168.1	45 24.4	59.4	168.6	43 26.7	59.4	169.0	41 28.9	59.5	169.3	39 30.9	59.6	169.6	2
46 22.7	59.3	168.4	44 25.1	59.4	168.8	42 27.3	59.5	169.1	40 29.4	59.6	169.5	38 31.3	59.5	169.8	3
45 23.4	59.3	168.6	43 25.7	59.4	169.0	41 27.8	59.4	169.3	39 29.8	59.6	169.6	37 31.8	59.6	169.9	4
44 24.1	−59.4	168.8	42 26.3	−59.4	169.2	40 28.4	−59.5	169.5	38 30.3	−59.5	169.8	36 32.2	−59.6	170.1	5
43 24.7	59.3	169.0	41 26.9	59.5	169.4	39 28.9	59.5	169.7	37 30.8	59.6	170.0	35 32.6	59.7	170.2	6
42 25.4	59.4	169.2	40 27.4	59.4	169.5	38 29.4	59.5	169.8	36 31.2	59.6	170.1	34 32.9	59.6	170.3	7
41 26.0	59.4	169.4	39 28.0	59.5	169.7	37 29.9	59.6	170.0	35 31.6	59.6	170.3	33 33.3	59.6	170.5	8
40 26.6	59.4	169.6	38 28.5	59.5	169.9	36 30.3	59.5	170.2	34 32.1	59.6	170.4	32 33.7	59.6	170.6	9
39 27.2	−59.5	169.8	37 29.0	−59.5	170.1	35 30.8	−59.6	170.3	33 32.5	−59.6	170.5	31 34.1	−59.7	170.7	10
38 27.7	59.4	170.0	36 29.5	59.5	170.2	34 31.2	59.5	170.5	32 32.9	59.6	170.7	30 34.4	59.6	170.9	11
37 28.3	59.5	170.1	35 30.0	59.5	170.4	33 31.7	59.6	170.6	31 33.3	59.7	170.8	29 34.8	59.7	171.0	12
36 28.8	59.5	170.3	34 30.5	59.5	170.5	32 32.1	59.6	170.7	30 33.6	59.6	170.9	28 35.1	59.7	171.1	13
35 29.4	59.5	170.5	33 31.0	59.6	170.7	31 32.5	59.6	170.9	29 34.0	59.6	171.1	27 35.4	59.6	171.2	14
34 29.9	−59.5	170.6	32 31.4	−59.5	170.8	30 32.9	−59.6	171.0	28 34.4	−59.7	171.2	26 35.8	−59.7	171.4	15
33 30.4	59.5	170.8	31 31.9	59.5	171.0	29 33.3	59.6	171.2	27 34.7	59.6	171.3	25 36.1	59.7	171.5	16
32 30.9	59.6	170.9	30 32.3	59.5	171.1	28 33.7	59.6	171.3	26 35.1	59.6	171.4	24 36.4	59.7	171.6	17
31 31.3	59.5	171.1	29 32.8	59.6	171.2	27 34.1	59.6	171.4	25 35.5	59.7	171.6	23 36.7	59.7	171.7	18
30 31.8	59.5	171.2	28 33.2	59.6	171.4	26 34.5	59.6	171.5	24 35.8	59.7	171.7	22 37.0	59.7	171.8	19
29 32.3	−59.6	171.4	27 33.6	−59.6	171.5	25 34.9	−59.6	171.7	23 36.1	−59.6	171.8	21 37.3	−59.7	171.9	20
28 32.7	59.6	171.5	26 34.0	59.6	171.6	24 35.3	59.7	171.8	22 36.5	59.7	171.9	20 37.6	59.7	172.0	21
27 33.1	59.5	171.6	25 34.4	59.6	171.8	23 35.6	59.6	171.9	21 36.8	59.7	172.0	19 37.9	59.7	172.1	22
26 33.6	59.6	171.8	24 34.8	59.6	171.9	22 36.0	59.7	172.0	20 37.1	59.7	172.1	18 38.2	59.7	172.2	23
25 34.0	59.6	171.9	23 35.2	59.6	172.0	21 36.3	59.6	172.1	19 37.4	59.7	172.2	17 38.5	59.7	172.3	24
24 34.4	−59.6	172.0	22 35.6	−59.7	172.1	20 36.7	−59.7	172.3	18 37.7	−59.6	172.4	16 38.8	−59.7	172.4	25
23 34.8	59.6	172.2	21 35.9	59.6	172.3	19 37.0	59.7	172.4	17 38.1	59.7	172.5	15 39.1	59.7	172.5	26
22 35.2	59.6	172.3	20 36.3	59.6	172.4	18 37.3	59.7	172.5	16 38.4	59.7	172.6	14 39.4	59.8	172.6	27
21 35.6	59.6	172.4	19 36.7	59.7	172.5	17 37.7	59.7	172.6	15 38.7	59.7	172.7	13 39.6	59.7	172.7	28
20 36.0	59.6	172.5	18 37.0	59.6	172.6	16 38.0	59.7	172.7	14 39.0	59.7	172.8	12 39.9	59.7	172.8	29

50° – 58°

50° Hc	d	Z	52° Hc	d	Z	54° Hc	d	Z	56° Hc	d	Z	58° Hc	d	Z	Dec.
39 32.0	−59.6	169.6	37 33.9	−59.6	169.9	35 35.8	−59.7	170.1	33 37.5	−59.8	170.4	31 39.1	−59.7	170.6	0
38 32.4	59.6	169.8	36 34.3	59.7	170.0	34 36.1	59.8	170.3	32 37.7	59.7	170.5	30 39.4	59.8	170.7	1
37 32.8	59.6	169.9	35 34.6	59.7	170.2	33 36.3	59.7	170.4	31 38.0	59.7	170.6	29 39.6	59.8	170.8	2
36 33.2	59.6	170.0	34 35.0	59.7	170.3	32 36.6	59.7	170.5	30 38.2	59.7	170.7	28 39.8	59.8	170.9	3
35 33.6	59.7	170.2	33 35.3	59.7	170.4	31 36.9	59.7	170.6	29 38.5	59.7	170.9	27 40.0	59.8	171.0	4
34 33.9	−59.7	170.3	32 35.6	−59.7	170.5	30 37.2	−59.7	170.7	28 38.7	−59.7	170.9	26 40.2	−59.8	171.1	5
33 34.3	59.7	170.4	31 35.9	59.7	170.6	29 37.5	59.8	170.8	27 39.0	59.8	171.0	25 40.4	59.8	171.2	6
32 34.6	59.7	170.6	30 36.2	59.7	170.8	28 37.7	59.7	170.9	26 39.2	59.7	171.1	24 40.6	59.8	171.3	7
31 34.9	59.7	170.7	29 36.5	59.7	170.9	27 38.0	59.8	171.1	25 39.4	59.8	171.2	23 40.8	59.8	171.3	8
30 35.3	59.7	170.8	28 36.8	59.7	171.0	26 38.2	59.7	171.2	24 39.6	59.7	171.3	22 41.0	59.8	171.4	9
29 35.6	−59.7	170.9	27 37.1	−59.8	171.1	25 38.5	−59.8	171.3	23 39.9	−59.8	171.4	21 41.2	−59.8	171.5	10
28 35.9	59.7	171.0	26 37.3	59.7	171.2	24 38.7	59.7	171.4	22 40.1	59.8	171.5	20 41.4	59.8	171.6	11
27 36.2	59.7	171.2	25 37.6	59.7	171.3	23 39.0	59.8	171.5	21 40.3	59.8	171.6	19 41.6	59.9	171.7	12
26 36.5	59.7	171.3	24 37.9	59.7	171.4	22 39.2	59.8	171.6	20 40.5	59.8	171.7	18 41.7	59.8	171.8	13
25 36.8	59.7	171.4	23 38.2	59.7	171.5	21 39.4	59.7	171.6	19 40.7	59.8	171.8	17 41.9	59.9	171.9	14
24 37.1	−59.7	171.5	22 38.4	−59.7	171.6	20 39.7	−59.8	171.7	18 40.9	−59.8	171.8	16 42.1	−59.8	171.9	15
23 37.4	59.7	171.6	21 38.7	59.8	171.7	19 39.9	59.8	171.8	17 41.1	59.8	171.9	15 42.3	59.8	172.0	16
22 37.7	59.7	171.7	20 38.9	59.7	171.8	18 40.1	59.7	171.9	16 41.3	59.8	172.0	14 42.5	59.9	172.1	17
21 38.0	59.7	171.8	19 39.2	59.8	171.9	17 40.4	59.8	172.0	15 41.5	59.8	172.1	13 42.6	59.8	172.2	18
20 38.2	59.7	171.9	18 39.4	59.7	172.0	16 40.6	59.8	172.1	14 41.7	59.8	172.2	12 42.8	59.8	172.2	19
19 38.5	−59.7	172.0	17 39.7	−59.8	172.1	15 40.8	−59.8	172.2	13 41.9	−59.8	172.3	11 43.0	−59.9	172.3	20
18 38.8	59.7	172.1	16 39.9	59.8	172.2	14 41.0	59.8	172.3	12 42.1	59.8	172.4	10 43.1	59.8	172.4	21
17 39.1	59.7	172.2	15 40.1	59.7	172.3	13 41.2	59.7	172.4	11 42.3	59.8	172.4	9 43.3	59.8	172.5	22
16 39.3	59.7	172.3	14 40.4	59.8	172.4	12 41.4	59.7	172.5	10 42.5	59.8	172.5	8 43.5	59.8	172.6	23
15 39.6	59.8	172.4	13 40.6	59.7	172.5	11 41.6	59.7	172.5	9 42.7	59.9	172.6	7 43.7	59.9	172.6	24
14 39.8	−59.7	172.5	12 40.9	−59.8	172.6	10 41.9	−59.8	172.6	8 42.8	−59.8	172.7	6 43.8	−59.9	172.7	25
13 40.1	59.8	172.6	11 41.1	59.8	172.7	9 42.1	59.8	172.7	7 43.0	59.8	172.7	5 44.0	59.9	172.8	26
12 40.3	59.7	172.7	10 41.3	59.8	172.8	8 42.3	59.8	172.8	6 43.2	59.8	172.8	4 44.1	59.8	172.9	27
11 40.6	59.8	172.8	9 41.5	59.7	172.8	7 42.5	59.8	172.9	5 43.4	59.8	172.9	3 44.3	59.8	172.9	28
10 40.8	59.7	172.9	8 41.8	59.8	172.9	6 42.7	59.8	173.0	4 43.6	59.8	173.0	2 44.5	59.9	173.0	29

Dec.	0° Hc	d	Z	2° Hc	d	Z	4° Hc	d	Z	6° Hc	d	Z	8° Hc	d	Z
°	° ′	′	°	° ′	′	°	° ′	′	°	° ′	′	°	° ′	′	°
0	80 00.0	− 3.0·	90.0	79 48.2	+ 9.0·	101.2	79 14.2	+ 20.0·	111.6	78 21.2	+29.2·	120.7	77 13.2	+36.2·	128.3
1	79 57.0	8.8·	84.3	79 57.2	+ 3.2·	95.6	79 34.2	14.8·	106.5	78 50.4	24.9·	116.2	77 49.4	33.1·	124.6
2	79 48.2	14.4·	78.6	80 00.4	− 2.8·	89.8	79 49.0	9.1·	101.0	79 15.3	20.1·	111.4	78 22.5	29.3·	120.5
3	79 33.8	19.6·	73.2	79 57.6	8.6·	84.1	79 58.1	+ 3.4·	95.4	79 35.4	15.0·	106.3	78 51.8	25.2·	116.1
4	79 14.2	24.3·	68.1	79 49.0	14.3·	78.4	80 01.5	− 2.6·	89.7	79 50.4	9.4·	100.9	79 17.0	20.4·	111.3
5	78 49.9	−28.7·	63.3	79 34.7	−19.4·	73.0	79 58.9	− 8.5·	83.9	79 59.8	+ 3.5·	95.2	79 37.4	+15.1·	106.2
6	78 21.2	32.4·	58.8	79 15.3	24.3·	67.9	79 50.4	14.1·	78.2	80 03.3	− 2.4·	89.5	79 52.5	9.6·	100.8
7	77 48.8	35.6·	54.7	78 51.0	28.5·	63.0	79 36.3	19.3·	72.8	80 00.9	8.4·	83.7	80 02.1	+ 3.8·	95.1
8	77 13.2	38.6·	51.0	78 22.5	32.3·	58.6	79 17.0	24.2·	67.6	79 52.5	13.9·	78.0	80 05.9	− 2.3·	89.3
9	76 34.6	41.0·	47.6	77 50.2	35.6·	54.5	78 52.8	28.4·	62.8	79 38.6	19.3·	72.6	80 03.6	8.2·	83.5
10	75 53.6	−43.1·	44.6	77 14.6	−38.5·	50.8	78 24.4	−32.3·	58.3	79 19.3	−24.0·	67.4	79 55.4	−13.9·	77.8
11	75 10.5	44.9	41.8	76 36.1	40.9·	47.4	77 52.1	35.5·	54.2	78 55.3	28.4·	62.5	79 41.5	19.1·	72.3
12	74 25.6	46.5	39.2	75 55.2	43.1·	44.3	77 16.6	38.4·	50.5	78 26.9	32.2·	58.0	79 22.4	24.0·	67.1
13	73 39.1	47.9	36.9	75 12.1	44.9	41.5	76 38.2	40.9·	47.1	77 54.7	35.6·	53.9	78 58.4	28.4·	62.2
14	72 51.2	49.0	34.9	74 27.2	46.4	39.0	75 57.3	43.1·	44.0	77 19.1	38.4·	50.1	78 30.0	32.2·	57.7
15	72 02.2	−50.1	32.9	73 40.8	−47.9	36.6	75 14.2	−44.9	41.2	76 40.7	−40.9·	46.7	77 57.8	−35.5·	53.5
16	71 12.1	51.0	31.2	72 52.9	49.0	34.5	74 29.3	46.4	38.6	75 59.8	43.0·	43.6	77 22.3	38.5·	49.8
17	70 21.1	51.7	29.6	72 03.9	50.1	32.6	73 42.9	47.9	36.3	75 16.8	44.0	40.8	76 43.8	40.9·	46.3
18	69 29.4	52.5	28.1	71 13.8	50.9	30.9	72 55.0	49.0	34.2	74 31.9	46.5	38.3	76 02.9	43.1·	43.2
19	68 36.9	53.0	26.8	70 22.9	51.8	29.3	72 06.0	50.0	32.3	73 45.4	47.8	35.9	75 19.8	44.9	40.4
20	67 43.9	−53.6	25.5	69 31.1	−52.4	27.8	71 16.0	−51.0	30.5	72 57.6	−49.1	33.8	74 34.9	−46.5	37.9
21	66 50.3	54.1	24.3	68 38.7	53.0	26.4	70 25.0	51.7	28.9	72 08.5	50.0	31.9	73 48.4	47.9	35.5
22	65 56.2	54.5	23.3	67 45.7	53.6	25.2	69 33.3	52.5	27.4	71 18.5	51.0	30.2	73 00.5	49.1	33.4
23	65 01.7	54.8	22.2	66 52.1	54.1	24.0	68 40.8	53.0	26.1	70 27.5	51.8	28.5	72 11.4	50.1	31.5
24	64 06.9	55.3	21.3	65 58.0	54.4	22.9	67 47.8	53.6	24.8	69 35.7	52.4	27.1	71 21.3	51.0	29.7
25	63 11.6	−55.5	20.4	65 03.6	−54.9	21.9	66 54.2	−54.1	23.7	68 43.3	−53.1	25.7	70 30.3	−51.8	28.1
26	62 16.1	55.8	19.6	64 08.7	55.2	21.0	66 00.1	54.4	22.6	67 50.2	53.6	24.4	69 38.5	52.5	26.7
27	61 20.3	56.0	18.8	63 13.5	55.5	20.1	65 05.7	54.9	21.6	66 56.6	54.1	23.3	68 46.0	53.1	25.3
28	60 24.3	56.3	18.1	62 18.0	55.8	19.3	64 10.8	55.2	20.6	66 02.5	54.5	22.2	67 52.9	53.6	24.0
29	59 28.0	56.5	17.4	61 22.2	56.1	18.5	63 15.6	55.6	19.7	65 08.0	54.9	21.2	66 59.3	54.1	22.9

Dec.	10° Hc	d	Z	12° Hc	d	Z	14° Hc	d	Z	16° Hc	d	Z	18° Hc	d	Z
°	° ′	′	°	° ′	′	°	° ′	′	°	° ′	′	°	° ′	′	°
0	75 53.6	+41.7·	134.6	74 25.6	+45.7	139.7	72 51.2	+48.7	143.9	71 12.1	+50.9	147.4	69 29.4	+52.6	150.3
1	76 35.3	39.3·	131.5	75 11.3	43.9	137.2	73 39.9	47.3	141.9	72 03.0	49.9	145.7	70 22.0	51.8	148.9
2	77 14.6	36.5·	128.2	75 55.2	41.9·	134.5	74 27.2	45.9	139.6	72 52.9	48.9	143.9	71 13.8	51.1	147.4
3	77 51.1	33.3·	124.5	76 37.1	39.5·	131.5	75 13.1	44.2	137.2	73 41.8	47.5	141.9	72 04.9	50.1	145.7
4	78 24.4	29.6·	120.5	77 16.6	36.7·	128.1	75 57.3	42.1·	134.5	74 29.3	46.1	139.6	72 55.0	49.1	143.9
5	78 54.0	+25.3·	116.0	77 53.3	+33.6·	124.5	76 39.4	+39.7·	131.4	75 15.4	+44.4	137.2	73 44.1	+47.8	141.9
6	79 19.3	20.7·	111.2	78 26.9	29.8·	120.4	77 19.1	37.1·	128.1	75 59.8	42.4·	134.5	74 31.9	46.3	139.6
7	79 40.0	15.4·	106.1	78 56.7	25.7·	116.0	77 56.2	33.8·	124.4	76 42.2	40.1·	131.5	75 18.2	44.7	137.2
8	79 55.4	9.8·	100.6	79 22.4	20.9·	111.2	78 30.0	30.1·	120.4	77 22.3	37.3·	128.1	76 02.9	42.7·	134.5
9	80 05.2	+ 3.9·	94.9	79 43.3	15.7·	106.0	79 00.1	26.0·	116.0	77 59.6	34.1·	124.5	76 45.6	40.3·	131.5
10	80 09.1	− 2.1·	89.1	79 59.0	+10.0·	100.5	79 26.1	+21.2·	111.1	78 33.7	+30.5·	120.4	77 25.9	+37.7·	128.2
11	80 07.0	8.0·	83.3	80 09.0	+ 4.1·	94.8	79 47.3	16.0·	106.0	79 04.2	26.3·	116.0	78 03.6	34.5·	124.5
12	79 59.0	13.8·	77.6	80 13.1	− 1.9·	89.0	80 03.3	10.2·	100.4	79 30.5	21.5·	111.1	78 38.1	30.8·	120.5
13	79 45.2	19.1·	72.0	80 11.2	7.9·	83.1	80 13.5	+ 4.4·	94.7	79 52.0	16.2·	105.9	79 08.9	26.6·	116.0
14	79 26.1	24.0·	66.8	80 03.3	13.7·	77.3	80 17.9	− 1.8·	88.8	80 08.2	10.6·	100.4	79 35.5	21.8·	111.2
15	79 02.1	−28.4·	61.9	79 49.6	−19.1·	71.7	80 16.1	− 9.2·	82.9	80 18.8	+ 4.5·	94.6	79 57.3	+16.6·	105.9
16	78 33.7	32.2·	57.3	79 30.5	24.0·	66.4	80 08.2	13.6·	77.0	80 23.3	− 1.6·	88.6	80 13.9	10.8·	100.3
17	78 01.5	35.6·	53.2	79 06.5	28.4·	61.5	79 54.6	19.1·	71.4	80 21.7	7.8·	82.6	80 24.7	+ 4.7·	94.5
18	77 25.9	38.5·	49.4	78 38.1	32.3·	56.9	79 35.5	24.1·	66.1	80 13.9	13.6·	76.8	80 29.4	− 1.5·	88.5
19	76 47.4	40.9·	45.9	78 05.8	35.7·	52.7	79 11.4	28.4·	61.1	80 00.3	19.1·	71.1	80 27.9	7.7·	82.4
20	76 06.5	−43.2·	42.8	77 30.1	−38.5·	48.9	78 43.0	−32.4·	56.5	79 41.2	−24.2·	65.7	80 20.2	−13.6·	76.5
21	75 23.3	45.0	40.0	76 51.6	41.1·	45.5	78 10.6	35.7·	52.3	79 17.0	28.5·	60.7	80 06.6	19.1·	70.7
22	74 38.3	46.5	37.4	76 10.5	43.2·	42.4	77 34.9	38.7·	48.5	78 48.5	32.5·	56.0	79 47.5	24.3·	65.3
23	73 51.8	48.0	35.1	75 27.3	45.1	39.5	76 56.2	41.2·	45.0	78 16.0	35.9·	51.8	79 23.2	28.7·	60.2
24	73 03.8	49.1	33.0	74 42.2	46.7	37.0	76 15.0	43.4	41.9	77 40.1	38.8·	48.0	78 54.5	32.6·	55.6
25	72 14.7	−50.2	31.1	73 55.5	−48.0	34.6	75 31.6	−45.1	39.0	77 01.3	−41.4·	44.5	78 21.9	−36.1·	51.3
26	71 24.5	51.1	29.3	73 07.5	49.2	32.5	74 46.5	46.8	36.5	76 19.9	44.5	41.3	77 45.8	39.0·	47.4
27	70 33.4	51.8	27.7	72 18.3	50.3	30.6	73 59.7	48.2	34.1	75 36.4	45.3	38.5	77 06.8	41.5·	43.9
28	69 41.6	52.6	26.2	71 28.0	51.1	28.8	73 11.5	49.3	32.0	74 51.1	46.9	35.9	76 25.3	43.7·	40.8
29	68 49.0	53.1	24.9	70 36.9	51.9	27.2	72 22.2	50.3	30.1	74 04.2	48.3	33.6	75 41.6	45.5	37.9

	0°			2°			4°			6°			8°		Dec.
	Hc	d	Z	Hc	d	Z	Hc	d	Z	Hc	d	Z	Hc	d	Z	
	80 00.0	– 3.0°	90.0	79 48.2	– 14.5°	101.2	79 14.2	– 24.7°	111.6	78 21.2	– 32.8°	120.7	77 13.2	– 39.1°	128.3	0
	79 57.0	8.8°	95.7	79 33.7	19.8°	106.6	78 49.5	28.9°	116.4	77 48.4	36.1°	124.7	76 34.1	41.5°	131.6	1
	79 48.2	14.4°	101.4	79 13.9	24.5°	111.7	78 20.6	32.7°	120.8	77 12.3	38.9°	128.4	75 52.6	43.6	134.7	2
	79 33.8	19.6°	106.8	78 49.4	28.8°	116.5	77 47.9	35.9°	124.9	76 33.4	41.3°	131.8	75 09.0	45.3	137.4	3
	79 14.2	24.3°	111.9	78 20.6	32.5°	121.0	77 12.0	38.7°	128.6	75 52.1	43.4	134.8	74 23.7	46.9	139.9	4
	78 49.9	– 28.7°	116.7	77 48.1	– 35.8°	125.0	76 33.3	– 41.2°	131.9	75 08.7	– 45.2	137.6	73 36.8	– 48.2	142.2	5
	78 21.2	32.4°	121.2	77 12.3	38.6°	128.8	75 52.1	43.3	135.0	74 23.5	46.8	140.1	72 48.6	49.3	144.2	6
	77 48.8	35.6°	125.3	76 33.7	41.1°	132.1	75 08.8	45.1	137.8	73 36.7	48.1	142.3	71 59.3	50.3	146.1	7
	77 13.2	38.6°	129.0	75 52.6	43.2	135.2	74 23.7	46.6	140.3	72 48.6	49.2	144.4	71 09.0	51.3	147.8	8
	76 34.6	41.0°	132.4	75 09.4	45.0	138.0	73 37.1	48.0	142.5	71 59.4	50.2	146.3	70 17.7	51.9	149.4	9
	75 53.6	– 43.1	135.4	74 24.4	– 46.5	140.5	72 49.1	– 49.2	144.6	71 09.2	– 51.2	148.0	69 25.8	– 52.7	150.9	10
	75 10.5	44.9	138.2	73 37.9	48.0	142.8	71 59.9	50.2	146.5	70 18.0	51.9	149.6	68 33.1	53.2	152.2	11
	74 25.6	46.5	140.8	72 49.9	49.1	144.9	71 09.7	51.0	148.3	69 26.1	52.5	151.1	67 39.9	53.8	153.5	12
	73 39.1	47.9	143.1	72 00.8	50.1	146.8	70 18.7	51.8	149.9	68 33.6	53.2	152.4	66 46.1	54.2	154.6	13
	72 51.2	49.0	145.1	71 10.7	51.0	148.5	69 26.9	52.6	151.3	67 40.4	53.7	153.7	65 51.9	54.6	155.7	14
	72 02.2	– 50.1	147.1	70 19.7	– 51.8	150.1	68 34.3	– 53.1	152.7	66 46.7	– 54.2	154.8	64 57.3	– 55.0	156.7	15
	71 12.1	51.0	148.8	69 27.9	52.4	151.6	67 41.2	53.6	153.9	65 52.5	54.5	155.9	64 02.3	55.4	157.6	16
	70 21.1	51.7	150.4	68 35.5	53.1	152.9	66 47.6	54.1	155.1	64 58.0	55.0	156.9	63 06.9	55.6	158.5	17
	69 29.4	52.5	151.9	67 42.4	53.6	154.2	65 53.5	54.6	156.2	64 03.0	55.3	157.8	62 11.3	55.9	159.3	18
	68 36.9	53.0	153.2	66 48.8	54.1	155.4	64 58.9	54.9	157.2	63 07.5	55.6	158.7	61 15.4	56.2	160.0	19
	67 43.9	– 53.6	154.5	65 54.7	– 54.5	156.4	64 04.0	– 55.3	158.1	62 12.1	– 55.9	159.5	60 19.2	– 56.3	160.8	20
	66 50.3	54.1	155.7	65 00.2	54.9	157.4	63 08.7	55.5	159.0	61 16.2	56.1	160.3	59 22.9	56.6	161.4	21
	65 56.2	54.5	156.7	64 05.3	55.2	158.4	62 13.2	55.8	159.8	60 20.1	56.3	161.0	58 26.3	56.8	162.1	22
	65 01.7	54.8	157.8	63 10.1	55.6	159.3	61 17.4	56.1	160.6	59 23.8	56.5	161.7	57 29.5	56.9	162.7	23
	64 06.9	55.3	158.7	62 14.5	55.8	160.1	60 21.3	56.3	161.3	58 27.3	56.8	162.3	56 32.6	57.1	163.3	24
	63 11.6	– 55.5	159.6	61 18.7	– 56.0	160.9	59 25.0	– 56.6	162.0	57 30.5	– 56.9	163.0	55 35.5	– 57.2	163.8	25
	62 16.1	55.8	160.4	60 22.7	56.3	161.6	58 28.4	56.7	162.6	56 33.6	57.0	163.5	54 38.3	57.4	164.4	26
	61 20.3	56.0	161.2	59 26.4	56.5	162.3	57 31.7	56.8	163.3	55 36.6	57.2	164.1	53 40.9	57.4	164.9	27
	60 24.3	56.3	161.9	58 29.9	56.7	162.9	56 34.9	57.1	163.8	54 39.4	57.3	164.6	52 43.5	57.6	165.3	28
	59 28.0	56.5	162.6	57 33.2	56.9	163.6	55 37.8	57.1	164.4	53 42.1	57.5	165.1	51 45.9	57.7	165.8	29

	10°			12°			14°			16°			18°			Dec.
	Hc	d	Z	Hc	d	Z	Hc	d	Z	Hc	d	Z	Hc	d	Z	
	75 53.6	– 43.7	134.6	74 25.6	– 47.2	139.7	72 51.2	– 49.7	143.9	71 12.1	– 51.7	147.4	69 29.4	– 53.2	150.3	0
	75 09.9	45.5	137.3	73 38.4	48.5	141.9	72 01.5	50.8	145.8	70 20.4	52.5	148.9	68 36.2	53.8	151.6	1
	74 24.4	47.0	139.8	72 49.9	49.6	144.0	71 10.7	51.5	147.5	69 27.9	53.0	150.3	67 42.4	54.3	152.8	2
	73 37.4	48.3	142.0	72 00.3	50.6	145.9	70 19.2	52.3	149.0	68 34.9	53.7	151.7	66 48.1	54.6	153.9	3
	72 49.1	49.5	144.1	71 09.7	51.4	147.6	69 26.9	53.0	150.4	67 41.2	54.1	152.9	65 53.5	55.1	154.9	4
	71 59.6	– 50.4	146.0	70 18.3	– 52.2	149.1	68 33.9	– 53.5	151.7	66 47.1	– 54.6	154.0	64 58.4	– 55.4	155.9	5
	71 09.2	51.4	147.7	69 26.1	52.8	150.6	67 40.4	54.0	153.0	65 52.5	54.9	155.0	64 03.0	55.7	156.8	6
	70 17.8	52.0	149.3	68 33.3	53.4	151.9	66 46.4	54.5	154.1	64 57.6	55.3	156.0	63 07.3	56.0	157.6	7
	69 25.8	52.8	150.7	67 39.9	53.9	153.1	65 51.9	54.8	155.1	64 02.3	55.6	156.9	62 11.3	56.2	158.4	8
	68 33.0	53.2	152.0	66 46.0	54.4	154.2	64 57.1	55.3	156.1	63 06.7	55.9	157.7	61 15.1	56.5	159.1	9
	67 39.7	– 53.8	153.3	65 51.6	– 54.8	155.3	64 01.8	– 55.5	157.0	62 10.8	– 56.2	158.5	60 18.6	– 56.7	159.8	10
	66 45.9	54.3	154.4	64 56.8	55.1	156.3	63 06.3	55.8	157.9	61 14.6	56.4	159.2	59 21.9	56.8	160.5	11
	65 51.6	54.7	155.5	64 01.7	55.5	157.2	62 10.5	56.1	158.7	60 18.2	56.6	159.9	58 25.1	57.0	161.1	12
	64 56.9	55.1	156.4	63 06.2	55.7	158.0	61 14.4	56.3	159.4	59 21.6	56.8	160.6	57 28.1	57.2	161.7	13
	64 01.8	55.4	157.4	62 10.5	56.0	158.8	60 18.1	56.5	160.1	58 24.8	56.9	161.2	56 30.9	57.3	162.2	14
	63 06.4	– 55.6	158.2	61 14.5	– 56.3	159.6	59 21.6	– 56.8	160.8	57 27.9	– 57.1	161.8	55 33.6	– 57.5	162.7	15
	62 10.8	56.0	159.0	60 18.2	56.4	160.3	58 24.8	56.9	161.4	56 30.8	57.3	162.4	54 36.1	57.5	163.3	16
	61 14.8	56.2	159.8	59 21.8	56.7	161.0	57 27.9	57.0	162.0	55 33.5	57.4	162.9	53 38.6	57.7	163.7	17
	60 18.6	56.4	160.5	58 25.1	56.9	161.6	56 30.9	57.2	162.6	54 36.1	57.5	163.4	52 40.9	57.8	164.2	18
	59 22.2	56.6	161.2	57 28.2	57.0	162.2	55 33.7	57.4	163.1	53 38.6	57.6	163.9	51 43.1	57.9	164.6	19
	58 25.6	– 56.8	161.8	56 31.2	– 57.1	162.8	54 36.3	– 57.4	163.6	52 41.0	– 57.7	164.4	50 45.2	– 57.9	165.1	20
	57 28.8	57.0	162.4	55 34.1	57.3	163.3	53 38.9	57.6	164.1	51 43.3	57.9	164.8	49 47.3	58.1	165.5	21
	56 31.8	57.1	163.0	54 36.8	57.4	163.9	52 41.3	57.7	164.6	50 45.4	57.9	165.3	48 49.2	58.1	165.8	22
	55 34.7	57.3	163.6	53 39.4	57.6	164.4	51 43.6	57.8	165.0	49 47.5	58.0	165.7	47 51.1	58.2	166.2	23
	54 37.4	57.3	164.1	52 41.8	57.6	164.8	50 45.8	57.9	165.5	48 49.5	58.1	166.1	46 52.9	58.2	166.6	24
	53 40.1	– 57.6	164.6	51 44.2	– 57.8	165.3	49 47.9	– 57.9	165.9	47 51.4	– 58.1	166.4	45 54.7	– 58.3	166.9	25
	52 42.5	57.6	165.1	50 46.4	57.8	165.7	48 50.0	58.1	166.3	46 53.3	58.2	166.8	44 56.3	58.3	167.3	26
	51 44.9	57.7	165.5	49 48.6	57.9	166.1	47 51.9	58.1	166.7	45 55.1	58.3	167.1	43 58.0	58.5	167.6	27
	50 47.2	57.8	166.0	48 50.7	58.1	166.5	46 53.8	58.1	167.0	44 56.8	58.3	167.5	42 59.5	58.5	167.9	28
	49 49.4	57.9	166.4	47 52.6	58.0	166.9	45 55.7	58.3	167.4	43 58.5	58.4	167.8	42 01.1	58.6	168.2	29

Dec.	20° Hc	d	Z	22° Hc	d	Z	24° Hc	d	Z	26° Hc	d	Z	28° Hc	d	Z
°	° ′	′	°	° ′	′	°	° ′	′	°	° ′	′	°	° ′	′	°
0	67 43.9	+53.9	152.7	65 56.2	+55.0	154.8	64 06.9	+55.7	156.6	62 16.1	+56.4	158.1	60 24.3	+56.9	159.4
1	68 37.8	53.3	151.5	66 51.2	54.5	153.8	65 02.6	55.4	155.7	63 12.5	56.2	157.3	61 21.2	56.8	158.8
2	69 31.1	52.8	150.3	67 45.7	54.0	152.7	65 58.0	55.1	154.8	64 08.7	55.9	156.6	62 18.0	56.5	158.1
3	70 23.9	52.1	148.9	68 39.7	53.6	151.5	66 53.1	54.7	153.8	65 04.6	55.5	155.7	63 14.5	56.3	157.3
4	71 16.0	51.2	147.4	69 33.3	52.9	150.3	67 47.8	54.2	152.7	66 00.1	55.3	154.8	64 10.8	56.0	156.6
5	72 07.2	+50.4	145.7	70 26.2	+52.3	148.9	68 42.0	+53.7	151.6	66 55.4	+54.8	153.8	65 06.8	+55.7	155.7
6	72 57.6	49.3	143.9	71 18.5	51.4	147.4	69 35.7	53.1	150.3	67 50.2	54.4	152.8	66 02.5	55.4	154.8
7	73 46.9	48.0	141.9	72 09.9	50.6	145.8	70 28.8	52.5	148.9	68 44.6	53.9	151.6	66 57.9	55.0	153.9
8	74 34.9	46.6	139.7	73 00.5	49.5	144.0	71 21.3	51.7	147.5	69 38.5	53.3	150.4	67 52.9	54.6	152.8
9	75 21.5	45.0	137.3	73 50.0	48.3	142.0	72 13.0	50.8	145.8	70 31.8	52.7	149.0	68 47.5	54.1	151.7
10	76 06.5	+42.9	134.6	74 38.3	+46.9	139.8	73 03.8	+49.8	144.1	71 24.5	+51.9	147.6	69 41.6	+53.5	150.5
11	76 49.4	40.7	131.6	75 25.2	45.3	137.4	73 53.6	48.6	142.1	72 16.4	51.1	146.0	70 35.1	52.9	149.1
12	77 30.1	38.0	128.3	76 10.5	43.3	134.7	74 42.2	47.2	139.9	73 07.5	50.1	144.2	71 28.0	52.2	147.7
13	78 08.1	34.9	124.6	76 53.8	41.1	131.7	75 29.4	45.6	137.5	73 57.6	48.9	142.2	72 20.2	51.3	146.1
14	78 43.0	31.2	120.6	77 34.9	38.3	128.4	76 15.0	43.7	134.9	74 46.5	47.5	140.1	73 11.5	50.4	144.4
15	79 14.2	+27.0	116.1	78 13.2	+35.3	124.8	76 58.7	+41.4	131.9	75 34.0	+45.9	137.7	74 01.9	+49.2	142.4
16	79 41.2	22.2	111.2	78 48.5	31.6	120.7	77 40.1	38.8	128.6	76 19.9	44.1	135.1	74 51.1	47.9	140.3
17	80 03.4	16.8	105.9	79 20.1	27.4	116.2	78 18.9	35.6	124.9	77 04.0	41.8	132.1	75 39.0	46.3	137.9
18	80 20.2	11.1	100.3	79 47.5	22.5	111.3	78 54.5	32.1	120.9	77 45.8	39.2	128.8	76 25.3	44.5	135.3
19	80 31.3	+5.0	94.4	80 10.0	17.3	106.0	79 26.6	27.8	116.3	78 25.0	36.1	125.1	77 09.8	42.2	132.4
20	80 36.3	-1.4	88.3	80 27.3	+11.3	100.3	79 54.4	+23.0	111.4	79 01.1	+32.5	121.1	77 52.0	+39.7	129.1
21	80 34.9	7.6	82.2	80 38.6	5.2	94.3	80 17.4	17.6	106.0	79 33.6	28.3	116.5	78 31.7	36.6	125.4
22	80 27.3	13.7	76.1	80 43.8	-1.3	88.1	80 35.0	11.6	100.3	80 01.9	23.4	111.5	79 08.3	33.0	121.3
23	80 13.6	19.2	70.3	80 42.5	7.5	81.9	80 46.6	+5.4	94.2	80 25.3	18.0	106.1	79 41.3	28.7	116.8
24	79 54.4	24.4	64.8	80 35.0	13.7	75.8	80 52.0	-1.1	88.0	80 43.3	12.0	100.3	80 10.0	23.9	111.7
25	79 30.0	-28.9	59.7	80 21.3	-19.4	69.9	80 50.9	-7.6	81.7	80 55.3	+5.6	94.1	80 33.9	+18.4	106.3
26	79 01.1	32.8	55.0	80 01.9	24.5	64.4	80 43.3	13.8	75.5	81 00.9	-1.1	87.8	80 52.3	12.3	100.3
27	78 28.3	36.3	50.7	79 37.4	29.1	59.2	80 29.5	19.5	69.5	80 59.8	7.5	81.4	81 04.6	+5.8	94.1
28	77 52.0	39.2	46.8	79 08.3	33.1	54.5	80 10.0	24.7	63.9	80 52.3	13.9	75.1	81 10.4	-0.9	87.6
29	77 12.8	41.7	43.3	78 35.2	36.5	50.1	79 45.3	29.3	58.6	80 38.4	19.7	69.0	81 09.5	7.6	81.1

Dec.	30° Hc	d	Z	32° Hc	d	Z	34° Hc	d	Z	36° Hc	d	Z	38° Hc	d	Z
°	° ′	′	°	° ′	′	°	° ′	′	°	° ′	′	°	° ′	′	°
0	58 31.5	+57.4	160.6	56 38.0	+57.7	161.6	54 43.8	+58.1	162.5	52 49.1	+58.3	163.3	50 54.0	+58.5	164.0
1	59 28.9	57.2	160.0	57 35.7	57.7	161.1	55 41.9	57.9	162.1	53 47.4	58.3	162.9	51 52.5	58.3	163.7
2	60 26.1	57.1	159.4	58 33.4	57.4	160.6	56 39.8	57.9	161.6	54 45.7	58.1	162.5	52 51.0	58.4	163.3
3	61 23.2	56.8	158.8	59 30.8	57.2	160.0	57 37.7	57.7	161.1	55 43.8	58.1	162.1	53 49.4	58.3	162.9
4	62 20.0	56.7	158.1	60 28.2	57.2	159.4	58 35.4	57.6	160.6	56 41.9	57.9	161.6	54 47.7	58.2	162.5
5	63 16.7	+56.4	157.4	61 25.4	+56.9	158.8	59 33.0	+57.5	160.0	57 39.8	+57.9	161.1	55 45.9	+58.2	162.1
6	64 13.1	56.2	156.6	62 22.3	56.8	158.1	60 30.5	57.3	159.5	58 37.7	57.7	160.6	56 44.1	58.0	161.6
7	65 09.3	55.9	155.8	63 19.1	56.6	157.4	61 27.8	57.1	158.9	59 35.4	57.5	160.1	57 42.1	57.9	161.2
8	66 05.2	55.5	154.9	64 15.7	56.3	156.7	62 24.9	56.9	158.2	60 32.9	57.5	159.5	58 40.1	57.8	160.7
9	67 00.7	55.2	153.9	65 12.0	56.1	155.9	63 21.8	56.7	157.5	61 30.4	57.2	158.9	59 37.9	57.7	160.2
10	67 55.9	+54.8	152.9	66 08.1	+55.7	155.0	64 18.5	+56.5	156.8	62 27.6	+57.1	158.3	60 35.6	+57.6	159.6
11	68 50.7	54.2	151.8	67 03.8	55.3	154.1	65 15.0	56.2	156.0	63 24.7	56.8	157.6	61 33.2	57.3	159.0
12	69 45.0	53.7	150.6	67 59.1	55.0	153.1	66 11.2	55.9	155.1	64 21.5	56.7	156.9	62 30.5	57.3	158.4
13	70 38.7	53.2	149.3	68 54.1	54.5	152.0	67 07.1	55.5	154.2	65 18.2	56.3	156.1	63 27.8	57.0	157.7
14	71 31.9	52.4	147.9	69 48.6	54.0	150.8	68 02.6	55.2	153.2	66 14.5	56.1	155.3	64 24.8	56.8	157.0
15	72 24.3	+51.6	146.3	70 42.6	+53.4	149.5	68 57.8	+54.8	152.1	67 10.6	+55.8	154.4	65 21.6	+56.5	156.3
16	73 15.9	50.7	144.6	71 36.0	52.7	148.1	69 52.6	54.2	151.0	68 06.4	55.4	153.4	66 18.1	56.3	155.5
17	74 06.6	49.5	142.7	72 28.7	51.9	146.5	70 46.8	53.6	149.7	69 01.8	54.9	152.4	67 14.4	55.9	154.6
18	74 56.1	48.3	140.5	73 20.6	51.0	144.8	71 40.4	53.0	148.3	69 56.7	54.5	151.2	68 10.3	55.6	153.6
19	75 44.4	46.7	138.2	74 11.6	49.9	142.9	72 33.4	52.3	146.8	70 51.2	53.9	150.0	69 05.9	55.2	152.6
20	76 31.1	+44.9	135.6	74 58.5	+48.7	140.8	73 25.7	+51.3	145.1	71 45.1	+53.3	148.6	70 01.1	+54.8	151.5
21	77 16.0	42.7	132.7	75 50.2	47.1	138.5	74 17.0	50.3	143.2	72 38.4	52.6	147.1	70 55.9	54.2	150.2
22	77 58.7	40.2	129.4	76 37.3	45.3	135.9	75 07.3	49.0	141.2	73 31.0	51.6	145.4	71 50.1	53.6	148.9
23	78 38.9	37.1	125.7	77 22.6	43.2	133.0	75 56.3	47.5	138.9	74 22.6	50.7	143.6	72 43.7	52.8	147.4
24	79 16.0	33.5	121.6	78 05.8	40.7	129.7	76 43.8	45.8	136.3	75 13.3	49.4	141.5	73 36.5	52.1	145.8
25	79 49.5	+29.2	117.0	78 46.5	+37.6	126.1	77 29.6	+43.8	133.4	76 02.7	+48.0	139.3	74 28.6	+51.0	144.0
26	80 18.7	24.4	112.0	79 24.1	34.1	121.9	78 13.4	41.2	130.1	76 50.7	46.3	136.7	75 19.6	49.9	142.0
27	80 43.1	18.8	106.4	79 58.2	29.8	117.3	78 54.6	38.2	126.5	77 37.0	44.3	133.8	76 09.5	48.5	139.7
28	81 01.9	12.6	100.4	80 28.0	24.9	112.2	79 32.8	34.6	122.3	78 21.3	41.8	130.6	76 58.0	46.8	137.2
29	81 14.5	+6.1	94.1	80 52.9	19.2	106.6	80 07.4	30.4	117.7	79 03.1	38.8	126.9	77 44.8	44.8	134.3

20°			22°			24°			26°			28°			Dec.
Hc	d	Z	Hc	d	Z	Hc	d	Z	Hc	d	Z	Hc	d	Z	
67 43.9	-54.4	152.7	65 56.2	-55.3	154.8	64 06.9	-56.1	156.6	62 16.1	-56.6	158.1	60 24.3	-57.2	159.4	0
66 49.5	54.4	153.8	65 00.9	55.6	155.7	63 10.8	56.3	157.4	61 19.5	56.8	158.8	59 27.1	57.2	160.0	1
65 54.7	55.2	154.8	64 05.3	55.9	156.6	62 14.5	56.5	158.1	60 22.7	57.1	159.4	58 29.9	57.5	160.6	2
64 59.5	55.5	155.8	63 09.4	56.2	157.4	61 18.0	56.7	158.8	59 25.6	57.2	160.1	57 32.4	57.5	161.1	3
64 04.0	55.8	156.7	62 13.2	56.4	158.2	60 21.3	57.0	159.5	58 28.4	57.3	160.7	56 34.9	57.7	161.7	4
63 08.2	-56.1	157.5	61 16.8	-56.7	158.9	59 24.3	-57.0	160.1	57 31.1	-57.5	161.2	55 37.2	-57.8	162.2	5
62 12.1	56.3	158.3	60 20.1	56.8	159.6	58 27.3	57.3	160.7	56 33.6	57.6	161.7	54 39.4	57.9	162.6	6
61 15.8	56.6	159.0	59 23.3	57.0	160.2	57 30.0	57.4	161.3	55 36.0	57.7	162.2	53 41.5	58.0	163.1	7
60 19.2	56.7	159.7	58 26.3	57.2	160.8	56 32.6	57.5	161.8	54 38.3	57.8	162.7	52 43.5	58.1	163.5	8
59 22.5	56.9	160.3	57 29.1	57.3	161.4	55 35.1	57.7	162.3	53 40.5	58.0	163.2	51 45.4	58.2	163.9	9
58 25.6	-57.1	160.9	56 31.8	-57.4	161.9	54 37.4	-57.7	162.8	52 42.5	-58.0	163.6	50 47.2	-58.2	164.3	10
57 28.5	57.3	161.5	55 34.4	57.6	162.5	53 39.7	57.9	163.3	51 44.5	58.1	164.0	49 49.0	58.3	164.7	11
56 31.2	57.3	162.1	54 36.8	57.7	162.9	52 41.8	57.9	163.7	50 46.4	58.2	164.4	48 50.7	58.4	165.0	12
55 33.9	57.6	162.6	53 39.1	57.8	163.4	51 43.9	58.1	164.1	49 48.2	58.2	164.8	47 52.3	58.5	165.4	13
54 36.3	57.6	163.1	52 41.3	57.9	163.9	50 45.8	58.1	164.6	48 50.0	58.3	165.2	46 53.8	58.5	165.7	14
53 38.7	-57.7	163.6	51 43.4	-58.0	164.3	49 47.7	-58.2	164.9	47 51.7	-58.4	165.5	45 55.3	-58.5	166.0	15
52 41.0	57.9	164.0	50 45.4	58.0	164.7	48 49.5	58.3	165.3	46 53.3	58.5	165.9	44 56.8	58.6	166.4	16
51 43.1	57.9	164.5	49 47.4	58.2	165.1	47 51.2	58.3	165.7	45 54.8	58.5	166.2	43 58.2	58.7	166.7	17
50 45.2	58.0	164.9	48 49.2	58.2	165.5	46 52.9	58.4	166.0	44 56.3	58.5	166.5	42 59.5	58.6	167.0	18
49 47.2	58.1	165.3	47 51.0	58.3	165.8	45 54.5	58.4	166.4	43 57.8	58.6	166.8	42 00.9	58.8	167.2	19
48 49.1	-58.1	165.7	46 52.7	-58.3	166.2	44 56.1	-58.5	166.7	42 59.2	-58.6	167.1	41 02.1	-58.7	167.5	20
47 51.0	58.3	166.0	45 54.4	58.4	166.5	43 57.6	58.6	167.0	42 00.6	58.7	167.4	40 03.4	58.8	167.8	21
46 52.7	58.3	166.4	44 56.0	58.5	166.9	42 59.0	58.6	167.3	41 01.9	58.7	167.7	39 04.6	58.9	168.0	22
45 54.4	58.3	166.7	43 57.5	58.5	167.2	42 00.4	58.6	167.6	40 03.2	58.8	167.9	38 05.7	58.8	168.3	23
44 56.1	58.4	167.1	42 59.0	58.5	167.5	41 01.8	58.7	167.9	39 04.4	58.8	168.2	37 06.9	58.9	168.5	24
43 57.7	-58.5	167.4	42 00.5	-58.6	167.8	40 03.1	-58.7	168.1	38 05.6	-58.8	168.5	36 08.0	-59.0	168.8	25
42 59.2	58.5	167.7	41 01.9	58.7	168.1	39 04.4	58.7	168.4	37 06.8	58.9	168.7	35 09.0	58.9	169.0	26
42 00.7	58.6	168.0	40 03.2	58.6	168.3	38 05.6	58.7	168.7	36 07.9	58.9	169.0	34 10.1	59.0	169.2	27
41 02.1	58.6	168.3	39 04.6	58.8	168.6	37 06.9	58.9	168.9	35 09.0	58.9	169.2	33 11.1	59.0	169.4	28
40 03.5	58.6	168.6	38 05.8	58.7	168.9	36 08.0	58.8	169.2	34 10.1	59.0	169.4	32 12.1	59.0	169.7	29

30°			32°			34°			36°			38°			Dec.
Hc	d	Z	Hc	d	Z	Hc	d	Z	Hc	d	Z	Hc	d	Z	
58 31.5	-57.5	160.6	56 38.0	-57.9	161.6	54 43.8	-58.1	162.5	52 49.1	-58.4	163.3	50 54.0	-58.6	164.0	0
57 34.0	57.7	161.1	55 40.1	58.0	162.1	53 45.7	58.3	162.9	51 50.7	58.4	163.7	49 55.4	58.7	164.4	1
56 36.3	57.8	161.6	54 42.1	58.0	162.5	52 47.4	58.3	163.3	50 52.3	58.6	164.0	48 56.7	58.7	164.7	2
55 38.5	57.8	162.1	53 44.1	58.2	163.0	51 49.1	58.4	163.7	49 53.7	58.5	164.4	47 58.0	58.8	165.0	3
54 40.7	58.0	162.6	52 45.9	58.2	163.4	50 50.7	58.4	164.1	48 55.2	58.7	164.7	46 59.2	58.8	165.3	4
53 42.7	-58.1	163.0	51 47.7	-58.3	163.8	49 52.3	-58.5	164.4	47 56.5	-58.7	165.0	46 00.4	-58.8	165.6	5
52 44.6	58.2	163.4	50 49.4	58.4	164.1	48 53.8	58.6	164.8	46 57.8	58.7	165.3	45 01.6	58.9	165.9	6
51 46.4	58.2	163.8	49 51.0	58.4	164.5	47 55.2	58.6	165.1	45 59.1	58.8	165.6	44 02.7	58.9	166.1	7
50 48.2	58.3	164.2	48 52.6	58.6	164.8	46 56.6	58.7	165.4	45 00.3	58.8	165.9	43 03.8	59.0	166.4	8
49 49.9	58.4	164.6	47 54.0	58.5	165.2	45 57.9	58.7	165.7	44 01.5	58.9	166.2	42 04.8	59.0	166.6	9
48 51.5	-58.4	164.9	46 55.5	-58.6	165.5	44 59.2	-58.8	166.0	43 02.6	-58.9	166.5	41 05.8	-59.0	166.9	10
47 53.1	58.5	165.3	45 56.9	58.7	165.8	44 00.4	58.8	166.3	42 03.7	58.9	166.7	40 06.8	59.0	167.1	11
46 54.6	58.6	165.6	44 58.2	58.7	166.1	43 01.6	58.8	166.6	41 04.8	59.0	167.0	39 07.8	59.1	167.4	12
45 56.0	58.6	165.9	43 59.5	58.8	166.4	42 02.8	58.9	166.8	40 05.8	59.0	167.2	38 08.7	59.1	167.6	13
44 57.4	58.6	166.2	43 00.7	58.7	166.7	41 03.9	58.9	167.1	39 06.8	59.0	167.5	37 09.6	59.1	167.8	14
43 58.8	-58.7	166.5	42 02.0	-58.9	166.9	40 05.0	-59.0	167.3	38 07.8	-59.0	167.7	36 10.5	-59.2	168.0	15
43 00.1	58.8	166.8	41 03.1	58.8	167.2	39 06.0	59.0	167.6	37 08.8	59.1	167.9	35 11.3	59.1	168.2	16
42 01.3	58.8	167.1	40 04.3	59.0	167.5	38 07.0	59.0	167.8	36 09.7	59.1	168.1	34 12.2	59.2	168.4	17
41 02.5	58.8	167.4	39 05.4	59.0	167.7	37 08.0	59.0	168.0	35 10.6	59.1	168.3	33 13.0	59.2	168.6	18
40 03.7	58.8	167.6	38 06.4	58.9	168.0	36 09.0	59.0	168.3	34 11.5	59.2	168.6	32 13.8	59.2	168.8	19
39 04.9	-58.9	167.9	37 07.5	-59.0	168.2	35 10.0	-59.1	168.5	33 12.3	-59.1	168.7	31 14.6	-59.3	169.0	20
38 06.0	58.9	168.1	36 08.5	59.0	168.4	34 10.9	59.1	168.7	32 13.2	59.2	169.0	30 15.3	59.3	169.2	21
37 07.1	58.9	168.4	35 09.5	59.0	168.6	33 11.8	59.1	168.9	31 14.0	59.2	169.1	29 16.1	59.3	169.4	22
36 08.2	59.0	168.6	34 10.5	59.2	168.9	32 12.7	59.1	169.1	30 14.8	59.2	169.3	28 16.8	59.3	169.5	23
35 09.2	59.0	168.8	33 11.4	59.1	169.1	31 13.6	59.2	169.3	29 15.6	59.2	169.5	27 17.6	59.3	169.7	24
34 10.2	-59.0	169.0	32 12.3	-59.0	169.3	30 14.4	-59.2	169.5	28 16.4	-59.3	169.7	26 18.3	-59.3	169.9	25
33 11.2	59.0	169.3	31 13.3	59.2	169.5	29 15.2	59.2	169.7	27 17.1	59.2	169.9	25 19.0	59.4	170.1	26
32 12.2	59.1	169.5	30 14.1	59.1	169.7	28 16.0	59.2	169.9	26 17.9	59.3	170.1	24 19.6	59.3	170.2	27
31 13.1	59.1	169.7	29 15.0	59.1	169.9	27 16.8	59.2	170.1	25 18.6	59.3	170.2	23 20.3	59.4	170.4	28
30 14.0	59.1	169.9	28 15.9	59.2	170.1	26 17.6	59.2	170.2	24 19.3	59.3	170.4	22 21.0	59.4	170.5	29

35

Dec.	40° Hc	d	Z	42° Hc	d	Z	44° Hc	d	Z	46° Hc	d	Z	48° Hc	d	Z
°	° ′	′	°	° ′	′	°	° ′	′	°	° ′	′	°	° ′	′	°
0	48 58.4	+58.7	164.7	47 02.5	+58.9	165.2	45 06.3	+59.1	165.8	43 09.9	+59.2	166.2	41 13.3	+59.2	166.7
1	49 57.1	58.7	164.3	48 01.4	58.9	165.0	46 05.4	59.0	165.5	44 09.1	59.1	166.0	42 12.5	59.3	166.4
2	50 55.8	58.6	164.0	49 00.3	58.8	164.7	47 04.4	58.9	165.2	45 08.2	59.1	165.8	43 11.8	59.2	166.2
3	51 54.4	58.6	163.7	49 59.1	58.7	164.4	48 03.3	59.0	165.0	46 07.3	59.1	165.5	44 11.0	59.2	166.0
4	52 53.0	58.5	163.3	50 57.8	58.7	164.0	49 02.3	58.8	164.7	47 06.4	59.0	165.3	45 10.2	59.2	165.8
5	53 51.5	+58.4	162.9	51 56.5	+58.5	163.7	50 01.1	+58.9	164.4	48 05.4	+59.0	165.0	46 09.4	+59.1	165.5
6	54 49.9	58.3	162.6	52 55.2	58.5	163.4	51 00.0	58.8	164.1	49 04.4	59.0	164.7	47 08.5	59.1	165.3
7	55 48.2	58.3	162.1	53 53.7	58.6	163.0	51 58.8	58.7	163.8	50 03.4	58.9	164.4	48 07.6	59.1	165.0
8	56 46.5	58.1	161.7	54 52.3	58.4	162.6	52 57.5	58.6	163.4	51 02.3	58.8	164.1	49 06.7	59.0	164.8
9	57 44.6	58.1	161.3	55 50.7	58.3	162.2	53 56.1	58.7	163.1	52 01.1	58.8	163.8	50 05.7	59.0	164.5
10	58 42.7	+57.9	160.8	56 49.0	+58.3	161.8	54 54.8	+58.5	162.7	52·59.9	+58.8	163.5	51 04.7	+58.9	164.2
11	59 40.6	57.9	160.3	57 47.3	58.2	161.4	55 53.3	58.4	162.3	53 58.7	58.7	163.2	52 03.6	58.9	163.9
12	60 38.5	57.6	159.7	58 45.5	58.0	160.9	56 51.7	58.4	161.9	54 57.4	58.6	162.8	53 02.5	58.8	163.6
13	61 36.1	57.6	159.2	59 43.5	58.0	160.4	57 50.1	58.3	161.5	55 56.0	58.6	162.4	54 01.3	58.8	163.3
14	62 33.7	57.3	158.6	60 41.5	57.8	159.9	58 48.4	58.2	161.0	56 54.6	58.4	162.0	55 00.1	58.8	162.9
15	63 31.0	+57.1	157.9	61 39.3	+57.6	159.3	59 46.6	+58.0	160.5	57 53.0	+58.4	161.6	55 58.9	+58.6	162.6
16	64 28.2	57.0	157.2	62 36.9	57.5	158.7	60 44.6	58.0	160.0	58 51.4	58.3	161.2	56 57.5	58.6	162.2
17	65 25.2	56.7	156.5	63 34.4	57.4	158.1	61 42.6	57.8	159.5	59 49.7	58.2	160.7	57 56.1	58.5	161.8
18	66 21.9	56.4	155.7	64 31.8	57.1	157.4	62 40.4	57.6	158.9	60 47.9	58.1	160.2	58 54.6	58.4	161.3
19	67 18.3	56.2	154.8	65 28.9	56.9	156.7	63 38.0	57.5	158.3	61 46.0	57.9	159.7	59 53.0	58.3	160.9
20	68 14.5	+55.8	153.9	66 25.8	+56.7	155.9	64 35.5	+57.3	157.6	62 43.9	+57.9	159.1	60 51.3	+58.2	160.4
21	69 10.3	55.5	152.9	67 22.5	56.4	155.1	65 32.8	57.1	156.9	63 41.8	57.6	158.5	61 49.5	58.1	159.9
22	70 05.8	55.0	151.8	68 18.9	56.0	154.2	66 29.9	56.9	156.2	64 39.4	57.5	157.9	62 47.6	58.0	159.4
23	71 00.8	54.5	150.6	69 14.9	55.7	153.2	67 26.8	56.6	155.4	65 36.9	57.3	157.2	63 45.6	57.8	158.8
24	71 55.3	53.9	149.3	70 10.6	55.3	152.1	68 23.4	56.3	154.5	66 34.2	57.0	156.5	64 43.4	57.7	158.2
25	72 49.2	+53.2	147.8	71 05.9	+54.7	150.9	69 19.7	+55.9	153.5	67 31.2	+56.8	155.7	65 41.1	+57.4	157.5
26	73 42.4	52.4	146.2	72 00.6	54.3	149.6	70 15.6	55.5	152.5	68 28.0	56.5	154.8	66 38.5	57.3	156.8
27	74 34.8	51.4	144.4	72 54.9	53.5	148.2	71 11.1	55.1	151.3	69 24.5	56.2	153.9	67 35.8	57.0	156.0
28	75 26.2	50.3	142.4	73 48.4	52.8	146.6	72 06.2	54.5	150.1	70 20.7	55.8	152.9	68 32.8	56.8	155.2
29	76 16.5	49.0	140.2	74 41.2	51.9	144.9	73 00.7	53.9	148.7	71 16.5	55.4	151.8	69 29.6	56.4	154.3

Dec.	50° Hc	d	Z	52° Hc	d	Z	54° Hc	d	Z	56° Hc	d	Z	58° Hc	d	Z
°	° ′	′	°	° ′	′	°	° ′	′	°	° ′	′	°	° ′	′	°
0	39 16.4	+59.4	167.0	37 19.4	+59.4	167.4	35 22.2	+59.5	167.7	33 24.9	+59.6	168.0	31 27.5	+59.6	168.3
1	40 15.8	59.3	166.8	38 18.8	59.5	167.2	36 21.7	59.5	167.5	34 24.5	59.6	167.9	32 27.1	59.6	168.1
2	41 15.1	59.3	166.7	39 18.3	59.4	167.0	37 21.2	59.5	167.4	35 24.1	59.5	167.7	33 26.7	59.7	168.0
3	42 14.4	59.3	166.5	40 17.7	59.4	166.9	38 20.7	59.5	167.2	36 23.6	59.6	167.6	34 26.4	59.6	167.9
4	43 13.7	59.3	166.2	41 17.1	59.4	166.7	39 20.2	59.5	167.1	37 23.2	59.5	167.4	35 26.0	59.6	167.7
5	44 13.0	+59.3	166.0	42 16.5	+59.3	166.5	40 19.7	+59.4	166.9	38 22.7	+59.6	167.3	36 25.6	+59.6	167.6
6	45 12.3	59.2	165.8	43 15.8	59.4	166.3	41 19.1	59.5	166.7	39 22.3	59.5	167.1	37 25.2	59.6	167.4
7	46 11.5	59.2	165.6	44 15.2	59.3	166.1	42 18.6	59.4	166.5	40 21.8	59.5	166.9	38 24.8	59.6	167.3
8	47 10.7	59.2	165.3	45 14.5	59.3	165.9	43 18.0	59.4	166.3	41 21.3	59.5	166.8	39 24.4	59.5	167.1
9	48 09.9	59.1	165.1	46 13.8	59.2	165.6	44 17.4	59.4	166.1	42 20.8	59.1	166.6	40 23.9	59.6	167.0
10	49 09.0	+59.1	164.8	47 13.0	+59.2	165.4	45 16.8	+59.3	165.9	43 20.2	+59.5	166.4	41 23.5	+59.5	166.7
11	50 08.1	59.1	164.6	48 12.3	59.2	165.2	46 16.1	59.3	165.7	44 19.7	59.4	166.2	42 23.0	59.6	166.6
12	51 07.2	59.0	164.3	49 11.5	59.2	164.9	47 15.4	59.3	165.5	45 19.1	59.4	166.0	43 22.6	59.5	166.5
13	52 06.2	59.0	164.0	50 10.7	59.1	164.6	48 14.7	59.3	165.3	46 18.5	59.4	165.8	44 22.1	59.5	166.3
14	53 05.2	58.9	163.7	51 09.8	59.1	164.4	49 14.0	59.3	165.0	47 17.9	59.3	165.6	45 21.6	59.4	166.1
15	54 04.1	+58.9	163.4	52 08.9	+59.1	164.1	50 13.3	+59.2	164.8	48 17.3	+59.3	165.4	46 21.0	+59.5	165.9
16	55 03.0	58.8	163.1	53 08.0	59.0	163.8	51 12.5	59.2	164.5	49 16.6	59.3	165.2	47 20.5	59.4	165.7
17	56 01.8	58.8	162.7	54 07.0	59.0	163.5	52 11.7	59.1	164.3	50 16.0	59.3	164.9	48 19.9	59.4	165.5
18	57 00.6	58.7	162.3	55 05.9	59.0	163.2	53 10.8	59.1	164.0	51 15.3	59.2	164.7	49 19.3	59.4	165.3
19	57 59.3	58.6	162.0	56 04.9	58.8	162.9	54 09.9	59.1	163.7	52 14.5	59.2	164.4	50 18.7	59.4	165.1
20	58 57.9	+58.5	161.5	57 03.7	+58.8	162.5	55 09.0	+59.0	163.4	53 13.7	+59.2	164.2	51 18.1	+59.3	164.9
21	59 56.4	58.5	161.1	58 02.5	58.7	162.2	56 08.0	58.9	163.1	54 12.9	59.2	163.9	52 17.4	59.3	164.6
22	60 54.9	58.3	160.7	59 01.2	58.7	161.8	57 06.9	58.9	162.8	55 12.1	59.1	163.6	53 16.7	59.3	164.3
23	61 53.2	58.2	160.2	59 59.9	58.6	161.4	58 05.8	58.9	162.4	56 11.2	59.0	163.3	54 16.0	59.2	164.1
24	62 51.4	58.1	159.7	60 58.5	58.4	160.9	59 04.7	58.7	162.0	57 10.2	59.0	163.0	55 15.2	59.2	163.8
25	63 49.5	+58.0	159.1	61 56.9	+58.4	160.4	60 03.4	+58.7	161.6	58 09.2	+59.0	162.6	56 14.4	+59.2	163.5
26	64 47.5	57.8	158.5	62 55.3	58.3	159.9	61 02.1	58.7	161.2	59 08.2	58.9	162.3	57 13.6	59.1	163.2
27	65 45.3	57.7	157.9	63 52.6	58.1	159.4	62 00.8	58.5	160.7	60 07.1	58.8	161.9	58 12.7	59.0	162.9
28	66 43.0	57.5	157.2	64 51.7	58.0	158.8	62 59.3	58.3	160.3	61 05.9	58.7	161.5	59 11.7	59.0	162.6
29	67 40.5	57.2	156.4	65 49.7	57.8	158.2	63 57.7	58.3	159.8	62 04.6	58.7	161.1	60 10.7	58.9	162.2

40°			42°			44°			46°			48°			Dec.
Hc	d	Z	Hc	d	Z	Hc	d	Z	Hc	d	Z	Hc	d	Z	
48 58.4	-58.8	164.7	47 02.5	-58.9	165.2	45 06.3	-59.0	165.8	43 09.9	-59.2	166.2	41 13.3	-59.3	166.7	0
47 59.6	58.8	165.0	46 03.6	59.0	165.5	44 07.3	59.1	166.0	42 10.7	59.2	166.5	40 14.0	59.3	166.9	1
47 00.8	58.9	165.3	45 04.6	59.0	165.8	43 08.2	59.1	166.2	41 11.5	59.2	166.7	39 14.7	59.4	167.1	2
46 01.9	58.9	165.5	44 05.6	59.0	166.0	42 09.1	59.2	166.5	40 12.3	59.3	166.9	38 15.3	59.3	167.2	3
45 03.0	58.9	165.8	43 06.6	59.1	166.3	41 09.9	59.2	166.7	39 13.0	59.3	167.1	37 16.0	59.4	167.4	4
44 04.1	-59.0	166.1	42 07.5	-59.1	166.5	40 10.7	-59.2	166.9	38 13.7	-59.3	167.3	36 16.6	-59.4	167.6	5
43 05.1	59.0	166.3	41 08.4	59.1	166.7	39 11.5	59.2	167.1	37 14.4	59.3	167.5	35 17.2	59.4	167.8	6
42 06.1	59.0	166.6	40 09.3	59.2	167.0	38 12.3	59.3	167.3	36 15.1	59.3	167.7	34 17.8	59.4	168.0	7
41 07.1	59.1	166.8	39 10.1	59.1	167.2	37 13.0	59.2	167.5	35 15.8	59.4	167.8	33 18.4	59.4	168.1	8
40 08.0	59.1	167.0	38 11.0	59.2	167.4	36 13.8	59.3	167.7	34 16.4	59.3	168.0	32 19.0	59.4	168.3	9
39 08.9	-59.1	167.3	37 11.8	-59.3	167.6	35 14.5	-59.3	167.9	33 17.1	-59.4	168.2	31 19.6	-59.5	168.5	10
38 09.8	59.2	167.5	36 12.5	59.2	167.8	34 15.2	59.3	168.1	32 17.7	59.4	168.4	30 20.1	59.4	168.6	11
37 10.6	59.2	167.7	35 13.3	59.3	168.0	33 15.9	59.4	168.3	31 18.3	59.4	168.5	29 20.7	59.5	168.8	12
36 11.4	59.1	167.9	34 14.0	59.2	168.2	32 16.5	59.3	168.5	30 18.9	59.4	168.7	28 21.2	59.5	168.9	13
35 12.3	59.1	168.1	33 14.8	59.3	168.4	31 17.2	59.4	168.6	29 19.5	59.4	168.9	27 21.7	59.5	169.1	14
34 13.0	-59.2	168.3	32 15.5	-59.3	168.6	30 17.8	-59.4	168.8	28 20.1	-59.5	169.0	26 22.2	-59.5	169.2	15
33 13.8	59.2	168.5	31 16.2	59.3	168.7	29 18.4	59.3	169.0	27 20.6	59.5	169.2	25 22.7	59.5	169.4	16
32 14.6	59.3	168.7	30 16.9	59.4	168.9	28 19.1	59.4	169.1	26 21.2	59.5	169.3	24 23.2	59.5	169.5	17
31 15.3	59.3	168.9	29 17.5	59.3	169.1	27 19.7	59.5	169.3	25 21.7	59.5	169.5	23 23.7	59.5	169.6	18
30 16.0	59.3	169.0	28 18.2	59.4	169.3	26 20.2	59.4	169.4	24 22.2	59.4	169.6	22 24.2	59.5	169.8	19
29 16.7	-59.3	169.2	27 18.8	-59.3	169.4	25 20.8	-59.4	169.6	23 22.8	-59.5	169.8	21 24.7	-59.6	169.9	20
28 17.4	59.3	169.4	26 19.5	59.4	169.6	24 21.4	59.4	169.7	22 23.3	59.5	169.9	20 25.1	59.5	170.0	21
27 18.1	59.3	169.6	25 20.1	59.4	169.7	23 22.0	59.5	169.9	21 23.8	59.5	170.0	19 25.6	59.6	170.2	22
26 18.8	59.3	169.7	24 20.7	59.4	169.9	22 22.5	59.4	170.0	20 24.3	59.5	170.2	18 26.0	59.5	170.3	23
25 19.5	59.4	169.9	23 21.3	59.4	170.0	21 23.1	59.5	170.2	19 24.8	59.5	170.3	17 26.5	59.6	170.4	24
24 20.1	-59.4	170.1	22 21.9	-59.4	170.2	20 23.6	-59.5	170.3	18 25.3	-59.5	170.5	16 26.9	-59.5	170.6	25
23 20.7	59.3	170.2	21 22.5	59.5	170.4	19 24.1	59.4	170.5	17 25.8	59.4	170.6	15 27.4	59.6	170.7	26
22 21.4	59.4	170.4	20 23.0	59.4	170.5	18 24.7	59.5	170.6	16 26.2	59.5	170.7	14 27.8	59.6	170.8	27
21 22.0	59.4	170.5	19 23.6	59.4	170.6	17 25.2	59.5	170.8	15 26.7	59.5	170.8	13 28.2	59.5	170.9	28
20 22.6	59.4	170.7	18 24.2	59.5	170.8	16 25.7	59.5	170.9	14 27.2	59.5	171.0	12 28.7	59.6	171.1	29

50°			52°			54°			56°			58°			Dec.
Hc	d	Z	Hc	d	Z	Hc	d	Z	Hc	d	Z	Hc	d	Z	
39 16.4	-59.4	167.0	37 19.4	-59.5	167.4	35 22.2	-59.5	167.7	33 24.9	-59.6	168.0	31 27.5	-59.7	168.3	0
38 17.0	59.4	167.2	36 19.9	59.5	167.6	34 22.7	59.6	167.9	32 25.3	59.6	168.1	30 27.8	59.6	168.4	1
37 17.6	59.4	167.4	35 20.4	59.4	167.7	33 23.1	59.5	168.0	31 25.7	59.6	168.3	29 28.1	59.6	168.5	2
36 18.2	59.4	167.7	34 21.0	59.5	167.9	32 23.6	59.6	168.1	30 26.1	59.6	168.4	28 28.5	59.7	168.6	3
35 18.8	59.5	167.7	33 21.5	59.6	168.0	31 24.0	59.6	168.3	29 26.5	59.7	168.5	27 28.8	59.7	168.7	4
34 19.3	-59.4	167.9	32 21.9	-59.5	168.2	30 24.4	-59.5	168.4	28 26.8	-59.6	168.7	26 29.1	-59.7	168.9	5
33 19.9	59.5	168.1	31 22.4	59.5	168.3	29 24.9	59.6	168.6	27 27.2	59.7	168.8	25 29.4	59.6	169.0	6
32 20.4	59.5	168.2	30 22.9	59.6	168.5	28 25.3	59.6	168.7	26 27.5	59.6	168.9	24 29.8	59.7	169.1	7
31 20.9	59.5	168.4	29 23.3	59.5	168.6	27 25.7	59.6	168.8	25 27.9	59.6	169.0	23 30.1	59.7	169.2	8
30 21.4	59.5	168.5	28 23.8	59.6	168.8	26 26.1	59.7	169.0	24 28.2	59.6	169.1	22 30.4	59.7	169.3	9
29 21.9	-59.5	168.7	27 24.2	-59.5	168.9	25 26.4	-59.6	169.1	23 28.6	-59.7	169.3	21 30.7	-59.8	169.4	10
28 22.4	59.5	168.8	26 24.7	59.6	169.0	24 26.8	59.6	169.2	22 28.9	59.7	169.4	20 30.9	59.7	169.5	11
27 22.9	59.5	169.0	25 25.1	59.6	169.2	23 27.2	59.6	169.3	21 29.2	59.6	169.5	19 31.2	59.7	169.6	12
26 23.4	59.5	169.1	24 25.5	59.6	169.3	22 27.6	59.7	169.5	20 29.6	59.7	169.6	18 31.5	59.7	169.7	13
25 23.9	59.6	169.3	23 25.9	59.6	169.4	21 27.9	59.6	169.6	19 29.9	59.7	169.7	17 31.8	59.7	169.8	14
24 24.3	-59.5	169.4	22 26.3	-59.6	169.5	20 28.3	-59.7	169.7	18 30.2	-59.7	169.8	16 32.1	-59.7	169.9	15
23 24.8	59.6	169.6	21 26.7	59.6	169.7	19 28.6	59.6	169.8	17 30.5	59.7	169.9	15 32.4	59.8	170.0	16
22 25.2	59.6	169.7	20 27.1	59.6	169.8	18 29.0	59.7	169.9	16 30.8	59.7	170.0	14 32.6	59.7	170.1	17
21 25.6	59.5	169.8	19 27.5	59.6	169.9	17 29.3	59.7	170.0	15 31.1	59.7	170.1	13 32.9	59.7	170.2	18
20 26.1	59.6	169.9	18 27.9	59.6	170.0	16 29.7	59.7	170.1	14 31.4	59.7	170.2	12 33.2	59.8	170.3	19
19 26.5	-59.6	170.0	17 28.3	-59.6	170.1	15 30.0	-59.6	170.3	13 31.7	-59.7	170.3	11 33.4	-59.7	170.4	20
18 26.9	59.6	170.2	16 28.7	59.7	170.3	14 30.4	59.7	170.4	12 32.0	59.6	170.4	10 33.7	59.7	170.5	21
17 27.3	59.6	170.3	15 29.0	59.6	170.4	13 30.7	59.7	170.5	11 32.3	59.7	170.5	9 34.0	59.8	170.6	22
16 27.7	59.6	170.4	14 29.4	59.7	170.5	12 31.0	59.6	170.6	10 32.6	59.7	170.6	8 34.2	59.7	170.7	23
15 28.1	59.6	170.5	13 29.8	59.7	170.6	11 31.4	59.7	170.7	9 32.9	59.7	170.7	7 34.5	59.8	170.8	24
14 28.5	-59.6	170.6	12 30.1	-59.6	170.7	10 31.7	-59.7	170.8	8 33.2	-59.7	170.8	6 34.7	-59.7	170.9	25
13 28.9	59.6	170.8	11 30.5	59.7	170.8	9 32.0	59.6	170.9	7 33.5	59.7	170.9	5 35.0	59.7	171.0	26
12 29.3	59.6	170.9	10 30.8	59.6	170.9	8 32.3	59.7	171.0	6 33.8	59.7	171.0	4 35.3	59.8	171.1	27
11 29.7	59.6	171.0	9 31.2	59.7	171.1	7 32.6	59.6	171.1	5 34.1	59.7	171.1	3 35.5	59.7	171.2	28
10 30.1	59.6	171.1	8 31.5	59.6	171.2	6 33.0	59.7	171.2	4 34.4	59.7	171.2	2 35.8	59.8	171.3	29

Dec.	0° Hc	d	Z	2° Hc	d	Z	4° Hc	d	Z	6° Hc	d	Z	8° Hc	d	Z
°	° ′	′	°	° ′	′	°	° ′	′	°	° ′	′	°	° ′	′	°
0	78 00.0	− 2.5*	90.0	77 50.2	+ 7.6*	99.3	77 21.6	+17.0*	108.2	76 36.2	+25.3*	116.2	75 36.6	+32.2*	123.2
1	77 57.5	7.3*	85.2	77 57.8	+ 2.6*	94.6	77 38.6	12.5*	103.7	77 01.5	21.4*	112.2	76 08.8	29.0*	119.8
2	77 50.2	12.0*	80.5	78 00.4	− 2.2*	89.8	77 51.1	7.8*	99.1	77 22.9	17.2*	108.0	76 37.8	25.5*	116.0
3	77 38.2	16.6*	75.9	77 58.2	7.1*	85.0	77 58.9	+ 2.9*	94.4	77 40.1	12.7*	103.6	77 03.3	21.7*	112.1
4	77 21.6	20.8*	71.4	77 51.1	11.9*	80.2	78 01.8	− 2.1*	89.6	77 52.8	8.0*	98.9	77 25.0	17.4*	107.8
5	77 00.8	−24.6*	67.2	77 39.2	−16.3*	75.6	77 59.7	− 6.9*	84.8	78 00.8	+ 3.2*	94.2	77 42.4	+13.0*	103.4
6	76 36.2	28.2*	63.2	77 22.9	20.6*	71.2	77 52.8	11.7*	80.0	78 04.0	− 1.9*	89.4	77 55.4	8.3*	98.8
7	76 08.0	31.4*	59.4	77 02.3	24.5*	66.9	77 41.1	16.1*	75.4	78 02.1	6.7*	84.5	78 03.7	+ 3.9*	94.0
8	75 36.6	34.2*	55.9	76 37.8	28.1*	62.9	77 25.0	20.5*	70.9	77 55.4	11.5*	79.8	78 07.0	− 1.6*	89.2
9	75 02.4	36.8*	52.7	76 09.7	31.2*	59.2	77 04.5	24.4*	66.6	77 43.9	16.0*	75.1	78 05.4	6.5*	84.3
10	74 25.6	−39.0*	49.7	75 38.5	−34.2*	55.7	76 40.1	−27.9*	62.6	77 27.9	−20.4*	70.6	77 58.9	−11.4*	79.5
11	73 46.6	41.1	46.9	75 04.3	36.7*	52.4	76 12.2	31.2*	58.8	77 07.5	24.2*	66.3	77 47.5	15.9*	74.8
12	73 05.5	42.8	44.4	74 27.6	38.9*	49.4	75 41.0	34.0*	55.3	76 43.3	27.9*	62.3	77 31.6	20.2*	70.3
13	72 22.7	44.3	42.0	73 48.7	41.0	46.6	75 07.0	36.7*	52.1	76 15.4	31.1*	58.5	77 11.4	24.2*	66.0
14	71 38.4	45.8	39.8	73 07.7	42.7	44.0	74 30.3	38.9*	49.0	75 44.3	34.0*	55.0	76 47.2	27.8*	62.0
15	70 52.6	−46.9	37.8	72 25.0	−44.3	41.7	73 51.4	−40.9	46.2	75 10.3	−36.6*	51.7	76 19.4	−31.1*	58.1
16	70 05.7	48.1	35.9	71 40.7	45.7	39.5	73 10.5	42.7	43.7	74 33.7	38.9*	48.7	75 48.3	34.0*	54.6
17	69 17.6	48.9	34.2	70 55.0	46.9	37.5	72 27.8	44.3	41.3	73 54.8	40.9	45.9	75 14.3	36.6*	51.3
18	68 28.7	49.9	32.6	70 08.1	48.0	35.6	71 43.5	45.7	39.1	73 13.9	42.7	43.3	74 37.7	38.9*	48.2
19	67 38.8	50.6	31.1	69 20.1	49.0	33.9	70 57.8	46.9	37.1	72 31.2	44.3	40.9	73 58.8	40.9	45.4
20	66 48.2	−51.3	29.7	68 31.1	−49.8	32.2	70 10.9	−47.9	35.2	71 46.9	−45.7	38.7	73 17.9	−42.7	42.8
21	65 56.9	51.9	28.4	67 41.3	50.6	30.7	69 23.0	49.0	33.5	71 01.2	46.9	36.6	72 35.2	44.3	40.4
22	65 05.0	52.4	27.2	66 50.7	51.3	29.4	68 34.0	49.8	31.8	70 14.3	48.0	34.8	71 50.9	45.7	38.2
23	64 12.6	53.0	26.1	65 59.4	51.9	28.1	67 44.2	50.6	30.3	69 26.3	48.9	33.0	71 05.2	47.0	36.2
24	63 19.6	53.4	25.0	65 07.5	52.4	26.8	66 53.6	51.2	28.9	68 37.4	49.8	31.4	70 18.2	48.0	34.3
25	62 26.2	−53.8	24.0	64 15.1	−52.9	25.7	66 02.4	−51.9	27.6	67 47.6	−50.6	29.9	69 30.2	−49.0	32.6
26	61 32.4	54.1	23.1	63 22.2	53.4	24.6	65 10.5	52.5	26.4	66 57.0	51.3	28.5	68 41.2	49.9	30.9
27	60 38.3	54.5	22.2	62 28.8	53.8	23.6	64 18.0	52.9	25.3	66 05.7	51.9	27.2	67 51.3	50.6	29.4
28	59 43.8	54.9	21.4	61 35.0	54.1	22.7	63 25.1	53.4	24.2	65 13.8	52.5	26.0	67 00.7	51.3	28.0
29	58 48.9	55.0	20.6	60 40.9	54.5	21.8	62 31.7	53.8	23.2	64 21.3	52.9	24.8	66 09.4	51.9	26.7

Dec.	10° Hc	d	Z	12° Hc	d	Z	14° Hc	d	Z	16° Hc	d	Z	18° Hc	d	Z
°	° ′	′	°	° ′	′	°	° ′	′	°	° ′	′	°	° ′	′	°
0	74 25.6	+37.7*	129.2	73 05.5	+42.0	134.4	71 38.4	+45.4	138.7	70 05.7	+48.0	142.4	68 28.7	+50.1	145.5
1	75 03.3	35.2*	126.3	73 47.5	40.1*	131.9	72 23.8	43.9	136.6	70 53.7	47.0	140.6	69 18.8	49.3	144.0
2	75 38.5	32.4*	123.1	74 27.6	38.0*	129.1	73 07.7	42.3	134.3	71 40.7	45.6	138.6	70 08.1	48.2	142.3
3	76 10.9	29.2*	119.6	75 05.6	35.4*	126.2	73 50.0	40.3*	131.8	72 26.3	44.2	136.5	70 56.3	47.2	140.5
4	76 40.1	25.8*	115.9	75 41.0	32.7*	123.0	74 30.3	38.2*	129.1	73 10.5	42.5	134.2	71 43.5	45.9	138.6
5	77 05.9	+22.0*	111.9	76 13.7	+29.6*	119.5	75 08.5	+35.8*	126.1	73 53.0	+40.7*	131.7	72 29.4	+44.5	136.5
6	77 27.9	17.7*	107.7	76 43.3	26.1*	115.8	75 44.3	33.0*	122.9	74 33.7	38.5*	129.0	73 13.9	42.8	134.2
7	77 45.6	13.3*	103.2	77 09.4	22.2*	111.8	76 17.3	29.9*	119.5	75 12.2	36.1*	126.1	73 56.7	41.0	131.9
8	77 58.9	8.5*	98.6	77 31.6	18.1*	107.6	76 47.2	26.4*	115.7	75 48.3	33.3*	122.9	74 37.7	38.9*	129.0
9	78 07.4	+ 3.6*	93.8	77 49.7	13.5*	103.1	77 13.6	22.6*	111.8	76 21.6	30.3*	119.4	75 16.6	36.4*	126.1
10	78 11.0	− 1.4*	89.0	78 03.2	+ 8.8*	98.5	77 36.2	+18.3*	107.5	76 51.9	+26.7*	115.7	75 53.0	+33.7*	122.9
11	78 09.6	6.4*	84.1	78 12.0	+ 3.8*	93.6	77 54.5	13.9*	103.0	77 18.6	22.9*	111.7	76 26.7	30.6*	119.5
12	78 03.2	11.2*	79.2	78 15.8	− 1.2*	88.7	78 08.4	9.0*	98.3	77 41.5	18.7*	107.4	76 57.3	27.1*	115.7
13	77 52.0	15.8*	74.5	78 14.6	6.2*	83.8	78 17.4	+ 4.1*	93.5	78 00.2	14.2*	102.9	77 24.4	23.3*	111.7
14	77 36.2	20.2*	70.0	78 08.4	11.1*	79.0	78 21.5	− 1.1*	88.5	78 14.4	9.3*	98.2	77 47.7	19.1*	107.4
15	77 16.0	−24.1*	65.7	77 57.3	−15.8*	74.2	78 20.4	− 6.0*	83.6	78 23.7	+ 4.3*	93.3	78 06.8	+14.4*	102.9
16	76 51.9	27.8*	61.6	77 41.5	20.1*	69.7	78 14.4	11.0*	78.7	78 28.0	− 0.8*	88.3	78 21.2	9.6*	98.1
17	76 24.1	31.1*	57.7	77 21.4	24.1*	65.3	78 03.4	15.7*	73.9	78 27.2	6.0*	83.3	78 30.8	+ 4.6*	93.2
18	75 53.0	34.0*	54.2	76 57.3	27.8*	61.2	77 47.7	20.1*	69.3	78 21.2	10.9*	78.4	78 35.4	− 0.7*	88.1
19	75 19.0	36.6*	50.9	76 29.5	31.1*	57.3	77 27.6	24.1*	64.9	78 10.3	15.6*	73.6	78 34.7	5.8*	83.1
20	74 42.4	−39.0*	47.8	75 58.4	−34.1*	53.7	77 03.5	−27.9*	60.7	77 54.7	−20.1*	68.9	78 28.9	−10.8*	78.1
21	74 03.4	40.9	45.0	75 24.3	36.7*	50.4	76 35.6	31.1*	56.8	77 34.6	24.2*	64.5	78 18.1	15.7*	73.2
22	73 22.5	42.8	42.4	74 47.6	39.0*	47.3	76 04.5	34.2*	53.2	77 10.4	27.9*	60.3	78 02.4	20.1*	68.5
23	72 39.7	44.4	40.0	74 08.6	41.0	44.5	75 30.3	36.8*	49.9	76 42.5	31.3*	56.3	77 42.3	24.3*	64.0
24	71 55.3	45.7	37.7	73 27.6	42.9	41.8	74 53.5	39.4*	46.9	76 11.2	34.3*	52.7	77 18.0	28.0*	59.8
25	71 09.6	−47.0	35.7	72 44.7	−44.4	39.4	74 14.4	−41.1	43.9	75 36.9	−36.9*	49.3	76 50.0	−31.4*	55.8
26	70 22.6	48.1	33.8	72 00.3	45.8	37.2	73 33.3	43.0	41.3	75 00.0	39.2*	46.2	76 18.6	34.4*	52.1
27	69 34.5	49.1	32.1	71 14.5	47.1	35.2	72 50.3	44.5	38.9	74 20.8	41.3	43.4	75 44.2	37.1*	48.8
28	68 45.4	49.9	30.4	70 27.4	48.2	33.3	72 05.8	46.0	36.7	73 39.5	43.1	40.7	75 07.1	39.4*	45.6
29	67 55.5	50.6	28.9	69 39.2	49.1	31.5	71 19.8	47.1	34.6	72 56.4	44.7	38.3	74 27.7	41.5	42.8

0°			2°			4°			6°			8°			Dec.
Hc	d	Z	Hc	d	Z	Hc	d	Z	Hc	d	Z	Hc	d	Z	
78 00.0	- 2.5•	90.0	77 50.2	- 12.3•	99.3	77 21.6	- 21.2•	108.2	76 36.2	- 28.8•	116.2	75 36.6	- 34.9•	123.2	0
77 57.5	7.3•	94.8	77 37.9	16.7•	103.9	77 00.4	25.0•	112.4	76 07.4	31.9•	119.9	75 01.7	37.5•	126.4	1
77 50.2	12.0•	99.5	77 21.2	21.0•	108.4	76 35.4	28.5•	116.4	75 35.5	34.7•	123.4	74 24.2	39.6•	129.4	2
77 38.2	16.6•	104.1	77 00.2	24.8•	112.6	76 06.9	31.7•	120.1	75 00.8	37.2•	126.6	73 44.6	41.6	132.1	3
77 21.6	20.8•	108.6	76 35.4	28.3•	116.6	75 35.2	34.6•	123.6	74 23.6	39.5•	129.6	73 03.0	43.3	134.6	4
77 00.0	- 24.6•	112.8	76 07.1	- 31.6•	120.3	75 00.6	- 37.0•	126.8	73 44.1	- 41.4	132.3	72 19.7	- 44.8	137.0	5
76 36.2	28.2•	116.8	75 35.5	34.4•	123.8	74 23.6	39.3•	129.8	73 02.7	43.1	134.8	71 34.9	46.2	139.1	6
76 08.0	31.4•	120.6	75 01.1	36.9•	127.0	73 44.3	41.3	132.5	72 19.6	44.7	137.2	70 48.7	47.3	141.1	7
75 36.6	34.2•	124.1	74 24.2	39.1•	130.0	73 03.0	43.0	135.1	71 34.9	46.0	139.3	70 01.4	48.4	142.9	8
75 02.4	36.8•	127.3	73 45.1	41.1	132.8	72 20.0	44.5	137.4	70 48.9	47.2	141.3	69 13.0	49.3	144.6	9
74 25.6	- 39.0•	130.3	73 04.0	- 42.9	135.3	71 35.5	- 45.9	139.6	70 01.7	- 48.3	143.2	68 23.7	- 50.1	146.2	10
73 46.6	41.1	133.1	72 21.1	44.5	137.7	70 49.6	47.1	141.6	69 13.4	49.2	144.9	67 33.6	50.9	147.7	11
73 05.5	42.8	135.6	71 36.6	45.8	139.9	70 02.5	48.2	143.4	68 24.2	50.0	146.5	66 42.7	51.6	149.0	12
72 22.7	44.3	138.0	70 50.8	47.0	141.9	69 14.3	49.1	145.1	67 34.2	50.8	147.9	65 51.1	52.1	150.3	13
71 38.4	45.8	140.2	70 03.8	48.1	143.7	68 25.2	50.0	146.7	66 43.4	51.5	149.3	64 59.0	52.6	151.5	14
70 52.6	- 46.9	142.2	69 15.7	- 49.0	145.4	67 35.2	- 50.7	148.2	65 51.9	- 52.0	150.6	64 06.4	- 53.2	152.6	15
70 05.7	48.1	144.1	68 26.7	49.9	147.0	66 44.5	51.3	149.6	64 59.9	52.6	151.8	63 13.2	53.6	153.7	16
69 17.6	48.9	145.8	67 36.8	50.7	148.5	65 53.2	52.0	150.9	64 07.3	53.1	152.9	62 19.6	53.9	154.7	17
68 28.7	49.9	147.4	66 46.1	51.3	149.9	65 01.2	52.6	152.1	63 14.2	53.5	154.0	61 25.7	54.4	155.6	18
67 38.8	50.6	148.9	65 54.8	51.9	151.2	64 08.6	53.0	153.2	62 20.7	53.9	154.9	60 31.3	54.6	156.5	19
66 48.2	- 51.3	150.3	65 02.9	- 52.5	152.4	63 15.6	- 53.4	154.3	61 26.8	- 54.3	155.9	59 36.7	- 55.0	157.3	20
65 56.9	51.9	151.6	64 10.4	53.0	153.5	62 22.2	53.9	155.3	60 32.5	54.6	156.8	58 41.7	55.2	158.1	21
65 05.0	52.4	152.8	63 17.4	53.4	154.6	61 28.3	54.2	156.2	59 37.9	54.9	157.6	57 46.5	55.5	158.8	22
64 12.6	53.0	153.9	62 24.0	53.8	155.6	60 34.1	54.6	157.1	58 43.0	55.1	158.4	56 51.0	55.7	159.5	23
63 19.6	53.4	155.0	61 30.2	54.2	156.5	59 39.5	54.8	157.9	57 47.9	55.5	159.1	55 55.3	55.9	160.2	24
62 26.2	- 53.8	156.0	60 36.0	- 54.5	157.4	58 44.7	- 55.2	158.7	56 52.4	- 55.9	159.8	54 59.4	- 56.1	160.8	25
61 32.4	54.1	156.9	59 41.5	54.8	158.3	57 49.5	55.3	159.5	55 56.8	55.9	160.5	54 03.3	56.2	161.4	26
60 38.3	54.5	157.8	58 46.7	55.2	159.1	56 54.2	55.7	160.2	55 00.9	56.0	161.1	53 07.1	56.5	162.0	27
59 43.8	54.9	158.6	57 51.5	55.3	159.8	55 58.5	55.8	160.8	54 04.9	56.3	161.8	52 10.6	56.6	162.6	28
58 48.9	55.0	159.4	56 56.2	55.6	160.5	55 02.7	56.0	161.5	53 08.6	56.4	162.4	51 14.0	56.7	163.1	29

10°			12°			14°			16°			18°			Dec.
Hc	d	Z	Hc	d	Z	Hc	d	Z	Hc	d	Z	Hc	d	Z	
74 25.6	- 39.9•	129.2	73 05.5	- 43.7	134.4	71 38.4	- 46.7	138.7	70 05.7	- 49.1	142.4	68 28.7	- 51.0	145.5	0
73 45.7	41.7	132.0	72 21.8	45.2	136.7	70 51.7	47.9	140.7	69 16.6	49.9	144.0	67 37.7	51.6	146.9	1
73 04.0	43.5	134.5	71 36.6	46.5	138.8	70 03.8	48.8	142.5	68 26.7	50.7	145.6	66 46.1	52.2	148.2	2
72 20.5	45.0	136.8	70 50.1	47.6	140.8	69 15.0	49.8	144.1	67 36.0	51.5	147.0	65 53.9	52.7	149.4	3
71 35.5	46.3	138.9	70 02.5	48.7	142.6	68 25.2	50.6	145.7	66 44.5	52.0	148.3	65 01.2	53.3	150.6	4
70 49.2	- 47.5	140.9	69 13.8	- 49.6	144.3	67 34.6	- 51.2	147.1	65 52.5	- 52.6	149.6	64 07.9	- 53.7	151.7	5
70 01.7	48.5	142.7	68 24.2	50.4	145.8	66 43.4	51.9	148.5	64 59.9	53.1	150.7	63 14.2	54.1	152.7	6
69 13.2	49.5	144.4	67 33.8	51.1	147.3	65 51.5	52.5	149.7	64 06.8	53.6	151.8	62 20.1	54.4	153.6	7
68 23.7	50.2	146.0	66 42.7	51.8	148.6	64 59.0	53.0	150.9	63 13.2	54.0	152.8	61 25.7	54.8	154.5	8
67 33.5	51.0	147.5	65 50.9	52.3	149.9	64 06.0	53.4	152.0	62 19.2	54.3	153.8	60 30.9	55.1	155.3	9
66 42.5	- 51.7	148.8	64 58.6	- 52.9	151.0	63 12.6	- 53.9	153.0	61 24.9	- 54.7	154.7	59 35.8	- 55.4	156.1	10
65 50.8	52.2	150.1	64 05.7	53.3	152.1	62 18.7	54.2	153.9	60 30.2	55.0	155.5	58 40.4	55.6	156.9	11
64 58.6	52.8	151.3	63 12.4	53.8	153.2	61 24.5	54.6	154.9	59 35.2	55.2	156.3	57 44.8	55.8	157.6	12
64 05.8	53.2	152.4	62 18.6	54.1	154.2	60 29.9	54.8	155.7	58 40.0	55.5	157.1	56 49.0	56.1	158.3	13
63 12.6	53.7	153.4	61 24.5	54.5	155.1	59 35.1	55.2	156.5	57 44.5	55.8	157.8	55 52.9	56.2	158.9	14
62 18.9	- 54.0	154.4	60 30.0	- 54.8	155.9	58 39.9	- 55.4	157.3	56 48.7	- 56.0	158.5	54 56.7	- 56.4	159.5	15
61 24.9	54.4	155.3	59 35.2	55.1	156.7	57 44.5	55.7	158.0	55 52.7	56.1	159.1	54 00.3	56.6	160.1	16
60 30.5	54.7	156.2	58 40.1	55.3	157.5	56 48.8	55.9	158.7	54 56.6	56.3	159.7	53 03.7	56.8	160.7	17
59 35.8	55.0	157.0	57 44.8	55.6	158.3	55 52.9	56.1	159.4	54 00.3	56.6	160.3	52 06.9	56.8	161.2	18
58 40.8	55.3	157.8	56 49.2	55.8	158.9	54 56.8	56.2	160.0	53 03.7	56.6	160.9	51 10.1	57.0	161.7	19
57 45.5	- 55.5	158.5	55 53.4	- 56.0	159.6	54 00.6	- 56.5	160.6	52 07.1	- 56.8	161.4	50 13.1	- 57.2	162.2	20
56 50.0	55.8	159.2	54 57.4	56.2	160.2	53 04.1	56.6	161.2	51 10.3	57.0	162.0	49 15.9	57.2	162.7	21
55 54.2	55.9	159.9	54 01.2	56.4	160.8	52 07.5	56.7	161.7	50 13.3	57.0	162.5	48 18.7	57.3	163.2	22
54 58.3	56.2	160.5	53 04.8	56.5	161.4	51 10.8	56.9	162.2	49 16.3	57.2	163.0	47 21.4	57.5	163.6	23
54 02.1	56.3	161.1	52 08.3	56.7	162.0	50 13.9	57.0	162.7	48 19.1	57.3	163.4	46 23.9	57.5	164.0	24
53 05.8	- 56.5	161.7	51 11.6	- 56.8	162.5	49 16.9	- 57.1	163.2	47 21.8	- 57.3	163.8	45 26.4	- 57.6	164.4	25
52 09.3	56.6	162.3	50 14.8	57.0	163.0	48 19.8	57.2	163.7	46 24.5	57.5	164.3	44 28.8	57.7	164.8	26
51 12.7	56.8	162.8	49 17.8	57.0	163.5	47 22.6	57.3	164.1	45 27.0	57.6	164.7	43 31.1	57.8	165.2	27
50 15.9	56.9	163.3	48 20.8	57.2	164.0	46 25.3	57.4	164.6	44 29.4	57.6	165.1	42 33.3	57.8	165.6	28
49 19.0	57.0	163.8	47 23.6	57.3	164.4	45 27.8	57.5	165.0	43 31.8	57.7	165.5	41 35.5	57.9	165.9	29

Dec.	20° Hc	d	Z	22° Hc	d	Z	24° Hc	d	Z	26° Hc	d	Z	28° Hc	d	Z
°	° ′	′	°	° ′	′	°	° ′	′	°	° ′	′	°	° ′	′	°
0	66 48.2	+51.8	148.1	65 05.0	+53.1	150.4	63 19.6	+54.2	152.4	61 32.4	+55.1	154.1	59 43.8	+55.7	155.6
1	67 40.0	51.1	146.8	65 58.1	52.6	149.3	64 13.8	53.7	151.4	62 27.5	54.7	153.3	60 39.5	55.5	154.9
2	68 31.1	50.4	145.4	66 50.7	52.0	148.1	65 07.5	53.3	150.4	63 22.2	54.3	152.4	61 35.0	55.2	154.1
3	69 21.5	49.4	143.9	67 42.7	51.3	146.8	66 00.8	52.8	149.3	64 16.5	54.0	151.4	62 30.2	54.9	153.3
4	70 10.9	48.6	142.3	68 34.0	50.6	145.4	66 53.6	52.2	148.1	65 10.5	53.5	150.4	63 25.1	54.5	152.4
5	70 59.5	+47.4	140.5	69 24.6	+49.7	143.9	67 45.8	+51.6	146.8	66 04.0	+53.0	149.3	64 19.6	+54.2	151.4
6	71 46.9	46.2	138.6	70 14.3	48.8	142.3	68 37.4	50.8	145.4	66 57.0	52.4	148.1	65 13.8	53.7	150.4
7	72 33.1	44.8	136.5	71 03.1	47.8	140.5	69 28.2	50.0	144.0	67 49.4	51.8	146.9	66 07.5	53.2	149.3
8	73 17.9	43.1	134.2	71 50.9	46.5	138.6	70 18.2	49.1	142.3	68 41.2	51.1	145.5	67 00.7	52.7	148.2
9	74 01.0	41.4	131.8	72 37.4	45.1	136.6	71 07.3	48.0	140.6	69 32.3	50.3	144.0	67 53.4	52.0	146.9
10	74 42.4	+39.2	129.1	73 22.5	+43.5	134.3	71 55.3	+46.8	138.7	70 22.6	+49.4	142.4	68 45.4	+51.4	145.6
11	75 21.6	36.8•	126.1	74 06.0	41.6	131.8	72 42.1	45.5	136.7	71 12.0	48.3	140.7	69 36.8	50.6	144.1
12	75 58.4	34.1•	123.0	74 47.6	39.6•	129.2	73 27.6	43.9	134.4	72 00.3	47.2	138.8	70 27.4	49.7	142.6
13	76 32.5	31.0•	119.5	75 27.2	37.3•	126.2	74 11.5	42.0	132.0	72 47.5	45.8	136.8	71 17.1	48.7	140.8
14	77 03.5	27.5•	115.7	76 04.5	34.5•	123.0	74 53.5	40.0•	129.3	73 33.3	44.2	134.6	72 05.8	47.5	139.0
15	77 31.0	+23.7•	111.7	76 39.0	+31.4•	119.6	75 33.5	+37.7•	126.4	74 17.5	+42.5	132.1	72 53.3	+46.2	137.0
16	77 54.7	19.4•	107.4	77 10.4	27.9•	115.8	76 11.2	34.9•	123.2	75 00.0	40.5•	129.4	73 39.5	44.7	134.7
17	78 14.1	14.8•	102.8	77 38.3	24.1•	111.8	76 46.1	31.9•	119.7	75 45.5	38.1•	125.6	74 24.2	42.9	132.3
18	78 28.9	9.9•	98.0	78 02.4	19.8•	107.4	77 18.0	28.4•	115.9	76 18.6	35.4•	123.3	75 07.1	40.9•	129.7
19	78 38.8	+ 4.8•	93.0	78 22.2	15.2•	102.8	77 46.4	24.5•	111.8	76 54.0	32.3•	119.8	75 48.0	38.6•	126.7
20	78 43.6	− 0.5•	87.9	78 37.4	+10.2•	97.9	78 10.9	+20.3•	107.4	77 26.3	+28.9•	116.1	76 26.6	+35.9•	123.5
21	78 43.1	5.7•	82.8	78 47.6	+ 5.0•	92.9	78 31.2	15.5•	102.8	77 55.2	25.0•	111.9	77 02.5	32.9•	120.1
22	78 37.4	10.8•	77.8	78 52.6	− 0.3•	87.7	78 46.7	10.5•	97.9	78 20.2	20.7•	107.5	77 35.4	29.4•	116.2
23	78 26.6	15.7•	72.8	78 52.3	5.6•	82.6	78 57.2	+ 5.2•	92.8	78 40.9	15.9•	102.8	78 04.8	25.4•	112.1
24	78 10.9	20.2•	68.0	78 46.7	10.8•	77.4	79 02.4	− 0.1•	87.6	78 56.8	10.8•	97.8	78 30.2	21.1•	107.6
25	77 50.7	−24.4•	63.5	78 35.9	−15.7•	72.4	79 02.3	− 5.5•	82.3	79 07.6	+ 5.5•	92.7	78 51.3	+16.3•	102.9
26	77 26.3	28.1•	59.2	78 20.2	20.3•	67.6	78 56.8	10.8•	77.1	79 13.1	0.0•	87.4	79 07.6	11.2•	97.8
27	76 58.2	31.6•	55.2	77 59.9	24.5•	63.0	78 46.0	15.8•	72.0	79 13.1	− 5.5•	82.0	79 18.8	5.7•	92.6
28	76 26.6	34.6•	51.5	77 35.4	28.4•	58.7	78 30.2	20.4•	67.1	79 07.6	10.8•	76.7	79 24.5	+ 0.2•	87.2
29	75 52.0	37.3•	48.1	77 07.0	31.8•	54.6	78 09.8	24.8•	62.4	78 56.8	15.9•	71.5	79 24.7	− 5.4•	81.7

Dec.	30° Hc	d	Z	32° Hc	d	Z	34° Hc	d	Z	36° Hc	d	Z	38° Hc	d	Z
°	° ′	′	°	° ′	′	°	° ′	′	°	° ′	′	°	° ′	′	°
0	57 53.9	+56.3	157.0	56 02.9	+56.9	158.1	54 11.2	+57.2	159.2	52 18.6	+57.7	160.1	50 25.5	+57.9	161.0
1	58 50.2	56.2	156.3	56 59.8	56.7	157.6	55 08.4	57.2	158.7	53 16.3	57.5	159.7	51 23.4	57.9	160.5
2	59 46.4	55.9	155.6	57 56.5	56.5	157.0	56 05.6	57.0	158.1	54 13.8	57.4	159.2	52 21.3	57.7	160.1
3	60 42.3	55.6	154.9	58 53.0	56.3	156.3	57 02.6	56.8	157.6	55 11.2	57.3	158.7	53 19.0	57.7	159.7
4	61 37.9	55.4	154.1	59 49.3	56.0	155.6	57 59.4	56.6	157.0	56 08.5	57.1	158.1	54 16.7	57.5	159.2
5	62 33.3	+55.1	153.3	60 45.3	+55.9	154.9	58 56.0	+56.5	156.3	57 05.6	+57.0	157.6	55 14.2	+57.4	158.7
6	63 28.4	54.7	152.4	61 41.2	55.5	154.2	59 52.5	56.2	155.7	58 02.6	56.8	157.0	56 11.6	57.3	158.2
7	64 23.1	54.4	151.5	62 36.7	55.3	153.3	60 48.7	56.0	155.0	58 59.4	56.6	156.4	57 08.9	57.1	157.6
8	65 17.5	53.9	150.5	63 32.0	54.9	152.5	61 44.7	55.8	154.2	59 56.0	56.4	155.7	58 06.0	57.0	157.1
9	66 11.4	53.5	149.4	64 26.9	54.6	151.6	62 40.5	55.4	153.4	60 52.4	56.3	154.9	59 03.0	56.8	156.5
10	67 04.9	+52.9	148.3	65 21.5	+54.2	150.6	63 35.9	+55.2	152.6	61 48.6	+55.9	154.3	59 59.8	+56.5	155.8
11	67 57.8	52.3	147.0	66 15.7	53.7	149.5	64 31.1	54.8	151.7	62 44.5	55.7	153.5	60 56.3	56.4	155.2
12	68 50.1	51.7	145.7	67 09.4	53.2	148.4	65 25.9	54.4	150.7	63 40.2	55.3	152.7	61 52.7	56.1	154.4
13	69 41.8	50.9	144.3	68 02.6	52.6	147.2	66 20.3	53.9	149.7	64 35.5	55.1	151.8	62 48.8	55.9	153.7
14	70 32.7	50.0	142.7	68 55.2	51.9	145.9	67 14.2	53.5	148.6	65 30.6	54.6	150.9	63 44.7	55.6	152.9
15	71 22.7	+49.0	141.0	69 47.1	+51.2	144.5	68 07.7	+52.9	147.4	66 25.2	+54.2	149.9	64 40.3	+55.3	152.0
16	72 11.7	47.9	139.2	70 38.3	50.4	142.9	69 00.6	52.3	146.1	67 19.4	53.8	148.8	65 35.6	54.9	151.1
17	72 59.6	46.6	137.2	71 28.7	49.4	141.3	69 52.9	51.5	144.7	68 13.2	53.2	147.6	66 30.5	54.4	150.1
18	73 46.2	45.1	135.0	72 18.1	48.3	139.4	70 44.4	50.7	143.2	69 06.4	52.6	146.3	67 24.9	54.1	149.0
19	74 31.3	43.4	132.6	73 06.4	47.0	137.4	71 35.1	49.8	141.5	69 59.0	51.9	144.9	68 19.0	53.5	147.9
20	75 14.7	+41.4•	129.9	73 53.4	+45.6	135.2	72 24.9	+48.7	139.7	70 50.9	+51.1	143.5	69 12.5	+52.9	146.6
21	75 56.1	39.1•	127.0	74 39.0	43.9	132.8	73 13.6	47.5	137.7	71 42.0	50.1	141.8	70 05.4	52.2	145.3
22	76 35.2	36.4•	123.8	75 22.9	41.9•	130.2	74 01.1	46.0	135.6	72 32.1	49.2	140.0	70 57.6	51.5	143.8
23	77 11.6	33.4•	120.3	76 04.8	39.6•	127.3	74 47.1	44.4	133.2	73 21.3	47.9	138.1	71 49.1	50.6	142.2
24	77 45.0	30.0•	116.5	76 44.4	37.0•	124.1	75 31.5	42.4•	130.5	74 09.2	46.5	135.9	72 39.7	49.6	140.4
25	78 15.0	+25.9•	112.3	77 21.4	+34.0•	120.6	76 13.9	+40.2•	127.6	74 55.7	+44.9	133.6	73 29.3	+48.4	138.5
26	78 40.9	21.6•	107.8	77 55.4	30.4•	116.7	76 54.1	37.6•	124.4	75 40.6	43.0•	130.9	74 17.7	47.1	136.3
27	79 02.5	16.8•	103.0	78 25.8	26.6•	112.5	77 31.7	34.6•	120.9	76 23.6	40.8•	128.0	75 04.8	45.4	134.0
28	79 19.3	11.5•	97.8	78 52.4	22.1•	108.0	78 06.3	31.1•	117.1	77 04.4	38.2•	124.9	75 50.2	43.6•	131.4
29	79 30.8	5.9•	92.5	79 14.5	17.1•	103.1	78 37.4	27.1•	112.8	77 42.6	35.2•	121.3	76 33.8	41.4•	128.5

20°			22°			24°			26°			28°			Dec.
Hc	d	Z	Hc	d	Z	Hc	d	Z	Hc	d	Z	Hc	d	Z	
66 48.2	-52.4	148.1	65 05.0	-53.6	150.4	63 19.6	-54.5	152.4	61 32.4	-55.3	154.1	59 43.8	-56.0	155.6	0
65 55.8	52.9	149.4	64 11.4	54.0	151.5	62 25.1	54.9	153.3	60 37.1	55.6	154.9	58 47.8	56.3	156.3	1
65 02.9	53.4	150.5	63 17.4	54.4	152.5	61 30.2	55.2	154.2	59 41.5	55.9	155.7	57 51.5	56.4	157.0	2
64 09.5	53.9	151.6	62 23.0	54.7	153.4	60 35.0	55.5	155.0	58 45.6	56.1	156.4	56 55.1	56.6	157.6	3
63 15.6	54.2	152.6	61 28.3	55.0	154.3	59 39.5	55.7	155.8	57 49.5	56.2	157.1	55 58.5	56.7	158.2	4
62 21.4	-54.6	153.5	60 33.3	-55.4	155.1	58 43.8	-55.9	156.5	56 53.3	-56.5	157.7	55 01.8	-56.9	158.8	5
61 26.8	54.9	154.4	59 37.9	55.6	155.9	57 47.9	56.2	157.2	55 56.8	56.7	158.3	54 04.9	57.1	159.4	6
60 31.9	55.2	155.2	58 42.3	55.8	156.6	56 51.7	56.4	157.8	55 00.1	56.8	158.9	53 07.8	57.2	159.9	7
59 36.7	55.5	156.0	57 46.5	56.0	157.3	55 55.3	56.5	158.4	54 03.3	56.9	159.5	52 10.6	57.3	160.4	8
58 41.2	55.7	156.7	56 50.5	56.3	157.9	54 58.8	56.7	159.0	53 06.4	57.1	160.0	51 13.3	57.4	160.9	9
57 45.5	-56.0	157.4	55 54.2	-56.4	158.6	54 02.1	-56.8	159.6	52 09.3	-57.2	160.5	50 15.9	-57.5	161.3	10
56 49.5	56.1	158.1	54 57.8	56.6	159.2	53 05.3	57.0	160.1	51 12.1	57.3	161.0	49 18.4	57.6	161.8	11
55 53.4	56.3	158.7	54 01.2	56.8	159.7	52 08.3	57.1	160.6	50 14.8	57.5	161.5	48 20.8	57.8	162.2	12
54 57.1	56.5	159.3	53 04.4	56.9	160.3	51 11.2	57.3	161.1	49 17.3	57.5	161.9	47 23.0	57.7	162.6	13
54 00.6	56.7	159.9	52 07.5	57.0	160.8	50 13.9	57.3	161.6	48 19.8	57.6	162.3	46 25.3	57.9	163.0	14
53 03.9	-56.8	160.5	51 10.5	-57.2	161.3	49 16.6	-57.5	162.1	47 22.2	-57.7	162.8	45 27.4	-58.0	163.4	15
52 07.1	57.0	161.0	50 13.3	57.2	161.8	48 19.1	57.5	162.5	46 24.5	57.8	163.2	44 29.4	58.0	163.7	16
51 10.1	57.0	161.5	49 16.1	57.4	162.3	47 21.6	57.7	162.9	45 26.7	57.9	163.5	43 31.4	58.1	164.1	17
50 13.1	57.2	162.0	48 18.7	57.5	162.7	46 23.9	57.7	163.3	44 28.8	57.9	163.9	42 33.3	58.1	164.4	18
49 15.9	57.3	162.5	47 21.2	57.5	163.1	45 26.2	57.8	163.7	43 30.9	58.0	164.3	41 35.2	58.2	164.8	19
48 18.6	-57.4	162.9	46 23.7	-57.7	163.5	44 28.4	-57.9	164.1	42 32.9	-58.1	164.6	40 37.0	-58.2	165.1	20
47 21.2	57.5	163.4	45 26.0	57.7	163.9	43 30.5	57.9	164.5	41 34.8	58.1	165.0	39 38.8	58.3	165.4	21
46 23.7	57.6	163.8	44 28.3	57.8	164.3	42 32.6	58.0	164.8	40 36.7	58.2	165.3	38 40.5	58.4	165.7	22
45 26.1	57.7	164.2	43 30.5	57.9	164.7	41 34.6	58.1	165.2	39 38.5	58.3	165.6	37 42.1	58.3	166.0	23
44 28.4	57.7	164.6	42 32.6	57.9	165.1	40 36.5	58.1	165.5	38 40.2	58.2	165.9	36 43.8	58.5	166.3	24
43 30.7	-57.8	164.9	41 34.7	-58.0	165.4	39 38.4	-58.2	165.8	37 42.0	-58.4	166.2	35 45.3	-58.4	166.5	25
42 32.9	57.9	165.3	40 36.7	58.1	165.7	38 40.2	58.2	166.2	36 43.6	58.3	166.5	34 46.9	58.5	166.8	26
41 35.0	58.0	165.7	39 38.6	58.1	166.1	37 42.0	58.2	166.5	35 45.3	58.4	166.8	33 48.4	58.6	167.1	27
40 37.0	58.0	166.0	38 40.5	58.2	166.4	36 43.8	58.4	166.8	34 46.9	58.5	167.1	32 49.8	58.5	167.4	28
39 39.0	58.1	166.3	37 42.3	58.2	166.7	35 45.4	58.3	167.1	33 48.4	58.5	167.4	31 51.3	58.6	167.6	29

30°			32°			34°			36°			38°			Dec.
Hc	d	Z	Hc	d	Z	Hc	d	Z	Hc	d	Z	Hc	d	Z	
57 53.9	-56.6	157.0	56 02.9	-57.0	158.1	54 11.2	-57.4	159.2	52 18.6	-57.7	160.1	50 25.5	-58.0	161.0	0
56 57.3	56.7	157.6	55 05.9	57.1	158.7	53 13.8	57.5	159.7	51 20.9	57.8	160.6	49 27.5	58.1	161.3	1
56 00.6	56.9	158.2	54 08.8	57.3	159.2	52 16.2	57.6	160.2	50 23.1	57.9	161.0	48 29.4	58.2	161.7	2
55 03.7	57.0	158.7	53 11.5	57.4	159.7	51 18.6	57.7	160.6	49 25.2	58.0	161.4	47 31.2	58.2	162.1	3
54 06.7	57.2	159.3	52 14.1	57.5	160.2	50 20.9	57.8	161.0	48 27.2	58.1	161.8	46 33.0	58.3	162.4	4
53 09.5	-57.3	159.8	51 16.6	-57.6	160.7	49 23.1	-57.9	161.4	47 29.1	-58.2	162.2	45 34.7	-58.4	162.8	5
52 12.2	57.4	160.3	50 19.0	57.7	161.1	48 25.2	58.0	161.8	46 30.9	58.2	162.5	44 36.3	58.5	163.1	6
51 14.8	57.6	160.8	49 21.3	57.8	161.5	47 27.2	58.0	162.2	45 32.7	58.2	162.9	43 37.9	58.5	163.4	7
50 17.3	57.6	161.2	48 23.5	57.9	161.9	46 29.2	58.2	162.6	44 34.5	58.4	163.2	42 39.4	58.5	163.7	8
49 19.7	57.7	161.6	47 25.6	58.0	162.3	45 31.0	58.2	163.0	43 36.1	58.4	163.5	41 40.9	58.6	164.0	9
48 22.0	-57.8	162.0	46 27.6	-58.0	162.7	44 32.8	-58.2	163.3	42 37.7	-58.4	163.8	40 42.3	-58.6	164.3	10
47 24.2	57.9	162.5	45 29.6	58.1	163.1	43 34.6	58.3	163.6	41 39.3	58.5	164.1	39 43.7	58.6	164.6	11
46 26.3	57.9	162.8	44 31.5	58.2	163.4	42 36.3	58.4	164.0	40 40.8	58.5	164.4	38 45.1	58.7	164.9	12
45 28.4	58.1	163.2	43 33.3	58.2	163.8	41 37.9	58.4	164.3	39 42.3	58.6	164.7	37 46.4	58.7	165.1	13
44 30.3	58.1	163.6	42 35.1	58.3	164.1	40 39.5	58.4	164.6	38 43.7	58.6	165.0	36 47.7	58.7	165.4	14
43 32.2	-58.1	163.9	41 36.8	-58.3	164.4	39 41.1	-58.5	164.9	37 45.1	-58.6	165.3	35 49.0	-58.8	165.7	15
42 34.1	58.2	164.3	40 38.5	58.4	164.7	38 42.6	58.6	165.2	36 46.5	58.7	165.6	34 50.2	58.8	165.9	16
41 35.9	58.3	164.6	39 40.1	58.4	165.0	37 44.0	58.5	165.5	35 47.8	58.7	165.8	33 51.4	58.9	166.1	17
40 37.6	58.3	164.9	38 41.6	58.4	165.3	36 45.5	58.7	165.7	34 49.1	58.8	166.1	32 52.5	58.8	166.4	18
39 39.3	58.4	165.2	37 43.2	58.5	165.6	35 46.8	58.6	166.0	33 50.3	58.7	166.3	31 53.7	58.9	166.6	19
38 40.9	-58.4	165.5	36 44.7	-58.6	165.9	34 48.2	-58.7	166.2	32 51.6	-58.8	166.6	30 54.8	-58.9	166.8	20
37 42.5	58.4	165.8	35 46.1	58.6	166.2	33 49.5	58.7	166.5	31 52.8	58.9	166.8	29 55.9	58.9	167.1	21
36 44.1	58.5	166.1	34 47.5	58.6	166.4	32 50.8	58.7	166.7	30 53.9	58.9	167.0	28 57.0	59.0	167.3	22
35 45.6	58.5	166.4	33 48.9	58.6	166.7	31 52.1	58.8	167.0	29 55.1	58.9	167.2	27 58.0	59.0	167.5	23
34 47.1	58.6	166.6	32 50.3	58.7	166.9	30 53.3	58.8	167.2	28 56.2	58.9	167.5	26 59.0	59.0	167.7	24
33 48.5	-58.6	166.9	31 51.6	-58.7	167.2	29 54.5	-58.8	167.4	27 57.3	-58.9	167.7	26 00.0	-59.0	167.9	25
32 49.9	58.6	167.2	30 52.9	58.7	167.4	28 55.7	58.8	167.7	26 58.4	58.9	167.9	25 01.0	59.0	168.1	26
31 51.3	58.6	167.4	29 54.2	58.8	167.7	27 56.9	58.9	167.9	25 59.5	59.0	168.1	24 02.0	59.0	168.3	27
30 52.7	58.7	167.6	28 55.4	58.8	167.9	26 58.0	58.9	168.1	25 00.5	58.9	168.3	23 03.0	59.1	168.5	28
29 54.0	58.7	167.9	27 56.6	58.8	168.1	25 59.1	58.9	168.3	24 01.6	59.0	168.5	22 03.9	59.0	168.7	29

Dec.	40° Hc	d	Z	42° Hc	d	Z	44° Hc	d	Z	46° Hc	d	Z	48° Hc	d	Z
0	48 31.8	+58.2	161.7	46 37.7	+58.4	162.4	44 43.1	+58.6	163.0	42 48.2	+58.8	163.5	40 52.9	+59.0	164.0
1	49 30.0	58.1	161.3	47 36.1	58.4	162.0	45 41.7	58.6	162.7	43 47.0	58.7	163.3	41 51.9	58.9	163.8
2	50 28.1	58.1	160.9	48 34.5	58.3	161.7	46 40.3	58.5	162.4	44 45.7	58.8	163.0	42 50.8	58.9	163.5
3	51 26.2	58.0	160.5	49 32.8	58.2	161.3	47 38.8	58.5	162.0	45 44.5	58.6	162.7	43 49.7	58.9	163.3
4	52 24.2	57.8	160.1	50 31.0	58.2	161.0	48 37.3	58.4	161.7	46 43.1	58.7	162.4	44 48.6	58.8	163.0
5	53 22.0	+57.8	159.7	51 29.2	+58.1	160.6	49 35.7	+58.4	161.4	47 41.8	+58.6	162.1	45 47.4	+58.8	162.7
6	54 19.8	57.7	159.2	52 27.3	57.9	160.2	50 34.1	58.2	161.0	48 40.4	58.5	161.8	46 46.2	58.7	162.4
7	55 17.5	57.5	158.8	53 25.2	57.9	159.7	51 32.3	58.2	160.6	49 38.9	58.4	161.4	47 44.9	58.7	162.1
8	56 15.0	57.4	158.2	54 23.1	57.8	159.3	52 30.5	58.2	160.2	50 37.3	58.4	161.1	48 43.6	58.6	161.8
9	57 12.4	57.3	157.7	55 20.9	57.7	158.8	53 28.7	58.0	159.8	51 35.7	58.3	160.7	49 42.2	58.6	161.5
10	58 09.7	+57.1	157.2	56 18.6	+57.6	158.3	54 26.7	+57.9	159.4	52 34.0	+58.3	160.3	50 40.8	+58.5	161.1
11	59 06.8	57.0	156.6	57 16.2	57.4	157.8	55 24.6	57.9	158.9	53 32.3	58.1	159.9	51 39.3	58.4	160.8
12	60 03.8	56.7	156.0	58 13.6	57.3	157.3	56 22.5	57.7	158.5	54 30.4	58.1	159.5	52 37.7	58.4	160.4
13	61 00.5	56.6	155.3	59 10.9	57.1	156.7	57 20.2	57.6	158.0	55 28.5	58.0	159.1	53 36.1	58.3	160.0
14	61 57.1	56.3	154.6	60 08.0	57.0	156.1	58 17.8	57.4	157.4	56 26.5	57.8	158.6	54 34.4	58.2	159.6
15	62 53.4	+56.1	153.9	61 05.0	+56.7	155.5	59 15.2	+57.3	156.9	57 24.3	+57.8	158.1	55 32.6	+58.1	159.2
16	63 49.5	55.8	153.1	62 01.7	56.6	154.8	60 12.5	57.1	156.3	58 22.1	57.6	157.6	56 30.7	58.0	158.8
17	64 45.3	55.5	152.2	62 58.3	56.3	154.1	61 09.6	57.0	155.7	59 19.7	57.5	157.1	57 28.7	57.9	158.3
18	65 40.8	55.2	151.3	63 54.6	56.0	153.3	62 06.6	56.7	155.0	60 17.2	57.3	156.5	58 26.6	57.8	157.8
19	66 36.0	54.7	150.3	64 50.6	55.8	152.5	63 03.3	56.5	154.3	61 14.5	57.1	155.9	59 24.4	57.6	157.3
20	67 30.7	+54.4	149.3	65 46.4	+55.4	151.6	63 59.8	+56.3	153.5	62 11.6	+57.0	155.2	60 22.0	+57.5	156.7
21	68 25.1	53.8	148.2	66 41.8	55.0	150.6	64 56.1	56.0	152.7	63 08.6	56.7	154.6	61 19.5	57.3	156.1
22	69 18.9	53.3	146.9	67 36.8	54.6	149.6	65 52.1	55.7	151.9	64 05.3	56.5	153.8	62 16.8	57.2	155.5
23	70 12.2	52.6	145.6	68 31.4	54.2	148.5	66 47.8	55.3	150.9	65 01.8	56.3	153.0	63 14.0	57.0	154.9
24	71 04.8	51.8	144.1	69 25.6	53.6	147.3	67 43.1	54.9	149.9	65 58.1	55.9	152.2	64 11.0	56.7	154.1
25	71 56.6	+51.1	142.6	70 19.2	+53.0	146.0	68 38.0	+54.5	148.9	66 54.0	+55.6	151.3	65 07.7	+56.5	153.4
26	72 47.7	50.0	140.8	71 12.2	52.3	144.6	69 32.5	54.0	147.7	67 49.6	55.3	150.3	66 04.2	56.2	152.6
27	73 37.7	48.9	138.9	72 04.5	51.4	143.0	70 26.5	53.3	146.4	68 44.9	54.8	149.3	67 00.4	55.9	151.7
28	74 26.6	47.6	136.8	72 55.9	50.5	141.3	71 19.8	52.7	145.0	69 39.7	54.3	148.1	67 56.3	55.6	150.7
29	75 14.2	46.0	134.5	73 46.4	49.4	139.4	72 12.5	51.9	143.5	70 34.0	53.7	146.9	68 51.9	55.1	149.7

Dec.	50° Hc	d	Z	52° Hc	d	Z	54° Hc	d	Z	56° Hc	d	Z	58° Hc	d	Z
0	38 57.4	+59.1	164.5	37 01.7	+59.2	164.9	35 05.7	+59.3	165.3	33 09.6	+59.4	165.6	31 13.3	+59.4	165.9
1	39 56.5	59.1	164.3	38 00.9	59.2	164.7	36 05.0	59.3	165.1	34 09.0	59.4	165.5	32 12.7	59.5	165.8
2	40 55.6	59.0	164.0	39 00.1	59.2	164.5	37 04.3	59.3	164.9	35 08.4	59.4	165.3	33 12.2	59.5	165.6
3	41 54.6	59.0	163.8	39 59.3	59.1	164.3	38 03.6	59.3	164.7	36 07.8	59.3	165.1	34 11.7	59.5	165.3
4	42 53.6	59.0	163.6	40 58.4	59.1	164.1	39 02.9	59.2	164.5	37 07.1	59.4	164.9	35 11.2	59.4	165.3
5	43 52.6	+59.0	163.3	41 57.5	+59.1	163.8	40 02.1	+59.3	164.3	38 06.5	+59.3	164.7	36 10.6	+59.4	165.1
6	44 51.6	58.9	163.0	42 56.6	59.1	163.6	41 01.4	59.2	164.1	39 05.8	59.3	164.5	37 10.0	59.5	165.0
7	45 50.5	58.8	162.8	43 55.7	59.0	163.3	42 00.6	59.1	163.9	40 05.1	59.3	164.4	38 09.5	59.4	164.8
8	46 49.3	58.9	162.5	44 54.7	59.0	163.1	42 59.7	59.2	163.7	41 04.4	59.3	164.2	39 08.9	59.3	164.6
9	47 48.2	58.7	162.2	45 53.7	59.0	162.8	43 58.9	59.1	163.4	42 03.7	59.2	163.9	40 08.2	59.4	164.4
10	48 46.9	+58.8	161.9	46 52.7	+58.9	162.6	44 58.0	+59.1	163.2	43 02.9	+59.3	163.7	41 07.6	+59.3	164.2
11	49 45.7	58.6	161.6	47 51.6	58.9	162.3	45 57.1	59.0	162.9	44 02.2	59.2	163.5	42 06.9	59.4	164.0
12	50 44.3	58.7	161.3	48 50.5	58.8	162.0	46 56.1	59.0	162.7	45 01.4	59.1	163.3	43 06.3	59.3	163.8
13	51 43.0	58.5	160.9	49 49.3	58.8	161.7	47 55.1	59.0	162.4	46 00.5	59.2	163.0	44 05.6	59.3	163.6
14	52 41.5	58.5	160.6	50 48.1	58.7	161.4	48 54.1	58.9	162.1	46 59.7	59.1	162.8	45 04.9	59.2	163.4
15	53 40.0	+58.4	160.2	51 46.8	+58.7	161.1	49 53.0	+58.9	161.8	47 58.8	+59.0	162.5	46 04.1	+59.2	163.2
16	54 38.4	58.4	159.8	52 45.5	58.6	160.7	50 51.9	58.9	161.5	48 57.8	59.1	162.3	47 03.3	59.2	162.9
17	55 36.8	58.2	159.4	53 44.1	58.5	160.4	51 50.8	58.7	161.2	49 56.9	59.0	162.0	48 02.5	59.2	162.7
18	56 35.0	58.2	159.0	54 42.6	58.5	160.0	52 49.5	58.7	160.9	50 55.9	58.9	161.7	49 01.7	59.1	162.4
19	57 33.2	58.0	158.5	55 41.1	58.4	159.6	53 48.3	58.6	160.6	51 54.8	58.9	161.4	50 00.8	59.1	162.2
20	58 31.2	+58.0	157.9	56 39.5	+58.3	159.2	54 46.9	+58.6	160.2	52 53.7	+58.8	161.0	50 59.9	+59.1	161.9
21	59 29.2	57.8	157.5	57 37.8	58.2	158.7	55 45.5	58.5	159.8	53 52.6	58.8	160.8	51 59.0	59.0	161.6
22	60 27.0	57.7	157.0	58 36.0	58.1	158.3	56 44.1	58.4	159.4	54 51.4	58.7	160.4	52 58.0	58.9	161.3
23	61 24.7	57.5	156.4	59 34.1	58.0	157.8	57 42.5	58.4	159.0	55 50.1	58.7	160.1	53 56.9	58.9	160.9
24	62 22.2	57.4	155.8	60 32.1	57.9	157.3	58 40.9	58.3	158.6	56 48.8	58.6	159.7	54 55.8	58.9	160.7
25	63 19.6	+57.2	155.2	61 30.0	+57.7	156.7	59 39.2	+58.1	158.1	57 47.4	+58.5	159.3	55 54.7	+58.8	160.4
26	64 16.8	56.9	154.5	62 27.7	57.6	156.2	60 37.3	58.1	157.6	58 45.9	58.4	158.9	56 53.5	58.7	160.0
27	65 13.7	56.8	153.6	63 25.3	57.4	155.5	61 35.4	57.9	157.1	59 44.3	58.3	158.4	57 52.2	58.7	159.6
28	66 10.5	56.5	153.0	64 22.7	57.2	154.9	62 33.3	57.8	156.5	60 42.6	58.3	158.0	58 50.9	58.6	159.2
29	67 07.0	56.2	152.1	65 19.9	57.0	154.2	63 31.1	57.6	155.9	61 40.9	58.1	157.5	59 49.5	58.5	158.8

LATITUDE **CONTRARY** NAME   L.H.A. 12°, 348°

40° Hc	d	Z	42° Hc	d	Z	44° Hc	d	Z	46° Hc	d	Z	48° Hc	d	Z	Dec.
48 31.8	−58.3	161.7	46 37.7	−58.5	162.4	44 43.1	−58.7	163.0	42 48.2	−58.9	163.5	40 52.9	−58.9	164.0	0
47 33.5	58.3	162.1	45 39.2	58.6	162.7	43 44.4	58.7	163.3	41 49.3	58.9	163.8	39 54.0	59.1	164.3	1
46 35.2	58.4	162.4	44 40.6	58.6	163.0	42 45.7	58.8	163.6	40 50.4	58.9	164.1	38 54.9	59.0	164.5	2
45 36.8	58.4	162.7	43 42.0	58.6	163.3	41 46.9	58.8	163.8	39 51.5	58.9	164.3	37 55.9	59.1	164.7	3
44 38.4	58.5	163.1	42 43.4	58.7	163.6	40 48.1	58.8	164.1	38 52.6	59.0	164.5	36 56.8	59.1	165.0	4
43 39.9	−58.6	163.4	41 44.7	−58.7	163.9	39 49.3	−58.9	164.4	37 53.6	−59.0	164.8	35 57.7	−59.1	165.2	5
42 41.3	58.6	163.7	40 46.0	58.8	164.2	38 50.4	58.9	164.6	36 54.6	59.0	165.0	34 58.6	59.1	165.4	6
41 42.7	58.6	164.0	39 47.2	58.6	164.4	37 51.5	58.9	164.8	35 55.6	59.1	165.2	33 59.5	59.2	165.6	7
40 44.1	58.7	164.2	38 48.5	58.9	164.7	36 52.6	59.0	165.1	34 56.5	59.0	165.5	33 00.3	59.2	165.8	8
39 45.4	58.7	164.5	37 49.6	58.8	164.9	35 53.6	58.9	165.3	33 57.5	59.1	165.7	32 01.1	59.2	166.0	9
38 46.7	−58.8	164.8	36 50.8	−58.9	165.2	34 54.7	−59.0	165.5	32 58.4	−59.1	165.9	31 01.9	−59.2	166.2	10
37 47.9	58.8	165.0	35 51.9	58.9	165.4	33 55.7	59.0	165.8	31 59.3	59.2	166.1	30 02.7	59.2	166.4	11
36 49.1	58.8	165.3	34 53.0	59.0	165.6	32 56.6	59.0	166.0	31 00.1	59.1	166.3	29 03.5	59.3	166.5	12
35 50.3	58.8	165.5	33 54.0	58.9	165.9	31 57.6	59.1	166.2	30 01.0	59.2	166.5	28 04.2	59.2	166.7	13
34 51.5	58.9	165.8	32 55.1	59.0	166.1	30 58.5	59.1	166.4	29 01.8	59.2	166.7	27 05.0	59.3	166.9	14
33 52.6	−58.9	166.0	31 56.1	−59.0	166.3	29 59.4	−59.1	166.6	28 02.6	−59.2	166.8	26 05.7	−59.3	167.1	15
32 53.7	58.9	166.2	30 57.1	59.1	166.5	29 00.3	59.1	166.8	27 03.4	59.2	167.0	25 06.4	59.3	167.2	16
31 54.8	59.0	166.5	29 58.0	59.0	166.7	28 01.2	59.2	167.0	26 04.2	59.2	167.2	24 07.1	59.3	167.4	17
30 55.8	59.0	166.7	28 59.0	59.1	166.9	27 02.0	59.2	167.2	25 05.0	59.2	167.4	23 07.8	59.3	167.5	18
29 56.9	59.0	166.9	27 59.9	59.0	167.1	26 02.9	59.2	167.4	24 05.8	59.3	167.6	22 08.5	59.3	167.7	19
28 57.9	−59.0	167.1	27 00.9	−59.1	167.3	25 03.7	−59.2	167.5	23 06.5	−59.3	167.7	21 09.2	−59.3	167.9	20
27 58.9	59.1	167.3	26 01.8	59.2	167.5	24 04.5	59.2	167.7	22 07.2	59.2	167.9	20 09.9	59.4	168.1	21
26 59.8	59.1	167.5	25 02.6	59.1	167.7	23 05.3	59.2	167.9	21 08.0	59.3	168.1	19 10.5	59.3	168.2	22
26 00.8	59.1	167.7	24 03.5	59.1	167.9	22 06.1	59.2	168.1	20 08.7	59.3	168.2	18 11.2	59.4	168.4	23
25 01.7	59.0	167.9	23 04.4	59.2	168.1	21 06.9	59.2	168.3	19 09.4	59.3	168.4	17 11.8	59.3	168.5	24
24 02.7	−59.1	168.1	22 05.2	−59.1	168.3	20 07.7	−59.2	168.4	18 10.1	−59.3	168.6	16 12.5	−59.4	168.7	25
23 03.6	59.1	168.3	21 06.1	59.2	168.4	19 08.5	59.3	168.6	17 10.8	59.3	168.7	15 13.1	59.4	168.8	26
22 04.5	59.1	168.5	20 06.9	59.2	168.6	18 09.2	59.3	168.8	16 11.5	59.3	168.9	14 13.7	59.4	169.0	27
21 05.4	59.2	168.7	19 07.7	59.2	168.8	17 09.9	59.2	168.9	15 12.2	59.4	169.0	13 14.3	59.4	169.1	28
20 06.2	59.1	168.8	18 08.5	59.2	169.0	16 10.7	59.3	169.1	14 12.8	59.3	169.2	12 14.9	59.3	169.3	29

50° Hc	d	Z	52° Hc	d	Z	54° Hc	d	Z	56° Hc	d	Z	58° Hc	d	Z	Dec.
38 57.4	−59.1	164.5	37 01.7	−59.2	164.9	35 05.7	−59.3	165.3	33 09.6	−59.4	165.6	31 13.3	−59.6	165.9	0
37 58.3	59.1	164.7	36 02.5	59.3	165.1	34 06.4	59.4	165.5	32 10.2	59.5	165.8	30 13.7	59.5	166.1	1
36 59.2	59.2	164.9	35 03.2	59.3	165.3	33 07.0	59.3	165.6	31 10.7	59.4	165.9	29 14.2	59.5	166.2	2
36 00.0	59.2	165.1	34 03.9	59.3	165.5	32 07.7	59.4	165.8	30 11.3	59.5	166.1	28 14.7	59.5	166.4	3
35 00.8	59.2	165.3	33 04.6	59.3	165.7	31 08.3	59.4	166.0	29 11.8	59.5	166.3	27 15.2	59.6	166.5	4
34 01.6	−59.2	165.5	32 05.3	−59.3	165.8	30 08.9	−59.4	166.1	28 12.3	−59.4	166.4	26 15.6	−59.5	166.6	5
33 02.4	59.2	165.7	31 06.0	59.3	166.0	29 09.5	59.4	166.3	27 12.9	59.5	166.6	25 16.1	59.6	166.8	6
32 03.2	59.3	165.9	30 06.7	59.4	166.2	28 10.1	59.4	166.5	26 13.4	59.5	166.7	24 16.5	59.6	166.9	7
31 03.9	59.3	166.1	29 07.3	59.3	166.4	27 10.7	59.5	166.6	25 13.9	59.5	166.8	23 17.0	59.6	167.0	8
30 04.6	59.3	166.3	28 08.0	59.4	166.5	26 11.2	59.4	166.8	24 14.4	59.6	167.0	22 17.4	59.6	167.2	9
29 05.3	−59.3	166.4	27 08.6	−59.4	166.7	25 11.8	−59.5	166.9	23 14.8	−59.5	167.1	21 17.8	−59.6	167.3	10
28 06.0	59.3	166.6	26 09.2	59.4	166.9	24 12.3	59.4	167.1	22 15.3	59.5	167.3	20 18.2	59.5	167.4	11
27 06.7	59.3	166.8	25 09.8	59.4	167.0	23 12.9	59.5	167.2	21 15.8	59.5	167.4	19 18.7	59.6	167.6	12
26 07.4	59.3	167.0	24 10.4	59.4	167.2	22 13.4	59.5	167.4	20 16.3	59.6	167.5	18 19.1	59.6	167.7	13
25 08.1	59.4	167.1	23 11.0	59.4	167.3	21 13.9	59.5	167.5	19 16.7	59.5	167.7	17 19.5	59.6	167.8	14
24 08.7	−59.3	167.3	22 11.6	−59.4	167.5	20 14.4	−59.5	167.6	18 17.2	−59.6	167.8	16 19.9	−59.6	167.9	15
23 09.4	59.4	167.4	21 12.2	59.5	167.6	19 14.9	59.5	167.8	17 17.6	59.5	167.9	15 20.3	59.7	168.0	16
22 10.0	59.4	167.6	20 12.7	59.4	167.8	18 15.4	59.5	167.9	16 18.1	59.6	168.0	14 20.6	59.6	168.3	17
21 10.6	59.4	167.8	19 13.3	59.4	167.9	17 15.9	59.5	168.0	15 18.5	59.6	168.2	13 21.0	59.6	168.3	18
20 11.2	59.4	167.9	18 13.9	59.5	168.1	16 16.4	59.5	168.2	14 18.9	59.5	168.3	12 21.4	59.6	168.4	19
19 11.8	−59.4	168.1	17 14.4	−59.5	168.2	15 16.9	−59.5	168.3	13 19.4	−59.6	168.4	11 21.8	−59.6	168.5	20
18 12.4	59.4	168.2	16 14.9	59.4	168.3	14 17.4	59.5	168.4	12 19.8	59.6	168.5	10 22.2	59.6	168.6	21
17 13.0	59.4	168.4	15 15.5	59.5	168.5	13 17.9	59.6	168.6	11 20.2	59.5	168.7	9 22.6	59.7	168.7	22
16 13.6	59.4	168.5	14 16.0	59.5	168.6	12 18.3	59.5	168.7	10 20.7	59.6	168.8	8 22.9	59.6	168.8	23
15 14.2	59.4	168.6	13 16.5	59.5	168.7	11 18.8	59.5	168.8	9 21.1	59.6	168.9	7 23.3	59.6	169.0	24
14 14.8	−59.5	168.8	12 17.0	−59.4	168.9	10 19.3	−59.6	169.0	8 21.5	−59.6	169.0	6 23.7	−59.7	169.1	25
13 15.3	59.4	168.9	11 17.6	59.5	169.0	9 19.7	59.5	169.1	7 21.9	59.6	169.1	5 24.0	59.6	169.2	26
12 15.9	59.4	169.1	10 18.1	59.5	169.2	8 20.2	59.5	169.2	6 22.3	59.6	169.3	4 24.4	59.6	169.3	27
11 16.5	59.5	169.2	9 18.6	59.5	169.3	7 20.7	59.6	169.3	5 22.7	59.6	169.4	3 24.8	59.7	169.4	28
10 17.0	59.4	169.3	8 19.1	59.5	169.4	6 21.1	59.5	169.5	4 23.1	59.6	169.5	2 25.1	59.6	169.5	29

Dec.	0° Hc	d	Z	2° Hc	d	Z	4° Hc	d	Z	6° Hc	d	Z	8° Hc	d	Z
°	° ′	′	°	° ′	′	°	° ′	′	°	° ′	′	°	° ′	′	°
0	76 00.0 − 2.1•		90.0	75 51.6 + 6.6•		98.0	75 27.0 +14.8•105.6			74 47.5 +22.3•112.7			73 54.9 +28.8•119.2		
1	75 57.9	6.3•	85.9	75 58.2 + 2.3•		93.9	75 41.8 10.9•101.7			75 09.8 18.7•109.2			74 23.7 25.7•116.0		
2	75 51.6	10.3•	81.8	76 00.5 − 1.8•		89.8	75 52.7 6.7•		97.7	75 28.5 15.1•105.4			74 49.4 22.6•112.6		
3	75 41.3	14.3•	77.8	75 58.7 6.0•		85.6	75 59.4 + 2.7•		93.6	75 43.6 11.1•101.5			75 12.0 19.0•109.0		
4	75 27.0	18.0•	73.9	75 52.7 10.1•		81.5	76 02.1 − 1.6•		89.5	75 54.7 7.0•	97.5		75 31.0 15.3•105.2		
5	75 09.0 −21.5•		70.1	75 42.6 −14.1•		77.5	76 00.5 − 5.8•		85.4	76 01.7 + 2.9•	93.4		75 46.3 +11.4•101.3		
6	74 47.5	24.8•	66.5	75 28.5 17.8•		73.6	75 54.7 9.9•		81.3	76 04.6 − 1.3•	89.3		75 57.7 7.4•	97.3	
7	74 22.7	27.8•	63.1	75 10.7 21.3•		69.8	75 44.8 13.8•		77.2	76 03.3 5.6•	85.1		76 05.1 + 3.1•	93.2	
8	73 54.9	30.6•	59.8	74 49.4 24.6•		66.2	75 31.0 17.6•		73.3	75 57.7 9.6•	81.0		76 08.2 − 1.1•	89.0	
9	73 24.3	33.1•	56.8	74 24.8 27.6•		62.8	75 13.4 21.1•		69.5	75 48.1 13.6•	76.9		76 07.1 5.3•	84.8	
10	72 51.2 −35.4•		53.9	73 57.2 −30.5•		59.5	74 52.3 −24.5•		65.9	75 34.5 −17.5•	73.0		76 01.8 − 9.5•	80.7	
11	72 15.8	37.4•	51.2	73 26.7 33.0•		56.5	74 27.8 27.5•		62.4	75 17.0 21.0•	69.2		75 52.3 13.4•	76.6	
12	71 38.4	39.4•	48.7	72 53.7 35.2•		53.6	74 00.3 30.3•		59.2	74 56.0 24.3•	65.6		75 38.9 17.3•	72.7	
13	70 59.0	41.0•	46.3	72 18.5 37.4•		50.9	73 30.0 32.9•		56.1	74 31.7 27.4•	62.1		75 21.6 20.9•	68.9	
14	70 18.0	42.5•	44.1	71 41.1 39.2•		48.3	72 57.1 35.2•		53.2	74 04.3 30.3•	58.8		75 00.7 24.2•	65.2	
15	69 35.5 −43.8•		42.1	71 01.9 −40.9•		46.0	72 21.9 −37.3•		50.5	73 34.0 −32.8•	55.7		74 36.5 −27.3•	61.7	
16	68 51.7	45.1•	40.2	70 21.0 42.5•		43.8	71 44.6 39.2•		47.9	73 01.2 35.1•	52.8		74 09.2 30.2•	58.4	
17	68 06.6	46.2•	38.4	69 38.5 43.8•		41.7	71 05.4 40.8•		45.6	72 26.1 37.2•	50.1		73 39.0 32.8•	55.3	
18	67 20.4	47.2•	36.7	68 54.7 45.0•		39.8	70 24.6 42.4•		43.3	71 48.9 39.2•	47.5		73 06.2 35.1•	52.3	
19	66 33.2	48.1•	35.1	68 09.7 46.1•		37.9	69 42.2 43.8•		41.3	71 09.7 40.8•	45.1		72 31.1 37.2•	49.6	
20	65 45.1 −48.8•		33.6	67 23.6 −47.2•		36.3	68 58.4 −45.0•		39.3	70 28.9 −42.4•	42.9		71 53.9 −39.1•	47.0	
21	64 56.3	49.6•	32.2	66 36.4 48.0•		34.7	68 13.4 46.1•		37.5	69 46.5 43.7•	40.8		71 14.8 40.9•	44.6	
22	64 06.7	50.3•	30.9	65 48.4 48.8•		33.2	67 27.3 47.1•		35.8	69 02.8 45.0•	38.8		70 33.9 42.4•	42.4	
23	63 16.4	50.9•	29.7	64 59.6 49.6•		31.8	66 40.2 48.0•		34.2	68 17.8 46.1•	37.0		69 51.5 43.7•	40.3	
24	62 25.5	51.4•	28.5	64 10.0 50.2•		30.5	65 52.2 48.8•		32.7	67 31.7 47.1•	35.3		69 07.8 45.0•	38.3	
25	61 34.1 −51.9•		27.4	63 19.8 −50.9•		29.2	65 03.4 −49.6•		31.3	66 44.6 −48.0•	33.7		68 22.8 −46.1•	36.5	
26	60 42.2	52.4•	26.4	62 28.9 51.4•		28.1	64 13.8 50.2•		30.0	65 56.6 48.8•	32.2		67 36.7 47.2•	34.8	
27	59 49.8	52.8•	25.4	61 37.5 51.9•		27.0	63 23.6 50.8•		28.8	65 07.8 49.6•	30.8		66 49.5 48.0•	33.2	
28	58 57.0	53.2•	24.5	60 45.6 52.3•		25.9	62 32.8 51.4•		27.6	64 18.2 50.3•	29.5		66 01.5 48.9•	31.7	
29	58 03.8	53.5•	23.6	59 53.3 52.8•		24.9	61 41.4 51.9•		26.5	63 27.9 50.8•	28.3		65 12.6 49.6•	30.3	

Dec.	10° Hc	d	Z	12° Hc	d	Z	14° Hc	d	Z	16° Hc	d	Z	18° Hc	d	Z
°	° ′	′	°	° ′	′	°	° ′	′	°	° ′	′	°	° ′	′	°
0	72 51.2 +34.2•124.9			71 38.4 +38.6 129.8			70 18.0 +42.4 134.1			68 51.7 +45.2 137.9			67 20.4 +47.7 141.1		
1	73 25.4 31.8•122.0			72 17.0 36.7•127.4			71 00.4 40.7 132.0			69 36.9 44.1 136.0			68 08.1 46.6 139.5		
2	73 57.2 29.0•119.0			72 53.7 34.5•124.7			71 41.1 39.0 129.7			70 21.0 42.6 134.0			68 54.7 45.6 137.8		
3	74 26.2 26.1•115.8			73 28.2 32.1•121.9			72 20.1 37.0•127.2			71 03.6 41.0 131.9			69 40.3 44.3 135.9		
4	74 52.3 22.8•112.4			74 00.3 29.3•118.9			72 57.1 34.8•124.6			71 44.6 39.3 129.6			70 24.6 42.9 134.0		
5	75 15.1 +19.4•108.8			74 29.6 +26.4•115.6			73 31.9 +32.4•121.8			72 23.9 +37.3•127.2			71 07.5 +41.4 131.8		
6	75 34.5 15.6•105.0			74 56.0 23.2•112.2			74 04.3 29.7•118.8			73 01.2 35.2•124.5			71 48.9 39.6 129.6		
7	75 50.1 11.7•101.1			75 19.2 19.7•108.6			74 34.0 26.7•115.5			73 36.4 32.8•121.7			72 28.5 37.7•127.1		
8	76 01.8 7.6• 97.1			75 38.9 15.9•104.9			75 00.7 23.6•112.1			74 09.2 30.0•118.7			73 06.2 35.6•124.5		
9	76 09.4 + 3.4• 93.0			75 54.8 12.1•101.0			75 24.3 20.0•108.5			74 39.2 27.1•115.5			73 41.8 33.1•121.7		
10	76 12.8 − 0.8• 88.8			76 06.9 + 7.9• 96.9			75 44.3 +16.3•104.7			75 06.3 +23.9•112.0			74 14.9 +30.5•119.5		
11	76 12.0 5.1• 84.6			76 14.8 + 3.6• 92.7			76 00.6 12.3•100.8			75 30.2 20.5•108.4			74 45.4 27.5•115.4		
12	76 06.9 9.3• 80.4			76 18.4 − 0.6• 88.5			76 12.9 8.2• 96.7			75 50.7 16.6•104.6			75 12.9 24.3•112.0		
13	75 57.6 13.3• 76.3			76 17.8 4.9• 84.3			76 21.1 + 4.0• 92.5			76 07.3 12.7•100.7			75 37.2 20.8•108.4		
14	75 44.3 17.2• 72.3			76 12.9 9.1• 80.1			76 25.1 − 0.4• 88.3			76 20.0 8.5• 96.6			75 58.0 17.0•104.5		
15	75 27.1 −20.8• 68.5			76 03.8 −13.1• 76.0			76 24.7 − 4.7• 84.0			76 28.5 + 4.2• 92.3			76 15.0 +13.0•100.5		
16	75 06.3 24.1• 64.8			75 50.7 17.1• 72.0			76 20.0 9.0• 79.8			76 32.7 − 0.2• 88.1			76 28.0 8.8• 96.4		
17	74 42.2 27.3• 61.3			75 33.6 20.7• 68.1			76 11.0 13.0• 75.6			76 32.5 4.5• 83.8			76 36.8 4.5• 92.1		
18	74 14.9 30.2• 57.9			75 12.9 24.1• 64.4			75 58.0 17.0• 71.6			76 28.0 8.8• 79.5			76 41.3 + 0.1• 87.8		
19	73 44.7 32.7• 54.8			74 48.8 27.3• 60.8			75 41.0 20.7• 67.7			76 19.2 13.0• 75.3			76 41.4 − 4.4• 83.5		
20	73 12.0 −35.1• 51.9			74 21.5 −30.2• 57.5			75 20.3 −24.1• 63.9			76 06.2 −16.9• 71.2			76 37.0 − 8.7• 79.2		
21	72 36.9 37.3• 49.1			73 51.3 32.8• 54.3			74 56.2 27.3• 60.3			75 49.3 20.7• 67.2			76 28.3 12.9• 74.9		
22	71 59.6 39.1• 46.5			73 18.5 35.1• 51.4			74 28.9 30.2• 57.0			75 28.6 24.1• 63.4			76 15.4 16.9• 70.8		
23	71 20.5 40.9• 44.1			72 43.4 37.3• 48.6			73 58.7 32.8• 53.8			75 04.5 27.4• 59.8			75 58.5 20.7• 66.8		
24	70 39.6 42.4• 41.9			72 06.1 39.2• 46.0			73 25.9 35.3• 50.8			74 37.1 30.2• 56.4			75 37.8 24.2• 62.9		
25	69 57.2 −43.8• 39.8			71 26.9 −40.9 43.6			72 50.6 −37.3• 48.0			74 06.9 −33.0• 53.2			75 13.6 −27.4• 59.3		
26	69 13.4 45.1• 37.8			70 46.0 42.5 41.3			72 13.3 39.3 45.4			73 33.9 35.3• 50.2			74 46.2 30.4• 55.9		
27	68 28.3 46.1• 36.0			70 03.5 43.9 39.2			71 34.0 41.1 43.0			72 58.6 37.5• 47.4			74 15.8 33.1• 52.6		
28	67 42.2 47.2 34.3			69 19.6 45.1 37.2			70 52.9 42.6 40.7			72 21.1 39.4 44.8			73 42.7 35.5• 49.6		
29	66 55.0 48.1 32.7			68 34.5 46.3 35.4			70 10.3 43.9 38.6			71 41.7 41.2 42.4			73 07.2 37.6• 46.8		

44

0°			2°			4°			6°			8°			Dec.
Hc	d	Z	Hc	d	Z	Hc	d	Z	Hc	d	Z	Hc	d	Z	
76 00.0	- 2.1•	90.0	75 51.6	- 10.5•	98.0	75 27.0	- 18.4•	105.6	74 47.5	- 25.5•	112.7	73 54.9	- 31.4•	119.2	0
75 57.9	6.3•	94.1	75 41.1	14.5•	102.0	75 08.6	22.0•	109.4	74 22.0	28.4•	116.2	73 23.5	34.0•	122.2	1
75 51.6	10.3•	98.2	75 26.6	18.3•	105.9	74 46.6	25.3•	113.0	73 53.6	31.2•	119.4	72 49.5	36.1•	125.0	2
75 41.3	14.3•	102.2	75 08.3	21.7•	109.6	74 21.3	28.2•	116.4	73 22.4	33.7•	122.4	72 13.4	38.2	127.7	3
75 27.0	18.0•	106.1	74 46.6	25.0•	113.2	73 53.1	30.9•	119.6	72 48.7	35.9•	125.2	71 35.2	40.0	130.2	4
75 09.0	- 21.5•	109.9	74 21.6	- 28.0•	116.6	73 22.2	- 33.5•	122.6	72 12.8	- 38.0	127.9	70 55.2	- 41.6	132.5	5
74 47.5	24.8•	113.5	73 53.6	30.8•	119.9	72 48.7	35.7•	125.5	71 34.8	39.8	130.4	70 13.6	43.0	134.7	6
74 22.7	27.8•	116.9	73 22.8	33.3•	122.9	72 13.0	37.8	128.2	70 55.0	41.4	132.7	69 30.6	44.4	136.7	7
73 54.9	30.6•	120.2	72 49.5	35.5•	125.8	71 35.2	39.6	130.7	70 13.6	42.9	134.9	68 46.2	45.6	138.6	8
73 24.3	33.1•	123.2	72 14.0	37.6•	128.5	70 55.6	41.2	133.0	69 30.7	44.2	136.9	68 00.6	46.6	140.3	9
72 51.2	- 35.4•	126.1	71 36.4	- 39.5	131.0	70 14.4	- 42.8	135.2	68 46.5	- 45.4	138.8	67 14.0	- 47.6	142.0	10
72 15.8	37.4•	128.8	70 56.9	41.1	133.3	69 31.6	44.0	137.2	68 01.1	46.5	140.6	66 26.4	48.4	143.5	11
71 38.4	39.4	131.3	70 15.8	42.6	135.5	68 47.6	45.3	139.1	67 14.6	47.4	142.3	65 38.0	49.3	145.0	12
70 59.0	41.0	133.7	69 33.2	43.9	137.6	68 02.3	46.4	140.9	66 27.2	48.3	143.8	64 48.7	49.9	146.4	13
70 18.0	42.5	135.9	68 49.3	45.2	139.5	67 15.9	47.3	142.6	65 38.9	49.1	145.3	63 58.8	50.6	147.6	14
69 35.5	- 43.8	137.9	68 04.1	- 46.3	141.3	66 28.6	- 48.2	144.2	64 49.8	- 49.9	146.7	63 08.2	- 51.1	148.9	15
68 51.7	45.1	139.8	67 17.8	47.2	142.9	65 40.4	49.0	145.6	63 59.9	50.4	148.0	62 17.1	51.7	150.0	16
68 06.6	46.2	141.6	66 30.6	48.1	144.5	64 51.4	49.8	147.0	63 09.5	51.1	149.2	61 25.4	52.2	151.1	17
67 20.4	47.2	143.3	65 42.5	49.0	146.0	64 01.6	50.4	148.3	62 18.4	51.6	150.3	60 33.2	52.6	152.1	18
66 33.2	48.1	144.9	64 53.5	49.6	147.4	63 11.2	50.9	149.5	61 26.8	52.1	151.4	59 40.6	53.0	153.1	19
65 45.1	- 48.8	146.4	64 03.9	- 50.3	148.7	62 20.3	- 51.5	150.7	60 34.7	- 52.5	152.4	58 47.6	- 53.4	154.0	20
64 56.3	49.6	147.8	63 13.6	51.0	149.9	61 28.8	52.1	151.8	59 42.2	52.9	153.4	57 54.2	53.7	154.8	21
64 06.7	50.3	149.1	62 22.6	51.4	151.1	60 36.7	52.4	152.8	58 49.3	53.3	154.3	57 00.5	54.0	155.7	22
63 16.4	50.9	150.3	61 31.2	52.0	152.2	59 44.3	52.9	153.8	57 56.0	53.7	155.2	56 06.5	54.3	156.5	23
62 25.5	51.4	151.5	60 39.2	52.4	153.2	58 51.4	53.2	154.7	57 02.3	53.9	156.0	55 12.2	54.6	157.2	24
61 34.1	- 51.9	152.6	59 46.8	- 52.8	154.2	57 58.2	- 53.6	155.6	56 08.4	- 54.3	156.8	54 17.6	- 54.9	157.9	25
60 42.2	52.4	153.6	58 54.0	53.2	155.1	57 04.6	54.0	156.4	55 14.1	54.5	157.6	53 22.7	55.0	158.6	26
59 49.8	52.8	154.6	58 00.8	53.6	156.0	56 10.6	54.2	157.2	54 19.6	54.8	158.3	52 27.7	55.3	159.3	27
58 57.0	53.2	155.5	57 07.2	53.8	156.8	55 16.4	54.4	158.0	53 24.8	55.0	159.0	51 32.4	55.5	159.9	28
58 03.8	53.5	156.4	56 13.4	54.2	157.6	54 22.0	54.8	158.7	52 29.8	55.2	159.7	50 36.9	55.6	160.5	29

10°			12°			14°			16°			18°			Dec.
Hc	d	Z	Hc	d	Z	Hc	d	Z	Hc	d	Z	Hc	d	Z	
72 51.2	- 36.4•	124.9	71 38.4	- 40.5	129.8	70 18.0	- 43.7	134.1	68 51.7	- 46.4	137.9	67 20.4	- 48.6	141.1	0
72 14.8	38.4	127.5	70 57.9	42.1	132.1	69 34.3	45.0	136.1	68 05.3	47.5	139.6	66 31.8	49.3	142.6	1
71 36.4	40.2	130.0	70 15.8	43.5	134.3	68 49.3	46.2	138.0	67 17.8	48.3	141.2	65 42.5	50.1	144.0	2
70 56.2	41.8	132.3	69 32.3	44.7	136.3	68 03.1	47.2	139.7	66 29.5	49.1	142.8	64 52.4	50.8	145.3	3
70 14.4	43.3	134.5	68 47.6	46.0	138.2	67 15.9	48.1	141.4	65 40.4	49.9	144.1	64 01.6	51.3	146.6	4
69 31.1	- 44.6	136.5	68 01.6	- 47.0	139.9	66 27.8	- 48.9	142.9	64 50.5	- 50.6	145.5	63 10.3	- 51.9	147.7	5
68 46.5	45.7	138.3	67 14.6	47.9	141.5	65 38.9	49.7	144.3	63 59.9	51.1	146.7	62 18.4	52.4	148.8	6
68 00.8	46.8	140.1	66 26.7	48.7	143.1	64 49.2	50.4	145.6	63 08.8	51.7	147.9	61 26.0	52.8	149.9	7
67 14.0	47.7	141.8	65 38.0	49.5	144.5	63 58.8	51.0	146.9	62 17.1	52.2	149.0	60 33.2	53.2	150.8	8
66 26.3	48.6	143.3	64 48.5	50.3	145.9	63 07.8	51.5	148.1	61 24.9	52.7	150.0	59 40.0	53.6	151.8	9
65 37.7	- 49.4	144.7	63 58.2	- 50.8	147.1	62 16.3	- 52.1	149.2	60 32.2	- 53.0	151.0	58 46.4	- 53.9	152.6	10
64 48.3	50.1	146.1	63 07.4	51.4	148.3	61 24.2	52.5	150.3	59 39.2	53.5	152.0	57 52.5	54.3	153.5	11
63 58.2	50.6	147.4	62 16.0	51.9	149.4	60 31.7	52.9	151.3	58 45.7	53.8	152.9	56 58.2	54.5	154.3	12
63 07.6	51.3	148.6	61 24.1	52.4	150.5	59 38.8	53.3	152.2	57 51.9	54.1	153.7	56 03.7	54.8	155.0	13
62 16.3	51.8	149.7	60 31.7	52.8	151.5	58 45.5	53.7	153.1	56 57.8	54.4	154.5	55 08.9	55.0	155.7	14
61 24.5	- 52.3	150.8	59 38.9	- 53.2	152.5	57 51.8	- 54.0	153.9	56 03.4	- 54.7	155.3	54 13.9	- 55.3	156.4	15
60 32.2	52.7	151.8	58 45.7	53.6	153.4	56 57.8	54.3	154.8	55 08.7	54.9	156.0	53 18.6	55.5	157.1	16
59 39.5	53.1	152.7	57 52.1	53.9	154.2	56 03.5	54.6	155.5	54 13.8	55.2	156.7	52 23.1	55.7	157.7	17
58 46.4	53.4	153.7	56 58.2	54.2	155.0	55 08.9	54.8	156.3	53 18.6	55.4	157.4	51 27.5	55.9	158.3	18
57 53.0	53.8	154.5	56 04.0	54.4	155.8	54 14.1	55.1	157.0	52 23.2	55.5	158.0	50 31.6	56.0	158.9	19
56 59.2	- 54.2	155.3	55 09.6	- 54.8	156.6	53 19.0	- 55.3	157.6	51 27.7	- 55.8	158.6	49 35.6	- 56.2	159.5	20
56 05.0	54.3	156.1	54 14.8	54.9	157.3	52 23.7	55.4	158.3	50 31.9	55.9	159.2	48 39.4	56.3	160.0	21
55 10.7	54.7	156.9	53 19.9	55.2	157.9	51 28.3	55.7	158.9	49 36.0	56.1	159.8	47 43.1	56.4	160.5	22
54 16.0	54.9	157.6	52 24.7	55.4	158.6	50 32.6	55.8	159.5	48 39.9	56.2	160.3	46 46.7	56.6	161.0	23
53 21.1	55.1	158.3	51 29.3	55.6	159.2	49 36.8	56.0	160.1	47 43.7	56.4	160.8	45 50.1	56.7	161.5	24
52 26.0	- 55.4	158.9	50 33.7	- 55.8	159.8	48 40.8	- 56.2	160.6	46 47.3	- 56.5	161.3	44 53.4	- 56.8	162.0	25
51 30.6	55.5	159.6	49 37.9	55.9	160.4	47 44.6	56.3	161.1	45 50.8	56.6	161.8	43 56.6	56.9	162.4	26
50 35.1	55.7	160.2	48 42.0	56.1	160.9	46 48.3	56.4	161.6	44 54.2	56.7	162.3	42 59.7	57.0	162.9	27
49 39.4	55.9	160.7	47 45.9	56.2	161.5	45 51.9	56.6	162.1	43 57.5	56.9	162.7	42 02.7	57.1	163.3	28
48 43.5	56.0	161.3	46 49.7	56.4	162.0	44 55.3	56.6	162.6	43 00.6	56.9	163.2	41 05.6	57.2	163.7	29

Dec.	20° Hc	d	Z	22° Hc	d	Z	24° Hc	d	Z	26° Hc	d	Z	28° Hc	d	Z
°	° ′	′	°	° ′	′	°	° ′	′	°	° ′	′	°	° ′	′	°
0	65 45.1	+49.6	143.9	64 06.7	+51.1	146.4	62 25.5	+52.5	148.5	60 42.2	+53.5	150.4	58 57.0	+54.5	152.0
1	66 34.7	48.9	142.5	64 57.8	50.6	145.1	63 18.0	52.0	147.4	61 35.7	53.2	149.4	59 51.5	54.1	151.2
2	67 23.6	47.9	141.0	65 48.4	49.9	143.8	64 10.0	51.4	146.3	62 28.9	52.7	148.4	60 45.6	53.8	150.3
3	68 11.5	46.9	139.4	66 38.3	49.0	142.5	65 01.4	50.8	145.1	63 21.6	52.2	147.4	61 39.4	53.4	149.4
4	68 58.4	45.9	137.7	67 27.3	48.2	141.0	65 52.2	50.1	143.8	64 13.8	51.7	146.3	62 32.8	52.9	148.4
5	69 44.3	+44.6	135.9	68 15.5	+47.3	139.4	66 42.3	+49.4	142.5	65 05.5	+51.1	145.1	63 25.7	+52.5	147.4
6	70 28.9	43.3	133.9	69 02.8	46.2	137.7	67 31.7	48.5	141.0	65 56.6	50.4	143.8	64 18.2	51.9	146.3
7	71 12.2	41.8	131.8	69 49.0	44.9	135.9	68 20.2	47.6	139.4	66 47.0	49.7	142.5	65 10.1	51.4	145.1
8	71 53.9	40.0	129.6	70 33.9	43.6	133.9	69 07.8	46.5	137.7	67 36.7	48.8	141.0	66 01.5	50.7	143.9
9	72 33.9	38.1*	127.1	71 17.5	42.1	131.8	69 54.3	45.3	135.9	68 25.5	47.9	139.5	66 52.2	50.0	142.5
10	73 12.0	+35.9*	124.5	71 59.6	+40.4	129.6	70 39.6	+44.0	134.0	69 13.4	+46.9	137.8	67 42.2	+49.1	141.1
11	73 47.9	33.6*	121.7	72 40.0	38.5*	127.1	71 23.6	42.5	131.9	70 00.3	45.7	136.0	68 31.3	48.3	139.6
12	74 21.5	30.9*	118.6	73 18.5	36.4*	124.5	72 06.1	40.8	129.6	70 46.0	44.4	134.1	69 19.6	47.2	137.9
13	74 52.4	27.9*	115.4	73 54.9	34.0*	121.7	72 46.9	39.0*	127.2	71 30.4	42.9	132.0	70 06.8	46.1	136.1
14	75 20.3	24.7*	112.0	74 28.9	31.3*	118.7	73 25.9	36.8*	124.6	72 13.3	41.2	129.8	70 52.9	44.8	134.2
15	75 45.0	+21.2*	108.3	75 00.2	+28.4*	115.4	74 02.7	+34.4*	121.8	72 54.5	+39.4	127.3	71 37.7	+43.4	132.1
16	76 06.2	17.4*	104.5	75 28.6	25.2*	112.0	74 37.1	31.8*	118.7	73 33.9	37.3*	124.7	72 21.1	41.7	129.9
17	76 23.6	13.4*	100.4	75 53.8	21.6*	108.3	75 08.9	28.9*	115.5	74 11.2	35.0*	121.9	73 02.8	39.9	127.5
18	76 37.0	9.1*	96.3	76 15.4	17.8*	104.4	75 37.8	25.6*	112.0	74 46.2	32.3*	118.9	73 42.7	37.8*	124.9
19	76 46.1	4.8*	92.0	76 33.2	13.8*	100.4	76 03.4	22.1*	108.3	75 18.5	29.3*	115.6	74 20.5	35.5*	122.1
20	76 50.9	+0.3*	87.6	76 47.0	+9.4*	96.1	76 25.5	+18.2*	104.4	75 47.8	+26.2*	112.1	74 56.0	+32.8*	119.0
21	76 51.2	-4.2*	83.2	76 56.4	5.0*	91.8	76 43.7	14.2*	100.3	76 14.0	22.5*	108.4	75 28.8	29.9*	115.7
22	76 47.0	8.6*	78.8	77 01.4	0.5*	87.4	76 57.9	9.8*	96.0	76 36.5	18.7*	104.4	75 58.7	26.6*	112.2
23	76 38.4	12.9*	74.5	77 01.9	-4.0*	82.9	77 07.7	5.2*	91.6	76 55.2	14.5*	100.3	76 25.3	23.1*	108.5
24	76 25.5	16.9*	70.3	76 57.9	8.5*	78.5	77 12.9	+0.7*	87.1	77 09.7	10.1*	95.9	76 48.4	19.1*	104.5
25	76 08.6	-20.8*	66.3	76 49.4	-12.9*	74.1	77 13.6	-3.9*	82.8	77 19.8	+5.6*	91.5	77 07.5	+14.9*	100.3
26	75 47.8	24.3*	62.4	76 36.5	17.0*	69.9	77 09.7	8.5*	78.1	77 25.4	+0.9*	86.9	77 22.4	10.5*	95.9
27	75 23.5	27.5*	58.7	76 19.5	20.8*	65.8	77 01.2	12.8*	73.7	77 26.3	-3.9*	82.3	77 32.9	5.8*	91.3
28	74 56.0	30.6*	55.3	75 58.7	24.4*	61.8	76 48.4	17.1*	69.4	77 22.4	8.4*	77.7	77 38.7	+1.1*	86.7
29	74 25.4	33.2*	52.0	75 34.3	27.8*	58.1	76 31.3	20.9*	65.2	77 14.0	12.9*	73.2	77 39.8	-3.7*	82.0

Dec.	30° Hc	d	Z	32° Hc	d	Z	34° Hc	d	Z	36° Hc	d	Z	38° Hc	d	Z
°	° ′	′	°	° ′	′	°	° ′	′	°	° ′	′	°	° ′	′	°
0	57 10.3	+55.2	153.5	55 22.3	+55.9	154.8	53 33.2	+56.4	156.0	51 43.2	+56.8	157.0	49 52.3	+57.3	158.0
1	58 05.5	55.0	152.8	56 18.2	55.6	154.2	54 29.6	56.2	155.4	52 40.0	56.7	156.5	50 49.6	57.1	157.5
2	59 00.5	54.6	152.0	57 13.8	55.4	153.5	55 25.8	56.1	154.8	53 36.7	56.6	155.9	51 46.7	57.0	157.0
3	59 55.1	54.4	151.2	58 09.2	55.1	152.8	56 21.9	55.8	154.1	54 33.3	56.4	155.4	52 43.7	56.9	156.5
4	60 49.5	54.0	150.3	59 04.3	54.9	152.0	57 17.7	55.6	153.5	55 29.7	56.2	154.8	53 40.6	56.7	156.0
5	61 43.5	+53.6	149.4	59 59.2	+54.6	151.2	58 13.3	+55.3	152.8	56 25.9	+56.0	154.2	54 37.3	+56.6	155.4
6	62 37.1	53.2	148.5	60 53.8	54.2	150.4	59 08.6	55.1	152.0	57 21.9	55.8	153.5	55 33.9	56.4	154.8
7	63 30.3	52.7	147.4	61 48.0	53.9	149.5	60 03.7	54.8	151.2	58 17.7	55.6	152.8	56 30.3	56.2	154.2
8	64 23.0	52.2	146.4	62 41.9	53.4	148.5	60 58.5	54.5	150.4	59 13.3	55.3	152.1	57 26.5	56.0	153.6
9	65 15.2	51.7	145.2	63 35.3	53.0	147.5	61 53.0	54.1	149.5	60 08.6	55.0	151.3	58 22.5	55.8	152.9
10	66 06.9	+51.0	144.0	64 28.3	+52.5	146.4	62 47.1	+53.7	148.6	61 03.6	+54.7	150.5	59 18.3	+55.5	152.2
11	66 57.9	50.3	142.6	65 20.8	52.0	145.3	63 40.8	53.3	147.6	61 58.3	54.4	149.6	60 13.8	55.3	151.4
12	67 48.2	49.5	141.2	66 12.8	51.3	144.1	64 34.1	52.8	146.6	62 52.7	54.0	148.7	61 09.1	55.0	150.6
13	68 37.7	48.7	139.7	67 04.1	50.7	142.8	65 26.9	52.3	145.4	63 46.7	53.6	147.8	62 04.1	54.6	149.8
14	69 26.4	47.6	138.1	67 54.8	49.9	141.4	66 19.2	51.6	144.2	64 40.3	53.1	146.7	62 58.7	54.3	148.9
15	70 14.0	+46.5	136.3	68 44.7	+49.0	139.9	67 10.8	+51.0	142.9	65 33.4	+52.6	145.6	63 53.0	+53.8	147.9
16	71 00.5	45.3	134.4	69 33.7	48.0	138.2	68 01.8	50.3	141.6	66 26.0	52.0	144.4	64 46.8	53.5	146.9
17	71 45.8	43.8	132.3	70 21.7	47.0	136.5	68 52.1	49.4	140.1	67 18.0	51.4	143.2	65 40.3	52.9	145.8
18	72 29.6	42.2	130.1	71 08.7	45.7	134.6	69 41.5	48.5	138.5	68 09.4	50.6	141.8	66 33.2	52.4	144.7
19	73 11.8	40.4	127.7	71 54.4	44.3	132.6	70 30.0	47.4	136.7	69 00.0	49.9	140.3	67 25.6	51.7	143.4
20	73 52.2	+38.3	125.1	72 38.7	+42.7	130.3	71 17.4	+46.2	134.9	69 49.9	+48.9	138.8	68 17.3	+51.1	142.1
21	74 30.5	36.0*	122.3	73 21.4	41.0	127.9	72 03.6	44.8	132.8	70 38.8	47.9	137.0	69 08.4	50.3	140.6
22	75 06.5	33.4*	119.2	74 02.4	38.9*	125.3	72 48.4	43.3	130.6	71 26.7	46.6	135.2	69 58.7	49.3	139.1
23	75 39.9	30.5*	115.9	74 41.3	36.5*	122.5	73 31.7	41.5	128.2	72 13.3	45.4	133.2	70 48.0	48.4	137.4
24	76 10.4	27.1*	112.4	75 17.8	33.8*	119.5	74 13.2	39.4*	125.6	72 58.7	43.8	131.0	71 36.4	47.2	135.5
25	76 37.5	+23.6*	108.6	75 51.8	+31.0*	116.1	74 52.6	+37.2*	122.8	73 42.5	+42.1	128.6	72 23.6	+45.9	133.5
26	77 01.1	19.6*	104.5	76 22.8	27.8*	112.6	75 29.8	34.6*	119.7	74 24.6	40.1*	126.0	73 09.5	44.4	131.4
27	77 20.7	15.4*	100.3	76 50.6	24.1*	108.7	76 04.4	31.6*	116.4	75 04.7	37.8*	123.2	73 53.9	42.7	129.0
28	77 36.1	10.8*	95.8	77 14.7	20.1*	104.7	76 36.0	28.4*	112.8	75 42.5	35.2*	120.1	74 36.6	40.7*	126.4
29	77 46.9	6.1*	91.2	77 34.8	15.8*	100.3	77 04.4	24.7*	108.9	76 17.7	32.3*	116.7	75 17.3	38.5*	123.6

LATITUDE **CONTRARY** NAME   L.H.A. 14°, 346°

20° Hc	d	Z	22° Hc	d	Z	24° Hc	d	Z	26° Hc	d	Z	28° Hc	d	Z	Dec.
65 45.1	−50.3	143.9	64 06.7	−51.8	146.4	62 25.5	−52.9	148.5	60 42.2	−53.9	150.4	58 57.0	−54.7	152.0	0
64 54.8	50.9	145.2	63 14.9	52.3	147.5	61 32.6	53.4	149.5	59 48.3	54.3	151.3	58 02.3	55.1	152.8	1
64 03.9	51.6	146.4	62 22.6	52.7	148.6	60 39.2	53.7	150.4	58 54.0	54.6	152.1	57 07.2	55.3	153.6	2
63 12.3	52.0	147.6	61 29.9	53.2	149.6	59 45.5	54.1	151.3	57 59.4	54.8	152.9	56 11.9	55.5	154.3	3
62 20.3	52.6	148.7	60 36.7	53.5	150.5	58 51.4	54.4	152.2	57 04.6	55.2	153.6	55 16.4	55.7	154.9	4
61 27.7	−53.0	149.7	59 43.2	−53.9	151.4	57 57.0	−54.7	153.0	56 09.4	−55.3	154.4	54 20.7	−55.9	155.6	5
60 34.7	53.3	150.7	58 49.3	54.3	152.3	57 02.3	54.9	153.8	55 14.1	55.6	155.0	53 24.8	56.1	156.2	6
59 41.4	53.8	151.6	57 55.0	54.5	153.1	56 07.4	55.2	154.5	54 18.5	55.8	155.7	52 28.7	56.3	156.8	7
58 47.6	54.1	152.5	57 00.5	54.8	153.9	55 12.2	55.5	155.2	53 22.7	55.9	156.3	51 32.4	56.4	157.3	8
57 53.5	54.3	153.3	56 05.7	55.0	154.6	54 16.7	55.6	155.8	52 26.8	56.2	156.9	50 36.0	56.6	157.9	9
56 59.2	−54.7	154.1	55 10.7	−55.3	155.3	53 21.1	−55.8	156.5	51 30.6	−56.3	157.5	49 39.4	−56.7	158.4	10
56 04.5	54.9	154.8	54 15.4	55.5	156.0	52 25.3	56.0	157.1	50 34.3	56.4	158.0	48 42.7	56.8	158.9	11
55 09.6	55.2	155.5	53 19.9	55.7	156.7	51 29.3	56.2	157.7	49 37.9	56.6	158.6	47 45.9	57.0	159.4	12
54 14.4	55.4	156.2	52 24.2	55.9	157.3	50 33.1	56.3	158.2	48 41.3	56.7	159.1	46 48.9	57.0	159.9	13
53 19.0	55.6	156.9	51 28.3	56.1	157.9	49 36.8	56.5	158.8	47 44.6	56.8	159.6	45 51.9	57.2	160.3	14
52 23.4	−55.7	157.5	50 32.2	−56.2	158.4	48 40.3	−56.6	159.3	46 47.8	−57.0	160.0	44 54.7	−57.2	160.7	15
51 27.7	56.0	158.1	49 36.0	56.4	159.0	47 43.7	56.8	159.8	45 50.8	57.0	160.5	43 57.5	57.4	161.2	16
50 31.7	56.1	158.7	48 39.6	56.5	159.5	46 46.9	56.8	160.3	44 53.8	57.2	160.9	43 00.1	57.4	161.6	17
49 35.6	56.3	159.2	47 43.1	56.6	160.0	45 50.1	57.0	160.7	43 56.6	57.2	161.4	42 02.7	57.5	162.0	18
48 39.3	56.4	159.7	46 46.5	56.8	160.5	44 53.1	57.0	161.2	42 59.4	57.4	161.8	41 05.2	57.6	162.3	19
47 42.9	−56.5	160.3	45 49.7	−56.8	161.0	43 56.1	−57.2	161.6	42 02.0	−57.4	162.2	40 07.6	−57.6	162.7	20
46 46.4	56.7	160.7	44 52.9	57.0	161.4	42 58.9	57.2	162.0	41 04.6	57.5	162.6	39 10.0	57.7	163.1	21
45 49.7	56.7	161.2	43 55.9	57.0	161.9	42 01.7	57.3	162.4	40 07.1	57.5	162.9	38 12.3	57.8	163.4	22
44 53.0	56.9	161.7	42 58.9	57.2	162.3	41 04.4	57.4	162.8	39 09.6	57.6	163.3	37 14.5	57.8	163.8	23
43 56.1	57.0	162.1	42 01.7	57.2	162.7	40 07.0	57.5	163.2	38 12.0	57.7	163.7	36 16.7	57.9	164.1	24
42 59.1	−57.1	162.6	41 04.5	−57.4	163.1	39 09.5	−57.5	163.6	37 14.3	−57.8	164.0	35 18.8	−57.9	164.4	25
42 02.0	57.1	163.0	40 07.1	57.4	163.5	38 12.0	57.6	163.9	36 16.5	57.8	164.4	34 20.9	58.0	164.7	26
41 04.9	57.3	163.4	39 09.7	57.4	163.9	37 14.3	57.6	164.3	35 18.7	57.8	164.7	33 22.9	58.0	165.0	27
40 07.6	57.3	163.8	38 12.3	57.6	164.2	36 16.7	57.8	164.6	34 20.9	57.9	165.0	32 24.9	58.1	165.3	28
39 10.3	57.4	164.2	37 14.7	57.6	164.6	35 18.9	57.7	165.0	33 23.0	58.0	165.3	31 26.8	58.1	165.6	29

30° Hc	d	Z	32° Hc	d	Z	34° Hc	d	Z	36° Hc	d	Z	38° Hc	d	Z	Dec.
57 10.3	−55.4	153.5	55 22.3	−56.0	154.8	53 33.2	−56.5	156.0	51 43.2	−57.0	157.0	49 52.3	−57.4	158.0	0
56 14.9	55.7	154.2	54 26.3	56.3	155.4	52 36.7	56.8	156.5	50 46.2	57.1	157.5	48 54.9	57.4	158.4	1
55 19.2	55.9	154.9	53 30.0	56.4	156.0	51 39.9	56.8	157.1	49 49.1	57.3	158.0	47 57.5	57.6	158.8	2
54 23.3	56.1	155.5	52 33.6	56.5	156.6	50 43.1	57.0	157.6	48 51.8	57.3	158.5	46 59.9	57.6	159.3	3
53 27.2	56.2	156.1	51 37.1	56.7	157.1	49 46.1	57.1	158.1	47 54.5	57.4	158.9	46 02.3	57.8	159.7	4
52 31.0	−56.4	156.7	50 40.4	−56.9	157.6	48 49.0	−57.2	158.5	46 57.1	−57.6	159.3	45 04.5	−57.8	160.0	5
51 34.6	56.6	157.2	49 43.5	56.9	158.1	47 51.8	57.3	159.0	45 59.5	57.6	159.7	44 06.7	57.9	160.4	6
50 38.0	56.7	157.8	48 46.6	57.1	158.6	46 54.5	57.4	159.4	45 01.9	57.7	160.1	43 08.8	57.9	160.8	7
49 41.3	56.8	158.3	47 49.5	57.2	159.1	45 57.1	57.5	159.8	44 04.2	57.7	160.5	42 10.9	58.0	161.1	8
48 44.5	57.0	158.8	46 52.3	57.3	159.5	44 59.6	57.5	160.3	43 06.5	57.9	160.9	41 12.9	58.1	161.5	9
47 47.5	−57.0	159.2	45 55.0	−57.3	160.0	44 02.1	−57.7	160.6	42 08.6	−57.9	161.3	40 14.8	−58.1	161.8	10
46 50.5	57.2	159.7	44 57.7	57.6	160.4	43 04.4	57.7	161.0	41 10.7	57.9	161.6	39 16.7	58.2	162.1	11
45 53.3	57.3	160.1	44 00.2	57.6	160.8	42 06.7	57.8	161.4	40 12.8	58.1	161.9	38 18.5	58.2	162.4	12
44 56.0	57.3	160.6	43 02.6	57.6	161.2	41 08.9	57.9	161.8	39 14.7	58.1	162.3	37 20.3	58.3	162.8	13
43 58.7	57.5	161.0	42 05.0	57.7	161.6	40 11.0	57.9	162.1	38 16.6	58.1	162.6	36 22.0	58.3	163.1	14
43 01.2	−57.5	161.4	41 07.3	−57.7	161.9	39 13.1	−58.0	162.4	37 18.5	−58.2	162.9	35 23.7	−58.4	163.3	15
42 03.7	57.6	161.7	40 09.6	57.9	162.3	38 15.1	58.0	162.8	36 20.3	58.2	163.2	34 25.3	58.4	163.6	16
41 06.1	57.7	162.1	39 11.7	57.9	162.6	37 17.1	58.1	163.1	35 22.1	58.3	163.5	33 26.9	58.4	163.9	17
40 08.4	57.7	162.5	38 13.8	58.0	163.0	36 19.0	58.2	163.4	34 23.8	58.3	163.8	32 28.5	58.5	164.2	18
39 10.7	57.8	162.8	37 15.9	58.0	163.3	35 20.8	58.1	163.7	33 25.5	58.3	164.1	31 30.0	58.5	164.4	19
38 12.9	−57.9	163.2	36 17.9	−58.0	163.6	34 22.7	−58.3	164.0	32 27.2	−58.4	164.4	30 31.5	−58.5	164.7	20
37 15.0	57.9	163.5	35 19.9	58.1	163.9	33 24.4	58.2	164.3	31 28.8	58.4	164.6	29 33.0	58.5	165.0	21
36 17.1	57.9	163.8	34 21.8	58.2	164.2	32 26.2	58.3	164.6	30 30.4	58.4	164.9	28 34.5	58.6	165.2	22
35 19.2	58.0	164.2	33 23.6	58.2	164.5	31 27.9	58.4	164.9	29 32.0	58.5	165.2	27 35.9	58.6	165.4	23
34 21.2	58.1	164.5	32 25.4	58.2	164.8	30 29.5	58.3	165.1	28 33.5	58.5	165.5	26 37.3	58.7	165.7	24
33 23.1	−58.1	164.8	31 27.2	−58.3	165.1	29 31.2	−58.4	165.4	27 35.0	−58.6	165.7	25 38.6	−58.6	165.9	25
32 25.0	58.1	165.1	30 29.0	58.3	165.4	28 32.8	58.5	165.7	26 36.4	58.5	165.9	24 40.0	58.7	166.2	26
31 26.9	58.2	165.4	29 30.7	58.4	165.7	27 34.3	58.4	165.9	25 37.9	58.6	166.2	23 41.3	58.7	166.4	27
30 28.7	58.2	165.6	28 32.3	58.3	165.9	26 35.9	58.5	166.2	24 39.3	58.6	166.4	22 42.6	58.7	166.6	28
29 30.5	58.3	165.9	27 34.0	58.4	166.2	25 37.4	58.5	166.4	23 40.7	58.6	166.6	21 43.9	58.7	166.8	29

Dec.	40° Hc	d	Z	42° Hc	d	Z	44° Hc	d	Z	46° Hc	d	Z	48° Hc	d	Z
°	° ′	′	°	° ′	′	°	° ′	′	°	° ′	′	°	° ′	′	°
0	48 00.7	+57.7	158.8	46 08.6	+57.9	159.6	44 15.9	+58.1	160.3	42 22.7	+58.4	160.9	40 29.1	+58.6	161.5
1	48 58.4	57.5	158.4	47 06.5	57.8	159.2	45 14.0	58.1	159.9	43 21.1	58.4	160.6	41 27.7	58.6	161.2
2	49 55.9	57.4	157.9	48 04.3	57.8	158.8	46 12.1	58.1	159.6	44 19.5	58.2	160.2	42 26.3	58.5	160.9
3	50 53.3	57.3	157.5	49 02.1	57.6	158.4	47 10.2	57.9	159.2	45 17.7	58.3	159.9	43 24.8	58.5	160.6
4	51 50.6	57.1	157.0	49 59.7	57.6	158.0	48 08.1	57.9	158.8	46 16.0	58.1	159.6	44 23.3	58.4	160.3
5	52 47.7	+57.1	156.5	50 57.3	+57.4	157.5	49 06.0	+57.8	158.4	47 14.1	+58.1	159.2	45 21.7	+58.3	159.9
6	53 44.8	56.9	156.0	51 54.7	57.4	157.0	50 03.8	57.7	158.0	48 12.2	58.1	158.8	46 20.0	58.3	159.6
7	54 41.7	56.7	155.5	52 52.1	57.2	156.6	51 01.5	57.6	157.6	49 10.3	57.9	158.5	47 18.3	58.3	159.3
8	55 38.4	56.5	154.9	53 49.3	57.0	156.1	51 59.1	57.5	157.1	50 08.2	57.9	158.1	48 16.6	58.1	158.9
9	56 35.0	56.4	154.3	54 46.3	57.0	155.5	52 56.6	57.4	156.6	51 06.1	57.7	157.6	49 14.7	58.1	158.5
10	57 31.4	+56.3	153.7	55 43.3	+56.8	155.0	53 54.0	+57.3	156.1	52 03.8	+57.7	157.2	50 12.8	+58.0	158.1
11	58 27.7	55.9	153.0	56 40.1	56.6	154.4	54 51.3	57.1	155.6	53 01.5	57.5	156.7	51 10.8	58.0	157.7
12	59 23.6	55.8	152.3	57 36.7	56.4	153.8	55 48.4	57.0	155.1	53 59.0	57.3	156.3	52 08.8	57.8	157.3
13	60 19.4	55.5	151.6	58 33.1	56.2	153.1	56 45.4	56.8	154.5	54 56.5	57.3	155.8	53 06.6	57.7	156.9
14	61 14.9	55.2	150.8	59 29.3	56.0	152.5	57 42.2	56.6	153.9	55 53.8	57.2	155.3	54 04.3	57.6	156.4
15	62 10.1	+54.9	150.0	60 25.3	+55.8	151.7	58 38.8	+56.5	153.3	56 51.0	+57.0	154.7	55 01.9	+57.5	155.9
16	63 05.0	54.6	149.1	61 21.1	55.5	151.0	59 35.3	56.2	152.7	57 48.0	56.8	154.1	55 59.4	57.4	155.4
17	63 59.6	54.2	148.2	62 16.6	55.1	150.2	60 31.5	56.0	152.0	58 44.8	56.7	153.5	56 56.8	57.2	154.9
18	64 53.8	53.7	147.2	63 11.7	54.9	149.3	61 27.5	55.8	151.2	59 41.5	56.5	152.9	57 54.0	57.1	154.3
19	65 47.5	53.3	146.1	64 06.6	54.5	148.4	62 23.3	55.4	150.4	60 38.0	56.2	152.2	58 51.1	56.9	153.8
20	66 40.8	+52.8	145.0	65 01.1	+54.1	147.4	63 18.7	+55.2	149.6	61 34.2	+56.0	151.5	59 48.0	+56.7	153.1
21	67 33.6	52.1	143.7	65 55.2	53.6	146.4	64 13.9	54.8	148.7	62 30.2	55.8	150.7	60 44.7	56.5	152.5
22	68 25.7	51.5	142.4	66 48.8	53.1	145.3	65 08.7	54.4	147.7	63 26.0	55.4	149.9	61 41.2	56.3	151.8
23	69 17.2	50.7	141.0	67 41.9	52.5	144.1	66 03.1	54.0	146.7	64 21.4	55.2	149.0	62 37.5	56.0	151.0
24	70 07.9	49.8	139.4	68 34.4	51.9	142.8	66 57.1	53.5	145.6	65 16.6	54.7	148.1	63 33.5	55.7	150.2
25	70 57.7	+48.9	137.8	69 26.3	+51.2	141.4	67 50.6	+52.9	144.5	66 11.3	+54.4	147.1	64 29.2	+55.5	149.4
26	71 46.6	47.7	135.9	70 17.5	50.3	139.9	68 43.5	52.3	143.2	67 05.7	53.8	146.0	65 24.7	55.1	148.5
27	72 34.3	46.5	134.0	71 07.8	49.4	138.2	69 35.8	51.7	141.8	67 59.5	53.4	144.9	66 19.8	54.7	147.5
28	73 20.8	45.0	131.8	71 57.2	48.3	136.4	70 27.5	50.8	140.3	68 52.9	52.8	143.6	67 14.5	54.3	146.5
29	74 05.8	43.3	129.4	72 45.5	47.1	134.5	71 18.3	49.9	138.7	69 45.7	52.1	142.3	68 08.8	53.7	145.4

Dec.	50° Hc	d	Z	52° Hc	d	Z	54° Hc	d	Z	56° Hc	d	Z	58° Hc	d	Z
°	° ′	′	°	° ′	′	°	° ′	′	°	° ′	′	°	° ′	′	°
0	38 35.2	+58.8	162.0	36 40.9	+59.0	162.4	34 46.4	+59.1	162.9	32 51.6	+59.2	163.3	30 56.6	+59.3	163.6
1	39 34.0	58.7	161.7	37 39.9	58.9	162.2	35 45.5	59.1	162.7	33 50.8	59.2	163.1	31 55.9	59.3	163.4
2	40 32.7	58.7	161.4	38 38.8	58.9	162.0	36 44.5	59.1	162.4	34 50.0	59.1	162.9	32 55.2	59.3	163.3
3	41 31.4	58.7	161.2	39 37.7	58.8	161.7	37 43.6	59.0	162.2	35 49.1	59.2	162.7	33 54.5	59.2	163.1
4	42 30.1	58.6	160.9	40 36.5	58.8	161.5	38 42.6	58.9	162.0	36 48.3	59.1	162.5	34 53.7	59.3	162.9
5	43 28.7	+58.6	160.6	41 35.3	+58.8	161.2	39 41.5	+59.0	161.7	37 47.4	+59.1	162.2	35 53.0	+59.2	162.7
6	44 27.3	58.5	160.3	42 34.1	58.7	160.9	40 40.5	58.9	161.5	38 46.5	59.1	162.0	36 52.2	59.2	162.5
7	45 25.8	58.5	160.0	43 32.8	58.7	160.7	41 39.4	58.9	161.3	39 45.6	59.0	161.8	37 51.4	59.2	162.3
8	46 24.3	58.5	159.7	44 31.5	58.7	160.4	42 38.3	58.9	161.0	40 44.6	59.1	161.6	38 50.6	59.2	162.1
9	47 22.8	58.3	159.3	45 30.2	58.6	160.1	43 37.2	58.8	160.7	41 43.7	59.0	161.3	39 49.8	59.1	161.9
10	48 21.1	+58.3	159.0	46 28.8	+58.6	159.8	44 36.0	+58.7	160.5	42 42.7	+58.9	161.1	40 48.9	+59.2	161.7
11	49 19.4	58.2	158.6	47 27.4	58.5	159.4	45 34.7	58.7	160.2	43 41.6	58.9	160.8	41 48.1	59.1	161.4
12	50 17.6	58.2	158.3	48 25.9	58.4	159.1	46 33.5	58.6	159.9	44 40.5	58.9	160.6	42 47.2	59.0	161.2
13	51 15.8	58.1	157.9	49 24.3	58.4	158.8	47 32.1	58.7	159.6	45 39.4	58.9	160.3	43 46.2	59.1	160.9
14	52 13.9	58.0	157.5	50 22.7	58.3	158.4	48 30.8	58.5	159.2	46 38.3	58.8	160.0	44 45.3	58.9	160.7
15	53 11.9	+57.9	157.0	51 21.0	+58.2	158.0	49 29.3	+58.6	158.9	47 37.1	+58.7	159.7	45 44.2	+59.0	160.4
16	54 09.8	57.8	156.6	52 19.2	58.2	157.6	50 27.9	58.4	158.6	48 35.8	58.7	159.4	46 43.2	58.9	160.2
17	55 07.6	57.6	156.1	53 17.4	58.0	157.2	51 26.3	58.4	158.2	49 34.5	58.7	159.1	47 42.1	58.9	159.9
18	56 05.2	57.6	155.6	54 15.4	58.0	156.8	52 24.7	58.3	157.8	50 33.2	58.6	158.8	48 41.0	58.8	159.6
19	57 02.8	57.4	155.1	55 13.4	57.9	156.4	53 23.0	58.2	157.4	51 31.8	58.5	158.4	49 39.8	58.8	159.3
20	58 00.2	+57.3	154.6	56 11.3	+57.7	155.9	54 21.2	+58.2	157.0	52 30.3	+58.5	158.1	50 38.6	+58.8	159.0
21	58 57.5	57.1	154.0	57 09.0	57.6	155.4	55 19.4	58.0	156.6	53 28.8	58.4	157.7	51 37.4	58.6	158.7
22	59 54.6	57.0	153.4	58 06.6	57.5	154.9	56 17.4	58.0	156.2	54 27.2	58.3	157.3	52 36.0	58.7	158.3
23	60 51.6	56.7	152.8	59 04.1	57.4	154.3	57 15.4	57.8	155.7	55 25.5	58.2	156.9	53 34.7	58.5	158.0
24	61 48.3	56.6	152.1	60 01.5	57.2	153.7	58 13.2	57.7	155.2	56 23.7	58.1	156.5	54 33.2	58.5	157.6
25	62 44.9	+56.3	151.4	60 58.7	+57.0	153.1	59 10.9	+57.6	154.7	57 21.8	+58.1	156.0	55 31.7	+58.4	157.2
26	63 41.2	56.1	150.6	61 55.7	56.8	152.5	60 08.5	57.4	154.1	58 19.9	57.9	155.5	56 30.1	58.3	156.8
27	64 37.3	55.7	149.8	62 52.5	56.6	151.8	61 05.9	57.3	153.5	59 17.8	57.8	155.0	57 28.4	58.2	156.4
28	65 33.0	55.5	148.9	63 49.1	56.3	151.0	62 03.2	57.0	152.9	60 15.6	57.6	154.5	58 26.6	58.1	155.9
29	66 28.5	55.0	148.0	64 45.4	56.1	150.3	63 00.2	56.9	152.2	61 13.2	57.5	153.9	59 24.7	58.1	155.4

LATITUDE **CONTRARY** NAME   L.H.A. 14°, 346°

40°			42°			44°			46°			48°			Dec.
Hc	d	Z	Hc	d	Z	Hc	d	Z	Hc	d	Z	Hc	d	Z	
° ′	′	°	° ′	′	°	° ′	′	°	° ′	′	°	° ′	′	°	°
48 00.7	-57.7	158.8	46 08.6	-58.0	159.6	44 15.9	-58.3	160.3	42 22.7	-58.4	160.9	40 29.1	-58.6	161.5	0
47 03.0	57.7	159.2	45 10.6	58.1	159.9	43 17.6	58.2	160.6	41 24.3	58.5	161.2	39 30.5	58.7	161.7	1
46 05.3	57.9	159.6	44 12.5	58.1	160.3	42 19.4	58.4	160.9	40 25.8	58.6	161.5	38 31.8	58.7	162.0	2
45 07.4	57.9	160.0	43 14.4	58.1	160.6	41 21.0	58.4	161.2	39 27.2	58.6	161.8	37 33.1	58.8	162.3	3
44 09.5	58.0	160.3	42 16.3	58.3	161.0	40 22.6	58.4	161.5	38 28.6	58.6	162.0	36 34.3	58.8	162.5	4
43 11.5	-58.1	160.7	41 18.0	-58.3	161.3	39 24.2	-58.5	161.8	37 30.0	-58.6	162.3	35 35.5	-58.8	162.8	5
42 13.4	58.1	161.0	40 19.7	58.3	161.6	38 25.7	58.5	162.1	36 31.4	58.7	162.6	34 36.7	58.8	163.0	6
41 15.3	58.2	161.4	39 21.4	58.4	161.9	37 27.2	58.6	162.4	35 32.7	58.8	162.8	33 37.9	58.9	163.2	7
40 17.1	58.2	161.7	38 23.0	58.4	162.2	36 28.6	58.6	162.7	34 33.9	58.7	163.1	32 39.0	58.9	163.5	8
39 18.9	58.3	162.0	37 24.6	58.4	162.5	35 30.0	58.6	162.9	33 35.2	58.8	163.3	31 40.1	58.9	163.7	9
38 20.6	-58.3	162.3	36 26.2	-58.6	162.8	34 31.4	-58.7	163.2	32 36.4	-58.8	163.6	30 41.2	-58.9	163.9	10
37 22.3	58.4	162.6	35 27.6	58.5	163.0	33 32.7	58.7	163.4	31 37.6	58.8	163.8	29 42.3	59.0	164.1	11
36 23.9	58.4	162.9	34 29.1	58.6	163.3	32 34.0	58.7	163.7	30 38.8	58.9	164.0	28 43.3	59.0	164.3	12
35 25.5	58.4	163.2	33 30.5	58.6	163.6	31 35.3	58.7	163.9	29 39.9	58.9	164.3	27 44.3	59.0	164.6	13
34 27.1	58.5	163.5	32 31.9	58.6	163.8	30 36.6	58.8	164.2	28 41.0	58.9	164.5	26 45.3	59.0	164.8	14
33 28.6	-58.5	163.7	31 33.3	-58.7	164.1	29 37.8	-58.8	164.4	27 42.1	-58.9	164.7	25 46.3	-59.0	165.0	15
32 30.1	58.6	164.0	30 34.6	58.7	164.3	28 39.0	58.9	164.6	26 43.2	58.9	164.9	24 47.3	59.1	165.2	16
31 31.5	58.5	164.3	29 35.9	58.7	164.6	27 40.2	58.9	164.9	25 44.3	58.9	165.1	23 48.2	59.0	165.4	17
30 33.0	58.6	164.5	28 37.2	58.8	164.8	26 41.3	58.8	165.1	24 45.3	59.0	165.3	22 49.2	59.1	165.5	18
29 34.3	58.6	164.8	27 38.5	58.8	165.0	25 42.5	59.0	165.3	23 46.4	59.0	165.5	21 50.1	59.1	165.7	19
28 35.7	-58.7	165.0	26 39.7	-58.8	165.3	24 43.6	-58.9	165.5	22 47.4	-59.0	165.7	20 51.0	-59.1	165.9	20
27 37.0	58.6	165.2	25 40.9	58.8	165.5	23 44.7	58.9	165.7	21 48.4	59.0	165.9	19 51.9	59.1	166.1	21
26 38.4	58.7	165.5	24 42.1	58.8	165.7	22 45.8	58.9	165.9	20 49.4	59.1	166.1	18 52.8	59.1	166.3	22
25 39.7	58.8	165.7	23 43.3	58.8	165.9	21 46.9	59.0	166.1	19 50.3	59.0	166.3	17 53.7	59.1	166.5	23
24 40.9	58.7	165.9	22 44.5	58.9	166.1	20 47.9	58.9	166.3	18 51.3	59.1	166.5	16 54.6	59.2	166.6	24
23 42.2	-58.8	166.1	21 45.6	-58.9	166.3	19 49.0	-59.0	166.5	17 52.2	-59.0	166.7	15 55.4	-59.1	166.8	25
22 43.4	58.8	166.4	20 46.7	58.8	166.6	18 50.0	59.0	166.7	16 53.2	59.1	166.9	14 56.3	59.2	167.0	26
21 44.6	58.8	166.6	19 47.9	58.9	166.8	17 51.0	59.0	166.9	15 54.1	59.1	167.0	13 57.1	59.1	167.2	27
20 45.8	58.8	166.8	18 49.0	59.0	167.0	16 52.0	59.0	167.1	14 55.0	59.1	167.2	12 58.0	59.2	167.3	28
19 47.0	58.8	167.0	17 50.0	58.9	167.2	15 53.0	59.0	167.3	13 55.9	59.1	167.4	11 58.8	59.2	167.5	29

50°			52°			54°			56°			58°			Dec.
Hc	d	Z	Hc	d	Z	Hc	d	Z	Hc	d	Z	Hc	d	Z	
° ′	′	°	° ′	′	°	° ′	′	°	° ′	′	°	° ′	′	°	°
38 35.2	-58.8	162.0	36 40.9	-58.9	162.4	34 46.4	-59.1	162.9	32 51.6	-59.2	163.3	30 56.6	-59.4	163.6	0
37 36.4	58.9	162.2	35 42.0	59.0	162.7	33 47.3	59.2	163.1	31 52.4	59.3	163.5	29 57.2	59.3	163.8	1
36 37.5	58.9	162.5	34 43.0	59.1	162.9	32 48.1	59.1	163.3	30 53.1	59.2	163.6	28 57.9	59.4	164.0	2
35 38.6	58.9	162.7	33 43.9	59.0	163.1	31 49.0	59.2	163.5	29 53.9	59.3	163.8	27 58.5	59.4	164.1	3
34 39.7	58.9	162.9	32 44.9	59.1	163.3	30 49.8	59.1	163.7	28 54.6	59.3	164.0	26 59.1	59.4	164.3	4
33 40.8	-58.9	163.2	31 45.8	-59.0	163.5	29 50.7	-59.2	163.9	27 55.3	-59.3	164.2	25 59.8	-59.4	164.4	5
32 41.9	59.0	163.4	30 46.8	59.1	163.7	28 51.5	59.2	164.1	26 56.0	59.3	164.3	25 00.4	59.4	164.6	6
31 42.9	59.0	163.6	29 47.7	59.2	163.9	27 52.3	59.3	164.2	25 56.7	59.3	164.5	24 01.0	59.4	164.8	7
30 43.9	59.0	163.8	28 48.5	59.1	164.1	26 53.0	59.2	164.4	24 57.4	59.4	164.7	23 01.6	59.5	164.9	8
29 44.9	59.1	164.0	27 49.4	59.2	164.3	25 53.8	59.3	164.6	23 58.0	59.3	164.8	22 02.1	59.4	165.1	9
28 45.8	-59.0	164.2	26 50.2	-59.1	164.5	24 54.5	-59.2	164.8	22 58.7	-59.4	165.0	21 02.7	-59.5	165.2	10
27 46.8	59.1	164.4	25 51.1	59.2	164.7	23 55.3	59.3	164.9	21 59.3	59.3	165.2	20 03.3	59.5	165.4	11
26 47.7	59.1	164.6	24 51.9	59.2	164.9	22 56.0	59.3	165.1	21 00.0	59.4	165.3	19 03.8	59.5	165.5	12
25 48.6	59.1	164.8	23 52.7	59.2	165.1	21 56.7	59.3	165.3	20 00.6	59.4	165.5	18 04.4	59.5	165.6	13
24 49.5	59.1	165.0	22 53.5	59.2	165.2	20 57.4	59.3	165.4	19 01.2	59.4	165.6	17 04.9	59.5	165.8	14
23 50.4	-59.2	165.2	21 54.3	-59.2	165.4	19 58.1	-59.3	165.6	18 01.8	-59.4	165.8	16 05.5	-59.5	165.9	15
22 51.2	59.1	165.4	20 55.1	59.3	165.6	18 58.8	59.3	165.8	17 02.4	59.4	165.9	15 06.0	59.5	166.1	16
21 52.1	59.2	165.5	19 55.8	59.2	165.8	17 59.5	59.4	165.9	16 03.0	59.4	166.1	14 06.5	59.4	166.2	17
20 52.9	59.1	165.7	18 56.6	59.3	165.9	17 00.1	59.3	166.1	15 03.6	59.4	166.2	13 07.1	59.5	166.3	18
19 53.8	59.2	165.9	17 57.3	59.2	166.1	16 00.8	59.3	166.2	14 04.2	59.4	166.4	12 07.6	59.5	166.5	19
18 54.6	-59.2	166.1	16 58.1	-59.3	166.3	15 01.5	-59.4	166.4	13 04.8	-59.4	166.5	11 08.1	-59.5	166.6	20
17 55.4	59.2	166.3	15 58.8	59.3	166.4	14 02.1	59.3	166.5	12 05.4	59.4	166.7	10 08.6	59.5	166.7	21
16 56.2	59.2	166.4	14 59.5	59.3	166.6	13 02.8	59.4	166.7	11 06.0	59.5	166.8	9 09.1	59.5	166.9	22
15 57.0	59.2	166.6	14 00.2	59.3	166.7	12 03.4	59.4	166.8	10 06.5	59.4	166.9	8 09.6	59.5	167.0	23
14 57.8	59.2	166.8	13 00.9	59.3	166.9	11 04.0	59.3	167.0	9 07.1	59.4	167.1	7 10.1	59.5	167.1	24
13 58.6	-59.3	166.9	12 01.6	-59.3	167.0	10 04.7	-59.4	167.1	8 07.7	-59.5	167.2	6 10.6	-59.5	167.3	25
12 59.3	59.2	167.1	11 02.3	59.3	167.2	9 05.3	59.4	167.3	7 08.2	59.4	167.3	5 11.1	59.5	167.4	26
12 00.1	59.2	167.3	10 03.0	59.3	167.4	8 05.9	59.4	167.4	6 08.8	59.5	167.5	4 11.6	59.5	167.5	27
11 00.9	59.3	167.4	9 03.7	59.3	167.5	7 06.5	59.3	167.6	5 09.3	59.4	167.6	3 12.1	59.5	167.6	28
10 01.6	59.2	167.6	8 04.4	59.3	167.7	6 07.2	59.4	167.7	4 09.9	59.4	167.8	2 12.6	59.5	167.8	29

	0°			2°			4°			6°			8°		
Dec.	Hc	d	Z	Hc	d	Z	Hc	d	Z	Hc	d	Z	Hc	d	Z
°	° ′	′	°	° ′	′	°	° ′	′	°	° ′	′	°	° ′	′	°
0	74 00.0 − 1.8° 90.0			73 52.7 + 5.8° 96.9			73 31.2 +13.1°103.7			72 56.4 +19.8°110.0			72 09.5 +25.9°115.9		
1	73 58.2 5.5° 86.4			73 58.5 + 2.1° 93.3			73 44.3 9.6°100.2			73 16.2 16.7°106.8			72 35.4 23.2°112.9		
2	73 52.7 9.0° 82.8			74 00.6 − 1.5° 89.7			73 53.9 6.0° 96.7			73 32.9 13.4°103.4			72 58.6 20.2°109.8		
3	73 43.7 12.5° 79.2			73 59.1 5.2° 86.1			73 59.9 + 2.5° 93.1			73 46.3 9.9°100.0			73 18.8 17.0°106.5		
4	73 31.2 15.8° 75.8			73 53.9 8.7° 82.5			74 02.4 − 1.3° 89.4			73 56.2 6.4° 96.4			73 35.8 13.7°103.2		
5	73 15.4 −19.0° 72.4			73 45.2 −12.3° 78.9			74 01.1 − 4.9° 85.8			74 02.6 + 2.7° 92.8			73 49.5 +10.2° 99.7		
6	72 56.4 22.1° 69.1			73 32.9 15.5° 75.5			73 56.2 8.4° 82.2			74 05.3 − 1.0° 89.2			73 59.7 6.7° 96.1		
7	72 34.3 24.8° 66.0			73 17.4 18.8° 72.1			73 47.8 12.0° 78.6			74 04.3 4.6° 85.5			74 06.4 + 3.0° 92.5		
8	72 09.5 27.5° 63.0			72 58.6 21.8° 68.8			73 35.8 15.4° 75.1			73 59.7 8.2° 81.9			74 09.4 − 0.7° 88.9		
9	71 42.0 29.9° 60.1			72 36.8 24.7° 65.7			73 20.4 18.5° 71.7			73 51.5 11.7° 78.3			74 08.7 4.3° 85.2		
10	71 12.1 −32.2° 57.4			72 12.1 −27.3° 62.6			73 01.9 −21.6° 68.5			73 39.8 −15.2° 74.8			74 04.4 − 8.0° 81.6		
11	70 39.9 34.2° 54.8			71 44.8 29.7° 59.8			72 40.3 24.5° 65.3			73 24.6 18.3° 71.4			73 56.4 11.5° 78.0		
12	70 05.7 36.2° 52.4			71 15.1 32.0° 57.0			72 15.8 27.1° 62.3			73 06.3 21.4° 68.1			73 44.9 14.9° 74.4		
13	69 29.5 37.8° 50.1			70 43.1 34.1° 54.4			71 48.7 29.6° 59.4			72 44.9 24.4° 64.9			73 30.0 18.2° 71.0		
14	68 51.7 39.5° 47.9			70 09.0 36.0° 52.0			71 19.1 31.9° 56.6			72 20.5 27.0° 61.9			73 11.8 21.3° 67.7		
15	68 12.2 −40.9° 45.8			69 33.0 −37.8° 49.6			70 47.2 −34.0° 54.0			71 53.5 −29.4° 58.9			72 50.5 −24.2° 64.5		
16	67 31.3 42.2° 43.9			68 55.2 39.3° 47.4			70 13.2 35.9° 51.5			71 24.1 31.8° 56.2			72 26.3 26.9° 61.4		
17	66 49.1 43.4° 42.0			68 15.9 40.8° 45.4			69 37.3 37.7° 49.2			70 52.3 33.9° 53.6			71 59.4 29.4° 58.5		
18	66 05.7 44.5° 40.3			67 35.1 42.2° 43.4			68 59.6 39.2° 47.0			70 18.4 35.9° 51.1			71 30.0 31.7° 55.7		
19	65 21.2 45.6° 38.7			66 52.9 43.3° 41.6			68 20.4 40.8° 44.9			69 42.5 37.6° 48.7			70 58.3 33.9° 53.1		
20	64 35.6 −46.4° 37.1			66 09.6 −44.5° 39.9			67 39.6 −42.0° 43.0			69 04.9 −39.2° 46.5			70 24.4 −35.8° 50.6		
21	63 49.2 47.2° 35.7			65 25.1 45.4° 38.2			66 57.6 43.3° 41.1			68 25.7 40.7° 44.4			69 48.6 37.5° 48.2		
22	63 02.0 48.0° 34.3			64 39.7 46.4° 36.7			66 14.3 44.4° 39.4			67 45.0 42.0° 42.4			69 11.1 39.3° 46.0		
23	62 14.0 48.8° 33.0			63 53.3 47.2° 35.2			65 29.9 45.4° 37.7			67 03.0 43.3° 40.6			68 31.8 40.6° 43.9		
24	61 25.2 49.3° 31.8			63 06.1 47.9° 33.8			64 44.5 46.4° 36.2			66 19.7 44.4° 38.8			67 51.2 42.1° 41.9		
25	60 35.9 −49.9° 30.6			62 18.2 −48.7° 32.5			63 58.1 − 47.1° 34.7			65 35.3 −45.4° 37.2			67 09.1 −43.3° 40.0		
26	59 46.0 50.5° 29.5			61 29.5 49.3° 31.3			63 11.0 48.0° 33.3			64 49.9 46.3° 35.6			66 25.8 44.3° 38.3		
27	58 55.5 51.0° 28.4			60 40.2 49.9° 30.1			62 23.0 48.6° 32.0			64 03.6 47.2° 34.2			65 41.5 45.4° 36.6		
28	58 04.5 51.4° 27.4			59 50.3 50.4° 29.0			61 34.4 49.3° 30.7			63 16.4 47.9° 32.8			64 56.1 46.4° 35.1		
29	57 13.1 51.9° 26.4			58 59.9 51.0° 27.9			60 45.1 49.9° 29.6			62 28.5 48.6° 31.4			64 09.7 47.2° 33.6		

	10°			12°			14°			16°			18°		
Dec.	Hc	d	Z	Hc	d	Z	Hc	d	Z	Hc	d	Z	Hc	d	Z
°	° ′	′	°	° ′	′	°	° ′	′	°	° ′	′	°	° ′	′	°
0	71 12.1 +31.2°121.2			70 05.7 +35.7 125.9			68 51.7 +39.4 130.2			67 31.3 +42.6 133.9			66 05.7 +45.2 137.1		
1	71 43.3 28.8°118.5			70 41.4 33.7°123.5			69 31.1 37.9 128.0			68 13.9 41.3 132.0			66 50.9 44.2 135.5		
2	72 12.1 26.3°115.7			71 15.1 31.5°121.0			70 09.0 36.0 125.8			68 55.2 39.8 130.0			67 35.1 42.9 133.7		
3	72 38.4 23.5°112.7			71 46.6 29.2°118.3			70 45.0 34.1°123.4			69 35.0 38.2 127.9			68 18.0 41.6 131.9		
4	73 01.9 20.5°109.6			72 15.8 26.6°115.5			71 19.1 31.9°120.9			70 13.2 36.4 125.7			68 59.6 40.2 129.9		
5	73 22.4 +17.4°106.3			72 42.4 +23.9°112.5			71 51.0 +29.5°118.2			70 49.6 +34.5°123.3			69 39.8 +38.6 127.8		
6	73 39.8 14.0°103.0			73 06.3 20.9°109.4			72 20.5 27.0°115.3			71 24.1 32.3°120.7			70 18.4 36.8 125.6		
7	73 53.8 10.6° 99.5			73 27.2 17.7°106.1			72 47.5 24.3°112.4			71 56.4 29.9°118.1			70 55.2 34.8°123.2		
8	74 04.4 7.0° 95.9			73 44.9 14.4°102.8			73 11.8 21.2°109.2			72 26.3 27.4°115.2			71 30.0 32.7°120.7		
9	74 11.4 + 3.3° 92.3			73 59.3 10.9° 99.3			73 33.0 18.1°106.0			72 53.7 24.6°112.2			72 02.7 30.4°118.0		
10	74 14.7 − 0.4° 88.6			74 10.2 + 7.3° 95.7			73 51.1 +14.8°102.6			73 18.3 +21.7°109.1			72 33.1 +27.8°115.1		
11	74 14.3 4.1° 84.9			74 17.5 + 3.6° 92.0			74 05.9 11.2° 99.1			73 40.0 18.5°105.8			73 00.9 25.1°112.1		
12	74 10.2 7.8° 81.3			74 21.1 − 0.1° 88.3			74 17.1 7.7° 95.5			73 58.5 15.1°102.4			73 26.0 22.0°109.0		
13	74 02.4 11.3° 77.6			74 21.0 3.9° 84.6			74 24.8 3.9° 91.8			74 13.6 11.6° 98.9			73 48.0 18.9°105.7		
14	73 51.1 14.7° 74.1			74 17.1 7.5° 80.9			74 28.7 + 0.1° 88.1			74 25.2 8.0° 95.2			74 06.9 15.6°102.3		
15	73 36.4 −18.1° 70.6			74 09.6 −11.1° 77.3			74 28.8 − 3.6° 84.3			74 33.2 + 4.2° 91.5			74 22.5 +12.0° 98.7		
16	73 18.3 21.1° 67.3			73 58.5 14.6° 73.7			74 25.2 7.3° 80.6			74 37.4 + 0.4° 87.8			74 34.5 8.3° 95.0		
17	72 57.2 24.1° 64.0			73 43.9 17.9° 70.2			74 17.9 11.0° 76.9			74 37.8 − 3.3° 84.0			74 42.8 4.5° 91.3		
18	72 33.1 26.8° 61.0			73 26.0 21.1° 66.8			74 06.9 14.4° 73.3			74 34.5 7.2° 80.2			74 47.3 + 0.6° 87.5		
19	72 06.3 29.4° 58.0			73 04.9 24.0° 63.6			73 52.5 17.9° 69.8			74 27.3 10.8° 76.5			74 47.9 − 3.1° 83.7		
20	71 36.9 −31.7° 55.2			72 40.9 −26.8° 60.5			73 34.6 −21.0° 66.4			74 16.5 −14.4° 72.9			74 44.8 − 7.0° 79.9		
21	71 05.2 33.8° 52.6			72 14.1 29.4° 57.5			73 13.6 24.0° 63.1			74 02.1 17.8° 69.3			74 37.8 10.7° 76.1		
22	70 31.4 35.8° 50.0			71 44.7 31.7° 54.7			72 49.6 26.8° 59.9			73 44.3 20.9° 65.9			74 27.1 14.3° 72.4		
23	69 55.6 37.6° 47.7			71 13.0 33.8° 52.0			72 22.8 29.3° 57.0			73 23.4 24.0° 62.6			74 12.8 17.7° 68.8		
24	69 18.0 39.2° 45.4			70 39.2 35.8° 49.5			71 53.5 31.7° 54.1			72 59.4 26.9° 59.4			73 55.1 21.0° 65.4		
25	68 38.8 −40.7° 43.3			70 03.4 −37.6° 47.1			71 21.8 −33.9° 51.4			72 32.5 −29.4° 56.4			73 34.1 −24.1° 62.0		
26	67 58.1 42.1° 41.3			69 25.8 39.3° 44.8			70 47.9 35.9° 48.9			72 03.1 31.7° 53.5			73 10.0 26.8° 58.8		
27	67 16.0 43.3° 39.5			68 46.5 40.8° 42.7			70 12.0 37.7° 46.5			71 31.4 34.0° 50.8			72 43.2 29.5° 55.8		
28	66 32.7 44.4° 37.7			68 05.7 42.1° 40.7			69 34.3 39.4° 44.2			70 57.4 36.0° 48.2			72 13.7 31.9° 52.9		
29	65 48.3 45.5° 36.0			67 23.6 43.4° 38.8			68 54.9 40.8° 42.1			70 21.4 37.8° 45.8			71 41.8 34.1° 50.1		

0°			2°			4°			6°			8°			Dec.
Hc	d	Z	Hc	d	Z	Hc	d	Z	Hc	d	Z	Hc	d	Z	
74 00.0	- 1.8°	90.0	73 52.7	- 9.3°	96.9	73 31.2	- 16.4°	103.7	72 56.4	- 22.9°	110.0	72 09.5	- 28.5°	115.9	0
73 58.2	5.5°	93.6	73 43.4	12.8°	100.5	73 14.8	19.5°	107.0	72 33.5	25.6°	113.1	71 41.0	30.9°	118.7	1
73 52.7	9.0°	97.2	73 30.6	16.1°	103.9	72 55.3	22.6°	110.3	72 07.9	28.2°	116.1	71 10.1	33.1°	121.4	2
73 43.7	12.5°	100.8	73 14.5	19.2°	107.3	72 32.7	25.3°	113.4	71 39.7	30.6°	119.0	70 37.0	35.1°	124.0	3
73 31.2	15.8°	104.2	72 55.3	22.3°	110.6	72 07.4	28.0°	116.4	71 09.1	32.8°	121.7	70 01.9	37.0°	126.4	4
73 15.4	- 19.0°	107.6	72 33.0	- 25.1°	113.7	71 39.4	- 30.3°	119.2	70 36.3	- 34.9°	124.2	69 24.9	- 38.6°	128.6	5
72 56.4	22.1°	110.9	72 07.9	27.7°	116.7	71 09.1	32.6°	121.9	70 01.4	36.7°	126.6	68 46.3	40.2°	130.8	6
72 34.3	24.8°	114.0	71 40.2	30.1°	119.5	70 36.5	34.6°	124.5	69 24.7	38.4°	128.9	68 06.1	41.5°	132.8	7
72 09.5	27.5°	117.0	71 10.1	32.4°	122.3	70 01.9	36.5°	126.9	68 46.3	40.0°	131.1	67 24.6	42.9°	134.7	8
71 42.0	29.9°	119.9	70 37.7	34.4°	124.8	69 25.4	38.2°	129.2	68 06.3	41.3°	133.1	66 41.7	44.0°	136.5	9
71 12.1	- 32.2°	122.6	70 03.3	- 36.3°	127.3	68 47.2	- 39.8°	131.4	67 25.0	- 42.7°	135.0	65 57.7	- 45.0°	138.2	10
70 39.9	34.2°	125.2	69 27.0	38.0°	129.6	68 07.4	41.1°	133.4	66 42.3	43.8°	136.8	65 12.7	46.0°	139.8	11
70 05.7	36.2°	127.6	68 49.0	39.6°	131.7	67 26.3	42.5°	135.4	65 58.5	44.8°	138.5	64 26.7	46.9°	141.3	12
69 29.5	37.8°	129.9	68 09.4	41.0°	133.8	66 43.8	43.7°	137.2	65 13.7	45.9°	140.1	63 39.8	47.7°	142.7	13
68 51.7	39.5°	132.1	67 28.4	42.4°	135.7	66 00.1	44.7°	138.9	64 27.8	46.7°	141.7	62 52.1	48.4°	144.1	14
68 12.2	- 40.9°	134.2	66 46.0	- 43.5°	137.6	65 15.4	- 45.7°	140.5	63 41.1	- 47.6°	143.1	62 03.7	- 49.1°	145.4	15
67 31.3	42.2°	136.1	66 02.5	44.6°	139.3	64 29.7	46.6°	142.0	62 53.5	48.3°	144.4	61 14.6	49.7°	146.6	16
66 49.1	43.4°	138.0	65 17.9	45.6°	140.9	63 43.1	47.5°	143.5	62 05.2	48.9°	145.7	60 24.9	50.3°	147.7	17
66 05.7	44.5°	139.7	64 32.3	46.5°	142.4	62 55.6	48.1°	144.8	61 16.3	49.6°	146.9	59 34.6	50.8°	148.8	18
65 21.2	45.6°	141.3	63 45.8	47.3°	143.9	62 07.5	48.9°	146.1	60 26.7	50.2°	148.1	58 43.8	51.2°	149.9	19
64 35.6	- 46.4°	142.9	62 58.5	- 48.1°	145.2	61 18.6	- 49.5°	147.3	59 36.5	- 50.7°	149.2	57 52.6	- 51.7°	150.9	20
63 49.2	47.2°	144.3	62 10.4	48.8°	146.5	60 29.1	50.0°	148.5	58 45.8	51.1°	150.2	57 00.9	52.2°	151.8	21
63 02.0	48.0°	145.7	61 21.6	49.4°	147.8	59 39.1	50.6°	149.6	57 54.7	51.6°	151.2	56 08.7	52.4°	152.7	22
62 14.0	48.8°	147.0	60 32.2	50.0°	148.9	58 48.5	51.1°	150.7	57 03.1	52.1°	152.2	55 16.3	52.9°	153.6	23
61 25.2	49.3°	148.2	59 42.2	50.5°	150.1	57 57.4	51.5°	151.7	56 11.0	52.4°	153.1	54 23.4	53.1°	154.4	24
60 35.9	- 49.9°	149.4	58 51.7	- 51.0°	151.1	57 05.9	- 52.0°	152.6	55 18.6	- 52.7°	154.0	53 30.3	- 53.5°	155.2	25
59 46.0	50.5°	150.5	58 00.7	51.5°	152.1	56 13.9	52.3°	153.5	54 25.9	53.1°	154.8	52 36.8	53.7°	155.9	26
58 55.5	51.0°	151.6	57 09.2	51.9°	153.1	55 21.6	52.7°	154.4	53 32.8	53.4°	155.6	51 43.1	54.0°	156.6	27
58 04.5	51.4°	152.6	56 17.3	52.3°	154.0	54 28.9	53.0°	155.2	52 39.4	53.6°	156.3	50 49.1	54.2°	157.3	28
57 13.1	51.9°	153.6	55 25.0	52.6°	154.9	53 35.9	53.3°	156.0	51 45.8	53.9°	157.1	49 54.9	54.5°	158.0	29

10°			12°			14°			16°			18°			Dec.
Hc	d	Z	Hc	d	Z	Hc	d	Z	Hc	d	Z	Hc	d	Z	
71 12.1	- 33.4°	121.2	70 05.7	- 37.5°	125.9	68 51.7	- 41.0°	130.2	67 31.3	- 43.8°	133.9	66 05.7	- 46.3°	137.1	0
70 38.7	35.4°	123.7	69 28.2	39.2°	128.2	68 10.7	42.3°	132.1	66 47.5	45.0°	135.6	65 19.4	47.1°	138.7	1
70 03.3	37.2°	126.1	68 49.0	40.7°	130.3	67 28.4	43.6°	134.0	66 02.5	45.9°	137.3	64 32.3	48.0°	140.2	2
69 26.1	38.9°	128.4	68 08.3	42.0°	132.3	66 44.8	44.7°	135.8	65 16.6	46.9°	138.8	63 44.3	48.7°	141.5	3
68 47.2	40.4°	130.5	67 26.3	43.3°	134.2	66 00.1	45.7°	137.5	64 29.7	47.7°	140.3	62 55.6	49.3°	142.8	4
68 06.8	- 41.8°	132.6	66 43.0	- 44.5°	136.0	65 14.4	- 46.6°	139.0	63 42.0	- 48.5°	141.7	62 06.3	- 50.0°	144.1	5
67 25.0	43.1°	134.5	65 58.5	45.4°	137.7	64 27.8	47.5°	140.5	62 53.5	49.1°	143.0	61 16.3	50.6°	145.3	6
66 41.9	44.2°	136.2	65 13.1	46.4°	139.3	63 40.3	48.2°	141.9	62 04.4	49.8°	144.3	60 25.7	51.1°	146.3	7
65 57.7	45.2°	137.9	64 26.7	47.3°	140.7	62 52.1	48.9°	143.2	61 14.6	50.4°	145.4	59 34.6	51.5°	147.4	8
65 12.5	46.2°	139.5	63 39.4	48.0°	142.2	62 03.2	49.6°	144.5	60 24.2	50.9°	146.5	58 43.1	52.1°	148.4	9
64 26.3	- 47.1°	141.0	62 51.4	- 48.7°	143.5	61 13.6	- 50.2°	145.7	59 33.3	- 51.3°	147.6	57 51.0	- 52.4°	149.3	10
63 39.2	47.8°	142.4	62 02.7	49.5°	144.7	60 23.4	50.7°	146.8	58 42.0	51.9°	148.6	56 58.6	52.7°	150.2	11
62 51.4	48.6°	143.8	61 13.2	49.9°	145.9	59 32.7	51.2°	147.9	57 50.1	52.2°	149.6	56 05.9	53.2°	151.1	12
62 02.8	49.2°	145.0	60 23.3	50.6°	147.1	58 41.5	51.7°	148.9	56 57.9	52.6°	150.5	55 12.7	53.4°	151.9	13
61 13.6	49.9°	146.2	59 32.7	51.1°	148.2	57 49.8	52.1°	149.8	56 05.3	53.0°	151.4	54 19.3	53.8°	152.7	14
60 23.7	- 50.4°	147.4	58 41.6	- 51.5°	149.2	56 57.7	- 52.4°	150.8	55 12.3	- 53.3°	152.2	53 25.5	- 54.0°	153.5	15
59 33.3	50.9°	148.5	57 50.1	51.9°	150.2	56 05.3	52.9°	151.6	54 19.0	53.6°	153.0	52 31.5	54.2°	154.2	16
58 42.4	51.4°	149.5	56 58.2	52.3°	151.1	55 12.4	53.1°	152.5	53 25.4	53.9°	153.7	51 37.3	54.6°	154.9	17
57 51.0	51.8°	150.5	56 05.9	52.8°	152.0	54 19.3	53.5°	153.3	52 31.5	54.1°	154.5	50 42.7	54.7°	155.5	18
56 59.2	52.2°	151.4	55 13.1	53.0°	152.8	53 25.8	53.7°	154.1	51 37.4	54.4°	155.2	49 48.0	54.9°	156.2	19
56 07.0	- 52.6°	152.3	54 20.1	- 53.3°	153.6	52 32.1	- 54.1°	154.8	50 43.0	- 54.6°	155.9	48 53.1	- 55.1°	156.8	20
55 14.4	52.9°	153.2	53 26.8	53.7°	154.4	51 38.0	54.2°	155.5	49 48.4	54.8°	156.5	47 58.0	55.3°	157.4	21
54 21.5	53.3°	154.0	52 33.1	53.9°	155.1	50 43.8	54.5°	156.2	48 53.6	55.0°	157.1	47 02.7	55.5°	158.0	22
53 28.2	53.5°	154.8	51 39.2	54.2°	155.9	49 49.3	54.7°	156.8	47 58.6	55.2°	157.7	46 07.2	55.6°	158.5	23
52 34.7	53.8°	155.6	50 45.0	54.3°	156.6	48 54.6	54.9°	157.5	47 03.4	55.4°	158.3	45 11.6	55.8°	159.1	24
51 40.9	- 54.1°	156.2	49 50.7	- 54.7°	157.2	47 59.7	- 55.1°	158.1	46 08.0	- 55.5°	158.9	44 15.8	- 55.9°	159.6	25
50 46.8	54.3°	156.9	48 56.0	54.8°	157.8	47 04.6	55.3°	158.7	45 12.5	55.7°	159.4	43 19.9	56.0°	160.1	26
49 52.5	54.5°	157.6	48 01.2	55.0°	158.5	46 09.3	55.4°	159.2	44 16.8	55.8°	159.9	42 23.9	56.2°	160.6	27
48 58.0	54.7°	158.2	47 06.2	55.2°	159.1	45 13.9	55.6°	159.8	43 21.0	55.9°	160.4	41 27.7	56.2°	161.0	28
48 03.3	55.0°	158.9	46 11.0	55.3°	159.6	44 18.3	55.7°	160.3	42 25.1	56.1°	160.9	40 31.5	56.4°	161.5	29

Dec.	20° Hc	d	Z	22° Hc	d	Z	24° Hc	d	Z	26° Hc	d	Z	28° Hc	d	Z
°	° ′	′	°	° ′	′	°	° ′	′	°	° ′	′	°	° ′	′	°
0	64 35.6	+ 47.5	140.0	63 02.0	+ 49.2	142.6	61 25.2	+ 50.8	144.8	59 46.0	+ 52.0	146.8	58 04.5	+ 53.1	148.6
1	65 23.1	46.5	138.6	63 51.2	48.5	141.3	62 16.0	50.1	143.7	60 38.0	51.5	145.8	58 57.6	52.7	147.7
2	66 09.6	45.5	137.0	64 39.7	47.7	139.9	63 06.1	49.6	142.5	61 29.5	51.0	144.7	59 50.3	52.3	146.8
3	66 55.1	44.5	135.4	65 27.4	46.9	138.5	63 55.7	48.8	141.2	62 20.5	50.5	143.6	60 42.6	51.8	145.8
4	67 39.6	43.3	133.7	66 14.3	45.9	137.0	64 44.5	48.0	139.9	63 11.0	49.8	142.4	61 34.4	51.3	144.7
5	68 22.9	+ 42.0	131.8	67 00.2	+ 44.8	135.3	65 32.5	+ 47.2	138.5	64 00.8	+ 49.1	141.2	62 25.7	+ 50.7	143.6
6	69 04.9	40.6	129.8	67 45.0	43.7	133.6	66 19.7	46.2	136.9	64 49.9	48.4	139.9	63 16.4	50.2	142.4
7	69 45.5	38.9	127.7	68 28.7	42.4	131.8	67 05.9	45.3	135.3	65 38.3	47.5	138.5	64 06.6	49.5	141.2
8	70 24.4	37.2	125.5	69 11.1	40.9	129.8	67 51.2	44.0	133.6	66 25.8	46.7	137.0	64 56.1	48.7	139.9
9	71 01.6	35.3•	123.1	69 52.0	39.4	127.7	68 35.2	42.8	131.8	67 12.5	45.6	135.4	65 44.8	47.9	138.5
10	71 36.9	+ 33.1•	120.6	70 31.4	+ 37.6	125.5	69 18.0	+ 41.4	129.8	67 58.1	+ 44.4	133.6	66 32.7	+ 47.0	137.0
11	72 10.0	30.9•	117.9	71 09.0	35.7•	123.1	69 59.4	39.8	127.7	68 42.5	43.3	131.8	67 19.7	46.0	135.4
12	72 40.9	28.2•	115.1	71 44.7	33.6•	120.6	70 39.2	38.1	125.5	69 25.8	41.8	129.9	68 05.7	44.9	133.7
13	73 09.1	25.5•	112.1	72 18.3	31.3•	117.9	71 17.3	36.2•	123.2	70 07.6	40.3	127.8	68 50.6	43.7	131.9
14	73 34.6	22.6•	108.9	72 49.6	28.8•	115.1	71 53.5	34.1•	120.6	70 47.9	38.6	125.6	69 34.3	42.3	130.0
15	73 57.2	+ 19.3•	105.6	73 18.4	+ 25.9•	112.1	72 27.6	+ 31.8•	117.9	71 26.5	+ 36.6•	123.2	70 16.6	+ 40.8	127.9
16	74 16.5	15.9•	102.1	73 44.3	23.0•	108.9	72 59.4	29.2•	115.1	72 03.1	34.6•	120.7	70 57.4	39.1	125.7
17	74 32.4	12.4•	98.6	74 07.3	19.8•	105.5	73 28.6	26.5•	112.1	72 37.7	32.3•	118.0	71 36.5	37.2•	123.3
18	74 44.8	8.6•	94.9	74 27.1	16.4•	102.0	73 55.1	23.4•	108.9	73 10.0	29.8•	115.1	72 13.7	35.1•	120.8
19	74 53.4	4.8•	91.1	74 43.5	12.7•	98.4	74 18.5	20.3•	105.5	73 39.8	27.0•	112.1	72 48.8	32.8•	118.1
20	74 58.2	+ 1.0•	87.2	74 56.2	+ 9.0•	94.7	74 38.8	+ 16.8•	102.0	74 06.8	+ 24.0•	108.9	73 21.6	+ 30.4•	115.2
21	74 59.2	− 3.0•	83.4	75 05.2	5.1•	90.9	74 55.6	13.1•	98.3	74 30.8	20.7•	105.5	73 52.0	27.5•	112.2
22	74 56.2	6.8•	79.5	75 10.3	+ 1.2•	87.0	75 08.7	9.4•	94.5	74 51.5	17.2•	101.9	74 19.5	24.5•	108.9
23	74 49.4	10.6•	75.7	75 11.5	− 2.8•	83.1	75 18.1	5.4•	90.7	75 08.7	13.6•	98.2	74 44.0	21.2•	105.5
24	74 38.8	14.3•	72.0	75 08.7	6.7•	79.2	75 23.5	+ 1.4•	86.7	75 22.3	9.7•	94.4	75 05.2	17.7•	101.9
25	74 24.5	− 17.7•	68.3	75 02.0	− 10.5•	75.3	75 24.9	− 2.6•	82.8	75 32.0	+ 5.7•	90.5	75 22.9	+ 14.0•	98.2
26	74 06.8	21.0•	64.8	74 51.5	14.2•	71.5	75 22.3	6.6•	78.8	75 37.7	+ 1.6•	86.5	75 36.9	10.1•	94.3
27	73 45.8	24.2•	61.4	74 37.3	17.8•	67.8	75 15.7	10.5•	74.9	75 39.3	− 2.4•	82.4	75 47.0	6.0•	90.3
28	73 21.6	26.9•	58.2	74 19.5	21.1•	64.3	75 05.2	14.2•	71.0	75 36.9	6.5•	78.4	75 53.0	+ 1.9•	86.2
29	72 54.7	29.7•	55.1	73 58.4	24.2•	60.8	74 51.0	17.9•	67.3	75 30.4	10.5•	74.4	75 54.9	− 2.3•	82.1

Dec.	30° Hc	d	Z	32° Hc	d	Z	34° Hc	d	Z	36° Hc	d	Z	38° Hc	d	Z
°	° ′	′	°	° ′	′	°	° ′	′	°	° ′	′	°	° ′	′	°
0	56 21.2	+ 54.0	150.2	54 36.4	+ 54.8	151.6	52 50.2	+ 55.5	152.9	51 02.9	+ 56.0	154.0	49 14.6	+ 56.5	155.0
1	57 15.2	53.7	149.4	55 31.2	54.5	150.9	53 45.7	55.2	152.2	51 58.9	55.9	153.4	50 11.1	56.4	154.5
2	58 08.9	53.3	148.5	56 25.7	54.2	150.1	54 40.9	55.0	151.5	52 54.8	55.6	152.8	51 07.5	56.2	154.0
3	59 02.2	53.0	147.7	57 19.9	53.9	149.3	55 35.9	54.7	150.8	53 50.4	55.5	152.2	52 03.7	56.0	153.4
4	59 55.2	52.6	146.7	58 13.8	53.6	148.5	56 30.6	54.5	150.1	54 45.9	55.2	151.5	52 59.7	55.9	152.8
5	60 47.8	+ 52.1	145.8	59 07.4	+ 53.3	147.7	57 25.1	+ 54.2	149.3	55 41.1	+ 55.0	150.9	53 55.6	+ 55.6	152.2
6	61 39.9	51.6	144.7	60 00.7	52.8	146.7	58 19.3	53.8	148.5	56 36.1	54.7	150.1	54 51.2	55.5	151.6
7	62 31.5	51.0	143.6	60 53.5	52.4	145.8	59 13.1	53.6	147.7	57 30.8	54.4	149.4	55 46.7	55.2	150.9
8	63 22.5	50.5	142.5	61 45.9	51.9	144.8	60 06.7	53.1	146.8	58 25.2	54.1	148.6	56 41.9	55.0	150.2
9	64 13.0	49.8	141.3	62 37.8	51.4	143.7	60 59.8	52.7	145.8	59 19.3	53.8	147.8	57 36.9	54.7	149.4
10	65 02.8	+ 49.1	140.0	63 29.2	+ 50.8	142.5	61 52.5	+ 52.2	144.8	60 13.1	+ 53.5	146.9	58 31.6	+ 54.4	148.7
11	65 51.9	48.3	138.6	64 20.0	50.2	141.3	62 44.7	51.8	143.8	61 06.6	53.0	145.9	59 26.0	54.1	147.9
12	66 40.2	47.4	137.1	65 10.2	49.5	140.1	63 36.5	51.1	142.7	61 59.6	52.6	145.0	60 20.1	53.7	147.0
13	67 27.6	46.5	135.5	65 59.7	48.7	138.7	64 27.6	50.6	141.5	62 52.2	52.0	143.9	61 13.8	53.4	146.1
14	68 14.1	45.3	133.8	66 48.4	47.8	137.2	65 18.2	49.9	140.2	63 44.2	51.6	142.8	62 07.2	52.9	145.1
15	68 59.4	+ 44.2	132.0	67 36.2	+ 46.9	135.7	66 08.1	+ 49.1	138.8	64 35.8	+ 50.9	141.6	63 00.1	+ 52.4	144.1
16	69 43.6	42.8	130.1	68 23.1	45.8	134.0	66 57.2	48.3	137.4	65 26.7	50.3	140.4	63 52.5	52.0	143.0
17	70 26.4	41.3	128.1	69 08.9	44.7	132.2	67 45.5	47.3	135.9	66 17.0	49.6	139.1	64 44.5	51.3	141.8
18	71 07.7	39.6	125.9	69 53.6	43.3	130.3	68 32.8	46.3	134.2	67 06.6	48.7	137.6	65 35.8	50.7	140.6
19	71 47.3	37.7	123.5	70 36.9	41.8	128.3	69 19.1	45.2	132.4	67 55.3	47.8	136.1	66 26.5	50.0	139.3
20	72 25.0	+ 35.7•	121.0	71 18.7	+ 40.2	126.1	70 04.3	+ 43.8	130.5	68 43.1	+ 46.9	134.5	67 16.5	+ 49.2	137.9
21	73 00.7	33.5•	118.3	71 58.9	38.3	123.7	70 48.1	42.4	128.5	69 30.0	45.6	132.7	68 05.7	48.3	136.4
22	73 34.2	30.8•	115.4	72 37.2	36.3•	121.2	71 30.5	40.8	126.3	70 15.6	44.4	130.8	68 54.0	47.4	134.8
23	74 05.0	28.1•	112.3	73 13.5	34.0•	118.5	72 11.3	38.9	124.0	71 00.0	43.0	128.8	69 41.4	46.2	133.0
24	74 33.1	25.1•	109.0	73 47.5	31.5•	115.6	72 50.2	36.9•	121.4	71 43.0	41.4	126.6	70 27.6	45.0	131.2
25	74 58.2	+ 21.7•	105.6	74 19.0	+ 28.7•	112.5	73 27.1	+ 34.7•	118.7	72 24.4	+ 39.5	124.3	71 12.6	+ 43.6	129.1
26	75 19.9	18.2•	101.9	74 47.7	25.6•	109.2	74 01.8	32.1•	115.8	73 03.9	37.6•	121.7	71 56.2	42.0	127.0
27	75 38.1	14.5•	98.1	75 13.3	22.3•	105.7	74 33.9	29.3•	112.7	73 41.5	35.3•	119.0	72 38.2	40.2	124.6
28	75 52.6	10.4•	94.2	75 35.6	18.7•	102.0	75 03.2	26.2•	109.3	74 16.8	32.8•	116.1	73 18.4	38.2•	122.1
29	76 03.0	6.3•	90.1	75 54.3	14.9•	98.1	75 29.4	22.9•	105.8	74 49.6	29.9•	112.9	73 56.6	36.0•	119.4

20°			22°			24°			26°			28°			Dec.
Hc	d	Z	Hc	d	Z	Hc	d	Z	Hc	d	Z	Hc	d	Z	
64 35.6	−48.2	140.0	63 02.0	−49.9	142.6	61 25.2	−51.2	144.8	59 46.0	−52.5	146.8	58 04.5	−53.4	148.6	0
63 47.4	48.9	141.4	62 12.1	50.5	143.8	60 34.0	51.8	145.9	58 53.5	52.8	147.8	57 11.1	53.8	149.4	1
62 58.5	49.7	142.7	61 21.6	51.0	144.9	59 42.2	52.2	146.9	58 00.7	53.2	148.7	56 17.3	54.1	150.2	2
62 08.8	50.2	143.9	60 30.6	51.5	146.0	58 50.0	52.6	147.9	57 07.5	53.6	149.5	55 23.2	54.3	151.0	3
61 18.6	50.8	145.1	59 39.1	52.0	147.0	57 57.4	53.0	148.8	56 13.9	53.9	150.4	54 28.9	54.6	151.8	4
60 27.8	−51.3	146.2	58 47.1	−52.4	148.0	57 04.4	−53.4	149.7	55 20.0	−54.1	151.1	53 34.3	−54.9	152.5	5
59 36.5	51.7	147.2	57 54.7	52.8	148.9	56 11.0	53.6	150.5	54 25.9	54.4	151.9	52 39.4	55.0	153.1	6
58 44.8	52.2	148.2	57 01.9	53.2	149.8	55 17.4	54.0	151.3	53 31.5	54.7	152.6	51 44.4	55.3	153.8	7
57 52.6	52.6	149.1	56 08.7	53.8	150.7	54 23.4	54.2	152.0	52 36.8	54.9	153.3	50 49.1	55.5	154.4	8
57 00.0	53.0	150.0	55 15.3	53.8	151.5	53 29.2	54.5	152.8	51 41.9	55.1	153.9	49 53.6	55.6	155.0	9
56 07.0	−53.3	150.9	54 21.5	−54.1	152.2	52 34.7	−54.7	153.5	50 46.8	−55.3	154.6	48 58.0	−55.8	155.6	10
55 13.7	53.6	151.7	53 27.4	54.3	153.0	51 40.0	55.0	154.1	49 51.5	55.5	155.2	48 02.2	56.0	156.1	11
54 20.1	53.9	152.5	52 33.1	54.5	153.7	50 45.0	55.1	154.8	48 56.0	55.6	155.8	47 06.2	56.1	156.7	12
53 26.2	54.1	153.2	51 38.6	54.8	154.4	49 49.9	55.3	155.4	48 00.4	55.8	156.3	46 10.1	56.2	157.2	13
52 32.1	54.5	153.9	50 43.8	55.0	155.0	48 54.6	55.5	156.0	47 04.6	56.0	156.9	45 13.9	56.4	157.7	14
51 37.6	−54.6	154.6	49 48.8	−55.2	155.6	47 59.1	−55.7	156.6	46 08.6	−56.1	157.4	44 17.5	−56.5	158.2	15
50 43.0	54.9	155.3	48 53.6	55.4	156.2	47 03.4	55.8	157.1	45 12.5	56.2	157.9	43 21.0	56.6	158.6	16
49 48.1	55.0	155.9	47 58.2	55.5	156.8	46 07.6	56.0	157.6	44 16.3	56.4	158.4	42 24.4	56.7	159.1	17
48 53.1	55.2	156.5	47 02.7	55.7	157.4	45 11.6	56.1	158.2	43 19.9	56.4	158.9	41 27.7	56.8	159.5	18
47 57.9	55.5	157.1	46 07.0	55.9	157.9	44 15.5	56.2	158.7	42 23.5	56.6	159.3	40 30.9	56.8	160.0	19
47 02.4	−55.5	157.7	45 11.1	−55.9	158.4	43 19.3	−56.4	159.1	41 26.9	−56.7	159.8	39 34.1	−57.0	160.4	20
46 06.9	55.8	158.2	44 15.2	56.2	158.9	42 22.9	56.5	159.6	40 30.2	56.8	160.2	38 37.1	57.1	160.8	21
45 11.1	55.8	158.7	43 19.0	56.2	159.4	41 26.4	56.5	160.1	39 33.4	56.8	160.6	37 40.0	57.1	161.2	22
44 15.3	56.0	159.3	42 22.8	56.4	159.9	40 29.9	56.7	160.5	38 36.6	57.0	161.1	36 42.9	57.2	161.5	23
43 19.3	56.2	159.8	41 26.4	56.4	160.4	39 33.2	56.7	160.9	37 39.6	57.0	161.5	35 45.7	57.3	161.9	24
42 23.1	−56.2	160.2	40 30.0	−56.6	160.8	38 36.5	−56.9	161.4	36 42.6	−57.1	161.8	34 48.4	−57.3	162.3	25
41 26.9	56.4	160.7	39 33.4	56.6	161.3	37 39.6	56.9	161.8	35 45.5	57.2	162.2	33 51.1	57.4	162.6	26
40 30.5	56.4	161.2	38 36.8	56.8	161.7	36 42.7	57.0	162.2	34 48.3	57.2	162.6	32 53.7	57.5	163.0	27
39 34.1	56.6	161.6	37 40.0	56.8	162.1	35 45.7	57.1	162.5	33 51.1	57.3	163.0	31 56.2	57.5	163.3	28
38 37.5	56.6	162.0	36 43.2	56.9	162.5	34 48.6	57.1	162.9	32 53.8	57.4	163.3	30 58.7	57.5	163.7	29

30°			32°			34°			36°			38°			Dec.
Hc	d	Z	Hc	d	Z	Hc	d	Z	Hc	d	Z	Hc	d	Z	
56 21.2	−54.2	150.2	54 36.4	−55.0	151.6	52 50.2	−55.6	152.9	51 02.9	−56.2	154.0	49 14.6	−56.7	155.0	0
55 27.0	54.6	150.9	53 41.4	55.2	152.3	51 54.6	55.8	153.5	50 06.7	56.3	154.5	48 17.9	56.7	155.5	1
54 32.4	54.8	151.7	52 46.2	55.5	152.9	50 58.8	56.0	154.1	49 10.4	56.5	155.1	47 21.2	56.9	156.0	2
53 37.6	55.0	152.3	51 50.7	55.6	153.5	50 02.8	56.2	154.6	48 13.9	56.6	155.6	46 24.3	57.0	156.5	3
52 42.6	55.3	153.0	50 55.1	55.8	154.1	49 06.6	56.3	155.2	47 17.3	56.7	156.1	45 27.3	57.1	156.9	4
51 47.3	−55.4	153.6	49 59.3	−56.0	154.7	48 10.3	−56.4	155.7	46 20.6	−56.8	156.6	44 30.2	−57.2	157.4	5
50 51.9	55.7	154.3	49 03.3	56.1	155.3	47 13.9	56.6	156.2	45 23.8	57.0	157.0	43 33.0	57.3	157.8	6
49 56.2	55.8	154.8	48 07.2	56.3	155.8	46 17.3	56.6	156.7	44 26.8	57.0	157.5	42 35.7	57.4	158.2	7
49 00.4	55.9	155.4	47 10.9	56.4	156.3	45 20.7	56.8	157.1	43 29.8	57.2	157.9	41 38.3	57.4	158.6	8
48 04.5	56.2	156.0	46 14.5	56.5	156.8	44 23.9	56.9	157.6	42 32.6	57.2	158.3	40 40.9	57.6	159.0	9
47 08.3	−56.2	156.5	45 18.0	−56.7	157.3	43 27.0	−57.0	158.0	41 35.4	−57.3	158.7	39 43.3	−57.5	159.3	10
46 12.1	56.4	157.0	44 21.3	56.7	157.8	42 30.0	57.1	158.5	40 38.1	57.4	159.1	38 45.8	57.7	159.7	11
45 15.7	56.5	157.5	43 24.6	56.9	158.2	41 32.9	57.2	158.9	39 40.7	57.5	159.5	37 48.1	57.7	160.0	12
44 19.2	56.6	158.0	42 27.7	57.0	158.7	40 35.7	57.3	159.3	38 43.2	57.5	159.9	36 50.4	57.8	160.4	13
43 22.6	56.7	158.4	41 30.7	57.0	159.1	39 38.4	57.3	159.7	37 45.7	57.6	160.2	35 52.6	57.8	160.7	14
42 25.9	−56.9	158.9	40 33.7	−57.1	159.5	38 41.1	−57.4	160.1	36 48.1	−57.6	160.6	34 54.8	−57.9	161.1	15
41 29.0	56.9	159.3	39 36.6	57.2	159.9	37 43.7	57.5	160.4	35 50.5	57.8	160.9	33 56.9	57.9	161.4	16
40 32.1	57.0	159.7	38 39.4	57.4	160.3	36 46.2	57.5	160.8	34 52.7	57.7	161.3	32 59.0	58.0	161.7	17
39 35.1	57.1	160.1	37 42.1	57.4	160.7	35 48.7	57.6	161.1	33 55.0	57.8	161.6	32 01.0	58.0	162.0	18
38 38.0	57.1	160.5	36 44.7	57.4	161.0	34 51.1	57.7	161.5	32 57.2	57.9	161.9	31 03.0	58.1	162.3	19
37 40.9	−57.3	160.9	35 47.3	−57.5	161.4	33 53.4	−57.7	161.8	31 59.3	−57.9	162.2	30 04.9	−58.1	162.6	20
36 43.6	57.3	161.3	34 49.8	57.5	161.7	32 55.7	57.7	162.1	31 01.4	58.0	162.5	29 06.8	58.1	162.9	21
35 46.3	57.4	161.6	33 52.3	57.6	162.1	31 58.0	57.8	162.5	30 03.4	58.0	162.8	28 08.7	58.2	163.2	22
34 48.9	57.4	162.0	32 54.7	57.7	162.4	31 00.2	57.9	162.8	29 05.4	58.0	163.1	27 10.5	58.2	163.4	23
33 51.5	57.5	162.3	31 57.0	57.7	162.7	30 02.3	57.9	163.1	28 07.4	58.1	163.4	26 12.3	58.2	163.7	24
32 54.0	−57.6	162.7	30 59.3	−57.7	163.1	29 04.4	−57.9	163.4	27 09.3	−58.1	163.7	25 14.1	−58.3	164.0	25
31 56.4	57.6	163.0	30 01.6	57.8	163.4	28 06.5	58.0	163.7	26 11.2	58.1	164.0	24 15.8	58.3	164.2	26
30 58.8	57.6	163.4	29 03.8	57.9	163.7	27 08.5	58.0	164.0	25 13.1	58.2	164.2	23 17.5	58.3	164.5	27
30 01.2	57.7	163.7	28 05.9	57.8	164.0	26 10.5	58.0	164.3	24 14.9	58.2	164.5	22 19.2	58.3	164.7	28
29 03.5	57.8	164.0	27 08.1	58.0	164.3	25 12.5	58.1	164.5	23 16.7	58.2	164.8	21 20.9	58.4	165.0	29

Dec.	40° Hc	d	Z	42° Hc	d	Z	44° Hc	d	Z	46° Hc	d	Z	48° Hc	d	Z
0	47 25.4	+56.9	156.0	45 35.4	+57.4	156.8	43 44.8	+57.7	157.6	41 53.6	+58.0	158.3	40 01.9	+58.2	158.9
1	48 22.3	56.9	155.5	46 32.8	57.2	156.4	44 42.5	57.5	157.2	42 51.6	57.8	157.9	41 00.1	58.2	158.6
2	49 19.2	56.7	155.0	47 30.0	57.1	155.9	45 40.0	57.5	156.8	43 49.4	57.9	157.6	41 58.3	58.0	158.3
3	50 15.9	56.5	154.5	48 27.1	57.0	155.5	46 37.5	57.4	156.4	44 47.3	57.7	157.2	42 56.3	58.1	157.9
4	51 12.4	56.4	154.0	49 24.1	56.9	154.0	47 34.9	57.3	155.9	45 45.0	57.6	156.8	43 54.4	57.9	157.6
5	52 08.8	+56.3	153.4	50 21.0	+56.8	154.5	48 32.2	+57.2	155.5	46 42.6	+57.6	156.4	44 52.3	+57.9	157.2
6	53 05.1	56.1	152.8	51 17.8	56.6	154.0	49 29.4	57.1	155.0	47 40.2	57.5	156.0	45 50.2	57.9	156.8
7	54 01.2	55.9	152.2	52 14.4	56.4	153.5	50 26.5	57.0	154.6	48 37.7	57.4	155.5	46 48.1	57.7	156.4
8	54 57.1	55.7	151.6	53 10.8	56.3	152.9	51 23.5	56.8	154.1	49 35.1	57.2	155.1	47 45.8	57.7	156.0
9	55 52.8	55.4	151.0	54 07.1	56.2	152.3	52 20.3	56.7	153.5	50 32.3	57.2	154.6	48 43.5	57.5	155.6
10	56 48.2	+55.3	150.3	55 03.3	+55.9	151.7	53 17.0	+56.5	153.0	51 29.5	+57.0	154.2	49 41.0	+57.5	155.2
11	57 43.5	54.9	149.6	55 59.2	55.7	151.1	54 13.5	56.3	152.4	52 26.5	56.9	153.6	50 38.5	57.3	154.7
12	58 38.4	54.7	148.8	56 54.9	55.5	150.4	55 09.8	56.2	151.8	53 23.4	56.8	153.1	51 35.8	57.3	154.3
13	59 33.1	54.4	148.0	57 50.4	55.3	149.7	56 06.0	56.0	151.2	54 20.2	56.6	152.6	52 33.1	57.1	153.8
14	60 27.5	54.1	147.2	58 45.7	55.0	149.0	57 02.0	55.8	150.6	55 16.8	56.4	152.0	53 30.2	56.9	153.3
15	61 21.6	+53.6	146.3	59 40.7	+54.7	148.2	57 57.8	+55.5	149.9	56 13.2	+56.2	151.4	54 27.1	+56.7	152.7
16	62 15.2	53.3	145.3	60 35.4	54.3	147.3	58 53.3	55.3	149.2	57 09.4	56.0	150.8	55 24.0	56.6	152.2
17	63 08.5	52.8	144.3	61 29.7	54.0	146.5	59 48.6	55.0	148.4	58 05.4	55.9	150.1	56 20.6	56.5	151.6
18	64 01.3	52.3	143.2	62 23.7	53.6	145.5	60 43.6	54.7	147.6	59 01.3	55.5	149.4	57 17.1	56.3	151.0
19	64 53.6	51.8	142.1	63 17.3	53.2	144.6	61 38.3	54.3	146.7	59 56.8	55.3	148.6	58 13.4	56.1	150.3
20	65 45.4	+51.1	140.9	64 10.5	+52.7	143.5	62 32.6	+54.0	145.8	60 52.1	+55.0	147.9	59 09.5	+55.9	149.7
21	66 36.5	50.5	139.6	65 03.2	52.2	142.4	63 26.6	53.5	144.9	61 47.1	54.7	147.0	60 05.4	55.6	148.9
22	67 27.0	49.7	138.2	65 55.4	51.6	141.2	64 20.1	53.1	143.8	62 41.8	54.4	146.1	61 01.0	55.3	148.2
23	68 16.7	48.8	136.7	66 47.0	50.9	139.9	65 13.2	52.6	142.7	63 36.2	53.9	145.2	61 56.3	55.1	147.4
24	69 05.5	47.9	135.1	67 37.9	50.2	138.6	66 05.8	52.1	141.6	64 30.1	53.5	144.2	62 51.4	54.7	146.5
25	69 53.4	+46.8	133.4	68 28.1	+49.3	137.1	66 57.9	+51.4	140.3	65 23.6	+53.1	143.1	63 46.1	+54.3	145.6
26	70 40.2	45.5	131.5	69 17.4	48.5	135.5	67 49.3	50.7	139.0	66 16.7	52.5	142.0	64 40.4	53.9	144.6
27	71 25.7	44.2	129.5	70 05.9	47.3	133.8	68 40.0	49.9	137.5	67 09.2	51.8	140.8	65 34.3	53.5	143.6
28	72 09.9	42.7	127.4	70 53.2	46.2	132.0	69 29.9	48.9	136.0	68 01.0	51.2	139.4	66 27.8	53.0	142.5
29	72 52.6	40.9	125.0	71 39.4	44.9	130.0	70 18.8	48.0	134.3	68 52.2	50.5	138.0	67 20.8	52.3	141.3

Dec.	50° Hc	d	Z	52° Hc	d	Z	54° Hc	d	Z	56° Hc	d	Z	58° Hc	d	Z
0	38 09.7	+58.5	159.5	36 17.1	+58.7	160.0	34 24.2	+58.8	160.5	32 30.9	+59.0	160.9	30 37.4	+59.1	161.3
1	39 08.2	58.3	159.2	37 15.8	58.6	159.7	35 23.0	58.8	160.2	33 29.9	59.0	160.7	31 36.5	59.1	161.1
2	40 06.5	58.4	158.9	38 14.4	58.5	159.5	36 21.8	58.8	160.0	34 28.9	59.0	160.5	32 35.6	59.1	160.9
3	41 04.9	58.3	158.6	39 12.9	58.6	159.2	37 20.6	58.7	159.7	35 27.8	58.9	160.2	33 34.7	59.1	160.7
4	42 03.2	58.2	158.3	40 11.5	58.4	158.9	38 19.3	58.7	159.5	36 26.7	58.9	160.0	34 33.8	59.0	160.5
5	43 01.4	+58.2	157.9	41 09.9	+58.5	158.6	39 18.0	+58.6	159.2	37 25.6	+58.8	159.8	35 32.8	+59.0	160.3
6	43 59.6	58.1	157.6	42 08.4	58.4	158.3	40 16.6	58.6	158.9	38 24.4	58.8	159.5	36 31.8	59.0	160.1
7	44 57.7	58.1	157.3	43 06.8	58.3	158.0	41 15.2	58.6	158.7	39 23.2	58.8	159.3	37 30.8	59.0	159.8
8	45 55.8	58.0	156.9	44 05.1	58.3	157.7	42 13.8	58.5	158.4	40 22.0	58.8	159.0	38 29.8	58.9	159.6
9	46 53.8	57.9	156.5	45 03.4	58.2	157.3	43 12.3	58.5	158.1	41 20.8	58.7	158.7	39 28.7	58.9	159.3
10	47 51.7	+57.8	156.1	46 01.6	+58.1	157.0	44 10.8	+58.4	157.8	42 19.5	+58.6	158.5	40 27.6	+58.9	159.1
11	48 49.5	57.7	155.7	46 59.7	58.1	156.6	45 09.2	58.4	157.4	43 18.1	58.6	158.2	41 26.5	58.8	158.8
12	49 47.2	57.7	155.3	47 57.8	58.0	156.3	46 07.6	58.3	157.1	44 16.7	58.6	157.9	42 25.3	58.8	158.6
13	50 44.9	57.5	154.9	48 55.8	57.9	155.9	47 05.9	58.2	156.8	45 15.3	58.5	157.6	43 24.1	58.7	158.3
14	51 42.4	57.5	154.4	49 53.7	57.9	155.5	48 04.1	58.2	156.4	46 13.8	58.5	157.3	44 22.8	58.7	158.0
15	52 39.9	+57.3	154.0	50 51.6	+57.7	155.1	49 02.3	+58.1	156.0	47 12.3	+58.4	156.9	45 21.5	+58.7	157.7
16	53 37.2	57.2	153.5	51 49.3	57.6	154.6	50 00.4	58.0	155.7	48 10.7	58.3	156.6	46 20.2	58.6	157.4
17	54 34.4	57.1	153.0	52 46.9	57.6	154.2	50 58.4	58.0	155.3	49 09.0	58.3	156.2	47 18.8	58.6	157.1
18	55 31.5	56.9	152.4	53 44.5	57.4	153.7	51 56.4	57.8	154.8	50 07.3	58.2	155.9	48 17.4	58.5	156.8
19	56 28.4	56.7	151.8	54 41.9	57.3	153.2	52 54.2	57.8	154.4	51 05.5	58.1	155.5	49 15.9	58.4	156.5
20	57 25.1	+56.6	151.2	55 39.2	+57.1	152.7	53 52.0	+57.6	153.9	52 03.6	+58.1	155.1	50 14.3	+58.4	156.1
21	58 21.7	56.4	150.6	56 36.3	57.0	152.1	54 49.6	57.5	153.5	53 01.7	57.9	154.7	51 12.7	58.3	155.7
22	59 18.1	56.1	150.0	57 33.3	56.9	151.6	55 47.1	57.4	153.0	53 59.6	57.9	154.2	52 11.0	58.3	155.4
23	60 14.2	55.9	149.3	58 30.2	56.6	150.9	56 44.5	57.3	152.4	54 57.5	57.7	153.8	53 09.3	58.1	155.0
24	61 10.1	55.7	148.5	59 26.8	56.5	150.3	57 41.8	57.1	151.9	55 55.2	57.6	153.3	54 07.4	58.1	154.6
25	62 05.8	+55.4	147.7	60 23.3	+56.2	149.6	58 38.9	+56.9	151.3	56 52.8	+57.5	152.8	55 05.5	+57.9	154.1
26	63 01.2	55.1	146.9	61 19.5	56.0	148.9	59 35.8	56.7	150.7	57 50.3	57.4	152.3	56 03.4	57.9	153.7
27	63 56.3	54.7	146.0	62 15.5	55.8	148.2	60 32.5	56.6	150.0	58 47.7	57.2	151.7	57 01.3	57.7	153.2
28	64 51.0	54.3	145.1	63 11.3	55.4	147.3	61 29.1	56.3	149.3	59 44.9	57.0	151.1	57 59.0	57.7	152.7
29	65 45.3	53.9	144.0	64 06.7	55.1	146.5	62 25.4	56.1	148.6	60 41.9	56.9	150.5	58 56.7	57.4	152.1

40°			42°			44°			46°			48°			Dec.
Hc	d	Z	Hc	d	Z	Hc	d	Z	Hc	d	Z	Hc	d	Z	
° ′	′	°	° ′	′	°	° ′	′	°	° ′	′	°	° ′	′	°	°
47 25.4	−57.1	156.0	45 35.4	−57.4	156.8	43 44.8	−57.7	157.6	41 53.6	−58.0	158.3	40 01.9	−58.3	158.9	0
46 28.3	57.1	156.4	44 38.0	57.5	157.2	42 47.1	57.8	157.9	40 55.6	58.1	158.6	39 03.6	58.3	159.2	1
45 31.2	57.3	156.8	43 40.5	57.6	157.6	41 49.3	57.9	158.3	39 57.5	58.1	158.9	38 05.3	58.3	159.5	2
44 33.9	57.3	157.3	42 42.9	57.6	158.0	40 51.4	57.9	158.7	38 59.4	58.2	159.3	37 07.0	58.4	159.8	3
43 36.6	57.5	157.7	41 45.3	57.8	158.4	39 53.5	58.0	159.0	38 01.2	58.2	159.6	36 08.6	58.4	160.1	4
42 39.1	−57.5	158.1	40 47.5	−57.8	158.7	38 55.5	−58.1	159.3	37 03.0	−58.3	159.9	35 10.2	−58.5	160.4	5
41 41.6	57.6	158.5	39 49.7	57.8	159.1	37 57.4	58.1	159.7	36 04.7	58.3	160.2	34 11.7	58.5	160.6	6
40 44.0	57.6	158.8	38 51.9	57.9	159.4	36 59.3	58.1	160.0	35 06.4	58.3	160.5	33 13.2	58.6	160.9	7
39 46.4	57.8	159.2	37 54.0	58.0	159.8	36 01.2	58.2	160.3	34 08.1	58.4	160.7	32 14.6	58.6	161.2	8
38 48.6	57.7	159.6	36 56.0	58.0	160.1	35 03.0	58.2	160.6	33 09.7	58.4	161.0	31 16.1	58.6	161.4	9
37 50.9	−57.9	159.9	35 58.0	−58.1	160.4	34 04.8	−58.3	160.9	32 11.3	−58.5	161.3	30 17.5	−58.7	161.7	10
36 53.0	57.9	160.2	34 59.9	58.1	160.7	33 06.5	58.3	161.2	31 12.8	58.5	161.6	29 18.8	58.6	161.9	11
35 55.1	57.9	160.6	34 01.8	58.2	161.0	32 08.2	58.4	161.4	30 14.3	58.6	161.8	28 20.2	58.7	162.2	12
34 57.2	58.0	160.9	33 03.6	58.2	161.3	31 09.8	58.4	161.7	29 15.8	58.6	162.1	27 21.5	58.7	162.4	13
33 59.2	58.1	161.2	32 05.4	58.2	161.6	30 11.4	58.4	162.0	28 17.2	58.6	162.3	26 22.8	58.7	162.6	14
33 01.1	−58.1	161.5	31 07.2	−58.3	161.9	29 13.0	−58.4	162.2	27 18.6	−58.6	162.6	25 24.1	−58.8	162.9	15
32 03.0	58.1	161.8	30 08.9	58.3	162.2	28 14.6	58.5	162.5	26 20.0	58.6	162.8	24 25.3	58.7	163.1	16
31 04.9	58.2	162.1	29 10.6	58.3	162.4	27 16.1	58.5	162.7	25 21.4	58.6	163.0	23 26.6	58.8	163.3	17
30 06.7	58.2	162.4	28 12.3	58.4	162.7	26 17.6	58.5	163.0	24 22.8	58.7	163.3	22 27.8	58.8	163.5	18
29 08.5	58.2	162.6	27 13.9	58.4	163.0	25 19.1	58.6	163.2	23 24.1	58.7	163.5	21 29.0	58.8	163.7	19
28 10.3	−58.3	162.9	26 15.5	−58.4	163.2	24 20.5	−58.5	163.5	22 25.4	−58.7	163.7	20 30.2	−58.9	163.9	20
27 12.0	58.3	163.2	25 17.1	58.5	163.5	23 22.0	58.6	163.7	21 26.7	58.7	164.0	19 31.3	58.8	164.2	21
26 13.7	58.3	163.4	24 18.6	58.5	163.7	22 23.4	58.6	164.0	20 28.0	58.7	164.2	18 32.5	58.9	164.4	22
25 15.4	58.4	163.7	23 20.1	58.5	164.0	21 24.8	58.7	164.2	19 29.2	58.7	164.4	17 33.6	58.9	164.6	23
24 17.0	58.3	164.0	22 21.6	58.5	164.2	20 26.1	58.6	164.4	18 30.5	58.8	164.6	16 34.7	58.8	164.8	24
23 18.7	−58.4	164.2	21 23.1	−58.5	164.4	19 27.5	−58.7	164.6	17 31.7	−58.8	164.8	15 35.9	−58.9	165.0	25
22 20.3	58.4	164.5	20 24.6	58.6	164.7	18 28.8	58.7	164.9	16 32.9	58.8	165.0	14 37.0	58.9	165.2	26
21 21.8	58.4	164.7	19 26.0	58.5	164.9	17 30.1	58.7	165.1	15 34.1	58.8	165.2	13 38.1	59.0	165.4	27
20 23.4	58.5	165.0	18 27.5	58.6	165.1	16 31.4	58.7	165.3	14 35.3	58.8	165.4	12 39.1	58.9	165.6	28
19 24.9	58.5	165.2	17 28.9	58.6	165.4	15 32.7	58.7	165.5	13 36.5	58.8	165.6	11 40.2	58.9	165.7	29

50°			52°			54°			56°			58°			Dec.
Hc	d	Z	Hc	d	Z	Hc	d	Z	Hc	d	Z	Hc	d	Z	
° ′	′	°	° ′	′	°	° ′	′	°	° ′	′	°	° ′	′	°	°
38 09.7	−58.5	159.5	36 17.1	−58.6	160.0	34 24.2	−58.8	160.5	32 30.9	−59.0	160.9	30 37.4	−59.1	161.3	0
37 11.2	58.5	159.8	35 18.5	58.7	160.3	33 25.4	58.9	160.7	31 31.9	59.0	161.1	29 38.3	59.2	161.5	1
36 12.7	58.5	160.0	34 19.8	58.8	160.5	32 26.5	58.9	160.9	30 32.9	59.0	161.3	28 39.1	59.2	161.7	2
35 14.2	58.6	160.3	33 21.0	58.8	160.8	31 27.6	58.9	161.2	29 33.9	59.1	161.6	27 39.9	59.2	161.9	3
34 15.6	58.6	160.6	32 22.3	58.8	161.0	30 28.7	59.0	161.4	28 34.8	59.1	161.8	26 40.7	59.2	162.1	4
33 17.0	−58.7	160.8	31 23.5	−58.8	161.2	29 29.7	−58.9	161.6	27 35.7	−59.1	162.0	25 41.5	−59.2	162.3	5
32 18.3	58.7	161.1	30 24.7	58.9	161.5	28 30.8	59.0	161.8	26 36.6	59.1	162.1	24 42.3	59.2	162.4	6
31 19.6	58.7	161.3	29 25.8	58.9	161.7	27 31.8	59.0	162.0	25 37.5	59.1	162.3	23 43.1	59.2	162.6	7
30 20.9	58.7	161.6	28 27.0	58.9	161.9	26 32.8	59.0	162.2	24 38.4	59.1	162.5	22 43.9	59.3	162.8	8
29 22.2	58.8	161.8	27 28.1	58.9	162.1	25 33.8	59.1	162.4	23 39.3	59.2	162.7	21 44.6	59.2	163.0	9
28 23.4	−58.8	162.0	26 29.2	−58.9	162.3	24 34.7	−59.0	162.6	22 40.1	−59.1	162.9	20 45.4	−59.3	163.1	10
27 24.6	58.8	162.3	25 30.3	59.0	162.6	23 35.7	59.1	162.8	21 41.0	59.2	163.1	19 46.1	59.3	163.3	11
26 25.8	58.8	162.5	24 31.3	58.9	162.8	22 36.6	59.0	163.0	20 41.8	59.2	163.2	18 46.8	59.3	163.5	12
25 27.0	58.8	162.7	23 32.4	59.0	163.0	21 37.6	59.1	163.2	19 42.6	59.2	163.4	17 47.5	59.3	163.6	13
24 28.2	58.9	162.9	22 33.4	59.0	163.2	20 38.5	59.1	163.4	18 43.4	59.2	163.6	16 48.2	59.3	163.8	14
23 29.3	−58.9	163.1	21 34.4	−59.0	163.4	19 39.4	−59.1	163.6	17 44.2	−59.2	163.8	15 48.9	−59.3	163.9	15
22 30.4	58.9	163.3	20 35.4	59.0	163.6	18 40.3	59.2	163.8	16 45.0	59.2	163.9	14 49.6	59.3	164.1	16
21 31.5	58.9	163.5	19 36.4	59.0	163.8	17 41.1	59.1	164.0	15 45.8	59.3	164.1	13 50.3	59.3	164.2	17
20 32.6	58.9	163.7	18 37.4	59.1	163.9	16 42.0	59.1	164.1	14 46.5	59.2	164.3	12 51.0	59.3	164.4	18
19 33.7	58.9	163.9	17 38.3	59.0	164.1	15 42.9	59.2	164.3	13 47.3	59.2	164.4	11 51.7	59.4	164.6	19
18 34.8	−59.0	164.1	16 39.3	−59.1	164.3	14 43.7	−59.1	164.5	12 48.1	−59.3	164.6	10 52.3	−59.3	164.7	20
17 35.8	58.9	164.3	15 40.2	59.1	164.5	13 44.6	59.2	164.6	11 48.8	59.2	164.8	9 53.0	59.3	164.9	21
16 36.9	59.0	164.5	14 41.2	59.1	164.7	12 45.4	59.2	164.8	10 49.6	59.3	164.9	8 53.7	59.4	165.0	22
15 37.9	59.0	164.7	13 42.1	59.1	164.9	11 46.2	59.1	165.0	9 50.3	59.2	165.1	7 54.3	59.3	165.2	23
14 38.9	59.0	164.9	12 43.0	59.1	165.0	10 47.1	59.2	165.1	8 51.0	59.2	165.2	6 55.0	59.4	165.4	24
13 39.9	−59.0	165.1	11 43.9	−59.1	165.2	9 47.9	−59.2	165.3	7 51.8	−59.3	165.4	5 55.6	−59.3	165.5	25
12 40.9	59.0	165.3	10 44.8	59.1	165.4	8 48.7	59.2	165.5	6 52.5	59.3	165.5	4 56.3	59.4	165.6	26
11 41.9	59.0	165.5	9 45.7	59.1	165.6	7 49.5	59.2	165.6	5 53.2	59.3	165.7	3 56.9	59.3	165.7	27
10 42.9	59.0	165.7	8 46.6	59.1	165.7	6 50.3	59.2	165.8	4 53.9	59.2	165.8	2 57.6	59.4	165.9	28
9 43.9	59.0	165.8	7 47.5	59.1	165.9	5 51.1	59.2	166.0	3 54.7	59.3	166.0	1 58.2	59.3	166.0	29

Dec.	0° Hc	d	Z	2° Hc	d	Z	4° Hc	d	Z	6° Hc	d	Z	8° Hc	d	Z
0	72 00.0	− 1.6°	90.0	71 53.6	+ 5.1°	96.1	71 34.5	+ 11.7°	102.1	71 03.5	+ 17.9°	107.8	70 21.4	+ 23.6°	113.2
1	71 58.4	4.8°	86.8	71 58.7	+ 2.0°	92.9	71 46.2	8.7°	99.0	71 21.4	15.1°	104.9	70 45.0	21.0°	110.4
2	71 53.6	8.0°	83.6	72 00.7	− 1.3°	89.7	71 54.9	5.5°	95.8	71 36.5	12.0°	101.8	71 06.0	18.3°	107.6
3	71 45.6	11.1°	80.4	71 59.4	4.5°	86.4	72 00.4	+ 2.3°	92.6	71 48.5	9.0°	98.7	71 24.3	15.4°	104.6
4	71 34.5	14.1°	77.2	71 54.9	7.7°	83.2	72 02.7	− 1.0°	89.4	71 57.5	5.9°	95.5	71 39.7	12.4°	101.5
5	71 20.4	− 16.9°	74.2	71 47.2	− 10.7°	80.0	72 01.7	− 4.2°	86.1	72 03.4	+ 2.6°	92.3	71 52.1	+ 9.4°	98.4
6	71 03.5	19.8°	71.2	71 36.5	13.8°	76.9	71 57.5	7.3°	82.9	72 06.0	− 0.7°	89.1	72 01.5	6.1°	95.2
7	70 43.7	22.3°	68.3	71 22.7	16.7°	73.8	71 50.2	10.5°	79.7	72 05.3	3.8°	85.8	72 07.6	+ 3.0°	92.0
8	70 21.4	24.9°	65.5	71 06.0	19.5°	70.9	71 39.7	13.5°	76.6	72 01.5	7.1°	82.6	72 10.6	− 0.3°	88.7
9	69 56.5	27.1°	62.9	70 46.5	22.1°	68.0	71 26.2	16.4°	73.5	71 54.4	10.2°	79.4	72 10.3	3.6°	85.5
10	69 29.4	− 29.4°	60.3	70 24.4	− 24.6°	65.2	71 09.8	− 19.3°	70.5	71 44.2	− 13.2°	76.2	72 06.7	− 6.7°	82.2
11	69 00.0	31.3°	57.8	69 59.8	26.9°	62.5	70 50.5	21.8°	67.6	71 31.0	16.2°	73.1	72 00.0	10.0°	79.0
12	68 28.7	33.3°	55.5	69 32.9	29.2°	59.9	70 28.7	24.4°	64.8	71 14.8	19.0°	70.1	71 50.0	13.0°	75.8
13	67 55.4	35.0°	53.2	69 03.7	31.2°	57.4	70 04.3	26.8°	62.0	70 55.8	21.7°	67.2	71 37.0	15.9°	72.7
14	67 20.4	36.6°	51.1	68 32.5	33.1°	55.0	69 37.5	29.0°	59.5	70 34.1	24.2°	64.3	71 21.1	18.9°	69.7
15	66 43.8	− 38.1	49.1	67 59.4	− 34.8	52.8	69 08.5	− 31.0	57.0	70 09.9	− 26.6°	61.6	71 02.2	− 21.5°	66.7
16	66 05.7	39.5	47.1	67 24.6	36.5	50.6	68 37.5	32.9	54.6	69 43.3	28.8°	59.0	70 40.7	24.0°	63.9
17	65 26.2	40.8	45.3	66 48.1	38.0	48.6	68 04.6	34.8	52.3	69 14.5	31.0°	56.5	70 16.7	26.5°	61.1
18	64 45.4	41.9	43.6	66 10.1	39.3	46.7	67 29.8	36.3	50.2	68 43.5	32.8	54.1	69 50.2	28.7°	58.5
19	64 03.5	43.0	41.9	65 30.8	40.7	44.8	66 53.5	37.9	48.1	68 10.7	34.6	51.8	69 21.5	30.8°	56.0
20	63 20.5	− 44.0	40.3	64 50.1	− 41.8	43.1	66 15.6	− 39.3	46.2	67 36.1	− 36.3	49.6	68 50.7	− 32.8	53.6
21	62 36.5	44.9	38.8	64 08.3	42.9	41.4	65 36.3	40.5	44.3	66 59.8	37.8	47.6	68 17.9	34.6	51.3
22	61 51.6	45.7	37.4	63 25.4	43.9	39.8	64 55.8	41.8	42.5	66 22.0	39.2	45.6	67 43.3	36.2	49.1
23	61 05.9	46.5	36.1	62 41.5	44.8	38.3	64 14.0	42.8	40.9	65 42.8	40.5	43.8	67 07.1	37.7	47.0
24	60 19.4	47.2	34.8	61 56.7	45.6	36.9	63 31.2	43.8	39.3	65 02.3	41.7	42.0	66 29.4	39.2	45.0
25	59 32.2	− 47.9	33.6	61 11.1	− 46.5	35.5	62 47.4	− 44.8	37.8	64 20.6	− 42.8	40.3	65 50.2	− 40.5	43.2
26	58 44.3	48.5	32.4	60 24.6	47.2	34.2	62 02.6	45.6	36.3	63 37.8	43.8	38.7	65 09.7	41.7	41.4
27	57 55.8	49.1	31.2	59 37.4	47.8	33.0	61 17.0	46.4	35.0	62 54.0	44.8	37.2	64 28.0	42.8	39.7
28	57 06.7	49.6	30.2	58 49.6	48.4	31.8	60 30.6	47.2	33.7	62 09.2	45.6	35.7	63 45.2	43.8	38.1
29	56 17.1	50.1	29.1	58 01.2	49.1	30.7	59 43.4	47.8	32.4	61 23.6	46.4	34.4	63 01.4	44.8	36.6

Dec.	10° Hc	d	Z	12° Hc	d	Z	14° Hc	d	Z	16° Hc	d	Z	18° Hc	d	Z
0	69 29.4	+ 28.6°	118.1	68 28.7	+ 33.0	122.6	67 20.4	+ 36.9	126.7	66 05.7	+ 40.1	130.3	64 45.4	+ 43.0	133.6
1	69 58.0	26.4°	115.6	69 01.7	31.2°	120.3	67 57.3	35.2	124.6	66 45.8	38.8	128.5	65 28.4	41.7	131.9
2	70 24.4	24.0°	112.9	69 32.9	29.0°	117.9	68 32.5	33.5	122.4	67 24.6	37.3	126.5	66 10.1	40.6	130.2
3	70 48.4	21.4°	110.2	70 01.9	26.8°	115.4	69 06.0	31.5°	120.1	68 01.9	35.6	124.4	66 50.7	39.3	128.3
4	71 09.8	18.6°	107.3	70 28.7	24.3°	112.7	69 37.5	29.4°	117.7	68 37.5	33.9	122.2	67 29.8	37.7	126.3
5	71 28.4	+ 15.8°	104.3	70 53.0	+ 21.8°	109.9	70 06.9	+ 27.2°	115.2	69 11.4	+ 31.9°	119.9	68 07.5	+ 36.0	124.3
6	71 44.2	12.8°	101.3	71 14.8	19.0°	107.1	70 34.1	24.8°	112.5	69 43.3	29.8°	117.5	68 43.5	34.3	122.1
7	71 57.0	9.7°	98.1	71 33.8	16.2°	104.1	70 58.9	22.2°	109.7	70 13.1	27.6°	115.0	69 17.8	32.4°	119.8
8	72 06.7	6.6°	94.9	71 50.0	13.2°	101.0	71 21.1	19.4°	106.9	70 40.7	25.2°	112.3	69 50.2	30.3°	117.4
9	72 13.3	3.2°	91.7	72 03.2	10.1°	97.9	71 40.5	16.6°	103.9	71 05.9	22.6°	109.6	70 20.5	28.0°	114.9
10	72 16.5	+ 0.1°	88.4	72 13.3	+ 6.9°	94.6	71 57.1	+ 13.6°	100.8	71 28.5	+ 19.9°	106.7	70 48.5	+ 25.7°	112.2
11	72 16.6	− 3.3°	85.1	72 20.2	3.6°	91.4	72 10.7	10.4°	97.6	71 48.4	17.0°	103.7	71 14.2	23.1°	109.4
12	72 13.3	6.5°	81.9	72 23.8	+ 0.3°	88.1	72 21.1	7.3°	94.4	72 05.4	14.0°	100.6	71 37.3	20.3°	106.5
13	72 06.8	9.7°	78.6	72 24.1	− 3.0°	84.8	72 28.4	3.9°	91.1	72 19.4	10.9°	97.4	71 57.6	17.2°	103.5
14	71 57.1	12.8°	75.4	72 21.1	6.2°	81.5	72 32.3	+ 0.7°	87.8	72 30.3	7.6°	94.2	72 15.0	14.4°	100.6
15	71 44.3	− 15.8°	72.3	72 14.9	− 9.5°	78.2	72 33.0	− 2.7°	84.5	72 37.9	+ 4.3°	90.8	72 29.4	+ 11.3°	97.2
16	71 28.5	18.6°	69.2	72 05.4	12.5°	75.0	72 30.3	6.0°	81.1	72 42.2	+ 0.9°	87.5	72 40.7	7.9°	93.9
17	71 09.9	21.4°	66.3	71 52.9	15.6°	71.8	72 24.3	9.3°	77.8	72 43.1	− 2.4°	84.1	72 48.6	4.7°	90.6
18	70 48.5	23.9°	63.4	71 37.3	18.5°	68.8	72 15.0	12.4°	74.6	72 40.7	5.8°	80.8	72 53.3	+ 1.2°	87.2
19	70 24.6	26.4°	60.6	71 18.8	21.3°	65.8	72 02.6	15.4°	71.4	72 34.9	9.0°	77.4	72 54.5	− 1.2°	83.8
20	69 58.2	− 28.6°	58.0	70 57.5	− 23.9°	62.9	71 47.2	− 18.4°	68.3	72 25.9	− 12.3°	74.2	72 52.3	− 5.5°	80.4
21	69 29.6	30.8°	55.4	70 33.6	26.3°	60.1	71 28.8	21.2°	65.3	72 13.6	15.3°	70.9	72 46.8	8.9°	77.0
22	68 58.8	32.7	53.0	70 07.3	28.6°	57.4	71 07.6	23.8°	62.3	71 58.3	18.3°	67.8	72 37.9	12.1°	73.7
23	68 26.1	34.5	50.7	69 38.7	30.7°	54.9	70 43.8	26.3°	59.5	71 40.0	21.2°	64.7	72 25.8	15.3°	70.4
24	67 51.6	36.2	48.5	69 08.0	32.7	52.4	70 17.5	28.6°	56.8	71 18.8	23.7°	61.8	72 10.5	18.2°	67.3
25	67 15.4	− 37.8	46.4	68 35.3	− 34.5	50.1	69 48.9	− 30.7°	54.3	70 55.1	− 26.3°	58.9	71 52.3	− 21.1°	64.2
26	66 37.6	39.2	44.4	68 00.8	36.3	47.9	69 18.2	32.7	51.8	70 28.8	28.6°	56.2	71 31.2	23.8°	61.2
27	65 58.4	40.5	42.6	67 24.5	37.8	45.8	68 45.5	34.6	49.5	70 00.2	30.8°	53.6	71 07.4	26.4°	58.3
28	65 17.9	41.7	40.8	66 46.7	39.2	43.8	68 10.9	36.3	47.2	69 29.4	32.8	51.1	70 41.0	28.6°	55.6
29	64 36.2	42.8	39.1	66 07.5	40.5	41.9	67 34.6	37.9	45.1	68 56.6	34.7	48.8	70 12.4	30.9°	52.9

0°			2°			4°			6°			8°			Dec.
Hc	d	Z	Hc	d	Z	Hc	d	Z	Hc	d	Z	Hc	d	Z	°
72 00.0	- 1.6·	90.0	71 53.6	- 8.3·	96.1	71 34.5	- 14.7·	102.1	71 03.5	- 20.7·	107.8	70 21.4	- 26.1·	113.2	0
71 58.4	4.8·	93.2	71 45.3	11.4·	99.3	71 19.8	17.6·	105.2	70 42.8	23.3·	110.7	69 55.3	28.3·	115.8	1
71 53.6	8.0·	96.4	71 33.9	14.4·	102.4	71 02.2	20.3·	108.1	70 19.5	25.6·	113.5	69 27.0	30.4·	118.4	2
71 45.6	11.1·	99.6	71 19.5	17.3·	105.5	70 41.9	23.0·	111.0	69 53.9	28.0·	116.1	68 56.6	32.4	120.8	3
71 34.5	14.1·	102.8	71 02.2	20.0·	108.4	70 18.9	25.3·	113.8	69 25.9	30.1·	118.7	68 24.2	34.2	123.1	4
71 20.4	- 16.9·	105.8	70 42.2	- 22.7·	111.3	69 53.6	- 27.7·	116.4	68 55.8	- 32.2	121.1	67 50.0	- 36.0	125.3	5
71 03.5	19.8·	108.8	70 19.5	25.0·	114.1	69 25.9	29.9·	119.0	68 23.6	33.9	123.4	67 14.0	37.4	127.4	6
70 43.7	22.3·	111.7	69 54.5	27.5·	116.8	68 56.0	31.8	121.4	67 49.7	35.7	125.6	66 36.6	39.0	129.4	7
70 21.4	24.9·	114.5	69 27.0	29.5·	119.3	68 24.2	33.7	123.8	67 14.0	37.2	127.7	65 57.6	40.2	131.3	8
69 56.5	27.1·	117.1	68 57.5	31.6·	121.8	67 50.5	35.4	126.0	66 36.8	38.7	129.7	65 17.4	41.5	133.1	9
69 29.4	- 29.4·	119.7	68 25.9	- 33.5	124.1	67 15.1	- 37.0	128.1	65 58.1	- 40.0	131.6	64 35.9	- 42.6	134.8	10
69 00.0	31.3	122.2	67 52.4	35.2	126.4	66 38.1	38.4	130.1	65 18.1	41.2	133.4	63 53.3	43.6	136.4	11
68 28.7	33.3	124.5	67 17.2	36.8	128.5	65 59.7	39.9	132.0	64 36.9	42.4	135.2	63 09.7	44.6	138.0	12
67 55.4	35.0	126.8	66 40.4	38.2	130.5	65 19.8	41.0	133.8	63 54.5	43.4	136.8	62 25.1	45.4	139.4	13
67 20.4	36.6	128.8	66 02.2	39.7	132.4	64 38.8	42.2	135.6	63 11.1	44.4	138.3	61 39.7	46.3	140.8	14
66 43.8	- 38.1	130.9	65 22.5	- 40.9	134.2	63 56.6	- 43.3	137.2	62 26.7	- 45.3	139.8	60 53.4	- 47.0	142.2	15
66 05.7	39.5	132.9	64 41.6	42.0	136.0	63 13.3	44.2	138.8	61 41.4	46.1	141.2	60 06.4	47.7	143.4	16
65 26.2	40.8	134.7	63 59.6	43.1	137.6	62 29.1	45.1	140.2	60 55.3	46.8	142.6	59 18.7	48.3	144.6	17
64 45.4	41.9	136.4	63 16.5	44.1	139.2	61 44.0	46.0	141.6	60 08.5	47.6	143.8	58 30.4	48.9	145.8	18
64 03.5	43.0	138.1	62 32.4	45.0	140.7	60 58.0	46.7	143.0	59 20.9	48.2	145.0	57 41.5	49.5	146.9	19
63 20.5	- 44.0	139.7	61 47.4	- 45.8	142.1	60 11.3	- 47.4	144.3	58 32.7	- 48.8	146.2	56 52.0	- 49.9	147.9	20
62 36.5	44.9	141.2	61 01.6	46.6	143.4	59 23.9	48.1	145.5	57 43.9	49.3	147.3	56 02.1	50.5	148.9	21
61 51.6	45.7	142.6	60 15.0	47.3	144.7	58 35.8	48.6	146.6	56 54.6	49.8	148.3	55 11.6	50.8	149.9	22
61 05.9	46.5	143.9	59 27.7	48.0	146.0	57 47.2	49.3	147.8	56 04.8	50.3	149.4	54 20.8	51.3	150.8	23
60 19.4	47.2	145.2	58 39.7	48.6	147.1	56 57.9	49.7	148.8	55 14.5	50.8	150.3	53 29.5	51.6	151.7	24
59 32.2	- 47.9	146.5	57 51.1	- 49.1	148.2	56 08.2	- 50.2	149.8	54 23.7	- 51.1	151.2	52 37.9	- 52.0	152.5	25
58 44.3	48.5	147.6	57 02.0	49.7	149.3	55 18.0	50.7	150.8	53 32.6	51.6	152.1	51 45.9	52.3	153.3	26
57 55.8	49.1	148.8	56 12.3	50.1	150.3	54 27.3	51.0	151.7	52 41.0	51.9	153.0	50 53.6	52.6	154.1	27
57 06.7	49.6	149.8	55 22.2	50.6	151.3	53 36.3	51.5	152.6	51 49.1	52.2	153.8	50 01.0	52.9	154.9	28
56 17.1	50.1	150.9	54 31.6	51.0	152.2	52 44.8	51.8	153.5	50 56.9	52.5	154.6	49 08.1	53.2	155.6	29

10°			12°			14°			16°			18°			Dec.
Hc	d	Z	Hc	d	Z	Hc	d	Z	Hc	d	Z	Hc	d	Z	°
69 29.4	- 30.8·	118.1	68 28.7	- 34.9	122.6	67 20.4	- 38.4	126.7	66 05.7	- 41.5	130.3	64 45.4	- 44.0	133.6	0
68 58.6	32.7	120.5	67 53.8	36.6	124.8	66 42.0	39.8	128.6	65 24.2	42.6	132.1	64 01.4	44.9	135.1	1
68 25.9	34.6	122.9	67 17.2	38.3	126.9	66 02.2	41.1	130.5	64 41.6	43.6	133.7	63 16.5	45.9	136.6	2
67 51.3	36.2	125.0	66 39.1	39.4	128.9	65 21.1	42.3	132.3	63 58.0	44.7	135.3	62 30.6	46.6	138.0	3
67 15.1	37.8	127.1	65 59.7	40.8	130.7	64 38.8	43.4	134.0	63 13.3	45.5	136.8	61 44.0	47.4	139.4	4
66 37.3	- 39.2	129.1	65 18.9	- 42.0	132.5	63 55.4	- 44.3	135.5	62 27.8	- 46.4	138.3	60 56.6	- 48.1	140.7	5
65 58.1	40.5	131.0	64 36.9	43.1	134.2	63 11.1	45.3	137.1	61 41.4	47.1	139.6	60 08.5	48.8	141.9	6
65 17.6	41.7	132.8	63 53.8	44.1	135.8	62 25.8	46.1	138.5	60 54.3	47.9	140.9	59 19.7	49.3	143.0	7
64 35.9	42.8	134.5	63 09.7	45.0	137.3	61 39.7	46.9	139.9	60 06.4	48.5	142.1	58 30.4	49.9	144.1	8
63 53.1	43.8	136.1	62 24.7	45.9	138.8	60 52.8	47.6	141.2	59 17.9	49.1	143.3	57 40.5	50.3	145.2	9
63 09.3	- 44.8	137.6	61 38.8	- 46.6	140.1	60 05.2	- 48.3	142.4	58 28.8	- 49.6	144.4	56 50.2	- 50.9	146.2	10
62 24.5	45.7	139.1	60 52.2	47.4	141.5	59 16.9	48.9	143.6	57 39.2	50.2	145.5	55 59.3	51.2	147.2	11
61 38.8	46.4	140.5	60 04.8	48.1	142.7	58 28.0	49.4	144.7	56 49.0	50.6	146.5	55 08.1	51.7	148.1	12
60 52.4	47.2	141.8	59 16.7	48.7	143.9	57 38.6	49.9	145.8	55 58.4	51.1	147.4	54 16.4	52.0	149.0	13
60 05.2	47.9	143.0	58 28.0	49.2	145.0	56 48.7	50.5	146.8	55 07.3	51.4	148.4	53 24.4	52.4	149.8	14
59 17.3	- 48.5	144.2	57 38.8	- 49.8	146.1	55 58.2	- 50.9	147.8	54 15.9	- 51.9	149.3	52 32.0	- 52.7	150.6	15
58 28.8	49.0	145.4	56 49.0	50.2	147.1	55 07.3	51.2	148.7	53 24.0	52.2	150.1	51 39.3	53.0	151.4	16
57 39.8	49.6	146.5	55 58.8	50.7	148.1	54 16.1	51.7	149.6	52 31.8	52.5	150.9	50 46.3	53.2	152.1	17
56 50.2	50.1	147.5	55 08.1	51.2	149.1	53 24.4	52.1	150.5	51 39.3	52.8	151.7	49 53.1	53.6	152.9	18
56 00.1	50.6	148.5	54 16.9	51.5	150.0	52 32.3	52.3	151.3	50 46.5	53.1	152.5	48 59.5	53.7	153.6	19
55 09.5	- 51.0	149.5	53 25.4	- 51.9	150.8	51 40.0	- 52.7	152.1	49 53.4	- 53.4	153.2	48 05.8	- 54.0	154.2	20
54 18.5	51.4	150.4	52 33.5	52.2	151.7	50 47.3	53.0	152.8	49 00.0	53.6	153.9	47 11.8	54.2	154.9	21
53 27.1	51.7	151.2	51 41.3	52.5	152.5	49 54.3	53.2	153.6	48 06.4	53.9	154.6	46 17.6	54.4	155.5	22
52 35.4	52.1	152.1	50 48.8	52.9	153.2	49 01.1	53.5	154.3	47 12.5	54.0	155.2	45 23.2	54.6	156.1	23
51 43.3	52.5	152.9	49 55.9	53.1	154.0	48 07.6	53.7	155.0	46 18.5	54.3	155.9	44 28.6	54.7	156.7	24
50 50.8	- 52.7	153.7	49 02.8	- 53.3	154.7	47 13.9	- 53.9	155.6	45 24.2	- 54.4	156.5	43 33.9	- 55.0	157.3	25
49 58.1	53.0	154.4	48 09.5	53.7	155.4	46 20.0	54.2	156.3	44 29.8	54.7	157.1	42 38.9	55.0	157.8	26
49 05.1	53.2	155.1	47 15.8	53.8	156.1	45 25.8	54.3	156.9	43 35.1	54.8	157.7	41 43.9	55.3	158.3	27
48 11.9	53.5	155.8	46 22.0	54.0	156.7	44 31.5	54.6	157.5	42 40.3	54.9	158.2	40 48.6	55.3	158.9	28
47 18.4	53.8	156.5	45 28.0	54.3	157.3	43 36.9	54.7	158.1	41 45.4	55.2	158.8	39 53.3	55.5	159.4	29

Dec.	20° Hc	d	Z	22° Hc	d	Z	24° Hc	d	Z	26° Hc	d	Z	28° Hc	d	Z
0	63 20.5	+45.3	136.5	61 51.6	+47.3	139.1	60 19.4	+49.0	141.4	58 44.3	+50.4	143.5	57 06.7	+51.7	145.3
1	64 05.8	44.3	135.0	62 38.9	46.5	137.7	61 08.4	48.3	140.2	59 34.7	49.9	142.4	57 58.4	51.2	144.4
2	64 50.1	43.3	133.4	63 25.4	45.7	136.3	61 56.7	47.6	139.0	60 24.6	49.3	141.3	58 49.6	50.7	143.4
3	65 33.4	42.2	131.8	64 11.1	44.7	134.9	62 44.3	46.9	137.6	61 13.9	48.7	140.1	59 40.3	50.3	142.3
4	66 15.6	40.9	130.0	64 55.8	43.7	133.3	63 31.2	46.0	136.3	62 02.6	48.0	138.9	60 30.6	49.6	141.2
5	66 56.5	+39.6	128.2	65 39.5	+42.5	131.7	64 17.2	+45.1	134.8	62 50.6	+47.2	137.6	61 20.2	+49.0	140.1
6	67 36.1	38.1	126.2	66 22.0	41.3	129.9	65 02.3	44.1	133.3	63 37.8	46.4	136.2	62 09.2	48.4	138.9
7	68 14.2	36.5	124.2	67 03.3	40.0	128.1	65 46.4	43.0	131.6	64 24.2	45.5	134.8	62 57.6	47.6	137.6
8	68 50.7	34.7	122.0	67 43.3	38.6	126.2	66 29.4	41.7	129.9	65 09.7	44.5	133.2	63 45.2	46.8	136.2
9	69 25.4	32.8	119.7	68 21.9	36.9	124.1	67 11.1	40.5	128.1	65 54.2	43.4	131.6	64 32.0	45.9	134.8
10	69 58.2	+30.8	117.3	68 58.8	+35.2	122.0	67 51.6	+39.0	126.1	66 37.6	+42.2	129.9	65 17.9	+45.0	133.3
11	70 29.0	28.5	114.8	69 34.0	33.3	119.7	68 30.6	37.4	124.1	67 19.8	41.0	128.1	66 02.9	43.8	131.7
12	70 57.5	26.1	112.1	70 07.3	31.3	117.3	69 08.0	35.7	121.9	68 00.8	39.5	126.2	66 46.7	42.8	129.9
13	71 23.6	23.6	109.3	70 38.6	29.0	114.7	69 43.7	33.8	119.7	68 40.3	37.9	124.1	67 29.5	41.4	128.1
14	71 47.2	20.8	106.4	71 07.6	26.6	112.0	70 17.5	31.8	117.2	69 18.2	36.2	122.0	68 10.9	40.0	126.2
15	72 08.0	+17.9	103.4	71 34.2	+24.1	109.2	70 49.3	+29.5	114.7	69 54.4	+34.4	119.7	68 50.9	+38.5	124.2
16	72 25.9	14.8	100.2	71 58.3	21.2	106.3	71 18.8	27.2	112.0	70 28.8	32.3	117.3	69 29.4	36.7	122.0
17	72 40.7	11.6	97.0	72 19.5	18.4	103.3	71 46.0	24.5	109.2	71 01.1	30.1	114.7	70 06.1	34.9	119.7
18	72 52.3	8.4	93.7	72 37.9	15.3	100.1	72 10.5	21.8	106.2	71 31.2	27.6	112.0	70 41.0	32.9	117.3
19	73 00.7	4.9	90.3	72 53.2	12.0	96.8	72 32.3	18.8	103.2	71 58.8	25.1	109.2	71 13.9	30.7	114.8
20	73 05.6	+ 1.5	86.9	73 05.2	+ 8.7	93.5	72 51.1	+15.8	100.0	72 23.9	+22.3	106.2	71 44.6	+28.2	112.0
21	73 07.1	- 1.9	83.5	73 13.9	5.3	90.1	73 06.9	12.4	96.7	72 46.2	19.4	103.1	72 12.8	25.7	109.2
22	73 05.2	5.3	80.0	73 19.2	1.8	86.6	73 19.3	9.1	93.3	73 05.6	16.2	99.9	72 38.5	22.8	106.2
23	72 59.9	8.8	76.6	73 21.0	- 1.7	83.1	73 28.4	5.6	89.8	73 21.8	12.9	96.5	73 01.3	19.9	103.1
24	72 51.1	12.0	73.2	73 19.3	5.1	79.6	73 34.0	+ 2.1	86.3	73 34.7	9.4	93.1	73 21.2	16.6	99.8
25	72 39.1	-15.2	69.9	73 14.2	- 8.6	76.2	73 36.1	- 1.4	82.8	73 44.1	+ 6.0	89.6	73 37.8	+13.4	96.4
26	72 23.9	18.2	66.7	73 05.6	12.0	72.8	73 34.7	5.1	79.2	73 50.1	+ 2.3	86.0	73 51.2	9.8	92.9
27	72 05.7	21.1	63.6	72 53.6	15.1	69.4	73 29.6	8.4	75.7	73 52.4	- 1.2	82.4	74 01.0	6.3	89.4
28	71 44.6	23.9	60.6	72 38.5	18.3	66.1	73 21.2	11.9	72.3	73 51.2	4.9	78.8	74 07.3	+ 2.6	85.7
29	71 20.7	26.4	57.7	72 20.2	21.2	63.0	73 09.3	15.2	68.8	73 46.3	8.4	75.3	74 09.9	- 1.1	82.1

Dec.	30° Hc	d	Z	32° Hc	d	Z	34° Hc	d	Z	36° Hc	d	Z	38° Hc	d	Z
0	55 27.0	+52.8	147.0	53 45.6	+53.6	148.5	52 02.5	+54.4	149.8	50 18.1	+55.1	151.1	48 32.5	+55.7	152.2
1	56 19.8	52.3	146.1	54 39.2	53.3	147.7	52 56.9	54.2	149.1	51 13.2	54.9	150.4	49 28.2	55.6	151.6
2	57 12.1	52.0	145.2	55 32.5	53.0	146.9	53 51.1	53.9	148.4	52 08.1	54.7	149.8	50 23.8	55.3	151.0
3	58 04.1	51.5	144.3	56 25.5	52.7	146.1	54 45.0	53.6	147.7	53 02.8	54.5	149.1	51 19.1	55.2	150.4
4	58 55.6	51.1	143.3	57 18.2	52.3	145.2	55 38.6	53.3	146.9	53 57.3	54.1	148.4	52 14.3	54.9	149.8
5	59 46.7	+50.5	142.3	58 10.5	+51.8	144.3	56 31.9	+53.0	146.1	54 51.4	+53.9	147.7	53 09.2	+54.7	149.1
6	60 37.2	50.0	141.2	59 02.3	51.4	143.3	57 24.9	52.6	145.2	55 45.3	53.6	146.9	54 03.9	54.5	148.4
7	61 27.2	49.4	140.1	59 53.7	50.9	142.3	58 17.5	52.2	144.3	56 38.9	53.3	146.1	54 58.4	54.2	147.7
8	62 16.6	48.8	138.9	60 44.6	50.4	141.2	59 09.7	51.7	143.3	57 32.2	52.9	145.2	55 52.6	53.9	146.9
9	63 05.4	48.0	137.6	61 35.0	49.8	140.1	60 01.4	51.3	142.3	58 25.1	52.5	144.4	56 46.5	53.6	146.1
10	63 53.4	+47.2	136.3	62 24.8	+49.1	138.9	60 52.7	+50.7	141.3	59 17.6	+52.1	143.4	57 40.1	+53.2	145.3
11	64 40.6	46.4	134.8	63 13.9	48.4	137.7	61 43.4	50.2	140.2	60 09.7	51.7	142.4	58 33.3	52.9	144.4
12	65 27.0	45.4	133.3	64 02.3	47.7	136.3	62 33.6	49.6	139.0	61 01.4	51.1	141.4	59 26.2	52.5	143.5
13	66 12.4	44.3	131.7	64 50.0	46.8	134.9	63 23.2	48.8	137.8	61 52.5	50.6	140.3	60 18.7	52.0	142.5
14	66 56.7	43.3	130.0	65 36.8	45.9	133.4	64 12.0	48.1	136.5	62 43.1	50.0	139.1	61 10.7	51.5	141.5
15	67 40.0	+41.9	128.2	66 22.7	+44.9	131.8	65 00.1	+47.3	135.1	63 33.1	+49.3	137.9	62 02.2	+51.0	140.5
16	68 21.9	40.6	126.3	67 07.6	43.7	130.2	65 47.4	46.4	133.6	64 22.4	48.6	136.6	62 53.2	50.4	139.3
17	69 02.5	39.0	124.3	67 51.3	42.5	128.4	66 33.8	45.4	132.0	65 11.0	47.8	135.2	63 43.6	49.8	138.1
18	69 41.5	37.3	122.1	68 33.8	41.1	126.5	67 19.2	44.3	130.3	65 58.8	46.9	133.8	64 33.4	49.1	136.8
19	70 18.8	35.5	119.8	69 14.9	39.6	124.4	68 03.5	43.0	128.6	66 45.7	45.9	132.2	65 22.5	48.3	135.5
20	70 54.3	+33.5	117.4	69 54.5	+37.9	122.3	68 46.5	+41.7	126.7	67 31.6	+44.8	130.6	66 10.8	+47.4	134.0
21	71 27.8	31.2	114.8	70 32.4	36.1	120.0	69 28.2	40.2	124.7	68 16.4	43.6	128.8	66 58.2	46.5	132.5
22	71 59.0	28.9	112.1	71 08.5	34.1	117.6	70 08.4	38.6	122.5	69 00.0	42.3	126.9	67 44.7	45.4	130.8
23	72 27.9	26.2	109.3	71 42.6	31.9	115.0	70 47.0	36.7	120.2	69 42.3	40.9	124.9	68 30.1	44.2	129.1
24	72 54.1	23.4	106.2	72 14.5	29.4	112.2	71 23.7	34.7	117.8	70 23.2	39.2	122.8	69 14.3	42.9	127.2
25	73 17.5	+20.4	103.1	72 43.9	+26.9	109.4	71 58.4	+32.5	115.2	71 02.4	+37.3	120.5	69 57.2	+41.5	125.2
26	73 37.9	17.1	99.8	73 10.8	24.0	106.3	72 30.9	30.1	112.4	71 39.7	35.4	118.0	70 38.7	39.9	123.1
27	73 55.0	13.8	96.3	73 34.8	20.9	103.1	73 01.0	27.5	109.4	72 15.1	33.2	115.4	71 18.6	38.0	120.8
28	74 08.8	10.3	92.8	73 55.7	17.7	99.7	73 28.5	24.6	106.4	72 48.3	30.8	112.6	71 56.6	36.1	118.3
29	74 19.1	6.6	89.2	74 13.4	14.2	96.3	73 53.1	21.5	103.2	73 19.1	28.1	109.7	72 32.7	33.9	115.7

20°			22°			24°			26°			28°			Dec.
Hc	d	Z	Hc	d	Z	Hc	d	Z	Hc	d	Z	Hc	d	Z	
63 20.5	-46.1	136.5	61 51.6	-48.0	139.1	60 19.4	-49.6	141.4	58 44.3	-50.9	143.5	57 06.7	-52.1	145.3	0
62 34.4	47.0	137.9	61 03.6	48.6	140.3	59 29.8	50.1	142.5	57 53.4	51.4	144.5	56 14.6	52.4	146.2	1
61 47.4	47.7	139.2	60 15.0	49.3	141.5	58 39.7	50.7	143.6	57 02.0	51.8	145.4	55 22.2	52.8	147.1	2
60 59.7	48.4	140.5	59 25.7	49.9	142.6	57 49.0	51.1	144.6	56 10.2	52.2	146.3	54 29.4	53.1	147.9	3
60 11.3	49.0	141.7	58 35.8	50.3	143.7	56 57.9	51.5	145.6	55 18.0	52.6	147.2	53 36.3	53.5	148.7	4
59 22.3	-49.6	142.8	57 45.5	-50.9	144.8	56 06.4	-51.9	146.5	54 25.4	-52.8	148.1	52 42.8	-53.7	149.5	5
58 32.7	50.1	143.9	56 54.6	51.3	145.7	55 14.5	52.3	147.4	53 32.6	53.2	148.9	51 49.1	53.9	150.2	6
57 42.6	50.6	145.0	56 03.3	51.7	146.7	54 22.2	52.7	148.2	52 39.4	53.5	149.6	50 55.2	54.2	150.9	7
56 52.0	51.0	146.0	55 11.6	52.1	147.6	53 29.5	53.0	149.0	51 45.9	53.8	150.4	50 01.0	54.5	151.6	8
56 01.0	51.5	146.9	54 19.5	52.4	148.4	52 36.5	53.2	149.8	50 52.1	54.0	151.1	49 06.5	54.6	152.2	9
55 09.5	-51.9	147.8	53 27.1	-52.7	149.3	51 43.3	-53.6	150.6	49 58.1	-54.2	151.8	48 11.9	-54.9	152.8	10
54 17.6	52.2	148.7	52 34.4	53.1	150.1	50 49.7	53.8	151.3	49 03.9	54.4	152.4	47 17.0	55.0	153.4	11
53 25.4	52.6	149.5	51 41.3	53.3	150.8	49 55.9	54.0	152.0	48 09.5	54.7	153.1	46 22.0	55.2	154.0	12
52 32.8	52.8	150.3	50 48.0	53.7	151.6	49 01.9	54.3	152.7	47 14.8	54.8	153.7	45 26.8	55.3	154.6	13
51 40.0	53.2	151.1	49 54.3	53.8	152.3	48 07.6	54.4	153.3	46 20.0	55.1	154.3	44 31.5	55.5	155.1	14
50 46.8	-53.4	151.8	49 00.5	-54.1	152.9	47 13.2	-54.7	153.9	45 24.9	-55.1	154.9	43 36.0	-55.6	155.7	15
49 53.4	53.7	152.5	48 06.4	54.3	153.6	46 18.5	54.9	154.5	44 29.8	55.4	155.4	42 40.3	55.8	156.2	16
48 59.7	53.9	153.2	47 12.1	54.5	154.2	45 23.6	55.0	155.1	43 34.4	55.5	155.9	41 44.5	55.9	156.7	17
48 05.8	54.2	153.9	46 17.6	54.7	154.8	44 28.6	55.2	155.7	42 38.9	55.6	156.4	40 48.6	56.0	157.2	18
47 11.6	54.3	154.5	45 22.9	54.9	155.4	43 33.4	55.3	156.2	41 43.3	55.8	157.0	39 52.6	56.1	157.6	19
46 17.3	-54.5	155.2	44 28.0	-55.0	156.0	42 38.1	-55.5	156.8	40 47.5	-55.8	157.4	38 56.5	-56.3	158.1	20
45 22.8	54.8	155.8	43 33.0	55.2	156.5	41 42.6	55.6	157.3	39 51.7	56.0	157.9	38 00.2	56.3	158.5	21
44 28.0	54.9	156.3	42 37.8	55.3	157.1	40 47.0	55.7	157.8	38 55.7	56.1	158.4	37 03.9	56.4	159.0	22
43 33.1	55.0	156.9	41 42.5	55.5	157.6	39 51.3	55.9	158.3	37 59.6	56.2	158.8	36 07.5	56.5	159.4	23
42 38.1	55.2	157.4	40 47.0	55.6	158.1	38 55.4	55.9	158.7	37 03.4	56.3	159.3	35 11.0	56.6	159.8	24
41 42.9	-55.4	158.0	39 51.4	-55.7	158.6	37 59.5	-56.1	159.2	36 07.1	-56.4	159.7	34 14.4	-56.7	160.2	25
40 47.5	55.4	158.5	38 55.7	55.9	159.1	37 03.4	56.2	159.6	35 10.7	56.5	160.1	33 17.7	56.8	160.6	26
39 52.1	55.6	159.0	37 59.8	55.9	159.5	36 07.2	56.2	160.1	34 14.2	56.5	160.5	32 20.9	56.8	161.0	27
38 56.5	55.7	159.5	37 03.9	56.1	160.0	35 11.0	56.4	160.5	33 17.7	56.7	160.9	31 24.1	56.9	161.4	28
38 00.8	55.9	159.9	36 07.8	56.1	160.4	34 14.6	56.4	160.9	32 21.0	56.7	161.3	30 27.2	56.9	161.7	29

30°			32°			34°			36°			38°			Dec.
Hc	d	Z	Hc	d	Z	Hc	d	Z	Hc	d	Z	Hc	d	Z	
55 27.0	-53.0	147.0	53 45.6	-54.0	148.5	52 02.5	-54.6	149.8	50 18.1	-55.3	151.1	48 32.5	-55.8	152.2	0
54 34.0	53.4	147.8	52 51.6	54.1	149.2	51 07.9	54.9	150.5	49 22.8	55.5	151.7	47 36.7	56.1	152.7	1
53 40.6	53.7	148.6	51 57.5	54.5	149.9	50 13.0	55.1	151.1	48 27.3	55.6	152.2	46 40.6	56.1	153.2	2
52 46.9	53.9	149.3	51 03.0	54.6	150.6	49 17.9	55.3	151.8	47 31.7	55.8	152.8	45 44.5	56.3	153.8	3
51 53.0	54.2	150.0	50 08.4	54.9	151.3	48 22.6	55.4	152.3	46 35.9	56.0	153.3	44 48.2	56.3	154.2	4
50 58.8	-54.4	150.7	49 13.5	-55.0	151.9	47 27.2	-55.6	152.9	45 39.9	-56.1	153.9	43 51.8	-56.6	154.7	5
50 04.4	54.7	151.4	48 18.5	55.3	152.5	46 31.6	55.8	153.5	44 43.8	56.2	154.4	42 55.2	56.6	155.2	6
49 09.7	54.8	152.0	47 23.2	55.4	153.1	45 35.8	55.9	154.0	43 47.6	56.4	154.9	41 58.6	56.7	155.6	7
48 14.9	55.0	152.6	46 27.8	55.5	153.6	44 39.9	56.0	154.5	42 51.2	56.4	155.3	41 01.9	56.9	156.1	8
47 19.9	55.3	153.2	45 32.3	55.7	154.2	43 43.9	56.2	155.0	41 54.8	56.6	155.8	40 05.0	56.9	156.5	9
46 24.6	-55.3	153.8	44 36.6	-55.9	154.7	42 47.7	-56.3	155.5	40 58.2	-56.7	156.3	39 08.1	-57.0	156.9	10
45 29.3	55.6	154.4	43 40.7	56.0	155.2	41 51.4	56.4	156.0	40 01.5	56.7	156.7	38 11.1	57.1	157.3	11
44 33.7	55.6	154.9	42 44.7	56.1	155.7	40 55.0	56.5	156.4	39 04.8	56.9	157.1	37 14.0	57.2	157.7	12
43 38.1	55.9	155.4	41 48.6	56.2	156.2	39 58.5	56.6	156.9	38 07.9	56.9	157.5	36 16.8	57.2	158.1	13
42 42.2	55.9	155.9	40 52.4	56.4	156.6	39 01.9	56.6	157.3	37 11.0	57.0	157.9	35 19.6	57.3	158.4	14
41 46.3	-56.1	156.4	39 56.0	-56.4	157.1	38 05.3	-56.8	157.7	36 14.0	-57.1	158.3	34 22.3	-57.4	158.8	15
40 50.2	56.1	156.9	38 59.6	56.5	157.5	37 08.5	56.9	158.1	35 16.9	57.1	158.7	33 24.9	57.4	159.2	16
39 54.1	56.3	157.3	38 03.1	56.6	158.0	36 11.6	56.9	158.5	34 19.8	57.3	159.0	32 27.5	57.5	159.5	17
38 57.8	56.4	157.8	37 06.5	56.8	158.4	35 14.7	57.0	158.9	33 22.5	57.2	159.4	31 30.1	57.6	159.9	18
38 01.4	56.5	158.2	36 09.7	56.7	158.8	34 17.7	57.1	159.3	32 25.3	57.4	159.7	30 32.5	57.5	160.2	19
37 04.9	-56.5	158.7	35 13.0	-56.9	159.2	33 20.6	-57.1	159.7	31 27.9	-57.4	160.1	29 35.0	-57.7	160.5	20
36 08.4	56.7	159.1	34 16.1	57.0	159.6	32 23.5	57.2	160.0	30 30.5	57.4	160.4	28 37.3	57.6	160.8	21
35 11.7	56.7	159.5	33 19.1	57.0	159.9	31 26.3	57.3	160.4	29 33.1	57.5	160.8	27 39.7	57.7	161.1	22
34 15.0	56.8	159.9	32 22.1	57.0	160.3	30 29.0	57.3	160.7	28 35.6	57.5	161.1	26 42.0	57.8	161.4	23
33 18.2	56.9	160.3	31 25.1	57.2	160.7	29 31.7	57.4	161.1	27 38.1	57.6	161.4	25 44.2	57.8	161.7	24
32 21.3	-57.0	160.6	30 27.9	-57.1	161.0	28 34.3	-57.4	161.4	26 40.5	-57.6	161.7	24 46.4	-57.8	162.0	25
31 24.3	57.0	161.0	29 30.8	57.3	161.4	27 36.9	57.5	161.7	25 42.9	57.7	162.0	23 48.6	57.8	162.3	26
30 27.3	57.0	161.4	28 33.5	57.3	161.7	26 39.4	57.5	162.1	24 45.2	57.7	162.4	22 50.8	57.9	162.6	27
29 30.3	57.1	161.7	27 36.2	57.3	162.1	25 41.9	57.5	162.4	23 47.5	57.7	162.7	21 52.9	57.9	162.9	28
28 33.2	57.2	162.1	26 38.9	57.4	162.4	24 44.4	57.6	162.7	22 49.8	57.8	162.9	20 55.0	58.0	163.2	29

59

Dec.	40° Hc	d	Z	42° Hc	d	Z	44° Hc	d	Z	46° Hc	d	Z	48° Hc	d	Z
0	46 45.9	+56.2	153.2	44 58.4	+56.7	154.1	43 10.0	+57.1	154.9	41 21.0	+57.5	155.7	39 31.3	+57.8	156.4
1	47 42.1	56.1	152.7	45 55.1	56.5	153.6	44 07.1	57.0	154.5	42 18.5	57.3	155.3	40 29.1	57.7	156.0
2	48 38.2	56.0	152.1	46 51.6	56.5	153.2	45 04.1	56.9	154.1	43 15.8	57.3	154.9	41 26.8	57.7	155.7
3	49 34.2	55.8	151.6	47 48.1	56.3	152.7	46 01.0	56.8	153.6	44 13.1	57.2	154.5	42 24.5	57.5	155.3
4	50 30.0	55.6	151.0	48 44.4	56.2	152.1	46 57.8	56.7	153.1	45 10.3	57.1	154.1	43 22.0	57.5	154.9
5	51 25.6	+55.4	150.4	49 40.6	+56.0	151.6	47 54.5	+56.5	152.7	46 07.4	+57.0	153.6	44 19.5	+57.4	154.5
6	52 21.0	55.2	149.8	50 36.6	55.8	151.0	48 51.0	56.4	152.2	47 04.4	56.9	153.2	45 16.9	57.3	154.1
7	53 16.2	55.0	149.1	51 32.4	55.7	150.5	49 47.4	56.3	151.6	48 01.3	56.8	152.7	46 14.2	57.2	153.7
8	54 11.2	54.7	148.5	52 28.1	55.5	149.8	50 43.7	56.1	151.1	48 58.1	56.6	152.2	47 11.4	57.1	153.2
9	55 05.9	54.5	147.8	53 23.6	55.3	149.2	51 39.8	55.9	150.5	49 54.7	56.5	151.7	48 08.5	57.0	152.8
10	56 00.4	+54.2	147.0	54 18.9	+55.0	148.6	52 35.7	+55.8	149.9	50 51.2	+56.4	151.2	49 05.5	+56.9	152.3
11	56 54.6	53.9	146.2	55 13.9	54.8	147.9	53 31.5	55.5	149.3	51 47.6	56.1	150.6	50 02.4	56.7	151.8
12	57 48.5	53.6	145.4	56 08.7	54.5	147.1	54 27.0	55.3	148.7	52 43.7	56.0	150.1	50 59.1	56.6	151.3
13	58 42.1	53.2	144.6	57 03.2	54.3	146.4	55 22.3	55.1	148.0	53 39.8	55.8	149.5	51 55.7	56.5	150.8
14	59 35.3	52.9	143.7	57 57.5	53.9	145.6	56 17.4	54.9	147.3	54 35.6	55.6	148.8	52 52.2	56.2	150.2
15	60 28.2	+52.4	142.7	58 51.4	+53.6	144.8	57 12.3	+54.6	146.6	55 31.2	+55.4	148.2	53 48.4	+56.2	149.6
16	61 20.6	51.9	141.7	59 45.0	53.2	143.9	58 06.9	54.2	145.8	56 26.6	55.2	147.5	54 44.6	55.9	149.0
17	62 12.5	51.4	140.7	60 38.2	52.8	142.9	59 01.1	54.0	145.0	57 21.8	54.9	146.8	55 40.5	55.7	148.4
18	63 03.9	50.9	139.5	61 31.0	52.3	142.0	59 55.1	53.6	144.1	58 16.7	54.6	146.0	56 36.2	55.5	147.7
19	63 54.8	50.2	138.4	62 23.3	51.9	140.9	60 48.7	53.2	143.2	59 11.3	54.3	145.2	57 31.7	55.1	147.0
20	64 45.0	+49.6	137.1	63 15.2	+51.3	139.8	61 41.9	+52.8	142.2	60 05.6	+54.0	144.4	58 26.9	+55.0	146.3
21	65 34.6	48.8	135.8	64 06.5	50.7	138.6	62 34.7	52.3	141.2	60 59.6	53.6	143.5	59 21.9	54.7	145.5
22	66 23.4	48.0	134.3	64 57.2	50.1	137.4	63 27.0	51.8	140.1	61 53.2	53.2	142.6	60 16.6	54.4	144.7
23	67 11.4	47.0	132.8	65 47.3	49.3	136.1	64 18.8	51.2	139.0	62 46.4	52.8	141.6	61 11.0	54.0	143.8
24	67 58.4	46.0	131.2	66 36.6	48.6	134.7	65 10.0	50.5	137.8	63 39.2	52.3	140.5	62 05.0	53.6	142.9
25	68 44.4	+44.9	129.4	67 25.2	+47.6	133.2	66 00.5	+49.9	136.5	64 31.5	+51.7	139.4	62 58.6	+53.2	141.9
26	69 29.3	43.5	127.6	68 12.8	46.6	131.6	66 50.4	49.1	135.1	65 23.2	51.1	138.2	63 51.8	52.8	140.9
27	70 12.8	42.2	125.6	68 59.4	45.5	129.8	67 39.5	48.2	133.6	66 14.3	50.4	136.9	64 44.6	52.2	139.8
28	70 55.0	40.6	123.4	69 44.9	44.2	128.0	68 27.7	47.3	132.0	67 04.7	49.7	135.5	65 36.8	51.6	138.6
29	71 35.6	38.7	121.1	70 29.1	42.9	126.0	69 15.0	46.1	130.3	67 54.4	48.8	134.1	66 28.4	51.0	137.4

Dec.	50° Hc	d	Z	52° Hc	d	Z	54° Hc	d	Z	56° Hc	d	Z	58° Hc	d	Z
0	37 41.1	+58.1	157.0	35 50.4	+58.3	157.6	33 59.3	+58.5	158.1	32 07.7	+58.8	158.6	30 15.8	+58.9	159.0
1	38 39.2	58.0	156.7	36 48.7	58.3	157.3	34 57.8	58.5	157.9	33 06.5	58.6	158.4	31 14.7	58.9	158.8
2	39 37.2	57.9	156.4	37 47.0	58.2	157.0	35 56.3	58.4	157.6	34 05.1	58.7	158.1	32 13.6	58.9	158.6
3	40 35.1	57.9	156.0	38 45.2	58.2	156.7	36 54.7	58.4	157.3	35 03.8	58.6	157.9	33 12.5	58.8	158.3
4	41 33.0	57.8	155.7	39 43.4	58.1	156.4	37 53.1	58.4	157.0	36 02.4	58.6	157.6	34 11.3	58.8	158.1
5	42 30.8	+57.8	155.3	40 41.5	+58.0	156.0	38 51.5	+58.3	156.7	37 01.0	+58.6	157.3	35 10.1	+58.8	157.9
6	43 28.6	57.6	154.9	41 39.5	58.0	155.7	39 49.8	58.3	156.4	37 59.6	58.5	157.0	36 08.9	58.7	157.6
7	44 26.2	57.6	154.6	42 37.5	57.9	155.4	40 48.1	58.2	156.1	38 58.1	58.5	156.8	37 07.6	58.7	157.4
8	45 23.8	57.5	154.2	43 35.4	57.9	155.0	41 46.3	58.2	155.8	39 56.6	58.4	156.5	38 06.3	58.7	157.1
9	46 21.3	57.4	153.8	44 33.3	57.8	154.6	42 44.5	58.1	155.4	40 55.0	58.4	156.2	39 05.0	58.6	156.8
10	47 18.7	+57.4	153.3	45 31.1	+57.7	154.3	43 42.6	+58.0	155.1	41 53.4	+58.3	155.9	40 03.6	+58.6	156.6
11	48 16.1	57.2	152.9	46 28.8	57.6	153.9	44 40.6	58.0	154.7	42 51.7	58.3	155.6	41 02.2	58.5	156.3
12	49 13.3	57.1	152.4	47 26.4	57.5	153.5	45 38.6	57.9	154.4	43 50.0	58.3	155.2	42 00.7	58.5	156.0
13	50 10.4	57.0	152.0	48 23.9	57.5	153.0	46 36.5	57.8	154.0	44 48.3	58.1	154.9	42 59.2	58.5	155.7
14	51 07.4	56.8	151.5	49 21.4	57.3	152.6	47 34.3	57.8	153.6	45 46.4	58.1	154.5	43 57.7	58.4	155.4
15	52 04.2	+56.7	150.9	50 18.7	+57.2	152.1	48 32.1	+57.6	153.2	46 44.5	+58.0	154.2	44 56.1	+58.3	155.1
16	53 00.9	56.6	150.4	51 15.9	57.1	151.7	49 29.7	57.6	152.8	47 42.5	58.0	153.8	45 54.4	58.3	154.7
17	53 57.5	56.4	149.9	52 13.0	57.0	151.2	50 27.3	57.3	152.3	48 40.5	57.9	153.4	46 52.7	58.2	154.4
18	54 53.9	56.2	149.3	53 10.0	56.8	150.6	51 24.8	57.3	151.9	49 38.4	57.7	153.0	47 50.9	58.2	154.0
19	55 50.1	56.0	148.6	54 06.8	56.7	150.1	52 22.1	57.2	151.4	50 36.1	57.7	152.6	48 49.1	58.1	153.7
20	56 46.1	+55.8	148.0	55 03.5	+56.5	149.5	53 19.3	+57.1	150.9	51 33.8	+57.6	152.2	49 47.2	+58.0	153.3
21	57 41.9	55.6	147.3	56 00.0	56.3	148.9	54 16.4	57.0	150.4	52 31.4	57.5	151.7	50 45.2	57.9	152.9
22	58 37.5	55.3	146.6	56 56.3	56.2	148.3	55 13.4	56.8	149.8	53 28.9	57.3	151.2	51 43.1	57.8	152.5
23	59 32.8	55.1	145.9	57 52.5	55.9	147.7	56 10.2	56.6	149.3	54 26.2	57.2	150.7	52 40.9	57.7	152.0
24	60 27.9	54.8	145.1	58 48.4	55.7	147.0	57 06.8	56.4	148.7	55 23.4	57.1	150.2	53 38.6	57.6	151.6
25	61 22.7	+54.4	144.2	59 44.1	+55.4	146.2	58 03.2	+56.3	148.0	56 20.5	+57.0	149.6	54 36.2	+57.5	151.1
26	62 17.1	54.0	143.3	60 39.5	55.1	145.5	58 59.5	56.0	147.4	57 17.5	56.7	149.1	55 33.7	57.4	150.6
27	63 11.1	53.7	142.4	61 34.6	54.9	144.7	59 55.5	55.8	146.7	58 14.2	56.6	148.5	56 31.1	57.2	150.1
28	64 04.8	53.2	141.4	62 29.5	54.5	143.8	60 51.3	55.6	145.9	59 10.8	56.4	147.8	57 28.3	57.1	149.5
29	64 58.0	52.7	140.3	63 24.0	54.1	142.9	61 46.9	55.2	145.1	60 07.2	56.2	147.1	58 25.4	56.9	148.9

40° Hc	d	Z	42° Hc	d	Z	44° Hc	d	Z	46° Hc	d	Z	48° Hc	d	Z	Dec.
46 45.9	-56.4	153.2	44 58.4	-56.8	154.1	43 10.0	-57.1	154.9	41 21.0	-57.5	155.7	39 31.3	-57.8	156.4	0
45 49.5	56.5	153.7	44 01.6	56.9	154.6	42 12.9	57.3	155.3	40 23.5	57.6	156.1	38 33.5	57.9	156.7	1
44 53.0	56.6	154.2	43 04.7	57.0	155.0	41 15.6	57.4	155.7	39 25.9	57.7	156.4	37 35.6	57.9	157.1	2
43 56.4	56.7	154.6	42 07.7	57.1	155.4	40 18.2	57.4	156.1	38 28.2	57.7	156.8	36 37.7	58.0	157.4	3
42 59.7	56.8	155.1	41 10.6	57.2	155.8	39 20.8	57.5	156.5	37 30.5	57.8	157.1	35 39.7	58.1	157.7	4
42 02.9	-56.9	155.5	40 13.4	-57.3	156.2	38 23.3	-57.6	156.9	36 32.7	-57.9	157.5	34 41.6	-58.1	158.0	5
41 06.0	57.0	155.9	39 16.1	57.3	156.6	37 25.7	57.6	157.2	35 34.8	57.9	157.8	33 43.5	58.1	158.3	6
40 09.0	57.1	156.3	38 18.8	57.4	157.0	36 28.1	57.7	157.6	34 36.9	57.9	158.1	32 45.4	58.2	158.6	7
39 11.9	57.2	156.7	37 21.4	57.5	157.4	35 30.4	57.7	157.9	33 39.0	58.0	158.4	31 47.2	58.2	158.9	8
38 14.7	57.2	157.1	36 23.9	57.5	157.7	34 32.7	57.8	158.3	32 41.0	58.0	158.7	30 49.0	58.3	159.2	9
37 17.5	-57.4	157.5	35 26.4	-57.6	158.1	33 34.9	-57.9	158.6	31 43.0	-58.1	159.0	29 50.7	-58.2	159.5	10
36 20.1	57.3	157.9	34 28.8	57.7	158.4	32 37.0	57.9	158.9	30 44.9	58.1	159.3	28 52.5	58.3	159.7	11
35 22.8	57.5	158.2	33 31.1	57.7	158.7	31 39.1	57.9	159.2	29 46.8	58.2	159.6	27 54.1	58.3	160.0	12
34 25.3	57.5	158.6	32 33.4	57.7	159.1	30 41.2	58.0	159.5	28 48.6	58.2	159.9	26 55.8	58.4	160.3	13
33 27.8	57.5	158.9	31 35.7	57.8	159.4	29 43.2	58.0	159.8	27 50.4	58.2	160.2	25 57.4	58.4	160.5	14
32 30.3	-57.7	159.3	30 37.9	-57.9	159.7	28 45.2	-58.1	160.1	26 52.2	-58.2	160.5	24 59.0	-58.4	160.8	15
31 32.6	57.6	159.6	29 40.0	57.9	160.0	27 47.1	58.1	160.4	25 54.0	58.3	160.7	24 00.6	58.5	161.0	16
30 35.0	57.7	159.9	28 42.1	57.9	160.3	26 49.0	58.1	160.7	24 55.7	58.3	161.0	23 02.1	58.5	161.3	17
29 37.3	57.8	160.2	27 44.2	58.0	160.6	25 50.9	58.2	160.9	23 57.4	58.4	161.2	22 03.6	58.5	161.5	18
28 39.5	57.8	160.6	26 46.2	58.0	160.9	24 52.7	58.2	161.2	22 59.0	58.3	161.5	21 05.1	58.5	161.8	19
27 41.7	-57.8	160.9	25 48.2	-58.0	161.2	23 54.5	-58.2	161.5	22 00.7	-58.4	161.7	20 06.6	-58.5	162.0	20
26 43.9	57.9	161.2	24 50.2	58.1	161.5	22 56.3	58.2	161.7	21 02.3	58.4	162.0	19 08.1	58.6	162.2	21
25 46.0	57.9	161.4	23 52.1	58.1	161.8	21 58.1	58.3	162.0	20 03.9	58.4	162.2	18 09.5	58.6	162.5	22
24 48.1	57.9	161.7	22 54.1	58.2	162.0	20 59.8	58.3	162.3	19 05.5	58.5	162.5	17 11.0	58.6	162.7	23
23 50.2	58.0	162.0	21 55.9	58.1	162.3	20 01.5	58.3	162.5	18 07.0	58.4	162.7	16 12.4	58.6	162.9	24
22 52.2	-58.0	162.3	20 57.8	-58.2	162.5	19 03.2	-58.3	162.8	17 08.6	-58.5	163.0	15 13.8	-58.6	163.1	25
21 54.2	58.0	162.6	19 59.6	58.2	162.8	18 04.9	58.3	163.0	16 10.1	58.5	163.2	14 15.2	58.7	163.3	26
20 56.2	58.1	162.9	19 01.4	58.2	163.1	17 06.6	58.4	163.3	15 11.6	58.5	163.4	13 16.5	58.6	163.6	27
19 58.1	58.1	163.1	18 03.2	58.2	163.3	16 08.2	58.4	163.5	14 13.1	58.5	163.7	12 17.9	58.6	163.8	28
19 00.0	58.1	163.4	17 05.0	58.3	163.6	15 09.8	58.4	163.7	13 14.6	58.5	163.9	11 19.3	58.7	164.0	29

50° Hc	d	Z	52° Hc	d	Z	54° Hc	d	Z	56° Hc	d	Z	58° Hc	d	Z	Dec.
37 41.1	-58.1	157.0	35 50.4	-58.3	157.6	33 59.3	-58.6	158.1	32 07.7	-58.7	158.6	30 15.8	-58.9	159.0	0
36 43.0	58.1	157.3	34 52.1	58.4	157.9	33 00.7	58.6	158.4	31 09.0	58.8	158.8	29 16.9	58.9	159.3	1
35 44.9	58.2	157.6	33 53.7	58.4	158.2	32 02.1	58.6	158.6	30 10.2	58.8	159.1	28 18.0	59.0	159.5	2
34 46.7	58.3	157.9	32 55.3	58.5	158.4	31 03.5	58.7	158.9	29 11.4	58.8	159.3	27 19.0	59.0	159.7	3
33 48.4	58.2	158.2	31 56.8	58.5	158.7	30 04.8	58.6	159.1	28 12.6	58.9	159.5	26 20.0	59.0	159.9	4
32 50.2	-58.4	158.5	30 58.3	-58.5	159.0	29 06.2	-58.7	159.4	27 13.7	-58.8	159.7	25 21.0	-59.0	160.1	5
31 51.8	58.3	158.8	29 59.8	58.5	159.2	28 07.5	58.8	159.6	26 14.9	58.9	160.0	24 22.0	59.0	160.3	6
30 53.5	58.4	159.1	29 01.3	58.6	159.5	27 08.7	58.7	159.9	25 16.0	58.9	160.2	23 23.0	59.1	160.5	7
29 55.1	58.4	159.3	28 02.7	58.6	159.7	26 10.0	58.8	160.1	24 17.1	58.9	160.4	22 23.9	59.0	160.7	8
28 56.7	58.5	159.6	27 04.1	58.6	160.0	25 11.2	58.8	160.3	23 18.2	59.0	160.6	21 24.9	59.1	160.9	9
27 58.2	-58.4	159.9	26 05.5	-58.7	160.2	24 12.4	-58.8	160.5	22 19.2	-58.9	160.8	20 25.8	-59.1	161.0	10
26 59.8	58.5	160.1	25 06.8	58.7	160.4	23 13.6	58.8	160.7	21 20.3	59.0	161.0	19 26.7	59.0	161.2	11
26 01.3	58.6	160.3	24 08.1	58.7	160.7	22 14.8	58.8	160.9	20 21.3	59.0	161.2	18 27.6	59.1	161.4	12
25 02.7	58.5	160.6	23 09.4	58.7	160.9	21 15.9	58.9	161.2	19 22.3	59.0	161.4	17 28.5	59.1	161.6	13
24 04.2	58.6	160.8	22 10.7	58.7	161.1	20 17.1	58.9	161.4	18 23.3	59.0	161.6	16 29.4	59.1	161.8	14
23 05.6	-58.6	161.1	21 12.0	-58.7	161.3	19 18.2	-58.8	161.6	17 24.3	-59.0	161.8	15 30.3	-59.1	162.0	15
22 07.0	58.6	161.3	20 13.3	58.8	161.5	18 19.4	58.9	161.8	16 25.3	59.0	162.0	14 31.2	59.2	162.1	16
21 08.4	58.6	161.5	19 14.5	58.8	161.8	17 20.5	59.0	162.0	15 26.3	59.0	162.1	13 32.0	59.1	162.3	17
20 09.8	58.7	161.8	18 15.7	58.8	162.0	16 21.5	58.9	162.2	14 27.3	59.1	162.3	12 32.9	59.1	162.5	18
19 11.1	58.7	162.0	17 16.9	58.8	162.2	15 22.6	58.9	162.4	13 28.2	59.0	162.5	11 33.7	59.1	162.6	19
18 12.4	-58.6	162.2	16 18.1	-58.8	162.4	14 23.7	-58.9	162.6	12 29.2	-59.1	162.7	10 34.6	-59.2	162.8	20
17 13.8	58.7	162.4	15 19.3	58.8	162.6	13 24.8	59.0	162.7	11 30.1	59.1	162.9	9 35.4	59.2	163.0	21
16 15.1	58.7	162.6	14 20.5	58.9	162.8	12 25.8	59.0	162.9	10 31.0	59.0	163.1	8 36.2	59.1	163.2	22
15 16.4	58.8	162.9	13 21.6	58.8	163.0	11 26.8	58.9	163.1	9 32.0	59.1	163.2	7 37.1	59.2	163.3	23
14 17.6	58.7	163.1	12 22.8	58.9	163.2	10 27.9	59.0	163.3	8 32.9	59.1	163.4	6 37.9	59.2	163.5	24
13 18.9	-58.7	163.3	11 23.9	-58.8	163.4	9 28.9	-59.0	163.5	7 33.8	-59.1	163.6	5 38.7	-59.2	163.7	25
12 20.2	58.8	163.5	10 25.1	58.9	163.6	8 29.9	58.9	163.7	6 34.7	59.0	163.8	4 39.5	59.2	163.8	26
11 21.4	58.7	163.7	9 26.2	58.9	163.8	7 31.0	59.0	163.9	5 35.7	59.1	163.9	3 40.3	59.2	164.0	27
10 22.7	58.8	163.9	8 27.3	58.9	164.0	6 32.0	59.0	164.1	4 36.6	59.1	164.1	2 41.1	59.1	164.1	28
9 23.9	58.8	164.1	7 28.5	58.9	164.2	5 33.0	59.0	164.2	3 37.5	59.1	164.3	1 42.0	59.2	164.3	29

Dec.	0° Hc	d	Z	2° Hc	d	Z	4° Hc	d	Z	6° Hc	d	Z	8° Hc	d	Z
°	° ′	′	°	° ′	′	°	° ′	′	°	° ′	′	°	° ′	′	°
0	70 00.0 -	1.4•	90.0	69 54.3 +	4.6•	95.5	69 37.2 +	10.7•	100.8	69 09.3 +	16.3•	106.0	68 31.2 +	21.7•	110.9
1	69 58.6	4.3•	87.1	69 58.9 +	1.8•	92.6	69 47.9	7.8•	98.0	69 25.6	13.8•	103.3	68 52.9	19.2•	108.4
2	69 54.3	7.2•	84.2	70 00.7 -	1.0•	89.6	69 55.7	5.1•	95.1	69 39.4	11.0•	100.5	69 12.1	16.8•	105.7
3	69 47.1	9.9•	81.3	69 59.7	4.0•	86.7	70 00.8 +	2.2•	92.2	69 50.4	8.3•	97.7	69 28.9	14.1•	103.0
4	69 37.2	12.6•	78.4	69 55.7	6.8•	83.8	70 03.0 -	0.8•	89.3	69 58.7	5.4•	94.8	69 43.0	11.4•	100.2
5	69 24.6 -	15.3•	75.7	69 48.9 -	9.5•	80.9	70 02.3 -	3.5•	86.4	70 04.1 +	2.5•	91.9	69 54.4 +	8.7•	97.4
6	69 09.3	17.8•	72.9	69 39.4	12.3•	78.1	69 58.7	6.5•	83.4	70 06.6 -	0.3•	88.9	70 03.1	5.8•	94.5
7	68 51.5	20.3•	70.3	69 27.1	15.0•	75.3	69 52.2	9.2•	80.5	70 06.3	3.2•	86.0	70 08.9 +	2.9•	91.5
8	68 31.2	22.6•	67.7	69 12.1	17.5•	72.5	69 43.0	12.0•	77.7	70 03.1	6.1•	83.1	70 11.8	0.0•	88.4
9	68 08.6	24.7•	65.2	68 54.6	19.9•	69.9	69 31.0	14.6•	74.9	69 57.0	8.9•	80.2	70 11.8 -	2.9•	85.6
10	67 43.9 -	26.9•	62.7	68 34.7 -	22.3•	67.2	69 16.4 -	17.3•	72.1	69 48.1 -	11.7•	77.3	70 08.9 -	5.7•	82.7
11	67 17.0	28.8	60.4	68 12.4	24.5•	64.7	68 59.1	19.6•	69.4	69 36.4	14.4•	74.5	70 03.2	8.7•	79.8
12	66 48.2	30.7	58.1	67 47.9	26.7•	62.3	68 39.5	22.1•	66.8	69 22.0	16.9•	71.7	69 54.5	11.4•	76.9
13	66 17.5	32.4	56.0	67 21.2	28.6	59.9	68 17.4	24.3•	64.3	69 05.1	19.5•	69.0	69 43.1	14.0•	74.0
14	65 45.1	34.0	53.9	66 52.6	30.4	57.7	67 53.1	26.4•	61.8	68 45.6	21.6•	66.4	69 29.1	16.8•	71.2
15	65 11.1 -	35.5	51.9	66 22.2 -	32.2	55.5	67 26.7 -	28.3	59.5	68 23.8 -	24.1•	63.8	69 12.3 -	19.2•	68.5
16	64 35.6	36.9	50.0	65 50.0	33.8	53.4	66 58.4	30.3	57.2	67 59.7	26.2•	61.3	68 53.1	21.6•	65.9
17	63 58.7	38.2	48.2	65 16.2	35.3	51.4	66 28.1	32.0	55.0	67 33.5	28.2	59.0	68 31.5	23.9•	63.3
18	63 20.5	39.4	46.5	64 40.9	36.8	49.4	65 56.1	33.7	52.9	67 05.3	30.1	56.7	68 07.6	26.0•	60.8
19	62 41.1	40.6	44.8	64 04.1	38.1	47.7	65 22.4	35.2	50.9	66 35.2	31.9	54.5	67 41.6	28.1•	58.4
20	62 00.5 -	41.6	43.2	63 26.0 -	39.2	45.9	64 47.2 -	36.6	49.0	66 03.3 -	33.5	52.4	67 13.5 -	30.0	56.1
21	61 18.9	42.5	41.7	62 46.8	40.5	44.3	64 10.6	38.0	47.1	65 29.8	35.1	50.3	66 43.5	31.8	53.9
22	60 36.4	43.5	40.2	62 06.3	41.5	42.7	63 32.6	39.1	45.4	64 54.7	36.6	48.4	66 11.7	33.5	51.8
23	59 52.9	44.3	38.9	61 24.8	42.4	41.1	62 53.5	40.4	43.7	64 18.1	37.8	46.6	65 38.2	35.0	49.7
24	59 08.6	45.1	37.5	60 42.4	43.4	39.7	62 13.1	41.4	42.1	63 40.3	39.1	44.8	65 03.2	36.4	47.8
25	58 23.5 -	45.8	36.3	59 59.0 -	44.2	38.3	61 31.7 -	42.4	40.6	63 01.2 -	40.3	43.1	64 26.8 -	37.9	45.9
26	57 37.7	46.5	35.0	59 14.8	45.0	37.0	60 49.3	43.3	39.1	62 20.9	41.3	41.5	63 48.9	39.0	44.2
27	56 51.2	47.1	33.9	58 29.8	45.8	35.7	60 06.0	44.1	37.7	61 39.6	42.4	39.9	63 09.9	40.3	42.5
28	56 04.1	47.7	32.8	57 44.0	46.4	34.4	59 21.9	45.0	36.3	60 57.2	43.2	38.5	62 29.6	41.3	40.8
29	55 16.4	48.3	31.7	56 57.6	47.0	33.3	58 36.9	45.7	35.1	60 14.0	44.2	37.1	61 48.3	42.3	39.3

Dec.	10° Hc	d	Z	12° Hc	d	Z	14° Hc	d	Z	16° Hc	d	Z	18° Hc	d	Z
°	° ′	′	°	° ′	′	°	° ′	′	°	° ′	′	°	° ′	′	°
0	67 43.9 +	26.4•	115.5	66 48.2 +	30.8	119.7	65 45.1 +	34.6	123.6	64 35.6 +	37.9	127.1	63 20.5 +	40.8	130.3
1	68 10.3	24.4•	113.1	67 19.0	28.9•	117.5	66 19.7	32.9	121.6	65 13.5	36.5	125.3	64 01.3	39.6	128.7
2	68 34.7	22.0•	110.6	67 47.9	26.8•	115.2	66 52.6	31.2	119.5	65 50.0	35.0	123.4	64 40.9	38.3	126.9
3	68 56.7	19.7•	108.1	68 14.7	24.8•	112.8	67 23.8	29.3	117.3	66 25.0	33.4	121.4	65 19.2	36.9	125.1
4	69 16.4	17.1•	105.4	68 39.5	22.4•	110.4	67 53.1	27.3•	115.0	66 58.4	31.6	119.3	65 56.1	35.4	123.2
5	69 33.5 +	14.6•	102.7	69 01.9 +	20.1•	107.8	68 20.4 +	25.2•	112.6	67 30.0 +	29.7	117.1	66 31.5 +	33.8	121.2
6	69 48.1	11.8•	99.9	69 22.0	17.6•	105.1	68 45.6	22.9•	110.1	67 59.7	27.8•	114.8	67 05.3	32.1	119.1
7	69 59.9	9.0•	97.0	69 39.6	14.9•	102.4	69 08.5	20.5•	107.6	68 27.5	25.6•	112.4	67 37.4	30.2	116.9
8	70 08.9	6.2•	94.1	69 54.5	12.3•	99.6	69 29.0	18.1•	104.9	68 53.1	23.4•	109.9	68 07.6	28.2•	114.6
9	70 15.1	3.3•	91.2	70 06.8	9.4•	96.7	69 47.1	15.4•	102.2	69 16.5	21.0•	107.3	68 35.8	26.2•	112.2
10	70 18.4 +	0.4•	88.2	70 16.2 +	6.6•	93.8	70 02.5 +	12.6•	99.3	69 37.5 +	18.4•	104.7	69 02.0 +	23.8•	109.7
11	70 18.8 -	2.6•	85.3	70 22.8	3.7•	90.9	70 15.1	9.9•	96.5	69 55.9	15.9•	101.9	69 25.8	21.5•	107.1
12	70 16.2	5.4•	82.3	70 26.5 +	0.7•	87.9	70 25.0	7.0•	93.5	70 11.8	13.1•	99.1	69 47.3	18.9•	104.5
13	70 10.8	8.3•	79.4	70 27.2 -	2.2•	84.9	70 32.0	4.0•	90.6	70 24.9	10.3•	96.2	70 06.2	16.3•	101.7
14	70 02.5	11.2•	76.5	70 25.0	5.2•	81.9	70 36.0	1.1•	87.6	70 35.2	7.3•	93.2	70 22.5	13.6•	98.9
15	69 51.3 -	13.8•	73.6	70 19.8 -	8.0•	79.0	70 37.1 -	1.9•	84.5	70 42.5 +	4.4•	90.2	70 36.1 +	10.7•	95.9
16	69 37.5	16.5•	70.8	70 11.8	10.9•	76.0	70 35.2	4.9•	81.5	70 46.9 +	1.4•	87.2	70 46.8	7.7•	93.0
17	69 21.0	19.0•	68.0	70 00.9	13.6•	73.1	70 30.3	7.8•	78.5	70 48.3 -	1.5•	84.2	70 54.5	4.8•	89.9
18	69 02.0	21.5•	65.4	69 47.3	16.3•	70.3	70 22.5	10.6•	75.6	70 46.8	4.6•	81.1	70 59.3 +	1.7•	86.9
19	68 40.5	23.7•	62.8	69 31.0	18.9•	67.5	70 11.9	13.5•	72.7	70 42.2	7.6•	78.1	71 01.0 -	1.3•	83.8
20	68 16.8 -	26.0•	60.3	69 12.1 -	21.3•	64.8	69 58.4 -	16.1•	69.8	70 34.6 -	10.4•	75.1	70 59.7 -	4.3•	80.7
21	67 50.8	28.0	57.9	68 50.8	23.6•	62.2	69 42.3	18.8•	67.0	70 24.2	13.3•	72.2	70 55.4	7.3•	77.7
22	67 22.8	29.9	55.5	68 27.2	25.9•	59.7	69 23.5	21.2•	64.3	70 10.9	16.0•	69.3	70 48.1	10.3•	74.7
23	66 52.9	31.7	53.3	68 01.3	27.9•	57.3	69 02.3	23.5•	61.7	69 54.9	18.6•	66.5	70 37.8	13.1•	71.7
24	66 21.2	33.4	51.2	67 33.4	29.9	54.9	68 38.8	25.8•	59.1	69 36.3	21.2•	63.7	70 24.7	15.9•	68.7
25	65 47.8 -	34.9	49.1	67 03.5 -	31.6	52.7	68 13.0 -	27.9•	56.6	69 15.1 -	23.5•	61.0	70 08.8 -	18.6•	65.9
26	65 12.9	36.5	47.2	66 31.9	33.4	50.5	67 45.1	29.8	54.3	68 51.6	25.7•	58.5	69 50.2	21.1•	63.1
27	64 36.4	37.8	45.3	65 58.5	35.0	48.5	67 15.3	31.7	52.0	68 25.9	27.9•	56.0	69 29.1	23.5•	60.4
28	63 58.6	39.0	43.5	65 23.5	36.4	46.5	66 43.6	33.4	49.8	67 58.0	29.9	53.6	69 05.6	25.8•	57.8
29	63 19.6	40.3	41.8	64 47.1	37.9	44.6	66 10.2	35.0	47.8	67 28.1	31.7	51.3	68 39.8	27.9•	55.3

0°			2°			4°			6°			8°			
Hc	d	Z	Hc	d	Z	Hc	d	Z	Hc	d	Z	Hc	d	Z	Dec.
° ′	′	°	° ′	′	°	° ′	′	°	° ′	′	°	° ′	′	°	°
70 00.0	1.4·	90.0	69 54.3	– 7.5·	95.5	69 37.2	– 13.4·	100.8	69 09.3	– 18.9·	106.0	68 31.2	– 23.9·	110.9	0
69 58.6	4.3·	92.9	69 46.8	10.3·	98.4	69 23.8	15.9·	103.6	68 50.4	21.2·	108.7	68 07.3	26.1·	113.4	1
69 54.3	7.2·	95.8	69 36.5	13.0·	101.2	69 07.9	18.5·	106.4	68 29.2	23.6·	111.2	67 41.2	28.1	115.8	2
69 47.1	9.9·	98.7	69 23.5	15.6·	104.0	68 49.4	20.9·	109.0	68 05.6	25.7·	113.7	67 13.1	30.0	118.1	3
69 37.2	12.6·	101.6	69 07.9	18.2·	106.7	68 28.5	23.2·	111.6	67 39.9	27.8	116.1	66 43.1	31.8	120.3	4
69 24.6	– 15.3·	104.3	68 49.7	– 20.5·	109.4	68 05.3	– 25.4·	114.1	67 12.1	– 29.6	118.4	66 11.3	– 33.5	122.4	5
69 09.3	17.8·	107.1	68 29.2	22.9·	111.9	67 39.9	27.4·	116.5	66 42.5	31.5	120.7	65 37.8	35.0	124.5	6
68 51.5	20.3·	109.7	68 06.3	25.1·	114.4	67 12.5	29.4·	118.8	66 11.0	33.2	122.8	65 02.8	36.5	126.4	7
68 31.2	22.6·	112.3	67 41.2	27.1·	116.9	66 43.1	31.2	121.0	65 37.8	34.7	124.8	64 26.3	37.8	128.3	8
68 08.6	24.7·	114.8	67 14.1	29.1	119.2	66 11.9	32.9	123.2	65 03.1	36.2	126.8	63 48.5	39.1	130.1	9
67 43.9	– 26.9·	117.3	66 45.0	– 30.9	121.4	65 39.0	– 34.4	125.2	64 26.9	– 37.6	128.7	63 09.4	– 40.3	131.8	10
67 17.0	28.8	119.6	66 14.1	32.6	123.6	65 04.6	36.0	127.2	63 49.3	38.8	130.4	62 29.1	41.3	133.4	11
66 48.2	30.7	121.9	65 41.5	34.2	125.6	64 28.6	37.3	129.1	63 10.5	40.0	132.2	61 47.8	42.3	134.9	12
66 17.5	32.4	124.0	65 07.3	35.7	127.6	63 51.3	38.6	130.9	62 30.5	41.1	133.8	61 05.5	43.3	136.4	13
65 45.1	34.1	126.1	64 31.6	37.1	129.5	63 12.7	39.7	132.6	61 49.4	42.1	135.3	60 22.2	44.1	137.8	14
65 11.1	– 35.5	128.1	63 54.5	– 38.4	131.3	62 33.0	– 40.9	134.2	61 07.3	– 43.1	136.8	59 38.1	– 45.0	139.2	15
64 35.6	36.9	130.0	63 16.1	39.6	133.0	61 52.1	41.9	135.8	60 24.2	43.9	138.3	58 53.1	45.6	140.5	16
63 58.7	38.2	131.8	62 36.5	40.7	134.7	61 10.2	42.9	137.3	59 40.3	44.7	139.6	58 07.5	46.4	141.7	17
63 20.5	39.4	133.5	61 55.8	41.8	136.3	60 27.3	43.8	138.7	58 55.6	45.5	140.9	57 21.1	47.0	142.9	18
62 41.1	40.6	135.2	61 14.0	42.7	137.8	59 43.5	44.5	140.1	58 10.1	46.2	142.2	56 34.1	47.6	144.1	19
62 00.5	– 41.6	136.8	60 31.3	– 43.6	139.2	58 59.0	– 45.4	141.4	57 23.9	– 46.9	143.4	55 46.5	– 48.2	145.2	20
61 18.9	42.5	138.3	59 47.7	44.4	140.6	58 13.6	46.0	142.7	56 37.0	47.4	144.5	54 58.3	48.7	146.2	21
60 36.4	43.5	139.8	59 03.3	45.2	141.9	57 27.6	46.7	143.9	55 49.6	48.0	145.6	54 09.6	49.2	147.2	22
59 52.9	44.3	141.1	58 18.1	45.9	143.2	56 40.9	47.3	145.0	55 01.6	48.6	146.7	53 20.4	49.6	148.2	23
59 08.6	45.1	142.5	57 32.2	46.6	144.4	55 53.6	47.9	146.1	54 13.0	49.0	147.7	52 30.8	50.1	149.1	24
58 23.5	– 45.8	143.7	56 45.6	– 47.2	145.6	55 05.7	– 48.5	147.2	53 24.0	– 49.5	148.7	51 40.7	– 50.4	150.0	25
57 37.7	46.5	145.0	55 58.4	47.8	146.7	54 17.2	48.9	148.2	52 34.5	50.0	149.6	50 50.3	50.9	150.9	26
56 51.2	47.1	146.1	55 10.6	48.3	147.7	53 28.3	49.4	149.2	51 44.5	50.3	150.5	49 59.4	51.1	151.7	27
56 04.1	47.7	147.2	54 22.3	48.8	148.8	52 38.9	49.8	150.1	50 54.2	50.7	151.4	49 08.3	51.5	152.5	28
55 16.4	48.3	148.3	53 33.5	49.4	149.8	51 49.1	50.2	151.1	50 03.5	51.1	152.2	48 16.8	51.8	153.3	29

10°			12°			14°			16°			18°			
Hc	d	Z	Hc	d	Z	Hc	d	Z	Hc	d	Z	Hc	d	Z	Dec.
° ′	′	°	° ′	′	°	° ′	′	°	° ′	′	°	° ′	′	°	°
67 43.9	– 28.5·	115.5	66 48.2	– 32.5	119.7	65 45.1	– 36.0	123.6	64 35.6	– 39.1	127.1	63 20.5	– 41.8	130.3	0
67 15.4	30.4	117.8	66 15.7	34.2	121.8	65 09.1	37.5	125.5	63 56.5	40.4	128.9	62 38.7	42.9	131.9	1
66 45.0	32.1	120.0	65 41.5	35.7	123.9	64 31.6	38.8	127.4	63 16.1	41.5	130.5	61 55.8	43.8	133.4	2
66 12.9	33.9	122.1	65 05.8	37.2	125.8	63 52.8	40.1	129.1	62 34.6	42.5	132.1	61 12.0	44.7	134.8	3
65 39.0	35.3	124.2	64 28.6	38.4	127.6	63 12.7	41.1	130.8	61 52.1	43.5	133.6	60 27.3	45.5	136.2	4
65 03.7	– 36.8	126.1	63 50.2	– 39.7	129.4	62 31.6	– 42.2	132.4	61 08.6	– 44.4	135.1	59 41.8	– 46.2	137.5	5
64 26.9	38.1	127.9	63 10.5	40.8	131.1	61 49.4	43.1	133.9	60 24.2	45.1	136.5	58 55.6	46.9	138.8	6
63 48.8	39.4	129.7	62 29.7	41.9	132.7	61 06.3	44.1	135.4	59 39.1	46.0	137.8	58 08.7	47.6	140.0	7
63 09.4	40.5	131.4	61 47.8	42.8	134.2	60 22.2	44.9	136.8	58 53.1	46.6	139.0	57 21.1	48.2	141.1	8
62 28.9	41.6	133.0	61 05.0	43.8	135.7	59 37.3	45.6	138.1	58 06.5	47.3	140.3	56 32.9	48.7	142.2	9
61 47.3	– 42.6	134.6	60 21.2	– 44.6	137.1	58 51.7	– 46.4	139.4	57 19.2	– 47.9	141.4	55 44.2	– 49.2	143.3	10
61 04.7	43.5	136.0	59 36.6	45.4	138.4	58 05.3	47.0	140.6	56 31.3	48.4	142.5	54 55.0	49.7	144.3	11
60 21.2	44.4	137.4	58 51.2	46.1	139.7	57 18.3	47.6	141.7	55 42.9	49.0	143.6	54 05.3	50.1	145.2	12
59 36.8	45.1	138.8	58 05.1	46.8	140.9	56 30.7	48.3	142.8	54 53.9	49.5	144.6	53 15.2	50.6	146.2	13
58 51.7	45.9	140.1	57 18.3	47.4	142.1	55 42.4	48.7	143.9	54 04.4	49.9	145.6	52 24.6	50.9	147.0	14
58 05.8	– 46.6	141.3	56 30.9	– 48.0	143.2	54 53.7	– 49.3	144.9	53 14.5	– 50.3	146.5	51 33.7	– 51.4	147.9	15
57 19.2	47.2	142.5	55 42.9	48.6	144.3	54 04.4	49.7	145.9	52 24.2	50.8	147.4	50 42.3	51.6	148.7	16
56 32.0	47.8	143.6	54 54.3	49.0	145.3	53 14.7	50.1	146.9	51 33.4	51.1	148.3	49 50.7	52.0	149.5	17
55 44.2	48.3	144.7	54 05.3	49.5	146.3	52 24.6	50.5	147.8	50 42.3	51.4	149.1	48 58.7	52.2	150.3	18
54 55.9	48.9	145.7	53 15.8	50.0	147.3	51 34.1	51.0	148.7	49 50.9	51.8	149.9	48 06.5	52.6	151.0	19
54 07.0	– 49.3	146.7	52 25.8	– 50.3	148.2	50 43.1	– 51.2	149.5	48 59.1	– 52.1	150.7	47 13.9	– 52.8	151.8	20
53 17.7	49.8	147.7	51 35.5	50.8	149.1	49 51.9	51.6	150.3	48 07.0	52.3	151.4	46 21.1	53.0	152.4	21
52 27.9	50.2	148.6	50 44.7	51.1	149.9	49 00.3	51.9	151.1	47 14.7	52.6	152.2	45 28.1	53.3	153.1	22
51 37.7	50.6	149.5	49 53.6	51.4	150.7	48 08.4	52.2	151.8	46 22.1	52.9	152.9	44 34.8	53.4	153.8	23
50 47.1	50.9	150.4	49 02.2	51.8	151.5	47 16.2	52.5	152.6	45 29.2	53.1	153.5	43 41.4	53.7	154.4	24
49 56.2	– 51.3	151.2	48 10.4	– 52.0	152.3	46 23.7	– 52.7	153.3	44 36.1	– 53.3	154.2	42 47.7	– 53.9	155.0	25
49 04.9	51.7	152.0	47 18.4	52.3	153.0	45 31.0	53.0	154.0	43 42.8	53.6	154.8	41 53.8	54.1	155.6	26
48 13.2	51.9	152.8	46 26.1	52.6	153.8	44 38.0	53.2	154.6	42 49.2	53.7	155.5	40 59.7	54.2	156.2	27
47 21.3	52.2	153.5	45 33.5	52.8	154.5	43 44.8	53.4	155.3	41 55.5	53.9	156.1	40 05.5	54.4	156.7	28
46 29.1	52.4	154.2	44 40.7	53.1	155.1	42 51.4	53.6	155.9	41 01.6	54.1	156.6	39 11.1	54.5	157.3	29

Dec.	20° Hc	d	Z	22° Hc	d	Z	24° Hc	d	Z	26° Hc	d	Z	28° Hc	d	Z
°	° ′	′	°	° ′	′	°	° ′	′	°	° ′	′	°	° ′	′	°
0	62 00.5	+43.3	133.2	60 36.4	+45.4	135.8	59 08.6	+47.2	138.2	57 37.7	+48.8	140.3	56 04.1	+50.2	142.2
1	62 43.8	42.2	131.7	61 21.8	44.5	134.5	59 55.8	46.6	137.0	58 26.5	48.3	139.2	56 54.3	49.7	141.2
2	63 26.0	41.2	130.2	62 06.3	43.7	133.1	60 42.4	45.8	135.7	59 14.8	47.6	138.1	57 44.0	49.2	140.2
3	64 07.2	40.0	128.5	62 50.0	42.6	131.6	61 28.2	44.9	134.3	60 02.4	46.9	136.8	58 33.2	48.7	139.1
4	64 47.2	38.7	126.8	63 32.6	41.6	130.0	62 13.1	44.1	132.9	60 49.3	46.2	135.6	59 21.9	48.0	138.0
5	65 25.9	+37.4	125.0	64 14.2	+40.5	128.4	62 57.2	+43.1	131.5	61 35.5	+45.4	134.3	60 09.9	+47.3	136.8
6	66 03.3	35.9	123.1	64 54.7	39.2	126.7	63 40.3	42.0	129.9	62 20.9	44.5	132.9	60 57.2	46.6	135.5
7	66 39.2	34.3	121.1	65 33.9	37.8	124.9	64 22.3	40.9	128.3	63 05.4	43.5	131.4	61 43.8	45.8	134.2
8	67 13.5	32.5	119.0	66 11.7	36.4	123.0	65 03.2	39.7	126.6	63 48.9	42.6	129.9	62 29.6	45.0	132.8
9	67 46.0	30.8	116.8	66 48.1	34.7	121.0	65 42.9	38.3	124.8	64 31.5	41.4	128.2	63 14.6	44.0	131.4
10	68 16.8	+28.7	114.5	67 22.8	+33.1	118.9	66 21.2	+36.9	122.9	65 12.9	+40.1	126.5	63 58.6	+43.0	129.9
11	68 45.5	26.6	112.1	67 55.9	31.3	116.7	66 58.1	35.3	120.9	65 53.0	38.9	124.7	64 41.6	41.9	128.2
12	69 12.1	24.4	109.6	68 27.2	29.2	114.4	67 33.4	33.6	118.8	66 31.9	37.4	122.9	65 23.5	40.7	126.5
13	69 36.5	21.9	107.0	68 56.4	27.1	112.0	68 07.0	31.8	116.6	67 09.3	35.8	120.9	66 04.2	39.4	124.8
14	69 58.4	19.4	104.3	69 23.5	24.9	109.5	68 38.8	29.8	114.3	67 45.1	34.2	118.8	66 43.6	38.0	122.9
15	70 17.8	+16.8	101.5	69 48.4	+22.5	106.8	69 08.6	+27.7	111.9	68 19.3	+32.3	116.6	67 21.6	+36.4	120.9
16	70 34.6	14.0	98.6	70 10.9	19.9	104.1	69 36.3	25.4	109.4	68 51.6	30.4	114.3	67 58.0	34.7	118.8
17	70 48.6	11.1	95.7	70 30.8	17.3	101.3	70 01.7	23.0	106.7	69 22.0	28.2	111.9	68 32.7	32.9	116.6
18	70 59.7	8.2	92.7	70 48.1	14.5	98.4	70 24.7	20.4	104.0	69 50.2	26.0	109.3	69 05.6	31.0	114.3
19	71 07.9	5.1	89.6	71 02.6	11.5	95.5	70 45.1	17.8	101.2	70 16.2	23.6	106.7	69 36.6	28.8	111.8
20	71 13.0	+2.1	86.5	71 14.1	+8.6	92.4	71 02.9	+14.9	98.3	70 39.8	+21.0	103.9	70 05.4	+26.6	109.3
21	71 15.1	-1.0	83.4	71 22.7	5.5	89.3	71 17.8	12.0	95.3	71 00.8	18.2	101.1	70 32.0	24.1	106.6
22	71 14.1	4.1	80.3	71 28.2	2.4	86.2	71 29.8	9.0	92.2	71 19.0	15.5	98.1	70 56.1	21.6	103.9
23	71 10.0	7.1	77.2	71 30.6	-0.8	83.1	71 38.8	5.9	89.1	71 34.5	12.4	95.1	71 17.7	18.8	101.1
24	71 02.9	10.1	74.2	71 29.8	3.8	79.9	71 44.7	+2.7	85.9	71 46.9	9.4	92.0	71 36.5	15.9	98.0
25	70 52.8	-13.0	71.1	71 26.0	-7.0	76.8	71 47.4	-0.5	82.7	71 56.3	+6.2	88.8	71 52.4	+12.9	94.9
26	70 39.8	15.9	68.2	71 19.0	9.9	73.7	71 46.9	3.6	79.5	72 02.5	+3.0	85.6	72 05.3	9.8	91.8
27	70 23.9	18.5	65.3	71 09.1	13.0	70.6	71 43.3	6.8	76.3	72 05.5	-0.2	82.3	72 15.1	6.6	88.5
28	70 05.4	21.1	62.5	70 56.1	15.8	67.6	71 36.5	9.9	73.2	72 05.3	3.5	79.1	72 21.7	+3.3	85.3
29	69 44.3	23.5	59.7	70 40.3	18.5	64.7	71 26.6	12.9	70.0	72 01.8	6.6	75.8	72 25.0	0.0	82.0

Dec.	30° Hc	d	Z	32° Hc	d	Z	34° Hc	d	Z	36° Hc	d	Z	38° Hc	d	Z
°	° ′	′	°	° ′	′	°	° ′	′	°	° ′	′	°	° ′	′	°
0	54 28.1	+51.4	143.9	52 50.1	+52.5	145.5	51 10.4	+53.3	146.9	49 29.1	+54.1	148.2	47 46.4	+54.8	149.4
1	55 19.5	51.1	143.1	53 42.6	52.1	144.7	52 03.7	53.1	146.2	50 23.2	54.0	147.6	48 41.2	54.7	148.8
2	56 10.6	50.5	142.1	54 34.7	51.8	143.9	52 56.8	52.8	145.4	51 17.2	53.6	146.9	49 35.9	54.5	148.2
3	57 01.1	50.1	141.1	55 26.5	51.3	143.0	53 49.6	52.5	144.6	52 10.8	53.4	146.1	50 30.4	54.2	147.5
4	57 51.2	49.6	140.1	56 17.8	51.0	142.1	54 42.1	52.1	143.8	53 04.2	53.1	145.4	51 24.6	54.0	146.8
5	58 40.8	+49.0	139.0	57 08.8	+50.4	141.1	55 34.2	+51.7	142.9	53 57.3	+52.8	144.6	52 18.6	+53.7	146.1
6	59 29.8	48.4	137.9	57 59.2	50.0	140.1	56 25.9	51.3	142.0	54 50.1	52.5	143.8	53 12.3	53.4	145.4
7	60 18.2	47.8	136.7	58 49.2	49.4	139.0	57 17.2	50.8	141.1	55 42.6	52.1	142.9	54 05.7	53.2	144.6
8	61 06.0	47.0	135.5	59 38.6	48.9	137.9	58 08.0	50.4	140.1	56 34.7	51.6	142.1	54 58.9	52.8	143.8
9	61 53.0	46.3	134.2	60 27.5	48.1	136.8	58 58.4	49.8	139.1	57 26.3	51.3	141.1	55 51.7	52.4	143.0
10	62 39.3	+45.4	132.8	61 15.6	+47.5	135.5	59 48.2	+49.3	138.0	58 17.6	+50.7	140.1	56 44.1	+52.1	142.1
11	63 24.7	44.5	131.4	62 03.1	46.8	134.2	60 37.5	48.6	136.8	59 08.3	50.3	139.1	57 36.2	51.6	141.2
12	64 09.2	43.6	129.9	62 49.9	45.9	132.9	61 26.1	48.0	135.6	59 58.6	49.7	138.0	58 27.8	51.2	140.2
13	64 52.8	42.3	128.3	63 35.8	45.0	131.5	62 14.1	47.2	134.3	60 48.3	49.1	136.9	59 19.0	50.7	139.2
14	65 35.2	41.2	126.6	64 20.8	44.1	130.0	63 01.3	46.4	133.0	61 37.4	48.5	135.7	60 09.7	50.2	138.2
15	66 16.4	+40.0	124.8	65 04.9	+42.9	128.4	63 47.7	+45.6	131.6	62 25.9	+47.7	134.5	60 59.9	+49.5	137.0
16	66 56.4	38.5	122.9	65 47.8	41.8	126.7	64 33.3	44.6	130.1	63 13.6	46.9	133.1	61 49.4	49.0	135.9
17	67 34.9	37.0	120.9	66 29.6	40.6	124.9	65 17.9	43.5	128.5	64 00.5	46.1	131.7	62 38.4	48.2	134.6
18	68 11.9	35.4	118.9	67 10.2	39.1	123.0	66 01.4	42.4	126.8	64 46.6	45.2	130.2	63 26.6	47.5	133.3
19	68 47.3	33.5	116.7	67 49.3	37.6	121.1	66 43.8	41.1	125.1	65 31.8	44.1	128.7	64 14.1	46.6	131.9
20	69 20.8	+31.6	114.3	68 26.9	+36.0	119.0	67 24.9	+39.8	123.2	66 15.9	+43.0	127.0	65 00.7	+45.8	130.5
21	69 52.4	29.4	111.9	69 02.9	34.1	116.8	68 04.7	38.2	121.2	66 58.9	41.7	125.3	65 46.5	44.7	128.9
22	70 21.8	27.2	109.3	69 37.0	32.3	114.4	68 42.9	36.7	119.1	67 40.6	40.4	123.4	66 31.2	43.6	127.3
23	70 49.0	24.7	106.6	70 09.3	30.1	112.0	69 19.6	34.8	116.9	68 21.0	39.0	121.4	67 14.8	42.4	125.5
24	71 13.7	22.1	103.8	70 39.4	27.8	109.4	69 54.4	32.9	114.6	69 00.0	37.3	119.3	67 57.2	41.1	123.7
25	71 35.8	+19.4	100.9	71 07.2	+25.3	106.7	70 27.3	+30.7	112.1	69 37.3	+35.5	117.1	68 38.3	+39.6	121.7
26	71 55.2	16.4	97.9	71 32.5	22.7	103.9	70 58.0	28.5	109.5	70 12.8	33.5	114.8	69 17.9	38.0	119.6
27	72 11.6	13.4	94.8	71 55.2	19.9	100.9	71 26.5	26.0	106.8	70 46.3	31.5	112.3	69 55.9	36.2	117.4
28	72 25.0	10.2	91.6	72 15.1	17.0	97.8	71 52.5	23.3	103.9	71 17.8	29.1	109.7	70 32.1	34.3	115.0
29	72 35.2	6.9	88.3	72 32.1	13.8	94.7	72 15.8	20.5	100.9	71 46.9	26.7	106.9	71 06.4	32.2	112.5

20°			22°			24°			26°			28°			Dec.
Hc	d	Z	Hc	d	Z	Hc	d	Z	Hc	d	Z	Hc	d	Z	
° ′	′	°	° ′	′	°	° ′	′	°	° ′	′	°	° ′	′	°	°
62 00.5	−44.1	133.2	60 36.4	−46.2	135.8	59 08.6	−47.9	138.2	57 37.7	−49.4	140.3	56 04.1	−50.7	142.2	0
61 16.4	45.1	134.6	59 50.2	46.9	137.1	58 20.7	48.5	139.3	56 48.3	49.9	141.3	55 13.4	51.1	143.2	1
60 31.3	45.8	136.0	59 03.3	47.5	138.3	57 32.2	49.1	140.4	55 58.4	50.4	142.3	54 22.3	51.5	144.1	2
59 45.5	46.5	137.3	58 15.8	48.2	139.5	56 43.1	49.5	141.5	55 08.0	50.8	143.3	53 30.8	51.9	144.9	3
58 59.0	47.3	138.5	57 27.6	48.8	140.6	55 53.6	50.1	142.5	54 17.2	51.2	144.2	52 38.9	52.2	145.8	4
58 11.7	−48.2	139.7	56 38.8	−49.2	141.7	55 03.5	−50.5	143.5	53 26.0	−51.5	145.1	51 46.7	−52.5	146.6	5
57 23.9	48.5	140.9	55 49.6	49.8	142.7	54 13.0	50.9	144.4	52 34.5	52.0	146.0	50 54.2	52.8	147.4	6
56 35.4	48.9	141.9	54 59.8	50.2	143.7	53 22.1	51.3	145.3	51 42.5	52.2	146.8	50 01.4	53.1	148.1	7
55 46.5	49.5	143.0	54 09.6	50.4	144.7	52 30.8	51.7	146.2	50 50.3	52.6	147.6	49 08.3	53.4	148.8	8
54 57.0	50.0	144.0	53 18.9	51.0	145.6	51 39.1	52.0	147.0	49 57.7	52.8	148.3	48 14.9	53.6	149.5	9
54 07.0	−50.4	144.9	52 27.9	−51.4	146.4	50 47.1	−52.3	147.8	49 04.9	−53.2	149.1	47 21.3	−53.8	150.2	10
53 16.6	50.8	145.8	51 36.5	51.8	147.3	49 54.8	52.6	148.6	48 11.7	53.3	149.8	46 27.5	54.0	150.8	11
52 25.8	51.1	146.7	50 44.7	52.0	148.1	49 02.2	52.9	149.3	47 18.4	53.6	150.4	45 33.5	54.2	151.5	12
51 34.7	51.6	147.6	49 52.7	52.4	148.9	48 09.3	53.1	150.0	46 24.8	53.8	151.1	44 39.3	54.5	152.1	13
50 43.1	51.8	148.4	49 00.3	52.7	149.6	47 16.2	53.4	150.7	45 31.0	54.0	151.7	43 44.8	54.6	152.7	14
49 51.3	−52.2	149.2	48 07.6	−52.9	150.3	46 22.8	−53.6	151.4	44 37.0	−54.2	152.3	42 50.2	−54.7	153.2	15
48 59.1	52.4	149.9	47 14.7	53.2	151.0	45 29.2	53.8	152.0	43 42.8	54.4	152.9	41 55.5	54.9	153.8	16
48 06.7	52.8	150.7	46 21.5	53.4	151.7	44 35.4	54.0	152.7	42 48.4	54.6	153.5	41 00.6	55.1	154.3	17
47 13.9	52.9	151.4	45 28.1	53.6	152.4	43 41.4	54.2	153.3	41 53.8	54.7	154.1	40 05.5	55.2	154.8	18
46 21.0	53.2	152.1	44 34.5	53.8	153.0	42 47.2	54.4	153.9	40 59.1	54.9	154.6	39 10.3	55.3	155.3	19
45 27.8	−53.5	152.7	43 40.7	−54.1	153.6	41 52.8	−54.6	154.4	40 04.2	−55.0	155.2	38 15.0	−55.4	155.8	20
44 34.3	53.6	153.4	42 46.6	54.2	154.2	40 58.2	54.7	155.0	39 09.2	55.2	155.7	37 19.6	55.6	156.3	21
43 40.7	53.9	154.0	41 52.4	54.3	154.8	40 03.5	54.8	155.5	38 14.0	55.2	156.2	36 24.0	55.7	156.8	22
42 46.8	54.0	154.6	40 58.1	54.6	155.4	39 08.7	55.0	156.0	37 18.8	55.5	156.7	35 28.3	55.8	157.3	23
41 52.8	54.2	155.2	40 03.5	54.6	155.9	38 13.7	55.1	156.6	36 23.4	55.5	157.2	34 32.5	55.8	157.7	24
40 58.6	−54.4	155.8	39 08.9	−54.9	156.4	37 18.6	−55.2	157.1	35 27.9	−55.7	157.6	33 36.7	−56.0	158.1	25
40 04.2	54.5	156.3	38 14.0	55.1	156.9	36 23.4	55.4	157.6	34 32.2	55.7	158.1	32 40.7	56.0	158.6	26
39 09.7	54.7	156.9	37 19.1	55.1	157.5	35 28.0	55.5	158.0	33 36.5	55.8	158.5	31 44.7	56.2	159.0	27
38 15.0	54.8	157.4	36 24.0	55.2	158.0	34 32.5	55.5	158.5	32 40.7	55.9	159.0	30 48.5	56.2	159.4	28
37 20.2	55.0	157.9	35 28.8	55.3	158.4	33 37.0	55.7	158.9	31 44.8	56.0	159.4	29 52.3	56.2	159.8	29

30°			32°			34°			36°			38°			Dec.
Hc	d	Z	Hc	d	Z	Hc	d	Z	Hc	d	Z	Hc	d	Z	
° ′	′	°	° ′	′	°	° ′	′	°	° ′	′	°	° ′	′	°	°
54 28.1	−51.8	143.9	52 50.1	−52.8	145.5	51 10.4	−53.7	146.9	49 29.1	−54.4	148.2	47 46.4	−55.1	149.4	0
53 36.3	52.2	144.8	51 57.3	53.0	146.3	50 16.7	53.9	147.6	48 34.7	54.6	148.9	46 51.3	55.2	150.0	1
52 44.1	52.4	145.6	51 04.3	53.4	147.0	49 22.8	54.1	148.3	47 40.1	54.8	149.5	45 56.1	55.4	150.6	2
51 51.7	52.8	146.4	50 10.9	53.6	147.8	48 28.7	54.3	149.0	46 45.3	55.0	150.1	45 00.7	55.5	151.1	3
50 58.9	53.1	147.2	49 17.3	53.9	148.5	47 34.4	54.6	149.6	45 50.3	55.2	150.7	44 05.2	55.7	151.6	4
50 05.8	−53.4	147.9	48 23.4	−54.1	149.1	46 39.8	−54.7	150.2	44 55.1	−55.3	151.2	43 09.5	−55.8	152.2	5
49 12.4	53.6	148.6	47 29.3	54.3	149.8	45 45.1	54.9	150.8	43 59.8	55.4	151.8	42 13.7	56.0	152.7	6
48 18.8	53.8	149.3	46 35.0	54.4	150.4	44 50.2	55.1	151.4	43 04.4	55.6	152.3	41 17.7	56.1	153.1	7
47 25.0	54.1	150.0	45 40.6	54.7	151.0	43 55.1	55.2	152.0	42 08.8	55.8	152.8	40 21.6	56.1	153.6	8
46 30.9	54.2	150.6	44 45.9	54.9	151.6	42 59.9	55.4	152.5	41 13.0	55.8	153.3	39 25.5	56.3	154.1	9
45 36.7	−54.5	151.2	43 51.0	−55.0	152.2	42 04.5	−55.5	153.0	40 17.2	−56.0	153.8	38 29.2	−56.4	154.5	10
44 42.2	54.6	151.8	42 56.0	55.2	152.7	41 09.0	55.7	153.5	39 21.2	56.1	154.3	37 32.8	56.5	155.0	11
43 47.6	54.8	152.4	42 00.8	55.3	153.2	40 13.3	55.7	154.0	38 25.1	56.1	154.7	36 36.3	56.7	155.4	12
42 52.8	55.0	152.9	41 05.5	55.4	153.8	39 17.6	55.9	154.5	37 29.0	56.3	155.2	35 39.8	56.7	155.8	13
41 57.8	55.1	153.5	40 10.1	55.6	154.3	38 21.7	56.0	155.0	36 32.7	56.4	155.6	34 43.1	56.8	156.2	14
41 02.7	−55.2	154.0	39 14.5	−55.7	154.8	37 25.7	−56.1	155.4	35 36.3	−56.5	156.0	33 46.4	−56.8	156.6	15
40 07.5	55.4	154.5	38 18.8	55.8	155.2	36 29.6	56.2	155.9	34 39.8	56.5	156.4	32 49.6	56.8	157.0	16
39 12.1	55.5	155.0	37 23.0	55.9	155.7	35 33.4	56.3	156.3	33 43.3	56.6	156.8	31 52.8	57.0	157.3	17
38 16.6	55.6	155.5	36 27.1	56.0	156.1	34 37.1	56.4	156.7	32 46.7	56.7	157.2	30 55.8	57.0	157.7	18
37 21.0	55.8	156.0	35 31.1	56.1	156.6	33 40.7	56.4	157.1	31 50.0	56.7	157.6	29 58.8	57.0	158.1	19
36 25.2	−55.8	156.5	34 35.0	−56.2	157.0	32 44.3	−56.5	157.5	30 53.2	−56.8	158.0	29 01.8	−57.1	158.4	20
35 29.4	55.9	156.9	33 38.8	56.3	157.4	31 47.8	56.6	157.9	29 56.4	56.9	158.4	28 04.7	57.2	158.8	21
34 33.5	56.1	157.4	32 42.5	56.3	157.9	30 51.2	56.7	158.3	28 59.5	56.9	158.7	27 07.5	57.2	159.1	22
33 37.4	56.1	157.8	31 46.2	56.5	158.3	29 54.5	56.7	158.7	28 02.6	57.0	159.1	26 10.3	57.2	159.5	23
32 41.3	56.2	158.2	30 49.7	56.5	158.7	28 57.8	56.8	159.1	27 05.6	57.1	159.5	25 13.1	57.3	159.8	24
31 45.1	−56.3	158.6	29 53.2	−56.6	159.1	28 01.0	−56.9	159.4	26 08.5	−57.1	159.8	24 15.8	−57.4	160.1	25
30 48.8	56.3	159.0	28 56.6	56.6	159.4	27 04.1	56.9	159.8	25 11.4	57.2	160.1	23 18.4	57.4	160.4	26
29 52.5	56.4	159.4	28 00.0	56.7	159.8	26 07.2	56.9	160.2	24 14.2	57.1	160.5	22 21.0	57.4	160.8	27
28 56.1	56.5	159.8	27 03.3	56.8	160.2	25 10.3	57.0	160.5	23 17.1	57.3	160.8	21 23.6	57.4	161.1	28
27 59.6	56.6	160.2	26 06.5	56.8	160.5	24 13.3	57.1	160.9	22 19.8	57.3	161.1	20 26.2	57.5	161.4	29

LATITUDE **SAME** NAME

Dec.	40° Hc	d	Z	42° Hc	d	Z	44° Hc	d	Z	46° Hc	d	Z	48° Hc	d	Z
°	° ′	′	°	° ′	′	°	° ′	′	°	° ′	′	°	° ′	′	°
0	46 02.5	+ 55.5	150.5	44 17.6	+ 56.0	151.5	42 31.7	+ 56.5	152.3	40 45.0	+ 57.0	153.2	38 57.6	+ 57.3	153.9
1	46 58.0	55.3	149.9	45 13.6	55.9	151.0	43 28.2	56.4	151.9	41 42.0	56.8	152.7	39 54.9	57.2	153.5
2	47 53.3	55.1	149.4	46 09.5	55.7	150.4	44 24.6	56.3	151.4	42 38.8	56.7	152.3	40 52.1	57.2	153.1
3	48 48.4	55.0	148.8	47 05.2	55.6	149.9	45 20.9	56.1	150.9	43 35.5	56.6	151.9	41 49.3	57.0	152.7
4	49 43.4	54.7	148.1	48 00.8	55.4	149.3	46 17.0	56.0	150.4	44 32.1	56.6	151.4	42 46.3	57.0	152.3
5	50 38.1	+ 54.6	147.5	48 56.2	+ 55.3	148.8	47 13.0	+ 55.9	149.9	45 28.7	+ 56.3	150.9	43 43.3	+ 56.9	151.9
6	51 32.7	54.3	146.8	49 51.5	55.0	148.2	48 08.9	55.7	149.3	46 25.0	56.3	150.4	44 40.2	56.7	151.4
7	52 27.0	54.0	146.2	50 46.5	54.8	147.5	49 04.6	55.5	148.8	47 21.3	56.1	149.9	45 36.9	56.6	151.0
8	53 21.0	53.8	145.4	51 41.3	54.6	146.9	50 00.1	55.3	148.2	48 17.4	56.0	149.4	46 33.5	56.5	150.5
9	54 14.8	53.5	144.7	52 35.9	54.4	146.2	50 55.4	55.1	147.6	49 13.4	55.8	148.9	47 30.1	56.3	150.0
10	55 08.3	+ 53.1	143.9	53 30.3	+ 54.1	145.5	51 50.5	+ 55.0	147.0	50 09.2	+ 55.6	148.3	48 26.4	+ 56.3	149.5
11	56 01.4	52.9	143.1	54 24.4	53.9	144.8	52 45.5	54.7	146.3	51 04.8	55.5	147.7	49 22.7	56.1	149.0
12	56 54.3	52.4	142.2	55 18.3	53.5	144.0	53 40.2	54.4	145.6	52 00.3	55.2	147.1	50 18.8	55.9	148.4
13	57 46.7	52.1	141.3	56 11.8	53.2	143.2	54 34.6	54.2	144.9	52 55.5	55.1	146.4	51 14.7	55.8	147.8
14	58 38.8	51.6	140.4	57 05.0	52.9	142.4	55 28.8	53.9	144.2	53 50.6	54.8	145.8	52 10.5	55.5	147.2
15	59 30.4	+ 51.1	139.4	57 57.9	+ 52.4	141.5	56 22.7	+ 53.6	143.4	54 45.4	+ 54.5	145.1	53 06.0	+ 55.4	146.6
16	60 21.5	50.6	138.3	58 50.3	52.1	140.6	57 16.3	53.3	142.5	55 39.9	54.3	144.3	54 01.4	55.2	146.0
17	61 12.1	50.1	137.2	59 42.4	51.6	139.6	58 09.6	52.9	141.7	56 34.2	54.0	143.6	54 56.6	54.9	145.3
18	62 02.2	49.4	136.1	60 34.0	51.1	138.6	59 02.5	52.4	140.8	57 28.2	53.6	142.8	55 51.5	54.6	144.6
19	62 51.6	48.8	134.9	61 25.1	50.5	137.5	59 54.9	52.1	139.8	58 21.8	53.3	141.9	56 46.1	54.4	143.8
20	63 40.4	+ 48.0	133.6	62 15.6	+ 50.0	136.3	60 47.0	+ 51.6	138.8	59 15.1	+ 53.0	141.1	57 40.5	+ 54.1	143.1
21	64 28.4	47.3	132.2	63 05.6	49.3	135.1	61 38.6	51.0	137.8	60 08.1	52.5	140.1	58 34.6	53.7	142.2
22	65 15.7	46.3	130.7	63 54.9	48.6	133.8	62 29.6	50.5	136.6	61 00.6	52.1	139.1	59 28.3	53.4	141.4
23	66 02.0	45.3	129.2	64 43.5	47.8	132.5	63 20.1	49.9	135.4	61 52.7	51.5	138.1	60 21.7	53.0	140.5
24	66 47.3	44.3	127.6	65 31.3	46.9	131.1	64 10.0	49.1	134.2	62 44.2	51.0	137.0	61 14.7	52.5	139.5
25	67 31.6	+ 43.1	125.9	66 18.2	+ 46.0	129.5	64 59.1	+ 48.4	132.9	63 35.2	+ 50.4	135.8	62 07.2	+ 52.1	138.5
26	68 14.7	41.7	124.0	67 04.2	44.9	127.9	65 47.5	47.6	131.4	64 25.6	49.8	134.6	62 59.3	51.6	137.4
27	68 56.4	40.3	122.0	67 49.1	43.8	126.2	66 35.1	46.6	129.9	65 15.4	49.0	133.3	63 50.9	50.9	136.3
28	69 36.7	38.8	119.9	68 32.9	42.5	124.3	67 21.7	45.7	128.3	66 04.4	48.2	131.9	64 41.8	50.4	135.0
29	70 15.5	36.9	117.7	69 15.4	41.0	122.4	68 07.4	44.4	126.6	66 52.6	47.3	130.4	65 32.2	49.6	133.8

Dec.	50° Hc	d	Z	52° Hc	d	Z	54° Hc	d	Z	56° Hc	d	Z	58° Hc	d	Z
°	° ′	′	°	° ′	′	°	° ′	′	°	° ′	′	°	° ′	′	°
0	37 09.5	+ 57.7	154.6	35 20.8	+ 58.0	155.2	33 31.7	+ 58.2	155.7	31 42.0	+ 58.4	156.3	29 51.9	+ 58.7	156.8
1	38 07.2	57.5	154.2	36 18.8	57.9	154.9	34 29.9	58.1	155.5	32 40.4	58.5	156.0	30 50.6	58.6	156.5
2	39 04.7	57.5	153.5	37 16.7	57.8	154.6	35 28.0	58.1	155.2	33 38.9	58.3	155.8	31 49.2	58.6	156.3
3	40 02.2	57.3	153.5	38 14.5	57.8	154.2	36 26.1	58.1	154.9	34 37.2	58.4	155.5	32 47.8	58.6	156.0
4	40 59.7	57.3	153.1	39 12.3	57.7	153.9	37 24.2	58.0	154.6	35 35.6	58.3	155.3	33 46.4	58.5	155.8
5	41 57.0	+ 57.3	152.7	40 10.0	+ 57.6	153.5	38 22.2	+ 58.0	154.2	36 33.9	+ 58.2	154.9	34 44.9	+ 58.5	155.5
6	42 54.3	57.2	152.3	41 07.6	57.6	153.2	39 20.2	57.9	153.9	37 32.1	58.2	154.6	35 43.4	58.5	155.2
7	43 51.5	57.1	151.9	42 05.2	57.5	152.8	40 18.1	57.9	153.6	38 30.3	58.2	154.3	36 41.9	58.4	155.0
8	44 48.6	57.0	151.5	43 02.7	57.4	152.4	41 16.0	57.7	153.2	39 28.5	58.1	154.0	37 40.3	58.4	154.7
9	45 45.6	56.9	151.0	44 00.1	57.3	152.0	42 13.7	57.8	152.9	40 26.6	58.0	153.6	38 38.7	58.3	154.4
10	46 42.5	+ 56.8	150.6	44 57.4	+ 57.3	151.6	43 11.5	+ 57.6	152.5	41 24.6	+ 58.0	153.3	39 37.0	+ 58.3	154.1
11	47 39.3	56.6	150.1	45 54.7	57.1	151.1	44 09.1	57.5	152.1	42 22.6	57.9	153.0	40 35.3	58.3	153.8
12	48 35.9	56.5	149.6	46 51.8	57.0	150.7	45 06.6	57.4	151.7	43 20.5	57.9	152.6	41 33.6	58.2	153.4
13	49 32.4	56.4	149.1	47 48.8	57.0	150.2	46 04.0	57.4	151.3	44 18.4	57.8	152.2	42 31.8	58.1	153.1
14	50 28.8	56.2	148.6	48 45.8	56.7	149.8	47 01.5	57.3	150.9	45 16.2	57.7	151.9	43 29.9	58.1	152.8
15	51 25.0	+ 56.1	148.0	49 42.5	+ 56.7	149.3	47 58.8	+ 57.1	150.4	46 13.9	+ 57.6	151.5	44 28.0	+ 58.0	152.4
16	52 21.1	55.9	147.4	50 39.2	56.5	148.8	48 55.9	57.1	150.0	47 11.5	57.5	151.1	45 26.0	57.9	152.1
17	53 17.0	55.7	146.8	51 35.7	56.4	148.2	49 53.0	57.0	149.5	48 09.0	57.4	150.6	46 23.9	57.8	151.7
18	54 12.7	55.5	146.2	52 32.1	56.2	147.7	50 50.0	56.8	149.0	49 06.4	57.4	150.2	47 21.7	57.8	151.3
19	55 08.2	55.3	145.5	53 28.3	56.0	147.1	51 46.8	56.6	148.5	50 03.8	57.2	149.8	48 19.5	57.7	150.9
20	56 03.5	+ 55.0	144.9	54 24.3	+ 55.9	146.5	52 43.4	+ 56.6	148.0	51 01.0	+ 57.1	149.3	49 17.2	+ 57.6	150.5
21	56 58.5	54.7	144.1	55 20.2	55.6	145.8	53 40.0	56.3	147.4	51 58.1	57.0	148.8	50 14.8	57.5	150.0
22	57 53.2	54.5	143.4	56 15.8	55.4	145.2	54 36.3	56.2	146.8	52 55.1	56.8	148.3	51 12.3	57.3	149.6
23	58 47.7	54.2	142.6	57 11.2	55.2	144.5	55 32.5	56.0	146.2	53 51.9	56.7	147.7	52 09.6	57.3	149.1
24	59 41.9	53.8	141.7	58 06.4	54.9	143.7	56 28.5	55.8	145.5	54 48.6	56.5	147.2	53 06.9	57.1	148.6
25	60 35.7	+ 53.5	140.9	59 01.3	+ 54.6	143.0	57 24.3	+ 55.5	144.9	55 45.1	+ 56.3	146.5	54 04.0	+ 57.0	148.1
26	61 29.2	53.0	139.9	59 55.9	54.2	142.2	58 19.8	55.3	144.2	56 41.4	56.1	146.0	55 01.0	56.9	147.6
27	62 22.2	52.6	138.9	60 50.1	54.0	141.3	59 15.1	55.0	143.4	57 37.6	55.9	145.3	55 57.9	56.7	147.0
28	63 14.8	52.1	137.9	61 44.1	53.5	140.4	60 10.1	54.8	142.6	58 33.5	55.7	144.6	56 54.6	56.5	146.4
29	64 06.9	51.6	136.7	62 37.6	53.1	139.4	61 04.9	54.4	141.8	59 29.2	55.5	143.9	57 51.1	56.3	145.8

40°			42°			44°			46°			48°			Dec.
Hc	d	Z	Hc	d	Z	Hc	d	Z	Hc	d	Z	Hc	d	Z	°
46 02.5	−55.6	150.5	44 17.6	−56.2	151.5	42 31.7	−56.6	152.3	40 45.0	−57.0	153.2	38 57.6	−57.4	153.9	0
45 06.9	55.8	151.0	43 21.4	56.2	151.9	41 35.1	56.7	152.8	39 48.0	57.1	153.6	38 00.2	57.4	154.3	1
44 11.1	55.9	151.5	42 25.2	56.4	152.4	40 38.4	56.8	153.2	38 50.9	57.2	154.0	37 02.8	57.5	154.6	2
43 15.2	56.1	152.0	41 28.8	56.5	152.9	39 41.6	56.9	153.6	37 53.7	57.2	154.4	36 05.3	57.6	155.0	3
42 19.1	56.1	152.5	40 32.3	56.6	153.3	38 44.7	57.0	154.1	36 56.5	57.3	154.7	35 07.7	57.6	155.3	4
41 23.0	−56.3	153.0	39 35.7	−56.7	153.8	37 47.7	−57.0	154.5	35 59.2	−57.4	155.1	34 10.1	−57.7	155.7	5
40 26.7	56.4	153.5	38 39.0	56.8	154.2	36 50.7	57.2	154.8	35 01.8	57.5	155.5	33 12.4	57.8	156.0	6
39 30.3	56.5	153.9	37 42.2	56.8	154.6	35 53.5	57.2	155.2	34 04.3	57.5	155.8	32 14.6	57.8	156.3	7
38 33.8	56.6	154.3	36 45.4	57.0	155.0	34 56.3	57.2	155.6	33 06.8	57.6	156.1	31 16.8	57.8	156.7	8
37 37.2	56.6	154.8	35 48.4	57.0	155.4	33 59.1	57.4	156.0	32 09.2	57.6	156.5	30 19.0	57.9	157.0	9
36 40.6	−56.8	155.2	34 51.4	−57.1	155.8	33 01.7	−57.3	156.3	31 11.6	−57.6	156.8	29 21.1	−57.9	157.3	10
35 43.8	56.8	155.6	33 54.3	57.1	156.1	32 04.4	57.5	156.7	30 14.0	57.7	157.1	28 23.2	57.9	157.6	11
34 47.0	56.9	156.0	32 57.2	57.2	156.5	31 06.9	57.5	157.0	29 16.3	57.8	157.4	27 25.3	58.0	157.9	12
33 50.1	57.0	156.3	32 00.0	57.3	156.9	30 09.4	57.5	157.3	28 18.5	57.8	157.8	26 27.3	58.0	158.1	13
32 53.1	57.0	156.7	31 02.7	57.3	157.2	29 11.9	57.6	157.7	27 20.7	57.8	158.1	25 29.3	58.1	158.4	14
31 56.1	−57.1	157.1	30 05.4	−57.4	157.6	28 14.3	−57.7	158.0	26 22.9	−57.9	158.4	24 31.2	−58.1	158.7	15
30 59.0	57.2	157.5	29 08.0	57.4	157.9	27 16.6	57.7	158.3	25 25.0	57.9	158.7	23 33.1	58.1	159.0	16
30 01.8	57.2	157.8	28 10.6	57.5	158.2	26 19.0	57.7	158.6	24 27.1	57.9	158.9	22 35.0	58.1	159.3	17
29 04.6	57.3	158.1	27 13.1	57.5	158.5	25 21.3	57.8	158.9	23 29.2	58.0	159.2	21 36.9	58.2	159.5	18
28 07.3	57.3	158.5	26 15.6	57.6	158.9	24 23.5	57.8	159.2	22 31.2	58.0	159.5	20 38.7	58.2	159.8	19
27 10.0	−57.3	158.8	25 18.0	−57.6	159.2	23 25.7	−57.8	159.5	21 33.2	−58.0	159.8	19 40.5	−58.2	160.0	20
26 12.7	57.4	159.2	24 20.4	57.6	159.5	22 27.9	57.9	159.8	20 35.2	58.1	160.1	18 42.3	58.2	160.3	21
25 15.3	57.5	159.5	23 22.8	57.7	159.8	21 30.0	57.9	160.1	19 37.1	58.1	160.3	17 44.1	58.3	160.6	22
24 17.8	57.5	159.8	22 25.1	57.7	160.1	20 32.2	57.9	160.4	18 39.1	58.1	160.6	16 45.8	58.3	160.8	23
23 20.3	57.5	160.1	21 27.4	57.7	160.4	19 34.3	58.0	160.6	17 41.0	58.1	160.9	15 47.5	58.2	161.1	24
22 22.8	−57.6	160.4	20 29.7	−57.8	160.7	18 36.3	−57.9	161.0	16 42.9	−58.2	161.1	14 49.3	−58.3	161.3	25
21 25.2	57.5	160.7	19 31.9	57.8	161.0	17 38.4	58.0	161.2	15 44.7	58.1	161.4	13 51.0	58.4	161.5	26
20 27.7	57.7	161.0	18 34.1	57.8	161.2	16 40.4	58.0	161.5	14 46.6	58.2	161.6	12 52.6	58.3	161.8	27
19 30.0	57.6	161.3	17 36.3	57.9	161.5	15 42.4	58.0	161.7	13 48.4	58.2	161.9	11 54.3	58.3	162.0	28
18 32.4	57.7	161.6	16 38.4	57.8	161.8	14 44.4	58.0	162.0	12 50.2	58.2	162.1	10 56.0	58.4	162.3	29

50°			52°			54°			56°			58°			Dec.
Hc	d	Z	Hc	d	Z	Hc	d	Z	Hc	d	Z	Hc	d	Z	°
37 09.5	−57.7	154.6	35 20.8	−57.9	155.2	33 31.7	−58.3	155.8	31 42.0	−58.5	156.3	29 51.9	−58.7	156.8	0
36 11.8	57.7	154.9	34 22.9	58.1	155.5	32 33.4	58.3	156.1	30 43.5	58.5	156.6	28 53.2	58.7	157.0	1
35 14.1	57.9	155.3	33 24.8	58.1	155.8	31 35.1	58.3	156.3	29 45.0	58.5	156.8	27 54.5	58.7	157.2	2
34 16.2	57.8	155.6	32 26.7	58.1	156.1	30 36.8	58.4	156.6	28 46.5	58.6	157.1	26 55.8	58.8	157.5	3
33 18.4	57.9	155.9	31 28.6	58.1	156.4	29 38.4	58.4	156.9	27 47.9	58.6	157.3	25 57.0	58.8	157.7	4
32 20.5	−58.0	156.2	30 30.5	−58.2	156.7	28 40.0	−58.4	157.2	26 49.3	−58.6	157.6	24 58.2	−58.8	157.9	5
31 22.5	58.0	156.5	29 32.3	58.3	157.0	27 41.6	58.4	157.4	25 50.7	58.7	157.8	23 59.4	58.8	158.1	6
30 24.5	58.0	156.8	28 34.0	58.2	157.3	26 43.2	58.5	157.7	24 52.0	58.6	158.0	23 00.6	58.8	158.4	7
29 26.5	58.1	157.1	27 35.8	58.3	157.5	25 44.7	58.5	157.9	23 53.4	58.7	158.3	22 01.8	58.9	158.6	8
28 28.4	58.1	157.4	26 37.5	58.4	157.8	24 46.2	58.5	158.2	22 54.7	58.7	158.5	21 02.9	58.8	158.8	9
27 30.3	−58.2	157.7	25 39.1	−58.3	158.1	23 47.7	−58.6	158.4	21 56.0	−58.7	158.7	20 04.1	−58.9	159.0	10
26 32.1	58.1	158.0	24 40.8	58.4	158.3	22 49.1	58.5	158.6	20 57.3	58.7	158.9	19 05.2	58.9	159.2	11
25 34.0	58.2	158.2	23 42.4	58.4	158.6	21 50.6	58.6	158.9	19 58.5	58.7	159.1	18 06.3	58.9	159.4	12
24 35.8	58.2	158.5	22 44.0	58.4	158.8	20 52.0	58.6	159.1	18 59.8	58.8	159.4	17 07.4	58.9	159.6	13
23 37.5	58.2	158.8	21 45.6	58.5	159.1	19 53.4	58.6	159.3	18 01.0	58.6	159.6	16 08.5	58.9	159.8	14
22 39.3	−58.3	159.0	20 47.1	−58.4	159.3	18 54.8	−58.7	159.6	17 02.2	−58.8	159.8	15 09.6	−59.0	160.0	15
21 41.0	58.3	159.3	19 48.7	58.5	159.5	17 56.1	58.6	159.8	16 03.4	58.8	160.0	14 10.6	58.9	160.2	16
20 42.7	58.3	159.5	18 50.2	58.5	159.8	16 57.5	58.7	160.0	15 04.6	58.8	160.2	13 11.7	59.0	160.4	17
19 44.4	58.4	159.8	17 51.7	58.6	160.0	15 58.8	58.7	160.2	14 05.8	58.8	160.4	12 12.7	59.0	160.6	18
18 46.0	58.4	160.0	16 53.1	58.5	160.2	15 00.1	58.7	160.4	13 07.0	58.8	160.6	11 13.8	59.0	160.7	19
17 47.6	−58.4	160.3	15 54.6	−58.6	160.5	14 01.4	−58.7	160.7	12 08.2	−58.9	160.8	10 14.8	−59.0	160.9	20
16 49.2	58.4	160.5	14 56.0	58.5	160.7	13 02.7	58.6	160.9	11 09.3	58.8	161.0	9 15.8	58.9	161.1	21
15 50.8	58.4	160.8	13 57.5	58.6	160.9	12 04.0	58.7	161.1	10 10.5	58.9	161.2	8 16.8	59.0	161.3	22
14 52.4	58.4	161.0	12 58.9	58.6	161.2	11 05.3	58.7	161.3	9 11.6	58.9	161.4	7 17.8	59.0	161.5	23
13 54.0	58.5	161.2	12 00.3	58.6	161.4	10 06.6	58.7	161.5	8 12.7	58.8	161.6	6 18.8	59.0	161.7	24
12 55.5	−58.4	161.5	11 01.7	−58.6	161.6	9 07.8	−58.7	161.7	7 13.9	−58.9	161.8	5 19.8	−59.0	161.9	25
11 57.1	58.5	161.7	10 03.1	58.6	161.8	8 09.1	58.8	161.9	6 15.0	58.9	162.0	4 20.8	59.0	162.0	26
10 58.6	58.5	161.9	9 04.5	58.6	162.0	7 10.3	58.7	162.1	5 16.1	58.9	162.2	3 21.8	59.0	162.2	27
10 00.1	58.5	162.1	8 05.9	58.7	162.2	6 11.6	58.8	162.3	4 17.2	58.9	162.4	2 22.8	59.0	162.4	28
9 01.6	58.5	162.4	7 07.2	58.6	162.5	5 12.8	58.8	162.5	3 18.3	58.9	162.6	1 23.8	59.0	162.6	29

Dec.	0° Hc	d	Z	2° Hc	d	Z	4° Hc	d	Z	6° Hc	d	Z	8° Hc	d	Z
°	° ′	′	°	° ′	′	°	° ′	′	°	° ′	′	°	° ′	′	°
0	68 00.0	- 1.3°	90.0	67 54.8	+ 4.3°	94.9	67 39.4	+ 9.8°	99.8	67 14.1	+15.1°	104.5	66 39.5	+20.0°	109.0
1	67 58.7	3.9°	87.3	67 59.1	+ 1.7°	92.3	67 49.2	7.2°	97.2	67 29.2	12.6°	102.0	66 59.5	17.8°	106.6
2	67 54.8	6.4°	84.7	68 00.8	- 0.9°	89.6	67 56.4	4.7°	94.6	67 41.8	10.2°	99.4	67 17.3	15.5°	104.2
3	67 48.4	9.0°	82.0	67 59.9	3.5°	86.9	68 01.1	+ 2.2°	91.9	67 52.0	7.7°	96.8	67 32.8	13.0°	101.6
4	67 39.4	11.4°	79.4	67 56.4	6.0°	84.3	68 03.3	- 0.5°	89.2	67 59.7	5.1°	94.2	67 45.8	10.6°	99.1
5	67 28.0	-13.9°	76.9	67 50.4	- 8.6°	81.6	68 02.8	- 3.1°	86.5	68 04.8	+ 2.5°	91.5	67 56.4	+ 8.1°	96.5
6	67 14.1	16.1°	74.3	67 41.8	11.0°	79.0	67 59.7	5.7°	83.9	68 07.3	- 0.1°	88.8	68 04.5	5.6°	93.8
7	66 58.0	18.5°	71.9	67 30.8	13.5°	76.4	67 54.0	8.2°	81.2	68 07.2	2.7°	86.2	68 10.1	2.9°	91.1
8	66 39.5	20.6°	69.4	67 17.3	15.8°	73.9	67 45.8	10.7°	78.6	68 04.5	5.2°	83.5	68 13.0	+ 0.3°	88.5
9	66 18.9	22.7°	67.1	67 01.5	18.1°	71.4	67 35.1	13.1°	76.0	67 59.3	7.9°	80.8	68 13.3	- 2.3°	85.8
10	65 56.2	-24.6	64.8	66 43.4	-20.3°	69.0	67 22.0	-15.5°	73.5	67 51.4	-10.3°	78.2	68 11.0	- 4.9°	83.1
11	65 31.6	26.6	62.6	66 23.1	22.4°	66.6	67 06.5	17.8°	71.0	67 41.1	12.8°	75.6	68 06.1	7.5°	80.4
12	65 05.0	28.3	60.4	66 00.7	24.4	64.3	66 48.7	20.0°	68.5	67 28.3	15.2°	73.0	67 58.6	10.0°	77.7
13	64 36.7	30.0	58.4	65 36.3	26.3	62.1	66 28.7	22.1°	66.1	67 13.1	17.5°	70.5	67 48.6	12.5°	75.1
14	64 06.7	31.6	56.4	65 10.0	28.0	59.9	66 06.6	24.1	63.8	66 55.6	19.7°	68.0	67 36.1	14.9°	72.5
15	63 35.1	-33.1	54.4	64 42.0	-29.8	57.9	65 42.5	-26.0	61.6	66 35.9	-21.9°	65.6	67 21.2	-17.2°	70.0
16	63 02.0	34.5	52.6	64 12.2	31.4	55.8	65 16.5	27.9	59.4	66 14.0	23.9	63.3	67 04.0	19.5°	67.5
17	62 27.5	35.9	50.8	63 40.8	32.9	53.9	64 48.6	29.5	57.3	65 50.1	25.8	61.1	66 44.5	21.6°	65.1
18	61 51.6	37.0	49.1	63 07.9	34.3	52.0	64 19.1	31.2	55.3	65 24.3	27.6	58.9	66 22.9	23.7°	62.8
19	61 14.6	38.2	47.4	62 33.6	35.6	50.2	63 47.9	32.7	53.3	64 56.7	29.4	56.8	65 59.2	25.7	60.5
20	60 36.4	-39.3	45.8	61 58.0	-36.9	48.5	63 15.2	-34.1	51.5	64 27.3	-31.0	54.7	65 33.5	-27.4	58.3
21	59 57.1	40.3	44.3	61 21.1	38.0	46.8	62 41.1	35.5	49.7	63 56.3	32.6	52.8	65 06.1	29.3	56.2
22	59 16.8	41.3	42.8	60 43.1	39.2	45.2	62 05.6	36.8	47.9	63 23.7	34.0	50.9	64 36.8	30.9	54.1
23	58 35.5	42.1	41.4	60 03.9	40.2	43.7	61 28.8	37.9	46.2	62 49.7	35.3	49.0	64 05.9	32.4	52.1
24	57 53.4	43.0	40.1	59 23.7	41.1	42.2	60 50.9	39.0	44.6	62 14.4	36.7	47.3	63 33.5	33.9	50.2
25	57 10.4	-43.8	38.8	58 42.6	-42.0	40.8	60 11.9	-40.1	43.1	61 37.7	-37.8	45.6	62 59.6	-35.3	48.4
26	56 26.6	44.4	37.5	58 00.6	42.9	39.5	59 31.8	41.0	41.6	60 59.9	39.0	44.0	62 24.3	36.5	46.6
27	55 42.2	45.2	36.3	57 17.7	43.6	38.2	58 50.8	42.0	40.2	60 20.9	39.9	42.4	61 47.8	37.8	44.9
28	54 57.0	45.8	35.2	56 34.1	44.4	36.9	58 08.8	42.7	38.8	59 41.0	41.0	40.9	61 10.0	38.9	43.3
29	54 11.2	46.4	34.1	55 49.7	45.1	35.7	57 26.1	43.6	37.5	59 00.0	41.9	39.5	60 31.1	39.9	41.7

Dec.	10° Hc	d	Z	12° Hc	d	Z	14° Hc	d	Z	16° Hc	d	Z	18° Hc	d	Z
°	° ′	′	°	° ′	′	°	° ′	′	°	° ′	′	°	° ′	′	°
0	65 56.2	+24.6	113.3	65 05.0	+28.8	117.2	64 06.7	+32.4	120.9	63 02.0	+35.8	124.3	61 51.6	+38.8	127.4
1	66 20.8	22.6°	111.0	65 33.8	26.9	115.1	64 39.1	30.9	119.0	63 37.8	34.4	122.5	62 30.4	37.5	125.8
2	66 43.4	20.4°	108.7	66 00.7	25.0	112.9	65 10.0	29.2	116.9	64 12.2	32.9	120.7	63 07.9	36.3	124.1
3	67 03.8	18.2°	106.3	66 25.7	23.0°	110.7	65 39.2	27.4	114.8	64 45.1	31.4	118.7	63 44.2	34.9	122.3
4	67 22.0	15.9°	103.8	66 48.7	20.9°	108.4	66 06.6	25.5	112.7	65 16.5	29.6	116.7	64 19.1	33.4	120.4
5	67 37.9	+13.5°	101.3	67 09.6	+18.7°	106.0	66 32.1	+23.5°	110.4	65 46.1	+27.9	114.6	64 52.5	+31.8	118.5
6	67 51.4	11.1°	98.7	67 28.3	16.3°	103.5	66 55.6	21.3°	108.1	66 14.0	26.0	112.4	65 24.3	30.2	116.5
7	68 02.5	8.5°	96.1	67 44.6	14.0°	101.0	67 16.9	19.2°	105.7	66 40.0	24.0°	110.2	65 54.5	28.4	114.4
8	68 11.0	6.0°	93.5	67 58.6	11.5°	98.4	67 36.1	16.8°	103.2	67 04.0	21.8°	107.8	66 22.9	26.4	112.2
9	68 17.0	3.3°	90.8	68 10.1	9.0°	95.8	67 52.9	14.5°	100.7	67 25.8	19.6°	105.4	66 49.3	24.5°	109.9
10	68 20.3	0.7°	88.1	68 19.1	+ 6.3°	93.1	68 07.4	+11.9°	98.1	67 45.4	+17.4°	102.9	67 13.8	+22.4°	107.6
11	68 21.0	- 1.9°	85.4	68 25.4	3.8°	90.4	68 19.3	9.4°	95.4	68 02.8	14.9°	100.4	67 36.2	20.1°	105.2
12	68 19.1	4.6°	82.6	68 29.2	+ 1.1°	87.7	68 28.7	6.8°	92.8	68 17.7	12.4°	97.8	67 56.3	17.8°	102.7
13	68 14.5	7.1°	80.0	68 30.3	- 1.6°	85.0	68 35.5	4.3°	90.0	68 30.1	9.9°	95.1	68 14.1	15.4°	100.1
14	68 07.4	9.7°	77.3	68 28.7	4.2°	82.2	68 39.7	+ 1.5°	87.3	68 40.0	7.2°	92.4	68 29.5	12.9°	97.5
15	67 57.7	-12.3°	74.6	68 24.5	- 6.8°	79.5	68 41.2	- 1.2°	84.6	68 47.2	+ 4.5°	89.7	68 42.4	+10.3°	94.8
16	67 45.4	14.6°	72.0	68 17.7	9.4°	76.8	68 40.0	3.9°	81.8	68 51.7	+ 1.9°	86.9	68 52.7	7.7°	92.1
17	67 30.8	17.0°	69.5	68 08.3	12.0°	74.2	68 36.1	6.6°	79.1	68 53.6	- 0.9°	84.2	69 00.4	5.0°	89.3
18	67 13.8	19.2°	67.0	67 56.3	14.4°	71.5	68 29.5	9.1°	76.4	68 52.7	3.5°	81.4	69 05.4	+ 2.3°	86.6
19	66 54.6	21.5°	64.6	67 41.9	16.8°	69.0	68 20.4	11.7°	73.7	68 49.2	6.3°	78.6	69 07.6	- 0.5°	83.8
20	66 33.1	-23.5°	62.2	67 25.1	-19.0°	66.5	68 08.7	-14.2°	71.0	68 42.9	- 8.9°	75.9	69 07.1	- 3.3°	81.0
21	66 09.6	25.5	59.9	67 06.1	21.3°	64.0	67 54.5	16.6°	68.4	68 34.0	11.4°	73.2	69 03.8	6.0°	78.2
22	65 44.1	27.3	57.7	66 44.8	23.4°	61.6	67 37.9	18.9°	65.9	68 22.6	14.0°	70.5	68 57.8	8.6°	75.4
23	65 16.8	29.1	55.5	66 21.4	25.3	59.3	67 19.0	21.1°	63.4	68 08.6	16.5°	67.9	68 49.2	11.3°	72.6
24	64 47.7	30.8	53.5	65 56.1	27.3	57.1	66 57.9	23.3°	61.0	67 52.1	18.8°	65.3	68 37.9	13.8°	69.9
25	64 16.9	-32.4	51.5	65 28.8	-29.0	54.9	66 34.6	-25.3	58.7	67 33.3	-21.0°	62.8	68 24.1	-16.4°	67.3
26	63 44.5	33.8	49.6	64 59.8	30.8	52.8	66 09.3	27.2	56.4	67 12.3	23.2°	60.3	68 07.7	18.7°	64.7
27	63 10.7	35.3	47.7	64 29.0	32.3	50.8	65 42.1	29.0	54.2	66 49.1	25.2°	58.0	67 49.0	21.0°	62.1
28	62 35.4	36.5	45.9	63 56.7	33.8	48.9	65 13.1	30.7	52.1	66 23.9	27.2	55.7	67 28.0	23.1°	59.7
29	61 58.9	37.7	44.2	63 22.9	35.2	47.0	64 42.4	32.3	50.1	65 56.7	29.0	53.5	67 04.9	25.3°	57.3

0°			2°			4°			6°			8°			Dec.
Hc	d	Z	Hc	d	Z	Hc	d	Z	Hc	d	Z	Hc	d	Z	
68 00.0 − 1.3° 90.0			67 54.8 − 6.8° 94.9			67 39.4 − 12.2° 99.8			67 14.1 − 17.3°104.5			66 39.5 − 22.1°109.0			0
67 58.7 3.9° 92.7			67 48.0 9.4° 97.6			67 27.2 14.6°102.4			66 56.8 19.6°107.0			66 17.4 24.2 111.3			1
67 54.8 6.4° 95.3			67 38.6 11.8°100.2			67 12.6 17.0°104.9			66 37.2 21.7°109.4			65 53.2 26.0 113.6			2
67 48.4 9.0° 98.0			67 26.8 14.2°102.7			66 55.6 19.2°107.3			66 15.5 23.7°111.7			65 27.2 27.9 115.8			3
67 39.4 11.4°100.6			67 12.6 16.6°105.3			66 36.4 21.3°109.7			65 51.8 25.7 114.0			64 59.3 29.7 117.9			4
67 28.0 −13.9°103.1			66 56.0 −18.8°107.7			66 15.1 −23.3°112.1			65 26.1 −27.6 116.2			64 29.6 −31.3 119.9			5
67 14.1 16.1°105.7			66 37.2 20.9°110.1			65 51.8 25.4 114.3			64 58.5 29.2 118.3			63 58.3 32.8 121.9			6
66 58.0 18.5°108.1			66 16.3 23.1°112.5			65 26.4 27.1 116.5			64 29.3 31.0 120.3			63 25.5 34.2 123.8			7
66 39.5 20.6°110.6			65 53.2 24.9 114.8			64 59.3 29.0 118.7			63 58.3 32.4 122.3			62 51.3 35.6 125.6			8
66 18.9 22.7°112.9			65 28.3 26.9 117.0			64 30.3 30.6 120.7			63 25.9 33.9 124.2			62 15.7 36.8 127.3			9
65 56.2 −24.6 115.2			65 01.4 −28.6 119.1			63 59.7 −32.1 122.7			62 52.0 −35.3 126.0			61 38.9 −38.1 129.0			10
65 31.6 26.6 117.4			64 32.8 30.3 121.2			63 27.6 33.6 124.6			62 16.7 36.6 127.8			61 00.8 39.1 130.6			11
65 05.0 28.3 119.6			64 02.5 31.8 123.2			62 54.0 35.0 126.5			61 40.1 37.7 129.5			60 21.7 40.2 132.2			12
64 36.7 30.0 121.6			63 30.7 33.4 125.1			62 19.0 36.3 128.2			61 02.4 38.9 131.1			59 41.5 41.2 133.7			13
64 06.7 31.6 123.6			62 57.3 34.7 126.9			61 42.7 37.5 129.9			60 23.5 39.9 132.6			59 00.3 42.0 135.1			14
63 35.1 −33.1 125.6			62 22.6 −36.1 128.7			61 05.2 −38.6 131.5			59 43.6 −40.9 134.1			58 18.3 −42.9 136.5			15
63 02.0 34.5 127.4			61 46.5 37.2 130.4			60 26.6 39.7 133.1			59 02.7 41.8 135.6			57 35.4 43.7 137.8			16
62 27.5 35.9 129.2			61 09.3 38.4 132.1			59 46.9 40.7 134.6			58 20.9 42.7 136.9			56 51.7 44.4 139.1			17
61 51.6 37.0 130.9			60 30.9 39.5 133.6			59 06.2 41.6 136.1			57 38.2 43.5 138.3			56 07.3 45.2 140.3			18
61 14.6 38.2 132.6			59 51.4 40.5 135.1			58 24.6 42.4 137.5			56 54.7 44.2 139.5			55 22.1 45.7 141.4			19
60 36.4 −39.3 134.2			59 10.9 −41.4 136.6			57 42.2 −43.3 138.8			56 10.5 −44.9 140.8			54 36.4 −46.4 142.6			20
59 57.1 40.3 135.7			58 29.5 42.3 138.0			56 58.9 44.1 140.1			55 25.6 45.6 142.0			53 50.0 47.0 143.7			21
59 16.8 41.3 137.2			57 47.2 43.1 139.3			56 14.8 44.7 141.3			54 40.0 46.2 143.1			53 03.0 47.4 144.7			22
58 35.5 42.1 138.6			57 04.1 43.9 140.6			55 30.1 45.4 142.5			53 53.8 46.7 144.2			52 15.6 48.0 145.7			23
57 53.4 43.0 139.9			56 20.2 44.6 141.9			54 44.7 46.0 143.6			53 07.1 47.3 145.2			51 27.6 48.4 146.7			24
57 10.4 −43.8 141.2			55 35.6 −45.2 143.1			53 58.7 −46.7 144.7			52 19.8 −47.9 146.3			50 39.2 −48.9 147.6			25
56 26.6 44.4 142.5			54 50.4 45.9 144.2			53 12.0 47.1 145.8			51 31.9 48.2 147.2			49 50.3 49.3 148.5			26
55 42.2 45.2 143.7			54 04.5 46.5 145.3			52 24.9 47.7 146.8			50 43.7 48.8 148.2			49 01.0 49.7 149.4			27
54 57.0 45.8 144.8			53 18.0 47.1 146.4			51 37.2 48.1 147.8			49 54.9 49.1 149.1			48 11.3 50.0 150.3			28
54 11.2 46.4 145.9			52 30.9 47.5 147.4			50 49.1 48.6 148.8			49 05.8 49.5 150.0			47 21.3 50.4 151.1			29

10°			12°			14°			16°			18°			Dec.
Hc	d	Z	Hc	d	Z	Hc	d	Z	Hc	d	Z	Hc	d	Z	
65 56.2 − 26.5 113.3			65 05.0 − 30.4 117.2			64 06.7 − 34.0 120.9			63 02.0 − 37.1 124.3			61 51.6 − 39.8 127.4			0
65 29.7 28.3 115.4			64 34.6 32.1 119.3			63 32.7 35.4 122.8			62 24.9 38.4 126.0			61 11.8 40.9 129.0			1
65 01.4 30.0 117.5			64 02.5 33.5 121.2			62 57.3 36.7 124.6			61 46.5 39.4 127.7			60 30.9 41.9 130.5			2
64 31.4 31.7 119.6			63 29.0 35.0 123.1			62 20.6 37.9 126.3			61 07.1 40.5 129.2			59 49.0 42.8 131.9			3
63 59.7 33.1 121.5			62 54.0 36.3 124.9			61 42.7 39.0 128.0			60 26.6 41.5 130.8			59 06.2 43.6 133.3			4
63 26.6 −34.6 123.4			62 17.7 −37.6 126.6			61 03.7 −40.2 129.5			59 45.1 −42.4 132.2			58 22.6 −44.4 134.6			5
62 52.0 36.0 125.2			61 40.1 38.6 128.3			60 23.5 41.1 131.1			59 02.7 43.3 133.6			57 38.2 45.1 135.9			6
62 16.0 37.1 127.0			61 01.5 39.8 129.9			59 42.4 42.1 132.5			58 19.4 44.0 134.9			56 53.1 45.8 137.1			7
61 38.9 38.4 128.6			60 21.7 40.8 131.4			59 00.3 42.9 133.9			57 35.4 44.8 136.2			56 07.3 46.5 138.3			8
61 00.5 39.4 130.2			59 40.9 41.7 132.9			58 17.4 43.7 135.3			56 50.6 45.5 137.4			55 20.8 47.1 139.4			9
60 21.1 −40.5 131.8			58 59.2 −42.7 134.3			57 33.7 −44.5 136.5			56 05.1 −46.2 138.6			54 33.7 −47.6 140.5			10
59 40.6 41.4 133.3			58 16.5 43.4 135.6			56 49.2 45.2 137.8			55 18.9 46.7 139.7			53 46.1 48.1 141.5			11
58 59.2 42.4 134.7			57 33.1 44.2 136.9			56 04.0 45.9 139.0			54 32.2 47.4 140.8			52 58.0 48.6 142.5			12
58 16.8 43.1 136.0			56 48.9 44.9 138.2			55 18.1 46.5 140.1			53 44.8 47.8 141.9			52 09.4 49.1 143.5			13
57 33.7 44.0 137.3			56 04.0 45.6 139.4			54 31.6 47.0 141.2			52 57.0 48.4 142.9			51 20.3 49.5 144.4			14
56 49.7 −44.6 138.6			55 18.4 −46.2 140.5			53 44.6 −47.6 142.3			52 08.6 −48.8 143.9			50 30.8 −49.9 145.3			15
56 05.1 45.4 139.8			54 32.2 46.8 141.6			52 57.0 48.1 143.3			51 19.8 49.2 144.8			49 40.9 50.2 146.2			16
55 19.7 46.0 141.0			53 45.4 47.4 142.7			52 08.9 48.6 144.3			50 30.6 49.7 145.7			48 50.7 50.7 147.0			17
54 33.7 46.5 142.1			52 58.0 47.9 143.7			51 20.3 49.0 145.2			49 40.9 50.0 146.6			48 00.0 50.9 147.8			18
53 47.2 47.2 143.2			52 10.1 48.3 144.7			50 31.3 49.4 146.1			48 50.9 50.4 147.4			47 09.1 51.3 148.6			19
53 00.0 −47.6 144.2			51 21.8 −48.8 145.7			49 41.9 −49.8 147.0			48 00.5 −50.7 148.3			46 17.8 −51.5 149.4			20
52 12.4 48.2 145.2			50 33.0 49.2 146.6			48 52.1 50.2 147.9			47 09.8 51.1 149.0			45 26.3 51.8 150.1			21
51 24.2 48.6 146.2			49 43.8 49.7 147.5			48 01.9 50.6 148.7			46 18.7 51.3 149.8			44 34.5 52.1 150.8			22
50 35.6 49.0 147.1			48 54.1 50.0 148.4			47 11.3 50.8 149.5			45 27.4 51.7 150.6			43 42.4 52.3 151.5			23
49 46.6 49.5 148.0			48 04.1 50.3 149.2			46 20.5 51.2 150.3			44 35.7 51.8 151.3			42 50.1 52.6 152.2			24
48 57.1 −49.8 148.9			47 13.8 −50.7 150.0			45 29.3 −51.4 151.0			43 43.9 −52.2 152.0			41 57.5 −52.8 152.8			25
48 07.3 50.2 149.7			46 23.1 51.0 150.8			44 37.9 51.7 151.8			42 51.7 52.4 152.7			41 04.7 52.9 153.5			26
47 17.1 50.5 150.5			45 32.1 51.3 151.5			43 46.2 52.0 152.5			41 59.3 52.6 153.3			40 11.8 53.2 154.1			27
46 26.6 50.8 151.3			44 40.8 51.5 152.3			42 54.2 52.2 153.2			41 06.7 52.8 154.0			39 18.6 53.4 154.7			28
45 35.8 51.2 152.1			43 49.3 51.8 153.0			42 02.0 52.5 153.8			40 13.9 53.0 154.6			38 25.2 53.5 155.3			29

69

	20°			22°			24°			26°			28°		
Dec.	Hc	d	Z	Hc	d	Z	Hc	d	Z	Hc	d	Z	Hc	d	Z
°	° ′	′	°	° ′	′	°	° ′	′	°	° ′	′	°	° ′	′	°
0	60 36.4	+41.3	130.2	59 16.8	+43.6	132.8	57 53.4	+45.5	135.2	56 26.6	+47.3	137.3	54 57.0	+48.8	139.3
1	61 17.7	40.3	128.8	60 00.4	42.7	131.5	58 38.9	44.8	134.0	57 13.9	46.7	136.2	55 45.8	48.3	138.3
2	61 58.0	39.2	127.2	60 43.1	41.7	130.1	59 23.7	44.1	132.7	58 00.6	46.0	135.0	56 34.1	47.7	137.2
3	62 37.2	38.0	125.6	61 24.8	40.8	128.6	60 07.8	43.1	131.3	58 46.6	45.2	133.8	57 21.8	47.0	136.1
4	63 15.2	36.7	123.9	62 05.6	39.6	127.0	60 50.9	42.2	129.9	59 31.8	44.5	132.5	58 08.8	46.5	134.9
5	63 51.9	+35.4	122.1	62 45.2	+38.5	125.4	61 33.1	+41.3	128.4	60 16.3	+43.6	131.2	58 55.3	+45.7	133.7
6	64 27.3	33.9	120.2	63 23.7	37.2	123.7	62 14.4	40.1	126.9	60 59.9	42.7	129.8	59 41.0	44.9	132.4
7	65 01.2	32.3	118.3	64 00.9	35.9	121.9	62 54.5	39.0	125.3	61 42.6	41.7	128.3	60 25.9	44.1	131.1
8	65 33.5	30.7	116.3	64 36.8	34.5	120.1	63 33.5	37.8	123.6	62 24.3	40.7	126.8	61 10.0	43.2	129.7
9	66 04.2	28.9	114.2	65 11.3	32.8	118.2	64 11.3	36.4	121.8	63 05.0	39.5	125.2	61 53.2	42.2	128.3
10	66 33.1	+27.0	112.0	65 44.1	+31.3	116.1	64 47.7	+34.9	120.0	63 44.5	+38.3	123.5	62 35.4	+41.2	126.7
11	67 00.1	25.0	109.7	66 15.4	29.4	114.0	65 22.6	33.5	118.0	64 22.8	37.0	121.7	63 16.6	40.1	125.1
12	67 25.1	22.9	107.4	66 44.8	27.6	111.9	65 56.1	31.8	116.0	64 59.8	35.5	119.9	63 56.7	38.9	123.5
13	67 48.0	20.7	105.0	67 12.4	25.5	109.6	66 27.9	30.0	113.9	65 35.3	34.0	118.0	64 35.6	37.5	121.7
14	68 08.7	18.3	102.5	67 37.9	23.5	107.2	66 57.9	28.1	111.7	66 09.3	32.4	116.0	65 13.1	36.1	119.9
15	68 27.0	+15.9	99.9	68 01.4	+21.2	104.8	67 26.0	+26.1	109.5	66 41.7	+30.6	113.9	65 49.2	+34.7	117.9
16	68 42.9	13.4	97.3	68 22.6	18.8	102.3	67 52.1	24.0	107.1	67 12.3	28.7	111.7	66 23.9	32.9	115.9
17	68 56.3	10.8	94.6	68 41.4	16.4	99.7	68 16.1	21.8	104.6	67 41.0	26.7	109.4	66 56.8	31.2	113.8
18	69 07.1	8.1	91.8	68 57.8	13.9	97.0	68 37.9	19.4	102.1	68 07.7	24.6	107.0	67 28.0	29.4	111.6
19	69 15.2	5.3	89.0	69 11.7	11.2	94.3	68 57.3	16.9	99.5	68 32.3	22.4	104.5	67 57.4	27.3	109.3
20	69 20.5	+2.6	86.2	69 22.9	+8.5	91.5	69 14.2	+14.4	96.8	68 54.7	+19.9	102.0	68 24.7	+25.2	106.9
21	69 23.1	-0.2	83.4	69 31.4	5.8	88.7	69 28.6	11.7	94.0	69 14.6	17.5	99.3	68 49.9	22.9	104.4
22	69 22.9	3.0	80.5	69 37.2	2.9	85.8	69 40.3	8.9	91.2	69 32.1	14.8	96.6	69 12.8	20.5	101.8
23	69 19.9	5.7	77.7	69 40.1	+0.2	83.0	69 49.2	6.2	88.4	69 46.9	12.2	93.8	69 33.3	18.1	99.2
24	69 14.2	8.4	74.9	69 40.3	-2.7	80.1	69 55.4	3.3	85.5	69 59.1	9.4	91.0	69 51.4	15.3	96.4
25	69 05.8	-11.1	72.1	69 37.6	-5.7	77.2	69 58.7	+0.4	82.6	70 08.5	+6.5	88.1	70 06.7	+12.7	93.6
26	68 54.7	13.8	69.3	69 32.1	8.3	74.4	69 59.1	-2.4	79.6	70 15.0	3.6	85.1	70 19.4	9.8	90.7
27	68 40.9	16.2	66.7	69 23.8	11.0	71.5	69 56.7	5.3	76.7	70 18.6	+0.8	82.2	70 29.2	6.9	87.8
28	68 24.7	18.6	64.0	69 12.8	13.6	68.8	69 51.4	8.2	73.8	70 19.4	-2.2	79.2	70 36.1	4.0	84.8
29	68 06.1	21.0	61.5	68 59.2	16.2	66.0	69 43.2	10.8	71.0	70 17.2	5.2	76.2	70 40.1	+1.0	81.8

	30°			32°			34°			36°			38°		
Dec.	Hc	d	Z	Hc	d	Z	Hc	d	Z	Hc	d	Z	Hc	d	Z
°	° ′	′	°	° ′	′	°	° ′	′	°	° ′	′	°	° ′	′	°
0	53 24.8	+50.2	141.1	51 50.4	+51.3	142.7	50 14.1	+52.3	144.2	48 36.0	+53.2	145.5	46 56.4	+54.0	146.7
1	54 15.0	49.6	140.1	52 41.7	50.9	141.8	51 06.4	52.0	143.4	49 29.2	52.9	144.8	47 50.4	53.7	146.1
2	55 04.6	49.2	139.2	53 32.6	50.5	140.9	51 58.4	51.6	142.6	50 22.1	52.7	144.1	48 44.1	53.6	145.4
3	55 53.8	48.7	138.1	54 23.1	50.1	140.0	52 50.0	51.3	141.7	51 14.8	52.3	143.3	49 37.7	53.2	144.7
4	56 42.5	48.1	137.1	55 13.2	49.6	139.1	53 41.3	50.9	140.9	52 07.1	52.0	142.5	50 30.9	53.0	144.0
5	57 30.6	+47.5	136.0	56 02.8	+49.1	138.1	54 32.2	+50.4	140.0	52 59.1	+51.7	141.7	51 23.9	+52.7	143.3
6	58 18.1	46.9	134.8	56 51.9	48.5	137.0	55 22.6	50.0	139.0	53 50.8	51.3	140.8	52 16.6	52.4	142.5
7	59 05.0	46.2	133.6	57 40.4	48.0	135.9	56 12.6	49.6	138.0	54 42.1	50.8	140.0	53 09.0	52.1	141.7
8	59 51.2	45.4	132.4	58 28.4	47.3	134.8	57 02.2	49.0	137.0	55 32.9	50.5	139.0	54 01.1	51.7	140.8
9	60 36.6	44.6	131.1	59 15.7	46.7	133.6	57 51.2	48.4	135.9	56 23.4	50.0	138.1	54 52.8	51.3	140.0
10	61 21.2	+43.7	129.7	60 02.4	+45.9	132.4	58 39.6	+47.8	134.8	57 13.4	+49.4	137.0	55 44.1	+50.9	139.1
11	62 04.9	42.8	128.2	60 48.3	45.1	131.1	59 27.4	47.2	133.6	58 02.8	48.9	136.0	56 35.0	50.4	138.1
12	62 47.7	41.7	126.7	61 33.4	44.3	129.7	60 14.6	46.4	132.4	58 51.7	48.3	134.9	57 25.4	49.9	137.1
13	63 29.4	40.7	125.1	62 17.7	43.3	128.3	61 01.0	45.7	131.1	59 40.0	47.7	133.7	58 15.3	49.4	136.1
14	64 10.1	39.4	123.5	63 01.0	42.3	126.8	61 46.7	44.8	129.8	60 27.7	47.0	132.5	59 04.7	48.8	135.0
15	64 49.5	+38.2	121.7	63 43.3	+41.3	125.2	62 31.5	+43.9	128.3	61 14.7	+46.2	131.2	59 53.5	+48.2	133.8
16	65 27.7	36.7	119.9	64 24.6	40.0	123.5	63 15.4	42.9	126.9	62 00.9	45.3	129.9	60 41.7	47.5	132.6
17	66 04.4	35.2	118.0	65 04.6	38.8	121.8	63 58.3	41.8	125.3	62 46.2	44.5	128.5	61 29.2	46.8	131.4
18	66 39.6	33.6	115.9	65 43.4	37.3	119.9	64 40.1	40.7	123.6	63 30.7	43.6	127.0	62 16.0	46.0	130.0
19	67 13.2	31.9	113.8	66 20.7	35.9	118.0	65 20.8	39.4	121.9	64 14.3	42.4	125.4	63 02.0	45.1	128.6
20	67 45.1	+30.0	111.6	66 56.6	+34.3	116.0	66 00.2	+38.0	120.1	64 56.7	+41.3	123.8	63 47.1	+44.1	127.2
21	68 15.1	27.9	109.3	67 30.9	32.5	113.9	66 38.2	36.6	118.1	65 38.0	40.1	122.0	64 31.2	43.1	125.6
22	68 43.0	25.8	106.9	68 03.4	30.6	111.7	67 14.8	34.9	116.1	66 18.1	38.7	120.2	65 14.3	42.0	124.0
23	69 08.8	23.6	104.4	68 34.0	28.6	109.3	67 49.7	33.2	114.0	66 56.8	37.3	118.3	65 56.3	40.8	122.2
24	69 32.4	21.1	101.8	69 02.6	26.5	106.9	68 22.9	31.3	111.7	67 34.1	35.6	116.3	66 37.1	39.4	120.4
25	69 53.5	+18.5	99.1	69 29.1	+24.2	104.4	68 54.2	+29.3	109.4	68 09.7	+33.9	114.1	67 16.5	+37.9	118.5
26	70 12.0	15.9	96.3	69 53.3	21.7	101.7	69 23.5	27.1	106.9	68 43.6	32.0	111.9	67 54.4	36.4	116.5
27	70 27.9	13.2	93.4	70 15.0	19.1	99.0	69 50.6	24.9	104.4	69 15.6	30.0	109.5	68 30.8	34.6	114.3
28	70 41.1	10.2	90.5	70 34.1	16.5	96.2	70 15.5	22.3	101.7	69 45.6	27.8	107.0	69 05.4	32.8	112.1
29	70 51.3	7.3	87.5	70 50.6	13.6	93.2	70 37.8	19.7	98.9	70 13.4	25.5	104.5	69 38.2	30.7	109.7

20°			22°			24°			26°			28°			Dec.
Hc	d	Z	Hc	d	Z	Hc	d	Z	Hc	d	Z	Hc	d	Z	
60 36.4	-42.3	130.2	59 16.8	-44.4	132.8	57 53.4	-46.3	135.2	56 26.6	-47.8	137.3	54 57.0	-49.3	139.3	0
59 54.1	43.2	131.7	58 32.4	45.2	134.1	57 07.1	46.9	136.4	55 38.8	48.4	138.4	54 07.7	49.7	140.3	1
59 10.9	44.0	133.0	57 47.2	45.8	135.4	56 20.2	47.5	137.5	54 50.4	49.0	139.5	53 18.0	50.2	141.2	2
58 26.9	44.7	134.4	57 01.4	46.6	136.6	55 32.7	48.0	138.6	54 01.4	49.4	140.4	52 27.8	50.6	142.1	3
57 42.2	45.5	135.6	56 14.8	47.1	137.7	54 44.7	48.6	139.7	53 12.0	49.8	141.4	51 37.2	51.0	143.0	4
56 56.7	-46.2	136.8	55 27.7	-47.7	138.8	53 56.1	-49.0	140.7	52 22.2	-50.3	142.3	50 46.2	-51.3	143.8	5
56 10.5	46.8	138.0	54 40.0	48.2	139.9	53 07.1	49.6	141.6	51 31.9	50.6	143.2	49 54.9	51.6	144.6	6
55 23.7	47.3	139.1	53 51.8	48.8	140.9	52 17.5	49.9	142.6	50 41.3	51.0	144.1	49 03.3	52.0	145.4	7
54 36.4	48.4	140.2	53 03.0	49.2	141.9	51 27.6	50.3	143.5	49 50.3	51.3	144.9	48 11.3	52.2	146.2	8
53 48.4	48.4	141.2	52 13.8	49.6	142.8	50 37.3	50.7	144.3	48 59.0	51.7	145.7	47 19.1	52.5	146.9	9
53 00.0	-48.9	142.2	51 24.2	-50.0	143.7	49 46.6	-51.1	145.2	48 07.3	-52.0	146.5	46 26.6	-52.8	147.6	10
52 11.1	49.3	143.1	50 34.2	50.4	144.6	48 55.5	51.4	146.0	47 15.3	52.2	147.2	45 33.8	53.0	148.3	11
51 21.8	49.8	144.1	49 43.8	50.8	145.5	48 04.1	51.6	146.7	46 23.1	52.5	147.9	44 40.8	53.2	149.0	12
50 32.0	50.1	145.0	48 53.0	51.1	146.3	47 12.5	52.0	147.5	45 30.6	52.7	148.6	43 47.6	53.4	149.6	13
49 41.9	50.5	145.8	48 01.9	51.5	147.1	46 20.5	52.3	148.2	44 37.9	53.0	149.3	42 54.2	53.6	150.3	14
48 51.4	-50.9	146.6	47 10.4	-51.7	147.8	45 28.2	-52.5	148.9	43 44.9	-53.2	149.9	42 00.6	-53.9	150.9	15
48 00.5	51.2	147.4	46 18.7	52.0	148.6	44 35.7	52.7	149.6	42 51.7	53.4	150.6	41 06.7	54.0	151.4	16
47 09.3	51.5	148.2	45 26.7	52.2	149.3	43 43.0	52.9	150.3	41 58.3	53.6	151.2	40 12.7	54.1	152.0	17
46 17.8	51.7	149.0	44 34.5	52.5	150.0	42 50.1	53.2	150.9	41 04.7	53.7	151.8	39 18.6	54.3	152.6	18
45 26.1	52.1	149.7	43 42.0	52.8	150.7	41 56.9	53.4	151.6	40 11.0	54.0	152.4	38 24.3	54.5	153.1	19
44 34.0	-52.3	150.4	42 49.2	-52.9	151.3	41 03.5	-53.5	152.2	39 17.0	-54.1	152.9	37 29.8	-54.6	153.7	20
43 41.7	52.5	151.1	41 56.3	53.2	152.0	40 10.0	53.8	152.8	38 22.9	54.3	153.5	36 35.2	54.7	154.2	21
42 49.2	52.7	151.7	41 03.1	53.3	152.6	39 16.2	53.9	153.3	37 28.6	54.4	154.0	35 40.5	54.9	154.7	22
41 56.5	53.0	152.4	40 09.8	53.6	153.2	38 22.3	54.0	153.9	36 34.2	54.5	154.6	34 45.6	55.0	155.2	23
41 03.5	53.1	153.0	39 16.2	53.7	153.8	37 28.3	54.2	154.5	35 39.7	54.7	155.1	33 50.6	55.1	155.7	24
40 10.4	-53.4	153.6	38 22.5	-53.9	154.3	36 34.1	-54.4	155.0	34 45.0	-54.8	155.6	32 55.5	-55.2	156.1	25
39 17.0	53.7	154.2	37 28.6	54.0	154.9	35 39.7	54.5	155.5	33 50.2	54.9	156.1	32 00.3	55.3	156.6	26
38 23.5	53.7	154.8	36 34.6	54.1	155.4	34 45.2	54.6	156.0	32 55.3	55.0	156.6	31 05.0	55.4	157.1	27
37 29.8	53.8	155.4	35 40.5	54.4	156.0	33 50.6	54.7	156.5	32 00.3	55.1	157.0	30 09.6	55.4	157.5	28
36 36.0	54.0	155.9	34 46.1	54.4	156.5	32 55.9	54.9	157.0	31 05.2	55.2	157.5	29 14.2	55.6	157.9	29

30°			32°			34°			36°			38°			Dec.
Hc	d	Z	Hc	d	Z	Hc	d	Z	Hc	d	Z	Hc	d	Z	
53 24.8	-50.5	141.1	51 50.4	-51.6	142.7	50 14.1	-52.6	144.2	48 36.0	-53.5	145.5	46 56.4	-54.2	146.7	0
52 34.3	50.9	142.0	50 58.8	52.0	143.5	49 21.5	52.9	144.9	47 42.5	53.7	146.2	46 02.2	54.4	147.3	1
51 43.4	51.3	142.8	50 06.8	52.2	144.3	48 28.6	53.1	145.6	46 48.8	53.9	146.8	45 07.8	54.6	148.0	2
50 52.1	51.6	143.6	49 14.6	52.6	145.0	47 35.5	53.4	146.3	45 54.9	54.1	147.5	44 13.2	54.8	148.5	3
50 00.5	52.0	144.4	48 22.0	52.8	145.8	46 42.1	53.6	147.0	45 00.8	54.3	148.1	43 18.4	54.9	149.1	4
49 08.5	-52.2	145.2	47 29.2	-53.1	146.5	45 48.5	-53.8	147.6	44 06.5	-54.4	148.7	42 23.5	-55.1	149.6	5
48 16.3	52.6	146.0	46 36.1	53.3	147.2	44 54.7	54.1	148.3	43 12.1	54.7	149.3	41 28.4	55.2	150.2	6
47 23.7	52.8	146.7	45 42.8	53.5	147.8	44 00.6	54.2	148.9	42 17.4	54.8	149.8	40 33.2	55.4	150.7	7
46 30.9	53.0	147.4	44 49.3	53.8	148.5	43 06.4	54.4	149.5	41 22.6	55.0	150.4	39 37.8	55.4	151.2	8
45 37.9	53.3	148.1	43 55.5	53.9	149.1	42 12.0	54.5	150.0	40 27.6	55.1	150.9	38 42.4	55.6	151.7	9
44 44.6	-53.4	148.7	43 01.6	-54.2	149.7	41 17.5	-54.7	150.6	39 32.5	-55.2	151.4	37 46.8	-55.8	152.2	10
43 51.2	53.9	149.4	42 07.4	54.3	150.3	40 22.8	54.9	151.1	38 37.3	55.4	151.9	36 51.0	55.8	152.6	11
42 57.5	53.9	150.0	41 13.1	54.4	150.8	39 27.9	55.0	151.7	37 41.9	55.5	152.4	35 55.2	55.9	153.1	12
42 03.6	54.1	150.6	40 18.7	54.7	151.4	38 32.9	55.1	152.2	36 46.4	55.6	152.9	34 59.3	56.0	153.5	13
41 09.5	54.2	151.3	39 24.0	54.7	151.9	37 37.8	55.3	152.7	35 50.8	55.7	153.4	34 03.3	56.1	154.0	14
40 15.3	-54.4	151.7	38 29.3	-54.9	152.5	36 42.5	-55.3	153.2	34 55.1	-55.8	153.8	33 07.2	-56.2	154.4	15
39 20.9	54.5	152.2	37 34.4	55.1	153.0	35 47.2	55.5	153.6	33 59.3	55.9	154.3	32 11.0	56.3	154.8	16
38 26.4	54.7	152.8	36 39.3	55.1	153.5	34 51.7	55.6	154.1	33 03.4	55.9	154.7	31 14.7	56.3	155.2	17
37 31.7	54.8	153.3	35 44.2	55.3	154.0	33 56.1	55.7	154.6	32 07.5	56.1	155.1	30 18.4	56.4	155.6	18
36 36.9	54.9	153.8	34 48.9	55.4	154.4	33 00.4	55.8	155.0	31 11.4	56.2	155.5	29 22.0	56.5	156.0	19
35 42.0	-55.1	154.3	33 53.5	-55.4	154.9	32 04.6	-55.8	155.5	30 15.2	-56.2	156.0	28 25.5	-56.6	156.4	20
34 46.9	55.2	154.8	32 58.1	55.6	155.4	31 08.8	56.0	155.9	29 19.0	56.3	156.4	27 28.9	56.6	156.8	21
33 51.7	55.3	155.3	32 02.5	55.7	155.8	30 12.8	56.0	156.3	28 22.7	56.3	156.7	26 32.3	56.7	157.2	22
32 56.4	55.4	155.7	31 06.8	55.8	156.2	29 16.8	56.1	156.7	27 26.4	56.5	157.1	25 35.6	56.7	157.5	23
32 01.0	55.4	156.2	30 11.0	55.8	156.7	28 20.7	56.2	157.1	26 29.9	56.4	157.5	24 38.9	56.8	157.9	24
31 05.6	-55.6	156.6	29 15.2	-55.9	157.1	27 24.5	-56.2	157.5	25 33.5	-56.6	157.9	23 42.1	-56.8	158.2	25
30 10.0	55.7	157.1	28 19.3	56.0	157.5	26 28.3	56.4	157.9	24 36.9	56.6	158.3	22 45.3	56.8	158.6	26
29 14.3	55.7	157.5	27 23.3	56.1	157.9	25 31.9	56.3	158.3	23 40.3	56.6	158.6	21 48.5	56.9	158.9	27
28 18.6	55.8	157.9	26 27.2	56.1	158.3	24 35.6	56.4	158.7	22 43.7	56.7	159.0	20 51.6	57.0	159.3	28
27 22.8	55.9	158.3	25 31.1	56.2	158.7	23 39.2	56.5	159.0	21 47.0	56.7	159.3	19 54.6	57.0	159.6	29

Dec.	40° Hc	d	Z	42° Hc	d	Z	44° Hc	d	Z	46° Hc	d	Z	48° Hc	d	Z
°	° ′	′	°	° ′	′	°	° ′	′	°	° ′	′	°	° ′	′	°
0	45 15.4	+54.7	147.8	43 33.2	+55.3	148.9	41 50.0	+55.8	149.8	40 05.8	+56.4	150.7	38 20.8	+56.8	151.5
1	46 10.1	54.5	147.3	44 28.5	55.2	148.3	42 45.8	55.8	149.3	41 02.2	56.2	150.2	39 17.6	56.7	151.1
2	47 04.6	54.3	146.7	45 23.7	55.0	147.8	43 41.6	55.6	148.8	41 58.4	56.2	149.8	40 14.3	56.6	150.6
3	47 58.9	54.1	146.0	46 18.7	54.8	147.2	44 37.2	55.5	148.3	42 54.6	56.0	149.3	41 10.9	56.5	150.2
4	48 53.0	53.9	145.4	47 13.5	54.6	146.6	45 32.7	55.3	147.8	43 50.6	55.9	148.8	42 07.4	56.4	149.7
5	49 46.9	+53.6	144.7	48 08.1	+54.5	146.0	46 28.0	+55.1	147.2	44 46.5	+55.7	148.3	43 03.8	+56.3	149.3
6	50 40.5	53.4	144.0	49 02.6	54.2	145.4	47 23.1	54.9	146.6	45 42.2	55.6	147.8	44 00.1	56.2	148.8
7	51 33.9	53.0	143.3	49 56.8	54.0	144.7	48 18.0	54.8	146.0	46 37.8	55.5	147.2	44 56.3	56.1	148.3
8	52 26.9	52.8	142.5	50 50.8	53.7	144.0	49 12.8	54.6	145.4	47 33.3	55.2	146.7	45 52.4	55.9	147.8
9	53 19.7	52.5	141.7	51 44.5	53.4	143.3	50 07.4	54.3	144.8	48 28.5	55.1	146.1	46 48.3	55.7	147.3
10	54 12.2	+52.1	140.9	52 37.9	+53.2	142.6	51 01.7	+54.1	144.1	49 23.6	+54.9	145.5	47 44.0	+55.6	146.7
11	55 04.3	51.7	140.0	53 31.1	52.9	141.8	51 55.8	53.8	143.4	50 18.5	54.7	144.8	48 39.6	55.4	146.2
12	55 56.0	51.3	139.1	54 24.0	52.5	141.0	52 49.6	53.6	142.7	51 13.2	54.5	144.2	49 35.0	55.3	145.6
13	56 47.3	50.9	138.2	55 16.5	52.2	140.2	53 43.2	53.2	141.9	52 07.7	54.2	143.5	50 30.3	55.0	145.0
14	57 38.2	50.4	137.2	56 08.7	51.7	139.3	54 36.4	53.0	141.1	53 01.9	54.0	142.8	51 25.3	54.9	144.3
15	58 28.6	+49.9	136.2	57 00.4	+51.4	138.4	55 29.4	+52.6	140.3	53 55.9	+53.6	142.1	52 20.2	+54.6	143.7
16	59 18.5	49.3	135.1	57 51.8	50.9	137.4	56 22.0	52.2	139.4	54 49.5	53.4	141.3	53 14.8	54.3	143.0
17	60 07.8	48.8	134.0	58 42.7	50.4	136.4	57 14.2	51.8	138.5	55 42.9	53.1	140.5	54 09.1	54.1	142.3
18	60 56.6	48.0	132.8	59 33.1	49.8	135.3	58 06.0	51.4	137.6	56 36.0	52.6	139.7	55 03.2	53.8	141.5
19	61 44.6	47.4	131.6	60 22.9	49.3	134.2	58 57.4	50.9	136.6	57 28.6	52.4	138.8	55 57.0	53.5	140.8
20	62 32.0	+46.5	130.3	61 12.2	+48.6	133.0	59 48.3	+50.4	135.6	58 21.0	+51.8	137.9	56 50.5	+53.2	139.9
21	63 18.5	45.8	128.9	62 00.8	48.0	131.8	60 38.7	49.9	134.5	59 12.8	51.5	136.9	57 43.7	52.7	139.1
22	64 04.3	44.8	127.4	62 48.8	47.2	130.5	61 28.6	49.2	133.3	60 04.3	50.9	135.9	58 36.4	52.4	138.2
23	64 49.1	43.7	125.9	63 36.0	46.3	129.1	62 17.8	48.5	132.1	60 55.2	50.4	134.8	59 28.8	52.0	137.2
24	65 32.8	42.7	124.2	64 22.3	45.5	127.7	63 06.3	47.8	130.8	61 45.6	49.8	133.7	60 20.8	51.5	136.2
25	66 15.5	+41.5	122.5	65 07.8	+44.4	126.2	63 54.1	+47.1	129.5	62 35.4	+49.2	132.5	61 12.3	+51.0	135.2
26	66 57.0	40.1	120.7	65 52.2	43.4	124.6	64 41.2	46.1	128.1	63 24.6	48.4	131.2	62 03.3	50.4	134.1
27	67 37.1	38.7	118.8	66 35.6	42.2	122.8	65 27.3	45.2	126.5	64 13.0	47.7	129.9	62 53.7	49.7	132.9
28	68 15.8	37.1	116.7	67 17.8	40.9	121.0	66 12.5	44.1	124.9	65 00.7	46.8	128.5	63 43.4	49.1	131.7
29	68 52.9	35.4	114.6	67 57.8	39.5	119.1	66 56.6	42.9	123.2	65 47.5	45.9	127.0	64 32.5	48.4	130.3

Dec.	50° Hc	d	Z	52° Hc	d	Z	54° Hc	d	Z	56° Hc	d	Z	58° Hc	d	Z
°	° ′	′	°	° ′	′	°	° ′	′	°	° ′	′	°	° ′	′	°
0	36 35.0	+57.2	152.2	34 48.5	+57.5	152.9	33 01.4	+57.9	153.5	31 13.8	+58.2	154.0	29 25.7	+58.4	154.5
1	37 32.2	57.1	151.8	35 46.0	57.5	152.5	33 59.3	57.8	153.1	32 12.0	58.1	153.7	30 24.1	58.4	154.3
2	38 29.3	57.0	151.4	36 43.5	57.5	152.2	34 57.1	57.8	152.8	33 10.1	58.0	153.4	31 22.5	58.3	154.0
3	39 26.3	57.0	151.0	37 41.0	57.3	151.8	35 54.9	57.7	152.5	34 08.1	58.1	153.1	32 20.8	58.3	153.7
4	40 23.3	56.9	150.6	38 38.3	57.3	151.4	36 52.6	57.6	152.2	35 06.2	57.9	152.8	33 19.1	58.2	153.4
5	41 20.2	+56.8	150.2	39 35.6	+57.2	151.0	37 50.2	+57.6	151.8	36 04.1	+58.0	152.5	34 17.4	+58.2	153.1
6	42 17.0	56.7	149.8	40 32.8	57.2	150.6	38 47.8	57.5	151.4	37 02.1	57.8	152.2	35 15.6	58.2	152.9
7	43 13.7	56.5	149.3	41 30.0	57.0	150.2	39 45.3	57.5	151.1	37 59.9	57.8	151.8	36 13.8	58.1	152.6
8	44 10.2	56.5	148.9	42 27.0	56.9	149.8	40 42.8	57.4	150.7	38 57.7	57.8	151.5	37 11.9	58.1	152.2
9	45 06.7	56.3	148.4	43 23.9	56.9	149.4	41 40.2	57.3	150.3	39 55.5	57.7	151.2	38 10.0	58.0	151.9
10	46 03.0	+56.2	147.9	44 20.8	+56.7	148.9	42 37.5	+57.2	149.9	40 53.2	+57.6	150.8	39 08.0	+58.0	151.6
11	46 59.2	56.1	147.4	45 17.5	56.5	148.5	43 34.7	57.1	149.4	41 50.8	57.5	150.4	40 06.0	57.9	151.3
12	47 55.3	55.9	146.9	46 14.2	56.5	148.0	44 31.8	57.0	149.1	42 48.3	57.5	150.0	41 03.9	57.9	150.9
13	48 51.2	55.8	146.3	47 10.7	56.3	147.5	45 28.8	56.9	148.6	43 45.8	57.4	149.6	42 01.8	57.7	150.6
14	49 47.0	55.6	145.7	48 07.0	56.3	147.0	46 25.7	56.8	148.2	44 43.2	57.3	149.2	42 59.5	57.7	150.2
15	50 42.6	+55.3	145.2	49 03.3	+56.1	146.5	47 22.5	+56.7	147.7	45 40.5	+57.1	148.8	43 57.2	+57.7	149.8
16	51 37.9	55.2	144.5	49 59.4	55.9	145.9	48 19.2	56.5	147.2	46 37.6	57.1	148.4	44 54.9	57.5	149.4
17	52 33.1	55.0	143.9	50 55.3	55.7	145.4	49 15.7	56.5	146.7	47 34.7	57.0	147.9	45 52.4	57.5	149.0
18	53 28.1	54.8	143.2	51 51.0	55.6	144.8	50 12.2	56.2	146.2	48 31.7	56.9	147.5	46 49.9	57.4	148.6
19	54 22.9	54.5	142.5	52 46.6	55.4	144.2	51 08.4	56.1	145.6	49 28.6	56.7	147.0	47 47.3	57.2	148.2
20	55 17.4	+54.2	141.8	53 42.0	+55.1	143.5	52 04.5	+55.9	145.1	50 25.3	+56.6	146.5	48 44.5	+57.2	147.7
21	56 11.6	54.0	141.1	54 37.1	54.9	142.8	53 00.4	55.8	144.5	51 21.9	56.4	145.9	49 41.7	57.0	147.3
22	57 05.6	53.6	140.3	55 32.0	54.7	142.1	53 56.2	55.5	143.8	52 18.3	56.3	145.4	50 38.7	57.0	146.8
23	57 59.2	53.3	139.4	56 26.7	54.4	141.4	54 51.7	55.4	143.2	53 14.6	56.1	144.8	51 35.7	56.7	146.3
24	58 52.5	52.9	138.5	57 21.1	54.1	140.6	55 47.1	55.0	142.5	54 10.7	56.0	144.2	52 32.4	56.7	145.8
25	59 45.4	+52.4	137.6	58 15.2	+53.7	139.8	56 42.1	+54.9	141.8	55 06.7	+55.5	143.6	53 29.1	+56.5	145.2
26	60 37.8	52.1	136.6	59 08.9	53.4	139.0	57 37.0	54.5	141.0	56 02.4	55.5	142.9	54 25.6	56.3	144.6
27	61 29.9	51.5	135.6	60 02.3	53.0	138.1	58 31.5	54.3	140.3	56 57.9	55.3	142.2	55 21.9	56.1	144.0
28	62 21.4	51.0	134.5	60 55.3	52.6	137.1	59 25.8	53.9	139.4	57 53.2	55.0	141.5	56 18.0	55.9	143.4
29	63 12.4	50.5	133.4	61 47.9	52.2	136.1	60 19.7	53.5	138.6	58 48.2	54.7	140.8	57 13.9	55.7	142.7

| 40° | | | 42° | | | 44° | | | 46° | | | 48° | | | Dec. |
Hc	d	Z	Hc	d	Z	Hc	d	Z	Hc	d	Z	Hc	d	Z	
45 15.4	-54.9	147.8	43 33.2	-55.5	148.9	41 50.0	-56.0	149.8	40 05.8	-56.5	150.7	38 20.8	-56.9	151.5	0
44 20.5	55.0	148.4	42 37.7	55.6	149.4	40 54.0	56.1	150.3	39 09.3	56.6	151.1	37 23.9	57.0	151.9	1
43 25.5	55.2	149.0	41 42.1	55.7	149.9	39 57.9	56.3	150.8	38 12.7	56.6	151.5	36 26.9	57.1	152.3	2
42 30.3	55.4	149.5	40 46.4	55.9	150.4	39 01.6	56.3	151.2	37 16.1	56.8	152.0	35 29.8	57.1	152.6	3
41 34.9	55.4	150.0	39 50.5	55.9	150.9	38 05.3	56.4	151.7	36 19.3	56.8	152.4	34 32.7	57.2	153.0	4
40 39.5	-55.6	150.5	38 54.6	-56.1	151.3	37 08.9	-56.5	152.1	35 22.5	-56.9	152.8	33 35.5	-57.2	153.4	5
39 43.9	55.8	151.0	37 58.5	56.2	151.8	36 12.4	56.5	152.5	34 25.6	56.9	153.1	32 38.3	57.3	153.7	6
38 48.1	55.8	151.5	37 02.3	56.3	152.2	35 15.8	56.7	152.9	33 28.7	57.1	153.5	31 41.0	57.4	154.1	7
37 52.3	56.0	152.0	36 06.0	56.3	152.7	34 19.1	56.7	153.3	32 31.6	57.1	153.9	30 43.6	57.4	154.4	8
36 56.3	56.0	152.4	35 09.7	56.5	153.1	33 22.4	56.9	153.7	31 34.5	57.2	154.3	29 46.2	57.5	154.8	9
36 00.3	-56.2	152.9	34 13.2	-56.5	153.5	32 25.5	-56.9	154.1	30 37.3	-57.2	154.6	28 48.7	-57.5	155.1	10
35 04.1	56.2	153.3	33 16.7	56.7	153.9	31 28.6	56.9	154.5	29 40.1	57.2	155.0	27 51.2	57.6	155.4	11
34 07.9	56.3	153.7	32 20.0	56.6	154.3	30 31.7	57.0	154.8	28 42.9	57.4	155.3	26 53.6	57.6	155.7	12
33 11.6	56.4	154.1	31 23.4	56.8	154.7	29 34.7	57.1	155.2	27 45.5	57.3	155.6	25 56.0	57.6	156.1	13
32 15.2	56.5	154.5	30 26.6	56.8	155.1	28 37.6	57.1	155.5	26 48.2	57.5	156.0	24 58.4	57.7	156.4	14
31 18.7	-56.5	154.9	29 29.8	-56.9	155.4	27 40.5	-57.2	155.9	25 50.7	-57.4	156.3	24 00.7	-57.7	156.7	15
30 22.2	56.7	155.3	28 32.9	56.9	155.8	26 43.3	57.3	156.2	24 53.3	57.5	156.6	23 03.0	57.7	157.0	16
29 25.5	56.6	155.7	27 36.0	57.0	156.2	25 46.0	57.2	156.6	23 55.8	57.5	156.9	22 05.3	57.8	157.3	17
28 28.9	56.8	156.1	26 39.0	57.1	156.5	24 48.8	57.3	156.9	22 58.3	57.6	157.2	21 07.5	57.8	157.5	18
27 32.1	56.8	156.5	25 41.9	57.0	156.9	23 51.5	57.4	157.2	22 00.7	57.6	157.5	20 09.7	57.9	157.8	19
26 35.3	-56.8	156.8	24 44.9	-57.2	157.2	22 54.1	-57.4	157.5	21 03.1	-57.7	157.8	19 11.8	-57.8	158.1	20
25 38.5	56.9	157.2	23 47.7	57.2	157.5	21 56.7	57.4	157.8	20 05.4	57.6	158.1	18 14.0	57.9	158.4	21
24 41.6	57.0	157.5	22 50.5	57.2	157.9	20 59.3	57.5	158.2	19 07.8	57.7	158.4	17 16.1	57.9	158.7	22
23 44.6	57.0	157.9	21 53.3	57.2	158.2	20 01.8	57.5	158.5	18 10.1	57.7	158.7	16 18.2	57.9	158.9	23
22 47.6	57.0	158.2	20 56.1	57.3	158.5	19 04.3	57.5	158.8	17 12.4	57.8	159.0	15 20.3	58.0	159.2	24
21 50.6	-57.1	158.5	19 58.8	-57.3	158.8	18 06.8	-57.6	159.1	16 14.6	-57.7	159.3	14 22.3	-58.0	159.5	25
20 53.5	57.1	158.9	19 01.5	57.4	159.1	17 09.2	57.5	159.4	15 16.9	57.8	159.6	13 24.3	57.9	159.7	26
19 56.4	57.2	159.2	18 04.1	57.4	159.4	16 11.7	57.6	159.7	14 19.1	57.8	159.9	12 26.4	58.0	160.0	27
18 59.2	57.2	159.5	17 06.7	57.4	159.8	15 14.1	57.7	160.0	13 21.3	57.9	160.1	11 28.4	58.0	160.3	28
18 02.0	57.2	159.8	16 09.3	57.4	160.1	14 16.4	57.6	160.2	12 23.4	57.8	160.4	10 30.4	58.1	160.5	29

| 50° | | | 52° | | | 54° | | | 56° | | | 58° | | | Dec. |
Hc	d	Z	Hc	d	Z	Hc	d	Z	Hc	d	Z	Hc	d	Z	
36 35.0	-57.3	152.2	34 48.5	-57.6	152.9	33 01.4	-57.9	153.5	31 13.8	-58.2	154.0	29 25.7	-58.4	154.5	0
35 37.7	57.4	152.6	33 50.9	57.7	153.2	32 03.5	58.0	153.8	30 15.6	58.2	154.3	28 27.3	58.5	154.8	1
34 40.3	57.4	152.9	32 53.2	57.7	153.5	31 05.5	58.0	154.1	29 17.4	58.3	154.6	27 28.8	58.5	155.0	2
33 42.9	57.4	153.3	31 55.5	57.8	153.8	30 07.5	58.0	154.4	28 19.1	58.3	154.9	26 30.3	58.5	155.3	3
32 45.5	57.5	153.6	30 57.7	57.8	154.2	29 09.5	58.1	154.7	27 20.8	58.3	155.1	25 31.8	58.5	155.5	4
31 48.0	-57.6	154.0	29 59.9	-57.9	154.5	28 11.4	-58.1	155.0	26 22.5	-58.3	155.4	24 33.2	-58.5	155.8	5
30 50.4	57.6	154.3	29 02.1	57.9	154.8	27 13.3	58.1	155.2	25 24.2	58.4	155.6	23 34.7	58.6	156.0	6
29 52.8	57.7	154.6	28 04.2	58.0	155.1	26 15.2	58.2	155.5	24 25.8	58.4	155.9	22 36.1	58.6	156.3	7
28 55.1	57.7	154.9	27 06.2	57.9	155.4	25 17.0	58.2	155.8	23 27.4	58.4	156.1	21 37.5	58.6	156.5	8
27 57.4	57.7	155.2	26 08.3	58.0	155.7	24 18.8	58.3	156.0	22 29.0	58.5	156.4	20 38.9	58.7	156.7	9
26 59.7	-57.8	155.5	25 10.3	-58.1	155.9	23 20.5	-58.2	156.3	21 30.5	-58.5	156.6	19 40.2	-58.6	156.9	10
26 01.9	57.8	155.8	24 12.2	58.0	156.2	22 22.3	58.3	156.6	20 32.0	58.5	156.9	18 41.6	58.7	157.2	11
25 04.1	57.9	156.1	23 14.2	58.1	156.5	21 24.0	58.3	156.8	19 33.5	58.5	157.1	17 42.9	58.7	157.4	12
24 06.2	57.9	156.4	22 16.1	58.1	156.8	20 25.7	58.4	157.1	18 35.0	58.5	157.4	16 44.2	58.7	157.6	13
23 08.3	57.9	156.7	21 18.0	58.2	157.0	19 27.3	58.3	157.3	17 36.5	58.6	157.6	15 45.5	58.7	157.8	14
22 10.4	-58.0	157.0	20 19.8	-58.2	157.3	18 29.0	-58.4	157.6	16 38.0	-58.6	157.8	14 46.8	-58.8	158.0	15
21 12.4	57.9	157.3	19 21.6	58.2	157.6	17 30.6	58.4	157.8	15 39.4	58.6	158.0	13 48.0	58.7	158.2	16
20 14.5	58.0	157.6	18 23.4	58.2	157.8	16 32.2	58.4	158.1	14 40.8	58.5	158.3	12 49.3	58.7	158.4	17
19 16.5	58.0	157.8	17 25.2	58.2	158.1	15 33.8	58.4	158.3	13 42.3	58.6	158.5	11 50.6	58.8	158.7	18
18 18.4	58.0	158.1	16 27.0	58.2	158.3	14 35.4	58.4	158.5	12 43.7	58.6	158.7	10 51.8	58.8	158.9	19
17 20.4	-58.1	158.4	15 28.8	-58.3	158.6	13 37.0	-58.5	158.8	11 45.1	-58.7	158.9	9 53.0	-58.7	159.1	20
16 22.3	58.1	158.6	14 30.5	58.3	158.8	12 38.5	58.4	159.0	10 46.4	58.6	159.1	8 54.3	58.8	159.3	21
15 24.2	58.1	158.9	13 32.2	58.3	159.1	11 40.1	58.5	159.2	9 47.8	58.6	159.4	7 55.5	58.8	159.5	22
14 26.1	58.1	159.1	12 33.9	58.3	159.3	10 41.6	58.5	159.5	8 49.2	58.7	159.6	6 56.7	58.8	159.7	23
13 28.0	58.1	159.4	11 35.6	58.3	159.6	9 43.1	58.5	159.7	7 50.5	58.6	159.8	5 57.9	58.8	159.9	24
12 29.9	-58.2	159.7	10 37.3	-58.3	159.8	8 44.6	-58.5	159.9	6 51.9	-58.6	160.0	4 59.1	-58.8	160.1	25
11 31.7	58.2	159.9	9 39.0	58.4	160.0	7 46.1	58.5	160.1	5 53.3	58.7	160.2	4 00.3	58.8	160.3	26
10 33.5	58.1	160.2	8 40.6	58.3	160.3	6 47.6	58.5	160.4	4 54.6	58.7	160.4	3 01.5	58.8	160.5	27
9 35.4	58.2	160.4	7 42.3	58.4	160.5	5 49.1	58.5	160.6	3 55.9	58.6	160.6	2 02.7	58.8	160.7	28
8 37.2	58.2	160.6	6 43.9	58.3	160.7	4 50.6	58.5	160.8	2 57.3	58.7	160.8	1 03.9	58.8	160.9	29

Dec.	0° Hc	d	Z	2° Hc	d	Z	4° Hc	d	Z	6° Hc	d	Z	8° Hc	d	Z
0	66 00.0	- 1.2	90.0	65 55.3	+ 4.0	94.5	65 41.3	+ 9.0	98.9	65 18.3	+13.9	103.2	64 46.6	+18.6	107.4
1	65 58.8	3.5	87.5	65 59.3	+ 1.6	92.0	65 50.3	6.8	96.5	65 32.2	11.7	100.9	65 05.2	16.5	105.1
2	65 55.3	5.8	85.1	66 00.9	- 0.7	89.6	65 57.1	4.4	94.1	65 43.9	9.5	98.5	65 21.7	14.4	102.8
3	65 49.5	8.2	82.7	66 00.2	3.1	87.1	66 01.5	+ 2.1	91.6	65 53.4	7.2	96.1	65 36.1	12.2	100.5
4	65 41.3	10.4	80.2	65 57.1	5.4	84.7	66 03.6	- 0.3	89.2	66 00.6	4.9	93.7	65 48.3	10.0	98.1
5	65 30.9	-12.6	77.9	65 51.7	- 7.8	82.2	66 03.3	- 2.7	86.7	66 05.5	+ 2.5	91.2	65 58.3	+ 7.6	95.7
6	65 18.3	14.8	75.5	65 43.9	10.0	79.8	66 00.6	5.0	84.2	66 08.0	+ 0.2	88.7	66 05.9	5.4	93.2
7	65 03.5	16.9	73.2	65 33.9	12.2	77.4	65 55.6	7.3	81.8	66 08.2	- 2.3	86.3	66 11.3	2.9	90.8
8	64 46.6	18.9	70.9	65 21.7	14.4	75.1	65 48.3	9.6	79.4	66 05.9	4.5	83.8	66 14.2	+ 0.6	88.3
9	64 27.7	20.8	68.7	65 07.3	16.5	72.7	65 38.7	11.8	77.0	66 01.4	6.9	81.3	66 14.8	- 1.8	85.8
10	64 06.9	-22.8	66.6	64 50.8	-18.5	70.5	65 26.9	-14.0	74.6	65 54.5	- 9.2	78.9	66 13.0	- 4.2	83.3
11	63 44.1	24.5	64.5	64 32.3	20.5	68.2	65 12.9	16.1	72.3	65 45.3	11.5	76.5	66 08.8	6.5	80.9
12	63 19.6	26.2	62.4	64 11.8	22.4	66.1	64 56.8	18.2	70.0	65 33.8	13.7	74.1	66 02.3	8.8	78.4
13	62 53.4	27.9	60.4	63 49.4	24.2	63.9	64 38.6	20.2	67.7	65 20.1	15.8	71.8	65 53.5	11.1	76.0
14	62 25.5	29.4	58.5	63 25.2	25.9	61.9	64 18.4	22.1	65.5	65 04.3	17.8	69.5	65 42.4	13.3	73.6
15	61 56.1	-30.9	56.6	62 59.3	-27.6	59.9	63 56.3	-23.9	63.4	64 46.5	-19.9	67.2	65 29.1	-15.5	71.2
16	61 25.2	32.2	54.8	62 31.7	29.1	57.9	63 32.4	25.7	61.3	64 26.6	21.8	65.0	65 13.6	17.6	68.9
17	60 53.0	33.6	53.1	62 02.6	30.6	56.1	63 06.7	27.3	59.3	64 04.8	23.7	62.9	64 56.0	19.6	66.6
18	60 19.4	34.8	51.4	61 32.0	32.1	54.2	62 39.4	28.9	57.4	63 41.1	25.4	60.8	64 36.4	21.6	64.4
19	59 44.6	36.0	49.8	60 59.9	33.3	52.5	62 10.5	30.4	55.5	63 15.7	27.1	58.7	64 14.8	23.4	62.3
20	59 08.6	-37.1	48.2	60 26.6	-34.6	50.8	61 40.1	-31.8	53.6	62 48.6	-28.7	56.8	63 51.4	-25.2	60.2
21	58 31.5	38.1	46.7	59 52.0	35.8	49.1	61 08.3	33.1	51.9	62 19.9	30.2	54.9	63 26.2	26.9	58.1
22	57 53.4	39.1	45.2	59 16.2	36.9	47.6	60 35.2	34.5	50.2	61 49.7	31.6	53.0	62 59.3	28.5	56.1
23	57 14.3	40.1	43.8	58 39.3	38.0	46.0	60 00.7	35.6	48.5	61 18.1	33.0	51.2	62 30.8	30.0	54.2
24	56 34.2	40.9	42.4	58 01.3	38.9	44.6	59 25.1	36.8	46.9	60 45.1	34.3	49.5	62 00.8	31.6	52.4
25	55 53.3	-41.7	41.1	57 22.4	-39.9	43.1	58 48.3	-37.8	45.4	60 10.8	-35.5	47.8	61 29.2	-32.8	50.6
26	55 11.6	42.4	39.8	56 42.5	40.4	41.8	58 10.5	38.8	43.9	59 35.3	36.6	46.2	60 56.4	34.2	48.8
27	54 29.2	43.2	38.6	56 01.8	41.6	40.4	57 31.7	39.7	42.5	58 58.7	37.7	44.7	60 22.2	35.4	47.1
28	53 46.0	43.9	37.4	55 20.2	42.4	39.2	56 52.0	40.7	41.1	58 21.0	38.7	43.2	59 46.8	36.5	45.5
29	53 02.1	44.5	36.3	54 37.8	43.0	37.9	56 11.3	41.4	39.7	57 42.3	39.7	41.7	59 10.3	37.7	44.0

Dec.	10° Hc	d	Z	12° Hc	d	Z	14° Hc	d	Z	16° Hc	d	Z	18° Hc	d	Z
0	64 06.9	+22.9	111.3	63 19.6	+27.0	115.0	62 25.5	+30.6	118.5	61 25.2	+34.0	121.8	60 19.4	+36.9	124.8
1	64 29.8	21.0	109.2	63 46.6	25.2	113.0	62 56.1	29.1	116.6	61 59.2	32.5	120.0	60 56.3	35.7	123.2
2	64 50.8	19.1	107.0	64 11.8	23.4	111.0	63 25.2	27.5	114.7	62 31.7	31.1	118.2	61 32.0	34.4	121.5
3	65 09.9	17.0	104.7	64 35.2	21.6	108.8	63 52.7	25.7	112.7	63 02.8	29.6	116.3	62 06.4	33.0	119.7
4	65 26.9	14.9	102.4	64 56.8	19.5	106.6	64 18.4	23.9	110.6	63 32.4	27.9	114.4	62 39.4	31.6	117.9
5	65 41.8	+12.7	100.1	65 16.3	+17.5	104.4	64 42.3	+22.0	108.5	64 00.3	+26.3	112.4	63 11.0	+30.1	116.1
6	65 54.5	10.4	97.7	65 33.8	15.4	102.1	65 04.3	20.1	106.3	64 26.6	24.4	110.3	63 41.1	28.5	114.1
7	66 04.9	8.1	95.3	65 49.2	13.1	99.7	65 24.4	18.0	104.1	64 51.0	22.6	108.2	64 09.6	26.8	112.1
8	66 13.0	5.8	92.8	66 02.3	10.9	97.4	65 42.4	15.9	101.8	65 13.6	20.6	106.0	64 36.4	25.0	110.1
9	66 18.8	3.4	90.4	66 13.2	8.6	94.9	65 58.3	13.6	99.4	65 34.2	18.5	103.8	65 01.4	23.1	107.9
10	66 22.2	+ 1.0	87.9	66 21.8	+ 6.3	92.5	66 11.9	+11.4	97.0	65 52.7	+16.4	101.4	65 24.5	+21.1	105.7
11	66 23.2	- 1.4	85.4	66 28.1	3.8	90.0	66 23.3	9.1	94.6	66 09.1	14.1	99.1	65 45.6	19.1	103.5
12	66 21.8	3.7	82.9	66 31.9	+ 1.5	87.5	66 32.4	6.7	92.1	66 23.2	11.9	96.7	66 04.7	16.9	101.1
13	66 18.1	6.2	80.4	66 33.4	- 1.0	85.0	66 39.1	4.3	89.6	66 35.1	9.6	94.2	66 21.6	14.6	98.8
14	66 11.9	8.4	77.9	66 32.4	3.4	82.4	66 43.4	+ 1.8	87.1	66 44.7	7.1	91.7	66 36.2	12.4	96.3
15	66 03.5	-10.8	75.5	66 29.0	- 5.8	79.9	66 45.2	- 0.5	84.5	66 51.8	+ 4.8	89.2	66 48.6	+10.1	93.9
16	65 52.7	13.0	73.1	66 23.2	8.1	77.5	66 44.7	3.0	82.0	66 56.6	+ 2.2	86.6	66 58.7	7.6	91.4
17	65 39.7	15.2	70.7	66 15.1	10.4	75.0	66 41.7	5.5	79.5	66 58.8	- 0.1	84.1	67 06.3	5.1	88.8
18	65 24.5	17.3	68.4	66 04.7	12.8	72.5	66 36.2	7.8	77.0	66 58.7	2.7	81.5	67 11.4	2.7	86.2
19	65 07.2	19.4	66.1	65 51.9	14.9	70.1	66 28.4	10.1	74.5	66 56.0	5.1	79.0	67 14.1	+ 0.2	83.7
20	64 47.8	-21.3	63.8	65 37.0	-17.1	67.8	66 18.3	-12.5	72.0	66 50.9	- 7.5	76.4	67 14.3	- 2.3	81.1
21	64 26.5	23.3	61.7	65 19.9	19.1	65.5	66 05.8	14.7	69.7	66 43.4	9.9	73.9	67 12.0	4.7	78.5
22	64 03.2	25.0	59.5	65 00.8	21.2	63.2	65 51.1	16.9	67.2	66 33.5	12.2	71.4	67 07.3	7.3	75.9
23	63 38.2	26.7	57.5	64 39.6	23.1	61.0	65 34.2	18.9	64.9	66 21.3	14.5	69.0	67 00.0	9.6	73.4
24	63 11.5	28.4	55.5	64 16.5	24.8	58.9	65 15.3	21.0	62.6	66 06.8	16.7	66.6	66 50.4	12.0	70.9
25	62 43.1	-29.9	53.5	63 51.7	-26.7	56.8	64 54.3	-23.0	60.4	65 50.1	-18.8	64.2	66 38.4	-14.4	68.4
26	62 13.2	31.4	51.7	63 25.0	28.2	54.8	64 31.3	24.8	58.2	65 31.3	20.9	61.9	66 24.0	16.5	65.9
27	61 41.8	32.8	49.8	62 56.8	29.9	52.8	64 06.5	26.5	56.1	65 10.4	22.9	59.7	66 07.5	18.8	63.6
28	61 09.0	34.1	48.1	62 26.9	31.3	50.9	63 40.0	28.2	54.1	64 47.5	24.7	57.5	65 48.7	20.8	61.2
29	60 34.9	35.4	46.4	61 55.6	32.8	49.1	63 11.8	29.8	52.1	64 22.8	26.5	55.4	65 27.9	22.7	58.9

0°			2°			4°			6°			8°			Dec.
Hc	d	Z	Hc	d	Z	Hc	d	Z	Hc	d	Z	Hc	d	Z	
66 00.0	- 1.2*	90.0	65 55.3	- 6.3*	94.5	65 41.3	- 11.3*	98.9	65 18.3	- 16.1*	103.2	64 46.6	- 20.6	107.4	0
65 58.8	3.5*	92.5	65 49.0	8.6*	96.9	65 30.0	13.5*	101.3	65 02.2	18.1*	105.5	64 26.0	22.4	109.5	1
65 55.3	5.8*	94.9	65 40.4	10.8*	99.3	65 16.5	15.6*	103.6	64 44.1	20.2	107.8	64 03.6	24.4	111.7	2
65 49.5	8.2*	97.3	65 29.6	13.1*	101.7	65 00.9	17.7*	105.9	64 23.9	22.0	109.9	63 39.2	26.0	113.8	3
65 41.3	10.4*	99.8	65 16.5	15.2*	104.0	64 43.2	19.7	108.2	64 01.9	23.9	112.1	63 13.2	27.7	115.8	4
65 30.9	-12.6*	102.1	65 01.3	-17.2*	106.3	64 23.5	-21.6	110.4	63 38.0	-25.6	114.2	62 45.5	-29.3	117.7	5
65 18.3	14.8*	104.5	64 44.1	19.3*	108.6	64 01.9	23.5	112.5	63 12.4	27.3	116.2	62 16.2	30.8	119.6	6
65 03.5	16.9*	106.8	64 24.8	21.2	110.8	63 38.4	25.2	114.6	62 45.1	28.9	118.1	61 45.4	32.2	121.4	7
64 46.6	18.9	109.1	64 03.6	23.1	113.0	63 13.2	26.9	116.6	62 16.2	30.4	120.0	61 13.2	33.5	123.2	8
64 27.7	20.8	111.3	63 40.5	24.9	115.1	62 46.3	28.5	118.6	61 45.8	31.8	121.9	60 39.7	34.8	124.9	9
64 06.9	-22.8	113.4	63 15.6	-26.6	117.1	62 17.8	-30.1	120.5	61 14.0	-33.2	123.7	60 04.9	-35.9	126.6	10
63 44.1	24.5	115.5	62 49.0	28.1	119.1	61 47.7	31.4	122.4	60 40.8	34.4	125.4	59 29.0	37.1	128.2	11
63 19.6	26.2	117.6	62 20.9	29.7	121.0	61 16.3	32.9	124.1	60 06.4	35.6	127.0	58 51.9	38.1	129.7	12
62 53.4	27.9	119.6	61 51.2	31.2	122.8	60 43.4	34.1	125.9	59 30.8	36.8	128.6	58 13.8	39.2	131.2	13
62 25.5	29.4	121.5	61 20.0	32.5	124.6	60 09.3	35.3	127.5	58 54.0	37.8	130.2	57 34.6	40.0	132.6	14
61 56.1	-30.9	123.4	60 47.5	-33.9	126.4	59 34.0	-36.5	129.1	58 16.2	-38.9	131.7	56 54.6	-41.0	134.0	15
61 25.2	32.2	125.2	60 13.6	35.0	128.1	58 57.5	37.6	130.7	57 37.3	39.8	133.1	56 13.6	41.7	135.3	16
60 53.0	33.6	126.9	59 38.6	36.2	129.7	58 19.9	38.5	132.2	56 57.5	40.6	134.5	55 31.9	42.6	136.6	17
60 19.4	34.8	128.6	59 02.4	37.4	131.2	57 41.4	39.6	133.6	56 16.9	41.5	135.8	54 49.3	43.2	137.8	18
59 44.6	36.0	130.2	58 25.0	38.3	132.8	57 01.8	40.4	135.0	55 35.4	42.3	137.1	54 06.1	43.9	139.0	19
59 08.6	-37.1	131.8	57 46.7	-39.3	134.2	56 21.4	-41.3	136.4	54 53.1	-43.0	138.4	53 22.2	-44.6	140.2	20
58 31.5	38.1	133.3	57 07.4	40.2	135.6	55 40.1	42.0	137.7	54 10.1	43.7	139.6	52 37.6	45.2	141.3	21
57 53.4	39.1	134.8	56 27.2	41.1	137.0	54 58.1	42.8	138.9	53 26.4	44.4	140.7	51 52.4	45.8	142.4	22
57 14.3	40.1	136.2	55 46.1	41.8	138.3	54 15.3	43.5	140.1	52 42.0	45.0	141.8	51 06.6	46.2	143.4	23
56 34.2	40.9	137.6	55 04.3	42.7	139.5	53 31.8	44.2	141.3	51 57.0	45.5	142.9	50 20.4	46.8	144.4	24
55 53.3	-41.7	138.9	54 21.6	-43.3	140.8	52 47.4	-44.8	142.4	51 11.5	-46.1	144.0	49 33.6	-47.3	145.4	25
55 11.6	42.4	140.2	53 38.3	44.0	141.9	52 02.8	45.3	143.5	50 25.4	46.6	145.0	48 46.3	47.7	146.3	26
54 29.2	43.2	141.4	52 54.3	44.6	143.1	51 17.4	45.9	144.6	49 38.8	47.1	146.0	47 58.6	48.1	147.2	27
53 46.0	43.9	142.6	52 09.7	45.3	144.2	50 31.5	46.5	145.6	48 51.7	47.6	146.9	47 10.5	48.6	148.1	28
53 02.1	44.5	143.7	51 24.4	45.8	145.2	49 45.0	46.9	146.6	48 04.1	47.9	147.8	46 21.9	48.9	149.0	29

10°			12°			14°			16°			18°			Dec.
Hc	d	Z	Hc	d	Z	Hc	d	Z	Hc	d	Z	Hc	d	Z	
64 06.9	- 24.8	111.3	63 19.6	- 28.6	115.0	62 25.5	- 32.0	118.5	61 25.2	- 35.2	121.8	60 19.4	- 38.0	124.8	0
63 42.1	26.5	113.4	62 51.0	30.1	117.0	61 53.5	33.5	120.3	60 50.0	36.4	123.4	59 41.4	39.0	126.3	1
63 15.6	28.1	115.4	62 20.9	31.6	118.9	61 20.0	34.7	122.1	60 13.6	37.5	125.1	59 02.4	40.1	127.8	2
62 47.5	29.7	117.3	61 49.3	33.0	120.7	60 45.3	36.0	123.8	59 36.1	38.6	126.6	58 22.3	40.9	129.2	3
62 17.8	31.2	119.2	61 16.3	34.4	122.4	60 09.3	37.1	125.4	58 57.5	39.6	128.1	57 41.4	41.9	130.6	4
61 46.6	-32.6	121.0	60 41.9	-35.5	124.1	59 32.2	-38.2	126.9	58 17.9	-40.6	129.6	56 59.5	-42.6	131.9	5
61 14.0	33.9	122.8	60 06.4	36.7	125.7	58 54.0	39.2	128.5	57 37.3	41.4	130.9	56 16.9	43.4	133.2	6
60 40.1	35.2	124.5	59 29.7	37.8	127.3	58 14.8	40.2	129.9	56 55.9	42.3	132.3	55 33.5	44.2	134.5	7
60 04.9	36.3	126.1	58 51.9	38.8	128.8	57 34.6	41.0	131.3	56 13.6	43.0	133.6	54 49.3	44.7	135.6	8
59 28.6	37.4	127.7	58 13.1	39.8	130.3	56 53.6	41.9	132.7	55 30.6	43.8	134.8	54 04.6	45.5	136.8	9
58 51.2	-38.5	129.2	57 33.3	-40.7	131.7	56 11.7	-42.7	134.0	54 46.8	-44.4	136.0	53 19.1	-46.0	137.9	10
58 12.7	39.4	130.7	56 52.6	41.6	133.1	55 29.0	43.4	135.2	54 02.4	45.1	137.2	52 33.1	46.5	139.0	11
57 33.3	40.4	132.1	56 11.0	42.3	134.4	54 45.6	44.1	136.4	53 17.3	45.7	138.3	51 46.6	47.1	140.0	12
56 52.9	41.2	133.5	55 28.7	43.1	135.6	54 01.5	44.8	137.6	52 31.6	46.2	139.4	50 59.5	47.6	141.0	13
56 11.7	42.1	134.8	54 45.6	43.8	136.8	53 16.7	45.4	138.7	51 45.4	46.8	140.4	50 11.9	48.0	141.9	14
55 29.6	-42.8	136.1	54 01.8	-44.5	138.0	52 31.3	-45.9	139.8	50 58.6	-47.3	141.4	49 23.9	-48.5	142.9	15
54 46.8	43.5	137.3	53 17.3	45.1	139.2	51 45.4	46.5	140.8	50 11.3	47.7	142.4	48 35.4	48.8	143.8	16
54 03.3	44.2	138.5	52 32.2	45.6	140.2	50 58.9	47.0	141.8	49 23.6	48.2	143.3	47 46.6	49.3	144.6	17
53 19.1	44.8	139.6	51 46.6	46.3	141.3	50 11.9	47.5	142.8	48 35.4	48.6	144.2	46 57.3	49.6	145.5	18
52 34.3	45.4	140.7	51 00.3	46.7	142.3	49 24.4	47.9	143.8	47 46.8	49.0	145.1	46 07.7	50.0	146.3	19
51 48.9	-46.0	141.8	50 13.6	-47.2	143.3	48 36.5	-48.3	144.7	46 57.8	-49.3	145.9	45 17.7	-50.2	147.1	20
51 02.9	46.5	142.8	49 26.4	47.7	144.3	47 48.2	48.8	145.6	46 08.5	49.7	146.8	44 27.5	50.6	147.9	21
50 16.4	47.0	143.8	48 38.7	48.1	145.2	46 59.4	49.1	146.4	45 18.8	50.1	147.6	43 36.9	50.9	148.6	22
49 29.4	47.4	144.8	47 50.6	48.5	146.1	46 10.3	49.5	147.3	44 28.7	50.3	148.3	42 46.0	51.1	149.3	23
48 42.0	47.9	145.7	47 02.1	48.9	147.0	45 20.8	49.8	148.1	43 38.4	50.6	149.1	41 54.9	51.4	150.0	24
47 54.1	-48.4	146.6	46 13.2	-49.3	147.8	44 31.0	-50.1	148.9	42 47.8	-50.9	149.8	41 03.5	-51.6	150.7	25
47 05.7	48.7	147.5	45 23.9	49.6	148.6	43 40.9	50.4	149.6	41 56.9	51.2	150.6	40 11.9	51.8	151.4	26
46 17.0	49.0	148.4	44 34.3	49.9	149.4	42 50.5	50.7	150.4	41 05.7	51.4	151.3	39 20.1	52.1	152.1	27
45 28.0	49.5	149.2	43 44.4	50.3	150.2	41 59.8	51.0	151.1	40 14.3	51.7	151.9	38 28.0	52.3	152.7	28
44 38.5	49.7	150.0	42 54.1	50.5	150.9	41 08.8	51.2	151.8	39 22.6	51.8	152.6	37 35.7	52.4	153.3	29

Dec.	20° Hc	d	Z	22° Hc	d	Z	24° Hc	d	Z	26° Hc	d	Z	28° Hc	d	Z
°	° ′	′	°	° ′	′	°	° ′	′	°	° ′	′	°	° ′	′	°
0	59 08.6	+39.5	127.5	57 53.4	+41.8	130.1	56 34.2	+44.0	132.4	55 11.6	+45.8	134.6	53 46.0	+47.4	136.5
1	59 48.1	38.5	126.0	58 35.2	41.0	128.7	57 18.2	43.1	131.2	55 57.4	45.1	133.4	54 33.4	46.8	135.5
2	60 26.6	37.3	124.5	59 16.2	40.0	127.3	58 01.3	42.4	129.9	56 42.5	44.4	132.2	55 20.2	46.2	134.4
3	61 03.9	36.2	122.9	59 56.2	39.0	125.8	58 43.7	41.4	128.5	57 26.9	43.6	131.0	56 06.4	45.6	133.2
4	61 40.1	34.9	121.2	60 35.2	37.8	124.3	59 25.1	40.5	127.1	58 10.5	42.9	129.7	56 52.0	44.9	132.1
5	62 15.0	+33.6	119.5	61 13.0	+36.7	122.7	60 05.6	+39.5	125.6	58 53.4	+41.9	128.4	57 36.9	+44.1	130.8
6	62 48.6	32.2	117.7	61 49.7	35.5	121.0	60 45.1	38.4	124.1	59 35.3	41.0	127.0	58 21.0	43.3	129.6
7	63 20.8	30.6	115.9	62 25.2	34.1	119.3	61 23.5	37.3	122.5	60 16.3	40.1	125.5	59 04.3	42.5	128.2
8	63 51.4	29.1	113.9	62 59.3	32.7	117.5	62 00.8	36.0	120.9	60 56.4	38.9	124.0	59 46.8	41.6	126.8
9	64 20.5	27.3	111.9	63 32.0	31.2	115.7	62 36.8	34.7	119.2	61 35.3	37.9	122.4	60 28.4	40.6	125.4
10	64 47.8	+25.5	109.8	64 03.2	+29.6	113.7	63 11.5	+33.3	117.4	62 13.2	+36.5	120.8	61 09.0	+39.5	123.9
11	65 13.3	23.7	107.7	64 32.8	28.0	111.7	63 44.8	31.7	115.5	62 49.7	35.3	119.0	61 48.5	38.4	122.3
12	65 37.0	21.7*	105.5	65 00.8	26.1	109.6	64 16.5	30.2	113.6	63 25.0	33.9	117.2	62 26.9	37.2	120.7
13	65 58.7	19.6*	103.2	65 26.9	24.2	107.5	64 46.7	28.6	111.6	63 58.9	32.4	115.4	63 04.1	35.9	119.0
14	66 18.3	17.4*	100.9	65 51.1	22.3*	105.3	65 15.3	26.7	109.5	64 31.3	30.8	113.4	63 40.0	34.5	117.2
15	66 35.7	+15.2*	98.5	66 13.4	+20.1*	103.0	65 42.0	+24.8	107.3	65 02.1	+29.2	111.1	64 14.5	+33.0	115.3
16	66 50.9	12.9*	96.0	66 33.5	18.0*	100.6	66 06.8	22.8*	105.1	65 31.3	27.3	109.3	64 47.5	31.5	113.4
17	67 03.8	10.5*	93.5	66 51.5	15.8*	98.2	66 29.6	20.8*	102.8	65 58.6	25.4	107.2	65 19.0	29.7	111.3
18	67 14.3	8.1*	91.0	67 07.3	13.4*	95.8	66 50.4	18.5*	100.4	66 24.0	23.5*	104.9	65 48.7	28.0	109.2
19	67 22.4	5.6*	88.4	67 20.7	11.0*	93.2	67 08.9	16.3*	98.0	66 47.5	21.3*	102.6	66 16.7	26.1*	107.1
20	67 28.0	+3.1*	85.8	67 31.7	+8.5*	90.7	67 25.2	+14.0*	95.5	67 08.8	+19.1*	100.2	66 42.8	+24.0*	104.8
21	67 31.1	0.6*	83.2	67 40.2	6.0*	88.1	67 39.2	11.5*	92.9	67 27.9	16.9*	97.8	67 06.8	22.0*	102.5
22	67 31.7	-2.2*	80.6	67 46.2	3.5*	85.4	67 50.7	9.0*	90.3	67 44.8	14.4*	95.2	67 28.8	19.7*	100.1
23	67 29.7	4.5*	78.0	67 49.7	+1.0*	82.8	67 59.7	6.4*	87.7	67 59.2	12.0*	92.7	67 48.5	17.4*	97.6
24	67 25.2	7.0*	75.4	67 50.7	-1.7*	80.2	68 06.1	3.9*	85.1	68 11.2	9.5*	90.0	68 05.9	15.0*	95.0
25	67 18.2	-9.4*	72.8	67 49.0	-4.2*	77.5	68 10.0	+1.2*	82.4	68 20.7	+6.9*	87.4	68 20.9	+12.5*	92.4
26	67 08.8	11.8*	70.3	67 44.8	6.8*	74.9	68 11.2	-1.3*	79.7	68 27.6	4.2*	84.7	68 33.4	9.9*	89.8
27	66 57.0	14.2*	67.8	67 38.0	9.2*	72.2	68 09.9	4.0*	77.0	68 31.8	+1.6*	82.0	68 43.3	7.3*	87.0
28	66 42.8	16.5*	65.3	67 28.8	11.7*	69.7	68 05.9	6.5*	74.3	68 33.4	-1.1*	79.2	68 50.6	4.6*	84.3
29	66 26.3	18.6*	62.9	67 17.1	14.1*	67.1	67 59.4	9.1*	71.7	68 32.3	3.7*	76.5	68 55.2	+1.9*	81.5

Dec.	30° Hc	d	Z	32° Hc	d	Z	34° Hc	d	Z	36° Hc	d	Z	38° Hc	d	Z
°	° ′	′	°	° ′	′	°	° ′	′	°	° ′	′	°	° ′	′	°
0	52 17.6	+48.8	138.3	50 46.8	+50.1	140.0	49 13.9	+51.3	141.5	47 39.2	+52.2	142.9	46 02.7	+53.1	144.1
1	53 06.4	48.4	137.4	51 36.9	49.7	139.1	50 05.2	50.8	140.7	48 31.4	51.9	142.1	46 55.8	52.8	143.5
2	53 54.8	47.8	136.4	52 26.6	49.3	138.2	50 56.0	50.5	139.8	49 23.3	51.6	141.4	47 48.6	52.6	142.8
3	54 42.6	47.3	135.3	53 15.9	48.7	137.2	51 46.5	50.1	139.0	50 14.9	51.3	140.6	48 41.2	52.4	142.0
4	55 29.9	46.7	134.2	54 04.6	48.3	136.2	52 36.6	49.7	138.1	51 06.2	50.9	139.7	49 33.6	52.0	141.3
5	56 16.6	+46.0	133.1	54 52.9	+47.8	135.2	53 26.3	+49.2	137.1	51 57.1	+50.5	138.9	50 25.6	+51.7	140.5
6	57 02.6	45.4	132.0	55 40.7	47.1	134.2	54 15.5	48.8	136.2	52 47.6	50.2	138.0	51 17.3	51.3	139.7
7	57 48.0	44.6	130.7	56 27.8	46.3	133.1	55 04.3	48.2	135.2	53 37.8	49.7	137.1	52 08.6	51.0	138.9
8	58 32.6	43.9	129.5	57 14.4	45.9	131.9	55 52.5	47.7	134.1	54 27.5	49.2	136.1	52 59.6	50.6	138.0
9	59 16.5	43.0	128.2	58 00.3	45.2	130.7	56 40.2	47.0	133.0	55 16.7	48.7	135.1	53 50.2	50.1	137.1
10	59 59.5	+42.2	126.8	58 45.5	+44.4	129.4	57 27.2	+46.5	131.9	56 05.4	+48.2	134.1	54 40.3	+49.7	136.2
11	60 41.7	41.1	125.3	59 29.9	43.6	128.1	58 13.7	45.7	130.7	56 53.6	47.6	133.0	55 30.0	49.2	135.2
12	61 22.8	40.2	123.8	60 13.5	42.7	126.8	58 59.4	45.0	129.4	57 41.2	46.9	131.9	56 19.2	48.7	134.2
13	62 03.0	39.0	122.3	60 56.2	41.7	125.3	59 44.4	44.1	128.1	58 28.1	46.3	130.7	57 07.9	48.2	133.1
14	62 42.0	37.8	120.6	61 37.9	40.8	123.8	60 28.5	43.4	126.7	59 14.4	45.6	129.5	57 56.1	47.5	132.0
15	63 19.8	+36.5	118.9	62 18.7	+39.6	122.3	61 11.9	+42.3	125.4	60 00.0	+44.7	128.2	58 43.6	+46.9	130.8
16	63 56.3	35.2	117.1	62 58.3	38.5	120.6	61 54.2	41.4	123.9	60 44.7	44.0	126.9	59 30.5	46.1	129.6
17	64 31.5	33.7	115.3	63 36.8	37.2	118.9	62 35.6	40.3	122.3	61 28.7	43.0	125.5	60 16.6	45.4	128.3
18	65 05.2	32.1	113.3	64 14.0	35.8	117.1	63 15.9	39.1	120.7	62 11.7	42.0	124.0	61 02.0	44.5	127.0
19	65 37.3	30.4	111.3	64 49.8	34.3	115.3	63 55.0	37.9	119.0	62 53.7	40.9	122.4	61 46.5	43.7	125.6
20	66 07.7	+28.6	109.2	65 24.1	+32.8	113.3	64 32.9	+36.5	117.2	63 34.6	+39.8	120.8	62 30.2	+42.7	124.1
21	66 36.3	26.7	107.0	65 56.9	31.1	111.3	65 09.4	35.0	115.3	64 14.4	38.6	119.1	63 12.9	41.6	122.6
22	67 03.0	24.7*	104.7	66 28.0	29.3	109.2	65 44.4	33.5	113.4	64 53.0	37.2	117.3	63 54.5	40.5	121.0
23	67 27.7	22.6*	102.4	66 57.3	27.4	107.0	66 17.9	31.8	111.3	65 30.2	35.8	115.4	64 35.0	39.3	119.3
24	67 50.3	20.3*	99.9	67 24.7	25.4*	104.7	66 49.7	30.0	109.2	66 06.0	34.2	113.5	65 14.3	37.9	117.5
25	68 10.6	+18.0*	97.4	67 50.1	+23.2*	102.3	67 19.7	+28.1*	107.0	66 40.2	+32.5	111.4	65 52.2	+36.6	115.6
26	68 28.6	15.6*	94.8	68 13.3	20.9*	99.8	67 47.8	26.0*	104.7	67 12.7	30.7	109.3	66 28.8	34.9	113.6
27	68 44.2	12.9*	92.2	68 34.2	18.6*	97.3	68 13.8	23.9*	102.3	67 43.4	28.8	107.1	67 03.7	33.3	111.6
28	68 57.1	10.4*	89.5	68 52.8	16.1*	94.7	68 37.7	21.6*	99.8	68 12.2	26.8*	104.7	67 37.0	31.5	109.4
29	69 07.5	7.7*	86.7	69 08.9	13.5*	92.0	68 59.3	19.2*	97.2	68 39.0	24.5*	102.3	68 08.5	29.5*	107.2

20°			22°			24°			26°			28°			Dec.
Hc	d	Z	Hc	d	Z	Hc	d	Z	Hc	d	Z	Hc	d	Z	
59 08.6	-40.5	127.5	57 53.4	-42.7	130.1	56 34.2	-44.6	132.4	55 11.6	-46.3	134.6	53 46.0	-47.9	136.5	0
58 28.1	41.4	129.0	57 10.7	43.5	131.4	55 49.6	45.3	133.6	54 25.3	47.0	135.7	52 58.1	48.4	137.5	1
57 46.7	42.2	130.3	56 27.2	44.2	132.6	55 04.3	46.0	134.8	53 38.3	47.5	136.7	52 09.7	48.9	138.5	2
57 04.5	43.1	131.6	55 43.0	44.9	133.9	54 18.3	46.5	135.9	52 50.8	48.0	137.7	51 20.8	49.3	139.4	3
56 21.4	43.8	132.9	54 58.1	45.6	135.0	53 31.8	47.2	137.0	52 02.8	48.5	138.7	50 31.5	49.7	140.3	4
55 37.6	-44.5	134.1	54 12.5	-46.1	136.1	52 44.6	-47.6	138.0	51 14.3	-48.9	139.7	49 41.8	-50.1	141.2	5
54 53.1	45.2	135.3	53 26.4	46.8	137.2	51 57.0	48.1	139.0	50 25.4	49.4	140.6	48 51.7	50.5	142.1	6
54 07.9	45.7	136.4	52 39.6	47.2	138.3	51 08.9	48.5	139.9	49 36.0	49.7	141.5	48 01.2	50.7	142.9	7
53 22.2	46.4	137.5	51 52.4	47.8	139.3	50 20.4	49.0	140.9	48 46.3	50.1	142.3	47 10.5	51.1	143.7	8
52 35.8	46.9	138.6	51 04.6	48.2	140.3	49 31.4	49.4	141.8	47 56.2	50.5	143.2	46 19.4	51.4	144.4	9
51 48.9	-47.4	139.6	50 16.4	-48.6	141.2	48 42.0	-49.8	142.6	47 05.7	-50.7	144.0	45 28.0	-51.7	145.2	10
51 01.5	47.9	140.6	49 27.8	49.1	142.1	47 52.2	50.1	143.5	46 15.0	51.1	144.7	44 36.3	51.9	145.9	11
50 13.6	48.3	141.5	48 38.7	49.5	143.0	47 02.1	50.5	144.3	45 23.9	51.4	145.5	43 44.4	52.2	146.6	12
49 25.3	48.8	142.5	47 49.2	49.8	143.8	46 11.6	50.8	145.1	44 32.5	51.6	146.2	42 52.2	52.4	147.3	13
48 36.5	49.1	143.4	46 59.4	50.1	144.6	45 20.8	51.1	145.8	43 40.9	51.9	146.9	41 59.8	52.7	147.9	14
47 47.4	-49.6	144.2	46 09.3	-50.5	145.4	44 29.7	-51.3	146.6	42 49.0	-52.1	147.6	41 07.1	-52.8	148.6	15
46 57.8	49.8	145.0	45 18.8	50.8	146.2	43 38.4	51.6	147.3	41 56.9	52.4	148.3	40 14.3	53.1	149.2	16
46 08.0	50.3	145.9	44 28.0	51.1	147.0	42 46.8	51.9	148.0	41 04.5	52.6	148.9	39 21.2	53.2	149.8	17
45 17.7	50.5	146.6	43 36.9	51.4	147.7	41 54.9	52.1	148.7	40 11.9	52.8	149.6	38 28.0	53.4	150.4	18
44 27.2	50.8	147.4	42 45.5	51.6	148.4	41 02.8	52.3	149.3	39 19.1	52.9	150.2	37 34.6	53.6	151.0	19
43 36.4	-51.1	148.1	41 53.9	-51.8	149.1	40 10.5	-52.5	150.0	38 26.2	-53.2	150.8	36 41.0	-53.7	151.5	20
42 45.3	51.4	148.9	41 02.1	52.1	149.8	39 18.0	52.8	150.6	37 33.0	53.3	151.4	35 47.3	53.9	152.1	21
41 53.9	51.6	149.6	40 10.0	52.3	150.4	38 25.2	52.9	151.2	36 39.7	53.5	152.0	34 53.4	54.0	152.6	22
41 02.3	51.8	150.2	39 17.7	52.5	151.1	37 32.3	53.1	151.8	35 46.2	53.6	152.5	33 59.4	54.1	153.2	23
40 10.5	52.1	150.9	38 25.2	52.7	151.7	36 39.2	53.2	152.4	34 52.6	53.8	153.1	33 05.3	54.3	153.7	24
39 18.4	-52.2	151.5	37 32.5	-52.8	152.3	35 46.0	-53.4	153.0	33 58.8	-54.0	153.6	32 11.0	-54.4	154.2	25
38 26.2	52.5	152.2	36 39.7	53.1	152.9	34 52.6	53.6	153.5	33 04.8	54.0	154.1	31 16.6	54.5	154.7	26
37 33.7	52.7	152.8	35 46.6	53.2	153.5	33 59.0	53.7	154.1	32 10.8	54.2	154.6	30 22.1	54.6	155.2	27
36 41.0	52.8	153.4	34 53.4	53.3	154.0	33 05.3	53.9	154.6	31 16.6	54.3	155.2	29 27.5	54.7	155.6	28
35 48.2	53.0	154.0	34 00.1	53.5	154.6	32 11.4	53.9	155.1	30 22.3	54.4	155.6	28 32.8	54.8	156.1	29

30°			32°			34°			36°			38°			Dec.
Hc	d	Z	Hc	d	Z	Hc	d	Z	Hc	d	Z	Hc	d	Z	
52 17.6	-49.3	138.3	50 46.8	-50.4	140.0	49 13.9	-51.5	141.5	47 39.2	-52.5	142.9	46 02.7	-53.3	144.1	0
51 28.3	49.7	139.2	49 56.4	50.9	140.8	48 22.4	51.8	142.3	46 46.7	52.8	143.6	45 09.4	53.6	144.8	1
50 38.6	50.0	140.1	49 05.5	51.1	141.6	47 30.6	52.2	143.0	45 53.9	53.0	144.3	44 15.8	53.7	145.4	2
49 48.6	50.5	141.0	48 14.4	51.5	142.4	46 38.4	52.4	143.7	45 00.9	53.2	144.9	43 22.1	54.0	146.0	3
48 58.1	50.8	141.8	47 22.9	51.8	143.2	45 46.0	52.6	144.4	44 07.7	53.4	145.6	42 28.1	54.1	146.6	4
48 07.3	-51.1	142.6	46 31.1	-52.0	143.9	44 53.4	-52.9	145.1	43 14.3	-53.6	146.2	41 34.0	-54.3	147.2	5
47 16.2	51.5	143.4	45 39.1	52.4	144.6	44 00.5	53.1	145.8	42 20.7	53.9	146.8	40 39.7	54.5	147.8	6
46 24.7	51.7	144.2	44 46.7	52.5	145.3	43 07.4	53.3	146.4	41 26.8	54.0	147.4	39 45.2	54.6	148.3	7
45 33.0	52.0	144.9	43 54.2	52.8	146.0	42 14.1	53.5	147.0	40 32.8	54.1	148.0	38 50.6	54.7	148.9	8
44 41.0	52.2	145.6	43 01.4	53.0	146.7	41 20.6	53.7	147.7	39 38.7	54.3	148.6	37 55.9	54.9	149.4	9
43 48.8	-52.5	146.3	42 08.4	-53.2	147.3	40 26.9	-53.9	148.2	38 44.4	-54.5	149.1	37 01.0	-55.1	149.9	10
42 56.3	52.7	146.9	41 15.2	53.4	147.9	39 33.0	54.0	148.8	37 49.9	54.6	149.6	36 05.9	55.1	150.4	11
42 03.6	52.9	147.6	40 21.8	53.6	148.5	38 39.0	54.2	149.4	36 55.3	54.8	150.2	35 10.8	55.2	150.9	12
41 10.7	53.1	148.2	39 28.2	53.8	149.1	37 44.8	54.4	149.9	36 00.5	54.8	150.7	34 15.6	55.4	151.3	13
40 17.6	53.3	148.8	38 34.4	53.9	149.7	36 50.4	54.5	150.5	35 05.7	55.0	151.2	33 20.2	55.5	151.8	14
39 24.2	-53.4	149.4	37 40.5	-54.1	150.2	35 55.9	-54.6	151.0	34 10.7	-55.1	151.6	32 24.7	-55.5	152.3	15
38 30.8	53.7	150.0	36 46.4	54.2	150.8	35 01.3	54.7	151.5	33 15.6	55.3	152.1	31 29.2	55.7	152.7	16
37 37.1	53.8	150.6	35 52.2	54.4	151.3	34 06.6	54.9	152.0	32 20.3	55.3	152.6	30 33.5	55.7	153.1	17
36 43.3	54.0	151.1	34 57.8	54.5	151.8	33 11.7	54.9	152.5	31 25.0	55.4	153.0	29 37.8	55.8	153.6	18
35 49.3	54.1	151.7	34 03.3	54.6	152.3	32 16.8	55.1	152.9	30 29.6	55.5	153.5	28 42.0	55.9	154.0	19
34 55.2	-54.3	152.2	33 08.7	-54.7	152.8	31 21.7	-55.2	153.4	29 34.1	-55.6	153.9	27 46.1	-55.9	154.4	20
34 00.9	54.3	152.7	32 14.0	54.8	153.3	30 26.5	55.3	153.9	28 38.5	55.6	154.4	26 50.2	56.1	154.8	21
33 06.6	54.5	153.2	31 19.2	55.0	153.8	29 31.2	55.3	154.3	27 42.9	55.8	154.8	25 54.1	56.1	155.2	22
32 12.1	54.6	153.7	30 24.2	55.0	154.3	28 35.9	55.5	154.8	26 47.1	55.8	155.2	24 58.0	56.1	155.6	23
31 17.5	54.8	154.2	29 29.2	55.2	154.7	27 40.4	55.5	155.2	25 51.3	55.8	155.6	24 01.9	56.2	156.0	24
30 22.7	-54.8	154.7	28 34.0	-55.2	155.2	26 44.9	-55.6	155.6	24 55.5	-56.0	156.0	23 05.7	-56.3	156.4	25
29 27.9	54.9	155.2	27 38.8	55.3	155.6	25 49.3	55.6	156.0	23 59.5	56.0	156.4	22 09.4	56.3	156.8	26
28 33.0	55.0	155.6	26 43.5	55.4	156.1	24 53.7	55.8	156.5	23 03.5	56.1	156.8	21 13.1	56.4	157.1	27
27 38.0	55.1	156.1	25 48.1	55.4	156.5	23 57.9	55.8	156.9	22 07.4	56.1	157.2	20 16.7	56.4	157.5	28
26 42.9	55.2	156.5	24 52.7	55.6	156.9	23 02.1	55.8	157.3	21 11.3	56.1	157.6	19 20.3	56.5	157.9	29

Dec.	40° Hc	d	Z	42° Hc	d	Z	44° Hc	d	Z	46° Hc	d	Z	48° Hc	d	Z
°	° ′	′	°	° ′	′	°	° ′	′	°	° ′	′	°	° ′	′	°
0	44 24.7	+53.9	145.3	42 45.4	+54.6	146.4	41 05.0	+55.2	147.3	39 23.4	+55.8	148.2	37 40.9	+56.3	149.1
1	45 18.6	53.7	144.7	43 40.0	54.5	145.8	42 00.2	55.1	146.8	40 19.2	55.7	147.8	38 37.2	56.2	148.6
2	46 12.3	53.5	144.0	44 34.5	54.2	145.2	42 55.3	54.9	146.3	41 14.9	55.5	147.3	39 33.4	56.1	148.2
3	47 05.8	53.2	143.4	45 28.7	54.0	144.6	43 50.2	54.8	145.7	42 10.4	55.4	146.8	40 29.5	56.0	147.7
4	47 59.0	53.0	142.7	46 22.7	53.9	144.0	44 45.0	54.5	145.2	43 05.8	55.3	146.2	41 25.5	55.8	147.2
5	48 52.0	+52.7	142.0	47 16.6	+53.6	143.3	45 39.5	+54.4	144.6	44 01.1	+55.1	145.7	42 21.3	+55.7	146.7
6	49 44.7	52.4	141.2	48 10.2	53.3	142.7	46 33.9	54.2	144.0	44 56.2	54.9	145.2	43 17.0	55.6	146.2
7	50 37.1	52.1	140.5	49 03.5	53.1	142.0	47 28.1	54.0	143.3	45 51.1	54.7	144.6	44 12.6	55.4	145.7
8	51 29.2	51.8	139.7	49 56.6	52.9	141.3	48 22.1	53.8	142.7	46 45.8	54.6	144.0	45 08.0	55.3	145.2
9	52 21.0	51.4	138.9	50 49.5	52.5	140.5	49 15.9	53.5	142.0	47 40.4	54.4	143.4	46 03.3	55.1	144.6
10	53 12.4	+51.1	138.0	51 42.0	+52.2	139.7	50 09.4	+53.2	141.3	48 34.8	+54.1	142.7	46 58.4	+54.9	144.1
11	54 03.5	50.6	137.1	52 34.2	51.9	138.9	51 02.6	53.0	140.6	49 28.9	53.9	142.1	47 53.3	54.8	143.5
12	54 54.1	50.2	136.2	53 26.1	51.5	138.1	51 55.6	52.6	139.8	50 22.8	53.7	141.4	48 48.1	54.5	142.8
13	55 44.3	49.7	135.3	54 17.6	51.1	137.2	52 48.2	52.4	139.0	51 16.5	53.4	140.7	49 42.6	54.3	142.2
14	56 34.0	49.3	134.2	55 08.7	50.7	136.3	53 40.6	52.0	138.2	52 09.9	53.1	140.0	50 36.9	54.1	141.5
15	57 23.3	+48.6	133.2	55 59.4	+50.3	135.4	54 32.6	+51.6	137.4	53 03.0	+52.8	139.2	51 31.0	+53.8	140.9
16	58 11.9	48.1	132.1	56 49.7	49.8	134.4	55 24.2	51.2	136.5	53 55.8	52.5	138.4	52 24.8	53.6	140.1
17	59 00.0	47.5	131.0	57 39.5	49.2	133.4	56 15.4	50.8	135.6	54 48.3	52.1	137.6	53 18.4	53.3	139.4
18	59 47.5	46.7	129.8	58 28.7	48.7	132.3	57 06.2	50.3	134.6	55 40.4	51.7	136.7	54 11.7	52.9	138.6
19	60 34.2	46.0	128.5	59 17.4	48.0	131.1	57 56.5	49.8	133.6	56 32.1	51.3	135.8	55 04.6	52.6	137.8
20	61 20.2	+45.2	127.2	60 05.4	+47.4	130.0	58 46.3	+49.2	132.5	57 23.4	+50.9	134.8	55 57.2	+52.3	136.9
21	62 05.4	44.4	125.8	60 52.8	46.6	128.7	59 35.5	48.7	131.4	58 14.3	50.3	133.8	56 49.5	51.8	136.1
22	62 49.8	43.3	124.3	61 39.4	45.9	127.4	60 24.2	48.0	130.2	59 04.6	49.9	132.8	57 41.3	51.4	135.1
23	63 33.1	42.4	122.8	62 25.3	45.0	126.0	61 12.2	47.3	129.0	59 54.5	49.3	131.7	58 32.7	51.0	134.2
24	64 15.5	41.2	121.2	63 10.3	44.1	124.6	61 59.5	46.5	127.7	60 43.8	48.6	130.5	59 23.7	50.4	133.1
25	64 56.7	+40.0	119.5	63 54.4	+43.0	123.1	62 46.0	+45.7	126.3	61 32.4	+48.0	129.3	60 14.1	+49.9	132.1
26	65 36.7	38.7	117.7	64 37.4	42.0	121.5	63 31.7	44.8	124.9	62 20.4	47.2	128.0	61 04.0	49.3	130.9
27	66 15.4	37.3	115.8	65 19.4	40.8	119.8	64 16.5	43.9	123.4	63 07.6	46.4	126.7	61 53.3	48.7	129.7
28	66 52.7	35.7	113.9	66 00.2	39.5	118.0	65 00.4	42.7	121.8	63 54.0	45.6	125.3	62 42.0	47.9	128.5
29	67 28.4	34.1	111.8	66 39.7	38.0	116.1	65 43.1	41.5	120.1	64 39.6	44.5	123.8	63 29.9	47.2	127.1

Dec.	50° Hc	d	Z	52° Hc	d	Z	54° Hc	d	Z	56° Hc	d	Z	58° Hc	d	Z
°	° ′	′	°	° ′	′	°	° ′	′	°	° ′	′	°	° ′	′	°
0	35 57.6	+56.7	149.8	34 13.5	+57.1	150.5	32 28.7	+57.5	151.2	30 43.2	+57.9	151.8	28 57.2	+58.2	152.3
1	36 54.3	56.6	149.4	35 10.6	57.1	150.2	33 26.2	57.4	150.8	31 41.1	57.8	151.5	29 55.4	58.1	152.0
2	37 51.0	56.6	149.0	36 07.7	57.0	149.8	34 23.6	57.4	150.5	32 38.9	57.7	151.1	30 53.5	58.0	151.7
3	38 47.6	56.4	148.6	37 04.7	56.9	149.4	35 21.0	57.3	150.1	33 36.6	57.7	150.8	31 51.5	58.0	151.4
4	39 44.0	56.4	148.2	38 01.6	56.9	149.0	36 18.3	57.3	149.8	34 34.3	57.6	150.5	32 49.5	58.0	151.1
5	40 40.4	+56.3	147.7	38 58.5	+56.7	148.6	37 15.6	+57.2	149.4	35 31.9	+57.5	150.1	33 47.5	+57.9	150.8
6	41 36.7	56.1	147.2	39 55.2	56.7	148.2	38 12.8	57.1	149.0	36 29.5	57.5	149.8	34 45.4	57.9	150.5
7	42 32.8	56.1	146.8	40 51.9	56.6	147.7	39 09.9	57.1	148.6	37 27.0	57.5	149.4	35 43.3	57.8	150.2
8	43 28.9	55.9	146.3	41 48.5	56.4	147.3	40 07.0	56.9	148.2	38 24.5	57.4	149.1	36 41.1	57.8	149.9
9	44 24.8	55.7	145.8	42 44.9	56.4	146.8	41 03.9	56.9	147.8	39 21.9	57.3	148.7	37 38.9	57.7	149.5
10	45 20.5	+55.6	145.3	43 41.3	+56.2	146.4	42 00.8	+56.7	147.4	40 19.2	+57.2	148.3	38 36.6	+57.6	149.2
11	46 16.1	55.5	144.7	44 37.5	56.1	145.9	42 57.5	56.7	146.9	41 16.4	57.1	147.9	39 34.2	57.6	148.8
12	47 11.6	55.3	144.2	45 33.6	55.9	145.4	43 54.2	56.5	146.5	42 13.5	57.1	147.5	40 31.8	57.5	148.4
13	48 06.9	55.1	143.6	46 29.5	55.9	144.9	44 50.7	56.4	146.0	43 10.6	56.9	147.1	41 29.3	57.4	148.1
14	49 02.0	54.9	143.0	47 25.4	55.6	144.3	45 47.1	56.3	145.4	44 07.5	56.9	146.6	42 26.7	57.4	147.7
15	49 56.9	+54.8	142.4	48 21.0	+55.5	143.8	46 43.4	+56.2	145.0	45 04.4	+56.8	146.2	43 24.1	+57.2	147.3
16	50 51.7	54.5	141.7	49 16.5	55.3	143.2	47 39.6	56.0	144.5	46 01.2	56.6	145.7	44 21.3	57.2	146.9
17	51 46.2	54.2	141.1	50 11.8	55.1	142.6	48 35.6	55.9	144.0	46 57.8	56.5	145.3	45 18.5	57.0	146.4
18	52 40.4	54.0	140.4	51 06.9	55.0	142.0	49 31.5	55.7	143.4	47 54.3	56.4	144.8	46 15.5	57.0	146.0
19	53 34.4	53.8	139.6	52 01.9	54.7	141.3	50 27.2	55.5	142.8	48 50.7	56.2	144.2	47 12.5	56.8	145.5
20	54 28.2	+53.4	138.9	52 56.6	+54.4	140.6	51 22.7	+55.3	142.2	49 46.9	+56.1	143.7	48 09.3	+56.8	145.0
21	55 21.6	53.1	138.1	53 51.0	54.2	139.9	52 18.0	55.1	141.6	50 43.0	55.9	143.2	49 06.1	56.5	144.6
22	56 14.7	52.8	137.3	54 45.2	53.9	139.2	53 13.1	54.9	141.0	51 38.9	55.7	142.6	50 02.6	56.5	144.0
23	57 07.5	52.4	136.4	55 39.1	53.6	138.4	54 08.0	54.7	140.3	52 34.6	55.6	142.0	50 59.1	56.3	143.5
24	57 59.9	51.9	135.5	56 32.7	53.3	137.6	55 02.7	54.4	139.6	53 30.2	55.3	141.3	51 55.4	56.1	143.0
25	58 51.8	+51.6	134.5	57 26.0	+52.9	136.8	55 57.1	+54.1	138.8	54 25.5	+55.1	140.7	52 51.5	+56.0	142.4
26	59 43.4	51.0	133.5	58 18.9	52.6	135.9	56 51.2	53.8	138.0	55 20.6	54.9	140.0	53 47.5	55.7	141.8
27	60 34.4	50.6	132.5	59 11.5	52.1	135.0	57 45.0	53.5	137.2	56 15.5	54.6	139.3	54 43.2	55.6	141.1
28	61 25.0	49.9	131.4	60 03.6	51.7	134.0	58 38.5	53.1	136.4	57 10.1	54.3	138.5	55 38.8	55.3	140.5
29	62 14.9	49.3	130.2	60 55.3	51.1	132.9	59 31.6	52.7	135.5	58 04.4	54.0	137.7	56 34.1	55.1	139.8

40°			42°			44°			46°			48°			Dec.
Hc	d	Z	Hc	d	Z	Hc	d	Z	Hc	d	Z	Hc	d	Z	
° ′	′	°	° ′	′	°	° ′	′	°	° ′	′	°	° ′	′	°	°
44 24.7	−54.1	145.3	42 45.4	−54.7	146.4	41 05.0	−55.4	147.3	39 23.4	−55.9	148.2	37 40.9	−56.4	149.1	0
43 30.6	54.2	145.9	41 50.7	54.9	146.9	40 09.6	55.5	147.9	38 27.5	56.0	148.7	36 44.5	56.4	149.5	1
42 36.4	54.5	146.5	40 55.8	55.1	147.5	39 14.1	55.6	148.3	37 31.5	56.1	149.2	35 48.1	56.6	149.9	2
41 41.9	54.6	147.0	40 00.7	55.2	148.0	38 18.5	55.7	148.8	36 35.4	56.2	149.6	34 51.5	56.6	150.3	3
40 47.3	54.7	147.6	39 05.5	55.3	148.5	37 22.8	55.9	149.3	35 39.2	56.3	150.0	33 54.9	56.8	150.7	4
39 52.6	−55.0	148.1	38 10.2	−55.5	149.0	36 26.9	−55.9	149.8	34 42.9	−56.4	150.5	32 58.1	−56.7	151.1	5
38 57.7	55.1	148.7	37 14.7	55.5	149.5	35 31.0	56.0	150.2	33 46.5	56.5	150.9	32 01.4	56.9	151.5	6
38 02.6	55.1	149.2	36 19.2	55.7	149.9	34 35.0	56.2	150.6	32 50.0	56.5	151.3	31 04.5	56.9	151.9	7
37 07.5	55.3	149.7	35 23.5	55.8	150.4	33 38.8	56.2	151.1	31 53.5	56.6	151.7	30 07.6	57.0	152.2	8
36 12.2	55.4	150.1	34 27.7	55.8	150.8	32 42.6	56.3	151.5	30 56.9	56.7	152.1	29 10.6	57.0	152.6	9
35 16.8	−55.5	150.6	33 31.9	−56.0	151.3	31 46.3	−56.4	151.9	30 00.2	−56.8	152.4	28 13.6	−57.1	153.0	10
34 21.3	55.7	151.1	32 35.9	56.0	151.7	30 49.9	56.4	152.3	29 03.4	56.8	152.8	27 16.5	57.2	153.3	11
33 25.6	55.7	151.5	31 39.9	56.2	152.1	29 53.5	56.5	152.7	28 06.6	56.8	153.2	26 19.3	57.2	153.6	12
32 29.9	55.8	152.0	30 43.7	56.2	152.5	28 57.0	56.6	153.1	27 09.8	57.0	153.5	25 22.1	57.2	154.0	13
31 34.1	55.8	152.4	29 47.5	56.3	153.0	28 00.4	56.6	153.4	26 12.8	56.9	153.9	24 24.9	57.3	154.3	14
30 38.3	−56.0	152.8	28 51.2	−56.3	153.3	27 03.8	−56.7	153.8	25 15.9	−57.0	154.3	23 27.6	−57.3	154.6	15
29 42.3	56.1	153.2	27 54.9	56.4	153.7	26 07.1	56.8	154.2	24 18.9	57.1	154.6	22 30.3	57.4	155.0	16
28 46.2	56.1	153.7	26 58.5	56.5	154.1	25 10.3	56.8	154.5	23 21.8	57.1	154.9	21 32.9	57.4	155.3	17
27 50.1	56.2	154.1	26 02.0	56.5	154.5	24 13.5	56.8	154.9	22 24.7	57.2	155.3	20 35.5	57.4	155.6	18
26 53.9	56.2	154.5	25 05.5	56.6	154.9	23 16.7	56.9	155.3	21 27.5	57.1	155.6	19 38.1	57.4	155.9	19
25 57.7	−56.3	154.8	24 08.9	−56.6	155.2	22 19.8	−57.0	155.6	20 30.3	−57.2	155.9	18 40.7	−57.5	156.2	20
25 01.4	56.4	155.2	23 12.3	56.7	155.6	21 22.8	57.0	155.9	19 33.1	57.2	156.2	17 43.2	57.5	156.5	21
24 05.0	56.4	155.6	22 15.6	56.8	156.0	20 25.8	57.0	156.3	18 35.9	57.3	156.6	16 45.7	57.6	156.8	22
23 08.6	56.5	156.0	21 18.8	56.8	156.3	19 28.8	57.0	156.6	17 38.6	57.3	156.9	15 48.1	57.5	157.1	23
22 12.1	56.5	156.3	20 22.1	56.9	156.6	18 31.8	57.1	156.9	16 41.3	57.4	157.2	14 50.6	57.6	157.4	24
21 15.6	−56.6	156.7	19 25.2	−56.8	157.0	17 34.7	−57.1	157.3	15 43.9	−57.3	157.5	13 53.0	−57.6	157.7	25
20 19.0	56.6	157.1	18 28.4	56.9	157.3	16 37.6	57.2	157.6	14 46.6	57.4	157.8	12 55.4	57.6	158.0	26
19 22.4	56.7	157.4	17 31.5	56.9	157.7	15 40.4	57.2	157.9	13 49.2	57.5	158.1	11 57.8	57.7	158.3	27
18 25.7	56.6	157.8	16 34.6	57.0	158.0	14 43.2	57.2	158.2	12 51.7	57.4	158.4	11 00.1	57.6	158.5	28
17 29.1	56.8	158.1	15 37.6	57.0	158.3	13 46.0	57.2	158.5	11 54.3	57.4	158.7	10 02.5	57.7	158.8	29

50°			52°			54°			56°			58°			Dec.
Hc	d	Z	Hc	d	Z	Hc	d	Z	Hc	d	Z	Hc	d	Z	
° ′	′	°	° ′	′	°	° ′	′	°	° ′	′	°	° ′	′	°	°
35 57.6	−56.8	149.8	34 13.5	−57.3	150.5	32 28.7	−57.6	151.2	30 43.2	−57.9	151.8	28 57.2	−58.1	152.3	0
35 00.8	56.9	150.2	33 16.2	57.2	150.9	31 31.1	57.6	151.5	29 45.3	57.9	152.1	27 59.1	58.2	152.6	1
34 03.9	57.0	150.6	32 19.0	57.4	151.3	30 33.5	57.7	151.8	28 47.4	58.0	152.4	27 00.9	58.2	152.9	2
33 06.9	57.0	151.0	31 21.6	57.4	151.6	29 35.8	57.7	152.2	27 49.4	58.0	152.7	26 02.6	58.2	153.1	3
32 09.9	57.1	151.4	30 24.2	57.4	151.9	28 38.1	57.8	152.5	26 51.4	58.0	153.0	25 04.4	58.3	153.4	4
31 12.8	−57.2	151.7	29 26.8	−57.5	152.3	27 40.3	−57.8	152.8	25 53.4	−58.1	153.2	24 06.1	−58.3	153.6	5
30 15.6	57.2	152.1	28 29.3	57.5	152.6	26 42.5	57.8	153.1	24 55.3	58.0	153.5	23 07.8	58.4	153.9	6
29 18.4	57.3	152.4	27 31.8	57.6	152.9	25 44.7	57.8	153.4	23 57.3	58.2	153.7	22 09.4	58.3	154.2	7
28 21.1	57.3	152.8	26 34.2	57.6	153.2	24 46.9	57.9	153.7	22 59.1	58.1	154.1	21 11.1	58.4	154.4	8
27 23.8	57.4	153.1	25 36.6	57.7	153.5	23 49.0	58.0	154.0	22 01.0	58.2	154.3	20 12.7	58.4	154.7	9
26 26.4	−57.4	153.4	24 38.9	−57.7	153.9	22 51.0	−57.9	154.2	21 02.8	−58.2	154.6	19 14.3	−58.5	154.9	10
25 29.0	57.4	153.7	23 41.2	57.7	154.2	21 53.1	58.0	154.5	20 04.6	58.2	154.8	18 15.8	58.4	155.1	11
24 31.6	57.5	154.1	22 43.5	57.8	154.4	20 55.1	58.0	154.8	19 06.4	58.3	155.1	17 17.4	58.5	155.4	12
23 34.1	57.5	154.4	21 45.7	57.8	154.7	19 57.1	58.1	155.1	18 08.1	58.2	155.4	16 18.9	58.4	155.6	13
22 36.6	57.6	154.7	20 47.9	57.8	155.0	18 59.0	58.0	155.3	17 09.9	58.3	155.6	15 20.5	58.5	155.8	14
21 39.0	−57.6	155.0	19 50.1	−57.9	155.3	18 01.0	−58.1	155.6	16 11.6	−58.3	155.9	14 22.0	−58.5	156.1	15
20 41.4	57.6	155.3	18 52.3	57.9	155.6	17 02.9	58.1	155.9	15 13.3	58.3	156.1	13 23.5	58.5	156.3	16
19 43.8	57.7	155.6	17 54.4	57.9	155.8	16 04.8	58.1	156.1	14 15.0	58.4	156.3	12 25.0	58.6	156.5	17
18 46.1	57.7	155.9	16 56.5	57.9	156.1	15 06.7	58.2	156.4	13 16.6	58.3	156.6	11 26.4	58.5	156.8	18
17 48.5	57.7	156.2	15 58.6	58.0	156.4	14 08.5	58.1	156.6	12 18.3	58.4	156.8	10 27.9	58.6	157.0	19
16 50.8	−57.8	156.5	15 00.6	−57.9	156.7	13 10.4	−58.2	156.9	11 19.9	−58.4	157.1	9 29.3	−58.5	157.2	20
15 53.0	57.7	156.7	14 02.7	58.0	157.0	12 12.2	58.2	157.1	10 21.5	58.3	157.3	8 30.8	58.6	157.4	21
14 55.3	57.8	157.0	13 04.7	58.0	157.2	11 14.0	58.2	157.4	9 23.2	58.4	157.5	7 32.2	58.6	157.6	22
13 57.5	57.8	157.3	12 06.7	58.0	157.5	10 15.8	58.2	157.6	8 24.8	58.4	157.8	6 33.7	58.6	157.9	23
12 59.7	57.8	157.6	11 08.7	58.0	157.7	9 17.6	58.2	157.9	7 26.4	58.4	158.0	5 35.1	58.6	158.1	24
12 01.9	−57.8	157.9	10 10.7	−58.0	158.0	8 19.4	−58.2	158.1	6 28.0	−58.4	158.2	4 36.5	−58.6	158.3	25
11 04.1	57.9	158.1	9 12.7	58.1	158.3	7 21.2	58.3	158.4	5 29.6	58.4	158.5	3 37.9	58.6	158.5	26
10 06.2	57.8	158.4	8 14.6	58.0	158.5	6 22.9	58.2	158.6	4 31.2	58.5	158.7	2 39.3	58.5	158.7	27
9 08.4	57.9	158.7	7 16.6	58.1	158.8	5 24.7	58.3	158.9	3 32.7	58.4	158.9	1 40.8	58.6	158.9	28
8 10.5	57.8	158.9	6 18.5	58.1	159.0	4 26.4	58.2	159.1	2 34.3	58.4	159.1	0 42.2	−58.6	159.2	29

Dec.	0° Hc	d	Z	2° Hc	d	Z	4° Hc	d	Z	6° Hc	d	Z	8° Hc	d	Z
0	64 00.0	- 1.1·	90.0	63 55.7	+ 3.7·	94.1	63 42.9	+ 8.4·	98.1	63 21.8	+13.0	102.1	62 52.7	+17.4	105.9
1	63 58.9	3.2·	87.7	63 59.4	+ 1.6·	91.8	63 51.3	6.3·	95.9	63 34.8	11.0·	99.9	63 10.1	15.5	103.8
2	63 55.7	5.3·	85.4	64 01.0	- 0.6·	89.5	63 57.6	4.2·	93.6	63 45.8	8.9·	97.7	63 25.6	13.5·	101.7
3	63 50.4	7.5·	83.2	64 00.4	2.8·	87.3	64 01.8	+ 2.1·	91.4	63 54.7	6.8·	95.5	63 39.1	11.5·	99.5
4	63 42.9	9.5·	80.9	63 57.6	4.8·	85.0	64 03.9	- 0.1·	89.1	64 01.5	4.7·	93.2	63 50.6	9.4·	97.3
5	63 33.4	-11.6·	78.7	63 52.8	- 7.0·	82.7	64 03.8	- 2.3·	86.8	64 06.2	+ 2.5·	90.9	64 00.0	+ 7.3·	95.0
6	63 21.8	13.5·	76.5	63 45.8	9.1·	80.5	64 01.5	4.4·	84.5	64 08.7	+ 0.4·	88.6	64 07.3	5.1·	92.7
7	63 08.3	15.6	74.4	63 36.7	11.1·	78.2	63 57.1	6.5·	82.2	64 09.1	- 1.8·	86.3	64 12.4	3.0·	90.5
8	62 52.7	17.3	72.2	63 25.6	13.1·	76.0	63 50.6	8.7·	80.0	64 07.3	4.0·	84.0	64 15.4	+ 0.9·	88.2
9	62 35.4	19.3	70.1	63 12.5	15.1	73.9	63 41.9	10.7·	77.7	64 03.3	6.1·	81.7	64 16.3	- 1.3·	85.9
10	62 16.1	-21.0	68.1	62 57.4	-17.0	71.7	63 31.2	-12.7	75.5	63 57.2	- 8.2·	79.5	64 15.0	- 3.5·	83.6
11	61 55.1	22.7	66.1	62 40.4	18.8	69.6	63 18.5	14.6·	73.3	63 49.0	10.2·	77.2	64 11.5	5.7·	81.3
12	61 32.4	24.3	64.1	62 21.6	20.7	67.6	63 03.9	16.7	71.2	63 38.8	12.3·	75.0	64 05.8	7.8·	79.0
13	61 08.1	25.9	62.2	62 00.9	22.3	65.5	62 47.2	18.4	69.1	63 26.5	14.3·	72.8	63 58.0	9.8·	76.7
14	60 42.2	27.4	60.4	61 38.6	24.0	63.6	62 28.8	20.3	67.0	63 12.2	16.3	70.6	63 48.2	12.0·	74.5
15	60 14.8	-28.8	58.6	61 14.6	-25.6	61.7	62 08.5	-22.0	65.0	62 55.9	-18.1	68.5	63 36.2	-13.9	72.3
16	59 46.0	30.2	56.8	60 49.0	27.0	59.8	61 46.5	23.7	63.0	62 37.8	19.9	66.4	63 22.3	15.9	70.1
17	59 15.8	31.5	55.1	60 22.0	28.6	58.0	61 22.8	25.2	61.1	62 17.9	21.7	64.4	63 06.4	17.8	67.9
18	58 44.3	32.7	53.5	59 53.4	29.9	56.2	60 57.6	26.8	59.2	61 56.2	23.4	62.4	62 48.6	19.7	65.8
19	58 11.6	33.9	51.9	59 23.5	31.2	54.5	60 30.8	28.3	57.4	61 32.8	25.0	60.5	62 28.9	21.4	63.8
20	57 37.7	-35.0	50.3	58 52.3	-32.5	52.8	60 02.5	-29.6	55.6	61 07.8	-26.6	58.6	62 07.5	-23.1	61.8
21	57 02.7	36.1	48.8	58 19.8	33.6	51.2	59 32.9	31.0	53.9	60 41.2	28.0	56.7	61 44.4	24.8	59.8
22	56 26.6	37.0	47.3	57 46.2	34.8	49.7	59 01.9	32.3	52.2	60 13.2	29.4	54.9	61 19.6	26.3	57.9
23	55 49.6	38.0	45.9	57 11.4	35.8	48.1	58 29.6	33.4	50.5	59 43.8	30.8	53.2	60 53.3	27.8	56.0
24	55 11.6	38.8	44.6	56 35.6	36.8	46.7	57 56.2	34.6	49.0	59 13.0	32.1	51.5	60 25.5	29.3	54.2
25	54 32.8	-39.7	43.2	55 58.8	-37.8	45.2	57 21.6	-35.6	47.4	58 40.9	-33.2	49.8	59 56.2	-30.6	52.5
26	53 53.1	40.5	41.9	55 21.0	38.7	43.9	56 46.0	36.7	46.0	58 07.7	34.4	48.3	59 25.6	31.9	50.8
27	53 12.6	41.3	40.7	54 42.3	39.5	42.5	56 09.3	37.6	44.5	57 33.3	35.6	46.7	58 53.7	33.1	49.1
28	52 31.3	41.9	39.5	54 02.8	40.4	41.2	55 31.7	38.6	43.1	56 57.7	36.5	45.2	58 20.6	34.3	47.5
29	51 49.4	42.7	38.3	53 22.4	41.1	40.0	54 53.1	39.4	41.8	56 21.2	37.5	43.8	57 46.3	35.4	46.0

Dec.	10° Hc	d	Z	12° Hc	d	Z	14° Hc	d	Z	16° Hc	d	Z	18° Hc	d	Z
0	62 16.1	+21.5	109.6	61 32.4	+25.4	113.1	60 42.2	+28.9	116.4	59 46.0	+32.2	119.5	58 44.3	+35.1	122.4
1	62 37.6	19.8	107.6	61 57.8	23.8	111.2	61 11.1	27.5	114.6	60 18.2	30.8	117.8	59 19.4	34.0	120.8
2	62 57.4	17.9	105.5	62 21.6	22.0	109.2	61 38.6	25.9	112.7	60 49.0	29.5	116.0	59 53.4	32.8	119.2
3	63 15.3	15.9	103.4	62 43.6	20.3	107.2	62 04.5	24.3	110.8	61 18.5	28.0	114.2	60 26.2	31.4	117.5
4	63 31.2	14.1·	101.3	63 03.9	18.4	105.1	62 28.8	22.6	108.8	61 46.5	26.5	112.4	60 57.6	30.0	115.7
5	63 45.3	+11.9·	99.1	63 22.3	+16.5	103.0	62 51.4	+20.8	106.8	62 13.0	+24.8	110.5	61 27.6	+28.6	113.9
6	63 57.2	10.0·	96.8	63 38.8	14.5·	100.9	63 12.2	18.9	104.8	62 37.8	23.1	108.5	61 56.2	27.0	112.1
7	64 07.2	7.8·	94.6	63 53.3	12.5·	98.7	63 31.1	17.1	102.6	63 00.9	21.4	106.5	62 23.2	25.4	110.2
8	64 15.0	5.6·	92.3	64 05.8	10.4·	96.4	63 48.2	15.0·	100.5	62 22.3	19.5	104.4	62 48.6	23.7	108.2
9	64 20.6	3.5·	90.0	64 16.2	8.3·	94.2	64 03.2	13.1·	98.3	63 41.8	17.6	102.3	63 12.3	21.9	106.2
10	64 24.1	+ 1.3·	87.7	64 24.5	+ 6.2·	91.9	64 16.3	+10.9·	96.0	63 59.4	+15.6·	100.1	63 34.2	+20.1	104.1
11	64 25.4	- 0.9·	85.4	64 30.7	4.0·	89.6	64 27.2	8.8·	93.8	64 15.0	13.8·	97.9	63 54.3	18.1	102.0
12	64 24.5	3.0·	83.1	64 34.7	+ 1.7·	87.3	64 36.0	6.7·	91.5	64 28.6	11.4·	95.7	64 12.4	16.2·	99.8
13	64 21.5	5.2·	80.8	64 36.4	- 0.4·	84.9	64 42.7	4.4·	89.1	64 40.0	9.4·	93.4	64 28.6	14.1·	97.6
14	64 16.3	7.4·	78.5	64 36.0	2.6·	82.6	64 47.1	2.2·	86.8	64 49.4	7.1·	91.1	64 42.7	12.0·	95.3
15	64 08.9	- 9.5·	76.2	64 33.4	- 4.8·	80.3	64 49.3	+ 0.1·	84.5	64 56.5	+ 4.9·	88.7	64 54.7	+ 9.9·	93.0
16	63 59.4	11.6·	73.9	64 28.6	7.0·	77.9	64 49.4	- 2.3·	82.1	65 01.4	2.7·	86.4	65 04.6	7.6·	90.7
17	63 47.8	13.6·	71.7	64 21.6	9.2·	75.6	64 47.1	4.4·	79.8	65 04.1	+ 0.5·	84.0	65 12.2	5.4·	88.3
18	63 34.2	15.6	69.5	64 12.4	11.2·	73.4	64 42.7	6.6·	77.4	65 04.6	- 1.9·	81.6	65 17.6	3.1·	85.9
19	63 18.6	17.5	67.3	64 01.2	13.3·	71.1	64 36.1	8.8·	75.1	65 02.7	4.0·	79.2	65 20.7	+ 0.9·	83.5
20	63 01.1	-19.4	65.2	63 47.9	-15.3·	68.9	64 27.3	-10.9·	72.8	64 58.7	- 6.3·	76.9	65 21.6	- 1.4·	81.1
21	62 41.7	21.2	63.1	63 32.6	17.3	66.7	64 16.4	13.1·	70.5	64 52.4	8.5·	74.5	65 20.2	3.7·	78.7
22	62 20.5	22.9	61.1	63 15.3	19.1	64.6	64 03.3	15.0	68.3	64 43.9	10.6·	72.2	65 16.5	6.0·	76.3
23	61 57.6	24.5	59.1	62 56.2	21.0	62.5	63 48.3	17.0·	66.1	64 33.3	12.8·	69.9	65 10.5	8.2·	74.0
24	61 33.1	26.2	57.2	62 35.2	22.7	60.4	63 31.3	19.0	63.9	64 20.5	14.8·	67.6	65 02.3	10.4·	71.6
25	61 06.9	-27.6	55.3	62 12.5	-24.4	58.4	63 12.3	-20.8	61.8	64 05.7	-16.8·	65.4	64 51.9	-12.5·	69.3
26	60 39.3	29.1	53.5	61 48.1	26.0	56.5	62 51.5	22.5	59.7	63 48.9	18.8	63.2	64 39.4	14.7·	67.0
27	60 10.2	30.5	51.7	61 22.1	27.5	54.6	62 29.0	24.3	57.7	63 30.1	20.7	61.1	64 24.7	16.6·	64.7
28	59 39.7	31.8	50.0	60 54.6	29.0	52.8	62 04.7	25.9	55.7	63 09.4	22.4	59.0	64 08.1	18.7	62.5
29	59 07.9	33.0	48.4	60 25.6	30.4	51.0	61 38.8	27.4	53.8	62 47.0	24.2	57.0	63 49.4	20.5	60.4

0°			2°			4°			6°			8°			Dec.
Hc	d	Z	Hc	d	Z	Hc	d	Z	Hc	d	Z	Hc	d	Z	
64 00.0	- 1.1•	90.0	63 55.7	- 5.8•	94.1	63 42.9	- 10.5•	98.1	63 21.8	- 14.9	102.1	62 52.7	- 19.2	105.9	0
63 58.9	3.2•	92.3	63 49.9	7.9•	96.4	63 32.4	12.5•	100.4	63 06.9	16.9	104.2	62 33.5	21.0	108.0	1
63 55.7	5.3•	94.6	63 42.0	10.0•	98.6	63 19.9	14.5	102.5	62 50.0	18.8	106.4	62 12.5	22.8	110.0	2
63 50.4	7.5•	96.8	63 32.0	12.1•	100.8	63 05.4	16.4	104.7	62 31.2	20.5	108.4	61 49.7	24.4	112.0	3
63 42.9	9.5•	99.1	63 19.9	14.0	103.0	62 49.0	18.2	106.8	62 10.7	22.3	110.5	61 25.3	25.9	113.9	4
63 33.4	-11.6•	101.3	63 05.9	-15.9	105.2	62 30.8	-20.1	108.9	61 48.4	-23.9	112.4	60 59.4	-27.5	115.8	5
63 21.8	13.5•	103.5	62 50.0	17.9	107.3	62 10.7	21.8	110.9	61 24.5	25.6	114.4	60 31.9	29.0	117.6	6
63 08.3	15.6	105.6	62 32.1	19.6	109.4	61 48.9	23.6	112.9	60 58.9	27.0	116.2	60 02.9	30.3	119.4	7
62 52.7	17.3	107.8	62 12.5	21.4	111.4	61 25.3	25.1	114.8	60 31.9	28.5	118.1	59 32.6	31.6	121.1	8
62 35.4	19.3	109.9	61 51.1	23.1	113.4	61 00.2	26.6	116.7	60 03.4	29.9	119.8	59 01.0	32.9	122.7	9
62 16.1	-21.0	111.9	61 28.0	-24.7	115.3	60 33.6	-28.1	118.6	59 33.5	-31.3	121.6	58 28.1	-34.0	124.4	10
61 55.1	22.7	113.9	61 03.3	26.3	117.2	60 05.5	29.5	120.3	59 02.2	32.4	123.2	57 54.1	35.1	125.9	11
61 32.4	24.3	115.9	60 37.0	27.7	119.1	59 36.0	30.9	122.1	58 29.8	33.7	124.9	57 19.0	36.2	127.4	12
61 08.1	25.9	117.8	60 09.3	29.2	120.9	59 05.1	32.1	123.8	57 56.1	34.8	126.4	56 42.8	37.2	128.9	13
60 42.2	27.4	119.6	59 40.1	30.5	122.6	58 33.0	33.3	125.4	57 21.3	35.8	128.0	56 05.6	38.2	130.3	14
60 14.8	-28.8	121.4	59 09.6	-31.8	124.3	57 59.7	-34.5	127.0	56 45.5	-36.9	129.4	55 27.4	-39.0	131.7	15
59 46.0	30.2	123.2	58 37.8	33.0	126.0	57 25.2	35.5	128.5	56 08.6	37.8	130.9	54 48.4	39.9	133.0	16
59 15.8	31.5	124.9	58 04.8	34.1	127.5	56 49.7	36.6	130.0	55 30.8	38.8	132.2	54 08.5	40.7	134.3	17
58 44.3	32.7	126.5	57 30.7	35.3	129.1	56 13.1	37.5	131.4	54 52.0	39.6	133.6	53 27.8	41.4	135.5	18
58 11.6	33.9	128.1	56 55.4	36.3	130.6	55 35.6	38.5	132.8	54 12.4	40.3	134.9	52 46.4	42.2	136.8	19
57 37.7	-35.0	129.7	56 19.1	-37.2	132.0	54 57.1	-39.3	134.2	53 32.1	-41.2	136.1	52 04.2	-42.8	137.9	20
57 02.7	36.1	131.2	55 41.9	38.2	133.4	54 17.8	40.1	135.5	52 50.9	41.9	137.3	51 21.4	43.4	139.1	21
56 26.6	37.0	132.7	55 03.7	39.1	134.8	53 37.7	40.9	136.7	52 09.0	42.5	138.5	50 38.0	44.0	140.1	22
55 49.6	38.0	134.1	54 24.6	39.9	136.1	52 56.8	41.6	138.0	51 26.5	43.2	139.7	49 54.0	44.6	141.2	23
55 11.6	38.8	135.4	53 44.7	40.7	137.4	52 15.2	42.4	139.1	50 43.3	43.8	140.8	49 09.4	45.2	142.2	24
54 32.8	-39.7	136.8	53 04.0	-41.4	138.6	51 32.8	-43.0	140.3	49 59.5	-44.4	141.8	48 24.2	-45.6	143.2	25
53 53.1	40.5	138.1	52 22.6	42.1	139.8	50 49.8	43.5	141.4	49 15.1	44.9	142.9	47 38.6	46.1	144.2	26
53 12.6	41.3	139.3	51 40.5	42.8	141.0	50 06.3	44.2	142.5	48 30.2	45.5	143.9	46 52.5	46.6	145.2	27
52 31.3	41.9	140.5	50 57.7	43.4	142.1	49 22.1	44.8	143.5	47 44.7	45.9	144.9	46 05.9	47.0	146.1	28
51 49.4	42.7	141.7	50 14.3	44.0	143.2	48 37.3	45.2	144.5	46 58.8	46.4	145.8	45 18.9	47.4	147.0	29

10°			12°			14°			16°			18°			Dec.
Hc	d	Z	Hc	d	Z	Hc	d	Z	Hc	d	Z	Hc	d	Z	
62 16.1	- 23.2	109.6	61 32.4	- 26.9	113.1	60 42.2	- 30.4	116.4	59 46.0	- 33.5	119.5	58 44.3	- 36.3	122.4	0
61 52.9	24.9	111.6	61 05.5	28.5	114.9	60 11.8	31.7	118.1	59 12.5	34.7	121.1	58 08.0	37.3	123.9	1
61 28.0	26.4	113.5	60 37.0	29.8	116.8	59 40.1	32.9	119.8	58 37.8	35.7	122.7	57 30.7	38.3	125.3	2
61 01.6	28.0	115.4	60 07.2	31.2	118.5	59 07.2	34.2	121.5	58 02.1	36.9	124.2	56 52.4	39.3	126.8	3
60 33.6	29.4	117.2	59 36.0	32.5	120.2	58 33.0	35.3	123.1	57 25.2	37.8	125.7	56 13.1	40.1	128.1	4
60 04.2	-30.7	118.9	59 03.5	-33.7	121.9	57 57.7	-36.4	124.6	56 47.4	-38.8	127.1	55 33.0	-41.0	129.5	5
59 33.5	32.1	120.6	58 29.8	34.9	123.5	57 21.3	37.4	126.1	56 08.6	39.7	128.5	54 52.0	41.7	130.7	6
59 01.4	33.3	122.3	57 54.9	35.9	125.0	56 43.9	38.3	127.5	55 28.9	40.5	129.8	54 10.3	42.5	132.0	7
58 28.1	34.4	123.9	57 19.0	37.0	126.5	56 05.6	39.3	128.9	54 48.4	41.4	131.1	53 27.8	43.2	133.2	8
57 53.7	35.5	125.4	56 42.0	38.0	127.9	55 26.3	40.1	130.3	54 07.0	42.0	132.4	52 44.6	43.8	134.3	9
57 18.2	-36.6	126.9	56 04.0	-38.8	129.3	54 46.2	-41.0	131.6	53 25.0	-42.8	133.6	52 00.8	-44.4	135.5	10
56 41.6	37.6	128.4	55 25.2	39.8	130.7	54 05.2	41.6	132.8	52 42.2	43.4	134.8	51 16.4	45.0	136.5	11
56 04.0	38.5	129.8	54 45.4	40.5	132.0	53 23.6	42.4	134.0	51 58.8	44.1	135.9	50 31.4	45.6	137.6	12
55 25.5	39.3	131.2	54 04.9	41.3	133.3	52 41.2	43.1	135.2	51 14.7	44.7	137.0	49 45.8	46.1	138.6	13
54 46.2	40.2	132.5	53 23.6	42.1	134.5	51 58.1	43.8	136.3	50 30.0	45.2	138.0	48 59.7	46.6	139.6	14
54 06.0	-41.0	133.8	52 41.5	-42.7	135.7	51 14.3	-44.3	137.4	49 44.8	-45.7	139.1	48 13.1	-47.0	140.5	15
53 25.0	41.8	135.0	51 58.8	43.4	136.8	50 30.0	44.9	138.5	48 59.1	46.3	140.1	47 26.1	47.4	141.5	16
52 43.2	42.4	136.2	51 15.4	44.0	137.9	49 45.1	45.4	139.5	48 12.8	46.7	141.0	46 38.7	47.9	142.4	17
52 00.8	43.1	137.4	50 31.4	44.6	139.0	48 59.7	45.9	140.5	47 26.1	47.1	141.9	45 50.8	48.3	143.2	18
51 17.7	43.7	138.5	49 46.8	45.2	140.1	48 13.8	46.4	141.5	46 39.0	47.6	142.9	45 02.5	48.6	144.1	19
50 34.0	-44.3	139.6	49 01.6	-45.6	141.1	47 27.4	-46.9	142.5	45 51.4	-48.0	143.7	44 13.9	-49.0	144.9	20
49 49.7	44.8	140.6	48 16.0	46.1	142.1	46 40.5	47.3	143.4	45 03.4	48.3	144.6	43 24.9	49.3	145.7	21
49 04.9	45.4	141.6	47 29.9	46.6	143.0	45 53.2	47.7	144.3	44 15.1	48.7	145.4	42 35.6	49.6	146.5	22
48 19.5	45.9	142.6	46 43.3	47.1	143.9	45 05.5	48.0	145.1	43 26.4	49.0	146.2	41 46.0	49.8	147.2	23
47 33.6	46.3	143.6	45 56.2	47.4	144.8	44 17.5	48.5	146.0	42 37.4	49.4	147.0	40 56.2	50.2	148.0	24
46 47.3	-46.8	144.5	45 08.8	-47.8	145.7	43 29.0	-48.8	146.8	41 48.0	-49.6	147.8	40 06.0	-50.5	148.7	25
46 00.5	47.2	145.4	44 21.0	48.2	146.6	42 40.2	49.1	147.6	40 58.4	49.9	148.5	39 15.5	50.6	149.4	26
45 13.3	47.6	146.3	43 32.8	48.6	147.4	41 51.1	49.4	148.4	40 08.5	50.2	149.3	38 24.9	51.0	150.1	27
44 25.7	48.0	147.2	42 44.2	48.8	148.2	41 01.7	49.7	149.1	39 18.3	50.5	150.0	37 33.9	51.1	150.8	28
43 37.7	48.4	148.0	41 55.4	49.2	149.0	40 12.0	49.9	149.9	38 27.8	50.7	150.7	36 42.8	51.3	151.4	29

Dec.	20° Hc	d	Z	22° Hc	d	Z	24° Hc	d	Z	26° Hc	d	Z	28° Hc	d	Z
°	° ′	′	°	° ′	′	°	° ′	′	°	° ′	′	°	° ′	′	°
0	57 37.7	+37.8	125.0	56 26.6	+40.3	127.5	55 11.6	+42.4	129.8	53 53.1	+44.3	131.9	52 31.3	+46.0	133.9
1	58 15.5	36.8	123.6	57 06.9	39.3	126.2	55 54.0	41.6	128.6	54 37.4	43.6	130.8	53 17.3	45.5	132.8
2	58 52.3	35.7	122.1	57 46.2	38.3	124.8	56 35.6	40.7	127.3	55 21.0	42.9	129.6	54 02.8	44.8	131.7
3	59 28.0	34.5	120.5	58 24.5	37.4	123.3	57 16.3	39.9	125.9	56 03.9	42.1	128.4	54 47.6	44.1	130.6
4	60 02.5	33.3	118.9	59 01.9	36.2	121.8	57 56.2	38.9	124.5	56 46.0	41.3	127.1	55 31.7	43.4	129.4
5	60 35.8	+32.0	117.2	59 38.1	+35.1	120.2	58 35.1	+37.9	123.1	57 27.3	+40.4	125.7	56 15.1	+42.6	128.2
6	61 07.8	30.6	115.5	60 13.2	33.9	118.6	59 13.0	36.8	121.6	58 07.7	39.4	124.3	56 57.7	41.9	126.9
7	61 38.4	29.1	113.7	60 47.1	32.5	116.9	59 49.8	35.7	120.0	58 47.1	38.5	122.9	57 39.6	41.0	125.6
8	62 07.5	27.6	111.8	61 19.6	31.2	115.2	60 25.5	34.4	118.4	59 25.6	37.4	121.4	58 20.6	40.0	124.2
9	62 35.1	26.0	109.9	61 50.8	29.7	113.4	60 59.9	33.2	116.7	60 03.0	36.3	119.9	59 00.6	39.1	122.8
10	63 01.1	+24.3	107.9	62 20.5	+28.2	111.6	61 33.1	+31.8	115.0	60 39.3	+35.0	118.2	59 39.7	+38.0	121.3
11	63 25.4	22.5	105.9	62 48.7	26.6	109.6	62 04.9	30.3	113.2	61 14.3	33.8	116.6	60 17.7	36.9	119.7
12	63 47.9	20.6	103.8	63 15.3	24.9	107.7	62 35.2	28.8	111.4	61 48.1	32.4	114.8	60 54.6	35.7	118.1
13	64 08.5	18.8	101.7	63 40.2	23.1	105.6	63 04.0	27.3	109.4	62 20.5	31.0	113.0	61 30.3	34.4	116.5
14	64 27.3	16.7*	99.5	64 03.3	21.3	103.5	63 31.3	25.5	107.5	62 51.5	29.5	111.2	62 04.7	33.1	114.7
15	64 44.0	+14.7*	97.2	64 24.6	+19.3*	101.4	63 56.8	+23.7	105.4	63 21.0	+27.9	109.3	62 37.8	+31.6	112.9
16	64 58.7	12.5*	94.9	64 43.9	17.3*	99.2	64 20.5	21.9	103.3	63 48.9	26.1	107.3	63 09.4	30.2	111.1
17	65 11.2	10.4*	92.6	65 01.2	15.3*	96.9	64 42.4	19.9*	101.1	64 15.0	24.4	105.2	63 39.6	28.5	109.1
18	65 21.6	8.1*	90.3	65 16.5	13.0*	94.6	65 02.3	17.9*	98.9	64 39.4	22.5	103.1	64 08.1	26.8	107.1
19	65 29.7	5.9*	87.9	65 29.5	10.9*	92.3	65 20.2	15.8*	96.6	65 01.9	20.5*	100.9	64 34.9	25.0	105.1
20	65 35.6	+3.6*	85.5	65 40.4	+8.6*	89.9	65 36.0	+13.6*	94.3	65 22.4	+18.5*	98.7	64 59.9	+23.2	102.9
21	65 39.2	+1.2*	83.1	65 49.0	6.4*	87.5	65 49.6	11.4*	91.9	65 40.9	16.4*	96.4	65 23.1	21.1*	100.7
22	65 40.4	-1.0*	80.6	65 55.4	4.0*	85.1	66 01.0	9.1*	89.5	65 57.3	14.2*	94.0	65 44.2	19.1*	98.5
23	65 39.4	3.4*	78.2	65 59.4	+1.6*	82.6	66 10.1	6.8*	87.1	66 11.5	11.9*	91.6	66 03.3	17.0*	96.1
24	65 36.0	5.7*	75.8	66 01.0	-0.7*	80.1	66 16.9	4.5*	84.6	66 23.4	9.6*	89.2	66 20.3	14.7*	93.8
25	65 30.3	-7.9*	73.4	66 00.3	-3.0*	77.7	66 21.4	+2.0*	82.2	66 33.0	+7.2*	86.7	66 35.0	+12.5*	91.3
26	65 22.4	10.1*	71.0	65 57.3	5.4*	75.2	66 23.4	-0.4*	79.7	66 40.2	4.9*	84.2	66 47.5	10.1*	88.9
27	65 12.3	12.4*	68.6	65 51.9	7.7*	72.8	66 23.0	2.7*	77.2	66 45.1	+2.4*	81.7	66 57.6	7.6*	86.4
28	64 59.9	14.5*	66.3	65 44.2	9.9*	70.4	66 20.3	5.1*	74.7	66 47.5	-0.1*	79.2	67 05.2	5.3*	83.8
29	64 45.4	16.5*	64.0	65 34.3	12.2*	68.0	66 15.2	7.5*	72.2	66 47.4	2.4*	76.6	67 10.5	2.7*	81.3

Dec.	30° Hc	d	Z	32° Hc	d	Z	34° Hc	d	Z	36° Hc	d	Z	38° Hc	d	Z
°	° ′	′	°	° ′	′	°	° ′	′	°	° ′	′	°	° ′	′	°
0	51 06.7	+47.6	135.7	49 39.6	+48.9	137.4	48 10.2	+50.2	138.9	46 38.8	+51.3	140.3	45 05.6	+52.2	141.6
1	51 54.3	47.0	134.7	50 28.5	48.5	136.5	49 00.4	49.7	138.1	47 30.1	50.9	139.6	45 57.8	51.9	140.9
2	52 41.3	46.5	133.7	51 17.0	48.0	135.5	49 50.1	49.4	137.2	48 21.0	50.5	138.8	46 49.7	51.7	140.2
3	53 27.8	45.9	132.7	52 05.0	47.5	134.6	50 39.5	48.9	136.3	49 11.5	50.2	137.9	47 41.4	51.3	139.4
4	54 13.7	45.4	131.6	52 52.5	47.0	133.6	51 28.4	48.5	135.4	50 01.7	49.9	137.1	48 32.7	51.0	138.7
5	54 59.1	+44.6	130.4	53 39.5	+46.5	132.5	52 16.9	+48.1	134.5	50 51.6	+49.4	136.2	49 23.7	+50.7	137.9
6	55 43.7	44.0	129.3	54 26.0	45.8	131.4	53 05.0	47.5	133.5	51 41.0	49.0	135.3	50 14.4	50.3	137.0
7	56 27.7	43.2	128.0	55 11.8	45.2	130.3	53 52.5	46.9	132.4	52 30.0	48.5	134.4	51 04.7	49.9	136.2
8	57 10.9	42.4	126.8	55 57.0	44.5	129.2	54 39.4	46.4	131.4	53 18.5	48.1	133.4	51 54.6	49.5	135.3
9	57 53.3	41.6	125.5	56 41.5	43.8	128.0	55 25.8	45.8	130.3	54 06.6	47.5	132.4	52 44.1	49.1	134.4
10	58 34.9	+40.6	124.1	57 25.3	+43.0	126.7	56 11.6	+45.1	129.1	54 54.1	+46.9	131.3	53 33.2	+48.6	133.4
11	59 15.5	39.7	122.7	58 08.3	42.2	125.4	56 56.7	44.3	127.9	55 41.0	46.3	130.2	54 21.8	48.0	132.5
12	59 55.2	38.6	121.2	58 50.5	41.3	124.0	57 41.0	43.7	126.7	56 27.3	45.7	129.1	55 09.8	47.5	131.4
13	60 33.8	37.6	119.6	59 31.8	40.3	122.6	58 24.7	42.5	125.4	57 13.0	45.0	127.9	55 57.3	46.9	130.3
14	61 11.4	36.3	118.0	60 12.1	39.3	121.1	59 07.4	42.0	124.0	57 58.0	44.2	126.7	56 44.2	46.3	129.1
15	61 47.7	+35.1	116.4	60 51.4	+38.2	119.6	59 49.4	+40.9	122.6	58 42.2	+43.5	125.4	57 30.5	+45.6	128.0
16	62 22.8	33.8	114.6	61 29.6	37.0	118.0	60 30.3	40.0	121.1	59 25.7	42.5	124.1	58 16.1	44.9	126.8
17	62 56.6	32.3	112.8	62 06.6	35.8	116.3	61 10.3	38.9	119.6	60 08.2	41.7	122.8	59 01.0	44.1	125.5
18	63 28.9	30.8	111.0	62 42.4	34.4	114.6	61 49.2	37.7	118.0	60 49.9	40.6	121.2	59 45.1	43.2	124.1
19	63 59.7	29.2	109.0	63 16.8	33.1	112.8	62 26.9	36.5	116.4	61 30.5	39.6	119.7	60 28.3	42.3	122.8
20	64 28.9	+27.5	107.0	63 49.9	+31.5	110.9	63 03.4	+35.1	114.6	62 10.1	+38.4	118.1	61 10.6	+41.4	121.3
21	64 56.4	25.7	104.9	64 21.4	29.9	109.0	63 38.5	33.8	112.8	62 48.5	37.2	116.4	61 52.0	40.3	119.8
22	65 22.1	23.8	102.8	64 51.3	28.1	107.0	64 12.3	32.2	110.9	63 25.7	35.9	114.7	62 32.3	39.2	118.2
23	65 45.9	21.8*	100.6	65 19.4	26.4	104.9	64 44.5	30.6	109.0	64 01.6	34.5	112.9	63 11.5	37.9	116.5
24	66 07.7	19.7*	98.3	65 45.8	24.5	102.7	65 15.1	28.9	106.9	64 36.1	33.0	111.0	63 49.4	36.7	114.8
25	66 27.4	+17.6*	95.9	66 10.3	+22.5*	100.4	65 44.0	+27.1	104.8	65 09.1	+31.3	109.0	64 26.1	+35.2	113.0
26	66 45.0	15.3*	93.5	66 32.8	20.3*	98.1	66 11.1	25.2*	102.6	65 40.4	29.7	107.0	65 01.3	33.7	111.1
27	67 00.3	12.9*	91.1	66 53.1	18.2*	95.8	66 36.3	23.1*	100.4	66 10.1	27.8	104.8	65 35.0	32.2	109.1
28	67 13.2	10.6*	88.6	67 11.3	15.9*	93.3	66 59.4	21.0*	98.0	66 37.9	25.9*	102.6	66 07.2	30.4	107.0
29	67 23.8	8.1*	86.0	67 27.2	13.5*	90.8	67 20.4	18.8*	95.6	67 03.8	23.8*	100.3	66 37.6	28.5	104.9

20°			22°			24°			26°			28°			Dec.
Hc	d	Z	Hc	d	Z	Hc	d	Z	Hc	d	Z	Hc	d	Z	
° ′	′	°	° ′	′	°	° ′	′	°	° ′	′	°	° ′	′	°	°
57 37.7	-38.8	125.0	56 26.6	-41.0	127.5	55 11.6	-43.1	129.8	53 53.1	-45.0	131.9	52 31.3	-46.5	133.9	0
56 58.9	39.8	126.5	55 45.6	41.9	128.8	54 28.5	43.8	131.0	53 08.1	45.5	133.1	51 44.8	47.1	134.9	1
56 19.1	40.5	127.8	55 03.7	42.7	130.1	53 44.7	44.5	132.2	52 22.6	46.1	134.1	50 57.7	47.6	135.9	2
55 38.6	41.5	129.1	54 21.0	43.3	131.3	53 00.2	45.0	133.3	51 36.5	46.7	135.2	50 10.1	48.0	136.9	3
54 57.1	42.1	130.4	53 37.7	44.0	132.5	52 15.2	45.7	134.4	50 49.8	47.1	136.2	49 22.1	48.5	137.8	4
54 15.0	-42.9	131.6	52 53.7	-44.7	133.6	51 29.5	-46.2	135.5	50 02.7	-47.6	137.2	48 33.6	-48.9	138.7	5
53 32.1	43.6	132.8	52 09.0	45.2	134.7	50 43.3	46.7	136.5	49 15.1	48.1	138.1	47 44.7	49.2	139.6	6
52 48.5	44.3	134.0	51 23.8	45.8	135.8	49 56.6	47.2	137.5	48 27.0	48.4	139.0	46 55.5	49.6	140.4	7
52 04.2	44.8	135.1	50 38.0	46.3	136.8	49 09.4	47.7	138.4	47 38.6	48.9	139.9	46 05.9	50.0	141.2	8
51 19.4	45.4	136.1	49 51.7	46.8	137.8	48 21.7	48.1	139.3	46 49.7	49.2	140.7	45 15.9	50.2	142.0	9
50 34.0	-45.9	137.2	49 04.9	-47.3	138.8	47 33.6	-48.5	140.2	46 00.5	-49.6	141.6	44 25.7	-50.6	142.8	10
49 48.1	46.5	138.2	48 17.6	47.7	139.7	46 45.1	48.9	141.1	45 10.9	49.9	142.4	43 35.1	50.9	143.6	11
49 01.6	46.9	139.2	47 29.9	48.2	140.6	45 56.2	49.2	141.9	44 21.0	50.2	143.2	42 44.2	51.1	144.3	12
48 14.7	47.3	140.1	46 41.7	48.5	141.5	45 07.0	49.5	142.7	43 30.8	50.6	143.9	41 53.1	51.4	145.0	13
47 27.4	47.8	141.0	45 53.2	48.9	142.3	44 17.5	49.9	143.5	42 40.2	50.8	144.7	41 01.7	51.6	145.7	14
46 39.6	-48.2	141.8	45 04.3	-49.2	143.2	43 27.6	-50.2	144.3	41 49.4	-51.0	145.4	40 10.1	-51.8	146.3	15
45 51.4	48.6	142.8	44 15.1	49.6	144.0	42 37.4	50.5	145.1	40 58.4	51.3	146.1	39 18.3	52.1	147.0	16
45 02.8	48.9	143.6	43 25.5	49.9	144.7	41 46.9	50.7	145.8	40 07.1	51.6	146.8	38 26.2	52.3	147.6	17
44 13.9	49.3	144.4	42 35.6	50.1	145.5	40 56.2	51.0	146.5	39 15.5	51.7	147.4	37 33.9	52.4	148.3	18
43 24.6	49.5	145.2	41 45.5	50.5	146.2	40 05.2	51.2	147.2	38 23.8	52.0	148.1	36 41.5	52.6	148.9	19
42 35.1	-49.9	146.0	40 55.0	-50.7	147.0	39 13.9	-51.5	147.9	37 31.8	-52.2	148.7	35 48.9	-52.9	149.5	20
41 45.2	50.2	146.7	40 04.3	50.9	147.7	38 22.4	51.7	148.5	36 39.6	52.3	149.3	34 56.0	52.9	150.1	21
40 55.0	50.4	147.5	39 13.4	51.2	148.4	37 30.7	51.8	149.2	35 47.3	52.5	149.9	34 03.1	53.1	150.6	22
40 04.6	50.7	148.2	38 22.2	51.5	149.0	36 38.9	52.1	149.8	34 54.8	52.7	150.5	33 10.0	53.3	151.2	23
39 13.9	50.9	148.9	37 30.7	51.6	149.7	35 46.8	52.3	150.4	34 02.1	52.9	151.1	32 16.7	53.4	151.7	24
38 23.0	-51.2	149.5	36 39.1	-51.8	150.3	34 54.5	-52.4	151.0	33 09.2	-53.0	151.7	31 23.3	-53.6	152.3	25
37 31.8	51.4	150.2	35 47.3	52.0	150.9	34 02.1	52.7	151.6	32 16.2	53.2	152.2	30 29.7	53.6	152.8	26
36 40.4	51.5	150.9	34 55.3	52.2	151.6	33 09.4	52.7	152.2	31 23.0	53.3	152.8	29 36.1	53.8	153.3	27
35 48.9	51.8	151.5	34 03.1	52.4	152.1	32 16.7	52.9	152.8	30 29.7	53.4	153.3	28 42.3	53.9	153.8	28
34 57.1	52.0	152.1	33 10.7	52.5	152.7	31 23.8	53.1	153.3	29 36.3	53.5	153.8	27 48.4	54.0	154.3	29

30°			32°			34°			36°			38°			Dec.
Hc	d	Z	Hc	d	Z	Hc	d	Z	Hc	d	Z	Hc	d	Z	
° ′	′	°	° ′	′	°	° ′	′	°	° ′	′	°	° ′	′	°	°
51 06.7	-48.0	135.7	49 39.6	-49.3	137.4	48 10.2	-50.4	138.9	46 38.8	-51.5	140.3	45 05.6	-52.4	141.6	0
50 18.7	48.4	136.7	48 50.3	49.7	138.2	47 19.8	50.8	139.7	45 47.3	51.8	141.1	44 13.2	52.7	142.3	1
49 30.3	48.9	137.6	48 00.6	50.1	139.1	46 29.0	51.2	140.5	44 55.5	52.0	141.8	43 20.5	52.9	143.0	2
48 41.4	49.3	138.5	47 10.5	50.4	139.9	45 37.8	51.4	141.2	44 03.5	52.4	142.5	42 27.6	53.2	143.6	3
47 52.1	49.7	139.3	46 20.1	50.7	140.7	44 46.4	51.6	142.0	43 11.1	52.5	143.1	41 34.4	53.3	144.2	4
47 02.4	-50.0	140.1	45 29.4	-51.0	141.5	43 54.8	-52.0	142.7	42 18.6	-52.7	143.8	40 41.1	-53.5	144.8	5
46 12.4	50.3	141.0	44 38.4	51.3	142.2	43 02.8	52.1	143.4	41 25.9	53.0	144.4	39 47.6	53.7	145.4	6
45 22.1	50.6	141.7	43 47.1	51.5	142.9	42 10.7	52.4	144.0	40 32.9	53.2	145.1	38 53.9	53.8	146.0	7
44 31.5	50.9	142.5	42 55.6	51.9	143.6	41 18.3	52.7	144.7	39 39.7	53.3	145.7	38 00.1	54.0	146.6	8
43 40.6	51.3	143.2	42 03.7	52.0	144.3	40 25.6	52.8	145.3	38 46.4	53.5	146.3	37 06.1	54.2	147.1	9
42 49.3	-51.4	143.9	41 11.7	-52.3	145.0	39 32.8	-53.0	146.0	37 52.9	-53.7	146.8	36 11.9	-54.3	147.7	10
41 57.9	51.7	144.6	40 19.4	52.5	145.6	38 39.8	53.2	146.6	36 59.2	53.9	147.4	35 17.6	54.4	148.2	11
41 06.2	52.0	145.3	39 26.9	52.7	146.3	37 46.6	53.4	147.1	36 05.3	53.9	148.0	34 23.2	54.5	148.7	12
40 14.2	52.1	146.0	38 34.2	52.8	146.9	36 53.2	53.5	147.7	35 11.4	54.2	148.5	33 28.7	54.7	149.2	13
39 22.1	52.4	146.6	37 41.4	53.1	147.5	35 59.7	53.7	148.3	34 17.2	54.2	149.0	32 34.0	54.8	149.7	14
38 29.7	-52.6	147.2	36 48.3	-53.2	148.1	35 06.0	-53.8	148.8	33 23.0	-54.4	149.5	31 39.2	-54.9	150.2	15
37 37.1	52.7	147.9	35 55.1	53.4	148.6	34 12.2	54.0	149.4	32 28.6	54.5	150.0	30 44.3	55.0	150.6	16
36 44.4	52.9	148.5	35 01.7	53.5	149.2	33 18.2	54.0	149.9	31 34.1	54.6	150.5	29 49.3	55.1	151.1	17
35 51.5	53.1	149.0	34 08.2	53.7	149.8	32 24.2	54.3	150.4	30 39.5	54.7	151.0	28 54.2	55.1	151.6	18
34 58.4	53.3	149.6	33 14.5	53.8	150.3	31 29.9	54.3	150.9	29 44.8	54.8	151.5	27 59.1	55.3	152.0	19
34 05.1	-53.4	150.2	32 20.7	-54.0	150.8	30 35.6	-54.4	151.4	28 50.0	-54.9	152.0	27 03.8	-55.3	152.4	20
33 11.7	53.5	150.7	31 26.7	54.0	151.3	29 41.2	54.6	151.9	27 55.1	55.0	152.4	26 08.5	55.4	152.9	21
32 18.2	53.7	151.3	30 32.7	54.2	151.8	28 46.6	54.6	152.4	27 00.1	55.1	152.9	25 13.1	55.5	153.3	22
31 24.5	53.8	151.8	29 38.5	54.3	152.3	27 52.0	54.8	152.8	26 05.0	55.2	153.3	24 17.6	55.6	153.7	23
30 30.7	53.9	152.3	28 44.2	54.4	152.8	26 57.2	54.8	153.3	25 09.8	55.2	153.7	23 22.0	55.6	154.1	24
29 36.8	-54.0	152.8	27 49.8	-54.5	153.3	26 02.4	-54.9	153.8	24 14.6	-55.3	154.2	22 26.4	-55.7	154.5	25
28 42.8	54.2	153.3	26 55.3	54.6	153.8	25 07.5	55.0	154.2	23 19.3	55.4	154.6	21 30.7	55.8	154.9	26
27 48.6	54.2	153.8	26 00.7	54.6	154.2	24 12.5	55.1	154.6	22 23.9	55.5	155.0	20 35.0	55.8	155.3	27
26 54.4	54.4	154.3	25 06.1	54.8	154.7	23 17.4	55.1	155.1	21 28.4	55.5	155.4	19 39.2	55.9	155.7	28
26 00.0	54.4	154.7	24 11.3	54.8	155.1	22 22.3	55.2	155.5	20 32.9	55.5	155.8	18 43.3	55.9	156.1	29

Dec.	40° Hc	d	Z	42° Hc	d	Z	44° Hc	d	Z	46° Hc	d	Z	48° Hc	d	Z
°	° ′	′	°	° ′	′	°	° ′	′	°	° ′	′	°	° ′	′	°
0	43 30.8	+53.0	142.8	41 54.5	+53.8	143.9	40 16.9	+54.5	144.9	38 38.1	+55.2	145.9	36 58.3	+55.7	146.7
1	44 23.8	52.9	142.2	42 48.3	53.7	143.3	41 11.4	54.4	144.4	39 33.3	55.0	145.4	37 54.0	55.7	146.3
2	45 16.7	52.6	141.5	43 42.0	53.4	142.7	42 05.8	54.2	143.8	40 28.3	54.8	144.8	38 49.7	55.5	145.8
3	46 09.3	52.3	140.8	44 35.4	53.3	142.1	43 00.0	54.1	143.2	41 23.2	54.8	144.3	39 45.2	55.3	145.3
4	47 01.6	52.1	140.1	45 28.7	53.0	141.4	43 54.1	53.8	142.6	42 18.0	54.6	143.8	40 40.6	55.2	144.8
5	47 53.7	+51.8	139.4	46 21.7	+52.8	140.7	44 47.9	+53.7	142.0	43 12.6	+54.4	143.2	41 35.8	+55.2	144.3
6	48 45.5	51.5	138.6	47 14.5	52.5	140.0	45 41.6	53.4	141.4	44 07.0	54.3	142.6	42 31.0	54.9	143.7
7	49 37.0	51.1	137.8	48 07.0	52.2	139.3	46 35.0	53.2	140.7	45 01.3	54.0	142.0	43 25.9	54.8	143.2
8	50 28.1	50.8	137.0	48 59.2	51.9	138.6	47 28.2	52.9	140.0	45 55.3	53.8	141.4	44 20.7	54.7	142.6
9	51 18.9	50.4	136.2	49 51.1	51.7	137.8	48 21.1	52.7	139.3	46 49.1	53.7	140.7	45 15.4	54.4	142.0
10	52 09.3	+50.0	135.3	50 42.8	+51.2	137.0	49 13.8	+52.4	138.6	47 42.8	+53.4	140.1	46 09.8	+54.3	141.4
11	52 59.3	49.6	134.4	51 34.0	51.0	136.2	50 06.2	52.1	137.9	48 36.2	53.1	139.4	47 04.1	54.0	140.8
12	53 48.9	49.1	133.4	52 25.0	50.5	135.3	50 58.3	51.8	137.1	49 29.3	52.8	138.7	47 58.1	53.8	140.2
13	54 38.0	48.6	132.4	53 15.5	50.1	134.4	51 50.1	51.4	136.3	50 22.1	52.6	138.0	48 51.9	53.6	139.5
14	55 26.6	48.1	131.4	54 05.6	49.6	133.5	52 41.5	51.1	135.4	51 14.7	52.3	137.2	49 45.5	53.3	138.8
15	56 14.7	+47.5	130.4	54 55.2	+49.2	132.5	53 32.6	+50.6	134.6	52 07.0	+51.9	136.4	50 38.8	+53.1	138.1
16	57 02.2	46.9	129.2	55 44.4	48.7	131.5	54 23.2	50.2	133.6	52 58.9	51.6	135.6	51 31.9	52.8	137.4
17	57 49.1	46.2	128.1	56 33.1	48.1	130.5	55 13.4	49.8	132.7	53 50.5	51.2	134.7	52 24.7	52.4	136.6
18	58 35.3	45.6	126.9	57 21.2	47.5	129.4	56 03.2	49.3	131.7	54 41.7	50.8	133.8	53 17.1	52.1	135.8
19	59 20.9	44.7	125.6	58 08.7	46.9	128.2	56 52.5	48.7	130.7	55 32.5	50.3	132.9	54 09.2	51.8	134.9
20	60 05.6	+43.9	124.3	58 55.6	+46.2	127.0	57 41.2	+48.1	129.6	56 22.8	+49.9	131.9	55 01.0	+51.3	134.1
21	60 49.5	43.1	122.9	59 41.8	45.4	125.8	58 29.3	47.6	128.5	57 12.7	49.3	130.9	55 52.3	50.9	133.2
22	61 32.6	42.0	121.5	60 27.2	44.7	124.5	59 16.9	46.8	127.3	58 02.0	48.8	129.8	56 43.2	50.5	132.2
23	62 14.6	41.1	119.9	61 11.9	43.7	123.1	60 03.7	46.2	126.0	58 50.8	48.2	128.7	57 33.7	50.0	131.2
24	62 55.7	39.9	118.4	61 55.6	42.8	121.7	60 49.9	45.3	124.7	59 39.0	47.6	127.6	58 23.7	49.4	130.2
25	63 35.6	+38.7	116.7	62 38.4	+41.8	120.2	61 35.2	+44.5	123.4	60 26.6	+46.8	126.4	59 13.1	+48.9	129.1
26	64 14.3	37.5	115.0	63 20.2	40.7	118.6	62 19.7	43.6	122.0	61 13.4	46.1	125.1	60 02.0	48.3	127.9
27	64 51.8	36.0	113.1	64 00.9	39.5	116.9	63 03.3	42.5	120.5	61 59.5	45.2	123.7	60 50.3	47.5	126.7
28	65 27.8	34.5	111.2	64 40.4	38.3	115.2	63 45.8	41.5	118.9	62 44.7	44.4	122.3	61 37.8	46.8	125.5
29	66 02.3	32.9	109.3	65 18.7	36.8	113.4	64 27.3	40.4	117.2	63 29.1	43.4	120.8	62 24.6	46.1	124.1

Dec.	50° Hc	d	Z	52° Hc	d	Z	54° Hc	d	Z	56° Hc	d	Z	58° Hc	d	Z
°	° ′	′	°	° ′	′	°	° ′	′	°	° ′	′	°	° ′	′	°
0	35 17.5	+56.2	147.5	33 35.8	+56.8	148.2	31 53.4	+57.2	148.9	30 10.3	+57.5	149.5	28 26.6	+57.8	150.1
1	36 13.7	56.2	147.1	34 32.6	56.6	147.9	32 50.6	57.0	148.6	31 07.8	57.5	149.2	29 24.4	57.8	149.8
2	37 09.9	56.1	146.6	35 29.2	56.6	147.4	33 47.6	57.1	148.2	32 05.3	57.4	148.9	30 22.2	57.8	149.5
3	38 06.0	56.0	146.2	36 25.8	56.5	147.0	34 44.7	56.9	147.8	33 02.7	57.4	148.5	31 20.0	57.7	149.2
4	39 02.0	55.8	145.7	37 22.3	56.3	146.6	35 41.6	56.9	147.4	34 00.1	57.2	148.2	32 17.7	57.7	148.8
5	39 57.8	+55.8	145.3	38 18.6	+56.3	146.2	36 38.5	+56.7	147.0	34 57.3	+57.3	147.8	33 15.4	+57.8	148.5
6	40 53.6	55.6	144.8	39 14.9	56.2	145.7	37 35.2	56.7	146.6	35 54.6	57.1	147.4	34 13.0	57.6	148.2
7	41 49.2	55.4	144.3	40 11.1	56.1	145.3	38 31.9	56.6	146.2	36 51.7	57.1	147.1	35 10.6	57.5	147.8
8	42 44.6	55.4	143.8	41 07.2	56.0	144.8	39 28.5	56.5	145.8	37 48.8	57.0	146.7	36 08.1	57.4	147.5
9	43 40.0	55.2	143.2	42 03.2	55.8	144.3	40 25.0	56.5	145.3	38 45.8	56.9	146.3	37 05.5	57.3	147.1
10	44 35.2	+55.0	142.7	42 59.0	+55.7	143.8	41 21.5	+56.3	144.9	39 42.7	+56.8	145.9	38 02.8	+57.3	146.8
11	45 30.2	54.8	142.1	43 54.7	55.5	143.3	42 17.8	56.1	144.4	40 39.5	56.8	145.4	39 00.1	57.3	146.4
12	46 25.0	54.7	141.5	44 50.2	55.5	142.8	43 13.9	56.1	143.9	41 36.3	56.6	145.0	39 57.4	57.1	146.0
13	47 19.7	54.5	140.9	45 45.7	55.2	142.2	44 10.0	55.9	143.5	42 32.9	56.5	144.6	40 54.5	57.0	145.6
14	48 14.2	54.2	140.3	46 40.9	55.1	141.7	45 05.9	55.8	142.9	43 29.4	56.4	144.1	41 51.5	57.0	145.2
15	49 08.4	+54.1	139.7	47 36.0	+54.9	141.1	46 01.7	+55.7	142.4	44 25.8	+56.3	143.6	42 48.5	+56.9	144.7
16	50 02.5	53.8	139.0	48 30.9	54.7	140.5	46 57.4	55.4	141.9	45 22.1	56.2	143.1	43 45.4	56.7	144.3
17	50 56.3	53.5	138.3	49 25.6	54.4	139.9	47 52.8	55.3	141.3	46 18.3	56.0	142.6	44 42.1	56.7	143.9
18	51 49.8	53.2	137.6	50 20.0	54.3	139.2	48 48.1	55.2	140.7	47 14.3	55.9	142.1	45 38.8	56.5	143.4
19	52 43.0	53.0	136.8	51 14.3	54.0	138.5	49 43.3	54.9	140.1	48 10.2	55.7	141.6	46 35.3	56.4	142.9
20	53 36.0	+52.6	136.0	52 08.3	+53.8	137.8	50 38.2	+54.7	139.5	49 05.9	+55.6	141.0	47 31.7	+56.3	142.4
21	54 28.6	52.3	135.2	53 02.1	53.4	137.1	51 32.9	54.5	138.8	50 01.5	55.3	140.4	48 28.0	56.1	141.9
22	55 20.9	52.0	134.4	53 55.5	53.2	136.3	52 27.4	54.2	138.2	50 56.8	55.2	139.8	49 24.1	56.0	141.3
23	56 12.9	51.5	133.5	54 48.7	52.9	135.6	53 21.6	54.0	137.5	51 52.0	55.0	139.2	50 20.1	55.8	140.8
24	57 04.4	51.1	132.5	55 41.6	52.5	134.7	54 15.6	53.7	136.7	52 47.0	54.7	138.5	51 15.9	55.6	140.2
25	57 55.5	+50.6	131.6	56 34.1	+52.1	133.9	55 09.3	+53.4	135.9	53 41.7	+54.5	137.9	52 11.5	+55.4	139.6
26	58 46.1	50.1	130.5	57 26.2	51.7	132.9	56 02.7	53.1	135.1	54 36.2	54.2	137.1	53 06.9	55.4	139.0
27	59 36.2	49.5	129.5	58 17.9	51.2	132.0	56 55.8	52.7	134.3	55 30.4	54.0	136.4	54 01.2	55.0	138.3
28	60 25.7	49.0	128.3	59 09.1	50.8	131.0	57 48.5	52.3	133.4	56 24.4	53.6	135.6	54 57.1	54.8	137.6
29	61 14.7	48.3	127.2	59 59.9	50.2	129.9	58 40.8	51.9	132.5	57 18.0	53.3	134.8	55 51.9	54.5	136.9

40°			42°			44°			46°			48°			Dec.
Hc	d	Z	Hc	d	Z	Hc	d	Z	Hc	d	Z	Hc	d	Z	
° ′	′	°	° ′	′	°	° ′	′	°	° ′	′	°	° ′	′	°	°
43 30.8	−53.3	142.8	41 54.5	−54.1	143.9	40 16.9	−54.7	144.9	38 38.1	−55.3	145.9	36 58.3	−55.9	146.7	0
42 37.5	53.5	143.4	41 00.4	54.2	144.5	39 22.2	54.9	145.5	37 42.8	55.5	146.4	36 02.4	56.0	147.2	1
41 44.0	53.7	144.1	40 06.2	54.3	145.1	38 27.3	55.0	146.0	36 47.3	55.5	146.8	35 06.4	56.0	147.6	2
40 50.3	53.8	144.6	39 11.9	54.5	145.6	37 32.3	55.1	146.5	35 51.8	55.7	147.3	34 10.4	56.2	148.1	3
39 56.5	54.1	145.2	38 17.4	54.7	146.1	36 37.2	55.2	147.0	34 56.1	55.7	147.8	33 14.2	56.2	148.5	4
39 02.4	−54.1	145.8	37 22.7	−54.8	146.7	35 42.0	−55.4	147.5	34 00.4	−55.9	148.2	32 18.0	−56.3	148.9	5
38 08.3	54.4	146.3	36 27.9	54.9	147.2	34 46.6	55.4	147.9	33 04.5	55.9	148.6	31 21.7	56.4	149.3	6
37 13.9	54.4	146.9	35 33.0	55.1	147.7	33 51.2	55.6	148.4	32 08.6	56.0	149.1	30 25.3	56.5	149.7	7
36 19.5	54.6	147.4	34 37.9	55.1	148.2	32 55.6	55.6	148.9	31 12.6	56.1	149.5	29 28.8	56.5	150.1	8
35 24.9	54.8	147.9	33 42.8	55.3	148.6	32 00.0	55.8	149.3	30 16.5	56.2	149.9	28 32.3	56.6	150.5	9
34 30.1	−54.8	148.4	32 47.5	−55.3	149.1	31 04.2	−55.8	149.7	29 20.3	−56.3	150.3	27 35.7	−56.6	150.8	10
33 35.3	55.0	148.9	31 52.2	55.5	149.6	30 08.4	55.9	150.2	28 24.0	56.3	150.7	26 39.1	56.7	151.2	11
32 40.3	55.1	149.4	30 56.7	55.5	150.0	29 12.5	56.0	150.6	27 27.7	56.4	151.1	25 42.4	56.8	151.6	12
31 45.2	55.1	149.8	30 01.2	55.7	150.4	28 16.5	56.1	151.0	26 31.3	56.4	151.5	24 45.6	56.8	151.9	13
30 50.1	55.3	150.3	29 05.5	55.7	150.9	27 20.4	56.1	151.4	25 34.9	56.6	151.9	23 48.8	56.8	152.3	14
29 54.8	−55.4	150.8	28 09.8	−55.8	151.3	26 24.3	−56.2	151.8	24 38.3	−56.5	152.2	22 52.0	−56.9	152.6	15
28 59.4	55.4	151.2	27 14.0	55.8	151.7	25 28.1	56.2	152.2	23 41.8	56.6	152.6	21 55.1	57.0	153.0	16
28 04.0	55.5	151.6	26 18.2	56.0	152.1	24 31.9	56.3	152.6	22 45.2	56.7	153.0	20 58.1	57.0	153.3	17
27 08.5	55.6	152.1	25 22.2	56.0	152.5	23 35.6	56.4	152.9	21 48.5	56.7	153.3	20 01.1	57.0	153.7	18
26 12.9	55.7	152.5	24 26.2	56.0	152.9	22 39.2	56.4	153.3	20 51.8	56.7	153.7	19 04.1	57.0	154.0	19
25 17.2	−55.7	152.9	23 30.2	−56.1	153.3	21 42.8	−56.5	153.7	19 55.1	−56.8	154.0	18 07.1	−57.1	154.3	20
24 21.5	55.8	153.3	22 34.1	56.2	153.7	20 46.3	56.5	154.0	18 58.3	56.8	154.4	17 10.0	57.1	154.6	21
23 25.7	55.9	153.7	21 37.9	56.2	154.1	19 49.8	56.5	154.4	18 01.5	56.9	154.7	16 12.9	57.2	155.0	22
22 29.8	55.9	154.1	20 41.7	56.3	154.4	18 53.3	56.6	154.8	17 04.6	56.9	155.0	15 15.7	57.2	155.3	23
21 33.9	56.0	154.5	19 45.4	56.3	154.8	17 56.7	56.6	155.1	16 07.7	56.9	155.4	14 18.5	57.2	155.6	24
20 37.9	−56.0	154.9	18 49.1	−56.4	155.2	17 00.1	−56.7	155.5	15 10.8	−57.0	155.7	13 21.3	−57.2	155.9	25
19 41.9	56.1	155.3	17 52.7	56.4	155.5	16 03.4	56.7	155.8	14 13.8	56.9	156.0	12 24.1	57.2	156.2	26
18 45.8	56.1	155.6	16 56.3	56.4	155.9	15 06.7	56.7	156.1	13 16.9	57.0	156.3	11 26.9	57.3	156.5	27
17 49.7	56.2	156.0	15 59.9	56.5	156.3	14 10.0	56.8	156.5	12 19.9	57.0	156.7	10 29.6	57.2	156.8	28
16 53.5	56.2	156.4	15 03.4	56.5	156.6	13 13.2	56.8	156.8	11 22.9	57.1	157.0	9 32.4	57.3	157.1	29

50°			52°			54°			56°			58°			Dec.
Hc	d	Z	Hc	d	Z	Hc	d	Z	Hc	d	Z	Hc	d	Z	
° ′	′	°	° ′	′	°	° ′	′	°	° ′	′	°	° ′	′	°	°
35 17.5	−56.4	147.5	33 35.8	−56.8	148.2	31 53.4	−57.2	148.9	30 10.3	−57.5	149.5	28 26.6	−57.9	150.1	0
34 21.1	56.4	147.9	32 39.0	56.8	148.6	30 56.2	57.2	149.3	29 12.8	57.6	149.9	27 28.7	57.9	150.4	1
33 24.7	56.5	148.3	31 42.2	57.0	149.0	29 59.0	57.3	149.6	28 15.2	57.7	150.2	26 30.8	58.0	150.7	2
32 28.2	56.6	148.7	30 45.2	57.0	149.4	29 01.7	57.4	150.0	27 17.5	57.7	150.5	25 32.8	58.0	151.0	3
31 31.6	56.7	149.1	29 48.2	57.0	149.7	28 04.3	57.4	150.3	26 19.8	57.7	150.8	24 34.8	58.0	151.3	4
30 34.9	−56.7	149.5	28 51.2	−57.1	150.1	27 06.9	−57.5	150.6	25 22.1	−57.8	151.1	23 36.8	−58.0	151.5	5
29 38.2	56.8	149.9	27 54.1	57.2	150.5	26 09.4	57.5	150.9	24 24.3	57.8	151.4	22 38.8	58.1	151.8	6
28 41.4	56.9	150.3	26 56.9	57.2	150.8	25 11.9	57.5	151.3	23 26.5	57.8	151.7	21 40.7	58.1	152.1	7
27 44.5	56.9	150.6	25 59.7	57.2	151.1	24 14.4	57.6	151.6	22 28.7	57.9	152.0	20 42.6	58.2	152.3	8
26 47.6	56.9	151.0	25 02.5	57.3	151.5	23 16.8	57.6	151.9	21 30.8	57.9	152.3	19 44.4	58.1	152.6	9
25 50.7	−57.0	151.3	24 05.2	−57.4	151.8	22 19.2	−57.6	152.2	20 32.9	−57.9	152.5	18 46.3	−58.2	152.9	10
24 53.7	57.1	151.7	23 07.8	57.3	152.1	21 21.6	57.7	152.5	19 35.0	57.9	152.8	17 48.1	58.2	153.1	11
23 56.6	57.1	152.0	22 10.5	57.5	152.4	20 23.9	57.7	152.8	18 37.1	58.0	153.1	16 49.9	58.2	153.4	12
22 59.5	57.1	152.4	21 13.0	57.4	152.7	19 26.2	57.7	153.1	17 39.1	58.0	153.4	15 51.7	58.2	153.6	13
22 02.4	57.2	152.7	20 15.6	57.5	153.0	18 28.5	57.8	153.4	16 41.1	58.0	153.6	14 53.5	58.3	153.9	14
21 05.2	−57.2	153.0	19 18.1	−57.5	153.3	17 30.7	−57.8	153.6	15 43.1	−58.1	153.9	13 55.2	−58.3	154.1	15
20 08.0	57.3	153.3	18 20.6	57.5	153.6	16 32.9	57.8	153.9	14 45.0	58.0	154.2	12 56.9	58.2	154.4	16
19 10.7	57.2	153.7	17 23.1	57.6	153.9	15 35.1	57.8	154.2	13 47.0	58.1	154.4	11 58.7	58.3	154.6	17
18 13.5	57.4	154.0	16 25.5	57.6	154.2	14 37.3	57.8	154.5	12 48.9	58.0	154.7	11 00.4	58.3	154.9	18
17 16.1	57.3	154.3	15 27.9	57.6	154.5	13 39.5	57.9	154.8	11 50.9	58.1	154.9	10 02.1	58.3	155.1	19
16 18.8	−57.4	154.6	14 30.3	−57.6	154.8	12 41.6	−57.9	155.0	10 52.8	−58.1	155.2	9 03.8	−58.4	155.3	20
15 21.4	57.4	154.9	13 32.7	57.7	155.1	11 43.7	57.9	155.3	9 54.7	58.1	155.5	8 05.4	58.3	155.5	21
14 24.0	57.4	155.2	12 35.0	57.6	155.4	10 45.8	57.9	155.6	8 56.5	58.1	155.7	7 07.1	58.3	155.8	22
13 26.6	57.5	155.5	11 37.4	57.7	155.7	9 47.9	57.9	155.9	7 58.4	58.1	156.0	6 08.8	58.4	156.1	23
12 29.2	57.5	155.8	10 39.7	57.7	156.0	8 50.0	57.9	156.1	7 00.3	58.2	156.2	5 10.4	58.3	156.3	24
11 31.7	−57.4	156.1	9 42.0	−57.7	156.2	7 52.1	−57.9	156.4	6 02.1	−58.1	156.5	4 12.1	−58.4	156.5	25
10 34.3	57.5	156.4	8 44.3	57.8	156.5	6 54.2	58.0	156.6	5 04.0	58.2	156.7	3 13.7	58.3	156.8	26
9 36.8	57.5	156.7	7 46.5	57.8	156.8	5 56.2	57.9	156.9	4 05.8	58.1	156.9	2 15.4	58.4	157.0	27
8 39.3	57.6	157.0	6 48.8	57.8	157.1	4 58.3	58.0	157.1	3 07.7	58.2	157.2	1 17.0	58.3	157.2	28
7 41.7	57.5	157.2	5 51.0	57.7	157.3	4 00.3	58.0	157.4	2 09.5	58.2	157.4	0 18.7	−58.4	157.5	29

Dec.	0° Hc	d	Z	2° Hc	d	Z	4° Hc	d	Z	6° Hc	d	Z	8° Hc	d	Z
°	° ′	′	°	° ′	′	°	° ′	′	°	° ′	′	°	° ′	′	°
0	62 00.0 − 1.0		90.0	61 56.1 + 3.4·		93.8	61 44.3 + 7.9		97.5	61 24.9 + 12.2		101.1	60 58.1 + 16.4		104.7
1	61 59.0 2.9		87.9	61 59.5 + 1.5		91.6	61 52.2 5.9		95.4	61 37.1 10.3		99.1	61 14.5 14.5		102.7
2	61 56.1 4.9·		85.7	62 01.0 − 0.4·		89.5	61 58.1 4.0		93.3	61 47.4 8.4		97.0	61 29.0 12.7		100.7
3	61 51.2 6.9		83.6	62 00.6 2.5		87.4	62 02.1 + 2.1·		91.1	61 55.8 6.5		94.9	61 41.7 10.9		98.6
4	61 44.3 8.7		81.5	61 58.1 4.3		85.2	62 04.2 0.0·		89.0	62 02.3 4.5		92.8	61 52.6 8.9		96.5
5	61 35.6 − 10.7		79.4	61 53.8 − 6.4		83.1	62 04.2 − 1.9		86.9	62 06.8 + 2.6		90.6	62 01.5 + 7.1		94.4
6	61 24.9 12.5		77.4	61 47.4 8.2		81.0	62 02.3 3.9		84.7	62 09.4 + 0.6·		88.5	62 08.6 5.0·		92.3
7	61 12.4 14.3		75.3	61 39.2 10.2		78.9	61 58.4 5.8		82.6	62 10.0 − 1.4·		86.4	62 13.6 3.1		90.2
8	60 58.1 16.0		73.3	61 29.0 12.0		76.9	61 52.6 7.8		80.5	62 08.6 3.4·		84.2	62 16.7 + 1.1·		88.0
9	60 42.1 17.8		71.4	61 17.0 13.8		74.8	61 44.8 9.7		78.4	62 05.2 5.4		82.1	62 17.8 − 0.9·		85.9
10	60 24.3 − 19.5		69.4	61 03.2 − 15.7		72.8	61 35.1 − 11.5		76.3	61 59.8 − 7.3		80.0	62 16.9 − 2.9·		83.7
11	60 04.8 21.0		67.5	60 47.5 17.3		70.8	61 23.6 13.4		74.3	61 52.5 9.2		77.9	62 14.0 4.9·		81.6
12	59 43.8 22.7		65.6	60 30.2 19.0		68.9	61 10.2 15.2		72.2	61 43.3 11.1		75.8	62 09.1 6.9		79.4
13	59 21.1 24.1		63.8	60 11.2 20.7		66.9	60 55.0 16.9		70.2	61 32.2 13.0		73.7	62 02.2 8.7		77.3
14	58 57.0 25.5		62.0	59 50.5 22.2		65.1	60 38.1 18.7		68.3	61 19.2 14.8		71.7	61 53.5 10.7		75.2
15	58 31.5 − 27.0		60.3	59 28.3 − 23.8		63.2	60 19.4 − 20.2		66.3	61 04.4 − 16.5		69.6	61 42.8 − 12.6		73.1
16	58 04.5 28.2		58.6	59 04.5 25.2		61.4	59 59.2 21.9		64.4	60 47.9 18.3		67.7	61 30.2 14.4		71.1
17	57 36.3 29.6		56.9	58 39.3 26.6		59.7	59 37.3 23.4		62.6	60 29.6 19.9		65.7	61 15.8 16.2		69.0
18	57 06.7 30.7		55.3	58 12.7 27.9		58.0	59 13.9 24.9		60.8	60 09.7 21.5		63.8	60 59.6 17.9		67.0
19	56 36.0 31.9		53.7	57 44.8 29.2		56.3	58 49.0 26.2		59.0	59 48.2 23.1		62.0	60 41.7 19.6		65.1
20	56 04.1 − 33.0		52.2	57 15.6 − 30.5		54.7	58 22.8 − 27.7		57.3	59 25.1 − 24.6		60.1	60 22.1 − 21.2		63.2
21	55 31.1 34.1		50.7	56 45.1 31.6		53.1	57 55.1 28.9		55.6	59 00.5 26.0		58.3	60 00.9 22.8		61.3
22	54 57.0 35.0		49.3	56 13.5 32.7		51.5	57 26.2 30.2		54.0	58 34.5 27.4		56.6	59 38.1 24.3		59.4
23	54 22.0 36.0		47.9	55 40.8 33.8		50.0	56 56.0 31.4		52.4	58 07.1 28.6		54.9	59 13.8 25.8		57.6
24	53 46.0 36.9		46.5	55 07.0 34.8		48.6	56 24.6 32.5		50.8	57 38.5 30.0		53.3	58 48.0 27.1		55.9
25	53 09.1 − 37.8		45.2	54 32.2 − 35.8		47.2	55 52.1 − 33.6		49.3	57 08.5 − 31.2		51.6	58 20.9 − 28.5		54.2
26	52 31.3 38.5		43.9	53 56.4 36.7		45.8	55 18.5 34.6		47.8	56 37.3 32.3		50.1	57 52.4 29.8		52.5
27	51 52.8 39.4		42.7	53 19.7 37.5		44.5	54 43.9 35.5		46.4	56 05.0 33.3		48.6	57 22.6 30.9		50.9
28	51 13.4 40.1		41.4	52 42.2 38.4		43.2	54 08.4 36.5		45.0	55 31.7 34.5		47.1	56 51.7 32.2		49.3
29	50 33.3 40.7		40.3	52 03.8 39.1		41.9	53 31.9 37.4		43.7	54 57.2 35.4		45.6	56 19.5 33.2		47.8

Dec.	10° Hc	d	Z	12° Hc	d	Z	14° Hc	d	Z	16° Hc	d	Z	18° Hc	d	Z
°	° ′	′	°	° ′	′	°	° ′	′	°	° ′	′	°	° ′	′	°
0	60 24.3 + 20.2		108.1	59 43.8 + 23.9		111.4	58 57.0 + 27.5		114.5	58 04.5 + 30.7		117.4	57 06.7 + 33.6		120.2
1	60 44.5 18.7		106.2	60 07.7 22.5		109.5	59 24.5 26.0		112.7	58 35.2 29.3		115.8	57 40.3 32.4		118.6
2	61 03.2 16.8		104.2	60 30.2 20.8		107.7	59 50.5 24.6		110.9	59 04.5 28.1		114.1	58 12.7 31.3		117.0
3	61 20.0 15.1		102.2	60 51.0 19.2		105.7	60 15.1 23.0		109.1	59 32.6 26.6		112.3	58 44.0 29.9		115.4
4	61 35.1 13.3		100.2	61 10.2 17.4		103.8	60 38.1 21.4		107.2	59 59.2 25.1		110.6	59 13.9 28.6		113.7
5	61 48.4 + 11.4		98.1	61 27.6 + 15.7		101.8	60 59.5 + 19.7		105.3	60 24.3 + 23.6		108.7	59 42.5 + 27.2		112.0
6	61 59.8 9.5		96.1	61 43.3 13.8		99.8	61 19.2 18.0		103.4	60 47.9 22.0		106.9	60 09.7 25.7		110.2
7	62 09.3 7.6·		93.9	61 57.1 12.0		97.7	61 37.2 16.3		101.4	61 09.9 20.3		104.9	60 35.4 24.2		108.4
8	62 16.9 5.5·		91.8	62 09.1 10.0		95.6	61 53.5 14.4		99.3	61 30.2 18.6		103.0	60 59.6 22.6		106.5
9	62 22.4 3.6		89.7	62 19.1 8.1		93.5	62 07.9 12.5		97.3	61 48.8 16.8		101.0	61 22.2 20.9		104.6
10	62 26.0 + 1.6·		87.5	62 27.2 + 6.1·		91.4	62 20.4 + 10.6		95.2	62 05.6 + 15.0		98.9	61 43.1 + 19.2		102.6
11	62 27.6 − 0.4·		85.4	62 33.3 4.1·		89.2	62 31.0 8.6·		93.0	62 20.6 13.1		96.9	62 02.3 17.5		100.6
12	62 27.2 2.4·		83.2	62 37.4 2.1·		87.0	62 39.6 6.6		90.9	62 33.7 11.1		94.8	62 19.8 15.5		98.6
13	62 24.8 4.4·		81.0	62 39.5 + 0.1·		84.9	62 46.2 4.7·		88.7	62 44.8 9.2		92.6	62 35.3 13.7		96.6
14	62 20.4 6.4·		78.9	62 39.6 − 1.9·		82.7	62 50.9 2.6·		86.5	62 54.0 7.2·		90.5	62 49.0 11.7·		94.4
15	62 14.0 − 8.4		76.7	62 37.7 − 4.0·		80.5	62 53.5 + 0.5·		84.4	63 01.2 + 5.1·		88.3	63 00.7 + 9.7·		92.2
16	62 05.6 10.3		74.6	62 33.7 6.0		78.3	62 54.0 − 1.5·		82.2	63 06.3 3.1·		86.1	63 10.4 7.7·		90.0
17	61 55.3 12.2		72.5	62 27.7 7.9		76.2	62 52.5 3.5·		80.0	63 09.4 + 1.0·		83.9	63 18.1 5.7·		87.8
18	61 43.1 14.0		70.5	62 19.8 9.9·		74.0	62 49.0 5.6·		77.8	63 10.4 − 1.0·		81.6	63 23.8 3.5·		85.6
19	61 29.1 15.8		68.4	62 09.9 11.9		71.9	62 43.4 7.5·		75.6	63 09.4 3.1·		79.4	63 27.3 + 1.5·		83.4
20	61 13.3 − 17.6		66.4	61 58.0 − 13.7		69.8	62 35.9 − 9.6·		73.4	63 06.3 − 5.2·		77.2	63 28.8 − 0.6·		81.1
21	60 55.7 19.3		64.4	61 44.3 15.5		67.8	62 26.3 11.5		71.3	62 57.2 7.2·		75.0	63 28.2 2.7·		78.9
22	60 36.4 21.0		62.5	61 28.8 17.3		65.7	62 14.8 13.4		69.2	62 53.9 9.2·		72.8	63 25.5 4.8·		76.7
23	60 15.4 22.5		60.6	61 11.5 19.1		63.7	62 01.4 15.2		67.1	62 44.7 11.2		70.7	63 20.7 6.9·		74.4
24	59 52.9 24.1		58.7	60 52.4 20.7		61.8	61 46.2 17.1		65.1	62 33.5 13.1		68.5	63 13.8 8.8		72.2
25	59 28.8 − 25.5		56.9	60 31.7 − 22.3		59.9	61 29.1 − 18.8		63.0	62 20.4 − 15.0		66.4	63 04.9 − 10.9·		70.0
26	59 03.3 27.0		55.1	60 09.4 23.9		58.0	61 10.3 20.5		61.1	62 05.4 16.9		64.3	62 54.0 12.9		67.9
27	58 36.3 28.3		53.4	59 45.5 25.4		56.2	60 49.8 22.2		59.1	61 48.5 18.6		62.3	62 41.1 14.8		65.7
28	58 08.0 29.6		51.7	59 20.1 26.8		54.4	60 27.6 23.7		57.2	61 29.9 20.4		60.3	62 26.3 16.7		63.6
29	57 38.4 30.9		50.1	58 53.3 28.2		52.6	60 03.9 25.3		55.4	61 09.5 22.0		58.3	62 09.6 18.4		61.6

LATITUDE **CONTRARY** NAME　　　　L.H.A. 28°, 332°

0° Hc	d	Z	2° Hc	d	Z	4° Hc	d	Z	6° Hc	d	Z	8° Hc	d	Z	Dec.
62 00.0	- 1.0	90.0	61 56.1	- 5.5	93.8	61 44.3	- 9.8	97.5	61 24.9	-14.0	101.1	60 58.1	-18.0	104.7	0
61 59.0	2.9	92.1	61 50.6	7.3	95.9	61 34.5	11.6	99.6	61 10.9	15.8	103.1	60 40.1	19.8	106.6	1
61 56.1	4.9*	94.3	61 43.3	9.3	98.0	61 22.9	13.5	101.6	60 55.1	17.5	105.1	60 20.3	21.3	108.5	2
61 51.2	6.9	96.4	61 34.0	11.1	100.0	61 09.4	15.3	103.6	60 37.6	19.3	107.1	59 59.0	23.0	110.4	3
61 44.3	8.7	98.5	61 22.9	13.0	102.1	60 54.1	17.0	105.6	60 18.3	20.8	109.0	59 36.0	24.4	112.3	4
61 35.6	-10.7	100.6	61 09.9	-14.8	104.1	60 37.1	-18.8	107.6	59 57.5	-22.4	110.9	59 11.6	-25.9	114.1	5
61 24.9	12.5	102.6	60 55.1	16.5	106.1	60 18.3	20.3	109.5	59 35.1	24.0	112.7	58 45.7	27.3	115.8	6
61 12.4	14.3	104.7	60 38.6	18.3	108.1	59 58.0	22.0	111.4	59 11.1	25.4	114.5	58 18.4	28.6	117.5	7
60 58.1	16.0	106.7	60 20.3	19.9	110.0	59 36.0	23.5	113.3	58 45.7	26.8	116.3	57 49.8	29.8	119.2	8
60 42.1	17.8	108.6	60 00.4	21.5	111.9	59 12.5	24.9	115.1	58 18.9	28.2	118.0	57 20.0	31.1	120.8	9
60 24.3	-19.5	110.6	59 38.9	-23.0	113.8	58 47.6	-26.4	116.8	57 50.7	-29.4	119.7	56 48.9	-32.3	122.4	10
60 04.8	21.0	112.5	59 15.9	24.5	115.6	58 21.2	27.7	118.6	57 21.3	30.6	121.3	56 16.6	33.3	123.9	11
59 43.8	22.7	114.4	58 51.4	26.0	117.4	57 53.5	29.0	120.2	56 50.7	31.9	122.9	55 43.3	34.4	125.4	12
59 21.1	24.1	116.2	58 25.4	27.3	119.1	57 24.5	30.3	121.9	56 18.8	32.9	124.4	55 08.9	35.4	126.8	13
58 57.0	25.5	118.0	57 58.1	28.6	120.8	56 54.2	31.4	123.5	55 45.9	34.0	125.9	54 33.5	36.3	128.2	14
58 31.5	-27.0	119.7	57 29.5	-29.9	122.5	56 22.8	-32.5	125.0	55 11.9	-35.0	127.4	53 57.2	-37.2	129.6	15
58 04.5	28.2	121.4	56 59.6	31.1	124.1	55 50.3	33.7	126.5	54 36.9	35.9	128.8	53 20.0	38.1	130.9	16
57 36.3	29.6	123.1	56 28.5	32.2	125.6	55 16.6	34.6	128.0	54 01.0	36.9	130.2	52 41.9	38.9	132.2	17
57 06.7	30.7	124.7	55 56.3	33.3	127.1	54 42.0	35.7	129.4	53 24.1	37.8	131.5	52 03.0	39.6	133.4	18
56 36.0	31.9	126.3	55 23.0	34.3	128.6	54 06.3	36.5	130.8	52 46.3	38.5	132.8	51 23.4	40.4	134.7	19
56 04.1	-33.0	127.8	54 48.7	-35.3	130.0	53 29.8	-37.4	132.1	52 07.8	-39.4	134.1	50 43.0	-41.1	135.8	20
55 31.1	34.1	129.3	54 13.4	36.3	131.4	52 52.4	38.3	133.4	51 28.4	40.0	135.3	50 01.9	41.7	137.0	21
54 57.0	35.0	130.7	53 37.1	37.2	132.8	52 14.1	39.1	134.7	50 48.4	40.8	136.5	49 20.2	42.3	138.1	22
54 22.0	36.0	132.1	52 59.9	37.9	134.1	51 35.0	39.8	135.9	50 07.6	41.4	137.6	48 37.9	43.0	139.2	23
53 46.0	36.9	133.5	52 22.0	38.8	135.4	50 55.2	40.5	137.1	49 26.2	42.1	138.7	47 54.9	43.5	140.2	24
53 09.1	-37.8	134.8	51 43.2	-39.6	136.6	50 14.7	-41.2	138.3	48 44.1	-42.7	139.8	47 11.4	-44.0	141.2	25
52 31.3	38.5	136.1	51 03.6	40.3	137.8	49 33.5	41.8	139.4	48 01.4	43.2	140.9	46 27.4	44.5	142.2	26
51 52.8	39.4	137.3	50 23.3	40.9	139.0	48 51.7	42.4	140.5	47 18.2	43.8	141.9	45 42.9	45.0	143.2	27
51 13.4	40.1	138.6	49 42.4	41.6	140.1	48 09.3	43.0	141.6	46 34.4	44.3	142.9	44 57.9	45.5	144.1	28
50 33.3	40.7	139.7	49 00.8	42.3	141.2	47 26.3	43.6	142.6	45 50.1	44.8	143.9	44 12.4	45.8	145.1	29

10° Hc	d	Z	12° Hc	d	Z	14° Hc	d	Z	16° Hc	d	Z	18° Hc	d	Z	Dec.
60 24.3	-21.9	108.1	59 43.8	-25.5	111.4	58 57.0	-28.8	114.5	58 04.5	-31.9	117.4	57 06.7	-34.7	120.2	0
60 02.4	23.5	110.0	59 18.3	26.9	113.1	58 28.2	30.1	116.2	57 32.6	33.0	119.0	56 32.0	35.7	121.7	1
59 38.9	24.9	111.8	58 51.4	28.3	114.9	57 58.1	31.3	117.8	56 59.6	34.1	120.5	55 56.3	36.7	123.1	2
59 14.0	26.4	113.6	58 23.1	29.6	116.6	57 26.8	32.6	119.4	56 25.5	35.2	122.0	55 19.6	37.6	124.5	3
58 47.6	27.8	115.3	57 53.5	30.8	118.2	56 54.2	33.6	120.9	55 50.3	36.2	123.5	54 42.0	38.6	125.9	4
58 19.8	-29.1	117.0	57 22.7	-32.0	119.8	56 20.6	-34.7	122.4	55 14.1	-37.2	124.9	54 03.4	-39.3	127.2	5
57 50.7	30.3	118.7	56 50.7	33.2	121.4	55 45.9	35.7	123.9	54 36.9	38.0	126.3	53 24.1	40.2	128.5	6
57 20.4	31.5	120.3	56 17.5	34.2	122.9	55 10.2	36.7	125.3	53 58.9	38.9	127.6	52 43.9	40.9	129.7	7
56 48.9	32.7	121.9	55 43.3	35.2	124.4	54 33.5	37.5	126.7	53 20.0	39.7	128.9	52 03.0	41.6	130.9	8
56 16.2	33.8	123.4	55 08.1	36.2	125.8	53 56.0	38.5	128.0	52 40.3	40.4	130.1	51 21.4	42.2	132.1	9
55 42.4	-34.8	124.9	54 31.9	-37.2	127.2	53 17.5	-39.2	129.3	51 59.9	-41.2	131.3	50 39.2	-43.0	133.2	10
55 07.6	35.7	126.3	53 54.7	38.0	128.5	52 38.3	40.0	130.6	51 18.7	41.9	132.5	49 56.2	43.5	134.3	11
54 31.9	36.8	127.7	53 16.7	38.8	129.8	51 58.3	40.8	131.8	50 36.8	42.5	133.6	49 12.7	44.0	135.3	12
53 55.1	37.6	129.0	52 37.9	39.6	131.1	51 17.5	41.4	133.0	49 54.3	43.1	134.7	48 28.7	44.7	136.4	13
53 17.5	38.4	130.4	51 58.3	40.4	132.3	50 36.1	42.1	134.1	49 11.2	43.7	135.8	47 44.0	45.1	137.4	14
52 39.1	-39.2	131.6	51 17.9	-41.1	133.5	49 54.0	-42.8	135.3	48 27.5	-44.2	136.9	46 58.9	-45.6	138.3	15
51 59.9	40.0	132.9	50 36.8	41.7	134.7	49 11.2	43.3	136.3	47 43.3	44.7	137.9	46 13.3	46.0	139.3	16
51 19.9	40.7	134.1	49 55.1	42.4	135.8	48 27.9	43.9	137.4	46 58.6	45.3	138.9	45 27.3	46.5	140.2	17
50 39.2	41.4	135.2	49 12.7	42.9	136.9	47 44.0	44.4	138.4	46 13.3	45.7	139.8	44 40.8	46.9	141.1	18
49 57.8	42.1	136.4	48 29.8	43.6	137.9	46 59.6	44.9	139.4	45 27.6	46.1	140.7	43 53.9	47.3	142.0	19
49 15.7	-42.6	137.5	47 46.2	-44.0	139.0	46 14.7	-45.3	140.4	44 41.5	-46.6	141.6	43 06.6	-47.7	142.8	20
48 33.1	43.2	138.5	47 02.2	44.6	140.0	45 29.4	45.9	141.3	43 54.9	47.0	142.5	42 18.9	47.9	143.6	21
47 49.9	43.8	139.6	46 17.6	45.1	141.0	44 43.5	46.2	142.2	43 07.9	47.3	143.4	41 31.0	48.4	144.5	22
47 06.1	44.3	140.6	45 32.5	45.5	141.9	43 57.3	46.7	143.1	42 20.6	47.7	144.2	40 42.6	48.6	145.2	23
46 21.8	44.8	141.6	44 47.0	46.0	142.8	43 10.6	47.0	144.0	41 32.9	48.0	145.0	39 54.0	49.0	146.0	24
45 37.0	-45.2	142.5	44 01.0	-46.4	143.7	42 23.6	-47.4	144.8	40 44.9	-48.4	145.8	39 05.0	-49.2	146.8	25
44 51.8	45.7	143.5	43 14.6	46.7	144.6	41 36.2	47.8	145.6	39 56.5	48.6	146.6	38 15.8	49.5	147.5	26
44 06.1	46.2	144.4	42 27.9	47.2	145.5	40 48.4	48.1	146.5	39 07.9	49.0	147.4	37 26.3	49.7	148.2	27
43 19.9	46.5	145.3	41 40.7	47.5	146.3	40 00.3	48.3	147.2	38 18.9	49.2	148.1	36 36.6	50.0	148.9	28
42 33.4	46.9	146.1	40 53.2	47.8	147.1	39 12.0	48.7	148.0	37 29.7	49.5	148.8	35 46.6	50.2	149.6	29

Dec.	20° Hc	d	Z	22° Hc	d	Z	24° Hc	d	Z	26° Hc	d	Z	28° Hc	d	Z
°	° ′	′	°	° ′	′	°	° ′	′	°	° ′	′	°	° ′	′	°
0	56 04.1	+36.2	122.8	54 57.0	+38.7	125.2	53 46.0	+40.9	127.4	52 31.3	+42.9	129.5	51 13.4	+44.7	131.4
1	56 40.3	35.3	121.3	55 35.7	37.8	123.8	54 26.9	40.1	126.2	53 14.2	42.2	128.3	51 58.1	44.1	130.4
2	57 15.6	34.1	119.8	56 13.5	36.8	122.4	55 07.0	39.2	124.9	53 56.4	41.5	127.1	52 42.2	43.4	129.3
3	57 49.7	33.1	118.3	56 50.3	35.9	121.0	55 46.2	38.4	123.5	54 37.9	40.6	125.9	53 25.6	42.8	128.1
4	58 22.8	31.8	116.7	57 26.2	34.7	119.5	56 24.6	37.4	122.2	55 18.5	39.9	124.6	54 08.4	42.0	126.9
5	58 54.6	+30.5	115.1	58 00.9	+33.6	118.0	57 02.0	+36.5	120.7	55 58.4	+38.9	123.3	54 50.4	+41.3	125.7
6	59 25.1	29.2	113.4	58 34.5	32.4	116.4	57 38.5	35.3	119.3	56 37.3	38.1	121.9	55 31.7	40.4	124.4
7	59 54.3	27.8	111.7	59 06.9	31.2	114.8	58 13.8	34.2	117.7	57 15.4	37.0	120.5	56 12.1	39.6	123.1
8	60 22.1	26.4	109.9	59 38.1	29.8	113.1	58 48.0	33.1	116.2	57 52.4	36.0	119.0	56 51.7	38.6	121.7
9	60 48.5	24.8	108.1	60 07.9	28.5	111.4	59 21.1	31.8	114.5	58 28.4	34.9	117.5	57 30.3	37.7	120.3
10	61 13.3	+23.2	106.2	60 36.4	+27.0	109.6	59 52.9	+30.5	112.9	59 03.3	+33.6	116.0	58 08.0	+36.6	118.9
11	61 36.5	21.5	104.3	61 03.4	25.4	107.8	60 23.4	29.0	111.1	59 36.9	32.5	114.3	58 44.6	35.5	117.4
12	61 58.0	19.8	102.3	61 28.8	23.8	105.9	60 52.4	27.7	109.4	60 09.4	31.1	112.7	59 20.1	34.4	115.8
13	62 17.8	18.1	100.3	61 52.6	22.2	104.0	61 20.1	26.1	107.5	60 40.5	29.8	110.9	59 54.5	33.1	114.2
14	62 35.9	16.1	98.2	62 14.8	20.5	102.0	61 46.2	24.5	105.6	61 10.3	28.3	109.1	60 27.6	31.8	112.5
15	62 52.0	+14.3	96.1	62 35.3	+18.6	99.9	62 10.7	+22.8	103.7	61 38.6	+26.8	107.3	60 59.4	+30.5	110.8
16	63 06.3	12.2*	94.0	62 53.9	16.7	97.9	62 33.5	21.1	101.7	62 05.4	25.1	105.4	61 29.9	29.0	109.0
17	63 18.5	10.3*	91.8	63 10.6	14.9	95.8	62 54.6	19.2	99.7	62 30.5	23.5	103.4	61 58.9	27.4	107.1
18	63 28.8	8.2*	89.6	63 25.5	12.8*	93.6	63 13.8	17.4	97.6	62 54.0	21.7	101.4	62 26.3	25.9	105.2
19	63 37.0	6.2*	87.4	63 38.3	10.9*	91.4	63 31.2	15.4*	95.4	63 15.7	19.9	99.4	62 52.2	24.1	103.2
20	63 43.2	+ 4.0*	85.1	63 49.2	+ 8.7*	89.2	63 46.6	+13.4*	93.2	63 35.6	+18.0	97.3	63 16.3	+22.4	101.2
21	63 47.2	2.0*	82.9	63 57.9	6.7*	86.9	64 00.0	11.4*	91.0	63 53.6	16.0*	95.1	63 38.7	20.5	99.1
22	63 49.2	- 0.3*	80.6	64 04.6	4.5*	84.7	64 11.4	9.3*	88.8	64 09.6	14.0*	92.9	63 59.2	18.7	97.0
23	63 48.9	2.3*	78.3	64 09.1	2.3*	82.4	64 20.7	7.1*	86.5	64 23.6	12.0*	90.7	64 17.9	16.6*	94.8
24	63 46.6	4.4*	76.1	64 11.4	+ 0.2*	80.1	64 27.8	5.0*	84.2	64 35.6	9.8*	88.4	64 34.5	14.6*	92.6
25	63 42.2	- 6.6*	73.8	64 11.6	- 2.0*	77.8	64 32.8	+ 2.8*	81.9	64 45.4	+ 7.6*	86.1	64 49.1	+12.5*	90.3
26	63 35.6	8.6*	71.6	64 09.6	4.1*	75.5	64 35.6	0.5*	79.6	64 53.0	5.4*	83.8	65 01.6	10.3*	88.0
27	63 27.0	10.7*	69.4	64 05.5	6.3*	73.2	64 36.1	- 1.6*	77.2	64 58.4	3.2*	81.4	65 11.9	8.1*	85.7
28	63 16.3	12.7	67.2	63 59.2	8.3*	70.9	64 34.5	3.8*	74.9	65 01.6	+ 0.9*	79.0	65 20.0	5.8*	83.3
29	63 03.6	14.6	65.0	63 50.9	10.5*	68.7	64 30.7	6.0*	72.6	65 02.5	- 1.3*	76.7	65 25.8	3.6*	80.9

Dec.	30° Hc	d	Z	32° Hc	d	Z	34° Hc	d	Z	36° Hc	d	Z	38° Hc	d	Z
°	° ′	′	°	° ′	′	°	° ′	′	°	° ′	′	°	° ′	′	°
0	49 52.6	+46 3	133.2	48 29.1	+47.8	134.9	47 03.2	+49.1	136.4	45 35.2	+50.3	137.9	44 05.3	+51.3	139.2
1	50 38.9	45.8	132.2	49 16.9	47.2	134.0	47 52.3	48.7	135.6	46 25.5	49.9	137.1	44 56.6	51.0	138.5
2	51 24.7	45.2	131.2	50 04.1	46.9	133.0	48 41.0	48.2	134.7	47 15.4	49.5	136.3	45 47.6	50.7	137.7
3	52 09.9	44.6	130.2	50 51.0	46.3	132.0	49 29.2	47.8	133.8	48 04.9	49.3	135.4	46 38.3	50.4	136.9
4	52 54.5	44.0	129.1	51 37.3	45.7	131.0	50 17.0	47.4	132.9	48 54.1	48.8	134.6	47 28.7	50.0	136.1
5	53 38.5	+43.3	127.9	52 23.0	+45.2	130.0	51 04.4	+46.8	131.9	49 42.9	+48.3	133.7	48 18.7	+49.7	135.3
6	54 21.8	42.6	126.7	53 08.2	44.6	128.9	51 51.2	46.4	130.9	50 31.2	47.9	132.7	49 08.4	49.3	134.5
7	55 04.4	41.9	125.5	53 52.8	43.9	127.8	52 37.6	45.7	129.9	51 19.1	47.4	131.8	49 57.7	48.9	133.6
8	55 46.3	41.0	124.3	54 36.7	43.2	126.6	53 23.3	45.2	128.8	52 06.5	46.9	130.8	50 46.6	48.4	132.7
9	56 27.3	40.2	123.0	55 19.9	42.5	125.4	54 08.5	44.5	127.7	52 53.4	46.3	129.8	51 35.0	48.0	131.7
10	57 07.5	+39.3	121.6	56 02.4	+41.7	124.1	54 53.0	+43.8	126.5	53 39.7	+45.8	128.7	52 23.0	+47.5	130.8
11	57 46.8	38.3	120.2	56 44.1	40.8	122.8	55 36.8	43.1	125.3	54 25.5	45.1	127.6	53 10.5	46.9	129.7
12	58 25.1	37.3	118.7	57 24.9	40.0	121.5	56 19.9	42.3	124.1	55 10.6	44.5	126.5	53 57.4	46.4	128.7
13	59 02.4	36.2	117.2	58 04.9	39.0	120.1	57 02.2	41.6	122.8	55 55.1	43.7	125.3	54 43.8	45.7	127.6
14	59 38.6	35.1	115.7	58 43.9	37.9	118.6	57 43.8	40.6	121.4	56 38.8	43.0	124.1	55 29.5	45.1	126.5
15	60 13.7	+33.8	114.0	59 21.8	+36.9	117.1	58 24.4	+39.7	120.1	57 21.8	+42.2	122.8	56 14.6	+44.4	125.3
16	60 47.5	32.5	112.4	59 58.7	35.8	115.6	59 04.1	38.6	118.6	58 04.0	41.3	121.4	56 59.0	43.7	124.1
17	61 20.0	31.2	110.6	60 34.5	34.5	114.0	59 42.7	37.7	117.1	58 45.3	40.4	120.1	57 42.7	42.9	122.8
18	61 51.2	29.7	108.8	61 09.0	33.3	112.3	60 20.4	36.4	115.5	59 25.7	39.4	118.6	58 25.6	42.0	121.5
19	62 20.9	28.1	107.0	61 42.3	31.8	110.5	60 56.8	35.3	113.9	60 05.1	38.3	117.1	59 07.6	41.1	120.1
20	62 49.0	+26.6	105.1	62 14.1	+30.4	108.7	61 32.1	+34.0	112.2	60 43.4	+37.3	115.6	59 48.7	+40.2	118.7
21	63 15.6	24.8	103.1	62 44.5	28.9	106.9	62 06.1	32.4	110.5	61 20.7	36.0	113.9	60 28.9	39.1	117.2
22	63 40.4	23.1	101.0	63 13.4	27.3	104.9	62 38.7	31.1	108.7	61 56.7	34.7	112.3	61 08.0	37.9	115.6
23	64 03.5	21.2	98.9	63 40.7	25.5	102.9	63 09.8	29.6	106.8	62 31.4	33.4	110.5	61 45.9	36.8	114.0
24	64 24.7	19.2	96.8	64 06.2	23.8	100.9	63 39.4	28.0	104.9	63 04.8	31.9	108.7	62 22.7	35.5	112.3
25	64 43.9	+17.3*	94.6	64 30.0	+21.8	98.8	64 07.4	+26.3	102.9	63 36.7	+30.4	106.8	62 58.2	+34.2	110.6
26	65 01.2	15.2*	92.3	64 51.8	20.0*	96.6	64 33.7	24.5	100.8	64 07.1	28.7	104.8	63 32.4	32.7	108.7
27	65 16.4	13.0*	90.0	65 11.8	17.8*	94.4	64 58.2	22.5	98.6	64 35.8	27.0	102.8	64 05.1	31.1	106.8
28	65 29.4	10.8*	87.7	65 29.6	15.8*	92.1	65 20.7	20.6*	96.4	65 02.8	25.2	100.7	64 36.2	29.6	104.9
29	65 40.2	8.6*	85.3	65 45.4	13.6*	89.7	65 41.3	18.5*	94.2	65 28.0	23.3*	98.5	65 05.8	27.7	102.8

20°			22°			24°			26°			28°			Dec.
Hc	d	Z	Hc	d	Z	Hc	d	Z	Hc	d	Z	Hc	d	Z	
° ′	′	°	° ′	′	°	° ′	′	°	° ′	′	°	° ′	′	°	°
56 04.1	−37.3	122.8	54 57.0	−39.5	125.2	53 46.0	−41.7	127.4	52 31.3	−43.5	129.5	51 13.4	−45.2	131.4	0
55 26.8	38.1	124.1	54 17.5	40.4	126.5	53 04.3	42.3	128.6	51 47.8	44.2	130.6	50 28.2	45.8	132.5	1
54 48.7	39.1	125.5	53 37.1	41.1	127.7	52 22.0	43.1	129.8	51 03.6	44.7	131.7	49 42.4	46.3	133.5	2
54 09.6	39.8	126.8	52 56.0	41.9	128.9	51 38.9	43.7	130.9	50 18.9	45.4	132.8	48 56.1	46.8	134.5	3
53 29.8	40.6	128.1	52 14.1	42.5	130.1	50 55.2	44.2	132.0	49 33.5	45.8	133.8	48 09.3	47.3	135.4	4
52 49.2	−41.4	129.3	51 31.6	−43.2	131.3	50 11.0	−44.8	133.1	48 47.7	−46.3	134.8	47 22.0	−47.6	136.3	5
52 07.8	42.1	130.5	50 48.4	43.8	132.4	49 26.2	45.4	134.1	48 01.4	46.8	135.7	46 34.4	48.1	137.2	6
51 25.7	42.7	131.6	50 04.6	44.4	133.4	48 40.8	45.9	135.1	47 14.6	47.2	136.7	45 46.3	48.4	138.1	7
50 43.0	43.3	132.8	49 20.2	44.9	134.5	47 54.9	46.3	136.1	46 27.4	47.6	137.6	44 57.9	48.8	138.9	8
49 59.7	44.0	133.8	48 35.3	45.4	135.5	47 08.6	46.8	137.0	45 39.8	48.0	138.4	44 09.1	49.2	139.7	9
49 15.7	−44.5	134.9	47 49.9	−46.0	136.5	46 21.8	−47.2	137.9	44 51.8	−48.4	139.3	43 19.9	−49.4	140.5	10
48 31.2	45.0	135.9	47 03.9	46.3	137.4	45 34.6	47.6	138.8	44 03.4	48.8	140.1	42 30.5	49.8	141.3	11
47 46.2	45.5	136.9	46 17.6	46.8	138.3	44 47.0	48.0	139.7	43 14.6	49.0	140.9	41 40.7	50.0	142.1	12
47 00.7	46.0	137.9	45 30.8	47.3	139.2	43 59.0	48.4	140.5	42 25.6	49.4	141.7	40 50.7	50.4	142.8	13
46 14.7	46.4	138.8	44 43.5	47.6	140.1	43 10.6	48.7	141.3	41 36.2	49.7	142.5	40 00.3	50.5	143.5	14
45 28.3	−46.8	139.7	43 55.9	−48.0	141.0	42 21.9	−49.0	142.1	40 46.5	−50.0	143.2	39 09.8	−50.9	144.2	15
44 41.5	47.3	140.6	43 07.9	48.3	141.8	41 32.9	49.3	142.9	39 56.5	50.2	143.9	38 18.9	51.0	144.9	16
43 54.2	47.6	141.5	42 19.6	48.6	142.6	40 43.6	49.6	143.7	39 06.3	50.5	144.7	37 27.9	51.3	145.6	17
43 06.6	48.0	142.3	41 31.0	49.0	143.4	39 54.0	49.9	144.4	38 15.8	50.7	145.3	36 36.6	51.5	146.2	18
42 18.6	48.3	143.1	40 42.0	49.3	144.2	39 04.1	50.1	145.1	37 25.1	50.9	146.0	35 45.1	51.7	146.8	19
41 30.3	−48.6	143.9	39 52.7	−49.5	144.9	38 14.0	−50.4	145.8	36 34.2	−51.2	146.7	34 53.4	−51.8	147.5	20
40 41.7	49.0	144.7	39 03.2	49.9	145.7	37 23.6	50.7	146.5	35 43.0	51.3	147.3	34 01.6	52.1	148.1	21
39 52.7	49.2	145.4	38 13.3	50.0	146.4	36 32.9	50.8	147.2	34 51.7	51.6	148.0	33 09.5	52.2	148.7	22
39 03.5	49.5	146.2	37 23.3	50.4	147.1	35 42.1	51.0	147.8	34 00.1	51.7	148.6	32 17.3	52.3	149.3	23
38 14.0	49.8	146.9	36 32.9	50.5	147.7	34 51.1	51.3	148.5	33 08.4	51.9	149.2	31 25.0	52.6	149.8	24
37 24.2	−50.0	147.6	35 42.4	−50.7	148.4	33 59.8	−51.4	149.1	32 16.5	−52.1	149.8	30 32.4	−52.6	150.4	25
36 34.2	50.3	148.3	34 51.7	51.0	149.1	33 08.4	51.7	149.7	31 24.4	52.3	150.4	29 39.8	52.8	150.9	26
35 43.9	50.5	149.0	34 00.7	51.2	149.7	32 16.7	51.7	150.3	30 32.1	52.3	150.9	28 47.0	53.0	151.5	27
34 53.4	50.6	149.6	33 09.5	51.3	150.3	31 25.0	52.0	150.9	29 39.8	52.6	151.5	27 54.0	53.0	152.0	28
34 02.8	50.9	150.3	32 18.2	51.5	150.9	30 33.0	52.1	151.5	28 47.2	52.6	152.1	27 01.0	53.2	152.6	29

30°			32°			34°			36°			38°			Dec.
Hc	d	Z	Hc	d	Z	Hc	d	Z	Hc	d	Z	Hc	d	Z	
° ′	′	°	° ′	′	°	° ′	′	°	° ′	′	°	° ′	′	°	°
49 52.6	−46.8	133.2	48 29.1	−48.2	134.9	47 03.2	−49.4	136.4	45 35.2	−50.5	137.9	44 05.3	−51.5	139.2	0
49 05.8	47.3	134.2	47 40.9	48.6	135.8	46 13.8	49.8	137.3	44 44.7	50.8	138.6	43 13.8	51.8	139.9	1
48 18.5	47.7	135.1	46 52.3	48.9	136.7	45 24.0	50.1	138.1	43 53.9	51.2	139.4	42 22.0	52.1	140.6	2
47 30.8	48.1	136.0	46 03.4	49.3	137.5	44 33.9	50.4	138.8	43 02.7	51.4	140.1	41 29.9	52.3	141.2	3
46 42.7	48.5	136.9	45 14.1	49.7	138.3	43 43.5	50.7	139.6	42 11.3	51.6	140.8	40 37.6	52.5	141.9	4
45 54.2	−48.9	137.8	44 24.4	−50.0	139.1	42 52.8	−50.9	140.3	41 19.7	−51.9	141.5	39 45.1	−52.7	142.5	5
45 05.3	49.2	138.6	43 34.4	50.2	139.9	42 01.9	51.3	141.1	40 27.8	52.1	142.1	38 52.4	52.9	143.2	6
44 16.1	49.5	139.4	42 44.2	50.6	140.6	41 10.6	51.4	141.8	39 35.7	52.3	142.8	37 59.5	53.0	143.8	7
43 26.6	49.9	140.2	41 53.6	50.8	141.4	40 19.2	51.7	142.4	38 43.4	52.5	143.4	37 06.5	53.3	144.3	8
42 36.7	50.2	140.9	41 02.8	51.1	142.1	39 27.5	52.0	143.1	37 50.9	52.7	144.0	36 13.2	53.4	144.9	9
41 46.5	−50.4	141.7	40 11.7	−51.3	142.8	38 35.5	−52.1	143.7	36 58.2	−52.9	144.6	35 19.8	−53.5	145.5	10
40 56.1	50.7	142.4	39 20.4	51.6	143.4	37 43.4	52.3	144.4	36 05.3	53.0	145.2	34 26.3	53.7	146.0	11
40 05.4	50.9	143.1	38 28.8	51.8	144.1	36 51.1	52.5	145.0	35 12.3	53.2	145.8	33 32.6	53.8	146.6	12
39 14.5	51.2	143.8	37 37.0	51.9	144.7	35 58.6	52.7	145.6	34 19.1	53.4	146.4	32 38.8	54.0	147.1	13
38 23.3	51.4	144.5	36 45.1	52.2	145.4	35 05.9	52.9	146.2	33 25.7	53.5	146.9	31 44.8	54.1	147.6	14
37 31.9	−51.7	145.1	35 52.9	−52.3	146.0	34 13.0	−53.0	146.7	32 32.2	−53.6	147.5	30 50.7	−54.2	148.1	15
36 40.2	51.8	145.8	35 00.6	52.6	146.6	33 20.0	53.2	147.3	31 38.6	53.8	148.0	29 56.5	54.3	148.6	16
35 48.4	52.0	146.4	34 08.0	52.6	147.2	32 26.8	53.3	147.9	30 44.8	53.8	148.5	29 02.2	54.4	149.1	17
34 56.4	52.2	147.0	33 15.4	52.9	147.7	31 33.5	53.4	148.4	29 51.0	54.0	149.0	28 07.8	54.5	149.6	18
34 04.2	52.3	147.6	32 22.5	53.0	148.3	30 40.1	53.6	148.9	28 57.0	54.1	149.5	27 13.3	54.6	150.1	19
33 11.9	−52.6	148.2	31 29.5	−53.1	148.8	29 46.5	−53.7	149.5	28 02.9	−54.2	150.0	26 18.7	−54.7	150.5	20
32 19.3	52.6	148.8	30 36.4	53.3	149.4	28 52.8	53.8	150.0	27 08.7	54.4	150.5	25 24.0	54.8	151.0	21
31 26.7	52.8	149.3	29 43.1	53.3	149.9	27 59.0	53.9	150.5	26 14.3	54.4	151.0	24 29.2	54.9	151.4	22
30 33.9	53.0	149.9	28 49.8	53.5	150.4	27 05.1	54.0	151.0	25 19.9	54.4	151.4	23 34.3	54.9	151.9	23
29 40.9	53.1	150.4	27 56.3	53.7	151.0	26 11.1	54.1	151.4	24 25.5	54.6	151.9	22 39.4	55.0	152.3	24
28 47.8	−53.2	151.0	27 02.6	−53.7	151.5	25 17.0	−54.2	151.9	23 30.9	−54.7	152.4	21 44.4	−55.1	152.7	25
27 54.6	53.3	151.5	26 08.9	53.8	152.0	24 22.8	54.3	152.4	22 36.2	54.7	152.8	20 49.3	55.1	153.2	26
27 01.3	53.5	152.0	25 15.1	53.9	152.5	23 28.5	54.4	152.9	21 41.5	54.8	153.3	19 54.2	55.2	153.6	27
26 07.8	53.5	152.5	24 21.2	54.0	152.9	22 34.1	54.4	153.3	20 46.7	54.8	153.7	18 59.0	55.2	154.0	28
25 14.3	53.7	153.0	23 27.2	54.1	153.4	21 39.7	54.6	153.8	19 51.9	55.0	154.1	18 03.8	55.3	154.4	29

Dec.	40° Hc	d	Z	42° Hc	d	Z	44° Hc	d	Z	46° Hc	d	Z	48° Hc	d	Z
°	° ′	′	°	° ′	′	°	° ′	′	°	° ′	′	°	° ′	′	°
0	42 33.7	+52.2	140.4	41 00.5	+53.1	141.5	39 25.8	+53.9	142.6	37 49.9	+54.6	143.5	36 12.9	+55.2	144.4
1	43 25.9	52.0	139.7	41 53.6	52.9	140.9	40 19.7	53.7	142.0	38 44.5	54.4	143.0	37 08.1	55.0	143.9
2	44 17.9	51.8	139.0	42 46.5	52.6	140.3	41 13.4	53.5	141.4	39 38.9	54.3	142.5	38 03.1	55.0	143.4
3	45 09.7	51.4	138.3	43 39.1	52.5	139.6	42 06.9	53.3	140.8	40 33.2	54.1	141.9	38 58.1	54.8	142.9
4	46 01.1	51.2	137.6	44 31.6	52.2	138.9	43 00.2	53.2	140.2	41 27.3	53.9	141.3	39 52.9	54.7	142.4
5	46 52.3	+50.9	136.8	45 23.8	+51.9	138.2	43 53.4	+52.8	139.5	42 21.2	+53.8	140.7	40 47.6	+54.5	141.8
6	47 43.2	50.5	136.1	46 15.7	51.7	137.5	44 46.2	52.7	138.9	43 15.0	53.5	140.1	41 42.1	54.3	141.3
7	48 33.7	50.2	135.2	47 07.4	51.3	136.8	45 38.9	52.4	138.2	44 08.5	53.4	139.5	42 36.4	54.2	140.7
8	49 23.9	49.8	134.4	47 58.7	51.1	136.0	46 31.3	52.1	137.5	45 01.9	53.1	138.9	43 30.6	54.0	140.1
9	50 13.7	49.4	133.5	48 49.8	50.7	135.2	47 23.4	51.9	136.8	45 55.0	52.9	138.2	44 24.6	53.8	139.5
10	51 03.1	+49.0	132.7	49 40.5	+50.3	134.4	48 15.3	+51.6	136.0	46 47.9	+52.6	137.5	45 18.4	+53.6	138.9
11	51 52.1	48.6	131.7	50 30.8	50.0	133.6	49 06.9	51.2	135.2	47 40.5	52.3	136.8	46 12.0	53.3	138.3
12	52 40.7	48.0	130.8	51 20.8	49.6	132.7	49 58.1	50.9	134.4	48 32.8	52.1	136.1	47 05.3	53.1	137.6
13	53 28.7	47.6	129.8	52 10.4	49.1	131.8	50 49.0	50.5	133.6	49 24.9	51.8	135.3	47 58.4	52.9	136.9
14	54 16.3	47.0	128.7	52 59.5	48.6	130.8	51 39.5	50.1	132.8	50 16.7	51.4	134.5	48 51.3	52.5	136.2
15	55 03.3	+46.4	127.7	53 48.1	+48.2	129.8	52 29.6	+49.7	131.9	51 08.1	+51.1	133.7	49 43.8	+52.3	135.4
16	55 49.7	45.7	126.5	54 36.3	47.6	128.8	53 19.3	49.3	130.9	51 59.2	50.7	132.9	50 36.1	52.0	134.7
17	56 35.4	45.1	125.4	55 23.9	47.1	127.8	54 08.6	48.8	130.0	52 49.9	50.3	132.0	51 28.1	51.7	133.9
18	57 20.5	44.4	124.2	56 11.0	46.4	126.7	54 57.4	48.2	129.0	53 40.2	49.9	131.1	52 19.8	51.2	133.1
19	58 04.9	43.6	122.9	56 57.4	45.8	125.5	55 45.6	47.7	127.9	54 30.1	49.4	130.1	53 11.0	50.9	132.2
20	58 48.5	+42.7	121.6	57 43.2	+45.0	124.3	56 33.3	+47.2	126.8	55 19.5	+48.9	129.2	54 01.9	+50.5	131.3
21	59 31.2	41.9	120.2	58 28.2	44.3	123.1	57 20.5	46.4	125.7	56 08.4	48.3	128.1	54 52.4	50.1	130.4
22	60 13.1	40.9	118.8	59 12.5	43.5	121.8	58 06.9	45.8	124.5	56 56.7	47.8	127.1	55 42.5	49.5	129.4
23	60 54.0	39.8	117.3	59 56.0	42.6	120.4	58 52.7	45.1	123.3	57 44.5	47.2	125.9	56 32.0	49.1	128.4
24	61 33.8	38.8	115.8	60 38.6	41.7	119.0	59 37.8	44.2	122.0	58 31.7	46.5	124.8	57 21.1	48.5	127.3
25	62 12.6	+37.6	114.1	61 20.3	+40.7	117.5	60 22.0	+43.4	120.6	59 18.2	+45.8	123.5	58 09.6	+47.9	126.2
26	62 50.2	36.3	112.4	62 01.0	39.5	115.9	61 05.4	42.4	119.2	60 04.0	45.0	122.3	58 57.5	47.2	125.1
27	63 26.5	34.9	110.7	62 40.5	38.4	114.3	61 47.8	41.5	117.7	60 49.0	44.2	120.9	59 44.7	46.6	123.9
28	64 01.4	33.5	108.8	63 18.9	37.1	112.6	62 29.3	40.4	116.2	61 33.2	43.3	119.5	60 31.3	45.8	122.6
29	64 34.9	32.0	106.9	63 56.0	35.8	110.9	63 09.7	39.2	114.6	62 16.5	42.3	118.0	61 17.1	44.9	121.3

Dec.	50° Hc	d	Z	52° Hc	d	Z	54° Hc	d	Z	56° Hc	d	Z	58° Hc	d	Z
°	° ′	′	°	° ′	′	°	° ′	′	°	° ′	′	°	° ′	′	°
0	34 34.8	+55.7	145.2	32 55.7	+56.3	146.0	31 15.8	+56.8	146.7	29 35.2	+57.2	147.3	27 53.8	+57.6	147.9
1	35 30.5	55.7	144.8	33 52.0	56.2	145.6	32 12.6	56.7	146.3	30 32.4	57.1	147.0	28 51.4	57.5	147.6
2	36 26.2	55.6	144.3	34 48.2	56.1	145.2	33 09.3	56.6	145.9	31 29.5	57.0	146.6	29 48.9	57.5	147.3
3	37 21.8	55.5	143.9	35 44.3	56.1	144.7	34 05.9	56.5	145.5	32 26.5	57.0	146.3	30 46.4	57.4	146.9
4	38 17.2	55.3	143.4	36 40.4	55.9	144.3	35 02.4	56.5	145.1	33 23.5	56.9	145.9	31 43.8	57.3	146.6
5	39 12.5	+55.2	142.9	37 36.3	+55.8	143.8	35 58.9	+56.3	144.7	34 20.4	+56.9	145.5	32 41.1	+57.3	146.2
6	40 07.7	55.1	142.4	38 32.1	55.7	143.4	36 55.2	56.3	144.3	35 17.3	56.8	145.1	33 38.4	57.2	145.9
7	41 02.8	54.9	141.8	39 27.8	55.5	142.9	37 51.5	56.2	143.8	36 14.1	56.7	144.7	34 35.6	57.2	145.5
8	41 57.7	54.8	141.3	40 23.4	55.4	142.4	38 47.7	56.0	143.4	37 10.8	56.6	144.3	35 32.8	57.1	145.2
9	42 52.5	54.6	140.7	41 18.8	55.3	141.9	39 43.7	56.0	142.9	38 07.4	56.5	143.9	36 29.9	57.0	144.8
10	43 47.1	+54.4	140.2	42 14.1	+55.2	141.4	40 39.7	+55.8	142.4	39 03.9	+56.4	143.5	37 26.9	+56.9	144.4
11	44 41.5	54.2	139.6	43 09.3	55.0	140.8	41 35.5	55.7	142.0	40 00.3	56.3	143.0	38 23.8	56.9	144.0
12	45 35.7	54.0	139.0	44 04.3	54.8	140.3	42 31.2	55.6	141.5	40 56.6	56.2	142.6	39 20.7	56.8	143.6
13	46 29.7	53.9	138.4	44 59.1	54.7	139.7	43 26.8	55.4	140.9	41 52.8	56.1	142.1	40 17.5	56.6	143.2
14	47 23.6	53.6	137.7	45 53.8	54.5	139.1	44 22.2	55.3	140.4	42 48.9	56.0	141.6	41 14.1	56.6	142.7
15	48 17.2	+53.3	137.0	46 48.3	+54.3	138.5	45 17.5	+55.1	139.9	43 44.9	+55.8	141.1	42 10.7	+56.5	142.3
16	49 10.5	53.1	136.3	47 42.6	54.1	137.9	46 12.6	54.9	139.3	44 40.7	55.7	140.6	43 07.2	56.3	141.8
17	50 03.6	52.8	135.6	48 36.7	53.8	137.2	47 07.5	54.8	138.7	45 36.4	55.5	140.1	44 03.5	56.2	141.3
18	50 56.4	52.5	134.9	49 30.5	53.6	136.6	48 02.3	54.5	138.1	46 31.9	55.4	139.5	44 59.7	56.1	140.8
19	51 48.9	52.2	134.1	50 24.1	53.3	135.9	48 56.8	54.3	137.5	47 27.3	55.2	139.0	45 55.8	56.0	140.3
20	52 41.1	+51.9	133.3	51 17.4	+53.1	135.1	49 51.1	+54.2	136.8	48 22.5	+55.0	138.4	46 51.8	+55.9	139.8
21	53 33.0	51.5	132.5	52 10.5	52.8	134.4	50 45.3	53.8	136.1	49 17.5	54.9	137.8	47 47.6	55.7	139.3
22	54 24.5	51.1	131.6	53 03.3	52.4	133.6	51 39.1	53.6	135.4	50 12.4	54.6	137.1	48 43.3	55.4	138.7
23	55 15.6	50.7	130.7	53 55.7	52.1	132.8	52 32.7	53.3	134.7	51 07.0	54.3	136.5	49 38.7	55.3	138.1
24	56 06.3	50.2	129.7	54 47.8	51.7	131.9	53 26.0	53.1	134.0	52 01.3	54.2	135.8	50 34.0	55.1	137.5
25	56 56.5	+49.7	128.7	55 39.5	+51.4	131.0	54 19.1	+52.7	133.2	52 55.5	+53.9	135.1	51 29.1	+54.9	136.9
26	57 46.2	49.2	127.7	56 30.9	50.8	130.1	55 11.8	52.3	132.3	53 49.4	53.6	134.4	52 24.0	54.7	136.2
27	58 35.4	48.7	126.6	57 21.7	50.5	129.1	56 04.1	52.0	131.5	54 43.0	53.2	133.6	53 18.7	54.3	135.6
28	59 24.1	48.0	125.5	58 12.2	49.9	128.1	56 56.1	51.5	130.6	55 36.2	53.0	132.8	54 13.1	54.2	134.8
29	60 12.1	47.3	124.3	59 02.1	49.3	127.1	57 47.6	51.1	129.6	56 29.2	52.6	132.0	55 07.3	53.9	134.1

40°			42°			44°			46°			48°			Dec.
Hc	d	Z	Hc	d	Z	Hc	d	Z	Hc	d	Z	Hc	d	Z	
° ′	′	°	° ′	′	°	° ′	′	°	° ′	′	°	° ′	′	°	°
42 33.7	−52.5	140.4	41 00.5	−53.3	141.5	39 25.8	−54.0	142.6	37 49.9	−54.7	143.5	36 12.9	−55.4	144.4	0
41 41.2	52.7	141.1	40 07.2	53.5	142.1	38 31.8	54.2	143.1	36 55.2	54.8	144.0	35 17.5	55.4	144.9	1
40 48.5	52.9	141.7	39 13.7	53.7	142.7	37 37.6	54.4	143.7	36 00.4	55.0	144.6	34 22.1	55.5	145.4	2
39 55.6	53.1	142.3	38 20.0	53.8	143.3	36 43.2	54.4	144.2	35 05.4	55.1	145.0	33 26.6	55.7	145.8	3
39 02.5	53.2	142.9	37 26.2	54.0	143.9	35 48.8	54.7	144.7	34 10.3	55.2	145.5	32 30.9	55.7	146.3	4
38 09.3	−53.5	143.5	36 32.2	−54.1	144.4	34 54.1	−54.7	145.2	33 15.1	−55.3	146.0	31 35.2	−55.8	146.7	5
37 15.8	53.6	144.1	35 38.1	54.3	144.9	33 59.4	54.9	145.7	32 19.8	55.4	146.5	30 39.4	55.9	147.1	6
36 22.2	53.7	144.6	34 43.8	54.3	145.5	33 04.5	54.9	146.2	31 24.4	55.5	146.9	29 43.5	56.0	147.5	7
35 28.5	54.0	145.2	33 49.5	54.6	146.0	32 09.6	55.1	146.7	30 28.9	55.6	147.4	28 47.5	56.0	148.0	8
34 34.5	54.0	145.7	32 54.9	54.6	146.5	31 14.5	55.2	147.2	29 33.3	55.6	147.8	27 51.5	56.1	148.4	9
33 40.5	−54.2	146.3	32 00.3	−54.7	147.0	30 19.3	−55.2	147.6	28 37.7	−55.8	148.2	26 55.4	−56.2	148.8	10
32 46.3	54.3	146.8	31 05.6	54.9	147.4	29 24.1	55.4	148.1	27 41.9	55.8	148.6	25 59.2	56.3	149.2	11
31 52.0	54.4	147.3	30 10.7	54.9	147.9	28 28.7	55.4	148.5	26 46.1	55.9	149.0	25 02.9	56.3	149.5	12
30 57.6	54.5	147.8	29 15.8	55.1	148.4	27 33.3	55.5	148.9	25 50.2	55.9	149.5	24 06.6	56.3	149.9	13
30 03.1	54.6	148.2	28 20.7	55.1	148.8	26 37.8	55.6	149.4	24 54.3	56.1	149.9	23 10.3	56.5	150.3	14
29 08.5	−54.8	148.7	27 25.6	−55.3	149.3	25 42.2	−55.7	149.8	23 58.2	−56.0	150.2	22 13.8	−56.4	150.7	15
28 13.7	54.8	149.2	26 30.4	55.3	149.7	24 46.5	55.7	150.2	23 02.2	56.2	150.6	21 17.4	56.5	151.0	16
27 18.9	54.9	149.6	25 35.1	55.4	150.1	23 50.8	55.8	150.6	22 06.0	56.2	151.0	20 20.9	56.6	151.4	17
26 24.0	55.0	150.1	24 39.7	55.4	150.6	22 55.0	55.8	151.0	21 09.8	56.2	151.4	19 24.3	56.6	151.7	18
25 29.0	55.0	150.5	23 44.3	55.5	151.0	21 59.2	56.0	151.4	20 13.6	56.3	151.8	18 27.7	56.6	152.1	19
24 34.0	−55.2	151.0	22 48.8	−55.6	151.4	21 03.2	−55.9	151.8	19 17.3	−56.3	152.1	17 31.1	−56.7	152.4	20
23 38.8	55.2	151.4	21 53.2	55.6	151.8	20 07.3	56.0	152.2	18 21.0	56.4	152.5	16 34.4	56.7	152.8	21
22 43.6	55.3	151.9	20 57.6	55.7	152.2	19 11.3	56.1	152.6	17 24.6	56.4	152.9	15 37.7	56.8	153.1	22
21 48.3	55.3	152.3	20 01.9	55.7	152.6	18 15.2	56.1	152.9	16 28.2	56.4	153.2	14 41.0	56.8	153.5	23
20 53.0	55.4	152.7	19 06.2	55.8	153.0	17 19.1	56.1	153.3	15 31.8	56.5	153.6	13 44.2	56.8	153.8	24
19 57.6	−55.5	153.1	18 10.4	−55.8	153.4	16 23.0	−56.2	153.7	14 35.3	−56.5	153.9	12 47.4	−56.8	154.1	25
19 02.1	55.5	153.5	17 14.6	55.9	153.8	15 26.8	56.2	154.0	13 38.8	56.5	154.3	11 50.6	56.9	154.5	26
18 06.6	55.6	153.9	16 18.7	55.9	154.2	14 30.6	56.3	154.4	12 42.3	56.6	154.6	10 53.8	56.9	154.8	27
17 11.0	55.6	154.3	15 22.8	56.0	154.5	13 34.3	56.2	154.8	11 45.7	56.6	155.0	9 56.9	56.9	155.1	28
16 15.4	55.6	154.7	14 26.8	56.0	154.9	12 38.1	56.3	155.1	10 49.1	56.6	155.3	9 00.0	56.8	155.4	29

50°			52°			54°			56°			58°			Dec.
Hc	d	Z	Hc	d	Z	Hc	d	Z	Hc	d	Z	Hc	d	Z	
° ′	′	°	° ′	′	°	° ′	′	°	° ′	′	°	° ′	′	°	°
34 34.8	−55.9	145.2	32 55.7	−56.3	146.0	31 15.8	−56.8	146.7	29 35.2	−57.2	147.3	27 53.8	−57.5	147.9	0
33 38.9	56.0	145.7	31 59.4	56.5	146.4	30 19.0	56.9	147.1	28 38.0	57.3	147.7	26 56.3	57.7	148.2	1
32 42.9	56.0	146.1	31 02.9	56.5	146.8	29 22.1	56.9	147.4	27 40.7	57.3	148.0	25 58.6	57.7	148.5	2
31 46.9	56.2	146.6	30 06.4	56.6	147.2	28 25.2	57.0	147.8	26 43.4	57.4	148.3	25 00.9	57.7	148.8	3
30 50.7	56.2	146.9	29 09.8	56.6	147.6	27 28.2	57.0	148.1	25 46.0	57.4	148.7	24 03.2	57.7	149.1	4
29 54.5	−56.2	147.3	28 13.2	−56.7	147.9	26 31.2	−57.1	148.5	24 48.6	−57.5	149.0	23 05.5	−57.8	149.4	5
28 58.3	56.4	147.7	27 16.5	56.8	148.3	25 34.1	57.2	148.8	23 51.1	57.5	149.3	22 07.7	57.8	149.7	6
28 01.9	56.4	148.1	26 19.7	56.8	148.7	24 36.9	57.2	149.2	22 53.6	57.5	149.6	21 09.9	57.8	150.0	7
27 05.5	56.5	148.5	25 22.9	56.9	149.0	23 39.7	57.2	149.5	21 56.1	57.6	149.9	20 12.1	57.9	150.3	8
26 09.0	56.5	148.9	24 26.0	56.9	149.4	22 42.5	57.3	149.8	20 58.5	57.6	150.2	19 14.2	57.9	150.6	9
25 12.5	−56.6	149.3	23 29.1	−57.0	149.7	21 45.2	−57.3	150.1	20 00.9	−57.6	150.5	18 16.3	−57.9	150.9	10
24 15.9	56.7	149.7	22 32.1	57.0	150.1	20 47.9	57.3	150.5	19 03.3	57.6	150.8	17 18.4	58.0	151.1	11
23 19.2	56.7	150.0	21 35.1	57.0	150.4	19 50.6	57.4	150.8	18 05.7	57.7	151.1	16 20.4	57.9	151.4	12
22 22.5	56.7	150.4	20 38.1	57.1	150.7	18 53.2	57.4	151.1	17 08.0	57.7	151.4	15 22.5	58.0	151.7	13
21 25.8	56.9	150.8	19 41.0	57.1	151.1	17 55.8	57.4	151.4	16 10.3	57.7	151.7	14 24.5	58.0	151.9	14
20 29.0	−56.8	151.0	18 43.8	−57.1	151.4	16 58.3	−57.4	151.7	15 12.6	−57.8	152.0	13 26.5	−58.0	152.2	15
19 32.2	56.9	151.4	17 46.7	57.2	151.7	16 00.9	57.5	152.0	14 14.8	57.8	152.3	12 28.5	58.0	152.5	16
18 35.3	56.8	151.8	16 49.5	57.2	152.0	15 03.4	57.5	152.3	13 17.0	57.7	152.5	11 30.5	58.1	152.7	17
17 38.5	57.0	152.1	15 52.3	57.2	152.3	14 05.9	57.5	152.6	12 19.3	57.8	152.8	10 32.4	58.0	153.0	18
16 41.5	56.9	152.4	14 55.1	57.3	152.7	13 08.4	57.6	152.9	11 21.5	57.9	153.1	9 34.4	58.1	153.2	19
15 44.6	−57.0	152.7	13 57.8	−57.3	153.0	12 10.8	−57.6	153.2	10 23.6	−57.8	153.4	8 36.3	−58.1	153.5	20
14 47.6	57.0	153.0	13 00.5	57.3	153.3	11 13.2	57.5	153.5	9 25.8	57.8	153.6	7 38.2	58.0	153.8	21
13 50.6	57.1	153.4	12 03.2	57.3	153.6	10 15.7	57.6	153.7	8 28.0	57.9	153.9	6 40.2	58.0	154.0	22
12 53.5	57.0	153.7	11 05.9	57.4	153.9	9 18.1	57.7	154.0	7 30.1	57.9	154.2	5 42.1	58.1	154.3	23
11 56.5	57.1	154.0	10 08.5	57.3	154.2	8 20.4	57.6	154.3	6 32.2	57.8	154.4	4 44.0	58.1	154.5	24
10 59.4	−57.1	154.3	9 11.2	−57.4	154.5	7 22.8	−57.6	154.6	5 34.4	−57.9	154.7	3 45.9	−58.1	154.8	25
10 02.3	57.2	154.6	8 13.8	57.4	154.8	6 25.2	57.7	154.9	4 36.5	57.9	155.0	2 47.8	58.2	155.0	26
9 05.1	57.1	154.9	7 16.4	57.4	155.1	5 27.5	57.6	155.2	3 38.6	57.9	155.2	1 49.6	58.1	155.3	27
8 08.0	57.3	155.2	6 19.0	57.4	155.3	4 29.9	57.7	155.4	2 40.7	57.9	155.5	0 51.5	−58.1	155.5	28
7 10.9	57.2	155.6	5 21.6	57.4	155.6	3 32.2	57.6	155.7	1 42.8	57.9	155.7	0 06.6	+58.1	24.2	29

LATITUDE **SAME** NAME   L.H.A. 152°, 208°

LATITUDE **SAME** NAME

Dec.	0° Hc	d	Z	2° Hc	d	Z	4° Hc	d	Z	6° Hc	d	Z	8° Hc	d	Z
0	60 00.0	− 0.9	90.0	59 56.4	+ 3.3	93.5	59 45.5	+ 7.5	96.9	59 27.6	+11.5	100.3	59 02.9	+15.4	103.6
1	59 59.1	2.7	88.0	59 59.7	+ 1.4	91.5	59 53.0	5.6	94.9	59 39.1	9.8	98.3	59 18.3	13.8	101.7
2	59 56.4	4.5	86.0	60 01.1	− 0.3	89.5	59 58.6	3.9	92.9	59 48.9	8.0	96.4	59 32.1	12.0	99.8
3	59 51.9	6.4	84.0	60 00.8	2.2	87.5	60 02.5	2.0	90.9	59 56.9	6.2	94.4	59 44.1	10.3	97.8
4	59 45.5	8.0	82.0	59 58.6	4.0	85.5	60 04.5	+ 0.2	88.9	60 03.1	4.4	92.4	59 54.4	8.6	95.9
5	59 37.5	− 9.9	80.1	59 54.6	− 5.7	83.5	60 04.7	− 1.6	86.9	60 07.5	+ 2.6	90.4	60 03.0	+ 6.8	93.9
6	59 27.6	11.5	78.1	59 48.9	7.6	81.5	60 03.1	3.4	84.9	60 10.1	+ 0.8	88.4	60 09.8	5.0	91.9
7	59 16.1	13.2	76.2	59 41.3	9.2	79.5	59 59.7	5.3	82.9	60 10.9	− 1.1	86.4	60 14.8	3.1	89.9
8	59 02.9	14.9	74.3	59 32.1	11.1	77.6	59 54.4	7.0	80.9	60 09.8	2.9	84.4	60 17.9	+ 1.3	87.9
9	58 48.0	16.5	72.4	59 21.0	12.7	75.6	59 47.4	8.7	79.0	60 06.9	4.7	82.4	60 19.2	− 0.5	85.8
10	58 31.5	−18.1	70.6	59 08.3	−14.4	73.7	59 38.7	−10.6	77.0	60 02.2	− 6.5	80.4	60 18.7	− 2.3	83.8
11	58 13.4	19.5	68.8	58 53.9	16.0	71.8	59 28.1	12.2	75.1	59 55.7	8.3	78.4	60 16.4	4.2	81.8
12	57 53.9	21.1	67.0	58 37.9	17.6	70.0	59 15.9	13.9	73.1	59 47.4	10.0	76.4	60 12.2	6.0	79.8
13	57 32.8	22.5	65.2	58 20.3	19.1	68.1	59 02.0	15.6	71.2	59 37.4	11.8	74.5	60 06.2	7.8	77.8
14	57 10.3	23.9	63.5	58 01.2	20.6	66.4	58 46.4	17.1	69.4	59 25.6	13.4	72.5	59 58.4	9.6	75.8
15	56 46.4	−25.2	61.8	57 40.6	−22.1	64.6	58 29.3	−18.7	67.5	59 12.2	−15.1	70.6	59 48.8	−11.3	73.8
16	56 21.2	26.4	60.2	57 18.5	23.5	62.9	58 10.6	20.2	65.7	58 57.1	16.8	68.7	59 37.5	13.0	71.9
17	55 54.8	27.8	58.6	56 55.0	24.8	61.2	57 50.4	21.7	63.9	58 40.3	18.3	66.9	59 24.5	14.7	70.0
18	55 27.0	28.9	57.0	56 30.2	26.1	59.5	57 28.7	23.1	62.2	58 22.0	19.8	65.1	59 09.8	16.3	68.1
19	54 58.1	30.0	55.4	56 04.1	27.3	57.9	57 05.6	24.4	60.5	58 02.2	21.3	63.3	58 53.5	18.0	66.2
20	54 28.1	−31.1	53.9	55 36.8	−28.6	56.3	56 41.2	−25.8	58.8	57 40.9	−22.7	61.5	58 35.5	−19.5	64.4
21	53 57.0	32.2	52.5	55 08.2	29.7	54.7	56 15.4	27.0	57.2	57 18.2	24.2	59.8	58 16.0	20.9	62.6
22	53 24.8	33.1	51.1	54 38.5	30.8	53.2	55 48.4	28.3	55.6	56 54.0	25.4	58.1	57 55.1	22.5	60.8
23	52 51.7	34.1	49.7	54 07.7	31.9	51.8	55 20.1	29.4	54.0	56 28.6	26.8	56.4	57 32.6	23.8	59.1
24	52 17.6	35.0	48.3	53 35.8	32.8	50.3	54 50.7	30.5	52.5	56 01.8	27.9	54.8	57 08.8	25.2	57.4
25	51 42.6	−35.9	47.0	53 03.0	−33.8	48.9	54 20.2	−31.6	51.0	55 33.9	−29.2	53.3	56 43.6	−26.5	55.7
26	51 06.7	36.6	45.7	52 29.2	34.8	47.6	53 48.6	32.6	49.6	55 04.7	30.3	51.7	56 17.1	27.7	54.1
27	50 30.1	37.5	44.5	51 54.4	35.6	46.2	53 16.0	33.6	48.1	54 34.4	31.3	50.2	55 49.4	28.9	52.5
28	49 52.6	38.2	43.2	51 18.8	36.5	44.9	52 42.4	34.5	46.8	54 03.1	32.4	48.8	55 20.5	30.1	50.9
29	49 14.4	39.0	42.1	50 42.3	37.2	43.7	52 07.9	35.5	45.4	53 30.7	33.4	47.3	54 50.4	31.2	49.4

Dec.	10° Hc	d	Z	12° Hc	d	Z	14° Hc	d	Z	16° Hc	d	Z	18° Hc	d	Z
0	58 31.5	+19.2	106.7	57 53.9	+22.7	109.8	57 10.3	+26.1	112.7	56 21.2	+29.3	115.5	55 27.0	+32.2	118.2
1	58 50.7	17.6	104.9	58 16.6	21.3	108.1	57 36.4	24.8	111.1	56 50.5	28.0	113.9	55 59.2	31.0	116.7
2	59 08.3	16.0	103.1	58 37.9	19.8	106.3	58 01.2	23.3	109.4	57 18.5	26.7	112.3	56 30.2	29.9	115.1
3	59 24.3	14.4	101.2	58 57.7	18.2	104.4	58 24.5	21.9	107.6	57 45.2	25.4	110.6	57 00.1	28.6	113.5
4	59 38.7	12.6	99.3	59 15.9	16.6	102.6	58 46.4	20.4	105.8	58 10.6	24.0	108.9	57 28.7	27.3	111.9
5	59 51.3	+10.9	97.3	59 32.5	+14.9	100.7	59 06.8	+18.8	104.0	58 34.6	+22.5	107.2	57 56.0	+26.0	110.2
6	60 02.2	9.2	95.4	59 47.4	13.3	98.8	59 25.6	17.2	102.1	58 57.1	21.0	105.4	58 22.0	24.6	108.5
7	60 11.4	7.3	93.4	60 00.7	11.5	96.8	59 42.8	15.6	100.2	59 18.1	19.4	103.6	58 46.6	23.2	106.8
8	60 18.7	5.6	91.4	60 12.2	9.7	94.9	59 58.4	13.8	98.3	59 37.5	17.8	101.7	59 09.8	21.6	105.0
9	60 24.3	3.7	89.4	60 21.9	8.0	92.9	60 12.2	12.1	96.4	59 55.3	16.2	99.8	59 31.4	20.1	103.2
10	60 28.0	+ 1.7	87.3	60 29.9	+ 6.1	90.9	60 24.3	+10.4	94.4	60 11.5	+14.5	97.9	59 51.5	+18.5	101.3
11	60 29.8	+ 0.1	85.3	60 36.0	4.2	88.8	60 34.7	8.5	92.4	60 26.0	12.7	95.9	60 10.0	16.7	99.4
12	60 29.9	− 1.9	83.3	60 40.2	2.4	86.8	60 43.2	6.6	90.4	60 38.7	10.9	93.9	60 26.7	15.1	97.5
13	60 28.0	3.7	81.2	60 42.6	+ 0.6	84.8	60 49.8	4.9	88.3	60 49.6	9.1	91.9	60 41.8	13.3	95.5
14	60 24.3	5.5	79.2	60 43.2	− 1.3	82.7	60 54.7	2.9	86.3	60 58.7	7.2	89.9	60 55.1	11.5	93.5
15	60 18.8	− 7.3	77.2	60 41.9	− 3.2	80.7	60 57.6	+ 1.1	84.2	61 05.9	+ 5.4	87.8	61 06.6	+ 9.7	91.5
16	60 11.5	9.1	75.2	60 38.7	5.1	78.6	60 58.7	− 0.9	82.2	61 11.3	3.4	85.8	61 16.3	7.8	89.4
17	60 02.4	10.9	73.2	60 33.6	6.9	76.6	60 57.8	2.7	80.1	61 14.7	+ 1.6	83.7	61 24.1	5.9	87.3
18	59 51.5	12.6	71.3	60 26.7	8.6	74.6	60 55.1	4.6	78.1	61 16.3	− 0.3	81.6	61 30.0	4.0	85.3
19	59 38.9	14.3	69.3	60 18.1	10.5	72.6	60 50.5	6.4	76.0	61 16.0	2.3	79.5	61 34.0	2.1	83.2
20	59 24.6	−16.0	67.4	60 07.6	−12.3	70.6	60 44.1	− 8.3	74.0	61 13.7	− 4.1	77.5	61 36.1	+ 0.1	81.1
21	59 08.6	17.6	65.5	59 55.3	13.9	68.7	60 35.8	10.1	71.9	61 09.6	6.1	75.4	61 36.2	− 1.8	79.0
22	58 51.0	19.2	63.7	59 41.4	15.7	66.7	60 25.7	11.9	69.9	61 03.5	7.9	73.3	61 34.4	3.8	76.9
23	58 31.8	20.6	61.8	59 25.7	17.3	64.8	60 13.8	13.6	68.0	60 55.6	9.7	71.3	61 30.6	5.6	74.8
24	58 11.2	22.2	60.1	59 08.4	18.8	62.9	60 00.2	15.4	66.0	60 45.9	11.6	69.3	61 25.0	7.6	72.7
25	57 49.0	−23.6	58.3	58 49.6	−20.4	61.1	59 44.8	−17.0	64.1	60 34.3	−13.3	67.3	61 17.4	− 9.4	70.6
26	57 25.4	24.9	56.6	58 29.2	22.0	59.3	59 27.8	18.6	62.2	60 21.0	15.1	65.3	61 08.0	11.3	68.6
27	57 00.5	26.3	54.9	58 07.2	23.3	57.5	59 09.2	20.3	60.3	60 05.9	16.8	63.3	60 56.7	13.0	66.5
28	56 34.2	27.5	53.3	57 43.9	24.8	55.8	58 49.0	21.7	58.5	59 49.1	18.4	61.4	60 43.7	14.9	64.5
29	56 06.7	28.8	51.7	57 19.1	26.1	54.1	58 27.3	23.2	56.7	59 30.7	20.0	59.5	60 28.8	16.6	62.6

0°			2°			4°			6°			8°			Dec.
Hc	d	Z	Hc	d	Z	Hc	d	Z	Hc	d	Z	Hc	d	Z	
60 00.0	- 0.9	90.0	59 56.4	- 5.1	93.5	59 45.5	- 9.1	96.9	59 27.6	-13.1	100.3	59 02.9	-17.1	103.6	0
59 59.1	2.7	92.0	59 51.3	6.9	95.4	59 36.4	11.0	98.8	59 14.5	14.9	102.2	58 45.8	18.6	105.4	1
59 56.4	4.5	94.0	59 44.4	8.6	97.4	59 25.4	12.6	100.8	58 59.6	16.5	104.1	58 27.2	20.1	107.2	2
59 51.9	6.4	96.0	59 35.8	10.4	99.4	59 12.8	14.3	102.7	58 43.1	18.0	105.9	58 07.1	21.6	109.0	3
59 45.5	8.0	98.0	59 25.4	12.0	101.3	58 58.5	15.9	104.6	58 25.1	19.6	107.8	57 45.5	23.1	110.8	4
59 37.5	- 9.9	99.9	59 13.4	-13.8	103.2	58 42.6	-17.5	106.5	58 05.5	-21.1	109.5	57 22.4	-24.4	112.5	5
59 27.6	11.5	101.9	58 59.6	15.4	105.1	58 25.1	19.1	108.3	57 44.4	22.5	111.3	56 58.0	25.8	114.2	6
59 16.1	13.2	103.8	58 44.2	17.0	107.0	58 06.0	20.5	110.1	57 21.9	23.9	113.0	56 32.2	27.0	115.8	7
59 02.9	14.9	105.7	58 27.2	18.5	108.8	57 45.5	22.0	111.9	56 58.0	25.3	114.7	56 05.2	28.3	117.4	8
58 48.0	16.5	107.6	58 08.7	20.1	110.7	57 23.5	23.5	113.6	56 32.7	26.5	116.4	55 36.9	29.4	119.0	9
58 31.5	-18.1	109.4	57 48.6	-21.5	112.4	57 00.0	-24.7	115.3	56 06.2	-27.8	118.0	55 07.5	-30.6	120.6	10
58 13.4	19.5	111.2	57 27.1	22.9	114.2	56 35.3	26.1	117.0	55 38.4	28.9	119.6	54 36.9	31.6	122.0	11
57 53.9	21.1	113.0	57 04.2	24.3	115.9	56 09.2	27.3	118.6	55 09.5	30.1	121.1	54 05.3	32.7	123.5	12
57 32.8	22.5	114.8	56 39.9	25.7	117.6	55 41.9	28.5	120.2	54 39.4	31.2	122.6	53 32.6	33.6	124.9	13
57 10.3	23.9	116.5	56 14.2	26.9	119.2	55 13.4	29.7	121.7	54 08.2	32.3	124.1	52 59.0	34.6	126.3	14
56 46.4	-25.2	118.2	55 47.3	-28.1	120.8	54 43.7	-30.8	123.2	53 35.9	-33.2	125.5	52 24.4	-35.5	127.7	15
56 21.2	26.4	119.8	55 19.2	29.2	122.4	54 12.9	31.8	124.7	53 02.7	34.2	126.9	51 48.9	36.4	129.0	16
55 54.8	27.8	121.4	54 50.0	30.4	123.9	53 41.1	32.9	126.2	52 28.5	35.1	128.3	51 12.5	37.1	130.3	17
55 27.0	28.9	123.0	54 19.6	31.5	125.4	53 08.2	33.8	127.6	51 53.4	36.0	129.6	50 35.4	38.0	131.5	18
54 58.1	30.0	124.6	53 48.1	32.5	126.8	52 34.4	34.7	128.9	51 17.4	36.8	130.9	49 57.4	38.6	132.7	19
54 28.1	-31.1	126.1	53 15.6	-33.4	128.2	51 59.7	-35.6	130.3	50 40.6	-37.5	132.1	49 18.8	-39.4	133.9	20
53 57.0	32.2	127.5	52 42.2	34.4	129.6	51 24.1	36.5	131.6	50 03.1	38.4	133.4	48 39.4	40.1	135.0	21
53 24.8	33.1	128.9	52 07.8	35.3	131.0	50 47.6	37.2	132.8	49 24.7	39.0	134.6	47 59.3	40.6	136.2	22
52 51.7	34.1	130.3	51 32.5	36.2	132.3	50 10.4	38.0	134.1	48 45.7	39.7	135.7	47 18.7	41.3	137.2	23
52 17.6	35.0	131.7	50 56.3	36.9	133.5	49 32.4	38.8	135.3	48 06.0	40.4	136.8	46 37.4	41.9	138.3	24
51 42.6	-35.9	133.0	50 19.4	-37.7	134.8	48 53.6	-39.4	136.4	47 25.6	-41.0	137.9	45 55.5	-42.4	139.3	25
51 06.7	36.6	134.3	49 41.7	38.5	136.0	48 14.2	40.1	137.6	46 44.6	41.6	139.0	45 13.1	42.9	140.4	26
50 30.1	37.5	135.5	49 03.2	39.2	137.2	47 34.1	40.7	138.7	46 03.0	42.1	140.1	44 30.2	43.5	141.3	27
49 52.6	38.2	136.8	48 24.0	39.8	138.3	46 53.4	41.3	139.8	45 20.9	42.7	141.1	43 46.7	43.9	142.3	28
49 14.4	39.0	137.9	47 44.2	40.5	139.4	46 12.1	41.9	140.8	44 38.2	43.1	142.1	43 02.8	44.3	143.2	29

10°			12°			14°			16°			18°			Dec.
Hc	d	Z	Hc	d	Z	Hc	d	Z	Hc	d	Z	Hc	d	Z	
58 31.5	-20.7	106.7	57 53.9	-24.2	109.8	57 10.3	-27.4	112.7	56 21.2	-30.4	115.5	55 27.0	-33.2	118.2	0
58 10.8	22.2	108.5	57 29.7	25.5	111.5	56 42.9	28.7	114.4	55 50.8	31.6	117.1	54 53.8	34.2	119.6	1
57 48.6	23.6	110.3	57 04.2	26.9	113.2	56 14.2	29.8	116.0	55 19.2	32.6	118.6	54 19.6	35.2	121.0	2
57 25.0	25.0	112.0	56 37.3	28.1	114.8	55 44.4	31.1	117.5	54 46.6	33.7	120.0	53 44.4	36.2	122.4	3
57 00.0	26.2	113.7	56 09.2	29.3	116.4	55 13.4	32.1	119.0	54 12.9	34.6	121.5	53 08.2	37.0	123.8	4
56 33.8	-27.6	115.3	55 39.9	-30.4	118.0	54 41.3	-33.1	120.5	53 38.3	-35.6	122.8	52 31.2	-37.8	125.1	5
56 06.2	28.8	116.9	55 09.5	31.6	119.5	54 08.2	34.2	121.9	53 02.7	36.5	124.2	51 53.4	38.6	126.3	6
55 37.4	29.9	118.5	54 37.9	32.6	121.0	53 34.0	35.0	123.3	52 26.2	37.3	125.5	51 14.8	39.4	127.6	7
55 07.5	31.0	120.0	54 05.3	33.6	122.4	52 59.0	36.0	124.7	51 48.9	38.2	126.8	50 35.4	40.1	128.7	8
54 36.5	32.2	121.5	53 31.7	34.6	123.8	52 23.0	36.8	126.0	51 10.7	38.9	128.0	49 55.3	40.8	129.9	9
54 04.3	-33.1	122.9	52 57.1	-35.5	125.2	51 46.2	-37.7	127.3	50 31.8	-39.6	129.2	49 14.5	-41.4	131.0	10
53 31.2	34.1	124.4	52 21.6	36.3	126.5	51 08.5	38.4	128.5	49 52.2	40.3	130.4	48 33.1	42.1	132.1	11
52 57.1	35.0	125.7	51 45.3	37.2	127.8	50 30.1	39.2	129.7	49 11.9	41.0	131.5	47 51.0	42.6	133.2	12
52 22.1	35.9	127.1	51 08.1	38.0	129.1	49 50.9	39.9	130.9	48 30.9	41.6	132.7	47 08.4	43.2	134.3	13
51 46.2	36.8	128.4	50 30.1	38.7	130.3	49 11.0	40.5	132.1	47 49.3	42.1	133.7	46 25.2	43.7	135.3	14
51 09.4	-37.6	129.6	49 51.4	-39.5	131.5	48 30.5	-41.2	133.2	47 07.2	-42.8	134.8	45 41.5	-44.2	136.3	15
50 31.8	38.3	130.9	49 11.9	40.1	132.6	47 49.3	41.7	134.3	46 24.4	43.3	135.8	44 57.3	44.6	137.2	16
49 53.5	39.0	132.1	48 31.8	40.8	133.8	47 07.6	42.4	135.4	45 41.1	43.8	136.8	44 12.7	45.2	138.2	17
49 14.5	39.8	133.3	47 51.0	41.4	134.9	46 25.2	42.9	136.4	44 57.3	44.3	137.8	43 27.5	45.5	139.1	18
48 34.7	40.4	134.4	47 09.6	41.9	135.9	45 42.3	43.4	137.4	44 13.0	44.7	138.7	42 42.0	45.9	140.0	19
47 54.3	-41.0	135.5	46 27.7	-42.6	137.0	44 58.9	-43.9	138.4	43 28.3	-45.2	139.7	41 56.1	-46.4	140.8	20
47 13.3	41.6	136.6	45 45.1	43.0	138.0	44 15.0	44.4	139.3	42 43.1	45.5	140.6	41 09.7	46.7	141.7	21
46 31.7	42.2	137.6	45 02.1	43.6	139.0	43 30.6	44.8	140.3	41 57.6	46.0	141.4	40 23.0	47.0	142.5	22
45 49.5	42.7	138.7	44 18.5	44.0	140.0	42 45.8	45.2	141.2	41 11.6	46.4	142.3	39 36.0	47.4	143.3	23
45 06.8	43.2	139.7	43 34.5	44.5	140.9	42 00.6	45.7	142.1	40 25.2	46.7	143.1	38 48.6	47.7	144.1	24
44 23.6	-43.7	140.6	42 50.0	-44.9	141.8	41 14.9	-46.0	142.9	39 38.5	-47.0	144.0	38 00.9	-48.0	144.9	25
43 39.9	44.2	141.6	42 05.1	45.4	142.7	40 28.9	46.4	143.8	38 51.5	47.4	144.8	37 12.9	48.2	145.6	26
42 55.7	44.7	142.5	41 19.7	45.7	143.6	39 42.5	46.7	144.6	38 04.1	47.6	145.5	36 24.7	48.6	146.4	27
42 11.0	45.0	143.4	40 34.0	46.1	144.5	38 55.8	47.1	145.4	37 16.5	48.0	146.3	35 36.1	48.8	147.1	28
41 26.0	45.4	144.3	39 47.9	46.4	145.3	38 08.7	47.4	146.2	36 28.5	48.3	147.1	34 47.3	49.0	147.8	29

Dec.	20° Hc	d	Z	22° Hc	d	Z	24° Hc	d	Z	26° Hc	d	Z	28° Hc	d	Z
°	° ′	′	°	° ′	′	°	° ′	′	°	° ′	′	°	° ′	′	°
0	54 28.1	+34.8	120.6	53 24.8	+37.3	123.0	52 17.6	+39.5	125.2	51 06.7	+41.6	127.2	49 52.6	+43.4	129.1
1	55 02.9	33.9	119.2	54 02.1	36.4	121.7	52 57.1	38.7	123.9	51 48.3	40.9	126.1	50 36.0	42.8	128.0
2	55 36.8	32.7	117.8	54 38.5	35.4	120.3	53 35.8	37.9	122.6	52 29.2	40.1	124.9	51 18.8	42.1	126.9
3	56 09.5	31.7	116.3	55 13.9	34.5	118.9	54 13.7	37.0	121.3	53 09.3	39.3	123.6	52 00.9	41.5	125.8
4	56 41.2	30.4	114.7	55 48.4	33.3	117.4	54 50.7	36.1	120.0	53 48.6	38.5	122.4	52 42.4	40.7	124.6
5	57 11.6	+29.3	113.2	56 21.7	+32.3	115.9	55 26.8	+35.0	118.6	54 27.1	+37.6	121.0	53 23.1	+40.0	123.4
6	57 40.9	28.0	111.5	56 54.0	31.2	114.4	56 01.8	34.1	117.1	55 04.7	36.7	119.7	54 03.1	39:1	122.1
7	58 08.9	26.6	109.9	57 25.2	29.9	112.8	56 35.9	32.9	115.6	55 41.4	35.7	118.3	54 42.2	38.3	120.8
8	58 35.5	25.3	108.2	57 55.1	28.6	111.2	57 08.8	31.8	114.1	56 17.1	34.7	116.9	55 20.5	37.3	119.5
9	59 00.8	23.8	106.4	58 23.7	27.3	109.6	57 40.6	30.6	112.5	56 51.8	33.6	115.4	55 57.8	36.4	118.1
10	59 24.6	+22.2	104.6	58 51.0	+25.9	107.8	58 11.2	+29.3	110.9	57 25.4	+32.5	113.9	56 34.2	+35.4	116.6
11	59 46.8	20.8	102.8	59 16.9	24.5	106.1	58 40.5	27.9	109.3	57 57.9	31.3	112.3	57 09.6	34.3	115.2
12	60 07.6	19.1	100.9	59 41.4	22.9	104.3	59 08.4	26.6	107.5	58 29.2	30.0	110.7	57 43.9	33.1	113.6
13	60 26.7	17.4	99.0	60 04.3	21.4	102.4	59 35.0	25.2	105.8	58 59.2	28.6	109.0	58 17.0	32.0	112.1
14	60 44.1	15.7	97.1	60 25.7	19.7	100.6	60 00.2	23.6	104.0	59 27.8	27.3	107.3	58 49.0	30.7	110.4
15	60 59.8	+13.9	95.1	60 45.4	+18.1	98.6	60 23.8	+22.1	102.1	59 55.1	+25.9	105.5	59 19.7	+29.4	108.8
16	61 13.7	12.1	93.1	61 03.5	16.3	96.7	60 45.9	20.4	100.2	60 21.0	24.3	103.7	59 49.1	28.0	107.1
17	61 25.8	10.3	91.0	61 19.8	14.6	94.7	61 06.3	18.7	98.3	60 45.3	22.7	101.8	60 17.1	26.6	105.3
18	61 36.1	8.3	89.0	61 34.4	12.7	92.7	61 25.0	17.0	96.3	61 08.0	21.1	99.9	60 43.7	25.0	103.5
19	61 44.4	6.5	86.9	61 47.1	10.8	90.6	61 42.0	15.1	94.3	61 29.1	19.4	98.0	61 08.7	23.4	101.6
20	61 50.9	+4.5*	84.8	61 57.9	+8.9	88.5	61 57.1	+13.3	92.3	61 48.5	+17.6	96.0	61 32.1	+21.8	99.7
21	61 55.4	2.5	82.6	62 06.8	7.0	86.4	62 10.4	11.4	90.2	62 06.1	15.8	94.0	61 53.9	20.0	97.7
22	61 57.9+	0.5	80.5	62 13.8	5.0*	84.3	62 21.8	9.5	88.1	62 21.9	13.9	91.9	62 13.9	18.3	95.7
23	61 58.5 −	1.4	78.4	62 18.8	3.0	82.1	62 31.3	7.5*	85.9	62 35.8	12.0	89.8	62 32.2	16.4	93.6
24	61 57.1	3.3	76.3	62 21.8+	1.1*	80.0	62 38.8	5.5*	83.8	62 47.8	10.0*	87.6	62 48.6	14.5	91.5
25	61 53.8 −	5.3*	74.1	62 22.9 −	1.0*	77.8	62 44.3+	3.5*	81.6	62 57.8+	8.0*	85.5	63 03.1	+12.6	89.4
26	61 48.5	7.3	72.0	62 21.9	3.0	75.7	62 47.8+	1.4*	79.4	63 05.8	6.0*	83.3	63 15.7	10.6*	87.2
27	61 41.2	9.1	69.9	62 18.9	5.0	73.5	62 49.2 −	0.6*	77.2	63 11.8	3.9*	81.1	63 26.3	8.5*	85.0
28	61 32.1	11.0	67.9	62 13.9	6.9	71.4	62 48.6	2.6*	75.1	63 15.7+	1.8*	78.9	63 34.8	6.4*	82.8
29	61 21.1	12.9	65.8	62 07.0	8.9	69.2	62 46.0	4.7*	72.9	63 17.5 −	0.2*	76.7	63 41.2	4.4*	80.6

Dec.	30° Hc	d	Z	32° Hc	d	Z	34° Hc	d	Z	36° Hc	d	Z	38° Hc	d	Z
°	° ′	′	°	° ′	′	°	° ′	′	°	° ′	′	°	° ′	′	°
0	48 35.4	+45.1	130.9	47 15.6	+46.6	132.5	45 53.2	+48.0	134.1	44 28.7	+49.2	135.5	43 02.1	+50.4	136.8
1	49 20.5	44.6	129.9	48 02.2	46.1	131.6	46 41.2	47.6	133.2	45 17.9	48.9	134.7	43 52.5	50.0	136.1
2	50 05.1	44.0	128.9	48 48.3	45.7	130.6	47 28.8	47.2	132.3	46 06.8	48.6	133.9	44 42.5	49.8	135.3
3	50 49.1	43.3	127.8	49 34.0	45.1	129.7	48 16.0	46.7	131.4	46 55.4	48.1	133.0	45 32.3	49.5	134.5
4	51 32.4	42.8	126.7	50 19.1	44.6	128.6	49 02.7	46.2	130.5	47 43.5	47.7	132.1	46 21.8	49.0	133.7
5	52 15.2	+42.1	125.5	51 03.7	+44.0	127.6	49 48.9	+45.8	129.5	48 31.2	+47.3	131.2	47 10.8	+48.7	132.9
6	52 57.3	41.3	124.4	51 47.7	43.3	126.5	50 34.7	45.1	128.5	49 18.5	46.8	130.3	47 59.5	48.3	132.0
7	53 38.6	40.6	123.2	52 31.0	42.7	125.4	51 19.8	44.6	127.4	50 05.3	46.3	129.3	48 47.8	47.9	131.1
8	54 19.2	39.8	121.9	53 13.7	42.0	124.2	52 04.4	44.0	126.3	50 51.6	45.8	128.3	49 35.7	47.4	130.2
9	54 59.0	38.9	120.6	53 55.7	41.3	123.0	52 48.4	43.4	125.2	51 37.4	45.3	127.3	50 23.1	46.9	129.2
10	55 37.9	+38.1	119.3	54 37.0	+40.4	121.7	53 31.8	+42.6	124.1	52 22.7	+44.6	126.2	51 10.0	+46.4	128.3
11	56 16.0	37.0	117.9	55 17.4	39.7	120.5	54 14.4	41.9	122.9	53 07.3	44.0	125.1	51 56.4	45.9	127.2
12	56 53.0	36.1	116.5	55 57.1	38.7	119.1	54 56.3	41.2	121.6	53 51.3	43.3	124.0	52 42.3	45.3	126.2
13	57 29.1	35.0	115.0	56 35.8	37.8	117.8	55 37.5	40.4	120.3	54 34.6	42.6	122.8	53 27.6	44.7	125.1
14	58 04.1	33.9	113.5	57 13.6	36.8	116.3	56 17.8	39.4	119.0	55 17.2	41.9	121.6	54 12.3	44.0	124.0
15	58 38.0	+32.7	111.9	57 50.4	+35.7	114.9	56 57.2	+38.6	117.7	55 59.1	+41.0	120.3	54 56.3	+43.3	122.8
16	59 10.7	31.4	110.3	58 26.1	34.6	113.3	57 35.8	37.5	116.2	56 40.1	40.2	119.0	55 39.6	42.5	121.6
17	59 42.1	30.1	108.6	59 00.7	33.4	111.8	58 13.3	36.5	114.8	57 20.3	39.2	117.6	56 22.1	41.8	120.3
18	60 12.2	28.8	106.9	59 34.1	32.2	110.1	58 49.8	35.3	113.3	57 59.5	38.3	116.2	57 03.9	40.9	119.0
19	60 41.0	27.2	105.1	60 06.3	30.9	108.5	59 25.1	34.2	111.7	58 37.8	37.2	114.7	57 44.8	40.0	117.6
20	61 08.2	+25.8	103.3	60 37.2	+29.5	106.7	59 59.3	+32.9	110.1	59 15.0	+36.2	113.2	58 24.8	+39.0	116.2
21	61 34.0	24.1	101.4	61 06.7	28.0	104.9	60 32.2	31.7	108.4	59 51.2	34.9	111.7	59 03.8	38.1	114.8
22	61 58.1	22.5	99.4	61 34.7	26.4	103.1	61 03.9	30.2	106.6	60 26.1	33.8	110.0	59 41.9	36.9	113.2
23	62 20.6	20.7	97.5	62 01.1	24.9	101.2	61 34.1	28.8	104.8	60 59.9	32.4	108.3	60 18.8	35.7	111.7
24	62 41.3	19.0	95.4	62 26.0	23.2	99.2	62 02.9	27.3	102.9	61 32.3	31.0	106.6	60 54.5	34.6	110.0
25	63 00.3	+17.0	93.3	62 49.2	+21.4	97.2	62 30.1	+25.6	101.1	62 03.3	+29.5	104.8	61 29.1	+33.2	108.3
26	63 17.3	15.1	91.2	63 10.6	19.6	95.2	62 55.7	23.9	99.1	62 32.8	28.0	102.9	62 02.3	31.8	106.6
27	63 32.4	13.2*	89.1	63 30.2	17.7	93.1	63 19.6	22.1	97.1	63 00.8	26.4	101.0	62 34.1	30.3	104.8
28	63 45.6	11.1*	86.9	63 47.9	15.7	90.9	63 41.7	20.3	95.0	63 27.2	24.6	99.0	63 04.4	28.8	102.9
29	63 56.7	9.0*	84.6	64 03.6	13.8*	88.7	64 02.0	18.4*	92.8	63 51.8	22.9	96.9	63 33.2	27.2	100.9

20°			22°			24°			26°			28°			Dec.
Hc	d	Z	Hc	d	Z	Hc	d	Z	Hc	d	Z	Hc	d	Z	
° ′	′	°	° ′	′	°	° ′	′	°	° ′	′	°	° ′	′	°	°
54 28.1	−35.8	120.6	53 24.8	−38.1	123.0	52 17.6	−40.3	125.2	51 06.7	−42.2	127.2	49 52.6	−44.0	129.1	0
53 52.3	36.7	122.0	52 46.7	38.9	124.3	51 37.3	41.0	126.4	50 24.5	42.8	128.3	49 08.6	44.6	130.2	1
53 15.6	37.5	123.3	52 07.8	39.7	125.5	50 56.3	41.6	127.5	49 41.7	43.5	129.4	48 24.0	45.0	131.2	2
52 38.1	38.4	124.6	51 28.1	40.5	126.7	50 14.7	42.3	128.7	48 58.2	44.0	130.5	47 39.0	45.6	132.2	3
51 59.7	39.2	125.9	50 47.6	41.1	127.9	49 32.4	42.9	129.8	48 14.2	44.5	131.5	46 53.4	46.0	133.1	4
51 20.5	−39.9	127.1	50 06.5	−41.8	129.0	48 49.5	−43.5	130.8	47 29.7	−45.1	132.5	46 07.4	−46.5	134.1	5
50 40.6	40.6	128.3	49 24.7	42.4	130.2	48 06.0	44.1	131.9	46 44.6	45.5	133.5	45 20.9	46.9	135.0	6
50 00.0	41.2	129.5	48 42.3	43.0	131.2	47 21.9	44.5	132.9	45 59.1	46.0	134.4	44 34.0	47.3	135.8	7
49 18.8	41.9	130.6	47 59.3	43.5	132.3	46 37.4	45.1	133.9	45 13.1	46.4	135.3	43 46.7	47.6	136.7	8
48 36.9	42.6	131.7	47 15.8	44.1	133.3	45 52.3	45.5	134.8	44 26.7	46.8	136.2	42 59.1	48.1	137.5	9
47 54.3	−43.0	132.7	46 31.7	−44.6	134.3	45 06.8	−45.9	135.8	43 39.9	−47.3	137.1	42 11.0	−48.3	138.4	10
47 11.3	43.6	133.8	45 47.1	45.0	135.3	44 20.9	46.4	136.7	42 52.6	47.5	138.0	41 22.7	48.7	139.1	11
46 27.7	44.2	134.8	45 02.1	45.5	136.2	43 34.5	46.8	137.5	42 05.1	47.9	138.8	40 34.0	49.0	139.9	12
45 43.5	44.6	135.7	44 16.6	46.0	137.1	42 47.7	47.1	138.4	41 17.2	48.3	139.6	39 45.0	49.2	140.7	13
44 58.9	45.1	136.7	43 30.6	46.3	138.0	42 00.6	47.5	139.2	40 28.9	48.6	140.4	38 55.8	49.5	141.5	14
44 13.8	−45.5	137.6	42 44.3	−46.7	138.9	41 13.1	−47.9	140.1	39 40.3	−48.8	141.1	38 06.2	−49.7	142.1	15
43 28.3	45.9	138.5	41 57.6	47.1	139.7	40 25.2	48.1	140.9	38 51.5	49.2	141.9	37 16.5	50.1	142.8	16
42 42.4	46.3	139.4	41 10.5	47.5	140.6	39 37.1	48.5	141.6	38 02.3	49.4	142.6	36 26.4	50.3	143.5	17
41 56.1	46.7	140.3	40 23.0	47.7	141.4	38 48.6	48.7	142.4	37 12.9	49.6	143.3	35 36.1	50.5	144.2	18
41 09.4	47.1	141.1	39 35.3	48.1	142.2	37 59.9	49.1	143.1	36 23.3	49.9	144.0	34 45.6	50.7	144.9	19
40 22.3	−47.4	141.9	38 47.2	−48.4	142.9	37 10.8	−49.3	143.9	35 33.4	−50.1	144.7	33 54.9	−50.9	145.5	20
39 34.9	47.7	142.7	37 58.8	48.7	143.7	36 21.5	49.5	144.6	34 43.3	50.4	145.4	33 04.0	51.1	146.2	21
38 47.2	48.0	143.5	37 10.1	48.9	144.4	35 32.0	49.8	145.3	33 52.9	50.5	146.1	32 12.9	51.2	146.8	22
37 59.2	48.4	144.3	36 21.2	49.2	145.1	34 42.2	50.0	146.0	33 02.4	50.8	146.7	31 21.7	51.5	147.4	23
37 10.8	48.6	145.0	35 32.0	49.4	145.9	33 52.2	50.2	146.6	32 11.6	50.9	147.3	30 30.2	51.6	148.0	24
36 22.2	−48.8	145.8	34 42.6	−49.7	146.5	33 02.0	−50.4	147.3	31 20.7	−51.1	148.0	29 38.6	−51.7	148.6	25
35 33.4	49.4	146.5	33 52.9	49.9	147.2	32 11.6	50.6	147.9	30 29.6	51.3	148.6	28 46.9	51.9	149.2	26
34 44.3	49.4	147.2	33 03.0	50.1	147.9	31 21.0	50.8	148.6	29 38.3	51.4	149.2	27 55.0	52.1	149.7	27
33 54.9	49.5	147.9	32 12.9	50.2	148.5	30 30.2	50.9	149.2	28 46.9	51.6	149.8	27 02.9	52.2	150.3	28
33 05.4	49.8	148.5	31 22.7	50.5	149.2	29 39.3	51.2	149.8	27 55.3	51.8	150.3	26 10.7	52.3	150.8	29

30°			32°			34°			36°			38°			Dec.
Hc	d	Z	Hc	d	Z	Hc	d	Z	Hc	d	Z	Hc	d	Z	
° ′	′	°	° ′	′	°	° ′	′	°	° ′	′	°	° ′	′	°	°
48 35.4	−45.6	130.9	47 15.6	−47.1	132.5	45 53.2	−48.4	134.1	44 28.7	−49.6	135.5	43 02.1	−50.7	136.8	0
47 49.8	46.1	131.9	46 28.5	47.5	133.5	45 04.8	48.7	134.9	43 39.1	49.9	136.3	42 11.4	51.0	137.6	1
47 03.7	46.5	132.8	45 41.0	47.9	134.3	44 16.1	49.1	135.7	42 49.2	50.2	137.1	41 20.4	51.2	138.3	2
46 17.2	47.0	133.7	44 53.1	48.2	135.2	43 27.0	49.4	136.5	41 59.0	50.5	137.8	40 29.2	51.4	139.0	3
45 30.2	47.4	134.6	44 04.9	48.6	136.0	42 37.6	49.8	137.3	41 08.5	50.8	138.5	39 37.8	51.7	139.6	4
44 42.8	−47.7	135.5	43 16.3	−49.0	136.8	41 47.8	−50.0	138.1	40 17.7	−50.9	139.2	38 46.1	−51.8	140.3	5
43 55.1	48.2	136.3	42 27.3	49.2	137.6	40 57.8	50.3	138.8	39 26.8	51.3	139.9	37 54.3	52.1	140.9	6
43 06.9	48.4	137.2	41 38.1	49.6	138.4	40 07.5	50.5	139.5	38 35.5	51.4	140.6	37 02.2	52.3	141.6	7
42 18.5	48.8	138.0	40 48.5	49.8	139.1	39 17.0	50.8	140.2	37 44.1	51.7	141.2	36 09.9	52.5	142.2	8
41 29.7	49.1	138.8	39 58.7	50.1	139.9	38 26.2	51.0	140.9	36 52.4	51.8	141.9	35 17.4	52.6	142.8	9
40 40.6	−49.4	139.5	39 08.6	−50.4	140.6	37 35.2	−51.3	141.6	36 00.6	−52.1	142.5	34 24.8	−52.8	143.4	10
39 51.2	49.7	140.3	38 18.2	50.7	141.3	36 43.9	51.4	142.2	35 08.5	52.2	143.1	33 32.0	52.9	143.9	11
39 01.5	50.0	141.0	37 27.6	50.8	142.0	35 52.5	51.7	142.9	34 16.3	52.4	143.7	32 39.1	53.1	144.5	12
38 11.5	50.2	141.7	36 36.8	51.1	142.6	35 00.8	51.8	143.5	33 23.9	52.6	144.3	31 46.0	53.3	145.0	13
37 21.3	50.4	142.4	35 45.7	51.3	143.3	34 09.0	52.0	144.1	32 31.3	52.7	144.9	30 52.7	53.3	145.6	14
36 30.9	−50.7	143.1	34 54.4	−51.4	143.9	33 17.0	−52.2	144.7	31 38.6	−52.9	145.4	29 59.4	−53.5	146.1	15
35 40.2	50.8	143.7	34 03.0	51.6	144.5	32 24.8	52.4	145.3	30 45.7	53.0	146.0	29 05.9	53.6	146.6	16
34 49.4	51.1	144.4	33 11.4	51.9	145.2	31 32.4	52.5	145.9	29 52.7	53.1	146.5	28 12.3	53.8	147.1	17
33 58.3	51.3	145.0	32 19.5	51.9	145.8	30 39.9	52.6	146.4	28 59.6	53.3	147.1	27 18.5	53.8	147.6	18
33 07.0	51.4	145.6	31 27.6	52.2	146.3	29 47.3	52.8	147.0	28 06.3	53.4	147.6	26 24.7	53.9	148.1	19
32 15.6	−51.6	146.2	30 35.4	−52.3	146.9	28 54.5	−52.9	147.5	27 12.9	−53.4	148.1	25 30.8	−54.1	148.6	20
31 24.0	51.8	146.8	29 43.1	52.4	147.5	28 01.6	53.0	148.1	26 19.5	53.6	148.6	24 36.7	54.1	149.1	21
30 32.2	52.0	147.4	28 50.7	52.6	148.0	27 08.6	53.2	148.6	25 25.9	53.7	149.1	23 42.6	54.2	149.6	22
29 40.2	52.1	148.0	27 58.1	52.7	148.6	26 15.4	53.2	149.1	24 32.2	53.8	149.6	22 48.4	54.3	150.0	23
28 48.1	52.2	148.6	27 05.4	52.8	149.1	25 22.2	53.4	149.6	23 38.4	53.9	150.1	21 54.1	54.3	150.5	24
27 55.9	−52.4	149.1	26 12.6	−52.9	149.7	24 28.8	−53.5	150.1	22 44.5	−54.0	150.6	20 59.8	−54.4	151.0	25
27 03.5	52.4	149.7	25 19.7	53.1	150.2	23 35.3	53.5	150.6	21 50.5	54.0	151.0	20 05.4	54.5	151.4	26
26 11.1	52.7	150.2	24 26.6	53.1	150.7	22 41.8	53.7	151.1	20 56.5	54.1	151.5	19 10.9	54.5	151.9	27
25 18.4	52.7	150.8	23 33.5	53.2	151.2	21 48.1	53.7	151.6	20 02.4	54.2	152.0	18 16.3	54.6	152.3	28
24 25.7	52.8	151.3	22 40.3	53.4	151.7	20 54.4	53.8	152.1	19 08.2	54.3	152.4	17 21.7	54.7	152.7	29

LATITUDE **SAME** NAME

Dec.	40° Hc	d	Z	42° Hc	d	Z	44° Hc	d	Z	46° Hc	d	Z	48° Hc	d	Z
°	° ′	′	°	° ′	′	°	° ′	′	°	° ′	′	°	° ′	′	°
0	41 33.6	+51.5	138.1	40 03.6	+52.3	139.2	38 32.0	+53.2	140.3	36 59.0	+54.0	141.2	35 24.9	+54.6	142.2
1	42 25.1	51.1	137.4	40 55.9	52.1	138.6	39 25.2	53.0	139.7	37 53.0	53.8	140.7	36 19.5	54.5	141.6
2	43 16.2	50.9	136.7	41 48.0	51.9	137.9	40 18.2	52.8	139.1	38 46.8	53.6	140.1	37 14.0	54.4	141.1
3	44 07.1	50.6	135.9	42 39.9	51.7	137.2	41 11.0	52.6	138.4	39 40.4	53.5	139.6	38 08.4	54.2	140.6
4	44 57.7	50.3	135.2	43 31.6	51.4	136.5	42 03.6	52.4	137.8	40 33.9	53.2	139.0	39 02.6	54.1	140.0
5	45 48.0	+50.0	134.4	44 23.0	+51.1	135.8	42 56.0	+52.1	137.1	41 27.1	+53.1	138.4	39 56.7	+53.9	139.5
6	46 38.0	49.6	133.6	45 14.1	50.8	135.1	43 48.1	51.9	136.5	42 20.2	52.9	137.7	40 50.6	53.7	138.9
7	47 27.6	49.3	132.8	46 04.9	50.5	134.3	44 40.0	51.6	135.8	43 13.1	52.6	137.1	41 44.3	53.5	138.3
8	48 16.9	48.8	131.9	46 55.4	50.2	133.5	45 31.6	51.4	135.0	44 05.7	52.4	136.4	42 37.8	53.4	137.7
9	49 05.7	48.5	131.0	47 45.6	49.8	132.7	46 23.0	51.0	134.3	44 58.1	52.1	135.7	43 31.2	53.1	137.1
10	49 54.2	+48.0	130.1	48 35.4	+49.5	131.9	47 14.0	+50.7	133.5	45 50.2	+51.9	135.0	44 24.3	+52.9	136.4
11	50 42.2	47.5	129.2	49 24.9	49.0	131.0	48 04.7	50.4	132.7	46 42.1	51.6	134.3	45 17.2	52.7	135.8
12	51 29.7	47.1	128.2	50 13.9	48.6	130.1	48 55.1	50.1	131.9	47 33.7	51.3	133.6	46 09.9	52.4	135.1
13	52 16.8	46.5	127.2	51 02.5	48.2	129.2	49 45.2	49.6	131.1	48 25.0	51.0	132.8	47 02.3	52.1	134.4
14	53 03.3	45.9	126.2	51 50.7	47.7	128.3	50 34.8	49.3	130.2	49 16.0	50.6	132.0	47 54.4	51.8	133.6
15	53 49.2	+45.4	125.1	52 38.4	+47.2	127.3	51 24.1	+48.8	129.3	50 06.6	+50.2	131.1	48 46.2	+51.6	132.9
16	54 34.6	44.7	124.0	53 25.6	46.6	126.2	52 12.9	48.3	128.3	50 56.8	49.9	130.3	49 37.8	51.2	132.1
17	55 19.3	44.0	122.8	54 12.2	46.0	125.2	53 01.2	47.8	127.4	51 46.7	49.4	129.4	50 29.0	50.8	131.3
18	56 03.3	43.3	121.6	54 58.2	45.4	124.1	53 49.0	47.3	126.3	52 36.1	49.0	128.5	51 19.8	50.5	130.4
19	56 46.6	42.5	120.4	55 43.6	44.8	122.9	54 36.3	46.8	125.3	53 25.1	48.5	127.5	52 10.3	50.1	129.6
20	57 29.1	+41.7	119.1	56 28.4	+44.0	121.7	55 23.1	+46.1	124.2	54 13.6	+48.0	126.5	53 00.4	+49.7	128.7
21	58 10.8	40.8	117.7	57 12.4	43.3	120.5	56 09.2	45.5	123.1	55 01.6	47.5	125.5	53 50.1	49.2	127.7
22	58 51.6	39.8	116.3	57 55.7	42.4	119.2	56 54.7	44.8	121.9	55 49.1	46.8	124.4	54 39.3	48.6	126.7
23	59 31.4	38.8	114.8	58 38.1	41.6	117.8	57 39.5	44.0	120.6	56 35.9	46.3	123.3	55 27.9	48.2	125.7
24	60 10.2	37.7	113.3	59 19.7	40.6	116.4	58 23.5	43.2	119.4	57 22.2	45.5	122.1	56 16.1	47.6	124.7
25	60 47.9	+36.6	111.7	60 00.3	+39.6	115.0	59 06.7	+42.4	118.0	58 07.7	+44.8	120.9	57 03.7	+47.0	123.5
26	61 24.5	35.3	110.1	60 39.9	38.6	113.5	59 49.1	41.5	116.6	58 52.5	44.1	119.6	57 50.7	46.3	122.4
27	61 59.8	34.1	108.4	61 18.5	37.4	111.9	60 30.6	40.4	115.2	59 36.6	43.1	118.3	58 37.0	45.6	121.2
28	62 33.9	32.6	106.6	61 55.9	36.2	110.2	61 11.0	39.4	113.7	60 19.7	42.3	116.9	59 22.6	44.9	119.9
29	63 06.5	31.2	104.8	62 32.1	34.9	108.5	61 50.4	38.3	112.1	61 02.0	41.4	115.4	60 07.5	44.0	118.6

Dec.	50° Hc	d	Z	52° Hc	d	Z	54° Hc	d	Z	56° Hc	d	Z	58° Hc	d	Z
°	° ′	′	°	° ′	′	°	° ′	′	°	° ′	′	°	° ′	′	°
0	33 49.6	+55.2	143.0	32 13.2	+55.9	143.8	30 36.0	+56.3	144.5	28 57.9	+56.8	145.1	27 19.1	+57.2	145.8
1	34 44.8	55.2	142.5	33 09.1	55.7	143.3	31 32.3	56.3	144.1	29 54.7	56.8	144.8	28 16.3	57.2	145.4
2	35 40.0	55.0	142.0	34 04.8	55.7	142.9	32 28.6	56.2	143.7	30 51.5	56.7	144.4	29 13.5	57.1	145.1
3	36 35.0	55.0	141.6	35 00.5	55.5	142.4	33 24.8	56.1	143.3	31 48.2	56.6	144.0	30 10.6	57.1	144.7
4	37 30.0	54.7	141.0	35 56.0	55.5	142.0	34 20.9	56.1	142.8	32 44.8	56.6	143.6	31 07.7	57.0	144.4
5	38 24.7	+54.7	140.5	36 51.5	+55.3	141.5	35 17.0	+55.9	142.4	33 41.4	+56.4	143.2	32 04.7	+57.0	144.0
6	39 19.4	54.5	140.0	37 46.8	55.2	141.0	36 12.9	55.8	142.0	34 37.8	56.4	142.8	33 01.7	56.9	143.6
7	40 13.9	54.3	139.5	38 42.0	55.1	140.5	37 08.7	55.7	141.5	35 34.2	56.3	142.4	33 58.6	56.8	143.2
8	41 08.2	54.2	138.9	39 37.1	54.9	140.0	38 04.4	55.6	141.0	36 30.5	56.2	142.0	34 55.4	56.8	142.9
9	42 02.4	54.0	138.3	40 32.0	54.8	139.5	39 00.0	55.5	140.5	37 26.7	56.1	141.5	35 52.2	56.6	142.5
10	42 56.4	+53.8	137.7	41 26.8	+54.5	138.9	39 55.5	+55.4	140.1	38 22.8	+56.0	141.1	36 48.8	+56.6	142.0
11	43 50.2	53.6	137.1	42 21.4	54.5	138.4	40 50.9	55.2	139.5	39 18.8	55.9	140.6	37 45.4	56.5	141.6
12	44 43.8	53.4	136.5	43 15.9	54.2	137.8	41 46.1	55.1	139.0	40 14.7	55.8	140.2	38 41.9	56.4	141.2
13	45 37.2	53.2	135.8	44 10.1	54.1	137.2	42 41.2	54.9	138.5	41 10.5	55.6	139.7	39 38.3	56.2	140.8
14	46 30.4	53.0	135.2	45 04.2	53.9	136.6	43 36.1	54.7	137.9	42 06.1	55.5	139.2	40 34.5	56.2	140.3
15	47 23.4	+52.6	134.5	45 58.1	+53.7	136.0	44 30.8	+54.6	137.4	43 01.6	+55.4	138.6	41 30.7	+56.1	139.8
16	48 16.0	52.4	133.8	46 51.8	53.5	135.3	45 25.4	54.4	136.8	43 57.0	55.2	138.1	42 26.8	55.9	139.4
17	49 08.4	52.1	133.0	47 45.3	53.2	134.7	46 19.8	54.2	136.2	44 52.2	55.1	137.6	43 22.7	55.8	138.9
18	50 00.5	51.8	132.3	48 38.5	53.0	134.0	47 14.0	54.0	135.5	45 47.3	54.8	137.0	44 18.5	55.7	138.4
19	50 52.3	51.5	131.5	49 31.5	52.6	133.3	48 08.0	53.7	134.9	46 42.1	54.7	136.4	45 14.2	55.5	137.8
20	51 43.8	+51.1	130.7	50 24.1	+52.4	132.5	49 01.7	+53.5	134.2	47 36.8	+54.5	135.8	46 09.7	+55.4	137.3
21	52 34.9	50.7	129.8	51 16.5	52.1	131.7	49 55.2	53.3	133.5	48 31.3	54.3	135.2	47 05.1	55.1	136.7
22	53 25.6	50.3	128.9	52 08.6	51.7	130.9	50 48.5	53.0	132.8	49 25.6	54.1	134.5	48 00.2	55.0	136.1
23	54 15.9	49.9	128.0	53 00.3	51.4	130.1	51 41.5	52.6	132.1	50 19.7	53.8	133.9	48 55.2	54.8	135.5
24	55 05.8	49.4	127.0	53 51.7	51.0	129.2	52 34.1	52.4	131.3	51 13.5	53.5	133.2	49 50.0	54.6	134.9
25	55 55.2	+48.9	126.0	54 42.7	+50.5	128.3	53 26.5	+52.0	130.5	52 07.0	+53.3	132.4	50 44.6	+54.4	134.3
26	56 44.1	48.3	125.0	55 33.2	50.1	127.4	54 18.5	51.6	129.6	53 00.3	53.0	131.7	51 39.0	54.1	133.6
27	57 32.4	47.8	123.9	56 23.3	49.7	126.4	55 10.1	51.3	128.7	53 53.3	52.6	130.9	52 33.1	53.9	132.9
28	58 20.2	47.1	122.8	57 13.0	49.0	125.4	56 01.4	50.8	127.8	54 45.9	52.3	130.1	53 27.0	53.8	132.2
29	59 07.3	46.4	121.6	58 02.0	48.6	124.3	56 52.2	50.4	126.9	55 38.2	52.0	129.2	54 20.6	53.3	131.4

40° Hc	d	Z	42° Hc	d	Z	44° Hc	d	Z	46° Hc	d	Z	48° Hc	d	Z	Dec.
° ′	′	°	° ′	′	°	° ′	′	°	° ′	′	°	° ′	′	°	°
41 33.6	− 51.6	138.1	40 03.6	− 52.6	139.2	38 32.0	− 53.4	140.3	36 59.0	− 54.1	141.2	35 24.9	− 54.8	142.2	0
40 42.0	51.9	138.7	39 11.0	52.7	139.8	37 38.6	53.5	140.8	36 04.9	54.2	141.8	34 30.1	54.9	142.7	1
39 50.1	52.1	139.4	38 18.3	53.0	140.4	36 45.1	53.7	141.4	35 10.7	54.4	142.3	33 35.2	55.0	143.1	2
38 58.0	52.3	140.0	37 25.3	53.1	141.0	35 51.4	53.9	142.0	34 16.3	54.5	142.8	32 40.2	55.1	143.6	3
38 05.7	52.5	140.7	36 32.2	53.3	141.6	34 57.5	53.9	142.5	33 21.8	54.6	143.3	31 45.1	55.2	144.1	4
37 13.2	− 52.7	141.3	35 38.9	− 53.4	142.2	34 03.6	− 54.2	143.0	32 27.2	− 54.8	143.8	30 49.9	− 55.3	144.5	5
36 20.5	52.9	141.9	34 45.5	53.6	142.8	33 09.4	54.2	143.6	31 32.4	54.8	144.3	29 54.6	55.4	145.0	6
35 27.6	53.0	142.5	33 51.9	53.7	143.3	32 15.2	54.4	144.1	30 37.6	54.9	144.8	28 59.2	55.5	145.4	7
34 34.6	53.2	143.0	32 58.2	53.9	143.8	31 20.8	54.4	144.6	29 42.7	55.1	145.2	28 03.7	55.6	145.9	8
33 41.4	53.4	143.6	32 04.3	54.0	144.4	30 26.4	54.6	145.1	28 47.6	55.1	145.7	27 08.1	55.6	146.3	9
32 48.0	− 53.4	144.1	31 10.3	− 54.1	144.9	29 31.8	− 54.7	145.5	27 52.5	− 55.2	146.1	26 12.5	− 55.7	146.7	10
31 54.6	53.7	144.7	30 16.2	54.2	145.4	28 37.1	54.8	146.0	26 57.3	55.3	146.6	25 16.8	55.8	147.1	11
31 00.9	53.7	145.2	29 22.0	54.3	145.9	27 42.3	54.9	146.5	26 02.0	55.4	147.0	24 21.0	55.8	147.5	12
30 07.2	53.8	145.7	28 27.7	54.4	146.3	26 47.5	55.0	146.9	25 06.6	55.4	147.5	23 25.2	55.9	147.9	13
29 13.4	54.0	146.2	27 33.3	54.6	146.8	25 52.5	55.0	147.4	24 11.2	55.6	147.9	22 29.3	56.0	148.3	14
28 19.4	− 54.1	146.7	26 38.7	− 54.6	147.3	24 57.5	− 55.2	147.8	23 15.6	− 55.5	148.3	21 33.3	− 56.0	148.7	15
27 25.3	54.2	147.2	25 44.1	54.7	147.8	24 02.3	55.1	148.2	22 20.1	55.7	148.7	20 37.3	56.1	149.1	16
26 31.1	54.2	147.7	24 49.4	54.8	148.2	23 07.2	55.3	148.7	21 24.4	55.7	149.1	19 41.2	56.1	149.5	17
25 36.9	54.4	148.2	23 54.6	54.8	148.7	22 11.9	55.3	149.1	20 28.7	55.7	149.5	18 45.1	56.1	149.9	18
24 42.5	54.4	148.6	22 59.8	55.0	149.1	21 16.6	55.4	149.5	19 33.0	55.8	149.9	17 49.0	56.2	150.2	19
23 48.1	− 54.6	149.1	22 04.8	− 55.0	149.5	20 21.2	− 55.4	149.9	18 37.2	− 55.9	150.3	16 52.8	− 56.2	150.6	20
22 53.5	54.6	149.6	21 09.8	55.0	150.0	19 25.8	55.5	150.3	17 41.3	55.9	150.7	15 56.6	56.3	151.0	21
21 58.9	54.7	150.0	20 14.8	55.1	150.4	18 30.3	55.6	150.7	16 45.4	55.9	151.0	15 00.3	56.3	151.3	22
21 04.2	54.7	150.4	19 19.7	55.2	150.8	17 34.7	55.6	151.1	15 49.5	56.0	151.4	14 04.0	56.3	151.7	23
20 09.5	54.8	150.9	18 24.5	55.3	151.2	16 39.1	55.6	151.5	14 53.5	56.0	151.8	13 07.7	56.4	152.0	24
19 14.7	− 54.9	151.3	17 29.2	− 55.2	151.6	15 43.5	− 55.7	151.9	13 57.5	− 56.0	152.2	11 13.3	− 56.4	152.4	25
18 19.8	54.9	151.7	16 34.0	55.4	152.0	14 47.8	55.7	152.3	13 01.5	56.1	152.5	11 14.9	56.4	152.7	26
17 24.9	55.0	152.2	15 38.6	55.4	152.4	13 52.1	55.7	152.7	12 05.4	56.1	152.9	10 18.5	56.4	153.1	27
16 29.9	55.0	152.6	14 43.3	55.5	152.8	12 56.4	55.8	153.1	11 09.3	56.1	153.3	9 22.1	56.5	153.4	28
15 34.9	55.1	153.0	13 47.8	55.4	153.2	12 00.6	55.8	153.4	10 13.2	56.2	153.6	8 25.6	56.5	153.8	29

50° Hc	d	Z	52° Hc	d	Z	54° Hc	d	Z	56° Hc	d	Z	58° Hc	d	Z	Dec.
° ′	′	°	° ′	′	°	° ′	′	°	° ′	′	°	° ′	′	°	°
33 49.6	− 55.4	143.0	32 13.2	− 55.9	143.8	30 36.0	− 56.4	144.5	28 57.9	− 56.9	145.1	27 19.1	− 57.3	145.8	0
32 54.2	55.5	143.5	31 17.3	56.0	144.2	29 39.6	56.5	144.9	28 01.0	56.9	145.5	26 21.8	57.4	146.1	1
31 58.7	55.6	143.9	30 21.3	56.1	144.6	28 43.1	56.6	145.3	27 04.1	57.0	145.9	25 24.4	57.4	146.4	2
31 03.1	55.8	144.3	29 25.2	56.2	145.0	27 46.5	56.6	145.6	26 07.1	57.1	146.2	24 27.0	57.4	146.7	3
30 07.5	55.8	144.8	28 29.0	56.3	145.4	26 49.9	56.7	146.0	25 10.0	57.0	146.6	23 29.6	57.4	147.1	4
29 11.7	− 55.8	145.2	27 32.8	− 56.3	145.8	25 53.2	− 56.7	146.4	24 13.0	− 57.2	146.9	22 32.2	− 57.5	147.4	5
28 15.9	55.9	145.6	26 36.5	56.4	146.2	24 56.5	56.8	146.7	23 15.8	57.1	147.2	21 34.7	57.6	147.7	6
27 20.0	56.0	146.0	25 40.1	56.4	146.6	23 59.7	56.9	147.1	22 18.7	57.3	147.6	20 37.1	57.5	148.0	7
26 24.0	56.0	146.4	24 43.7	56.5	147.0	23 02.8	56.8	147.5	21 21.4	57.2	147.9	19 39.6	57.6	148.3	8
25 28.0	56.1	146.8	23 47.2	56.5	147.3	22 06.0	57.0	147.8	20 24.2	57.3	148.2	18 42.0	57.6	148.6	9
24 31.9	− 56.2	147.2	22 50.7	− 56.6	147.7	21 09.0	− 56.9	148.1	19 26.9	− 57.3	148.5	17 44.4	− 57.7	148.9	10
23 35.7	56.2	147.6	21 54.1	56.6	148.1	20 12.1	57.0	148.5	18 29.6	57.4	148.8	16 46.7	57.6	149.2	11
22 39.5	56.3	148.0	20 57.5	56.7	148.4	19 15.1	57.1	148.8	17 32.2	57.3	149.1	15 49.1	57.7	149.4	12
21 43.2	56.3	148.4	20 00.8	56.7	148.8	18 18.0	57.0	149.1	16 34.9	57.4	149.4	14 51.4	57.7	149.7	13
20 46.9	56.4	148.7	19 04.1	56.7	149.1	17 21.0	57.1	149.5	15 37.5	57.5	149.8	13 53.7	57.8	150.0	14
19 50.5	− 56.4	149.1	18 07.4	− 56.8	149.5	16 23.9	− 57.2	149.8	14 40.0	− 57.4	150.1	12 55.9	− 57.7	150.3	15
18 54.1	56.4	149.5	17 10.6	56.8	149.8	15 26.7	57.1	150.1	13 42.6	57.5	150.3	11 58.2	57.8	150.6	16
17 57.7	56.5	149.8	16 13.8	56.9	150.1	14 29.6	57.2	150.4	12 45.1	57.5	150.6	11 00.4	57.8	150.8	17
17 01.2	56.5	150.2	15 16.9	56.9	150.5	13 32.4	57.2	150.7	11 47.6	57.5	150.9	10 02.6	57.8	151.1	18
16 04.7	56.6	150.5	14 20.1	56.9	150.8	12 35.2	57.2	151.0	10 50.1	57.5	151.2	9 04.8	57.8	151.4	19
15 08.1	− 56.6	150.9	13 23.2	− 57.0	151.1	11 38.0	− 57.3	151.3	9 52.6	− 57.6	151.5	8 07.0	− 57.8	151.7	20
14 11.5	56.6	151.2	12 26.2	56.9	151.4	10 40.7	57.2	151.6	8 55.0	57.5	151.8	7 09.2	57.8	151.9	21
13 14.9	56.7	151.6	11 29.3	57.0	151.8	9 43.5	57.2	151.9	7 57.5	57.6	152.1	6 11.4	57.8	152.2	22
12 18.2	56.6	151.9	10 32.3	57.0	152.1	8 46.2	57.3	152.2	6 59.9	57.6	152.4	5 13.6	57.9	152.5	23
11 21.6	56.7	152.2	9 35.3	57.0	152.4	7 48.9	57.3	152.5	6 02.3	57.6	152.7	4 15.7	57.8	152.7	24
10 24.9	− 56.7	152.6	8 38.3	− 57.0	152.7	6 51.6	− 57.3	152.8	5 04.8	− 57.6	152.9	3 17.9	− 57.9	153.0	25
9 28.2	56.8	152.9	7 41.3	57.1	153.0	5 54.3	57.4	153.1	4 07.2	57.6	153.2	2 20.0	57.8	153.3	26
8 31.4	56.7	153.2	6 44.2	57.0	153.3	4 56.9	57.3	153.4	3 09.6	57.6	153.5	1 22.2	57.9	153.5	27
7 34.7	56.8	153.6	5 47.2	57.1	153.7	3 59.6	57.3	153.7	2 12.0	57.6	153.8	0 24.3	− 57.8	153.8	28
6 37.9	56.8	153.9	4 50.1	57.0	154.0	3 02.3	57.4	154.0	1 14.4	57.6	154.1	0 33.5	+ 57.9	25.9	29

Dec.	0° Hc	d	Z	2° Hc	d	Z	4° Hc	d	Z	6° Hc	d	Z	8° Hc	d	Z
°	° ′	′	°	° ′	′	°	° ′	′	°	° ′	′	°	° ′	′	°
0	58 00.0 − 0.8	90.0		57 56.7 + 3.1	93.2		57 46.6 + 7.1	96.4		57 30.1 + 10.8	99.5		57 07.1 + 14.6	102.6
1	57 59.2	2.5	88.1	57 59.8 + 1.4	91.3	57 53.7	5.3	94.5	57 40.9	9.3	97.7	57 21.7	13.1	100.8
2	57 56.7	4.2	86.2	58 01.2 − 0.2	89.4	57 59.0	3.8	92.6	57 50.2	7.7	95.8	57 34.8	11.5	98.9
3	57 52.5	5.9	84.4	58 01.0	2.0	87.5	58 02.8	2.0	90.7	57 57.9	5.9	93.9	57 46.3	9.9	97.1
4	57 46.6	7.4	82.5	58 01.0	3.5	85.7	58 04.8 + 0.4	88.9	58 03.8	4.4	92.1	57 56.2	8.2	95.3
5	57 39.2 − 9.1	80.6		57 55.5 − 3.8	83.8		58 05.2 − 1.4	87.0		58 08.2 + 2.6	90.2		58 04.4 + 6.6	93.4
6	57 30.1	10.7	78.8	57 50.2	6.9	81.9	58 03.8	3.0	85.1	58 10.8 + 1.0	88.3	58 11.0	4.9	91.5
7	57 19.4	12.3	77.0	57 43.3	8.5	80.0	58 00.8	4.6	83.2	58 11.8 − 0.8	86.4	58 15.9	3.3	89.6
8	57 07.1	13.8	75.1	57 34.8	10.1	78.2	57 56.2	6.4	81.3	58 11.0	2.4	84.5	58 19.2 + 1.5	87.7
9	56 53.3	15.3	73.4	57 24.7	11.8	76.3	57 49.8	7.9	79.4	58 08.6	4.1	82.6	58 20.7 − 0.1	85.8
10	56 38.0 − 16.8	71.6		57 12.9 − 13.2	74.5		57 41.9 − 9.6	77.6		58 04.5 − 5.8	80.7		58 20.6 − 1.9	83.9
11	56 21.2	18.3	69.9	56 59.7	14.8	72.7	57 32.3	11.2	75.7	57 58.7	7.4	78.8	58 18.7	3.5	82.0
12	56 02.9	19.6	68.1	56 44.9	16.3	71.0	57 21.1	12.7	73.9	57 51.3	9.1	77.0	58 15.2	5.3	80.1
13	55 43.3	21.0	66.5	56 28.6	17.7	69.2	57 08.4	14.3	72.1	57 42.2	10.6	75.1	58 09.9	6.8	78.2
14	55 22.3	22.3	64.8	56 10.9	19.2	67.5	56 54.1	15.8	70.3	57 31.6	12.3	73.3	58 03.1	8.6	76.3
15	55 00.0 − 23.6	63.2		55 51.7 − 20.5	65.8		56 38.3 − 17.3	68.5		57 19.3 − 13.8	71.4		57 54.5 − 10.2	74.5
16	54 36.4	24.8	61.6	55 31.2	21.9	64.1	56 21.0	18.7	66.8	57 05.5	15.3	69.7	57 44.3	11.7	72.6
17	54 11.6	26.0	60.0	55 09.3	23.1	62.5	56 02.3	20.1	65.1	56 50.2	16.8	67.9	57 32.6	13.4	70.8
18	53 45.6	27.2	58.5	54 46.2	24.5	60.9	55 42.2	21.4	63.4	56 33.4	18.3	66.1	57 19.2	14.9	69.0
19	53 18.4	28.3	57.0	54 21.7	25.6	59.3	55 20.8	22.8	61.8	56 15.1	19.7	64.4	57 04.3	16.4	67.2
20	52 50.1 − 29.3	55.5		53 56.1 − 26.7	57.8		54 58.0 − 24.0	60.2		55 55.4 − 21.0	62.7		56 47.9 − 17.9	65.4
21	52 20.8	30.4	54.1	53 29.4	27.9	56.3	54 34.0	25.2	58.6	55 34.4	22.4	61.1	56 30.0	19.3	63.7
22	51 50.4	31.3	52.7	53 01.5	29.0	54.8	54 08.8	26.5	57.0	55 12.0	23.7	59.4	56 10.7	20.7	62.0
23	51 19.1	32.3	51.3	52 32.5	30.0	53.3	53 42.3	27.5	55.5	54 48.3	24.9	57.8	55 50.0	22.0	60.3
24	50 46.8	33.1	50.0	52 02.5	31.0	51.9	53 14.8	28.7	54.0	54 23.4	26.1	56.2	55 28.0	23.3	58.6
25	50 13.7 − 34.1	48.7		51 31.5 − 32.0	50.5		52 46.1 − 29.7	52.5		53 57.3 − 27.2	54.7		55 04.7 − 24.6	57.0
26	49 39.6	34.8	47.4	50 59.5	32.9	49.2	52 16.4	30.7	51.1	53 30.1	28.4	53.2	54 40.1	25.9	55.4
27	49 04.8	35.7	46.1	50 26.6	33.7	47.9	51 45.7	31.7	49.7	53 01.7	29.4	51.7	54 14.2	26.9	53.9
28	48 29.1	36.4	44.9	49 52.9	34.6	46.6	51 14.0	32.6	48.4	52 32.3	30.5	50.3	53 47.3	28.2	52.4
29	47 52.7	37.1	43.7	49 18.3	35.4	45.3	50 41.4	33.5	47.0	52 01.8	31.4	48.9	53 19.1	29.2	50.9

Dec.	10° Hc	d	Z	12° Hc	d	Z	14° Hc	d	Z	16° Hc	d	Z	18° Hc	d	Z
°	° ′	′	°	° ′	′	°	° ′	′	°	° ′	′	°	° ′	′	°
0	56 38.0 + 18.2	105.5		56 02.9 + 21.7	108.4		55 22.3 + 24.9	111.2		54 36.4 + 28.0	113.8		53 45.6 + 30.8	116.3
1	56 56.2	16.7	103.8	56 24.6	20.3	106.7	55 47.2	23.7	109.6	55 04.4	26.8	112.3	54 16.4	29.8	114.9
2	57 12.9	15.3	102.0	56 44.9	18.8	105.0	56 10.9	22.2	107.9	55 31.2	25.5	110.7	54 46.2	28.6	113.4
3	57 28.2	13.7	100.2	57 03.7	17.4	103.3	56 33.1	21.0	106.2	55 56.7	24.3	109.1	55 14.8	27.4	111.8
4	57 41.9	12.1	98.4	57 21.1	15.9	101.5	56 54.1	19.5	104.5	56 21.0	22.9	107.4	55 42.2	26.2	110.3
5	57 54.0 + 10.5	96.6		57 37.0 + 14.3	99.7		57 13.6 + 18.0	102.8		56 43.9 + 21.6	105.8		56 08.4 + 25.0	108.7
6	58 04.5	8.9	94.7	57 51.3	12.7	97.9	57 31.6	16.5	101.0	57 05.5	20.2	104.1	56 33.4	23.6	107.0
7	58 13.4	7.2	92.8	58 04.0	11.2	96.1	57 48.1	15.0	99.2	57 25.7	18.6	102.3	56 57.0	22.2	105.3
8	58 20.6	5.5	91.0	58 15.2	9.5	94.2	58 03.1	13.3	97.4	57 44.3	17.2	100.5	57 19.2	20.8	103.6
9	58 26.1	3.8	89.1	58 24.7	7.8	92.3	58 16.4	11.8	95.5	58 01.5	15.6	98.7	57 40.0	19.4	101.9
10	58 29.9 + 2.2	87.1		58 32.5 + 6.1	90.4		58 28.2 + 10.1	93.7		58 17.1 + 14.0	96.9		57 59.4 + 17.8	100.1
11	58 32.1 + 0.4	85.2	58 38.6	4.4	88.5	58 38.3	8.4	91.8	58 31.1	12.4	95.1	58 17.2	16.3	98.3
12	58 32.5 − 1.3	83.3	58 43.0	2.8	86.6	58 46.7	6.8	89.9	58 43.5	10.8	93.2	58 33.5	14.6	96.4
13	58 31.2	3.0	81.4	58 45.8 + 0.9	84.7	58 53.5	5.0	88.0	58 54.3	9.0	91.3	58 48.1	13.1	94.6
14	58 28.2	4.7	79.5	58 46.7 − 0.7	82.7	58 58.5	3.3	86.0	59 03.3	7.4	89.4	59 01.2	11.3	92.7
15	58 23.5 − 6.4	77.6		58 46.0 − 2.5	80.8		59 01.8 + 1.5	84.1		59 10.7 + 5.6	87.4		59 12.5 + 9.7	90.8
16	58 17.1	8.0	75.7	58 43.5	4.2	78.9	59 03.3 − 0.2	82.1	59 16.3	3.8	85.5	59 22.2	7.9	88.8
17	58 09.1	9.7	73.8	58 39.3	5.8	77.0	59 03.1	1.9	80.2	59 20.1	2.1	83.5	59 30.1	6.2	86.9
18	57 59.4	11.4	71.9	58 33.5	7.6	75.0	59 01.2	3.7	78.3	59 22.2 + 0.3	81.6	59 36.3	4.4	84.9
19	57 48.0	12.9	70.1	58 25.9	9.3	73.2	58 57.5	5.4	76.3	59 22.5 − 1.4	79.6	59 40.7	2.6	83.0
20	57 35.1 − 14.5	68.3		58 16.6 − 10.9	71.3		58 52.1 − 7.2	74.4		59 21.1 − 3.2	77.6		59 43.3 + 0.9	81.0
21	57 20.6	16.0	66.5	58 05.7	12.5	69.4	58 44.9	8.8	72.5	59 17.9	5.0	75.7	59 44.2 − 1.0	79.0
22	57 04.6	17.5	64.7	57 53.2	14.1	67.6	58 36.1	10.5	70.6	59 12.9	6.7	73.7	59 43.2	2.7	77.0
23	56 47.1	18.9	62.9	57 39.1	15.7	65.7	58 25.6	12.1	68.7	59 06.2	8.4	71.8	59 40.5	4.6	75.0
24	56 28.2	20.4	61.2	57 23.4	17.1	63.9	58 13.5	13.8	66.8	58 57.8	10.2	69.9	59 35.9	6.3	73.1
25	56 07.8 − 21.7	59.5		57 06.3 − 18.7	62.2		57 59.7 − 15.3	65.0		58 47.6 − 11.8	68.0		59 29.6 − 8.1	71.1
26	55 46.1	23.1	57.9	56 47.6	20.0	60.4	57 44.4	16.9	63.2	58 35.8	13.6	66.1	59 21.5	9.7	69.2
27	55 23.0	24.3	56.2	56 27.6	21.5	58.7	57 27.5	18.4	61.4	58 22.4	15.0	64.2	59 11.8	11.5	67.2
28	54 58.7	25.6	54.6	56 06.1	22.8	57.0	57 09.1	19.8	59.6	58 07.4	16.7	62.4	59 00.3	13.2	65.3
29	54 33.1	26.8	53.0	55 43.3	24.1	55.4	56 49.3	21.2	57.9	57 50.7	18.1	60.6	58 47.1	14.8	63.4

0°			2°			4°			6°			8°			
Hc	d	Z	Hc	d	Z	Hc	d	Z	Hc	d	Z	Hc	d	Z	Dec.
° ′	′	°	° ′	′	°	° ′	′	°	° ′	′	°	° ′	′	°	°
58 00.0 –	0.8	90.0	57 56.7 –	4.8	93.2	57 46.6 –	8.6	96.4	57 30.1 –	12.5	99.5	57 07.1 –	16.1	102.6	0
57 59.2	2.5	91.9	57 51.9	6.5	95.1	57 38.0	10.3	98.2	57 17.6	14.0	101.3	56 51.0	17.6	104.3	1
57 56.7	4.2	93.8	57 45.4	8.0	96.9	57 27.7	11.9	100.1	57 03.6	15.5	103.1	56 33.4	19.1	106.1	2
57 52.5	5.9	95.6	57 37.4	9.7	98.8	57 15.8	13.4	101.9	56 48.1	17.0	104.9	56 14.3	20.4	107.8	3
57 46.6	7.4	97.5	57 27.7	11.3	100.6	57 02.4	14.9	103.7	56 31.1	18.5	106.6	55 53.9	21.8	109.5	4
57 39.2 –	9.1	99.4	57 16.4 –	12.8	102.5	56 47.5 –	16.4	105.4	56 12.6 –	19.9	108.3	55 32.1 –	23.1	111.1	5
57 30.1	10.7	101.2	57 03.6	14.4	104.3	56 31.1	17.9	107.2	55 52.7	21.2	110.0	55 09.0	24.4	112.7	6
57 19.4	12.3	103.0	56 49.2	15.8	106.0	56 13.2	19.3	108.9	55 31.5	22.5	111.7	54 44.6	25.6	114.3	7
57 07.1	13.8	104.9	56 33.4	17.4	107.8	55 53.9	20.7	110.6	55 09.0	23.8	113.3	54 19.0	26.8	115.9	8
56 53.3	15.3	106.9	56 16.0	18.7	109.5	55 33.2	22.0	112.3	54 45.2	25.1	114.9	53 52.2	27.9	117.4	9
56 38.0 –	16.8	108.4	55 57.3 –	20.2	111.2	55 11.2 –	23.3	113.9	54 20.1 –	26.3	116.5	53 24.3 –	29.0	118.9	10
56 21.2	18.3	110.1	55 37.1	21.4	112.9	54 47.9	24.5	115.5	53 53.8	27.4	118.0	52 55.3	30.1	120.4	11
56 02.9	19.6	111.9	55 15.7	22.8	114.5	54 23.4	25.8	117.1	53 26.4	28.5	119.5	52 25.2	31.0	121.8	12
55 43.3	21.0	113.5	54 52.9	24.1	116.2	53 57.6	26.9	118.6	52 57.9	29.5	121.0	51 54.2	32.1	123.2	13
55 22.3	22.3	115.2	54 28.8	25.3	117.7	53 30.7	28.0	120.2	52 28.4	30.6	122.4	51 22.1	32.9	124.6	14
55 00.0 –	23.6	116.8	54 03.5 –	26.4	119.3	53 02.7 –	29.1	121.6	51 57.8 –	31.6	123.8	50 49.2 –	33.9	125.9	15
54 36.4	24.8	118.4	53 37.1	27.6	120.8	52 33.6	30.2	123.1	51 26.2	32.5	125.2	50 15.3	34.7	127.2	16
54 11.6	26.0	120.0	53 09.5	28.7	122.3	52 03.4	31.1	124.5	50 53.7	33.4	126.5	49 40.6	35.5	128.5	17
53 45.6	27.2	121.5	52 40.8	29.7	123.8	51 32.3	32.1	125.9	50 20.3	34.3	127.8	49 05.1	36.3	129.7	18
53 18.4	28.3	123.0	52 11.1	30.7	125.2	51 00.2	33.0	127.2	49 46.0	35.1	129.1	48 28.8	37.0	130.9	19
52 50.1 –	29.3	124.5	51 40.4 –	31.7	126.6	50 27.2 –	33.9	128.5	49 10.9 –	35.9	130.4	47 51.8 –	37.7	132.1	20
52 20.8	30.4	125.9	51 08.7	32.6	127.9	49 53.3	34.7	129.8	48 35.0	36.6	131.6	47 14.1	38.4	133.2	21
51 50.4	31.3	127.3	50 36.1	33.6	129.3	49 18.6	35.5	131.1	47 58.4	37.4	132.8	46 35.7	39.1	134.4	22
51 19.1	32.3	128.7	50 02.5	34.3	130.6	48 43.1	36.3	132.3	47 21.0	38.0	133.9	45 56.6	39.7	135.5	23
50 46.8	33.1	130.0	49 28.2	35.2	131.8	48 06.8	37.0	133.5	46 43.0	38.7	135.1	45 16.9	40.2	136.5	24
50 13.7 –	34.1	131.3	48 53.0 –	35.9	133.1	47 29.8 –	37.7	134.7	46 04.3 –	39.3	136.2	44 36.7 –	40.8	137.6	25
49 39.6	34.8	132.6	48 17.1	36.7	134.3	46 52.1	38.4	135.8	45 25.0	40.0	137.3	43 55.9	41.4	138.6	26
49 04.8	35.7	133.9	47 40.4	37.4	135.5	46 13.7	39.0	137.0	44 45.0	40.5	138.3	43 14.5	41.9	139.6	27
48 29.1	36.4	135.1	47 03.0	38.1	136.6	45 34.7	39.6	138.1	44 04.5	41.0	139.4	42 32.6	42.3	140.6	28
47 52.7	37.1	136.3	46 24.9	38.8	137.8	44 55.1	40.2	139.1	43 23.5	41.6	140.4	41 50.3	42.8	141.5	29

10°			12°			14°			16°			18°			
Hc	d	Z	Hc	d	Z	Hc	d	Z	Hc	d	Z	Hc	d	Z	Dec.
° ′	′	°	° ′	′	°	° ′	′	°	° ′	′	°	° ′	′	°	°
56 38.0 –	19.7	105.5	56 02.9 –	23.0	108.4	55 22.3 –	26.1	111.2	54 36.4 –	29.1	113.8	53 45.6 –	31.9	116.3	0
56 18.3	21.0	107.2	55 39.9	24.2	110.0	54 56.2	27.4	112.7	54 07.3	30.2	115.3	53 13.7	32.9	117.7	1
55 57.3	22.4	108.9	55 15.7	25.6	111.7	54 28.8	28.5	114.3	53 37.1	31.3	116.8	52 40.8	33.8	119.1	2
55 34.9	23.7	110.6	54 50.1	26.7	113.2	54 00.3	29.6	115.8	53 05.8	32.2	118.2	52 07.0	34.7	120.5	3
55 11.2	24.9	112.2	54 23.4	27.9	114.8	53 30.7	30.7	117.3	52 33.6	33.3	119.6	51 32.3	35.6	121.8	4
54 46.3 –	26.2	113.8	53 55.5 –	29.1	116.3	53 00.0 –	31.6	118.7	52 00.3 –	34.1	121.0	50 56.7 –	36.4	123.1	5
54 20.1	27.3	115.3	53 26.4	30.1	117.8	52 28.4	32.7	120.1	51 26.2	35.0	122.3	50 20.3	37.2	124.3	6
53 52.8	28.5	116.8	52 56.3	31.1	119.2	51 55.7	33.6	121.5	50 51.2	35.9	123.6	49 43.1	38.0	125.6	7
53 24.3	29.5	118.3	52 25.2	32.1	120.6	51 22.1	34.4	122.8	50 15.3	36.6	124.8	49 05.1	38.7	126.8	8
52 54.8	30.6	119.8	51 53.1	33.0	122.0	50 47.7	35.4	124.1	49 38.7	37.5	126.1	48 26.4	39.3	127.9	9
52 24.2 –	31.6	121.2	51 20.1 –	34.0	123.4	50 12.3 –	36.1	125.4	49 01.2 –	38.1	127.3	47 47.1 –	40.0	129.0	10
51 52.6	32.5	122.6	50 46.1	34.8	124.7	49 36.2	36.9	126.6	48 23.1	38.8	128.4	47 07.1	40.6	130.1	11
51 20.1	33.4	123.9	50 11.3	35.6	125.9	48 59.3	37.6	127.8	47 44.3	39.5	129.6	46 26.5	41.2	131.2	12
50 46.7	34.4	125.3	49 35.7	36.4	127.2	48 21.7	38.4	129.0	47 04.8	40.2	130.7	45 45.3	41.8	132.3	13
50 12.3	35.1	126.5	48 59.3	37.2	128.4	47 43.3	39.0	130.2	46 24.6	40.7	131.8	45 03.5	42.3	133.3	14
49 37.2 –	36.0	127.8	48 22.1 –	37.8	129.6	47 04.3 –	39.7	131.3	45 43.9 –	41.3	132.8	44 21.2 –	42.8	134.3	15
49 01.2	36.7	129.0	47 44.3	38.6	130.8	46 24.6	40.2	132.4	45 02.6	41.9	133.9	43 38.4	43.3	135.3	16
48 24.5	37.4	130.2	47 05.7	39.2	131.9	45 44.4	40.9	133.4	44 20.7	42.3	134.9	42 55.1	43.8	136.3	17
47 47.1	38.1	131.4	46 26.5	39.9	133.0	45 03.5	41.4	134.5	43 38.4	42.9	135.9	42 11.3	44.2	137.1	18
47 09.0	38.8	132.5	45 46.6	40.4	134.1	44 22.1	42.0	135.5	42 55.5	43.3	136.8	41 27.1	44.6	138.0	19
46 30.2 –	39.5	133.7	45 06.2 –	41.0	135.1	43 40.1 –	42.4	136.5	42 12.2 –	43.8	137.8	40 42.5 –	45.0	138.9	20
45 50.7	40.0	134.7	44 25.2	41.6	136.2	42 57.7	42.9	137.5	41 28.4	44.2	138.7	39 57.5	45.4	139.8	21
45 10.7	40.6	135.8	43 43.6	42.0	137.2	42 14.8	43.4	138.4	40 44.2	44.6	139.6	39 12.1	45.8	140.7	22
44 30.1	41.2	136.8	43 01.6	42.6	138.1	41 31.4	43.9	139.3	39 59.6	45.0	140.5	38 26.3	46.1	141.5	23
43 48.9	41.7	137.9	42 19.0	43.0	139.1	40 47.5	44.2	140.3	39 14.6	45.4	141.3	37 40.2	46.4	142.3	24
43 07.2 –	42.2	138.9	41 36.0 –	43.5	140.0	40 03.3 –	44.6	141.1	38 29.2 –	45.7	142.2	36 53.8 –	46.7	143.1	25
42 25.0	42.7	139.8	40 52.5	43.8	141.0	39 18.7	45.1	142.0	37 43.5	46.1	143.0	36 07.1	47.1	143.9	26
41 42.3	43.1	140.8	40 08.7	44.3	141.9	38 33.6	45.3	142.9	36 57.4	46.4	143.8	35 20.0	47.3	144.6	27
40 59.2	43.6	141.7	39 24.4	44.7	142.7	37 48.3	45.8	143.7	36 11.0	46.7	144.6	34 32.7	47.6	145.4	28
40 15.6	43.9	142.6	38 39.7	45.1	143.6	37 02.5	46.0	144.5	35 24.3	47.0	145.3	33 45.1	47.8	146.1	29

Dec.	20° Hc	d	Z	22° Hc	d	Z	24° Hc	d	Z	26° Hc	d	Z	28° Hc	d	Z
°	° '	'	°	° '	'	°	° '	'	°	° '	'	°	° '	'	°
0	52 50.1	+33.5	118.7	51 50.4	+36.0	120.9	50 46.8	+38.3	123.1	49 39.6	+40.3	125.1	48 29.1	+42.2	126.9
1	53 23.6	32.5	117.3	52 26.4	35.1	119.6	51 25.1	37.4	121.8	50 19.9	39.6	123.9	49 11.3	41.6	125.8
2	53 56.1	31.5	115.9	53 01.5	34.1	118.3	52 02.5	36.6	120.6	50 59.5	38.9	122.7	49 52.9	40.9	124.7
3	54 27.6	30.4	114.4	53 35.6	33.2	116.9	52 39.1	35.7	119.3	51 38.4	38.0	121.5	50 33.8	40.2	123.6
4	54 58.0	29.3	112.9	54 08.8	32.1	115.5	53 14.8	34.8	117.9	52 16.4	37.3	120.2	51 14.0	39.5	122.4
5	55 27.3	+28.1	111.4	54 40.9	+31.1	114.1	53 49.6	+33.8	116.6	52 53.7	+36.4	118.9	51 53.5	+38.8	121.2
6	55 55.4	26.9	109.8	55 12.0	29.9	112.6	54 23.4	32.8	115.2	53 30.1	35.4	117.6	52 32.3	37.9	120.0
7	56 22.3	25.6	108.2	55 41.9	28.8	111.0	54 56.2	31.8	113.7	54 05.5	34.6	116.3	53 10.2	37.1	118.7
8	56 47.9	24.3	106.6	56 10.7	27.6	109.5	55 28.0	30.7	112.2	54 40.1	33.5	114.9	53 47.3	36.1	117.3
9	57 12.2	22.9	104.9	56 38.3	26.3	107.9	55 58.7	29.5	110.7	55 13.6	32.5	113.4	54 23.4	35.3	116.0
10	57 35.1	+21.5	103.2	57 04.6	+25.0	106.2	56 28.2	+28.2	109.1	55 46.1	+31.3	111.9	54 58.7	+34.2	114.6
11	57 56.6	20.0	101.5	57 29.6	23.6	104.5	56 56.4	27.0	107.5	56 17.4	30.2	110.4	55 32.9	33.2	113.1
12	58 16.6	18.5	99.7	57 53.2	22.2	102.8	57 23.4	25.7	105.9	56 47.6	29.0	108.8	56 06.1	32.1	111.7
13	58 35.1	17.0	97.9	58 15.4	20.7	101.1	57 49.1	24.4	104.2	57 16.6	27.8	107.2	56 38.2	30.9	110.1
14	58 52.1	15.3	96.0	58 36.1	19.2	99.3	58 13.5	22.8	102.5	57 44.4	26.4	105.6	57 09.1	29.8	108.6
15	59 07.4	+13.7	94.1	58 55.3	+17.6	97.4	58 36.3	+21.5	100.7	58 10.8	+25.0	103.9	57 38.9	+28.5	107.0
16	59 21.1	12.0	92.2	59 12.9	16.0	95.6	58 57.8	19.8	98.9	58 35.8	23.6	102.1	58 07.4	27.1	105.5
17	59 33.1	10.2	90.3	59 28.9	14.3	93.7	59 17.6	18.3	97.1	58 59.4	22.1	100.4	58 34.5	25.8	103.6
18	59 43.3	8.6	88.3	59 43.2	12.6	91.8	59 35.9	16.7	95.2	59 21.5	20.6	98.6	59 00.3	24.3	101.9
19	59 51.9	6.7	86.4	59 55.8	10.9	89.8	59 52.6	14.9	93.3	59 42.1	19.0	96.7	59 24.6	22.8	100.1
20	59 58.6	+ 5.0	84.4	60 06.7	+ 9.1	87.9	60 07.5	+13.3	91.3	60 01.1	+17.3	94.8	59 47.4	+21.3	98.2
21	60 03.6	3.1	82.4	60 15.8	7.3	85.9	60 20.8	11.5	89.4	60 18.4	15.7	92.9	60 08.7	19.7	96.4
22	60 06.7	+ 1.3	80.4	60 23.1	5.5	83.9	60 32.3	9.7	87.4	60 34.1	13.8	90.9	60 28.4	18.0	94.5
23	60 08.0	- 0.5	78.4	60 28.6	3.7	81.9	60 42.0	7.9	85.4	60 47.9	12.1	88.9	60 46.4	16.3	92.5
24	60 07.5	2.3	76.4	60 32.3	+ 1.8	79.8	60 49.9	6.0	83.3	61 00.0	10.3	86.9	61 02.7	14.5	90.5
25	60 05.2	- 4.1	74.4	60 34.1	0.0	77.8	60 55.9	+ 4.1	81.3	61 10.3	+ 8.4	84.9	61 17.2	+12.7	88.5
26	60 01.1	5.9	72.4	60 34.1	- 2.0	75.8	61 00.0	2.3	79.2	61 18.7	6.6	82.8	61 29.9	10.9	86.5
27	59 55.2	7.8	70.4	60 32.1	3.7	73.7	61 02.3	+ 0.4	77.2	61 25.3	4.6	80.8	61 40.8	8.9	84.4
28	59 47.4	9.4	68.4	60 28.4	5.6	71.7	61 02.7	- 1.5	75.1	61 29.9	2.7	78.7	61 49.7	7.1	82.3
29	59 38.0	11.2	66.5	60 22.8	7.4	69.7	61 01.2	3.4	73.1	61 32.6	+ 0.8	76.6	61 56.8	5.0	80.2

Dec.	30° Hc	d	Z	32° Hc	d	Z	34° Hc	d	Z	36° Hc	d	Z	38° Hc	d	Z
°	° '	'	°	° '	'	°	° '	'	°	° '	'	°	° '	'	°
0	47 15.6	+43.9	128.7	45 59.2	+45.6	130.3	44 40.4	+47.0	131.8	43 19.3	+48.3	133.2	41 56.0	+49.5	134.6
1	47 59.5	43.4	127.7	46 44.8	45.0	129.4	45 27.4	46.5	130.9	44 07.6	47.9	132.4	42 45.5	49.2	133.8
2	48 42.9	42.8	126.6	47 29.8	44.6	128.4	46 13.9	46.2	130.0	44 55.5	47.6	131.6	43 34.7	48.9	133.0
3	49 25.7	42.2	125.5	48 14.4	44.0	127.4	47 00.1	45.6	129.1	45 43.1	47.1	130.7	44 23.6	48.5	132.2
4	50 07.9	41.6	124.4	48 58.4	43.4	126.4	47 45.7	45.2	128.1	46 30.2	46.7	129.8	45 12.1	48.1	131.4
5	50 49.5	+40.9	123.3	49 41.8	+42.9	125.3	48 30.9	+44.6	127.2	47 16.9	+46.3	128.9	46 00.2	+47.8	130.5
6	51 30.4	40.1	122.1	50 24.7	42.2	124.2	49 15.5	44.1	126.1	48 03.2	45.8	128.0	46 48.0	47.3	129.7
7	52 10.5	39.4	120.9	51 06.9	41.5	123.1	49 59.6	43.5	125.1	48 49.0	45.3	127.0	47 35.3	46.9	128.8
8	52 49.9	38.7	119.7	51 48.4	40.9	121.9	50 43.1	42.9	124.0	49 34.3	44.7	126.0	48 22.2	46.4	127.8
9	53 28.6	37.7	118.4	52 29.3	40.1	120.7	51 26.0	42.2	122.9	50 19.0	44.2	124.9	49 08.6	46.0	126.9
10	54 06.3	+36.9	117.1	53 09.4	+39.3	119.5	52 08.2	+41.6	121.8	51 03.2	+43.6	123.9	49 54.6	+45.4	125.9
11	54 43.2	36.0	115.8	53 48.7	38.5	118.2	52 49.8	40.8	120.6	51 46.8	42.9	122.8	50 40.0	44.8	124.8
12	55 19.2	34.9	114.4	54 27.2	37.6	116.9	53 30.6	40.1	119.4	52 29.7	42.3	121.6	51 24.8	44.3	123.8
13	55 54.1	34.0	112.9	55 04.8	36.7	115.6	54 10.7	39.2	118.1	53 12.0	41.5	120.5	52 09.1	43.6	122.7
14	56 28.1	32.8	111.4	55 41.5	35.8	114.2	54 49.9	38.3	116.8	53 53.5	40.8	119.2	52 52.7	43.0	121.6
15	57 00.9	+31.7	109.9	56 17.3	+34.6	112.7	55 28.2	+37.5	115.4	54 34.3	+40.0	118.0	53 35.7	+42.3	120.4
16	57 32.6	30.5	108.3	56 51.9	33.6	111.3	56 05.7	36.5	114.1	55 14.3	39.1	116.7	54 18.0	41.5	119.2
17	58 03.1	29.2	106.7	57 25.5	32.5	109.7	56 42.2	35.4	112.6	55 53.4	38.2	115.4	54 59.5	40.8	118.0
18	58 32.3	27.9	105.1	57 58.0	31.3	108.2	57 17.6	34.4	111.1	56 31.6	37.3	114.0	55 40.3	39.9	116.7
19	59 00.2	26.6	103.4	58 29.3	30.0	106.5	57 52.0	33.3	109.6	57 08.9	36.2	112.5	56 20.2	39.0	115.3
20	59 26.8	+25.0	101.6	58 59.3	+28.6	104.9	58 25.3	+32.0	108.0	57 45.1	+35.2	111.1	56 59.2	+38.0	113.9
21	59 51.8	23.6	99.8	59 27.9	27.3	103.2	58 57.3	30.8	106.4	58 20.3	34.0	109.5	57 37.2	37.1	112.5
22	60 15.4	22.0	98.0	59 55.2	25.8	101.4	59 28.1	29.4	104.7	58 54.3	32.9	107.9	58 14.3	36.0	111.0
23	60 37.4	20.4	96.1	60 21.0	24.4	99.6	59 57.5	28.1	103.0	59 27.2	31.6	106.3	58 50.3	34.8	109.5
24	60 57.8	18.7	94.1	60 45.4	22.7	97.7	60 25.6	26.6	101.2	59 58.8	30.2	104.6	59 25.1	33.7	107.9
25	61 16.5	+16.9	92.2	61 08.1	+21.1	95.8	60 52.2	+25.1	99.4	60 29.0	+28.9	102.9	59 58.8	+32.4	106.3
26	61 33.4	15.1	90.2	61 29.2	19.3	93.9	61 17.3	23.4	97.5	60 57.9	27.3	101.1	60 31.2	31.1	104.6
27	61 48.5	13.3	88.1	61 48.5	17.6	91.9	61 40.7	21.8	95.6	61 25.2	25.9	99.2	61 02.3	29.6	102.8
28	62 01.8	11.5	86.1	62 06.1	15.8	89.8	62 02.5	20.1	93.6	61 51.1	24.2	97.3	61 31.9	28.2	101.0
29	62 13.3	9.5*	84.0	62 21.9	13.9	87.8	62 22.6	18.3	91.6	62 15.3	22.5	95.4	62 00.1	26.6	99.1

20° Hc	d	Z	22° Hc	d	Z	24° Hc	d	Z	26° Hc	d	Z	28° Hc	d	Z	Dec.
52 50.1	−34.4	118.7	51 50.4	−36.7	120.9	50 46.8	−38.9	123.1	49 39.6	−40.9	125.1	48 29.1	−42.8	126.9	0
52 15.7	35.3	120.0	51 13.7	37.6	122.2	50 07.9	39.7	124.3	48 58.7	41.6	126.2	47 46.3	43.3	128.0	1
51 40.4	36.2	121.4	50 36.1	38.4	123.4	49 28.2	40.4	125.4	48 17.1	42.2	127.3	47 03.0	43.9	129.0	2
51 04.2	37.0	122.6	49 57.7	39.1	124.7	48 47.8	41.0	126.5	47 34.9	42.8	128.3	46 19.1	44.4	130.0	3
50 27.2	37.8	123.9	49 18.6	39.8	125.8	48 06.8	41.6	127.6	46 52.1	43.3	129.4	45 34.7	44.9	131.0	4
49 49.4	−38.5	125.1	48 38.8	−40.4	127.0	47 25.2	−42.2	128.7	46 08.8	−43.8	130.4	44 49.8	−45.3	131.9	5
49 10.9	39.2	126.3	47 58.4	41.1	128.1	46 43.0	42.8	129.8	45 25.0	44.4	131.3	44 04.5	45.7	132.8	6
48 31.7	39.9	127.4	47 17.3	41.6	129.2	46 00.2	43.3	130.8	44 40.6	44.7	132.3	43 18.8	46.2	133.7	7
47 51.8	40.5	128.5	46 35.7	42.3	130.2	45 16.9	43.7	131.8	43 55.9	45.3	133.2	42 32.6	46.5	134.6	8
47 11.3	41.1	129.6	45 53.4	42.7	131.2	44 33.2	44.3	132.7	43 10.6	45.6	134.1	41 46.1	46.9	135.4	9
46 30.2	−41.7	130.7	45 10.7	−43.3	132.2	43 48.9	−44.7	133.7	42 25.0	−46.0	135.0	40 59.2	−47.3	136.3	10
45 48.5	42.3	131.7	44 27.4	43.8	133.2	43 04.2	45.2	134.6	41 39.0	46.5	135.9	40 11.9	47.5	137.1	11
45 06.2	42.8	132.7	43 43.6	44.2	134.2	42 19.0	45.5	135.5	40 52.5	46.7	136.7	39 24.4	47.9	137.9	12
44 23.4	43.3	133.7	42 59.4	44.6	135.1	41 33.5	46.0	136.4	40 05.8	47.1	137.5	38 36.5	48.2	138.6	13
43 40.1	43.7	134.7	42 14.8	45.1	136.0	40 47.5	46.3	137.2	39 18.7	47.5	138.4	37 48.3	48.5	139.4	14
42 56.4	−44.2	135.6	41 29.7	−45.5	136.9	40 01.2	−46.6	138.1	38 31.2	−47.7	139.1	36 59.8	−48.8	140.1	15
42 12.2	44.6	136.6	40 44.2	45.9	137.8	39 14.6	47.0	138.9	37 43.5	48.1	139.9	36 11.0	49.0	140.9	16
41 27.6	45.1	137.5	39 58.3	46.2	138.6	38 27.6	47.4	139.7	36 55.4	48.3	140.7	35 22.0	49.3	141.6	17
40 42.5	45.4	138.3	39 12.1	46.6	139.4	37 40.2	47.6	140.5	36 07.1	48.6	141.4	34 32.7	49.5	142.3	18
39 57.1	45.8	139.2	38 25.5	46.9	140.2	36 52.6	47.9	141.2	35 18.5	48.9	142.1	33 43.2	49.7	143.0	19
39 11.3	−46.2	140.0	37 38.6	−47.2	141.0	36 04.7	−48.2	142.0	34 29.6	−49.0	142.8	32 53.5	−49.9	143.6	20
38 25.1	46.5	140.8	36 51.4	47.5	141.8	35 16.5	48.4	142.7	33 40.6	49.4	143.5	32 03.6	50.1	144.3	21
37 38.6	46.8	141.6	36 03.9	47.7	142.6	34 28.1	48.7	143.4	32 51.2	49.5	144.2	31 13.5	50.4	144.9	22
36 51.8	47.1	142.4	35 16.2	48.1	143.3	33 39.4	48.9	144.1	32 01.7	49.7	144.9	30 23.1	50.4	145.6	23
36 04.7	47.4	143.2	34 28.1	48.3	144.0	32 50.5	49.2	144.8	31 12.0	50.0	145.5	29 32.7	50.7	146.2	24
35 17.3	−47.6	144.0	33 39.8	−48.6	144.8	32 01.3	−49.3	145.5	30 22.0	−50.1	146.2	28 42.0	−50.8	146.8	25
34 29.6	47.9	144.7	32 51.2	48.7	145.5	31 12.0	49.6	146.2	29 31.9	50.3	146.8	27 51.2	51.0	147.4	26
33 41.7	48.2	145.4	32 02.5	49.0	146.2	30 22.4	49.7	146.8	28 41.6	50.4	147.4	27 00.2	51.2	148.0	27
32 53.5	48.4	146.1	31 13.5	49.2	146.8	29 32.7	50.0	147.5	27 51.2	50.7	148.0	26 09.0	51.2	148.6	28
32 05.1	48.7	146.8	30 24.3	49.5	147.5	28 42.7	50.1	148.1	27 00.5	50.8	148.7	25 17.8	51.4	149.2	29

30° Hc	d	Z	32° Hc	d	Z	34° Hc	d	Z	36° Hc	d	Z	38° Hc	d	Z	Dec.
47 15.6	−44.5	128.7	45 59.2	−45.9	130.3	44 40.4	−47.4	131.8	43 19.3	−48.7	133.2	41 56.0	−49.8	134.6	0
46 31.1	45.0	129.6	45 13.3	46.5	131.2	43 53.0	47.7	132.7	42 30.6	49.0	134.0	41 06.2	50.1	135.3	1
45 46.1	45.4	130.6	44 26.8	46.8	132.1	43 05.3	48.1	133.5	41 41.6	49.2	134.8	40 16.1	50.3	136.0	2
45 00.7	45.8	131.5	43 40.0	47.2	133.0	42 17.2	48.5	134.3	40 52.4	49.6	135.6	39 25.8	50.6	136.8	3
44 14.9	46.3	132.4	42 52.8	47.6	133.8	41 28.7	48.7	135.1	40 02.8	49.8	136.3	38 35.2	50.8	137.4	4
43 28.6	−46.7	133.3	42 05.2	−47.9	134.7	40 40.0	−49.1	135.9	39 13.0	−50.1	137.0	37 44.4	−51.1	138.1	5
42 41.9	47.0	134.2	41 17.3	48.2	135.5	39 50.9	49.3	136.7	38 22.9	50.4	137.8	36 53.3	51.3	138.8	6
41 54.9	47.4	135.0	40 29.1	48.6	136.2	39 01.6	49.7	137.4	37 32.5	50.6	138.4	36 02.0	51.5	139.4	7
41 07.5	47.8	135.8	39 40.5	48.8	137.0	38 11.9	49.8	138.1	36 41.9	50.8	139.1	35 10.5	51.6	140.1	8
40 19.7	48.0	136.6	38 51.7	49.2	137.8	37 22.1	50.1	138.8	35 51.1	51.0	139.8	34 18.9	51.9	140.7	9
39 31.7	−48.4	137.4	38 02.5	−49.4	138.5	36 32.0	−50.4	139.5	35 00.1	−51.2	140.4	33 27.0	−52.0	141.3	10
38 43.3	48.7	138.2	37 13.1	49.6	139.2	35 41.6	50.6	140.2	34 08.9	51.5	141.1	32 35.0	52.2	141.9	11
37 54.6	48.9	138.9	36 23.5	49.9	139.9	34 51.0	50.7	140.8	33 17.4	51.6	141.7	31 42.8	52.4	142.5	12
37 05.7	49.2	139.7	35 33.6	50.2	140.6	34 00.3	51.0	141.5	32 25.8	51.7	142.3	30 50.4	52.5	143.1	13
36 16.5	49.5	140.4	34 43.4	50.3	141.3	33 09.3	51.2	142.1	31 34.1	52.0	142.9	29 57.9	52.6	143.6	14
35 27.0	−49.7	141.1	33 53.1	−50.6	141.9	32 18.1	−51.3	142.7	30 42.1	−52.0	143.5	29 05.3	−52.8	144.1	15
34 37.3	49.9	141.8	33 02.5	50.7	142.6	31 26.8	51.6	143.3	29 50.1	52.3	144.0	28 12.5	52.9	144.7	16
33 47.4	50.1	142.4	32 11.8	50.9	143.2	30 35.2	51.6	143.9	28 57.8	52.4	144.6	27 19.6	53.0	145.2	17
32 57.3	50.3	143.1	31 20.9	51.1	143.8	29 43.6	51.9	144.5	28 05.4	52.5	145.2	26 26.6	53.1	145.7	18
32 07.0	50.6	143.7	30 29.8	51.3	144.4	28 51.7	51.9	145.1	27 12.9	52.6	145.7	25 33.5	53.3	146.3	19
31 16.4	−50.7	144.4	29 38.5	−51.4	145.0	27 59.8	−52.2	145.7	26 20.3	−52.7	146.2	24 40.2	−53.3	146.8	20
30 25.7	50.9	145.0	28 47.1	51.6	145.6	27 07.6	52.2	146.2	25 27.6	52.9	146.8	23 46.9	53.4	147.3	21
29 34.8	51.0	145.6	27 55.5	51.8	146.2	26 15.4	52.4	146.8	24 34.7	53.0	147.3	22 53.5	53.6	147.8	22
28 43.8	51.2	146.2	27 03.7	51.8	146.8	25 23.0	52.5	147.3	23 41.7	53.0	147.8	21 59.9	53.6	148.3	23
27 52.6	51.4	146.8	26 11.9	52.0	147.3	24 30.5	52.6	147.9	22 48.7	53.2	148.3	21 06.3	53.7	148.7	24
27 01.2	−51.5	147.4	25 19.9	−52.1	147.9	23 37.9	−52.7	148.4	21 55.5	−53.2	148.8	20 12.6	−53.7	149.2	25
26 09.7	51.6	148.0	24 27.8	52.3	148.4	22 45.2	52.8	148.9	21 02.3	53.4	149.3	19 18.9	53.9	149.7	26
25 18.1	51.7	148.5	23 35.5	52.3	149.0	21 52.4	52.9	149.4	20 08.9	53.4	149.8	18 25.0	53.9	150.2	27
24 26.4	51.9	149.1	22 43.2	52.5	149.5	20 59.5	52.9	149.9	19 15.5	53.5	150.3	17 31.1	54.0	150.6	28
23 34.5	52.0	149.6	21 50.7	52.5	150.0	20 06.6	53.1	150.4	18 22.0	53.6	150.8	16 37.1	54.0	151.1	29

Dec.	40° Hc	d	Z	42° Hc	d	Z	44° Hc	d	Z	46° Hc	d	Z	48° Hc	d	Z
°	° ′	′	°	° ′	′	°	° ′	′	°	° ′	′	°	° ′	′	°
0	40 30.9	+50.6	135.8	39 04.0	+51.6	137.0	37 35.5	+52.5	138.0	36 05.6	+53.3	139.0	34 34.4	+54.1	139.9
1	41 21.5	50.3	135.1	39 55.6	51.4	136.3	38 28.0	52.3	137.4	36 58.9	53.2	138.4	35 28.5	53.9	139.4
2	42 11.8	50.1	134.4	40 47.0	51.1	135.6	39 20.3	52.1	136.8	37 52.1	53.0	137.9	36 22.4	53.8	138.9
3	43 01.9	49.7	133.6	41 38.1	50.8	134.9	40 12.4	51.9	136.1	38 45.1	52.8	137.3	37 16.2	53.6	138.3
4	43 51.6	49.4	132.8	42 28.9	50.6	134.2	41 04.3	51.7	135.5	39 37.9	52.6	136.7	38 09.8	53.5	137.8
5	44 41.0	+49.1	132.1	43 19.5	+50.3	133.5	41 56.0	+51.4	134.8	40 30.5	+52.4	136.0	39 03.3	+53.3	137.2
6	45 30.1	48.7	131.2	44 09.8	50.0	132.7	42 47.4	51.1	134.1	41 22.9	52.2	135.4	39 56.6	53.1	136.6
7	46 18.8	48.4	130.4	44 59.8	49.7	131.9	43 38.5	50.9	133.4	42 15.1	51.9	134.7	40 49.7	52.9	136.0
8	47 07.2	47.9	129.5	45 49.5	49.3	131.1	44 29.4	50.5	132.6	43 07.0	51.7	134.0	41 42.6	52.7	135.3
9	47 55.1	47.6	128.6	46 38.8	49.0	130.3	45 19.9	50.3	131.9	43 58.7	51.4	133.3	42 35.3	52.5	134.7
10	48 42.7	+47.0	127.7	47 27.8	+48.6	129.5	46 10.2	+49.9	131.1	44 50.1	+51.1	132.6	43 27.8	+52.2	134.0
11	49 29.7	46.6	126.8	48 16.4	48.1	128.6	47 00.1	49.6	130.3	45 41.2	50.9	131.9	44 20.0	52.0	133.3
12	50 16.3	46.1	125.8	49 04.5	47.7	127.7	47 49.7	49.2	129.5	46 32.1	50.5	131.1	45 12.0	51.7	132.6
13	51 02.4	45.6	124.8	49 52.2	47.3	126.8	48 38.9	48.8	128.6	47 22.6	50.2	130.3	46 03.7	51.4	131.9
14	51 48.0	44.9	123.8	50 39.5	46.6	125.8	49 27.7	48.4	127.7	48 12.8	49.8	129.5	46 55.1	51.1	131.2
15	52 32.9	+44.4	122.7	51 26.3	+46.2	124.8	50 16.1	+47.9	126.8	49 02.6	+49.5	128.7	47 46.2	+50.8	130.4
16	53 17.3	43.7	121.6	52 12.5	45.7	123.8	51 04.0	47.5	125.8	49 52.1	49.0	127.8	48 37.0	50.5	129.6
17	54 01.0	43.0	120.4	52 58.2	45.1	122.7	51 51.5	46.9	124.9	50 41.1	48.6	126.9	49 27.5	50.1	128.8
18	54 44.0	42.3	119.2	53 43.3	44.4	121.6	52 38.4	46.4	123.8	51 29.7	48.2	126.0	50 17.6	49.7	127.9
19	55 26.3	41.5	118.0	54 27.7	43.8	120.5	53 24.8	45.8	122.8	52 17.9	47.6	125.0	51 07.3	49.3	127.0
20	56 07.8	+40.7	116.7	55 11.5	+43.1	119.3	54 10.6	+45.3	121.7	53 05.5	+47.2	124.0	51 56.6	+48.9	126.1
21	56 48.5	39.8	115.4	55 54.6	42.3	118.0	54 55.9	44.5	120.6	53 52.7	46.6	122.9	52 45.5	48.3	125.2
22	57 28.3	38.9	114.0	56 36.9	41.5	116.8	55 40.4	43.9	119.4	54 39.3	45.9	121.9	53 33.8	47.9	124.2
23	58 07.2	37.9	112.5	57 18.4	40.6	115.4	56 24.3	43.1	118.2	55 25.2	45.4	120.7	54 21.7	47.4	123.2
24	58 45.1	36.8	111.1	57 59.0	39.7	114.1	57 07.4	42.3	116.9	56 10.6	44.6	119.6	55 09.1	46.7	122.1
25	59 21.9	+35.7	109.5	58 38.7	+38.7	112.6	57 49.7	+41.4	115.6	56 55.2	+44.0	118.4	55 55.8	+46.1	121.0
26	59 57.6	34.5	107.9	59 17.4	37.7	111.1	58 31.1	40.6	114.2	57 39.2	43.1	117.1	56 41.9	45.5	119.8
27	60 32.1	33.2	106.3	59 55.1	36.5	109.6	59 11.7	39.6	112.8	58 22.3	42.3	115.8	57 27.4	44.8	118.6
28	61 05.3	31.9	104.6	60 31.6	35.4	108.0	59 51.3	38.5	111.3	59 04.6	41.4	114.4	58 12.2	44.0	117.4
29	61 37.2	30.5	102.8	61 07.0	34.1	106.4	60 29.8	37.4	109.8	59 46.0	40.5	113.0	58 56.2	43.1	116.1

Dec.	50° Hc	d	Z	52° Hc	d	Z	54° Hc	d	Z	56° Hc	d	Z	58° Hc	d	Z
°	° ′	′	°	° ′	′	°	° ′	′	°	° ′	′	°	° ′	′	°
0	33 02.0	+54.7	140.8	31 28.4	+55.4	141.6	29 53.9	+56.0	142.3	28 18.5	+56.5	143.0	26 42.3	+56.9	143.6
1	33 56.7	54.7	140.3	32 23.8	55.3	141.1	30 49.9	55.9	141.9	29 15.0	56.4	142.6	27 39.2	56.9	143.3
2	34 51.4	54.5	139.8	33 19.1	55.2	140.7	31 45.8	55.7	141.5	30 11.4	56.3	142.2	28 36.1	56.8	142.9
3	35 45.9	54.4	139.3	34 14.3	55.1	140.2	32 41.5	55.7	141.0	31 07.7	56.3	141.8	29 32.9	56.8	142.5
4	36 40.3	54.2	138.8	35 09.4	54.9	139.7	33 37.2	55.6	140.6	32 04.0	56.1	141.4	30 29.7	56.7	142.2
5	37 34.5	+54.1	138.2	36 04.3	+54.9	139.2	34 32.8	+55.5	140.1	33 00.1	+56.1	141.0	31 26.4	+56.6	141.8
6	38 28.6	54.0	137.7	36 59.2	54.7	138.7	35 28.3	55.4	139.7	33 56.2	56.0	140.6	32 23.0	56.5	141.4
7	39 22.6	53.7	137.1	37 53.9	54.5	138.2	36 23.7	55.3	139.2	34 52.2	55.9	140.1	33 19.5	56.5	141.0
8	40 16.3	53.6	136.5	38 48.4	54.4	137.7	37 19.0	55.1	138.7	35 48.1	55.8	139.7	34 16.0	56.4	140.6
9	41 09.9	53.5	136.0	39 42.8	54.3	137.1	38 14.1	55.0	138.2	36 43.9	55.7	139.2	35 12.4	56.3	140.2
10	42 03.4	+53.2	135.3	40 37.1	+54.1	136.6	39 09.1	+54.9	137.7	37 39.6	+55.6	138.8	36 08.7	+56.2	139.7
11	42 56.6	53.0	134.7	41 31.2	53.9	136.0	40 04.0	54.7	137.2	38 35.2	55.5	138.3	37 04.9	56.1	139.3
12	43 49.6	52.7	134.1	42 25.1	53.7	135.4	40 58.7	54.6	136.6	39 30.7	55.3	137.8	38 01.0	56.0	138.9
13	44 42.3	52.6	133.4	43 18.8	53.6	134.8	41 53.3	54.4	136.1	40 26.0	55.2	137.3	38 57.0	55.9	138.4
14	45 34.9	52.3	132.7	44 12.4	53.3	134.2	42 47.7	54.3	135.5	41 21.2	55.0	136.8	39 52.9	55.8	137.9
15	46 27.2	+52.0	132.0	45 05.7	+53.1	133.5	43 42.0	+54.0	134.9	42 16.2	+54.9	136.2	40 48.7	+55.7	137.4
16	47 19.2	51.7	131.3	45 58.8	52.8	132.9	44 36.0	53.9	134.3	43 11.1	54.8	135.7	41 44.4	55.5	136.9
17	48 10.9	51.4	130.5	46 51.6	52.6	132.2	45 29.9	53.6	133.7	44 05.9	54.5	135.1	42 39.9	55.4	136.4
18	49 02.3	51.1	129.8	47 44.2	52.3	131.5	46 23.5	53.4	133.1	45 00.4	54.4	134.5	43 35.3	55.2	135.9
19	49 53.4	50.8	128.9	48 36.5	52.1	130.7	47 16.9	53.2	132.4	45 54.8	54.2	133.9	44 30.5	55.1	135.4
20	50 44.2	+50.4	128.1	49 28.6	+51.7	130.0	48 10.1	+52.9	131.7	46 49.0	+54.0	133.3	45 25.6	+54.9	134.8
21	51 34.6	49.9	127.2	50 20.3	51.4	129.2	49 03.0	52.7	131.0	47 43.0	53.7	132.7	46 20.5	54.7	134.2
22	52 24.5	49.6	126.3	51 11.7	51.1	128.4	49 55.7	52.3	130.2	48 36.7	53.6	132.0	47 15.2	54.5	133.6
23	53 14.1	49.1	125.4	52 02.8	50.6	127.5	50 48.0	52.1	129.5	49 30.3	53.2	131.3	48 09.7	54.3	133.0
24	54 03.2	48.6	124.4	52 53.4	50.3	126.6	51 40.1	51.7	128.7	50 23.5	53.0	130.6	49 04.0	54.1	132.4
25	54 51.8	+48.1	123.4	53 43.7	+49.8	125.7	52 31.8	+51.4	127.9	51 16.5	+52.7	129.9	49 58.1	+53.9	131.7
26	55 39.9	47.6	122.4	54 33.5	49.4	124.8	53 23.2	50.9	127.0	52 09.2	52.4	129.1	50 52.0	53.6	131.0
27	56 27.5	46.9	121.3	55 22.9	48.9	123.8	54 14.1	50.6	126.1	53 01.6	52.0	128.3	51 45.6	53.3	130.3
28	57 14.4	46.3	120.2	56 11.8	48.3	122.8	55 04.7	50.1	125.2	53 53.6	51.7	127.4	52 38.9	53.0	129.5
29	58 00.7	45.6	119.0	57 00.1	47.7	121.7	55 54.8	49.6	124.2	54 45.3	51.3	126.6	53 31.9	52.8	128.8

40°			42°			44°			46°			48°			Dec.
Hc	d	Z	Hc	d	Z	Hc	d	Z	Hc	d	Z	Hc	d	Z	
40 30.9	-50.9	135.8	39 04.0	-51.8	137.0	37 35.5	-52.7	138.0	36 05.6	-53.5	139.0	34 34.4	-54.2	139.9	0
39 40.0	51.1	136.5	38 12.2	52.0	137.6	36 42.8	52.8	138.6	35 12.1	53.6	139.6	33 40.2	54.4	140.5	1
38 48.9	51.3	137.2	37 20.2	52.3	138.2	35 50.0	53.1	139.2	34 18.5	53.8	140.1	32 45.8	54.4	141.0	2
37 57.6	51.5	137.8	36 27.9	52.4	138.9	34 56.9	53.2	139.8	33 24.7	53.9	140.7	31 51.4	54.6	141.5	3
37 06.1	51.8	138.5	35 35.5	52.6	139.5	34 03.7	53.3	140.3	32 30.8	54.1	141.2	30 56.8	54.7	141.9	4
36 14.3	-51.9	139.1	34 42.9	-52.7	140.0	33 10.4	-53.5	140.9	31 36.7	-54.1	141.7	30 02.1	-54.8	142.4	5
35 22.4	52.2	139.7	33 50.2	52.9	140.6	32 16.9	53.6	141.4	30 42.6	54.3	142.2	29 07.3	54.9	142.9	6
34 30.2	52.3	140.3	32 57.3	53.1	141.2	31 23.3	53.8	142.0	29 48.3	54.4	142.7	28 12.4	55.0	143.4	7
33 37.9	52.4	140.9	32 04.2	53.2	141.7	30 29.5	53.8	142.5	28 53.9	54.5	143.2	27 17.4	55.0	143.8	8
32 45.5	52.7	141,5	31 11.0	53.3	142.3	29 35.7	54.0	143.0	27 59.4	54.6	143.6	26 22.4	55.2	144.3	9
31 52.8	-52.7	142.1	30 17.7	-53.4	142.8	28 41.7	-54.1	143.5	27 04.8	-54.6	144.1	25 27.2	-55.2	144.7	10
31 00.1	52.9	142.6	29 24.3	53.6	143.3	27 47.6	54.2	144.0	26 10.2	54.8	144.6	24 32.0	55.3	145.1	11
30 07.2	53.1	143.2	28 30.7	53.7	143.9	26 53.4	54.3	144.5	25 15.4	54.9	145.0	23 36.7	55.3	145.5	12
29 14.1	53.2	143.7	27 37.0	53.8	144.4	25 59.1	54.4	144.9	24 20.5	54.9	145.5	22 41.4	55.4	146.0	13
28 20.9	53.3	144.3	26 43.2	53.9	144.9	25 04.7	54.5	145.4	23 25.6	55.0	145.9	21 46.0	55.4	146.4	14
27 27.6	-53.4	144.8	25 49.3	-54.0	145.3	24 10.2	-54.5	145.8	22 30.6	-55.0	146.4	20 50.5	-55.6	146.8	15
26 34.2	53.5	145.3	24 55.3	54.1	145.8	23 15.7	54.6	146.3	21 35.6	55.2	146.8	19 54.9	55.6	147.2	16
25 40.7	53.6	145.8	24 01.2	54.2	146.3	22 21.1	54.7	146.8	20 40.4	55.2	147.2	18 59.3	55.6	147.6	17
24 47.1	53.7	146.3	23 07.0	54.3	146.8	21 26.4	54.8	147.2	19 45.2	55.2	147.6	18 03.7	55.7	148.0	18
23 53.4	53.8	146.8	22 12.7	54.3	147.2	20 31.6	54.8	147.7	18 50.0	55.3	148.0	17 08.0	55.7	148.4	19
22 59.6	-53.9	147.3	21 18.4	-54.4	147.7	19 36.8	-54.9	148.1	17 54.7	-55.4	148.4	16 12.3	-55.8	148.8	20
22 05.7	54.0	147.7	20 24.0	54.5	148.1	18 41.9	55.0	148.5	16 59.3	55.4	148.8	15 16.5	55.8	149.1	21
21 11.7	54.0	148.2	19 29.5	54.5	148.6	17 46.9	55.0	148.9	16 03.9	55.4	149.2	14 20.7	55.9	149.5	22
20 17.7	54.2	148.7	18 35.0	54.6	149.0	16 51.9	55.1	149.4	15 08.5	55.5	149.6	13 24.8	55.9	149.9	23
19 23.5	54.2	149.1	17 40.4	54.7	149.5	15 56.8	55.1	149.8	14 13.0	55.5	150.0	12 28.9	55.9	150.3	24
18 29.3	-54.2	149.6	16 45.7	-54.7	149.9	15 01.7	-55.1	150.2	13 17.5	-55.6	150.4	11 33.0	-55.9	150.6	25
17 35.1	54.3	150.0	15 51.0	54.8	150.3	14 06.6	55.2	150.6	12 21.9	55.6	150.8	10 37.1	56.0	151.0	26
16 40.8	54.4	150.5	14 56.2	54.8	150.7	13 11.4	55.2	151.0	11 26.3	55.6	151.2	9 41.1	56.0	151.4	27
15 46.4	54.4	150.9	14 01.4	54.9	151.2	12 16.2	55.3	151.4	10 30.7	55.6	151.6	8 45.1	56.0	151.7	28
14 52.0	54.5	151.3	13 06.5	54.9	151.6	11 20.9	55.3	151.8	9 35.1	55.7	152.0	7 49.1	56.1	152.1	29

50°			52°			54°			56°			58°			Dec.
Hc	d	Z	Hc	d	Z	Hc	d	Z	Hc	d	Z	Hc	d	Z	
33 02.0	-54.9	140.8	31 28.4	-55.4	141.6	29 53.9	-56.0	142.3	28 18.5	-56.5	143.0	26 42.3	-57.0	143.6	0
32 07.1	55.0	141.3	30 33.0	55.6	142.0	28 57.9	56.1	142.7	27 22.0	56.6	143.4	25 45.3	57.0	144.0	1
31 12.1	55.1	141.7	29 37.4	55.7	142.5	28 01.8	56.2	143.1	26 25.4	56.6	143.7	24 48.3	57.1	144.3	2
30 17.0	55.2	142.2	28 41.7	55.7	142.9	27 05.6	56.2	143.5	25 28.8	56.7	144.1	23 51.2	57.1	144.6	3
29 21.8	55.3	142.7	27 46.0	55.8	143.3	26 09.4	56.3	143.9	24 32.1	56.8	144.5	22 54.1	57.2	145.0	4
28 26.5	-55.3	143.1	26 50.2	-55.9	143.7	25 13.1	-56.4	144.3	23 35.3	-56.8	144.8	21 56.9	-57.2	145.3	5
27 31.2	55.4	143.5	25 54.3	55.9	144.1	24 16.7	56.4	144.7	22 38.5	56.8	145.2	20 59.7	57.2	145.6	6
26 35.8	55.4	144.0	24 58.4	56.1	144.5	23 20.3	56.5	145.1	21 41.7	56.9	145.5	20 02.5	57.3	146.0	7
25 40.2	55.5	144.4	24 02.3	56.0	144.9	22 23.8	56.5	145.4	20 44.8	57.0	145.9	19 05.2	57.3	146.3	8
24 44.7	55.7	144.8	23 06.3	56.2	145.3	21 27.3	56.5	145.8	19 47.8	56.9	146.2	18 07.9	57.3	146.6	9
23 49.0	-55.7	145.2	22 10.1	-56.1	145.7	20 30.8	-56.7	146.1	18 50.9	-57.0	146.5	17 10.6	-57.4	146.9	10
22 53.3	55.8	145.6	21 14.0	56.3	146.1	19 34.1	56.6	146.5	17 53.9	57.1	146.9	16 13.2	57.4	147.2	11
21 57.5	55.8	146.0	20 17.7	56.2	146.5	18 37.5	56.7	146.8	16 56.8	57.1	147.2	15 15.8	57.4	147.5	12
21 01.7	55.9	146.4	19 21.5	56.4	146.8	17 40.8	56.7	147.2	15 59.8	57.1	147.5	14 18.4	57.4	147.8	13
20 05.8	56.0	146.8	18 25.1	56.3	147.2	16 44.1	56.8	147.5	15 02.7	57.1	147.8	13 21.0	57.5	148.1	14
19 09.8	-55.9	147.2	17 28.8	-56.4	147.5	15 47.3	-56.9	147.9	14 05.6	-57.2	148.1	12 23.5	-57.5	148.4	15
18 13.9	56.1	147.6	16 32.4	56.5	147.9	14 50.6	56.9	148.2	13 08.4	57.1	148.5	11 26.0	57.5	148.7	16
17 17.8	56.0	147.9	15 35.9	56.4	148.3	13 53.7	56.8	148.5	12 11.3	57.2	148.8	10 28.5	57.5	149.0	17
16 21.8	56.2	148.3	14 39.5	56.5	148.6	12 56.9	56.9	148.9	11 14.1	57.2	149.1	9 31.0	57.5	149.3	18
15 25.6	56.1	148.7	13 43.0	56.6	149.0	12 00.0	56.8	149.2	10 16.9	57.3	149.4	8 33.5	57.5	149.6	19
14 29.5	-56.2	149.0	12 46.4	-56.5	149.3	11 03.2	-57.0	149.5	9 19.6	-57.2	149.7	7 36.0	-57.6	149.8	20
13 33.3	56.2	149.4	11 49.9	56.6	149.6	10 06.2	56.9	149.8	8 22.4	57.2	150.0	6 38.4	57.5	150.1	21
12 37.1	56.2	149.8	10 53.3	56.6	150.0	9 09.3	56.9	150.2	7 25.2	57.3	150.3	5 40.9	57.6	150.4	22
11 40.9	56.3	150.1	9 56.7	56.6	150.3	8 12.4	57.0	150.5	6 27.9	57.3	150.6	4 43.3	57.6	150.7	23
10 44.6	56.3	150.5	9 00.1	56.7	150.7	7 15.4	57.0	150.8	5 30.6	57.3	150.9	3 45.7	57.6	151.0	24
9 48.3	-56.3	150.8	8 03.4	-56.6	151.0	6 18.4	-56.9	151.1	4 33.3	-57.3	151.2	2 48.1	-57.5	151.3	25
8 52.0	56.3	151.2	7 06.8	56.7	151.3	5 21.5	57.0	151.4	3 36.0	57.3	151.5	1 50.6	57.6	151.5	26
7 55.7	56.4	151.5	6 10.1	56.7	151.6	4 24.5	57.0	151.7	2 38.7	57.3	151.8	0 53.0	-57.6	151.8	27
6 59.3	56.3	151.9	5 13.4	56.7	152.0	3 27.5	57.0	152.0	1 41.4	57.3	152.1	0 04.6	+57.6	27.9	28
6 03.0	56.4	152.2	4 16.7	56.7	152.3	2 30.5	57.1	152.4	0 44.1	-57.3	152.4	1 02.2	57.6	27.6	29

Dec.	0° Hc	d	Z	2° Hc	d	Z	4° Hc	d	Z	6° Hc	d	Z	8° Hc	d	Z
0	56 00.0	− 0.8	90.0	55 56.9	+ 3.0	93.0	55 47.6	+ 6.7	95.9	55 32.2	+ 10.4	98.8	55 10.9	+ 13.9	101.7
1	55 59.2	2.3	88.2	55 59.9	+ 1.4	91.2	55 54.3	5.2	94.1	55 42.6	8.8	97.1	55 24.8	12.5	99.9
2	55 56.9	3.9	86.4	56 01.3	− 0.2	89.4	55 59.5	3.6	92.4	55 51.4	7.4	95.3	55 37.3	11.0	98.2
3	55 53.0	5.4	84.6	56 01.1	1.6	87.6	56 03.1	2.0	90.6	55 58.8	5.8	93.5	55 48.3	9.5	96.5
4	55 47.6	6.9	82.9	55 59.5	3.3	85.8	56 05.1	+ 0.5	88.8	56 04.6	4.2	91.8	55 57.8	8.0	94.7
5	55 40.7	− 8.5	81.1	55 56.2	− 4.8	84.0	56 05.6	− 1.0	87.0	56 08.8	+ 2.7	90.0	56 05.8	+ 6.4	92.9
6	55 32.2	9.9	79.4	55 51.4	6.3	82.2	56 04.6	2.6	85.2	56 11.5	+ 1.1	88.2	56 12.2	4.9	91.2
7	55 22.3	11.4	77.6	55 45.1	7.8	80.5	56 02.0	4.2	83.4	56 12.6	− 0.4	86.4	56 17.1	3.3	89.4
8	55 10.9	12.8	75.9	55 37.3	9.3	78.7	55 57.8	5.7	81.6	56 12.2	2.0	84.6	56 20.4	1.8	87.6
9	54 58.1	14.3	74.2	55 28.0	10.8	77.0	55 52.1	7.2	79.8	56 10.2	3.5	82.8	56 22.2	+ 0.2	85.8
10	54 43.8	− 15.6	72.5	55 17.2	− 12.3	75.2	55 44.9	− 8.8	78.1	56 06.7	− 5.1	81.0	56 22.4	− 1.4	84.0
11	54 28.2	17.0	70.8	55 04.9	13.7	73.5	55 36.1	10.2	76.3	56 01.6	6.7	79.2	56 21.0	2.9	82.1
12	54 11.2	18.4	69.2	54 51.2	15.1	71.8	55 25.9	11.7	74.6	55 54.9	8.1	77.4	56 18.1	4.6	80.3
13	53 52.8	19.6	67.6	54 36.1	16.4	70.2	55 14.2	13.1	72.9	55 46.8	9.7	75.7	56 13.5	6.0	78.6
14	53 33.2	20.9	66.0	54 19.7	17.8	68.5	55 01.1	14.6	71.2	55 37.1	11.2	73.9	56 07.5	7.6	76.8
15	53 12.3	− 22.1	64.4	54 01.9	− 19.2	66.9	54 46.5	− 16.0	69.5	55 25.9	− 12.6	72.2	55 59.9	− 9.2	75.0
16	52 50.2	23.3	62.9	53 42.7	20.3	65.3	54 30.5	17.3	67.8	55 13.3	14.0	70.5	55 50.7	10.6	73.2
17	52 26.9	24.4	61.3	53 22.4	21.7	63.7	54 13.2	18.6	66.2	54 59.3	15.5	68.8	55 40.1	12.1	71.5
18	52 02.5	25.5	59.8	53 00.7	22.8	62.1	53 54.6	19.9	64.5	54 43.8	16.8	67.1	55 28.0	13.6	69.7
19	51 37.0	26.6	58.4	52 37.9	24.0	60.6	53 34.7	21.2	62.9	54 27.0	18.2	65.4	55 14.4	15.0	68.0
20	51 10.4	− 27.7	56.9	52 13.9	− 25.1	59.1	53 13.5	− 22.3	61.4	54 08.8	− 19.4	63.8	54 59.4	− 16.3	66.3
21	50 42.7	28.6	55.5	51 48.8	26.1	57.6	52 51.2	23.6	59.8	53 49.4	20.8	62.2	54 43.1	17.8	64.7
22	50 14.1	29.6	54.2	51 22.7	27.3	56.2	52 27.6	24.7	58.3	53 28.6	22.0	60.6	54 25.3	19.0	63.0
23	49 44.5	30.6	52.8	50 55.4	28.2	54.7	52 02.9	25.8	56.8	53 06.6	23.1	59.0	54 06.3	20.4	61.4
24	49 13.9	31.4	51.5	50 27.2	29.3	53.4	51 37.1	26.9	55.4	52 43.5	24.4	57.5	53 45.9	21.6	59.8
25	48 42.5	− 32.3	50.2	49 57.9	− 30.2	52.0	51 10.2	− 27.9	53.9	52 19.1	− 25.4	56.0	53 24.3	− 22.8	58.2
26	48 10.2	33.1	48.9	49 27.7	31.0	50.7	50 42.3	28.9	52.5	51 53.7	26.6	54.5	53 01.5	24.0	56.7
27	47 37.1	33.9	47.7	48 56.7	32.0	49.3	50 13.4	29.8	51.1	51 27.1	27.6	53.1	52 37.5	25.2	55.2
28	47 03.2	34.6	46.4	48 24.7	32.8	48.1	49 43.6	30.8	49.8	50 59.5	28.6	51.7	52 12.3	26.2	53.7
29	46 28.6	35.4	45.3	47 51.9	33.6	46.8	49 12.8	31.7	48.5	50 30.9	29.5	50.3	51 46.1	27.3	52.2

Dec.	10° Hc	d	Z	12° Hc	d	Z	14° Hc	d	Z	16° Hc	d	Z	18° Hc	d	Z
0	54 43.8	+ 17.4	104.4	54 11.2	+ 20.6	107.1	53 33.2	+ 23.8	109.7	52 50.2	+ 26.9	112.2	52 02.5	+ 29.7	114.6
1	55 01.2	16.0	102.8	54 31.8	19.4	105.5	53 57.0	22.7	108.2	53 17.1	25.6	110.7	52 32.2	28.5	113.2
2	55 17.2	14.5	101.1	54 51.2	18.0	103.9	54 19.7	21.3	106.6	53 42.7	24.6	109.2	53 00.7	27.5	111.7
3	55 31.7	13.2	99.4	55 09.2	16.7	102.2	54 41.0	20.1	105.0	54 07.3	23.2	107.7	53 28.2	26.4	110.3
4	55 44.9	11.6	97.6	55 25.9	15.2	100.5	55 01.1	18.7	103.4	54 30.5	22.1	106.1	53 54.6	25.2	108.7
5	55 56.5	+ 10.2	95.9	55 41.1	+ 13.8	98.8	55 19.8	+ 17.3	101.7	54 52.6	+ 20.7	104.5	54 19.8	+ 24.0	107.2
6	56 06.7	8.6	94.1	55 54.9	12.3	97.1	55 37.1	15.9	100.0	55 13.3	19.4	102.8	54 43.8	22.8	105.6
7	56 15.3	7.1	92.4	56 07.2	10.9	95.3	55 53.0	14.5	98.3	55 32.7	18.0	101.2	55 06.6	21.4	104.0
8	56 22.4	5.5	90.6	56 18.1	9.3	93.6	56 07.5	13.0	96.5	55 50.7	16.6	99.5	55 28.0	20.1	102.4
9	56 27.9	4.0	88.8	56 27.4	7.7	91.8	56 20.5	11.5	94.8	56 07.3	15.2	97.8	55 48.1	18.7	100.7
10	56 31.9	+ 2.4	87.0	56 35.1	+ 6.2	90.0	56 32.0	+ 9.9	93.0	56 22.5	+ 13.7	96.0	56 06.8	+ 17.3	99.0
11	56 34.3	+ 0.8	85.1	56 41.3	4.6	88.2	56 41.9	8.4	91.2	56 36.2	12.1	94.3	56 24.1	15.9	97.3
12	56 35.1	− 0.8	83.3	56 45.9	3.0	86.4	56 50.3	6.8	89.4	56 48.3	10.6	92.5	56 40.0	14.3	95.5
13	56 34.3	2.3	81.5	56 48.9	+ 1.4	84.5	56 57.1	5.3	87.6	56 58.9	9.1	90.7	56 54.3	12.8	93.7
14	56 32.0	4.0	79.7	56 50.3	− 0.2	82.7	57 02.4	3.6	85.8	57 08.0	7.4	88.9	57 07.1	11.3	92.0
15	56 28.0	− 5.5	77.9	56 50.1	− 1.8	80.9	57 06.0	+ 1.8	83.9	57 15.4	+ 5.9	87.0	57 18.4	+ 9.7	90.1
16	56 22.5	7.1	76.1	56 48.3	3.4	79.1	57 08.0	+ 0.4	82.1	57 21.3	4.2	85.2	57 28.1	8.1	88.3
17	56 15.4	8.6	74.3	56 44.9	4.9	77.2	57 08.4	− 1.3	80.3	57 25.5	2.6	83.3	57 36.2	6.5	86.5
18	56 06.8	10.1	72.5	56 40.0	6.6	75.4	57 07.1	2.8	78.4	57 28.1	+ 1.0	81.5	57 42.7	4.8	84.6
19	55 56.7	11.7	70.8	56 33.4	8.1	73.6	57 04.3	4.5	76.6	57 29.1	− 0.7	79.6	57 47.5	3.1	82.7
20	55 45.0	− 13.1	69.0	56 25.3	− 9.7	71.8	56 59.8	− 6.0	74.7	57 28.4	− 2.4	77.8	57 50.6	+ 1.5	80.9
21	55 31.9	14.5	67.3	56 15.6	11.2	70.0	56 53.8	7.7	72.9	57 26.0	3.9	75.9	57 52.1	− 0.1	79.0
22	55 17.4	16.0	65.6	56 04.4	12.6	68.3	56 46.1	9.2	71.1	57 22.1	5.6	74.0	57 52.0	1.9	77.1
23	55 01.4	17.3	63.9	55 51.8	14.2	66.5	56 36.9	10.8	69.3	57 16.5	7.2	72.2	57 50.1	3.4	75.2
24	54 44.1	18.7	62.3	55 37.6	15.6	64.8	56 26.1	12.2	67.5	57 09.3	8.8	70.4	57 46.7	5.2	73.3
25	54 25.4	− 20.0	60.6	55 22.0	− 17.0	63.1	56 13.9	− 13.8	65.8	57 00.5	− 10.4	68.5	57 41.5	− 6.8	71.5
26	54 05.4	21.3	59.0	55 05.0	18.3	61.4	56 00.1	15.2	64.0	56 50.1	11.9	66.7	57 34.7	8.4	69.6
27	53 44.1	22.5	57.4	54 46.7	19.7	59.8	55 44.9	16.7	62.3	56 38.2	13.4	65.0	57 26.3	10.0	67.8
28	53 21.6	23.7	55.8	54 27.0	21.0	58.1	55 28.2	18.1	60.6	56 24.8	15.0	63.2	57 16.3	11.6	66.0
29	52 57.9	24.9	54.3	54 06.0	22.2	56.5	55 10.1	19.4	58.9	56 09.8	16.3	61.4	57 04.7	13.1	64.1

0°			2°			4°			6°			8°			Dec.
Hc	d	Z	Hc	d	Z	Hc	d	Z	Hc	d	Z	Hc	d	Z	
° ′	′	°	° ′	′	°	° ′	′	°	° ′	′	°	° ′	′	°	°
56 00.0 –	0.8	90.0	55 56.9 –	4.5	93.0	55 47.6 –	8.2	95.9	55 32.2 –	11.8	98.8	55 10.9 –	15.3	101.7	0
55 59.2	2.3	91.8	55 52.4	6.1	94.7	55 39.4	9.7	97.7	55 20.4	13.2	100.5	54 55.6	16.7	103.3	1
55 56.9	3.9	93.6	55 46.3	7.5	96.5	55 29.7	11.2	99.4	55 07.2	14.7	102.2	54 38.9	18.1	105.0	2
55 53.0	5.4	95.4	55 38.8	9.1	98.3	55 18.5	12.6	101.1	54 52.5	16.1	103.9	54 20.8	19.4	106.7	3
55 47.6	6.9	97.1	55 29.7	10.5	100.0	55 05.9	14.0	102.9	54 36.4	17.4	105.6	54 01.4	20.6	108.3	4
55 40.7 –	8.5	98.9	55 19.2 –	12.0	101.8	54 51.9 –	15.5	104.5	54 19.0 –	18.8	107.3	53 40.8 –	21.9	109.9	5
55 32.2	9.9	100.6	55 07.2	13.5	103.5	54 36.4	16.8	106.2	54 00.2	20.0	108.9	53 18.9	23.2	111.4	6
55 22.3	11.4	102.4	54 53.7	14.8	105.2	54 19.6	18.2	107.9	53 40.2	21.3	110.5	52 55.7	24.2	113.0	7
55 10.9	12.8	104.1	54 38.9	16.2	106.9	54 01.4	19.4	109.5	53 18.9	22.6	112.0	52 31.5	25.5	114.5	8
54 58.1	14.3	105.8	54 22.7	17.6	108.5	53 42.0	20.7	111.1	52 56.3	23.7	113.6	52 06.0	26.5	116.0	9
54 43.8 –	15.6	107.5	54 05.1 –	18.9	110.1	53 21.3 –	22.0	112.7	52 32.6 –	24.8	115.1	51 39.5 –	27.5	117.4	10
54 28.2	17.0	109.2	53 46.2	20.2	111.8	52 59.3	23.1	114.2	52 07.8	26.0	116.6	51 12.0	28.6	118.8	11
54 11.2	18.4	110.8	53 26.0	21.4	113.3	52 36.2	24.3	115.8	51 41.8	27.0	118.1	50 43.4	29.6	120.2	12
53 52.8	19.6	112.4	53 04.6	22.6	114.9	52 11.9	25.5	117.3	51 14.8	28.0	119.5	50 13.8	30.5	121.6	13
53 33.2	20.9	114.0	52 42.0	23.7	116.4	51 46.4	26.5	118.7	50 46.8	29.1	120.9	49 43.3	31.4	122.9	14
53 12.3 –	22.1	115.6	52 18.3 –	25.0	118.0	51 19.9 –	27.5	120.2	50 17.7 –	30.0	122.3	49 11.9 –	32.3	124.3	15
52 50.2	23.3	117.1	51 53.3	26.0	119.4	50 52.4	28.5	121.6	49 47.7	30.9	123.6	48 39.6	33.1	125.5	16
52 26.9	24.4	118.7	51 27.3	27.0	120.9	50 23.9	29.6	123.0	49 16.8	31.8	124.9	48 06.5	33.9	126.8	17
52 02.5	25.5	120.2	51 00.3	28.1	122.3	49 54.3	30.4	124.3	48 45.0	32.6	126.2	47 32.6	34.7	128.0	18
51 37.0	26.6	121.6	50 32.2	29.1	123.7	49 23.9	31.4	125.7	48 12.4	33.5	127.5	46 57.9	35.5	129.2	19
51 10.4 –	27.7	123.1	50 03.1 –	30.0	125.1	48 52.5 –	32.2	127.0	47 38.9 –	34.3	128.7	46 22.4 –	36.1	130.4	20
50 42.7	28.6	124.5	49 33.1	30.9	126.4	48 20.3	33.0	128.2	47 04.6	35.0	130.0	45 46.3	36.8	131.5	21
50 14.1	29.6	125.8	49 02.2	31.8	127.7	47 47.3	33.8	129.5	46 29.6	35.7	131.1	45 09.5	37.5	132.7	22
49 44.5	30.6	127.2	48 30.4	32.6	129.0	47 13.5	34.6	130.7	45 53.9	36.4	132.3	44 32.0	38.1	133.8	23
49 13.9	31.4	128.5	47 57.8	33.5	130.3	46 38.9	35.4	131.9	45 17.5	37.1	133.4	43 53.9	38.7	134.9	24
48 42.5 –	32.3	129.8	47 24.3 –	34.2	131.5	46 03.5 –	36.0	133.1	44 40.4 –	37.7	134.5	43 15.2 –	39.2	135.9	25
48 10.2	33.1	131.1	46 50.1	35.0	132.7	45 27.5	36.7	134.2	44 02.7	38.3	135.6	42 36.0	39.8	136.9	26
47 37.1	33.9	132.3	46 15.1	35.7	133.9	44 50.8	37.4	135.4	43 24.4	38.9	136.7	41 56.2	40.3	137.9	27
47 03.2	34.6	133.6	45 39.4	36.4	135.1	44 13.4	37.9	136.5	42 45.5	39.4	137.7	41 15.9	40.9	138.9	28
46 28.6	35.4	134.7	45 03.0	37.0	136.2	43 35.5	38.6	137.5	42 06.1	40.0	138.8	40 35.0	41.3	139.9	29

10°			12°			14°			16°			18°			Dec.
Hc	d	Z	Hc	d	Z	Hc	d	Z	Hc	d	Z	Hc	d	Z	
° ′	′	°	° ′	′	°	° ′	′	°	° ′	′	°	° ′	′	°	°
54 43.8 –	18.7	104.4	54 11.2 –	22.0	107.1	53 33.2 –	25.0	109.7	52 50.2 –	27.9	112.2	52 02.5 –	30.6	114.6	0
54 25.1	20.0	106.1	53 49.2	23.2	108.7	53 08.2	26.2	111.3	52 22.3	29.0	113.7	51 31.9	31.6	116.0	1
54 05.1	21.3	107.7	53 26.0	24.3	110.3	52 42.0	27.2	112.7	51 53.3	29.9	115.1	51 00.3	32.5	117.4	2
53 43.8	22.5	109.3	53 01.7	25.5	111.8	52 14.8	28.4	114.2	51 23.4	31.0	116.5	50 27.8	33.5	118.7	3
53 21.3	23.8	110.8	52 36.2	26.7	113.3	51 46.4	29.3	115.6	50 52.4	31.9	117.9	49 54.3	34.2	120.0	4
52 57.5 –	24.9	112.4	52 09.5 –	27.7	114.8	51 17.1 –	30.3	117.0	50 20.5 –	32.8	119.2	49 20.1 –	35.1	121.3	5
52 32.6	26.0	113.9	51 41.8	28.7	116.2	50 46.8	31.3	118.4	49 47.7	33.6	120.5	48 45.0	35.8	122.5	6
52 06.6	27.1	115.3	51 13.1	29.7	117.6	50 15.5	32.2	119.8	49 14.1	34.5	121.8	48 09.2	36.6	123.7	7
51 39.5	28.1	116.8	50 43.4	30.7	119.0	49 43.3	33.0	121.1	48 39.6	35.2	123.0	47 32.6	37.3	124.9	8
51 11.4	29.2	118.2	50 12.7	31.6	120.3	49 10.3	33.9	122.4	48 04.4	36.1	124.3	46 55.3	38.0	126.0	9
50 42.2 –	30.1	119.6	49 41.1 –	32.5	121.7	48 36.4 –	34.7	123.6	47 28.3 –	36.7	125.4	46 17.3 –	38.6	127.2	10
50 12.1	31.0	121.0	49 08.6	33.3	123.0	48 01.7	35.5	124.8	46 51.6	37.4	126.6	45 38.7	39.3	128.3	11
49 41.1	31.9	122.3	48 35.3	34.2	124.2	47 26.2	36.2	126.0	46 14.2	38.1	127.7	44 59.4	39.8	129.3	12
49 09.2	32.8	123.6	48 01.1	34.9	125.5	46 50.0	36.9	127.2	45 36.1	38.7	128.9	44 19.6	40.4	130.4	13
48 36.4	33.7	124.9	47 26.2	35.6	126.7	46 13.1	37.5	128.4	44 57.4	39.3	129.9	43 39.2	41.0	131.4	14
48 02.7 –	34.4	126.1	46 50.6 –	36.4	127.8	45 35.6 –	38.2	129.5	44 18.1 –	39.9	131.0	42 58.2 –	41.5	132.4	15
47 28.3	35.1	127.3	46 14.2	37.1	129.0	44 57.4	38.8	130.6	43 38.2	40.5	132.0	42 16.7	41.9	133.4	16
46 53.2	35.9	128.5	45 37.1	37.7	130.1	44 18.6	39.4	131.6	42 57.7	41.0	133.1	41 34.8	42.4	134.4	17
46 17.3	36.6	129.7	44 59.4	38.3	131.2	43 39.2	40.0	132.7	42 16.7	41.4	134.0	40 52.4	42.9	135.3	18
45 40.7	37.3	130.8	44 21.1	39.0	132.3	42 59.2	40.5	133.7	41 35.3	42.0	135.0	40 09.5	43.3	136.2	19
45 03.4 –	37.9	131.9	43 42.1 –	39.5	133.4	42 18.7 –	41.0	134.7	40 53.3 –	42.4	136.0	39 26.2 –	43.7	137.1	20
44 25.5	38.5	133.0	43 02.6	40.1	134.4	41 37.7	41.6	135.7	40 10.9	42.9	136.9	38 42.5	44.1	138.0	21
43 47.0	39.3	134.1	42 22.5	40.6	135.4	40 56.1	41.9	136.7	39 28.0	43.2	137.8	37 58.4	44.5	138.9	22
43 08.0	39.7	135.1	41 41.9	41.0	136.4	40 14.2	42.5	137.6	38 44.8	43.7	138.7	37 13.9	44.8	139.7	23
42 28.3	40.2	136.2	41 00.9	41.6	137.4	39 31.7	42.8	138.5	38 01.1	44.1	139.6	36 29.1	45.2	140.6	24
41 48.1 –	40.7	137.2	40 19.3 –	42.0	138.3	38 48.9 –	43.3	139.4	37 17.0 –	44.4	140.4	35 43.9 –	45.5	141.4	25
41 07.4	41.1	138.1	39 37.3	42.5	139.3	38 05.6	43.6	140.3	36 32.6	44.7	141.3	34 58.4	45.8	142.2	26
40 26.3	41.7	139.1	38 54.8	42.9	140.2	37 22.0	44.1	141.2	35 47.9	45.1	142.1	34 12.6	46.1	143.0	27
39 44.6	42.1	140.0	38 11.9	43.2	141.1	36 37.9	44.3	142.0	35 02.8	45.4	142.9	33 26.5	46.3	143.7	28
39 02.5	42.5	141.0	37 28.7	43.7	142.0	35 53.6	44.8	142.9	34 17.4	45.8	143.7	32 40.2	46.7	144.5	29

Dec.	20° Hc	d	Z	22° Hc	d	Z	24° Hc	d	Z	26° Hc	d	Z	28° Hc	d	Z
°	° ′	′	°	° ′	′	°	° ′	′	°	° ′	′	°	° ′	′	°
0	51 10.4	+32.2	116.9	50 14.1	+34.7	119.0	49 13.9	+37.0	121.1	48 10.2	+39.1	123.0	47 03.2	+41.1	124.8
1	51 42.6	31.3	115.5	50 48.8	33.9	117.8	49 50.9	36.3	119.9	48 49.3	38.4	121.9	47 44.3	40.4	123.8
2	52 13.9	30.4	114.2	51 22.7	32.9	116.4	50 27.2	35.3	118.6	49 27.7	37.7	120.7	48 24.7	39.8	122.7
3	52 44.3	29.2	112.7	51 55.6	32.0	115.1	51 02.5	34.6	117.4	50 05.4	36.9	119.5	49 04.5	39.1	121.5
4	53 13.5	28.2	111.3	52 27.6	31.0	113.7	51 37.1	33.6	116.0	50 42.3	36.1	118.3	49 43.6	38.3	120.4
5	53 41.7	+27.1	109.8	52 58.6	+30.0	112.3	52 10.7	+32.8	114.7	51 18.4	+35.3	117.0	50 21.9	+37.6	119.2
6	54 08.8	25.9	108.3	53 28.6	28.9	110.9	52 43.5	31.7	113.3	51 53.7	34.3	115.7	50 59.5	36.8	117.9
7	54 34.7	24.7	106.7	53 57.5	27.8	109.4	53 15.2	30.7	111.9	52 28.0	33.5	114.3	51 36.3	36.0	116.7
8	54 59.4	23.5	105.2	54 25.3	26.7	107.9	53 45.9	29.6	110.5	53 01.5	32.4	113.0	52 12.3	35.1	115.4
9	55 22.9	22.1	103.5	54 52.0	25.4	106.3	54 15.5	28.6	109.0	53 33.9	31.5	111.6	52 47.4	34.2	114.0
10	55 45.0	+20.8	101.9	55 17.4	+24.2	104.7	54 44.1	+27.3	107.5	54 05.4	+30.4	110.1	53 21.6	+33.2	112.7
11	56 05.8	19.5	100.2	55 41.6	22.8	103.1	55 11.4	26.2	105.9	54 35.8	29.2	108.6	53 54.8	32.2	111.3
12	56 25.3	18.0	98.5	56 04.4	21.6	101.5	55 37.6	24.9	104.3	55 05.0	28.2	107.1	54 27.0	31.2	109.8
13	56 43.3	16.5	96.8	56 26.0	20.1	99.8	56 02.5	23.6	102.7	55 33.2	26.9	105.6	54 58.2	30.0	108.3
14	56 59.8	15.1	95.0	56 46.1	18.7	98.1	56 26.1	22.3	101.1	56 00.1	25.7	104.0	55 28.2	28.9	106.8
15	57 14.9	+13.5	93.3	57 04.8	+17.3	96.3	56 48.4	+20.9	99.4	56 25.8	+24.3	102.4	55 57.1	+27.7	105.3
16	57 28.4	11.9	91.4	57 22.1	15.7	94.6	57 09.3	19.4	97.7	56 50.1	23.0	100.7	56 24.8	26.4	103.7
17	57 40.3	10.3	89.6	57 37.8	14.2	92.8	57 28.7	18.0	95.9	57 13.1	21.6	99.0	56 51.2	25.1	102.0
18	57 50.6	8.8	87.8	57 52.0	12.6	91.0	57 46.7	16.4	94.1	57 34.7	20.2	97.3	57 16.3	23.8	100.4
19	57 59.4	7.0	85.9	58 04.6	11.0	89.1	58 03.1	14.8	92.3	57 54.9	18.6	95.5	57 40.1	22.3	98.7
20	58 06.4	+5.4	84.0	58 15.6	+9.3	87.2	58 17.9	+13.3	90.5	58 13.5	+17.2	93.7	58 02.4	+20.9	96.9
21	58 11.8	3.8	82.1	58 24.9	7.7	85.4	58 31.2	11.6	88.6	58 30.7	15.5	91.9	58 23.3	19.4	95.1
22	58 15.6	2.0	80.2	58 32.6	5.9	83.5	58 42.8	10.0	86.7	58 46.2	13.9	90.0	58 42.7	17.8	93.3
23	58 17.6	+0.3	78.3	58 38.5	4.3	81.6	58 52.8	8.2	84.8	59 00.1	12.3	88.1	59 00.5	16.2	91.5
24	58 17.9	-1.3	76.4	58 42.8	2.6	79.6	59 01.0	6.6	82.9	59 12.4	10.5	86.2	59 16.7	14.6	89.6
25	58 16.6	-3.1	74.5	58 45.4	+0.8	77.7	59 07.6	+4.8	81.0	59 22.9	+8.9	84.3	59 31.3	+12.9	87.7
26	58 13.5	4.7	72.6	58 46.2	-0.9	75.8	59 12.4	3.0	79.0	59 31.8	7.1	82.4	59 44.2	11.2	85.8
27	58 08.8	6.4	70.8	58 45.3	2.6	73.9	59 15.4	1.3	77.1	59 38.9	5.3	80.4	59 55.4	9.4	83.8
28	58 02.4	8.0	68.9	58 42.7	4.3	71.9	59 16.7	-0.4	75.1	59 44.2	3.5	78.4	60 04.8	7.6	81.8
29	57 54.4	9.7	67.0	58 38.4	6.1	70.0	59 16.3	2.3	73.2	59 47.7	+1.8	76.4	60 12.4	5.8	79.8

Dec.	30° Hc	d	Z	32° Hc	d	Z	34° Hc	d	Z	36° Hc	d	Z	38° Hc	d	Z
°	° ′	′	°	° ′	′	°	° ′	′	°	° ′	′	°	° ′	′	°
0	45 53.2	+42.8	126.5	44 40.4	+44.5	128.2	43 25.0	+46.0	129.7	42 07.3	+47.4	131.1	40 47.4	+48.6	132.4
1	46 36.0	42.3	125.5	45 24.9	44.0	127.2	44 11.0	45.6	128.8	42 54.7	47.0	130.2	41 36.0	48.4	131.6
2	47 18.3	41.7	124.5	46 08.9	43.4	126.2	44 56.6	45.1	127.9	43•41.7	46.6	129.4	42 24.4	47.9	130.8
3	48 00.0	41.1	123.4	46 52.3	43.0	125.2	45 41.7	44.6	126.9	44 28.3	46.2	128.5	43 12.3	47.6	130.0
4	48 41.1	40.5	122.3	47 35.3	42.4	124.2	46 26.3	44.2	126.0	45 14.5	45.7	127.6	43 59.9	47.3	129.2
5	49 21.6	+39.8	121.2	48 17.7	+41.7	123.1	47 10.5	+43.6	125.0	46 00.2	+45.3	126.7	44 47.2	+46.8	128.3
6	50 01.4	39.0	120.0	48 59.4	41.2	122.1	47 54.1	43.0	123.9	46 45.5	44.8	125.7	45 34.0	46.4	127.4
7	50 40.4	38.4	118.9	49 40.6	40.5	120.9	48 37.1	42.5	122.9	47 30.3	44.3	124.8	46 20.4	46.0	126.5
8	51 18.8	37.5	117.6	50 21.1	39.8	119.8	49 19.6	41.9	121.8	48 14.6	43.8	123.7	47 06.4	45.5	125.6
9	51 56.3	36.7	116.4	51 00.9	39.0	118.6	50 01.5	41.2	120.7	48 58.4	43.2	122.7	47 51.9	44.9	124.6
10	52 33.0	+35.8	115.1	51 39.9	+38.3	117.4	50 42.7	+40.5	119.6	49 41.6	+42.5	121.6	48 36.8	+44.5	123.6
11	53 08.8	35.0	113.8	52 18.2	37.5	116.1	51 23.2	39.8	118.4	50 24.1	42.0	120.5	49 21.3	43.9	122.6
12	53 43.8	34.0	112.4	52 55.7	36.6	114.9	52 03.0	39.0	117.2	51 06.1	41.2	119.4	50 05.2	43.3	121.5
13	54 17.8	32.9	111.0	53 32.3	35.7	113.5	52 42.0	38.3	116.0	51 47.3	40.6	118.3	50 48.5	42.7	120.5
14	54 50.7	31.9	109.6	54 08.0	34.7	112.2	53 20.3	37.3	114.7	52 27.9	39.8	117.1	51 31.2	42.0	119.3
15	55 22.6	+30.9	108.1	54 42.7	+33.8	110.8	53 57.6	+36.5	113.4	53 07.7	+39.0	115.8	52 13.2	+41.4	118.2
16	55 53.5	29.6	106.6	55 16.5	32.7	109.3	54 34.1	35.6	112.0	53 46.7	38.2	114.5	52 54.6	40.5	117.0
17	56 23.1	28.5	105.0	55 49.2	31.6	107.8	55 09.7	34.5	110.6	54 24.9	37.3	113.2	53 35.1	39.9	115.7
18	56 51.6	27.2	103.4	56 20.8	30.5	106.3	55 44.2	33.5	109.2	55 02.2	36.3	111.9	54 15.0	38.8	114.3
19	57 18.8	25.9	101.8	56 51.3	29.2	104.8	56 17.7	32.5	107.7	55 38.5	35.4	110.5	54 53.9	38.1	113.1
20	57 44.7	+24.5	100.1	57 20.5	+28.0	103.2	56 50.2	+31.2	106.1	56 13.9	+34.3	109.0	55 32.0	+37.2	111.8
21	58 09.2	23.1	98.4	57 48.5	26.7	101.5	57 21.4	30.1	104.6	56 48.2	33.3	107.5	56 09.2	36.2	110.4
22	58 32.3	21.6	96.6	58 15.2	25.3	99.8	57 51.5	28.8	103.0	57 21.5	32.1	106.0	56 45.4	35.2	109.0
23	58 53.9	20.1	94.8	58 40.5	23.8	98.1	58 20.3	27.5	101.3	57 53.6	30.8	104.4	57 20.6	34.1	107.5
24	59 14.0	18.6	93.0	59 04.3	22.4	96.3	58 47.8	26.0	99.6	58 24.4	29.6	102.8	57 54.7	32.9	105.9
25	59 32.6	+16.9	91.1	59 26.7	+20.9	94.5	59 13.8	+24.7	97.8	58 54.0	+28.3	101.1	58 27.6	+31.7	104.3
26	59 49.5	15.2	89.2	59 47.6	19.2	92.6	59 38.5	23.1	96.0	59 22.3	26.9	99.4	58 59.3	30.4	102.7
27	60 04.7	13.5	87.3	60 06.8	17.6	90.7	60 01.6	21.6	94.2	59 49.2	25.4	97.6	59 29.7	29.1	101.0
28	60 18.2	11.8	85.3	60 24.4	15.9	88.8	60 23.2	19.9	92.3	60 14.6	23.9	95.8	59 58.8	27.7	99.3
29	60 30.0	10.0	83.3	60 40.3	14.1	86.9	60 43.1	18.3	90.4	60 38.5	22.4	94.0	60 26.5	26.3	97.5

20°			22°			24°			26°			28°			Dec.
Hc	d	Z	Hc	d	Z	Hc	d	Z	Hc	d	Z	Hc	d	Z	Dec.
° ′	′	°	° ′	′	°	° ′	′	°	° ′	′	°	° ′	′	°	°
51 10.4	−33.2	116.9	50 14.1	−35.6	119.0	49 13.9	−37.7	121.1	48 10.2	−39.7	123.0	47 03.2	−41.6	124.8	0
50 37.2	34.1	118.2	49 38.5	36.3	120.3	48 36.2	38.4	122.3	47 30.5	40.4	124.1	46 21.6	42.2	125.9	1
50 03.1	34.9	119.5	49 02.2	37.1	121.5	47 57.8	39.2	123.4	46 50.1	41.0	125.2	45 39.4	42.7	126.9	2
49 28.2	35.7	120.8	48 25.1	37.8	122.7	47 18.6	39.7	124.6	46 09.1	41.6	126.3	44 56.7	43.3	127.9	3
48 52.5	36.4	122.0	47 47.3	38.5	123.9	46 38.9	40.4	125.6	45 27.5	42.1	127.3	44 13.4	43.7	128.9	4
48 16.1	−37.2	123.2	47 08.8	−39.2	125.0	45 58.5	−41.0	126.7	44 45.4	−42.7	128.3	43 29.7	−44.2	129.8	5
47 38.9	37.9	124.4	46 29.6	39.7	126.1	45 17.5	41.5	127.8	44 02.7	43.1	129.3	42 45.5	44.6	130.8	6
47 01.0	38.6	125.5	45 49.9	40.4	127.2	44 36.0	42.1	128.8	43 19.6	43.6	130.3	42 00.9	45.0	131.7	7
46 22.4	39.2	126.6	45 09.5	41.0	128.3	43 53.9	42.5	129.8	42 36.0	44.1	131.2	41 15.9	45.5	132.5	8
45 43.2	39.8	127.7	44 28.5	41.5	129.3	43 11.4	43.1	130.8	41 51.9	44.5	132.1	40 30.4	45.8	133.4	9
45 03.4	−40.3	128.8	43 47.0	−42.0	130.3	42 28.3	−43.5	131.7	41 07.4	−44.8	133.0	39 44.6	−46.2	134.3	10
44 23.1	41.0	129.8	43 05.0	42.5	131.3	41 44.8	43.9	132.6	40 22.6	45.3	133.9	38 58.4	46.5	135.1	11
43 42.1	41.5	130.8	42 22.5	42.9	132.2	41 00.9	44.4	133.5	39 37.3	45.7	134.8	38 11.9	46.8	135.9	12
43 00.6	41.9	131.8	41 39.6	43.5	133.2	40 16.5	44.8	134.4	38 51.6	46.0	135.6	37 25.1	47.2	136.7	13
42 18.7	42.5	132.8	40 56.1	43.8	134.1	39 31.7	45.1	135.3	38 05.6	46.3	136.4	36 37.9	47.4	137.4	14
41 36.2	−42.9	133.8	40 12.3	−44.3	135.0	38 46.6	−45.5	136.1	37 19.3	−46.7	137.2	35 50.5	−47.7	138.2	15
40 53.3	43.3	134.7	39 28.0	44.6	135.9	38 01.1	45.8	137.0	36 32.6	46.9	138.0	35 02.8	48.0	139.0	16
40 10.0	43.8	135.6	38 43.4	45.0	136.7	37 15.3	46.2	137.8	35 45.7	47.3	138.8	34 14.8	48.3	139.7	17
39 26.2	44.2	136.5	37 58.4	45.4	137.6	36 29.1	46.5	138.6	34 58.4	47.5	139.5	33 26.5	48.5	140.4	18
38 42.0	44.5	137.4	37 13.0	45.7	138.4	35 42.6	46.8	139.4	34 10.9	47.8	140.3	32 38.0	48.7	141.1	19
37 57.5	−44.9	138.2	36 27.3	−46.0	139.2	34 55.8	−47.1	140.1	33 23.1	−48.0	141.0	31 49.3	−48.9	141.8	20
37 12.6	45.3	139.0	35 41.3	46.4	140.0	34 08.7	47.3	140.9	32 35.1	48.3	141.7	31 00.4	49.2	142.5	21
36 27.3	45.6	139.9	34 54.9	46.6	140.8	33 21.4	47.6	141.6	31 46.8	48.5	142.4	30 11.2	49.3	143.1	22
35 41.7	45.9	140.7	34 08.3	46.9	141.5	32 33.8	47.8	142.4	30 58.3	48.7	143.1	29 21.9	49.5	143.8	23
34 55.8	46.2	141.5	33 21.4	47.2	142.3	31 46.0	48.1	143.1	30 09.6	48.9	143.8	28 32.4	49.8	144.4	24
34 09.6	−46.5	142.2	32 34.2	−47.4	143.0	30 57.9	−48.3	143.8	29 20.7	−49.2	144.5	27 42.6	−49.8	145.1	25
33 23.1	46.8	143.0	31 46.8	47.7	143.8	30 09.6	48.5	144.5	28 31.5	49.3	145.1	26 52.8	50.1	145.7	26
32 36.3	47.0	143.7	30 59.1	47.9	144.5	29 21.1	48.7	145.1	27 42.2	49.4	145.8	26 02.7	50.2	146.3	27
31 49.3	47.2	144.5	30 11.2	48.1	145.2	28 32.4	49.0	145.8	26 52.8	49.7	146.4	25 12.5	50.3	146.9	28
31 02.1	47.6	145.2	29 23.1	48.3	145.9	27 43.4	49.0	146.5	26 03.1	49.8	147.0	24 22.2	50.5	147.5	29

30°			32°			34°			36°			38°			Dec.
Hc	d	Z	Hc	d	Z	Hc	d	Z	Hc	d	Z	Hc	d	Z	Dec.
° ′	′	°	° ′	′	°	° ′	′	°	° ′	′	°	° ′	′	°	°
45 53.2	−43.3	126.5	44 40.4	−44.9	128.2	43 25.0	−46.4	129.7	42 07.3	−47.7	131.1	40 47.4	−48.9	132.4	0
45 09.9	43.9	127.5	43 55.5	45.4	129.1	42 38.6	46.7	130.5	41 19.6	48.1	131.9	39 58.5	49.3	133.1	1
44 26.0	44.3	128.5	43 10.1	45.8	130.0	41 51.9	47.2	131.4	40 31.5	48.4	132.7	39 09.2	49.5	133.9	2
43 41.7	44.8	129.4	42 24.3	46.2	130.9	41 04.7	47.5	132.2	39 43.1	48.6	133.4	38 19.7	49.7	134.6	3
42 56.9	45.2	130.4	41 38.1	46.5	131.7	40 17.2	47.8	133.0`	38 54.5	49.0	134.2	37 30.0	50.1	135.3	4
42 11.7	−45.6	131.2	40 51.6	−47.0	132.6	39 29.4	−48.1	133.8	38 05.5	−49.2	134.9	36 39.9	−50.2	136.0	5
41 26.1	46.0	132.1	40 04.6	47.2	133.4	38 41.3	48.4	134.6	37 16.3	49.5	135.7	35 49.7	50.5	136.7	6
40 40.1	46.4	133.0	39 17.4	47.6	134.2	37 52.9	48.7	135.3	36 26.8	49.7	136.4	34 59.2	50.7	137.4	7
39 53.7	46.7	133.8	38 29.8	47.9	135.0	37 04.2	49.0	136.1	35 37.1	50.0	137.1	34 08.5	50.9	138.0	8
39 07.0	47.0	134.6	37 41.9	48.1	135.7	36 15.2	49.2	136.8	34 47.1	50.2	137.7	33 17.6	51.0	138.6	9
38 20.0	−47.4	135.4	36 53.8	−48.5	136.5	35 26.0	−49.4	137.5	33 56.9	−50.4	138.4	32 26.6	−51.3	139.3	10
37 32.6	47.6	136.2	36 05.3	48.7	137.2	34 36.6	49.7	138.2	33 06.5	50.6	139.1	31 35.3	51.4	139.9	11
36 45.0	48.0	136.9	35 16.6	49.0	137.9	33 46.9	49.9	138.8	32 15.9	50.8	139.7	30 43.9	51.6	140.5	12
35 57.0	48.2	137.7	34 27.6	49.2	138.6	32 57.0	50.2	139.5	31 25.1	50.9	140.3	29 52.3	51.8	141.1	13
35 08.8	48.4	138.4	33 38.4	49.4	139.3	32 06.8	50.3	140.2	30 34.2	51.2	140.9	29 00.5	51.9	141.7	14
34 20.4	−48.8	139.1	32 49.0	−49.6	140.0	31 16.5	−50.5	140.8	29 43.0	−51.3	141.5	28 08.6	−52.0	142.2	15
33 31.6	48.9	139.8	31 59.4	49.9	140.7	30 26.0	50.6	141.4	28 51.7	51.4	142.1	27 16.6	52.2	142.8	16
32 42.7	49.2	140.5	31 09.5	50.0	141.3	29 35.4	50.9	142.1	28 00.3	51.6	142.7	26 24.4	52.3	143.3	17
31 53.5	49.4	141.2	30 19.5	50.2	142.0	28 44.5	51.0	142.7	27 08.7	51.7	143.3	25 32.1	52.4	143.9	18
31 04.1	49.6	141.9	29 29.3	50.4	142.6	27 53.5	51.2	143.3	26 17.0	51.9	143.9	24 39.7	52.5	144.4	19
30 14.5	−49.7	142.5	28 38.9	−50.6	143.2	27 02.3	−51.3	143.8	25 25.1	−52.0	144.4	23 47.2	−52.7	145.0	20
29 24.8	50.0	143.2	27 48.3	50.7	143.8	26 11.0	51.4	144.4	24 33.1	52.1	145.0	22 54.5	52.7	145.5	21
28 34.8	50.1	143.8	26 57.6	50.9	144.4	25 19.6	51.6	145.0	23 41.0	52.2	145.5	22 01.8	52.8	146.0	22
27 44.7	50.3	144.4	26 06.7	51.0	145.0	24 28.0	51.7	145.6	22 48.8	52.4	146.1	21 09.0	53.0	146.5	23
26 54.4	50.5	145.1	25 15.7	51.2	145.6	23 36.3	51.8	146.1	21 56.4	52.4	146.6	20 16.0	53.0	147.0	24
26 03.9	−50.6	145.7	24 24.5	−51.3	146.2	22 44.5	−51.9	146.7	21 04.0	−52.5	147.1	19 23.0	−53.1	147.5	25
25 13.3	50.8	146.3	23 33.2	51.4	146.8	21 52.6	52.0	147.2	20 11.5	52.6	147.6	18 29.9	53.1	148.0	26
24 22.5	50.8	146.8	22 41.8	51.5	147.3	21 00.6	52.2	147.7	19 18.9	52.7	148.1	17 36.8	53.3	148.5	27
23 31.7	51.0	147.4	21 50.3	51.6	147.9	20 08.4	52.2	148.3	18 26.2	52.8	148.6	16 43.5	53.3	149.0	28
22 40.7	51.2	148.0	20 58.7	51.8	148.4	19 16.2	52.3	148.8	17 33.4	52.9	149.1	15 50.2	53.3	149.4	29

Dec.	40° Hc	d	Z	42° Hc	d	Z	44° Hc	d	Z	46° Hc	d	Z	48° Hc	d	Z
°	° ′	′	°	° ′	′	°	° ′	′	°	° ′	′	°	° ′	′	°
0	39 25.6	+49.7	133.6	38 01.9	+50.8	134.8	36 36.6	+51.8	135.8	35 09.8	+52.7	136.8	33 41.5	+53.6	137.8
1	40 15.3	49.6	132.9	38 52.7	50.7	134.1	37 28.4	51.6	135.2	36 02.5	52.5	136.3	34 35.1	53.3	137.2
2	41 04.9	49.2	132.1	39 43.4	50.3	133.4	38 20.0	51.4	134.6	36 55.0	52.3	135.7	35 28.4	53.2	136.7
3	41 54.1	48.9	131.4	40 33.7	50.1	132.7	39 11.4	51.2	133.9	37 47.3	52.2	135.0	36 21.6	53.1	136.1
4	42 43.0	48.6	130.6	41 23.8	49.8	132.0	40 02.6	50.9	133.2	38 39.5	51.9	134.4	37 14.7	52.9	135.5
5	43 31.6	+48.2	129.8	42 13.6	+49.5	131.2	40 53.5	+50.7	132.5	39 31.4	+51.8	133.8	38 07.6	+52.6	134.9
6	44 19.8	47.9	129.0	43 03.1	49.2	130.4	41 44.2	50.4	131.8	40 23.2	51.5	133.1	39 00.2	52.5	134.3
7	45 07.7	47.4	128.1	43 52.3	48.9	129.7	42 34.6	50.1	131.1	41 14.7	51.2	132.4	39 52.7	52.3	133.7
8	45 55.1	47.1	127.3	44 41.2	48.5	128.8	43 24.7	49.8	130.3	42 05.9	51.0	131.7	40 45.0	52.1	133.0
9	46 42.2	46.6	126.4	45 29.7	48.1	128.0	44 14.5	49.5	129.6	42 56.9	50.7	131.0	41 37.1	51.8	132.4
10	47 28.8	+46.2	125.4	46 17.8	+47.7	127.2	45 04.0	+49.1	128.8	43 47.6	+50.4	130.3	42 28.9	+51.6	131.7
11	48 15.0	45.7	124.5	47 05.5	47.4	126.3	45 53.1	48.8	127.9	44 38.0	50.1	129.5	43 20.5	51.3	131.0
12	49 00.7	45.2	123.5	47 52.9	46.8	125.4	46 41.9	48.4	127.1	45 28.1	49.8	128.7	44 11.8	51.0	130.3
13	49 45.9	44.6	122.5	48 39.7	46.4	124.4	47 30.3	48.0	126.2	46 17.9	49.5	127.9	45 02.8	50.8	129.5
14	50 30.5	44.1	121.4	49 26.1	45.9	123.5	48 18.3	47.6	125.3	47 07.4	49.1	127.1	45 53.6	50.4	128.8
15	51 14.6	+43.4	120.4	50 12.0	+45.4	122.5	49 05.9	+47.1	124.4	47 56.5	+48.6	126.3	46 44.0	+50.1	128.0
16	51 58.0	42.8	119.3	50 57.4	44.8	121.4	49 53.0	46.6	123.5	48 45.1	48.3	125.4	47 34.1	49.8	127.2
17	52 40.8	42.1	118.1	51 42.2	44.2	120.4	50 39.6	46.1	122.5	49 33.4	47.8	124.5	48 23.9	49.3	126.4
18	53 22.9	41.4	116.9	52 26.4	43.6	119.3	51 25.7	45.6	121.5	50 21.2	47.4	123.5	49 13.2	49.0	125.5
19	54 04.3	40.6	115.7	53 10.0	42.9	118.1	52 11.3	45.0	120.4	51 08.6	46.9	122.6	50 02.2	48.6	124.6
20	54 44.9	+39.8	114.4	53 52.9	+42.2	116.9	52 56.3	+44.3	119.3	51 55.5	+46.3	121.6	50 50.8	+48.1	123.7
21	55 24.7	38.9	113.1	54 35.1	41.4	115.7	53 40.6	43.7	118.2	52 41.8	45.7	120.5	51 38.9	47.6	122.7
22	56 03.6	38.0	111.8	55 16.5	40.6	114.5	54 24.3	43.1	117.0	53 27.5	45.2	119.4	52 26.5	47.1	121.7
23	56 41.6	37.1	110.4	55 57.1	39.8	113.2	55 07.4	42.2	115.8	54 12.7	44.5	118.3	53 13.6	46.5	120.7
24	57 18.7	36.0	108.9	56 36.9	38.9	111.8	55 49.6	41.5	114.6	54 57.2	43.9	117.2	54 00.1	46.0	119.6
25	57 54.7	+34.9	107.4	57 15.8	+37.9	110.4	56 31.1	+40.5	113.3	55 41.1	+43.1	116.0	54 46.1	+45.4	118.5
26	58 29.6	33.8	105.9	57 53.7	36.8	109.0	57 11.7	39.8	111.9	56 24.2	42.3	114.7	55 31.5	44.6	117.4
27	59 03.4	32.6	104.3	58 30.5	35.9	107.5	57 51.5	38.7	110.5	57 06.5	41.5	113.4	56 16.1	44.0	116.2
28	59 36.0	31.3	102.7	59 06.4	34.6	105.9	58 30.2	37.8	109.1	57 48.0	40.6	112.1	57 00.1	43.2	115.0
29	60 07.3	29.9	101.0	59 41.0	33.4	104.3	59 08.0	36.7	107.6	58 28.6	39.7	110.7	57 43.3	42.4	113.7

Dec.	50° Hc	d	Z	52° Hc	d	Z	54° Hc	d	Z	56° Hc	d	Z	58° Hc	d	Z
°	° ′	′	°	° ′	′	°	° ′	′	°	° ′	′	°	° ′	′	°
0	32 12.1	+54.2	138.6	30 41.5	+54.9	139.4	29 09.8	+55.5	140.2	27 37.1	+56.2	140.9	26 03.6	+56.7	141.5
1	33 06.3	54.2	138.1	31 36.4	54.8	139.0	30 05.3	55.5	139.7	28 33.3	56.0	140.5	27 00.3	56.5	141.1
2	34 00.5	54.0	137.6	32 31.2	54.7	138.5	31 00.8	55.3	139.3	29 29.3	55.9	140.1	27 56.8	56.5	140.8
3	34 54.5	53.8	137.1	33 25.9	54.6	138.0	31 56.1	55.3	138.9	30 25.2	55.9	139.6	28 53.3	56.4	140.4
4	35 48.3	53.7	136.5	34 20.5	54.5	137.5	32 51.4	55.2	138.4	31 21.1	55.8	139.2	29 49.7	56.4	140.0
5	36 42.0	+53.6	136.0	35 15.0	+54.3	137.0	33 46.6	+55.0	137.9	32 16.9	+55.7	138.8	30 46.1	+56.3	139.6
6	37 35.6	53.4	135.4	36 09.3	54.2	136.5	34 41.6	55.0	137.4	33 12.6	55.6	138.3	31 42.4	56.2	139.2
7	38 29.0	53.2	134.8	37 03.5	54.1	135.9	35 36.6	54.8	136.9	34 08.2	55.5	137.9	32 38.6	56.1	138.8
8	39 22.2	53.0	134.3	37 57.6	53.9	135.4	36 31.4	54.7	136.4	35 03.7	55.4	137.4	33 34.7	56.0	138.3
9	40 15.2	52.8	133.6	38 51.5	53.7	134.8	37 26.1	54.5	135.9	35 59.1	55.3	137.0	34 30.7	56.0	137.9
10	41 08.0	+52.7	133.0	39 45.2	+53.6	134.2	38 20.6	+54.4	135.4	36 54.4	+55.1	136.5	35 26.7	+55.8	137.5
11	42 00.7	52.4	132.4	40 38.8	53.4	133.7	39 15.0	54.3	134.9	37 49.5	55.1	136.0	36 22.5	55.7	137.0
12	42 53.1	52.1	131.7	41 32.2	53.1	133.1	40 09.3	54.1	134.3	38 44.6	54.9	135.5	37 18.2	55.7	136.6
13	43 45.2	51.9	131.0	42 25.3	53.0	132.4	41 03.4	53.9	133.7	39 39.5	54.7	134.9	38 13.9	55.5	136.1
14	44 37.1	51.7	130.3	43 18.3	52.8	131.8	41 57.3	53.7	133.1	40 34.2	54.6	134.4	39 09.4	55.3	135.6
15	45 28.8	+51.4	129.6	44 11.1	+52.5	131.1	42 51.0	+53.5	132.5	41 28.8	+54.5	133.9	40 04.7	+55.3	135.1
16	46 20.2	51.0	128.9	45 03.6	52.2	130.4	43 44.5	53.4	131.9	42 23.3	54.2	133.3	41 00.0	55.1	134.6
17	47 11.2	50.8	128.1	45 55.8	52.0	129.7	44 37.9	53.1	131.3	43 17.5	54.1	132.7	41 55.1	55.0	134.1
18	48 02.0	50.4	127.3	46 47.8	51.7	129.0	45 31.0	52.8	130.6	44 11.6	53.9	132.1	42 50.1	54.8	133.5
19	48 52.4	50.1	126.5	47 39.5	51.5	128.3	46 23.8	52.6	129.9	45 05.5	53.7	131.5	43 44.9	54.6	133.0
20	49 42.5	+49.7	125.7	48 31.0	+51.1	127.5	47 16.4	+52.4	129.2	45 59.2	+53.5	130.9	44 39.5	+54.5	132.4
21	50 32.2	49.2	124.8	49 22.1	50.7	126.7	48 08.8	52.1	128.5	46 52.7	53.2	130.2	45 34.0	54.2	131.8
22	51 21.4	48.9	123.9	50 12.8	50.4	125.9	49 00.9	51.7	127.8	47 45.9	53.0	129.5	46 28.2	54.1	131.2
23	52 10.3	48.4	122.9	51 03.2	50.0	125.0	49 52.6	51.5	127.0	48 38.9	52.7	128.8	47 22.3	53.8	130.5
24	52 58.7	47.9	122.0	51 53.2	49.6	124.1	50 44.1	51.1	126.2	49 31.6	52.5	128.1	48 16.1	53.6	129.9
25	53 46.6	+47.3	121.0	52 42.8	+49.1	123.2	51 35.2	+50.7	125.3	50 24.1	+52.1	127.3	49 09.7	+53.4	129.2
26	54 33.9	46.8	119.9	53 31.9	48.7	122.3	52 25.9	50.3	124.5	51 16.2	51.8	126.6	50 03.1	53.1	128.5
27	55 20.7	46.2	118.8	54 20.6	48.2	121.3	53 16.2	50.0	123.6	52 08.0	51.4	125.7	50 56.2	52.8	127.8
28	56 06.9	45.5	117.7	55 08.8	47.6	120.2	54 06.2	49.4	122.6	52 59.4	51.1	124.9	51 49.0	52.5	127.0
29	56 52.4	44.9	116.5	55 56.4	47.0	119.2	54 55.6	49.0	121.7	53 50.5	50.7	124.0	52 41.5	52.2	126.2

40°			42°			44°			46°			48°			Dec.
Hc	d	Z	Hc	d	Z	Hc	d	Z	Hc	d	Z	Hc	d	Z	
39 25.6	−50.1	133.6	38 01.9	−51.1	134.8	36 36.6	−52.0	135.8	35 09.8	−52.9	136.8	33 41.5	−53.6	137.8	0
38 35.5	50.3	134.3	37 10.8	51.3	135.4	35 44.6	52.2	136.5	34 16.9	53.1	137.4	32 47.9	53.8	138.3	1
37 45.2	50.6	135.0	36 19.5	51.5	136.1	34 52.4	52.4	137.1	33 23.8	53.1	138.0	31 54.1	53.9	138.8	2
36 54.6	50.7	135.7	35 28.0	51.7	136.7	34 00.0	52.6	137.7	32 30.7	53.4	138.5	31 00.2	54.1	139.3	3
36 03.9	51.0	136.4	34 36.3	51.9	137.3	33 07.4	52.7	138.2	31 37.3	53.4	139.1	30 06.1	54.1	139.8	4
35 12.9	−51.2	137.0	33 44.4	−52.0	137.9	32 14.7	−52.8	138.8	30 43.9	−53.6	139.6	29 12.0	−54.3	140.3	5
34 21.7	51.4	137.6	32 52.4	52.3	138.5	31 21.9	53.0	139.4	29 50.3	53.7	140.1	28 17.7	54.3	140.8	6
33 30.3	51.6	138.3	32 00.1	52.3	139.1	30 28.9	53.2	139.9	28 56.6	53.8	140.6	27 23.4	54.5	141.3	7
32 38.7	51.7	138.9	31 07.8	52.6	139.7	29 35.7	53.2	140.4	28 02.8	54.0	141.1	26 28.9	54.6	141.8	8
31 47.0	51.9	139.5	30 15.2	52.6	140.3	28 42.5	53.4	141.0	27 08.8	54.0	141.6	25 34.3	54.6	142.2	9
30 55.1	−52.1	140.1	29 22.6	−52.8	140.8	27 49.1	−53.5	141.5	26 14.8	−54.1	142.1	24 39.7	−54.7	142.7	10
30 03.0	52.2	140.6	28 29.8	53.0	141.3	26 55.6	53.6	142.0	25 20.7	54.2	142.6	23 45.0	54.8	143.2	11
29 10.8	52.3	141.2	27 36.8	53.0	141.9	26 02.0	53.7	142.5	24 26.5	54.4	143.1	22 50.2	54.9	143.6	12
28 18.5	52.5	141.8	26 43.8	53.2	142.4	25 08.3	53.8	143.0	23 32.1	54.3	143.5	21 55.3	54.9	144.0	13
27 26.0	52.6	142.3	25 50.6	53.3	142.9	24 14.5	53.9	143.5	22 37.8	54.5	144.0	21 00.4	55.0	144.5	14
26 33.4	−52.8	142.9	24 57.3	−53.4	143.4	23 20.6	−53.9	144.0	21 43.3	−54.5	144.4	20 05.4	−55.1	144.9	15
25 40.6	52.8	143.4	24 04.0	53.5	143.9	22 26.7	54.1	144.4	20 48.8	54.7	144.9	19 10.3	55.1	145.3	16
24 47.8	53.0	143.9	23 10.5	53.6	144.4	21 32.6	54.1	144.9	19 54.1	54.6	145.3	18 15.2	55.2	145.7	17
23 54.8	53.0	144.4	22 16.9	53.8	144.9	20 38.5	54.3	145.4	18 59.5	54.8	145.8	17 20.0	55.2	146.1	18
23 01.8	53.2	144.9	21 23.3	53.8	145.4	19 44.2	54.2	145.8	18 04.7	54.8	146.2	16 24.8	55.3	146.6	19
22 08.6	−53.2	145.4	20 29.5	−53.8	145.9	18 50.0	−54.4	146.3	17 09.9	−54.8	146.6	15 29.5	−55.3	147.0	20
21 15.4	53.3	145.9	19 35.7	53.8	146.3	17 55.6	54.4	146.7	16 15.1	54.9	147.1	14 34.2	55.3	147.4	21
20 22.1	53.4	146.4	18 41.9	54.0	146.8	17 01.2	54.4	147.2	15 20.2	54.9	147.5	13 38.9	55.4	147.8	22
19 28.7	53.5	146.9	17 47.9	54.0	147.3	16 06.8	54.6	147.6	14 25.3	55.0	147.9	12 43.5	55.4	148.1	23
18 35.2	53.6	147.4	16 53.9	54.1	147.7	15 12.2	54.5	148.0	13 30.3	55.0	148.3	11 48.1	55.5	148.5	24
17 41.6	−53.6	147.9	15 59.8	−54.1	148.2	14 17.7	−54.6	148.5	12 35.3	−55.1	148.7	10 52.6	−55.5	148.9	25
16 48.0	53.7	148.3	15 05.7	54.2	148.6	13 23.1	54.7	148.9	11 40.2	55.1	149.1	9 57.1	55.5	149.3	26
15 54.3	53.8	148.8	14 11.5	54.2	149.1	12 28.4	54.7	149.3	10 45.1	55.1	149.5	9 01.6	55.5	149.7	27
15 00.5	53.8	149.3	13 17.3	54.3	149.5	11 33.7	54.7	149.7	9 50.0	55.2	149.9	8 06.1	55.6	150.1	28
14 06.7	53.8	149.7	12 23.0	54.3	150.0	10 39.0	54.8	150.2	8 54.8	55.1	150.3	7 10.5	55.6	150.5	29

50°			52°			54°			56°			58°			Dec.
Hc	d	Z	Hc	d	Z	Hc	d	Z	Hc	d	Z	Hc	d	Z	
32 12.1	−54.4	138.6	30 41.5	−55.1	139.4	29 09.8	−55.6	140.2	27 37.1	−56.1	140.9	26 03.6	−56.6	141.5	0
31 17.7	54.5	139.1	29 46.4	55.1	139.9	28 14.2	55.8	140.6	26 41.0	56.3	141.3	25 07.0	56.7	141.9	1
30 23.2	54.6	139.6	28 51.3	55.2	140.4	27 18.4	55.7	141.0	25 44.7	56.3	141.7	24 10.3	56.8	142.2	2
29 28.6	54.7	140.1	27 56.1	55.3	140.8	26 22.7	55.9	141.4	24 48.4	56.3	142.0	23 13.5	56.8	142.6	3
28 33.9	54.8	140.6	27 00.8	55.3	141.2	25 26.8	55.9	141.8	23 52.1	56.4	142.4	22 16.7	56.9	142.9	4
27 39.1	−54.9	141.0	26 05.4	−55.4	141.7	24 30.9	−56.0	142.2	22 55.7	−56.5	142.8	21 19.8	−56.9	143.3	5
26 44.2	54.9	141.5	25 10.0	55.6	142.1	23 34.9	56.0	142.6	21 59.2	56.5	143.1	20 22.9	56.9	143.6	6
25 49.3	55.1	141.9	24 14.4	55.6	142.5	22 38.9	56.1	143.0	21 02.7	56.6	143.5	19 26.0	57.0	144.0	7
24 54.2	55.1	142.4	23 18.8	55.6	142.9	21 42.8	56.2	143.4	20 06.1	56.5	143.9	18 29.0	57.0	144.3	8
23 59.1	55.2	142.8	22 23.2	55.7	143.3	20 46.6	56.1	143.8	19 09.6	56.7	144.2	17 32.0	57.1	144.6	9
23 03.9	−55.3	143.2	21 27.5	−55.8	143.7	19 50.5	−56.3	144.2	18 12.9	−56.7	144.6	16 34.9	−57.1	144.9	10
22 08.6	55.3	143.7	20 31.7	55.8	144.1	18 54.2	56.3	144.5	17 16.2	56.7	144.9	15 37.8	57.1	145.2	11
21 13.3	55.4	144.1	19 35.9	55.9	144.5	17 57.9	56.3	144.9	16 19.5	56.7	145.3	14 40.7	57.1	145.6	12
20 17.9	55.4	144.5	18 40.0	55.9	144.9	17 01.6	56.4	145.3	15 22.8	56.8	145.6	13 43.6	57.1	145.9	13
19 22.5	55.4	144.9	17 44.1	56.0	145.3	16 05.2	56.4	145.6	14 26.0	56.8	145.9	12 46.5	57.2	146.2	14
18 27.0	−55.6	145.3	16 48.1	−56.0	145.7	15 08.8	−56.4	146.0	13 29.2	−56.8	146.3	11 49.3	−57.2	146.5	15
17 31.4	55.6	145.7	15 52.1	56.0	146.0	14 12.4	56.4	146.3	12 32.4	56.9	146.6	10 52.1	57.2	146.8	16
16 35.8	55.6	146.1	14 56.1	56.1	146.4	13 16.0	56.5	146.7	11 35.5	56.8	146.9	9 54.9	57.2	147.1	17
15 40.2	55.7	146.5	14 00.0	56.1	146.8	12 19.5	56.6	147.0	10 38.7	56.9	147.2	8 57.7	57.3	147.4	18
14 44.5	55.7	146.9	13 03.9	56.2	147.1	11 22.9	56.5	147.4	9 41.8	56.9	147.6	8 00.4	57.2	147.7	19
13 48.8	−55.8	147.2	12 07.7	−56.1	147.5	10 26.4	−56.6	147.7	8 44.9	−57.0	147.9	7 03.2	−57.3	148.0	20
12 53.0	55.8	147.6	11 11.6	56.2	147.8	9 29.8	56.5	148.1	7 47.9	56.9	148.2	6 05.9	57.3	148.3	21
11 57.2	55.8	148.0	10 15.4	56.3	148.2	8 33.3	56.6	148.4	6 51.0	56.9	148.5	5 08.6	57.3	148.6	22
11 01.4	55.8	148.4	9 19.1	56.2	148.6	7 36.7	56.6	148.7	5 54.1	57.0	148.8	4 11.3	57.3	148.9	23
10 05.6	55.9	148.7	8 22.9	56.3	148.9	6 40.1	56.7	149.0	4 57.1	57.0	149.2	3 14.0	57.3	149.2	24
9 09.7	−55.9	149.1	7 26.6	−56.2	149.3	5 43.4	−56.6	149.4	4 00.1	−57.0	149.5	2 16.7	−57.3	149.5	25
8 13.8	55.9	149.5	6 30.4	56.3	149.6	4 46.8	56.6	149.7	3 03.1	56.9	149.8	1 19.4	57.3	149.8	26
7 17.9	55.9	149.8	5 34.1	56.3	150.0	3 50.2	56.7	150.0	2 06.2	57.0	150.1	0 22.1	−57.3	150.1	27
6 22.0	56.0	150.2	4 37.8	56.3	150.3	2 53.5	56.7	150.4	1 09.2	57.0	150.4	0 35.2	+57.3	29.6	28
5 26.0	55.9	150.6	3 41.5	56.4	150.7	1 56.8	56.6	150.7	0 12.2	−57.0	150.7	1 32.5	57.3	29.3	29

LATITUDE **SAME** NAME   L.H.A. 146°, 214°

LATITUDE **SAME** NAME

Dec.	0° Hc	d	Z	2° Hc	d	Z	4° Hc	d	Z	6° Hc	d	Z	8° Hc	d	Z
0	54 00.0	- 0.7	90.0	53 57.1	+ 2.9	92.8	53 48.5	+ 6.4	95.5	53 34.2	+ 9.9	98.2	53 14.4	+13.3	100.8
1	53 59.3	2.2	88.3	54 00.0	+ 1.4	91.1	53 54.9	4.9	93.8	53 44.1	8.5	96.5	53 27.7	11.9	99.2
2	53 57.1	3.6	86.6	54 01.4	- 0.1	89.4	53 59.8	3.6	92.1	53 52.6	7.0	94.8	53 39.6	10.5	97.6
3	53 53.5	5.0	84.9	54 01.3	1.5	87.6	54 03.4	2.0	90.4	53 59.6	5.7	93.2	53 50.1	9.2	95.9
4	53 48.5	6.4	83.2	53 59.8	2.9	85.9	54 05.4	+ 0.7	88.7	54 05.3	4.2	91.5	53 59.3	7.8	94.2
5	53 42.1	- 7.9	81.5	53 56.9	- 4.3	84.2	54 06.1	- 0.8	87.0	54 09.5	+ 2.7	89.8	54 07.1	+ 6.3	92.5
6	53 34.2	9.2	79.9	53 52.6	5.8	82.6	54 05.3	2.3	85.3	54 12.2	+ 1.3	88.1	54 13.4	4.9	90.8
7	53 25.0	10.6	78.2	53 46.8	7.2	80.9	54 03.0	3.7	83.6	54 13.5	- 0.1	86.3	54 18.3	3.4	89.1
8	53 14.4	12.0	76.6	53 39.6	8.6	79.2	53 59.3	5.1	81.9	54 13.4	1.6	84.6	54 21.7	2.0	87.4
9	53 02.4	13.3	74.9	53 31.0	10.0	77.5	53 54.2	6.6	80.2	54 11.8	3.0	82.9	54 23.7	+ 0.5	85.7
10	52 49.1	-14.6	73.3	53 21.0	-11.3	75.9	53 47.6	- 7.9	78.5	54 08.8	- 4.5	81.2	54 24.2	- 0.9	84.0
11	52 34.5	15.9	71.7	53 09.7	12.7	74.2	53 39.7	9.4	76.8	54 04.3	5.9	79.5	54 23.3	2.4	82.3
12	52 18.6	17.1	70.1	52 57.0	14.0	72.6	53 30.3	10.7	75.2	53 58.4	7.4	77.8	54 20.9	3.9	80.5
13	52 01.5	18.3	68.6	52 43.0	15.3	71.0	53 19.6	12.1	73.5	53 51.0	8.7	76.1	54 17.0	5.3	78.8
14	51 43.2	19.6	67.0	52 27.7	16.5	69.4	53 07.5	13.4	71.9	53 42.3	10.2	74.5	54 11.7	6.7	77.1
15	51 23.6	-20.7	65.5	52 11.2	-17.8	67.8	52 54.1	-14.7	70.3	53 32.1	-11.5	72.8	54 05.0	- 8.2	75.4
16	51 02.9	21.8	64.0	51 53.4	19.0	66.3	52 39.4	16.0	68.7	53 20.6	12.9	71.2	53 56.8	9.6	73.7
17	50 41.1	23.0	62.5	51 34.4	20.2	64.7	52 23.4	17.3	67.1	53 07.7	14.1	69.5	53 47.2	10.9	72.1
18	50 18.1	24.0	61.1	51 14.2	21.3	63.2	52 06.1	18.5	65.5	52 53.6	15.5	67.9	53 36.3	12.4	70.4
19	49 54.1	25.0	59.6	50 52.9	22.5	61.7	51 47.6	19.7	64.0	52 38.1	16.8	66.3	53 23.9	13.6	68.8
20	49 29.1	-26.1	58.2	50 30.4	-23.5	60.3	51 27.9	-20.8	62.4	52 21.3	-18.0	64.7	53 10.3	-15.0	67.1
21	49 03.0	27.0	56.8	50 06.9	24.6	58.8	51 07.1	22.0	60.9	52 03.3	19.2	63.2	52 55.3	16.3	65.5
22	48 36.0	28.0	55.5	49 42.3	25.6	57.4	50 45.1	23.1	59.5	51 44.1	20.4	61.6	52 39.0	17.6	63.9
23	48 08.0	28.8	54.2	49 16.7	26.6	56.0	50 22.0	24.1	58.0	51 23.7	21.5	60.1	52 21.4	18.7	62.4
24	47 39.2	29.8	52.9	48 50.1	27.5	54.7	49 57.9	25.2	56.6	51 02.2	22.7	58.6	52 02.7	20.0	60.8
25	47 09.4	-30.6	51.6	48 22.6	-28.5	53.3	49 32.7	-26.2	55.2	50 39.5	-23.8	57.2	51 42.7	-21.2	59.3
26	46 38.8	31.4	50.3	47 54.1	29.4	52.0	49 06.5	27.2	53.8	50 15.7	24.8	55.7	51 21.5	22.3	57.8
27	46 07.4	32.2	49.1	47 24.7	30.2	50.7	48 39.3	28.1	52.4	49 50.9	25.8	54.3	50 59.2	23.4	56.3
28	45 35.2	32.9	47.9	46 54.5	31.0	49.4	48 11.2	29.0	51.1	49 25.1	26.8	52.9	50 35.8	24.4	54.8
29	45 02.3	33.6	46.7	46 23.5	31.8	48.2	47 42.2	29.8	49.8	48 58.3	27.8	51.6	50 11.4	25.5	53.4

Dec.	10° Hc	d	Z	12° Hc	d	Z	14° Hc	d	Z	16° Hc	d	Z	18° Hc	d	Z
0	52 49.1	+16.6	103.4	52 18.6	+19.8	106.0	51 43.2	+22.8	108.4	51 02.9	+25.8	110.8	50 18.1	+28.6	113.0
1	53 05.7	15.3	101.8	52 38.4	18.6	104.4	52 06.0	21.7	106.9	51 28.7	24.7	109.3	50 46.7	27.5	111.7
2	53 21.0	14.0	100.2	52 57.0	17.3	102.8	52 27.7	20.5	105.4	51 53.4	23.6	107.9	51 14.2	26.5	110.2
3	53 35.0	12.6	98.6	53 14.3	16.0	101.3	52 48.2	19.3	103.8	52 17.0	22.4	106.4	51 40.7	25.4	108.8
4	53 47.6	11.3	96.9	53 30.3	14.7	99.6	53 07.5	18.0	102.3	52 39.4	21.2	104.8	52 06.1	24.3	107.3
5	53 58.9	+ 9.9	95.3	53 45.0	+13.4	98.0	53 25.5	+16.8	100.7	53 00.6	+20.0	103.3	52 30.4	+23.2	105.8
6	54 08.8	8.4	93.6	53 58.4	11.9	96.3	53 42.3	15.4	99.1	53 20.6	18.8	101.7	52 53.6	21.9	104.3
7	54 17.2	7.0	91.9	54 10.3	10.6	94.7	53 57.7	14.0	97.4	53 39.4	17.4	100.1	53 15.5	20.8	102.8
8	54 24.2	5.6	90.2	54 20.9	9.1	93.0	54 11.7	12.7	95.8	53 56.8	16.1	98.5	53 36.3	19.4	101.2
9	54 29.8	4.1	88.5	54 30.0	7.7	91.3	54 24.4	11.3	94.1	54 12.9	14.8	96.9	53 55.7	18.2	99.6
10	54 33.9	+ 2.7	86.8	54 37.7	+ 6.3	89.6	54 35.7	+ 9.8	92.4	54 27.7	+13.4	95.2	54 13.9	+16.9	98.0
11	54 36.6	+ 1.1	85.0	54 44.0	4.8	87.9	54 45.5	8.4	90.7	54 41.1	12.0	93.5	54 30.8	15.5	96.3
12	54 37.7	- 0.3	83.3	54 48.8	3.3	86.1	54 53.9	6.9	89.0	54 53.1	10.5	91.8	54 46.3	14.1	94.7
13	54 37.4	1.7	81.6	54 52.1	1.8	84.4	55 00.8	5.5	87.2	55 03.6	9.1	90.1	55 00.4	12.7	93.0
14	54 35.7	3.3	79.9	54 53.9	+ 0.3	82.7	55 06.3	3.9	85.5	55 12.7	7.6	88.4	55 13.1	11.2	91.3
15	54 32.4	- 4.7	78.1	54 54.2	- 1.1	80.9	55 10.2	+ 2.5	83.8	55 20.3	+ 6.1	86.6	55 24.3	+ 9.7	89.5
16	54 27.7	6.2	76.4	54 53.1	2.7	79.2	55 12.7	+ 0.9	82.0	55 26.4	4.6	84.9	55 34.0	8.3	87.8
17	54 21.5	7.6	74.7	54 50.4	4.1	77.5	55 13.6	- 0.5	80.3	55 31.0	3.0	83.1	55 42.3	6.8	86.0
18	54 13.9	9.0	73.0	54 46.3	5.6	75.7	55 13.1	2.1	78.5	55 34.0	+ 1.6	81.4	55 49.1	5.2	84.3
19	54 04.9	10.4	71.3	54 40.7	7.1	74.0	55 11.0	3.6	76.8	55 35.6	0.0	79.6	55 54.3	3.7	82.5
20	53 54.5	-11.9	69.7	54 33.6	- 8.5	72.3	55 07.4	- 5.0	75.0	55 35.6	- 1.5	77.8	55 58.0	+ 2.1	80.7
21	53 42.6	13.2	68.0	54 25.1	9.9	70.6	55 02.4	6.6	73.3	55 34.1	3.0	76.1	56 00.1	+ 0.6	78.9
22	53 29.4	14.5	66.4	54 15.2	11.4	68.9	54 55.8	8.0	71.5	55 31.1	4.6	74.3	56 00.7	- 0.9	77.1
23	53 14.9	15.8	64.7	54 03.8	12.7	67.2	54 47.8	9.5	69.8	55 26.5	6.0	72.5	55 59.8	2.6	75.3
24	52 59.1	17.1	63.1	53 51.1	14.1	65.5	54 38.3	10.9	68.1	55 20.5	7.6	70.8	55 57.2	4.0	73.6
25	52 42.0	-18.4	61.5	53 37.0	-15.4	63.9	54 27.4	-12.3	66.4	55 12.9	- 9.0	69.0	55 53.2	- 5.6	71.8
26	52 23.6	19.6	60.0	53 21.6	16.8	62.3	54 15.1	13.7	64.7	55 03.9	10.5	67.3	55 47.6	7.1	70.0
27	52 04.0	20.8	58.4	53 04.8	18.0	60.7	54 01.4	15.1	63.1	54 53.4	11.9	65.6	55 40.5	8.6	68.2
28	51 43.2	22.0	56.9	52 46.8	19.3	59.1	53 46.3	16.3	61.4	54 41.5	13.3	63.9	55 31.9	10.1	66.5
29	51 21.2	23.0	55.4	52 27.5	20.4	57.5	53 30.0	17.7	59.8	54 28.2	14.8	62.2	55 21.8	11.6	64.8

0°			2°			4°			6°			8°			Dec.
Hc	d	Z	Hc	d	Z	Hc	d	Z	Hc	d	Z	Hc	d	Z	
54 00.0	− 0.7	90.0	53 57.1	− 4.3	92.8	53 48.5	− 7.8	95.5	53 34.2	−11.2	98.2	53 14.4	−14.6	100.8	0
53 59.3	2.2	91.7	53 52.8	5.7	94.4	53 40.7	9.2	97.2	53 23.0	12.6	99.8	52 59.8	16.0	102.5	1
53 57.1	3.6	93.4	53 47.1	7.1	96.1	53 31.5	10.5	98.8	53 10.4	14.0	101.5	52 43.8	17.1	104.1	2
53 53.5	5.0	95.1	53 40.0	8.5	97.8	53 21.0	12.0	100.5	52 56.4	15.2	103.1	52 26.7	18.5	105.6	3
53 48.5	6.4	96.8	53 31.5	9.9	99.5	53 09.0	13.2	102.1	52 41.2	16.5	104.7	52 08.2	19.6	107.2	4
53 42.1	− 7.9	98.5	53 21.6	−11.2	101.1	52 55.8	−14.6	103.7	52 24.7	−17.8	106.3	51 48.6	−20.8	108.7	5
53 34.2	9.2	100.1	53 10.4	12.6	102.8	52 41.2	15.8	105.3	52 06.9	18.9	107.8	51 27.8	22.0	110.2	6
53 25.0	10.6	101.8	52 57.8	14.0	104.4	52 25.4	17.2	106.9	51 48.0	20.2	109.4	51 05.8	23.1	111.7	7
53 14.4	12.0	103.4	52 43.8	15.2	106.0	52 08.2	18.5	108.5	51 27.8	21.3	110.9	50 42.7	24.1	113.2	8
53 02.4	13.3	105.1	52 28.6	16.5	107.6	51 49.9	19.5	110.0	51 06.5	22.5	112.4	50 18.6	25.2	114.6	9
52 49.1	−14.6	106.7	52 12.1	−17.7	109.2	51 30.4	−20.8	111.6	50 44.0	−23.5	113.9	49 53.4	−26.2	116.0	10
52 34.5	15.9	108.3	51 54.4	18.9	110.7	51 09.6	21.8	113.1	50 20.5	24.6	115.3	49 27.2	27.2	117.4	11
52 18.6	17.1	109.9	51 35.5	20.1	112.3	50 47.8	23.0	114.5	49 55.9	25.7	116.7	49 00.0	28.2	118.8	12
52 01.5	18.3	111.4	51 15.4	21.3	113.8	50 24.8	24.0	116.0	49 30.2	26.6	118.1	48 31.8	29.1	120.1	13
51 43.2	19.6	113.0	50 54.1	22.4	115.3	50 00.8	25.0	117.4	49 03.6	27.6	119.5	48 02.7	29.9	121.5	14
51 23.6	−20.7	114.5	50 31.7	−23.5	116.7	49 35.8	−26.1	118.8	48 36.0	−28.5	120.8	47 32.8	−30.8	122.7	15
51 02.9	21.8	116.0	50 08.2	24.5	118.2	49 09.7	27.1	120.2	48 07.5	29.4	122.2	47 02.0	31.6	124.0	16
50 41.1	23.0	117.5	49 43.7	25.5	119.6	48 42.6	27.9	121.6	47 38.1	30.3	123.5	46 30.4	32.4	125.2	17
50 18.1	24.0	119.0	49 18.2	26.6	121.0	48 14.7	28.9	122.9	47 07.8	31.1	124.7	45 58.0	33.2	126.5	18
49 54.1	25.0	120.4	48 51.6	27.4	122.4	47 45.8	29.8	124.2	46 36.7	31.9	126.0	45 24.8	33.9	127.7	19
49 29.1	−26.1	121.8	48 24.2	−28.5	123.7	47 16.0	−30.6	125.5	46 04.8	−32.7	127.2	44 50.9	−34.6	128.8	20
49 03.0	27.0	123.1	47 55.7	29.3	125.0	46 45.4	31.5	126.8	45 32.1	33.4	128.4	44 16.3	35.3	130.0	21
48 36.0	28.0	124.5	47 26.4	30.1	126.3	46 13.9	32.2	128.0	44 58.7	34.1	129.6	43 41.0	35.9	131.1	22
48 08.0	28.8	125.8	46 56.3	31.0	127.6	45 41.7	33.0	129.2	44 24.6	34.9	130.8	43 05.1	36.6	132.2	23
47 39.2	29.8	127.1	46 25.3	31.8	128.8	45 08.7	33.7	130.4	43 49.7	35.4	131.9	42 28.5	37.1	133.3	24
47 09.4	−30.6	128.4	45 53.5	−32.6	130.1	44 35.0	−34.4	131.6	43 14.3	−36.2	133.0	41 51.4	−37.7	134.3	25
46 38.8	31.4	129.7	45 20.9	33.3	131.3	44 00.6	35.1	132.7	42 38.1	36.7	134.1	41 13.7	38.3	135.4	26
46 07.4	32.2	130.9	44 47.6	34.0	132.4	43 25.5	35.7	133.9	42 01.4	37.3	135.2	40 35.4	38.8	136.4	27
45 35.2	32.9	132.1	44 13.6	34.7	133.6	42 49.8	36.3	135.0	41 24.1	37.9	136.2	39 56.6	39.3	137.4	28
45 02.3	33.6	133.3	43 38.9	35.4	134.7	42 13.5	37.0	136.0	40 46.2	38.4	137.2	39 17.3	39.8	138.4	29

10°			12°			14°			16°			18°			Dec.
Hc	d	Z	Hc	d	Z	Hc	d	Z	Hc	d	Z	Hc	d	Z	
52 49.1	−17.9	103.4	52 18.6	−21.0	106.0	51 43.2	−24.0	108.4	51 02.9	−26.8	110.8	50 18.1	−29.5	113.0	0
52 31.2	19.1	105.0	51 57.6	22.1	107.5	51 19.2	25.1	109.9	50 36.1	27.9	112.2	49 48.6	30.4	114.4	1
52 12.1	20.3	106.6	51 35.5	23.3	109.0	50 54.1	26.1	111.3	50 08.2	28.8	113.6	49 18.2	31.4	115.7	2
51 51.8	21.4	108.1	51 12.2	24.4	110.5	50 28.0	27.2	112.8	49 39.4	29.7	114.9	48 46.8	32.1	117.0	3
51 30.4	22.7	109.6	50 47.8	25.5	111.9	50 00.8	28.1	114.2	49 09.7	30.7	116.3	48 14.7	33.1	118.3	4
51 07.7	−23.7	111.1	50 22.3	−26.4	113.4	49 32.7	−29.1	115.5	48 39.0	−31.5	117.6	47 41.6	−33.8	119.5	5
50 44.0	24.8	112.5	49 55.9	27.5	114.8	49 03.6	30.0	116.9	48 07.5	32.3	118.9	47 07.8	34.5	120.8	6
50 19.2	25.8	114.0	49 28.4	28.4	116.1	48 33.6	30.9	118.2	47 35.2	33.2	120.1	46 33.3	35.3	122.0	7
49 53.4	26.9	115.4	49 00.0	29.4	117.5	48 02.7	31.7	119.5	47 02.0	34.0	121.4	45 58.0	36.1	123.1	8
49 26.5	27.8	116.8	48 30.6	30.3	118.8	47 31.0	32.5	120.7	46 28.0	34.6	122.6	45 21.9	36.6	124.3	9
48 58.7	−28.7	118.1	48 00.3	−31.1	120.1	46 58.5	−33.4	122.0	45 53.4	−35.4	123.7	44 45.3	−37.3	125.4	10
48 30.0	29.7	119.5	47 29.2	31.9	121.4	46 25.1	34.0	123.2	45 18.0	36.1	124.9	44 08.0	38.0	126.5	11
48 00.3	30.5	120.8	46 57.3	32.7	122.6	45 51.1	34.8	124.4	44 41.9	36.7	126.0	43 30.0	38.5	127.6	12
47 29.8	31.3	122.0	46 24.6	33.5	123.8	45 16.3	35.5	125.5	44 05.2	37.4	127.1	42 51.5	39.1	128.6	13
46 58.5	32.2	123.3	45 51.1	34.2	125.0	44 40.8	36.2	126.7	43 27.8	37.9	128.2	42 12.4	39.6	129.6	14
46 26.3	−32.9	124.5	45 16.8	−34.9	126.2	44 04.6	−36.8	127.8	42 49.9	−38.6	129.3	41 32.8	−40.2	130.7	15
45 53.4	33.7	125.7	44 41.9	35.6	127.4	43 27.8	37.4	128.9	42 11.3	39.1	130.3	40 52.6	40.6	131.6	16
45 19.7	34.4	126.9	44 06.3	36.3	128.5	42 50.4	38.0	130.0	41 32.2	39.6	131.3	40 12.0	41.1	132.6	17
44 45.3	35.1	128.1	43 30.0	36.9	129.6	42 12.4	38.6	131.0	40 52.6	40.1	132.3	39 30.9	41.6	133.6	18
44 10.2	35.8	129.2	42 53.1	37.5	130.7	41 33.8	39.1	132.0	40 12.5	40.6	133.3	38 49.3	42.0	134.5	19
43 34.4	−36.4	130.3	42 15.6	−38.0	131.7	40 54.7	−39.6	133.0	39 31.9	−41.1	134.3	38 07.3	−42.4	135.4	20
42 58.0	37.0	131.4	41 37.6	38.6	132.8	40 15.1	40.1	134.0	38 50.8	41.5	135.2	37 24.9	42.9	136.3	21
42 21.0	37.6	132.5	40 59.0	39.2	133.8	39 35.0	40.6	135.0	38 09.3	41.9	136.1	36 42.0	43.2	137.2	22
41 43.4	38.1	133.5	40 19.8	39.6	134.8	38 54.4	41.0	135.9	37 27.4	42.4	137.0	35 58.8	43.5	138.0	23
41 05.3	38.7	134.6	39 40.2	40.2	135.8	38 13.4	41.5	136.9	36 45.0	42.7	137.9	35 15.3	43.9	138.9	24
40 26.6	−39.2	135.6	39 00.0	−40.6	136.7	37 31.9	−41.9	137.8	36 02.3	−43.1	138.8	34 31.4	−44.3	139.7	25
39 47.4	39.7	136.6	38 19.4	41.0	137.7	36 50.0	42.3	138.7	35 19.2	43.5	139.6	33 47.1	44.5	140.5	26
39 07.7	40.2	137.5	37 38.4	41.5	138.6	36 07.7	42.7	139.6	34 35.7	43.8	140.5	33 02.6	44.9	141.3	27
38 27.5	40.6	138.5	36 56.9	41.8	139.5	35 25.0	43.0	140.4	33 51.9	44.1	141.3	32 17.7	45.1	142.1	28
37 46.9	41.1	139.4	36 15.1	42.3	140.4	34 42.0	43.4	141.3	33 07.8	44.4	142.1	31 32.6	45.5	142.9	29

Dec.	20° Hc	d	Z	22° Hc	d	Z	24° Hc	d	Z	26° Hc	d	Z	28° Hc	d	Z
0	49 29.1	+31.1	115.2	48 36.0	+33.6	117.3	47 39.2	+35.8	119.2	46 38.8	+38.0	121.1	45 35.2	+40.0	122.9
1	50 00.2	30.2	113.9	49 09.6	32.7	116.0	48 15.0	35.1	118.0	47 16.8	37.3	120.0	46 15.2	39.3	121.8
2	50 30.4	29.3	112.5	49 42.3	31.9	114.7	48 50.1	34.3	116.8	47 54.1	36.6	118.8	46 54.5	38.7	120.7
3	50 59.7	28.2	111.2	50 14.2	30.9	113.4	49 24.4	33.5	115.6	48 30.7	35.8	117.6	47 33.2	38.0	119.6
4	51 27.9	27.3	109.7	50 45.1	30.0	112.1	49 57.9	32.6	114.3	49 06.5	35.0	116.4	48 11.2	37.3	118.4
5	51 55.2	+26.1	108.3	51 15.1	+29.0	110.7	50 30.5	+31.7	113.0	49 41.5	+34.2	115.2	48 48.5	+36.6	117.2
6	52 21.3	25.1	106.8	51 44.1	28.0	109.3	51 02.2	30.7	111.6	50 15.7	33.4	113.9	49 25.1	35.8	116.0
7	52 46.4	23.9	105.3	52 12.1	26.9	107.8	51 32.9	29.8	110.3	50 49.1	32.4	112.6	50 00.9	34.9	114.8
8	53 10.3	22.7	103.8	52 39.0	25.8	106.4	52 02.7	28.7	108.8	51 21.5	31.5	111.2	50 35.8	34.2	113.5
9	53 33.0	21.5	102.3	53 04.8	24.6	104.9	52 31.4	27.7	107.4	51 53.0	30.6	109.9	51 10.0	33.2	112.2
10	53 54.5	+20.2	100.7	53 29.4	+23.5	103.4	52 59.1	+26.6	105.9	52 23.6	+29.5	108.5	51 43.2	+32.3	110.9
11	54 14.7	18.9	99.1	53 52.9	22.3	101.8	53 25.7	25.4	104.5	52 53.1	28.5	107.0	52 15.5	31.3	109.5
12	54 33.6	17.6	97.5	54 15.2	20.9	100.2	53 51.1	24.2	102.9	53 21.6	27.3	105.6	52 46.8	30.3	108.1
13	54 51.2	16.2	95.8	54 36.1	19.7	98.6	54 15.3	23.0	101.4	53 48.9	26.2	104.1	53 17.1	29.2	106.7
14	55 07.4	14.8	94.1	54 55.8	18.3	97.0	54 38.3	21.8	99.8	54 15.1	25.0	102.5	53 46.3	28.2	105.2
15	55 22.2	+13.4	92.4	55 14.1	+17.0	95.3	55 00.1	+20.4	98.2	54 40.1	+23.8	101.0	54 14.5	+27.0	103.7
16	55 35.6	11.9	90.7	55 31.1	15.5	93.6	55 20.5	19.1	96.5	55 03.9	22.5	99.4	54 41.5	25.8	102.2
17	55 47.5	10.5	89.0	55 46.6	14.1	91.9	55 39.6	17.6	94.8	55 26.4	21.2	97.7	55 07.3	24.6	100.6
18	55 58.0	8.9	87.2	56 00.7	12.6	90.2	55 57.2	16.3	93.1	55 47.6	19.8	96.1	55 31.9	23.2	99.0
19	56 06.9	7.4	85.4	56 13.3	11.1	88.4	56 13.5	14.8	91.4	56 07.4	18.5	94.4	55 55.1	22.0	97.3
20	56 14.3	+ 5.9	83.7	56 24.4	+ 9.6	86.7	56 28.3	+13.3	89.7	56 25.9	+16.9	92.7	56 17.1	+20.6	95.7
21	56 20.2	4.2	81.9	56 34.0	8.1	84.9	56 41.6	11.8	87.9	56 42.8	15.5	90.9	56 37.7	19.2	94.0
22	56 24.4	2.8	80.1	56 42.1	6.4	83.1	56 53.4	10.2	86.1	56 58.3	14.0	89.2	56 56.9	17.7	92.2
23	56 27.2	+ 1.1	78.3	56 48.5	4.9	81.2	57 03.6	8.7	84.3	57 12.3	12.5	87.4	57 14.6	16.2	90.5
24	56 28.3	- 0.4	76.4	56 53.4	3.3	79.4	57 12.3	7.0	82.5	57 24.8	10.9	85.6	57 30.8	14.7	88.7
25	56 27.9	- 2.0	74.6	56 56.7	+ 1.6	77.6	57 19.3	+ 5.5	80.6	57 35.7	+ 9.2	83.7	57 45.5	+13.1	86.9
26	56 25.9	3.6	72.8	56 58.3	+ 0.1	75.8	57 24.8	3.8	78.8	57 44.9	7.7	81.9	57 58.6	11.5	85.1
27	56 22.3	5.2	71.0	56 58.4	- 1.5	73.9	57 28.6	2.2	76.9	57 52.6	6.0	80.0	58 10.1	9.9	83.2
28	56 17.1	6.7	69.2	56 56.9	3.2	72.1	57 30.8	+ 0.5	75.1	57 58.6	4.3	78.2	58 20.0	8.2	81.3
29	56 10.4	8.3	67.4	56 53.7	4.8	70.3	57 31.3	- 1.1	73.2	58 02.9	2.7	76.3	58 28.2	6.5	79.4

Dec.	30° Hc	d	Z	32° Hc	d	Z	34° Hc	d	Z	36° Hc	d	Z	38° Hc	d	Z
0	44 28.7	+41.7	124.5	43 19.3	+43.4	126.1	42 07.3	+45.0	127.6	40 52.9	+46.5	129.0	39 36.4	+47.8	130.3
1	45 10.4	41.3	123.5	44 02.7	43.0	125.2	42 52.3	44.6	126.7	41 39.4	46.1	128.1	40 24.2	47.4	129.5
2	45 51.7	40.6	122.5	44 45.7	42.5	124.2	43 36.9	44.2	125.8	42 25.5	45.7	127.3	41 11.6	47.2	128.7
3	46 32.3	40.1	121.4	45 28.2	41.9	123.2	44 21.1	43.6	124.8	43 11.2	45.3	126.4	41 58.8	46.7	127.9
4	47 12.4	39.4	120.3	46 10.1	41.4	122.1	45 04.7	43.2	123.9	43 56.5	44.8	125.5	42 45.5	46.4	127.0
5	47 51.8	+38.7	119.2	46 51.5	+40.7	121.1	45 47.9	+42.6	122.9	44 41.3	+44.4	124.6	43 31.9	+45.9	126.1
6	48 30.5	38.1	118.1	47 32.2	40.2	120.0	46 30.5	42.1	121.9	45 25.7	43.8	123.6	44 17.8	45.5	125.2
7	49 08.6	37.3	116.9	48 12.4	39.5	118.9	47 12.6	41.5	120.8	46 09.5	43.4	122.6	45 03.3	45.1	124.3
8	49 45.9	36.5	115.7	48 51.9	38.8	117.8	47 54.1	40.9	119.7	46 52.9	42.8	121.6	45 48.4	44.6	123.4
9	50 22.4	35.8	114.5	49 30.7	38.1	116.6	48 35.0	40.3	118.6	47 35.7	42.3	120.6	46 33.0	44.1	122.4
10	50 58.2	+34.9	113.2	50 08.8	+37.3	115.4	49 15.3	+39.6	117.5	48 18.0	+41.6	119.5	47 17.1	+43.6	121.4
11	51 33.1	34.0	111.9	50 46.1	36.5	114.2	49 54.9	38.8	116.4	48 59.6	41.0	118.4	48 00.7	43.0	120.4
12	52 07.1	33.1	110.6	51 22.6	35.7	112.9	50 33.7	38.1	115.2	49 40.6	40.4	117.3	48 43.7	42.4	119.4
13	52 40.2	32.1	109.2	51 58.3	34.8	111.6	51 11.8	37.3	113.9	50 21.0	39.6	116.2	49 26.1	41.8	118.3
14	53 12.3	31.1	107.8	52 33.1	33.9	110.3	51 49.1	36.5	112.6	51 00.6	39.0	115.0	50 07.9	41.1	117.2
15	53 43.4	+30.0	106.4	53 07.0	+32.9	108.9	52 25.6	+35.7	111.4	51 39.6	+38.1	113.8	50 49.0	+40.5	116.0
16	54 13.4	29.0	104.9	53 39.9	32.0	107.5	53 01.3	34.7	110.1	52 17.7	37.3	112.5	51 29.5	39.7	114.8
17	54 42.4	27.8	103.4	54 11.9	30.8	106.1	53 36.0	33.7	108.7	52 55.0	36.5	111.2	52 09.2	39.0	113.6
18	55 10.2	26.6	101.8	54 42.7	29.8	104.6	54 09.7	32.8	107.3	53 31.5	35.5	109.9	52 48.2	38.1	112.4
19	55 36.8	25.3	100.3	55 12.5	28.6	103.1	54 42.5	31.7	105.9	54 07.0	34.6	108.5	53 26.3	37.3	111.1
20	56 02.1	+24.1	98.6	55 41.1	+27.4	101.5	55 14.2	+30.6	104.4	54 41.6	+33.6	107.1	54 03.6	+36.4	109.8
21	56 26.2	22.7	97.0	56 08.5	26.2	100.0	55 44.8	29.4	102.9	55 15.2	32.5	105.7	54 40.0	35.5	108.4
22	56 48.9	21.4	95.3	56 34.7	24.9	98.3	56 14.2	28.3	101.3	55 47.7	31.5	104.2	55 15.5	34.4	107.0
23	57 10.3	19.9	93.6	56 59.6	23.5	96.7	56 42.5	26.9	99.7	56 19.2	30.3	102.7	55 49.9	33.4	105.6
24	57 30.2	18.5	91.8	57 23.1	22.1	95.0	57 09.4	25.7	98.1	56 49.5	29.0	101.1	56 23.3	32.3	104.1
25	57 48.7	+16.9	90.1	57 45.2	+20.7	93.2	57 35.1	+24.3	96.4	57 18.5	+27.8	99.5	56 55.6	+31.1	102.5
26	58 05.6	15.3	88.3	58 05.9	19.1	91.5	57 59.4	22.9	94.7	57 46.3	26.5	97.8	57 26.7	30.0	101.0
27	58 20.9	13.8	86.4	58 25.0	17.7	89.7	58 22.3	21.4	92.9	58 12.8	25.1	96.1	57 56.7	28.6	99.3
28	58 34.7	12.1	84.6	58 42.7	16.0	87.8	58 43.7	20.0	91.1	58 37.9	23.7	94.4	58 25.3	27.3	97.7
29	58 46.8	10.5	82.7	58 58.7	14.4	86.0	59 03.7	18.3	89.3	59 01.6	22.2	92.6	58 52.6	26.0	96.0

20°			22°			24°			26°			28°			Dec.
Hc	d	Z	Hc	d	Z	Hc	d	Z	Hc	d	Z	Hc	d	Z	
° ′	′	°	° ′	′	°	° ′	′	°	° ′	′	°	° ′	′	°	°
49 29.1	-32.1	115.2	48 36.0	-34.4	117.3	47 39.2	-36.6	119.2	46 38.8	-38.6	121.1	45 35.2	-40.5	122.9	0
48 57.0	32.8	116.5	48 01.6	35.2	118.5	47 02.6	37.3	120.4	46 00.2	39.3	122.2	44 54.7	41.1	123.9	1
48 24.2	33.7	117.8	47 26.4	35.9	119.7	46 25.3	38.0	121.6	45 20.9	39.8	123.3	44 13.6	41.6	124.9	2
47 50.5	34.5	119.0	46 50.5	36.6	120.9	45 47.3	38.6	122.7	44 41.1	40.5	124.4	43 32.0	42.2	125.9	3
47 16.0	35.2	120.2	46 13.9	37.3	122.0	45 08.7	39.2	123.8	44 00.6	41.0	125.4	42 49.8	42.6	126.9	4
46 40.8	-36.0	121.4	45 36.6	-37.9	123.2	44 29.5	-39.8	124.8	43 19.6	-41.5	126.4	42 07.2	-43.1	127.9	5
46 04.8	36.6	122.6	44 58.7	38.5	124.3	43 49.7	40.3	125.9	42 38.1	42.0	127.4	41 24.1	43.5	128.8	6
45 28.2	37.3	123.7	44 20.2	39.2	125.3	43 09.4	40.9	126.9	41 56.1	42.4	128.3	40 40.6	44.0	129.7	7
44 50.9	37.9	124.8	43 41.0	39.7	126.4	42 28.5	41.4	127.9	41 13.7	43.0	129.3	39 56.6	44.4	130.6	8
44 13.0	38.6	125.9	43 01.3	40.3	127.4	41 47.1	41.8	128.9	40 30.7	43.3	130.2	39 12.2	44.7	131.5	9
43 34.4	-39.1	127.0	42 21.0	-40.8	128.4	41 05.3	-42.4	129.8	39 47.4	-43.8	131.1	38 27.5	-45.1	132.3	10
42 55.3	39.7	128.0	41 40.2	41.2	129.4	40 22.9	42.7	130.8	39 03.6	44.2	132.0	37 42.4	45.5	133.2	11
42 15.6	40.2	129.0	40 59.0	41.8	130.4	39 40.2	43.2	131.7	38 19.4	44.5	132.9	36 56.9	45.8	134.0	12
41 35.4	40.7	130.0	40 17.2	42.2	131.3	38 57.0	43.6	132.6	37 34.9	44.9	133.7	36 11.1	46.1	134.8	13
40 54.7	41.2	131.0	39 35.0	42.6	132.3	38 13.4	44.0	133.5	36 50.0	45.2	134.6	35 25.0	46.4	135.6	14
40 13.5	-41.6	132.0	38 52.4	-43.1	133.2	37 29.4	-44.4	134.3	36 04.8	-45.6	135.4	34 38.6	-46.7	136.4	15
39 31.9	42.1	132.9	38 09.3	43.4	134.1	36 45.0	44.7	135.2	35 19.2	45.9	136.2	33 51.9	46.9	137.1	16
38 49.8	42.5	133.8	37 25.9	43.9	134.9	36 00.3	45.0	136.0	34 33.3	46.2	137.0	33 05.0	47.3	137.9	17
38 07.3	42.9	134.7	36 42.0	44.1	135.8	35 15.3	45.4	136.8	33 47.1	46.4	137.7	32 17.7	47.5	138.6	18
37 24.4	43.4	135.6	35 57.9	44.6	136.6	34 29.9	45.6	137.6	33 00.7	46.8	138.5	31 30.2	47.7	139.3	19
36 41.0	-43.6	136.5	35 13.3	-44.8	137.5	33 44.3	-46.0	138.4	32 13.9	-46.9	139.2	30 42.5	-47.9	140.0	20
35 57.4	44.1	137.3	34 28.5	45.2	138.3	32 58.3	46.2	139.1	31 27.0	47.3	140.0	29 54.6	48.2	140.7	21
35 13.3	44.3	138.2	33 43.3	45.5	139.1	32 12.1	46.5	139.9	30 39.7	47.4	140.7	29 06.4	48.4	141.4	22
34 29.0	44.7	139.0	32 57.8	45.7	139.8	31 25.6	46.8	140.6	29 52.3	47.7	141.4	28 18.0	48.5	142.1	23
33 44.3	45.1	139.8	32 12.1	46.1	140.6	30 38.8	47.0	141.4	29 04.6	47.9	142.1	27 29.5	48.8	142.7	24
32 59.2	-45.3	140.6	31 26.0	-46.3	141.4	29 51.8	-47.2	142.1	28 16.7	-48.1	142.8	26 40.7	-48.9	143.4	25
32 13.9	45.5	141.4	30 39.7	46.5	142.1	29 04.6	47.5	142.8	27 28.6	48.3	143.5	25 51.8	49.1	144.0	26
31 28.4	45.9	142.1	29 53.2	46.8	142.8	28 17.1	47.6	143.5	26 40.3	48.5	144.1	25 02.7	49.3	144.7	27
30 42.5	46.1	142.9	29 06.4	47.0	143.6	27 29.5	47.9	144.2	25 51.8	48.7	144.8	24 13.4	49.4	145.3	28
29 56.4	46.3	143.6	28 19.4	47.2	144.3	26 41.6	48.0	144.9	25 03.1	48.8	145.4	23 24.0	49.5	145.9	29

30°			32°			34°			36°			38°			Dec.
Hc	d	Z	Hc	d	Z	Hc	d	Z	Hc	d	Z	Hc	d	Z	
° ′	′	°	° ′	′	°	° ′	′	°	° ′	′	°	° ′	′	°	°
44 28.7	-42.4	124.5	43 19.3	-44.0	126.1	42 07.3	-45.4	127.6	40 52.9	-46.8	129.0	39 36.4	-48.1	130.3	0
43 46.3	42.8	125.5	42 35.3	44.3	127.0	41 21.9	45.9	128.5	40 06.1	47.1	129.8	38 48.3	48.4	131.0	1
43 03.5	43.2	126.5	41 51.0	44.8	127.9	40 36.0	46.2	129.3	39 19.0	47.5	130.6	37 59.9	48.7	131.8	2
42 20.3	43.8	127.4	41 06.2	45.2	128.8	39 49.8	46.5	130.2	38 31.5	47.8	131.4	37 11.2	48.9	132.5	3
41 36.5	44.1	128.4	40 21.0	45.6	129.7	39 03.3	46.9	131.0	37 43.7	48.1	132.2	36 22.3	49.2	133.3	4
40 52.4	-44.6	129.3	39 35.4	-45.9	130.6	38 16.4	-47.2	131.8	36 55.6	-48.4	132.9	35 33.1	-49.5	134.0	5
40 07.8	44.9	130.1	38 49.5	46.3	131.4	37 29.2	47.5	132.5	36 07.2	48.6	133.6	34 43.6	49.7	134.7	6
39 22.9	45.4	131.0	38 03.2	46.6	132.2	36 41.7	47.8	133.3	35 18.6	48.9	134.4	33 53.9	49.9	135.3	7
38 37.5	45.7	131.8	37 16.6	47.0	133.0	35 53.9	48.0	134.1	34 29.7	49.1	135.1	33 04.0	50.1	136.0	8
37 51.8	46.0	132.7	36 29.6	47.2	133.8	35 05.9	48.4	134.8	33 40.6	49.4	135.8	32 13.9	50.3	136.7	9
37 05.8	-46.4	133.5	35 42.4	-47.5	134.5	34 17.5	-48.5	135.5	32 51.2	-49.5	136.4	31 23.6	-50.5	137.3	10
36 19.4	46.6	134.3	34 54.9	47.7	135.3	33 29.0	48.9	136.2	32 01.7	49.8	137.1	30 33.1	50.6	137.9	11
35 32.8	47.0	135.0	34 07.2	48.1	136.0	32 40.1	49.0	136.9	31 11.9	50.0	137.8	29 42.5	50.9	138.6	12
34 45.8	47.2	135.8	33 19.1	48.3	136.7	31 51.1	49.2	137.6	30 21.9	50.1	138.4	28 51.6	51.0	139.2	13
33 58.6	47.5	136.5	32 30.8	48.5	137.4	31 01.9	49.5	138.3	29 31.8	50.4	139.0	28 00.6	51.1	139.8	14
33 11.1	-47.7	137.3	31 42.3	-48.7	138.1	30 12.4	-49.6	138.9	28 41.4	-50.5	139.7	27 09.5	-51.3	140.3	15
32 23.4	48.0	138.0	30 53.6	48.9	138.8	29 22.8	49.9	139.6	27 50.9	50.6	140.3	26 18.2	51.5	140.9	16
31 35.4	48.3	138.7	30 04.7	49.2	139.5	28 32.9	50.0	140.2	27 00.3	50.9	140.9	25 26.7	51.5	141.5	17
30 47.1	48.4	139.4	29 15.5	49.3	140.2	27 42.9	50.2	140.8	26 09.4	50.9	141.5	24 35.2	51.7	142.1	18
29 58.7	48.6	140.1	28 26.2	49.5	140.8	26 52.7	50.3	141.5	25 18.5	51.1	142.1	23 43.5	51.8	142.6	19
29 10.1	-48.9	140.8	27 36.7	-49.7	141.4	26 02.4	-50.5	142.1	24 27.4	-51.2	142.6	22 51.7	-52.0	143.2	20
28 21.2	49.0	141.4	26 47.0	49.9	142.1	25 11.9	50.6	142.7	23 36.2	51.4	143.2	21 59.7	52.0	143.7	21
27 32.2	49.2	142.1	25 57.1	50.0	142.7	24 21.3	50.8	143.3	22 44.8	51.5	143.8	21 07.7	52.1	144.2	22
26 43.0	49.4	142.7	25 07.1	50.2	143.3	23 30.5	50.8	143.8	21 53.3	51.5	144.3	20 15.6	52.2	144.8	23
25 53.6	49.6	143.4	24 16.9	50.3	143.9	22 39.7	51.1	144.4	21 01.8	51.7	144.9	19 23.4	52.4	145.3	24
25 04.0	-49.7	144.0	23 26.6	-50.4	144.5	21 48.6	-51.1	145.0	20 10.1	-51.8	145.4	18 31.0	-52.3	145.8	25
24 14.3	49.8	144.6	22 36.2	50.6	145.1	20 57.5	51.2	145.5	19 18.3	51.9	146.0	17 38.7	52.5	146.3	26
23 24.5	50.0	145.2	21 45.6	50.7	145.7	20 06.3	51.4	146.1	18 26.4	51.9	146.5	16 46.2	52.6	146.8	27
22 34.5	50.2	145.8	20 54.9	50.8	146.2	19 14.9	51.4	146.7	17 34.5	52.1	147.0	15 53.6	52.6	147.3	28
21 44.3	50.2	146.4	20 04.1	50.9	146.8	18 23.5	51.5	147.2	16 42.4	52.1	147.5	15 01.0	52.7	147.8	29

Dec.	40° Hc	d	Z	42° Hc	d	Z	44° Hc	d	Z	46° Hc	d	Z	48° Hc	d	Z
°	° ′	′	°	° ′	′	°	° ′	′	°	° ′	′	°	° ′	′	°
0	38 17.8	+49.0	131.5	36 57.4	+50.1	132.6	35 35.3	+51.2	133.7	34 11.6	+52.1	134.7	32 46.5	+52.9	135.6
1	39 06.8	48.8	130.8	37 47.5	49.9	132.0	36 26.5	50.9	133.1	35 03.7	51.9	134.1	33 39.4	52.8	135.1
2	39 55.6	48.4	130.0	38 37.4	49.6	131.2	37 17.4	50.7	132.4	35 55.6	51.7	133.5	34 32.2	52.7	134.5
3	40 44.0	48.1	129.2	39 27.0	49.4	130.5	38 08.1	50.5	131.7	36 47.3	51.5	132.9	35 24.9	52.4	133.9
4	41 32.1	47.7	128.4	40 16.4	49.0	129.8	38 58.6	50.2	131.0	37 38.8	51.3	132.2	36 17.3	52.3	133.3
5	42 19.8	+47.4	127.6	41 05.4	+48.8	129.0	39 48.8	+50.0	130.3	38 30.1	+51.1	131.6	37 09.6	+52.1	132.7
6	43 07.2	47.1	126.8	41 54.2	48.4	128.2	40 38.8	49.6	129.6	39 21.2	50.8	130.9	38 01.7	51.9	132.1
7	43 54.3	46.6	125.9	42 42.6	48.0	127.4	41 28.4	49.4	128.9	40 12.0	50.6	130.2	38 53.6	51.7	131.4
8	44 40.9	46.2	125.1	43 30.6	47.8	126.6	42 17.8	49.1	128.1	41 02.6	50.3	129.5	39 45.3	51.4	130.8
9	45 27.1	45.8	124.1	44 18.4	47.3	125.8	43 06.9	48.7	127.3	41 52.9	50.1	128.8	40 36.7	51.2	130.1
10	46 12.9	+45.3	123.2	45 05.7	+46.9	124.9	43 55.6	+48.4	126.5	42 43.0	+49.7	128.0	41 27.9	+50.9	129.4
11	46 58.2	44.9	122.3	45 52.6	46.5	124.0	44 44.0	48.1	125.7	43 32.7	49.4	127.2	42 18.8	50.7	128.7
12	47 43.1	44.3	121.3	46 39.1	46.1	123.1	45 32.1	47.6	124.8	44 22.1	49.1	126.5	43 09.5	50.4	128.0
13	48 27.4	43.8	120.3	47 25.2	45.6	122.2	46 19.7	47.2	124.0	45 11.2	48.7	125.6	43 59.9	50.1	127.2
14	49 11.2	43.2	119.2	48 10.8	45.0	121.2	47 06.9	46.8	123.1	45 59.9	48.4	124.8	44 50.0	49.7	126.5
15	49 54.4	+42.6	118.2	48 55.8	+44.6	120.2	47 53.7	+46.3	122.1	46 48.3	+47.9	124.0	45 39.7	+49.5	125.7
16	50 37.0	41.9	117.1	49 40.4	44.0	119.2	48 40.0	45.9	121.2	47 36.2	47.5	123.1	46 29.2	49.0	124.9
17	51 18.9	41.3	115.9	50 24.4	43.4	118.1	49 25.9	45.3	120.2	48 23.7	47.1	122.2	47 18.2	48.7	124.0
18	52 00.2	40.5	114.8	51 07.8	42.7	117.0	50 11.2	44.8	119.2	49 10.8	46.6	121.2	48 06.9	48.3	123.1
19	52 40.7	39.8	113.6	51 50.5	42.1	115.9	50 56.0	44.2	118.1	49 57.4	46.2	120.2	48 55.2	47.8	122.2
20	53 20.5	+39.0	112.3	52 32.6	+41.4	114.7	51 40.2	+43.6	117.1	50 43.6	+45.5	119.2	49 43.0	+47.4	121.3
21	53 59.5	38.2	111.0	53 14.0	40.6	113.5	52 23.8	42.9	115.9	51 29.1	45.0	118.2	50 30.4	46.9	120.4
22	54 37.7	37.2	109.7	53 54.6	39.9	112.3	53 06.7	42.2	114.8	52 14.1	44.5	117.1	51 17.3	46.4	119.4
23	55 14.9	36.3	108.3	54 34.5	39.0	111.0	53 48.9	41.5	113.6	52 58.6	43.7	116.0	52 03.7	45.8	118.4
24	55 51.2	35.4	106.9	55 13.5	38.1	109.7	54 30.4	40.8	112.4	53 42.3	43.1	114.9	52 49.5	45.3	117.3
25	56 26.6	+34.2	105.5	55 51.6	+37.2	108.3	55 11.2	+39.8	111.1	54 25.4	+42.4	113.7	53 34.8	+44.6	116.2
26	57 00.8	33.2	104.0	56 28.8	36.2	106.9	55 51.0	39.1	109.8	55 07.8	41.6	112.5	54 19.4	44.0	115.1
27	57 34.0	32.0	102.4	57 05.0	35.2	105.5	56 30.1	38.1	108.4	55 49.4	40.8	111.2	55 03.4	43.2	113.9
28	58 06.0	30.8	100.9	57 40.2	34.0	104.0	57 08.2	37.1	107.0	56 30.2	39.9	109.9	55 46.6	42.5	112.7
29	58 36.8	29.5	99.2	58 14.2	32.9	102.4	57 45.3	36.0	105.5	57 10.1	39.0	108.5	56 29.1	41.7	111.4

Dec.	50° Hc	d	Z	52° Hc	d	Z	54° Hc	d	Z	56° Hc	d	Z	58° Hc	d	Z
°	° ′	′	°	° ′	′	°	° ′	′	°	° ′	′	°	° ′	′	°
0	31 20.0	+53.8	136.5	29 52.4	+54.5	137.3	28 23.6	+55.2	138.1	26 53.9	+55.7	138.8	25 23.2	+56.2	139.4
1	32 13.8	53.6	136.0	30 46.9	54.3	136.8	29 18.8	55.0	137.6	27 49.6	55.7	138.4	26 19.4	56.3	139.0
2	33 07.4	53.5	135.5	31 41.2	54.3	136.3	30 13.8	54.9	137.2	28 45.3	55.5	137.9	27 15.7	56.1	138.6
3	34 00.9	53.3	134.9	32 35.5	54.1	135.8	31 08.7	54.9	136.7	29 40.8	55.5	137.5	28 11.8	56.1	138.2
4	34 54.2	53.2	134.4	33 29.6	54.0	135.3	32 03.6	54.7	136.2	30 36.3	55.4	137.1	29 07.9	56.0	137.8
5	35 47.4	+53.0	133.8	34 23.6	+53.8	134.8	32 58.3	+54.6	135.7	31 31.7	+55.4	136.6	30 03.9	+56.0	137.4
6	36 40.4	52.8	133.2	35 17.4	53.7	134.3	33 52.9	54.5	135.2	32 27.1	55.2	136.2	30 59.9	55.8	137.0
7	37 33.2	52.7	132.6	36 11.1	53.6	133.7	34 47.4	54.4	134.7	33 22.3	55.1	135.7	31 55.7	55.8	136.6
8	38 25.9	52.4	132.0	37 04.7	53.4	133.1	35 41.8	54.2	134.2	34 17.4	55.0	135.2	32 51.5	55.7	136.1
9	39 18.3	52.3	131.4	37 58.1	53.2	132.6	36 36.0	54.1	133.7	35 12.4	54.8	134.7	33 47.2	55.6	135.7
10	40 10.6	+52.0	130.7	38 51.3	+53.0	132.0	37 30.1	+54.0	133.1	36 07.2	+54.8	134.2	34 42.8	+55.5	135.2
11	41 02.6	51.9	130.1	39 44.3	52.9	131.4	38 24.1	53.7	132.6	37 02.0	54.6	133.7	35 38.2	55.4	134.8
12	41 54.5	51.5	129.4	40 37.2	52.6	130.8	39 17.8	53.6	132.0	37 56.6	54.4	133.2	36 33.6	55.2	134.3
13	42 46.0	51.3	128.7	41 29.8	52.4	130.1	40 11.4	53.4	131.4	38 51.0	54.4	132.7	37 28.8	55.2	133.8
14	43 37.3	51.1	128.0	42 22.2	52.2	129.5	41 04.8	53.3	130.8	39 45.4	54.1	132.1	38 24.0	55.0	133.3
15	44 28.4	+50.7	127.3	43 14.4	+52.0	128.8	41 58.1	+53.0	130.2	40 39.5	+54.0	131.5	39 19.0	+54.8	132.8
16	45 19.1	50.5	126.5	44 06.4	51.7	128.1	42 51.1	52.8	129.6	41 33.5	53.8	131.0	40 13.8	54.7	132.3
17	46 09.6	50.1	125.8	44 58.1	51.4	127.4	43 43.9	52.6	128.9	42 27.3	53.6	130.4	41 08.5	54.6	131.7
18	46 59.7	49.8	125.0	45 49.5	51.1	126.7	44 36.5	52.3	128.3	43 20.9	53.5	129.8	42 03.1	54.3	131.2
19	47 49.5	49.4	124.1	46 40.6	50.8	125.9	45 28.8	52.1	127.6	44 14.4	53.2	129.1	42 57.4	54.2	130.6
20	48 38.9	+49.0	123.3	47 31.4	+50.5	125.1	46 20.9	+51.8	126.9	45 07.6	+52.9	128.5	43 51.6	+54.1	130.0
21	49 27.9	48.6	122.4	48 21.9	50.2	124.3	47 12.7	51.5	126.1	46 00.5	52.8	127.8	44 45.7	53.8	129.4
22	50 16.5	48.2	121.5	49 12.1	49.7	123.5	48 04.2	51.2	125.4	46 53.3	52.4	127.1	45 39.5	53.6	128.8
23	51 04.7	47.7	120.5	50 01.8	49.4	122.6	48 55.4	50.9	124.6	47 45.7	52.2	126.4	46 33.1	53.4	128.1
24	51 52.4	47.2	119.6	50 51.2	48.9	121.7	49 46.3	50.5	123.8	48 37.9	51.9	125.7	47 26.5	53.1	127.4
25	52 39.6	+46.7	118.6	51 40.1	+48.5	120.8	50 36.8	+50.1	122.9	49 29.8	+51.6	124.9	48 19.6	+52.9	126.8
26	53 26.3	46.1	117.5	52 28.6	48.1	119.8	51 26.9	49.8	122.0	50 21.4	51.3	124.1	49 12.5	52.6	126.0
27	54 12.4	45.4	116.4	53 16.7	47.5	118.9	52 16.7	49.3	121.1	51 12.7	50.9	123.3	50 05.1	52.3	125.3
28	54 57.8	44.9	115.3	54 04.2	46.9	117.8	53 06.0	48.8	120.2	52 03.6	50.5	122.4	50 57.4	52.0	124.5
29	55 42.7	44.1	114.1	54 51.1	46.4	116.7	53 54.8	48.3	119.2	52 54.1	50.1	121.5	51 49.4	51.6	123.7

40° Hc	d	Z	42° Hc	d	Z	44° Hc	d	Z	46° Hc	d	Z	48° Hc	d	Z	Dec.
38 17.8	-49.2	131.5	36 57.4	-50.3	132.6	35 35.3	-51.3	133.7	34 11.6	-52.3	134.7	32 46.5	-53.1	135.6	0
37 28.6	49.6	132.2	36 07.1	50.6	133.3	34 44.0	51.6	134.3	33 19.3	52.4	135.3	31 53.4	53.3	136.2	1
36 39.0	49.7	132.9	35 16.5	50.8	134.0	33 52.4	51.7	135.0	32 26.9	52.6	135.9	31 00.1	53.3	136.7	2
35 49.3	50.1	133.6	34 25.7	51.0	134.6	33 00.7	51.9	135.6	31 34.3	52.7	136.5	30 06.8	53.5	137.3	3
34 59.2	50.2	134.3	33 34.7	51.2	135.3	32 08.8	52.1	136.2	30 41.6	52.9	137.0	29 13.3	53.7	137.8	4
34 09.0	-50.4	135.0	32 43.5	-51.4	135.9	31 16.7	-52.2	136.8	29 48.7	-53.0	137.6	28 19.6	-53.7	138.3	5
33 18.6	50.7	135.6	31 52.1	51.5	136.5	30 24.5	52.4	137.3	28 55.7	53.1	138.1	27 25.9	53.8	138.8	6
32 27.9	50.8	136.3	31 00.6	51.7	137.1	29 32.1	52.5	137.9	28 02.6	53.3	138.6	26 32.1	54.0	139.3	7
31 37.1	51.0	136.9	30 08.9	51.9	137.7	28 39.6	52.6	138.4	27 09.3	53.3	139.1	25 38.1	54.0	139.8	8
30 46.1	51.2	137.5	29 17.0	52.0	138.3	27 47.0	52.8	139.0	26 16.0	53.5	139.7	24 44.1	54.1	140.3	9
29 54.9	-51.4	138.1	28 25.0	-52.1	138.8	26 54.2	-52.9	139.5	25 22.5	-53.6	140.2	23 50.0	-54.2	140.7	10
29 03.5	51.5	138.7	27 32.9	52.3	139.4	26 01.3	53.0	140.1	24 28.9	53.6	140.7	22 55.8	54.3	141.2	11
28 12.0	51.6	139.3	26 40.6	52.4	140.0	25 08.3	-53.1	140.6	23 35.3	53.8	141.1	22 01.5	54.4	141.7	12
27 20.4	51.8	139.9	25 48.2	52.5	140.5	24 15.2	53.2	141.1	22 41.5	53.9	141.6	21 07.1	54.5	142.1	13
26 28.6	51.9	140.4	24 55.7	52.6	141.0	23 22.0	53.3	141.6	21 47.6	53.9	142.1	20 12.6	54.5	142.6	14
25 36.7	-52.1	141.0	24 03.1	-52.8	141.6	22 28.7	-53.4	142.1	20 53.7	-54.0	142.6	19 18.1	-54.5	143.0	15
24 44.6	52.1	141.5	23 10.3	52.8	142.1	21 35.3	53.5	142.6	19 59.7	54.1	143.0	18 23.6	54.7	143.5	16
23 52.5	52.3	142.1	22 17.5	53.0	142.6	20 41.8	53.5	143.1	19 05.6	54.1	143.5	17 28.9	54.7	143.9	17
23 00.2	52.4	142.6	21 24.5	53.0	143.1	19 48.3	53.7	143.5	18 11.5	54.2	144.0	16 34.2	54.7	144.3	18
22 07.8	52.5	143.1	20 31.5	53.1	143.6	18 54.6	53.7	144.0	17 17.3	54.3	144.4	15 39.5	54.8	144.7	19
21 15.3	-52.6	143.7	19 38.4	-53.2	144.1	18 00.9	-53.7	144.5	16 23.0	-54.3	144.9	14 44.7	-54.8	145.2	20
20 22.7	52.6	144.2	18 45.2	53.3	144.6	17 07.2	53.9	145.0	15 28.7	-54.4	145.3	13 49.9	54.9	145.6	21
19 30.1	52.8	144.7	17 51.9	53.3	145.1	16 13.3	53.9	145.4	14 34.3	54.4	145.7	12 55.0	54.9	146.0	22
18 37.3	52.8	145.2	16 58.6	53.4	145.5	15 19.4	53.9	145.9	13 39.9	54.5	146.2	12 00.1	55.0	146.4	23
17 44.5	52.9	145.7	16 05.2	53.5	146.0	14 25.5	54.0	146.3	12 45.4	54.5	146.6	11 05.1	55.0	146.8	24
16 51.6	-53.0	146.2	15 11.7	-53.5	146.5	13 31.5	-54.1	146.8	11 50.9	-54.5	147.0	10 10.1	-55.0	147.2	25
15 58.6	53.1	146.7	14 18.2	53.6	147.0	12 37.4	54.1	147.2	10 56.4	54.6	147.4	9 15.1	55.0	147.6	26
15 05.5	53.1	147.2	13 24.6	53.7	147.4	11 43.3	54.1	147.7	10 01.8	54.6	147.9	8 20.1	55.1	148.0	27
14 12.4	53.1	147.6	12 30.9	53.6	147.9	10 49.2	54.2	148.1	9 07.2	54.7	148.3	7 25.0	55.1	148.4	28
13 19.3	53.2	148.1	11 37.3	53.8	148.3	9 55.0	54.2	148.5	8 12.5	54.6	148.7	6 29.9	55.1	148.8	29

50° Hc	d	Z	52° Hc	d	Z	54° Hc	d	Z	56° Hc	d	Z	58° Hc	d	Z	Dec.
31 20.0	-53.8	136.5	29 52.4	-54.6	137.3	28 23.6	-55.2	138.1	26 53.9	-55.9	138.8	25 23.2	-56.4	139.4	0
30 26.2	54.0	137.0	28 57.8	54.7	137.8	27 28.4	55.3	138.5	25 58.0	55.8	139.2	24 26.8	56.4	139.8	1
29 32.2	54.1	137.5	28 03.1	54.7	138.3	26 33.1	55.4	139.0	25 02.2	56.0	139.6	23 30.4	56.5	140.2	2
28 38.1	54.2	138.0	27 08.4	54.9	138.7	25 37.7	55.4	139.4	24 06.2	56.0	140.0	22 33.9	56.5	140.5	3
27 43.9	54.3	138.5	26 13.5	54.9	139.2	24 42.3	55.6	139.8	23 10.2	56.1	140.4	21 37.4	56.5	140.9	4
26 49.6	-54.4	139.0	25 18.6	-55.1	139.6	23 46.7	-55.6	140.2	22 14.1	-56.1	140.8	20 40.9	-56.6	141.3	5
25 55.2	54.5	139.5	24 23.5	55.1	140.1	22 51.1	55.6	140.6	21 18.0	56.1	141.1	19 44.3	56.7	141.6	6
25 00.7	54.6	139.9	23 28.4	55.1	140.5	21 55.5	55.7	141.0	20 21.9	56.2	141.5	18 47.6	56.6	142.0	7
24 06.1	54.7	140.4	22 33.3	55.3	140.9	20 59.8	55.8	141.4	19 25.7	56.3	141.9	17 51.0	56.8	142.3	8
23 11.4	54.7	140.8	21 38.0	55.3	141.4	20 04.0	55.8	141.8	18 29.4	56.3	142.3	16 54.2	56.7	142.6	9
22 16.7	-54.8	141.3	20 42.7	-55.3	141.8	19 08.2	-55.9	142.2	17 33.1	-56.4	142.6	15 57.5	-56.8	143.0	10
21 21.9	54.9	141.7	19 47.4	55.4	142.2	18 12.3	55.9	142.6	16 36.7	56.3	143.0	15 00.7	56.8	143.3	11
20 27.0	54.9	142.1	18 52.0	55.5	142.6	17 16.4	55.9	143.0	15 40.4	56.4	143.3	14 03.9	56.8	143.7	12
19 32.1	55.0	142.6	17 56.5	55.5	143.0	16 20.5	56.0	143.4	14 44.0	56.5	143.7	13 07.1	56.9	144.0	13
18 37.1	55.1	143.0	17 01.0	55.6	143.4	15 24.5	56.1	143.7	13 47.5	56.5	144.0	12 10.2	56.9	144.3	14
17 42.0	-55.1	143.4	16 05.4	-55.6	143.8	14 28.4	-56.0	144.1	12 51.0	-56.5	144.4	11 13.3	-56.9	144.6	15
16 46.9	55.1	143.8	15 09.8	55.6	144.2	13 32.4	56.1	144.5	11 54.5	56.5	144.7	10 16.4	56.9	145.0	16
15 51.8	55.2	144.2	14 14.2	55.7	144.6	12 36.3	56.2	144.8	10 58.0	56.5	145.1	9 19.5	56.9	145.3	17
14 56.6	55.3	144.6	13 18.5	55.7	144.9	11 40.1	56.1	145.2	10 01.5	56.6	145.4	8 22.6	57.0	145.6	18
14 01.3	55.3	145.1	12 22.8	55.7	145.3	10 44.0	56.2	145.6	9 04.9	56.6	145.7	7 25.6	57.0	145.9	19
13 06.0	-55.3	145.5	11 27.1	-55.8	145.7	9 47.8	-56.2	145.9	8 08.3	-56.6	146.1	6 28.6	-56.9	146.2	20
12 10.7	55.3	145.8	10 31.3	55.8	146.1	8 51.6	56.2	146.3	7 11.7	56.6	146.4	5 31.7	57.0	146.5	21
11 15.4	55.4	146.2	9 35.5	55.8	146.4	7 55.4	56.3	146.6	6 15.1	56.6	146.8	4 34.7	57.0	146.9	22
10 20.0	55.4	146.6	8 39.7	55.9	146.8	6 59.1	56.2	147.0	5 18.5	56.7	147.1	3 37.7	57.0	147.2	23
9 24.6	55.5	147.0	7 43.8	55.9	147.2	6 02.9	56.3	147.3	4 21.8	56.6	147.4	2 40.7	57.1	147.5	24
8 29.1	-55.4	147.4	6 47.9	-55.8	147.6	5 06.6	-56.3	147.7	3 25.2	-56.7	147.7	1 43.6	-57.0	147.8	25
7 33.7	55.5	147.8	5 52.1	55.9	147.9	4 10.3	56.3	148.0	2 28.5	56.7	148.1	0 46.6	-57.0	148.1	26
6 38.2	55.5	148.2	4 56.2	55.9	148.3	3 14.0	56.3	148.4	1 31.8	56.9	148.4	0 10.4	+57.0	31.6	27
5 42.7	55.5	148.6	4 00.3	56.0	148.7	2 17.7	56.3	148.7	0 35.2	-56.7	148.7	1 07.4	57.0	31.3	28
4 47.2	55.5	148.9	3 04.3	55.9	149.0	1 21.4	56.3	149.1	0 21.5	+56.7	30.9	2 04.4	57.0	31.0	29

	0°			2°			4°			6°			8°		
Dec.	Hc	d	Z	Hc	d	Z	Hc	d	Z	Hc	d	Z	Hc	d	Z
°	° ′	′	°	° ′	′	°	° ′	′	°	° ′	′	°	° ′	′	°
0	52 00.0	− 0.7	90.0	51 57.3	+ 2.8	92.6	51 49.3	+ 6.1	95.1	51 36.0	+ 9.5	97.6	51 17.5	+ 12.7	100.1
1	51 59.3	2.0	88.4	52 00.1	1.3	90.9	51 55.4	4.8	93.5	51 45.5	8.1	96.0	51 30.2	11.5	98.5
2	51 57.3	3.3	86.8	52 01.4	+ 0.1	89.3	52 00.2	3.5	91.9	51 53.6	6.8	94.4	51 41.7	10.2	97.0
3	51 54.0	4.7	85.1	52 01.5	− 1.3	87.7	52 03.7	2.1	90.3	52 00.4	5.6	92.8	51 51.9	8.9	95.4
4	51 49.3	6.0	83.5	52 00.2	2.6	86.1	52 05.8	+ 0.7	88.6	52 06.0	4.1	91.2	52 00.8	7.5	93.8
5	51 43.3	− 7.3	81.9	51 57.6	− 4.0	84.4	52 06.5	− 0.5	87.0	52 10.1	+ 2.9	89.6	52 08.3	+ 6.3	92.1
6	51 36.0	8.6	80.3	51 53.6	5.3	82.8	52 06.0	2.0	85.4	52 13.0	1.4	87.9	52 14.6	4.9	90.5
7	51 27.4	9.9	78.7	51 48.3	6.6	81.2	52 04.0	3.2	83.7	52 14.4	+ 0.2	86.3	52 19.5	3.5	88.9
8	51 17.5	11.1	77.1	51 41.7	7.9	79.6	52 00.8	4.6	82.1	52 14.6	− 1.2	84.7	52 23.0	2.2	87.3
9	51 06.4	12.4	75.6	51 33.8	9.2	78.0	51 56.2	5.9	80.5	52 13.4	2.6	83.0	52 25.2	+ 0.9	85.6
10	50 54.0	− 13.7	74.0	51 24.6	− 10.5	76.4	51 50.3	− 7.3	78.9	52 10.8	− 3.9	81.4	52 26.1	− 0.6	84.0
11	50 40.3	14.8	72.5	51 14.1	11.7	74.8	51 43.0	8.5	77.3	52 06.9	5.3	79.8	52 25.5	1.9	82.3
12	50 25.5	16.0	71.0	51 02.4	13.0	73.3	51 34.5	9.9	75.7	52 01.6	6.6	78.2	52 23.6	3.2	80.7
13	50 09.5	17.2	69.4	50 49.4	14.2	71.7	51 24.6	11.1	74.1	51 55.0	7.9	76.6	52 20.4	4.6	79.1
14	49 52.3	18.3	68.0	50 35.2	15.4	70.2	51 13.5	12.3	72.5	51 47.1	9.2	74.9	52 15.8	5.9	77.4
15	49 34.0	− 19.4	66.5	50 19.8	− 16.6	68.7	51 01.2	− 13.6	71.0	51 37.9	− 10.4	73.4	52 09.9	− 7.3	75.8
16	49 14.6	20.5	65.0	50 03.2	17.7	67.2	50 47.6	14.8	69.4	51 27.5	11.8	71.8	52 02.6	8.6	74.2
17	48 54.1	21.6	63.6	49 45.5	18.9	65.7	50 32.8	16.0	67.9	51 15.7	13.0	70.2	51 54.0	9.9	72.6
18	48 32.5	22.5	62.2	49 26.6	19.9	64.2	50 16.8	17.2	66.4	51 02.7	14.2	68.6	51 44.1	11.2	71.0
19	48 10.0	23.6	60.8	49 06.7	21.0	62.8	49 59.6	18.3	64.9	50 48.5	15.5	67.1	51 32.9	12.4	69.4
20	47 46.4	− 24.6	59.4	48 45.7	− 22.1	61.4	49 41.3	− 19.4	63.4	50 33.0	− 16.6	65.6	51 20.5	− 13.7	67.8
21	47 21.8	25.4	58.1	48 23.6	23.0	60.0	49 21.9	20.5	62.0	50 16.4	17.8	64.1	51 06.8	14.9	66.3
22	46 56.4	26.4	56.7	47 59.8	24.1	58.6	49 01.4	21.5	60.5	49 58.6	18.9	62.6	50 51.9	16.1	64.7
23	46 30.0	27.3	55.4	47 36.5	25.0	57.2	48 39.9	22.6	59.1	49 39.7	20.0	61.1	50 35.8	17.3	63.2
24	46 02.7	28.1	54.1	47 11.5	25.9	55.9	48 17.3	23.6	57.7	49 19.7	21.1	59.7	50 18.5	18.5	61.7
25	45 34.6	− 29.0	52.9	46 45.6	− 26.8	54.5	47 53.7	− 24.5	56.3	48 58.6	− 22.1	58.2	50 00.0	− 19.6	60.2
26	45 05.6	29.7	51.6	46 18.8	27.7	53.2	47 29.2	25.5	55.0	48 36.5	23.2	56.8	49 40.4	20.6	58.8
27	44 35.9	30.6	50.4	45 51.1	28.5	52.0	47 03.7	26.4	53.6	48 13.3	24.1	55.4	49 19.8	21.7	57.3
28	44 05.3	31.2	49.2	45 22.6	29.4	50.7	46 37.3	27.3	52.3	47 49.2	25.1	54.1	48 58.1	22.8	55.9
29	43 34.1	32.0	48.0	44 53.2	30.1	49.5	46 10.0	28.2	51.0	47 24.1	26.1	52.7	48 35.3	23.8	54.5

	10°			12°			14°			16°			18°		
Dec.	Hc	d	Z	Hc	d	Z	Hc	d	Z	Hc	d	Z	Hc	d	Z
°	° ′	′	°	° ′	′	°	° ′	′	°	° ′	′	°	° ′	′	°
0	50 54.0	+ 15.9	102.5	50 25.5	+ 19.0	104.9	49 52.3	+ 22.0	107.2	49 14.6	+ 24.8	109.4	48 32.5	+ 27.6	111.6
1	51 09.9	14.7	101.0	50 44.5	17.9	103.4	50 14.3	20.9	105.8	49 39.4	23.8	108.0	49 00.1	26.5	110.2
2	51 24.6	13.4	99.4	51 02.4	16.6	101.9	50 35.2	19.7	104.3	50 03.2	22.7	106.6	49 26.6	25.6	108.9
3	51 38.0	12.3	97.9	51 19.0	15.5	100.4	50 54.9	18.6	102.8	50 25.9	21.7	105.2	49 52.2	24.6	107.5
4	51 50.3	10.9	96.3	51 34.5	14.2	98.8	51 13.5	17.4	101.3	50 47.6	20.5	103.7	50 16.8	23.5	106.0
5	52 01.2	+ 9.6	94.7	51 48.7	+ 12.9	97.2	51 30.9	+ 16.2	99.7	51 08.1	+ 19.4	102.2	50 40.3	+ 22.4	104.6
6	52 10.8	8.3	93.1	52 01.6	11.7	95.7	51 47.1	15.0	98.2	51 27.5	18.1	100.7	51 02.7	21.3	103.1
7	52 19.1	7.0	91.5	52 13.3	10.3	94.1	52 02.1	13.7	96.6	51 45.6	17.0	99.2	51 24.0	20.1	101.6
8	52 26.1	5.6	89.9	52 23.6	9.1	92.5	52 15.8	12.4	95.0	52 02.6	15.7	97.6	51 44.1	19.0	100.1
9	52 31.7	4.2	88.2	52 32.7	7.7	90.8	52 28.2	11.1	93.4	52 18.3	14.5	96.0	52 03.1	17.7	98.6
10	52 35.9	+ 2.9	86.6	52 40.4	+ 6.3	89.2	52 39.3	+ 9.8	91.8	52 32.8	+ 13.1	94.4	52 20.8	+ 16.5	97.0
11	52 38.8	1.6	84.9	52 46.7	5.0	87.6	52 49.1	8.4	90.2	52 45.9	11.8	92.8	52 37.3	15.2	95.4
12	52 40.4	+ 0.1	83.3	52 51.7	3.6	85.9	52 57.5	7.0	88.5	52 57.7	10.5	91.2	52 52.5	13.9	93.8
13	52 40.5	− 1.2	81.6	52 55.3	2.2	84.3	53 04.5	5.7	86.9	53 08.2	9.2	89.6	53 06.4	12.5	92.2
14	52 39.3	2.6	80.0	52 57.5	+ 0.8	82.6	53 10.2	4.3	85.2	53 17.4	7.7	87.9	53 18.9	11.3	90.6
15	52 36.7	− 3.9	78.3	52 58.3	− 0.6	80.9	53 14.5	+ 2.9	83.6	53 25.1	+ 6.4	86.2	53 30.2	+ 9.8	88.9
16	52 32.8	5.4	76.7	52 57.7	1.9	79.3	53 17.4	1.5	81.9	53 31.5	5.0	84.6	53 40.0	8.5	87.3
17	52 27.4	6.6	75.1	52 55.8	3.3	77.6	53 18.9	0.0	80.2	53 36.5	3.5	82.9	53 48.5	7.0	85.6
18	52 20.8	8.0	73.4	52 52.5	4.7	76.0	53 18.9	− 1.3	78.6	53 40.0	2.2	81.2	53 55.5	5.7	83.9
19	52 12.8	9.3	71.8	52 47.8	6.1	74.3	53 17.6	2.7	76.9	53 42.2	+ 0.7	79.5	54 01.2	4.2	82.2
20	52 03.5	− 10.7	70.2	52 41.7	− 7.5	72.7	53 14.9	− 4.1	75.2	53 42.9	− 0.8	77.8	54 05.4	+ 2.7	80.5
21	51 52.8	11.9	68.6	52 34.2	8.7	71.0	53 10.8	5.6	73.5	53 42.1	2.1	76.2	54 08.1	+ 1.3	78.8
22	51 40.9	13.2	67.0	52 25.5	10.1	69.4	53 05.2	6.8	71.9	53 40.0	3.6	74.5	54 09.5	− 0.2	77.1
23	51 27.7	14.4	65.5	52 15.4	11.4	67.8	52 58.4	8.3	70.2	53 36.4	4.9	72.8	54 09.3	1.6	75.4
24	51 13.3	15.6	63.9	52 04.0	12.8	66.2	52 50.1	9.6	68.6	53 31.5	6.4	71.1	54 07.7	3.0	73.7
25	50 57.7	− 16.9	62.4	51 51.2	− 13.9	64.6	52 40.5	− 11.0	67.0	53 25.1	− 7.8	69.4	54 04.7	− 4.5	72.0
26	50 40.8	18.0	60.8	51 37.3	15.2	63.0	52 29.5	12.2	65.3	53 17.3	9.1	67.8	54 00.2	5.9	70.3
27	50 22.8	19.2	59.3	51 22.1	16.5	61.5	52 17.3	13.6	63.7	53 08.2	10.6	66.1	53 54.3	7.3	68.6
28	50 03.6	20.2	57.9	51 05.6	17.6	59.9	52 03.7	14.8	62.2	52 57.6	11.8	64.5	53 47.0	8.7	66.9
29	49 43.4	21.4	56.4	50 48.0	18.8	58.4	51 48.9	16.0	60.6	52 45.8	13.2	62.9	53 38.3	10.1	65.3

0°			2°			4°			6°			8°			Dec.
Hc	d	Z	Hc	d	Z	Hc	d	Z	Hc	d	Z	Hc	d	Z	
° ′	′	°	° ′	′	°	° ′	′	°	° ′	′	°	° ′	′	°	°
52 00.0	− 0.7	90.0	51 57.3	− 4.0	92.6	51 49.3	− 7.4	95.1	51 36.0	− 10.7	97.6	51 17.5	− 14.0	100.1	0
51 59.3	2.0	91.6	51 53.3	5.4	94.2	51 41.9	8.8	96.7	51 25.3	12.0	99.2	51 03.5	15.1	101.7	1
51 57.3	3.3	93.2	51 47.9	6.7	95.8	51 33.1	10.0	98.3	51 13.3	13.3	100.8	50 48.4	16.4	103.2	2
51 54.0	4.7	94.9	51 41.2	8.1	97.4	51 23.1	11.3	99.9	51 00.0	14.5	102.3	50 32.0	17.6	104.7	3
51 49.3	6.0	96.5	51 33.1	9.3	99.0	51 11.8	12.5	101.5	50 45.5	15.6	103.9	50 14.4	18.7	106.2	4
51 43.3	− 7.3	98.1	51 23.8	− 10.5	100.6	50 59.3	− 13.8	103.0	50 29.9	− 16.9	105.4	49 55.7	− 19.8	107.7	5
51 36.0	8.6	99.7	51 13.3	11.9	102.1	50 45.5	14.9	104.6	50 13.0	18.0	106.9	49 35.9	20.9	109.1	6
51 27.4	9.9	101.3	51 01.4	13.0	103.7	50 30.6	16.2	106.1	49 55.0	19.1	108.4	49 15.0	22.0	110.6	7
51 17.5	11.1	102.9	50 48.4	14.3	105.3	50 14.4	17.3	107.6	49 35.9	20.2	109.8	48 53.0	23.0	112.0	8
51 06.4	12.4	104.4	50 34.1	15.5	106.8	49 57.1	18.5	109.1	49 15.7	21.3	111.3	48 30.0	24.0	113.4	9
50 54.0	− 13.7	106.0	50 18.6	− 16.7	108.3	49 38.6	− 19.5	110.6	48 54.4	− 22.4	112.7	48 06.0	− 24.9	114.8	10
50 40.3	14.8	107.5	50 01.9	17.8	109.8	49 19.1	20.7	112.0	48 32.0	23.3	114.1	47 41.1	25.9	116.1	11
50 25.5	16.0	109.0	49 44.1	18.9	111.3	48 58.4	21.7	113.4	48 08.7	24.3	115.5	47 15.2	26.9	117.5	12
50 09.5	17.2	110.6	49 25.2	20.0	112.8	48 36.7	22.7	114.9	47 44.4	25.3	116.9	46 48.3	27.7	118.8	13
49 52.3	18.3	112.0	49 05.2	21.1	114.2	48 14.0	23.7	116.3	47 19.1	26.2	118.2	46 20.6	28.5	120.1	14
49 34.0	− 19.4	113.5	48 44.1	− 22.1	115.6	47 50.3	− 24.7	117.6	46 52.9	− 27.1	119.5	45 52.1	− 29.4	121.3	15
49 14.6	20.5	115.0	48 22.0	23.2	117.0	47 25.6	25.6	119.0	46 25.8	28.0	120.8	45 22.7	30.2	122.6	16
48 54.1	21.6	116.4	47 58.8	24.1	118.4	47 00.0	26.6	120.3	45 57.8	28.9	122.1	44 52.5	31.0	123.8	17
48 32.5	22.5	117.8	47 34.7	25.1	119.8	46 33.4	27.4	121.6	45 28.9	29.6	123.4	44 21.5	31.7	125.0	18
48 10.0	23.6	119.2	47 09.6	26.0	121.1	46 06.0	28.3	122.9	44 59.3	30.4	124.6	43 49.8	32.4	126.2	19
47 46.4	− 24.6	120.6	46 43.6	− 26.8	122.4	45 37.7	− 29.1	124.2	44 28.9	− 31.2	125.8	43 17.4	− 33.2	127.4	20
47 21.8	25.4	121.9	46 16.8	27.8	123.7	45 08.6	29.9	125.4	43 57.7	31.9	127.0	42 44.2	33.8	128.5	21
46 56.4	26.4	123.3	45 49.0	28.6	125.0	44 38.7	30.6	126.6	43 25.8	32.6	128.2	42 10.4	34.4	129.6	22
46 30.0	27.3	124.6	45 20.4	29.4	126.3	44 08.1	31.4	127.8	42 53.2	33.3	129.3	41 36.0	35.0	130.7	23
46 02.7	28.1	125.9	44 51.0	30.2	127.5	43 36.7	32.2	129.0	42 19.9	33.9	130.5	41 01.0	35.7	131.8	24
45 34.6	− 29.0	127.1	44 20.8	− 31.0	128.7	43 04.5	− 32.8	130.2	41 46.0	− 34.6	131.6	40 25.3	− 36.2	132.9	25
45 05.6	29.7	128.4	43 49.8	31.6	129.9	42 31.7	33.5	131.3	41 11.4	35.2	132.7	39 49.1	36.8	133.9	26
44 35.9	30.6	129.6	43 18.2	32.4	131.1	41 58.2	34.1	132.5	40 36.2	35.8	133.7	39 12.3	37.3	134.9	27
44 05.3	31.2	130.8	42 45.8	33.1	132.2	41 24.1	34.8	133.6	40 00.4	36.3	134.8	38 35.0	37.8	135.9	28
43 34.1	32.0	132.0	42 12.7	33.7	133.4	40 49.3	35.3	134.6	39 24.1	36.8	135.8	37 57.2	38.2	136.9	29

10°			12°			14°			16°			18°			Dec.
Hc	d	Z	Hc	d	Z	Hc	d	Z	Hc	d	Z	Hc	d	Z	
° ′	′	°	° ′	′	°	° ′	′	°	° ′	′	°	° ′	′	°	°
50 54.0	− 17.2	102.5	50 25.5	− 20.1	104.9	49 52.3	− 23.0	107.2	49 14.6	− 25.8	109.4	48 32.5	− 28.4	111.6	0
50 36.8	18.2	104.0	50 05.4	21.3	106.4	49 29.3	24.1	108.6	48 48.8	26.8	110.8	48 04.1	29.4	112.9	1
50 18.6	19.4	105.5	49 44.1	22.3	107.8	49 05.2	25.1	110.0	48 22.0	27.8	112.2	47 34.7	30.2	114.2	2
49 59.2	20.6	107.0	49 21.8	23.4	109.3	48 40.1	26.1	111.4	47 54.2	28.6	113.5	47 04.5	31.1	115.5	3
49 38.6	21.6	108.5	48 58.4	24.3	110.7	48 14.0	27.0	112.8	47 25.6	29.5	114.8	46 33.4	31.8	116.7	4
49 17.0	− 22.6	109.9	48 34.1	− 25.4	112.1	47 47.0	− 27.9	114.1	46 56.1	− 30.3	116.1	46 01.6	− 32.7	118.0	5
48 54.4	23.7	111.3	48 08.7	26.3	113.4	47 19.1	28.8	115.4	46 25.8	31.2	117.3	45 28.9	33.3	119.2	6
48 30.7	24.7	112.7	47 42.4	27.2	114.8	46 50.3	29.7	116.7	45 54.6	31.9	118.6	44 55.6	34.1	120.3	7
48 06.0	25.6	114.1	47 15.2	28.2	116.1	46 20.6	30.5	118.0	45 22.7	32.7	119.8	44 21.5	34.8	121.5	8
47 40.4	26.5	115.4	46 47.0	28.9	117.4	45 50.1	31.2	119.2	44 50.0	33.5	121.0	43 46.7	35.4	122.6	9
47 13.9	− 27.5	116.8	46 18.1	− 29.9	118.6	45 18.9	− 32.1	120.4	44 16.5	− 34.1	122.1	43 11.3	− 36.1	123.7	10
46 46.4	28.3	118.1	45 48.2	30.6	119.9	44 46.8	32.7	121.6	43 42.4	34.8	123.3	42 35.2	36.6	124.8	11
46 18.1	29.2	119.3	45 17.6	31.4	121.1	44 14.1	33.5	122.8	43 07.6	35.4	124.4	41 58.6	37.3	125.9	12
45 48.9	30.0	120.6	44 46.2	32.1	122.3	43 40.6	34.2	124.0	42 32.2	36.0	125.5	41 21.3	37.8	126.9	13
45 18.9	30.8	121.8	44 14.1	32.8	123.5	43 06.4	34.8	125.1	41 56.2	36.7	126.6	40 43.5	38.4	128.0	14
44 48.1	− 31.6	123.1	43 41.2	− 33.6	124.7	42 31.6	− 35.4	126.2	41 19.5	− 37.2	127.6	40 05.1	− 38.9	129.0	15
44 16.5	32.2	124.3	43 07.6	34.2	125.8	41 56.2	36.1	127.3	40 42.3	37.8	128.7	39 26.2	39.3	130.0	16
43 44.3	33.0	125.4	42 33.4	34.8	126.9	41 20.1	36.6	128.4	40 04.5	38.3	129.7	38 46.9	39.9	131.0	17
43 11.3	33.7	126.6	41 58.6	35.5	128.0	40 43.5	37.2	129.4	39 26.2	38.8	130.7	38 07.0	40.3	131.9	18
42 37.6	34.3	127.7	41 23.1	36.1	129.1	40 06.3	37.8	130.4	38 47.4	39.2	131.7	37 26.7	40.7	132.8	19
42 03.3	− 34.9	128.8	40 47.0	− 36.7	130.2	39 28.5	− 38.2	131.5	38 08.2	− 39.8	132.6	36 46.0	− 41.2	133.8	20
41 28.4	35.6	129.9	40 10.3	37.2	131.2	38 50.3	38.8	132.4	37 28.4	40.2	133.6	36 04.8	41.5	134.7	21
40 52.8	36.1	131.0	39 33.1	37.7	132.2	38 11.5	39.2	133.4	36 48.2	40.6	134.5	35 23.3	42.0	135.6	22
40 16.7	36.7	132.0	38 55.4	38.2	133.2	37 32.3	39.7	134.4	36 07.6	41.1	135.4	34 41.3	42.3	136.4	23
39 40.0	37.2	133.1	38 17.2	38.8	134.2	36 52.6	40.1	135.3	35 26.5	41.4	136.3	33 59.0	42.6	137.3	24
39 02.8	− 37.8	134.1	37 38.4	− 39.2	135.2	36 12.5	− 40.5	136.2	34 45.1	− 41.8	137.2	33 16.4	− 43.0	138.1	25
38 25.0	38.2	135.1	36 59.2	39.6	136.2	35 32.0	41.0	137.2	34 03.3	42.2	138.1	32 33.4	43.3	139.0	26
37 46.8	38.8	136.0	36 19.6	40.1	137.1	34 51.0	41.3	138.1	33 21.1	42.5	139.0	31 50.1	43.7	139.8	27
37 08.0	39.2	137.0	35 39.5	40.4	138.0	34 09.7	41.7	138.9	32 38.6	42.8	139.8	31 06.4	43.9	140.6	28
36 28.8	39.6	138.0	34 59.1	40.9	138.9	33 28.0	42.1	139.8	31 55.8	43.2	140.6	30 22.5	44.2	141.4	29

Dec.	20° Hc	d	Z	22° Hc	d	Z	24° Hc	d	Z	26° Hc	d	Z	28° Hc	d	Z
°	° ′	′	°	° ′	′	°	° ′	′	°	° ′	′	°	° ′	′	°
0	47 46.4	+30.1	113.6	46 56.4	+32.5	115.6	46 02.7	+34.8	117.5	45 05.6	+36.9	119.3	44 05.3	+38.9	121.0
1	48 16.5	29.2	112.3	47 28.9	31.7	114.4	46 37.5	34.0	116.3	45 42.5	36.3	118.2	44 44.2	38.4	119.9
2	48 45.7	28.3	111.0	48 00.6	30.8	113.1	47 11.5	33.3	115.1	46 18.8	35.5	117.0	45 22.6	37.6	118.8
3	49 14.0	27.3	109.7	48 31.4	30.0	111.8	47 44.8	32.5	113.9	46 54.3	34.9	115.9	46 00.2	37.1	117.7
4	49 41.3	26.4	108.3	49 01.4	29.1	110.5	48 17.3	31.6	112.6	47 29.2	34.0	114.7	46 37.3	36.3	116.6
5	50 07.7	+25.3	106.9	49 30.5	+28.1	109.2	48 48.9	+30.8	111.3	48 03.2	+33.3	113.4	47 13.6	+35.6	115.4
6	50 33.0	24.3	105.5	49 58.6	27.2	107.8	49 19.7	29.8	110.0	48 36.5	32.4	112.2	47 49.2	34.8	114.2
7	50 57.3	23.2	104.1	50 25.8	26.1	106.4	49 49.5	29.0	108.7	49 08.9	31.5	110.9	48 24.0	34.1	113.0
8	51 20.5	22.0	102.6	50 51.9	25.0	105.0	50 18.5	27.9	107.3	49 40.4	30.7	109.6	48 58.1	33.2	111.8
9	51 42.5	21.0	101.1	51 16.9	24.0	103.5	50 46.4	26.9	105.9	50 11.1	29.7	108.3	49 31.3	32.3	110.5
10	52 03.5	+19.7	99.6	51 40.9	+22.9	102.1	51 13.3	+25.9	104.5	50 40.8	+28.8	106.9	50 03.6	+31.5	109.2
11	52 23.2	18.5	98.0	52 03.8	21.7	100.6	51 39.2	24.8	103.1	51 09.6	27.7	105.5	50 35.1	30.5	107.9
12	52 41.7	17.2	96.5	52 25.5	20.5	99.1	52 04.0	23.6	101.6	51 37.3	26.7	104.1	51 05.6	29.6	106.5
13	52 58.9	16.0	94.9	52 46.0	19.2	97.5	52 27.6	22.5	100.1	52 04.0	25.5	102.6	51 35.2	28.5	105.1
14	53 14.9	14.6	93.3	53 05.2	18.1	95.9	52 50.1	21.3	98.6	52 29.5	24.5	101.2	52 03.7	27.5	103.7
15	53 29.5	+13.4	91.6	53 23.3	+16.7	94.3	53 11.4	+20.1	97.0	52 54.0	+23.3	99.6	52 31.2	+26.4	102.2
16	53 42.9	11.9	90.0	53 40.0	15.4	92.7	53 31.5	18.7	95.4	53 17.3	22.1	98.1	52 57.6	25.3	100.7
17	53 54.8	10.6	88.3	53 55.4	14.1	91.1	53 50.2	17.5	93.8	53 39.4	20.8	96.5	53 22.9	24.1	99.2
18	54 05.4	9.1	86.7	54 09.5	12.6	89.4	54 07.7	16.2	92.2	54 00.2	19.6	95.0	53 47.0	22.9	97.7
19	54 14.5	7.8	85.0	54 22.1	11.3	87.8	54 23.9	14.8	90.6	54 19.8	18.3	93.3	54 09.9	21.7	96.1
20	54 22.3	+6.3	83.3	54 33.4	+9.9	86.1	54 38.7	+13.4	88.9	54 38.1	+16.9	91.7	54 31.6	+20.3	94.5
21	54 28.6	4.8	81.6	54 43.3	8.4	84.4	54 52.1	12.0	87.2	54 55.0	15.5	90.0	54 51.9	19.1	92.9
22	54 33.4	3.4	79.9	54 51.7	6.9	82.7	55 04.1	10.5	85.5	55 10.5	14.1	88.4	55 11.0	17.6	91.2
23	54 36.8	1.9	78.1	54 58.6	5.5	80.9	55 14.6	9.1	83.8	55 24.6	12.7	86.6	55 28.6	16.3	89.5
24	54 38.7	+0.4	76.4	55 04.1	3.9	79.2	55 23.7	7.5	82.0	55 37.3	11.2	84.9	55 44.9	14.8	87.8
25	54 39.1	-1.0	74.7	55 08.0	+2.5	77.4	55 31.2	+6.1	80.3	55 48.5	+9.7	83.2	55 59.7	+13.4	86.1
26	54 38.1	2.5	73.0	55 10.5	+1.0	75.7	55 37.3	4.6	78.5	55 58.2	8.2	81.4	56 13.1	11.8	84.4
27	54 35.6	4.0	71.2	55 11.5	-0.5	73.9	55 41.9	3.0	76.8	56 06.4	6.7	79.6	56 24.9	10.4	82.6
28	54 31.6	5.5	69.5	55 11.0	2.1	72.2	55 44.9	+1.5	75.0	56 13.1	5.1	77.9	56 35.3	8.8	80.8
29	54 26.1	6.9	67.8	55 08.9	3.5	70.4	55 46.4	-0.1	73.2	56 18.2	3.5	76.1	56 44.1	7.2	79.0

Dec.	30° Hc	d	Z	32° Hc	d	Z	34° Hc	d	Z	36° Hc	d	Z	38° Hc	d	Z
°	° ′	′	°	° ′	′	°	° ′	′	°	° ′	′	°	° ′	′	°
0	43 02.1	+40.7	122.6	41 56.0	+42.5	124.1	40 47.4	+44.1	125.6	39 36.4	+45.6	127.0	38 23.2	+46.9	128.2
1	43 42.8	40.3	121.6	42 38.5	42.0	123.2	41 31.5	43.7	124.7	40 22.0	45.2	126.1	39 10.1	46.7	127.4
2	44 23.1	39.6	120.6	43 20.5	41.6	122.2	42 15.2	43.2	123.8	41 07.2	44.8	125.2	39 56.8	46.3	126.4
3	45 02.7	39.1	119.5	44 02.1	40.9	121.2	42 58.4	42.8	122.8	41 52.0	44.4	124.4	40 43.1	45.9	125.8
4	45 41.8	38.4	118.4	44 43.0	40.2	120.2	43 41.2	42.2	121.9	42 36.4	44.0	123.4	41 29.0	45.5	124.9
5	46 20.2	+37.8	117.3	45 23.4	+39.9	119.2	44 23.4	+41.7	120.9	43 20.4	+43.4	122.5	42 14.5	+45.1	124.1
6	46 58.0	37.1	116.2	46 03.3	39.2	118.1	45 05.1	41.2	119.9	44 03.8	43.0	121.6	42 59.6	44.7	123.2
7	47 35.1	36.4	115.0	46 42.5	38.6	117.0	45 46.3	40.6	118.8	44 46.8	42.5	120.6	43 44.3	44.2	122.2
8	48 11.5	35.7	113.9	47 21.1	37.9	115.9	46 26.9	40.0	117.8	45 29.3	42.0	119.6	44 28.5	43.8	121.3
9	48 47.2	34.8	112.6	47 59.0	37.1	114.7	47 06.9	39.4	116.7	46 11.3	41.4	118.6	45 12.3	43.2	120.3
10	49 22.0	+34.0	111.4	48 36.1	+36.5	113.5	47 46.3	+38.7	115.6	46 52.7	+40.8	117.5	45 55.5	+42.8	119.4
11	49 56.0	33.2	110.1	49 12.6	35.7	112.3	48 25.0	38.0	114.4	47 33.5	40.1	116.4	46 38.3	42.1	118.3
12	50 29.2	32.3	108.8	49 48.3	34.8	111.1	49 03.0	37.2	113.2	48 13.6	39.5	115.3	47 20.4	41.6	117.3
13	51 01.5	31.4	107.5	50 23.1	34.0	109.8	49 40.2	36.5	112.0	48 53.1	38.9	114.2	48 02.0	41.0	116.2
14	51 32.9	30.4	106.1	50 57.1	33.2	108.5	50 16.7	35.7	110.8	49 32.0	38.1	113.0	48 43.0	40.3	115.1
15	52 03.3	+29.3	104.7	51 30.3	+32.1	107.2	50 52.4	+34.9	109.5	50 10.1	+37.3	111.8	49 23.3	+39.7	114.0
16	52 32.6	28.4	103.3	52 02.4	31.3	105.8	51 27.3	34.0	108.2	50 47.4	36.5	110.6	50 03.0	38.9	112.8
17	53 01.0	27.2	101.9	52 33.7	30.2	104.4	52 01.3	33.0	106.9	51 23.9	35.7	109.3	50 41.9	38.2	111.6
18	53 28.2	26.1	100.4	53 03.9	29.2	103.0	52 34.3	32.1	105.5	51 59.6	34.9	108.0	51 20.1	37.4	110.4
19	53 54.3	24.9	98.8	53 33.1	28.0	101.5	53 06.4	31.1	104.1	52 34.5	33.9	106.7	51 57.5	36.6	109.2
20	54 19.2	+23.7	97.3	54 01.1	+27.0	100.0	53 37.5	+30.0	102.7	53 08.4	+32.9	105.3	52 34.1	+35.7	107.9
21	54 42.9	22.5	95.7	54 28.1	25.7	98.5	54 07.5	28.9	101.2	53 41.3	32.0	103.9	53 09.8	34.8	106.5
22	55 05.4	21.1	94.1	54 53.8	24.6	96.9	54 36.4	27.8	99.7	54 13.3	30.9	102.5	53 44.6	33.8	105.2
23	55 26.5	19.8	92.5	55 18.4	23.2	95.3	55 04.2	26.6	98.2	54 44.2	29.7	101.0	54 18.4	32.8	103.8
24	55 46.3	18.4	90.8	55 41.6	21.9	93.7	55 30.8	25.3	96.6	55 13.9	28.7	99.5	54 51.2	31.8	102.3
25	56 04.7	+17.0	89.1	56 03.5	+20.6	92.1	55 56.1	+24.1	95.0	55 42.6	+27.4	97.9	55 23.0	+30.7	100.8
26	56 21.7	15.6	87.4	56 24.1	19.2	90.4	56 20.2	22.7	93.4	56 10.0	26.2	96.4	55 53.7	29.5	99.3
27	56 37.3	14.0	85.6	56 43.3	17.7	88.6	56 42.9	21.4	91.7	56 36.2	24.9	94.7	56 23.2	28.2	97.7
28	56 51.3	12.5	83.8	57 01.0	16.3	86.9	57 04.3	19.9	90.0	57 01.1	23.5	93.1	56 51.4	27.1	96.1
29	57 03.8	11.0	82.0	57 17.3	14.7	85.1	57 24.2	18.4	88.2	57 24.6	22.1	91.4	57 18.5	25.7	94.5

20°			22°			24°			26°			28°			Dec.
Hc	d	Z	Hc	d	Z	Hc	d	Z	Hc	d	Z	Hc	d	Z	
° ′	′	°	° ′	′	°	° ′	′	°	° ′	′	°	° ′	′	°	°
47 46.4	-31.0	113.6	46 56.4	-33.3	115.6	46 02.7	-35.5	117.5	45 05.6	-37.6	119.3	44 05.3	-39.5	121.0	0
47 15.4	31.8	114.9	46 23.1	34.1	116.8	45 27.2	36.2	118.7	44 28.0	38.2	120.4	43 25.8	40.0	122.0	1
46 43.6	32.5	116.2	45 49.0	34.8	118.0	44 51.0	36.9	119.8	43 49.8	38.7	121.5	42 45.8	40.6	123.1	2
46 11.1	33.4	117.4	45 14.2	35.5	119.2	44 14.1	37.4	120.9	43 11.1	39.4	122.5	42 05.2	41.1	124.1	3
45 37.7	34.0	118.6	44 38.7	36.1	120.3	43 36.7	38.1	122.0	42 31.7	39.9	123.6	41 24.1	41.6	125.0	4
45 03.7	-34.8	119.7	44 02.6	-36.8	121.4	42 58.6	-38.7	123.0	41 51.8	-40.4	124.6	40 42.5	-42.1	126.0	5
44 28.9	35.4	120.9	43 25.8	37.4	122.5	42 19.9	39.2	124.1	41 11.4	40.9	125.5	40 00.4	42.4	126.9	6
43 53.5	36.1	122.0	42 48.4	38.0	123.6	41 40.7	39.7	125.1	40 30.5	41.4	126.5	39 18.0	43.0	127.8	7
43 17.4	36.8	123.1	42 10.4	38.5	124.6	41 01.0	40.3	126.1	39 49.1	41.8	127.5	38 35.0	43.3	128.7	8
42 40.6	37.3	124.2	41 31.9	39.1	125.7	40 20.7	40.7	127.1	39 07.3	42.3	128.4	37 51.7	43.7	129.6	9
42 03.3	-37.9	125.3	40 52.8	-39.6	126.7	39 40.0	-41.2	128.0	38 25.0	-42.7	129.3	37 08.0	-44.0	130.5	10
41 25.4	38.4	126.3	40 13.2	40.1	127.7	38 58.8	41.6	129.0	37 42.3	43.1	130.2	36 24.0	44.5	131.3	11
40 47.0	39.0	127.3	39 33.1	40.5	128.6	38 17.2	42.1	129.9	36 59.2	43.4	131.1	35 39.5	44.7	132.2	12
40 08.0	39.5	128.3	38 52.6	41.1	129.6	37 35.1	42.5	130.8	36 15.8	43.8	131.9	34 54.8	45.1	133.0	13
39 28.5	39.9	129.3	38 11.5	41.4	130.5	36 52.6	42.8	131.7	35 32.0	44.2	132.8	34 09.7	45.4	133.8	14
38 48.6	-40.4	130.3	37 30.1	-41.9	131.4	36 09.8	-43.3	132.6	34 47.8	-44.5	133.6	33 24.3	-45.7	134.6	15
38 08.2	40.9	131.2	36 48.2	42.3	132.3	35 26.5	43.5	133.4	34 03.3	44.8	134.4	32 38.6	45.9	135.3	16
37 27.3	41.3	132.1	36 05.9	42.6	133.2	34 43.0	44.0	134.3	33 18.5	45.1	135.2	31 52.7	46.3	136.1	17
36 46.0	41.7	133.0	35 23.3	43.0	134.1	33 59.0	44.2	135.1	32 33.4	45.4	136.0	31 06.4	46.4	136.9	18
36 04.3	42.1	133.9	34 40.3	43.4	134.9	33 14.8	44.6	135.9	31 48.0	45.7	136.8	30 20.0	46.8	137.6	19
35 22.2	-42.5	134.8	33 56.9	-43.7	135.8	32 30.2	-44.8	136.7	31 02.3	-45.9	137.5	29 33.2	-46.9	138.3	20
34 39.7	42.8	135.7	33 13.2	44.0	136.6	31 45.4	45.2	137.5	30 16.4	46.2	138.3	28 46.3	47.2	139.0	21
33 56.9	43.2	136.5	32 29.2	44.3	137.4	31 00.2	45.5	138.2	29 30.2	46.4	139.0	27 59.1	47.4	139.7	22
33 13.7	43.5	137.4	31 44.9	44.7	138.2	30 14.8	45.6	139.0	28 43.8	46.7	139.7	27 11.7	47.6	140.4	23
32 30.2	43.8	138.2	31 00.2	44.9	139.0	29 29.2	46.0	139.8	27 57.1	46.9	140.5	26 24.1	47.8	141.1	24
31 46.4	-44.1	139.0	30 15.3	-45.1	139.8	28 43.2	-46.1	140.5	27 10.2	-47.1	141.2	25 36.3	-47.9	141.8	25
31 02.3	44.4	139.8	29 30.2	45.4	140.5	27 57.1	46.4	141.2	26 23.1	47.2	141.9	24 48.4	48.2	142.4	26
30 17.9	44.7	140.6	28 44.8	45.7	141.3	27 10.7	46.6	141.9	25 35.9	47.5	142.5	24 00.2	48.3	143.1	27
29 33.2	44.9	141.3	27 59.1	45.9	142.0	26 24.1	46.8	142.6	24 48.4	47.7	143.2	23 11.9	48.4	143.7	28
28 48.3	45.2	142.1	27 13.2	46.1	142.7	25 37.3	47.0	143.3	24 00.7	47.8	143.9	22 23.5	48.6	144.4	29

30°			32°			34°			36°			38°			Dec.
Hc	d	Z	Hc	d	Z	Hc	d	Z	Hc	d	Z	Hc	d	Z	
° ′	′	°	° ′	′	°	° ′	′	°	° ′	′	°	° ′	′	°	°
43 02.1	-41.3	122.6	41 56.0	-42.9	124.1	40 47.4	-44.5	125.6	39 36.4	-46.0	127.0	38 23.2	-47.3	128.2	0
42 20.8	41.8	123.6	41 13.1	43.5	125.1	40 02.9	44.9	126.5	38 50.4	46.2	127.8	37 35.9	47.6	129.0	1
41 39.0	42.3	124.6	40 29.6	43.8	126.0	39 18.0	45.3	127.3	38 04.2	46.7	128.6	36 48.3	47.9	129.8	2
40 56.7	42.7	125.5	39 45.8	44.2	126.9	38 32.7	45.6	128.2	37 17.5	46.9	129.4	36 00.4	48.1	130.5	3
40 14.0	43.2	126.4	39 01.6	44.6	127.8	37 47.1	46.0	129.0	36 30.6	47.3	130.2	35 12.3	48.4	131.3	4
39 30.8	-43.5	127.3	38 17.0	-45.0	128.6	37 01.1	-46.3	129.8	35 43.3	-47.5	130.9	34 23.9	-48.7	132.0	5
38 47.3	44.0	128.2	37 32.0	45.4	129.5	36 14.8	46.6	130.6	34 55.8	47.8	131.7	33 35.2	48.9	132.7	6
38 03.3	44.3	129.1	36 46.6	45.6	130.3	35 28.2	46.9	131.4	34 08.0	48.0	132.4	32 46.3	49.1	133.4	7
37 19.0	44.7	130.0	36 01.0	46.0	131.1	34 41.3	47.2	132.1	33 20.0	48.3	133.1	31 57.2	49.3	134.1	8
36 34.3	45.1	130.8	35 15.0	46.3	131.9	33 54.1	47.4	132.9	32 31.7	48.5	133.8	31 07.9	49.5	134.7	9
35 49.2	-45.3	131.6	34 28.7	-46.6	132.6	33 06.7	-47.7	133.6	31 43.2	-48.8	134.5	30 18.4	-49.8	135.4	10
35 03.9	45.7	132.4	33 42.1	46.8	133.4	32 19.0	48.0	134.3	30 54.4	48.9	135.2	29 28.6	49.9	136.0	11
34 18.2	46.0	133.2	32 55.3	47.1	134.2	31 31.0	48.1	135.1	30 05.5	49.2	135.9	28 38.7	50.1	136.7	12
33 32.2	46.3	134.0	32 08.2	47.4	134.9	30 42.9	48.4	135.8	29 16.3	49.3	136.6	27 48.6	50.2	137.3	13
32 45.9	46.5	134.7	31 20.8	47.6	135.6	29 54.5	48.6	136.4	28 27.0	49.6	137.2	26 58.4	50.4	137.9	14
31 59.4	-46.8	135.5	30 33.2	-47.8	136.3	29 05.9	-48.8	137.1	27 37.4	-49.7	137.8	26 08.0	-50.6	138.5	15
31 12.6	47.0	136.2	29 45.4	48.0	137.0	28 17.1	49.0	137.8	26 47.7	49.9	138.5	25 17.4	50.7	139.1	16
30 25.6	47.3	136.9	28 57.4	48.3	137.7	27 28.1	49.2	138.4	25 57.8	50.0	139.1	24 26.7	50.8	139.7	17
29 38.3	47.5	137.6	28 09.1	48.4	138.4	26 38.9	49.3	139.1	25 07.8	50.2	139.7	23 35.9	51.0	140.3	18
28 50.8	47.7	138.3	27 20.7	48.7	139.1	25 49.6	49.5	139.7	24 17.6	50.3	140.3	22 44.9	51.1	140.9	19
28 03.1	-47.9	139.0	26 32.0	-48.8	139.7	25 00.1	-49.7	140.3	23 27.3	-50.4	140.9	21 53.8	-51.2	141.4	20
27 15.2	48.1	139.7	25 43.2	49.0	140.4	24 10.4	49.8	140.9	22 36.9	50.6	141.5	21 02.6	51.3	142.0	21
26 27.1	48.3	140.4	24 54.2	49.1	141.0	23 20.6	49.9	141.6	21 46.3	50.7	142.1	20 11.3	51.4	142.5	22
25 38.8	48.5	141.0	24 05.1	49.3	141.7	22 30.7	50.1	142.2	20 55.6	50.8	142.6	19 19.9	51.5	143.1	23
24 50.3	48.6	141.7	23 15.8	49.4	142.3	21 40.6	50.2	142.8	20 04.8	50.9	143.2	18 28.4	51.6	143.6	24
24 01.7	-48.8	142.3	22 26.4	-49.6	142.9	20 50.4	-50.3	143.3	19 13.9	-51.1	143.8	17 36.8	-51.7	144.2	25
23 12.9	48.9	143.0	21 36.8	49.7	143.5	20 00.1	50.5	143.9	18 22.8	51.1	144.3	16 45.1	51.8	144.7	26
22 24.0	49.1	143.6	20 47.1	49.9	144.1	19 09.6	50.5	144.5	17 31.7	51.2	144.9	15 53.3	51.8	145.2	27
21 34.9	49.2	144.2	19 57.2	49.9	144.7	18 19.1	50.6	145.1	16 40.5	51.3	145.4	15 01.5	51.9	145.7	28
20 45.7	49.4	144.8	19 07.3	50.1	145.3	17 28.5	50.8	145.6	15 49.2	51.4	146.0	14 09.6	52.0	146.3	29

Dec.	40° Hc	d	Z	42° Hc	d	Z	44° Hc	d	Z	46° Hc	d	Z	48° Hc	d	Z
°	° ′	′	°	° ′	′	°	° ′	′	°	° ′	′	°	° ′	′	°
0	37 07.9	+48.2	129.4	35 50.7	+49.5	130.6	34 31.8	+50.5	131.6	33 11.3	+51.5	132.6	31 49.3	+52.4	133.6
1	37 56.1	48.0	128.7	36 40.2	49.1	129.9	35 22.3	50.3	131.0	34 02.8	51.3	132.0	32 41.7	52.3	133.0
2	38 44.1	47.6	127.9	37 29.3	48.9	129.2	36 12.6	50.0	130.3	34 54.1	51.1	131.4	33 34.0	52.0	132.4
3	39 31.7	47.3	127.1	38 18.2	48.6	128.4	37 02.6	49.8	129.6	35 45.2	50.9	130.7	34 26.0	51.9	131.8
4	40 19.0	47.0	126.3	39 06.8	48.3	127.7	37 52.4	49.6	128.9	36 36.1	50.6	130.1	35 17.9	51.7	131.2
5	41 06.0	+46.6	125.5	39 55.1	+48.0	126.9	38 42.0	+49.2	128.2	37 26.7	+50.5	129.4	36 09.6	+51.5	130.6
6	41 52.6	46.3	124.7	40 43.1	47.7	126.1	39 31.2	49.0	127.5	38 17.2	50.2	128.7	37 01.1	51.3	129.9
7	42 38.9	45.8	123.8	41 30.8	47.3	125.3	40 20.2	48.7	126.7	39 07.4	49.9	128.0	37 52.4	51.1	129.3
8	43 24.7	45.4	122.9	42 18.1	46.9	124.5	41 08.9	48.4	125.9	39 57.3	49.7	127.3	38 43.5	50.8	128.6
9	44 10.1	45.0	122.0	43 05.0	46.6	123.6	41 57.3	48.0	125.1	40 46.9	49.4	126.6	39 34.3	50.6	127.9
10	44 55.1	+44.5	121.1	43 51.6	+46.2	122.8	42 45.3	+47.7	124.3	41 36.3	+49.1	125.8	40 24.9	+50.3	127.2
11	45 39.6	44.1	120.2	44 37.8	45.7	121.9	43 33.0	47.3	123.5	42 25.4	48.7	125.0	41 15.2	50.1	126.5
12	46 23.7	43.5	119.2	45 23.5	45.3	121.0	44 20.3	46.9	122.7	43 14.1	48.4	124.3	42 05.3	49.7	125.8
13	47 07.2	43.0	118.2	46 08.8	44.8	120.0	45 07.2	46.5	121.8	44 02.5	48.1	123.4	42 55.0	49.5	125.0
14	47 50.2	42.4	117.1	46 53.6	44.3	119.1	45 53.7	46.0	120.9	44 50.6	47.6	122.6	43 44.5	49.1	124.2
15	48 32.6	+41.8	116.1	47 37.9	+43.8	118.1	46 39.7	+45.6	119.9	45 38.2	+47.3	121.7	44 33.6	+48.8	123.4
16	49 14.4	41.1	115.0	48 21.7	43.2	117.0	47 25.3	45.2	119.0	46 25.5	46.8	120.8	45 22.4	48.4	122.6
17	49 55.5	40.5	113.9	49 04.9	42.7	116.0	48 10.5	44.6	118.0	47 12.3	46.4	119.9	46 10.8	48.0	121.8
18	50 36.0	39.8	112.7	49 47.6	42.0	114.9	48 55.1	44.0	117.0	47 58.7	45.9	119.0	46 58.8	47.6	120.9
19	51 15.8	39.1	111.5	50 29.6	41.3	113.8	49 39.1	43.5	116.0	48 44.6	45.4	118.0	47 46.4	47.2	120.0
20	51 54.9	+38.3	110.3	51 10.9	+40.7	112.6	50 22.6	+42.8	114.9	49 30.0	+44.9	117.0	48 33.6	+46.7	119.1
21	52 33.2	37.4	109.0	51 51.6	39.9	111.5	51 05.4	42.3	113.8	50 14.9	44.3	116.0	49 20.3	46.3	118.1
22	53 10.6	36.6	107.7	52 31.5	39.2	110.2	51 47.7	41.5	112.6	50 59.2	43.8	114.9	50 06.6	45.7	117.1
23	53 47.2	35.7	106.4	53 10.7	38.3	109.0	52 29.2	40.8	111.5	51 43.0	43.1	113.8	50 52.3	45.2	116.1
24	54 22.9	34.7	105.0	53 49.0	37.5	107.7	53 10.0	40.1	110.2	52 26.1	42.4	112.7	51 37.5	44.6	115.0
25	54 57.6	+33.7	103.6	54 26.5	+36.6	106.4	53 50.1	+39.2	109.0	53 08.5	+41.7	111.5	52 22.1	+43.9	114.0
26	55 31.3	32.6	102.2	55 03.1	35.6	105.0	54 29.3	38.4	107.7	53 50.2	40.9	110.3	53 06.0	43.4	112.8
27	56 03.9	31.6	100.7	55 38.7	34.6	103.6	55 07.7	37.5	106.4	54 31.1	40.2	109.1	53 49.4	42.6	111.7
28	56 35.5	30.3	99.2	56 13.3	33.6	102.1	55 45.2	36.5	105.0	55 11.3	39.3	107.8	54 32.0	41.8	110.5
29	57 05.8	29.2	97.6	56 46.9	32.4	100.6	56 21.7	35.5	103.6	55 50.6	38.4	106.5	55 13.8	41.1	109.2

Dec.	50° Hc	d	Z	52° Hc	d	Z	54° Hc	d	Z	56° Hc	d	Z	58° Hc	d	Z
°	° ′	′	°	° ′	′	°	° ′	′	°	° ′	′	°	° ′	′	°
0	30 26.0	+53.2	134.4	29 01.3	+54.0	135.2	27 35.6	+54.7	136.0	26 08.7	+55.4	136.7	24 40.9	+56.0	137.3
1	31 19.2	53.1	133.9	29 55.3	53.9	134.7	28 30.3	54.6	135.5	27 04.1	55.3	136.3	25 36.9	55.9	136.9
2	32 12.3	53.0	133.4	30 49.2	53.8	134.2	29 24.9	54.5	135.1	27 59.4	55.2	135.8	26 32.8	55.8	136.5
3	33 05.3	52.8	132.8	31 43.0	53.7	133.7	30 19.4	54.4	134.6	28 54.6	55.1	135.4	27 28.6	55.8	136.1
4	33 58.1	52.6	132.2	32 36.7	53.5	133.2	31 13.8	54.4	134.1	29 49.7	55.0	134.9	28 24.4	55.7	135.7
5	34 50.7	+52.5	131.6	33 30.2	+53.4	132.6	32 08.2	+54.1	133.6	30 44.7	+55.0	134.5	29 20.1	+55.6	135.3
6	35 43.2	52.3	131.0	34 23.6	53.2	132.1	33 02.3	54.1	133.1	31 39.7	54.8	134.0	30 15.7	55.5	134.9
7	36 35.5	52.1	130.4	35 16.8	53.0	131.5	33 56.4	53.9	132.6	32 34.5	54.7	133.5	31 11.2	55.4	134.4
8	37 27.6	51.9	129.8	36 09.8	52.9	131.0	34 50.3	53.8	132.0	33 29.2	54.6	133.0	32 06.6	55.3	134.0
9	38 19.5	51.7	129.2	37 02.7	52.7	130.4	35 44.1	53.6	131.5	34 23.8	54.4	132.5	33 01.9	55.2	133.5
10	39 11.2	+51.5	128.5	37 55.4	+52.6	129.8	36 37.7	+53.5	130.9	35 18.2	+54.4	132.0	33 57.1	+55.1	133.0
11	40 02.7	51.2	127.9	38 48.0	52.3	129.2	37 31.2	53.3	130.4	36 12.6	54.2	131.5	34 52.2	55.0	132.6
12	40 53.9	51.0	127.2	39 40.3	52.1	128.5	38 24.5	53.1	129.8	37 06.8	54.0	131.0	35 47.2	54.9	132.1
13	41 44.9	50.7	126.5	40 32.4	51.9	127.9	39 17.6	53.0	129.2	38 00.8	53.9	130.4	36 42.1	54.7	131.6
14	42 35.6	50.5	125.8	41 24.3	51.6	127.2	40 10.6	52.7	128.6	38 54.7	53.7	129.9	37 36.8	54.6	131.1
15	43 26.1	+50.2	125.0	42 15.9	+51.4	126.5	41 03.3	+52.6	127.9	39 48.4	+53.6	129.3	38 31.4	+54.5	130.5
16	44 16.3	49.8	124.3	43 07.3	51.2	125.8	41 55.9	52.3	127.3	40 42.0	53.3	128.7	39 25.9	54.3	130.0
17	45 06.1	49.5	123.5	43 58.5	50.8	125.1	42 48.2	52.0	126.6	41 35.3	53.2	128.1	40 20.2	54.2	129.4
18	45 55.6	49.2	122.7	44 49.3	50.6	124.4	43 40.2	51.9	126.0	42 28.5	53.0	127.5	41 14.4	53.9	128.9
19	46 44.8	48.8	121.8	45 39.9	50.3	123.6	44 32.1	51.5	125.3	43 21.5	52.7	126.8	42 08.3	53.8	128.3
20	47 33.6	+48.4	121.0	46 30.2	+49.9	122.8	45 23.6	+51.3	124.5	44 14.2	+52.5	126.1	43 02.1	+53.6	127.7
21	48 22.0	48.0	120.1	47 20.1	49.5	122.0	46 14.9	51.0	123.8	45 06.7	52.2	125.5	43 55.7	53.4	127.1
22	49 10.0	47.5	119.2	48 09.6	49.2	121.2	47 05.9	50.6	123.0	45 58.9	52.0	124.8	44 49.1	53.2	126.4
23	49 57.5	47.1	118.2	48 58.8	48.8	120.3	47 56.5	50.3	122.2	46 50.9	51.7	124.0	45 42.3	52.9	125.7
24	50 44.6	46.5	117.3	49 47.6	48.3	119.4	48 46.8	50.0	121.4	47 42.6	51.4	123.3	46 35.2	52.7	125.1
25	51 31.1	+46.0	116.3	50 35.9	+47.9	118.5	49 36.8	+49.6	120.6	48 34.0	+51.1	122.5	47 27.9	+52.4	124.4
26	52 17.1	45.5	115.2	51 23.8	47.4	117.5	50 26.4	49.1	119.7	49 25.1	50.7	121.7	48 20.3	52.1	123.6
27	53 02.6	44.9	114.2	52 11.2	46.9	116.5	51 15.5	48.8	118.8	50 15.8	50.4	120.9	49 12.4	51.8	122.9
28	53 47.5	44.2	113.0	52 58.1	46.4	115.5	52 04.3	48.2	117.8	51 06.2	50.0	120.0	50 04.2	51.6	122.1
29	54 31.7	43.5	111.9	53 44.5	45.7	114.4	52 52.5	47.8	116.9	51 56.2	49.5	119.1	50 55.8	51.1	121.3

40°			42°			44°			46°			48°			Dec.
Hc	d	Z	Hc	d	Z	Hc	d	Z	Hc	d	Z	Hc	d	Z	°
37 07.9	−48.5	129.4	35 50.7	−49.6	130.6	34 31.8	−50.7	131.6	33 11.3	−51.6	132.6	31 49.3	−52.5	133.6	0
36 19.4	48.8	130.2	35 01.1	49.9	131.3	33 41.1	50.8	132.3	32 19.7	51.9	133.2	30 56.8	52.7	134.1	1
35 30.6	49.0	130.9	34 11.2	50.1	131.9	32 50.3	51.1	132.9	31 27.8	52.0	133.8	30 04.1	52.9	134.7	2
34 41.6	49.3	131.6	33 21.1	50.3	132.6	31 59.2	51.3	133.5	30 35.8	52.1	134.4	29 11.2	52.9	135.2	3
33 52.3	49.5	132.3	32 30.8	50.5	133.3	31 07.9	51.4	134.2	29 43.7	52.3	135.0	28 18.3	53.1	135.8	4
33 02.8	−49.7	133.0	31 40.3	−50.7	133.9	30 16.5	−51.6	134.8	28 51.4	−52.4	135.6	27 25.2	−53.2	136.3	5
32 13.1	49.9	133.6	30 49.6	50.8	134.5	29 24.9	51.7	135.3	27 59.0	52.6	136.1	26 32.0	53.3	136.8	6
31 23.2	50.1	134.3	29 58.8	51.0	135.1	28 33.2	51.9	135.9	27 06.4	52.7	136.6	25 38.7	53.5	137.3	7
30 33.1	50.3	134.9	29 07.8	51.2	135.7	27 41.3	52.1	136.5	26 13.7	52.8	137.2	24 45.2	53.5	137.8	8
29 42.8	50.5	135.6	28 16.6	51.4	136.3	26 49.2	52.1	137.0	25 20.9	52.9	137.7	23 51.7	53.6	138.3	9
28 52.3	−50.6	136.2	27 25.2	−51.5	136.9	25 57.1	−52.3	137.6	24 28.0	−53.0	138.2	22 58.1	−53.7	138.8	10
28 01.7	50.8	136.8	26 33.7	51.6	137.5	25 04.8	52.4	138.1	23 35.0	53.1	138.7	22 04.4	53.8	139.3	11
27 10.9	50.9	137.4	25 42.1	51.7	138.1	24 12.4	52.5	138.7	22 41.9	53.2	139.2	21 10.6	53.8	139.8	12
26 20.0	51.1	138.0	24 50.4	51.9	138.6	23 19.9	52.6	139.2	21 48.7	53.3	139.7	20 16.8	54.0	140.2	13
25 28.9	51.3	138.6	23 58.5	52.0	139.2	22 27.3	52.7	139.7	20 55.4	53.4	140.2	19 22.8	54.0	140.7	14
24 37.6	−51.4	139.1	23 06.5	−52.1	139.7	21 34.6	−52.8	140.2	20 02.0	−53.5	140.7	18 28.8	−54.1	141.2	15
23 46.3	51.5	139.7	22 14.4	52.2	140.3	20 41.8	52.9	140.8	19 08.5	53.5	141.2	17 34.7	54.1	141.6	16
22 54.8	51.6	140.3	21 22.2'	52.3	140.8	19 48.9	53.0	141.3	18 15.0	53.6	141.7	16 40.6	54.2	142.1	17
22 03.2	51.7	140.8	20 29.9	52.4	141.3	18 55.9	53.0	141.8	17 21.4	53.7	142.2	15 46.4	54.3	142.5	18
21 11.5	51.8	141.4	19 37.5	52.5	141.8	18 02.9	53.2	142.2	16 27.7	53.7	142.6	14 52.1	54.3	143.0	19
20 19.7	−51.9	141.9	18 45.0	−52.6	142.3	17 09.7	−53.2	142.7	15 34.0	−53.8	143.1	13 57.8	−54.3	143.4	20
19 27.8	52.0	142.4	17 52.4	52.6	142.8	16 16.5	53.2	143.2	14 40.2	53.8	143.5	13 03.5	54.4	143.8	21
18 35.8	52.1	143.0	16 59.8	52.8	143.4	15 23.3	53.4	143.7	13 46.4	53.9	144.0	12 09.1	54.4	144.3	22
17 43.7	52.2	143.5	16 07.0	52.8	143.8	14 29.9	53.3	144.2	12 52.5	54.0	144.5	11 14.7	54.5	144.7	23
16 51.5	52.2	144.0	15 14.2	52.8	144.3	13 36.6	53.5	144.6	11 58.5	54.0	144.9	10 20.2	54.5	145.1	24
15 59.3	−52.3	144.5	14 21.4	−52.9	144.8	12 43.1	−53.5	145.1	11 04.5	−54.0	145.3	9 25.7	−54.5	145.6	25
15 07.0	52.4	145.0	13 28.5	53.0	145.3	11 49.6	53.5	145.6	10 10.5	54.0	145.8	8 31.2	54.6	146.0	26
14 14.6	52.5	145.5	12 35.5	53.0	145.8	10 56.1	53.6	146.0	9 16.5	54.1	146.2	7 36.6	54.6	146.4	27
13 22.1	52.5	146.0	11 42.5	53.1	146.3	10 02.5	53.6	146.5	8 22.4	54.1	146.7	6 42.0	54.6	146.8	28
12 29.6	52.5	146.5	10 49.4	53.1	146.8	9 08.9	53.6	146.9	7 28.3	54.2	147.1	5 47.4	54.6	147.2	29

50°			52°			54°			56°			58°			Dec.
Hc	d	Z	Hc	d	Z	Hc	d	Z	Hc	d	Z	Hc	d	Z	°
30 26.0	−53.4	134.4	29 01.3	−54.1	135.2	27 35.6	−54.9	136.0	26 08.7	−55.4	136.7	24 40.9	−56.0	137.3	0
29 32.6	53.5	135.0	28 07.2	54.2	135.7	26 40.7	54.9	136.5	25 13.3	55.5	137.1	23 44.9	56.1	137.7	1
28 39.1	53.6	135.5	27 13.0	54.3	136.2	25 45.8	54.9	136.9	24 17.8	55.6	137.5	22 48.8	56.1	138.1	2
27 45.5	53.7	136.0	26 18.7	54.5	136.7	24 50.9	55.1	137.3	23 22.2	55.7	138.0	21 52.7	56.2	138.5	3
26 51.8	53.9	136.5	25 24.2	54.5	137.2	23 55.8	55.1	137.8	22 26.5	55.9	138.4	20 56.5	56.3	138.9	4
25 57.9	−53.9	137.0	24 29.7	−54.6	137.6	23 00.7	−55.2	138.2	21 30.8	−55.8	138.8	20 00.2	−56.3	139.3	5
25 04.0	54.0	137.5	23 35.1	54.6	138.1	22 05.5	55.3	138.6	20 35.0	55.8	139.2	19 03.9	56.3	139.6	6
24 10.0	54.1	138.0	22 40.5	54.8	138.5	21 10.2	55.3	139.1	19 39.2	55.9	139.5	18 07.6	56.4	140.0	7
23 15.9	54.2	138.4	21 45.7	54.8	139.0	20 14.9	55.4	139.5	18 43.3	55.9	139.9	17 11.2	56.4	140.3	8
22 21.7	54.3	138.9	20 50.9	54.8	139.4	19 19.5	55.5	139.9	17 47.4	55.9	140.3	16 14.8	56.4	140.7	9
21 27.4	−54.3	139.3	19 56.1	−55.0	139.8	18 24.0	−55.5	140.3	16 51.5	−56.0	140.7	15 18.4	−56.5	141.1	10
20 33.1	54.4	139.8	19 01.1	55.0	140.3	17 28.5	55.6	140.7	15 55.5	56.1	141.1	14 21.9	56.5	141.4	11
19 38.7	54.5	140.3	18 06.1	55.0	140.7	16 33.0	55.6	141.1	14 59.4	56.1	141.4	13 25.4	56.6	141.7	12
18 44.2	54.5	140.7	17 11.1	55.2	141.1	15 37.4	55.6	141.5	14 03.3	56.1	141.8	12 28.8	56.5	142.1	13
17 49.7	54.6	141.1	16 16.0	55.2	141.5	14 41.8	55.7	141.9	13 07.2	56.1	142.2	11 32.3	56.6	142.4	14
16 55.1	−54.7	141.6	15 20.8	−55.2	141.9	13 46.1	−55.7	142.2	12 11.1	−56.2	142.5	10 35.7	−56.6	142.8	15
16 00.4	54.7	142.0	14 25.6	55.2	142.3	12 50.4	55.7	142.6	11 14.9	56.2	142.9	9 39.1	56.6	143.1	16
15 05.7	54.7	142.4	13 30.4	55.3	142.7	11 54.7	55.7	143.0	10 18.7	56.2	143.2	8 42.5	56.7	143.4	17
14 11.0	54.8	142.8	12 35.1	55.3	143.1	10 59.0	55.8	143.4	9 22.5	56.2	143.6	7 45.8	56.7	143.8	18
13 16.2	54.9	143.3	11 39.8	55.3	143.5	10 03.2	55.8	143.8	8 26.3	56.3	144.0	6 49.1	56.6	144.1	19
12 21.3	−54.9	143.7	10 44.5	−55.4	143.9	9 07.4	−55.9	144.1	7 30.0	−56.3	144.3	5 52.5	−56.7	144.4	20
11 26.4	54.9	144.1	9 49.1	55.4	144.3	8 11.5	55.8	144.5	6 33.7	56.3	144.7	4 55.8	56.7	144.8	21
10 31.5	54.9	144.5	8 53.7	55.4	144.7	7 15.7	55.9	144.9	5 37.4	56.3	145.0	3 59.1	56.7	145.1	22
9 36.6	55.0	144.9	7 58.3	55.5	145.1	6 19.8	55.9	145.2	4 41.1	56.3	145.3	3 02.4	56.7	145.4	23
8 41.6	55.0	145.3	7 02.8	55.4	145.5	5 23.9	55.9	145.6	3 44.8	56.3	145.7	2 05.7	56.7	145.7	24
7 46.6	−55.0	145.7	6 07.4	−55.5	145.9	4 28.0	−55.9	146.0	2 48.5	−56.3	146.0	1 09.0	−56.8	146.1	25
6 51.6	55.0	146.1	5 11.9	55.5	146.2	3 32.1	55.9	146.3	1 52.2	56.3	146.4	0 12.2	−56.7	146.4	26
5 56.6	55.1	146.5	4 16.4	55.5	146.6	2 36.2	56.0	146.7	0 55.9	−56.4	146.7	0 44.5	+56.7	33.3	27
5 01.5	55.1	146.9	3 20.9	55.5	147.0	1 40.2	55.9	147.1	0 00.5	+56.3	32.9	1 41.2	56.7	32.9	28
4 06.5	55.1	147.3	2 25.4	55.5	147.4	0 44.3	−55.9	147.4	0 56.8	56.3	32.6	2 37.9	56.7	32.6	29

LATITUDE **SAME** NAME   L.H.A. 142°, 218°

Dec.	0° Hc	d	Z	2° Hc	d	Z	4° Hc	d	Z	6° Hc	d	Z	8° Hc	d	Z
0	50 00.0	− 0.6	90.0	49 57.5	+ 2.6	92.4	49 50.0	+ 5.9	94.8	49 37.6	+ 9.1	97.1	49 20.4	+12.2	99.4
1	49 59.4	1.9	88.4	50 00.1	1.4	90.8	49 55.9	4.7	93.2	49 46.7	7.9	95.6	49 32.6	11.1	97.9
2	49 57.5	3.1	86.9	50 01.5	+ 0.2	89.3	50 00.6	3.3	91.7	49 54.6	6.6	94.0	49 43.7	9.8	96.4
3	49 54.4	4.4	85.3	50 01.7	− 1.1	87.7	50 03.9	2.2	90.1	50 01.2	5.4	92.5	49 53.5	8.7	94.9
4	49 50.0	5.5	83.8	50 00.6	2.4	86.2	50 06.1	+ 0.9	88.5	50 06.6	4.2	90.9	50 02.2	7.4	93.3
5	49 44.5	− 6.9	82.2	49 58.2	− 3.6	84.6	50 07.0	− 0.4	87.0	50 10.8	+ 2.9	89.4	50 09.6	+ 6.1	91.8
6	49 37.6	8.0	80.7	49 54.6	4.9	83.1	50 06.6	1.6	85.4	50 13.7	1.7	87.8	50 15.7	5.0	90.2
7	49 29.6	9.2	79.2	49 49.7	6.0	81.5	50 05.0	2.8	83.9	50 15.4	+ 0.3	86.3	50 20.7	3.6	88.7
8	49 20.4	10.4	77.7	49 43.7	7.3	80.0	50 02.2	4.1	82.3	50 15.7	− 0.8	84.7	50 24.3	2.4	87.1
9	49 10.0	11.6	76.2	49 36.4	8.5	78.4	49 58.1	5.4	80.8	50 14.9	2.1	83.1	50 26.7	+ 1.2	85.5
10	48 58.4	−12.7	74.7	49 27.9	− 9.7	76.9	49 52.7	− 6.6	79.2	50 12.8	− 3.4	81.6	50 27.9	− 0.2	84.0
11	48 45.7	13.9	73.2	49 18.2	10.9	75.4	49 46.1	7.7	77.7	50 09.4	4.6	80.0	50 27.7	1.4	82.4
12	48 31.8	15.0	71.7	49 07.3	12.0	73.9	49 38.4	9.0	76.1	50 04.8	5.9	78.5	50 26.3	2.6	80.8
13	48 16.8	16.1	70.2	48 55.3	13.2	72.4	49 29.4	10.2	74.6	49 58.9	7.1	76.9	50 23.7	3.9	79.3
14	48 00.7	17.1	68.8	48 42.1	14.3	70.9	49 19.2	11.4	73.1	49 51.8	8.3	75.4	50 19.8	5.2	77.7
15	47 43.6	−18.2	67.4	48 27.8	−15.5	69.4	49 07.8	−12.5	71.6	49 43.5	− 9.6	73.8	50 14.6	− 6.5	76.1
16	47 25.4	19.3	66.0	48 12.3	16.5	68.0	48 55.3	13.7	70.1	49 33.9	10.7	72.3	50 08.1	7.6	74.6
17	47 06.1	20.2	64.6	47 55.8	17.6	66.6	48 41.6	14.8	68.6	49 23.2	11.9	70.8	50 00.5	8.9	73.0
18	46 45.9	21.2	63.2	47 38.2	18.6	65.1	48 26.8	15.9	67.2	49 11.3	13.1	69.3	49 51.6	10.1	71.5
19	46 24.7	22.2	61.8	47 19.6	19.6	63.7	48 10.9	17.0	65.7	48 58.2	14.2	67.8	49 41.5	11.3	70.0
20	46 02.5	−23.1	60.5	47 00.0	−20.7	62.3	47 53.9	−18.1	64.3	48 44.0	−15.3	66.3	49 30.2	−12.5	68.5
21	45 39.4	24.0	59.2	46 39.3	21.6	61.0	47 35.8	19.1	62.9	48 28.7	16.4	64.9	49 17.7	13.6	66.9
22	45 15.4	24.9	57.8	46 17.7	22.6	59.6	47 16.7	20.1	61.5	48 12.3	17.5	63.4	49 04.1	14.8	65.5
23	44 50.5	25.8	56.6	45 55.1	23.5	58.3	46 56.6	21.1	60.1	47 54.8	18.6	62.0	48 49.3	15.9	64.0
24	44 24.7	26.5	55.3	45 31.6	24.3	57.0	46 35.5	22.0	58.7	47 36.2	19.6	60.6	48 33.4	17.0	62.5
25	43 58.2	−27.4	54.0	45 07.3	−25.3	55.7	46 13.5	−23.0	57.4	47 16.6	−20.6	59.2	48 16.4	−18.0	61.1
26	43 30.8	28.2	52.8	44 42.0	26.1	54.4	45 50.5	23.9	56.0	46 56.0	21.5	57.8	47 58.4	19.2	59.6
27	43 02.6	28.9	51.6	44 15.9	26.9	53.1	45 26.6	24.8	54.7	46 34.5	22.6	56.4	47 39.2	20.1	58.2
28	42 33.7	29.7	50.4	43 49.0	27.7	51.9	45 01.8	25.7	53.4	46 11.9	23.4	55.1	47 19.1	21.1	56.8
29	42 04.0	30.4	49.2	43 21.3	28.5	50.6	44 36.1	26.4	52.1	45 48.5	24.4	53.8	46 58.0	22.2	55.5

Dec.	10° Hc	d	Z	12° Hc	d	Z	14° Hc	d	Z	16° Hc	d	Z	18° Hc	d	Z
0	48 58.4	+15.3	101.7	48 31.8	+18.3	103.9	48 00.7	+21.2	106.1	47 25.4	+23.9	108.2	46 45.9	+26.6	110.2
1	49 13.7	14.2	100.2	48 50.1	17.2	102.5	48 21.9	20.2	104.7	47 49.3	23.0	106.8	47 12.5	25.7	108.9
2	49 27.9	13.0	98.7	49 07.3	16.1	101.0	48 42.1	19.1	103.3	48 12.3	22.0	105.4	47 38.2	24.8	107.6
3	49 40.9	11.8	97.2	49 23.4	15.0	99.5	49 01.2	18.0	101.8	48 34.3	21.0	104.0	48 03.0	23.8	106.2
4	49 52.7	10.6	95.7	49 38.4	13.7	98.0	49 19.2	16.8	100.4	48 55.3	19.8	102.6	48 26.8	22.7	104.8
5	50 03.3	+ 9.5	94.2	49 52.1	+12.7	96.5	49 36.0	+15.8	98.9	49 15.1	+18.8	101.2	48 49.5	+21.8	103.4
6	50 12.8	8.1	92.6	50 04.8	11.4	95.0	49 51.8	14.6	97.4	49 33.9	17.7	99.7	49 11.3	20.7	102.0
7	50 20.9	7.0	91.1	50 16.2	10.1	93.5	50 06.4	13.4	95.9	49 51.6	16.5	98.2	49 32.0	19.6	100.6
8	50 27.9	5.7	89.5	50 26.3	9.0	91.9	50 19.8	12.1	94.4	50 08.1	15.4	96.7	49 51.6	18.5	99.1
9	50 33.6	4.4	88.0	50 35.3	7.7	90.4	50 31.9	11.0	92.8	50 23.5	14.2	95.2	50 10.1	17.3	97.6
10	50 38.0	+ 3.1	86.4	50 43.0	+ 6.4	88.8	50 42.9	+ 9.7	91.3	50 37.7	+13.0	93.7	50 27.4	+16.2	96.1
11	50 41.1	1.9	84.8	50 49.4	5.2	87.3	50 52.6	8.5	89.7	50 50.7	11.7	92.2	50 43.6	14.9	94.6
12	50 43.0	+ 0.6	83.2	50 54.6	3.9	85.7	51 01.1	7.2	88.1	51 02.4	10.5	90.6	50 58.5	13.8	93.1
13	50 43.6	− 0.7	81.7	50 58.5	2.6	84.1	51 08.3	5.9	86.6	51 12.9	9.2	89.0	51 12.3	12.5	91.5
14	50 42.9	2.0	80.1	51 01.1	+ 1.3	82.5	51 14.2	4.6	85.0	51 22.1	8.0	87.5	51 24.8	11.3	90.0
15	50 40.9	− 3.2	78.5	51 02.4	0.0	80.9	51 18.8	+ 3.3	83.4	51 30.1	+ 6.6	85.9	51 36.1	+ 9.9	88.4
16	50 37.7	4.5	76.9	51 02.4	− 1.3	79.3	51 22.1	2.0	81.8	51 36.7	5.3	84.3	51 46.0	8.7	86.8
17	50 33.2	5.8	75.3	51 01.1	2.6	77.7	51 24.1	+ 0.7	80.2	51 42.0	4.0	82.7	51 54.7	7.4	85.2
18	50 27.4	7.0	73.8	50 58.5	3.8	76.1	51 24.8	− 0.6	78.6	51 46.0	2.7	81.1	52 02.1	6.0	83.6
19	50 20.4	8.3	72.2	50 54.7	5.2	74.6	51 24.2	1.9	77.0	51 48.7	+ 1.4	79.4	52 08.1	4.7	82.0
20	50 12.1	− 9.5	70.7	50 49.5	− 6.4	73.0	51 22.3	− 3.3	75.4	51 50.1	0.0	77.8	52 12.8	+ 3.4	80.3
21	50 02.6	10.7	69.1	50 43.1	7.7	71.4	51 19.0	4.5	73.8	51 50.1	− 1.3	76.2	52 16.2	2.0	78.7
22	49 51.9	11.9	67.6	50 35.4	8.9	69.8	51 14.5	5.8	72.2	51 48.8	2.6	74.6	52 18.2	+ 0.7	77.1
23	49 40.0	13.1	66.1	50 26.5	10.2	68.3	51 08.7	7.2	70.6	51 46.2	4.0	73.0	52 18.9	− 0.7	75.4
24	49 26.9	14.3	64.6	50 16.3	11.4	66.7	51 01.5	8.4	69.0	51 42.2	5.2	71.4	52 18.2	2.1	73.8
25	49 12.6	−15.4	63.1	50 04.9	−12.5	65.2	50 53.1	− 9.6	67.4	51 37.0	− 6.6	69.8	52 16.1	− 3.4	72.2
26	48 57.2	16.5	61.6	49 52.4	13.8	63.7	50 43.5	10.9	65.9	51 30.4	7.9	68.2	52 12.7	4.7	70.5
27	48 40.7	17.6	60.3	49 38.6	14.9	62.2	50 32.6	12.1	64.3	51 22.5	9.2	66.6	52 08.0	6.1	68.9
28	48 23.1	18.7	58.7	49 23.7	16.1	60.7	50 20.5	13.3	62.8	51 13.3	10.4	65.0	52 01.9	7.4	67.3
29	48 04.4	19.7	57.3	49 07.6	17.2	59.2	50 07.2	14.5	61.3	51 02.9	11.7	63.4	51 54.5	8.7	65.7

0°			2°			4°			6°			8°			Dec.
Hc	d	Z	Hc	d	Z	Hc	d	Z	Hc	d	Z	Hc	d	Z	
50 00.0	- 0.6	90.0	49 57.5	- 3.9	92.4	49 50.0	- 7.1	94.8	49 37.6	-10.2	97.1	49 20.4	-13.4	99.4	0
49 59.4	1.9	91.6	49 53.6	5.1	93.9	49 42.9	8.3	96.3	49 27.4	11.5	98.6	49 07.0	14.5	100.9	1
49 57.5	3.1	93.1	49 48.5	6.3	95.5	49 34.6	9.5	97.8	49 15.9	12.6	100.1	48 52.5	15.7	102.4	2
49 54.4	4.4	94.7	49 42.2	7.6	97.0	49 25.1	10.7	99.3	49 03.3	13.8	101.6	48 36.8	16.8	103.9	3
49 50.0	5.5	96.2	49 34.6	8.7	98.5	49 14.4	11.9	100.8	48 49.5	14.9	103.1	48 20.0	17.8	105.3	4
49 44.5	- 6.9	97.8	49 25.9	-10.0	100.1	49 02.5	-13.0	102.3	48 34.6	-16.0	104.6	48 02.2	-18.9	106.7	5
49 37.6	8.0	99.3	49 15.9	11.1	101.6	48 49.5	14.2	103.8	48 18.6	17.1	106.0	47 43.3	19.9	108.1	6
49 29.6	9.2	100.8	49 04.8	12.3	103.1	48 35.3	15.3	105.3	48 01.5	18.2	107.5	47 23.4	21.0	109.5	7
49 20.4	10.4	102.3	48 52.5	13.5	104.6	48 20.0	16.3	106.8	47 43.3	19.2	108.9	47 02.4	21.9	110.9	8
49 10.0	11.6	103.8	48 39.0	14.5	106.1	48 03.7	17.5	108.2	47 24.1	20.2	110.3	46 40.5	22.8	112.3	9
48 58.4	-12.7	105.3	48 24.5	-15.7	107.5	47 46.2	-18.5	109.6	47 03.9	-21.2	111.7	46 17.7	-23.8	113.6	10
48 45.7	13.9	106.8	48 08.8	16.8	109.0	47 27.7	19.5	111.0	46 42.7	22.2	113.0	45 53.9	24.8	115.0	11
48 31.8	15.0	108.3	47 52.0	17.8	110.4	47 08.2	20.5	112.4	46 20.5	23.1	114.4	45 29.1	25.5	116.3	12
48 16.8	16.1	109.8	47 34.2	18.8	111.8	46 47.7	21.5	113.8	45 57.4	24.1	115.7	45 03.6	26.5	117.5	13
48 00.7	17.1	111.2	47 15.4	19.9	113.2	46 26.2	22.5	115.1	45 33.3	24.9	117.0	44 37.1	27.2	118.8	14
47 43.6	-18.2	112.6	46 55.5	-20.9	114.6	46 03.7	-23.4	116.5	45 08.4	-25.8	118.3	44 09.9	-28.1	120.1	15
47 25.4	19.3	114.0	46 34.6	21.8	116.0	45 40.3	24.3	117.8	44 42.6	26.6	119.6	43 41.8	28.8	121.3	16
47 06.1	20.2	115.4	46 12.8	22.8	117.3	45 16.0	25.2	119.1	44 16.0	27.4	120.9	43 13.0	29.6	122.5	17
46 45.9	21.2	116.8	45 50.0	23.7	118.7	44 50.8	26.0	120.4	43 48.6	28.3	122.1	42 43.4	30.3	123.7	18
46 24.7	22.2	118.2	45 26.3	24.5	120.0	44 24.8	26.8	121.7	43 20.3	29.0	123.3	42 13.1	31.1	124.9	19
46 02.5	-23.1	119.5	45 01.8	-25.5	121.3	43 58.0	-27.7	122.9	42 51.3	-29.7	124.5	41 42.0	-31.6	126.0	20
45 39.4	24.0	120.8	44 36.3	26.3	122.6	43 30.3	28.4	124.2	42 21.6	30.4	125.7	41 10.4	32.4	127.1	21
45 15.4	24.9	122.2	44 10.0	27.1	123.8	43 01.9	29.2	125.4	41 51.2	31.2	126.9	40 38.0	33.0	128.2	22
44 50.5	25.8	123.4	43 42.9	27.8	125.1	42 32.7	29.9	126.6	41 20.0	31.8	128.0	40 05.0	33.6	129.3	23
44 24.7	26.5	124.7	43 15.1	28.7	126.3	42 02.8	30.6	127.7	40 48.2	32.4	129.1	39 31.4	34.2	130.4	24
43 58.2	-27.4	126.0	42 46.4	-29.4	127.5	41 32.2	-31.3	128.9	40 15.8	-33.1	130.2	38 57.2	-34.7	131.5	25
43 30.8	28.2	127.2	42 17.0	30.1	128.7	41 00.9	31.9	130.0	39 42.7	33.7	131.3	38 22.5	35.3	132.5	26
43 02.6	28.9	128.4	41 46.9	30.8	129.8	40 29.0	32.6	131.1	39 09.0	34.2	132.4	37 47.2	35.8	133.6	27
42 33.7	29.7	129.6	41 16.1	31.5	131.0	39 56.4	33.2	132.2	38 34.8	34.8	133.4	37 11.4	36.3	134.6	28
42 04.0	30.4	130.8	40 44.6	32.1	132.1	39 23.2	33.8	133.3	38 00.0	35.4	134.5	36 35.1	36.9	135.6	29

10°			12°			14°			16°			18°			Dec.
Hc	d	Z	Hc	d	Z	Hc	d	Z	Hc	d	Z	Hc	d	Z	
48 58.4	-16.4	101.7	48 31.8	-19.4	103.9	48 00.7	-22.2	106.1	47 25.4	-24.9	108.2	46 45.9	-27.5	110.2	0
48 42.0	17.5	103.2	48 12.4	20.4	105.3	47 38.5	23.1	107.5	47 00.5	25.9	109.5	46 18.4	28.4	111.5	1
48 24.5	18.6	104.6	47 52.0	21.4	106.7	47 15.4	24.2	108.8	46 34.6	26.7	110.8	45 50.0	29.2	112.8	2
48 05.9	19.7	106.0	47 30.6	22.4	108.1	46 51.2	25.0	111.5	46 07.9	27.6	112.1	45 20.8	30.0	114.0	3
47 46.2	20.7	107.4	47 08.2	23.4	109.5	46 26.2	26.0	111.5	45 40.3	28.4	113.4	44 50.8	30.7	115.3	4
47 25.5	-21.6	108.8	46 44.8	-24.3	110.9	46 00.2	-26.9	112.8	45 11.9	-29.3	114.7	44 20.1	-31.5	116.5	5
47 03.9	22.7	110.2	46 20.5	25.2	112.2	45 33.3	27.7	114.1	44 42.6	30.0	115.9	43 48.6	32.3	117.6	6
46 41.2	23.5	111.6	45 55.3	26.2	113.5	45 05.6	28.5	115.3	44 12.6	30.8	117.1	43 16.3	32.9	118.8	7
46 17.7	24.6	112.9	45 29.1	26.9	114.8	44 37.1	29.3	116.6	43 41.8	31.5	118.3	42 43.4	33.6	120.0	8
45 53.1	25.3	114.2	45 02.2	27.8	116.0	44 07.8	30.0	117.8	43 10.3	32.2	119.5	42 09.8	34.3	121.1	9
45 27.8	-26.3	115.5	44 34.4	-28.6	117.3	43 37.8	-30.9	119.0	42 38.1	-32.9	120.6	41 35.5	-34.8	122.2	10
45 01.5	27.1	116.8	44 05.8	29.4	118.5	43 06.9	31.5	120.2	42 05.2	33.6	121.8	41 00.7	35.5	123.3	11
44 34.4	27.9	118.0	43 36.4	30.1	119.7	42 35.4	32.2	121.3	41 31.6	34.2	122.9	40 25.2	36.1	124.3	12
44 06.5	28.7	119.3	43 06.3	30.9	120.9	42 03.2	32.9	122.5	40 57.4	34.8	124.0	39 49.1	36.6	125.4	13
43 37.8	29.5	120.5	42 35.4	31.6	122.1	41 30.3	33.5	123.6	40 22.6	35.4	125.0	39 12.5	37.1	126.4	14
43 08.3	-30.2	121.7	42 03.8	-32.2	123.2	40 56.8	-34.2	124.7	39 47.2	-35.9	126.1	38 35.4	-37.6	127.4	15
42 38.1	31.0	122.9	41 31.6	32.9	124.4	40 22.6	34.7	125.8	39 11.3	36.5	127.1	37 57.8	38.2	128.4	16
42 07.1	31.6	124.0	40 58.7	33.5	125.5	39 47.9	35.4	126.9	38 34.8	37.0	128.2	37 19.6	38.6	129.4	17
41 35.5	32.3	125.2	40 25.2	34.1	126.6	39 12.5	35.8	127.9	37 57.8	37.5	129.2	36 41.0	39.0	130.3	18
41 03.2	32.9	126.3	39 51.1	34.8	127.7	38 36.7	36.4	128.9	37 20.3	38.0	130.1	36 02.0	39.5	131.3	19
40 30.3	-33.5	127.4	39 16.3	-35.2	128.7	38 00.3	-37.0	130.0	36 42.3	-38.5	131.1	35 22.5	-39.9	132.2	20
39 56.8	34.2	128.5	38 41.1	35.9	129.8	37 23.3	37.4	131.0	36 03.8	38.9	132.1	34 42.6	40.3	133.1	21
39 22.6	34.7	129.6	38 05.2	36.3	130.8	36 45.9	37.9	131.9	35 24.9	39.3	133.0	34 02.3	40.7	134.0	22
38 47.9	35.3	130.6	37 28.9	36.9	131.8	36 08.0	38.3	132.9	34 45.6	39.8	133.9	33 21.6	41.1	134.9	23
38 12.6	35.8	131.6	36 52.0	37.3	132.8	35 29.7	38.8	133.8	34 05.8	40.1	134.8	32 40.5	41.4	135.8	24
37 36.8	-36.3	132.7	36 14.7	-37.8	133.8	34 50.9	-39.2	134.8	33 25.7	-40.5	135.7	31 59.1	-41.8	136.6	25
37 00.5	36.8	133.7	35 36.9	38.3	134.7	34 11.7	39.6	135.7	32 45.2	40.9	136.6	31 17.3	42.1	137.5	26
36 23.7	37.3	134.6	34 58.6	38.7	135.7	33 32.1	40.0	136.6	32 04.3	41.3	137.5	30 35.2	42.3	138.3	27
35 46.4	37.8	135.6	34 19.9	39.1	136.6	32 52.1	40.4	137.5	31 23.0	41.5	138.3	29 52.9	42.7	139.1	28
35 08.6	38.2	136.6	33 40.8	39.5	137.5	32 11.7	40.7	138.4	30 41.5	41.9	139.2	29 10.2	43.0	139.9	29

Dec.	20° Hc	d	Z	22° Hc	d	Z	24° Hc	d	Z	26° Hc	d	Z	28° Hc	d	Z
°	° ′	′	°	° ′	′	°	° ′	′	°	° ′	′	°	° ′	′	°
0	46 02.5	+29.2	112.2	45 15.4	+31.5	114.1	44 24.7	+33.8	115.9	43 30.8	+35.9	117.6	42 33.7	+37.9	119.2
1	46 31.7	28.3	110.9	45 46.9	30.8	112.8	44 58.5	33.1	114.7	44 06.7	35.3	116.5	43 11.6	37.4	118.2
2	47 00.0	27.4	109.6	46 17.7	29.9	111.6	45 31.6	32.4	113.5	44 42.0	34.6	115.3	43 49.0	36.7	117.1
3	47 27.4	26.5	108.3	46 47.6	29.1	110.3	46 04.0	31.5	112.3	45 16.6	33.9	114.2	44 25.7	36.1	116.0
4	47 53.9	25.5	107.0	47 16.7	28.3	109.1	46 35.5	30.8	111.1	45 50.5	33.2	113.0	45 01.8	35.4	114.9
5	48 19.4	+24.6	105.6	47 45.0	+27.3	107.8	47 06.3	+29.9	109.8	46 23.7	+32.3	111.8	45 37.2	+34.7	113.7
6	48 44.0	23.6	104.2	48 12.3	26.4	106.4	47 36.2	29.1	108.5	46 56.0	31.6	110.6	46 11.9	34.0	112.5
7	49 07.6	22.6	102.8	48 38.7	25.4	105.1	48 05.3	28.1	107.2	47 27.6	30.8	109.3	46 45.9	33.2	111.3
8	49 30.2	21.5	101.4	49 04.1	24.4	103.7	48 33.4	27.2	105.9	47 58.4	29.8	108.1	47 19.1	32.4	110.1
9	49 51.7	20.4	100.0	49 28.5	23.4	102.3	49 00.6	26.3	104.6	48 28.2	29.0	106.7	47 51.5	31.6	108.9
10	50 12.1	+19.3	98.5	49 51.9	+22.3	100.9	49 26.9	+25.2	103.2	48 57.2	+28.1	105.4	48 23.1	+30.7	107.6
11	50 31.4	18.1	97.0	50 14.2	21.2	99.4	49 52.1	24.2	101.8	49 25.3	27.1	104.1	48 53.8	29.9	106.3
12	50 49.5	17.0	95.5	50 35.4	20.1	98.0	50 16.3	23.2	100.4	49 52.4	26.0	102.7	49 23.7	28.9	105.0
13	51 06.5	15.8	94.0	50 55.5	19.0	96.5	50 39.5	22.0	98.9	50 18.4	25.1	101.3	49 52.6	27.9	103.6
14	51 22.3	14.5	92.5	51 14.5	17.8	95.0	51 01.5	21.0	97.4	50 43.5	24.0	99.9	50 20.5	26.9	102.2
15	51 36.8	+13.3	90.9	51 32.3	+16.5	93.4	51 22.5	+19.7	95.9	51 07.5	+22.9	98.4	50 47.4	+25.9	100.8
16	51 50.1	12.0	89.3	51 48.8	15.3	91.9	51 42.2	18.6	94.4	51 30.4	21.7	96.9	51 13.3	24.9	99.4
17	52 02.1	10.7	87.7	52 04.1	14.1	90.3	52 00.8	17.4	92.9	51 52.1	20.6	95.4	51 38.2	23.7	97.9
18	52 12.8	9.4	86.1	52 18.2	12.8	88.7	52 18.2	16.1	91.3	52 12.7	19.4	93.9	52 01.9	22.6	96.5
19	52 22.2	8.1	84.5	52 31.0	11.5	87.1	52 34.3	14.8	89.7	52 32.1	18.1	92.3	52 24.5	21.4	94.9
20	52 30.3	+6.8	82.9	52 42.5	+10.1	85.5	52 49.1	+13.5	88.1	52 50.2	+16.9	90.8	52 45.9	+20.2	93.4
21	52 37.1	5.4	81.3	52 52.6	8.8	83.9	53 02.6	12.2	86.5	53 07.1	15.6	89.2	53 06.1	18.9	91.8
22	52 42.5	4.0	79.6	53 01.4	7.4	82.2	53 14.8	10.9	84.9	53 22.7	14.3	87.6	53 25.0	17.7	90.3
23	52 46.5	2.6	78.0	53 08.8	6.0	80.6	53 25.7	9.5	83.2	53 37.0	12.9	85.9	53 42.7	16.3	88.6
24	52 49.1	+1.3	76.3	53 14.8	4.7	78.9	53 35.2	8.0	81.6	53 49.9	11.6	84.3	53 59.0	15.1	87.0
25	52 50.4	−0.2	74.7	53 19.5	+3.2	77.3	53 43.2	+6.7	79.9	54 01.5	+10.1	82.6	54 14.1	+13.6	85.4
26	52 50.2	1.5	73.0	53 22.7	1.9	75.6	53 49.9	5.3	78.2	54 11.6	8.8	80.9	54 27.7	12.2	83.7
27	52 48.7	2.8	71.4	53 24.6	+0.4	73.9	53 55.2	3.8	76.5	54 20.4	7.3	79.2	54 39.9	10.9	82.0
28	52 45.9	4.3	69.7	53 25.0	−1.0	72.2	53 59.0	2.4	74.8	54 27.7	5.9	77.5	54 50.8	9.4	80.3
29	52 41.6	5.6	68.1	53 24.0	2.3	70.6	54 01.4	+1.0	73.1	54 33.6	4.4	75.8	55 00.2	7.9	78.6

Dec.	30° Hc	d	Z	32° Hc	d	Z	34° Hc	d	Z	36° Hc	d	Z	38° Hc	d	Z
°	° ′	′	°	° ′	′	°	° ′	′	°	° ′	′	°	° ′	′	°
0	41 33.6	+39.9	120.8	40 30.9	+41.6	122.3	39 25.6	+43.2	123.7	38 17.8	+44.8	125.0	37 07.9	+46.2	126.3
1	42 13.5	39.3	119.8	41 12.5	41.1	121.3	40 08.8	42.8	122.8	39 02.6	44.4	124.2	37 54.1	45.8	125.5
2	42 52.8	38.7	118.8	41 53.6	40.6	120.3	40 51.6	42.3	121.9	39 47.0	43.9	123.3	38 39.9	45.5	124.6
3	43 31.5	38.2	117.7	42 34.2	40.1	119.4	41 33.9	41.9	120.9	40 30.9	43.6	122.4	39 25.4	45.1	123.8
4	44 09.7	37.5	116.6	43 14.3	39.5	118.3	42 15.8	41.4	120.0	41 14.5	43.1	121.5	40 10.5	44.7	122.9
5	44 47.2	+36.9	115.5	43 53.8	+38.9	117.3	42 57.2	+40.9	119.0	41 57.6	+42.7	120.6	40 55.2	+44.4	122.1
6	45 24.1	36.2	114.4	44 32.7	38.4	116.2	43 38.1	40.3	118.0	42 40.3	42.1	119.6	41 39.6	43.8	121.2
7	46 00.3	35.5	113.3	45 11.1	37.7	115.2	44 18.4	39.7	116.9	43 22.4	41.7	118.6	42 23.4	43.5	120.3
8	46 35.8	34.9	112.1	45 48.8	37.0	114.0	44 58.1	39.2	115.9	44 04.1	41.1	117.6	43 06.9	42.9	119.3
9	47 10.7	34.0	110.9	46 25.8	36.4	112.9	45 37.3	38.5	114.8	44 45.2	40.6	116.6	43 49.8	42.5	118.3
10	47 44.7	+33.3	109.7	47 02.2	+35.7	111.7	46 15.8	+37.9	113.7	45 25.8	+40.0	115.6	44 32.3	+42.0	117.4
11	48 18.0	32.4	108.5	47 37.9	34.9	110.6	46 53.7	37.3	112.6	46 05.8	39.4	114.5	45 14.3	41.4	116.4
12	48 50.4	31.6	107.2	48 12.8	34.1	109.3	47 31.0	36.5	111.4	46 45.2	38.7	113.4	45 55.7	40.8	115.3
13	49 22.0	30.7	105.9	48 46.9	33.3	108.1	48 07.5	35.7	110.2	47 23.9	38.1	112.3	46 36.5	40.2	114.3
14	49 52.7	29.7	104.6	49 20.2	32.4	106.8	48 43.2	35.0	109.0	48 02.0	37.4	111.1	47 16.7	39.6	113.2
15	50 22.4	+28.8	103.2	49 52.6	+31.6	105.5	49 18.2	+34.2	107.8	48 39.4	+36.6	110.0	47 56.3	+38.9	112.1
16	50 51.2	27.8	101.8	50 24.2	30.6	104.2	49 52.4	33.3	106.5	49 16.0	35.8	108.8	48 35.2	38.3	110.9
17	51 19.0	26.8	100.4	50 54.8	29.6	102.9	50 25.7	32.4	105.2	49 51.8	35.1	107.5	49 13.5	37.5	109.7
18	51 45.8	25.6	99.0	51 24.4	28.7	101.5	50 58.1	31.5	103.9	50 26.9	34.2	106.3	49 51.0	36.7	108.5
19	52 11.4	24.6	97.5	51 53.1	27.6	100.1	51 29.6	30.5	102.5	51 01.1	33.3	105.0	50 27.7	36.0	107.3
20	52 36.0	+23.4	96.0	52 20.7	+26.6	98.6	52 00.1	+29.6	101.1	51 34.4	+32.4	103.6	51 03.7	+35.1	106.0
21	52 59.4	22.3	94.5	52 47.3	25.4	97.1	52 29.7	28.5	99.7	52 06.8	31.4	102.3	51 38.8	34.2	104.7
22	53 21.7	21.0	93.0	53 12.7	24.2	95.6	52 58.2	27.4	98.3	52 38.2	30.4	100.9	52 13.0	33.2	103.4
23	53 42.7	19.7	91.4	53 36.9	23.1	94.1	53 25.6	26.2	96.8	53 08.6	29.4	99.4	52 46.2	32.4	102.0
24	54 02.4	18.4	89.8	54 00.0	21.8	92.5	53 51.8	25.1	95.3	53 38.0	28.3	98.0	53 18.6	31.3	100.6
25	54 20.8	+17.2	88.1	54 21.8	+20.5	90.9	54 16.9	+23.9	93.7	54 06.3	+27.1	96.5	53 49.9	+30.2	99.2
26	54 38.0	15.7	86.5	54 42.3	19.3	89.3	54 40.8	22.7	92.1	54 33.4	26.0	95.0	54 20.1	29.2	97.7
27	54 53.7	14.4	84.8	55 01.6	17.8	87.7	55 03.5	21.3	90.5	54 59.4	24.7	93.4	54 49.3	28.0	96.2
28	55 08.1	12.9	83.1	55 19.4	16.5	86.0	55 24.8	20.0	88.9	55 24.1	23.4	91.8	55 17.3	26.8	94.7
29	55 21.0	11.5	81.4	55 35.9	15.1	84.3	55 44.8	18.6	87.2	55 47.5	22.2	90.2	55 44.1	25.6	93.1

20°			22°			24°			26°			28°			Dec.
Hc	d	Z	Hc	d	Z	Hc	d	Z	Hc	d	Z	Hc	d	Z	
° ′	′	°	° ′	′	°	° ′	′	°	° ′	′	°	° ′	′	°	°
46 02.5	−30.0	112.2	45 15.4	−32.3	114.1	44 24.7	−34.5	115.9	43 30.8	−36.6	117.6	42 33.7	−38.6	119.2	0
45 32.5	30.7	113.4	44 43.1	33.1	115.2	43 50.2	35.1	117.0	42 54.2	37.2	118.7	41 55.1	39.0	120.3	1
45 01.8	31.6	114.6	44 10.0	33.7	116.4	43 15.1	35.9	118.1	42 17.0	37.8	119.7	41 16.1	39.6	121.3	2
44 30.2	32.2	115.8	43 36.3	34.4	117.6	42 39.2	36.4	119.2	41 39.2	38.3	120.8	40 36.5	40.1	122.3	3
43 58.0	33.0	117.0	43 01.9	35.1	118.7	42 02.8	37.0	120.3	41 00.9	38.8	121.8	39 56.4	40.6	123.2	4
43 25.0	−33.7	118.2	42 26.8	−35.6	119.8	41 25.8	−37.6	121.3	40 22.1	−39.4	122.8	39 15.8	−41.0	124.2	5
42 51.3	34.3	119.3	41 51.2	36.3	120.9	40 48.2	38.1	122.4	39 42.7	39.9	123.8	38 34.8	41.5	125.1	6
42 17.0	35.0	120.4	41 14.9	36.9	121.9	40 10.1	38.7	123.4	39 02.8	40.3	124.8	37 53.3	41.9	126.1	7
41 42.0	35.5	121.5	40 38.0	37.4	123.0	39 31.4	39.1	124.4	38 22.5	40.8	125.7	37 11.4	42.3	127.0	8
41 06.5	36.2	122.6	40 00.6	38.0	124.0	38 52.3	39.7	125.4	37 41.7	41.2	126.6	36 29.1	42.7	127.8	9
40 30.3	−36.7	123.6	39 22.6	−38.4	125.0	38 12.6	−40.0	126.3	37 00.5	−41.6	127.6	35 46.4	−43.1	128.7	10
39 53.6	37.3	124.7	38 44.2	39.0	126.0	37 32.6	40.6	127.3	36 18.9	42.0	128.5	35 03.3	43.4	129.6	11
39 16.3	37.8	125.7	38 05.2	39.4	127.0	36 52.0	40.9	128.2	35 36.9	42.4	129.3	34 19.9	43.7	130.4	12
38 38.5	38.2	126.7	37 25.8	39.9	127.9	36 11.1	41.4	129.1	34 54.5	42.8	130.2	33 36.2	44.1	131.2	13
38 00.3	38.8	127.7	36 45.9	40.3	128.9	35 29.7	41.8	130.0	34 11.7	43.1	131.1	32 52.1	44.4	132.0	14
37 21.5	−39.2	128.6	36 05.6	−40.7	129.8	34 47.9	−42.1	130.9	33 28.6	−43.4	131.9	32 07.7	−44.7	132.8	15
36 42.3	39.7	129.6	35 24.9	41.1	130.7	34 05.8	42.5	131.7	32 45.2	43.8	132.7	31 23.0	44.9	133.6	16
36 02.6	40.1	130.5	34 43.8	41.5	131.6	33 23.3	42.8	132.6	32 01.4	44.1	133.5	30 38.1	45.2	134.4	17
35 22.5	40.5	131.4	34 02.3	41.9	132.5	32 40.5	43.1	133.4	31 17.3	44.3	134.3	29 52.9	45.5	135.2	18
34 42.0	40.9	132.3	33 20.4	42.2	133.3	31 57.4	43.5	134.2	30 33.0	44.7	135.1	29 07.4	45.8	135.9	19
34 01.1	−41.3	133.2	32 38.2	−42.6	134.2	31 13.9	−43.8	135.1	29 48.3	−44.9	135.9	28 21.6	−45.9	136.7	20
33 19.8	41.6	134.1	31 55.6	42.8	135.0	30 30.1	44.0	135.9	29 03.4	45.1	136.6	27 35.7	46.2	137.4	21
32 38.2	42.0	134.9	31 12.8	43.2	135.8	29 46.1	44.4	136.6	28 18.3	45.4	137.4	26 49.5	46.4	138.1	22
31 56.2	42.3	135.8	30 29.6	43.5	136.6	29 01.8	44.6	137.4	27 32.9	45.6	138.1	26 03.1	46.7	138.8	23
31 13.9	42.6	136.6	29 46.1	43.8	137.4	28 17.2	44.9	138.2	26 47.3	45.9	138.9	25 16.4	46.8	139.5	24
30 31.3	−43.0	137.4	29 02.3	−44.0	138.2	27 32.3	−45.0	138.9	26 01.4	−46.0	139.6	24 29.6	−46.9	140.2	25
29 48.3	43.2	138.3	28 18.3	44.3	139.0	26 47.3	45.3	139.7	25 15.4	46.3	140.3	23 42.7	47.2	140.9	26
29 05.1	43.5	139.1	27 34.0	44.5	139.8	26 02.0	45.6	140.4	24 29.1	46.4	141.0	22 55.5	47.4	141.5	27
28 21.6	43.7	139.8	26 49.5	44.8	140.5	25 16.4	45.7	141.1	23 42.7	46.7	141.7	22 08.1	47.5	142.2	28
27 37.9	44.1	140.6	26 04.7	45.0	141.3	24 30.7	45.9	141.8	22 56.0	46.8	142.4	21 20.6	47.6	142.9	29

30°			32°			34°			36°			38°			Dec.
Hc	d	Z	Hc	d	Z	Hc	d	Z	Hc	d	Z	Hc	d	Z	
° ′	′	°	° ′	′	°	° ′	′	°	° ′	′	°	° ′	′	°	°
41 33.6	−40.3	120.8	40 30.9	−42.1	122.3	39 25.6	−43.7	123.7	38 17.8	45.1	125.0	37 07.9	−46.5	126.3	0
40 53.3	40.8	121.8	39 48.8	42.5	123.2	38 41.9	44.0	124.6	37 32.7	45.4	125.8	36 21.4	46.8	127.1	1
40 12.5	41.3	122.7	39 06.3	42.9	124.1	37 57.9	44.4	125.4	36 47.3	45.8	126.7	35 34.6	47.1	127.8	2
39 31.2	41.8	123.7	38 23.4	43.3	125.0	37 13.5	44.6	126.3	36 01.5	46.1	127.5	34 47.5	47.3	128.6	3
38 49.4	42.2	124.6	37 40.1	43.7	125.9	36 28.7	45.1	127.1	35 15.4	46.4	128.3	34 00.2	47.7	129.3	4
38 07.2	−42.6	125.5	36 56.4	−44.0	126.8	35 43.6	−45.4	127.9	34 29.0	−46.7	129.0	33 12.5	−47.8	130.1	5
37 24.6	43.0	126.4	36 12.4	44.4	127.6	34 58.2	45.7	128.7	33 42.3	47.0	129.8	32 24.7	48.2	130.8	6
36 41.6	43.4	127.3	35 28.0	44.8	128.4	34 12.5	46.1	129.5	32 55.3	47.2	130.5	31 36.5	48.3	131.5	7
35 58.2	43.7	128.1	34 43.2	45.0	129.2	33 26.4	46.3	130.3	32 08.1	47.5	131.3	30 48.2	48.6	132.2	8
35 14.5	44.1	129.0	33 58.2	45.4	130.0	32 40.1	46.5	131.0	31 20.6	47.7	132.0	29 59.6	48.7	132.9	9
34 30.4	−44.4	129.8	33 12.8	−45.7	130.8	31 53.6	−46.9	131.8	30 32.9	−48.0	132.7	29 10.9	−49.0	133.5	10
33 46.0	44.7	130.6	32 27.1	45.9	131.6	31 06.7	47.1	132.5	29 44.9	48.1	133.4	28 21.9	49.2	134.2	11
33 01.3	45.0	131.4	31 41.2	46.2	132.4	30 19.6	47.3	133.2	28 56.8	48.4	134.1	27 32.7	49.3	134.8	12
32 16.3	45.3	132.2	30 55.0	46.5	133.1	29 32.3	47.5	134.0	28 08.4	48.5	134.7	26 43.4	49.5	135.5	13
31 31.0	45.6	133.0	30 08.5	46.7	133.8	28 44.8	47.8	134.7	27 19.9	48.8	135.4	25 53.9	49.7	136.1	14
30 45.4	−45.8	133.7	29 21.8	−46.9	134.6	27 57.0	−47.9	135.3	26 31.1	−48.9	136.1	25 04.2	−49.8	136.7	15
29 59.6	46.1	134.5	28 34.9	47.1	135.3	27 09.1	48.2	136.0	25 42.2	49.1	136.7	24 14.4	49.9	137.3	16
29 13.5	46.3	135.2	27 47.8	47.4	136.0	26 20.9	48.3	136.7	24 53.1	49.2	137.3	23 24.5	50.1	137.9	17
28 27.2	46.6	135.9	27 00.4	47.6	136.7	25 32.6	48.5	137.3	24 03.9	49.4	138.0	22 34.4	50.3	138.5	18
27 40.6	46.8	136.7	26 12.8	47.7	137.4	24 44.1	48.7	138.0	23 14.5	49.5	138.6	21 44.1	50.3	139.1	19
26 53.8	−47.1	137.4	25 25.1	−47.9	138.0	23 55.4	−48.8	138.6	22 25.0	−49.7	139.2	20 53.8	−50.5	139.7	20
26 06.9	47.2	138.1	24 37.2	48.1	138.7	23 06.6	49.0	139.3	21 35.3	49.8	139.8	20 03.3	50.6	140.3	21
25 19.7	47.4	138.7	23 49.1	48.3	139.3	22 17.6	49.1	139.9	20 45.5	49.9	140.4	19 12.7	50.7	140.9	22
24 32.3	47.5	139.4	23 00.8	48.4	140.0	21 28.5	49.2	140.5	19 55.6	50.1	141.0	18 22.0	50.8	141.4	23
23 44.8	47.7	140.1	22 12.4	48.6	140.6	20 39.3	49.4	141.1	19 05.5	50.1	141.6	17 31.2	50.8	142.0	24
22 57.1	−47.9	140.8	21 23.8	−48.7	141.3	19 49.9	−49.5	141.7	18 15.4	−50.3	142.2	16 40.4	−51.0	142.5	25
22 09.2	48.0	141.4	20 35.1	48.9	141.9	19 00.4	49.6	142.3	17 25.1	50.3	142.7	15 49.4	51.1	143.1	26
21 21.2	48.2	142.1	19 46.2	48.9	142.5	18 10.8	49.8	142.9	16 34.8	50.5	143.3	14 58.3	51.1	143.6	27
20 33.0	48.3	142.7	18 57.3	49.1	143.1	17 21.0	49.8	143.5	15 44.3	50.5	143.9	14 07.2	51.2	144.2	28
19 44.7	48.5	143.3	18 08.2	49.2	143.7	16 31.2	49.9	144.1	14 53.8	50.6	144.4	13 16.0	51.3	144.7	29

Dec.	40° Hc	d	Z	42° Hc	d	Z	44° Hc	d	Z	46° Hc	d	Z	48° Hc	d	Z
0	35 55.9	+47.5	127.5	34 42.0	+48.7	128.6	33 26.3	+49.9	129.6	32 09.0	+50.9	130.6	30 50.2	+51.8	131.5
1	36 43.4	47.2	126.7	35 30.7	48.5	127.9	34 16.2	49.6	128.9	32 59.9	50.7	130.0	31 42.0	51.7	130.9
2	37 30.6	46.9	125.9	36 19.2	48.2	127.1	35 05.8	49.4	128.3	33 50.6	50.5	129.3	32 33.7	51.5	130.3
3	38 17.5	46.5	125.1	37 07.4	47.8	126.4	35 55.2	49.1	127.6	34 41.1	50.2	128.7	33 25.2	51.3	129.7
4	39 04.0	46.3	124.3	37 55.2	47.6	125.6	36 44.3	48.9	126.9	35 31.3	50.1	128.0	34 16.5	51.2	129.1
5	39 50.3	+45.8	123.5	38 42.8	+47.3	124.8	37 33.2	+48.6	126.1	36 21.4	+49.8	127.3	35 07.7	+50.9	128.5
6	40 36.1	45.5	122.7	39 30.1	47.0	124.1	38 21.8	48.3	125.4	37 11.2	49.6	126.6	35 58.6	50.7	127.8
7	41 21.6	45.1	121.8	40 17.1	46.6	123.2	39 10.1	48.0	124.6	38 00.8	49.3	125.9	36 49.3	50.5	127.2
8	42 06.7	44.6	120.9	41 03.7	46.2	122.4	39 58.1	47.7	123.8	38 50.1	49.0	125.2	37 39.8	50.3	126.5
9	42 51.3	44.3	120.0	41 49.9	45.9	121.6	40 45.8	47.3	123.0	39 39.1	48.7	124.5	38 30.1	50.0	125.8
10	43 35.6	+43.7	119.1	42 35.8	+45.4	120.7	41 33.1	+47.0	122.2	40 27.8	+48.4	123.7	39 20.1	+49.7	125.1
11	44 19.3	43.3	118.1	43 21.2	45.0	119.8	42 20.1	46.6	121.3	41 16.2	48.1	122.9	40 09.8	49.4	124.3
12	45 02.6	42.8	117.1	44 06.2	44.6	118.9	43 06.7	46.3	120.5	42 04.3	47.8	122.1	40 59.2	49.2	123.6
13	45 45.4	42.2	116.1	44 50.8	44.1	117.9	43 53.0	45.8	119.7	42 52.1	47.4	121.3	41 48.4	48.8	122.8
14	46 27.6	41.7	115.1	45 34.9	43.6	117.0	44 38.8	45.4	118.8	43 39.5	47.0	120.4	42 37.2	48.6	122.1
15	47 09.3	+41.1	114.1	46 18.5	+43.1	116.0	45 24.2	+44.9	117.8	44 26.5	+46.6	119.6	43 25.8	+48.1	121.2
16	47 50.4	40.4	113.0	47 01.6	42.5	115.0	46 09.1	44.4	116.9	45 13.1	46.2	118.7	44 13.9	47.8	120.4
17	48 30.8	39.8	111.9	47 44.1	41.9	113.9	46 53.5	43.9	115.9	45 59.3	45.8	117.8	45 01.7	47.4	119.6
18	49 10.6	39.1	110.7	48 26.0	41.4	112.9	47 37.4	43.4	114.9	46 45.1	45.2	116.8	45 49.1	47.0	118.7
19	49 49.7	38.4	109.6	49 07.4	40.7	111.8	48 20.8	42.8	113.9	47 30.3	44.8	115.9	46 36.1	46.6	117.8
20	50 28.1	+37.7	108.4	49 48.1	+40.0	110.6	49 03.6	+42.2	112.8	48 15.1	+44.2	114.9	47 22.7	+46.1	116.9
21	51 05.8	36.8	107.1	50 28.1	39.3	109.5	49 45.8	41.6	111.7	48 59.3	43.7	113.9	48 08.8	45.6	115.9
22	51 42.6	36.0	105.9	51 07.4	38.5	108.3	50 27.4	40.9	110.6	49 43.0	43.1	112.8	48 54.4	45.1	114.9
23	52 18.6	35.1	104.6	51 45.9	37.7	107.1	51 08.3	40.2	109.4	50 26.1	42.5	111.7	49 39.5	44.6	113.9
24	52 53.7	34.2	103.2	52 23.6	36.9	105.8	51 48.5	39.5	108.2	51 08.6	41.8	110.6	50 24.1	44.0	112.9
25	53 27.9	+33.2	101.9	53 00.5	+36.1	104.5	52 28.0	+38.6	107.0	51 50.4	+41.1	109.5	51 08.1	+43.4	111.8
26	54 01.1	32.3	100.5	53 36.6	35.1	103.1	53 06.6	37.9	105.8	52 31.5	40.4	108.3	51 51.5	42.7	110.7
27	54 33.4	31.1	99.0	54 11.7	34.1	101.8	53 44.5	36.9	104.4	53 11.9	39.6	107.0	52 34.2	42.0	109.6
28	55 04.5	30.1	97.5	54 45.8	33.2	100.4	54 21.4	36.1	103.1	53 51.5	38.8	105.8	53 16.2	41.4	108.4
29	55 34.6	28.9	96.0	55 19.0	32.0	98.9	54 57.5	35.1	101.7	54 30.3	37.9	104.5	53 57.6	40.5	107.2

Dec.	50° Hc	d	Z	52° Hc	d	Z	54° Hc	d	Z	56° Hc	d	Z	58° Hc	d	Z
0	29 29.9	+52.8	132.4	28 08.4	+53.5	133.2	26 45.7	+54.3	134.0	25 21.8	+55.0	134.7	23 57.0	+55.7	135.3
1	30 22.7	52.6	131.8	29 01.9	53.5	132.7	27 40.0	54.2	133.5	26 16.8	55.0	134.2	24 52.7	55.5	134.9
2	31 15.3	52.4	131.3	29 55.4	53.3	132.2	28 34.2	54.1	133.0	27 11.8	54.8	133.8	25 48.2	55.5	134.5
3	32 07.7	52.3	130.7	30 48.7	53.2	131.6	29 28.3	54.0	132.5	28 06.6	54.8	133.3	26 43.7	55.3	134.1
4	33 00.0	52.1	130.1	31 41.9	53.0	131.1	30 22.3	53.9	132.0	29 01.4	54.6	132.8	27 39.2	55.3	133.6
5	33 52.1	+52.0	129.5	32 34.9	+52.9	130.5	31 16.2	+53.7	131.5	29 56.0	+54.5	132.4	28 34.5	+55.3	133.2
6	34 44.1	51.8	128.9	33 27.8	52.8	130.0	32 09.9	53.7	131.0	30 50.5	54.5	131.9	29 29.8	55.1	132.7
7	35 35.9	51.5	128.3	34 20.6	52.5	129.4	33 03.6	53.4	130.4	31 45.0	54.3	131.4	30 24.9	55.1	132.3
8	36 27.4	51.4	127.7	35 13.1	52.4	128.8	33 57.0	53.4	129.9	32 39.3	54.2	130.9	31 20.0	55.0	131.8
9	37 18.8	51.2	127.0	36 05.5	52.3	128.2	34 50.4	53.2	129.3	33 33.5	54.1	130.4	32 15.0	54.8	131.4
10	38 10.0	+50.9	126.4	36 57.8	+52.0	127.6	35 43.6	+53.0	128.8	34 27.6	+53.9	129.8	33 09.8	+54.8	130.9
11	39 00.9	50.7	125.7	37 49.8	51.8	127.0	36 36.6	52.8	128.2	35 21.5	53.8	129.3	34 04.6	54.6	130.4
12	39 51.6	50.4	125.0	38 41.6	51.6	126.3	37 29.4	52.7	127.6	36 15.3	53.6	128.8	34 59.2	54.5	129.9
13	40 42.0	50.2	124.3	39 33.2	51.3	125.7	38 22.1	52.5	127.0	37 08.9	53.5	128.2	35 53.7	54.4	129.3
14	41 32.2	49.9	123.6	40 24.6	51.1	125.0	39 14.6	52.3	126.4	38 02.4	53.3	127.6	36 48.1	54.2	128.8
15	42 22.1	+49.6	122.8	41 15.7	+50.9	124.3	40 06.9	+52.0	125.7	38 55.7	+53.1	127.0	37 42.3	+54.1	128.3
16	43 11.7	49.3	122.1	42 06.6	50.8	123.6	40 58.9	51.9	125.1	39 48.8	52.9	126.4	38 36.4	53.9	127.7
17	44 01.0	48.9	121.3	42 57.2	50.4	122.9	41 50.8	51.5	124.4	40 41.7	52.7	125.8	39 30.3	53.8	127.2
18	44 49.9	48.6	120.5	43 47.6	50.0	122.1	42 42.3	51.4	123.7	41 34.4	52.6	125.2	40 24.1	53.5	126.6
19	45 38.5	48.2	119.6	44 37.6	49.7	121.4	43 33.7	51.0	123.0	42 27.0	52.2	124.5	41 17.6	53.4	126.0
20	46 26.7	+47.8	118.8	45 27.3	+49.3	120.6	44 24.7	+50.8	122.3	43 19.2	+52.1	123.9	42 11.0	+53.2	125.4
21	47 14.5	47.4	117.9	46 16.7	49.0	119.7	45 15.5	50.5	121.5	44 11.3	51.8	123.2	43 04.2	53.0	124.8
22	48 01.9	46.9	117.0	47 05.7	48.6	118.9	46 06.0	50.1	120.7	45 03.1	51.5	122.5	43 57.2	52.7	124.1
23	48 48.8	46.5	116.0	47 54.3	48.2	118.0	46 56.1	49.8	119.9	45 54.6	51.2	121.7	44 49.9	52.5	123.5
24	49 35.3	46.0	115.1	48 42.5	47.8	117.1	47 45.9	49.5	119.1	46 45.8	50.9	121.0	45 42.4	52.3	122.8
25	50 21.3	+45.5	114.1	49 30.3	+47.3	116.2	48 35.4	+49.0	118.3	47 36.7	+50.6	120.2	46 34.7	+51.9	122.1
26	51 06.8	44.8	113.0	50 17.6	46.9	115.3	49 24.4	48.7	117.4	48 27.3	50.3	119.4	47 26.6	51.7	121.3
27	51 51.6	44.3	112.0	51 04.5	46.3	114.3	50 13.1	48.2	116.5	49 17.6	49.8	118.6	48 18.3	51.4	120.6
28	52 35.9	43.7	110.9	51 50.8	45.8	113.3	51 01.3	47.7	115.5	50 07.4	49.5	117.7	49 09.7	51.1	119.8
29	53 19.6	43.0	109.7	52 36.6	45.2	112.2	51 49.0	47.2	114.6	50 56.9	49.1	116.8	50 00.8	50.7	119.0

40°			42°			44°			46°			48°			Dec.
Hc	d	Z	Hc	d	Z	Hc	d	Z	Hc	d	Z	Hc	d	Z	
° ′	′	°	° ′	′	°	° ′	′	°	° ′	′	°	° ′	′	°	°
35 55.9	−47.8	127.5	34 42.0	−48.9	128.6	33 26.3	−50.0	129.6	32 09.0	−51.1	130.6	30 50.2	−52.0	131.5	0
35 08.1	48.0	128.2	33 53.1	49.2	129.3	32 36.3	50.3	130.3	31 17.9	51.2	131.2	29 58.2	52.2	132.1	1
34 20.1	48.3	128.9	33 03.9	49.4	130.0	31 46.0	50.4	130.9	30 26.7	51.4	131.8	29 06.0	52.3	132.7	2
33 31.8	48.5	129.6	32 14.5	49.7	130.6	30 55.6	50.6	131.6	29 35.3	51.6	132.4	28 13.7	52.4	133.2	3
32 43.3	48.8	130.3	31 24.8	49.8	131.3	30 05.0	50.8	132.2	28 43.7	51.7	133.0	27 21.3	52.6	133.8	4
31 54.5	−49.0	131.0	30 35.0	−50.0	131.9	29 14.2	−51.0	132.8	27 52.0	−51.8	133.6	26 28.7	−52.7	134.3	5
31 05.5	49.1	131.7	29 45.0	50.2	132.6	28 23.2	51.1	133.4	27 00.2	52.0	134.2	25 36.0	52.8	134.9	6
30 16.4	49.4	132.4	28 54.8	50.3	133.2	27 32.1	51.3	134.0	26 08.2	52.1	134.7	24 43.2	52.9	135.4	7
29 27.0	49.6	133.0	28 04.5	50.6	133.8	26 40.8	51.4	134.6	25 16.1	52.3	135.3	23 50.3	53.0	135.9	8
28 37.4	49.8	133.7	27 13.9	50.6	134.4	25 49.4	51.6	135.1	24 23.8	52.3	135.8	22 57.3	53.1	136.4	9
27 47.6	−49.9	134.3	26 23.3	−50.9	135.0	24 57.8	−51.6	135.7	23 31.5	−52.5	136.3	22 04.2	−53.1	136.9	10
26 57.7	50.1	134.9	25 32.4	50.9	135.6	24 06.2	51.8	136.3	22 39.0	52.5	136.9	21 11.1	53.3	137.4	11
26 07.6	50.2	135.5	24 41.5	51.2	136.2	23 14.4	51.9	136.8	21 46.5	52.7	137.4	20 17.8	53.4	137.9	12
25 17.4	50.4	136.2	23 50.3	51.2	136.8	22 22.5	52.0	137.4	20 53.8	52.7	137.9	19 24.4	53.4	138.4	13
24 27.0	50.6	136.8	22 59.1	51.3	137.4	21 30.5	52.2	137.9	20 01.1	52.9	138.4	18 31.0	53.5	138.9	14
23 36.4	−50.8	137.3	22 07.8	−51.5	137.9	20 38.3	−52.2	138.4	19 08.2	−52.9	138.9	17 37.5	−53.6	139.3	15
22 45.8	50.8	137.9	21 16.3	51.6	138.5	19 46.1	52.3	139.0	18 15.3	53.0	139.4	16 43.9	53.6	139.8	16
21 55.0	50.9	138.5	20 24.7	51.6	139.0	18 53.8	52.4	139.5	17 22.3	53.0	139.9	15 50.3	53.7	140.3	17
21 04.1	51.1	139.1	19 33.1	51.8	139.6	18 01.4	52.4	140.0	16 29.3	53.2	140.4	14 56.6	53.8	140.7	18
20 13.0	51.1	139.6	18 41.3	51.9	140.1	17 09.0	52.6	140.5	15 36.1	53.2	140.9	14 02.8	53.8	141.2	19
19 21.9	−51.2	140.2	17 49.4	−51.9	140.6	16 16.4	−52.6	141.0	14 42.9	−53.2	141.4	13 09.0	−53.9	141.7	20
18 30.7	51.3	140.7	16 57.5	52.0	141.1	15 23.8	52.7	141.5	13 49.7	53.3	141.8	12 15.1	53.9	142.1	21
17 39.4	51.5	141.3	16 05.5	52.1	141.7	14 31.1	52.7	142.0	12 56.4	53.4	142.3	11 21.2	53.9	142.6	22
16 47.9	51.4	141.8	15 13.4	52.2	142.2	13 38.4	52.8	142.5	12 03.0	53.4	142.8	10 27.3	54.0	143.0	23
15 56.5	51.6	142.4	14 21.2	52.2	142.7	12 45.6	52.9	143.0	11 09.6	53.4	143.2	9 33.3	54.0	143.5	24
15 04.9	−51.7	142.9	13 29.0	−52.3	143.2	11 52.7	−52.9	143.5	10 16.2	−53.5	143.7	8 39.3	−54.0	143.9	25
14 13.2	51.7	143.4	12 36.7	52.3	143.7	10 59.8	52.9	143.9	9 22.7	53.5	144.2	7 45.3	54.1	144.3	26
13 21.5	51.8	143.9	11 44.3	52.4	144.2	10 06.9	53.0	144.4	8 29.2	53.6	144.6	6 51.2	54.1	144.8	27
12 29.7	51.8	144.5	10 51.9	52.4	144.7	9 13.9	53.0	144.9	7 35.6	53.6	145.1	5 57.1	54.1	145.2	28
11 37.9	51.9	145.0	9 59.5	52.5	145.2	8 20.9	53.1	145.4	6 42.0	53.6	145.5	5 03.0	54.1	145.6	29

50°			52°			54°			56°			58°			Dec.
Hc	d	Z	Hc	d	Z	Hc	d	Z	Hc	d	Z	Hc	d	Z	
° ′	′	°	° ′	′	°	° ′	′	°	° ′	′	°	° ′	′	°	°
29 29.9	−52.9	132.4	28 08.4	−53.7	133.2	26 45.7	−54.5	134.0	25 21.8	−55.1	134.7	23 57.0	−55.7	135.3	0
28 37.0	53.0	132.9	27 14.7	53.8	133.7	25 51.2	54.5	134.4	24 26.7	55.1	135.1	23 01.3	55.8	135.7	1
27 44.0	53.1	133.5	26 20.9	53.8	134.2	24 56.7	54.5	134.9	23 31.6	55.2	135.5	22 05.5	55.8	136.1	2
26 50.9	53.2	134.0	25 27.1	54.0	134.7	24 02.2	54.7	135.3	22 36.4	55.3	135.9	21 09.7	55.9	136.5	3
25 57.7	53.3	134.5	24 33.1	54.1	135.2	23 07.5	54.7	135.8	21 41.1	55.4	136.4	20 13.8	55.9	136.9	4
25 04.4	−53.5	135.0	23 39.0	−54.1	135.6	22 12.8	−54.8	136.2	20 45.7	−55.4	136.8	19 17.9	−56.0	137.3	5
24 10.9	53.5	135.5	22 44.9	54.3	136.1	21 18.0	54.9	136.7	19 50.3	55.5	137.2	18 21.9	56.0	137.7	6
23 17.4	53.7	136.0	21 50.6	54.3	136.6	20 23.1	55.0	137.1	18 54.8	55.5	137.6	17 25.9	56.1	138.0	7
22 23.7	53.7	136.5	20 56.3	54.4	137.0	19 28.1	55.0	137.5	17 59.3	55.6	138.0	16 29.8	56.1	138.4	8
21 30.0	53.8	137.0	20 01.9	54.4	137.5	18 33.1	55.0	138.0	17 03.7	55.6	138.4	15 33.7	56.1	138.8	9
20 36.2	−53.9	137.4	19 07.5	−54.5	137.9	17 38.1	−55.1	138.4	16 08.1	−55.7	138.8	14 37.6	−56.2	139.1	10
19 42.3	53.9	137.9	18 13.0	54.6	138.4	16 43.0	55.2	138.8	15 12.4	55.7	139.2	13 41.4	56.2	139.5	11
18 48.4	54.0	138.4	17 18.4	54.6	138.8	15 47.8	55.2	139.2	14 16.7	55.7	139.6	12 45.2	56.2	139.9	12
17 54.4	54.1	138.8	16 23.8	54.7	139.2	14 52.6	55.2	139.6	13 21.0	55.8	139.9	11 49.0	56.3	140.2	13
17 00.3	54.1	139.3	15 29.1	54.8	139.7	13 57.4	55.3	140.0	12 25.2	55.8	140.3	10 52.7	56.3	140.6	14
16 06.2	−54.2	139.7	14 34.3	−54.7	140.1	13 02.1	−55.4	140.4	11 29.4	−55.8	140.7	9 56.4	−56.3	140.9	15
15 12.0	54.3	140.2	13 39.6	54.9	140.5	12 06.7	55.3	140.8	10 33.6	55.9	141.1	9 00.1	56.3	141.3	16
14 17.7	54.3	140.6	12 44.7	54.8	140.9	11 11.4	55.4	141.2	9 37.7	55.9	141.4	8 03.8	56.4	141.6	17
13 23.4	54.3	141.1	11 49.9	54.9	141.3	10 16.0	55.4	141.6	8 41.8	55.9	141.8	7 07.4	56.3	142.0	18
12 29.1	54.4	141.5	10 55.0	54.9	141.8	9 20.6	55.4	142.0	7 45.9	55.9	142.2	6 11.1	56.4	142.3	19
11 34.7	−54.4	141.9	10 00.1	−55.0	142.2	8 25.2	−55.5	142.4	6 50.0	−55.9	142.5	5 14.7	−56.4	142.7	20
10 40.3	54.5	142.4	9 05.1	55.0	142.6	7 29.7	55.5	142.8	5 54.1	55.9	142.9	4 18.3	56.4	143.0	21
9 45.8	54.5	142.8	8 10.1	55.0	143.0	6 34.2	55.5	143.1	4 58.1	55.9	143.3	3 21.9	56.4	143.3	22
8 51.3	54.5	143.2	7 15.1	55.0	143.4	5 38.7	55.5	143.5	4 02.2	56.0	143.6	2 25.5	56.4	143.7	23
7 56.8	54.5	143.6	6 20.1	55.1	143.8	4 43.2	55.5	143.9	3 06.2	56.0	144.0	1 29.1	56.4	144.0	24
7 02.3	−54.6	144.1	5 25.0	−55.0	144.2	3 47.7	−55.6	144.3	2 10.2	−56.0	144.3	0 32.7	−56.4	144.4	25
6 07.7	54.6	144.5	4 30.0	55.1	144.6	2 52.1	55.5	144.7	1 14.2	56.0	144.7	0 23.7	+56.4	35.3	26
5 13.1	54.6	144.9	3 34.9	55.1	145.0	1 56.6	55.6	145.0	0 18.2	−56.0	145.1	1 20.1	56.4	35.0	27
4 18.5	54.6	145.3	2 39.8	55.1	145.4	1 01.0	55.5	145.4	0 37.8	+56.0	34.6	2 16.5	56.4	34.6	28
3 23.9	54.6	145.7	1 44.7	55.1	145.8	0 05.5	−55.6	145.8	1 33.8	55.9	34.2	3 12.9	56.4	34.3	29

Dec.	0° Hc	d	Z	2° Hc	d	Z	4° Hc	d	Z	6° Hc	d	Z	8° Hc	d	Z
°	° ′	′	°	° ′	′	°	° ′	′	°	° ′	′	°	° ′	′	°
0	48 00.0	− 0.6	90.0	47 57.7	+ 2.5	92.2	47 50.7	+ 5.7	94.4	47 39.2	+ 8.7	96.6	47 23.1	+ 11.7	98.8
1	47 59.4	1.7	88.5	48 00.2	1.4	90.7	47 56.4	4.5	92.9	47 47.9	7.6	95.2	47 34.8	10.7	97.3
2	47 57.7	2.9	87.0	48 01.6	+ 0.2	89.2	48 00.9	3.3	91.5	47 55.5	6.5	93.7	47 45.5	9.6	95.9
3	47 54.8	4.1	85.5	48 01.8	− 0.9	87.7	48 04.2	2.2	90.0	48 02.0	5.3	92.2	47 55.1	8.4	94.4
4	47 50.7	5.2	84.0	48 00.9	2.1	86.2	48 06.4	+ 1.1	88.5	48 07.3	4.2	90.7	48 03.5	7.3	92.9
5	47 45.5	− 6.3	82.6	47 58.8	− 3.3	84.7	48 07.5	− 0.2	87.0	48 11.5	+ 3.0	89.2	48 10.8	+ 6.1	91.4
6	47 39.2	7.5	81.1	47 55.5	4.4	83.3	48 07.3	1.3	85.5	48 14.5	1.8	87.7	48 16.9	5.0	89.9
7	47 31.7	8.6	79.6	47 51.1	5.6	81.8	48 06.0	2.5	84.0	48 16.3	+ 0.6	86.2	48 21.9	3.8	88.4
8	47 23.1	9.8	78.1	47 45.5	6.7	80.3	48 03.5	3.6	82.5	48 16.9	− 0.5	84.7	48 25.7	2.6	86.9
9	47 13.3	10.8	76.7	47 38.8	7.8	78.8	47 59.9	4.8	81.0	48 16.4	1.7	83.2	48 28.3	1.4	85.4
10	47 02.5	− 11.9	75.2	47 31.0	− 9.0	77.3	47 55.1	− 6.0	79.5	48 14.7	− 2.9	81.7	48 29.7	+ 0.3	83.9
11	46 50.6	12.9	73.8	47 22.0	10.1	75.9	47 49.1	7.1	78.0	48 11.8	4.0	80.2	48 30.0	− 1.0	82.4
12	46 37.7	14.1	72.4	47 11.9	11.1	74.4	47 42.0	8.2	76.5	48 07.8	5.2	78.7	48 29.0	2.1	80.9
13	46 23.6	15.0	71.0	47 00.8	12.3	73.0	47 33.8	9.3	75.1	48 02.6	6.4	77.2	48 26.9	3.3	79.4
14	46 08.6	16.1	69.6	46 48.5	13.3	71.5	47 24.5	10.5	73.6	47 56.2	7.5	75.7	48 23.6	4.5	77.9
15	45 52.5	− 17.1	68.2	46 35.2	− 14.3	70.1	47 14.0	− 11.5	72.2	47 48.7	− 8.6	74.2	48 19.1	− 5.6	76.4
16	45 35.4	18.0	66.8	46 20.9	15.4	68.7	47 02.5	12.7	70.7	47 40.1	9.8	72.8	48 13.5	6.8	74.9
17	45 17.4	19.0	65.4	46 05.5	16.4	67.3	46 49.8	13.6	69.3	47 30.3	10.8	71.3	48 06.7	8.0	73.4
18	44 58.4	20.0	64.1	45 49.1	17.4	65.9	46 36.2	14.8	67.9	47 19.5	12.0	69.9	47 58.7	9.0	71.9
19	44 38.4	20.8	62.8	45 31.7	18.4	64.6	46 21.4	15.7	66.4	47 07.5	13.0	68.4	47 49.7	10.3	70.5
20	44 17.6	− 21.8	61.5	45 13.3	− 19.3	63.2	46 05.7	− 16.8	65.1	46 54.5	− 14.1	67.0	47 39.4	− 11.3	69.0
21	43 55.8	22.6	60.2	44 54.0	20.3	61.9	45 48.9	17.8	63.7	46 40.4	15.2	65.6	47 28.1	12.4	67.5
22	43 33.2	23.5	58.9	44 33.7	21.1	60.5	45 31.1	18.7	62.3	46 25.2	16.2	64.2	47 15.7	13.5	66.1
23	43 09.7	24.3	57.6	44 12.6	22.1	59.2	45 12.4	19.6	61.0	46 09.0	17.1	62.8	47 02.2	14.6	64.7
24	42 45.4	25.1	56.4	43 50.5	22.9	57.9	44 52.8	20.6	59.6	45 51.9	18.2	61.4	46 47.6	15.6	63.2
25	42 20.3	− 25.8	55.1	43 27.6	− 23.7	56.7	44 32.2	− 21.5	58.3	45 33.7	− 19.1	60.0	46 32.0	− 16.6	61.8
26	41 54.5	26.7	53.9	43 03.9	24.6	55.4	44 10.7	22.4	57.0	45 14.6	20.1	58.7	46 15.4	17.6	60.4
27	41 27.8	27.3	52.7	42 39.3	25.3	54.2	43 48.3	23.3	55.7	44 54.5	21.0	57.3	45 57.8	18.7	59.1
28	41 00.5	28.1	51.5	42 14.0	26.2	52.9	43 25.0	24.0	54.4	44 33.5	21.9	56.0	45 39.1	19.6	57.7
29	40 32.4	28.8	50.4	41 47.8	26.9	51.7	43 01.0	24.9	53.2	44 11.6	22.8	54.7	45 19.5	20.5	56.3

Dec.	10° Hc	d	Z	12° Hc	d	Z	14° Hc	d	Z	16° Hc	d	Z	18° Hc	d	Z
°	° ′	′	°	° ′	′	°	° ′	′	°	° ′	′	°	° ′	′	°
0	47 02.5	+ 14.8	100.9	46 37.7	+ 17.6	103.0	46 08.6	+ 20.4	105.0	45 35.4	+ 23.2	107.0	44 58.4	+ 25.8	108.9
1	47 17.3	13.7	99.5	46 55.3	16.6	101.6	46 29.0	19.5	103.7	45 58.6	22.3	105.7	45 24.2	24.9	107.7
2	47 31.0	12.6	98.1	47 11.9	15.6	100.2	46 48.5	18.5	102.3	46 20.9	21.3	104.4	45 49.1	24.0	106.4
3	47 43.6	11.5	96.6	47 27.5	14.5	98.8	47 07.0	17.5	100.9	46 42.2	20.3	103.0	46 13.1	23.1	105.0
4	47 55.1	10.3	95.1	47 42.0	13.5	97.3	47 24.5	16.4	99.5	47 02.5	19.3	101.6	46 36.2	22.1	103.7
5	48 05.4	+ 9.3	93.7	47 55.5	+ 12.3	95.9	47 40.9	+ 15.3	98.1	47 21.8	+ 18.3	100.2	46 58.3	+ 21.2	102.3
6	48 14.7	8.1	92.2	48 07.8	11.2	94.4	47 56.2	14.3	96.6	47 40.1	17.2	98.8	47 19.5	20.1	101.0
7	48 22.8	6.9	90.7	48 19.0	10.0	92.9	48 10.5	13.1	95.2	47 57.3	16.2	97.4	47 39.6	19.1	99.6
8	48 29.7	5.8	89.2	48 29.0	8.9	91.5	48 23.6	12.0	93.7	48 13.5	15.1	96.0	47 58.7	18.1	98.2
9	48 35.5	4.6	87.7	48 37.9	7.8	90.0	48 35.6	10.9	92.2	48 28.6	13.9	94.5	48 16.8	17.0	96.7
10	48 40.1	+ 3.3	86.2	48 45.7	+ 6.5	88.5	48 46.5	+ 9.7	90.7	48 42.5	+ 12.9	93.0	48 33.8	+ 16.0	95.3
11	48 43.4	2.3	84.7	48 52.2	5.4	87.0	48 56.2	8.5	89.2	48 55.4	11.7	91.5	48 49.8	14.7	93.8
12	48 45.7	+ 1.0	83.2	48 57.6	4.2	85.4	49 04.7	7.4	87.7	49 07.1	10.5	90.0	49 04.5	13.7	92.4
13	48 46.7	− 0.2	81.6	49 01.8	2.9	83.9	49 12.1	6.1	86.2	49 17.6	9.3	88.5	49 18.2	12.5	90.9
14	48 46.5	1.4	80.1	49 04.7	1.8	82.4	49 18.2	5.0	84.7	49 26.9	8.1	87.0	49 30.7	11.3	89.4
15	48 45.1	− 2.6	78.6	49 06.5	+ 0.6	80.9	49 23.2	+ 3.7	83.2	49 35.0	+ 7.0	85.5	49 42.0	+ 10.1	87.8
16	48 42.5	3.7	77.1	49 07.1	− 0.7	79.3	49 26.9	2.5	81.6	49 42.0	5.7	84.0	49 52.1	8.9	86.3
17	48 38.8	5.0	75.6	49 06.4	1.9	77.8	49 29.4	+ 1.3	80.1	49 47.7	4.4	82.4	50 01.0	7.7	84.8
18	48 33.8	6.1	74.1	49 04.5	3.0	76.3	49 30.7	0.0	78.6	49 52.1	3.3	80.9	50 08.7	6.5	83.2
19	48 27.7	7.3	72.6	49 01.5	4.3	74.8	49 30.7	− 1.1	77.0	49 55.4	2.0	79.3	50 15.2	5.2	81.7
20	48 20.4	− 8.4	71.1	48 57.2	− 5.4	73.2	49 29.6	− 2.4	75.5	49 57.4	+ 0.7	77.8	50 20.4	+ 3.9	80.1
21	48 12.0	9.6	69.6	48 51.8	6.7	71.7	49 27.2	3.6	73.9	49 58.1	− 0.5	76.2	50 24.3	2.7	78.6
22	48 02.4	10.7	68.1	48 45.1	7.8	70.2	49 23.6	4.9	72.4	49 57.6	1.7	74.7	50 27.0	1.4	77.0
23	47 51.7	11.8	66.6	48 37.3	6.9	68.7	49 18.7	6.0	70.9	49 55.9	3.0	73.1	50 28.4	+ 0.2	75.4
24	47 39.9	13.0	65.2	48 28.3	10.1	67.2	49 12.7	7.2	69.3	49 52.9	4.3	71.6	50 28.6	− 1.2	73.8
25	47 26.9	− 14.0	63.7	48 18.2	− 11.3	65.7	49 05.5	− 8.5	67.8	49 48.6	− 5.4	70.0	50 27.4	− 2.4	72.3
26	47 12.9	15.1	62.3	48 06.9	12.4	64.3	48 57.0	9.6	66.3	49 43.2	6.7	68.5	50 25.0	3.6	70.7
27	46 57.8	16.1	60.9	47 54.5	13.5	62.8	48 47.4	10.7	64.8	49 36.5	7.9	66.9	50 21.4	4.9	69.1
28	46 41.7	17.2	59.5	47 41.0	14.6	61.3	48 36.7	11.9	63.3	49 28.6	9.1	65.4	50 16.5	6.2	67.6
29	46 24.5	18.1	58.1	47 26.4	15.7	59.9	48 24.8	13.1	61.8	49 19.5	10.3	63.9	50 10.3	7.4	66.0

0°			2°			4°			6°			8°			Dec.
Hc	d	Z	Hc	d	Z	Hc	d	Z	Hc	d	Z	Hc	d	Z	°
48 00.0	-0.6	90.0	47 57.7	-3.7	92.2	47 50.7	-6.8	94.4	47 39.2	-9.9	96.6	47 23.1	-12.9	98.8	0
47 59.4	1.7	91.5	47 54.0	4.9	93.7	47 43.9	7.9	95.9	47 29.3	11.0	98.1	47 10.2	14.0	100.2	1
47 57.7	2.9	93.0	47 49.1	6.0	95.2	47 36.0	9.1	97.4	47 18.3	12.1	99.5	46 56.2	15.0	101.7	2
47 54.8	4.1	94.5	47 43.1	7.1	96.7	47 26.9	10.2	98.8	47 06.2	13.1	101.0	46 41.2	16.0	103.1	3
47 50.7	5.2	96.0	47 36.0	8.3	98.1	47 16.7	11.3	100.3	46 53.1	14.2	102.4	46 25.2	17.1	104.5	4
47 45.5	-6.3	97.4	47 27.7	-9.4	99.6	47 05.4	-12.3	101.7	46 38.9	-15.3	103.8	46 08.1	-18.0	105.9	5
47 39.2	7.5	98.9	47 18.3	10.5	101.1	46 53.1	13.4	103.2	46 23.6	16.2	105.2	45 50.1	19.0	107.2	6
47 31.7	8.6	100.4	47 07.8	11.6	102.5	46 39.7	14.5	104.6	46 07.4	17.3	106.6	45 31.1	20.0	108.6	7
47 23.1	9.8	101.9	46 56.2	12.6	104.0	46 25.2	15.5	106.0	45 50.1	18.3	108.0	45 11.1	20.9	109.9	8
47 13.3	10.8	103.3	46 43.6	13.7	105.4	46 09.7	16.5	107.4	45 31.8	19.2	109.4	44 50.2	21.9	111.3	9
47 02.5	-11.9	104.8	46 29.9	-14.8	106.8	45 53.2	-17.5	108.8	45 12.6	-20.2	110.7	44 28.3	-22.7	112.6	10
46 50.6	12.9	106.2	46 15.1	15.8	108.2	45 35.7	18.5	110.2	44 52.4	21.0	112.0	44 05.6	23.5	113.9	11
46 37.7	14.1	107.6	45 59.3	16.7	109.6	45 17.2	19.5	111.5	44 31.4	22.0	113.4	43 42.1	24.5	115.1	12
46 23.6	15.0	109.0	45 42.6	17.8	111.0	44 57.7	20.3	112.9	44 09.4	22.9	114.7	43 17.6	25.2	116.4	13
46 08.6	16.1	110.4	45 24.8	18.7	112.3	44 37.4	21.3	114.2	43 46.5	23.7	116.0	42 52.4	26.0	117.6	14
45 52.5	-17.1	111.8	45 06.1	-19.7	113.7	44 16.1	-22.2	115.5	43 22.8	-24.5	117.2	42 26.4	-26.8	118.9	15
45 35.4	18.0	113.2	44 46.4	20.6	115.0	43 53.9	23.0	116.8	42 58.3	25.4	118.5	41 59.6	27.6	120.1	16
45 17.4	19.0	114.6	44 25.8	21.5	116.4	43 30.9	23.9	118.1	42 32.9	26.1	119.7	41 32.0	28.2	121.3	17
44 58.4	20.0	115.9	44 04.3	22.4	117.7	43 07.0	24.6	119.3	42 06.8	26.9	120.9	41 03.8	29.0	122.4	18
44 38.4	20.8	117.2	43 41.9	23.2	118.9	42 42.4	25.5	120.6	41 39.9	27.6	122.1	40 34.8	29.7	123.6	19
44 17.6	-21.8	118.5	43 18.7	-24.1	120.2	42 16.9	-26.3	121.8	41 12.3	-28.4	123.3	40 05.1	-30.3	124.7	20
43 55.8	22.6	119.8	42 54.6	24.8	121.5	41 50.6	27.0	123.0	40 43.9	29.0	124.5	39 34.8	30.9	125.9	21
43 33.2	23.5	121.1	42 29.8	25.7	122.7	41 23.6	27.8	124.2	40 14.9	29.7	125.6	39 03.9	31.6	127.0	22
43 09.7	24.3	122.4	42 04.1	26.4	123.9	40 55.8	28.4	125.4	39 45.2	30.4	126.8	38 32.3	32.2	128.1	23
42 45.4	25.1	123.6	41 37.7	27.2	125.1	40 27.4	29.2	126.5	39 14.8	31.0	127.9	38 00.1	32.8	129.1	24
42 20.3	-25.8	124.9	41 10.5	-27.9	126.3	39 58.2	-29.8	127.7	38 43.8	-31.6	129.0	37 27.3	-33.3	130.2	25
41 54.5	26.7	126.1	40 42.6	28.6	127.5	39 28.4	30.4	128.8	38 12.2	32.2	130.1	36 54.0	33.8	131.2	26
41 27.8	27.3	127.3	40 14.0	29.3	128.7	38 58.0	31.1	129.9	37 40.0	32.8	131.1	36 20.2	34.4	132.3	27
41 00.5	28.1	128.5	39 44.7	29.9	129.8	38 26.9	31.7	131.0	37 07.2	33.3	132.2	35 45.8	34.9	133.3	28
40 32.4	28.8	129.6	39 14.8	30.6	130.9	37 55.2	32.2	132.1	36 33.9	33.9	133.2	35 10.9	35.4	134.3	29

10°			12°			14°			16°			18°			Dec.
Hc	d	Z	Hc	d	Z	Hc	d	Z	Hc	d	Z	Hc	d	Z	°
47 02.5	-15.8	100.9	46 37.7	-18.7	103.0	46 08.6	-21.4	105.0	45 35.4	-24.1	107.0	44 58.4	-26.7	108.9	0
46 46.7	16.8	102.3	46 19.0	19.7	104.4	45 47.2	22.4	106.4	45 11.3	24.9	108.3	44 31.7	27.4	110.2	1
46 29.9	17.9	103.7	45 59.3	20.6	105.7	45 24.8	23.3	107.7	44 46.4	25.8	109.6	44 04.3	28.2	111.4	2
46 12.0	18.8	105.1	45 38.7	21.5	107.1	45 01.5	24.1	109.0	44 20.6	26.7	110.9	43 36.1	29.1	112.7	3
45 53.2	19.8	106.5	45 17.2	22.5	108.4	44 37.4	25.0	110.3	43 53.9	27.4	112.1	43 07.0	29.7	113.9	4
45 33.4	-20.8	107.8	44 54.7	-23.3	109.7	44 12.4	-25.9	111.6	43 26.5	-28.2	113.4	42 37.3	-30.5	115.1	5
45 12.6	21.7	109.2	44 31.4	24.3	111.0	43 46.5	26.6	112.8	42 58.3	29.0	114.6	42 06.8	31.2	116.3	6
44 50.9	22.6	110.5	44 07.1	25.0	112.3	43 19.9	27.5	114.1	42 29.3	29.7	115.8	41 35.6	31.8	117.4	7
44 28.3	23.4	111.8	43 42.1	25.9	113.6	42 52.4	28.2	115.3	41 59.6	30.4	116.9	41 03.8	32.5	118.5	8
44 04.9	24.3	113.1	43 16.2	26.7	114.8	42 24.2	28.9	116.5	41 29.2	31.1	118.1	40 31.3	33.2	119.6	9
43 40.6	-25.2	114.3	42 49.5	-27.5	116.0	41 55.3	-29.7	117.7	40 58.1	-31.8	119.2	39 58.1	-33.7	120.7	10
43 15.4	25.9	115.6	42 22.0	28.2	117.3	41 25.6	30.4	118.8	40 26.3	32.4	120.3	39 24.4	34.3	121.8	11
42 49.5	26.7	116.8	41 53.8	28.9	118.4	40 55.2	31.0	120.0	39 53.9	33.0	121.4	38 50.1	34.9	122.8	12
42 22.8	27.5	118.0	41 24.9	29.7	119.6	40 24.2	31.7	121.1	39 20.9	33.6	122.5	38 15.2	35.4	123.9	13
41 55.3	28.3	119.2	40 55.2	30.3	120.8	39 52.5	32.3	122.2	38 47.3	34.1	123.6	37 39.8	35.9	124.9	14
41 27.0	-28.9	120.4	40 24.9	-31.0	121.9	39 20.2	-32.9	123.3	38 13.2	-34.8	124.6	37 03.9	-36.5	125.9	15
40 58.1	29.6	121.6	39 53.9	31.6	123.0	38 47.3	33.4	124.4	37 38.4	35.2	125.7	36 27.4	36.9	126.9	16
40 28.5	30.4	122.7	39 22.3	32.2	124.1	38 13.9	34.1	125.5	37 03.2	35.8	126.7	35 50.5	37.4	127.9	17
39 58.1	30.9	123.9	38 50.1	32.8	125.2	37 39.8	34.6	126.5	36 27.4	36.3	127.7	35 13.1	37.9	128.8	18
39 27.2	31.6	125.0	38 17.3	33.4	126.3	37 05.2	35.1	127.5	35 51.1	36.7	128.7	34 35.2	38.2	129.8	19
38 55.6	-32.2	126.1	37 43.9	-34.0	127.3	36 30.1	-35.6	128.5	35 14.4	-37.2	129.7	33 57.0	-38.7	130.7	20
38 23.4	32.7	127.2	37 09.9	34.5	128.4	35 54.5	36.2	129.5	34 37.2	37.6	130.6	33 18.3	39.1	131.6	21
37 50.6	33.3	128.2	36 35.4	35.0	129.4	35 18.3	36.5	130.5	33 59.6	38.1	131.6	32 39.2	39.5	132.5	22
37 17.3	33.9	129.3	36 00.4	35.5	130.4	34 41.8	37.1	131.5	33 21.5	38.5	132.5	31 59.7	39.8	133.4	23
36 43.4	34.4	130.3	35 24.9	36.0	131.4	34 04.7	37.4	132.4	32 43.0	38.9	133.4	31 19.9	40.2	134.3	24
36 09.0	-34.9	131.3	34 48.9	-36.4	132.4	33 27.3	-37.9	133.4	32 04.1	-39.2	134.3	30 39.7	-40.6	135.2	25
35 34.1	35.5	132.3	34 12.5	36.9	133.3	32 49.4	38.3	134.3	31 24.9	39.6	135.2	29 59.1	40.8	136.0	26
34 58.6	35.9	133.3	33 35.6	37.4	134.3	32 11.1	38.7	135.2	30 45.3	40.0	136.1	29 18.3	41.2	136.9	27
34 22.7	36.3	134.3	32 58.2	37.7	135.2	31 32.4	39.1	136.1	30 05.3	40.3	136.9	28 37.1	41.5	137.7	28
33 46.4	36.8	135.2	32 20.5	38.1	136.2	30 53.3	39.4	137.0	29 25.0	40.6	137.8	27 55.6	41.8	138.5	29

42°, 318° L.H.A. LATITUDE **SAME** NAME

Dec.	20° Hc	d	Z	22° Hc	d	Z	24° Hc	d	Z	26° Hc	d	Z	28° Hc	d	Z
0	44 17.6	+28.3	110.8	44 33.2	+30.7	112.6	42 45.4	+32.9	114.3	41 54.5	+35.0	116.0	41 00.5	+37.0	117.5
1	44 45.9	27.4	109.6	44 03.9	29.8	111.4	43 18.3	32.2	113.2	42 29.5	34.4	114.9	41 37.5	36.5	116.5
2	45 13.3	26.6	108.3	44 33.7	29.2	110.2	43 50.5	31.5	112.0	43 03.9	33.7	113.7	42 14.0	35.8	115.4
3	45 39.9	25.8	107.0	45 02.9	28.2	109.0	44 22.0	30.8	110.8	43 37.6	33.1	112.6	42 49.8	35.2	114.3
4	46 05.7	24.8	105.7	45 31.1	27.5	107.7	44 52.8	29.9	109.6	44 10.7	32.3	111.5	43 25.0	34.6	113.2
5	46 30.5	+24.0	104.4	45 58.6	+26.6	106.4	45 22.7	+29.2	108.4	44 43.0	+31.6	110.3	43 59.6	+33.9	112.1
6	46 54.5	22.9	103.1	46 25.2	25.7	105.1	45 51.9	28.3	107.1	45 14.6	30.8	109.1	44 33.5	33.2	110.9
7	47 17.4	22.0	101.7	46 50.9	24.8	103.8	46 20.2	27.4	105.9	45 45.4	30.0	107.8	45 06.7	32.4	109.8
8	47 39.4	21.1	100.3	47 15.7	23.8	102.5	46 47.6	26.6	104.6	46 15.4	29.2	106.6	45 39.1	31.7	108.6
9	48 00.5	19.9	98.9	47 39.5	22.9	101.1	47 14.2	25.7	103.3	46 44.6	28.3	105.3	46 10.8	30.9	107.3
10	48 20.4	+19.0	97.5	48 02.4	+21.9	99.7	47 39.9	+24.7	101.9	47 12.9	+27.4	104.0	46 41.7	+30.1	106.1
11	48 39.4	17.8	96.1	48 24.3	20.8	98.3	48 04.6	23.7	100.6	47 40.3	26.6	102.7	47 11.8	29.2	104.8
12	48 57.2	16.8	94.7	48 45.1	19.8	96.9	48 28.3	22.7	99.2	48 06.9	25.5	101.4	47 41.0	28.3	103.5
13	49 14.0	15.6	93.2	49 04.9	18.7	95.5	48 51.0	21.7	97.8	48 32.4	24.6	100.0	48 09.3	27.4	102.2
14	49 29.6	14.5	91.7	49 23.6	17.6	94.0	49 12.7	20.6	96.4	48 57.0	23.6	98.6	48 36.7	26.4	100.9
15	49 44.1	+13.3	90.2	49 41.2	+16.4	92.6	49 33.3	+19.6	94.9	49 20.6	+22.6	97.2	49 03.1	+25.5	99.5
16	49 57.4	12.1	88.7	49 57.6	15.3	91.1	49 52.9	18.4	93.4	49 43.2	21.5	95.8	49 28.6	24.5	98.1
17	50 09.5	10.9	87.2	50 12.9	14.1	89.6	50 11.3	17.3	92.0	50 04.7	20.3	94.4	49 53.1	23.4	96.7
18	50 20.4	9.6	85.6	50 27.0	12.9	88.0	50 28.6	16.1	90.5	50 25.0	19.3	92.9	50 16.5	22.3	95.3
19	50 30.0	8.5	84.1	50 39.9	11.7	86.5	50 44.7	14.9	88.9	50 44.3	18.1	91.4	50 38.8	21.3	93.8
20	50 38.5	+7.2	82.5	50 51.6	+10.4	85.0	50 59.6	+13.7	87.4	51 02.4	+16.9	89.9	51 00.1	+20.0	92.4
21	50 45.7	5.9	81.0	51 02.0	9.2	83.4	51 13.3	12.4	85.9	51 19.3	15.7	88.4	51 20.1	19.0	90.9
22	50 51.6	4.6	79.4	51 11.2	7.9	81.8	51 25.7	11.2	84.3	51 35.0	14.5	86.8	51 39.1	17.7	89.3
23	50 56.2	3.4	77.8	51 19.1	6.6	80.2	51 36.9	9.9	82.7	51 49.5	13.2	85.2	51 56.8	16.5	87.8
24	50 59.6	2.0	76.2	51 25.7	5.3	78.6	51 46.8	8.6	81.1	52 02.7	11.9	83.7	52 13.3	15.2	86.2
25	51 01.6	+0.8	74.6	51 31.0	+4.0	77.0	51 55.4	+7.3	79.5	52 14.6	+10.6	82.1	52 28.5	+14.0	84.6
26	51 02.4	-0.5	73.0	51 35.0	2.7	75.4	52 02.7	5.9	77.9	52 25.2	9.3	80.4	52 42.5	12.6	83.0
27	51 01.9	1.8	71.4	51 37.7	+1.4	73.8	52 08.6	4.7	76.3	52 34.5	8.0	78.8	52 55.1	11.3	81.4
28	51 00.1	3.2	69.9	51 39.1	0.0	72.2	52 13.3	3.3	74.7	52 42.5	6.6	77.2	53 06.4	10.0	79.8
29	50 56.9	4.4	68.3	51 39.1	-1.3	70.6	52 16.6	1.9	73.0	52 49.1	5.2	75.5	53 16.4	8.6	78.1

Dec.	30° Hc	d	Z	32° Hc	d	Z	34° Hc	d	Z	36° Hc	d	Z	38° Hc	d	Z
0	40 03.6	+38.9	119.0	39 04.0	+40.7	120.5	38 01.9	+42.4	121.8	36 57.4	+44.0	123.1	35 50.7	+45.5	124.4
1	40 42.5	38.4	118.0	39 44.7	40.3	119.5	38 44.3	41.9	120.9	37 41.4	43.5	122.3	36 36.2	45.0	123.6
2	41 20.9	37.9	117.0	40 25.0	39.7	118.6	39 26.2	41.6	120.0	38 24.9	43.2	121.4	37 21.2	44.8	122.7
3	41 58.8	37.3	116.0	41 04.7	39.2	117.6	40 07.8	41.0	119.1	39 08.1	42.8	120.5	38 06.0	44.3	121.9
4	42 36.1	36.7	114.9	41 43.9	38.7	116.6	40 48.8	40.6	118.1	39 50.9	42.3	119.6	38 50.3	44.0	121.0
5	43 12.8	+36.0	113.8	42 22.6	+38.2	115.5	41 29.4	+40.1	117.1	40 33.2	+41.9	118.7	39 34.3	+43.5	120.1
6	43 48.8	35.5	112.7	43 00.8	37.5	114.5	42 09.5	39.5	116.1	41 15.1	41.4	117.7	40 17.8	43.2	119.2
7	44 24.3	34.7	111.6	43 38.3	36.9	113.4	42 49.0	39.0	115.1	41 56.5	40.9	116.8	41 01.0	42.7	118.3
8	44 59.0	34.1	110.5	44 15.2	36.3	112.3	43 28.0	38.4	114.1	42 37.4	40.3	115.8	41 43.7	42.2	117.4
9	45 33.1	33.3	109.3	44 51.5	35.6	111.2	44 06.4	37.7	113.0	43 17.7	39.9	114.8	42 25.9	41.7	116.4
10	46 06.4	+32.5	108.1	45 27.1	+35.0	110.1	44 44.1	+37.2	111.9	43 57.6	+39.2	113.7	43 07.6	+41.2	115.5
11	46 38.9	31.8	106.9	46 02.1	34.2	108.9	45 21.3	36.5	110.8	44 36.8	38.7	112.7	43 48.8	40.7	114.5
12	47 10.7	31.0	105.7	46 36.3	33.4	107.7	45 57.8	35.8	109.7	45 15.5	38.0	111.6	44 29.5	40.2	113.4
13	47 41.7	30.0	104.4	47 09.7	32.7	106.5	46 33.6	35.3	108.5	45 53.5	37.4	110.5	45 09.7	39.5	112.4
14	48 11.7	29.2	103.1	47 42.4	31.8	105.2	47 08.7	34.3	107.3	46 30.9	36.7	109.4	45 49.2	38.9	111.3
15	48 40.9	+28.3	101.8	48 14.2	+31.0	104.0	47 43.0	+33.6	106.1	47 07.6	+36.0	108.2	46 28.1	+38.3	110.2
16	49 09.2	27.4	100.4	48 45.2	30.1	102.7	48 16.6	32.7	104.9	47 43.6	35.2	107.0	47 06.4	37.6	109.1
17	49 36.6	26.3	99.1	49 15.3	29.2	101.4	48 49.3	31.9	103.6	48 18.8	34.5	105.8	47 44.0	36.9	107.9
18	50 02.9	25.4	97.7	49 44.5	28.2	100.0	49 21.2	31.0	102.3	48 53.3	33.6	104.6	48 20.9	36.1	106.8
19	50 28.3	24.2	96.3	50 12.7	27.2	98.7	49 52.2	30.1	101.0	49 26.9	32.8	103.3	48 57.0	35.4	105.5
20	50 52.5	+23.2	94.8	50 39.9	+26.2	97.3	50 22.3	+29.1	99.7	49 59.7	+31.9	102.0	49 32.4	+34.6	104.3
21	51 15.7	22.1	93.3	51 06.1	25.2	95.8	50 51.4	28.1	98.3	50 31.6	31.0	100.7	50 07.0	33.7	103.0
22	51 37.8	20.9	91.9	51 31.3	24.1	94.4	51 19.5	27.1	96.9	51 02.6	30.1	99.3	50 40.7	32.8	101.7
23	51 58.7	19.8	90.3	51 55.4	22.9	92.9	51 46.6	26.1	95.4	51 32.7	29.0	97.9	51 13.5	31.9	100.4
24	52 18.5	18.5	88.8	52 18.3	21.7	91.4	52 12.7	24.9	94.0	52 01.7	28.0	96.5	51 45.4	30.9	99.1
25	52 37.0	+17.3	87.2	52 40.0	+20.6	89.9	52 37.6	+23.8	92.5	52 29.7	+26.9	95.1	52 16.3	+30.0	97.7
26	52 54.3	16.0	85.7	53 00.6	19.3	88.3	53 01.4	22.6	91.0	52 56.6	25.8	93.6	52 46.3	28.9	96.2
27	53 10.3	14.7	84.1	53 19.9	18.1	86.7	53 24.0	21.3	89.4	53 22.4	24.6	92.1	53 15.2	27.8	94.8
28	53 25.0	13.3	82.4	53 38.0	16.7	85.1	53 45.3	20.2	87.8	53 47.0	23.3	90.6	53 43.0	26.6	93.3
29	53 38.3	12.0	80.8	53 54.7	15.4	83.5	54 05.5	18.8	86.2	54 10.5	22.1	89.0	54 09.6	25.5	91.8

20°			22°			24°			26°			28°			Dec.
Hc	d	Z	Hc	d	Z	Hc	d	Z	Hc	d	Z	Hc	d	Z	
° ′	′	°	° ′	′	°	° ′	′	°	° ′	′	°	° ′	′	°	°
44 17.6	−29.1	110.8	43 33.2	−31.4	112.6	42 45.4	−33.5	114.3	41 54.5	−35.7	116.0	41 00.5	−37.7	117.5	0
43 48.5	29.8	112.0	43 01.8	32.0	113.8	42 11.9	34.2	115.4	41 18.8	36.2	117.0	40 22.8	38.1	118.6	1
43 18.7	30.6	113.2	42 29.8	32.8	114.9	41 37.7	34.9	116.5	40 42.6	36.8	118.1	39 44.7	38.6	119.6	2
42 48.1	31.2	114.4	41 57.0	33.4	116.0	41 02.8	35.4	117.6	40 05.8	37.4	119.1	39 06.1	39.2	120.6	3
42 16.9	32.0	115.6	41 23.6	34.1	117.2	40 27.4	36.0	118.7	39 28.4	37.8	120.1	38 26.9	39.6	121.5	4
41 44.9	−32.6	116.7	40 49.5	−34.6	118.2	39 51.4	−36.6	119.7	38 50.6	−38.4	121.1	37 47.3	−40.1	122.5	5
41 12.3	33.3	117.8	40 14.9	35.2	119.3	39 14.8	37.1	120.8	38 12.2	38.9	122.1	37 07.2	40.5	123.4	6
40 39.0	33.9	118.9	39 39.7	35.8	120.4	38 37.7	37.8	121.8	37 33.3	39.3	123.1	36 26.7	40.9	124.3	7
40 05.1	34.4	120.0	39 03.9	36.4	121.4	38 00.1	38.1	122.8	36 54.0	39.7	124.0	35 45.8	41.3	125.3	8
39 30.7	35.1	121.1	38 27.5	36.9	122.4	37 22.0	38.6	123.7	36 14.3	40.2	125.0	35 04.5	41.8	126.1	9
38 55.6	−35.6	122.1	37 50.6	−37.3	123.4	36 43.4	−39.0	124.7	35 34.1	−40.6	125.9	34 22.7	−42.0	127.0	10
38 20.0	36.1	123.1	37 13.3	37.9	124.4	36 04.4	39.5	125.6	34 53.5	41.0	126.8	33 40.7	42.5	127.9	11
37 43.9	36.7	124.2	36 35.4	38.3	125.4	35 24.9	39.9	126.6	34 12.5	41.4	127.7	32 58.2	42.7	128.7	12
37 07.2	37.1	125.1	35 57.1	38.8	126.4	34 45.0	40.3	127.5	33 31.1	41.7	128.6	32 15.5	43.1	129.6	13
36 30.1	37.6	126.1	35 18.3	39.1	127.3	34 04.7	40.7	128.4	32 49.4	42.1	129.4	31 32.4	43.4	130.4	14
35 52.5	−38.1	127.1	34 39.2	−39.6	128.2	33 24.0	−41.0	129.3	32 07.3	−42.4	130.3	30 49.0	−43.7	131.2	15
35 14.4	38.5	128.0	33 59.6	40.0	129.1	32 43.0	41.4	130.1	31 24.9	42.7	131.1	30 05.3	44.0	132.0	16
34 35.9	38.9	129.0	33 19.6	40.4	130.0	32 01.6	41.7	131.0	30 42.2	43.1	131.9	29 21.3	44.2	132.8	17
33 57.0	39.4	129.9	32 39.2	40.8	130.9	31 19.9	42.1	131.8	29 59.1	43.3	132.7	28 37.1	44.5	133.5	18
33 17.6	39.7	130.8	31 58.4	41.1	131.8	30 37.8	42.4	132.7	29 15.8	43.6	133.5	27 52.6	44.8	134.3	19
32 37.9	−40.1	131.7	31 17.3	−41.4	132.6	29 55.4	−42.7	133.5	28 32.2	−43.9	134.3	27 07.8	−45.0	135.0	20
31 57.8	40.5	132.6	30 35.9	41.7	133.5	29 12.7	42.9	134.3	27 48.3	44.1	135.1	26 22.8	45.2	135.8	21
31 17.3	40.8	133.4	29 54.2	42.1	134.3	28 29.8	43.3	135.1	27 04.2	44.4	135.8	25 37.6	45.4	136.5	22
30 36.5	41.1	134.3	29 12.1	42.3	135.1	27 46.5	43.5	135.9	26 19.8	44.6	136.6	24 52.2	45.6	137.2	23
29 55.4	41.4	135.1	28 29.8	42.7	135.9	27 03.0	43.8	136.7	25 35.2	44.8	137.3	24 06.6	45.9	138.0	24
29 14.0	−41.8	136.0	27 47.1	−42.9	136.7	26 19.2	−44.0	137.4	24 50.4	−45.0	138.1	23 20.7	−46.0	138.7	25
28 32.2	42.0	136.8	27 04.2	43.2	137.5	25 35.2	44.2	138.2	24 05.4	45.3	138.8	22 34.7	46.2	139.4	26
27 50.2	42.4	137.6	26 21.0	43.4	138.3	24 51.0	44.4	138.9	23 20.1	45.4	139.5	21 48.5	46.4	140.0	27
27 07.8	42.6	138.4	25 37.6	43.6	139.1	24 06.6	44.7	139.7	22 34.7	45.6	140.2	21 02.1	46.5	140.7	28
26 25.2	42.8	139.2	24 54.0	43.9	139.8	23 21.9	44.9	140.4	21 49.1	45.8	140.9	20 15.6	46.7	141.4	29

30°			32°			34°			36°			38°			Dec.
Hc	d	Z	Hc	d	Z	Hc	d	Z	Hc	d	Z	Hc	d	Z	
° ′	′	°	° ′	′	°	° ′	′	°	° ′	′	°	° ′	′	°	°
40 03.6	−39.5	119.0	39 04.0	−41.2	120.5	38 01.9	−42.8	121.8	36 57.4	−44.3	123.1	35 50.7	−45.7	124.4	0
39 24.1	39.9	120.0	38 22.8	41.6	121.4	37 19.1	43.2	122.7	36 13.1	44.6	124.0	35 05.0	46.0	125.2	1
38 44.2	40.4	121.0	37 41.2	42.0	122.3	36 35.9	43.5	123.6	35 28.5	45.0	124.8	34 19.0	46.3	125.9	2
38 03.8	40.8	121.9	36 59.2	42.4	123.2	35 52.4	44.0	124.4	34 43.5	45.3	125.6	33 32.7	46.6	126.7	3
37 23.0	41.3	122.9	36 16.8	42.8	124.1	35 08.4	44.2	125.3	33 58.2	45.6	126.4	32 46.1	46.9	127.5	4
36 41.7	−41.7	123.8	35 34.0	−43.2	125.0	34 24.2	−44.6	126.1	33 12.6	−45.9	127.2	31 59.2	−47.1	128.2	5
36 00.0	42.0	124.7	34 50.8	43.5	125.8	33 39.6	44.9	126.9	32 26.7	46.2	127.9	31 12.1	47.4	128.9	6
35 18.0	42.4	125.5	34 07.3	43.9	126.7	32 54.7	45.1	127.7	31 40.5	46.4	128.7	30 24.7	47.6	129.6	7
34 35.5	42.8	126.4	33 23.4	44.2	127.5	32 09.6	45.5	128.5	30 54.1	46.7	129.4	29 37.1	47.8	130.3	8
33 52.7	43.1	127.2	32 39.2	44.4	128.3	31 24.1	45.7	129.3	30 07.4	46.9	130.2	28 49.3	48.0	131.0	9
33 09.6	−43.5	128.1	31 54.8	−44.8	129.1	30 38.4	−46.0	130.0	29 20.5	−47.1	130.9	28 01.3	−48.2	131.7	10
32 26.1	43.7	128.9	31 10.0	45.0	129.9	29 52.4	46.3	130.8	28 33.4	47.4	131.6	27 13.1	48.4	132.4	11
31 42.4	44.1	129.7	30 25.0	45.4	130.6	29 06.1	46.4	131.5	27 46.0	47.6	132.3	26 24.7	48.6	133.0	12
30 58.3	44.4	130.5	29 39.6	45.5	131.4	28 19.7	46.7	132.2	26 58.4	47.7	133.0	25 36.1	48.8	133.7	13
30 13.9	44.6	131.3	28 54.1	45.8	132.1	27 33.0	46.9	132.9	26 10.7	48.0	133.7	24 47.3	48.9	134.3	14
29 29.3	−44.9	132.1	28 08.3	−46.1	132.9	26 46.1	−47.2	133.6	25 22.7	−48.1	134.3	23 58.4	−49.1	135.0	15
28 44.4	45.2	132.8	27 22.2	46.3	133.6	25 58.9	47.3	134.3	24 34.6	48.3	135.0	23 09.3	49.2	135.6	16
27 59.2	45.4	133.6	26 36.0	46.5	134.3	25 11.6	47.5	135.0	23 46.3	48.4	135.6	22 20.1	49.4	136.2	17
27 13.8	45.6	134.3	25 49.5	46.7	135.0	24 24.1	47.6	135.7	22 57.9	48.7	136.3	21 30.7	49.5	136.8	18
26 28.2	45.8	135.0	25 02.8	46.8	135.7	23 36.5	47.9	136.3	22 09.2	48.7	136.9	20 41.2	49.6	137.4	19
25 42.4	−46.1	135.7	24 16.0	−47.1	136.4	22 48.6	−48.0	137.0	21 20.5	−48.9	137.5	19 51.6	−49.7	138.0	20
24 56.3	46.2	136.5	23 28.9	47.2	137.1	22 00.6	48.1	137.6	20 31.6	49.0	138.2	19 01.9	49.9	138.6	21
24 10.1	46.4	137.2	22 41.7	47.4	137.7	21 12.5	48.3	138.3	19 42.6	49.2	138.8	18 12.0	50.0	139.2	22
23 23.7	46.7	137.8	21 54.3	47.6	138.4	20 24.2	48.4	138.9	18 53.4	49.2	139.4	17 22.0	50.0	139.8	23
22 37.0	46.8	138.5	21 06.7	47.7	139.1	19 35.8	48.6	139.5	18 04.2	49.4	140.0	16 32.0	50.2	140.4	24
21 50.2	−46.9	139.2	20 19.0	−47.8	139.7	18 47.2	−48.7	140.2	17 14.8	−49.5	140.6	15 41.8	−50.2	141.0	25
21 03.3	47.1	139.9	19 31.2	48.0	140.4	17 58.5	48.8	140.8	16 25.3	49.6	141.2	14 51.6	50.4	141.5	26
20 16.2	47.3	140.5	18 43.2	48.1	141.0	17 09.7	48.9	141.4	15 35.7	49.7	141.8	14 01.2	50.4	142.1	27
19 28.9	47.4	141.2	17 55.1	48.2	141.6	16 20.8	49.0	142.0	14 46.0	49.7	142.3	13 10.8	50.4	142.6	28
18 41.5	47.5	141.8	17 06.9	48.3	142.2	15 31.8	49.1	142.6	13 56.3	49.9	142.9	12 20.4	50.6	143.2	29

Dec.	40° Hc	d	Z	42° Hc	d	Z	44° Hc	d	Z	46° Hc	d	Z	48° Hc	d	Z
0	34 42.0	+46.8	125.5	33 31.3	+48.1	126.6	32 18.9	+49.2	127.7	31 04.8	+50.3	128.6	29 49.1	+51.3	129.5
1	35 28.8	46.4	124.8	34 19.4	47.8	125.9	33 08.1	49.0	127.0	31 55.1	50.1	128.0	30 40.4	51.2	128.9
2	36 15.2	46.2	124.0	35 07.2	47.5	125.2	33 57.1	48.7	126.3	32 45.2	49.9	127.3	31 31.6	51.0	128.3
3	37 01.4	45.8	123.2	35 54.7	47.2	124.4	34 45.8	48.5	125.6	33 35.1	49.7	126.7	32 22.6	50.7	127.7
4	37 47.2	45.5	122.4	36 41.9	46.9	123.6	35 34.3	48.3	124.9	34 24.8	49.4	126.0	33 13.3	50.6	127.1
5	38 32.7	+45.2	121.5	37 28.8	+46.6	122.9	36 22.6	+47.9	124.1	35 14.2	+49.2	125.3	34 03.9	+50.4	126.4
6	39 17.9	44.7	120.7	38 15.4	46.3	122.1	37 10.5	47.7	123.4	36 03.4	49.0	124.6	34 54.3	50.2	125.8
7	40 02.6	44.4	119.8	39 01.7	45.9	121.2	37 58.2	47.4	122.6	36 52.4	48.7	123.9	35 44.5	49.9	125.1
8	40 47.0	44.0	118.9	39 47.6	45.5	120.4	38 45.6	47.0	121.8	37 41.1	48.4	123.1	36 34.4	49.7	124.4
9	41 31.0	43.5	118.0	40 33.1	45.2	119.6	39 32.6	46.7	121.0	38 29.5	48.1	122.4	37 24.1	49.4	123.7
10	42 14.5	+43.0	117.1	41 18.3	+44.8	118.7	40 19.3	+46.4	120.2	39 17.6	+47.9	121.6	38 13.5	+49.2	123.0
11	42 57.5	42.6	116.2	42 03.1	44.3	117.8	41 05.7	45.9	119.4	40 05.5	47.5	120.8	39 02.7	48.9	122.3
12	43 40.1	42.1	115.2	42 47.4	43.9	116.9	41 51.6	45.6	118.5	40 53.0	47.1	120.0	39 51.6	48.5	121.5
13	44 22.2	41.5	114.2	43 31.3	43.4	116.0	42 37.2	45.2	117.6	41 40.1	46.8	119.2	40 40.1	48.3	120.7
14	45 03.7	41.0	113.0	44 14.7	43.0	115.0	43 22.4	44.7	116.7	42 26.9	46.4	118.4	41 28.4	47.9	119.9
15	45 44.7	+40.5	112.2	44 57.7	+42.4	114.0	44 07.1	+44.3	115.8	43 13.3	+46.0	117.5	42 16.3	+47.6	119.1
16	46 25.2	39.8	111.1	45 40.1	41.9	113.0	44 51.4	43.8	114.9	43 59.3	45.6	116.6	43 03.9	47.3	118.3
17	47 05.0	39.1	110.0	46 22.0	41.3	112.0	45 35.2	43.3	113.9	44 44.9	45.1	115.7	43 51.2	46.8	117.5
18	47 44.1	38.6	108.9	47 03.3	40.7	110.9	46 18.5	42.8	112.9	45 30.0	44.7	114.8	44 38.0	46.4	116.6
19	48 22.7	37.8	107.7	47 44.0	40.1	109.8	47 01.3	42.2	111.9	46 14.7	44.2	113.8	45 24.4	46.0	115.7
20	49 00.5	+37.0	106.6	48 24.1	+39.4	108.7	47 43.5	+41.6	110.8	46 58.9	+43.6	112.8	46 10.4	+45.6	114.8
21	49 37.5	36.3	105.3	49 03.5	38.7	107.6	48 25.1	41.0	109.7	47 42.5	43.1	111.8	46 56.0	45.0	113.8
22	50 13.8	35.5	104.1	49 42.2	38.0	106.4	49 06.1	40.3	108.6	48 25.6	42.5	110.8	47 41.0	44.6	112.8
23	50 49.3	34.6	102.8	50 20.2	37.2	105.2	49 46.4	39.7	107.5	49 08.1	42.0	109.7	48 25.6	44.0	111.8
24	51 23.9	33.8	101.5	50 57.4	36.5	104.0	50 26.1	38.9	106.3	49 50.1	41.2	108.6	49 09.6	43.4	110.8
25	51 57.7	+32.8	100.2	51 33.9	+35.5	102.7	51 05.0	+38.2	105.1	50 31.3	+40.6	107.5	49 53.0	+42.9	109.8
26	52 30.5	31.9	98.8	52 09.4	34.7	101.4	51 43.2	37.3	103.9	51 11.9	39.9	106.3	50 35.9	42.2	108.7
27	53 02.4	30.8	97.4	52 44.1	33.8	100.1	52 20.5	36.6	102.6	51 51.8	39.1	105.1	51 18.1	41.5	107.5
28	53 33.2	29.8	96.0	53 17.9	32.8	98.7	52 57.1	35.6	101.3	52 30.9	38.3	103.9	51 59.6	40.8	106.4
29	54 03.0	28.7	94.5	53 50.7	31.8	97.3	53 32.7	34.7	100.0	53 09.2	37.5	102.6	52 40.4	40.1	105.2

Dec.	50° Hc	d	Z	52° Hc	d	Z	54° Hc	d	Z	56° Hc	d	Z	58° Hc	d	Z
0	28 32.1	+52.2	130.4	27 13.7	+53.1	131.2	25 54.0	+53.9	131.9	24 33.3	+54.6	132.6	23 11.5	+55.3	133.3
1	29 24.3	52.1	129.8	28 06.8	53.0	130.7	26 47.9	53.9	131.5	25 27.9	54.6	132.2	24 06.8	55.3	132.9
2	30 16.4	52.0	129.3	28 59.8	52.8	130.1	27 41.8	53.7	131.0	26 22.5	54.5	131.7	25 02.1	55.1	132.4
3	31 08.4	51.8	128.7	29 52.6	52.7	129.6	28 35.5	53.5	130.4	27 17.0	54.3	131.2	25 57.2	55.1	132.0
4	32 00.2	51.6	128.1	30 45.3	52.6	129.0	29 29.0	53.5	129.9	28 11.3	54.3	130.8	26 52.3	55.1	131.6
5	32 51.8	+51.4	127.5	31 37.9	+52.5	128.5	30 22.5	+53.3	129.4	29 05.6	+54.2	130.3	27 47.4	+54.9	131.1
6	33 43.2	51.3	126.9	32 30.4	52.2	127.9	31 15.8	53.2	128.9	29 59.8	54.0	129.8	28 42.3	54.8	130.6
7	34 34.5	51.0	126.2	33 22.6	52.1	127.3	32 09.0	53.1	128.3	30 53.8	54.0	129.3	29 37.1	54.7	130.2
8	35 25.5	50.9	125.6	34 14.7	52.0	126.7	33 02.1	52.9	127.8	31 47.8	53.8	128.8	30 31.8	54.7	129.7
9	36 16.4	50.6	124.9	35 06.7	51.7	126.1	33 55.0	52.8	127.2	32 41.6	53.6	128.3	31 26.5	54.5	129.2
10	37 07.0	+50.4	124.3	35 58.4	+51.6	125.5	34 47.8	+52.6	126.6	33 35.2	+53.6	127.7	32 21.0	+54.4	128.7
11	37 57.4	50.2	123.6	36 50.0	51.3	124.9	35 40.4	52.4	126.0	34 28.8	53.4	127.2	33 15.4	54.3	128.2
12	38 47.6	49.9	122.9	37 41.3	51.1	124.2	36 32.8	52.2	125.4	35 22.2	53.2	126.6	34 09.7	54.1	127.7
13	39 37.5	49.7	122.2	38 32.4	50.9	123.5	37 25.0	52.0	124.8	36 15.4	53.1	126.0	35 03.8	54.0	127.2
14	40 27.2	49.3	121.4	39 23.3	50.6	122.9	38 17.0	51.8	124.2	37 08.5	52.9	125.5	35 57.8	53.9	126.7
15	41 16.5	+49.1	120.7	40 13.9	+50.4	122.2	39 08.8	+51.6	123.5	38 01.4	+52.7	124.9	36 51.7	+53.7	126.1
16	42 05.6	48.7	119.9	41 04.3	50.1	121.4	40 00.4	51.4	122.9	38 54.1	52.5	124.3	37 45.4	53.5	125.6
17	42 54.3	48.4	119.1	41 54.4	49.9	120.7	40 51.8	51.1	122.2	39 46.6	52.3	123.6	38 38.9	53.4	125.0
18	43 42.7	48.0	118.3	42 44.3	49.5	120.0	41 42.9	50.9	121.5	40 38.9	52.1	123.0	39 32.3	53.2	124.4
19	44 30.7	47.7	117.5	43 33.8	49.2	119.2	42 33.8	50.6	120.8	41 31.0	51.8	122.3	40 25.5	53.0	123.8
20	45 18.4	+47.3	116.6	44 23.0	+48.8	118.4	43 24.4	+50.3	120.1	42 22.8	+51.6	121.7	41 18.5	+52.8	123.2
21	46 05.7	46.8	115.7	45 11.8	48.5	117.6	44 14.7	50.0	119.3	43 14.4	51.0	121.0	42 11.3	52.5	122.5
22	46 52.5	46.4	114.8	46 00.3	48.1	116.7	45 04.7	49.6	118.5	44 05.8	51.0	120.2	43 03.8	52.4	121.9
23	47 38.9	46.0	113.9	46 48.4	47.7	115.9	45 54.3	49.4	117.7	44 56.8	50.8	119.5	43 56.2	52.1	121.2
24	48 24.9	45.4	112.9	47 36.1	47.3	115.0	46 43.7	48.9	116.9	45 47.6	50.5	118.8	44 48.3	51.8	120.5
25	49 10.3	+44.9	111.9	48 23.4	+46.9	114.0	47 32.6	+48.6	116.1	46 38.1	+50.1	118.0	45 40.1	+51.6	119.8
26	49 55.2	44.4	110.9	49 10.3	46.3	113.1	48 21.2	48.1	115.2	47 28.2	49.8	117.2	46 31.7	51.2	119.1
27	50 39.6	43.8	109.9	49 56.6	45.8	112.1	49 09.3	47.7	114.3	48 18.0	49.4	116.3	47 22.9	51.0	118.3
28	51 23.4	43.1	108.8	50 42.4	45.3	111.1	49 57.0	47.3	113.3	49 07.4	49.1	115.5	48 13.9	50.6	117.5
29	52 06.5	42.5	107.7	51 27.7	44.7	110.1	50 44.3	46.7	112.4	49 56.5	48.6	114.6	49 04.5	50.3	116.7

LATITUDE **CONTRARY** NAME L.H.A. 42°, 318°

40°			42°			44°			46°			48°			Dec.
Hc	d	Z	Hc	d	Z	Hc	d	Z	Hc	d	Z	Hc	d	Z	°
34 42.0	− 47.0	125.5	33 31.3	− 48.2	126.6	32 18.9	− 49.4	127.7	31 04.8	− 50.5	128.6	29 49.1	− 51.4	129.5	0
33 55.0	47.4	126.3	32 43.1	48.5	127.3	31 29.5	49.7	128.3	30 14.3	50.7	129.2	28 57.7	51.7	130.1	1
33 07.6	47.5	127.0	31 54.6	48.8	128.0	30 39.8	49.8	129.0	29 23.6	50.8	129.9	28 06.0	51.7	130.7	2
32 20.1	47.8	127.7	31 05.8	48.9	128.7	29 50.0	50.0	129.6	28 32.8	51.0	130.5	27 14.3	51.9	131.3	3
31 32.3	48.1	128.4	30 16.9	49.2	129.4	29 00.0	50.2	130.3	27 41.8	51.1	131.1	26 22.4	52.1	131.8	4
30 44.2	− 48.3	129.1	29 27.7	− 49.3	130.0	28 09.8	− 50.3	130.9	26 50.7	− 51.3	131.7	25 30.3	− 52.1	132.4	5
29 55.9	48.5	129.8	28 38.4	49.6	130.7	27 19.5	50.5	131.5	25 59.4	51.4	132.2	24 38.2	52.3	132.9	6
29 07.4	48.6	130.5	27 48.8	49.7	131.3	26 29.0	50.7	132.1	25 08.0	51.6	132.8	23 45.9	52.4	133.5	7
28 18.8	48.9	131.2	26 59.1	49.8	132.0	25 38.3	50.8	132.7	24 16.4	51.7	133.4	22 53.5	52.5	134.0	8
27 29.9	49.1	131.8	26 09.3	50.1	132.6	24 47.5	50.9	133.3	23 24.7	51.7	133.9	22 01.0	52.6	134.5	9
26 40.8	− 49.2	132.5	25 19.2	− 50.2	133.2	23 56.6	− 51.1	133.9	22 33.0	− 51.9	134.5	21 08.4	− 52.6	135.0	10
25 51.6	49.5	133.2	24 29.0	50.3	133.8	23 05.5	51.2	134.4	21 41.1	52.1	135.0	20 15.8	52.8	135.5	11
25 02.2	49.5	133.7	23 38.7	50.4	134.4	22 14.3	51.3	135.0	20 49.0	52.1	135.6	19 23.0	52.9	136.1	12
24 12.7	49.8	134.4	22 48.3	50.6	135.0	21 23.0	51.4	135.6	19 56.9	52.2	136.1	18 30.1	52.9	136.6	13
23 22.9	49.8	135.0	21 57.7	50.7	135.6	20 31.6	51.5	136.1	19 04.7	52.2	136.6	17 37.2	53.0	137.1	14
22 33.1	− 50.0	135.6	21 07.0	− 50.8	136.1	19 40.1	− 51.6	136.7	18 12.5	− 52.4	137.1	16 44.2	− 53.1	137.6	15
21 43.1	50.1	136.2	20 16.2	51.0	136.7	18 48.5	51.8	137.2	17 20.1	52.4	137.6	15 51.1	53.1	138.0	16
20 53.0	50.2	136.8	19 25.2	51.0	137.3	17 56.7	51.7	137.7	16 27.7	52.6	138.1	14 58.0	53.2	138.5	17
20 02.8	50.3	137.4	18 34.2	51.1	137.8	17 05.0	51.8	138.3	15 35.1	52.6	138.6	14 04.8	53.2	139.0	18
19 12.5	50.5	137.9	17 43.1	51.3	138.4	16 13.1	52.0	138.8	14 42.5	52.6	139.1	13 11.6	53.3	139.5	19
18 22.0	− 50.5	138.5	16 51.8	− 51.3	138.9	15 21.1	− 52.0	139.3	13 49.9	− 52.7	139.6	12 18.3	− 53.4	139.9	20
17 31.5	50.7	139.1	16 00.5	51.3	139.5	14 29.1	52.1	139.8	12 57.2	52.8	140.1	11 24.9	53.4	140.4	21
16 40.8	50.7	139.6	15 09.2	51.5	140.0	13 37.0	52.2	140.3	12 04.4	52.8	140.6	10 31.5	53.4	140.9	22
15 50.1	50.8	140.2	14 17.7	51.5	140.5	12 44.8	52.2	140.8	11 11.6	52.8	141.1	9 38.1	53.5	141.3	23
14 59.3	50.9	140.7	13 26.2	51.6	141.1	11 52.6	52.2	141.3	10 18.8	52.9	141.6	8 44.6	53.5	141.8	24
14 08.4	− 51.0	141.3	12 34.6	− 51.7	141.6	11 00.4	− 52.4	141.8	9 25.9	− 53.0	142.1	7 51.1	− 53.6	142.3	25
13 17.4	51.0	141.8	11 42.9	51.7	142.1	10 08.0	52.4	142.3	8 32.9	53.0	142.5	6 57.6	53.6	142.7	26
12 26.4	51.1	142.4	10 51.2	51.8	142.6	9 15.7	52.4	142.8	7 39.9	53.0	143.0	6 04.0	53.6	143.2	27
11 35.3	51.2	142.9	9 59.4	51.8	143.1	8 23.3	52.4	143.3	6 46.9	53.0	143.5	5 10.4	53.6	143.6	28
10 44.1	51.2	143.4	9 07.6	51.8	143.6	7 30.9	52.5	143.8	5 53.9	53.1	144.0	4 16.8	53.6	144.1	29

50°			52°			54°			56°			58°			Dec.
Hc	d	Z	Hc	d	Z	Hc	d	Z	Hc	d	Z	Hc	d	Z	°
28 32.1	− 52.4	130.4	27 13.7	− 53.3	131.2	25 54.0	− 54.0	131.9	24 33.3	− 54.7	132.6	23 11.5	− 55.4	133.3	0
27 39.7	52.5	130.9	26 20.4	53.3	131.7	25 00.0	54.1	132.4	23 38.6	54.9	133.1	22 16.1	55.4	133.7	1
26 47.2	52.7	131.5	25 27.1	53.5	132.2	24 05.9	54.2	132.9	22 43.7	54.8	133.5	21 20.7	55.6	134.1	2
25 54.5	52.7	132.0	24 33.6	53.5	132.7	23 11.7	54.2	133.4	21 48.9	55.0	134.0	20 25.1	55.6	134.5	3
25 01.8	52.9	132.6	23 40.1	53.6	133.2	22 17.5	54.4	133.8	20 53.9	55.0	134.4	19 29.6	55.6	134.9	4
24 08.9	− 53.0	133.1	22 46.5	− 53.8	133.7	21 23.1	− 54.4	134.3	19 58.9	− 55.1	134.8	18 34.0	− 55.7	135.3	5
23 15.9	53.0	133.6	21 52.7	53.8	134.2	20 28.7	54.5	134.7	19 03.8	55.1	135.2	17 38.3	55.7	135.7	6
22 22.9	53.2	134.1	20 58.9	53.8	134.7	19 34.2	54.6	135.2	18 08.7	55.2	135.7	16 42.6	55.8	136.1	7
21 29.7	53.2	134.6	20 05.1	54.0	135.1	18 39.6	54.6	135.6	17 13.5	55.2	136.1	15 46.8	55.8	136.5	8
20 36.5	53.4	135.1	19 11.1	54.0	135.6	17 45.0	54.6	136.1	16 18.3	55.3	136.5	14 51.0	55.8	136.9	9
19 43.1	− 53.4	135.6	18 17.1	− 54.1	136.1	16 50.4	− 54.8	136.5	15 23.0	− 55.3	136.9	13 55.2	− 55.9	137.2	10
18 49.7	53.5	136.1	17 23.0	54.2	136.5	15 55.6	54.7	136.9	14 27.7	55.4	137.3	12 59.3	55.9	137.6	11
17 56.2	53.5	136.5	16 28.8	54.2	137.0	15 00.9	54.9	137.3	13 32.4	55.4	137.7	12 03.4	55.9	138.0	12
17 02.7	53.6	137.0	15 34.6	54.2	137.4	14 06.0	54.8	137.8	12 37.0	55.5	138.1	11 07.5	56.0	138.3	13
16 09.1	53.7	137.5	14 40.4	54.3	137.8	13 11.2	54.9	138.2	11 41.5	55.4	138.5	10 11.5	56.0	138.7	14
15 15.4	− 53.7	137.9	13 46.1	− 54.4	138.3	12 16.3	− 55.0	138.6	10 46.1	− 55.5	138.9	9 15.5	− 56.0	139.1	15
14 21.7	53.8	138.4	12 51.7	54.4	138.7	11 21.3	55.0	139.0	9 50.6	55.5	139.3	8 19.5	56.0	139.5	16
13 27.9	53.8	138.9	11 57.3	54.4	139.2	10 26.3	55.0	139.4	8 55.1	55.6	139.6	7 23.5	56.0	139.8	17
12 34.0	53.9	139.3	11 02.9	54.5	139.6	9 31.3	55.0	139.8	7 59.5	55.5	140.0	6 27.5	56.1	140.2	18
11 40.1	53.9	139.8	10 08.4	54.5	140.0	8 36.3	55.1	140.2	7 04.0	55.6	140.4	5 31.4	56.1	140.5	19
10 46.2	− 53.9	140.2	9 13.9	− 54.6	140.4	7 41.2	− 55.0	140.6	6 08.4	− 55.6	140.8	4 35.3	− 56.0	140.9	20
9 52.3	54.0	140.6	8 19.3	54.6	140.9	6 46.2	55.1	141.0	5 12.8	55.6	141.2	3 39.3	56.1	141.2	21
8 58.3	54.1	141.1	7 24.8	54.6	141.3	5 51.1	55.2	141.4	4 17.2	55.6	141.5	2 43.2	56.1	141.6	22
8 04.2	54.0	141.5	6 30.2	54.6	141.7	4 55.9	55.1	141.8	3 21.6	55.7	141.9	1 47.1	56.1	142.0	23
7 10.2	54.1	142.0	5 35.6	54.7	142.1	4 00.8	55.1	142.2	2 25.9	55.6	142.3	0 51.0	− 56.1	142.3	24
6 16.1	− 54.1	142.4	4 40.9	− 54.6	142.5	3 05.7	− 55.2	142.6	1 30.3	− 55.7	142.7	0 05.1	+ 56.1	37.3	25
5 22.0	54.1	142.8	3 46.3	54.7	142.9	2 10.5	55.2	143.0	0 34.6	− 55.6	143.0	1 01.2	56.1	37.0	26
4 27.9	54.2	143.3	2 51.6	54.6	143.3	1 15.3	55.1	143.4	0 21.0	+ 55.6	36.6	1 57.3	56.1	36.6	27
3 33.7	54.1	143.7	1 57.0	54.7	143.8	0 20.2	− 55.2	143.8	1 16.6	55.7	36.2	2 53.4	56.1	36.3	28
2 39.6	54.2	144.1	1 02.3	54.7	144.2	0 35.0	+ 55.1	35.8	2 12.3	55.6	35.9	3 49.5	56.1	35.9	29

LATITUDE **SAME** NAME L.H.A. 138°, 222°

Dec.	0° Hc	d	Z	2° Hc	d	Z	4° Hc	d	Z	6° Hc	d	Z	8° Hc	d	Z
0	46 00.0	− 0.5	90.0	45 57.8	+ 2.5	92.1	45 51.3	+ 5.5	94.1	45 40.6	+ 8.4	96.2	45 25.5	+11.4	98.2
1	45 59.5	1.7	88.6	46 00.3	1.4	90.6	45 56.8	4.4	92.7	45 49.0	7.4	94.8	45 36.9	10.4	96.8
2	45 57.8	2.7	87.1	46 01.7	+ 0.3	89.2	46 01.2	3.3	91.3	45 56.4	6.3	93.3	45 47.3	9.3	95.4
3	45 55.1	3.8	85.7	46 02.0	− 0.8	87.8	46 04.5	2.3	89.8	46 02.7	5.3	91.9	45 56.6	8.2	94.0
4	45 51.3	4.8	84.3	46 01.2	1.9	86.3	46 06.8	1.1	88.4	46 08.0	4.1	90.5	46 04.8	7.2	92.5
5	45 46.5	− 5.9	82.8	45 59.3	− 2.9	84.9	46 07.9	+ 0.1	86.9	46 12.1	+ 3.1	89.0	46 12.0	+ 6.1	91.1
6	45 40.6	7.0	81.4	45 56.4	4.0	83.4	46 08.0	− 1.1	85.5	46 15.2	2.0	87.6	46 18.1	5.0	89.7
7	45 33.6	8.1	80.0	45 52.4	5.1	82.0	46 06.9	2.1	84.1	46 17.2	+ 0.7	86.1	46 23.1	3.9	88.2
8	45 25.5	9.0	78.6	45 47.3	6.2	80.6	46 04.8	3.2	82.6	46 18.1	− 0.2	84.7	46 27.0	2.8	86.8
9	45 16.5	10.2	77.2	45 41.1	7.2	79.1	46 01.6	4.3	81.2	46 17.9	1.3	83.2	46 29.8	1.7	85.3
10	45 06.3	−11.1	75.8	45 33.9	− 8.3	77.7	45 57.3	− 5.3	79.7	46 16.6	− 2.4	81.8	46 31.5	+ 0.7	83.9
11	44 55.2	12.1	74.4	45 25.6	9.3	76.3	45 52.0	6.5	78.3	46 14.2	3.5	80.3	46 32.2	− 0.5	82.4
12	44 43.1	13.1	73.0	45 16.3	10.4	74.9	45 45.5	7.5	76.9	46 10.7	4.6	78.9	46 31.7	1.6	81.0
13	44 30.0	14.1	71.6	45 05.9	11.3	73.5	45 38.0	8.5	75.5	46 06.1	5.6	77.5	46 30.1	2.7	79.5
14	44 15.9	15.1	70.3	44 54.6	12.4	72.1	45 29.5	9.6	74.0	46 00.5	6.7	76.0	46 27.4	3.8	78.1
15	44 00.8	−16.0	68.9	44 42.2	−13.3	70.7	45 19.9	−10.6	72.6	45 53.8	− 7.8	74.6	46 23.6	− 4.9	76.6
16	43 44.8	16.9	67.6	44 28.9	14.4	69.4	45 09.3	11.6	71.2	45 46.0	8.9	73.2	46 18.7	6.0	75.2
17	43 27.9	17.9	66.2	44 14.5	15.3	68.0	44 57.7	12.7	69.9	45 37.1	9.9	71.8	46 12.7	7.0	73.7
18	43 10.0	18.7	64.9	43 59.2	16.2	66.7	44 45.0	13.6	68.5	45 27.2	10.9	70.4	46 05.7	8.2	72.3
19	42 51.3	19.6	63.6	43 43.0	17.1	65.3	44 31.4	14.6	67.1	45 16.3	11.9	69.0	45 57.5	9.2	70.9
20	42 31.7	−20.4	62.3	43 25.9	−18.1	64.0	44 16.8	−15.5	65.8	45 04.4	−13.0	67.6	45 48.3	−10.2	69.5
21	42 11.3	21.3	61.1	43 07.8	18.9	62.7	44 01.3	16.5	64.4	44 51.4	13.9	66.2	45 38.1	11.3	68.0
22	41 50.0	22.1	59.8	42 48.9	19.8	61.4	43 44.8	17.4	63.1	44 37.5	14.9	64.8	45 26.8	12.3	66.6
23	41 27.9	22.9	58.6	42 29.1	20.7	60.1	43 27.4	18.3	61.7	44 22.6	15.9	63.5	45 14.5	13.3	65.3
24	41 05.0	23.7	57.3	42 08.4	21.5	58.9	43 09.1	19.3	60.4	44 06.7	16.8	62.1	45 01.2	14.3	63.9
25	40 41.3	−24.4	56.1	41 46.9	−22.3	57.6	42 49.8	−20.0	59.1	43 49.9	−17.7	60.8	44 46.9	−15.2	62.5
26	40 16.9	25.2	54.9	41 24.6	23.1	56.4	42 29.8	20.9	57.9	43 32.2	18.6	59.5	44 31.7	16.3	61.1
27	39 51.7	25.9	53.7	41 01.5	23.9	55.1	42 08.9	21.8	56.6	43 13.6	19.5	58.2	44 15.4	17.1	59.8
28	39 25.8	26.6	52.6	40 37.6	24.6	53.9	41 47.1	22.5	55.3	42 54.1	20.4	56.9	43 58.3	18.1	58.5
29	38 59.2	27.2	51.4	40 13.0	25.3	52.7	41 24.6	23.4	54.1	42 33.7	21.2	55.6	43 40.2	19.0	57.1

Dec.	10° Hc	d	Z	12° Hc	d	Z	14° Hc	d	Z	16° Hc	d	Z	18° Hc	d	Z
0	45 06.3	+14.3	100.2	44 43.1	+17.1	102.2	44 15.9	+19.8	104.1	43 44.8	+22.5	105.9	43 10.0	+25.1	107.7
1	45 20.6	13.3	98.8	45 00.2	16.1	100.8	44 35.7	18.9	102.7	44 07.3	21.6	104.6	43 35.1	24.1	106.5
2	45 33.9	12.2	97.4	45 16.3	15.1	99.4	44 54.6	17.9	101.4	44 28.9	20.6	103.3	43 59.2	23.4	105.2
3	45 46.1	11.2	96.0	45 31.4	14.1	98.1	45 12.5	17.0	100.1	44 49.5	19.8	102.0	44 22.6	22.4	103.9
4	45 57.3	10.2	94.6	45 45.5	13.1	96.7	45 29.5	16.0	98.7	45 09.3	18.8	100.7	44 45.0	21.6	102.6
5	46 07.5	+ 9.1	93.2	45 58.6	+12.1	95.3	45 45.5	+15.0	97.3	45 28.1	+17.9	99.3	45 06.6	+20.6	101.3
6	46 16.6	8.0	91.8	46 10.7	11.0	93.9	46 00.5	13.9	95.9	45 46.0	16.8	98.0	45 27.2	19.7	100.0
7	46 24.6	6.9	90.3	46 21.7	10.0	92.4	46 14.4	13.0	94.5	46 02.8	15.9	96.6	45 46.9	18.8	98.6
8	46 31.5	5.9	88.9	46 31.7	8.8	91.0	46 27.4	11.9	93.1	46 18.7	14.8	95.2	46 05.7	17.7	97.3
9	46 37.4	4.8	87.4	46 40.5	7.8	89.6	46 39.3	10.8	91.7	46 33.5	13.8	93.8	46 23.4	16.7	95.9
10	46 42.2	+ 3.6	86.0	46 48.3	+ 6.7	88.1	46 50.1	+ 9.7	90.2	46 47.3	+12.7	92.4	46 40.1	+15.7	94.5
11	46 45.8	2.5	84.5	46 55.0	5.6	86.7	46 59.8	8.6	88.8	47 00.0	11.7	90.9	46 55.8	14.7	93.1
12	46 48.3	1.5	83.1	47 00.6	4.5	85.2	47 08.4	7.5	87.3	47 11.7	10.6	89.5	47 10.5	13.6	91.7
13	46 49.8	+ 0.3	81.6	47 05.1	3.3	83.7	47 15.9	6.4	85.9	47 22.3	9.4	88.1	47 24.1	12.5	90.2
14	46 50.1	− 0.9	80.1	47 08.4	2.2	82.3	47 22.3	5.3	84.4	47 31.7	8.4	86.6	47 36.6	11.4	88.8
15	46 49.2	− 1.9	78.7	47 10.6	+ 1.1	80.8	47 27.6	+ 4.1	82.9	47 40.1	+ 7.2	85.1	47 48.0	+10.3	87.3
16	46 47.3	3.0	77.2	47 11.7	0.0	79.3	47 31.7	3.0	81.5	47 47.3	6.0	83.6	47 58.3	9.1	85.8
17	46 44.3	4.2	75.8	47 11.7	− 1.2	77.9	47 34.7	1.9	80.0	47 53.3	5.0	82.2	48 07.4	8.0	84.4
18	46 40.1	5.2	74.3	47 10.5	2.3	76.4	47 36.6	+ 0.7	78.5	47 58.3	3.7	80.7	48 15.4	6.9	82.9
19	46 34.9	6.4	72.9	47 08.2	3.4	74.9	47 37.3	− 0.5	77.0	48 02.0	2.6	79.2	48 22.3	5.7	81.4
20	46 28.5	− 7.4	71.4	47 04.8	− 4.6	73.4	47 36.8	− 1.5	75.5	48 04.6	+ 1.1	77.7	48 28.0	+ 4.5	79.9
21	46 21.1	8.5	70.0	47 00.2	5.7	72.0	47 35.3	2.8	74.1	48 06.1	+ 0.2	76.2	48 32.5	3.3	78.4
22	46 12.6	9.6	68.5	46 54.5	6.7	70.5	47 32.5	3.8	72.6	48 06.3	− 0.8	74.7	48 35.8	2.2	76.9
23	46 03.0	10.6	67.1	46 47.8	7.9	69.1	47 28.7	5.1	71.1	48 05.5	2.1	73.2	48 38.0	+ 0.9	75.4
24	45 52.4	11.7	65.7	46 39.9	9.0	67.6	47 23.6	6.1	69.6	48 03.4	3.2	71.7	48 38.9	− 0.2	73.9
25	45 40.7	−12.7	64.3	46 30.9	−10.0	66.2	47 17.5	− 7.2	68.2	48 00.2	− 4.4	70.2	48 38.7	− 1.4	72.3
26	45 28.0	13.7	62.9	46 20.9	11.1	64.8	47 10.3	8.4	66.7	47 55.8	5.5	68.7	48 37.3	2.6	70.8
27	45 14.3	14.8	61.5	46 09.8	12.1	63.3	47 01.9	9.5	65.2	47 50.3	6.7	67.2	48 34.7	3.8	69.3
28	44 59.5	15.7	60.1	45 57.7	13.2	61.9	46 52.4	10.5	63.8	47 43.6	7.8	65.8	48 30.9	5.0	67.8
29	44 43.8	16.6	58.8	45 44.5	14.2	60.5	46 41.9	11.7	62.4	47 35.8	9.0	64.3	48 25.9	6.1	66.3

0° Hc	d	Z	2° Hc	d	Z	4° Hc	d	Z	6° Hc	d	Z	8° Hc	d	Z	Dec.
46 00.0	−0.5	90.0	45 57.8	−3.5	92.1	45 51.3	−6.5	94.1	45 40.6	−9.5	96.2	45 25.5	−12.4	98.2	0
45 59.5	1.7	91.4	45 54.3	4.6	93.5	45 44.8	7.6	95.6	45 31.1	10.6	97.6	45 13.1	13.4	99.6	1
45 57.8	2.7	92.9	45 49.7	5.7	94.9	45 37.2	8.7	97.0	45 20.5	11.5	99.0	44 59.7	14.4	101.0	2
45 55.1	3.8	94.3	45 44.0	6.8	96.4	45 28.5	9.6	98.4	45 09.0	12.6	100.4	44 45.3	15.4	102.3	3
45 51.3	4.8	95.7	45 37.2	7.8	97.8	45 18.9	10.8	99.8	44 56.4	13.6	101.8	44 29.9	16.3	103.7	4
45 46.5	−5.9	97.2	45 29.4	−8.9	99.2	45 08.1	−11.7	101.2	44 42.8	−14.5	103.1	44 13.6	−17.3	105.0	5
45 40.6	7.0	98.6	45 20.5	9.9	100.6	44 56.4	12.7	102.6	44 28.3	15.5	104.5	43 56.3	18.2	106.4	6
45 33.6	8.1	100.0	45 10.6	10.9	102.0	44 43.7	13.8	104.0	44 12.8	16.5	105.9	43 38.1	19.1	107.7	7
45 25.5	9.0	101.4	44 59.7	11.9	103.4	44 29.9	14.7	105.3	43 56.3	17.4	107.2	43 19.0	19.9	109.0	8
45 16.5	10.2	102.8	44 47.8	12.9	104.8	44 15.2	15.6	106.7	43 38.9	18.2	108.5	42 59.1	20.9	110.3	9
45 06.3	−11.1	104.2	44 34.9	−13.9	106.2	43 59.6	−16.6	108.0	43 20.7	−19.2	109.8	42 38.2	−21.7	111.6	10
44 55.2	12.1	105.6	44 21.0	14.9	107.5	43 43.0	17.5	109.4	43 01.5	20.1	111.1	42 16.5	22.5	112.8	11
44 43.1	13.1	107.0	44 06.1	15.8	108.9	43 25.5	18.4	110.7	42 41.4	20.9	112.4	41 54.0	23.3	114.1	12
44 30.0	14.1	108.4	43 50.3	16.7	110.2	43 07.1	19.3	112.0	42 20.5	21.7	113.7	41 30.7	24.1	115.3	13
44 15.9	15.1	109.7	43 33.6	17.7	111.5	42 47.8	20.2	113.3	41 58.8	22.6	114.9	41 06.6	24.8	116.5	14
44 00.8	−16.0	111.1	43 15.9	−18.6	112.9	42 27.6	−21.0	114.6	41 36.2	−23.4	116.2	40 41.8	−25.6	117.7	15
43 44.8	16.9	112.4	42 57.3	19.4	114.2	42 06.6	21.8	115.8	41 12.8	24.1	117.4	40 16.2	26.3	118.9	16
43 27.9	17.9	113.8	42 37.9	20.3	115.5	41 44.8	22.6	117.1	40 48.7	24.9	118.6	39 49.9	27.1	120.1	17
43 10.0	18.7	115.1	42 17.6	21.1	116.7	41 22.2	23.5	118.3	40 23.8	25.6	119.8	39 22.8	27.7	121.3	18
42 51.3	19.6	116.4	41 56.5	22.0	118.0	40 58.7	24.2	119.5	39 58.2	26.3	121.0	38 55.1	28.3	122.4	19
42 31.7	−20.4	117.7	41 34.5	−22.7	119.2	40 34.5	−24.9	120.7	39 31.9	−27.0	122.2	38 26.8	−29.0	123.5	20
42 11.3	21.3	118.9	41 11.8	23.5	120.5	40 09.6	25.6	121.9	39 04.9	27.7	123.3	37 57.8	29.7	124.7	21
41 50.0	22.1	120.2	40 48.3	24.3	121.7	39 44.0	26.4	123.1	38 37.2	28.4	124.5	37 28.1	30.2	125.8	22
41 27.9	22.9	121.4	40 24.0	25.0	122.9	39 17.6	27.1	124.3	38 08.8	28.9	125.6	36 57.9	30.8	126.8	23
41 05.0	23.7	122.7	39 59.0	25.8	124.1	38 50.5	27.7	125.4	37 39.9	29.6	126.7	36 27.1	31.4	127.9	24
40 41.3	−24.4	123.9	39 33.2	−26.4	125.3	38 22.8	−28.4	126.6	37 10.3	−30.2	127.8	35 55.7	−31.9	129.0	25
40 16.9	25.2	125.1	39 06.8	27.2	126.4	37 54.4	29.0	127.7	36 40.1	30.8	128.9	35 23.8	32.4	130.0	26
39 51.7	25.9	126.3	38 39.6	27.8	127.6	37 25.4	29.6	128.8	36 09.3	31.3	130.0	34 51.4	33.0	131.0	27
39 25.8	26.6	127.4	38 11.8	28.4	128.7	36 55.8	30.2	129.9	35 38.0	31.9	131.0	34 18.4	33.5	132.1	28
38 59.2	27.2	128.6	37 43.4	29.1	129.8	36 25.6	30.8	131.0	35 06.1	32.4	132.0	33 44.9	33.9	133.1	29

10° Hc	d	Z	12° Hc	d	Z	14° Hc	d	Z	16° Hc	d	Z	18° Hc	d	Z	Dec.
45 06.3	−15.2	100.2	44 43.1	−18.0	102.2	44 15.9	−20.7	104.1	43 44.8	−23.3	105.9	43 10.0	−25.8	107.7	0
44 51.1	16.2	101.6	44 25.1	19.0	103.5	43 55.2	21.6	105.4	43 21.5	24.2	107.2	42 44.2	26.6	109.0	1
44 34.9	17.2	102.9	44 06.1	19.9	104.8	43 33.6	22.5	106.7	42 57.3	24.9	108.5	42 17.6	27.3	110.2	2
44 17.7	18.1	104.3	43 46.2	20.7	106.1	43 11.1	23.3	107.9	42 32.4	25.8	109.7	41 50.3	28.1	111.4	3
43 59.6	19.0	105.6	43 25.5	21.6	107.4	42 47.8	24.1	109.2	42 06.6	26.5	110.9	41 22.2	28.9	112.6	4
43 40.6	−19.9	106.9	43 03.9	−22.5	108.7	42 23.7	−24.9	110.4	41 40.1	−27.3	112.1	40 53.3	−29.5	113.7	5
43 20.7	20.8	108.2	42 41.4	23.3	110.0	41 58.8	25.7	111.7	41 12.8	27.9	113.3	40 23.8	30.1	114.9	6
42 59.9	21.7	109.5	42 18.1	24.1	111.2	41 33.1	26.5	112.9	40 44.9	28.7	114.5	39 53.7	30.9	116.0	7
42 38.2	22.5	110.8	41 54.0	24.9	112.5	41 06.6	27.2	114.1	40 16.2	29.4	115.6	39 22.8	31.4	117.1	8
42 15.7	23.3	112.0	41 29.1	25.6	113.7	40 39.4	27.8	115.3	39 46.8	30.0	116.8	38 51.4	32.1	118.2	9
41 52.4	−24.0	113.3	41 03.5	−26.4	114.9	40 11.6	−28.6	116.4	39 16.8	−30.7	117.9	38 19.3	−32.6	119.3	10
41 28.4	24.9	114.5	40 37.1	27.1	116.1	39 43.0	29.3	117.6	38 46.1	31.3	119.0	37 46.7	33.3	120.4	11
41 03.5	25.6	115.7	40 10.0	27.8	117.2	39 13.7	29.8	118.7	38 14.8	31.8	120.1	37 13.4	33.7	121.4	12
40 37.9	26.3	116.9	39 42.2	28.5	118.4	38 43.9	30.6	119.8	37 43.0	32.5	121.2	36 39.7	34.3	122.5	13
40 11.6	27.1	118.1	39 13.7	29.1	119.5	38 13.3	31.1	120.9	37 10.5	33.0	122.2	36 05.4	34.8	123.5	14
39 44.5	−27.7	119.2	38 44.6	−29.8	120.7	37 42.2	−31.7	122.0	36 37.5	−33.6	123.3	35 30.6	−35.3	124.5	15
39 16.8	28.4	120.4	38 14.8	30.4	121.8	37 10.5	32.3	123.1	36 03.9	34.0	124.3	34 55.3	35.8	125.5	16
38 48.4	29.1	121.5	37 44.4	31.0	122.9	36 38.2	32.8	124.1	35 29.9	34.6	125.3	34 19.5	36.2	126.4	17
38 19.3	29.7	122.6	37 13.4	31.5	123.9	36 05.4	33.4	125.2	34 55.3	35.1	126.3	33 43.3	36.7	127.4	18
37 49.6	30.3	123.7	36 41.9	32.2	125.0	35 32.0	33.8	126.2	34 20.2	35.5	127.3	33 06.6	37.1	128.4	19
37 19.3	−30.8	124.8	36 09.7	−32.6	126.0	34 58.2	−34.4	127.2	33 44.7	−36.0	128.3	32 29.5	−37.5	129.3	20
36 48.5	31.5	125.9	35 37.1	33.2	127.1	34 23.8	34.9	128.2	33 08.7	36.4	129.2	31 52.0	37.9	130.2	21
36 17.0	32.0	127.0	35 03.9	33.7	128.1	33 48.9	35.3	129.2	32 32.3	36.8	130.2	31 14.1	38.2	131.1	22
35 45.0	32.6	128.0	34 30.2	34.2	129.1	33 13.6	35.7	130.1	31 55.5	37.3	131.1	30 35.9	38.7	132.0	23
35 12.4	33.0	129.0	33 56.0	34.7	130.1	32 37.9	36.2	131.1	31 18.2	37.6	132.0	29 57.2	39.0	132.9	24
34 39.4	−33.6	130.1	33 21.3	−35.1	131.1	32 01.7	−36.6	132.0	30 40.6	−38.0	132.9	29 18.2	−39.3	133.8	25
34 05.8	34.0	131.1	32 46.2	35.6	132.1	31 25.1	37.0	133.0	30 02.6	38.3	133.8	28 38.9	39.7	134.6	26
33 31.8	34.6	132.1	32 10.6	35.9	133.0	30 48.1	37.4	133.9	29 24.3	38.7	134.7	27 59.2	39.9	135.5	27
32 57.2	34.9	133.0	31 34.7	36.4	133.9	30 10.7	37.7	134.8	28 45.6	39.1	135.6	27 19.3	40.3	136.3	28
32 22.3	35.4	134.0	30 58.3	36.8	134.9	29 33.0	38.1	135.7	28 06.5	39.3	136.5	26 39.0	40.5	137.2	29

Dec.	20° Hc	d	Z	22° Hc	d	Z	24° Hc	d	Z	26° Hc	d	Z	28° Hc	d	Z
0	42 31.7	+27.5	109.5	41 50.0	+29.8	111.2	41 05.0	+32.0	112.8	40 16.9	+34.1	114.4	39 25.8	+36.2	115.9
1	42 59.2	26.7	108.3	42 19.8	29.1	110.0	41 37.0	31.4	111.7	40 51.0	33.6	113.3	40 02.0	35.6	114.9
2	43 25.9	25.9	107.1	42 48.9	28.3	108.8	42 08.4	30.7	110.6	41 24.6	32.9	112.2	40 37.6	35.1	113.8
3	43 51.8	25.0	105.8	43 17.2	27.6	107.6	42 39.1	30.0	109.4	41 57.5	32.3	111.1	41 12.7	34.4	112.8
4	44 16.8	24.2	104.6	43 44.8	26.8	106.4	43 09.1	29.2	108.2	42 29.8	31.5	110.0	41 47.1	33.8	111.7
5	44 41.0	+23.4	103.3	44 11.6	+25.9	105.2	43 38.3	+28.4	107.0	43 01.3	+30.9	108.8	42 20.9	+33.2	110.6
6	45 04.4	22.4	102.0	44 37.5	25.1	103.9	44 06.7	27.7	105.8	43 32.2	30.1	107.6	42 54.1	32.4	109.4
7	45 26.8	21.5	100.7	45 02.6	24.2	102.6	44 34.4	26.8	104.6	44 02.3	29.4	106.4	43 26.5	31.8	108.3
8	45 48.3	20.6	99.3	45 26.8	23.4	101.3	45 01.2	26.0	103.3	44 31.7	28.5	105.2	43 58.3	31.0	107.1
9	46 08.9	19.6	98.0	45 50.2	22.4	100.0	45 27.2	25.2	102.0	45 00.2	27.8	104.0	44 29.3	30.2	105.9
10	46 28.5	+18.7	96.6	46 12.6	+21.4	98.7	45 52.4	+24.2	100.7	45 28.0	+26.9	102.7	44 59.5	+29.5	104.7
11	46 47.2	17.6	95.2	46 34.0	20.5	97.3	46 16.6	23.3	99.4	45 54.9	26.0	101.4	45 29.0	28.7	103.4
12	47 04.8	16.5	93.8	46 54.5	19.5	95.9	46 39.9	22.4	98.1	46 20.9	25.1	100.1	45 57.7	27.8	102.2
13	47 21.3	15.5	92.4	47 14.0	18.5	94.6	47 02.3	21.3	96.7	46 46.0	24.3	98.8	46 25.5	26.9	100.9
14	47 36.8	14.5	91.0	47 32.5	17.5	93.2	47 23.6	20.4	95.3	47 10.3	23.2	97.5	46 52.4	26.1	99.6
15	47 51.3	+13.3	89.5	47 50.0	+16.3	91.7	47 44.0	+19.4	93.9	47 33.5	+22.3	96.1	47 18.5	+25.1	98.3
16	48 04.6	12.3	88.1	48 06.3	15.3	90.3	48 03.4	18.3	92.5	47 55.8	21.3	94.7	47 43.6	24.1	96.9
17	48 16.9	11.1	86.6	48 21.6	14.2	88.8	48 21.7	17.2	91.1	48 17.1	20.2	93.3	48 07.7	23.2	95.6
18	48 28.0	9.9	85.1	48 35.8	13.1	87.4	48 38.9	16.2	89.6	48 37.3	19.2	91.9	48 30.9	22.1	94.2
19	48 37.9	8.8	83.6	48 48.9	11.9	85.9	48 55.1	15.0	88.2	48 56.5	18.0	90.5	48 53.0	21.2	92.8
20	48 46.7	+7.7	82.1	49 00.8	+10.7	84.4	49 10.1	+13.9	86.7	49 14.5	+17.0	89.0	49 14.2	+20.0	91.3
21	48 54.4	6.4	80.6	49 11.5	9.6	82.9	49 24.0	12.7	85.2	49 31.5	15.9	87.6	49 34.2	18.9	89.9
22	49 00.8	5.2	79.1	49 21.1	8.4	81.4	49 36.7	11.5	83.7	49 47.4	14.6	86.1	49 53.1	17.8	88.4
23	49 06.0	4.1	77.6	49 29.5	7.2	79.9	49 48.2	10.3	82.2	50 02.0	13.5	84.6	50 10.9	16.7	86.9
24	49 10.1	2.8	76.1	49 36.7	5.9	78.3	49 58.5	9.2	80.7	50 15.5	12.3	83.0	50 27.6	15.5	85.4
25	49 12.9	+1.6	74.5	49 42.6	+4.8	76.8	50 07.7	+7.8	79.1	50 27.8	+11.1	81.5	50 43.1	+14.3	83.9
26	49 14.5	+0.5	73.0	49 47.4	3.5	75.3	50 15.5	6.7	77.6	50 38.9	9.9	80.0	50 57.4	13.0	82.4
27	49 15.0	-0.8	71.5	49 50.9	2.2	73.7	50 22.2	5.4	76.0	50 48.8	8.6	78.4	51 10.4	11.8	80.8
28	49 14.2	2.1	69.9	49 53.1	+1.0	72.2	50 27.6	4.1	74.5	50 57.4	7.3	76.8	51 22.2	10.6	79.3
29	49 12.1	3.2	68.4	49 54.1	-0.2	70.6	50 31.7	2.9	72.9	51 04.7	6.0	75.3	51 32.8	9.2	77.7

Dec.	30° Hc	d	Z	32° Hc	d	Z	34° Hc	d	Z	36° Hc	d	Z	38° Hc	d	Z
0	38 32.0	+38.1	117.4	37 35.5	+39.9	118.8	36 36.6	+41.6	120.1	35 35.3	+43.2	121.3	34 31.8	+44.7	122.5
1	39 10.1	37.6	116.4	38 15.4	39.5	117.8	37 18.2	41.1	119.2	36 18.5	42.8	120.5	35 16.5	44.4	121.7
2	39 47.7	37.0	115.4	38 54.9	38.9	116.8	37 59.3	40.8	118.3	37 01.3	42.4	119.6	36 00.9	44.0	120.9
3	40 24.7	36.5	114.3	39 33.8	38.5	115.9	38 40.1	40.3	117.3	37 43.7	42.0	118.7	36 44.9	43.6	120.0
4	41 01.2	35.9	113.3	40 12.3	37.9	114.9	39 20.4	39.8	116.4	38 25.7	41.6	117.8	37 28.5	43.2	119.2
5	41 37.1	+35.4	112.2	40 50.2	+37.3	113.8	40 00.2	+39.3	115.4	39 07.3	+41.2	116.9	38 11.7	+42.9	118.3
6	42 12.5	34.6	111.1	41 27.5	36.8	112.8	40 39.5	38.8	114.4	39 48.5	40.6	115.9	38 54.6	42.4	117.4
7	42 47.1	34.1	110.0	42 04.3	36.2	111.7	41 18.3	38.2	113.4	40 29.1	40.2	115.0	39 37.0	42.0	116.5
8	43 21.2	33.3	108.9	42 40.5	35.6	110.7	41 56.5	37.7	112.4	41 09.3	39.7	114.0	40 19.0	41.5	115.6
9	43 54.5	32.7	107.8	43 16.1	35.0	109.6	42 34.2	37.1	111.3	41 49.0	39.1	113.0	41 00.5	41.1	114.6
10	44 27.2	+31.9	106.6	43 51.1	+34.2	108.4	43 11.3	+36.5	110.2	42 28.1	+38.6	112.0	41 41.6	+40.6	113.6
11	44 59.1	31.2	105.4	44 25.3	33.6	107.3	43 47.8	35.8	109.1	43 06.7	38.0	110.9	42 22.2	40.0	112.6
12	45 30.3	30.4	104.2	44 58.9	32.8	106.1	44 23.6	35.2	108.0	43 44.7	37.4	109.9	43 02.2	39.5	111.6
13	46 00.7	29.5	102.9	45 31.7	32.1	104.9	44 58.8	34.5	106.9	44 22.1	36.7	108.8	43 41.7	38.9	110.6
14	46 30.2	28.8	101.7	46 03.8	31.3	103.7	45 33.3	33.8	105.7	44 58.8	36.1	107.7	44 20.6	38.3	109.5
15	46 59.0	+27.8	100.4	46 35.1	+30.5	102.5	46 07.1	+33.0	104.5	45 34.9	+35.5	106.5	44 58.9	+37.7	108.4
16	47 26.8	27.0	99.1	47 05.6	29.7	101.2	46 40.1	32.2	103.3	46 10.4	34.7	105.4	45 36.6	37.0	107.3
17	47 53.8	26.0	97.8	47 35.3	28.7	100.0	47 12.3	31.4	102.1	46 45.1	33.9	104.2	46 13.6	36.3	106.2
18	48 19.8	25.0	96.4	48 04.0	27.9	98.6	47 43.7	30.6	100.8	47 19.0	33.2	103.0	46 49.9	35.7	105.1
19	48 44.8	24.1	95.1	48 31.9	26.9	97.3	48 14.3	29.7	99.5	47 52.2	32.3	101.7	47 25.6	34.8	103.9
20	49 08.9	+23.0	93.7	48 58.8	+26.0	96.0	48 44.0	+28.6	98.2	48 24.5	+31.5	100.5	48 00.4	+34.1	102.7
21	49 31.9	22.0	92.2	49 24.8	25.0	94.6	49 12.8	27.8	96.9	48 56.0	30.6	99.2	48 34.5	33.3	101.4
22	49 53.9	20.9	90.8	49 49.8	23.9	93.2	49 40.6	26.9	95.5	49 26.6	29.7	97.9	49 07.8	32.5	100.2
23	50 14.8	19.8	89.3	50 13.7	22.8	91.7	50 07.5	25.9	94.1	49 56.3	28.8	96.5	49 40.3	31.5	98.9
24	50 34.6	18.6	87.9	50 36.5	21.8	90.3	50 33.4	24.8	92.7	50 25.1	27.8	95.2	50 11.8	30.7	97.5
25	50 53.2	+17.5	86.4	50 58.3	+20.6	88.8	50 58.2	+23.7	91.3	50 52.9	+26.7	93.8	50 42.5	+29.7	96.2
26	51 10.7	16.3	84.8	51 18.9	19.5	87.3	51 21.9	22.6	89.8	51 19.6	25.7	92.3	51 12.2	28.7	94.8
27	51 27.0	15.0	83.3	51 38.4	18.3	85.8	51 44.5	21.5	88.3	51 45.3	24.6	90.9	51 40.9	27.6	93.4
28	51 42.0	13.8	81.7	51 56.7	17.0	84.3	52 06.0	20.3	86.8	52 09.9	23.5	89.4	52 08.5	26.6	92.0
29	51 55.8	12.6	80.2	52 13.7	15.8	82.7	52 26.3	19.0	85.3	52 33.4	22.3	87.9	52 35.1	25.5	90.5

20°			22°			24°			26°			28°			Dec.
Hc	d	Z	Hc	d	Z	Hc	d	Z	Hc	d	Z	Hc	d	Z	
42 31.7	−28.2	109.5	41 50.0	−30.5	111.2	41 05.0	−32.7	112.8	40 16.9	−34.8	114.4	39 25.8	−36.7	115.9	0
42 03.5	29.0	110.7	41 19.5	31.2	112.4	40 32.3	33.3	113.9	39 42.1	35.3	115.5	38 49.1	37.3	116.9	1
41 34.5	29.6	111.9	40 48.3	31.9	113.5	39 59.0	34.0	115.0	39 06.8	35.9	116.5	38 11.8	37.7	117.9	2
41 04.9	30.4	113.0	40 16.4	32.4	114.6	39 25.0	34.5	116.1	38 30.9	36.5	117.6	37 34.1	38.3	118.9	3
40 34.5	31.0	114.2	39 44.0	33.1	115.7	38 50.5	35.0	117.2	37 54.4	36.9	118.6	36 55.8	38.7	119.9	4
40 03.5	−31.6	115.3	39 10.9	−33.7	116.8	38 15.5	−35.6	118.2	37 17.5	−37.4	119.6	36 17.1	−39.1	120.9	5
39 31.9	32.3	116.4	38 37.2	34.3	117.8	37 39.9	36.2	119.2	36 40.1	37.9	120.5	35 38.0	39.6	121.8	6
38 59.6	32.8	117.5	38 02.9	34.8	118.9	37 03.7	36.6	120.2	36 02.2	38.4	121.5	34 58.4	40.0	122.7	7
38 26.8	33.4	118.6	37 28.1	35.3	119.9	36 27.1	37.1	121.2	35 23.8	38.8	122.4	34 18.4	40.4	123.6	8
37 53.3	34.0	119.6	36 52.8	35.8	120.9	35 50.0	37.6	122.2	34 45.0	39.2	123.4	33 38.0	40.8	124.5	9
37 19.3	−34.5	120.7	36 17.0	−36.3	121.9	35 12.4	−38.0	123.1	34 05.8	−39.6	124.3	32 57.2	−41.1	125.4	10
36 44.8	35.1	121.7	35 40.7	36.8	122.9	34 34.4	38.4	124.1	33 26.2	40.0	125.2	32 16.1	41.4	126.2	11
36 09.7	35.5	122.7	35 03.9	37.3	123.9	33 56.0	38.9	125.0	32 46.2	40.4	126.1	31 34.7	41.9	127.1	12
35 34.2	36.0	123.7	34 26.6	37.7	124.8	33 17.1	39.2	125.9	32 05.8	40.7	127.0	30 52.8	42.1	127.9	13
34 58.2	36.5	124.7	33 48.9	38.1	125.8	32 37.9	39.7	126.8	31 25.1	41.1	127.8	30 10.7	42.4	128.8	14
34 21.7	−37.0	125.6	33 10.8	−38.5	126.7	31 58.2	−40.0	127.7	30 44.0	−41.4	128.7	29 28.3	−42.7	129.6	15
33 44.7	37.4	126.6	32 32.3	38.9	127.6	31 18.2	40.3	128.6	30 02.6	41.7	129.5	28 45.6	43.0	130.4	16
33 07.3	37.8	127.5	31 53.4	39.3	128.5	30 37.9	40.7	129.5	29 20.9	42.0	130.3	28 02.6	43.3	131.2	17
32 29.5	38.2	128.4	31 14.1	39.6	129.4	29 57.2	41.0	130.3	28 38.9	42.3	131.2	27 19.3	43.6	132.0	18
31 51.3	38.5	129.4	30 34.5	40.0	130.3	29 16.2	41.3	131.2	27 56.6	42.6	132.0	26 35.7	43.7	132.7	19
31 12.8	−39.0	130.2	29 54.5	−40.3	131.1	28 34.9	−41.6	132.0	27 14.0	−42.8	132.8	25 52.0	−44.1	133.5	20
30 33.8	39.3	131.1	29 14.2	40.7	132.0	27 53.3	41.9	132.8	26 31.2	43.2	133.5	25 07.9	44.2	134.2	21
29 54.5	39.6	132.0	28 33.5	40.9	132.8	27 11.4	42.2	133.6	25 48.0	43.3	134.3	24 23.7	44.5	135.0	22
29 14.9	40.0	132.9	27 52.6	41.2	133.7	26 29.2	42.5	134.4	25 04.7	43.6	135.1	23 39.2	44.6	135.7	23
28 34.9	40.3	133.7	27 11.4	41.6	134.5	25 46.7	42.7	135.2	24 21.1	43.8	135.8	22 54.6	44.9	136.5	24
27 54.6	−40.6	134.6	26 29.8	−41.8	135.3	25 04.0	−42.9	136.0	23 37.3	−44.0	136.6	22 09.7	−45.0	137.2	25
27 14.0	40.9	135.4	25 48.0	42.3	136.1	24 21.1	43.1	136.7	22 53.3	44.2	137.3	21 24.7	45.3	137.9	26
26 33.1	41.1	136.2	25 06.0	42.3	136.9	23 38.0	43.4	137.5	22 09.1	44.4	138.1	20 39.4	45.4	138.6	27
25 52.0	41.5	137.0	24 23.7	42.5	137.7	22 54.6	43.6	138.3	21 24.7	44.6	138.8	19 54.0	45.5	139.3	28
25 10.5	41.7	137.8	23 41.2	42.8	138.4	22 11.0	43.8	139.0	20 40.1	44.8	139.5	19 08.5	45.7	140.0	29

30°			32°			34°			36°			38°			Dec.
Hc	d	Z	Hc	d	Z	Hc	d	Z	Hc	d	Z	Hc	d	Z	
38 32.0	−38.6	117.4	37 35.5	−40.3	118.8	36 36.6	−42.0	120.1	35 35.3	−43.5	121.3	34 31.8	−45.0	122.5	0
37 53.4	39.1	118.3	36 55.2	40.8	119.7	35 54.6	42.4	121.0	34 51.8	43.9	122.2	33 46.8	45.3	123.3	1
37 14.3	39.5	119.3	36 14.4	41.2	120.6	35 12.2	42.7	121.8	34 07.9	44.2	123.0	33 01.5	45.5	124.1	2
36 34.8	40.0	120.2	35 33.2	41.6	121.5	34 29.5	43.1	122.7	33 23.7	44.6	123.8	32 16.0	45.9	124.9	3
35 54.8	40.3	121.2	34 51.6	41.9	122.4	33 46.4	43.5	123.5	32 39.1	44.8	124.6	31 30.1	46.1	125.6	4
35 14.5	−40.8	122.1	34 09.7	−42.3	123.2	33 02.9	−43.7	124.4	31 54.3	−45.1	125.4	30 44.0	−46.4	126.4	5
34 33.7	41.2	123.0	33 27.4	42.7	124.1	32 19.2	44.1	125.2	31 09.2	45.4	126.2	29 57.6	46.7	127.1	6
33 52.5	41.5	123.9	32 44.7	43.0	124.9	31 35.1	44.3	126.0	30 23.8	45.6	126.9	29 10.9	46.8	127.8	7
33 11.0	41.9	124.7	32 01.7	43.3	125.8	30 50.8	44.7	126.8	29 38.2	45.9	127.7	28 24.1	47.1	128.6	8
32 29.1	42.2	125.6	31 18.4	43.6	126.6	30 06.1	44.9	127.5	28 52.3	46.4	128.4	27 37.0	47.3	129.3	9
31 46.9	−42.6	126.4	30 34.8	−43.9	127.4	29 21.2	−45.2	128.3	28 06.1	−46.3	129.1	26 49.7	−47.5	129.9	10
31 04.3	42.8	127.2	29 50.9	44.1	128.2	28 36.0	45.4	129.0	27 19.8	46.6	129.9	26 02.2	47.6	130.6	11
30 21.5	43.2	128.1	29 06.8	44.5	128.9	27 50.6	45.6	129.8	26 33.2	46.8	130.6	25 14.6	47.9	131.3	12
29 38.3	43.4	128.9	28 22.3	44.7	129.7	27 05.0	45.9	130.5	25 46.4	46.9	131.3	24 26.7	48.0	132.0	13
28 54.9	43.8	129.6	27 37.6	44.9	130.5	26 19.1	46.1	131.2	24 59.5	47.2	132.0	23 38.7	48.2	132.6	14
28 11.1	−43.9	130.4	26 52.7	−45.2	131.2	25 33.0	−46.2	132.0	24 12.3	−47.4	132.6	22 50.5	−48.3	133.3	15
27 27.2	44.3	131.2	26 07.5	45.4	131.9	24 46.8	46.5	132.7	23 24.9	47.5	133.3	22 02.2	48.5	133.9	16
26 42.9	44.4	132.0	25 22.1	45.6	132.7	24 00.3	46.7	133.3	22 37.4	47.7	134.0	21 13.7	48.7	134.5	17
25 58.5	44.7	132.7	24 36.5	45.8	133.4	23 13.6	46.8	134.0	21 49.7	47.8	134.6	20 25.0	48.7	135.2	18
25 13.8	45.0	133.4	23 50.7	46.0	134.1	22 26.8	47.0	134.7	21 01.9	48.0	135.3	19 36.3	48.9	135.8	19
24 28.8	−45.1	134.2	23 04.7	−46.1	134.8	21 39.8	−47.2	135.4	20 13.9	−48.1	135.9	18 47.4	−49.0	136.4	20
23 43.7	45.3	134.9	22 18.6	46.4	135.5	20 52.6	47.3	136.0	19 25.8	48.2	136.6	17 58.4	49.2	137.0	21
22 58.4	45.5	135.6	21 32.2	46.5	136.2	20 05.3	47.5	136.7	18 37.6	48.4	137.2	17 09.2	49.2	137.6	22
22 12.9	45.7	136.3	20 45.7	46.7	136.9	19 17.8	47.6	137.4	17 49.2	48.5	137.8	16 20.0	49.3	138.2	23
21 27.2	45.9	137.0	19 59.0	46.8	137.5	18 30.2	47.7	138.0	17 00.7	48.6	138.4	15 30.7	49.4	138.8	24
20 41.3	−46.0	137.7	19 12.2	−46.9	138.2	17 42.5	−47.9	138.6	16 12.1	−48.7	139.0	14 41.3	−49.6	139.4	25
19 55.3	46.2	138.4	18 25.3	47.1	138.8	16 54.6	48.0	139.3	15 23.4	48.8	139.6	13 51.7	49.6	140.0	26
19 09.1	46.3	139.1	17 38.2	47.3	139.5	16 06.6	48.0	139.9	14 34.6	48.9	140.2	13 02.1	49.6	140.6	27
18 22.8	46.5	139.7	16 50.9	47.3	140.1	15 18.6	48.2	140.5	13 45.7	49.0	140.8	12 12.5	49.8	141.1	28
17 36.3	46.6	140.4	16 03.6	47.5	140.8	14 30.4	48.3	141.1	12 56.7	49.0	141.4	11 22.7	49.8	141.7	29

Dec.	40° Hc	d	Z	42° Hc	d	Z	44° Hc	d	Z	46° Hc	d	Z	48° Hc	d	Z
°	° ′	′	°	° ′	′	°	° ′	′	°	° ′	′	°	° ′	′	°
0	33 26.3	+46.1	123.6	32 18.9	+47.4	124.7	31 09.7	+48.6	125.7	29 58.8	+49.7	126.7	28 46.3	+50.8	127.6
1	34 12.4	45.8	122.9	33 06.3	47.1	124.0	31 58.3	48.3	125.0	30 48.5	49.6	126.0	29 37.1	50.7	127.0
2	34 58.2	45.5	122.1	33 53.4	46.8	123.2	32 46.6	48.2	124.3	31 38.1	49.3	125.4	30 27.8	50.4	126.3
3	35 43.7	45.1	121.3	34 40.2	46.6	122.5	33 34.8	47.9	123.6	32 27.4	49.1	124.7	31 18.2	50.2	125.7
4	36 28.8	44.8	120.5	35 26.8	46.3	121.7	34 22.7	47.6	122.9	33 16.5	48.9	124.0	32 08.4	50.1	125.1
5	37 13.6	+44.5	119.6	36 13.1	+45.9	120.9	35 10.3	+47.3	122.2	34 05.4	+48.6	123.3	32 58.5	+49.8	124.4
6	37 58.1	44.0	118.8	36 59.0	45.6	120.1	35 57.6	47.1	121.4	34 54.0	48.4	122.6	33 48.3	49.7	123.8
7	38 42.1	43.7	117.9	37 44.6	45.3	119.3	36 44.7	46.7	120.6	35 42.4	48.1	121.9	34 38.0	49.3	123.1
8	39 25.8	43.3	117.1	38 29.9	44.9	118.5	37 31.4	46.5	119.8	36 30.5	47.9	121.1	35 27.3	49.2	122.4
9	40 09.1	42.9	116.1	39 14.8	44.6	117.6	38 17.9	46.1	119.0	37 18.4	47.5	120.4	36 16.5	48.9	121.7
10	40 52.0	+42.4	115.2	39 59.4	+44.1	116.8	39 04.0	+45.7	118.2	38 05.9	+47.3	119.6	37 05.4	+48.6	121.0
11	41 34.4	41.9	114.3	40 43.5	43.7	115.9	39 49.7	45.4	117.4	38 53.2	46.9	118.8	37 54.0	48.4	120.2
12	42 16.3	41.4	113.3	41 27.2	43.3	115.0	40 35.1	45.0	116.5	39 40.1	46.5	118.0	38 42.4	48.0	119.5
13	42 57.7	41.0	112.3	42 10.5	42.8	114.0	41 20.1	44.5	115.7	40 26.6	46.3	117.2	39 30.4	47.7	118.7
14	43 38.7	40.4	111.3	42 53.3	42.1	113.0	42 04.6	44.2	114.8	41 12.9	45.8	116.4	40 18.1	47.4	117.9
15	44 19.1	+39.8	110.3	43 35.6	+41.9	112.1	42 48.8	+43.7	113.8	41 58.7	+45.1	115.5	41 05.5	+47.1	117.1
16	44 58.9	39.2	109.3	44 17.5	41.3	111.1	43 32.5	43.2	112.9	42 44.1	44.8	114.6	41 52.6	46.7	116.3
17	45 38.1	38.6	108.2	44 58.8	40.7	110.1	44 15.7	42.7	111.9	43 29.2	44.5	113.7	42 39.3	46.3	115.4
18	46 16.7	38.0	107.1	45 39.5	40.1	109.1	44 58.4	42.2	111.0	44 13.7	44.2	112.8	43 25.6	45.9	114.5
19	46 54.7	37.2	106.0	46 19.6	39.6	108.0	45 40.6	41.7	109.9	44 57.9	43.6	111.8	44 11.5	45.4	113.6
20	47 31.9	+36.6	104.8	46 59.2	+38.9	106.9	46 22.3	+41.1	108.9	45 41.5	+43.1	110.9	44 56.9	+45.0	112.7
21	48 08.5	35.8	103.6	47 38.1	38.2	105.8	47 03.4	40.5	107.8	46 24.6	42.6	109.9	45 41.9	44.6	111.8
22	48 44.3	35.1	102.4	48 16.3	37.5	104.6	47 43.9	39.8	106.7	47 07.2	42.0	108.8	46 26.5	44.0	110.8
23	49 19.4	34.2	101.2	48 53.8	36.8	103.4	48 23.7	39.2	105.6	47 49.2	41.4	107.8	47 10.5	43.5	109.8
24	49 53.6	33.4	99.9	49 30.6	36.0	102.2	49 02.9	38.4	104.5	48 30.6	40.8	106.7	47 54.0	43.0	108.8
25	50 27.0	+32.5	98.6	50 06.6	+35.2	101.0	49 41.3	+37.8	103.3	49 11.4	+40.1	105.6	48 37.0	+42.4	107.8
26	50 59.5	31.6	97.3	50 41.8	34.3	99.7	50 19.1	36.9	102.1	49 51.5	39.5	104.4	49 19.4	41.7	106.7
27	51 31.1	30.6	95.9	51 16.1	33.5	98.4	50 56.0	36.2	100.9	50 31.0	38.7	103.2	50 01.1	41.1	105.6
28	52 01.7	29.6	94.5	51 49.6	32.5	97.1	51 32.2	35.3	99.6	51 09.7	37.9	102.0	50 42.2	40.4	104.4
29	52 31.3	28.6	93.1	52 22.1	31.5	95.7	52 07.5	34.4	98.3	51 47.6	37.1	100.8	51 22.6	39.7	103.3

Dec.	50° Hc	d	Z	52° Hc	d	Z	54° Hc	d	Z	56° Hc	d	Z	58° Hc	d	Z
°	° ′	′	°	° ′	′	°	° ′	′	°	° ′	′	°	° ′	′	°
0	27 32.5	+51.7	128.4	26 17.2	+52.7	129.2	25 00.8	+53.5	130.0	23 43.1	+54.3	130.6	22 24.5	+55.0	131.3
1	28 24.2	51.6	127.9	27 09.9	52.6	128.7	25 54.3	53.4	129.5	24 37.4	54.2	130.2	23 19.5	54.9	130.9
2	29 15.8	51.5	127.3	28 02.5	52.4	128.1	26 47.7	53.3	128.9	25 31.6	54.1	129.7	24 14.4	54.8	130.4
3	30 07.3	51.3	126.7	28 54.9	52.3	127.6	27 41.0	53.2	128.4	26 25.7	54.0	129.2	25 09.2	54.8	130.0
4	30 58.6	51.2	126.1	29 47.2	52.1	127.0	28 34.2	53.0	127.9	27 19.7	54.0	128.7	26 04.0	54.7	129.5
5	31 49.8	+50.9	125.5	30 39.3	+52.0	126.4	29 27.2	+52.9	127.4	28 13.7	+53.8	128.2	26 58.7	+54.6	129.1
6	32 40.7	50.8	124.8	31 31.3	51.8	125.9	30 20.1	52.8	126.8	29 07.5	53.6	127.7	27 53.3	54.5	128.6
7	33 31.5	50.5	124.2	32 23.1	51.6	125.3	31 12.9	52.7	126.3	30 01.1	53.6	127.2	28 47.8	54.3	128.1
8	34 22.0	50.4	123.6	33 14.7	51.5	124.7	32 05.6	52.5	125.7	30 54.7	53.4	126.7	29 42.2	54.3	127.6
9	35 12.4	50.1	122.9	34 06.2	51.3	124.0	32 58.1	52.3	125.1	31 48.1	53.3	126.2	30 36.5	54.2	127.1
10	36 02.5	+49.9	122.3	34 57.5	+51.1	123.4	33 50.4	+52.2	124.5	32 41.4	+53.2	125.6	31 30.7	+54.0	126.6
11	36 52.4	49.7	121.5	35 48.6	50.8	122.8	34 42.6	52.0	124.0	33 34.6	53.0	125.1	32 24.7	54.0	126.1
12	37 42.1	49.4	120.8	36 39.4	50.7	122.1	35 34.6	51.8	123.3	34 27.6	52.8	124.5	33 18.7	53.7	125.6
13	38 31.5	49.1	120.1	37 30.1	50.4	121.4	36 26.4	51.5	122.7	35 20.4	52.7	123.9	34 12.4	53.7	125.1
14	39 20.6	48.9	119.4	38 20.5	50.2	120.8	37 17.9	51.4	122.1	36 13.1	52.5	123.3	35 06.1	53.5	124.5
15	40 09.5	+48.5	118.6	39 10.7	+49.9	120.1	38 09.3	+51.2	121.4	37 05.6	+52.3	122.7	35 59.6	+53.4	124.0
16	40 58.0	48.2	117.8	40 00.6	49.6	119.3	39 00.5	50.9	120.8	37 57.9	52.1	122.1	36 53.0	53.1	123.4
17	41 46.2	47.9	117.0	40 50.2	49.4	118.6	39 51.4	50.7	120.1	38 50.0	51.9	121.5	37 46.1	53.1	122.8
18	42 34.1	47.6	116.2	41 39.6	49.0	117.8	40 42.1	50.4	119.4	39 41.9	51.7	120.8	38 39.2	52.8	122.2
19	43 21.7	47.1	115.4	42 28.6	48.7	117.1	41 32.5	50.2	118.7	40 33.6	51.4	120.2	39 32.0	52.6	121.6
20	44 08.8	+46.8	114.5	43 17.3	+48.4	116.3	42 22.7	+49.8	117.9	41 25.0	+51.2	119.5	40 24.6	+52.4	121.0
21	44 55.6	46.3	113.7	44 05.7	48.0	115.4	43 12.5	49.6	117.2	42 16.2	51.0	118.8	41 17.0	52.2	120.3
22	45 41.9	45.9	112.8	44 53.7	47.7	114.6	44 02.1	49.2	116.4	43 07.2	50.6	118.1	42 09.2	52.0	119.7
23	46 27.8	45.5	111.8	45 41.4	47.2	113.7	44 51.3	48.9	115.6	43 57.8	50.4	117.3	43 01.2	51.7	119.0
24	47 13.3	45.0	110.9	46 28.6	46.8	112.9	45 40.2	48.5	114.8	44 48.2	50.0	116.6	43 52.9	51.4	118.3
25	47 58.3	+44.4	109.9	47 15.4	+46.4	111.9	46 28.7	+48.1	113.9	45 38.2	+49.8	115.8	44 44.3	+51.2	117.6
26	48 42.7	43.9	108.9	48 01.8	45.9	111.0	47 16.8	47.7	113.0	46 28.0	49.3	115.0	45 35.5	50.9	116.8
27	49 26.6	43.3	107.8	48 47.7	45.3	110.0	48 04.5	47.3	112.1	47 17.3	49.0	114.1	46 26.4	50.5	116.1
28	50 09.9	42.7	106.8	49 33.0	44.9	109.0	48 51.8	46.8	111.2	48 06.3	48.6	113.3	47 16.9	50.3	115.3
29	50 52.6	42.1	105.7	50 17.9	44.3	108.0	49 38.6	46.3	110.2	48 54.9	48.2	112.4	48 07.2	49.8	114.5

40° Hc	d	Z	42° Hc	d	Z	44° Hc	d	Z	46° Hc	d	Z	48° Hc	d	Z	Dec.
33 26.3	–46.3	123.6	32 18.9	–47.6	124.7	31 09.7	–48.8	125.7	29 58.8	–49.9	126.7	28 46.3	–50.9	127.6	0
32 40.0	46.7	124.4	31 31.3	47.9	125.4	30 20.9	49.1	126.4	29 08.9	50.1	127.3	27 55.4	51.1	128.2	1
31 53.3	46.8	125.2	30 43.4	48.1	126.1	29 31.8	49.2	127.1	28 18.8	50.3	127.9	27 04.3	51.3	128.8	2
31 06.5	47.2	125.9	29 55.3	48.3	126.8	28 42.6	49.4	127.7	27 28.5	50.4	128.6	26 13.0	51.3	129.4	3
30 19.3	47.3	126.6	29 07.0	48.5	127.5	27 53.2	49.5	128.4	26 38.1	50.6	129.2	25 21.7	51.6	129.9	4
29 32.0	–47.6	127.3	28 18.5	–48.7	128.2	27 03.7	–49.8	129.0	25 47.5	–50.7	129.8	24 30.1	–51.6	130.5	5
28 44.4	47.8	128.0	27 29.8	48.9	128.8	26 13.9	49.9	129.6	24 56.8	50.9	130.4	23 38.5	51.8	131.0	6
27 56.6	48.0	128.7	26 40.9	49.0	129.5	25 24.0	50.1	130.2	24 05.9	51.0	130.9	22 46.7	51.8	131.6	7
27 08.6	48.2	129.4	25 51.9	49.2	130.1	24 33.9	50.2	130.9	23 14.9	51.1	131.5	21 54.9	52.0	132.1	8
26 20.4	48.3	130.0	25 02.7	49.4	130.8	23 43.7	50.3	131.5	22 23.8	51.2	132.1	21 02.9	52.1	132.7	9
25 32.1	–48.6	130.7	24 13.3	–49.6	131.4	22 53.4	–50.5	132.0	21 32.6	–51.4	132.7	20 10.8	–52.2	133.2	10
24 43.5	48.7	131.3	23 23.7	49.6	132.0	22 02.9	50.6	132.6	20 41.2	51.5	133.2	19 18.6	52.2	133.7	11
23 54.8	48.8	132.0	22 34.1	49.9	132.6	21 12.3	50.7	133.2	19 49.7	51.5	133.8	18 26.4	52.4	134.3	12
23 06.0	49.1	132.6	21 44.2	49.9	133.2	20 21.6	50.8	133.8	18 58.2	51.7	134.3	17 34.0	52.4	134.8	13
22 16.9	49.1	133.2	20 54.3	50.1	133.8	19 30.8	50.9	134.3	18 06.5	51.7	134.8	16 41.6	52.5	135.3	14
21 27.8	–49.3	133.9	20 04.2	–50.2	134.4	18 39.9	–51.0	134.9	17 14.8	–51.8	135.4	15 49.1	–52.6	135.8	15
20 38.5	49.4	134.5	19 14.0	50.2	135.0	17 48.9	51.2	135.5	16 23.0	51.9	135.9	14 56.5	52.6	136.3	16
19 49.1	49.6	135.1	18 23.8	50.4	135.6	16 57.7	51.2	136.0	15 31.1	52.0	136.4	14 03.9	52.7	136.8	17
18 59.5	49.6	135.7	17 33.4	50.5	136.1	16 06.5	51.3	136.6	14 39.1	52.0	136.9	13 11.2	52.7	137.3	18
18 09.9	49.8	136.3	16 42.9	50.6	136.7	15 15.2	51.3	137.1	13 47.1	52.1	137.4	12 18.5	52.8	137.8	19
17 20.1	–49.8	136.9	15 52.3	–50.7	137.3	14 23.9	–51.5	137.6	12 55.0	–52.2	138.0	11 25.7	–52.9	138.2	20
16 30.3	50.0	137.4	15 01.6	50.7	137.8	13 32.4	51.5	138.2	12 02.8	52.2	138.5	10 32.8	52.9	138.7	21
15 40.3	50.0	138.0	14 10.9	50.9	138.4	12 40.9	51.5	138.7	11 10.6	52.2	139.0	9 39.9	52.9	139.2	22
14 50.3	50.2	138.6	13 20.0	50.9	138.9	11 49.4	51.6	139.2	10 18.4	52.4	139.5	8 47.0	53.0	139.7	23
14 00.1	50.2	139.2	12 29.1	50.9	139.5	10 57.8	51.7	139.7	9 26.0	52.3	140.0	7 54.0	53.0	140.2	24
13 09.9	–50.3	139.7	11 38.2	–51.0	140.0	10 06.1	–51.7	140.2	8 33.7	–52.4	140.5	7 01.0	–53.0	140.6	25
12 19.6	50.3	140.3	10 47.2	51.1	140.5	9 14.4	51.8	140.8	7 41.3	52.4	140.9	6 08.0	53.0	141.1	26
11 29.3	50.4	140.8	9 56.1	51.1	141.1	8 22.6	51.8	141.3	6 48.9	52.5	141.4	5 15.0	53.1	141.6	27
10 38.9	50.5	141.4	9 05.0	51.2	141.6	7 30.8	51.8	141.8	5 56.4	52.4	141.9	4 21.9	53.1	142.0	28
9 48.4	50.5	141.9	8 13.8	51.2	142.1	6 39.0	51.9	142.3	5 04.0	52.5	142.4	3 28.8	53.1	142.5	29

50° Hc	d	Z	52° Hc	d	Z	54° Hc	d	Z	56° Hc	d	Z	58° Hc	d	Z	Dec.
27 32.5	–51.9	128.4	26 17.2	–52.8	129.2	25 00.8	–53.7	130.0	23 43.1	–54.3	130.6	22 24.5	–55.1	131.3	0
26 40.6	52.1	129.0	25 24.4	52.9	129.7	24 07.1	53.7	130.4	22 48.8	54.5	131.1	21 29.4	55.2	131.7	1
25 48.5	52.1	129.5	24 31.5	53.0	130.3	23 13.4	53.8	130.9	21 54.3	54.5	131.6	20 34.2	55.2	132.1	2
24 56.4	52.3	130.1	23 38.5	53.1	130.8	22 19.6	53.8	131.4	20 59.8	54.6	132.0	19 39.0	55.2	132.6	3
24 04.1	52.3	130.6	22 45.4	53.2	131.3	21 25.8	54.0	131.9	20 05.2	54.7	132.5	18 43.8	55.3	133.0	4
23 11.7	–52.5	131.2	21 52.2	–53.3	131.8	20 31.8	–54.0	132.4	19 10.5	–54.7	132.9	17 48.5	–55.4	133.4	5
22 19.2	52.6	131.7	20 58.9	53.4	132.3	19 37.8	54.1	132.8	18 15.8	54.8	133.3	16 53.1	55.4	133.8	6
21 26.6	52.7	132.2	20 05.5	53.4	132.8	18 43.7	54.2	133.3	17 21.0	54.8	133.8	15 57.7	55.4	134.2	7
20 33.9	52.8	132.7	19 12.1	53.5	133.2	17 49.5	54.2	133.7	16 26.2	54.9	134.2	15 02.3	55.5	134.6	8
19 41.1	52.8	133.2	18 18.6	53.6	133.7	16 55.3	54.3	134.2	15 31.3	54.9	134.6	14 06.8	55.5	135.0	9
18 48.3	–53.0	133.7	17 25.0	–53.7	134.2	16 01.0	–54.4	134.6	14 36.4	–55.0	135.0	13 11.3	–55.6	135.4	10
17 55.3	53.0	134.2	16 31.3	53.7	134.7	15 06.6	54.4	135.1	13 41.4	55.0	135.4	12 15.7	55.6	135.7	11
17 02.3	53.1	134.7	15 37.6	53.8	135.1	14 12.2	54.4	135.5	12 46.4	55.1	135.8	11 20.1	55.6	136.1	12
16 09.2	53.2	135.2	14 43.8	53.9	135.6	13 17.8	54.5	136.0	11 51.3	55.0	136.2	10 24.5	55.7	136.5	13
15 16.0	53.2	135.7	13 49.9	53.9	136.0	12 23.3	54.5	136.4	10 56.3	55.2	136.6	9 28.8	55.7	136.9	14
14 22.8	–53.2	136.2	12 56.0	–53.9	136.5	11 28.8	–54.6	136.8	10 01.1	–55.1	137.0	8 33.1	–55.7	137.3	15
13 29.6	53.4	136.6	12 02.1	54.0	136.9	10 34.2	54.6	137.2	9 06.0	55.2	137.4	7 37.4	55.7	137.6	16
12 36.2	53.3	137.1	11 08.1	54.0	137.4	9 39.6	54.6	137.7	8 10.8	55.2	137.8	6 41.7	55.7	138.0	17
11 42.9	53.5	137.6	10 14.1	54.1	137.8	8 45.0	54.7	138.1	7 15.6	55.2	138.2	5 46.0	55.8	138.4	18
10 49.4	53.4	138.0	9 20.0	54.0	138.3	7 50.3	54.6	138.5	6 20.4	55.2	138.6	4 50.2	55.7	138.8	19
9 56.0	–53.5	138.5	8 26.0	–54.2	138.7	6 55.7	–54.7	138.9	5 25.2	–55.3	139.0	3 54.5	–55.8	139.1	20
9 02.5	53.6	139.0	7 31.8	54.1	139.1	6 01.0	54.8	139.3	4 29.9	55.3	139.4	2 58.7	55.8	139.5	21
8 08.9	53.6	139.4	6 37.7	54.2	139.6	5 06.2	54.7	139.7	3 34.6	55.3	139.8	2 02.9	55.8	139.9	22
7 15.4	53.6	139.9	5 43.5	54.2	140.0	4 11.5	54.7	140.1	2 39.4	55.3	140.2	1 07.1	55.7	140.2	23
6 21.8	53.6	140.3	4 49.3	54.2	140.4	3 16.8	54.8	140.5	1 44.1	55.3	140.6	0 11.4	–55.8	140.6	24
5 28.2	–53.7	140.8	3 55.1	–54.2	140.9	2 22.0	–54.8	140.9	0 48.8	–55.3	141.0	0 44.4	+55.8	39.0	25
4 34.5	53.6	141.2	3 00.9	54.2	141.3	1 27.2	54.7	141.4	0 06.5	+55.3	38.6	1 40.2	55.8	38.7	26
3 40.9	53.7	141.7	2 06.7	54.2	141.7	0 32.5	–54.8	141.8	1 01.8	55.3	38.2	2 36.0	55.8	38.3	27
2 47.2	53.7	142.1	1 12.5	54.3	142.2	0 22.3	+54.8	37.8	1 57.1	55.2	37.9	3 31.8	55.7	37.9	28
1 53.5	53.6	142.6	0 18.2	–54.2	142.6	1 17.1	54.7	37.4	2 52.3	55.3	37.5	4 27.5	55.8	37.5	29

Dec.	0° Hc	d	Z	2° Hc	d	Z	4° Hc	d	Z	6° Hc	d	Z	8° Hc	d	Z
°	° ′	′	°	° ′	′	°	° ′	′	°	° ′	′	°	° ′	′	°
0	44 00.0	- 0.5	90.0	43 58.0	+ 2.4	91.9	43 51.9	+ 5.3	93.9	43 41.9	+ 8.1	95.8	43 27.8	+11.1	97.7
1	43 59.5	1.5	88.6	44 00.4	1.4	90.5	43 57.2	4.3	92.5	43 50.0	7.2	94.4	43 38.9	10.0	96.3
2	43 58.0	2.5	87.2	44 01.8	+ 0.4	89.2	44 01.5	3.3	91.1	43 57.2	6.2	93.0	43 48.9	9.1	94.9
3	43 55.5	3.6	85.8	44 02.2	- 0.7	87.8	44 04.8	2.3	89.7	44 03.4	5.2	91.6	43 58.0	8.1	93.6
4	43 51.9	4.5	84.4	44 01.5	1.6	86.4	44 07.1	1.3	88.3	44 08.6	4.2	90.2	44 06.1	7.1	92.2
5	43 47.4	- 5.5	83.1	43 59.9	- 2.7	85.0	44 08.4	+ 0.2	86.9	44 12.8	+ 3.2	88.9	44 13.2	+ 6.1	90.8
6	43 41.9	6.6	81.7	43 57.2	3.6	83.6	44 08.6	- 0.7	85.5	44 16.0	2.1	87.5	44 19.3	5.0	89.4
7	43 35.3	7.5	80.3	43 53.6	4.7	82.2	44 07.9	1.8	84.1	44 18.1	1.2	86.1	44 24.3	4.1	88.0
8	43 27.8	8.4	78.9	43 48.9	5.6	80.8	44 06.1	2.8	82.7	44 19.3	+ 0.1	84.7	44 28.4	3.0	86.6
9	43 19.4	9.5	77.6	43 43.3	6.7	79.4	44 03.3	3.8	81.3	44 19.4	- 1.0	83.3	44 31.4	2.0	85.2
10	43 09.9	- 10.4	76.2	43 36.6	- 7.6	78.1	43 59.5	- 4.8	80.0	44 18.4	- 1.9	81.9	44 33.4	+ 1.0	83.8
11	42 59.5	11.3	74.9	43 29.0	8.6	76.7	43 54.7	5.8	78.6	44 16.5	2.9	80.5	44 34.4	- 0.1	82.4
12	42 48.2	12.3	73.5	43 20.4	9.6	75.3	43 48.9	6.8	77.2	44 13.6	4.0	79.1	44 34.3	1.1	81.0
13	42 35.9	13.2	72.2	43 10.8	10.5	74.0	43 42.1	7.8	75.8	44 09.6	5.0	77.7	44 33.2	2.1	79.6
14	42 22.7	14.1	70.9	43 00.3	11.5	72.6	43 34.3	8.8	74.4	44 04.6	6.0	76.3	44 31.1	3.2	78.2
15	42 08.6	- 15.0	69.6	42 48.8	- 12.4	71.3	43 25.5	- 9.9	73.1	43 58.6	- 7.0	74.9	44 27.9	- 4.2	76.8
16	41 53.6	15.9	68.3	42 36.4	13.3	70.0	43 15.8	10.7	71.7	43 51.6	8.0	73.5	44 23.7	5.1	75.4
17	41 37.7	16.7	67.0	42 23.1	14.3	68.6	43 05.1	11.6	70.4	43 43.6	8.9	72.2	44 18.6	6.3	74.0
18	41 21.0	17.6	65.7	42 08.8	15.1	67.3	42 53.5	12.6	69.0	43 34.7	10.0	70.8	44 12.3	7.2	72.6
19	41 03.4	18.4	64.4	41 53.7	16.0	66.0	42 40.9	13.5	67.7	43 24.7	10.8	69.4	44 05.1	8.2	71.2
20	40 45.0	- 19.2	63.2	41 37.7	- 16.8	64.7	42 27.4	- 14.4	66.4	43 13.9	- 11.9	68.1	43 56.9	- 9.2	69.9
21	40 25.8	20.0	61.9	41 20.9	17.7	63.5	42 13.0	15.3	65.1	43 02.0	12.8	66.7	43 47.7	10.2	68.5
22	40 05.8	20.8	60.7	41 03.2	18.5	62.2	41 57.7	16.1	63.8	42 49.2	13.7	65.4	43 37.5	11.1	67.1
23	39 45.0	21.6	59.5	40 44.7	19.4	60.9	41 41.6	17.1	62.5	42 35.5	14.6	64.1	43 26.4	12.1	65.8
24	39 23.4	22.3	58.2	40 25.3	20.1	59.7	41 24.5	17.8	61.2	42 20.9	15.5	62.8	43 14.3	13.0	64.4
25	39 01.1	- 23.0	57.0	40 05.2	- 20.9	58.4	41 06.7	- 18.7	59.9	42 05.4	- 16.4	61.5	43 01.3	- 14.0	63.1
26	38 38.1	23.8	55.9	39 44.3	21.7	57.2	40 48.0	19.5	58.7	41 49.0	17.2	60.2	42 47.3	14.9	61.8
27	38 14.3	24.4	54.7	39 22.6	22.4	56.0	40 28.5	20.4	57.4	41 31.8	18.1	58.9	42 32.4	15.8	60.4
28	37 49.9	25.1	53.5	39 00.2	23.2	54.8	40 08.1	21.0	56.2	41 13.7	18.9	57.6	42 16.6	16.6	59.1
29	37 24.8	25.8	52.4	38 37.0	23.8	53.6	39 47.1	21.9	55.0	40 54.8	19.8	56.4	42 00.0	17.6	57.8

Dec.	10° Hc	d	Z	12° Hc	d	Z	14° Hc	d	Z	16° Hc	d	Z	18° Hc	d	Z
°	° ′	′	°	° ′	′	°	° ′	′	°	° ′	′	°	° ′	′	°
0	43 09.9	+13.8	99.5	42 48.2	+16.5	101.4	42 22.7	+19.2	103.1	41 53.6	+21.8	104.9	41 21.0	+24.3	106.6
1	43 23.7	12.9	98.2	43 04.7	15.7	100.0	42 41.9	18.4	101.9	42 15.4	21.0	103.7	41 45.3	23.5	105.4
2	43 36.6	11.9	96.8	43 20.4	14.7	98.7	43 00.3	17.4	100.6	42 36.4	20.1	102.4	42 08.8	22.8	104.2
3	43 48.5	11.0	95.5	43 35.1	13.8	97.4	43 17.7	16.6	99.3	42 56.5	19.3	101.1	42 31.6	21.9	102.9
4	43 59.5	10.0	94.1	43 48.9	12.8	96.0	43 34.3	15.6	97.9	43 15.8	18.0	99.8	42 53.5	21.0	101.6
5	44 09.5	+ 8.9	92.7	44 01.7	+11.9	94.7	43 49.9	+14.7	96.6	43 34.2	+17.4	98.5	43 14.5	+20.2	100.4
6	44 18.4	8.0	91.4	44 13.6	10.8	93.3	44 04.6	13.7	95.2	43 51.6	16.6	97.2	43 34.7	19.3	99.1
7	44 26.4	7.0	90.0	44 24.4	9.9	91.9	44 18.3	12.8	93.9	44 08.2	15.5	95.8	43 54.0	18.3	97.7
8	44 33.4	6.0	88.6	44 34.3	8.9	90.6	44 31.1	11.8	92.5	44 23.7	14.7	94.5	44 12.3	17.5	96.4
9	44 39.4	4.9	87.2	44 43.2	7.8	89.2	44 42.9	10.7	91.1	44 38.4	13.6	93.1	44 29.8	16.5	95.1
10	44 44.3	+ 3.9	85.8	44 51.0	+ 6.9	87.8	44 53.6	+ 9.8	89.8	44 52.0	+12.7	91.7	44 46.3	+15.5	93.7
11	44 48.2	2.8	84.4	44 57.9	5.8	86.4	45 03.4	8.7	88.4	45 04.7	11.7	90.4	45 01.8	14.6	92.4
12	44 51.0	1.8	83.0	45 03.7	4.7	85.0	45 12.1	7.7	87.0	45 16.4	10.6	89.0	45 16.4	13.6	91.0
13	44 52.8	+ 0.8	81.6	45 08.4	3.7	83.5	45 19.8	6.7	85.6	45 27.0	9.6	87.6	45 30.0	12.5	89.6
14	44 53.6	- 0.2	80.1	45 12.1	2.7	82.1	45 26.5	5.6	84.1	45 36.6	8.6	86.2	45 42.5	11.5	88.2
15	44 53.4	- 1.4	78.7	45 14.8	+ 1.6	80.7	45 32.1	+ 4.5	82.7	45 45.2	+ 7.5	84.8	45 54.0	+10.5	86.8
16	44 52.0	2.3	77.3	45 16.4	+ 0.5	79.3	45 36.6	3.5	81.3	45 52.7	6.4	83.3	46 04.5	9.4	85.4
17	44 49.7	3.4	75.9	45 16.9	- 0.5	77.9	45 40.1	2.4	79.9	45 59.1	5.4	81.9	46 13.9	8.3	84.0
18	44 46.3	4.4	74.5	45 16.4	1.6	76.4	45 42.5	1.3	78.4	46 04.5	4.3	80.5	46 22.2	7.3	82.5
19	44 41.9	5.5	73.1	45 14.8	2.6	75.0	45 43.8	+ 0.3	77.0	46 08.8	3.2	79.0	46 29.5	6.2	81.1
20	44 36.4	- 6.5	71.7	45 12.2	- 3.7	73.6	45 44.1	- 0.8	75.6	46 12.0	+ 2.1	77.6	46 35.7	+ 5.0	79.6
21	44 29.9	7.5	70.3	45 08.5	4.7	72.2	45 43.3	1.9	74.1	46 14.1	+ 1.0	76.1	46 40.7	4.0	78.2
22	44 22.4	8.4	68.9	45 03.8	5.8	70.8	45 41.4	3.0	72.7	46 15.1	- 0.1	74.7	46 44.7	2.9	76.7
23	44 14.0	9.5	67.5	44 58.0	6.8	69.4	45 38.4	4.0	71.3	46 15.0	1.2	73.2	46 47.6	1.7	75.3
24	44 05.5	10.5	66.2	44 51.2	7.8	68.0	45 34.4	5.1	69.9	46 13.8	2.2	71.8	46 49.3	+ 0.7	73.8
25	43 54.0	- 11.5	64.8	44 43.4	- 8.8	66.6	45 29.3	- 6.1	68.4	46 11.6	- 3.4	70.4	46 50.0	- 0.5	72.4
26	43 42.5	12.4	63.4	44 34.6	9.9	65.2	45 23.2	7.2	67.0	46 08.2	4.4	68.9	46 49.5	1.6	70.9
27	43 30.1	13.4	62.1	44 24.7	10.8	63.8	45 16.0	8.2	65.6	46 03.8	5.5	67.5	46 47.9	2.7	69.4
28	43 16.7	14.3	60.7	44 13.9	11.9	62.4	45 07.8	9.3	64.2	45 58.3	6.6	66.0	46 45.2	3.9	68.0
29	43 02.4	15.2	59.4	44 02.0	12.8	61.1	44 58.5	10.3	62.8	45 51.7	7.7	64.6	46 41.3	4.9	66.5

LATITUDE **CONTRARY** NAME   L.H.A. 46°, 314°

0° Hc	d	Z	2° Hc	d	Z	4° Hc	d	Z	6° Hc	d	Z	8° Hc	d	Z	Dec.
44 00.0	- 0.5	90.0	43 58.0	- 3.4	91.9	43 51.9	- 6.3	93.9	43 41.9	- 9.2	95.8	43 27.8	- 11.9	97.7	0
43 59.5	1.5	91.4	43 54.6	4.5	93.3	43 45.6	7.3	95.2	43 32.7	10.1	97.1	43 15.9	13.0	99.0	1
43 58.0	2.5	92.8	43 50.1	5.4	94.7	43 38.3	8.2	96.6	43 22.6	11.1	98.5	43 02.9	13.8	100.3	2
43 55.5	3.6	94.2	43 44.7	6.4	96.1	43 30.1	9.3	98.0	43 11.5	12.1	99.8	42 49.1	14.8	101.7	3
43 51.9	4.5	95.6	43 38.3	7.4	97.5	43 20.8	10.2	99.3	42 59.4	12.9	101.2	42 34.3	15.7	103.0	4
43 47.4	- 5.5	96.9	43 30.9	- 8.3	98.8	43 10.6	- 11.2	100.7	42 46.5	- 13.9	102.5	42 18.6	- 16.5	104.3	5
43 41.9	6.6	98.3	43 22.6	9.4	100.2	42 59.4	12.1	102.0	42 32.6	14.8	103.8	42 02.1	17.4	105.6	6
43 35.3	7.5	99.7	43 13.2	10.3	101.5	42 47.3	13.0	103.4	42 17.8	15.7	105.1	41 44.7	18.3	106.9	7
43 27.8	8.4	101.1	43 02.9	11.2	102.9	42 34.3	13.9	104.7	42 02.1	16.6	106.4	41 26.4	19.1	108.2	8
43 19.4	9.5	102.4	42 51.7	12.2	104.2	42 20.4	14.9	106.0	41 45.5	17.4	107.7	41 07.3	19.9	109.4	9
43 09.9	- 10.4	103.8	42 39.5	- 13.1	105.6	42 05.5	- 15.7	107.3	41 28.1	- 18.3	109.0	40 47.4	- 20.8	110.7	10
42 59.5	11.3	105.1	42 26.4	14.0	106.9	41 49.8	16.6	108.6	41 09.8	19.1	110.3	40 26.6	21.5	111.9	11
42 48.2	12.3	106.5	42 12.4	14.9	108.2	41 33.2	17.4	109.9	40 50.7	19.9	111.5	40 05.1	22.2	113.1	12
42 35.9	13.2	107.8	41 57.5	15.8	109.5	41 15.8	18.3	111.2	40 30.8	20.7	112.8	39 42.9	23.1	114.3	13
42 22.7	14.1	109.1	41 41.7	16.6	110.8	40 57.5	19.1	112.4	40 10.1	21.4	114.0	39 19.8	23.7	115.5	14
42 08.6	- 15.0	110.4	41 25.1	- 17.5	112.1	40 38.4	- 19.9	113.7	39 48.7	- 22.3	115.2	38 56.1	- 24.5	116.7	15
41 53.6	15.9	111.7	41 07.6	18.3	113.4	40 18.5	20.7	114.9	39 26.4	22.9	116.4	38 31.6	25.1	117.9	16
41 37.7	16.7	113.0	40 49.3	19.2	114.6	39 57.8	21.5	116.2	39 03.5	23.7	117.6	38 06.5	25.8	119.0	17
41 21.0	17.6	114.3	40 30.1	19.9	115.9	39 36.3	22.2	117.4	38 39.8	24.4	118.8	37 40.7	26.5	120.2	18
41 03.4	18.4	115.6	40 10.2	20.8	117.1	39 14.1	23.0	118.6	38 15.4	25.1	120.0	37 14.2	27.1	121.3	19
40 45.0	- 19.2	116.8	39 49.4	- 21.5	118.3	38 51.1	- 23.6	119.8	37 50.3	- 25.7	121.1	36 47.1	- 27.7	122.4	20
40 25.8	20.0	118.1	39 27.9	22.2	119.6	38 27.5	24.4	121.0	37 24.6	26.4	122.3	36 19.4	28.4	123.5	21
40 05.8	20.8	119.3	39 05.7	23.0	120.8	38 03.1	25.0	122.1	36 58.2	27.1	123.4	35 51.0	28.9	124.6	22
39 45.0	21.6	120.5	38 42.7	23.6	121.9	37 38.1	25.7	123.3	36 31.1	27.6	124.5	35 22.1	29.5	125.7	23
39 23.4	22.3	121.8	38 19.1	24.4	123.1	37 12.4	26.4	124.4	36 03.5	28.2	125.6	34 52.6	30.0	126.8	24
39 01.1	- 23.0	123.0	37 54.7	- 25.1	124.3	36 46.0	- 27.0	125.5	35 35.3	- 28.9	126.7	34 22.6	- 30.6	127.8	25
38 38.1	23.8	124.1	37 29.6	25.7	125.4	36 19.0	27.6	126.6	35 06.4	29.3	127.8	33 52.0	31.1	128.9	26
38 14.3	24.4	125.3	37 03.9	26.3	126.6	35 51.4	28.1	127.7	34 37.1	30.0	128.8	33 20.9	31.5	129.9	27
37 49.9	25.1	126.5	36 37.6	27.0	127.7	35 23.3	28.8	128.8	34 07.1	30.4	129.9	32 49.4	32.1	130.9	28
37 24.8	25.8	127.6	36 10.6	27.6	128.8	34 54.5	29.3	129.9	33 36.7	31.0	130.9	32 17.3	32.6	131.9	29

10° Hc	d	Z	12° Hc	d	Z	14° Hc	d	Z	16° Hc	d	Z	18° Hc	d	Z	Dec.
43 09.9	- 14.7	99.5	42 48.2	- 17.5	101.4	42 22.7	- 20.1	103.1	41 53.6	- 22.6	104.9	41 21.0	- 25.1	106.6	0
42 55.2	15.7	100.8	42 30.7	18.3	102.7	42 02.6	20.9	104.4	41 31.0	23.4	106.1	40 55.9	25.8	107.8	1
42 39.5	16.5	102.2	42 12.4	19.2	103.9	41 41.7	21.7	105.7	41 07.6	24.2	107.4	40 30.1	26.5	109.0	2
42 23.0	17.5	103.5	41 53.2	20.0	105.2	41 20.0	22.5	106.9	40 43.4	24.9	108.6	40 03.6	27.3	110.2	3
42 05.5	18.3	104.8	41 33.2	20.8	106.5	40 57.5	23.3	108.2	40 18.5	25.7	109.8	39 36.3	27.9	111.3	4
41 47.2	- 19.1	106.0	41 12.4	- 21.7	107.7	40 34.2	- 24.1	109.4	39 52.8	- 26.4	111.0	39 08.4	- 28.6	112.5	5
41 28.1	20.0	107.3	40 50.7	22.4	109.0	40 10.1	24.8	110.6	39 26.4	27.0	112.1	38 39.8	29.3	113.6	6
41 08.1	20.7	108.6	40 28.3	23.2	110.2	39 45.3	25.5	111.8	38 59.4	27.8	113.3	38 10.5	29.8	114.7	7
40 47.4	21.6	109.8	40 05.1	23.9	111.4	39 19.8	26.2	112.9	38 31.6	28.3	114.4	37 40.7	30.5	115.8	8
40 25.8	22.3	111.0	39 41.2	24.7	112.6	38 53.6	26.8	114.1	38 03.3	29.1	115.5	37 10.2	31.0	116.9	9
40 03.5	- 23.1	112.2	39 16.5	- 25.3	113.8	38 26.8	- 27.6	115.2	37 34.2	- 29.6	116.6	36 39.2	- 31.7	118.0	10
39 40.4	23.9	113.5	38 51.2	26.1	114.9	37 59.2	28.2	116.4	37 04.6	30.2	117.7	36 07.5	32.1	119.0	11
39 16.5	24.5	114.6	38 25.1	26.7	116.1	37 31.0	28.8	117.5	36 34.4	30.8	118.8	35 35.4	32.7	120.1	12
38 52.0	25.2	115.8	37 58.4	27.4	117.2	37 02.2	29.4	118.6	36 03.6	31.4	119.9	35 02.7	33.2	121.1	13
38 26.8	26.0	117.0	37 31.0	28.0	118.4	36 32.8	30.0	119.7	35 32.2	31.9	120.9	34 29.5	33.7	122.1	14
38 00.8	- 26.6	118.1	37 03.0	- 28.6	119.5	36 02.8	- 30.6	120.8	35 00.3	- 32.4	122.0	33 55.8	- 34.2	123.1	15
37 34.2	27.2	119.3	36 34.4	29.2	120.6	35 32.2	31.1	121.8	34 27.9	32.9	123.0	33 21.6	34.7	124.1	16
37 07.0	27.8	120.4	36 05.2	29.8	121.7	35 01.1	31.6	122.9	33 55.0	33.4	124.0	32 46.9	35.1	125.1	17
36 39.2	28.5	121.5	35 35.4	30.4	122.7	34 29.5	32.2	123.9	33 21.6	33.9	125.0	32 11.8	35.5	126.1	18
36 10.7	29.1	122.6	35 05.0	30.9	123.8	33 57.3	32.7	124.9	32 47.7	34.4	126.0	31 36.3	35.9	127.0	19
35 41.6	- 29.6	123.7	34 34.1	- 31.4	124.8	33 24.6	- 33.1	125.9	32 13.3	- 34.8	127.0	31 00.4	- 36.4	127.9	20
35 12.0	30.2	124.7	34 02.7	32.0	125.9	32 51.5	33.6	126.9	31 38.5	35.2	127.9	30 24.0	36.7	128.9	21
34 41.8	30.7	125.8	33 30.7	32.4	126.9	32 17.9	34.1	127.9	31 03.3	35.6	128.9	29 47.3	37.1	129.8	22
34 11.1	31.2	126.8	32 58.3	32.9	127.9	31 43.8	34.5	128.9	30 27.7	36.0	129.8	29 10.2	37.5	130.7	23
33 39.9	31.8	127.9	32 25.4	33.4	128.9	31 09.3	34.9	129.8	29 51.7	36.4	130.7	28 32.7	37.8	131.8	24
33 08.1	- 32.2	128.9	31 52.0	- 33.8	129.9	30 34.4	- 35.4	130.8	29 15.3	- 36.8	131.6	27 54.9	- 38.1	132.5	25
32 35.9	32.7	129.9	31 18.2	34.3	130.8	29 59.0	35.7	131.7	28 38.5	37.1	132.6	27 16.8	38.5	133.3	26
32 03.2	33.2	130.9	30 43.9	34.6	131.8	29 23.3	36.1	132.6	28 01.4	37.5	133.4	26 38.3	38.8	134.2	27
31 30.0	33.6	131.8	30 09.3	35.1	132.7	28 47.2	36.5	133.6	27 23.9	37.8	134.3	25 59.5	39.0	135.0	28
30 56.4	34.0	132.8	29 34.2	35.5	133.7	28 10.7	36.8	134.5	26 46.1	38.1	135.2	25 20.5	39.4	135.9	29

	20°			22°			24°			26°			28°		
Dec.	Hc	d	Z	Hc	d	Z	Hc	d	Z	Hc	d	Z	Hc	d	Z
°	° ′	′	°	° ′	′	°	° ′	′	°	° ′	′	°	° ′	′	°
0	40 45.0	+26.8	108.3	40 05.8	+29.0	109.9	39 23.4	+31.3	111.4	38 38.1	+33.4	112.9	37 49.9	+35.4	114.4
1	41 11.8	25.9	107.1	40 34.8	28.4	108.7	39 54.7	30.6	110.3	39 11.5	32.8	111.9	38 25.3	34.9	113.4
2	41 37.7	25.3	105.9	41 03.2	27.6	107.6	40 25.3	30.0	109.2	39 44.3	32.1	110.8	39 00.2	34.3	112.3
3	42 03.0	24.4	104.7	41 30.8	26.9	106.4	40 55.3	29.2	108.1	40 16.4	31.6	109.7	39 34.5	33.6	111.3
4	42 27.4	23.6	103.4	41 57.7	26.2	105.2	41 24.5	28.6	106.9	40 48.0	30.8	108.6	40 08.1	33.1	110.2
5	42 51.0	+22.9	102.2	42 23.9	+25.3	104.0	41 53.1	+27.8	105.7	41 18.8	+30.2	107.4	40 41.2	+32.5	109.1
6	43 13.9	21.9	100.9	42 49.2	24.6	102.8	42 20.9	27.1	104.5	41 49.0	29.5	106.3	41 13.7	31.8	108.0
7	43 35.8	21.1	99.6	43 13.8	23.7	101.5	42 48.0	26.3	103.3	42 18.5	28.8	105.1	41 45.5	31.1	106.8
8	43 56.9	20.2	98.3	43 37.5	22.9	100.2	43 14.3	25.5	102.1	42 47.3	28.0	103.9	42 16.6	30.4	105.7
9	44 17.1	19.3	97.0	44 00.4	22.0	99.0	43 39.8	24.7	100.8	43 15.3	27.2	102.7	42 47.0	29.7	104.5
10	44 36.4	+18.4	95.7	44 22.4	+21.2	97.7	44 04.5	+23.8	99.6	43 42.5	+26.5	101.5	43 16.7	+29.0	103.3
11	44 54.8	17.4	94.4	44 43.6	20.2	96.3	44 28.3	22.9	98.3	44 09.0	25.6	100.2	43 45.7	28.2	102.1
12	45 12.2	16.4	93.0	45 03.8	19.3	95.0	44 51.2	22.1	97.0	44 34.6	24.7	99.0	44 13.9	27.3	100.9
13	45 28.6	15.5	91.6	45 23.1	18.3	93.7	45 13.3	21.1	95.7	44 59.3	23.9	97.7	44 41.2	26.6	99.6
14	45 44.1	14.4	90.3	45 41.4	17.3	92.3	45 34.4	20.2	94.4	45 23.2	23.0	96.4	45 07.8	25.7	98.4
15	45 58.5	+13.5	88.9	45 58.7	+16.4	90.9	45 54.6	+19.2	93.0	45 46.2	+22.0	95.1	45 33.5	+24.8	97.1
16	46 12.0	12.3	87.5	46 15.1	15.3	89.6	46 13.8	18.3	91.6	46 08.2	21.1	93.7	45 58.3	23.9	95.8
17	46 24.3	11.4	86.0	46 30.4	14.3	88.1	46 32.1	17.2	90.3	46 29.3	20.2	92.4	46 22.2	23.0	94.5
18	46 35.7	10.2	84.6	46 44.7	13.2	86.7	46 49.3	16.2	88.9	46 49.5	19.1	91.0	46 45.2	22.0	93.1
19	46 45.9	9.2	83.2	46 57.9	12.2	85.3	47 05.5	15.2	87.5	47 08.6	18.1	89.6	47 07.2	21.0	91.8
20	46 55.1	+8.0	81.7	47 10.1	+11.1	83.9	47 20.7	+14.1	86.0	47 26.7	+17.1	88.2	47 28.2	+20.0	90.4
21	47 03.1	7.0	80.3	47 21.2	10.0	82.4	47 34.8	13.0	84.6	47 43.8	16.0	86.8	47 48.2	19.0	89.0
22	47 10.1	5.9	78.8	47 31.2	8.8	81.0	47 47.8	11.9	83.1	47 59.8	14.9	85.3	48 07.2	18.0	87.6
23	47 16.0	4.7	77.4	47 40.0	7.8	79.5	47 59.7	10.7	81.7	48 14.7	13.9	83.9	48 25.2	16.8	86.1
24	47 20.7	3.6	75.9	47 47.8	6.6	78.0	48 10.4	9.7	80.2	48 28.6	12.7	82.4	48 42.0	15.8	84.7
25	47 24.3	+2.4	74.4	47 54.4	+5.4	76.5	48 20.1	+8.5	78.7	48 41.3	+11.5	80.9	48 57.8	+14.6	83.2
26	47 26.7	1.3	72.9	47 59.8	4.3	75.1	48 28.6	7.3	77.2	48 52.8	10.4	79.5	49 12.4	13.5	81.7
27	47 28.0	+ 0.2	71.5	48 04.1	3.1	73.6	48 35.9	6.1	75.7	49 03.2	9.2	78.0	49 25.9	12.3	80.2
28	47 28.2	− 1.0	70.0	48 07.2	2.0	72.1	48 42.0	5.0	74.2	49 12.4	8.1	76.4	49 38.2	11.2	78.7
29	47 27.2	2.1	68.5	48 09.2	+ 0.8	70.6	48 47.0	3.8	72.7	49 20.5	6.8	74.9	49 49.4	9.9	77.2

	30°			32°			34°			36°			38°		
Dec.	Hc	d	Z	Hc	d	Z	Hc	d	Z	Hc	d	Z	Hc	d	Z
°	° ′	′	°	° ′	′	°	° ′	′	°	° ′	′	°	° ′	′	°
0	36 59.0	+37.4	115.8	36 05.6	+39.1	117.1	35 09.8	+40.8	118.4	34 11.6	+42.5	119.6	33 11.3	+44.0	120.7
1	37 36.4	36.8	114.8	36 44.7	38.7	116.2	35 50.6	40.4	117.5	34 54.1	42.1	118.7	33 55.3	43.7	119.9
2	38 13.2	36.3	113.8	37 23.4	38.2	115.2	36 31.0	40.0	116.6	35 36.2	41.7	117.8	34 39.0	43.3	119.1
3	38 49.5	35.7	112.8	38 01.6	37.7	114.2	37 11.0	39.6	115.6	36 17.9	41.3	117.0	35 22.3	42.9	118.2
4	39 25.2	35.2	111.7	38 39.3	37.2	113.2	37 50.6	39.1	114.7	36 59.2	40.9	116.1	36 05.2	42.6	117.4
5	40 00.4	+34.6	110.7	39 16.5	+36.7	112.2	38 29.7	+38.6	113.7	37 40.1	+40.4	115.1	36 47.8	+42.2	116.5
6	40 35.0	34.0	109.6	39 53.2	36.1	111.2	39 08.3	38.1	112.7	38 20.5	40.0	114.2	37 30.0	41.7	115.6
7	41 09.0	33.4	108.5	40 29.3	35.5	110.2	39 46.4	37.6	111.7	39 00.5	39.5	113.2	38 11.7	41.4	114.7
8	41 42.4	32.8	107.4	41 04.8	35.0	109.1	40 24.0	37.0	110.7	39 40.0	39.0	112.3	38 53.1	40.9	113.8
9	42 15.2	32.0	106.3	41 39.8	34.3	108.0	41 01.0	36.5	109.7	40 19.0	38.5	111.3	39 34.0	40.4	112.8
10	42 47.2	+31.4	105.1	42 14.1	+33.7	106.9	41 37.5	+35.9	108.6	40 57.5	+38.0	110.3	40 14.4	+39.9	111.9
11	43 18.6	30.6	104.0	42 47.8	33.0	105.8	42 13.4	35.2	107.5	41 35.5	37.4	109.2	40 54.3	39.5	110.9
12	43 49.2	29.9	102.8	43 20.8	32.3	104.6	42 48.6	34.6	106.4	42 12.9	36.8	108.2	41 33.8	38.9	109.9
13	44 19.1	29.1	101.6	43 53.1	31.6	103.5	43 23.2	34.0	105.3	42 49.7	36.2	107.1	42 12.7	38.3	108.9
14	44 48.2	28.3	100.4	44 24.7	30.8	102.3	43 57.2	33.3	104.2	43 25.9	35.6	106.0	42 51.0	37.8	107.8
15	45 16.5	+27.5	99.1	44 55.5	+30.1	101.1	44 30.5	+32.5	103.0	44 01.5	+34.9	104.9	43 28.8	+37.1	106.8
16	45 44.0	26.7	97.8	45 25.6	29.2	99.9	45 03.0	31.8	101.8	44 36.4	34.2	103.8	44 05.9	36.5	105.7
17	46 10.7	25.7	96.5	45 54.8	28.5	98.6	45 34.8	31.0	100.6	45 10.6	33.5	102.6	44 42.4	35.9	104.6
18	46 36.4	24.8	95.2	46 23.3	27.5	97.3	46 05.8	30.2	99.4	45 44.1	32.8	101.4	45 18.3	35.2	103.4
19	47 01.2	23.9	93.9	46 50.8	26.7	96.0	46 36.0	29.4	98.1	46 16.9	31.9	100.2	45 53.5	34.4	102.3
20	47 25.1	+23.0	92.6	47 17.5	+25.8	94.7	47 05.4	+28.5	96.9	46 48.8	+31.2	99.0	46 27.9	+33.7	101.1
21	47 48.1	21.9	91.2	47 43.3	24.8	93.4	47 33.9	27.6	95.6	47 20.0	30.3	97.7	47 01.6	32.9	99.9
22	48 10.0	20.9	89.8	48 08.1	23.8	92.0	48 01.5	26.7	94.3	47 50.3	29.5	96.5	47 34.5	32.2	98.6
23	48 30.9	19.9	88.4	48 31.9	22.9	90.6	48 28.2	25.7	92.9	48 19.8	28.5	95.2	48 06.7	31.2	97.4
24	48 50.8	18.8	87.0	48 54.8	21.8	89.2	48 53.9	24.8	91.5	48 48.3	27.6	93.8	48 37.9	30.5	96.1
25	49 09.6	+17.7	85.5	49 16.6	+20.7	87.8	49 18.7	+23.7	90.1	49 15.9	+26.7	92.5	49 08.4	+29.4	94.8
26	49 27.3	16.6	84.0	49 37.3	19.6	86.4	49 42.4	22.7	88.7	49 42.6	25.7	91.1	49 37.8	28.6	93.4
27	49 43.9	15.4	82.6	49 56.9	18.6	84.9	50 05.1	21.6	87.3	50 08.3	24.6	89.7	50 06.4	27.6	92.1
28	49 59.3	14.2	81.1	50 15.5	17.4	83.4	50 26.7	20.5	85.8	50 32.9	23.5	88.3	50 34.0	26.5	90.7
29	50 13.5	13.1	79.5	50 32.9	16.2	81.9	50 47.2	19.3	84.4	50 56.4	22.5	86.8	51 00.5	25.5	89.3

20°			22°			24°			26°			28°			Dec.
Hc	d	Z	Hc	d	Z	Hc	d	Z	Hc	d	Z	Hc	d	Z	
40 45.0	-27.4	108.3	40 05.8	-29.7	109.9	39 23.4	-31.9	111.4	38 38.1	-34.0	112.9	37 49.9	-35.9	114.4	0
40 17.6	28.2	109.4	39 36.1	30.4	111.0	38 51.5	32.4	112.5	38 04.1	34.5	114.0	37 14.0	36.4	115.4	1
39 49.4	28.8	110.6	39 05.7	31.0	112.1	38 19.1	33.1	113.6	37 29.6	35.0	115.0	36 37.6	37.0	116.4	2
39 20.6	29.5	111.7	38 34.7	31.6	113.2	37 46.0	33.6	114.7	36 54.6	35.6	116.0	36 00.6	37.3	117.4	3
38 51.1	30.1	112.9	38 03.1	32.2	114.3	37 12.4	34.2	115.7	36 19.0	36.0	117.1	35 23.3	37.9	118.3	4
38 21.0	-30.7	114.0	37 30.9	-32.7	115.4	36 38.2	-34.7	116.7	35 43.0	-36.6	118.0	34 45.4	-38.3	119.3	5
37 50.3	31.3	115.1	36 58.2	33.3	116.4	36 03.5	35.2	117.8	35 06.4	36.9	119.0	34 07.1	38.6	120.2	6
37 19.0	31.9	116.1	36 24.9	33.9	117.5	35 28.3	35.7	118.8	34 29.5	37.5	120.0	33 28.5	39.1	121.1	7
36 47.1	32.5	117.2	35 51.0	34.3	118.5	34 52.6	36.1	119.7	33 52.0	37.8	120.9	32 49.4	39.5	122.0	8
36 14.6	33.0	118.2	35 16.7	34.9	119.5	34 16.5	36.6	120.7	33 14.2	38.3	121.8	32 09.9	39.9	122.9	9
35 41.6	-33.5	119.3	34 41.8	-35.3	120.5	33 39.9	-37.1	121.7	32 35.9	-38.7	122.8	31 30.0	-40.2	123.8	10
35 08.1	34.0	120.3	34 06.5	35.8	121.5	33 02.8	37.4	122.6	31 57.2	39.0	123.7	30 49.8	40.5	124.7	11
34 34.1	34.5	121.3	33 30.7	36.2	122.4	32 25.4	37.9	123.5	31 18.2	39.4	124.6	30 09.3	40.9	125.5	12
33 59.6	35.0	122.3	32 54.5	36.6	123.4	31 47.5	38.2	124.4	30 38.8	39.8	125.4	29 28.4	41.2	126.4	13
33 24.6	35.4	123.3	32 17.9	37.1	124.3	31 09.3	38.6	125.4	29 59.0	40.1	126.3	28 47.2	41.5	127.2	14
32 49.2	-35.9	124.2	31 40.8	-37.5	125.3	30 30.7	-39.0	126.2	29 18.9	-40.4	127.2	28 05.7	-41.8	128.0	15
32 13.3	36.3	125.2	31 03.3	37.8	126.2	29 51.7	39.3	127.1	28 38.5	40.7	128.0	27 23.9	42.0	128.8	16
31 37.0	36.6	126.1	30 25.5	38.2	127.1	29 12.4	39.7	128.0	27 57.8	41.0	128.8	26 41.9	42.4	129.6	17
31 00.4	37.1	127.0	29 47.3	38.6	128.0	28 32.7	40.0	128.8	27 16.8	41.3	129.7	25 59.5	42.5	130.4	18
30 23.3	37.5	128.0	29 08.7	38.9	128.9	27 52.7	40.2	129.7	26 35.5	41.6	130.5	25 17.0	42.9	131.2	19
29 45.8	-37.8	128.9	28 29.8	-39.2	129.7	27 12.5	-40.6	130.5	25 53.9	-41.9	131.3	24 34.1	-43.0	132.0	20
29 08.0	38.2	129.8	27 50.6	39.6	130.6	26 31.9	40.9	131.4	25 12.0	42.1	132.1	23 51.1	43.3	132.8	21
28 29.8	38.5	130.6	27 11.0	39.8	131.4	25 51.0	41.1	132.2	24 29.9	42.3	132.9	23 07.8	43.5	133.5	22
27 51.3	38.8	131.5	26 31.2	40.2	132.3	25 09.9	41.4	133.0	23 47.6	42.6	133.6	22 24.3	43.7	134.3	23
27 12.5	39.2	132.4	25 51.0	40.4	133.1	24 28.5	41.6	133.8	23 05.0	42.8	134.4	21 40.6	43.9	135.0	24
26 33.3	-39.4	133.2	25 10.6	-40.7	133.9	23 46.9	-41.9	134.6	22 22.2	-43.0	135.2	20 56.7	-44.1	135.7	25
25 53.9	39.8	134.1	24 29.9	40.9	134.7	23 05.0	42.1	135.3	21 39.2	43.2	135.9	20 12.6	44.2	136.5	26
25 14.1	40.0	134.9	23 49.0	41.2	135.5	22 22.9	42.3	136.1	20 56.0	43.4	136.7	19 28.4	44.5	137.2	27
24 34.1	40.2	135.7	23 07.8	41.4	136.3	21 40.6	42.5	136.9	20 12.6	43.5	137.4	18 43.9	44.5	137.9	28
23 53.9	40.6	136.5	22 26.4	41.7	137.1	20 58.1	42.7	137.6	19 29.1	43.8	138.1	17 59.4	44.8	138.6	29

30°			32°			34°			36°			38°			Dec.
Hc	d	Z	Hc	d	Z	Hc	d	Z	Hc	d	Z	Hc	d	Z	
36 59.0	-37.8	115.8	36 05.6	-39.6	117.1	35 09.8	-41.3	118.4	34 11.6	42.8	119.6	33 11.3	-44.3	120.7	0
36 21.2	38.2	116.7	35 26.0	39.9	118.0	34 28.5	41.6	119.3	33 28.8	43.1	120.4	32 27.0	44.6	121.5	1
35 43.0	38.7	117.7	34 46.1	40.4	118.9	33 46.9	42.0	120.1	32 45.7	43.5	121.3	31 42.4	44.9	122.3	2
35 04.3	39.1	118.6	34 05.7	40.8	119.8	33 04.9	42.3	121.0	32 02.2	43.8	122.1	30 57.5	45.1	123.1	3
34 25.2	39.6	119.6	33 24.9	41.1	120.7	32 22.6	42.6	121.8	31 18.4	44.1	122.9	30 12.4	45.4	123.9	4
33 45.6	-39.9	120.5	32 43.8	-41.5	121.6	31 40.0	-43.0	122.7	30 34.3	-44.3	123.7	29 27.0	-45.7	124.6	5
33 05.7	40.3	121.4	32 02.3	41.8	122.4	30 57.0	43.3	123.5	29 50.0	44.7	124.4	28 41.3	45.9	125.4	6
32 25.4	40.7	122.2	31 20.5	42.2	123.3	30 13.7	43.5	124.3	29 05.3	44.8	125.2	27 55.4	46.1	126.1	7
31 44.7	41.0	123.1	30 38.3	42.5	124.1	29 30.2	43.9	125.1	28 20.5	45.2	126.0	27 09.3	46.4	126.8	8
31 03.7	41.3	124.0	29 55.8	42.7	124.9	28 46.3	44.1	125.8	27 35.3	45.3	126.7	26 22.9	46.6	127.5	9
30 22.4	-41.7	124.8	29 13.1	-43.1	125.7	28 02.2	-44.3	126.6	26 50.0	-45.6	127.4	25 36.3	-46.7	128.2	10
29 40.7	42.0	125.6	28 30.0	43.3	126.5	27 17.9	44.6	127.4	26 04.4	45.9	128.2	24 49.6	47.0	128.9	11
28 58.7	42.2	126.5	27 46.7	43.6	127.3	26 33.3	44.9	128.1	25 18.5	46.0	128.9	24 02.6	47.1	129.6	12
28 16.5	42.6	127.3	27 03.1	43.8	128.1	25 48.4	45.0	128.9	24 32.5	46.2	129.6	23 15.5	47.3	130.3	13
27 33.9	42.8	128.1	26 19.3	44.1	128.9	25 03.4	45.3	129.6	23 46.3	46.4	130.3	22 28.2	47.5	130.9	14
26 51.1	-43.1	128.8	25 35.2	-44.3	129.6	24 18.1	-45.5	130.3	22 59.9	-46.6	131.0	21 40.7	-47.6	131.6	15
26 08.0	43.3	129.6	24 50.9	44.5	130.4	23 32.6	45.6	131.0	22 13.3	46.7	131.7	20 53.1	47.8	132.3	16
25 24.7	43.6	130.4	24 06.4	44.8	131.1	22 47.0	45.9	131.7	21 26.6	46.9	132.3	20 05.3	47.9	132.9	17
24 41.1	43.8	131.2	23 21.6	44.9	131.8	22 01.1	46.0	132.4	20 39.7	47.1	133.0	19 17.4	48.0	133.5	18
23 57.3	44.0	131.9	22 36.7	45.1	132.5	21 15.1	46.2	133.1	19 52.6	47.2	133.7	18 29.4	48.2	134.2	19
23 13.3	-44.2	132.6	21 51.6	-45.3	133.3	20 28.9	-46.3	133.8	19 05.4	-47.3	134.3	17 41.2	-48.3	134.8	20
22 29.1	44.4	133.4	21 06.3	45.4	134.0	19 42.6	46.5	134.5	18 18.1	47.5	135.0	16 52.9	48.4	135.4	21
21 44.7	44.6	134.1	20 20.8	45.7	134.7	18 56.1	46.7	135.2	17 30.6	47.6	135.6	16 04.5	48.5	136.0	22
21 00.1	44.7	134.8	19 35.1	45.8	135.3	18 09.4	46.8	135.8	16 43.0	47.7	136.3	15 16.0	48.6	136.7	23
20 15.4	45.0	135.5	18 49.3	45.9	136.0	17 22.6	46.9	136.5	15 55.3	47.8	136.9	14 27.4	48.6	137.3	24
19 30.4	-45.1	136.2	18 03.4	-46.1	136.7	16 35.7	-47.0	137.1	15 07.5	-47.9	137.5	13 38.8	-48.8	137.9	25
18 45.3	45.3	136.9	17 17.3	46.2	137.4	15 48.7	47.1	137.8	14 19.6	48.0	138.1	12 50.0	48.9	138.5	26
18 00.0	45.4	137.6	16 31.1	46.4	138.0	15 01.6	47.3	138.4	13 31.6	48.1	138.8	12 01.1	48.9	139.1	27
17 14.6	45.5	138.3	15 44.7	46.6	138.7	14 14.3	47.3	139.1	12 43.5	48.2	139.4	11 12.2	49.0	139.6	28
16 29.1	45.7	139.0	14 58.3	46.6	139.4	13 27.0	47.5	139.7	11 55.3	48.3	140.0	10 23.2	49.1	140.2	29

Dec.	40° Hc	d	Z	42° Hc	d	Z	44° Hc	d	Z	46° Hc	d	Z	48° Hc	d	Z
0	32 09.0	+45.4	121.8	31 04.8	+46.7	122.9	29 58.8	+48.0	123.9	28 51.1	+49.2	124.8	27 41.9	+50.3	125.7
1	32 54.4	45.1	121.1	31 51.5	46.5	122.1	30 46.8	47.8	123.2	29 40.3	49.0	124.1	28 32.2	50.1	125.0
2	33 39.5	44.8	120.3	32 38.0	46.3	121.4	31 34.6	47.5	122.5	30 29.3	48.8	123.5	29 22.3	49.9	124.4
3	34 24.3	44.5	119.5	33 24.3	45.9	120.6	32 22.1	47.3	121.7	31 18.1	48.5	122.8	30 12.2	49.7	123.8
4	35 08.8	44.2	118.6	34 10.2	45.6	119.9	33 09.4	47.1	121.0	32 06.6	48.4	122.1	31 01.9	49.6	123.1
5	35 53.0	+43.8	117.8	34 55.8	+45.4	119.1	33 56.5	+46.7	120.3	32 55.0	+48.0	121.4	31 51.5	+49.3	122.5
6	36 36.8	43.4	117.0	35 41.2	45.0	118.3	34 43.2	46.5	119.5	33 43.0	47.9	120.7	32 40.8	49.1	121.8
7	37 20.2	43.1	116.1	36 26.2	44.7	117.4	35 29.7	46.2	118.7	34 30.9	47.6	119.9	33 29.9	48.9	121.1
8	38 03.3	42.7	115.2	37 10.9	44.3	116.6	36 15.9	45.8	117.9	35 18.5	47.3	119.2	34 18.8	48.6	120.4
9	38 46.0	42.2	114.3	37 55.2	43.9	115.8	37 01.7	45.5	117.1	36 05.8	47.0	118.4	35 07.4	48.4	119.7
10	39 28.2	+41.8	113.4	38 39.1	+43.5	114.9	37 47.2	+45.2	116.3	36 52.8	+46.7	117.7	35 55.8	+48.1	119.0
11	40 10.0	41.3	112.5	39 22.6	43.2	114.0	38 32.4	44.8	115.5	37 39.5	46.3	116.9	36 43.9	47.9	118.2
12	40 51.3	40.9	111.5	40 05.8	42.7	113.1	39 17.2	44.4	114.6	38 25.8	46.1	116.1	37 31.8	47.5	117.5
13	41 32.2	40.3	110.5	40 48.5	42.2	112.2	40 01.6	44.1	113.7	39 11.9	45.6	115.3	38 19.3	47.2	116.7
14	42 12.5	39.9	109.6	41 30.7	41.8	111.2	40 45.7	43.6	112.9	39 57.5	45.4	114.4	39 06.5	46.9	115.9
15	42 52.4	+39.2	108.5	42 12.5	+41.3	110.3	41 29.3	+43.1	111.9	40 42.9	+44.9	113.6	39 53.4	+46.6	115.1
16	43 31.6	38.7	107.5	42 53.8	40.7	109.3	42 12.4	42.7	111.0	41 27.8	44.5	112.7	40 40.0	46.0	114.3
17	44 10.3	38.1	106.4	43 34.5	40.2	108.3	42 55.1	42.2	110.1	42 12.3	44.0	111.8	41 26.2	45.8	113.4
18	44 48.4	37.5	105.4	44 14.7	39.7	107.2	43 37.3	41.7	109.1	42 56.3	43.7	110.9	42 12.0	45.4	112.6
19	45 25.9	36.8	104.3	44 54.4	39.1	106.2	44 19.0	41.2	108.1	43 40.0	43.1	109.9	42 57.4	44.9	111.7
20	46 02.7	+36.2	103.1	45 33.5	+38.4	105.1	45 00.2	+40.6	107.1	44 23.1	+42.6	108.9	43 42.3	+44.6	110.8
21	46 38.9	35.4	102.0	46 11.9	37.8	104.0	45 40.8	40.0	106.0	45 05.7	42.2	108.0	44 26.9	44.1	109.8
22	47 14.3	34.7	100.8	46 49.7	37.1	102.9	46 20.8	39.4	104.9	45 47.9	41.5	106.9	45 11.0	43.5	108.9
23	47 49.0	33.9	99.6	47 26.8	36.4	101.7	47 00.2	38.8	103.8	46 29.4	41.0	105.9	45 54.5	43.1	107.9
24	48 22.9	33.0	98.3	48 03.2	35.6	100.5	47 39.0	38.0	102.7	47 10.4	40.4	104.8	46 37.6	42.5	106.9
25	48 55.9	+32.3	97.1	48 38.8	+34.9	99.3	48 17.0	+37.4	101.6	47 50.8	+39.7	103.7	47 20.1	+42.0	105.8
26	49 28.2	31.3	95.8	49 13.7	34.0	98.1	48 54.4	36.6	100.4	48 30.5	39.0	102.6	48 02.1	41.3	104.8
27	49 59.5	30.5	94.5	49 47.7	33.2	96.8	49 31.0	35.9	99.2	49 09.5	38.4	101.5	48 43.4	40.7	103.7
28	50 30.0	29.5	93.1	50 20.9	32.3	95.5	50 06.9	35.0	97.9	49 47.9	37.6	100.3	49 24.1	40.1	102.6
29	50 59.5	28.5	91.7	50 53.2	31.4	94.2	50 41.9	34.2	96.6	50 25.5	36.8	99.1	50 04.2	39.3	101.4

Dec.	50° Hc	d	Z	52° Hc	d	Z	54° Hc	d	Z	56° Hc	d	Z	58° Hc	d	Z
0	26 31.2	+51.3	126.5	25 19.2	+52.2	127.3	24 05.9	+53.1	128.0	22 51.5	+53.9	128.7	21 36.0	+54.6	129.3
1	27 22.5	51.2	125.9	26 11.4	52.2	126.7	24 59.0	53.1	127.5	23 45.4	53.9	128.2	22 30.6	54.7	128.9
2	28 13.7	51.0	125.3	27 03.6	52.0	126.2	25 52.1	52.9	127.0	24 39.3	53.7	127.7	23 25.3	54.5	128.4
3	29 04.7	50.8	124.7	27 55.6	51.8	125.6	26 45.0	52.8	126.4	25 33.0	53.7	127.2	24 19.8	54.5	128.0
4	29 55.5	50.7	124.1	28 47.4	51.7	125.0	27 37.8	52.6	125.9	26 26.7	53.5	126.7	25 14.3	54.3	127.5
5	30 46.2	+50.4	123.5	29 39.1	+51.5	124.5	28 30.4	+52.6	125.4	27 20.2	+53.5	126.2	26 08.6	+54.3	127.0
6	31 36.6	50.3	122.9	30 30.6	51.4	123.9	29 23.0	52.3	124.8	28 13.7	53.3	125.7	27 02.9	54.2	126.5
7	32 26.9	50.1	122.2	31 22.0	51.2	123.3	30 15.3	52.3	124.3	29 07.0	53.2	125.2	27 57.1	54.0	126.1
8	33 17.0	49.9	121.6	32 13.2	51.1	122.6	31 07.6	52.1	123.7	30 00.2	53.1	124.7	28 51.1	54.0	125.6
9	34 06.9	49.7	120.9	33 04.3	50.8	122.0	31 59.7	51.9	123.1	30 53.3	52.9	124.1	29 45.1	53.9	125.1
10	34 56.6	+49.4	120.2	33 55.1	+50.7	121.4	32 51.6	+51.8	122.5	31 46.2	+52.8	123.6	30 39.0	+53.7	124.6
11	35 46.0	49.2	119.5	34 45.8	50.4	120.7	33 43.4	51.5	121.9	32 39.0	52.6	123.0	31 32.7	53.6	124.0
12	36 35.2	48.9	118.8	35 36.2	50.2	120.1	34 34.9	51.4	121.3	33 31.6	52.5	122.4	32 26.3	53.4	123.5
13	37 24.1	48.6	118.1	36 26.4	50.0	119.4	35 26.3	51.2	120.7	34 24.1	52.3	121.8	33 19.7	53.3	123.0
14	38 12.7	48.4	117.3	37 16.4	49.7	118.7	36 17.5	51.0	120.0	35 16.4	52.1	121.2	34 13.1	53.1	122.4
15	39 01.1	+48.1	116.6	38 06.1	+49.4	118.0	37 08.5	+50.7	119.3	36 08.5	+51.9	120.6	35 06.2	+53.0	121.9
16	39 49.2	47.7	115.8	38 55.5	49.2	117.3	37 59.2	50.6	118.7	37 00.4	51.8	120.0	35 59.2	52.9	121.3
17	40 36.9	47.4	115.0	39 44.7	48.9	116.5	38 49.8	50.2	118.0	37 52.2	51.5	119.4	36 52.1	52.6	120.7
18	41 24.3	47.1	114.2	40 33.6	48.6	115.8	39 40.0	50.0	117.3	38 43.7	51.3	118.7	37 44.7	52.5	120.1
19	42 11.4	46.7	113.4	41 22.2	48.3	115.0	40 30.0	49.8	116.6	39 35.0	51.0	118.1	38 37.2	52.3	119.5
20	42 58.1	+46.3	112.5	42 10.5	+47.9	114.2	41 19.8	+49.4	115.8	40 26.0	+50.8	117.4	39 29.5	+52.0	118.8
21	43 44.4	45.9	111.6	42 58.4	47.6	113.4	42 09.2	49.1	115.1	41 16.8	50.6	116.7	40 21.5	51.9	118.2
22	44 30.3	45.5	110.7	43 46.0	47.2	112.5	42 58.3	48.8	114.3	42 07.4	50.3	115.9	41 13.4	51.6	117.5
23	45 15.8	45.0	109.8	44 33.2	46.8	111.7	43 47.1	48.5	113.5	42 57.7	49.9	115.2	42 05.0	51.3	116.9
24	46 00.8	44.5	108.9	45 20.0	46.4	110.8	44 35.6	48.1	112.7	43 47.6	49.7	114.4	42 56.3	51.1	116.1
25	46 45.3	+44.0	107.9	46 06.4	+45.9	109.9	45 23.7	+47.7	111.8	44 37.3	+49.3	113.7	43 47.4	+50.8	115.4
26	47 29.3	43.5	106.9	46 52.3	45.5	109.0	46 11.4	47.3	110.9	45 26.6	49.0	112.9	44 38.2	50.6	114.7
27	48 12.8	42.9	105.9	47 37.8	45.0	108.0	46 58.7	46.9	110.0	46 15.6	48.7	112.0	45 28.8	50.2	113.9
28	48 55.7	42.3	104.8	48 22.8	44.4	107.0	47 45.6	46.4	109.1	47 04.2	48.2	111.2	46 19.0	49.8	113.1
29	49 38.0	41.7	103.7	49 07.2	43.9	106.0	48 32.0	45.9	108.2	47 52.4	47.8	110.3	47 08.8	49.5	112.3

40°			42°			44°			46°			48°			Dec.
Hc	d	Z	Hc	d	Z	Hc	d	Z	Hc	d	Z	Hc	d	Z	
32 09.0	-45.7	121.8	31 04.8	-47.0	122.9	29 58.8	-48.2	123.9	28 51.1	-49.3	124.8	27 41.9	-50.4	125.7	0
31 23.3	45.9	122.6	30 17.8	47.2	123.6	29 10.6	48.5	124.5	28 01.8	49.6	125.4	26 51.5	50.6	126.3	1
30 37.4	46.2	123.3	29 30.6	47.5	124.3	28 22.1	48.6	125.2	27 12.2	49.7	126.1	26 00.9	50.8	126.9	2
29 51.2	46.5	124.1	28 43.1	47.7	125.0	27 33.5	48.8	125.9	26 22.5	49.9	126.7	25 10.1	50.8	127.5	3
29 04.7	46.7	124.8	27 55.4	47.8	125.7	26 44.7	49.0	126.5	25 32.6	50.0	127.3	24 19.3	51.1	128.1	4
28 18.0	-46.9	125.5	27 07.6	-48.1	126.4	25 55.7	-49.1	127.2	24 42.6	-50.2	127.9	23 28.2	-51.1	128.6	5
27 31.1	47.1	126.2	26 19.5	48.3	127.0	25 06.6	49.4	127.8	23 52.4	50.3	128.5	22 37.1	51.3	129.2	6
26 44.0	47.3	126.9	25 31.2	48.4	127.7	24 17.2	49.4	128.4	23 02.1	50.5	129.1	21 45.8	51.3	129.8	7
25 56.7	47.5	127.6	24 42.8	48.6	128.4	23 27.8	49.6	129.1	22 11.6	50.5	129.7	20 54.5	51.5	130.3	8
25 09.2	47.7	128.3	23 54.2	48.7	129.0	22 38.2	49.8	129.7	21 21.1	50.7	130.3	20 03.0	51.6	130.9	9
24 21.5	-47.9	129.0	23 05.5	-48.9	129.6	21 48.4	-49.9	130.3	20 30.4	-50.8	130.9	19 11.4	-51.6	131.4	10
23 33.6	48.0	129.6	22 16.6	49.1	130.3	20 58.5	50.0	130.9	19 39.6	50.9	131.4	18 19.8	51.8	131.9	11
22 45.6	48.2	130.3	21 27.5	49.2	130.9	20 08.5	50.1	131.5	18 48.7	51.1	132.0	17 28.0	51.8	132.5	12
21 57.4	48.3	130.9	20 38.3	49.3	131.5	19 18.4	50.2	132.0	17 57.6	51.1	132.5	16 36.2	52.0	133.0	13
21 09.1	48.5	131.5	19 49.0	49.4	132.1	18 28.2	50.4	132.6	17 06.5	51.1	133.1	15 44.2	52.0	133.5	14
20 20.6	-48.6	132.2	18 59.6	-49.7	132.7	17 37.8	-50.4	133.2	16 15.4	-51.3	133.6	14 52.2	-52.0	134.0	15
19 32.0	48.8	132.8	18 10.1	49.7	133.3	16 47.4	50.5	133.8	15 24.1	51.4	134.2	14 00.2	52.1	134.5	16
18 43.2	48.8	133.4	17 20.4	49.8	133.9	15 56.9	50.6	134.3	14 32.7	51.4	134.7	13 08.1	52.2	135.1	17
17 54.4	49.0	134.0	16 30.6	49.8	134.5	15 06.3	50.7	134.9	13 41.3	51.5	135.2	12 15.9	52.3	135.6	18
17 05.4	49.1	134.6	15 40.8	50.0	135.1	14 15.6	50.8	135.4	12 49.8	51.5	135.8	11 23.6	52.3	136.1	19
16 16.3	-49.1	135.2	14 50.8	-50.0	135.6	13 24.8	-50.8	136.0	11 58.3	-51.6	136.3	10 31.3	-52.3	136.6	20
15 27.2	49.3	135.8	14 00.8	50.1	136.2	12 34.0	51.0	136.5	11 06.7	51.7	136.8	9 39.0	52.4	137.1	21
14 37.9	49.4	136.4	13 10.7	50.2	136.8	11 43.0	50.9	137.1	10 15.0	51.7	137.3	8 46.6	52.4	137.6	22
13 48.5	49.4	137.0	12 20.5	50.2	137.3	10 52.1	51.0	137.6	9 23.3	51.8	137.8	7 54.2	52.5	138.0	23
12 59.1	49.6	137.6	11 30.3	50.4	137.9	10 01.1	51.1	138.1	8 31.5	51.8	138.4	7 01.7	52.5	138.5	24
12 09.5	-49.5	138.2	10 39.9	-50.3	138.4	9 10.0	-51.1	138.7	7 39.7	-51.8	138.9	6 09.2	-52.5	139.0	25
11 20.0	49.7	138.7	9 49.6	50.5	139.0	8 18.9	51.2	139.2	6 47.9	51.9	139.4	5 16.7	52.5	139.5	26
10 30.3	49.7	139.3	8 59.1	50.6	139.5	7 27.7	51.2	139.7	5 56.0	51.9	139.9	4 24.2	52.6	140.0	27
9 40.6	49.8	139.9	8 08.7	50.6	140.1	6 36.5	51.2	140.3	5 04.1	51.9	140.4	3 31.6	52.5	140.5	28
8 50.8	49.8	140.5	7 18.1	50.5	140.6	5 45.3	51.3	140.8	4 12.2	51.9	140.9	2 39.1	52.6	141.0	29

50°			52°			54°			56°			58°			Dec.
Hc	d	Z	Hc	d	Z	Hc	d	Z	Hc	d	Z	Hc	d	Z	
26 31.2	-51.4	126.5	25 19.2	-52.4	127.3	24 05.9	-53.2	128.0	22 51.5	-54.0	128.7	21 36.0	-54.8	129.3	0
25 39.8	51.6	127.1	24 26.8	52.4	127.8	23 12.7	53.3	128.5	21 57.5	54.1	129.2	20 41.2	54.8	129.8	1
24 48.2	51.7	127.6	23 34.4	52.6	128.3	22 19.4	53.4	129.0	21 03.4	54.2	129.6	19 46.4	54.9	130.2	2
23 56.5	51.8	128.2	22 41.8	52.7	128.9	21 26.0	53.5	129.5	20 09.2	54.3	130.1	18 51.5	55.0	130.6	3
23 04.7	51.9	128.7	21 49.1	52.8	129.4	20 32.5	53.6	130.0	19 14.9	54.3	130.5	17 56.5	55.0	131.0	4
22 12.8	-52.0	129.3	20 56.3	-52.9	129.9	19 38.9	-53.7	130.5	18 20.6	-54.4	131.0	17 01.5	-55.0	131.5	5
21 20.8	52.2	129.8	20 03.4	52.9	130.4	18 45.2	53.7	130.9	17 26.2	54.4	131.4	16 06.5	55.1	131.9	6
20 28.6	52.3	130.3	19 10.5	53.0	130.9	17 51.5	53.8	131.4	16 31.8	54.5	131.9	15 11.4	55.2	132.3	7
19 36.4	52.3	130.9	18 17.5	53.2	131.4	16 57.7	53.8	131.9	15 37.3	54.5	132.3	14 16.2	55.2	132.7	8
18 44.1	52.4	131.4	17 24.3	53.1	131.9	16 03.9	53.9	132.3	14 42.8	54.6	132.7	13 21.1	55.3	133.1	9
17 51.7	-52.5	131.9	16 31.2	-53.3	132.4	15 10.0	-54.0	132.8	13 48.2	-54.6	133.2	12 25.8	-55.2	133.5	10
16 59.2	52.6	132.4	15 37.9	53.3	132.8	14 16.0	54.0	133.2	12 53.6	54.7	133.6	11 30.6	55.3	133.9	11
16 06.6	52.6	132.9	14 44.6	53.4	133.3	13 22.0	54.1	133.7	11 58.9	54.7	134.0	10 35.3	55.3	134.3	12
15 14.0	52.7	133.4	13 51.2	53.4	133.8	12 27.9	54.1	134.1	11 04.2	54.8	134.4	9 40.0	55.3	134.7	13
14 21.3	52.9	133.9	12 57.8	53.4	134.3	11 33.8	54.1	134.6	10 09.4	54.8	134.8	8 44.6	55.3	135.1	14
13 28.6	-52.9	134.4	12 04.4	-53.6	134.7	10 39.7	-54.2	135.0	9 14.6	-54.8	135.3	7 49.3	-55.4	135.5	15
12 35.7	52.8	134.9	11 10.8	53.5	135.2	9 45.5	54.2	135.4	8 19.8	54.8	135.7	6 53.9	55.4	135.9	16
11 42.9	52.9	135.4	10 17.3	53.6	135.6	8 51.3	54.2	135.9	7 25.0	54.8	136.1	5 58.5	55.5	136.2	17
10 50.0	53.0	135.8	9 23.7	53.7	136.1	7 57.1	54.3	136.3	6 30.2	54.9	136.5	5 03.0	55.4	136.6	18
9 57.0	53.0	136.3	8 30.0	53.6	136.6	7 02.8	54.3	136.7	5 35.3	54.9	136.9	4 07.6	55.5	137.0	19
9 04.0	-53.0	136.8	7 36.4	-53.7	137.0	6 08.5	-54.3	137.2	4 40.4	-54.9	137.3	3 12.1	-55.4	137.4	20
8 11.0	53.1	137.3	6 42.7	53.7	137.5	5 14.2	54.4	137.6	3 45.5	54.9	137.7	2 16.7	55.5	137.8	21
7 17.9	53.1	137.7	5 49.0	53.8	137.9	4 19.8	54.4	138.0	2 50.6	54.9	138.1	1 21.2	55.4	138.2	22
6 24.8	53.1	138.2	4 55.2	53.7	138.3	3 25.5	54.4	138.4	1 55.7	55.0	138.5	0 25.8	-55.5	138.5	23
5 31.7	53.2	138.7	4 01.5	53.8	138.8	2 31.1	54.3	138.9	1 00.7	54.9	138.9	0 29.7	+55.5	40.7	24
4 38.5	-53.1	139.1	3 07.7	-53.8	139.2	1 36.8	-54.4	139.3	0 05.8	-54.9	139.3	1 25.2	+55.5	40.7	25
3 45.4	53.2	139.6	2 13.9	53.8	139.7	0 42.4	-54.4	139.7	0 49.1	+55.0	40.3	2 20.7	55.4	40.3	26
2 52.2	53.2	140.1	1 20.1	53.7	140.1	0 12.0	+54.3	39.9	1 44.1	54.9	39.9	3 16.1	55.5	39.9	27
1 59.0	53.2	140.5	0 26.4	-53.8	140.6	1 06.3	54.4	39.4	2 39.0	54.9	39.5	4 11.6	55.4	39.6	28
1 05.8	53.2	141.0	0 27.4	+53.8	39.0	2 00.7	54.4	39.0	3 33.9	54.9	39.1	5 07.0	55.4	39.2	29

Dec.	0° Hc	d	Z	2° Hc	d	Z	4° Hc	d	Z	6° Hc	d	Z	8° Hc	d	Z
°	° ′	′	°	° ′	′	°	° ′	′	°	° ′	′	°	° ′	′	°
0	42 00.0	- 0.5	90.0	41 58.1	+ 2.4	91.8	41 52.5	+ 5.1	93.6	41 43.1	+ 7.9	95.4	41 30.0	+ 10.7	97.1
1	41 59.5	1.4	88.7	42 00.5	1.4	90.5	41 57.6	4.2	92.3	41 51.0	7.0	94.0	41 40.7	9.8	95.8
2	41 58.1	2.3	87.3	42 01.9	+ 0.4	89.1	42 01.8	3.3	90.9	41 58.0	6.1	92.7	41 50.5	8.9	94.5
3	41 55.8	3.3	86.0	42 02.3	- 0.5	87.8	42 05.1	2.4	89.6	42 04.1	5.2	91.4	41 59.4	7.9	93.2
4	41 52.5	4.3	84.6	42 01.8	1.4	86.4	42 07.5	1.3	88.2	42 09.3	4.2	90.0	42 07.3	7.1	91.8
5	41 48.2	- 5.1	83.3	42 00.4	- 2.4	85.1	42 08.8	+ 0.5	86.9	42 13.5	+ 3.3	88.7	42 14.4	+ 4.0	90.5
6	41 43.1	6.1	81.9	41 58.0	3.3	83.7	42 09.3	- 0.5	85.5	42 16.8	2.3	87.3	42 20.4	5.2	89.2
7	41 37.0	7.0	80.6	41 54.7	4.2	82.4	42 08.8	1.5	84.2	42 19.1	1.3	86.0	42 25.6	4.2	87.8
8	41 30.0	7.9	79.3	41 50.5	5.2	81.0	42 07.3	2.4	82.8	42 20.4	+ 0.4	84.6	42 29.8	3.2	86.5
9	41 22.1	8.8	78.0	41 45.3	6.1	79.7	42 04.9	3.3	81.5	42 20.8	- 0.5	83.3	42 33.0	2.3	85.1
10	41 13.3	- 9.8	76.7	41 39.2	- 7.0	78.4	42 01.6	- 4.3	80.1	42 20.3	- 1.5	81.9	42 35.3	+ 1.3	83.7
11	41 03.5	10.6	75.3	41 32.2	8.0	77.0	41 57.3	5.2	78.8	42 18.8	2.5	80.6	42 36.6	+ 0.3	82.4
12	40 52.9	11.4	74.0	41 24.2	8.8	75.7	41 52.1	6.2	77.5	42 16.3	3.4	79.2	42 36.9	- 0.6	81.0
13	40 41.5	12.4	72.7	41 15.4	9.7	74.4	41 45.9	7.0	76.1	42 12.9	4.3	77.9	42 36.3	1.6	79.7
14	40 29.1	13.2	71.5	41 05.7	10.7	73.1	41 38.9	8.0	74.8	42 08.6	5.3	76.5	42 34.7	2.5	78.3
15	40 15.9	- 14.0	70.2	40 55.0	- 11.5	71.8	41 30.9	- 8.9	73.5	42 03.3	- 6.2	75.2	42 32.2	- 3.5	77.0
16	40 01.9	14.9	68.9	40 43.5	12.3	70.5	41 22.0	9.8	72.1	41 57.1	7.2	73.8	42 28.7	4.5	75.6
17	39 47.0	15.7	67.6	40 31.2	13.3	69.2	41 12.2	10.7	70.8	41 49.9	8.1	72.5	42 24.2	5.4	74.2
18	39 31.3	16.4	66.4	40 17.9	14.0	67.9	41 01.5	11.6	69.5	41 41.8	9.0	71.2	42 18.8	6.3	72.9
19	39 14.9	17.3	65.1	40 03.9	14.9	66.7	40 49.9	12.4	68.2	41 32.8	9.8	69.9	42 12.5	7.3	71.6
20	38 57.6	- 18.0	63.9	39 49.0	- 15.7	65.4	40 37.5	- 13.3	66.9	41 23.0	- 10.8	68.5	42 05.2	- 8.2	70.2
21	38 39.6	18.8	62.7	39 33.3	16.5	64.1	40 24.2	14.1	65.7	41 12.2	11.7	67.2	41 57.0	9.1	68.9
22	38 20.8	19.6	61.5	39 16.8	17.3	62.9	40 10.1	15.0	64.3	41 00.5	12.6	65.9	41 47.9	10.1	67.6
23	38 01.2	20.3	60.3	38 59.5	18.1	61.7	39 55.1	15.8	63.1	40 47.9	13.4	64.6	41 37.8	10.9	66.2
24	37 40.9	21.0	59.1	38 41.4	18.8	60.4	39 39.3	16.6	61.9	40 34.5	14.2	63.4	41 26.9	11.9	64.9
25	37 19.9	- 21.6	57.9	38 22.6	- 19.6	59.2	39 22.7	- 17.4	60.6	40 20.3	- 15.1	62.1	41 15.0	- 12.7	63.6
26	36 58.3	22.4	56.7	38 03.0	20.3	58.0	39 05.3	18.1	59.4	40 05.2	16.0	60.8	41 02.3	13.6	62.3
27	36 35.9	23.0	55.6	37 42.7	21.1	56.8	38 47.2	18.9	58.2	39 49.2	16.7	59.6	40 48.7	14.4	61.0
28	36 12.9	23.7	54.4	37 21.6	21.7	55.6	38 28.3	19.7	56.9	39 32.5	17.5	58.3	40 34.3	15.3	59.7
29	35 49.2	24.3	53.3	36 59.9	22.4	54.5	38 08.6	20.4	55.7	39 15.0	18.3	57.1	40 19.0	16.1	58.5

Dec.	10° Hc	d	Z	12° Hc	d	Z	14° Hc	d	Z	16° Hc	d	Z	18° Hc	d	Z
°	° ′	′	°	° ′	′	°	° ′	′	°	° ′	′	°	° ′	′	°
0	41 13.3	+ 13.4	98.9	40 52.9	+ 16.1	100.6	40 29.1	+ 18.7	102.3	40 01.9	+ 21.2	103.9	39 31.3	+ 23.7	105.5
1	41 26.7	12.5	97.6	41 09.0	15.2	99.3	40 47.8	17.9	101.0	40 23.1	20.4	102.7	39 55.0	22.9	104.4
2	41 39.2	11.6	96.3	41 24.2	14.4	98.0	41 05.7	17.0	99.8	40 43.5	19.7	101.5	40 17.9	22.2	103.1
3	41 50.8	10.8	95.0	41 38.6	13.5	96.7	41 22.7	16.2	98.5	41 03.2	18.8	100.2	40 40.1	21.4	101.9
4	42 01.6	9.8	93.6	41 52.1	12.6	95.4	41 38.9	15.3	97.2	41 22.0	18.0	99.0	41 01.5	20.6	100.7
5	42 11.4	+ 8.9	92.3	42 04.7	+ 11.6	94.1	41 54.2	+ 14.4	95.9	41 40.0	+ 17.1	97.7	41 22.1	+ 19.7	99.4
6	42 20.3	8.0	91.0	42 16.3	10.8	92.8	42 08.6	13.5	94.6	41 57.1	16.2	96.4	41 41.8	19.0	98.2
7	42 28.3	7.0	89.6	42 27.1	9.8	91.5	42 22.1	12.6	93.3	42 13.3	15.4	95.1	42 00.8	18.0	96.9
8	42 35.3	6.0	88.3	42 36.9	8.9	90.1	42 34.7	11.7	92.0	42 28.7	14.5	93.8	42 18.8	17.3	95.6
9	42 41.3	5.1	86.9	42 45.8	8.0	88.8	42 46.4	10.8	90.6	42 43.2	13.5	92.5	42 36.1	16.3	94.3
10	42 46.4	+ 4.2	85.6	42 53.8	+ 6.9	87.4	42 57.2	+ 9.8	89.3	42 56.7	+ 12.7	91.2	42 52.4	+ 15.4	93.0
11	42 50.6	3.2	84.2	43 00.7	6.1	86.1	43 07.0	8.9	87.9	43 09.4	11.6	89.8	43 07.8	14.5	91.7
12	42 53.8	2.2	82.9	43 06.8	5.0	84.7	43 15.9	7.9	86.6	43 21.0	10.8	88.5	43 22.3	13.5	90.4
13	42 56.0	1.2	81.5	43 11.8	4.1	83.3	43 23.8	6.9	85.2	43 31.8	9.7	87.1	43 35.8	12.6	89.0
14	42 57.2	+ 0.2	80.1	43 15.9	3.0	82.0	43 30.7	5.9	83.9	43 41.5	8.8	85.7	43 48.4	11.7	87.7
15	42 57.4	- 0.7	78.8	43 18.9	+ 2.1	80.6	43 36.6	+ 4.9	82.5	43 50.3	+ 7.8	84.4	44 00.1	+ 10.7	86.3
16	42 56.7	1.7	77.4	43 21.0	1.2	79.2	43 41.5	4.0	81.1	43 58.1	6.8	83.0	44 10.8	9.6	84.9
17	42 55.0	2.6	76.0	43 22.2	+ 0.1	77.9	43 45.5	2.9	79.7	44 04.9	5.9	81.6	44 20.4	8.7	83.6
18	42 52.4	3.7	74.7	43 22.3	- 0.9	76.5	43 48.4	2.0	78.3	44 10.8	4.8	80.2	44 29.1	7.7	82.2
19	42 48.7	4.6	73.3	43 21.4	1.8	75.1	43 50.4	+ 0.9	77.0	44 15.6	3.7	78.8	44 36.8	6.6	80.8
20	42 44.1	- 5.5	71.9	43 19.6	- 2.9	73.7	43 51.3	0.0	75.6	44 19.3	+ 2.8	77.4	44 43.4	+ 5.7	79.4
21	42 38.6	6.5	70.6	43 16.7	3.8	72.4	43 51.3	- 1.1	74.2	44 22.1	1.7	76.1	44 49.1	4.6	78.0
22	42 32.1	7.5	69.2	43 12.9	4.8	71.0	43 50.2	2.1	72.8	44 23.8	+ 0.8	74.7	44 53.7	3.5	76.6
23	42 24.6	8.4	67.9	43 08.1	5.8	69.6	43 48.1	3.1	71.4	44 24.6	- 0.4	73.3	44 57.2	2.5	75.2
24	42 16.2	9.3	66.6	43 02.3	6.7	68.3	43 45.0	4.0	70.0	44 24.2	1.3	71.9	44 59.7	1.5	73.7
25	42 06.9	- 10.3	65.2	42 55.6	- 7.7	66.9	43 41.0	- 5.1	68.6	44 22.9	- 2.4	70.5	45 01.2	+ 0.4	72.3
26	41 56.6	11.2	63.9	42 47.9	8.7	65.5	43 35.9	6.1	67.3	44 20.5	3.3	69.1	45 01.6	- 0.6	70.9
27	41 45.4	12.0	62.6	42 39.2	9.6	64.2	43 29.8	7.0	65.9	44 17.2	4.4	67.7	45 01.0	1.7	69.5
28	41 33.4	13.0	61.3	42 29.6	10.5	62.9	43 22.8	8.0	64.5	44 12.8	5.4	66.3	44 59.3	2.7	68.1
29	41 20.4	13.8	60.0	42 19.1	11.5	61.5	43 14.8	9.0	63.2	44 07.4	6.5	64.9	44 56.6	3.8	66.7

0°			2°			4°			6°			8°			Dec.
Hc	d	Z	Hc	d	Z	Hc	d	Z	Hc	d	Z	Hc	d	Z	
42 00.0	− 0.5	90.0	41 58.1	− 3.3	91.8	41 52.5	− 6.1	93.6	41 43.1	− 8.9	95.4	41 30.0	−11.6	97.1	0
41 59.5	1.4	91.3	41 54.8	4.2	93.1	41 46.4	7.0	94.9	41 34.2	9.7	96.7	41 18.4	12.5	98.5	1
41 58.1	2.3	92.7	41 50.6	5.1	94.5	41 39.4	8.0	96.3	41 24.5	10.7	98.0	41 05.9	13.3	99.8	2
41 55.8	3.3	94.0	41 45.5	6.1	95.8	41 31.4	8.8	97.6	41 13.8	11.6	99.3	40 52.6	14.2	101.0	3
41 52.5	4.3	95.4	41 39.4	7.0	97.2	41 22.6	9.7	98.9	41 02.2	12.4	100.6	40 38.4	15.1	102.3	4
41 48.2	− 5.1	96.7	41 32.4	− 7.9	98.5	41 12.9	−10.7	100.2	40 49.8	−13.3	101.9	40 23.3	−15.9	103.6	5
41 43.1	6.1	98.1	41 24.5	8.9	99.8	41 02.2	11.5	101.5	40 36.5	14.1	103.2	40 07.4	16.7	104.9	6
41 37.0	7.0	99.4	41 15.6	9.7	101.1	40 50.7	12.3	102.8	40 22.4	15.0	104.5	39 50.7	17.5	106.1	7
41 30.0	7.9	100.7	41 05.9	10.6	102.4	40 38.4	13.3	104.1	40 07.4	15.8	105.8	39 33.2	18.3	107.4	8
41 22.1	8.8	102.0	40 55.3	11.5	103.7	40 25.1	14.0	105.4	39 51.6	16.6	107.0	39 14.9	19.0	108.6	9
41 13.3	− 9.8	103.3	40 43.8	−12.3	105.0	40 11.1	−15.0	106.7	39 35.0	−17.4	108.3	38 55.9	−19.9	109.8	10
41 03.5	10.6	104.7	40 31.5	13.2	106.3	39 56.1	15.7	107.9	39 17.6	18.2	109.5	38 36.0	20.5	111.0	11
40 52.9	11.4	106.0	40 18.3	14.1	107.6	39 40.4	16.5	109.2	38 59.4	18.9	110.7	38 15.5	21.3	112.2	12
40 41.5	12.4	107.3	40 04.2	14.8	108.9	39 23.9	17.4	110.4	38 40.5	19.7	112.0	37 54.2	22.0	113.4	13
40 29.1	13.2	108.5	39 49.4	15.7	110.1	39 06.5	18.1	111.7	38 20.8	20.5	113.2	37 32.2	22.7	114.6	14
40 15.9	−14.0	109.8	39 33.7	−16.5	111.4	38 48.4	−18.8	112.9	38 00.3	−21.1	114.4	37 09.5	−23.4	115.8	15
40 01.9	14.9	111.1	39 17.2	17.3	112.6	38 29.6	19.7	114.1	37 39.2	21.9	115.5	36 46.1	24.0	116.9	16
39 47.0	15.7	112.4	38 59.9	18.0	113.9	38 09.9	20.3	115.3	37 17.3	22.6	116.7	36 22.1	24.7	118.0	17
39 31.3	16.4	113.6	38 41.9	18.9	115.1	37 49.6	21.1	116.5	36 54.7	23.2	117.9	35 57.4	25.3	119.2	18
39 14.9	17.3	114.9	38 23.0	19.5	116.3	37 28.5	21.7	117.7	36 31.5	23.9	119.0	35 32.1	25.9	120.3	19
38 57.6	−18.0	116.1	38 03.5	−20.3	117.5	37 06.8	−22.5	118.9	36 07.6	−24.5	120.2	35 06.2	−26.5	121.4	20
38 39.6	18.8	117.3	37 43.2	21.0	118.7	36 44.3	23.1	120.0	35 43.1	25.1	121.3	34 39.7	27.1	122.5	21
38 20.8	19.6	118.5	37 22.2	21.7	119.9	36 21.2	23.8	121.2	35 18.0	25.8	122.4	34 12.6	27.6	123.6	22
38 01.2	20.3	119.7	37 00.5	22.4	121.1	35 57.4	24.4	122.3	34 52.2	26.3	123.5	33 45.0	28.2	124.6	23
37 40.9	21.0	120.9	36 38.1	23.1	122.2	35 33.0	25.0	123.4	34 25.9	26.9	124.6	33 16.8	28.8	125.7	24
37 19.9	−21.6	122.1	36 15.0	−23.7	123.4	35 08.0	−25.6	124.6	33 59.0	−27.5	125.7	32 48.0	−29.2	126.7	25
36 58.3	22.4	123.3	35 51.3	24.3	124.5	34 42.4	26.3	125.7	33 31.5	28.1	126.8	32 18.8	29.8	127.8	26
36 35.9	23.0	124.4	35 27.0	25.0	125.6	34 16.1	26.8	126.8	33 03.4	28.5	127.8	31 49.0	30.2	128.8	27
36 12.9	23.7	125.6	35 02.0	25.5	126.7	33 49.3	27.3	127.8	32 34.9	29.1	128.9	31 18.8	30.7	129.8	28
35 49.2	24.3	126.7	34 36.5	26.2	127.8	33 22.0	27.9	128.9	32 05.8	29.6	129.9	30 48.1	31.2	130.8	29

10°			12°			14°			16°			18°			Dec.
Hc	d	Z	Hc	d	Z	Hc	d	Z	Hc	d	Z	Hc	d	Z	
41 13.3	−14.3	98.9	40 52.9	−16.9	100.6	40 29.1	−19.5	102.3	40 01.9	−22.0	103.9	39 31.3	−24.3	105.5	0
40 59.0	15.2	100.2	40 36.0	17.7	101.9	40 09.6	20.2	103.5	39 39.9	22.7	105.2	39 07.0	25.1	106.7	1
40 43.8	15.9	101.5	40 18.3	18.6	103.1	39 49.4	21.1	104.8	39 17.2	23.5	106.3	38 41.9	25.8	107.9	2
40 27.9	16.8	102.7	39 59.7	19.3	104.4	39 28.3	21.8	106.0	38 53.7	24.1	107.5	38 16.1	26.5	109.1	3
40 11.1	17.7	104.0	39 40.4	20.1	105.6	39 06.5	22.5	107.2	38 29.6	24.9	108.7	37 49.6	27.1	110.2	4
39 53.4	−18.4	105.2	39 20.3	−20.9	106.8	38 44.0	−23.2	108.4	38 04.7	−25.5	109.9	37 22.5	−27.8	111.3	5
39 35.0	19.2	106.5	38 59.4	21.6	108.0	38 20.8	24.0	109.5	37 39.2	26.2	111.0	36 54.7	28.3	112.4	6
39 15.8	19.9	107.7	38 37.8	22.3	109.2	37 56.8	24.6	110.7	37 13.0	26.9	112.1	36 26.4	29.0	113.5	7
38 55.9	20.7	108.9	38 15.5	23.1	110.4	37 32.2	25.3	111.9	36 46.1	27.4	113.3	35 57.4	29.5	114.6	8
38 35.2	21.5	110.1	37 52.4	23.7	111.6	37 06.9	25.9	113.0	36 18.7	28.1	114.4	35 27.9	30.1	115.7	9
38 13.7	−22.1	111.3	37 28.7	−24.4	112.7	36 41.0	−26.6	114.1	35 50.6	−28.6	115.5	34 57.8	−30.6	116.7	10
37 51.6	22.9	112.5	37 04.3	25.1	113.9	36 14.4	27.2	115.2	35 22.0	29.3	116.5	34 27.2	31.2	117.8	11
37 28.7	23.5	113.7	36 39.2	25.7	115.0	35 47.2	27.8	116.4	34 52.7	29.7	117.6	33 56.0	31.7	118.8	12
37 05.2	24.2	114.8	36 13.5	26.3	116.2	35 19.4	28.3	117.4	34 23.0	30.3	118.7	33 24.3	32.2	119.8	13
36 41.0	24.9	116.0	35 47.2	26.9	117.3	34 51.1	29.0	118.5	33 52.7	30.9	119.7	32 52.1	32.6	120.9	14
36 16.1	−25.5	117.1	35 20.3	−27.6	118.4	34 22.1	−29.4	119.6	33 21.8	−31.3	120.7	32 19.5	−33.1	121.8	15
35 50.6	26.1	118.2	34 52.7	28.1	119.5	33 52.7	30.0	120.6	32 50.5	31.8	121.8	31 46.4	33.6	122.8	16
35 24.5	26.7	119.3	34 24.6	28.6	120.5	33 22.7	30.6	121.7	32 18.7	32.3	122.8	31 12.8	34.0	123.8	17
34 57.8	27.3	120.4	33 56.0	29.2	121.6	32 52.1	31.0	122.7	31 46.4	32.8	123.8	30 38.8	34.4	124.8	18
34 30.5	27.8	121.5	33 26.8	29.7	122.6	32 21.1	31.5	123.7	31 13.6	33.2	124.7	30 04.4	34.8	125.7	19
34 02.7	−28.5	122.6	32 57.1	−30.2	123.7	31 49.6	−31.9	124.7	30 40.4	−33.6	125.7	29 29.6	−35.3	126.7	20
33 34.2	28.9	123.6	32 26.9	30.8	124.7	31 17.7	32.5	125.7	30 06.8	34.1	126.7	28 54.3	35.5	127.6	21
33 05.3	29.5	124.7	31 56.1	31.2	125.7	30 45.2	32.8	126.7	29 32.7	34.4	127.6	28 18.8	36.0	128.5	22
32 35.8	29.9	125.7	31 24.9	31.6	126.7	30 12.4	33.3	127.7	28 58.3	34.8	128.6	27 42.8	36.3	129.4	23
32 05.9	30.5	126.7	30 53.3	32.1	127.7	29 39.1	33.7	128.6	28 23.5	35.2	129.5	27 06.5	36.6	130.3	24
31 35.4	−30.9	127.8	30 21.2	−32.6	128.7	29 05.4	−34.1	129.6	27 48.3	−35.6	130.4	26 29.9	−37.0	131.2	25
31 04.5	31.4	128.8	29 48.6	33.0	129.7	28 31.3	34.5	130.5	27 12.7	35.9	131.3	25 52.9	37.3	132.1	26
30 33.1	31.9	129.7	29 15.6	33.3	130.6	27 56.8	34.8	131.4	26 36.8	36.2	132.2	25 15.6	37.6	132.9	27
30 01.2	32.3	130.7	28 42.3	33.8	131.6	27 22.0	35.2	132.4	26 00.6	36.6	133.1	24 38.0	37.8	133.8	28
29 28.9	32.6	131.7	28 08.5	34.2	132.5	26 46.8	35.6	133.3	25 24.0	36.9	134.0	24 00.2	38.2	134.6	29

Dec.	20° Hc	d	Z	22° Hc	d	Z	24° Hc	d	Z	26° Hc	d	Z	28° Hc	d	Z
°	° ′	′	°	° ′	′	°	° ′	′	°	° ′	′	°	° ′	′	°
0	38 57.6	+26.0	107.1	38 20.8	+28.3	108.6	37 40.9	+30.6	110.1	36 58.3	+32.6	111.5	36 12.9	+34.6	112.9
1	39 23.6	25.4	106.0	38 49.1	27.7	107.5	38 11.5	29.9	109.0	37 30.9	32.1	110.5	36 47.5	34.1	111.9
2	39 49.0	24.6	104.8	39 16.8	27.0	106.4	38 41.4	29.3	107.9	38 03.0	31.5	109.4	37 21.6	33.6	110.9
3	40 13.6	23.9	103.6	39 43.8	26.3	105.2	39 10.7	28.6	106.8	38 34.5	30.8	108.3	37 55.2	33.1	109.8
4	40 37.5	23.1	102.4	40 10.1	25.5	104.0	39 39.3	28.0	105.7	39 05.3	30.3	107.2	38 28.3	32.4	108.8
5	41 00.6	+22.4	101.2	40 35.6	+24.9	102.9	40 07.3	+27.2	104.5	39 35.6	+29.6	106.1	39 00.7	+31.8	107.7
6	41 23.0	21.5	99.9	41 00.5	24.1	101.6	40 34.5	26.6	103.3	40 05.2	28.9	105.0	39 32.5	31.2	106.6
7	41 44.5	20.7	98.7	41 24.6	23.3	100.4	41 01.1	25.8	102.1	40 34.1	28.2	103.8	40 03.7	30.6	105.5
8	42 05.2	19.9	97.4	41 47.9	22.5	99.2	41 26.9	25.0	100.9	41 02.3	27.5	102.7	40 34.3	29.9	104.3
9	42 25.1	19.0	96.1	42 10.4	21.7	98.0	41 51.9	24.3	99.7	41 29.8	26.8	101.5	41 04.2	29.2	103.2
10	42 44.1	+18.2	94.9	42 32.1	+20.8	96.7	42 16.2	+23.5	98.5	41 56.6	+26.0	100.3	41 33.4	+28.5	102.0
11	43 02.3	17.3	93.6	42 52.9	20.0	95.4	42 39.7	22.6	97.3	42 22.6	25.3	99.1	42 01.9	27.7	100.9
12	43 19.6	16.3	92.2	43 12.9	19.1	94.1	43 02.3	21.8	96.0	42 47.9	24.4	97.8	42 29.6	27.0	99.7
13	43 35.9	15.4	90.9	43 32.0	18.2	92.8	43 24.1	20.9	94.7	43 12.3	23.6	96.6	42 56.6	26.2	98.4
14	43 51.3	14.5	89.6	43 50.2	17.3	91.5	43 45.0	20.1	93.4	43 35.9	22.8	95.3	43 22.8	25.4	97.2
15	44 05.8	+13.5	88.2	44 07.5	+16.3	90.2	44 05.1	+19.1	92.1	43 58.7	+21.8	94.0	43 48.2	+24.6	96.0
16	44 19.3	12.6	86.9	44 23.8	15.4	88.8	44 24.2	18.3	90.8	44 20.5	21.0	92.7	44 12.8	23.7	94.7
17	44 31.9	11.5	85.5	44 39.2	14.5	87.5	44 42.5	17.2	89.4	44 41.5	20.1	91.4	44 36.5	22.8	93.4
18	44 43.4	10.6	84.1	44 53.7	13.8	86.1	44 59.7	16.3	88.1	45 01.6	19.2	90.1	44 59.3	22.0	92.1
19	44 54.0	9.5	82.7	45 07.1	12.4	84.7	45 16.0	15.4	86.7	45 20.8	18.2	88.8	45 21.3	21.0	90.8
20	45 03.5	+8.6	81.3	45 19.5	+11.5	83.3	45 31.4	+14.3	85.4	45 39.0	+17.2	87.4	45 42.3	+20.0	89.4
21	45 12.1	7.4	79.9	45 31.0	10.4	81.9	45 45.7	13.3	84.0	45 56.2	16.2	86.0	46 02.3	19.1	88.1
22	45 19.5	6.5	78.5	45 41.4	9.3	80.5	45 59.0	12.3	82.6	46 12.4	15.2	84.6	46 21.4	18.1	86.7
23	45 26.0	5.4	77.1	45 50.7	8.3	79.1	46 11.3	11.2	81.2	46 27.6	14.1	83.2	46 39.5	17.1	85.3
24	45 31.4	4.3	75.7	45 59.0	7.2	77.7	46 22.5	10.1	79.7	46 41.7	13.1	81.8	46 56.6	16.1	83.9
25	45 35.7	+3.3	74.3	46 06.2	+6.2	76.3	46 32.6	+9.1	78.3	46 54.8	+12.1	80.4	47 12.7	+15.0	82.5
26	45 39.0	2.1	72.8	46 12.4	5.0	74.8	46 41.7	8.0	76.9	47 06.9	10.9	79.0	47 27.7	13.9	81.1
27	45 41.1	1.2	71.4	46 17.4	4.0	73.4	46 49.7	6.9	75.4	47 17.8	9.9	77.5	47 41.6	12.8	79.6
28	45 42.3	0.0	70.0	46 21.4	2.9	71.9	46 56.6	5.8	74.0	47 27.7	8.7	76.1	47 54.4	11.7	78.2
29	45 42.3	−1.0	68.5	46 24.3	1.8	70.5	47 02.4	4.7	72.5	47 36.4	7.6	74.6	48 06.1	10.6	76.7

Dec.	30° Hc	d	Z	32° Hc	d	Z	34° Hc	d	Z	36° Hc	d	Z	38° Hc	d	Z
°	° ′	′	°	° ′	′	°	° ′	′	°	° ′	′	°	° ′	′	°
0	35 24.9	+36.5	114.2	34 34.4	+38.4	115.5	33 41.5	+40.2	116.7	32 46.5	+41.8	117.9	31 49.3	+43.3	119.0
1	36 01.4	36.1	113.3	35 12.8	37.9	114.6	34 21.7	39.7	115.8	33 28.3	41.4	117.0	32 32.6	43.0	118.2
2	36 37.5	35.6	112.3	35 50.7	37.5	113.6	35 01.4	39.3	114.9	34 09.7	41.0	116.2	33 15.6	42.7	117.4
3	37 13.1	35.1	111.3	36 28.2	37.1	112.7	35 40.7	38.9	114.0	34 50.7	40.6	115.3	33 58.3	42.3	116.5
4	37 48.2	34.5	110.2	37 05.3	36.5	111.7	36 19.6	38.4	113.0	35 31.3	40.3	114.4	34 40.6	41.9	115.7
5	38 22.7	+34.0	109.2	37 41.8	+36.0	110.7	36 58.0	+38.0	112.1	36 11.6	+39.8	113.5	35 22.5	+41.6	114.8
6	38 56.7	33.4	108.1	38 17.8	35.5	109.7	37 36.0	37.5	111.1	36 51.4	39.4	112.5	36 04.1	41.1	113.9
7	39 30.1	32.8	107.1	38 53.3	34.9	108.6	38 13.5	37.0	110.1	37 30.8	38.9	111.6	36 45.2	40.8	113.0
8	40 02.9	32.2	106.0	39 28.2	34.4	107.6	38 50.5	36.4	109.1	38 09.7	38.1	110.6	37 26.0	40.3	112.1
9	40 35.1	31.5	104.9	40 02.6	33.8	106.5	39 26.9	35.9	108.1	38 48.1	37.9	109.6	38 06.3	39.8	111.1
10	41 06.6	+30.9	103.8	40 36.4	+33.1	105.4	40 02.8	+35.3	107.1	39 26.0	+37.4	108.6	38 46.1	+39.4	110.2
11	41 37.5	30.1	102.6	41 09.5	32.5	104.3	40 38.1	34.7	106.0	40 03.4	36.9	107.6	39 25.5	38.9	109.2
12	42 07.6	29.5	101.4	41 42.0	31.8	103.2	41 12.8	34.2	104.9	40 40.3	36.3	106.6	40 04.4	38.3	108.2
13	42 37.1	28.7	100.3	42 13.8	31.2	102.1	41 47.0	33.4	103.8	41 16.6	35.7	105.5	40 42.7	37.9	107.2
14	43 05.8	28.0	99.1	42 45.0	30.4	100.9	42 20.4	32.9	102.7	41 52.3	35.1	104.5	41 20.6	37.2	106.2
15	43 33.8	+27.1	97.9	43 15.4	+29.7	99.7	42 53.3	+32.1	101.6	42 27.4	+34.4	103.4	41 57.8	+36.7	105.1
16	44 00.9	26.4	96.6	43 45.1	29.0	98.5	43 25.4	31.4	100.4	43 01.8	33.8	102.2	42 34.5	36.1	104.1
17	44 27.3	25.5	95.4	44 14.1	28.1	97.3	43 56.8	30.7	99.2	43 35.6	33.1	101.1	43 10.6	35.4	103.0
18	44 52.8	24.7	94.1	44 42.2	27.3	96.1	44 27.5	29.8	98.0	44 08.7	32.4	100.0	43 46.0	34.8	101.8
19	45 17.5	23.8	92.8	45 09.5	26.5	94.8	44 57.4	29.1	96.8	44 41.1	31.7	98.8	44 20.8	34.1	100.7
20	45 41.3	+22.9	91.5	45 36.0	+25.6	93.5	45 26.5	+28.3	95.6	45 12.8	+30.8	97.6	44 54.9	+33.4	99.6
21	46 04.2	21.9	90.2	46 01.6	24.8	92.2	45 54.8	27.4	94.3	45 43.6	30.1	96.4	45 28.3	32.6	98.4
22	46 26.1	21.0	88.8	46 26.4	23.8	90.9	46 22.2	26.6	93.0	46 13.7	29.3	95.1	46 00.9	31.8	97.2
23	46 47.1	20.0	87.5	46 50.2	22.8	89.6	46 48.8	25.7	91.7	46 43.0	28.4	93.8	46 32.7	31.1	96.0
24	47 07.1	18.9	86.1	47 13.0	21.9	88.2	47 14.5	24.7	90.4	47 11.4	27.5	92.6	47 03.8	30.2	94.7
25	47 26.0	+18.0	84.7	47 34.9	+20.9	86.9	47 39.2	+23.8	89.0	47 38.9	+26.6	91.2	47 34.0	+29.4	93.4
26	47 44.0	16.9	83.3	47 55.8	19.9	85.5	48 03.0	22.8	87.7	48 05.5	25.7	89.9	48 03.4	28.5	92.1
27	48 00.9	15.8	81.8	48 15.7	18.8	84.0	48 25.8	21.7	86.3	48 31.2	24.7	88.5	48 31.9	27.5	90.8
28	48 16.7	14.7	80.4	48 34.5	17.7	82.6	48 47.5	20.8	84.9	48 55.9	23.7	87.2	48 59.4	26.6	89.5
29	48 31.4	13.6	78.9	48 52.2	16.6	81.2	49 08.3	19.6	83.4	49 19.6	22.6	85.8	49 26.0	25.6	88.1

20° Hc	d	Z	22° Hc	d	Z	24° Hc	d	Z	26° Hc	d	Z	28° Hc	d	Z	Dec.
38 57.6	−26.7	107.1	38 20.8	−29.0	108.6	37 40.9	−31.1	110.1	36 58.3	−33.2	111.5	36 12.9	−35.2	112.9	0
38 30.9	27.4	108.3	37 51.8	29.6	109.8	37 09.8	31.7	111.2	36 25.1	33.8	112.6	35 37.7	35.7	113.9	1
38 03.5	28.1	109.4	37 22.2	30.2	110.9	36 38.1	32.3	112.3	35 51.3	34.2	113.6	35 02.0	36.1	114.9	2
37 35.4	28.6	110.5	36 52.0	30.8	111.9	36 05.8	32.8	113.3	35 17.1	34.7	114.6	34 25.9	36.6	115.9	3
37 06.8	29.3	111.6	36 21.2	31.3	113.0	35 33.0	33.3	114.3	34 42.4	35.3	115.6	33 49.3	37.0	116.8	4
36 37.5	−29.9	112.7	35 49.9	−31.9	114.1	34 59.7	−33.8	115.4	34 07.1	−35.6	116.6	33 12.3	−37.4	117.8	5
36 07.6	30.4	113.8	35 18.0	32.4	115.1	34 25.9	34.3	116.4	33 31.5	36.2	117.6	32 34.9	37.9	118.7	6
35 37.2	31.0	114.9	34 45.6	33.0	116.1	33 51.6	34.8	117.3	32 55.3	36.5	118.5	31 57.0	38.2	119.6	7
35 06.2	31.5	115.9	34 12.6	33.4	117.1	33 16.8	35.3	118.3	32 18.8	37.0	119.5	31 18.8	38.6	120.5	8
34 34.7	32.0	116.9	33 39.2	33.9	118.1	32 41.5	35.6	119.3	31 41.8	37.3	120.4	30 40.2	39.0	121.4	9
34 02.7	−32.6	118.0	33 05.3	−34.4	119.1	32 05.9	−36.1	120.2	31 04.5	−37.8	121.3	30 01.2	−39.3	122.3	10
33 30.1	33.0	119.0	32 30.9	34.8	120.1	31 29.8	36.5	121.2	30 26.7	38.1	122.2	29 21.9	39.6	123.2	11
32 57.1	33.5	120.0	31 56.1	35.2	121.1	30 53.3	36.9	122.1	29 48.6	38.5	123.1	28 42.3	40.0	124.0	12
32 23.6	34.0	121.0	31 20.9	35.7	122.0	30 16.4	37.3	123.0	29 10.1	38.8	124.0	28 02.3	40.3	124.9	13
31 49.6	34.4	121.9	30 45.2	36.0	123.0	29 39.1	37.6	123.9	28 31.3	39.1	124.8	27 22.0	40.6	125.7	14
31 15.2	−34.8	122.9	30 09.2	−36.5	123.9	29 01.5	−38.0	124.8	27 52.2	−39.5	125.7	26 41.4	−40.8	126.5	15
30 40.4	35.2	123.8	29 32.7	36.8	124.8	28 23.5	38.4	125.7	27 12.7	39.8	126.6	26 00.6	41.2	127.4	16
30 05.2	35.6	124.8	28 55.9	37.1	125.7	27 45.1	38.6	126.6	26 32.9	40.0	127.4	25 19.4	41.4	128.2	17
29 29.6	36.0	125.7	28 18.8	37.6	126.6	27 06.5	39.0	127.4	25 52.9	40.3	128.2	24 38.0	41.6	129.0	18
28 53.6	36.4	126.6	27 41.2	37.8	127.5	26 27.5	39.2	128.3	25 12.6	40.6	129.0	23 56.4	41.9	129.8	19
28 17.2	−36.7	127.5	27 03.4	−38.2	128.4	25 48.3	−39.6	129.1	24 32.0	−40.9	129.9	23 14.5	−42.1	130.5	20
27 40.5	37.1	128.4	26 25.2	38.5	129.2	25 08.7	39.8	130.0	23 51.1	41.1	130.7	22 32.4	42.4	131.3	21
27 03.4	37.4	129.3	25 46.7	38.7	130.1	24 28.9	40.1	130.8	23 10.0	41.4	131.5	21 50.0	42.5	132.1	22
26 26.0	37.7	130.2	25 08.0	39.1	130.9	23 48.8	40.6	131.6	22 28.6	41.5	132.2	21 07.5	42.7	132.8	23
25 48.3	38.0	131.1	24 28.9	39.3	131.8	23 08.5	40.6	132.4	21 47.1	41.8	133.0	20 24.8	43.0	133.6	24
25 10.3	−38.3	131.9	23 49.6	−39.6	132.6	22 27.9	−40.8	133.2	21 05.3	−42.0	133.8	19 41.8	−43.1	134.3	25
24 32.0	38.6	132.8	23 10.0	39.9	133.4	21 47.1	41.1	134.0	20 23.3	42.2	134.6	18 58.7	43.3	135.1	26
23 53.4	38.9	133.6	22 30.1	40.1	134.2	21 06.0	41.2	134.8	19 41.1	42.4	135.3	18 15.4	43.4	135.8	27
23 14.5	39.1	134.4	21 50.0	40.3	135.0	20 24.8	41.5	135.6	18 58.7	42.6	136.1	17 32.0	43.7	136.5	28
22 35.4	39.4	135.3	21 09.7	40.5	135.8	19 43.3	41.7	136.3	18 16.1	42.7	136.8	16 48.3	43.7	137.2	29

30° Hc	d	Z	32° Hc	d	Z	34° Hc	d	Z	36° Hc	d	Z	38° Hc	d	Z	Dec.
35 24.9	−37.1	114.2	34 34.4	−38.8	115.5	33 41.5	−40.5	116.7	32 46.5	−42.1	117.9	31 49.3	−43.6	119.0	0
34 47.8	37.5	115.2	33 55.6	39.3	116.4	33 01.0	40.8	117.6	32 04.4	42.5	118.7	31 05.7	43.9	119.8	1
34 10.3	37.9	116.1	33 16.3	39.6	117.3	32 20.2	41.3	118.5	31 21.9	42.7	119.6	30 21.8	44.2	120.6	2
33 32.4	38.3	117.1	32 36.7	40.0	118.2	31 38.9	41.6	119.3	30 39.2	43.1	120.4	29 37.6	44.5	121.4	3
32 54.1	38.7	118.0	31 56.7	40.3	119.1	30 57.3	41.9	120.2	29 56.1	43.4	121.2	28 53.1	44.7	122.1	4
32 15.4	−39.2	118.9	31 16.4	−40.7	120.0	30 15.4	−42.2	121.0	29 12.7	−43.6	122.0	28 08.4	−45.0	122.9	5
31 36.2	39.4	119.8	30 35.7	41.1	120.8	29 33.2	42.5	121.8	28 29.1	43.9	122.8	27 23.4	45.2	123.7	6
30 56.8	39.9	120.7	29 54.6	41.3	121.7	28 50.7	42.8	122.6	27 45.2	44.1	123.5	26 38.2	45.5	124.4	7
30 16.9	40.1	121.5	29 13.3	41.7	122.5	28 07.9	43.0	123.4	27 01.1	44.4	124.3	25 52.7	45.6	125.1	8
29 36.8	40.5	122.4	28 31.6	41.9	123.3	27 24.9	43.3	124.2	26 16.7	44.7	125.1	25 07.1	45.9	125.9	9
28 56.3	−40.9	123.3	27 49.7	−42.3	124.2	26 41.6	−43.6	125.0	25 32.0	−44.6	125.8	24 21.2	−46.1	126.6	10
28 15.4	41.1	124.1	27 07.4	42.5	125.0	25 58.0	43.8	125.8	24 47.2	45.1	126.5	23 35.1	46.2	127.3	11
27 34.3	41.4	124.9	26 24.9	42.7	125.7	25 14.2	44.1	126.5	24 02.1	45.2	127.3	22 48.9	46.4	127.9	12
26 52.9	41.7	125.7	25 42.2	43.0	126.5	24 30.1	44.2	127.3	23 16.9	45.5	128.0	22 02.5	46.6	128.6	13
26 11.2	41.9	126.5	24 59.2	43.3	127.3	23 45.9	44.5	128.0	22 31.4	45.6	128.7	21 15.9	46.8	129.3	14
25 29.3	−42.2	127.3	24 15.9	−43.4	128.1	23 01.4	−44.7	128.7	21 45.8	−45.9	129.4	20 29.1	−46.9	130.0	15
24 47.1	42.4	128.1	23 32.5	43.7	128.8	22 16.7	44.8	129.5	20 59.9	45.9	130.1	19 42.2	47.0	130.6	16
24 04.7	42.7	128.9	22 48.8	43.9	129.6	21 31.9	45.1	130.2	20 14.0	46.2	130.8	18 55.2	47.2	131.3	17
23 22.0	42.9	129.7	22 04.9	44.1	130.3	20 46.8	45.2	130.9	19 27.8	46.3	131.4	18 08.0	47.3	132.0	18
22 39.1	43.1	130.4	21 20.8	44.3	131.0	20 01.6	45.4	131.6	18 41.5	46.4	132.1	17 20.7	47.5	132.6	19
21 56.0	−43.3	131.2	20 36.5	−44.4	131.7	19 16.2	−45.5	132.3	17 55.1	−46.6	132.8	16 33.2	−47.5	133.3	20
21 12.7	43.5	131.9	19 52.1	44.6	132.5	18 30.7	45.7	133.0	17 08.5	46.7	133.4	15 45.7	47.7	133.9	21
20 29.2	43.7	132.6	19 07.5	44.8	133.2	17 45.0	45.8	133.7	16 21.8	46.8	134.1	14 58.0	47.8	134.5	22
19 45.5	43.9	133.4	18 22.7	44.9	133.9	16 59.2	46.0	134.3	15 35.0	46.9	134.8	14 10.2	47.8	135.1	23
19 01.6	44.0	134.1	17 37.8	45.1	134.6	16 13.2	46.1	135.0	14 48.1	47.1	135.4	13 22.4	48.0	135.7	24
18 17.6	−44.2	134.8	16 52.7	−45.2	135.3	15 27.1	−46.2	135.7	14 01.0	−47.1	136.0	12 34.4	−48.0	136.4	25
17 33.4	44.3	135.5	16 07.5	45.4	135.9	14 40.9	46.3	136.3	13 13.9	47.3	136.7	11 46.4	48.2	137.0	26
16 49.1	44.5	136.2	15 22.1	45.6	136.6	13 54.6	46.4	137.0	12 26.6	47.3	137.3	10 58.2	48.1	137.6	27
16 04.6	44.6	136.9	14 36.6	45.5	137.3	13 08.2	46.5	137.6	11 39.3	47.4	137.9	10 10.1	48.3	138.2	28
15 20.0	44.8	137.6	13 51.1	45.7	138.0	12 21.7	46.6	138.3	10 51.9	47.5	138.6	9 21.8	48.3	138.8	29

Dec.	40° Hc	d	Z	42° Hc	d	Z	44° Hc	d	Z	46° Hc	d	Z	48° Hc	d	Z
°	° ′	′	°	° ′	′	°	° ′	′	°	° ′	′	°	° ′	′	°
0	30 50.2	+44.7	120.1	29 49.1	+46.2	121.1	28 46.3	+47.5	122.0	27 41.9	+48.7	122.9	26 35.9	+49.8	123.8
1	31 34.9	44.5	119.3	30 35.3	45.9	120.3	29 33.8	47.2	121.3	28 30.6	48.4	122.3	27 25.7	49.6	123.2
2	32 19.4	44.2	118.5	31 21.2	45.6	119.6	30 21.0	47.0	120.6	29 19.0	48.3	121.6	28 15.3	49.4	122.5
3	33 03.6	43.9	117.7	32 06.8	45.4	118.8	31 08.0	46.7	119.9	30 07.3	48.0	120.9	29 04.7	49.3	121.9
4	33 47.5	43.5	116.9	32 52.2	45.0	118.0	31 54.7	46.5	119.2	30 55.3	47.8	120.2	29 54.0	49.0	121.2
5	34 31.0	+43.2	116.0	33 37.2	+44.8	117.2	32 41.2	+46.2	118.4	31 43.1	+47.6	119.5	30 43.0	+48.9	120.6
6	35 14.2	42.9	115.2	34 22.0	44.4	116.4	33 27.4	45.9	117.6	32 30.7	47.3	118.8	31 31.9	48.6	119.9
7	35 57.1	42.5	114.3	35 06.4	44.1	115.6	34 13.3	45.6	116.9	33 18.0	47.0	118.1	32 20.5	48.4	119.2
8	36 39.6	42.0	113.5	35 50.5	43.7	114.8	34 58.9	45.4	116.1	34 05.0	46.8	117.3	33 08.9	48.1	118.5
9	37 21.6	41.7	112.6	36 34.2	43.4	113.9	35 44.3	44.9	115.3	34 51.8	46.5	116.5	33 57.0	47.9	117.8
10	38 03.3	+41.2	111.7	37 17.6	+43.0	113.1	36 29.2	+44.7	114.5	35 38.3	+46.2	115.8	34 44.9	+47.7	117.0
11	38 44.5	40.8	110.7	38 00.6	42.6	112.2	37 13.9	44.3	113.6	36 24.5	45.9	115.0	35 32.6	47.3	116.3
12	39 25.3	40.3	109.8	38 43.2	42.2	111.3	37 58.2	43.9	112.8	37 10.4	45.5	114.2	36 19.9	47.1	115.5
13	40 05.6	39.9	108.8	39 25.4	41.7	110.4	38 42.1	43.5	111.9	37 55.9	45.2	113.4	37 07.0	46.7	114.8
14	40 45.5	39.3	107.8	40 07.1	41.3	109.5	39 25.6	43.1	111.0	38 41.1	44.8	112.5	37 53.7	46.4	113.9
15	41 24.8	+38.8	106.8	40 48.4	+40.8	108.5	40 08.7	+42.7	110.1	39 25.9	+44.4	111.7	38 40.1	+46.1	113.2
16	42 03.6	38.2	105.8	41 29.2	40.2	107.5	40 51.4	42.2	109.2	40 10.3	44.1	110.8	39 26.2	45.7	112.3
17	42 41.8	37.7	104.8	42 09.4	39.8	106.5	41 33.6	41.7	108.2	40 54.4	43.6	109.9	40 11.9	45.4	111.5
18	43 19.5	37.0	103.7	42 49.2	39.2	105.5	42 15.3	41.3	107.3	41 38.0	43.1	109.0	40 57.3	45.0	110.6
19	43 56.5	36.4	102.6	43 28.4	38.6	104.5	42 56.6	40.7	106.3	42 21.1	42.7	108.0	41 42.3	44.5	109.8
20	44 32.9	+35.8	101.5	44 07.0	+38.1	103.4	43 37.3	+40.2	105.3	43 03.8	+42.2	107.1	42 26.8	+44.1	108.9
21	45 08.7	35.1	100.4	44 45.1	37.4	102.3	44 17.5	39.6	104.2	43 46.0	41.7	106.1	43 10.9	43.7	107.9
22	45 43.8	34.3	99.2	45 22.5	36.7	101.2	44 57.1	39.0	103.2	44 27.7	41.2	105.1	43 54.6	43.1	107.0
23	46 18.1	33.6	98.0	45 59.2	36.1	100.1	45 36.1	38.4	102.1	45 08.9	40.6	104.1	44 37.7	42.7	106.0
24	46 51.7	32.9	96.8	46 35.3	35.3	98.9	46 14.5	37.7	101.0	45 49.5	40.0	103.0	45 20.4	42.1	105.0
25	47 24.6	+32.0	95.6	47 10.6	+34.6	97.8	46 52.2	+37.1	99.9	46 29.5	+39.4	102.0	46 02.5	+41.6	104.0
26	47 56.6	31.2	94.3	47 45.2	33.9	96.5	47 29.3	36.3	98.7	47 08.9	38.7	100.9	46 44.1	41.0	103.0
27	48 27.8	30.3	93.1	48 19.1	33.0	95.3	48 05.6	35.6	97.5	47 47.6	38.1	99.7	47 25.1	40.4	101.9
28	48 58.1	29.5	91.8	48 52.1	32.1	94.0	48 41.2	34.8	96.3	48 25.7	37.3	98.6	48 05.5	39.7	100.8
29	49 27.6	28.4	90.4	49 24.2	31.3	92.8	49 16.0	34.0	95.1	49 03.0	36.6	97.4	48 45.2	39.1	99.6

Dec.	50° Hc	d	Z	52° Hc	d	Z	54° Hc	d	Z	56° Hc	d	Z	58° Hc	d	Z
°	° ′	′	°	° ′	′	°	° ′	′	°	° ′	′	°	° ′	′	°
0	25 28.5	+50.8	124.6	24 19.7	+51.8	125.4	23 09.6	+52.8	126.1	21 58.4	+53.6	126.7	20 46.1	+54.4	127.4
1	26 19.3	50.7	124.0	25 11.5	51.7	124.8	24 02.4	52.6	125.6	22 52.0	53.5	126.3	21 40.5	54.3	126.9
2	27 10.0	50.5	123.4	26 03.2	51.6	124.2	24 55.0	52.5	125.0	23 45.5	53.4	125.8	22 34.8	54.2	126.5
3	28 00.5	50.5	122.8	26 54.8	51.4	123.7	25 47.5	52.4	124.5	24 38.9	53.3	125.3	23 29.0	54.1	126.0
4	28 50.9	50.2	122.2	27 46.2	51.3	123.1	26 39.9	52.3	123.9	25 32.2	53.2	124.8	24 23.1	54.1	125.5
5	29 41.1	+50.0	121.6	28 37.5	+51.1	122.5	27 32.2	+52.2	123.4	26 25.4	+53.1	124.2	25 17.2	+54.0	125.0
6	30 31.1	49.9	120.9	29 28.6	51.0	121.9	28 24.4	52.0	122.8	27 18.5	53.0	123.7	26 11.2	53.8	124.6
7	31 21.0	49.6	120.3	30 19.6	50.8	121.3	29 16.4	51.8	122.3	28 11.5	52.8	123.2	27 05.0	53.8	124.1
8	32 10.6	49.4	119.6	31 10.4	50.6	120.7	30 08.2	51.7	121.7	29 04.3	52.7	122.6	27 58.8	53.6	123.6
9	33 00.0	49.2	118.9	32 01.0	50.4	120.0	30 59.9	51.6	121.1	29 57.0	52.6	122.1	28 52.4	53.6	123.0
10	33 49.2	+49.0	118.2	32 51.4	+50.2	119.4	31 51.5	+51.3	120.5	30 49.6	+52.5	121.5	29 46.0	+53.2	122.5
11	34 38.2	48.7	117.5	33 41.6	50.0	118.7	32 42.8	51.1	119.9	31 42.1	52.2	121.0	30 39.4	53.3	122.0
12	35 26.9	48.5	116.8	34 31.6	49.8	118.1	33 34.0	51.0	119.3	32 34.3	52.2	120.4	31 32.7	53.1	121.5
13	36 15.4	48.2	116.1	35 21.4	49.5	117.4	34 25.0	50.8	118.6	33 26.5	51.9	119.8	32 25.8	53.0	120.9
14	37 03.6	47.9	115.4	36 10.9	49.3	116.7	35 15.8	50.6	118.0	34 18.4	51.8	119.2	33 18.8	52.8	120.4
15	37 51.5	+47.7	114.6	37 00.2	+49.1	116.0	36 06.4	+50.4	117.3	35 10.2	+51.5	118.6	34 11.6	+52.7	119.8
16	38 39.2	47.3	113.8	37 49.3	48.8	115.3	36 56.8	50.1	116.6	36 01.7	51.4	118.0	35 04.3	52.5	119.2
17	39 26.5	46.9	113.0	38 38.1	48.5	114.5	37 46.9	49.9	115.9	36 53.1	51.2	117.3	35 56.8	52.4	118.6
18	40 13.4	46.7	112.2	39 26.6	48.1	113.8	38 36.8	49.6	115.2	37 44.3	50.9	116.7	36 49.2	52.1	118.0
19	41 00.1	46.2	111.4	40 14.7	47.9	113.0	39 26.4	49.3	114.5	38 35.2	50.7	116.0	37 41.3	51.9	117.4
20	41 46.3	+45.9	110.6	41 02.6	+47.5	112.2	40 15.7	+49.1	113.8	39 25.9	+50.4	115.3	38 33.2	+51.8	116.8
21	42 32.2	45.5	109.7	41 50.1	47.2	111.4	41 04.8	48.7	113.0	40 16.3	50.2	114.6	39 25.0	51.5	116.1
22	43 17.7	45.1	108.8	42 37.3	46.8	110.5	41 53.5	48.4	112.2	41 06.5	49.9	113.9	40 16.5	51.2	115.4
23	44 02.8	44.6	107.9	43 24.1	46.4	109.7	42 41.9	48.1	111.4	41 56.4	49.6	113.1	41 07.7	51.1	114.7
24	44 47.4	44.1	106.9	44 10.5	46.0	108.8	43 30.0	47.7	110.6	42 46.0	49.3	112.4	41 58.8	50.7	114.0
25	45 31.5	+43.6	106.0	44 56.5	+45.6	107.9	44 17.7	+47.4	109.8	43 35.3	+49.0	111.6	42 49.5	+50.5	113.3
26	46 15.1	43.2	105.0	45 42.1	45.1	107.0	45 05.1	46.9	108.9	44 24.3	48.7	110.8	43 40.0	50.2	112.6
27	46 58.3	42.5	104.0	46 27.2	44.6	106.0	45 52.0	46.5	108.0	45 13.0	48.2	110.0	44 30.2	49.8	111.8
28	47 40.8	42.0	102.9	47 11.8	44.1	105.1	46 38.5	46.1	107.1	46 01.2	47.9	109.1	45 20.0	49.6	111.0
29	48 22.8	41.4	101.9	47 55.9	43.5	104.1	47 24.6	45.6	106.2	46 49.1	47.4	108.2	46 09.6	49.1	110.2

40°			42°			44°			46°			48°			Dec.
Hc	d	Z	Hc	d	Z	Hc	d	Z	Hc	d	Z	Hc	d	Z	
° ′	′	°	° ′	′	°	° ′	′	°	° ′	′	°	° ′	′	°	°
30 50.2	−45.1	120.1	29 49.1	−46.4	121.1	28 46.3	−47.6	122.0	27 41.9	−48.8	122.9	26 35.9	−49.9	123.8	0
30 05.1	45.3	120.8	29 02.7	46.6	121.8	27 58.7	47.9	122.7	26 53.1	49.1	123.6	25 46.0	50.1	124.4	1
29 19.8	45.6	121.6	28 16.1	46.8	122.5	27 10.8	48.0	123.4	26 04.0	49.1	124.2	24 55.9	50.3	125.0	2
28 34.2	45.8	122.3	27 29.3	47.1	123.2	26 22.8	48.3	124.1	25 14.9	49.4	124.9	24 05.6	50.4	125.6	3
27 48.4	46.0	123.1	26 42.2	47.3	123.9	25 34.5	48.4	124.7	24 25.5	49.5	125.5	23 15.2	50.5	126.2	4
27 02.4	−46.3	123.8	25 54.9	−47.4	124.6	24 46.1	−48.6	125.4	23 36.0	−49.6	126.1	22 24.7	−50.6	126.8	5
26 16.1	46.4	124.5	25 07.5	47.6	125.3	23 57.5	48.7	126.0	22 46.4	49.8	126.7	21 34.1	50.8	127.4	6
25 29.7	46.7	125.2	24 19.9	47.8	126.0	23 08.8	48.9	126.7	21 56.6	49.9	127.3	20 43.3	50.9	127.9	7
24 43.0	46.8	125.9	23 32.1	48.0	126.6	22 19.9	49.0	127.3	21 06.7	50.1	127.9	19 52.4	50.9	128.5	8
23 56.2	47.1	126.6	22 44.1	48.2	127.3	21 30.9	49.2	127.9	20 16.6	50.1	128.5	19 01.5	51.1	129.1	9
23 09.1	−47.2	127.3	21 55.9	−48.2	127.9	20 41.7	−49.3	128.5	19 26.5	−50.3	129.1	18 10.4	−51.2	129.6	10
22 21.9	47.3	127.9	21 07.7	48.3	128.6	19 52.4	49.4	129.1	18 36.2	50.3	129.7	17 19.2	51.3	130.2	11
21 34.6	47.5	128.6	20 19.2	48.5	129.2	19 03.0	49.6	129.7	17 45.9	50.5	130.2	16 27.9	51.3	130.7	12
20 47.1	47.7	129.2	19 30.7	48.7	129.8	18 13.4	49.6	130.3	16 55.4	50.6	130.8	15 36.6	51.4	131.3	13
19 59.4	47.8	129.9	18 42.0	48.8	130.4	17 23.8	49.8	130.9	16 04.8	50.6	131.4	14 45.2	51.5	131.8	14
19 11.6	−48.0	130.5	17 53.2	−48.9	131.0	16 34.0	−49.8	131.5	15 14.2	−50.8	131.9	13 53.7	−51.6	132.3	15
18 23.6	48.1	131.2	17 04.3	49.1	131.6	15 44.2	50.0	132.1	14 23.4	50.8	132.5	13 02.1	51.6	132.8	16
17 35.6	48.2	131.8	16 15.2	49.1	132.2	14 54.2	50.0	132.7	13 32.6	50.8	133.0	12 10.5	51.7	133.4	17
16 47.4	48.3	132.4	15 26.1	49.2	132.8	14 04.2	50.1	133.2	12 41.8	51.0	133.6	11 18.8	51.7	133.9	18
15 59.1	48.4	133.0	14 36.9	49.3	133.4	13 14.1	50.2	133.8	11 50.8	51.0	134.1	10 27.1	51.8	134.4	19
15 10.7	−48.5	133.7	13 47.6	−49.4	134.0	12 23.9	−50.2	134.4	10 59.8	−51.0	134.7	9 35.3	−51.8	134.9	20
14 22.2	48.6	134.3	12 58.2	49.5	134.6	11 33.7	50.3	134.9	10 08.8	51.2	135.2	8 43.5	51.9	135.4	21
13 33.6	48.7	134.9	12 08.7	49.5	135.2	10 43.4	50.4	135.5	9 17.6	51.1	135.7	7 51.6	51.9	135.9	22
12 44.9	48.8	135.5	11 19.2	49.6	135.8	9 53.0	50.4	136.0	8 26.5	51.3	136.2	6 59.7	52.0	136.4	23
11 56.2	48.9	136.1	10 29.6	49.7	136.3	9 02.6	50.5	136.6	7 35.3	51.3	136.8	6 07.7	51.9	136.9	24
11 07.3	−48.9	136.7	9 39.9	−49.7	136.9	8 12.1	−50.5	137.1	6 44.0	−51.2	137.3	5 15.8	−52.0	137.4	25
10 18.4	48.9	137.2	8 50.2	49.8	137.5	7 21.6	50.6	137.7	5 52.8	51.3	137.8	4 23.8	52.1	137.9	26
9 29.5	49.1	137.8	8 00.4	49.8	138.0	6 31.0	50.6	138.2	5 01.5	51.4	138.3	3 31.7	52.0	138.4	27
8 40.4	49.0	138.4	7 10.6	49.9	138.6	5 40.4	50.6	138.7	4 10.1	51.3	138.9	2 39.7	52.0	138.9	28
7 51.4	49.2	139.0	6 20.7	49.9	139.2	4 49.8	50.6	139.3	3 18.8	51.4	139.4	1 47.7	52.1	139.4	29

50°			52°			54°			56°			58°			Dec.
Hc	d	Z	Hc	d	Z	Hc	d	Z	Hc	d	Z	Hc	d	Z	
° ′	′	°	° ′	′	°	° ′	′	°	° ′	′	°	° ′	′	°	°
25 28.5	−51.0	124.6	24 19.7	−52.0	125.4	23 09.6	−52.8	126.1	21 58.4	−53.7	126.7	20 46.1	−54.5	127.4	0
24 37.5	51.1	125.2	23 27.7	52.0	125.9	22 16.8	53.0	126.6	21 04.7	53.7	127.2	19 51.6	54.5	127.8	1
23 46.4	51.3	125.8	22 35.7	52.2	126.4	21 23.8	53.0	127.1	20 11.0	53.9	127.7	18 57.1	54.6	128.3	2
22 55.1	51.3	126.3	21 43.5	52.3	127.0	20 30.8	53.1	127.6	19 17.1	53.9	128.2	18 02.5	54.6	128.7	3
22 03.8	51.5	126.9	20 51.2	52.3	127.5	19 37.7	53.2	128.1	18 23.2	54.0	128.6	17 07.9	54.7	129.1	4
21 12.3	−51.6	127.4	19 58.9	−52.5	128.0	18 44.5	−53.3	128.6	17 29.2	−54.0	129.1	16 13.2	−54.8	129.6	5
20 20.7	51.7	128.0	19 06.4	52.5	128.5	17 51.2	53.3	129.1	16 35.2	54.1	129.5	15 18.4	54.8	130.0	6
19 29.0	51.7	128.5	18 13.9	52.6	129.1	16 57.9	53.4	129.5	15 41.1	54.1	130.0	14 23.6	54.8	130.4	7
18 37.3	51.9	129.1	17 21.3	52.7	129.6	16 04.5	53.5	130.0	14 47.0	54.2	130.4	13 28.8	54.9	130.8	8
17 45.4	51.9	129.6	16 28.6	52.8	130.1	15 11.0	53.5	130.5	13 52.8	54.3	130.9	12 33.9	54.9	131.2	9
16 53.5	−52.1	130.1	15 35.8	−52.8	130.6	14 17.5	−53.6	131.0	12 58.5	−54.3	131.3	11 39.0	−54.9	131.6	10
16 01.4	52.1	130.6	14 43.0	52.9	131.0	13 23.9	53.7	131.4	12 04.2	54.3	131.8	10 44.1	55.0	132.1	11
15 09.3	52.1	131.1	13 50.1	53.0	131.5	12 30.2	53.6	131.9	11 09.9	54.4	132.2	9 49.1	55.0	132.5	12
14 17.2	52.3	131.7	12 57.1	53.0	132.0	11 36.6	53.8	132.3	10 15.5	54.4	132.6	8 54.1	55.1	132.9	13
13 24.9	52.3	132.2	12 04.1	53.0	132.5	10 42.8	53.7	132.8	9 21.1	54.4	133.0	7 59.0	55.0	133.3	14
12 32.6	−52.3	132.7	11 11.1	−53.1	133.0	9 49.1	−53.8	133.2	8 26.7	−54.5	133.5	7 04.0	−55.1	133.7	15
11 40.3	52.4	133.2	10 18.0	53.2	133.4	8 55.3	53.9	133.7	7 32.2	54.5	133.9	6 08.9	55.1	134.1	16
10 47.9	52.5	133.7	9 24.8	53.1	133.9	8 01.4	53.8	134.1	6 37.7	54.5	134.3	5 13.8	55.1	134.5	17
9 55.4	52.5	134.2	8 31.7	53.3	134.4	7 07.6	53.9	134.6	5 43.2	54.5	134.7	4 18.7	55.2	134.9	18
9 02.9	52.5	134.6	7 38.4	53.2	134.9	6 13.7	53.9	135.0	4 48.7	54.5	135.2	3 23.5	55.1	135.3	19
8 10.4	−52.6	135.1	6 45.2	−53.3	135.3	5 19.8	−53.9	135.5	3 54.2	−54.6	135.6	2 28.4	−55.2	135.7	20
7 17.8	52.6	135.6	5 51.9	53.3	135.8	4 25.9	54.0	135.9	2 59.6	54.6	136.0	1 33.2	55.1	136.0	21
6 25.2	52.6	136.1	4 58.7	53.3	136.2	3 31.9	53.9	136.3	2 05.0	54.5	136.4	0 38.1	−55.2	136.4	22
5 32.6	52.6	136.6	4 05.4	53.4	136.7	2 38.0	54.0	136.8	1 10.5	54.6	136.8	0 17.1	+55.2	43.2	23
4 40.0	52.7	137.1	3 12.0	53.3	137.2	1 44.0	54.0	137.2	0 15.9	−54.6	137.2	1 12.2	55.2	42.8	24
3 47.3	−52.7	137.5	2 18.7	−53.4	137.6	0 50.0	−54.0	137.7	0 38.7	+54.5	42.3	2 07.4	+55.1	42.4	25
2 54.6	52.7	138.0	1 25.3	53.3	138.1	0 04.0	+53.9	41.9	1 33.2	54.6	41.9	3 02.5	55.1	42.0	26
2 01.9	52.7	138.5	0 32.0	−53.4	138.5	0 57.9	54.0	41.5	2 27.8	54.6	41.5	3 57.6	55.1	41.6	27
1 09.2	52.7	139.0	0 21.4	+53.3	41.0	1 51.9	54.0	41.0	3 22.4	54.5	41.1	4 52.7	55.2	41.2	28
0 16.5	−52.7	139.5	1 14.7	53.3	40.6	2 45.9	53.9	40.6	4 16.9	54.6	40.7	5 47.9	55.0	40.8	29

LATITUDE **SAME** NAME   L.H.A. 132°, 228°

Dec.	Hc	d	Z	Hc	d	Z	Hc	d	Z	Hc	d	Z	Hc	d	Z
	0°			**2°**			**4°**			**6°**			**8°**		
°	° ′	′	°	° ′	′	°	° ′	′	°	° ′	′	°	° ′	′	°
0	40 00.0−	0.4	90.0	39 58.2+	2.3	91.7	39 53.0+	5.0	93.3	39 44.2+	7.8	95.0	39 32.0+	10.4	96.7
1	39 59.6	1.4	88.7	40 00.5	1.5	90.4	39 58.0	4.1	92.1	39 52.0	6.8	93.7	39 42.4	9.6	95.4
2	39 58.2	2.2	87.4	40 02.0+	0.5	89.1	40 02.1	3.3	90.7	39 58.8	6.0	92.4	39 52.0	8.7	94.1
3	39 56.0	3.0	86.1	40 02.5−	0.4	87.8	40 05.4	2.4	89.4	40 04.8	5.1	91.1	40 00.7	7.8	92.8
4	39 53.0	4.0	84.8	40 02.1	1.2	86.5	40 07.8	1.5	88.1	40 09.9	4.3	89.8	40 08.5	7.0	91.5
5	39 49.0−	4.8	83.5	40 00.9−	2.1	85.1	40 09.3+	0.6	86.8	40 14.2+	3.4	88.5	40 15.5+	6.1	90.2
6	39 44.2	5.6	82.2	39 58.8	3.0	83.8	40 09.9−	0.2	85.5	40 17.6	2.4	87.2	40 21.6	5.2	88.9
7	39 38.6	6.6	80.9	39 55.8	3.8	82.5	40 09.7	1.2	84.2	40 20.0	1.6	85.9	40 26.8	4.4	87.6
8	39 32.0	7.4	79.6	39 52.0	4.7	81.2	40 08.5	2.0	82.9	40 21.6+	0.7	84.6	40 31.2	3.4	86.3
9	39 24.6	8.2	78.3	39 47.3	5.6	79.9	40 06.5	2.9	81.6	40 22.3−	0.2	83.3	40 34.6	2.6	85.0
10	39 16.4−	9.1	77.0	39 41.7−	6.5	78.6	40 03.6−	3.8	80.3	40 22.1−	1.0	82.0	40 37.2+	1.6	83.7
11	39 07.3	9.9	75.8	39 35.2	7.3	77.4	39 59.8	4.6	79.0	40 21.1	2.0	80.7	40 38.8+	0.8	82.3
12	38 57.4	10.7	74.5	39 27.9	8.1	76.1	39 55.2	5.5	77.7	40 19.1	2.9	79.3	40 39.6−	0.2	81.0
13	38 46.7	11.5	73.2	39 19.8	9.0	74.8	39 49.7	6.4	76.4	40 16.2	3.7	78.0	40 39.4	1.0	79.7
14	38 35.2	12.4	72.0	39 10.8	9.8	73.5	39 43.3	7.3	75.1	40 12.5	4.6	76.7	40 38.4	1.8	78.4
15	38 22.8−	13.1	70.7	39 01.0−	10.7	72.2	39 36.0−	8.1	73.8	40 07.9−	5.5	75.4	40 36.4−	2.8	77.1
16	38 09.7	13.9	69.5	38 50.3	11.4	71.0	39 27.9	8.9	72.5	40 02.4	6.4	74.1	40 33.6	3.8	75.8
17	37 55.8	14.7	68.2	38 38.9	12.3	69.7	39 19.0	9.8	71.2	39 56.0	7.2	72.8	40 29.8	4.6	74.4
18	37 41.1	15.4	67.0	38 26.6	13.1	68.5	39 09.2	10.6	70.0	39 48.8	8.1	71.5	40 25.2	5.5	73.1
19	37 25.7	16.2	65.8	38 13.5	13.8	67.2	38 58.6	11.5	68.7	39 40.7	9.0	70.2	40 19.7	6.4	71.8
20	37 09.5−	16.9	64.6	37 59.7−	14.6	66.0	38 47.1−	12.2	67.4	39 31.7−	9.8	69.0	40 13.3−	7.3	70.5
21	36 52.6	17.6	63.4	37 45.1	15.4	64.8	38 34.9	13.0	66.2	39 21.9	10.6	67.7	40 06.0	8.1	69.2
22	36 35.0	18.4	62.2	37 29.7	16.1	63.5	38 21.9	13.9	64.9	39 11.3	11.4	66.4	39 57.9	9.0	67.9
23	36 16.6	19.0	61.0	37 13.6	16.9	62.3	38 08.0	14.6	63.7	38 59.9	12.3	65.1	39 48.9	9.8	66.6
24	35 57.6	19.7	59.8	36 56.7	17.6	61.1	37 53.4	15.3	62.5	38 47.6	13.1	63.9	39 39.1	10.7	65.4
25	35 37.9−	20.4	58.7	36 39.1−	18.3	59.9	37 38.1−	16.1	61.2	38 34.5−	13.8	62.6	39 28.4−	11.6	64.1
26	35 17.5	21.1	57.5	36 20.8	18.9	58.7	37 22.0	16.9	60.0	38 20.7	14.7	61.4	39 16.8	12.3	62.8
27	34 56.4	21.6	56.4	36 01.9	19.7	57.6	37 05.1	17.6	58.8	38 06.0	15.4	60.2	39 04.5	13.2	61.5
28	34 34.8	22.3	55.2	35 42.2	20.3	56.4	36 47.5	18.3	57.6	37 50.6	16.1	58.9	38 51.3	13.9	60.3
29	34 12.5	22.9	54.1	35 21.9	21.0	55.2	36 29.2	19.0	56.4	37 34.5	16.9	57.7	38 37.4	14.8	59.0

Dec.	Hc	d	Z	Hc	d	Z	Hc	d	Z	Hc	d	Z	Hc	d	Z
	10°			**12°**			**14°**			**16°**			**18°**		
°	° ′	′	°	° ′	′	°	° ′	′	°	° ′	′	°	° ′	′	°
0	39 16.4+	13.1	98.3	38 57.4+	15.7	99.9	38 35.2+	18.2	101.5	38 09.7+	20.7	103.0	37 41.1+	23.1	104.5
1	39 29.5	12.2	97.0	39 13.1	14.8	98.7	38 53.4	17.4	100.3	38 30.4	19.9	101.8	38 04.2	22.4	103.4
2	39 41.7	11.4	95.8	39 27.9	14.1	97.4	39 10.8	16.6	99.0	38 50.3	19.2	100.6	38 26.6	21.7	102.2
3	39 53.1	10.5	94.5	39 42.0	13.2	96.1	39 27.4	15.9	97.8	39 09.5	18.4	99.4	38 48.3	20.9	101.0
4	40 03.6	9.7	93.2	39 55.2	12.4	94.9	39 43.3	15.0	96.5	39 27.9	17.6	98.2	39 09.2	20.2	99.8
5	40 13.3+	8.8	91.9	40 07.6+	11.5	93.6	39 58.3+	14.2	95.3	39 45.5+	16.9	96.9	39 29.4+	19.4	98.6
6	40 22.1	8.0	90.6	40 19.1	10.6	92.3	40 12.5	13.3	94.0	40 02.4	16.0	95.7	39 48.8	18.6	97.3
7	40 30.1	7.1	89.3	40 29.7	9.9	91.0	40 25.8	12.6	92.7	40 18.4	15.2	94.4	40 07.4	17.8	96.1
8	40 37.2	6.1	88.0	40 39.6	8.9	89.7	40 38.4	11.6	91.4	40 33.6	14.3	93.1	40 25.2	17.0	94.8
9	40 43.3	5.3	86.7	40 48.5	8.0	88.4	40 50.0	10.8	90.1	40 47.9	13.5	91.9	40 42.2	16.2	93.6
10	40 48.6+	4.4	85.4	40 56.5+	7.2	87.1	41 00.8+	9.9	88.8	41 01.4+	12.6	90.6	40 58.4+	15.3	92.3
11	40 53.0	3.5	84.1	41 03.7	6.2	85.8	41 10.7	9.0	87.5	41 14.0	11.7	89.3	41 13.7	14.4	91.0
12	40 56.5	2.6	82.7	41 09.9	5.3	84.5	41 19.7	8.0	86.2	41 25.7	10.9	88.0	41 28.1	13.6	89.7
13	40 59.1	1.7	81.4	41 15.2	4.5	83.1	41 27.7	7.2	84.9	41 36.6	9.9	86.7	41 41.7	12.7	88.4
14	41 00.8+	0.7	80.1	41 19.7	3.5	81.8	41 34.9	6.3	83.6	41 46.5	9.1	85.3	41 54.4	11.8	87.1
15	41 01.5−	0.1	78.8	41 23.2+	2.5	80.5	41 41.2+	5.3	82.2	41 55.6+	8.1	84.0	42 06.2+	10.9	85.8
16	41 01.4	1.1	77.4	41 25.7	1.7	79.1	41 46.5	4.5	80.9	42 03.7	7.2	82.7	42 17.1	10.0	84.5
17	41 00.3	1.9	76.1	41 27.4+	0.7	77.8	41 51.0	3.4	79.6	42 10.9	6.2	81.3	42 27.1	9.0	83.1
18	40 58.4	2.9	74.8	41 28.1−	0.1	76.5	41 54.4	2.6	78.2	42 17.1	5.3	80.0	42 36.1	8.1	81.8
19	40 55.5	3.8	73.5	41 28.0	1.2	75.1	41 57.0	1.6	76.9	42 22.4	4.4	78.6	42 44.2	7.1	80.5
20	40 51.7−	4.7	72.1	41 26.8−	2.0	73.8	41 58.6+	0.6	75.5	42 26.8+	3.4	77.3	42 51.3+	6.2	79.1
21	40 47.0	5.5	70.8	41 24.8	2.9	72.5	41 59.2−	0.2	74.2	42 30.2	2.4	75.9	42 57.5	5.2	77.7
22	40 41.5	6.5	69.5	41 21.9	3.9	71.1	41 59.0	1.3	72.8	42 32.6	1.5	74.6	43 02.7	4.2	76.4
23	40 35.0	7.4	68.2	41 18.0	4.8	69.8	41 57.7	2.1	71.5	42 34.1+	0.5	73.2	43 06.9	3.3	75.0
24	40 27.6	8.2	66.9	41 13.2	5.7	68.5	41 55.6	3.1	70.2	42 34.6−	0.4	71.9	43 10.2	2.3	73.6
25	40 19.4−	9.1	65.6	41 07.5−	6.6	67.2	41 52.5−	4.1	68.8	42 34.2−	1.4	70.5	43 12.5+	1.3	72.3
26	40 10.3	10.0	64.3	41 00.9	7.5	65.9	41 48.4	4.9	67.5	42 32.8	2.4	69.2	43 13.8+	0.3	70.9
27	40 00.3	10.8	63.0	40 53.4	8.4	64.5	41 43.5	5.9	66.1	42 30.4	3.3	67.8	43 14.1−	0.7	69.5
28	39 49.5	11.6	61.7	40 45.0	9.3	63.2	41 37.6	6.9	64.8	42 27.1	4.3	66.4	43 13.4	1.7	68.2
29	39 37.9	12.5	60.5	40 35.7	10.2	61.9	41 30.7	7.7	63.5	42 22.8	5.2	65.1	43 11.7	2.6	66.8

0°			2°			4°			6°			8°			Dec.
Hc	d	Z	Hc	d	Z	Hc	d	Z	Hc	d	Z	Hc	d	Z	
° ′	′	°	° ′	′	°	° ′	′	°	° ′	′	°	° ′	′	°	°
40 00.0	− 0.4	90.0	39 58.2	− 3.1	91.7	39 53.0	− 5.9	93.3	39 44.2	− 8.6	95.0	39 32.0	−11.2	96.7	0
39 59.6	1.4	91.3	39 55.1	4.1	93.0	39 47.1	6.8	94.6	39 35.6	9.4	96.3	39 20.8	12.1	97.9	1
39 58.2	2.2	92.6	39 51.0	4.9	94.3	39 40.3	7.6	95.9	39 26.2	10.2	97.6	39 08.7	12.9	99.2	2
39 56.0	3.0	93.9	39 46.1	5.8	95.6	39 32.7	8.4	97.2	39 16.0	11.1	98.9	38 55.8	13.7	100.5	3
39 53.0	4.0	95.2	39 40.3	6.6	96.9	39 24.3	9.3	98.5	39 04.9	12.0	100.1	38 42.1	14.4	101.7	4
39 49.0	− 4.8	96.5	39 33.7	− 7.5	98.2	39 15.0	−10.1	99.8	38 52.9	−12.7	101.4	38 27.7	−15.3	102.9	5
39 44.2	5.6	97.8	39 26.2	8.3	99.4	39 04.9	11.0	101.1	38 40.2	13.5	102.6	38 12.4	16.0	104.2	6
39 38.6	6.6	99.1	39 17.9	9.2	100.7	38 53.9	11.8	102.3	38 26.7	14.3	103.9	37 56.4	16.8	105.4	7
39 32.0	7.4	100.4	39 08.7	10.0	102.0	38 42.1	12.5	103.6	38 12.4	15.1	105.1	37 39.6	17.6	106.6	8
39 24.6	8.2	101.7	38 58.7	10.8	103.3	38 29.6	13.4	104.8	37 57.3	15.8	106.3	37 22.0	18.2	107.8	9
39 16.4	− 9.1	103.0	38 47.9	−11.7	104.5	38 16.2	−14.2	106.1	37 41.5	−16.6	107.6	37 03.8	−19.0	109.0	10
39 07.3	9.9	104.2	38 36.2	12.4	105.8	38 02.0	14.9	107.3	37 24.9	17.4	108.8	36 44.8	19.7	110.2	11
38 57.4	10.7	105.5	38 23.8	13.2	107.0	37 47.1	15.7	108.5	37 07.5	18.0	110.0	36 25.1	20.3	111.4	12
38 46.7	11.5	106.8	38 10.6	14.0	108.3	37 31.4	16.4	109.8	36 49.5	18.8	111.2	36 04.8	21.0	112.5	13
38 35.2	12.4	108.0	37 56.6	14.8	109.5	37 15.0	17.1	111.0	36 30.7	19.4	112.4	35 43.8	21.7	113.7	14
38 22.8	−13.1	109.3	37 41.8	−15.6	110.7	36 57.9	−17.9	112.2	36 11.3	−20.2	113.5	35 22.1	−22.4	114.9	15
38 09.7	13.9	110.5	37 26.2	16.3	112.0	36 40.0	18.6	113.4	35 51.1	20.8	114.7	34 59.7	22.9	116.0	16
37 55.8	14.7	111.8	37 09.9	17.0	113.2	36 21.4	19.3	114.5	35 30.3	21.5	115.9	34 36.8	23.6	117.1	17
37 41.1	15.4	113.0	36 52.9	17.7	114.4	36 02.1	19.9	115.7	35 08.8	22.1	117.0	34 13.2	24.2	118.2	18
37 25.7	16.2	114.2	36 35.2	18.5	115.6	35 42.2	20.7	116.9	34 46.7	22.7	118.1	33 49.0	24.7	119.3	19
37 09.5	−16.9	115.4	36 16.7	−19.1	116.8	35 21.5	−21.3	118.0	34 24.0	−23.4	119.3	33 24.3	−25.4	120.4	20
36 52.6	17.6	116.6	35 57.6	19.8	117.9	35 00.2	21.9	119.2	34 00.6	23.9	120.4	32 58.9	25.9	121.5	21
36 35.0	18.4	117.8	35 37.8	20.5	119.1	34 38.3	22.5	120.3	33 36.7	24.5	121.5	32 33.0	26.4	122.6	22
36 16.6	19.0	119.0	35 17.3	21.1	120.2	34 15.8	23.2	121.4	33 12.2	25.1	122.6	32 06.6	26.9	123.6	23
35 57.6	19.7	120.2	34 56.2	21.8	121.4	33 52.6	23.7	122.6	32 47.1	25.7	123.7	31 39.7	27.5	124.7	24
35 37.9	−20.4	121.3	34 34.4	−22.4	122.5	33 28.9	−24.4	123.7	32 21.4	−26.2	124.7	31 12.2	−28.0	125.7	25
35 17.5	21.1	122.5	34 12.0	23.0	123.6	33 04.5	24.9	124.7	31 55.2	26.7	125.8	30 44.2	28.4	126.8	26
34 56.4	21.6	123.6	33 49.0	23.6	124.8	32 39.6	25.4	125.8	31 28.5	27.2	126.8	30 15.8	28.9	127.8	27
34 34.8	22.3	124.8	33 25.4	24.2	125.9	32 14.2	26.0	126.9	31 01.3	27.7	127.9	29 46.9	29.4	128.8	28
34 12.5	22.9	125.9	33 01.2	24.7	127.0	31 48.2	26.5	128.0	30 33.6	28.2	128.9	29 17.5	29.8	129.8	29

10°			12°			14°			16°			18°			Dec.
Hc	d	Z	Hc	d	Z	Hc	d	Z	Hc	d	Z	Hc	d	Z	
° ′	′	°	° ′	′	°	° ′	′	°	° ′	′	°	° ′	′	°	°
39 16.4	−13.9	98.3	38 57.4	−16.4	99.9	38 35.2	−19.0	101.5	38 09.7	−21.4	103.0	37 41.1	−23.7	104.5	0
39 02.5	14.6	99.5	38 41.0	17.2	101.1	38 16.2	19.6	102.7	37 48.3	22.1	104.2	37 17.4	24.5	105.7	1
38 47.9	15.5	100.8	38 23.8	18.0	102.4	37 56.6	20.5	103.9	37 26.2	22.8	105.4	36 52.9	25.1	106.8	2
38 32.4	16.2	102.0	38 05.8	18.7	103.6	37 36.1	21.1	105.1	37 03.4	23.4	106.5	36 27.8	25.7	108.0	3
38 16.2	17.0	103.3	37 47.1	19.4	104.8	37 15.0	21.8	106.3	36 40.0	24.1	107.7	36 02.1	26.3	109.1	4
37 59.2	−17.7	104.5	37 27.7	−20.2	106.0	36 53.2	−22.5	107.4	36 15.9	−24.8	108.8	35 35.8	−27.0	110.2	5
37 41.5	18.5	105.7	37 07.5	20.8	107.2	36 30.7	23.1	108.6	35 51.1	25.4	110.0	35 08.8	27.5	111.3	6
37 23.0	19.2	106.9	36 46.7	21.6	108.3	36 07.6	23.8	109.7	35 25.7	26.0	111.1	34 41.3	28.1	112.4	7
37 03.8	19.9	108.1	36 25.1	22.2	109.5	35 43.8	24.5	110.9	34 59.7	26.6	112.2	34 13.2	28.7	113.5	8
36 43.9	20.6	109.3	36 02.9	22.8	110.6	35 19.3	25.0	112.0	34 33.1	27.1	113.3	33 44.5	29.1	114.5	9
36 23.3	−21.3	110.4	35 40.1	−23.5	111.8	34 54.3	−25.7	113.1	34 06.0	−27.7	114.3	33 15.4	−29.8	115.6	10
36 02.0	21.6	111.6	35 16.6	24.2	112.9	34 28.6	26.2	114.2	33 38.3	28.3	115.4	32 45.6	30.2	116.6	11
35 40.1	22.6	112.7	34 52.4	24.7	114.0	34 02.4	26.8	115.3	33 10.0	28.8	116.5	32 15.4	30.7	117.6	12
35 17.5	23.2	113.9	34 27.7	25.3	115.1	33 35.6	27.4	116.4	32 41.2	29.3	117.5	31 44.7	31.2	118.6	13
34 54.3	23.9	115.0	34 02.4	25.9	116.2	33 08.2	27.9	117.4	32 11.9	29.8	118.6	31 13.6	31.6	119.6	14
34 30.4	−24.4	116.1	33 36.5	−26.5	117.3	32 40.3	−28.4	118.5	31 42.1	−30.3	119.7	30 41.9	−32.1	120.6	15
34 06.0	25.0	117.2	33 10.0	27.0	118.4	32 11.9	28.9	119.5	31 11.8	30.8	120.6	30 09.8	32.5	121.6	16
33 41.0	25.6	118.3	32 43.0	27.6	119.5	31 43.0	29.5	120.6	30 41.0	31.2	121.6	29 37.3	33.0	122.6	17
33 15.4	26.2	119.4	32 15.4	28.0	120.5	31 13.5	29.9	121.6	30 09.8	31.7	122.6	29 04.3	33.3	123.5	18
32 49.2	26.7	120.5	31 47.4	28.6	121.6	30 43.6	30.3	122.6	29 38.1	32.0	123.6	28 31.0	33.7	124.5	19
32 22.5	−27.2	121.5	31 18.8	−29.1	122.6	30 13.3	−30.9	123.6	29 06.1	−32.5	124.5	27 57.3	−34.1	125.4	20
31 55.3	27.8	122.6	30 49.7	29.5	123.6	29 42.4	31.2	124.6	28 33.6	32.9	125.5	27 23.2	34.5	126.3	21
31 27.5	28.3	123.6	30 20.2	30.0	124.6	29 11.2	31.7	125.6	28 00.7	33.3	126.4	26 48.7	34.9	127.2	22
30 59.2	28.7	124.7	29 50.2	30.5	125.6	28 39.5	32.1	126.5	27 27.4	33.7	127.4	26 13.8	35.1	128.2	23
30 30.5	29.2	125.7	29 19.7	30.9	126.6	28 07.4	32.5	127.5	26 53.7	34.0	128.3	25 38.7	35.5	129.1	24
30 01.3	−29.7	126.7	28 48.8	−31.3	127.6	27 34.9	−32.9	128.4	26 19.7	−34.4	129.2	25 03.2	−35.8	130.0	25
29 31.6	30.1	127.7	28 17.5	31.7	128.6	27 02.0	33.2	129.4	25 45.3	34.7	130.1	24 27.4	36.2	130.9	26
29 01.5	30.5	128.7	27 45.8	32.1	129.5	26 28.8	33.6	130.3	25 10.6	35.1	131.0	23 51.2	36.4	131.7	27
28 31.0	31.0	129.7	27 13.7	32.5	130.5	25 55.2	34.0	131.2	24 35.5	35.3	131.9	23 14.8	36.7	132.6	28
28 00.0	31.4	130.6	26 41.2	32.9	131.4	25 21.2	34.3	132.1	24 00.2	35.7	132.8	22 38.1	37.0	133.5	29

Dec.	20° Hc	d	Z	22° Hc	d	Z	24° Hc	d	Z	26° Hc	d	Z	28° Hc	d	Z
0	37 09.5	+25.4	106.0	36 35.0	+27.6	107.4	35 57.6	+29.8	108.8	35 17.5	+31.9	110.2	34 34.8	+33.9	111.5
1	37 34.9	24.8	104.9	37 02.6	27.1	106.3	36 27.4	29.3	107.8	35 49.4	31.4	109.2	35 08.7	33.5	110.5
2	37 59.7	24.1	103.7	37 29.7	26.4	105.2	36 56.7	28.7	106.7	36 20.8	30.9	108.1	35 42.2	32.9	109.5
3	38 23.8	23.3	102.6	37 56.1	25.8	104.1	37 25.4	28.0	105.6	36 51.7	30.3	107.0	36 15.1	32.4	108.4
4	38 47.1	22.7	101.4	38 21.9	25.0	102.9	37 53.4	27.5	104.5	37 22.0	29.6	105.9	36 47.5	31.9	107.4
5	39 09.8	+21.9	100.2	38 46.9	+24.4	101.8	38 20.9	+26.7	103.3	37 51.6	+29.1	104.9	37 19.4	+31.2	106.3
6	39 31.7	21.2	99.0	39 11.3	23.7	100.6	38 47.6	26.1	102.2	38 20.7	28.4	103.7	37 50.6	30.7	105.3
7	39 52.9	20.4	97.8	39 35.0	22.9	99.4	39 13.7	25.4	101.0	38 49.1	27.7	102.6	38 21.3	30.0	104.2
8	40 13.3	19.6	96.5	39 57.9	22.2	98.2	39 39.1	24.6	99.9	39 16.8	27.1	101.5	38 51.3	29.5	103.1
9	40 32.9	18.8	95.3	40 20.1	21.4	97.0	40 03.7	23.9	98.7	39 43.9	26.4	100.3	39 20.8	28.7	101.9
10	40 51.7	+18.0	94.0	40 41.5	+20.6	95.8	40 27.6	+23.2	97.5	40 10.3	+25.7	99.1	39 49.5	+28.1	100.8
11	41 09.7	17.1	92.8	41 02.1	19.8	94.5	40 50.8	22.4	96.2	40 36.0	24.9	98.0	40 17.6	27.4	99.6
12	41 26.8	16.3	91.5	41 21.9	18.9	93.3	41 13.2	21.6	95.0	41 00.9	24.1	96.8	40 45.0	26.6	98.5
13	41 43.1	15.5	90.2	41 40.8	18.2	92.0	41 34.8	20.8	93.8	41 25.0	23.4	95.5	41 11.6	26.0	97.3
14	41 58.6	14.5	88.9	41 59.0	17.2	90.7	41 55.6	19.9	92.5	41 48.4	22.6	94.3	41 37.6	25.1	96.1
15	42 13.1	+13.7	87.6	42 16.2	+16.4	89.4	42 15.5	+19.1	91.2	42 11.0	+21.8	93.1	42 02.7	+24.4	94.9
16	42 26.8	12.7	86.3	42 32.6	15.5	88.1	42 34.6	18.2	90.0	42 32.8	20.9	91.8	42 27.1	23.6	93.6
17	42 39.5	11.8	85.0	42 48.1	14.6	86.8	42 52.8	17.4	88.7	42 53.7	20.1	90.5	42 50.7	22.7	92.4
18	42 51.3	10.9	83.6	43 02.7	13.7	85.5	43 10.2	16.4	87.4	43 13.8	19.2	89.2	43 13.4	21.9	91.1
19	43 02.2	9.9	82.3	43 16.4	12.7	84.2	43 26.6	15.6	86.0	43 33.0	18.2	87.9	43 35.3	21.0	89.8
20	43 12.1	+9.0	80.9	43 29.1	+11.8	82.8	43 42.2	+14.5	84.7	43 51.2	+17.4	86.6	43 56.3	+20.2	88.5
21	43 21.1	8.0	79.6	43 40.9	10.8	81.5	43 56.7	13.7	83.4	44 08.6	16.5	85.3	44 16.5	19.2	87.2
22	43 29.1	7.0	78.2	43 51.7	9.8	80.1	44 10.4	12.6	82.0	44 25.1	15.4	83.9	44 35.7	18.3	85.9
23	43 36.1	6.1	76.8	44 01.5	8.9	78.7	44 23.0	11.7	80.6	44 40.5	14.5	82.6	44 54.0	17.3	84.6
24	43 42.2	5.0	75.5	44 10.4	7.8	77.3	44 34.7	10.7	79.3	44 55.0	13.6	81.2	45 11.3	16.4	83.2
25	43 47.2	+4.0	74.1	44 18.2	+6.9	76.0	44 45.4	+9.6	77.9	45 08.6	+12.5	79.8	45 27.7	+15.4	81.8
26	43 51.2	3.1	72.7	44 25.1	5.8	74.6	44 55.0	8.7	76.5	45 21.1	11.5	78.4	45 43.1	14.4	80.5
27	43 54.3	2.0	71.3	44 30.9	4.8	73.2	45 03.7	7.6	75.1	45 32.6	10.5	77.0	45 57.5	13.3	79.1
28	43 56.3	+1.1	69.9	44 35.7	3.8	71.8	45 11.3	6.6	73.7	45 43.1	9.4	75.6	46 10.8	12.3	77.7
29	43 57.4	0.0	68.5	44 39.5	2.7	70.4	45 17.9	5.5	72.3	45 52.5	8.4	74.2	46 23.1	11.3	76.2

Dec.	30° Hc	d	Z	32° Hc	d	Z	34° Hc	d	Z	36° Hc	d	Z	38° Hc	d	Z
0	33 49.6	+35.8	112.8	33 02.0	+37.7	114.0	32 12.1	+39.4	115.1	31 20.0	+41.2	116.3	30 26.0	+42.6	117.3
1	34 25.4	35.5	111.8	33 39.7	37.3	113.0	32 51.5	39.1	114.2	32 01.2	40.7	115.4	31 08.6	42.4	116.5
2	35 00.9	34.9	110.8	34 17.0	36.8	112.1	33 30.6	38.7	113.3	32 41.9	40.4	114.5	31 51.0	42.1	115.7
3	35 35.8	34.4	109.8	34 53.8	36.4	111.1	34 09.3	38.2	112.4	33 22.3	40.1	113.6	32 33.1	41.7	114.8
4	36 10.2	34.0	108.8	35 30.2	35.9	110.2	34 47.5	37.9	111.5	34 02.4	39.6	112.8	33 14.8	41.3	114.0
5	36 44.2	+33.4	107.8	36 06.1	+35.5	109.2	35 25.4	+37.3	110.5	34 42.0	+39.2	111.8	33 56.1	+41.0	113.1
6	37 17.6	32.8	106.7	36 41.6	34.9	108.2	36 02.7	36.9	109.6	35 21.2	38.8	110.9	34 37.1	40.6	112.2
7	37 50.4	32.2	105.7	37 16.5	34.3	107.2	36 39.6	36.4	108.6	36 00.0	38.3	110.0	35 17.7	40.1	111.3
8	38 22.6	31.7	104.6	37 50.8	33.9	106.1	37 16.0	35.9	107.6	36 38.3	37.9	109.0	35 57.8	39.8	110.4
9	38 54.3	31.1	103.5	38 24.7	33.2	105.1	37 51.9	35.4	106.6	37 16.2	37.4	108.1	36 37.6	39.3	109.5
10	39 25.4	+30.4	102.4	38 57.9	+32.7	104.0	38 27.3	+34.8	105.6	37 53.6	+36.9	107.1	37 16.9	+38.9	108.5
11	39 55.8	29.7	101.3	39 30.6	32.1	102.9	39 02.1	34.3	104.5	38 30.5	36.4	106.1	37 55.8	38.3	107.6
12	40 25.5	29.1	100.2	40 02.7	31.4	101.8	39 36.4	33.7	103.5	39 06.9	35.8	105.0	38 34.1	37.9	106.6
13	40 54.6	28.4	99.0	40 34.1	30.7	100.7	40 10.1	33.0	102.4	39 42.7	35.2	104.0	39 12.0	37.4	105.6
14	41 23.0	27.7	97.8	41 04.8	30.1	99.6	40 43.1	32.5	101.3	40 17.9	34.7	102.9	39 49.4	36.8	104.6
15	41 50.7	+26.9	96.7	41 34.9	+29.4	98.4	41 15.6	+31.7	100.2	40 52.6	+34.1	101.9	40 26.2	+36.3	103.5
16	42 17.6	26.1	95.4	42 04.3	28.7	97.2	41 47.3	31.1	99.0	41 26.7	33.4	100.8	41 02.5	35.6	102.5
17	42 43.7	25.4	94.2	42 33.0	27.9	96.1	42 18.4	30.4	97.9	42 00.1	32.8	99.7	41 38.1	35.1	101.4
18	43 09.1	24.6	93.0	43 00.9	27.1	94.9	42 48.8	29.7	96.7	42 32.9	32.1	98.5	42 13.2	34.5	100.3
19	43 33.7	23.7	91.7	43 28.0	26.4	93.6	43 18.5	28.9	95.5	43 05.0	31.4	97.4	42 47.7	33.7	99.2
20	43 57.4	+22.8	90.5	43 54.4	+25.5	92.4	43 47.4	+28.1	94.3	43 36.4	+30.6	96.2	43 21.4	+33.1	98.1
21	44 20.2	22.0	89.2	44 19.9	24.7	91.1	44 15.5	27.3	93.1	44 07.0	29.9	95.0	43 54.5	32.4	96.9
22	44 42.2	21.1	87.9	44 44.6	23.8	89.8	44 42.8	26.5	91.8	44 36.9	29.2	93.8	44 26.9	31.7	95.8
23	45 03.3	20.1	86.5	45 08.4	22.9	88.6	45 09.3	25.7	90.6	45 06.1	28.3	92.6	44 58.6	30.9	94.6
24	45 23.4	19.2	85.2	45 31.3	22.1	87.2	45 35.0	24.8	89.3	45 34.4	27.4	91.3	45 29.5	30.1	93.4
25	45 42.6	+18.3	83.9	45 53.4	+21.0	85.9	45 59.8	+23.8	88.0	46 01.8	+26.7	90.0	45 59.6	+29.3	92.1
26	46 00.9	17.2	82.5	46 14.4	20.1	84.6	46 23.6	23.0	86.6	46 28.5	25.7	88.7	46 28.9	28.4	90.9
27	46 18.1	16.3	81.1	46 34.5	19.1	83.2	46 46.6	21.9	85.3	46 54.2	24.8	87.4	46 57.3	27.6	89.6
28	46 34.4	15.2	79.7	46 53.6	18.1	81.8	47 08.5	21.0	83.9	47 19.0	23.8	86.1	47 24.9	26.6	88.3
29	46 49.6	14.1	78.3	47 11.7	17.1	80.4	47 29.5	20.0	82.6	47 42.8	22.9	84.7	47 51.5	25.7	86.9

20° Hc	d	Z	22° Hc	d	Z	24° Hc	d	Z	26° Hc	d	Z	28° Hc	d	Z	Dec.
37 09.5	−26.1	106.0	36 35.0	−28.3	107.4	35 57.6	−30.5	108.8	35 17.5	−32.5	110.2	34 34.8	−34.5	111.5	0
36 43.4	26.7	107.1	36 06.7	28.9	108.5	35 27.1	30.9	109.9	34 45.0	33.0	111.2	34 00.3	34.9	112.5	1
36 16.7	27.3	108.3	35 37.8	29.5	109.6	34 56.2	31.5	111.0	34 12.0	33.5	112.2	33 25.4	35.4	113.5	2
35 49.4	27.9	109.4	35 08.3	30.0	110.7	34 24.7	32.1	112.0	33 38.5	34.0	113.2	32 50.0	35.8	114.4	3
35 21.5	28.5	110.4	34 38.3	30.5	111.8	33 52.6	32.5	113.0	33 04.5	34.4	114.2	32 14.2	36.2	115.4	4
34 53.0	−29.0	111.5	34 07.8	−31.1	112.8	33 20.1	−33.0	114.0	32 30.1	−34.9	115.2	31 38.0	−36.7	116.3	5
34 24.0	29.6	112.6	33 36.7	31.6	113.8	32 47.1	33.5	115.0	31 55.2	35.3	116.2	31 01.3	37.0	117.3	6
33 54.4	30.1	113.6	33 05.1	32.1	114.8	32 13.6	33.9	116.0	31 19.9	35.7	117.1	30 24.3	37.4	118.2	7
33 24.3	30.7	114.7	32 33.0	32.5	115.8	31 39.7	34.4	117.0	30 44.2	36.1	118.0	29 46.9	37.8	119.1	8
32 53.6	31.1	115.7	32 00.5	33.0	116.8	31 05.3	34.8	117.9	30 08.1	36.5	119.0	29 09.1	38.1	120.0	9
32 22.5	−31.6	116.7	31 27.5	−33.4	117.8	30 30.5	−35.2	118.9	29 31.6	−36.8	119.9	28 31.0	−38.5	120.8	10
31 50.9	32.1	117.7	30 54.1	33.9	118.8	29 55.3	35.6	119.8	28 54.8	37.3	120.8	27 52.5	38.8	121.7	11
31 18.8	32.6	118.7	30 20.2	34.3	119.8	29 19.7	36.0	120.7	28 17.5	37.5	121.7	27 13.7	39.1	122.6	12
30 46.2	32.9	119.7	29 45.9	34.7	120.7	28 43.7	36.3	121.7	27 40.0	38.0	122.6	26 34.6	39.4	123.4	13
30 13.3	33.4	120.7	29 11.2	35.1	121.6	28 07.4	36.7	122.6	27 02.0	38.2	123.4	25 55.2	39.7	124.3	14
29 39.9	−33.8	121.6	28 36.1	−35.4	122.6	27 30.7	−37.0	123.5	26 23.8	−38.5	124.3	25 15.5	−40.0	125.1	15
29 06.1	34.2	122.6	28 00.7	35.9	123.5	26 53.7	37.4	124.3	25 45.3	38.8	125.2	24 35.5	40.2	125.9	16
28 31.9	34.6	123.5	27 24.8	36.1	124.4	26 16.3	37.6	125.2	25 06.5	39.1	126.0	23 55.3	40.5	126.7	17
27 57.3	35.0	124.4	26 48.7	36.5	125.3	25 38.7	38.0	126.1	24 27.4	39.4	126.8	23 14.8	40.7	127.5	18
27 22.3	35.3	125.4	26 12.2	36.8	126.2	25 00.7	38.3	126.9	23 48.0	39.7	127.7	22 34.1	41.0	128.3	19
26 47.0	−35.7	126.3	25 35.4	−37.2	127.0	24 22.4	−38.5	127.8	23 08.3	−39.9	128.5	21 53.1	−41.2	129.1	20
26 11.3	35.9	127.2	24 58.2	37.4	127.9	23 43.9	38.8	128.6	22 28.4	40.1	129.3	21 11.9	41.4	129.9	21
25 35.4	36.3	128.0	24 20.8	37.7	128.8	23 05.1	39.1	129.5	21 48.3	40.4	130.1	20 30.5	41.6	130.7	22
24 59.1	36.7	128.9	23 43.1	38.0	129.6	22 26.0	39.3	130.3	21 07.9	40.6	130.9	19 48.9	41.8	131.5	23
24 22.4	36.9	129.8	23 05.1	38.3	130.5	21 46.7	39.6	131.1	20 27.3	40.8	131.7	19 07.1	42.0	132.2	24
23 45.5	−37.2	130.7	22 26.8	−38.5	131.3	21 07.1	−39.8	131.9	19 46.5	−40.9	132.5	18 25.1	−42.1	133.0	25
23 08.3	37.4	131.5	21 48.3	38.8	132.1	20 27.3	40.0	132.7	19 05.6	41.2	133.2	17 43.0	42.3	133.7	26
22 30.9	37.8	132.4	21 09.5	39.0	133.0	19 47.3	40.4	133.5	18 24.4	41.4	134.0	17 00.7	42.5	134.5	27
21 53.1	38.0	133.2	20 30.5	39.2	133.8	19 07.1	40.4	134.3	17 43.0	41.6	134.8	16 18.2	42.7	135.2	28
21 15.1	38.2	134.0	19 51.3	39.4	134.6	18 26.7	40.6	135.1	17 01.4	41.7	135.5	15 35.5	42.8	135.9	29

30° Hc	d	Z	32° Hc	d	Z	34° Hc	d	Z	36° Hc	d	Z	38° Hc	d	Z	Dec.
33 49.6	−36.4	112.8	33 02.0	−38.2	114.0	32 12.1	−39.9	115.1	31 20.0	−41.4	116.3	30 26.0	−43.0	117.3	0
33 13.2	36.7	113.7	32 23.8	38.5	114.9	31 32.2	40.1	116.0	30 38.6	41.8	117.1	29 43.0	43.3	118.1	1
32 36.5	37.2	114.7	31 45.3	38.9	115.8	30 52.1	40.6	116.9	29 56.8	42.1	117.9	28 59.7	43.6	118.9	2
31 59.3	37.6	115.6	31 06.4	39.3	116.7	30 11.5	40.8	117.7	29 14.7	42.4	118.7	28 16.1	43.8	119.7	3
31 21.7	38.0	116.5	30 27.1	39.6	117.6	29 30.7	41.2	118.6	28 32.3	42.6	119.6	27 32.3	44.1	120.5	4
30 43.7	−38.3	117.4	29 47.5	−39.9	118.4	28 49.5	−41.5	119.4	27 49.7	−43.0	120.4	26 48.2	−44.3	121.2	5
30 05.4	38.7	118.3	29 07.6	40.3	119.3	28 08.0	41.8	120.2	27 06.7	43.2	121.1	26 03.9	44.5	122.0	6
29 26.7	39.0	119.2	28 27.3	40.6	120.1	27 26.2	42.0	121.1	26 23.5	43.4	121.9	25 19.4	44.8	122.7	7
28 47.7	39.4	120.0	27 46.7	40.9	121.0	26 44.2	42.3	121.9	25 40.1	43.7	122.7	24 34.6	45.0	123.5	8
28 08.3	39.7	120.9	27 05.8	41.1	121.8	26 01.9	42.6	122.6	24 56.4	43.9	123.4	23 49.6	45.2	124.2	9
27 28.6	−40.0	121.8	26 24.7	−41.5	122.6	25 19.3	−42.8	123.4	24 12.5	−44.1	124.2	23 04.4	−45.3	124.9	10
26 48.6	40.3	122.6	25 43.2	41.7	123.4	24 36.5	43.1	124.2	23 28.4	44.4	124.9	22 19.1	45.6	125.6	11
26 08.3	40.5	123.4	25 01.5	41.9	124.2	23 53.4	43.3	125.0	22 44.0	44.5	125.7	21 33.5	45.7	126.3	12
25 27.8	40.9	124.2	24 19.6	42.2	125.0	23 10.1	43.4	125.7	21 59.5	44.7	126.4	20 47.8	45.9	127.0	13
24 46.9	41.0	125.0	23 37.4	42.4	125.8	22 26.7	43.7	126.5	21 14.8	44.9	127.1	20 01.9	46.1	127.7	14
24 05.9	−41.4	125.8	22 55.0	−42.7	126.5	21 43.0	−43.9	127.2	20 29.9	−45.1	127.8	19 15.8	−46.2	128.4	15
23 24.5	41.6	126.6	22 12.3	42.8	127.3	20 59.1	44.1	127.9	19 44.8	45.2	128.5	18 29.6	46.3	129.1	16
22 42.9	41.8	127.4	21 29.5	43.1	128.1	20 15.0	44.2	128.7	18 59.6	45.4	129.2	17 43.3	46.5	129.7	17
22 01.1	42.0	128.2	20 46.4	43.2	128.8	19 30.8	44.5	129.4	18 14.2	45.6	129.9	16 56.8	46.6	130.4	18
21 19.1	42.2	129.0	20 03.2	43.4	129.6	18 46.3	44.5	130.1	17 28.6	45.6	130.6	16 10.2	46.7	131.0	19
20 36.9	−42.4	129.7	19 19.8	−43.6	130.3	18 01.8	−44.8	130.8	16 43.0	−45.8	131.3	15 23.5	−46.9	131.7	20
19 54.5	42.6	130.5	18 36.2	43.8	131.0	17 17.0	44.9	131.5	15 57.2	46.0	131.9	14 36.6	46.9	132.3	21
19 11.9	42.8	131.2	17 52.4	43.9	131.7	16 32.1	45.0	132.2	15 11.2	46.0	132.6	13 49.7	47.1	133.0	22
18 29.1	43.0	132.0	17 08.5	44.1	132.4	15 47.1	45.1	132.9	14 25.2	46.2	133.3	13 02.6	47.1	133.6	23
17 46.1	43.1	132.7	16 24.4	44.2	133.2	15 02.0	45.3	133.6	13 39.0	46.3	133.9	12 15.5	47.2	134.3	24
17 03.0	−43.3	133.4	15 40.2	−44.4	133.9	14 16.7	−45.3	134.3	12 52.7	−46.3	134.6	11 28.3	−47.3	134.9	25
16 19.7	43.4	134.2	14 55.8	44.5	134.6	13 31.4	45.5	134.9	12 06.4	46.5	135.2	10 41.0	47.4	135.5	26
15 36.3	43.6	134.9	14 11.3	44.6	135.2	12 45.9	45.6	135.6	11 19.9	46.5	135.9	9 53.6	47.5	136.1	27
14 52.7	43.7	135.6	13 26.7	44.7	135.9	12 00.3	45.7	136.3	10 33.4	46.6	136.5	9 06.1	47.5	136.8	28
14 09.0	43.8	136.3	12 42.0	44.8	136.6	11 14.6	45.8	136.9	9 46.8	46.7	137.2	8 18.6	47.5	137.4	29

Dec.	Hc (40°)	d	Z	Hc (42°)	d	Z	Hc (44°)	d	Z	Hc (46°)	d	Z	Hc (48°)	d	Z
°	° '	'	°	° '	'	°	° '	'	°	° '	'	°	° '	'	°
0	29 29.9	+44.2	118.3	28 32.1	+45.5	119.3	27 32.5	+46.9	120.2	26 31.2	+48.2	121.1	25 28.5	+49.3	121.9
1	30 14.1	43.9	117.6	29 17.6	45.4	118.6	28 19.4	46.6	119.5	27 19.4	47.9	120.4	26 17.8	49.1	121.3
2	30 58.0	43.6	116.8	30 03.0	45.0	117.8	29 06.0	46.5	118.8	28 07.3	47.8	119.8	27 06.9	49.0	120.7
3	31 41.6	43.3	116.0	30 48.0	44.8	117.1	29 52.5	46.2	118.1	28 55.1	47.5	119.1	27 55.9	48.8	120.0
4	32 24.9	43.0	115.1	31 32.8	44.5	116.3	30 38.7	45.9	117.3	29 42.6	47.3	118.4	28 44.7	48.5	119.4
5	33 07.9	+42.6	114.3	32 17.3	+44.2	115.5	31 24.6	+45.7	116.6	30 29.9	+47.1	117.7	29 33.2	+48.4	118.7
6	33 50.5	42.3	113.5	33 01.5	43.9	114.7	32 10.3	45.4	115.8	31 17.0	46.8	116.9	30 21.6	48.2	118.0
7	34 32.8	41.9	112.6	33 45.4	43.6	113.9	32 55.7	45.1	115.1	32 03.8	46.6	116.2	31 09.8	47.9	117.3
8	35 14.7	41.5	111.7	34 29.0	43.2	113.0	33 40.8	44.8	114.3	32 50.4	46.3	115.5	31 57.7	47.7	116.6
9	35 56.2	41.2	110.9	35 12.2	42.9	112.2	34 25.6	44.5	113.5	33 36.7	46.0	114.7	32 45.4	47.4	115.9
10	36 37.4	+40.7	110.0	35 55.1	+42.4	111.3	35 10.1	+44.2	112.7	34 22.7	+45.7	113.9	33 32.8	+47.2	115.2
11	37 18.1	40.3	109.0	36 37.5	42.1	110.5	35 54.3	43.8	111.8	35 08.4	45.4	113.1	34 20.0	46.9	114.4
12	37 58.4	39.8	108.1	37 19.6	41.7	109.6	36 38.1	43.4	111.0	35 53.8	45.0	112.3	35 06.9	46.6	113.6
13	38 38.2	39.4	107.1	38 01.3	41.3	108.6	37 21.5	43.0	110.1	36 38.8	44.8	111.5	35 53.5	46.3	112.9
14	39 17.6	38.8	106.2	38 42.6	40.8	107.7	38 04.5	42.7	109.2	37 23.6	44.3	110.7	36 39.8	46.0	112.1
15	39 56.4	+38.4	105.2	39 23.4	+40.3	106.8	38 47.2	+42.2	108.3	38 07.9	+44.0	109.8	37 25.8	+45.7	111.3
16	40 34.8	37.8	104.2	40 03.7	39.9	105.8	39 29.4	41.8	107.4	38 51.9	43.6	109.0	38 11.5	45.3	110.5
17	41 12.6	37.3	103.2	40 43.6	39.3	104.8	40 11.2	41.3	106.5	39 35.5	43.2	108.1	38 56.8	44.9	109.6
18	41 49.9	36.6	102.1	41 22.9	38.8	103.8	40 52.5	40.9	105.5	40 18.7	42.8	107.2	39 41.7	44.6	108.8
19	42 26.5	36.1	101.0	42 01.7	38.3	102.8	41 33.4	40.3	104.6	41 01.5	42.3	106.2	40 26.3	44.1	107.9
20	43 02.6	+35.5	99.9	42 40.0	+37.7	101.8	42 13.7	+39.8	103.6	41 43.8	+41.8	105.3	41 10.4	+43.7	107.0
21	43 38.1	34.7	98.8	43 17.7	37.1	100.7	42 53.5	39.3	102.5	42 25.6	41.3	104.3	41 54.1	43.3	106.1
22	44 12.8	34.1	97.7	43 54.8	36.4	99.6	43 32.8	38.6	101.5	43 06.9	40.8	103.3	42 37.4	42.8	105.1
23	44 46.9	33.4	96.6	44 31.2	35.8	98.5	44 11.4	38.1	100.4	43 47.7	40.3	102.3	43 20.2	42.3	104.2
24	45 20.3	32.7	95.4	45 07.0	35.1	97.4	44 49.5	37.5	99.4	44 28.0	39.7	101.3	44 02.5	41.8	103.2
25	45 53.0	+31.9	94.2	45 42.1	+34.4	96.2	45 27.0	+36.8	98.3	45 07.7	+39.1	100.2	44 44.3	+41.3	102.2
26	46 24.9	31.1	93.0	46 16.5	33.7	95.0	46 03.8	36.1	97.1	45 46.8	38.5	99.2	45 25.6	40.7	101.2
27	46 56.0	30.2	91.7	46 50.2	32.8	93.8	46 39.9	35.4	96.0	46 25.3	37.8	98.1	46 06.3	40.1	100.1
28	47 26.2	29.4	90.4	47 23.0	32.1	92.6	47 15.3	34.7	94.8	47 03.1	37.1	96.9	46 46.4	39.5	99.0
29	47 55.6	28.6	89.1	47 55.1	31.3	91.4	47 50.0	33.8	93.6	47 40.2	36.4	95.8	47 25.9	38.8	97.9

Dec.	Hc (50°)	d	Z	Hc (52°)	d	Z	Hc (54°)	d	Z	Hc (56°)	d	Z	Hc (58°)	d	Z
°	° '	'	°	° '	'	°	° '	'	°	° '	'	°	° '	'	°
0	24 24.3	+50.4	122.7	23 18.7	+51.4	123.5	22 11.9	+52.4	124.2	21 04.0	+53.2	124.8	19 54.9	+54.1	125.4
1	25 14.7	50.2	122.1	24 10.1	51.3	122.9	23 04.3	52.3	123.6	21 57.2	53.2	124.3	20 49.0	54.0	125.0
2	26 04.9	50.1	121.5	25 01.4	51.2	122.3	23 56.6	52.1	123.1	22 50.4	53.1	123.8	21 43.0	53.9	124.5
3	26 55.0	50.0	120.9	25 52.6	51.0	121.8	24 48.7	52.1	122.6	23 43.5	52.9	123.3	22 36.9	53.9	124.0
4	27 45.0	49.7	120.3	26 43.6	50.9	121.2	25 40.8	51.9	122.0	24 36.4	52.9	122.8	23 30.8	53.7	123.6
5	28 34.7	+49.6	119.7	27 34.5	+50.7	120.6	26 32.7	+51.8	121.5	25 29.3	+52.8	122.3	24 24.5	+53.7	123.1
6	29 24.3	49.4	119.0	28 25.2	50.6	120.0	27 24.5	51.6	120.9	26 22.1	52.6	121.8	25 18.2	53.5	122.6
7	30 13.7	49.2	118.4	29 15.8	50.4	119.4	28 16.1	51.5	120.3	27 14.7	52.5	121.2	26 11.7	53.5	122.1
8	31 02.9	49.0	117.7	30 06.2	50.2	118.7	29 07.6	51.3	119.7	28 07.2	52.4	120.7	27 05.2	53.3	121.6
9	31 51.9	48.8	117.0	30 56.4	50.0	118.1	29 58.9	51.2	119.1	28 59.6	52.2	120.1	27 58.5	53.3	121.0
10	32 40.7	+48.5	116.3	31 46.4	+49.8	117.5	30 50.1	+51.0	118.5	29 51.8	+52.1	119.6	28 51.8	+53.1	120.5
11	33 29.2	48.3	115.6	32 36.2	49.6	116.8	31 41.1	50.8	117.9	30 43.9	52.0	119.0	29 44.9	52.9	120.0
12	34 17.5	48.1	114.9	33 25.8	49.4	116.1	32 31.9	50.6	117.3	31 35.9	51.7	118.4	30 37.8	52.9	119.4
13	35 05.6	47.8	114.2	34 15.2	49.2	115.4	33 22.5	50.5	116.6	32 27.6	51.7	117.8	31 30.7	52.7	118.9
14	35 53.4	47.5	113.4	35 04.4	48.9	114.7	34 13.0	50.2	116.0	33 19.3	51.4	117.2	32 23.4	52.5	118.3
15	36 40.9	+47.2	112.7	35 53.3	+48.7	114.0	35 03.2	+50.0	115.3	34 10.7	+51.2	116.6	33 15.9	+52.4	117.8
16	37 28.1	46.9	111.9	36 42.0	48.3	113.3	35 53.2	49.7	114.6	35 01.9	51.0	115.9	34 08.3	52.2	117.2
17	38 15.0	46.6	111.1	37 30.3	48.1	112.6	36 42.9	49.6	114.0	35 52.9	50.9	115.3	35 00.5	52.0	116.6
18	39 01.6	46.2	110.3	38 18.4	47.8	111.8	37 32.5	49.2	113.2	36 43.8	50.6	114.6	35 52.5	51.8	116.0
19	39 47.8	45.9	109.5	39 06.2	47.5	111.0	38 21.7	49.0	112.5	37 34.4	50.3	114.0	36 44.3	51.6	115.3
20	40 33.7	+45.5	108.6	39 53.7	+47.2	110.2	39 10.7	+48.7	111.8	38 24.7	+50.1	113.3	37 35.9	+51.5	114.7
21	41 19.2	45.1	107.8	40 40.9	46.8	109.4	39 59.4	48.1	111.0	39 14.8	49.9	112.6	38 27.4	51.2	114.0
22	42 04.3	44.7	106.9	41 27.7	46.4	108.6	40 47.8	48.1	110.2	40 04.7	49.6	111.8	39 18.6	50.9	113.4
23	42 49.0	44.2	106.0	42 14.1	46.1	107.7	41 35.9	47.7	109.5	40 54.3	49.2	111.1	40 09.5	50.7	112.7
24	43 33.2	43.8	105.1	43 00.2	45.7	106.9	42 23.6	47.4	108.6	41 43.5	49.0	110.3	41 00.2	50.5	112.0
25	44 17.0	+43.3	104.1	43 45.8	+45.3	106.0	43 11.0	+47.0	107.8	42 32.5	+48.7	109.6	41 50.7	+50.1	111.3
26	45 00.3	42.8	103.1	44 31.1	44.7	105.1	43 58.0	46.6	106.9	43 21.2	48.3	108.8	42 40.8	49.9	110.5
27	45 43.1	42.3	102.1	45 15.8	44.3	104.1	44 44.6	46.2	106.1	44 09.5	47.9	107.9	43 30.7	49.6	109.8
28	46 25.4	41.7	101.1	46 00.1	43.8	103.2	45 30.8	45.7	105.2	44 57.4	47.6	107.1	44 20.3	49.2	109.0
29	47 07.1	41.1	100.1	46 43.9	43.3	102.2	46 16.5	45.3	104.2	45 45.0	47.2	106.2	45 09.5	48.9	108.2

40°			42°			44°			46°			48°			Dec.
Hc	d	Z	Hc	d	Z	Hc	d	Z	Hc	d	Z	Hc	d	Z	
29 29.9	−44.4	118.3	28 32.1	−45.9	119.3	27 32.5	−47.2	120.2	26 31.2	−48.3	121.1	25 28.5	−49.5	121.9	0
28 45.5	44.7	119.1	27 46.2	46.0	120.0	26 45.3	47.3	120.9	25 42.9	48.5	121.8	24 39.0	49.6	122.6	1
28 00.8	45.0	119.9	27 00.2	46.3	120.8	25 58.0	47.5	121.6	24 54.4	48.7	122.4	23 49.4	49.8	123.2	2
27 15.8	45.2	120.6	26 13.9	46.4	121.5	25 10.5	47.7	122.3	24 05.7	48.8	123.1	22 59.6	49.9	123.8	3
26 30.6	45.4	121.4	25 27.5	46.7	122.2	24 22.8	47.8	123.0	23 16.9	49.0	123.7	22 09.7	50.0	124.4	4
25 45.2	−45.6	122.1	24 40.8	−46.9	122.9	23 35.0	−48.0	123.6	22 27.9	−49.1	124.3	21 19.7	−50.2	125.0	5
24 59.6	45.8	122.8	23 53.9	47.0	123.6	22 47.0	48.2	124.3	21 38.8	49.3	124.9	20 29.5	50.3	125.6	6
24 13.8	46.0	123.5	23 06.9	47.2	124.2	21 58.8	48.3	124.9	20 49.5	49.4	125.6	19 39.2	50.4	126.2	7
23 27.8	46.2	124.2	22 19.7	47.4	124.9	21 10.5	48.5	125.6	20 00.1	49.5	126.2	18 48.8	50.5	126.7	8
22 41.6	46.4	124.9	21 32.3	47.5	125.6	20 22.0	48.6	126.2	19 10.6	49.6	126.8	17 58.3	50.5	127.3	9
21 55.2	−46.6	125.6	20 44.8	−47.7	126.2	19 33.4	−48.8	126.8	18 21.0	−49.7	127.4	17 07.8	−50.7	127.9	10
21 08.6	46.7	126.3	19 57.1	47.8	126.9	18 44.6	48.8	127.4	17 31.3	49.9	127.9	16 17.1	50.8	128.4	11
20 21.9	46.9	126.9	19 09.3	47.9	127.5	17 55.8	49.0	128.0	16 41.4	49.9	128.5	15 26.3	50.9	129.0	12
19 35.0	47.0	127.6	18 21.4	48.1	128.1	17 06.8	49.1	128.6	15 51.5	50.0	129.1	14 35.4	50.9	129.5	13
18 48.0	47.1	128.3	17 33.3	48.2	128.8	16 17.7	49.1	129.2	15 01.5	50.1	129.7	13 44.5	51.0	130.1	14
18 00.9	−47.3	128.9	16 45.1	−48.3	129.4	15 28.6	−49.3	129.8	14 11.4	−50.2	130.3	12 53.5	−51.1	130.6	15
17 13.6	47.4	129.6	15 56.8	48.4	130.0	14 39.3	49.4	130.4	13 21.2	50.3	130.8	12 02.4	51.1	131.2	16
16 26.2	47.5	130.2	15 08.4	48.5	130.6	13 49.9	49.4	131.0	12 30.9	50.3	131.4	11 11.3	51.2	131.7	17
15 38.7	47.6	130.8	14 19.9	48.6	131.2	13 00.5	49.5	131.6	11 40.6	50.4	131.9	10 20.1	51.2	132.2	18
14 51.1	47.8	131.5	13 31.3	48.7	131.8	12 11.0	49.6	132.2	10 50.2	50.5	132.5	9 28.9	51.3	132.7	19
14 03.3	−47.8	132.1	12 42.6	−48.7	132.4	11 21.4	−49.7	132.8	9 59.7	−50.5	133.0	8 37.6	−51.3	133.3	20
13 15.5	47.9	132.7	11 53.9	48.9	133.0	10 31.7	49.7	133.3	9 09.2	50.6	133.6	7 46.3	51.4	133.8	21
12 27.6	48.0	133.3	11 05.0	48.9	133.6	9 42.0	49.8	133.9	8 18.6	50.6	134.1	6 54.9	51.4	134.3	22
11 39.6	48.1	133.9	10 16.1	49.0	134.2	8 52.2	49.8	134.5	7 28.0	50.6	134.7	6 03.5	51.4	134.8	23
10 51.5	48.1	134.6	9 27.1	49.0	134.8	8 02.4	49.9	135.0	6 37.4	50.7	135.2	5 12.1	51.5	135.4	24
10 03.4	−48.2	135.2	8 38.1	−49.1	135.4	7 12.5	−49.9	135.6	5 46.7	−50.7	135.7	4 20.6	−51.5	135.9	25
9 15.2	48.3	135.8	7 49.0	49.2	136.0	6 22.6	49.9	136.1	4 56.0	50.8	136.3	3 29.2	51.5	136.4	26
8 26.9	48.3	136.4	6 59.9	49.2	136.6	5 32.7	50.0	136.7	4 05.2	50.7	136.8	2 37.7	51.5	136.9	27
7 38.6	48.4	137.0	6 10.7	49.2	137.1	4 42.7	50.0	137.3	3 14.5	50.8	137.4	1 46.2	51.5	137.4	28
6 50.2	48.4	137.6	5 21.5	49.2	137.7	3 52.7	50.0	137.8	2 23.7	50.8	137.9	0 54.7	51.6	137.9	29

50°			52°			54°			56°			58°			Dec.
Hc	d	Z	Hc	d	Z	Hc	d	Z	Hc	d	Z	Hc	d	Z	
24 24.3	−50.6	122.7	23 18.7	−51.5	123.5	22 11.9	−52.4	124.2	21 04.0	−53.4	124.8	19 54.9	−54.2	125.4	0
23 33.7	50.6	123.3	22 27.2	51.7	124.0	21 19.5	52.6	124.7	20 10.6	53.4	125.3	19 00.7	54.2	125.9	1
22 43.1	50.8	123.9	21 35.5	51.7	124.6	20 26.9	52.7	125.2	19 17.2	53.5	125.8	18 06.5	54.3	126.3	2
21 52.3	51.0	124.5	20 43.8	51.9	125.1	19 34.2	52.7	125.7	18 23.7	53.6	126.3	17 12.2	54.3	126.8	3
21 01.3	51.0	125.0	19 51.9	52.0	125.7	18 41.5	52.9	126.2	17 30.1	53.6	126.7	16 17.9	54.4	127.2	4
20 10.3	−51.1	125.6	18 59.9	−52.0	126.2	17 48.6	−52.9	126.7	16 36.5	−53.7	127.2	15 23.5	−54.4	127.7	5
19 19.2	51.3	126.2	18 07.9	52.1	126.7	16 55.7	52.9	127.2	15 42.8	53.8	127.7	14 29.1	54.5	128.1	6
18 27.9	51.3	126.8	17 15.8	52.2	127.2	16 02.8	53.1	127.7	14 49.0	53.8	128.1	13 34.6	54.6	128.5	7
17 36.6	51.4	127.3	16 23.6	52.3	127.7	15 09.7	53.1	128.2	13 55.2	53.9	128.6	12 40.0	54.6	129.0	8
16 45.2	51.5	127.8	15 31.3	52.4	128.3	14 16.6	53.1	128.7	13 01.3	53.9	129.1	11 45.4	54.6	129.4	9
15 53.7	−51.6	128.3	14 38.9	−52.4	128.8	13 23.5	−53.2	129.2	12 07.4	−53.9	129.5	10 50.8	−54.6	129.8	10
15 02.1	51.6	128.8	13 46.5	52.5	129.3	12 30.3	53.3	129.6	11 13.5	54.0	129.9	9 56.2	54.7	130.2	11
14 10.5	51.7	129.4	12 54.0	52.5	129.8	11 37.0	53.3	130.1	10 19.5	54.1	130.4	9 01.5	54.7	130.7	12
13 18.8	51.8	129.9	12 01.5	52.6	130.3	10 43.7	53.4	130.6	9 25.4	54.0	130.8	8 06.8	54.8	131.1	13
12 27.0	51.9	130.4	11 08.9	52.6	130.7	9 50.3	53.3	131.0	8 31.4	54.1	131.3	7 12.0	54.7	131.5	14
11 35.1	−51.9	130.9	10 16.3	−52.7	131.2	8 57.0	−53.5	131.5	7 37.3	−54.1	131.7	6 17.3	−54.8	131.9	15
10 43.2	51.9	131.5	9 23.6	52.7	131.7	8 03.5	53.4	132.0	6 43.2	54.2	132.1	5 22.5	54.8	132.3	16
9 51.3	52.0	132.0	8 30.9	52.8	132.2	7 10.1	53.5	132.4	5 49.0	54.2	132.6	4 27.7	54.8	132.7	17
8 59.3	52.0	132.5	7 38.1	52.8	132.7	6 16.6	53.5	132.9	4 54.8	54.1	133.0	3 32.9	54.8	133.1	18
8 07.3	52.1	133.0	6 45.3	52.8	133.2	5 23.1	53.5	133.3	4 00.7	54.2	133.4	2 38.1	54.8	133.5	19
7 15.2	−52.1	133.5	5 52.5	−52.8	133.6	4 29.6	−53.6	133.8	3 06.5	−54.2	133.9	1 43.3	−54.8	133.9	20
6 23.1	52.1	134.0	4 59.7	52.9	134.1	3 36.0	53.5	134.2	2 12.3	54.2	134.3	0 48.4	−54.8	134.3	21
5 31.0	52.2	134.5	4 06.8	52.9	134.6	2 42.5	53.6	134.7	1 18.1	54.3	134.7	0 06.4	+54.8	45.3	22
4 38.8	52.2	135.0	3 13.9	52.9	135.1	1 48.9	53.6	135.1	0 23.8	−54.2	135.2	1 01.2	54.9	44.9	23
3 46.6	52.2	135.5	2 21.0	52.9	135.5	0 55.3	53.5	135.6	0 30.4	+54.2	44.4	1 56.1	54.8	44.4	24
2 54.4	−52.2	136.0	1 28.1	−52.9	136.0	0 01.8	−53.6	136.0	1 24.6	+54.2	44.0	2 50.9	+54.8	44.0	25
2 02.2	52.2	136.5	0 35.2	−52.9	136.5	0 51.8	+53.6	43.5	2 18.8	54.2	43.6	3 45.7	54.8	43.6	26
1 10.0	52.2	136.9	0 17.7	+52.9	43.0	1 45.4	53.5	43.1	3 13.0	54.2	43.1	4 40.5	54.8	43.2	27
0 17.8	−52.2	137.4	1 10.6	52.9	42.6	2 38.9	53.6	42.6	4 07.2	54.2	42.7	5 35.3	54.8	42.8	28
0 34.4	+52.2	42.1	2 03.5	52.9	42.1	3 32.5	53.5	42.2	5 01.4	54.1	42.3	6 30.1	54.7	42.4	29

Dec.	0° Hc	d	Z	2° Hc	d	Z	4° Hc	d	Z	6° Hc	d	Z	8° Hc	d	Z
°	° ′	′	°	° ′	′	°	° ′	′	°	° ′	′	°	° ′	′	°
0	38 00.0	− 0.4	90.0	37 58.4	+ 2.2	91.6	37 53.5	+ 4.9	93.1	37 45.3	+ 7.5	94.7	37 33.9	+10.2	96.2
1	37 59.6	1.2	88.7	38 00.6	1.4	90.3	37 58.4	4.0	91.9	37 52.8	6.8	93.4	37 44.1	9.3	95.0
2	37 58.4	2.1	87.5	38 02.0	+ 0.7	89.0	38 02.4	3.3	90.6	37 59.6	5.9	92.2	37 53.4	8.6	93.7
3	37 56.3	2.8	86.2	38 02.7	− 0.3	87.8	38 05.7	2.5	89.3	38 05.5	5.1	90.9	38 02.0	7.7	92.5
4	37 53.5	3.7	84.9	38 02.4	1.0	86.5	38 08.2	1.6	88.1	38 10.6	4.3	89.6	38 09.7	7.0	91.2
5	37 49.8	− 4.5	83.7	38 01.4	− 1.8	85.2	38 09.8	+ 0.8	86.8	38 14.9	+ 3.5	88.4	38 16.7	+ 6.1	89.9
6	37 45.3	5.3	82.4	37 59.6	2.7	83.9	38 10.6	0.0	85.5	38 18.4	2.6	87.1	38 22.8	5.3	88.7
7	37 40.0	6.1	81.1	37 56.9	3.5	82.7	38 10.6	− 0.9	84.2	38 21.0	1.8	85.8	38 28.1	4.5	87.4
8	37 33.9	7.2	79.9	37 53.4	4.3	81.4	38 09.7	1.6	83.0	38 22.8	1.0	84.5	38 32.6	3.6	86.1
9	37 27.1	7.7	78.6	37 49.1	5.0	80.2	38 08.1	2.5	81.7	38 23.8	+ 0.2	83.3	38 36.2	2.9	84.8
10	37 19.4	− 8.5	77.4	37 44.1	− 5.9	78.9	38 05.6	− 3.3	80.4	38 24.0	− 0.7	82.0	38 39.1	+ 1.9	83.6
11	37 10.9	9.2	76.1	37 38.2	6.7	77.6	38 02.3	4.1	79.2	38 23.3	1.5	80.7	38 41.0	1.2	82.3
12	37 01.7	10.0	74.9	37 31.5	7.5	76.4	37 58.2	5.0	77.9	38 21.8	2.4	79.4	38 42.2	+ 0.3	81.0
13	36 51.7	10.8	73.7	37 24.0	8.3	75.1	37 53.2	5.7	76.6	38 19.4	3.1	78.2	38 42.5	− 0.6	79.7
14	36 40.9	11.5	72.4	37 15.7	9.1	73.9	37 47.5	6.5	75.4	38 16.3	4.0	76.9	38 41.9	1.3	78.4
15	36 29.4	−12.3	71.2	37 06.6	− 9.8	72.6	37 41.0	− 7.4	74.1	38 12.3	− 4.8	75.6	38 40.6	− 2.3	77.2
16	36 17.1	13.0	70.0	36 56.8	10.6	71.4	37 33.6	8.1	72.9	38 07.5	5.6	74.3	38 38.3	3.0	75.9
17	36 04.1	13.7	68.8	36 46.2	11.3	70.2	37 25.5	8.9	71.6	38 01.9	6.4	73.1	38 35.3	3.9	74.6
18	35 50.4	14.4	67.6	36 34.9	12.1	69.0	37 16.6	9.7	70.4	37 55.5	7.3	71.8	38 31.4	4.7	73.3
19	35 36.0	15.2	66.4	36 22.8	12.9	67.7	37 06.9	10.5	69.1	37 48.2	8.0	70.6	38 26.7	5.5	72.0
20	35 20.8	−15.8	65.2	36 09.9	−13.5	66.5	36 56.4	−11.2	67.9	37 40.2	− 8.8	69.3	38 21.2	− 6.4	70.8
21	35 05.0	16.5	64.0	35 56.4	14.3	65.3	36 45.2	12.0	66.7	37 31.4	9.6	68.1	38 14.8	7.2	69.5
22	34 48.5	17.2	62.9	35 42.1	15.0	64.1	36 33.2	12.7	65.4	37 21.8	10.4	66.8	38 07.6	7.9	68.2
23	34 31.3	17.8	61.7	35 27.1	15.7	62.9	36 20.5	13.5	64.2	37 11.4	11.2	65.6	37 59.7	8.8	67.0
24	34 13.5	18.5	60.5	35 11.4	16.4	61.7	36 07.0	14.2	63.0	37 00.2	11.9	64.3	37 50.9	9.6	65.7
25	33 55.0	−19.2	59.4	34 55.0	−17.0	60.6	35 52.8	−14.8	61.8	36 48.3	−12.6	63.1	37 41.3	−10.4	64.5
26	33 35.8	19.7	58.2	34 38.0	17.7	59.4	35 38.0	15.6	60.6	36 35.7	13.5	61.9	37 30.9	11.1	63.2
27	33 16.1	20.4	57.1	34 20.3	18.4	58.2	35 22.4	16.3	59.4	36 22.2	14.1	60.7	37 19.8	11.9	62.0
28	32 55.7	20.9	56.0	34 01.9	19.0	57.1	35 06.1	17.0	58.3	36 08.1	14.8	59.5	37 07.9	12.7	60.8
29	32 34.8	21.6	54.9	33 42.9	19.6	56.0	34 49.1	17.6	57.1	35 53.3	15.6	58.3	36 55.2	13.4	59.6

Dec.	10° Hc	d	Z	12° Hc	d	Z	14° Hc	d	Z	16° Hc	d	Z	18° Hc	d	Z
°	° ′	′	°	° ′	′	°	° ′	′	°	° ′	′	°	° ′	′	°
0	37 19.4	+12.7	97.7	37 01.7	+15.2	99.2	36 40.9	+17.8	100.7	36 17.1	+20.2	102.2	35 50.4	+22.6	103.6
1	37 32.1	12.0	96.5	37 16.9	14.6	98.0	36 58.7	17.0	99.5	36 37.3	19.5	101.0	36 13.0	21.9	102.4
2	37 44.1	11.1	95.3	37 31.5	13.7	96.8	37 15.7	16.3	98.3	36 56.8	18.8	99.8	36 34.9	21.2	101.3
3	37 55.2	10.4	94.0	37 45.2	13.0	95.6	37 32.0	15.5	97.1	37 15.6	18.0	98.6	36 56.1	20.5	100.1
4	38 05.6	9.6	92.8	37 58.2	12.2	94.3	37 47.5	14.8	95.9	37 33.6	17.3	97.4	37 16.6	19.8	98.9
5	38 15.2	+ 8.8	91.5	38 10.4	+11.4	93.1	38 02.3	+14.0	94.6	37 50.9	+16.6	96.2	37 36.4	+19.1	97.7
6	38 24.0	7.9	90.2	38 21.8	10.6	91.8	38 16.3	13.2	93.4	38 07.5	15.8	95.0	37 55.5	18.3	96.5
7	38 31.9	7.2	89.0	38 32.4	9.8	90.6	38 29.5	12.4	92.2	38 23.3	15.0	93.8	38 13.8	17.6	95.3
8	38 39.1	6.3	87.7	38 42.2	9.0	89.3	38 41.9	11.7	90.9	38 38.3	14.3	92.5	38 31.4	16.9	94.1
9	38 45.4	5.5	86.4	38 51.2	8.1	88.0	38 53.6	10.8	89.7	38 52.6	13.4	91.3	38 48.3	16.0	92.9
10	38 50.9	+ 4.6	85.2	38 59.3	+ 7.3	86.8	39 04.4	+10.0	88.4	39 06.0	+12.7	90.0	39 04.3	+15.3	91.6
11	38 55.5	3.8	83.9	39 06.6	6.5	85.3	39 14.4	9.1	87.1	39 18.7	11.8	88.8	39 19.6	14.4	90.4
12	38 59.3	3.0	82.6	39 13.1	5.6	84.2	39 23.5	8.3	85.8	39 30.5	11.0	87.5	39 34.0	13.7	89.1
13	39 02.3	2.1	81.3	39 18.7	4.8	82.9	39 31.8	7.5	84.6	39 41.5	10.1	86.2	39 47.7	12.8	87.9
14	39 04.4	1.2	80.0	39 23.5	3.9	81.6	39 39.3	6.6	83.3	39 51.6	9.3	84.9	40 00.5	11.9	86.6
15	39 05.6	+ 0.4	78.7	39 27.4	+ 3.1	80.3	39 45.9	+ 5.7	82.0	40 00.9	+ 8.4	83.6	40 12.4	+11.2	85.3
16	39 06.0	− 0.4	77.4	39 30.5	2.2	79.0	39 51.6	4.9	80.7	40 09.3	7.6	82.3	40 23.6	10.2	84.0
17	39 05.6	1.3	76.2	39 32.7	1.3	77.8	39 56.5	4.0	79.4	40 16.9	6.7	81.0	40 33.8	9.4	82.7
18	39 04.3	2.1	74.9	39 34.0	+ 0.5	76.5	40 00.5	3.1	78.1	40 23.6	5.8	79.7	40 43.2	8.5	81.4
19	39 02.2	3.0	73.6	39 34.5	− 0.4	75.2	40 03.6	2.2	76.8	40 29.4	4.9	78.4	40 51.7	7.6	80.1
20	38 59.2	− 3.9	72.3	39 34.1	− 1.2	73.9	40 05.8	+ 1.4	75.5	40 34.3	+ 4.0	77.1	40 59.3	+ 6.7	78.8
21	38 55.3	4.6	71.0	39 32.9	2.2	72.6	40 07.2	+ 0.5	74.2	40 38.3	3.1	75.8	41 06.0	5.8	77.5
22	38 50.7	5.5	69.7	39 30.7	3.0	71.3	40 07.7	− 0.4	72.9	40 41.4	2.3	74.5	41 11.8	4.9	76.2
23	38 45.2	6.4	68.5	39 27.7	3.8	70.0	40 07.3	1.3	71.5	40 43.7	1.3	73.2	41 16.7	4.0	74.8
24	38 38.8	7.2	67.2	39 23.9	4.7	68.7	40 06.0	2.2	70.2	40 45.0	+ 0.4	71.9	41 20.7	3.1	73.5
25	38 31.6	− 7.9	65.9	39 19.2	− 5.5	67.4	40 03.8	− 3.0	68.9	40 45.4	− 0.5	70.5	41 23.8	+ 2.1	72.2
26	38 23.7	8.9	64.6	39 13.7	6.4	66.1	40 00.8	3.9	67.6	40 44.9	1.3	69.2	41 25.9	1.3	70.9
27	38 14.8	9.6	63.4	39 07.3	7.3	64.8	39 56.9	4.8	66.3	40 43.6	2.3	67.9	41 27.2	+ 0.3	69.5
28	38 05.2	10.4	62.1	39 00.0	8.0	63.5	39 52.1	5.7	65.0	40 41.3	3.2	66.6	41 27.5	− 0.7	68.2
29	37 54.8	11.2	60.9	38 52.0	8.9	62.3	39 46.4	6.5	63.7	40 38.1	4.1	65.3	41 26.8	1.5	66.8

0°			2°			4°			6°			8°			Dec.
Hc	d	Z	Hc	d	Z	Hc	d	Z	Hc	d	Z	Hc	d	Z	
38 00.0 - 0.4 90.0			37 58.4 - 3.1 91.6			37 53.5 - 5.7 93.1			37 45.3 - 8.3 94.7			37 33.9 - 10.9 96.2			0
37 59.6 1.2 91.3			37 55.3 3.9 92.8			37 47.8 6.6 94.4			37 37.0 9.1 95.9			37 23.0 11.7 97.4			1
37 58.4 2.1 92.5			37 51.4 4.7 94.1			37 41.2 7.3 95.6			37 27.9 9.9 97.2			37 11.3 12.4 98.7			2
37 56.3 2.8 93.8			37 46.7 5.5 95.4			37 33.9 8.1 96.9			37 18.0 10.7 98.4			36 58.9 13.2 99.9			3
37 53.5 3.7 95.1			37 41.2 6.2 96.6			37 25.8 8.9 98.1			37 07.3 11.5 99.6			36 45.7 14.0 101.1			4
37 49.8 - 4.5 96.3			37 35.0 - 7.1 97.9			37 16.9 - 9.6 99.4			36 55.8 - 12.2 100.9			36 31.7 - 14.7 102.3			5
37 45.3 5.3 97.6			37 27.9 7.9 99.1			37 07.3 10.5 100.6			36 43.6 12.9 102.1			36 17.0 15.4 103.5			6
37 40.0 6.1 98.9			37 20.0 8.7 100.4			36 56.8 11.1 101.9			36 30.7 13.7 103.3			36 01.6 16.1 104.7			7
37 33.9 6.8 100.1			37 11.3 9.4 101.6			36 45.7 12.0 103.1			36 17.0 14.4 104.5			35 45.5 16.8 105.9			8
37 27.1 7.7 101.4			37 01.9 10.2 102.9			36 33.7 12.7 104.3			36 02.6 15.1 105.7			35 28.7 17.5 107.1			9
37 19.4 - 8.5 102.6			36 51.7 - 11.0 104.1			36 21.0 - 13.4 105.5			35 47.5 - 15.8 106.9			35 11.2 - 18.2 108.3			10
37 10.9 9.2 103.9			36 40.7 11.7 105.3			36 07.6 14.2 106.7			35 31.7 16.6 108.1			34 53.0 18.8 109.4			11
37 01.7 10.0 105.1			36 29.0 12.5 106.5			35 53.4 14.8 107.9			35 15.1 17.2 109.3			34 34.2 19.5 110.6			12
36 51.7 10.8 106.3			36 16.5 13.2 107.7			35 38.6 15.6 109.1			34 57.9 17.8 110.5			34 14.7 20.1 111.7			13
36 40.9 11.5 107.6			36 03.3 13.9 109.0			35 23.0 16.3 110.3			34 40.1 18.6 111.6			33 54.6 20.7 112.9			14
36 29.4 - 12.3 108.8			35 49.4 - 14.6 110.2			35 06.7 - 16.9 111.5			34 21.5 - 19.2 112.8			33 33.9 - 21.4 114.0			15
36 17.1 13.0 110.0			35 34.8 15.4 111.4			34 49.8 17.6 112.7			34 02.3 19.8 113.9			33 12.5 21.9 115.1			16
36 04.1 13.7 111.2			35 19.4 16.0 112.5			34 32.2 18.9 113.8			33 42.5 20.4 115.1			32 50.6 22.5 116.2			17
35 50.4 14.4 112.4			35 03.4 16.7 113.7			34 13.9 18.9 115.0			33 22.1 21.0 116.2			32 28.1 23.1 117.3			18
35 36.0 15.2 113.6			34 46.7 17.4 114.9			33 55.0 19.5 116.1			33 01.1 21.7 117.3			32 05.0 23.7 118.4			19
35 20.8 - 15.8 114.8			34 29.3 - 18.0 116.1			33 35.5 - 20.2 117.3			32 39.4 - 22.2 118.4			31 41.3 - 24.2 119.5			20
35 05.0 16.5 116.0			34 11.3 18.7 117.2			33 15.3 20.7 118.4			32 17.2 22.8 119.5			31 17.1 24.7 120.6			21
34 48.5 17.2 117.1			33 52.6 19.3 118.4			32 54.6 21.4 119.5			31 54.4 23.3 120.6			30 52.4 25.2 121.7			22
34 31.3 17.8 118.3			33 33.3 19.9 119.5			32 33.2 21.9 120.6			31 31.1 23.9 121.7			30 27.2 25.8 122.7			23
34 13.5 18.5 119.5			33 13.4 20.6 120.6			32 11.3 22.6 121.7			31 07.2 24.4 122.8			30 01.4 26.2 123.8			24
33 55.0 - 19.2 120.6			32 52.8 - 21.1 121.7			31 48.7 - 23.0 122.8			30 42.8 - 24.9 123.8			29 35.2 - 26.7 124.8			25
33 35.8 19.7 121.8			32 31.7 21.7 122.9			31 25.7 23.6 123.9			30 17.9 25.4 124.9			29 08.5 27.2 125.8			26
33 16.1 20.4 122.9			32 10.0 22.3 124.0			31 02.1 24.2 125.0			29 52.5 26.0 125.9			28 41.3 27.7 126.8			27
32 55.7 20.9 124.0			31 47.7 22.8 125.1			30 37.9 24.6 126.0			29 26.5 26.4 127.0			28 13.6 28.0 127.8			28
32 34.8 21.6 125.1			31 24.9 23.4 126.1			30 13.3 25.2 127.1			29 00.1 26.8 128.0			27 45.6 28.6 128.8			29

10°			12°			14°			16°			18°			Dec.
Hc	d	Z	Hc	d	Z	Hc	d	Z	Hc	d	Z	Hc	d	Z	
37 19.4 - 13.5 97.7			37 01.7 - 16.0 99.2			36 40.9 - 18.4 100.7			36 17.1 - 20.8 102.2			35 50.4 - 23.2 103.6			0
37 05.9 14.2 98.9			36 45.7 16.7 100.4			36 22.5 19.2 101.9			35 56.3 21.5 103.3			35 27.2 23.8 104.7			1
36 51.7 15.0 100.2			36 29.0 17.4 101.6			36 03.3 19.8 103.1			35 34.8 22.2 104.5			35 03.4 24.4 105.8			2
36 36.7 15.7 101.4			36 11.6 18.2 102.8			35 43.5 20.5 104.2			35 12.6 22.8 105.6			34 39.0 25.1 106.9			3
36 21.0 16.4 102.6			35 53.4 18.8 104.0			35 23.0 21.2 105.4			34 49.8 23.4 106.7			34 13.9 25.6 108.0			4
36 04.6 - 17.1 103.8			35 34.6 - 19.5 105.2			35 01.8 - 21.7 106.5			34 26.4 - 24.1 107.9			33 48.3 - 26.2 109.1			5
35 47.5 17.8 105.0			35 15.1 20.1 106.3			34 40.1 22.5 107.7			34 02.3 24.6 109.0			33 22.1 26.7 110.2			6
35 29.7 18.5 106.1			34 55.0 20.8 107.5			34 17.6 23.0 108.8			33 37.7 25.2 110.1			32 55.4 27.3 111.3			7
35 11.2 19.2 107.3			34 34.2 21.4 108.6			33 54.6 23.6 109.9			33 12.5 25.7 111.1			32 28.1 27.9 112.3			8
34 52.0 19.8 108.4			34 12.8 22.1 109.8			33 31.0 24.2 111.0			32 46.8 26.3 112.2			32 00.2 28.3 113.4			9
34 32.2 - 20.4 109.6			33 50.7 - 22.6 110.9			33 06.8 - 24.8 112.1			32 20.5 - 26.9 113.3			31 31.9 - 28.8 114.4			10
34 11.8 20.7 110.7			33 28.1 23.3 112.0			32 42.0 25.3 113.2			31 53.6 27.3 114.3			31 03.1 29.3 115.5			11
33 50.7 21.7 111.9			33 04.8 23.8 113.1			32 16.7 25.9 114.3			31 26.3 27.9 115.4			30 33.8 29.8 116.5			12
33 29.0 22.2 113.0			32 41.0 24.3 114.2			31 50.8 26.4 115.3			30 58.4 28.4 116.4			30 04.0 30.2 117.5			13
33 06.8 22.9 114.1			32 16.7 25.0 115.3			31 24.4 26.9 116.4			30 30.0 28.8 117.5			29 33.8 30.7 118.5			14
32 43.9 - 23.4 115.2			31 51.7 - 25.4 116.3			30 57.5 - 27.5 117.4			30 01.2 - 29.3 118.5			29 03.1 - 31.1 119.5			15
32 20.5 24.0 116.3			31 26.3 26.0 117.4			30 30.0 27.9 118.5			29 31.9 29.7 119.5			28 32.0 31.5 120.4			16
31 56.5 24.6 117.4			31 00.3 26.5 118.5			30 02.1 28.3 119.5			29 02.2 30.2 120.5			28 00.5 31.9 121.4			17
31 31.9 25.1 118.4			30 33.8 27.0 119.5			29 33.8 28.9 120.5			28 32.0 30.6 121.5			27 28.6 32.3 122.4			18
31 06.8 25.6 119.5			30 06.8 27.5 120.5			29 04.9 29.2 121.5			28 01.4 31.0 122.4			26 56.3 32.7 123.3			19
30 41.2 - 26.1 120.6			29 39.3 - 27.9 121.6			28 35.7 - 29.7 122.5			27 30.4 - 31.4 123.4			26 23.6 - 33.1 124.2			20
30 15.1 26.6 121.6			29 11.4 28.4 122.6			28 06.0 30.2 123.5			26 59.0 31.8 124.4			25 50.5 33.4 125.2			21
29 48.5 27.0 122.6			28 43.0 28.9 123.6			27 35.8 30.5 124.5			26 27.2 32.2 125.3			25 17.1 33.7 126.1			22
29 21.5 27.6 123.7			28 14.1 29.2 124.6			27 05.3 31.0 125.4			25 55.0 32.5 126.2			24 43.4 34.1 127.0			23
28 53.9 28.0 124.7			27 44.9 29.7 125.6			26 34.3 31.3 126.4			25 22.5 32.9 127.2			24 09.3 34.3 127.9			24
28 25.9 - 28.4 125.7			27 15.2 - 30.1 126.5			26 03.0 - 31.7 127.4			24 49.6 - 33.2 128.1			23 35.0 - 34.7 128.8			25
27 57.5 28.9 126.7			26 45.1 30.5 127.5			25 31.3 32.0 128.3			24 16.4 33.6 129.0			23 00.3 35.0 129.7			26
27 28.6 29.3 127.7			26 14.6 30.9 128.5			24 59.3 32.4 129.2			23 42.8 33.8 129.9			22 25.3 35.3 130.6			27
26 59.3 29.7 128.7			25 43.7 31.2 129.4			24 26.9 32.7 130.2			23 09.0 34.2 130.8			21 50.0 35.5 131.4			28
26 29.6 30.0 129.6			25 12.5 31.6 130.4			23 54.2 33.1 131.1			22 34.8 34.4 131.7			21 14.5 35.8 132.3			29

Dec.	20° Hc	d	Z	22° Hc	d	Z	24° Hc	d	Z	26° Hc	d	Z	28° Hc	d	Z
0	35 20.8	+24.9	105.0	34 48.5	+27.1	106.3	34 13.5	+29.2	107.6	33 35.8	+31.4	108.9	32 55.7	+33.4	110.1
1	35 45.7	24.2	103.8	35 15.6	26.5	105.2	34 42.7	28.7	106.6	34 07.2	30.8	107.9	33 29.1	32.8	109.1
2	36 09.9	23.6	102.7	35 42.1	25.8	104.1	35 11.4	28.1	105.5	34 38.0	30.2	106.8	34 01.9	32.3	108.1
3	36 33.5	22.9	101.6	36 07.9	25.3	103.0	35 39.5	27.5	104.4	35 08.2	29.8	105.8	34 34.2	31.9	107.1
4	36 56.4	22.3	100.4	36 33.2	24.6	101.9	36 07.0	26.9	103.3	35 38.0	29.1	104.7	35 06.1	31.3	106.1
5	37 18.7	+21.5	99.3	36 57.8	+24.0	100.7	36 33.9	+26.3	102.2	36 07.1	+28.6	103.6	35 37.4	+30.7	105.0
6	37 40.2	20.8	98.1	37 21.8	23.3	99.6	37 00.2	25.7	101.1	36 35.7	27.9	102.6	36 08.1	30.2	104.0
7	38 01.0	20.2	96.9	37 45.1	22.5	98.4	37 25.9	25.0	100.0	37 03.6	27.3	101.4	36 38.3	29.6	102.9
8	38 21.2	19.4	95.7	38 07.6	21.9	97.3	37 50.9	24.3	98.8	37 30.9	26.7	100.3	37 07.9	29.0	101.8
9	38 40.6	18.6	94.5	38 29.5	21.2	96.1	38 15.2	23.6	97.6	37 57.6	26.1	99.2	37 36.9	28.3	100.7
10	38 59.2	+17.8	93.3	38 50.7	+20.4	94.9	38 38.8	+22.9	96.5	38 23.7	+25.3	98.0	38 05.2	+27.8	99.6
11	39 17.0	17.1	92.0	39 11.1	19.6	93.7	39 01.7	22.2	95.3	38 49.0	24.7	96.9	38 33.0	27.0	98.5
12	39 34.1	16.3	90.8	39 30.7	18.9	92.4	39 23.9	21.4	94.1	39 13.7	23.9	95.7	39 00.0	26.4	97.3
13	39 50.4	15.4	89.5	39 49.6	18.1	91.2	39 45.3	20.7	92.9	39 37.6	23.2	94.5	39 26.4	25.7	96.2
14	40 05.8	14.7	88.3	40 07.7	17.3	90.0	40 06.0	19.9	91.6	40 00.8	22.5	93.3	39 52.1	25.0	95.0
15	40 20.5	+13.8	87.0	40 25.0	+16.4	88.7	40 25.9	+19.1	90.4	40 23.3	+21.6	92.1	40 17.1	+24.2	93.8
16	40 34.3	12.9	85.7	40 41.4	15.7	87.4	40 45.0	18.3	89.2	40 44.9	20.9	90.9	40 41.3	23.5	92.6
17	40 47.2	12.1	84.4	40 57.1	14.7	86.2	41 03.3	17.4	87.9	41 05.8	20.1	89.6	41 04.8	22.7	91.4
18	40 59.3	11.2	83.1	41 11.8	13.9	84.9	41 20.7	16.6	86.6	41 25.9	19.3	88.4	41 27.5	21.9	90.2
19	41 10.5	10.3	81.8	41 25.7	13.1	83.6	41 37.3	15.8	85.3	41 45.2	18.4	87.1	41 49.4	21.0	88.9
20	41 20.8	+9.5	80.5	41 38.8	+12.1	82.3	41 53.1	+14.8	84.1	42 03.6	+17.6	85.8	42 10.4	+20.3	87.7
21	41 30.3	8.5	79.2	41 50.9	11.3	81.0	42 07.9	14.0	82.7	42 21.2	16.7	84.6	42 30.7	19.4	86.4
22	41 38.8	7.6	77.9	42 02.2	10.3	79.6	42 21.9	13.0	81.4	42 37.9	15.8	83.3	42 50.1	18.5	85.1
23	41 46.4	6.7	76.6	42 12.5	9.4	78.3	42 34.9	12.2	80.1	42 53.7	14.8	81.9	43 08.6	17.6	83.8
24	41 53.1	5.7	75.2	42 21.9	8.4	77.0	42 47.1	11.2	78.8	43 08.5	14.0	80.6	43 26.2	16.7	82.5
25	41 58.8	+4.8	73.9	42 30.3	+7.6	75.6	42 58.3	+10.2	77.4	43 22.5	+13.0	79.3	43 42.9	+15.8	81.2
26	42 03.6	3.9	72.5	42 37.9	6.5	74.3	43 08.5	9.4	76.1	43 35.5	12.1	77.9	43 58.7	14.8	79.8
27	42 07.5	2.9	71.2	42 44.4	5.7	72.9	43 17.9	8.3	74.7	43 47.6	11.1	76.6	44 13.5	13.9	78.5
28	42 10.4	2.0	69.9	42 50.1	4.6	71.6	43 26.2	7.4	73.4	43 58.7	10.1	75.2	44 27.4	12.9	77.1
29	42 12.4	+1.1	68.5	42 54.7	3.7	70.2	43 33.6	6.3	72.0	44 08.8	9.1	73.8	44 40.3	11.9	75.7

Dec.	30° Hc	d	Z	32° Hc	d	Z	34° Hc	d	Z	36° Hc	d	Z	38° Hc	d	Z
0	32 13.2	+35.3	111.3	31 28.4	+37.1	112.5	30 41.5	+38.8	113.6	29 52.4	+40.5	114.7	29 01.3	+42.1	115.7
1	32 48.5	34.8	110.4	32 05.5	36.7	111.6	31 20.3	38.5	112.7	30 32.9	40.2	113.8	29 43.4	41.8	114.9
2	33 23.3	34.3	109.4	32 42.2	36.2	110.6	31 58.8	38.0	111.8	31 13.1	39.8	112.9	30 25.2	41.5	114.0
3	33 57.6	33.9	108.4	33 18.4	35.8	109.7	32 36.8	37.7	110.9	31 52.9	39.4	112.1	31 06.7	41.1	113.2
4	34 31.5	33.3	107.4	33 54.2	35.4	108.7	33 14.5	37.2	110.0	32 32.3	39.1	111.2	31 47.8	40.8	112.3
5	35 04.8	+32.9	106.4	34 29.6	+34.9	107.7	33 51.7	+36.9	109.0	33 11.4	+38.7	110.3	32 28.6	+40.4	111.5
6	35 37.7	32.3	105.4	35 04.5	34.4	106.7	34 28.6	36.3	108.1	33 50.1	38.2	109.4	33 09.0	40.1	110.6
7	36 10.0	31.8	104.3	35 38.9	33.8	105.7	35 04.9	35.9	107.1	34 28.3	37.8	108.4	33 49.1	39.7	109.7
8	36 41.8	31.2	103.3	36 12.7	33.4	104.7	35 40.8	35.4	106.1	35 06.1	37.4	107.5	34 28.8	39.2	108.8
9	37 13.0	30.6	102.2	36 46.1	32.8	103.7	36 16.2	34.9	105.1	35 43.5	36.9	106.5	35 08.0	38.8	107.9
10	37 43.6	+30.1	101.1	37 18.9	+32.3	102.6	36 51.1	+34.4	104.1	36 20.4	+36.5	105.5	35 46.8	+38.4	106.9
11	38 13.7	29.4	100.0	37 51.2	31.6	101.6	37 25.5	33.9	103.1	36 56.9	35.9	104.6	36 25.2	38.0	106.0
12	38 43.1	28.7	98.9	38 22.8	31.1	100.5	37 59.4	33.2	102.0	37 32.8	35.4	103.6	37 03.2	37.4	105.0
13	39 11.8	28.1	97.8	38 53.9	30.4	99.4	38 32.6	32.7	101.0	38 08.2	34.9	102.5	37 40.6	37.0	104.0
14	39 39.9	27.4	96.7	39 24.3	29.8	98.3	39 05.3	32.1	99.9	38 43.1	34.3	101.5	38 17.6	36.4	103.0
15	40 07.3	+26.7	95.5	39 54.1	+29.1	97.2	39 37.4	+31.5	98.8	39 17.4	+33.7	100.4	38 54.0	+35.9	102.0
16	40 34.0	26.0	94.3	40 23.2	28.5	96.0	40 08.9	30.8	97.7	39 51.1	33.1	99.4	39 29.9	35.3	101.0
17	41 00.0	25.3	93.1	40 51.7	27.7	94.9	40 39.7	30.2	96.6	40 24.2	32.5	98.3	40 05.2	34.8	99.9
18	41 25.3	24.5	91.9	41 19.4	27.0	93.7	41 09.9	29.5	95.4	40 56.7	31.9	97.2	40 40.0	34.1	98.9
19	41 49.8	23.7	90.7	41 46.4	26.3	92.5	41 39.3	28.8	94.3	41 28.6	31.2	96.0	41 14.1	33.6	97.8
20	42 13.5	+22.8	89.5	42 12.7	+25.5	91.3	42 08.1	+28.0	93.1	41 59.8	+30.4	94.9	41 47.7	+32.8	96.7
21	42 36.3	22.1	88.2	42 38.2	24.6	90.1	42 36.1	27.3	91.9	42 30.2	29.8	93.7	42 20.5	32.2	95.5
22	42 58.4	21.2	86.9	43 02.8	23.9	88.8	43 03.4	26.5	90.7	43 00.0	29.0	92.5	42 52.7	31.5	94.4
23	43 19.6	20.3	85.7	43 26.7	23.0	87.5	43 29.9	25.6	89.4	43 29.0	28.3	91.3	43 24.2	30.8	93.2
24	43 39.9	19.5	84.4	43 49.7	22.2	86.3	43 55.5	24.9	88.2	43 57.3	27.5	90.1	43 55.0	30.1	92.0
25	43 59.4	+18.5	83.1	44 11.9	+21.3	85.0	44 20.4	+24.0	86.9	44 24.8	+26.6	88.9	44 25.1	+29.2	90.8
26	44 17.9	17.7	81.7	44 33.2	20.4	83.7	44 44.4	23.1	85.6	44 51.4	25.8	87.6	44 54.3	28.5	89.6
27	44 35.6	16.6	80.4	44 53.6	19.4	82.3	45 07.5	22.2	84.3	45 17.2	25.0	86.3	45 22.8	27.6	88.4
28	44 52.2	15.7	79.0	45 13.0	18.5	81.0	45 29.7	21.3	83.0	45 42.2	24.0	85.0	45 50.4	26.8	87.1
29	45 07.9	14.7	77.7	45 31.5	17.5	79.7	45 51.0	20.3	81.7	46 06.2	23.1	83.7	46 17.2	25.8	85.8

20° Hc d Z	22° Hc d Z	24° Hc d Z	26° Hc d Z	28° Hc d Z	Dec.
35 20.8 −25.4 105.0	34 48.5 −27.7 106.3	34 13.5 −29.8 107.6	33 35.8 −31.8 108.9	32 55.7 −33.8 110.1	0
34 55.4 26.1 106.1	34 20.8 28.2 107.4	33 43.7 30.3 108.7	33 04.0 32.3 109.9	32 21.9 34.2 111.1	1
34 29.3 26.6 107.2	33 52.6 28.8 108.5	33 13.4 30.8 109.7	32 31.7 32.8 110.9	31 47.7 34.7 112.1	2
34 02.7 27.2 108.2	33 23.8 29.2 109.5	32 42.6 31.3 110.7	31 58.9 33.2 111.9	31 13.0 35.1 113.1	3
33 35.5 27.8 109.3	32 54.6 29.9 110.6	32 11.3 31.8 111.7	31 25.7 33.7 112.9	30 37.9 35.5 114.0	4
33 07.7 −28.3 110.4	32 24.7 −30.3 111.6	31 39.5 −32.3 112.7	30 52.0 −34.1 113.9	30 02.4 −35.9 114.9	5
32 39.4 28.8 111.4	31 54.4 30.7 112.6	31 07.2 32.7 113.7	30 17.9 34.5 114.8	29 26.5 36.2 115.9	6
32 10.6 29.3 112.5	31 23.7 31.3 113.6	30 34.5 33.1 114.7	29 43.4 34.9 115.8	28 50.3 36.7 116.8	7
31 41.3 29.8 113.5	30 52.4 31.7 114.6	30 01.4 33.5 115.7	29 08.5 35.3 116.7	28 13.6 37.0 117.7	8
31 11.5 30.3 114.5	30 20.7 32.2 115.6	29 27.9 34.0 116.6	28 33.2 35.7 117.6	27 36.6 37.3 118.6	9
30 41.2 −30.7 115.5	29 48.5 −32.5 116.6	28 53.9 −34.3 117.6	27 57.5 −36.1 118.5	26 59.3 −37.6 119.4	10
30 10.5 31.2 116.5	29 16.0 33.0 117.5	28 19.6 34.7 118.5	27 21.4 36.3 119.4	26 21.7 38.0 120.3	11
29 39.3 31.6 117.5	28 43.0 33.4 118.5	27 44.9 35.1 119.4	26 45.1 36.7 120.3	25 43.7 38.2 121.2	12
29 07.7 32.0 118.5	28 09.6 33.8 119.4	27 09.8 35.5 120.3	26 08.4 37.1 121.2	25 05.5 38.6 122.0	13
28 35.7 32.5 119.4	27 35.8 34.1 120.4	26 34.3 35.7 121.3	25 31.3 37.3 122.1	24 26.9 38.8 122.9	14
28 03.2 −32.8 120.4	27 01.7 −34.5 121.3	25 58.6 −36.1 122.1	24 54.0 −37.6 122.9	23 48.1 −39.1 123.7	15
27 30.4 33.2 121.3	26 27.2 34.9 122.2	25 22.5 36.4 123.0	24 16.4 37.9 123.8	23 09.0 39.4 124.5	16
26 57.2 33.6 122.3	25 52.3 35.2 123.1	24 46.1 36.8 123.9	23 38.5 38.2 124.7	22 29.6 39.6 125.4	17
26 23.6 34.0 123.2	25 17.1 35.5 124.0	24 09.3 37.0 124.8	23 00.3 38.5 125.5	21 50.0 39.8 126.2	18
25 49.6 34.2 124.1	24 41.6 35.8 124.9	23 32.3 37.3 125.6	22 21.8 38.7 126.3	21 10.2 40.1 127.0	19
25 15.4 −34.6 125.0	24 05.8 −36.1 125.8	22 55.0 −37.5 126.5	21 43.1 −38.9 127.1	20 30.1 −40.2 127.8	20
24 40.8 35.0 125.9	23 29.7 36.4 126.7	22 17.5 37.8 127.3	21 04.2 39.2 128.0	19 49.9 40.5 128.6	21
24 05.8 35.2 126.8	22 53.3 36.7 127.5	21 39.7 38.1 128.2	20 25.0 39.4 128.8	19 09.4 40.7 129.3	22
23 30.6 35.6 127.7	22 16.6 36.9 128.4	21 01.6 38.3 129.0	19 45.6 39.6 129.6	18 28.7 40.9 130.1	23
22 55.0 35.8 128.6	21 39.7 37.2 129.2	20 23.3 38.6 129.8	19 06.0 39.8 130.4	17 47.8 41.0 130.9	24
22 19.2 −36.1 129.5	21 02.5 −37.5 130.1	19 44.7 −38.7 130.6	18 26.2 −40.1 131.2	17 06.8 −41.2 131.6	25
21 43.1 36.3 130.3	20 25.0 37.7 130.9	19 06.0 39.0 131.5	17 46.1 40.2 131.9	16 25.6 41.4 132.4	26
21 06.8 36.7 131.2	19 47.3 37.9 131.7	18 27.0 39.2 132.3	17 05.9 40.3 132.7	15 44.2 41.5 133.2	27
20 30.1 36.8 132.0	19 09.4 38.2 132.6	17 47.8 39.3 133.1	16 25.6 40.6 133.5	15 02.7 41.7 133.9	28
19 53.3 37.1 132.9	18 31.2 38.3 133.4	17 08.5 39.6 133.8	15 45.0 40.7 134.3	14 21.0 41.8 134.7	29

30° Hc d Z	32° Hc d Z	34° Hc d Z	36° Hc d Z	38° Hc d Z	Dec.
32 13.2 −35.6 111.3	31 28.4 −37.4 112.5	30 41.5 −39.2 113.6	29 52.4 −40.8 114.7	29 01.3 −42.4 115.7	0
31 37.6 36.1 112.3	30 51.0 37.9 113.4	30 02.3 39.6 114.5	29 11.6 41.2 115.5	28 18.9 42.6 116.5	1
31 01.5 36.5 113.2	30 13.1 38.2 114.3	29 22.7 39.8 115.3	28 30.4 41.4 116.3	27 36.3 43.0 117.3	2
30 25.0 36.9 114.1	29 34.9 38.6 115.2	28 42.9 40.2 116.2	27 49.0 41.8 117.2	26 53.3 43.2 118.1	3
29 48.1 37.2 115.1	28 56.3 38.9 116.1	28 02.7 40.5 117.0	27 07.2 42.0 118.0	26 10.1 43.4 118.9	4
29 10.9 −37.6 116.0	28 17.4 −39.2 116.9	27 22.2 −40.8 117.9	26 25.2 −42.2 118.8	25 26.7 −43.7 119.6	5
28 33.3 38.0 116.8	27 38.2 39.6 117.8	26 41.4 41.1 118.7	25 43.0 42.6 119.6	24 43.0 43.9 120.4	6
27 55.3 38.3 117.7	26 58.6 39.8 118.6	26 00.3 41.3 119.5	25 00.4 42.7 120.3	23 59.1 44.1 121.1	7
27 17.0 38.5 118.6	26 18.8 40.1 119.5	25 19.0 41.6 120.3	24 17.7 43.0 121.1	23 15.0 44.3 121.9	8
26 38.5 38.9 119.5	25 38.7 40.4 120.3	24 37.4 41.9 121.1	23 34.7 43.2 121.9	22 30.7 44.5 122.6	9
25 59.6 −39.2 120.3	24 58.3 −40.7 121.1	23 55.5 −42.0 121.9	22 51.5 −43.5 122.6	21 46.2 −44.8 123.3	10
25 20.4 39.5 121.1	24 17.6 40.9 121.9	23 13.5 42.4 122.7	22 08.0 43.6 123.4	21 01.4 44.8 124.0	11
24 40.9 39.8 122.0	23 36.7 41.2 122.7	22 31.1 42.5 123.4	21 24.4 43.8 124.1	20 16.6 45.1 124.7	12
24 01.1 40.0 122.8	22 55.5 41.4 123.5	21 48.6 42.7 124.2	20 40.6 44.0 124.8	19 31.5 45.2 125.4	13
23 21.1 40.2 123.6	22 14.1 41.6 124.3	21 05.9 43.0 125.0	19 56.6 44.2 125.6	18 46.3 45.4 126.1	14
22 40.9 −40.5 124.4	21 32.5 −41.9 125.1	20 22.9 −43.1 125.7	19 12.4 −44.3 126.3	18 00.9 −45.5 126.8	15
22 00.4 40.8 125.2	20 50.6 42.0 125.9	19 39.8 43.3 126.4	18 28.1 44.5 127.0	17 15.4 45.6 127.5	16
21 19.6 41.0 126.0	20 08.6 42.3 126.6	18 56.5 43.4 127.2	17 43.6 44.7 127.7	16 29.8 45.8 128.2	17
20 38.7 41.2 126.8	19 26.3 42.4 127.4	18 13.1 43.7 127.9	16 58.9 44.8 128.4	15 44.0 45.9 128.9	18
19 57.5 41.3 127.6	18 43.9 42.6 128.1	17 29.4 43.8 128.6	16 14.1 44.9 129.1	14 58.1 46.1 129.5	19
19 16.2 −41.6 128.3	18 01.3 −42.8 128.9	16 45.6 −43.9 129.3	15 29.2 −45.1 129.8	14 12.0 −46.1 130.2	20
18 34.6 41.7 129.1	17 18.5 42.9 129.6	16 01.7 44.1 130.1	14 44.1 45.2 130.5	13 25.9 46.2 130.9	21
17 52.9 41.9 129.9	16 35.6 43.1 130.3	15 17.6 44.2 130.8	13 58.9 45.2 131.2	12 39.7 46.3 131.5	22
17 11.0 42.1 130.6	15 52.5 43.2 131.1	14 33.4 44.3 131.5	13 13.7 45.4 131.8	11 53.4 46.5 132.2	23
16 28.9 42.2 131.3	15 09.3 43.3 131.8	13 49.1 44.5 132.2	12 28.3 45.5 132.5	11 06.9 46.4 132.8	24
15 46.7 −42.4 132.1	14 26.0 −43.5 132.5	13 04.6 −44.5 132.8	11 42.8 −45.6 133.2	10 20.5 −46.6 133.5	25
15 04.3 42.5 132.8	13 42.5 43.6 133.2	12 20.1 44.7 133.5	10 57.2 45.7 133.8	9 33.9 46.7 134.1	26
14 21.8 42.6 133.5	12 58.9 43.8 133.9	11 35.4 44.8 134.2	10 11.5 45.7 134.5	8 47.2 46.7 134.7	27
13 39.2 42.8 134.3	12 15.1 43.8 134.6	10 50.6 44.8 134.9	9 25.8 45.9 135.1	8 00.5 46.7 135.4	28
12 56.4 42.9 135.0	11 31.3 43.9 135.3	10 05.8 44.9 135.6	8 39.9 45.9 135.8	7 13.8 46.9 136.0	29

Dec.	40° Hc	d	Z	42° Hc	d	Z	44° Hc	d	Z	46° Hc	d	Z	48° Hc	d	Z
°	° ′	′	°	° ′	′	°	° ′	′	°	° ′	′	°	° ′	′	°
0	28 08.4	+ 43.6	116.7	27 13.7	+ 45.0	117.6	26 17.2	+ 46.4	118.5	25 19.2	+ 47.7	119.3	24 19.7	+ 48.8	120.1
1	28 52.0	43.3	115.9	27 58.7	44.8	116.9	27 03.6	46.2	117.8	26 06.9	47.4	118.7	25 08.5	48.7	119.5
2	29 35.3	43.1	115.1	28 43.5	44.5	116.1	27 49.8	45.9	117.1	26 54.3	47.3	118.0	25 57.2	48.5	118.9
3	30 18.4	42.7	114.3	29 28.0	44.3	115.3	28 35.7	45.7	116.3	27 41.6	47.0	117.3	26 45.7	48.4	118.2
4	31 01.1	42.4	113.5	30 12.3	44.0	114.6	29 21.4	45.5	115.6	28 28.6	46.9	116.6	27 34.1	48.1	117.5
5	31 43.5	+ 42.1	112.6	30 56.3	+ 43.6	113.8	30 06.9	+ 45.2	114.8	29 15.5	+ 46.6	115.9	28 22.2	+ 47.9	116.9
6	32 25.6	41.8	111.8	31 39.9	43.4	113.0	30 52.1	44.9	114.1	30 02.1	46.3	115.1	29 10.1	47.7	116.2
7	33 07.4	41.4	110.9	32 23.3	43.1	112.1	31 37.0	44.6	113.3	30 48.4	46.1	114.4	29 57.8	47.5	115.5
8	33 48.8	41.1	110.1	33 06.4	42.7	111.3	32 21.6	44.3	112.5	31 34.5	45.9	113.7	30 45.3	47.3	114.8
9	34 29.9	40.6	109.2	33 49.1	42.4	110.5	33 05.9	44.1	111.7	32 20.4	45.5	112.9	31 32.6	47.0	114.0
10	35 10.5	+ 40.3	108.3	34 31.5	+ 42.0	109.6	33 50.0	+ 43.6	110.9	33 05.9	+ 45.3	112.1	32 19.6	+ 46.8	113.3
11	35 50.8	39.8	107.4	35 13.5	41.7	108.8	34 33.6	43.4	110.1	33 51.2	45.0	111.3	33 06.4	46.4	112.6
12	36 30.6	39.4	106.5	35 55.2	41.2	107.9	35 17.0	43.0	109.2	34 36.2	44.6	110.5	33 52.8	46.2	111.8
13	37 10.0	38.9	105.5	36 36.4	40.8	107.0	36 00.0	42.6	108.4	35 20.8	44.3	109.7	34 39.0	45.9	111.0
14	37 48.9	38.5	104.6	37 17.2	40.4	106.0	36 42.6	42.2	107.5	36 05.1	44.0	108.9	35 24.9	45.6	110.2
15	38 27.4	+ 38.0	103.6	37 57.6	+ 40.0	105.1	37 24.8	+ 41.9	106.6	36 49.1	+ 43.6	108.0	36 10.5	+ 45.3	109.4
16	39 05.4	37.4	102.6	38 37.6	39.5	104.2	38 06.7	41.4	105.7	37 32.7	43.2	107.2	36 55.8	44.9	108.6
17	39 42.8	36.9	101.6	39 17.1	38.9	103.2	38 48.1	40.9	104.8	38 15.9	42.8	106.3	37 40.7	44.6	107.8
18	40 19.7	36.4	100.6	39 56.0	38.5	102.2	39 29.0	40.5	103.8	38 58.7	42.4	105.4	38 25.3	44.2	106.9
19	40 56.1	35.8	99.5	40 34.5	38.0	101.2	40 09.5	40.0	102.9	39 41.1	42.0	104.5	39 09.5	43.8	106.1
20	41 31.9	+ 35.2	98.4	41 12.5	+ 37.3	100.2	40 49.5	+ 39.5	101.9	40 23.1	+ 41.4	103.6	39 53.3	+ 43.3	105.2
21	42 07.1	34.5	97.4	41 49.8	36.8	99.1	41 29.0	38.9	100.9	41 04.5	41.1	102.6	40 36.6	43.0	104.3
22	42 41.6	33.9	96.2	42 26.6	36.3	98.1	42 07.9	38.4	99.9	41 45.6	40.5	101.6	41 19.6	42.5	103.4
23	43 15.5	33.2	95.1	43 02.9	35.5	97.0	42 46.3	37.9	98.8	42 26.1	39.9	100.6	42 02.1	42.0	102.4
24	43 48.7	32.5	94.0	43 38.4	34.9	95.9	43 24.2	37.2	97.8	43 06.0	39.5	99.6	42 44.1	41.5	101.5
25	44 21.2	+ 31.8	92.8	44 13.3	+ 34.3	94.7	44 01.4	+ 36.6	96.7	43 45.5	+ 38.8	98.6	43 25.6	+ 41.0	100.5
26	44 53.0	31.1	91.6	44 47.6	33.5	93.6	44 38.0	35.9	95.6	44 24.3	38.3	97.5	44 06.6	40.4	99.5
27	45 24.1	30.2	90.4	45 21.1	32.8	92.4	45 13.9	35.3	94.4	45 02.6	37.6	96.4	44 47.0	39.9	98.4
28	45 54.3	29.4	89.2	45 53.9	32.0	91.2	45 49.2	34.5	93.3	45 40.2	36.9	95.3	45 26.9	39.3	97.4
29	46 23.7	28.6	87.9	46 25.9	31.3	90.0	46 23.7	33.8	92.1	46 17.1	36.3	94.2	46 06.2	38.6	96.3

Dec.	50° Hc	d	Z	52° Hc	d	Z	54° Hc	d	Z	56° Hc	d	Z	58° Hc	d	Z
°	° ′	′	°	° ′	′	°	° ′	′	°	° ′	′	°	° ′	′	°
0	23 18.7	+ 50.0	120.9	22 16.5	+ 51.0	121.6	21 12.9	+ 52.0	122.3	20 08.2	+ 53.0	122.9	19 02.5	+ 53.8	123.5
1	24 08.7	49.8	120.3	23 07.5	50.9	121.0	22 04.9	52.0	121.8	21 01.2	52.8	122.4	19 56.3	53.7	123.1
2	24 58.5	49.7	119.7	23 58.4	50.8	120.5	22 56.9	51.8	121.2	21 54.0	52.8	121.9	20 50.0	53.6	122.6
3	25 48.2	49.5	119.1	24 49.2	50.6	119.9	23 48.7	51.6	120.7	22 46.8	52.6	121.4	21 43.6	53.6	122.1
4	26 37.7	49.4	118.4	25 39.8	50.5	119.3	24 40.3	51.6	120.1	23 39.4	52.6	120.9	22 37.2	53.4	121.6
5	27 27.1	+ 49.2	117.8	26 30.3	+ 50.3	118.7	25 31.9	+ 51.4	119.5	24 32.0	+ 52.4	120.4	23 30.6	+ 53.4	121.1
6	28 16.3	49.0	117.1	27 20.6	50.2	118.1	26 23.3	51.3	119.0	25 24.4	52.3	119.8	24 24.0	53.3	120.6
7	29 05.3	48.8	116.5	28 10.8	50.0	117.5	27 14.6	51.2	118.4	26 16.7	52.2	119.3	25 17.3	53.2	120.1
8	29 54.1	48.5	115.8	29 00.8	49.9	116.8	28 05.8	50.9	117.8	27 08.9	52.1	118.7	26 10.5	53.0	119.6
9	30 42.6	48.3	115.1	29 50.7	49.6	116.2	28 56.7	50.9	117.2	28 01.0	51.9	118.2	27 03.5	52.9	119.1
10	31 31.0	+ 48.2	114.4	30 40.3	+ 49.4	115.5	29 47.6	+ 50.6	116.6	28 52.9	+ 51.8	117.6	27 56.4	+ 52.8	118.5
11	32 19.2	47.9	113.7	31 29.7	49.3	114.9	30 38.2	50.5	116.0	29 44.7	51.6	117.0	28 49.2	52.7	118.0
12	33 07.1	47.6	113.0	32 19.0	49.0	114.2	31 28.7	50.3	115.3	30 36.3	51.5	116.4	29 41.9	52.6	117.5
13	33 54.7	47.4	112.3	33 08.0	48.8	113.5	32 19.0	50.1	114.7	31 27.8	51.2	115.8	30 34.5	52.4	116.9
14	34 42.1	47.1	111.6	33 56.8	48.5	112.8	33 09.1	49.8	114.0	32 19.0	51.2	115.2	31 26.9	52.2	116.3
15	35 29.2	+ 46.9	110.8	34 45.3	+ 48.3	112.1	33 58.9	+ 49.7	113.4	33 10.2	+ 50.9	114.6	32 19.1	+ 52.1	115.8
16	36 16.1	46.5	110.0	35 33.6	48.1	111.4	34 48.6	49.4	112.7	34 01.1	50.7	114.0	33 11.2	51.9	115.2
17	37 02.6	46.2	109.2	36 21.7	47.7	110.6	35 38.0	49.2	112.0	34 51.8	50.5	113.3	34 03.1	51.7	114.6
18	37 48.8	45.9	108.4	37 09.4	47.5	109.9	36 27.2	48.9	111.3	35 42.3	50.3	112.6	34 54.8	51.6	113.9
19	38 34.7	45.5	107.6	37 56.9	47.1	109.1	37 16.1	48.7	110.6	36 32.6	50.0	112.0	35 46.4	51.3	113.3
20	39 20.2	+ 45.2	106.8	38 44.0	+ 46.8	108.3	38 04.8	+ 48.5	109.8	37 22.6	+ 49.8	111.3	36 37.7	+ 51.1	112.7
21	40 05.4	44.7	105.9	39 30.8	46.5	107.5	38 53.1	48.1	109.1	38 12.4	49.6	110.6	37 28.8	51.0	112.0
22	40 50.1	44.4	105.1	40 17.3	46.1	106.7	39 41.2	47.8	108.3	39 02.0	49.3	109.8	38 19.8	50.6	111.3
23	41 34.5	43.9	104.2	41 03.4	45.8	105.9	40 29.0	47.4	107.5	39 51.3	48.9	109.1	39 10.4	50.5	110.6
24	42 18.4	43.5	103.2	41 49.2	45.3	105.0	41 16.4	47.1	106.7	40 40.2	48.7	108.4	40 00.9	50.1	110.0
25	43 01.9	+ 43.0	102.3	42 34.5	+ 44.9	104.1	42 03.5	+ 46.7	105.9	41 28.9	+ 48.4	107.6	40 51.0	+ 49.9	109.2
26	43 44.9	42.6	101.3	43 19.4	44.5	103.2	42 50.2	46.3	105.0	42 17.3	48.0	106.8	41 40.9	49.6	108.5
27	44 27.5	42.0	100.4	44 03.9	44.0	102.3	43 36.5	45.9	104.2	43 05.3	47.7	106.0	42 30.5	49.3	107.7
28	45 09.5	41.4	99.4	44 47.9	43.6	101.3	44 22.4	45.5	103.2	43 53.0	47.3	105.1	43 19.8	49.0	107.0
29	45 50.9	40.9	98.3	45 31.5	43.0	100.3	45 07.9	45.0	102.3	44 40.3	46.8	104.3	44 08.8	48.6	106.2

162

40° Hc	d	Z	42° Hc	d	Z	44° Hc	d	Z	46° Hc	d	Z	48° Hc	d	Z	Dec.
28 08.4	43.9	116.7	27 13.7	45.3	117.6	26 17.2	46.6	118.5	25 19.2	47.8	119.3	24 19.7	49.0	120.1	0
27 24.5	44.1	117.4	26 28.4	45.5	118.3	25 30.6	46.7	119.2	24 31.4	48.0	120.0	23 30.7	49.2	120.8	1
26 40.4	44.4	118.2	25 42.9	45.7	119.1	24 43.9	47.0	119.9	23 43.4	48.2	120.7	22 41.5	49.3	121.4	2
25 56.0	44.5	118.9	24 57.2	45.9	119.8	23 56.9	47.2	120.6	22 55.2	48.3	121.3	21 52.2	49.3	122.0	3
25 11.5	44.8	119.7	24 11.3	46.1	120.5	23 09.7	47.3	121.2	22 06.9	48.5	121.9	21 02.8	49.6	122.6	4
24 26.7	45.1	120.4	23 25.2	46.3	121.2	22 22.4	47.5	121.9	21 18.4	48.6	122.6	20 13.2	49.7	123.2	5
23 41.6	45.2	121.1	22 38.9	46.5	121.9	21 34.9	47.6	122.6	20 29.8	48.8	123.2	19 23.5	49.8	123.8	6
22 56.4	45.3	121.8	21 52.4	46.6	122.6	20 47.3	47.8	123.2	19 41.0	48.9	123.8	18 33.7	49.9	124.4	7
22 11.0	45.6	122.6	21 05.8	46.8	123.2	19 59.5	47.9	123.9	18 52.1	49.0	124.4	17 43.8	50.1	125.0	8
21 25.4	45.7	123.3	20 19.0	46.9	123.9	19 11.6	48.1	124.5	18 03.1	49.1	125.1	16 53.7	50.1	125.6	9
20 39.7	46.0	124.0	19 32.1	47.1	124.6	18 23.5	48.2	125.1	17 14.0	49.2	125.7	16 03.6	50.2	126.1	10
19 53.7	46.0	124.7	18 45.0	47.2	125.2	17 35.3	48.3	125.8	16 24.8	49.3	126.3	15 13.4	50.3	126.7	11
19 07.7	46.3	125.3	17 57.8	47.3	125.9	16 47.0	48.4	126.4	15 35.5	49.5	126.8	14 23.1	50.3	127.3	12
18 21.4	46.3	126.0	17 10.5	47.5	126.5	15 58.6	48.5	127.0	14 46.0	49.5	127.4	13 32.8	50.5	127.8	13
17 35.1	46.5	126.7	16 23.0	47.6	127.2	15 10.1	48.5	127.6	13 56.5	49.5	128.0	12 42.3	50.5	128.4	14
16 48.6	46.7	127.3	15 35.4	47.7	127.8	14 21.5	48.7	128.2	13 07.0	49.7	128.6	11 51.8	50.6	128.9	15
16 01.9	46.7	128.0	14 47.7	47.8	128.4	13 32.8	48.8	128.8	12 17.3	49.7	129.2	11 01.2	50.6	129.5	16
15 15.2	46.9	128.6	13 59.9	47.9	129.0	12 44.0	48.8	129.4	11 27.6	49.8	129.7	10 10.6	50.7	130.0	17
14 28.3	46.9	129.3	13 12.0	47.9	129.7	11 55.2	49.0	130.0	10 37.8	49.9	130.3	9 19.9	50.7	130.6	18
13 41.4	47.1	129.9	12 24.1	48.1	130.3	11 06.2	49.0	130.6	9 47.9	49.9	130.9	8 29.2	50.8	131.1	19
12 54.3	47.2	130.6	11 36.0	48.1	130.9	10 17.2	49.1	131.2	8 58.0	50.0	131.4	7 38.4	50.8	131.7	20
12 07.1	47.2	131.2	10 47.9	48.2	131.5	9 28.1	49.1	131.8	8 08.0	50.0	132.0	6 47.6	50.9	132.2	21
11 19.9	47.3	131.8	9 59.7	48.3	132.1	8 39.0	49.2	132.4	7 18.0	50.1	132.6	5 56.7	50.9	132.7	22
10 32.6	47.4	132.5	9 11.4	48.3	132.7	7 49.8	49.2	132.9	6 27.9	50.1	133.1	5 05.8	50.9	133.3	23
9 45.2	47.5	133.1	8 23.1	48.4	133.3	7 00.6	49.3	133.5	5 37.8	50.1	133.7	4 14.9	50.9	133.8	24
8 57.7	47.5	133.7	7 34.7	48.5	133.9	6 11.3	49.3	134.1	4 47.7	50.1	134.2	3 24.0	51.0	134.3	25
8 10.2	47.6	134.3	6 46.2	48.4	134.5	5 22.0	49.3	134.7	3 57.6	50.2	134.8	2 33.0	51.0	134.8	26
7 22.6	47.6	134.9	5 57.8	48.6	135.1	4 32.7	49.4	135.2	3 07.4	50.2	135.3	1 42.0	51.0	135.3	27
6 35.0	47.7	135.5	5 09.2	48.5	135.7	3 43.3	49.4	135.8	2 17.2	50.2	135.9	0 51.1	51.0	135.9	28
5 47.3	47.7	136.2	4 20.7	48.6	136.3	2 53.9	49.4	136.4	1 27.0	50.2	136.4	0 00.1 –	51.0	136.4	29

50° Hc	d	Z	52° Hc	d	Z	54° Hc	d	Z	56° Hc	d	Z	58° Hc	d	Z	Dec.
23 18.7	50.1	120.9	22 16.5	51.2	121.6	21 12.9	52.1	122.3	20 08.2	53.0	122.9	19 02.5	53.9	123.5	0
22 28.6	50.2	121.5	21 25.3	51.3	122.2	20 20.8	52.2	122.8	19 15.2	53.1	123.4	18 08.6	53.9	124.0	1
21 38.4	50.4	122.1	20 34.0	51.3	122.7	19 28.6	52.3	123.3	18 22.1	53.2	123.9	17 14.7	54.0	124.5	2
20 48.0	50.5	122.7	19 42.7	51.5	123.3	18 36.3	52.4	123.9	17 28.9	53.2	124.4	16 20.7	54.0	124.9	3
19 57.5	50.6	123.2	18 51.2	51.6	123.8	17 43.9	52.5	124.4	16 35.7	53.3	124.9	15 26.7	54.2	125.4	4
19 06.9	50.7	123.8	17 59.6	51.6	124.4	16 51.4	52.5	124.9	15 42.4	53.4	125.4	14 32.5	54.1	125.8	5
18 16.2	50.8	124.4	17 08.0	51.7	124.9	15 58.9	52.6	125.4	14 49.0	53.4	125.8	13 38.4	54.2	126.3	6
17 25.4	50.9	124.9	16 16.3	51.9	125.4	15 06.3	52.7	125.9	13 55.6	53.5	126.3	12 44.2	54.3	126.7	7
16 34.5	51.0	125.5	15 24.4	51.8	126.0	14 13.6	52.7	126.4	13 02.1	53.5	126.8	11 49.9	54.2	127.1	8
15 43.5	51.0	126.0	14 32.6	52.0	126.5	13 20.9	52.8	126.9	12 08.6	53.6	127.2	10 55.7	54.2	127.6	9
14 52.5	51.2	126.6	13 40.6	52.0	127.0	12 28.1	52.9	127.4	11 15.0	53.7	127.7	10 01.3	54.3	128.0	10
14 01.3	51.2	127.1	12 48.6	52.1	127.5	11 35.2	52.9	127.8	10 21.3	53.6	128.2	9 07.0	54.4	128.4	11
13 10.1	51.2	127.7	11 56.5	52.1	128.0	10 42.3	52.9	128.3	9 27.7	53.7	128.6	8 12.6	54.4	128.9	12
12 18.9	51.4	128.2	11 04.4	52.2	128.5	9 49.4	53.0	128.8	8 34.0	53.7	129.1	7 18.2	54.4	129.3	13
11 27.5	51.4	128.7	10 12.2	52.2	129.0	8 56.4	53.0	129.3	7 40.3	53.8	129.5	6 23.8	54.5	129.7	14
10 36.1	51.4	129.3	9 20.0	52.3	129.5	8 03.4	53.0	129.8	6 46.5	53.8	130.0	5 29.3	54.5	130.1	15
9 44.7	51.5	129.8	8 27.7	52.3	130.0	7 10.4	53.1	130.2	5 52.7	53.8	130.4	4 34.8	54.5	130.5	16
8 53.2	51.6	130.3	7 35.4	52.3	130.5	6 17.3	53.1	130.7	4 58.9	53.8	130.8	3 40.3	54.5	131.0	17
8 01.7	51.6	130.8	6 43.1	52.4	131.0	5 24.2	53.1	131.2	4 05.1	53.8	131.3	2 45.8	54.5	131.4	18
7 10.1	51.6	131.3	5 50.7	52.4	131.5	4 31.1	53.2	131.7	3 11.3	53.9	131.7	1 51.3	54.5	131.8	19
6 18.5	51.7	131.8	4 58.3	52.4	132.0	3 37.9	53.1	132.1	2 17.4	53.8	132.2	0 56.8	54.5	132.2	20
5 26.8	51.6	132.4	4 05.9	52.4	132.5	2 44.8	53.2	132.6	1 23.6	53.9	132.6	0 02.3 –	54.5	132.6	21
4 35.2	51.7	132.9	3 13.5	52.5	133.0	1 51.6	53.2	133.0	0 29.7 –	53.9	133.1	0 52.2 +	54.5	46.9	22
3 43.5	51.7	133.4	2 21.0	52.4	133.4	0 58.4	53.1	133.5	0 24.2 +	53.8	46.5	1 46.7	54.5	46.5	23
2 51.8	51.7	133.9	1 28.6	52.5	133.9	0 05.3 –	53.2	134.0	1 18.0	53.9	46.1	2 41.2	54.5	46.1	24
2 00.1	51.8	134.4	0 36.1 –	52.5	134.4	0 47.9 +	53.2	45.6	2 11.9 +	53.8	45.6	3 35.7 +	54.5	45.7	25
1 08.3	51.7	134.9	0 16.4 +	52.4	45.1	1 41.1	53.1	45.1	3 05.7	53.8	45.2	4 30.2	54.5	45.3	26
0 16.6 –	51.7	135.4	1 08.8	52.4	44.6	2 34.2	53.2	44.7	3 59.5	53.9	44.7	5 24.7	54.5	44.9	27
0 35.1 +	51.8	44.1	2 01.3	52.4	44.1	3 27.4	53.1	44.2	4 53.4	53.8	44.3	6 19.2	54.4	44.4	28
1 26.9	51.7	43.6	2 53.7	52.5	43.6	4 20.5	53.2	43.7	5 47.2	53.8	43.8	7 13.6	54.4	44.0	29

LATITUDE **SAME** NAME L.H.A. 128°, 232°

Dec.	0° Hc	d	Z	2° Hc	d	Z	4° Hc	d	Z	6° Hc	d	Z	8° Hc	d	Z
0	36 00.0	- 0.4	90.0	35 58.5	+ 2.2	91.5	35 53.9	+ 4.8	92.9	35 46.3	+ 7.4	94.3	35 35.8	+ 9.9	95.8
1	35 59.6	1.1	88.8	36 00.7	1.4	90.2	35 58.7	4.0	91.7	35 53.7	6.6	93.1	35 45.7	9.1	94.6
2	35 58.5	1.9	87.5	36 02.1	+ 0.7	89.0	36 02.7	3.3	90.4	36 00.3	5.9	91.9	35 54.8	8.5	93.3
3	35 56.6	2.7	86.3	36 02.8	- 0.1	87.7	36 06.0	2.5	89.2	36 06.2	5.1	90.7	36 03.3	7.6	92.1
4	35 53.9	3.4	85.1	36 02.7	0.8	86.5	36 08.5	1.8	88.0	36 11.3	4.3	89.4	36 10.9	7.0	90.9
5	35 50.5	- 4.2	83.8	36 01.9	- 1.6	85.3	36 10.3	+ 1.0	86.7	36 15.6	+ 3.6	88.2	36 17.9	+ 6.1	89.7
6	35 46.3	4.9	82.6	36 00.3	2.4	84.0	36 11.3	+ 0.2	85.5	36 19.2	2.8	87.0	36 24.0	5.4	88.4
7	35 41.4	5.6	81.4	35 57.9	3.1	82.8	36 11.5	- 0.6	84.2	36 22.0	2.0	85.7	36 29.4	4.7	87.2
8	35 35.8	6.5	80.1	35 54.8	3.8	81.6	36 10.9	1.3	83.0	36 24.0	1.3	84.5	36 34.1	3.8	85.9
9	35 29.3	7.1	78.9	35 51.0	4.7	80.3	36 09.6	2.1	81.8	36 25.3	+ 0.5	83.2	36 37.9	3.1	84.7
10	35 22.2	- 7.9	77.7	35 46.3	- 5.3	79.1	36 07.5	- 2.8	80.5	36 25.8	- 0.3	82.0	36 41.0	+ 2.3	83.5
11	35 14.3	8.6	76.5	35 41.0	6.2	77.9	36 04.7	3.6	79.3	36 25.5	1.1	80.7	36 43.3	1.5	82.2
12	35 05.7	9.3	75.3	35 34.8	6.8	76.7	36 01.1	4.4	78.1	36 24.4	1.8	79.5	36 44.8	+ 0.8	81.0
13	34 56.4	10.0	74.1	35 28.0	7.6	75.4	35 56.7	5.1	76.8	36 22.6	2.6	78.3	36 45.6	- 0.1	79.7
14	34 46.4	10.8	72.9	35 20.4	8.4	74.2	35 51.6	5.8	75.6	36 20.0	3.3	77.0	36 45.5	0.8	78.5
15	34 35.6	- 11.4	71.7	35 12.0	- 9.0	73.0	35 45.8	- 6.7	74.4	36 16.7	- 4.2	75.8	36 44.7	- 1.6	77.2
16	34 24.2	12.1	70.5	35 03.0	9.8	71.8	35 39.1	7.3	73.1	36 12.5	4.9	74.5	36 43.1	2.4	76.0
17	34 12.1	12.8	69.3	34 53.2	10.4	70.6	35 31.8	8.1	71.9	36 07.6	5.6	73.3	36 40.7	3.2	74.7
18	33 59.3	13.5	68.1	34 42.8	11.2	69.4	35 23.7	8.8	70.7	36 02.0	6.4	72.1	36 37.5	3.9	73.5
19	33 45.8	14.1	66.9	34 31.6	11.9	68.2	35 14.9	9.6	69.5	35 55.6	7.2	70.8	36 33.6	4.7	72.2
20	33 31.7	- 14.8	65.8	34 19.7	- 12.5	67.0	35 05.3	- 10.2	68.3	35 48.4	- 7.9	69.6	36 28.9	- 5.5	71.0
21	33 16.9	15.5	64.6	34 07.2	13.3	65.8	34 55.1	11.0	67.1	35 40.5	8.6	68.4	36 23.4	6.2	69.8
22	33 01.4	16.1	63.5	33 53.9	13.9	64.7	34 44.1	11.6	65.9	35 31.9	9.3	67.2	36 17.2	7.0	68.5
23	32 45.3	16.6	62.3	33 40.0	14.5	63.5	34 32.5	12.4	64.7	35 22.6	10.1	66.0	36 10.2	7.8	67.3
24	32 28.7	17.4	61.2	33 25.5	15.2	62.3	34 20.1	13.0	63.5	35 12.5	10.8	64.8	36 02.4	8.5	66.1
25	32 11.3	- 17.9	60.0	33 10.3	- 15.9	61.2	34 07.1	- 13.7	62.3	35 01.7	- 11.6	63.6	35 53.9	- 9.3	64.8
26	31 53.4	18.5	58.9	32 54.4	16.5	60.0	33 53.4	14.4	61.2	34 50.1	12.2	62.4	35 44.6	9.9	63.6
27	31 34.9	19.1	57.8	32 37.9	17.1	58.9	33 39.0	15.1	60.0	34 37.9	12.9	61.2	35 34.7	10.7	62.4
28	31 15.8	19.6	56.7	32 20.8	17.7	57.7	33 23.9	15.6	58.8	34 25.0	13.6	60.0	35 24.0	11.5	61.2
29	30 56.2	20.2	55.6	32 03.1	18.3	56.6	33 08.3	16.3	57.7	34 11.4	14.2	58.8	35 12.5	12.1	60.0

Dec.	10° Hc	d	Z	12° Hc	d	Z	14° Hc	d	Z	16° Hc	d	Z	18° Hc	d	Z
0	35 22.2	+ 12.4	97.2	35 05.7	+ 14.9	98.6	34 46.4	+ 17.3	100.0	34 24.2	+ 19.7	101.3	33 59.3	+ 22.0	102.7
1	35 34.6	11.7	96.0	35 20.6	14.2	97.4	35 03.7	16.7	98.8	34 43.9	19.1	100.2	34 21.3	21.5	101.5
2	35 46.3	11.0	94.8	35 34.8	13.5	96.2	35 20.4	15.9	97.6	35 03.0	18.4	99.0	34 42.8	20.8	100.4
3	35 57.3	10.2	93.6	35 48.3	12.8	95.0	35 36.3	15.3	96.4	35 21.4	17.7	97.9	35 03.6	20.1	99.3
4	36 07.5	9.5	92.4	36 01.1	12.0	93.8	35 51.6	14.6	95.3	35 39.1	17.1	96.7	35 23.7	19.5	98.1
5	36 17.0	+ 8.8	91.1	36 13.1	+ 11.3	92.6	36 06.2	+ 13.8	94.1	35 56.2	+ 16.3	95.5	35 43.2	+ 18.8	96.9
6	36 25.8	8.0	89.9	36 24.4	10.6	91.4	36 20.0	13.1	92.8	36 12.5	15.7	94.3	36 02.0	18.1	95.8
7	36 33.8	7.2	88.7	36 35.0	9.8	90.1	36 33.1	12.4	91.6	36 28.2	14.9	93.1	36 20.1	17.4	94.6
8	36 41.0	6.4	87.4	36 44.8	9.1	88.9	36 45.5	11.6	90.4	36 43.1	14.2	91.9	36 37.5	16.7	93.4
9	36 47.4	5.7	86.2	36 53.9	8.2	87.7	36 57.1	10.9	89.2	36 57.3	13.4	90.7	36 54.2	16.0	92.2
10	36 53.1	+ 4.9	84.9	37 02.1	+ 7.5	86.4	37 08.0	+ 10.1	88.0	37 10.7	+ 12.7	89.5	37 10.2	+ 15.3	91.0
11	36 58.0	4.1	83.7	37 09.6	6.7	85.2	37 18.1	9.3	86.7	37 23.4	11.9	88.2	37 25.4	14.5	89.8
12	37 02.1	3.4	82.4	37 16.3	6.0	84.0	37 27.4	8.5	85.5	37 35.3	11.1	87.0	37 39.9	13.7	88.5
13	37 05.5	2.5	81.2	37 22.3	5.1	82.7	37 35.9	7.8	84.2	37 46.4	10.3	85.8	37 53.6	13.0	87.3
14	37 08.0	1.7	79.9	37 27.4	4.3	81.4	37 43.7	6.9	83.0	37 56.7	9.6	84.5	38 06.6	12.1	86.1
15	37 09.7	+ 1.0	78.7	37 31.7	+ 3.6	80.2	37 50.6	+ 6.1	81.7	38 06.3	+ 8.7	83.3	38 18.7	+ 11.4	84.8
16	37 10.7	+ 0.1	77.4	37 35.3	2.7	78.9	37 56.7	5.4	80.5	38 15.0	8.0	82.0	38 30.1	10.6	83.6
17	37 10.8	- 0.6	76.2	37 38.0	1.9	77.7	38 02.1	4.5	79.2	38 23.0	7.1	80.7	38 40.7	9.7	82.3
18	37 10.2	1.4	74.9	37 39.9	1.1	76.4	38 06.6	3.7	77.9	38 30.1	6.3	79.5	38 50.4	8.9	81.1
19	37 08.8	2.2	73.7	37 41.0	+ 0.4	75.1	38 10.3	2.9	76.7	38 36.4	5.5	78.2	38 59.3	8.1	79.8
20	37 06.6	- 3.1	72.4	37 41.4	- 0.6	73.9	38 13.2	+ 2.0	75.4	38 41.9	+ 4.6	76.9	39 07.4	+ 7.3	78.5
21	37 03.5	3.8	71.2	37 40.8	1.3	72.6	38 15.2	1.2	74.1	38 46.5	3.8	75.6	39 14.7	6.6	77.2
22	36 59.7	4.5	69.9	37 39.5	2.1	71.4	38 16.4	+ 0.4	72.8	38 50.3	3.0	74.4	39 21.1	5.5	75.9
23	36 55.2	5.4	68.7	37 37.4	2.9	70.1	38 16.8	- 0.4	71.6	38 53.3	2.1	73.1	39 26.6	4.7	74.7
24	36 49.8	6.2	67.4	37 34.5	3.8	68.8	38 16.4	1.2	70.3	38 55.4	1.3	71.8	39 31.3	3.9	73.4
25	36 43.6	- 6.9	66.2	37 30.8	- 4.5	67.6	38 15.2	- 2.1	69.0	38 56.7	+ 0.4	70.5	39 35.2	+ 2.9	72.1
26	36 36.7	7.7	64.9	37 26.3	5.4	66.3	38 13.1	2.9	67.7	38 57.1	- 0.4	69.2	39 38.1	2.2	70.8
27	36 29.0	8.3	63.7	37 20.9	6.1	65.1	38 10.2	3.7	66.5	38 56.7	1.3	67.9	39 40.3	1.2	69.5
28	36 20.6	9.2	62.5	37 14.8	6.9	63.8	38 06.5	4.6	65.2	38 55.4	2.1	66.7	39 41.5	+ 0.4	68.2
29	36 11.4	9.9	61.3	37 07.9	7.7	62.6	38 01.9	5.3	63.9	38 53.3	3.0	65.4	39 41.9	- 0.5	66.9

0°			2°			4°			6°			8°			Dec.
Hc	d	Z	Hc	d	Z	Hc	d	Z	Hc	d	Z	Hc	d	Z	
° ′	′	°	° ′	′	°	° ′	′	°	° ′	′	°	° ′	′	°	°
36 00.0	- 0.4	90.0	35 58.5	- 3.0	91.5	35 53.9	- 5.5	92.9	35 46.3	- 8.1	94.3	35 35.8	- 10.7	95.8	0
35 59.6	1.1	91.2	35 55.5	3.7	92.7	35 48.4	6.3	94.1	35 38.2	8.8	95.6	35 25.1	11.3	97.0	1
35 58.5	1.9	92.5	35 51.8	4.5	93.9	35 42.1	7.0	95.4	35 29.4	9.6	96.8	35 13.8	12.1	98.2	2
35 56.6	2.7	93.7	35 47.3	5.2	95.1	35 35.1	7.8	96.6	35 19.8	10.3	98.0	35 01.7	12.8	99.4	3
35 53.9	3.4	94.9	35 42.1	6.0	96.4	35 27.3	8.5	97.8	35 09.5	11.0	99.2	34 48.9	13.4	100.6	4
35 50.5	- 4.2	96.2	35 36.1	- 6.7	97.6	35 18.8	- 9.3	99.0	34 58.5	- 11.7	100.4	34 35.5	- 14.2	101.8	5
35 46.3	4.9	97.4	35 29.4	7.4	98.8	35 09.5	9.9	100.2	34 46.8	12.4	101.6	34 21.3	14.8	102.9	6
35 41.4	5.6	98.6	35 22.0	8.2	100.0	34 59.6	10.7	101.4	34 34.4	13.1	102.8	34 06.5	15.5	104.1	7
35 35.8	6.5	99.9	35 13.8	8.9	101.3	34 48.9	11.3	102.6	34 21.3	13.7	104.0	33 51.0	16.1	105.3	8
35 29.3	7.1	101.1	35 04.9	9.7	102.5	34 37.6	12.1	103.8	34 07.6	14.5	105.1	33 34.9	16.8	106.4	9
35 22.2	- 7.9	102.3	34 55.2	- 10.3	103.7	34 25.5	- 12.7	105.0	33 53.1	- 15.1	106.3	33 18.1	- 17.4	107.6	10
35 14.3	8.6	103.5	34 44.9	11.0	104.9	34 12.8	13.4	106.2	33 38.0	15.7	107.5	33 00.7	18.0	108.7	11
35 05.7	9.3	104.7	34 33.9	11.8	106.1	33 59.4	14.1	107.4	33 22.3	16.4	108.6	32 42.7	18.6	109.9	12
34 56.4	10.0	105.9	34 22.1	12.4	107.3	33 45.3	14.8	108.5	33 05.9	17.1	109.8	32 24.1	19.3	111.0	13
34 46.4	10.8	107.1	34 09.7	13.1	108.4	33 30.5	15.4	109.7	32 48.8	17.6	110.9	32 04.8	19.8	112.1	14
34 35.6	- 11.4	108.3	33 56.6	- 13.7	109.6	33 15.1	- 16.0	110.9	32 31.2	- 18.3	112.1	31 45.0	- 20.4	113.2	15
34 24.2	12.1	109.5	33 42.9	14.5	110.8	32 59.1	16.7	112.0	32 12.9	18.8	113.2	31 24.6	21.0	114.3	16
34 12.1	12.8	110.7	33 28.4	15.0	112.0	32 42.4	17.3	113.2	31 54.1	19.4	114.3	31 03.6	21.5	115.4	17
33 59.3	13.5	111.9	33 13.4	15.8	113.1	32 25.1	17.9	114.3	31 34.7	20.0	115.4	30 42.1	22.0	116.5	18
33 45.8	14.1	113.1	32 57.6	16.3	114.3	32 07.2	18.5	115.4	31 14.7	20.6	116.5	30 20.1	22.6	117.6	19
33 31.7	- 14.8	114.2	32 41.3	- 17.0	115.4	31 48.7	- 19.1	116.5	30 54.1	- 21.1	117.6	29 57.5	- 23.1	118.7	20
33 16.9	15.5	115.4	32 24.3	17.6	116.5	31 29.6	19.6	117.7	30 33.0	21.7	118.7	29 34.4	23.6	119.7	21
33 01.4	16.1	116.5	32 06.7	18.1	117.7	31 10.0	20.2	118.8	30 11.3	22.2	119.8	29 10.8	24.1	120.8	22
32 45.3	16.6	117.7	31 48.6	18.8	118.8	30 49.8	20.8	119.9	29 49.1	22.7	120.9	28 46.7	24.6	121.8	23
32 28.7	17.4	118.8	31 29.8	19.4	119.9	30 29.0	21.3	120.9	29 26.4	23.2	121.9	28 22.1	25.1	122.9	24
32 11.3	- 17.9	120.0	31 10.4	- 19.9	121.0	30 07.7	- 21.8	122.0	29 03.2	- 23.7	123.0	27 57.0	- 25.5	123.9	25
31 53.4	18.5	121.1	30 50.5	20.4	122.1	29 45.9	22.4	123.1	28 39.5	24.2	124.0	27 31.5	25.9	124.9	26
31 34.9	19.1	122.2	30 30.1	21.0	123.2	29 23.5	22.9	124.2	28 15.3	24.7	125.1	27 05.6	26.4	125.9	27
31 15.8	19.6	123.3	30 09.1	21.6	124.3	29 00.6	23.3	125.2	27 50.6	25.1	126.1	26 39.2	26.8	126.9	28
30 56.2	20.2	124.4	29 47.5	22.0	125.4	28 37.3	23.9	126.3	27 25.5	25.5	127.1	26 12.4	27.2	127.9	29

10°			12°			14°			16°			18°			Dec.
Hc	d	Z	Hc	d	Z	Hc	d	Z	Hc	d	Z	Hc	d	Z	
° ′	′	°	° ′	′	°	° ′	′	°	° ′	′	°	° ′	′	°	°
35 22.2	- 13.1	97.2	35 05.7	- 15.6	98.6	34 46.4	- 18.0	100.0	34 24.2	- 20.4	101.3	33 59.3	- 22.7	102.7	0
35 09.1	13.9	98.4	34 50.1	16.2	99.8	34 28.4	18.7	101.1	34 03.8	20.9	102.5	33 36.6	23.2	103.8	1
34 55.2	14.5	99.6	34 33.9	17.0	100.9	34 09.7	19.3	102.3	33 42.9	21.6	103.6	33 13.4	23.9	104.9	2
34 40.7	15.2	100.8	34 16.9	17.5	102.1	33 50.4	19.9	103.4	33 21.3	22.2	104.7	32 49.5	24.4	106.0	3
34 25.5	15.8	101.9	33 59.4	18.3	103.3	33 30.5	20.5	104.6	32 59.1	22.8	105.8	32 25.1	24.9	107.1	4
34 09.7	- 16.6	103.1	33 41.1	- 18.8	104.4	33 10.0	- 21.2	105.7	32 36.3	- 23.4	106.9	32 00.2	- 25.5	108.1	5
33 53.1	17.2	104.3	33 22.3	19.5	105.5	32 48.8	21.7	106.8	32 12.9	23.9	108.0	31 34.7	26.1	109.2	6
33 35.9	17.8	105.4	33 02.8	20.1	106.7	32 27.1	22.3	107.9	31 49.0	24.4	109.1	31 08.6	26.5	110.2	7
33 18.1	18.4	106.6	32 42.7	20.7	107.8	32 04.8	22.9	109.0	31 24.6	25.0	110.2	30 42.1	27.0	111.3	8
32 59.7	19.1	107.7	32 22.0	21.3	108.9	31 41.9	23.4	110.1	30 59.6	25.5	111.2	30 15.1	27.5	112.3	9
32 40.6	- 19.6	108.8	32 00.7	- 21.8	110.0	31 18.5	- 23.9	111.2	30 34.1	- 26.0	112.3	29 47.6	- 28.0	113.4	10
32 21.0	20.3	109.9	31 38.9	22.4	111.1	30 54.6	24.5	112.2	30 08.1	26.5	113.3	29 19.6	28.5	114.4	11
32 00.7	20.8	111.1	31 16.5	22.9	112.2	30 30.1	25.0	113.3	29 41.6	27.0	114.4	28 51.1	28.9	115.4	12
31 39.9	21.4	112.2	30 53.6	23.5	113.3	30 05.1	25.5	114.4	29 14.6	27.4	115.4	28 22.2	29.3	116.4	13
31 18.5	21.9	113.3	30 30.1	24.0	114.3	29 39.6	26.0	115.4	28 47.2	27.9	116.4	27 52.9	29.7	117.4	14
30 56.6	- 22.5	114.3	30 06.1	- 24.5	115.4	29 13.6	- 26.4	116.4	28 19.3	- 28.3	117.4	27 23.2	- 30.2	118.3	15
30 34.1	23.0	115.4	29 41.6	25.0	116.5	28 47.2	26.9	117.5	27 51.0	28.8	118.4	26 53.0	30.5	119.3	16
30 11.1	23.5	116.5	29 16.6	25.5	117.5	28 20.3	27.4	118.5	27 22.2	29.2	119.4	26 22.5	30.9	120.3	17
29 47.6	24.1	117.6	28 51.1	25.9	118.5	27 52.9	27.8	119.5	26 53.0	29.5	120.4	25 51.6	31.3	121.2	18
29 23.5	24.5	118.6	28 25.2	26.4	119.6	27 25.1	28.2	120.5	26 23.5	30.0	121.4	25 20.3	31.7	122.2	19
28 59.0	- 25.0	119.6	27 58.8	- 26.9	120.6	26 56.9	- 28.6	121.5	25 53.5	- 30.4	122.3	24 48.6	- 32.0	123.1	20
28 34.0	25.5	120.7	27 31.9	27.3	121.6	26 28.3	29.1	122.5	25 23.1	30.7	123.3	24 16.6	32.3	124.0	21
28 08.5	25.9	121.7	27 04.6	27.7	122.6	25 59.2	29.4	123.4	24 52.4	31.1	124.2	23 44.3	32.7	125.0	22
27 42.6	26.4	122.7	26 36.9	28.1	123.6	25 29.8	29.8	124.4	24 21.3	31.4	125.2	23 11.6	33.0	125.9	23
27 16.2	26.8	123.7	26 08.8	28.5	124.6	25 00.0	30.2	125.4	23 49.9	31.7	126.1	22 38.6	33.3	126.8	24
26 49.4	- 27.3	124.8	25 40.3	- 28.9	125.6	24 29.8	- 30.5	126.3	23 18.2	- 32.1	127.0	22 05.3	- 33.5	127.7	25
26 22.1	27.6	125.7	25 11.4	29.3	126.5	23 59.3	30.9	127.3	22 46.1	32.4	127.9	21 31.8	33.9	128.6	26
25 54.5	28.1	126.7	24 42.1	29.7	127.5	23 28.4	31.2	128.2	22 13.7	32.7	128.9	20 57.9	34.1	129.5	27
25 26.4	28.4	127.7	24 12.4	30.0	128.4	22 57.2	31.5	129.1	21 41.0	33.0	129.8	20 23.8	34.4	130.4	28
24 58.0	28.8	128.7	23 42.4	30.3	129.4	22 25.7	31.8	130.0	21 08.0	33.3	130.7	19 49.4	34.7	131.2	29

Dec.	20° Hc	d	Z	22° Hc	d	Z	24° Hc	d	Z	26° Hc	d	Z	28° Hc	d	Z
°	° ′	′	°	° ′	′	°	° ′	′	°	° ′	′	°	° ′	′	°
0	33 31.7	+24.3	104.0	33 01.4	+26.6	105.2	32 28.7	+28.6	106.5	31 53.4	+30.8	107.7	31 15.8	+32.8	108.8
1	33 56.0	23.7	102.9	33 28.0	25.9	104.2	32 57.3	28.2	105.4	32 24.2	30.2	106.7	31 48.6	32.2	107.9
2	34 19.7	23.1	101.7	33 53.9	25.4	103.1	33 25.5	27.6	104.4	32 54.4	29.7	105.6	32 20.8	31.8	106.9
3	34 42.8	22.5	100.6	34 19.3	24.8	102.0	33 53.1	27.0	103.3	33 24.1	29.3	104.6	32 52.6	31.3	105.8
4	35 05.3	21.9	99.5	34 44.1	24.2	100.9	34 20.1	26.5	102.2	33 53.4	28.6	103.5	33 23.9	30.8	104.8
5	35 27.2	+21.2	98.4	35 08.3	+23.6	99.8	34 46.6	+25.9	101.1	34 22.0	+28.1	102.5	33 54.7	+30.3	103.8
6	35 48.4	20.6	97.2	35 31.9	23.0	98.6	35 12.5	25.2	100.0	34 50.1	27.6	101.4	34 25.0	29.8	102.8
7	36 09.0	19.9	96.0	35 54.9	22.3	97.5	35 37.7	24.7	98.9	35 17.7	26.9	100.3	34 54.8	29.2	101.7
8	36 28.9	19.2	94.9	36 17.2	21.6	96.3	36 02.4	24.0	97.8	35 44.6	26.4	99.2	35 24.0	28.6	100.6
9	36 48.1	18.5	93.7	36 38.8	20.9	95.2	36 26.4	23.4	96.7	36 11.0	25.7	98.1	35 52.6	28.0	99.5
10	37 06.6	+17.7	92.5	36 59.7	+20.3	94.0	36 49.8	+22.7	95.5	36 36.7	+25.1	97.0	36 20.6	+27.4	98.5
11	37 24.3	17.1	91.3	37 20.0	19.5	92.8	37 12.5	22.0	94.3	37 01.8	24.5	95.9	36 48.0	26.8	97.3
12	37 41.4	16.2	90.1	37 39.5	18.9	91.6	37 34.5	21.3	93.2	37 26.3	23.7	94.7	37 14.8	26.2	96.2
13	37 57.6	15.6	88.9	37 58.4	18.0	90.4	37 55.8	20.6	92.0	37 50.0	23.1	93.5	37 41.0	25.5	95.1
14	38 13.2	14.7	87.6	38 16.4	17.4	89.2	38 16.4	19.9	90.8	38 13.1	22.4	92.4	38 06.5	24.8	93.9
15	38 27.9	+14.0	86.4	38 33.8	+16.5	88.0	38 36.3	+19.1	89.6	38 35.5	+21.6	91.2	38 31.3	+24.1	92.8
16	38 41.9	13.1	85.2	38 50.3	15.8	86.8	38 55.4	18.4	88.4	38 57.1	20.9	90.0	38 55.4	23.4	91.6
17	38 55.0	12.4	83.9	39 06.1	15.0	85.5	39 13.8	17.5	87.2	39 18.0	20.1	88.8	39 18.8	22.7	90.4
18	39 07.4	11.6	82.7	39 21.1	14.1	84.3	39 31.3	16.8	85.9	39 38.1	19.4	87.6	39 41.5	21.9	89.2
19	39 19.0	10.7	81.4	39 35.2	13.4	83.0	39 48.1	16.0	84.7	39 57.5	18.6	86.3	40 03.4	21.2	88.0
20	39 29.7	+ 9.9	80.1	39 48.6	+12.5	81.8	40 04.1	+15.1	83.4	40 16.1	+17.8	85.1	40 24.6	+20.4	86.8
21	39 39.6	9.0	78.8	40 01.1	11.7	80.5	40 19.2	14.4	82.1	40 33.9	16.9	83.8	40 45.0	19.6	85.5
22	39 48.6	8.2	77.5	40 12.8	10.8	79.2	40 33.6	13.4	80.9	40 50.8	16.2	82.6	41 04.6	18.7	84.3
23	39 56.8	7.3	76.3	40 23.6	10.0	77.9	40 47.0	12.6	79.6	41 07.0	15.2	81.3	41 23.3	17.9	83.0
24	40 04.1	6.4	75.0	40 33.6	9.0	76.6	40 59.6	11.8	78.3	41 22.2	14.4	80.0	41 41.2	17.1	81.8
25	40 10.5	+ 5.6	73.7	40 42.6	+ 8.2	75.3	41 11.4	+10.8	77.0	41 36.6	+13.6	78.7	41 58.3	+16.2	80.5
26	40 16.1	4.7	72.4	40 50.8	7.4	74.0	41 22.2	10.0	75.7	41 50.2	12.6	77.4	42 14.5	15.3	79.2
27	40 20.8	3.8	71.1	40 58.2	6.4	72.7	41 32.2	9.0	74.4	42 02.8	11.7	76.1	42 29.8	14.4	77.9
28	40 24.6	2.9	69.7	41 04.6	5.5	71.4	41 41.2	8.2	73.0	42 14.5	10.8	74.8	42 44.2	13.5	76.5
29	40 27.5	2.0	68.4	41 10.1	4.6	70.0	41 49.4	7.2	71.7	42 25.3	9.9	73.4	42 57.7	12.6	75.2

Dec.	30° Hc	d	Z	32° Hc	d	Z	34° Hc	d	Z	36° Hc	d	Z	38° Hc	d	Z
°	° ′	′	°	° ′	′	°	° ′	′	°	° ′	′	°	° ′	′	°
0	30 36.0	+34.6	110.0	29 53.9	+36.5	111.1	29 09.8	+38.2	112.1	28 23.6	+40.0	113.1	27 35.6	+41.5	114.1
1	31 10.6	34.2	109.0	30 30.4	36.1	110.1	29 48.0	37.9	111.2	29 03.6	39.6	112.3	28 17.1	41.2	113.3
2	31 44.8	33.8	108.1	31 06.5	35.7	109.2	30 25.9	37.5	110.3	29 43.2	39.2	111.4	28 58.3	41.0	112.5
3	32 18.6	33.4	107.1	31 42.2	35.3	108.3	31 03.4	37.2	109.4	30 22.4	38.9	110.5	29 39.3	40.6	111.6
4	32 52.0	32.8	106.1	32 17.5	34.8	107.3	31 40.6	36.7	108.5	31 01.3	38.6	109.7	30 19.9	40.3	110.8
5	33 24.8	+32.4	105.1	32 52.3	+34.4	106.3	32 17.3	+36.3	107.6	31 39.9	+38.1	108.8	31 00.2	+39.9	109.9
6	33 57.2	31.8	104.1	33 26.7	33.9	105.4	32 53.6	35.9	106.6	32 18.0	37.8	107.8	31 40.1	39.6	109.0
7	34 29.0	31.4	103.1	34 00.6	33.4	104.4	33 29.5	35.4	105.7	32 55.8	37.4	106.9	32 19.7	39.1	108.1
8	35 00.4	30.8	102.0	34 34.0	32.9	103.4	34 04.9	35.0	104.7	33 33.2	36.9	106.0	32 58.8	38.8	107.2
9	35 31.2	30.3	101.0	35 06.9	32.5	102.4	34 39.9	34.5	103.7	34 10.1	36.5	105.0	33 37.6	38.4	106.3
10	36 01.5	+29.6	99.9	35 39.4	+31.8	101.3	35 14.4	+34.0	102.7	34 46.6	+36.0	104.1	34 16.0	+38.0	105.4
11	36 31.1	29.1	98.8	36 11.2	31.4	100.3	35 48.4	33.4	101.7	35 22.6	35.5	103.1	34 54.0	37.5	104.5
12	37 00.2	28.5	97.7	36 42.6	30.7	99.2	36 21.8	33.0	100.7	35 58.1	35.1	102.1	35 31.5	37.1	103.5
13	37 28.7	27.9	96.6	37 13.3	30.2	98.1	36 54.8	32.3	99.6	36 33.2	34.5	101.1	36 08.6	36.6	102.5
14	37 56.6	27.2	95.5	37 43.5	29.5	97.0	37 27.1	31.9	98.6	37 07.7	34.0	100.1	36 45.2	36.1	101.6
15	38 23.8	+26.5	94.4	38 13.0	+28.9	95.9	37 59.0	+31.2	97.5	37 41.7	+33.4	99.0	37 21.3	+35.5	100.6
16	38 50.3	25.9	93.2	38 41.9	28.3	94.8	38 30.2	30.6	96.4	38 15.1	32.9	98.0	37 56.8	35.1	99.5
17	39 16.2	25.2	92.1	39 10.2	27.6	93.7	39 00.8	29.9	95.3	38 48.0	32.3	96.9	38 31.9	34.5	98.5
18	39 41.4	24.4	90.9	39 37.8	26.9	92.5	39 30.7	29.4	94.2	39 20.3	31.6	95.8	39 06.4	33.9	97.5
19	40 05.8	23.7	89.7	40 04.7	26.2	91.4	40 00.1	28.6	93.1	39 51.9	31.0	94.7	39 40.3	33.3	96.4
20	40 29.5	+23.0	88.5	40 30.9	+25.5	90.2	40 28.7	+28.0	91.9	40 22.9	+30.4	93.6	40 13.6	+32.7	95.3
21	40 52.5	22.2	87.3	40 56.4	24.7	89.0	40 56.7	27.2	90.7	40 53.3	29.7	92.5	40 46.3	32.1	94.2
22	41 14.7	21.3	86.0	41 21.1	24.0	87.8	41 23.9	26.5	89.6	41 23.0	29.0	91.3	41 18.4	31.4	93.1
23	41 36.0	20.6	84.8	41 45.1	23.2	86.6	41 50.4	25.7	88.4	41 52.0	28.2	90.1	41 49.8	30.7	91.9
24	41 56.6	19.7	83.5	42 08.3	22.3	85.3	42 16.1	25.0	87.1	42 20.2	27.5	89.0	42 20.5	30.0	90.8
25	42 16.3	+18.9	82.3	42 30.6	+21.5	84.1	42 41.1	+24.1	85.9	42 47.7	+26.8	87.8	42 50.5	+29.3	89.6
26	42 35.2	18.0	81.0	42 52.1	20.7	82.8	43 05.2	23.4	84.7	43 14.5	25.9	86.5	43 19.8	28.5	88.4
27	42 53.2	17.1	79.7	43 12.8	19.8	81.5	43 28.6	22.4	83.4	43 40.4	25.1	85.3	43 48.3	27.7	87.2
28	43 10.3	16.2	78.4	43 32.6	18.9	80.2	43 51.0	21.7	82.1	44 05.5	24.3	84.0	44 16.0	26.9	86.0
29	43 26.5	15.3	77.0	43 51.5	18.0	78.9	44 12.7	20.7	80.8	44 29.8	23.4	82.7	44 42.9	26.1	84.7

20°			22°			24°			26°			28°			Dec.
Hc	d	Z	Hc	d	Z	Hc	d	Z	Hc	d	Z	Hc	d	Z	
° ′	′	°	° ′	′	°	° ′	′	°	° ′	′	°	° ′	′	°	°
33 31.7	−25.0	104.0	33 01.4	−27.1	105.2	32 28.7	−29.2	106.5	31 53.4	−31.2	107.7	31 15.8	−33.1	108.8	0
33 06.7	25.4	105.0	32 34.3	27.6	106.3	31 59.5	29.7	107.5	31 22.2	31.7	108.7	30 42.7	33.6	109.8	1
32 41.3	26.0	106.1	32 06.7	28.1	107.3	31 29.8	30.2	108.5	30 50.5	32.1	109.7	30 09.1	34.0	110.8	2
32 15.3	26.6	107.2	31 38.6	28.6	108.4	30 59.6	30.6	109.5	30 18.4	32.5	110.6	29 35.1	34.5	111.7	3
31 48.7	27.0	108.2	31 10.0	29.1	109.4	30 29.0	31.1	110.5	29 45.9	33.0	111.6	29 00.6	34.8	112.7	4
31 21.7	−27.6	109.3	30 40.9	−29.6	110.4	29 57.9	−31.5	111.5	29 12.9	−33.4	112.6	28 25.8	−35.2	113.6	5
30 54.1	28.1	110.3	30 11.3	30.0	111.4	29 26.4	31.9	112.5	28 39.5	33.8	113.5	27 50.6	35.5	114.5	6
30 26.0	28.5	111.4	29 41.3	30.5	112.4	28 54.5	32.4	113.5	28 05.7	34.2	114.5	27 15.1	35.9	115.4	7
29 57.5	29.0	112.4	29 10.8	31.0	113.4	28 22.1	32.8	114.4	27 31.5	34.5	115.4	26 39.2	36.2	116.3	8
29 28.5	29.5	113.4	28 39.8	31.3	114.4	27 49.3	33.1	115.4	26 57.0	34.9	116.3	26 03.0	36.6	117.2	9
28 59.0	−29.9	114.4	28 08.5	−31.7	115.4	27 16.2	−33.5	116.3	26 22.1	−35.2	117.2	25 26.4	−36.8	118.1	10
28 29.1	30.3	115.4	27 36.8	32.2	116.3	26 42.7	33.9	117.2	25 46.9	35.5	118.1	24 49.6	37.2	119.0	11
27 58.8	30.8	116.4	27 04.6	32.5	117.3	26 08.8	34.2	118.2	25 11.4	35.9	119.0	24 12.4	37.4	119.8	12
27 28.0	31.1	117.3	26 32.1	32.9	118.2	25 34.6	34.6	119.1	24 35.5	36.2	119.9	23 35.0	37.8	120.7	13
26 56.9	31.5	118.3	25 59.2	33.2	119.2	25 00.0	34.9	120.0	23 59.3	36.5	120.8	22 57.2	38.0	121.5	14
26 25.4	−31.9	119.2	25 26.0	−33.6	120.1	24 25.1	−35.2	120.9	23 22.8	−36.7	121.6	22 19.2	−38.2	122.4	15
25 53.5	32.3	120.2	24 52.4	33.9	121.0	23 49.9	35.5	121.8	22 46.1	37.0	122.5	21 41.0	38.5	123.2	16
25 21.2	32.6	121.1	24 18.5	34.2	121.9	23 14.4	35.8	122.6	22 09.1	37.3	123.4	21 02.5	38.7	124.0	17
24 48.6	32.9	122.0	23 44.3	34.6	122.8	22 38.6	36.1	123.5	21 31.8	37.6	124.2	20 23.8	39.0	124.8	18
24 15.7	33.3	123.0	23 09.7	34.8	123.7	22 02.5	36.3	124.4	20 54.2	37.8	125.0	19 44.8	39.2	125.6	19
23 42.4	−33.6	123.9	22 34.9	−35.1	124.6	21 26.2	−36.6	125.2	20 16.4	−38.0	125.9	19 05.6	−39.4	126.4	20
23 08.8	33.9	124.8	21 59.8	35.5	125.5	20 49.6	36.9	126.1	19 38.4	38.2	126.7	18 26.2	39.5	127.2	21
22 34.9	34.2	125.7	21 24.3	35.6	126.3	20 12.7	37.0	126.9	19 00.2	38.5	127.5	17 46.7	39.8	128.0	22
22 00.7	34.5	126.6	20 48.7	36.0	127.2	19 35.7	37.4	127.8	18 21.7	38.7	128.3	17 06.9	40.0	128.8	23
21 26.2	34.8	127.4	20 12.7	36.1	128.0	18 58.3	37.5	128.6	17 43.0	38.8	129.1	16 26.9	40.1	129.6	24
20 51.4	−35.0	128.3	19 36.6	−36.4	128.9	18 20.8	−37.8	129.4	17 04.2	−39.1	129.9	15 46.8	−40.3	130.4	25
20 16.4	35.3	129.2	19 00.2	36.7	129.7	17 43.0	37.9	130.2	16 25.1	39.2	130.7	15 06.5	40.4	131.1	26
19 41.1	35.5	130.0	18 23.5	36.8	130.6	17 05.1	38.2	131.1	15 45.9	39.4	131.5	14 26.1	40.6	131.9	27
19 05.6	35.7	130.9	17 46.7	37.1	131.4	16 26.9	38.3	131.9	15 06.5	39.5	132.3	13 45.5	40.7	132.7	28
18 29.9	36.0	131.7	17 09.6	37.3	132.2	15 48.6	38.5	132.7	14 27.0	39.7	133.1	13 04.8	40.9	133.4	29

30°			32°			34°			36°			38°			Dec.
Hc	d	Z	Hc	d	Z	Hc	d	Z	Hc	d	Z	Hc	d	Z	
° ′	′	°	° ′	′	°	° ′	′	°	° ′	′	°	° ′	′	°	°
30 36.0	−35.1	110.0	29 53.9	−36.8	111.1	29 09.8	−38.6	112.1	28 23.6	−40.2	113.1	27 35.6	−41.9	114.1	0
30 00.9	35.4	110.9	29 17.1	37.3	112.0	28 31.2	38.9	113.0	27 43.4	40.6	114.0	26 53.7	42.1	114.9	1
29 25.5	35.9	111.8	28 39.8	37.5	112.9	27 52.3	39.3	113.8	27 02.8	40.8	114.8	26 11.6	42.3	115.7	2
28 49.6	36.2	112.8	28 02.3	37.9	113.7	27 13.0	39.5	114.7	26 22.0	41.1	115.6	25 29.3	42.6	116.5	3
28 13.4	36.5	113.7	27 24.4	38.3	114.6	26 33.5	39.9	115.5	25 40.9	41.4	116.4	24 46.7	42.8	117.3	4
27 36.9	−36.9	114.6	26 46.1	−38.5	115.5	25 53.6	−40.1	116.4	24 59.5	−41.6	117.2	24 03.9	−43.1	118.0	5
27 00.0	37.3	115.4	26 07.6	38.9	116.3	25 13.5	40.4	117.2	24 17.9	41.9	118.0	23 20.8	43.3	118.8	6
26 22.7	37.5	116.3	25 28.7	39.1	117.2	24 33.1	40.7	118.0	23 36.0	42.1	118.8	22 37.5	43.5	119.5	7
25 45.2	37.9	117.2	24 49.6	39.4	118.0	23 52.4	40.9	118.8	22 53.9	42.3	119.6	21 54.0	43.7	120.3	8
25 07.3	38.1	118.0	24 10.2	39.7	118.8	23 11.5	41.1	119.6	22 11.6	42.6	120.3	21 10.3	43.9	121.0	9
24 29.2	−38.4	118.9	23 30.5	−40.0	119.7	22 30.4	−41.4	120.4	21 29.0	−42.7	121.1	20 26.4	−44.0	121.8	10
23 50.8	38.7	119.7	22 50.5	40.1	120.5	21 49.0	41.6	121.2	20 46.3	43.0	121.9	19 42.4	44.3	122.5	11
23 12.1	39.0	120.6	22 10.4	40.4	121.3	21 07.4	41.8	122.0	20 03.3	43.1	122.6	18 58.1	44.4	123.2	12
22 33.1	39.2	121.4	21 30.0	40.7	122.1	20 25.6	42.0	122.7	19 20.2	43.3	123.3	18 13.7	44.5	123.9	13
21 53.9	39.5	122.2	20 49.3	40.8	122.9	19 43.6	42.2	123.5	18 36.9	43.5	124.1	17 29.2	44.7	124.6	14
21 14.4	−39.7	123.0	20 08.5	−41.1	123.7	19 01.4	−42.3	124.2	17 53.4	−43.6	124.8	16 44.5	−44.9	125.3	15
20 34.7	39.9	123.8	19 27.4	41.3	124.4	18 19.1	42.6	125.0	17 09.8	43.8	125.5	15 59.6	44.9	125.9	16
19 54.8	40.1	124.6	18 46.1	41.4	125.2	17 36.5	42.7	125.7	16 26.0	43.9	126.2	15 14.7	45.1	126.7	17
19 14.7	40.3	125.4	18 04.7	41.6	126.0	16 53.8	42.9	126.5	15 42.1	44.1	126.9	14 29.6	45.2	127.4	18
18 34.4	40.5	126.2	17 23.1	41.8	126.7	16 10.9	43.0	127.2	14 58.0	44.2	127.6	13 44.4	45.4	128.0	19
17 53.9	−40.7	127.0	16 41.3	−41.9	127.5	15 27.9	−43.1	127.9	14 13.8	−44.3	128.3	12 59.0	−45.4	128.7	20
17 13.2	40.9	127.7	15 59.4	42.2	128.2	14 44.8	43.3	128.6	13 29.5	44.4	129.0	12 13.6	45.5	129.4	21
16 32.3	41.0	128.5	15 17.2	42.2	129.0	14 01.5	43.4	129.4	12 45.1	44.6	129.7	11 28.1	45.6	130.1	22
15 51.3	41.2	129.3	14 35.0	42.4	129.7	13 18.1	43.6	130.1	12 00.5	44.6	130.4	10 42.5	45.7	130.7	23
15 10.1	41.4	130.0	13 52.6	42.5	130.4	12 34.5	43.6	130.8	11 15.9	44.7	131.1	9 56.8	45.8	131.4	24
14 28.8	−41.5	130.8	13 10.1	−42.6	131.1	11 50.9	−43.8	131.5	10 31.2	−44.9	131.8	9 11.0	−45.8	132.0	25
13 47.3	41.6	131.5	12 27.5	42.8	131.9	11 07.1	43.8	132.2	9 46.3	44.9	132.5	8 25.2	46.0	132.7	26
13 05.7	41.8	132.3	11 44.7	42.8	132.6	10 23.3	43.9	132.9	9 01.4	44.9	133.1	7 39.2	45.9	133.3	27
12 23.9	41.8	133.0	11 01.9	43.0	133.3	9 39.4	44.1	133.6	8 16.5	45.1	133.8	6 53.3	46.0	134.0	28
11 42.1	42.0	133.7	10 18.9	43.0	134.0	8 55.3	44.0	134.3	7 31.4	45.1	134.5	6 07.3	46.1	134.6	29

Dec.	40° Hc	d	Z	42° Hc	d	Z	44° Hc	d	Z	46° Hc	d	Z	48° Hc	d	Z
0	26 45.7	+43.0	115.0	25 54.0	+44.5	115.9	25 00.8	+45.8	116.8	24 05.9	+47.2	117.6	23 09.6	+48.4	118.4
1	27 28.7	42.8	114.3	26 38.5	44.3	115.2	25 46.6	45.7	116.1	24 53.1	47.0	116.9	23 58.0	48.3	117.7
2	28 11.5	42.5	113.5	27 22.8	44.1	114.4	26 32.3	45.5	115.3	25 40.1	46.8	116.2	24 46.3	48.1	117.1
3	28 54.0	42.3	112.7	28 06.9	43.7	113.7	27 17.8	45.2	114.6	26 26.9	46.6	115.5	25 34.4	47.9	116.4
4	29 36.3	41.9	111.8	28 50.6	43.5	112.9	28 03.0	45.0	113.9	27 13.5	46.4	114.8	26 22.3	47.7	115.7
5	30 18.2	+41.6	111.0	29 34.1	+43.2	112.1	28 48.0	+44.7	113.1	27 59.9	+46.2	114.1	27 10.0	+47.5	115.1
6	30 59.8	41.3	110.2	30 17.3	42.9	111.3	29 32.7	44.5	112.4	28 46.1	45.9	113.4	27 57.5	47.3	114.4
7	31 41.1	40.9	109.3	31 00.2	42.7	110.5	30 17.2	44.2	111.6	29 32.0	45.7	112.6	28 44.8	47.1	113.7
8	32 22.0	40.6	108.5	31 42.9	42.2	109.6	31 01.4	43.9	110.8	30 17.7	45.4	111.9	29 31.9	46.9	113.0
9	33 02.6	40.2	107.6	32 25.1	42.0	108.8	31 45.3	43.6	110.0	31 03.1	45.2	111.1	30 18.8	46.6	112.2
10	33 42.8	+39.9	106.7	33 07.1	+41.6	108.0	32 28.9	+43.2	109.2	31 48.3	+44.8	110.4	31 05.4	+46.3	111.5
11	34 22.7	39.4	105.8	33 48.7	41.2	107.1	33 12.1	43.0	108.4	32 33.1	44.6	109.6	31 51.7	46.1	110.8
12	35 02.1	39.0	104.9	34 29.9	40.9	106.2	33 55.1	42.6	107.5	33 17.7	44.2	108.8	32 37.8	45.9	110.0
13	35 41.1	38.5	104.0	35 10.8	40.4	105.3	34 37.7	42.2	106.7	34 01.9	44.0	108.0	33 23.7	45.5	109.2
14	36 19.6	38.2	103.0	35 51.2	40.0	104.4	35 19.9	41.9	105.8	34 45.9	43.6	107.1	34 09.2	45.2	108.5
15	36 57.8	+37.6	102.0	36 31.2	+39.6	103.5	36 01.8	+41.4	104.9	35 29.5	+43.2	106.3	34 54.4	+44.9	107.7
16	37 35.4	37.1	101.1	37 10.8	39.2	102.6	36 43.2	41.1	104.0	36 12.7	42.9	105.5	35 39.3	44.6	106.8
17	38 12.5	36.6	100.1	37 50.0	38.6	101.6	37 24.3	40.6	103.1	36 55.6	42.4	104.6	36 23.9	44.2	106.0
18	38 49.1	36.1	99.1	38 28.6	38.2	100.6	38 04.9	40.2	102.2	37 38.0	42.1	103.7	37 08.1	43.9	105.2
19	39 25.2	35.6	98.0	39 06.8	37.7	99.6	38 45.1	39.7	101.2	38 20.1	41.6	102.8	37 52.0	43.5	104.3
20	40 00.8	+34.9	97.0	39 44.5	+37.1	98.6	39 24.8	+39.2	100.3	39 01.7	+41.2	101.9	38 35.5	+43.0	103.4
21	40 35.7	34.4	95.9	40 21.6	36.6	97.6	40 04.0	38.7	99.3	39 42.9	40.8	100.9	39 18.5	42.7	102.5
22	41 10.1	33.8	94.8	40 58.2	36.0	96.6	40 42.7	38.2	98.3	40 23.7	40.2	100.0	40 01.2	42.2	101.6
23	41 43.9	33.1	93.7	41 34.2	35.4	95.5	41 20.9	37.6	97.3	41 03.9	39.8	99.0	40 43.4	41.8	100.7
24	42 17.0	32.4	92.6	42 09.6	34.8	94.4	41 58.5	37.0	96.2	41 43.7	39.2	98.0	41 25.2	41.2	99.7
25	42 49.4	+31.7	91.5	42 44.4	+34.1	93.3	42 35.5	+36.5	95.1	42 22.9	+38.6	97.0	42 06.4	+40.8	98.8
26	43 21.1	31.0	90.3	43 18.5	33.5	92.2	43 12.0	35.8	94.1	43 01.5	38.1	95.9	42 47.2	40.3	97.8
27	43 52.1	30.3	89.1	43 52.0	32.7	91.0	43 47.8	35.2	93.0	43 39.6	37.5	94.9	43 27.5	39.7	96.8
28	44 22.4	29.5	87.9	44 24.7	32.1	89.9	44 23.0	34.4	91.8	44 17.1	36.8	93.8	44 07.2	39.1	95.7
29	44 51.9	28.7	86.7	44 56.8	31.3	88.7	44 57.4	33.8	90.7	44 53.9	36.2	92.7	44 46.3	38.5	94.7

Dec.	50° Hc	d	Z	52° Hc	d	Z	54° Hc	d	Z	56° Hc	d	Z	58° Hc	d	Z
0	22 11.9	+49.6	119.1	21 12.9	+50.7	119.8	20 12.7	+51.7	120.4	19 11.3	+52.7	121.1	18 08.9	+53.5	121.6
1	23 01.5	49.4	118.5	22 03.6	50.5	119.2	21 04.4	51.6	119.9	20 04.0	52.5	120.6	19 02.4	53.4	121.2
2	23 50.9	49.3	117.9	22 54.1	50.3	118.6	21 56.0	51.4	119.4	20 56.5	52.4	120.0	19 55.8	53.4	120.7
3	24 40.2	49.0	117.2	23 44.5	50.3	118.0	22 47.4	51.4	118.8	21 48.9	52.4	119.5	20 49.2	53.3	120.2
4	25 29.3	49.0	116.6	24 34.8	50.1	117.4	23 38.8	51.2	118.2	22 41.3	52.2	119.0	21 42.5	53.2	119.7
5	26 18.3	+48.8	116.0	25 24.9	+50.0	116.8	24 30.0	+51.1	117.7	23 33.5	+52.2	118.5	22 35.7	+53.1	119.2
6	27 07.1	48.6	115.3	26 14.9	49.8	116.2	25 21.1	50.9	117.1	24 25.7	52.0	117.9	23 28.8	52.9	118.7
7	27 55.7	48.4	114.7	27 04.7	49.7	115.6	26 12.0	50.8	116.5	25 17.7	51.9	117.4	24 21.7	52.9	118.2
8	28 44.1	48.2	114.0	27 54.4	49.4	115.0	27 02.8	50.7	115.9	26 09.6	51.7	116.8	25 14.6	52.8	117.7
9	29 32.3	48.0	113.3	28 43.8	49.3	114.3	27 53.5	50.5	115.3	27 01.3	51.6	116.2	26 07.4	52.7	117.1
10	30 20.3	+47.8	112.6	29 33.1	+49.1	113.7	28 44.0	+50.3	114.7	27 52.9	+51.5	115.7	27 00.1	+52.5	116.6
11	31 08.1	47.5	111.9	30 22.2	48.9	113.0	29 34.3	50.1	114.1	28 44.4	51.3	115.1	27 52.6	52.4	116.1
12	31 55.6	47.3	111.2	31 11.1	48.7	112.3	30 24.4	50.0	113.4	29 35.7	51.2	114.5	28 45.0	52.3	115.5
13	32 42.9	47.0	110.5	31 59.8	48.4	111.6	31 14.4	49.8	112.8	30 26.9	51.0	113.9	29 37.3	52.1	114.9
14	33 29.9	46.8	109.7	32 48.2	48.2	110.9	32 04.2	49.5	112.1	31 17.9	50.8	113.3	30 29.4	52.0	114.4
15	34 16.7	+46.5	109.0	33 36.4	+48.0	110.2	32 53.7	+49.4	111.5	32 08.7	+50.6	112.6	31 21.4	+51.8	113.8
16	35 03.2	46.2	108.2	34 24.4	47.7	109.5	33 43.1	49.1	110.8	32 59.3	50.4	112.0	32 13.2	51.6	113.2
17	35 49.4	45.9	107.4	35 12.1	47.4	108.8	34 32.2	48.9	110.1	33 49.7	50.2	111.4	33 04.8	51.5	112.6
18	36 35.3	45.5	106.6	35 59.5	47.2	108.0	35 21.1	48.6	109.4	34 39.9	50.0	110.7	33 56.3	51.3	112.0
19	37 20.8	45.2	105.8	36 46.7	46.8	107.2	36 09.7	48.3	108.7	35 29.9	49.8	110.0	34 47.6	51.0	111.3
20	38 06.0	+44.9	105.0	37 33.5	+46.5	106.5	36 58.0	+48.1	107.9	36 19.7	+49.5	109.3	35 38.6	+50.9	110.7
21	38 50.9	44.4	104.1	38 20.0	46.2	105.7	37 46.1	47.8	107.2	37 09.2	49.3	108.6	36 29.5	50.6	110.0
22	39 35.3	44.1	103.3	39 06.2	45.8	104.8	38 33.9	47.5	106.4	37 58.5	49.0	107.9	37 20.1	50.4	109.4
23	40 19.4	43.7	102.5	39 52.0	45.5	104.0	39 21.4	47.1	105.6	38 47.5	48.7	107.2	38 10.5	50.2	108.7
24	41 03.1	43.2	101.5	40 37.5	45.1	103.2	40 08.5	46.8	104.8	39 36.2	48.4	106.4	39 00.7	49.9	108.0
25	41 46.3	+42.8	100.5	41 22.6	+44.6	102.3	40 55.3	+46.4	104.0	40 24.6	+48.1	105.6	39 50.6	+49.7	107.3
26	42 29.1	42.3	99.6	42 07.2	44.3	101.4	41 41.7	46.1	103.1	41 12.7	47.8	104.9	40 40.3	49.3	106.5
27	43 11.4	41.8	98.6	42 51.5	43.8	100.5	42 27.8	45.7	102.3	42 00.5	47.4	104.0	41 29.6	49.1	105.8
28	43 53.2	41.3	97.6	43 35.3	43.3	99.5	43 13.5	45.2	101.4	42 47.9	47.1	103.2	42 18.7	48.7	105.0
29	44 34.5	40.7	96.6	44 18.6	42.8	98.6	43 58.7	44.8	100.5	43 35.0	46.6	102.4	43 07.4	48.4	104.2

40° Hc	d	Z	42° Hc	d	Z	44° Hc	d	Z	46° Hc	d	Z	48° Hc	d	Z	Dec.
26 45.7	−43.4	115.0	25 54.0	−44.7	115.9	25 00.8	−46.1	116.8	24 05.9	−47.3	117.6	23 09.6	−48.6	118.4	0
26 02.3	43.5	115.8	25 09.3	45.0	116.7	24 14.7	46.3	117.5	23 18.6	47.6	118.3	22 21.0	48.7	119.0	1
25 18.8	43.8	116.6	24 24.3	45.1	117.4	23 28.4	46.5	118.2	22 31.0	47.7	118.9	21 32.3	48.8	119.6	2
24 35.0	44.0	117.3	23 39.2	45.4	118.1	22 41.9	46.6	118.9	21 43.3	47.8	119.6	20 43.5	49.0	120.3	3
23 51.0	44.3	118.1	22 53.8	45.6	118.8	21 55.3	46.8	119.5	20 55.5	48.0	120.2	19 54.5	49.2	120.9	4
23 06.7	−44.4	118.8	22 08.2	−45.7	119.5	21 08.5	−47.0	120.2	20 07.5	−48.2	120.9	19 05.3	−49.2	121.5	5
22 22.3	44.6	119.5	21 22.5	45.9	120.2	20 21.5	47.1	120.9	19 19.3	48.2	121.5	18 16.1	49.3	122.1	6
21 37.7	44.8	120.3	20 36.6	46.1	120.9	19 34.4	47.3	121.5	18 31.1	48.4	122.1	17 26.8	49.5	122.7	7
20 52.9	45.0	121.0	19 50.5	46.2	121.6	18 47.1	47.4	122.2	17 42.7	48.5	122.8	16 37.3	49.6	123.3	8
20 07.9	45.2	121.7	19 04.3	46.3	122.3	17 59.7	47.5	122.8	16 54.2	48.6	123.4	15 47.7	49.6	123.9	9
19 22.7	−45.3	122.4	18 18.0	−46.6	122.9	17 12.2	−47.6	123.5	16 05.6	−48.7	124.0	14 58.1	−49.7	124.4	10
18 37.4	45.5	123.1	17 31.4	46.6	123.6	16 24.6	47.8	124.1	15 16.9	48.8	124.6	14 08.4	49.9	125.0	11
17 51.9	45.6	123.8	16 44.8	46.7	124.3	15 36.8	47.9	124.7	14 28.0	48.9	125.2	13 18.5	49.9	125.6	12
17 06.3	45.7	124.4	15 58.1	46.9	124.9	14 49.0	48.0	125.4	13 39.1	49.0	125.8	12 28.6	49.9	126.2	13
16 20.6	45.9	125.1	15 11.2	47.0	125.6	14 01.0	48.1	126.0	12 50.1	49.0	126.4	11 38.7	50.1	126.7	14
15 34.7	−46.0	125.8	14 24.2	−47.1	126.2	13 12.9	−48.1	126.6	12 01.1	−49.2	127.0	10 48.6	−50.1	127.3	15
14 48.7	46.1	126.4	13 37.1	47.2	126.9	12 24.8	48.2	127.2	11 11.9	49.2	127.6	9 58.5	50.1	127.9	16
14 02.6	46.2	127.1	12 49.9	47.3	127.5	11 36.6	48.3	127.8	10 22.7	49.2	128.1	9 08.4	50.2	128.4	17
13 16.4	46.3	127.8	12 02.6	47.3	128.1	10 48.3	48.4	128.4	9 33.5	49.4	128.7	8 18.2	50.3	129.0	18
12 30.1	46.4	128.4	11 15.3	47.5	128.7	9 59.9	48.4	129.0	8 44.1	49.4	129.3	7 27.9	50.2	129.5	19
11 43.7	−46.5	129.1	10 27.8	−47.5	129.4	9 11.5	−48.5	129.6	7 54.7	−49.4	129.9	6 37.7	−50.4	130.1	20
10 57.2	46.6	129.7	9 40.3	47.6	130.0	8 23.0	48.6	130.2	7 05.3	49.5	130.4	5 47.3	50.3	130.6	21
10 10.6	46.6	130.4	8 52.7	47.6	130.6	7 34.4	48.6	130.8	6 15.8	49.5	131.0	4 57.0	50.4	131.2	22
9 24.0	46.7	131.0	8 05.1	47.7	131.2	6 45.8	48.6	131.4	5 26.3	49.5	131.6	4 06.6	50.4	131.7	23
8 37.3	46.8	131.6	7 17.4	47.8	131.8	5 57.2	48.7	132.0	4 36.8	49.6	132.1	3 16.2	50.4	132.2	24
7 50.5	−46.9	132.3	6 29.6	−47.8	132.4	5 08.5	−48.7	132.6	3 47.2	−49.6	132.7	2 25.8	−50.5	132.8	25
7 03.6	46.8	132.9	5 41.8	47.8	133.1	4 19.8	48.7	133.2	2 57.6	49.6	133.3	1 35.3	50.4	133.3	26
6 16.8	47.0	133.5	4 54.0	47.8	133.7	3 31.1	48.8	133.8	2 08.0	49.6	133.8	0 44.9	−50.5	133.9	27
5 29.8	46.9	134.1	4 06.2	47.9	134.3	2 42.3	48.7	134.3	1 18.4	49.6	134.4	0 05.6	+50.4	45.6	28
4 42.9	47.1	134.8	3 18.3	47.9	134.9	1 53.6	48.8	134.9	0 28.8	−49.6	135.0	0 56.0	50.5	45.0	29

50° Hc	d	Z	52° Hc	d	Z	54° Hc	d	Z	56° Hc	d	Z	58° Hc	d	Z	Dec.
22 11.9	−49.7	119.1	21 12.9	−50.7	119.8	20 12.7	−51.8	120.4	19 11.3	−52.7	121.1	18 08.9	−53.6	121.6	0
21 22.2	49.8	119.7	20 22.2	50.9	120.4	19 20.9	51.8	121.0	18 18.6	52.8	121.6	17 15.3	53.6	122.1	1
20 32.4	50.0	120.3	19 31.3	51.0	120.9	18 29.1	52.0	121.5	17 25.8	52.8	122.1	16 21.7	53.7	122.6	2
19 42.4	50.0	120.9	18 40.3	51.1	121.5	17 37.1	52.0	122.0	16 33.0	53.0	122.6	15 28.0	53.8	123.0	3
18 52.4	50.2	121.5	17 49.2	51.2	122.0	16 45.1	52.1	122.6	15 40.0	52.9	123.1	14 34.2	53.8	123.5	4
18 02.2	−50.3	122.0	16 58.0	−51.2	122.6	15 53.0	−52.2	123.1	14 47.1	−53.1	123.5	13 40.4	−53.9	124.0	5
17 11.9	50.4	122.6	16 06.8	51.4	123.1	15 00.8	52.3	123.6	13 54.0	53.1	124.0	12 46.5	53.9	124.4	6
16 21.5	50.5	123.2	15 15.4	51.4	123.7	14 08.5	52.3	124.1	13 00.9	53.2	124.5	11 52.6	54.0	124.9	7
15 31.0	50.5	123.8	14 24.0	51.5	124.2	13 16.2	52.4	124.6	12 07.7	53.2	125.0	10 58.6	54.0	125.3	8
14 40.5	50.7	124.3	13 32.5	51.6	124.7	12 23.8	52.4	125.1	11 14.5	53.3	125.4	10 04.6	54.0	125.7	9
13 49.9	−50.7	124.9	12 40.9	−51.6	125.2	11 31.4	−52.5	125.6	10 21.2	−53.3	125.9	9 10.6	−54.0	126.2	10
12 59.2	50.8	125.4	11 49.3	51.7	125.8	10 38.9	52.5	126.1	9 27.9	53.3	126.4	8 16.6	54.1	126.6	11
12 08.4	50.9	126.0	10 57.6	51.7	126.3	9 46.4	52.6	126.6	8 34.6	53.4	126.8	7 22.5	54.2	127.1	12
11 17.5	50.9	126.5	10 05.9	51.8	126.8	8 53.8	52.6	127.1	7 41.2	53.4	127.3	6 28.3	54.1	127.5	13
10 26.6	50.9	127.0	9 14.1	51.8	127.3	8 01.2	52.7	127.6	6 47.8	53.4	127.8	5 34.2	54.1	127.9	14
9 35.7	−51.0	127.6	8 22.3	−51.9	127.8	7 08.5	−52.7	128.0	5 54.4	−53.4	128.2	4 40.1	−54.2	128.4	15
8 44.7	51.1	128.1	7 30.4	51.9	128.3	6 15.8	52.7	128.5	5 01.0	53.5	128.7	3 45.9	54.2	128.8	16
7 53.6	51.0	128.6	6 38.5	51.9	128.8	5 23.1	52.7	129.0	4 07.5	53.5	129.1	2 51.7	54.2	129.2	17
7 02.6	51.2	129.2	5 46.6	51.9	129.3	4 30.4	52.7	129.5	3 14.0	53.5	129.6	1 57.5	54.2	129.7	18
6 11.4	51.1	129.7	4 54.7	52.0	129.8	3 37.7	52.8	130.0	2 20.5	53.5	130.0	1 03.3	54.2	130.1	19
5 20.3	−51.2	130.2	4 02.7	−52.0	130.3	2 44.9	−52.7	130.4	1 27.0	−53.5	130.5	0 09.1	−54.2	130.5	20
4 29.1	51.2	130.7	3 10.7	52.0	130.8	1 52.2	52.8	130.9	0 33.5	−53.5	130.9	0 45.1	+54.2	49.1	21
3 37.9	51.2	131.3	2 18.7	52.0	131.3	0 59.4	52.8	131.4	0 20.0	+53.5	48.6	1 39.3	54.2	48.6	22
2 46.7	51.2	131.8	1 26.7	52.1	131.8	0 06.6	−52.8	131.9	1 13.5	53.5	48.1	2 33.5	54.2	48.2	23
1 55.5	51.3	132.3	0 34.6	−52.0	132.3	0 46.2	+52.8	47.7	2 07.0	53.5	47.7	3 27.7	54.2	47.8	24
1 04.2	−51.2	132.8	0 17.4	+52.0	47.2	1 39.0	+52.7	47.2	3 00.5	+53.5	47.2	4 21.9	+54.1	47.3	25
0 13.0	−51.3	133.4	1 09.4	52.0	46.7	2 31.7	52.8	46.7	3 54.0	53.4	46.8	5 16.0	54.2	46.9	26
0 38.3	+51.2	46.1	2 01.4	52.0	46.2	3 24.5	52.7	46.2	4 47.4	53.5	46.3	6 10.2	54.1	46.5	27
1 29.5	51.3	45.6	2 53.4	52.0	45.7	4 17.2	52.8	45.8	5 40.9	53.4	45.9	7 04.3	54.1	46.0	28
2 20.8	51.2	45.1	3 45.4	52.0	45.2	5 10.0	52.7	45.3	6 34.3	53.4	45.4	7 58.4	54.1	45.6	29

Dec.	0° Hc	d	Z	2° Hc	d	Z	4° Hc	d	Z	6° Hc	d	Z	8° Hc	d	Z
0	34 00.0	- 0.4	90.0	33 58.6	+ 2.2	91.3	33 54.4	+ 4.6	92.7	33 47.3	+ 7.2	94.0	33 37.5	+ 9.7	95.4
1	33 59.6	1.0	88.8	34 00.8	1.4	90.1	33 59.0	4.0	91.5	33 54.5	6.5	92.8	33 47.2	9.0	94.2
2	33 58.6	1.8	87.6	34 02.2	+ 0.8	88.9	34 03.0	3.3	90.3	34 01.0	5.8	91.6	33 56.2	8.3	93.0
3	33 56.8	2.4	86.4	34 03.0	0.0	87.7	34 06.3	2.6	89.1	34 06.8	5.1	90.4	34 04.5	7.6	91.8
4	33 54.4	3.2	85.2	34 03.0	- 0.6	86.5	34 08.9	1.9	87.9	34 11.9	4.4	89.2	34 12.1	6.9	90.6
5	33 51.2	- 3.9	84.0	34 02.4	- 1.4	85.3	34 10.8	+ 1.1	86.7	34 16.3	+ 3.7	88.0	34 19.0	+ 6.2	89.4
6	33 47.3	4.6	82.8	34 01.0	2.0	84.1	34 11.9	+ 0.5	85.5	34 20.0	3.0	86.8	34 25.2	5.5	88.2
7	33 42.7	5.2	81.6	33 59.0	2.8	82.9	34 12.4	- 0.3	84.3	34 23.0	2.2	85.6	34 30.7	4.8	87.0
8	33 37.5	6.0	80.4	33 56.2	3.5	81.7	34 12.1	1.0	83.0	34 25.2	1.6	84.4	34 35.5	4.1	85.8
9	33 31.5	6.6	79.2	33 52.7	4.2	80.5	34 11.1	1.7	81.8	34 26.8	0.8	83.2	34 39.6	3.3	84.6
10	33 24.9	- 7.3	78.0	33 48.5	- 4.8	79.3	34 09.4	- 2.3	80.6	34 27.6	+ 0.1	82.0	34 42.9	+ 2.7	83.3
11	33 17.6	8.0	76.8	33 43.7	5.6	78.1	34 07.1	3.2	79.4	34 27.7	- 0.6	80.8	34 45.6	1.9	82.1
12	33 09.6	8.7	75.6	33 38.1	6.3	76.9	34 03.9	3.8	78.2	34 27.1	1.3	79.5	34 47.5	1.1	80.9
13	33 00.9	9.3	74.4	33 31.8	6.9	75.7	34 00.1	4.5	77.0	34 25.8	2.1	78.3	34 48.6	+ 0.5	79.7
14	32 51.6	10.0	73.3	33 24.9	7.6	74.5	33 55.6	5.2	75.8	34 23.7	2.8	77.1	34 49.1	- 0.3	78.5
15	32 41.6	-10.7	72.1	33 17.3	- 8.3	73.3	33 50.4	- 5.9	74.6	34 20.9	- 3.4	75.9	34 48.8	- 1.0	77.3
16	32 30.9	11.2	70.9	33 09.0	9.0	72.1	33 44.5	6.6	73.4	34 17.5	4.2	74.7	34 47.8	1.8	76.0
17	32 19.7	12.0	69.8	33 00.0	9.6	71.0	33 37.9	7.3	72.2	34 13.3	4.9	73.5	34 46.0	2.4	74.8
18	32 07.7	12.5	68.6	32 50.4	10.3	69.8	33 30.6	8.0	71.0	34 08.4	5.6	72.3	34 43.6	3.2	73.6
19	31 55.2	13.2	67.4	32 40.1	11.0	68.6	33 22.6	8.6	69.8	34 02.8	6.3	71.1	34 40.4	3.9	72.4
20	31 42.0	-13.8	66.3	32 29.1	-11.6	67.5	33 14.0	- 9.3	68.6	33 56.5	- 7.0	69.9	34 36.5	- 4.7	71.2
21	31 28.2	14.4	65.2	32 17.5	12.2	66.3	33 04.7	10.0	67.5	33 49.5	7.7	68.7	34 31.8	5.3	70.0
22	31 13.8	15.0	64.0	32 05.3	12.8	65.1	32 54.7	10.7	66.3	33 41.8	8.4	67.5	34 26.5	6.1	68.8
23	30 58.8	15.6	62.9	31 52.5	13.5	64.0	32 44.0	11.2	65.1	33 33.4	9.1	66.3	34 20.4	6.7	67.6
24	30 43.2	16.1	61.8	31 39.0	14.1	62.8	32 32.8	12.0	64.0	33 24.3	9.7	65.1	34 13.7	7.5	66.3
25	30 27.1	-16.8	60.6	31 24.9	-14.6	61.7	32 20.8	-12.5	62.8	33 14.6	-10.4	63.9	34 06.2	- 8.2	65.2
26	30 10.3	17.3	59.5	31 10.3	15.3	60.6	32 08.3	13.2	61.6	33 04.2	11.0	62.8	33 58.0	8.8	64.0
27	29 53.0	17.8	58.4	30 55.0	15.9	59.4	31 55.1	13.9	60.5	32 53.2	11.7	61.6	33 49.2	9.6	62.8
28	29 35.2	18.4	57.3	30 39.1	16.4	58.3	31 41.2	14.4	59.3	32 41.5	12.4	60.4	33 39.6	10.2	61.6
29	29 16.8	18.9	56.2	30 22.7	17.0	57.2	31 26.8	15.0	58.2	32 29.1	13.0	59.3	33 29.4	10.9	60.4

Dec.	10° Hc	d	Z	12° Hc	d	Z	14° Hc	d	Z	16° Hc	d	Z	18° Hc	d	Z
0	33 24.9	+12.1	96.7	33 09.6	+14.6	98.0	32 51.6	+16.9	99.3	32 30.9	+19.4	100.5	32 07.7	+21.6	101.8
1	33 37.0	11.5	95.5	33 24.2	13.9	96.8	33 08.5	16.4	98.1	32 50.3	18.7	99.4	32 29.3	21.1	100.7
2	33 48.5	10.8	94.3	33 38.1	13.2	95.7	33 24.9	15.7	97.0	33 09.0	18.0	98.3	32 50.4	20.4	99.6
3	33 59.3	10.1	93.1	33 51.3	12.6	94.5	33 40.6	15.0	95.8	33 27.0	17.5	97.1	33 10.8	19.8	98.4
4	34 09.4	9.5	92.0	34 03.9	12.0	93.3	33 55.6	14.4	94.7	33 44.5	16.8	96.0	33 30.6	19.2	97.3
5	34 18.9	+ 8.7	90.8	34 15.9	+11.2	92.1	34 10.0	+13.7	93.5	34 01.3	+16.2	94.8	33 49.8	+18.6	96.2
6	34 27.6	8.0	89.6	34 27.1	10.5	90.9	34 23.7	13.0	92.3	34 17.5	15.5	93.7	34 08.4	17.9	95.0
7	34 35.6	7.3	88.4	34 37.6	9.9	89.7	34 36.7	12.4	91.1	34 33.0	14.8	92.5	34 26.3	17.3	93.9
8	34 42.9	6.6	87.1	34 47.5	9.1	88.5	34 49.1	11.6	89.9	34 47.8	14.1	91.3	34 43.6	16.6	92.7
9	34 49.5	5.9	85.9	34 56.6	8.4	87.3	35 00.7	10.9	88.7	35 01.9	13.5	90.1	35 00.2	15.9	91.5
10	34 55.4	+ 5.2	84.7	35 05.0	+ 7.7	86.1	35 11.6	+10.3	87.5	35 15.4	+12.7	88.9	35 16.1	+15.2	90.4
11	35 00.6	4.4	83.5	35 12.7	6.9	84.9	35 21.9	9.5	86.3	35 28.1	12.0	87.7	35 31.3	14.6	89.2
12	35 05.0	3.7	82.3	35 19.6	6.3	83.7	35 31.4	8.7	85.1	35 40.1	11.3	86.5	35 45.9	13.8	88.0
13	35 08.7	2.9	81.1	35 25.9	5.5	82.5	35 40.1	8.0	83.9	35 51.4	10.6	85.3	35 59.7	13.1	86.8
14	35 11.6	2.3	79.8	35 31.4	4.7	81.2	35 48.1	7.3	82.7	36 02.0	9.8	84.1	36 12.8	12.3	85.6
15	35 13.9	+ 1.5	78.6	35 36.1	+ 4.0	80.0	35 55.4	+ 6.6	81.4	36 11.8	+ 9.1	82.9	36 25.1	+11.6	84.3
16	35 15.4	+ 0.7	77.4	35 40.1	3.3	78.8	36 02.0	5.7	80.2	36 20.9	8.3	81.7	36 36.7	10.9	83.1
17	35 16.1	0.0	76.2	35 43.4	2.5	77.6	36 07.7	5.1	79.0	36 29.2	7.5	80.4	36 47.6	10.1	81.9
18	35 16.1	- 0.7	75.0	35 45.9	1.7	76.3	36 12.8	4.2	77.8	36 36.7	6.8	79.2	36 57.7	9.4	80.7
19	35 15.4	1.5	73.7	35 47.6	1.0	75.1	36 17.0	3.5	76.5	36 43.5	6.1	78.0	37 07.1	8.5	79.4
20	35 13.9	- 2.2	72.5	35 48.6	+ 0.2	73.9	36 20.5	+ 2.7	75.3	36 49.6	+ 5.2	76.7	37 15.6	+ 7.8	78.2
21	35 11.7	3.0	71.3	35 48.8	- 0.5	72.6	36 23.2	2.0	74.0	36 54.8	4.5	75.5	37 23.4	7.0	76.9
22	35 08.7	3.7	70.1	35 48.3	1.3	71.4	36 25.2	1.2	72.8	36 59.3	3.6	74.2	37 30.4	6.2	75.7
23	35 05.0	4.4	68.8	35 47.0	2.0	70.2	36 26.4	+ 0.4	71.6	37 02.9	2.9	73.0	37 36.6	5.4	74.4
24	35 00.6	5.2	67.6	35 45.0	2.8	68.9	36 26.8	- 0.4	70.3	37 05.8	2.1	71.7	37 42.0	4.6	73.2
25	34 55.4	- 5.8	66.4	35 42.2	- 3.5	67.7	36 26.4	- 1.1	69.1	37 07.9	+ 1.3	70.5	37 46.6	+ 3.8	71.9
26	34 49.6	6.6	65.2	35 38.7	4.3	66.5	36 25.3	1.9	67.8	37 09.2	+ 0.6	69.2	37 50.4	3.0	70.7
27	34 43.0	7.4	64.0	35 34.4	5.0	65.3	36 23.4	2.7	66.6	37 09.8	- 0.3	68.0	37 53.4	2.2	69.4
28	34 35.6	8.0	62.8	35 29.4	5.8	64.0	36 20.7	3.4	65.3	37 09.5	1.1	66.7	37 55.6	1.3	68.1
29	34 27.6	8.7	61.6	35 23.6	6.5	62.8	36 17.3	4.3	64.1	37 08.4	1.9	65.4	37 56.9	+ 0.6	66.9

0°			2°			4°			6°			8°			Dec.
Hc	d	Z	Hc	d	Z	Hc	d	Z	Hc	d	Z	Hc	d	Z	
° ′	′	°	° ′	′	°	° ′	′	°	° ′	′	°	° ′	′	°	°
34 00.0	- 0.4	90.0	33 58.6	- 2.9	91.3	33 54.4	- 5.4	92.7	33 47.3	- 7.9	94.0	33 37.5	- 10.4	95.4	0
33 59.6	1.0	91.2	33 55.7	3.6	92.6	33 49.0	6.1	93.9	33 39.4	8.6	95.2	33 27.1	11.0	96.5	1
33 58.6	1.8	92.4	33 52.1	4.2	93.8	33 42.9	6.8	95.1	33 30.8	9.2	96.4	33 16.1	11.7	97.7	2
33 56.8	2.4	93.6	33 47.9	5.0	95.0	33 36.1	7.5	96.3	33 21.6	9.9	97.6	33 04.4	12.4	98.9	3
33 54.4	3.2	94.8	33 42.9	5.7	96.2	33 28.6	8.1	97.5	33 11.7	10.6	98.8	32 52.0	13.0	100.1	4
33 51.2	- 3.9	96.0	33 37.2	- 6.4	97.4	33 20.5	- 8.8	98.7	33 01.1	- 11.3	100.0	32 39.0	- 13.6	101.2	5
33 47.3	4.6	97.2	33 30.8	7.0	98.5	33 11.7	9.5	99.8	32 49.8	11.9	101.1	32 25.4	14.3	102.4	6
33 42.7	5.2	98.4	33 23.8	7.7	99.7	33 02.2	10.2	101.0	32 37.9	12.5	102.3	32 11.1	14.9	103.5	7
33 37.5	6.0	99.6	33 16.1	8.4	100.9	32 52.0	10.8	102.2	32 25.4	13.2	103.4	31 56.2	15.5	104.7	8
33 31.5	6.6	100.8	33 07.7	9.1	102.1	32 41.2	11.4	103.4	32 12.2	13.8	104.6	31 40.7	16.0	105.8	9
33 24.9	- 7.3	102.0	32 58.6	- 9.7	103.3	32 29.8	- 12.1	104.5	31 58.4	- 14.4	105.7	31 24.7	- 16.7	106.9	10
33 17.6	8.0	103.2	32 48.9	10.4	104.5	32 17.7	12.8	105.7	31 44.0	15.0	106.9	31 08.0	17.3	108.1	11
33 09.6	8.7	104.4	32 38.5	11.0	105.6	32 04.9	13.3	106.8	31 29.0	15.7	108.0	30 50.7	17.9	109.2	12
33 00.9	9.3	105.6	32 27.5	11.7	106.8	31 51.6	14.0	108.0	31 13.3	16.2	109.2	30 32.8	18.4	110.3	13
32 51.6	10.0	106.8	32 15.8	12.3	108.0	31 37.6	14.6	109.1	30 57.1	16.8	110.3	30 14.4	18.9	111.4	14
32 41.6	- 10.7	107.9	32 03.5	- 13.0	109.1	31 23.0	- 15.2	110.3	30 40.3	- 17.3	111.4	29 55.5	- 19.5	112.5	15
32 30.9	11.2	109.1	31 50.5	13.5	110.3	31 07.8	15.7	111.4	30 23.0	18.0	112.5	29 36.0	20.0	113.6	16
32 19.7	12.0	110.2	31 37.0	14.2	111.4	30 52.1	16.4	112.5	30 05.0	18.4	113.6	29 16.0	20.6	114.7	17
32 07.7	12.5	111.4	31 22.8	14.8	112.5	30 35.7	16.9	113.7	29 46.6	19.1	114.7	28 55.4	21.0	115.7	18
31 55.2	13.2	112.6	31 08.0	15.3	113.7	30 18.8	17.5	114.8	29 27.5	19.5	115.8	28 34.4	21.6	116.8	19
31 42.0	- 13.8	113.7	30 52.7	- 16.0	114.8	30 01.3	- 18.0	115.9	29 08.0	- 20.1	116.9	28 12.8	- 22.0	117.9	20
31 28.2	14.4	114.8	30 36.7	16.5	115.9	29 43.3	18.6	117.0	28 47.9	20.6	118.0	27 50.8	22.6	118.9	21
31 13.8	15.0	116.0	30 20.2	17.1	117.0	29 24.7	19.1	118.1	28 27.3	21.0	119.0	27 28.2	22.9	120.0	22
30 58.8	15.6	117.1	30 03.1	17.6	118.2	29 05.6	19.6	119.2	28 06.3	21.6	120.1	27 05.3	23.5	121.0	23
30 43.2	16.1	118.2	29 45.5	18.2	119.3	28 46.0	20.2	120.2	27 44.7	22.1	121.2	26 41.8	23.9	122.0	24
30 27.1	- 16.8	119.4	29 27.3	- 18.7	120.4	28 25.8	- 20.6	121.3	27 22.6	- 22.5	122.2	26 17.9	- 24.3	123.1	25
30 10.3	17.3	120.5	29 08.6	19.3	121.4	28 05.2	21.2	122.4	27 00.1	22.9	123.2	25 53.6	24.7	124.1	26
29 53.0	17.8	121.6	28 49.3	19.7	122.5	27 44.0	21.6	123.4	26 37.2	23.5	124.3	25 28.9	25.2	125.1	27
29 35.2	18.4	122.7	28 29.6	20.3	123.6	27 22.4	22.1	124.5	26 13.7	23.8	125.3	25 03.7	25.6	126.1	28
29 16.8	18.9	123.8	28 09.3	20.7	124.7	27 00.3	22.5	125.5	25 49.9	24.3	126.3	24 38.1	25.9	127.1	29

10°			12°			14°			16°			18°			Dec.
Hc	d	Z	Hc	d	Z	Hc	d	Z	Hc	d	Z	Hc	d	Z	
° ′	′	°	° ′	′	°	° ′	′	°	° ′	′	°	° ′	′	°	°
33 24.9	- 12.8	96.7	33 09.6	- 15.2	98.0	32 51.6	- 17.6	99.3	32 30.9	- 19.9	100.5	32 07.7	- 22.1	101.8	0
33 12.1	13.5	97.8	32 54.4	15.9	99.1	32 34.0	18.2	100.4	32 11.0	20.5	101.6	31 45.6	22.8	102.9	1
32 58.6	14.1	99.0	32 38.5	16.5	100.3	32 15.8	18.8	101.5	31 50.5	21.0	102.8	31 22.8	23.3	104.0	2
32 44.5	14.7	100.2	32 22.0	17.1	101.4	31 57.0	19.4	102.7	31 29.5	21.7	103.9	30 59.5	23.8	105.0	3
32 29.8	15.4	101.3	32 04.9	17.6	102.6	31 37.6	19.9	103.8	31 07.8	22.1	104.9	30 35.7	24.3	106.1	4
32 14.4	- 16.0	102.5	31 47.3	- 18.3	103.7	31 17.7	- 20.6	104.9	30 45.7	- 22.7	106.0	30 11.4	- 24.8	107.2	5
31 58.4	16.6	103.6	31 29.0	18.9	104.8	30 57.1	21.0	106.0	30 23.0	23.3	107.1	29 46.6	25.4	108.2	6
31 41.8	17.1	104.7	31 10.1	19.4	105.9	30 36.1	21.7	107.1	29 59.7	23.7	108.2	29 21.2	25.8	109.3	7
31 24.7	17.8	105.9	30 50.7	20.0	107.0	30 14.4	22.1	108.1	29 36.0	24.3	109.2	28 55.4	26.3	110.3	8
31 06.9	18.4	107.0	30 30.7	20.5	108.1	29 52.3	22.7	109.2	29 11.7	24.7	110.3	28 29.1	26.7	111.3	9
30 48.5	- 18.9	108.1	30 10.2	- 21.1	109.2	29 29.6	- 23.1	110.3	28 47.0	- 25.2	111.3	28 02.4	- 27.2	112.3	10
30 29.6	19.4	109.2	29 49.1	21.6	110.3	29 06.5	23.7	111.3	28 21.8	25.7	112.4	27 35.2	27.6	113.3	11
30 10.2	20.0	110.3	29 27.5	22.1	111.4	28 42.8	24.1	112.4	27 56.1	26.1	113.4	27 07.6	28.1	114.3	12
29 50.2	20.6	111.4	29 05.4	22.6	112.4	28 18.7	24.7	113.4	27 30.0	26.6	114.4	26 39.5	28.4	115.3	13
29 29.6	21.0	112.5	28 42.8	23.1	113.5	27 54.0	25.0	114.5	27 03.4	27.0	115.4	26 11.1	28.9	116.3	14
29 08.6	- 21.6	113.5	28 19.7	- 23.6	114.5	27 29.0	- 25.6	115.5	26 36.4	- 27.4	116.4	25 42.2	- 29.2	117.3	15
28 47.0	22.1	114.6	27 56.1	24.0	115.6	27 03.4	25.9	116.5	26 09.0	27.8	117.4	25 13.0	29.6	118.3	16
28 24.9	22.5	115.7	27 32.1	24.4	116.6	26 37.5	26.4	117.5	25 41.2	28.2	118.4	24 43.4	30.0	119.2	17
28 02.4	23.0	116.7	27 07.6	25.0	117.6	26 11.1	26.8	118.5	25 13.0	28.6	119.4	24 13.4	30.3	120.2	18
27 39.4	23.5	117.8	26 42.6	25.3	118.7	25 44.3	27.2	119.5	24 44.4	28.9	120.3	23 43.1	30.7	121.1	19
27 15.9	- 24.0	118.8	26 17.3	- 25.9	119.7	25 17.1	- 27.6	120.5	24 15.5	- 29.4	121.3	23 12.4	- 30.9	122.0	20
26 51.9	24.4	119.8	25 51.5	26.3	120.7	24 49.5	28.0	121.5	23 46.1	29.6	122.3	22 41.5	31.4	123.0	21
26 27.5	24.8	120.8	25 25.2	26.6	121.7	24 21.5	28.3	122.5	23 16.5	30.1	123.2	22 10.1	31.6	123.9	22
26 02.7	25.3	121.9	24 58.6	27.0	122.7	23 53.2	28.7	123.4	22 46.4	30.3	124.1	21 38.5	31.9	124.8	23
25 37.4	25.6	122.9	24 31.6	27.4	123.6	23 24.5	29.1	124.4	22 16.1	30.7	125.1	21 06.6	32.2	125.7	24
25 11.8	- 26.1	123.9	24 04.2	- 27.7	124.6	22 55.4	- 29.4	125.3	21 45.4	- 30.9	126.0	20 34.4	- 32.5	126.6	25
24 45.7	26.5	124.9	23 36.5	28.1	125.6	22 26.0	29.7	126.3	21 14.5	31.3	126.9	20 01.9	32.8	127.5	26
24 19.2	26.8	125.8	23 08.4	28.5	126.5	21 56.3	30.0	127.2	20 43.2	31.5	127.8	19 29.1	33.0	128.4	27
23 52.4	27.2	126.8	22 39.9	28.8	127.5	21 26.3	30.4	128.1	20 11.7	31.9	128.7	18 56.1	33.3	129.3	28
23 25.2	27.6	127.8	22 11.1	29.1	128.5	20 55.9	30.6	129.1	19 39.8	32.1	129.6	18 22.8	33.5	130.2	29

Dec.	20° Hc	d	Z	22° Hc	d	Z	24° Hc	d	Z	26° Hc	d	Z	28° Hc	d	Z
°	° ′	′	°	° ′	′	°	° ′	′	°	° ′	′	°	° ′	′	°
0	31 42.0	+23.8	103.0	31 13.8	+26.0	104.2	30 43.2	+28.2	105.3	30 10.3	+30.2	106.5	29 35.2	+32.2	107.6
1	32 05.8	23.3	101.9	31 39.8	25.5	103.1	31 11.4	27.6	104.3	30 40.5	29.8	105.5	30 07.4	31.7	106.6
2	32 29.1	22.8	100.8	32 05.3	25.0	102.1	31 39.0	27.1	103.3	31 10.3	29.2	104.5	30 39.1	31.3	105.6
3	32 51.9	22.1	99.7	32 30.3	24.4	101.0	32 06.1	26.7	102.2	31 39.5	28.8	103.4	31 10.4	30.8	104.6
4	33 14.0	21.5	98.6	32 54.7	23.8	99.9	32 32.8	26.0	101.2	32 08.3	28.2	102.4	31 41.2	30.4	103.6
5	33 35.5	+21.0	97.5	33 18.5	+23.3	98.8	32 58.8	+25.5	100.1	32 36.5	+27.7	101.4	32 11.6	+29.9	102.6
6	33 56.5	20.3	96.4	33 41.8	22.6	97.7	33 24.3	25.0	99.0	33 04.2	27.2	100.3	32 41.5	29.3	101.6
7	34 16.8	19.7	95.2	34 04.4	22.1	96.6	33 49.3	24.4	97.9	33 31.4	26.6	99.2	33 10.8	28.8	100.5
8	34 36.5	19.0	94.1	34 26.5	21.4	95.5	34 13.7	23.7	96.8	33 58.0	26.1	98.2	33 39.6	28.3	99.5
9	34 55.5	18.4	92.9	34 47.9	20.8	94.3	34 37.4	23.2	95.7	34 24.1	25.5	97.1	34 07.9	27.7	98.4
10	35 13.9	+17.7	91.8	35 08.7	+20.1	93.2	35 00.6	+22.5	94.6	34 49.6	+24.8	96.0	34 35.6	+27.2	97.3
11	35 31.6	17.0	90.6	35 28.8	19.5	92.0	35 23.1	21.9	93.4	35 14.4	24.3	94.9	35 02.8	26.6	96.3
12	35 48.6	16.3	89.4	35 48.3	18.8	90.9	35 45.0	21.2	92.3	35 38.7	23.6	93.7	35 29.4	26.0	95.2
13	36 04.9	15.6	88.2	36 07.1	18.1	89.7	36 06.2	20.6	91.1	36 02.3	23.0	92.6	35 55.4	25.3	94.0
14	36 20.5	14.9	87.0	36 25.2	17.4	88.5	36 26.8	19.9	90.0	36 25.3	22.3	91.5	36 20.7	24.7	92.9
15	36 35.4	+14.2	85.8	36 42.6	+16.7	87.3	36 46.7	+19.1	88.8	36 47.6	+21.6	90.3	36 45.4	+24.1	91.8
16	36 49.6	13.4	84.6	36 59.3	15.9	86.1	37 05.8	18.5	87.6	37 09.2	21.0	89.1	37 09.5	23.4	90.6
17	37 03.0	12.6	83.4	37 15.2	15.2	84.9	37 24.3	17.7	86.4	37 30.2	20.2	88.0	37 32.9	22.7	89.5
18	37 15.6	11.9	82.2	37 30.4	14.5	83.7	37 42.0	17.0	85.2	37 50.4	19.5	86.8	37 55.6	22.0	88.3
19	37 27.5	11.2	80.9	37 44.9	13.7	82.5	37 59.0	16.3	84.0	38 09.9	18.8	85.6	38 17.6	21.3	87.1
20	37 38.7	+10.3	79.7	37 58.6	+12.9	81.2	38 15.3	+15.4	82.8	38 28.7	+18.0	84.4	38 38.9	+20.5	85.9
21	37 49.0	9.6	78.4	38 11.5	12.1	80.0	38 30.7	14.7	81.5	38 46.7	17.3	83.1	38 59.4	19.8	84.7
22	37 58.6	8.7	77.2	38 23.6	11.3	78.7	38 45.4	13.9	80.3	39 04.0	16.4	81.9	39 19.2	19.0	83.5
23	38 07.3	8.0	75.9	38 34.9	10.5	77.5	38 59.3	13.1	79.1	39 20.4	15.7	80.7	39 38.2	18.3	82.3
24	38 15.3	7.1	74.7	38 45.4	9.7	76.2	39 12.4	12.3	77.8	39 36.1	14.9	79.4	39 56.5	17.4	81.0
25	38 22.4	+6.3	73.4	38 55.1	+8.9	75.0	39 24.7	+11.4	76.5	39 51.0	+14.0	78.1	40 13.9	+16.7	79.8
26	38 28.7	5.5	72.1	39 04.0	8.0	73.7	39 36.1	10.6	75.3	40 05.0	13.2	76.9	40 30.6	15.8	78.5
27	38 34.2	4.7	70.9	39 12.0	7.2	72.4	39 46.7	9.8	74.0	40 18.2	12.4	75.6	40 46.4	14.9	77.3
28	38 38.9	3.8	69.6	39 19.2	6.4	71.1	39 56.5	8.9	72.7	40 30.6	11.5	74.3	41 01.3	14.1	76.0
29	38 42.7	3.0	68.3	39 25.6	5.5	69.8	40 05.4	8.0	71.4	40 42.1	10.6	73.0	41 15.4	13.2	74.7

Dec.	30° Hc	d	Z	32° Hc	d	Z	34° Hc	d	Z	36° Hc	d	Z	38° Hc	d	Z
°	° ′	′	°	° ′	′	°	° ′	′	°	° ′	′	°	° ′	′	°
0	28 57.9	+34.1	108.6	28 18.5	+36.0	109.7	27 37.1	+37.7	110.7	26 53.9	+39.3	111.6	26 08.7	+41.0	112.6
1	29 32.0	33.7	107.7	28 54.5	35.5	108.8	28 14.8	37.4	109.8	27 33.2	39.1	110.8	26 49.7	40.8	111.7
2	30 05.7	33.2	106.7	29 30.0	35.2	107.8	28 52.2	37.0	108.9	28 12.3	38.8	109.9	27 30.5	40.4	110.9
3	30 38.9	32.9	105.8	30 05.2	34.8	106.9	29 29.2	36.6	108.0	28 51.1	38.4	109.1	28 10.9	40.1	110.1
4	31 11.8	32.4	104.8	30 40.0	34.3	106.0	30 05.8	36.3	107.1	29 29.5	38.1	108.2	28 51.0	39.8	109.2
5	31 44.2	+31.9	103.8	31 14.3	+33.9	105.0	30 42.1	+35.8	106.2	30 07.6	+37.7	107.3	29 30.8	+39.5	108.4
6	32 16.1	31.5	102.8	31 48.2	33.5	104.0	31 17.9	35.5	105.2	30 45.3	37.3	106.4	30 10.3	39.1	107.5
7	32 47.6	30.9	101.8	32 21.7	33.1	103.1	31 53.4	35.0	104.3	31 22.6	36.9	105.5	30 49.4	38.8	106.6
8	33 18.5	30.5	100.8	32 54.8	32.5	102.1	32 28.4	34.6	103.3	31 59.5	36.5	104.5	31 28.2	38.4	105.7
9	33 49.0	29.9	99.7	33 27.3	32.1	101.1	33 03.0	34.1	102.3	32 36.0	36.1	103.6	32 06.6	37.9	104.8
10	34 18.9	+29.4	98.7	33 59.4	+31.5	100.0	33 37.1	+33.6	101.4	33 12.1	+35.7	102.6	32 44.5	+37.6	103.9
11	34 48.3	28.8	97.6	34 30.9	31.0	99.0	34 10.7	33.2	100.4	33 47.8	35.2	101.7	33 22.1	37.2	103.0
12	35 17.1	28.3	96.6	35 01.9	30.5	98.0	34 43.9	32.6	99.3	34 23.0	34.7	100.7	33 59.3	36.7	102.0
13	35 45.4	27.6	95.5	35 32.4	29.9	96.9	35 16.5	32.1	98.3	34 57.7	34.2	99.7	34 36.0	36.3	101.1
14	36 13.0	27.1	94.4	36 02.3	29.4	95.8	35 48.6	31.6	97.3	35 31.9	33.7	98.7	35 12.3	35.8	100.1
15	36 40.1	+26.4	93.3	36 31.7	+28.7	94.8	36 20.2	+31.0	96.2	36 05.6	+33.2	97.7	35 48.1	+35.3	99.1
16	37 06.5	25.8	92.2	37 00.4	28.2	93.7	36 51.2	30.4	95.2	36 38.8	32.7	96.7	36 23.4	34.8	98.1
17	37 32.3	25.2	91.0	37 28.6	27.5	92.6	37 21.6	29.9	94.1	37 11.5	32.1	95.6	36 58.2	34.3	97.1
18	37 57.5	24.4	89.9	37 56.1	26.9	91.4	37 51.5	29.2	93.0	37 43.6	31.5	94.5	37 32.5	33.7	96.1
19	38 21.9	23.8	88.7	38 23.0	26.2	90.3	38 20.7	28.6	91.9	38 15.1	30.9	93.5	38 06.2	33.2	95.0
20	38 45.7	+23.0	87.5	38 49.2	+25.5	89.1	38 49.3	+27.9	90.8	38 46.0	+30.3	92.4	38 39.4	+32.5	94.0
21	39 08.7	22.4	86.4	39 14.7	24.8	88.0	39 17.2	27.2	89.6	39 16.3	29.6	91.3	39 11.9	32.0	92.9
22	39 31.1	21.5	85.2	39 39.5	24.1	86.8	39 44.4	26.6	88.5	39 45.9	29.0	90.1	39 43.9	31.3	91.8
23	39 52.6	20.8	83.9	40 03.6	23.3	85.6	40 11.0	25.8	87.3	40 14.9	28.3	89.0	40 15.2	30.7	90.7
24	40 13.4	20.1	82.7	40 26.9	22.6	84.4	40 36.8	25.1	86.1	40 43.2	27.6	87.8	40 45.9	30.1	89.5
25	40 33.5	+19.2	81.5	40 49.5	+21.8	83.2	41 01.9	+24.4	84.9	41 10.8	+26.8	86.6	41 16.0	+29.3	88.4
26	40 52.7	18.4	80.2	41 11.3	21.0	81.9	41 26.3	23.5	83.7	41 37.6	26.1	85.5	41 45.3	28.6	87.2
27	41 11.1	17.5	79.0	41 32.3	20.1	80.7	41 49.8	22.8	82.5	42 03.7	25.4	84.2	42 13.9	27.9	86.1
28	41 28.6	16.8	77.7	41 52.4	19.4	79.4	42 12.6	22.0	81.2	42 29.1	24.5	83.0	42 41.8	27.1	84.8
29	41 45.4	15.8	76.4	42 11.8	18.5	78.2	42 34.6	21.1	80.0	42 53.6	23.7	81.8	43 08.9	26.3	83.6

20° Hc	d	Z	22° Hc	d	Z	24° Hc	d	Z	26° Hc	d	Z	28° Hc	d	Z	Dec.
31 42.0	−24.4	103.0	31 13.8	−26.5	104.2	30 43.2	−28.6	105.3	30 10.3	−30.6	106.5	29 35.2	−32.6	107.6	0
31 17.6	24.9	104.1	30 47.3	27.1	105.2	30 14.6	29.1	106.4	29 39.7	31.1	107.5	29 02.6	33.0	108.5	1
30 52.7	25.4	105.1	30 20.2	27.5	106.3	29 45.5	29.6	107.4	29 08.6	31.5	108.4	28 29.6	33.4	109.5	2
30 27.3	26.0	106.2	29 52.7	28.0	107.3	29 15.9	29.9	108.4	28 37.1	31.9	109.4	27 56.2	33.8	110.4	3
30 01.3	26.4	107.2	29 24.7	28.5	108.3	28 46.0	30.5	109.4	28 05.2	32.4	110.4	27 22.4	34.2	111.4	4
29 34.9	−26.9	108.3	28 56.2	−28.9	109.3	28 15.5	−30.8	110.3	27 32.8	−32.7	111.3	26 48.2	−34.5	112.3	5
29 08.0	27.4	109.3	28 27.3	29.3	110.3	27 44.7	31.3	111.3	27 00.1	33.1	112.3	26 13.7	34.8	113.2	6
28 40.6	27.8	110.3	27 58.0	29.8	111.3	27 13.4	31.6	112.3	26 27.0	33.4	113.2	25 38.9	35.2	114.1	7
28 12.8	28.3	111.3	27 28.2	30.1	112.3	26 41.8	32.0	113.2	25 53.6	33.8	114.1	25 03.7	35.5	115.0	8
27 44.5	28.6	112.3	26 58.1	30.6	113.3	26 09.8	32.4	114.2	25 19.8	34.1	115.1	24 28.2	35.8	115.9	9
27 15.9	−29.1	113.3	26 27.5	−30.9	114.2	25 37.4	−32.7	115.1	24 45.7	−34.5	116.0	23 52.4	−36.1	116.8	10
26 46.8	29.4	114.3	25 56.6	31.4	115.2	25 04.7	33.1	116.0	24 11.2	34.7	116.9	23 16.3	36.4	117.6	11
26 17.3	29.9	115.2	25 25.2	31.6	116.1	24 31.6	33.4	117.0	23 36.5	35.1	117.8	22 39.9	36.7	118.5	12
25 47.4	30.3	116.2	24 53.6	32.1	117.1	23 58.2	33.7	117.9	23 01.4	35.4	118.6	22 03.2	36.9	119.4	13
25 17.1	30.6	117.2	24 21.5	32.3	118.0	23 24.5	34.1	118.8	22 26.0	35.6	119.5	21 26.3	37.2	120.2	14
24 46.5	−31.0	118.1	23 49.2	−32.7	118.9	22 50.4	−34.3	119.7	21 50.4	−35.9	120.4	20 49.1	−37.4	121.0	15
24 15.5	31.4	119.1	23 16.5	33.0	119.8	22 16.1	34.6	120.6	21 14.5	36.2	121.2	20 11.7	37.7	121.9	16
23 44.1	31.7	120.0	22 43.5	33.4	120.7	21 41.5	34.9	121.4	20 38.3	36.4	122.1	19 34.0	37.9	122.7	17
23 12.4	31.9	120.9	22 10.1	33.6	121.6	21 06.6	35.2	122.3	20 01.9	36.7	122.9	18 56.1	38.1	123.5	18
22 40.5	32.4	121.8	21 36.5	33.9	122.5	20 31.4	35.4	123.2	19 25.2	36.9	123.8	18 18.0	38.3	124.3	19
22 08.1	−32.6	122.8	21 02.6	−34.1	123.4	19 56.0	−35.7	124.0	18 48.3	−37.1	124.6	17 39.7	−38.5	125.2	20
21 35.5	32.9	123.4	20 28.5	34.5	124.3	19 20.3	35.9	124.9	18 11.2	37.3	125.4	17 01.2	38.7	126.0	21
21 02.6	33.1	124.6	19 54.0	34.6	125.2	18 44.4	36.1	125.7	17 33.9	37.5	126.3	16 22.5	38.9	126.8	22
20 29.5	33.5	125.4	19 19.4	35.0	126.0	18 08.3	36.3	126.6	16 56.4	37.8	127.1	15 43.6	39.0	127.6	23
19 56.0	33.7	126.3	18 44.4	35.1	126.9	17 32.0	36.6	127.4	16 18.6	37.9	127.9	15 04.6	39.2	128.3	24
19 22.3	−34.0	127.2	18 09.3	−35.4	127.7	16 55.4	−36.8	128.2	15 40.7	−38.0	128.7	14 25.4	−39.4	129.1	25
18 48.3	34.2	128.1	17 33.9	35.6	128.6	16 18.6	36.9	129.1	15 02.7	38.3	129.5	13 46.0	39.5	129.9	26
18 14.1	34.4	128.9	16 58.3	35.8	129.4	15 41.7	37.1	129.9	14 24.4	38.4	130.3	13 06.5	39.7	130.7	27
17 39.7	34.7	129.8	16 22.5	36.0	130.3	15 04.6	37.3	130.7	13 46.0	38.6	131.1	12 26.8	39.7	131.4	28
17 05.0	34.8	130.7	15 46.5	36.2	131.1	14 27.3	37.5	131.5	13 07.4	38.7	131.9	11 47.1	39.9	132.2	29

30° Hc	d	Z	32° Hc	d	Z	34° Hc	d	Z	36° Hc	d	Z	38° Hc	d	Z	Dec.
28 57.9	−34.5	108.6	28 18.5	−36.3	109.7	27 37.1	−38.0	110.7	26 53.9	−39.7	111.6	26 08.7	−41.3	112.6	0
28 23.4	34.8	109.6	27 42.2	36.6	110.6	26 59.1	38.3	111.5	26 14.2	40.0	112.5	25 27.4	41.5	113.4	1
27 48.6	35.3	110.5	27 05.6	37.0	111.5	26 20.8	38.7	112.4	25 34.2	40.3	113.3	24 45.9	41.8	114.2	2
27 13.3	35.5	111.4	26 28.6	37.3	112.3	25 42.1	38.9	113.2	24 53.9	40.5	114.1	24 04.1	42.0	114.9	3
26 37.8	36.0	112.3	25 51.3	37.6	113.2	25 03.2	39.3	114.1	24 13.4	40.8	114.9	23 22.1	42.3	115.7	4
26 01.8	−36.2	113.2	25 13.7	−37.9	114.1	24 23.9	−39.4	114.9	23 32.6	−41.0	115.7	22 39.8	−42.5	116.5	5
25 25.6	36.5	114.1	24 35.8	38.2	114.9	23 44.5	39.8	115.7	22 51.6	41.3	116.5	21 57.3	42.7	117.3	6
24 49.1	36.9	115.0	23 57.6	38.4	115.8	23 04.7	40.0	116.6	22 10.3	41.4	117.3	21 14.6	42.9	118.0	7
24 12.2	37.1	115.8	23 19.2	38.8	116.6	22 24.7	40.3	117.4	21 28.9	41.7	118.1	20 31.7	43.1	118.8	8
23 35.1	37.5	116.7	22 40.4	38.9	117.4	21 44.4	40.4	118.2	20 47.2	41.9	118.9	19 48.6	43.2	119.5	9
22 57.6	−37.7	117.5	22 01.5	−39.3	118.3	21 04.0	−40.7	119.0	20 05.3	−42.1	119.6	19 05.4	−43.5	120.2	10
22 19.9	37.9	118.4	21 22.2	39.4	119.1	20 23.3	40.9	119.8	19 23.2	42.3	120.4	18 21.9	43.6	121.0	11
21 42.0	38.2	119.2	20 42.8	39.7	119.9	19 42.4	41.1	120.5	18 40.9	42.5	121.1	17 38.3	43.7	121.7	12
21 03.8	38.5	120.0	20 03.1	39.9	120.7	19 01.3	41.3	121.3	17 58.4	42.6	121.9	16 54.6	43.9	122.4	13
20 25.3	38.7	120.9	19 23.2	40.1	121.5	18 20.0	41.5	122.1	17 15.8	42.8	122.6	16 10.7	44.1	123.1	14
19 46.6	−38.9	121.7	18 43.1	−40.3	122.3	17 38.5	−41.6	122.8	16 33.0	−42.9	123.3	15 26.6	−44.2	123.8	15
19 07.7	39.1	122.5	18 02.8	40.5	123.1	16 56.9	41.9	123.6	15 50.1	43.1	124.1	14 42.4	44.3	124.5	16
18 28.6	39.3	123.3	17 22.3	40.8	123.8	16 15.0	41.9	124.3	15 07.0	43.3	124.8	13 58.1	44.4	125.2	17
17 49.3	39.5	124.1	16 41.6	40.8	124.6	15 33.1	42.1	125.1	14 23.7	43.3	125.5	13 13.7	44.5	125.9	18
17 09.8	39.6	124.9	16 00.8	41.0	125.4	14 51.0	42.3	125.8	13 40.4	43.5	126.2	12 29.2	44.7	126.6	19
16 30.2	−39.9	125.7	15 19.8	−41.1	126.1	14 08.7	−42.4	126.5	12 56.9	−43.6	126.9	11 44.5	−44.7	127.3	20
15 50.3	40.0	126.4	14 38.7	41.3	126.9	13 26.3	42.5	127.3	12 13.3	43.7	127.6	10 59.8	44.8	128.0	21
15 10.3	40.2	127.2	13 57.4	41.5	127.6	12 43.8	42.6	128.0	11 29.6	43.7	128.3	10 15.0	44.9	128.6	22
14 30.1	40.3	128.0	13 15.9	41.5	128.4	12 01.2	42.8	128.7	10 45.9	43.9	129.0	9 30.1	45.0	129.3	23
13 49.8	40.5	128.7	12 34.4	41.7	129.1	11 18.4	42.8	129.4	10 02.0	44.0	129.7	8 45.1	45.1	130.0	24
13 09.3	−40.6	129.5	11 52.7	−41.8	129.8	10 35.6	−43.0	130.1	9 18.0	−44.1	130.4	8 00.0	−45.1	130.6	25
12 28.7	40.7	130.3	11 10.9	41.9	130.6	9 52.6	43.0	130.9	8 33.9	44.1	131.1	7 14.9	45.2	131.3	26
11 48.0	40.8	131.0	10 29.0	42.0	131.3	9 09.6	43.1	131.6	7 49.8	44.2	131.8	6 29.7	45.2	132.0	27
11 07.2	41.0	131.8	9 47.0	42.1	132.0	8 26.5	43.2	132.3	7 05.6	44.2	132.5	5 44.5	45.3	132.6	28
10 26.2	41.0	132.5	9 04.9	42.1	132.8	7 43.3	43.2	133.0	6 21.4	44.3	133.1	4 59.2	45.3	133.3	29

Dec.	40° Hc	d	Z	42° Hc	d	Z	44° Hc	d	Z	46° Hc	d	Z	48° Hc	d	Z
°	° ′	′	°	° ′	′	°	° ′	′	°	° ′	′	°	° ′	′	°
0	25 21.8	+42.6	113.4	24 33.3	+44.0	114.3	23 43.1	+45.5	115.1	22 51.5	+46.7	115.9	21 58.4	+48.0	116.6
1	26 04.4	42.3	112.7	25 17.3	43.8	113.5	24 28.6	45.2	114.4	23 38.2	46.6	115.2	22 46.4	47.8	116.0
2	26 46.7	42.0	111.9	26 01.1	43.6	112.8	25 13.8	45.0	113.7	24 24.8	46.4	114.5	23 34.2	47.7	115.3
3	27 28.7	41.8	111.1	26 44.7	43.3	112.0	25 58.8	44.8	112.9	25 11.2	46.2	113.8	24 21.9	47.5	114.7
4	28 10.5	41.4	110.3	27 28.0	43.0	111.2	26 43.6	44.5	112.2	25 57.4	45.9	113.1	25 09.4	47.3	114.0
5	28 51.9	+41.2	109.4	28 11.0	+42.8	110.5	27 28.1	+44.3	111.4	26 43.3	+45.8	112.4	25 56.7	+47.2	113.3
6	29 33.1	40.8	108.6	28 53.8	42.5	109.7	28 12.4	44.1	110.7	27 29.1	45.5	111.7	26 43.9	46.9	112.6
7	30 13.9	40.6	107.8	29 36.3	42.2	108.8	28 56.5	43.7	109.9	28 14.6	45.3	110.9	27 30.8	46.7	111.9
8	30 54.5	40.1	106.9	30 18.5	41.8	108.0	29 40.2	43.5	109.1	28 59.9	45.0	110.2	28 17.5	46.5	111.2
9	31 34.6	39.8	106.0	31 00.3	41.6	107.2	30 23.7	43.2	108.3	29 44.9	44.8	109.4	29 04.0	46.2	110.5
10	32 14.4	+39.5	105.1	31 41.9	+41.2	106.3	31 06.9	+42.9	107.5	30 29.7	+44.5	108.6	29 50.2	+46.0	109.7
11	32 53.9	39.0	104.2	32 23.1	40.8	105.5	31 49.8	42.6	106.7	31 14.2	44.0	107.9	30 36.2	45.8	109.0
12	33 32.9	38.7	103.3	33 03.9	40.5	104.6	32 32.4	42.2	105.9	31 58.4	43.9	107.1	31 22.0	45.4	108.2
13	34 11.6	38.2	102.4	33 44.4	40.1	103.7	33 14.6	41.9	105.0	32 42.3	43.6	106.3	32 07.4	45.2	107.5
14	34 49.8	37.8	101.5	34 24.5	39.3	102.8	33 56.5	41.5	104.2	33 25.9	43.2	105.4	32 52.6	44.9	106.7
15	35 27.6	+37.3	100.5	35 04.2	+39.3	101.9	34 38.0	+41.2	103.3	34 09.1	+42.9	104.6	33 37.5	+44.6	105.9
16	36 04.9	36.9	99.6	35 43.5	38.9	101.0	35 19.2	40.7	102.4	34 52.0	42.6	103.8	34 22.1	44.3	105.1
17	36 41.8	36.4	98.6	36 22.4	38.4	100.1	35 59.9	40.4	101.5	35 34.6	42.2	102.9	35 06.4	43.9	104.3
18	37 18.2	35.9	97.6	37 00.8	37.9	99.1	36 40.3	39.9	100.6	36 16.8	41.8	102.0	35 50.3	43.6	103.4
19	37 54.1	35.3	96.6	37 38.7	37.4	98.1	37 20.2	39.4	99.6	36 58.6	41.3	101.1	36 33.9	43.2	102.6
20	38 29.4	+34.8	95.6	38 16.1	+37.0	97.1	37 59.6	+39.0	98.7	37 39.9	+41.0	100.2	37 17.1	+42.8	101.7
21	39 04.2	34.2	94.5	38 53.1	36.4	96.1	38 38.6	38.5	97.7	38 20.9	40.5	99.3	37 59.9	42.4	100.8
22	39 38.4	33.7	93.4	39 29.5	35.8	95.1	39 17.1	38.0	96.7	39 01.4	40.0	98.3	38 42.3	42.0	99.9
23	40 12.1	33.0	92.4	40 05.3	35.3	94.1	39 55.1	37.5	95.7	39 41.4	39.6	97.4	39 24.3	41.5	99.0
24	40 45.1	32.4	91.3	40 40.6	34.7	93.0	40 32.6	36.9	94.7	40 21.0	39.0	96.4	40 05.8	41.1	98.1
25	41 17.5	+31.7	90.2	41 15.3	+34.1	91.9	41 09.5	+36.3	93.7	41 00.0	+38.5	95.4	40 46.9	+40.6	97.1
26	41 49.2	31.1	89.0	41 49.4	33.4	90.8	41 45.8	35.7	92.6	41 38.5	38.0	94.4	41 27.5	40.1	96.1
27	42 20.3	30.3	87.9	42 22.8	32.8	89.7	42 21.5	35.2	91.5	42 16.5	37.3	93.3	42 07.6	39.6	95.1
28	42 50.6	29.6	86.7	42 55.6	32.1	88.6	42 56.7	34.4	90.4	42 53.8	36.8	92.3	42 47.2	39.0	94.1
29	43 20.2	28.9	85.5	43 27.7	31.3	87.4	43 31.1	33.8	89.3	43 30.6	36.2	91.2	43 26.2	38.4	93.1

Dec.	50° Hc	d	Z	52° Hc	d	Z	54° Hc	d	Z	56° Hc	d	Z	58° Hc	d	Z
°	° ′	′	°	° ′	′	°	° ′	′	°	° ′	′	°	° ′	′	°
0	21 04.0	+49.1	117.3	20 08.2	+50.3	118.0	19 11.3	+51.4	118.6	18 13.3	+52.3	119.2	17 14.2	+53.3	119.8
1	21 53.1	49.1	116.7	20 58.5	50.2	117.4	20 02.7	51.2	118.1	19 05.6	52.3	118.7	18 07.5	53.1	119.3
2	22 42.2	48.9	116.1	21 48.7	50.1	116.8	20 53.9	51.2	117.5	19 57.9	52.1	118.2	19 00.6	53.1	118.8
3	23 31.1	48.7	115.5	22 38.8	49.9	116.2	21 45.1	51.0	117.0	20 50.0	52.1	117.6	19 53.7	53.0	118.3
4	24 19.8	48.6	114.8	23 28.7	49.8	115.6	22 36.1	50.9	116.4	21 42.1	51.9	117.1	20 46.7	53.0	117.8
5	25 08.4	+48.4	114.2	24 18.5	+49.6	115.0	23 27.0	+50.8	115.8	22 34.0	+51.9	116.6	21 39.7	+52.8	117.3
6	25 56.8	48.3	113.5	25 08.1	49.5	114.4	24 17.8	50.6	115.2	23 25.9	51.7	116.0	22 32.5	52.7	116.8
7	26 45.1	48.0	112.9	25 57.6	49.3	113.8	25 08.4	50.5	114.6	24 17.6	51.6	115.5	23 25.2	52.6	116.3
8	27 33.1	47.9	112.2	26 46.9	49.1	113.1	25 58.9	50.3	114.0	25 09.2	51.4	114.9	24 17.8	52.5	115.7
9	28 21.0	47.6	111.5	27 36.0	49.0	112.5	26 49.2	50.2	113.4	26 00.6	51.4	114.3	25 10.3	52.4	115.2
10	29 08.6	+47.5	110.8	28 25.0	+48.8	111.8	27 39.4	+50.0	112.8	26 52.0	+51.2	113.8	26 02.7	+52.3	114.7
11	29 56.1	47.2	110.1	29 13.8	48.5	111.2	28 29.4	49.9	112.2	27 43.2	51.0	113.2	26 55.0	52.2	114.1
12	30 43.3	46.9	109.4	30 02.3	48.4	110.5	29 19.3	49.6	111.6	28 34.2	50.9	112.6	27 47.2	52.0	113.6
13	31 30.2	46.7	108.7	30 50.7	48.1	109.8	30 08.9	49.5	110.9	29 25.1	50.7	112.0	28 39.2	51.8	113.0
14	32 16.9	46.5	107.9	31 38.8	47.9	109.1	30 58.4	49.3	110.2	30 15.8	50.5	111.4	29 31.0	51.8	112.4
15	33 03.4	+46.1	107.2	32 26.7	+47.7	108.4	31 47.7	+49.0	109.6	31 06.3	+50.4	110.7	30 22.8	+51.5	111.8
16	33 49.5	45.9	106.4	33 14.4	47.4	107.7	32 36.7	48.8	108.9	31 56.7	50.1	110.1	31 14.3	51.4	111.2
17	34 35.4	45.6	105.6	34 01.8	47.1	106.9	33 25.5	48.6	108.2	32 46.8	50.0	109.4	32 05.7	51.2	110.6
18	35 21.0	45.3	104.8	34 48.9	46.9	106.2	34 14.1	48.4	107.5	33 36.8	49.7	108.8	32 56.9	51.0	110.0
19	36 06.3	44.9	104.0	35 35.8	46.5	105.4	35 02.5	48.1	106.8	34 26.5	49.5	108.1	33 47.9	50.9	109.4
20	36 51.2	+44.6	103.2	36 22.3	+46.3	104.6	35 50.6	+47.8	106.0	35 16.0	+49.3	107.4	34 38.8	+50.6	108.7
21	37 35.8	44.2	102.4	37 08.6	45.9	103.8	36 38.4	47.5	105.3	36 05.3	49.0	106.7	35 29.4	50.4	108.0
22	38 20.0	43.8	101.5	37 54.5	45.6	103.0	37 25.9	47.2	104.5	36 54.3	48.8	106.0	36 19.8	50.2	107.4
23	39 03.8	43.5	100.7	38 40.1	45.2	102.2	38 13.1	46.9	103.8	37 43.1	48.4	105.3	37 10.0	49.9	106.7
24	39 47.3	43.0	99.7	39 25.3	44.8	101.4	39 00.0	46.6	102.9	38 31.5	48.2	104.5	37 59.9	49.7	106.0
25	40 30.3	+42.6	98.8	40 10.1	+44.5	100.5	39 46.6	+46.2	102.1	39 19.7	+47.9	103.7	38 49.6	+49.4	105.3
26	41 12.9	42.1	97.9	40 54.6	44.0	99.6	40 32.8	45.9	101.3	40 07.6	47.5	103.0	39 39.0	49.1	104.6
27	41 55.0	41.6	96.9	41 38.6	43.6	98.7	41 18.7	45.4	100.5	40 55.1	47.2	102.2	40 28.1	48.9	103.8
28	42 36.6	41.1	96.0	42 22.2	43.2	97.8	42 04.1	45.1	99.6	41 42.3	46.9	101.3	41 17.0	48.5	103.1
29	43 17.7	40.6	95.0	43 05.4	42.7	96.8	42 49.2	44.6	98.7	42 29.2	46.5	100.5	42 05.5	48.2	102.3

40°			42°			44°			46°			48°			Dec.
Hc	d	Z	Hc	d	Z	Hc	d	Z	Hc	d	Z	Hc	d	Z	
° ′	′	°	° ′	′	°	° ′	′	°	° ′	′	°	° ′	′	°	°
25 21.8	−42.8	113.4	24 33.3	−44.3	114.3	23 43.1	−45.6	115.1	22 51.5	−46.9	115.9	21 58.4	−48.2	116.6	0
24 39.0	43.0	114.2	23 49.0	44.4	115.0	22 57.5	45.8	115.8	22 04.6	47.1	116.6	21 10.2	48.3	117.3	1
23 56.0	43.3	115.0	23 04.6	44.7	115.8	22 11.7	46.0	116.5	21 17.5	47.3	117.2	20 21.9	48.4	117.9	2
23 12.7	43.4	115.7	22 19.9	44.8	116.5	21 25.7	46.1	117.2	20 30.2	47.4	117.9	19 33.5	48.6	118.5	3
22 29.3	43.7	116.5	21 35.1	45.1	117.2	20 39.6	46.3	117.9	19 42.8	47.5	118.5	18 44.9	48.6	119.1	4
21 45.6	−43.9	117.2	20 50.0	−45.2	117.9	19 53.3	−46.5	118.6	18 55.3	−47.7	119.2	17 56.3	−48.8	119.8	5
21 01.7	44.1	118.0	20 04.8	45.3	118.6	19 06.8	46.6	119.2	18 07.6	47.8	119.8	17 07.5	49.0	120.4	6
20 17.6	44.2	118.7	19 19.5	45.5	119.3	18 20.2	46.8	119.9	17 19.8	47.9	120.5	16 18.5	49.0	121.0	7
19 33.4	44.4	119.4	18 33.9	45.6	120.0	17 33.4	46.8	120.6	16 31.9	48.0	121.1	15 29.5	49.1	121.6	8
18 49.0	44.6	120.1	17 48.3	45.8	120.7	16 46.6	47.0	121.2	15 43.9	48.1	121.7	14 40.4	49.2	122.2	9
18 04.4	−44.7	120.8	17 02.5	−46.0	121.4	15 59.6	−47.2	121.9	14 55.8	−48.2	122.3	13 51.2	−49.3	122.8	10
17 19.7	44.9	121.5	16 16.5	46.1	122.0	15 12.4	47.2	122.5	14 07.6	48.4	122.9	13 01.9	49.3	123.4	11
16 34.8	45.0	122.2	15 30.4	46.2	122.7	14 25.2	47.3	123.1	13 19.2	48.4	123.6	12 12.6	49.5	123.9	12
15 49.8	45.1	122.9	14 44.2	46.3	123.4	13 37.9	47.4	123.8	12 30.8	48.5	124.2	11 23.1	49.5	124.5	13
15 04.7	45.3	123.6	13 57.9	46.4	124.0	12 50.5	47.5	124.4	11 42.3	48.5	124.8	10 33.6	49.5	125.1	14
14 19.4	−45.3	124.3	13 11.5	−46.5	124.7	12 03.0	−47.6	125.0	10 53.8	−48.6	125.4	9 44.1	−49.6	125.7	15
13 34.1	45.5	124.9	12 25.0	46.6	125.3	11 15.4	47.7	125.7	10 05.2	48.7	126.0	8 54.5	49.7	126.2	16
12 48.6	45.6	125.6	11 38.4	46.7	126.0	10 27.7	47.8	126.3	9 16.5	48.8	126.6	8 04.8	49.7	126.8	17
12 03.0	45.7	126.3	10 51.7	46.9	126.6	9 39.9	47.8	126.9	8 27.7	48.8	127.1	7 15.1	49.8	127.4	18
11 17.3	45.7	126.9	10 05.0	46.9	127.2	8 52.1	47.8	127.5	7 38.9	48.9	127.7	6 25.3	49.8	127.9	19
10 31.6	−45.9	127.6	9 18.1	−46.9	127.9	8 04.3	−47.9	128.1	6 50.0	−48.9	128.3	5 35.5	−49.8	128.5	20
9 45.7	45.9	128.2	8 31.2	46.9	128.5	7 16.4	48.0	128.7	6 01.1	48.9	128.9	4 45.7	49.9	129.0	21
8 59.8	46.0	128.9	7 44.3	47.0	129.1	6 28.4	48.0	129.3	5 12.2	49.0	129.5	3 55.8	49.9	129.6	22
8 13.8	46.0	129.5	6 57.3	47.1	129.8	5 40.4	48.1	129.9	4 23.2	48.9	130.1	3 05.9	49.9	130.2	23
7 27.8	46.1	130.2	6 10.2	47.1	130.4	4 52.3	48.1	130.5	3 34.3	49.1	130.6	2 16.0	49.9	130.7	24
6 41.7	−46.2	130.8	5 23.1	−47.2	131.0	4 04.2	−48.1	131.1	2 45.2	−49.0	131.2	1 26.1	−49.9	131.3	25
5 55.5	46.2	131.5	4 35.9	47.2	131.6	3 16.1	48.1	131.7	1 56.2	49.0	131.8	0 36.2	−49.9	131.8	26
5 09.3	46.2	132.1	3 48.7	47.2	132.2	2 28.0	48.1	132.3	1 07.2	49.1	132.4	0 13.7	+49.9	47.6	27
4 23.1	46.3	132.8	3 01.5	47.2	132.9	1 39.9	48.2	132.9	0 18.1	−49.0	132.9	1 03.6	50.0	47.1	28
3 36.8	46.3	133.4	2 14.3	47.2	133.5	0 51.7	48.2	133.5	0 30.9	+49.1	46.5	1 53.6	49.9	46.5	29

50°			52°			54°			56°			58°			Dec.
Hc	d	Z	Hc	d	Z	Hc	d	Z	Hc	d	Z	Hc	d	Z	
° ′	′	°	° ′	′	°	° ′	′	°	° ′	′	°	° ′	′	°	°
21 04.0	−49.4	117.3	20 08.2	−50.4	118.0	19 11.3	−51.4	118.6	18 13.3	−52.4	119.2	17 14.2	−53.3	119.8	0
20 14.6	49.4	117.9	19 17.8	50.5	118.6	18 19.9	51.5	119.2	17 20.9	52.5	119.7	16 20.9	53.4	120.2	1
19 25.2	49.6	118.5	18 27.3	50.6	119.1	17 28.4	51.7	119.7	16 28.4	52.5	120.2	15 27.5	53.4	120.7	2
18 35.6	49.6	119.1	17 36.7	50.7	119.7	16 36.7	51.7	120.2	15 35.9	52.7	120.7	14 34.1	53.5	121.2	3
17 46.0	49.8	119.7	16 46.0	50.8	120.3	15 45.0	51.7	120.8	14 43.2	52.7	121.2	13 40.6	53.5	121.7	4
16 56.2	−49.9	120.3	15 55.2	−50.9	120.8	14 53.3	−51.9	121.3	13 50.5	−52.7	121.7	12 47.1	−53.6	122.1	5
16 06.3	50.0	120.9	15 04.3	51.0	121.4	14 01.4	51.9	121.8	12 57.8	52.8	122.2	11 53.5	53.6	122.6	6
15 16.3	50.0	121.5	14 13.3	51.0	121.9	13 09.5	52.0	122.3	12 05.0	52.9	122.7	10 59.9	53.7	123.0	7
14 26.3	50.2	122.0	13 22.3	51.2	122.5	12 17.5	52.0	122.8	11 12.1	52.9	123.2	10 06.2	53.7	123.5	8
13 36.1	50.2	122.6	12 31.1	51.1	123.0	11 25.5	52.1	123.3	10 19.2	52.9	123.7	9 12.5	53.8	124.0	9
12 45.9	−50.3	123.2	11 40.0	−51.3	123.5	10 33.4	−52.1	123.8	9 26.3	−53.0	124.1	8 18.7	−53.8	124.4	10
11 55.6	50.3	123.7	10 48.7	51.3	124.1	9 41.3	52.2	124.4	8 33.3	53.0	124.6	7 24.9	53.8	124.8	11
11 05.3	50.4	124.3	9 57.4	51.3	124.6	8 49.1	52.2	124.9	7 40.3	53.0	125.1	6 31.1	53.8	125.3	12
10 14.9	50.5	124.8	9 06.1	51.4	125.1	7 56.9	52.3	125.4	6 47.3	53.1	125.6	5 37.3	53.8	125.7	13
9 24.4	50.5	125.4	8 14.7	51.4	125.6	7 04.6	52.3	125.8	5 54.2	53.1	126.0	4 43.5	53.9	126.2	14
8 33.9	−50.6	125.9	7 23.3	−51.5	126.1	6 12.3	−52.3	126.3	5 01.1	−53.1	126.5	3 49.6	−53.9	126.6	15
7 43.3	50.6	126.5	6 31.8	51.5	126.7	5 20.0	52.3	126.8	4 08.0	53.2	127.0	2 55.7	53.9	127.1	16
6 52.7	50.6	127.0	5 40.3	51.5	127.2	4 27.7	52.4	127.3	3 14.8	53.1	127.4	2 01.8	53.9	127.5	17
6 02.1	50.7	127.5	4 48.8	51.5	127.7	3 35.3	52.4	127.8	2 21.7	53.2	127.9	1 07.9	53.9	127.9	18
5 11.4	50.7	128.1	3 57.3	51.6	128.2	2 43.0	52.4	128.3	1 28.5	53.1	128.4	0 14.0	−53.9	128.4	19
4 20.7	−50.7	128.6	3 05.7	−51.6	128.7	1 50.6	−52.4	128.8	0 35.4	−53.2	128.8	0 39.9	+53.9	51.2	20
3 30.0	50.8	129.2	2 14.1	51.5	129.2	0 58.2	52.4	129.3	0 17.8	+53.1	50.7	1 33.8	53.8	50.7	21
2 39.2	50.7	129.7	1 22.6	51.6	129.7	0 05.8	−52.4	129.8	1 10.9	53.2	50.2	2 27.6	53.9	50.3	22
1 48.5	50.8	130.2	0 31.0	−51.6	130.3	0 46.6	+52.4	49.7	2 04.1	53.2	49.8	3 21.5	53.9	49.9	23
0 57.7	50.8	130.8	0 20.6	+51.6	49.2	1 39.0	52.4	49.2	2 57.3	53.1	49.3	4 15.4	53.9	49.4	24
0 06.9	−50.7	131.3	1 12.2	+51.6	48.7	2 31.4	+52.3	48.8	3 50.4	+53.1	48.9	5 09.3	+53.8	49.0	25
0 43.8	+50.8	48.2	2 03.8	51.6	48.2	3 23.7	52.4	48.3	4 43.5	53.1	48.4	6 03.1	53.8	48.5	26
1 34.6	50.7	47.6	2 55.4	51.6	47.7	4 16.1	52.3	47.8	5 36.6	53.1	47.9	6 56.9	53.8	48.1	27
2 25.3	50.8	47.1	3 47.0	51.5	47.2	5 08.4	52.3	47.3	6 29.7	53.0	47.5	7 50.7	53.8	47.6	28
3 16.1	50.7	46.6	4 38.5	51.5	46.7	6 00.7	52.3	46.8	7 22.7	53.1	47.0	8 44.5	53.7	47.2	29

Dec.	0° Hc	d	Z	2° Hc	d	Z	4° Hc	d	Z	6° Hc	d	Z	8° Hc	d	Z
°	° ′	′	°	° ′	′	°	° ′	′	°	° ′	′	°	° ′	′	°
0	32 00.0 − 0.3	90.0		31 58.7 + 2.1	91.2		31 54.8 + 4.6	92.5		31 48.2 + 7.1	93.7		31 39.1 + 9.5	95.0
1	31 59.7	1.0	88.8	32 00.8	1.5	90.1	31 59.4	3.9	91.3	31 55.3	6.4	92.6	31 48.6	8.9	93.8
2	31 58.7	1.6	87.6	32 02.3	0.9	88.9	32 03.3	3.3	90.1	32 01.7	5.8	91.4	31 57.5	8.2	92.6
3	31 57.1	2.3	86.5	32 03.2 + 0.1	87.7		32 06.6	2.7	89.0	32 07.5	5.1	90.2	32 05.7	7.6	91.5
4	31 54.8	3.0	85.3	32 03.3 − 0.4	86.5		32 09.3	2.0	87.8	32 12.6	4.5	89.0	32 13.3	6.9	90.3
5	31 51.8 − 3.6	84.1		32 02.9 − 1.2	85.4		32 11.3 + 1.3	86.6		32 17.1 + 3.8	87.9		32 20.2 + 6.3	89.1
6	31 48.2	4.2	82.9	32 01.7	1.8	84.2	32 12.6 + 0.7	85.4		32 20.9	3.1	86.7	32 26.5	5.6	88.0
7	31 44.0	4.9	81.8	31 59.9	2.4	83.0	32 13.3	0.0	84.2	32 24.0	2.5	85.5	32 32.1	4.9	86.8
8	31 39.1	5.5	80.6	31 57.5	3.1	81.8	32 13.3 − 0.7	83.1		32 26.5	1.8	84.3	32 37.0	4.3	-85.6
9	31 33.6	6.1	79.4	31 54.4	3.7	80.6	32 12.6	1.3	81.9	32 28.3	1.1	83.1	32 41.3	3.6	84.4
10	31 27.5 − 6.8	78.3		31 50.7 − 4.4	79.5		32 11.3 − 1.9	80.7		32 29.4 + 0.5	81.9		32 44.9 + 3.0	83.2
11	31 20.7	7.4	77.1	31 46.3	5.1	78.3	32 09.4	2.7	79.5	32 29.9 − 0.2	80.8		32 47.9	2.2	82.0
12	31 13.3	8.1	75.9	31 41.2	5.7	77.1	32 06.7	3.2	78.3	32 29.7	0.8	79.6	32 50.1	1.6	80.8
13	31 05.2	8.6	74.8	31 35.5	6.3	75.9	32 03.5	4.0	77.2	32 28.9	1.5	78.4	32 51.7	0.9	79.7
14	30 56.6	9.3	73.6	31 29.2	6.9	74.8	31 59.5	4.6	76.0	32 27.4	2.2	77.2	32 52.6 + 0.3	78.5
15	30 47.3 − 9.9	72.5		31 22.3 − 7.6	73.6		31 54.9 − 5.2	74.8		32 25.2 − 2.9	76.0		32 52.9 − 0.5	77.3
16	30 37.4	10.5	71.3	31 14.7	8.2	72.5	31 49.7	5.9	73.6	32 22.3	3.5	74.8	32 52.4	1.1	76.1
17	30 26.9	11.1	70.2	31 06.5	8.8	71.3	31 43.8	6.5	72.5	32 18.8	4.2	73.7	32 51.3	1.8	74.9
18	30 15.8	11.6	69.0	30 57.7	9.4	70.1	31 37.3	7.1	71.3	32 14.6	4.8	72.5	32 49.5	2.4	73.7
19	30 04.2	12.3	67.9	30 48.3	10.1	69.0	31 30.2	7.8	70.1	32 09.8	5.5	71.3	32 47.1	3.2	72.5
20	29 51.9 − 12.8	66.8		30 38.2 − 10.6	67.8		31 22.4 − 8.4	69.0		32 04.3 − 6.1	70.1		32 43.9 − 3.8	71.3
21	29 39.1	13.4	65.6	30 27.6	11.3	66.7	31 14.0	9.1	67.8	31 58.2	6.8	69.0	32 40.1	4.4	70.1
22	29 25.7	14.0	64.5	30 16.3	11.8	65.6	31 04.9	9.6	66.7	31 51.4	7.4	67.8	32 35.7	5.2	69.0
23	29 11.7	14.5	63.4	30 04.5	12.4	64.4	30 55.3	10.3	65.5	31 44.0	8.1	66.6	32 30.5	5.8	67.8
24	28 57.2	15.0	62.3	29 52.1	13.0	63.3	30 45.0	10.8	64.4	31 35.9	8.7	65.4	32 24.7	6.5	66.6
25	28 42.2 − 15.6	61.2		29 39.1 − 13.5	62.2		30 34.2 − 11.5	63.2		31 27.2 − 9.3	64.3		32 18.2 − 7.1	65.4
26	28 26.6	16.1	60.1	29 25.6	14.2	61.1	30 22.7	12.1	62.1	31 17.9	9.9	63.1	32 11.1	7.7	64.2
27	28 10.5	16.7	59.0	29 11.4	14.6	59.9	30 10.6	12.6	60.9	31 08.0	10.6	62.0	32 03.4	8.4	63.1
28	27 53.8	17.1	57.9	28 56.8	15.2	58.8	29 58.0	13.2	59.8	30 57.4	11.1	60.8	31 55.0	9.1	61.9
29	27 36.7	17.6	56.8	28 41.6	15.8	57.7	29 44.8	13.8	58.7	30 46.3	11.8	59.7	31 45.9	9.7	60.7

Dec.	10° Hc	d	Z	12° Hc	d	Z	14° Hc	d	Z	16° Hc	d	Z	18° Hc	d	Z
°	° ′	′	°	° ′	′	°	° ′	′	°	° ′	′	°	° ′	′	°
0	31 27.5 + 11.9	96.2		31 13.3 + 14.2	97.4		30 56.6 + 16.6	98.6		30 37.4 + 18.9	99.8		30 15.8 + 21.2	100.9
1	31 39.4	11.3	95.0	31 27.5	13.7	96.3	31 13.2	16.0	97.5	30 56.3	18.4	98.7	30 37.0	20.7	99.8
2	31 50.7	10.6	93.9	31 41.2	13.1	95.1	31 29.2	15.5	96.3	31 14.7	17.8	97.6	30 57.7	20.1	98.8
3	32 01.3	10.0	92.7	31 54.3	12.4	94.0	31 44.7	14.8	95.2	31 32.5	17.2	96.4	31 17.8	19.5	97.7
4	32 11.3	9.4	91.6	32 06.7	11.8	92.8	31 59.5	14.2	94.1	31 49.7	16.6	95.3	31 37.3	19.0	96.5
5	32 20.7 + 8.7	90.4		32 18.5 + 11.2	91.7		32 13.7 + 13.7	92.9		32 06.3 + 16.0	94.2		31 56.3 + 18.3	95.4
6	32 29.4	8.1	89.2	32 29.7	10.6	90.5	32 27.4	12.9	91.8	32 22.3	15.4	93.0	32 14.6	17.8	94.3
7	32 37.5	7.4	88.0	32 40.3	9.8	89.3	32 40.3	12.3	90.6	32 37.7	14.7	91.9	32 32.4	17.1	93.2
8	32 44.9	6.8	86.9	32 50.1	9.3	88.2	32 52.6	11.7	89.4	32 52.4	14.2	90.7	32 49.5	16.6	92.0
9	32 51.7	6.1	85.7	32 59.4	8.5	87.0	33 04.3	11.0	88.3	33 06.6	13.4	89.6	33 06.1	15.9	90.9
10	32 57.8 + 5.4	84.5		33 07.9 + 7.9	85.8		33 15.3 + 10.4	87.1		33 20.0 + 12.8	88.4		33 22.0 + 15.2	89.7
11	33 03.2	4.7	83.3	33 15.8	7.2	84.6	33 25.7	9.7	85.9	33 32.8	12.2	87.2	33 37.2	14.6	88.6
12	33 07.9	4.1	82.1	33 23.0	6.5	83.4	33 35.4	9.0	84.7	33 45.0	11.5	86.1	33 51.8	14.0	87.4
13	33 12.0	3.3	80.9	33 29.5	5.9	82.2	33 44.4	8.3	83.6	33 56.5	10.8	84.9	34 05.8	13.2	86.2
14	33 15.3	2.7	79.7	33 35.4	5.1	81.0	33 52.7	7.6	82.4	34 07.3	10.1	83.7	34 19.0	12.6	85.1
15	33 18.0 + 2.0	78.5		33 40.5 + 4.5	79.8		34 00.3 + 7.0	81.2		34 17.4 + 9.4	82.5		34 31.6 + 11.9	83.9
16	33 20.0	1.3	77.3	33 45.0	3.8	78.6	34 07.3	6.2	80.0	34 26.8	8.7	81.3	34 43.5	11.2	82.7
17	33 21.3 + 0.7	76.0		33 48.8	3.0	77.4	34 13.5	5.5	78.8	34 35.5	8.0	80.1	34 54.7	10.5	81.5
18	33 22.0 − 0.1	75.0		33 51.8	2.4	76.2	34 19.0	4.8	77.6	34 43.5	7.3	78.9	35 05.2	9.7	80.3
19	33 21.9	0.8	73.8	33 54.2	1.6	75.0	34 23.8	4.1	76.4	34 50.8	6.5	77.7	35 14.9	9.1	79.1
20	33 21.1 − 1.4	72.6		33 55.8 + 1.0	73.8		34 27.9 + 3.4	75.1		34 57.3 + 5.9	76.5		35 24.0 + 8.3	77.9
21	33 19.7	2.1	71.4	33 56.8 + 0.2	72.6		34 31.3	2.7	73.9	35 03.2	5.1	75.3	35 32.3	7.6	76.6
22	33 17.6	2.9	70.2	33 57.0 − 0.4	71.4		34 34.0	1.9	72.7	35 08.3	4.4	74.1	35 39.9	6.8	75.4
23	33 14.7	3.5	69.0	33 56.6	1.2	70.2	34 35.9	1.3	71.5	35 12.7	3.6	72.8	35 46.7	6.1	74.2
24	33 11.2	4.1	67.8	33 55.4	1.8	69.0	34 37.2 + 0.5	70.3		35 16.3	3.0	71.6	35 52.8	5.4	73.0
25	33 07.1 − 4.9	66.6		33 53.6 − 2.6	67.8		34 37.7 − 0.2	69.1		35 19.3 + 2.1	70.4		35 58.2 + 4.6	71.7
26	33 02.2	5.5	65.4	33 51.0	3.3	66.6	34 37.5	1.0	67.9	35 21.4	1.4	69.2	36 02.8	3.8	70.5
27	32 56.7	6.3	64.2	33 47.7	3.9	65.4	34 36.5	1.7	66.6	35 22.8 + 0.7	67.9		36 06.6	3.1	69.3
28	32 50.4	6.8	63.0	33 43.8	4.7	64.2	34 34.8	2.3	65.4	35 23.5	0.0	66.7	36 09.7	2.3	68.0
29	32 43.6	7.6	61.8	33 39.1	5.3	63.0	34 32.5	3.1	64.2	35 23.5 − 0.8	65.5		36 12.0	1.6	66.8

0°			2°			4°			6°			8°			Dec.
Hc	d	Z	Hc	d	Z	Hc	d	Z	Hc	d	Z	Hc	d	Z	
32 00.0	− 0.3	90.0	31 58.7	− 2.8	91.2	31 54.8	− 5.3	92.5	31 48.2	− 7.7	93.7	31 39.1	− 10.1	95.0	0
31 59.7	1.0	91.2	31 55.9	3.4	92.4	31 49.5	5.9	93.7	31 40.5	8.3	94.9	31 29.0	10.7	96.1	1
31 58.7	1.6	92.4	31 52.5	4.1	93.6	31 43.6	6.5	94.8	31 32.2	8.9	96.1	31 18.3	11.4	97.3	2
31 57.1	2.3	93.5	31 48.4	4.8	94.8	31 37.1	7.2	96.0	31 23.3	9.6	97.2	31 06.9	12.0	98.4	3
31 54.8	3.0	94.7	31 43.6	5.4	95.9	31 29.9	7.8	97.2	31 13.7	10.2	98.4	30 54.9	12.5	99.6	4
31 51.8	− 3.6	95.9	31 38.2	− 6.0	97.1	31 22.1	− 8.4	98.3	31 03.5	− 10.9	99.5	30 42.4	− 13.2	100.7	5
31 48.2	4.2	97.1	31 32.2	6.6	98.3	31 13.7	9.1	99.5	30 52.6	11.4	100.7	30 29.2	13.7	101.8	6
31 44.0	4.9	98.2	31 25.6	7.3	99.5	31 04.6	9.7	100.6	30 41.2	12.0	101.8	30 15.5	14.4	103.0	7
31 39.1	5.5	99.4	31 18.3	7.9	100.6	30 54.9	10.2	101.8	30 29.2	12.6	103.0	30 01.1	14.9	104.1	8
31 33.6	6.1	100.6	31 10.4	8.6	101.8	30 44.7	10.9	102.9	30 16.6	13.2	104.1	29 46.2	15.4	105.2	9
31 27.5	− 6.8	101.7	31 01.8	− 9.1	102.9	30 33.8	− 11.5	104.1	30 03.4	− 13.8	105.2	29 30.8	− 16.0	106.3	10
31 20.7	7.4	102.9	30 52.7	9.8	104.1	30 22.3	12.1	105.2	29 49.6	14.3	106.3	29 14.8	16.6	107.4	11
31 13.3	8.1	104.1	30 42.9	10.4	105.2	30 10.2	12.6	106.4	29 35.3	14.9	107.5	28 58.2	17.1	108.5	12
31 05.2	8.6	105.2	30 32.5	10.9	106.4	29 57.6	13.3	107.5	29 20.4	15.4	108.6	28 41.1	17.6	109.6	13
30 56.6	9.3	106.4	30 21.6	11.6	107.5	29 44.3	13.8	108.6	29 05.0	16.0	109.7	28 23.5	18.1	110.7	14
30 47.3	− 9.9	107.5	30 10.0	− 12.1	108.7	29 30.5	− 14.3	109.7	28 49.0	− 16.5	110.8	28 05.4	− 18.6	111.8	15
30 37.4	10.5	108.7	29 57.9	12.8	109.8	29 16.2	14.9	110.9	28 32.5	17.1	111.9	27 46.8	19.1	112.9	16
30 26.9	11.1	109.8	29 45.1	13.3	110.9	29 01.3	15.5	112.0	28 15.4	17.5	113.0	27 27.7	19.7	113.9	17
30 15.8	11.6	111.0	29 31.8	13.8	112.0	28 45.8	16.0	113.1	27 57.9	18.1	114.1	27 08.0	20.1	115.0	18
30 04.2	12.3	112.1	29 18.0	14.4	113.2	28 29.8	16.5	114.2	27 39.8	18.6	115.1	26 47.9	20.5	116.1	19
29 51.9	− 12.8	113.2	29 03.6	− 15.0	114.3	28 13.3	− 17.0	115.3	27 21.2	− 19.0	116.2	26 27.4	− 21.0	117.1	20
29 39.1	13.4	114.4	28 48.6	15.5	115.4	27 56.3	17.6	116.3	27 02.2	19.6	117.3	26 06.4	21.5	118.2	21
29 25.7	14.0	115.5	28 33.1	16.0	116.5	27 38.7	18.0	117.4	26 42.6	20.0	118.3	25 44.9	21.9	119.2	22
29 11.7	14.5	116.6	28 17.1	16.5	117.6	27 20.7	18.5	118.5	26 22.6	20.4	119.4	25 23.0	22.4	120.2	23
28 57.2	15.0	117.7	28 00.6	17.1	118.7	27 02.2	19.0	119.6	26 02.2	20.9	120.4	25 00.6	22.7	121.3	24
28 42.2	− 15.6	118.8	27 43.5	− 17.6	119.7	26 43.2	− 19.5	120.6	25 41.3	− 21.4	121.5	24 37.9	− 23.2	122.3	25
28 26.6	16.1	119.9	27 25.9	18.0	120.8	26 23.7	20.0	121.7	25 19.9	21.8	122.5	24 14.7	23.6	123.3	26
28 10.5	16.7	121.0	27 07.9	18.6	121.9	26 03.7	20.4	122.7	24 58.1	22.2	123.5	23 51.1	23.9	124.3	27
27 53.8	17.1	122.1	26 49.3	19.0	123.0	25 43.3	20.8	123.8	24 35.9	22.6	124.6	23 27.2	24.3	125.3	28
27 36.7	17.6	123.2	26 30.3	19.5	124.0	25 22.5	21.3	124.8	24 13.3	23.0	125.6	23 02.9	24.8	126.3	29

10°			12°			14°			16°			18°			Dec.
Hc	d	Z	Hc	d	Z	Hc	d	Z	Hc	d	Z	Hc	d	Z	
31 27.5	− 12.6	96.2	31 13.3	− 14.9	97.4	30 56.6	− 17.3	98.6	30 37.4	− 19.5	99.8	30 15.8	− 21.7	100.9	0
31 14.9	13.1	97.3	30 58.4	15.5	98.5	30 39.3	17.7	99.7	30 17.9	20.0	100.9	29 54.1	22.3	102.0	1
31 01.8	13.7	98.5	30 42.9	16.1	99.7	30 21.6	18.4	100.8	29 57.9	20.6	102.0	29 31.8	22.7	103.1	2
30 48.1	14.3	99.6	30 26.8	16.6	100.8	30 03.2	18.9	101.9	29 37.3	21.1	103.0	29 09.1	23.3	104.1	3
30 33.8	14.8	100.7	30 10.2	17.2	101.9	29 44.3	19.4	103.0	29 16.2	21.6	104.1	28 45.8	23.7	105.2	4
30 18.9	− 15.5	101.9	29 53.0	− 17.7	103.0	29 24.9	− 19.9	104.1	28 54.6	− 22.1	105.2	28 22.1	− 24.2	106.2	5
30 03.4	16.0	103.0	29 35.3	18.3	104.1	29 05.0	20.5	105.2	28 32.5	22.6	106.2	27 57.9	24.7	107.3	6
29 47.4	16.6	104.1	29 17.0	18.8	105.2	28 44.5	21.0	106.3	28 09.9	23.1	107.3	27 33.2	25.2	108.3	7
29 30.8	17.1	105.2	28 58.2	19.3	106.3	28 23.5	21.4	107.3	27 46.8	23.6	108.3	27 08.0	25.5	109.3	8
29 13.7	17.7	106.3	28 38.9	19.8	107.4	28 02.1	22.0	108.4	27 23.2	24.0	109.4	26 42.5	26.1	110.3	9
28 56.0	− 18.2	107.4	28 19.1	− 20.4	108.4	27 40.1	− 22.4	109.4	26 59.2	− 24.4	110.4	26 16.4	− 26.4	111.3	10
28 37.8	18.7	108.5	27 58.7	20.8	109.5	27 17.7	22.9	110.5	26 34.8	24.9	111.4	25 50.0	26.8	112.3	11
28 19.1	19.3	109.6	27 37.9	21.3	110.6	26 54.8	23.3	111.5	26 09.9	25.3	112.4	25 23.2	27.2	113.3	12
27 59.8	19.7	110.6	27 16.6	21.8	111.6	26 31.5	23.8	112.6	25 44.6	25.8	113.5	24 56.0	27.7	114.3	13
27 40.1	20.2	111.7	26 54.8	22.2	112.7	26 07.7	24.2	113.6	25 18.8	26.1	114.5	24 28.3	27.9	115.3	14
27 19.9	− 20.7	112.8	26 32.6	− 22.7	113.7	25 43.5	− 24.7	114.6	24 52.7	− 26.5	115.5	24 00.4	− 28.4	116.3	15
26 59.2	21.1	113.8	26 09.9	23.2	114.7	25 18.8	25.0	115.6	24 26.2	26.9	116.4	23 32.0	28.7	117.2	16
26 38.1	21.7	114.9	25 46.7	23.5	115.8	24 53.8	25.5	116.6	23 59.3	27.3	117.4	23 03.3	29.1	118.2	17
26 16.4	22.0	115.9	25 23.2	24.0	116.8	24 28.3	25.8	117.6	23 32.0	27.6	118.4	22 34.2	29.3	119.1	18
25 54.4	22.5	116.9	24 59.2	24.4	117.8	24 02.5	26.2	118.6	23 04.4	28.0	119.4	22 04.9	29.7	120.1	19
25 31.9	− 22.9	118.0	24 34.8	− 24.8	118.8	23 36.3	− 26.6	119.6	22 36.4	− 28.3	120.3	21 35.2	− 30.0	121.0	20
25 09.0	23.4	119.0	24 10.0	25.1	119.8	23 09.7	26.9	120.6	22 08.1	28.7	121.3	21 05.2	30.4	121.9	21
24 45.6	23.8	120.0	23 44.9	25.6	120.8	22 42.8	27.3	121.5	21 39.4	29.0	122.2	20 34.8	30.6	122.9	22
24 21.8	24.1	121.0	23 19.3	25.9	121.8	22 15.5	27.7	122.5	21 10.4	29.3	123.2	20 04.2	30.9	123.8	23
23 57.7	24.6	122.0	22 53.4	26.3	122.8	21 47.8	27.9	123.4	20 41.1	29.5	124.1	19 33.3	31.1	124.7	24
23 33.1	− 24.9	123.0	22 27.1	− 26.6	123.7	21 19.9	− 28.3	124.4	20 11.6	− 29.9	125.0	19 02.2	− 31.4	125.6	25
23 08.2	25.3	124.0	22 00.5	27.0	124.7	20 51.6	28.6	125.3	19 41.7	30.2	125.9	18 30.8	31.7	126.5	26
22 42.9	25.6	125.0	21 33.5	27.3	125.7	20 23.0	28.9	126.3	19 11.5	30.4	126.9	17 59.1	31.9	127.4	27
22 17.3	26.0	126.0	21 06.2	27.6	126.6	19 54.1	29.1	127.2	18 41.1	30.7	127.8	17 27.2	32.2	128.3	28
21 51.3	26.4	127.0	20 38.6	27.9	127.6	19 25.0	29.5	128.1	18 10.4	30.9	128.7	16 55.0	32.4	129.2	29

Dec.	20° Hc	d	Z	22° Hc	d	Z	24° Hc	d	Z	26° Hc	d	Z	28° Hc	d	Z
°	° ′	′	°	° ′	′	°	° ′	′	°	° ′	′	°	° ′	′	°
0	29 51.9	+23.4	102.1	29 25.7	+25.6	103.2	28 57.2	+27.7	104.3	28 26.6	+29.7	105.3	27 53.8	+31.7	106.3
1	30 15.3	22.9	101.0	29 51.3	25.0	102.1	29 24.9	27.2	103.2	28 56.3	29.3	104.3	28 25.5	31.3	105.4
2	30 38.2	22.4	99.9	30 16.3	24.6	101.1	29 52.1	26.7	102.2	29 25.6	28.8	103.3	28 56.8	30.8	104.4
3	31 00.6	21.8	98.8	30 40.9	24.0	100.0	30 18.8	26.2	101.2	29 54.4	28.3	102.3	29 27.6	30.4	103.4
4	31 22.4	21.2	97.8	31 04.9	23.5	99.0	30 45.0	25.7	100.1	30 22.7	27.9	101.3	29 58.0	30.0	102.4
5	31 43.6	+20.7	96.7	31 28.4	+23.0	97.9	31 10.7	+25.2	99.1	30 50.6	+27.3	100.3	30 28.0	+29.4	101.4
6	32 04.3	20.1	95.6	31 51.4	22.4	96.8	31 35.9	24.7	98.0	31 17.9	26.9	99.2	30 57.4	29.0	100.4
7	32 24.4	19.5	94.4	32 13.8	21.9	95.7	32 00.6	24.1	96.9	31 44.8	26.3	98.2	31 26.4	28.6	99.4
8	32 43.9	19.0	93.3	32 35.7	21.2	94.6	32 24.7	23.6	95.9	32 11.1	25.8	97.1	31 55.0	28.0	98.4
9	33 02.9	18.2	92.2	32 56.9	20.7	93.5	32 48.3	22.9	94.8	32 36.9	25.3	96.1	32 23.0	27.4	97.3
10	33 21.1	+17.7	91.1	33 17.6	+20.0	92.4	33 11.2	+22.4	93.7	33 02.2	+24.7	95.0	32 50.4	+27.0	96.3
11	33 38.8	17.0	89.9	33 37.6	19.4	91.2	33 33.6	21.8	92.6	33 26.9	24.1	93.9	33 17.4	26.4	95.2
12	33 55.8	16.4	88.8	33 57.0	18.8	90.1	33 55.4	21.2	91.4	33 51.0	23.5	92.8	33 43.8	25.8	94.1
13	34 12.2	15.7	87.6	34 15.8	18.2	88.9	34 16.6	20.6	90.3	34 14.5	23.0	91.7	34 09.6	25.2	93.0
14	34 27.9	15.1	86.4	34 34.0	17.5	87.8	34 37.2	19.9	89.2	34 37.5	22.3	90.6	34 34.8	24.7	91.9
15	34 43.0	+14.3	85.2	34 51.5	+16.8	86.6	34 57.1	+19.2	88.0	34 59.8	+21.6	89.4	34 59.5	+24.0	90.8
16	34 57.3	13.7	84.1	35 08.3	16.2	85.5	35 16.3	18.6	86.9	35 21.4	21.0	88.3	35 23.5	23.4	89.7
17	35 11.0	13.0	82.9	35 24.5	15.4	84.3	35 34.9	17.9	85.7	35 42.4	20.4	87.1	35 46.9	22.8	88.6
18	35 24.0	12.3	81.7	35 39.9	14.7	83.1	35 52.8	17.3	84.5	36 02.8	19.7	86.0	36 09.7	22.1	87.4
19	35 36.3	11.5	80.5	35 54.6	14.1	81.9	36 10.1	16.5	83.3	36 22.5	18.9	84.8	36 31.8	21.4	86.3
20	35 47.8	+10.8	79.3	36 08.7	+13.3	80.7	36 26.6	+15.8	82.1	36 41.4	+18.3	83.6	36 53.2	+20.8	85.1
21	35 58.6	10.1	78.1	36 22.0	12.5	79.5	36 42.4	15.0	80.9	36 59.7	17.6	82.4	37 14.0	20.0	83.9
22	36 08.7	9.3	76.8	36 34.5	11.9	78.3	36 57.4	14.4	79.7	37 17.3	16.8	81.2	37 34.0	19.3	82.7
23	36 18.0	8.6	75.6	36 46.4	11.0	77.0	37 11.8	13.5	78.5	37 34.1	16.1	80.0	37 53.3	18.6	81.5
24	36 26.6	7.8	74.4	36 57.4	10.4	75.8	37 25.3	12.9	77.3	37 50.2	15.3	78.8	38 11.9	17.9	80.3
25	36 34.4	+7.0	73.1	37 07.8	+9.5	74.6	37 38.2	+12.0	76.1	38 05.5	+14.6	77.6	38 29.8	+17.0	79.1
26	36 41.4	6.3	71.9	37 17.3	8.7	73.3	37 50.2	11.3	74.8	38 20.1	13.8	76.3	38 46.8	16.3	77.9
27	36 47.5	5.5	70.7	37 26.0	8.0	72.1	38 01.5	10.4	73.6	38 33.9	12.9	75.1	39 03.1	15.5	76.7
28	36 53.2	4.8	69.4	37 34.0	7.2	70.9	38 11.9	9.7	72.3	38 46.8	12.2	73.8	39 18.6	14.8	75.4
29	36 58.0	3.9	68.2	37 41.2	6.4	69.6	38 21.6	8.8	71.1	38 59.0	11.4	72.6	39 33.4	13.8	74.2

Dec.	30° Hc	d	Z	32° Hc	d	Z	34° Hc	d	Z	36° Hc	d	Z	38° Hc	d	Z
°	° ′	′	°	° ′	′	°	° ′	′	°	° ′	′	°	° ′	′	°
0	27 19.1	+33.5	107.4	26 42.3	+35.4	108.3	26 03.6	+37.2	109.3	25 23.2	+38.8	110.2	24 40.9	+40.5	111.0
1	27 52.6	33.2	106.4	27 17.7	35.1	107.4	26 40.8	36.9	108.4	26 02.0	38.6	109.3	25 21.4	40.3	110.2
2	28 25.8	32.8	105.5	27 52.8	34.7	106.5	27 17.7	36.5	107.5	26 40.6	38.3	108.5	26 01.7	40.0	109.4
3	28 58.6	32.4	104.5	28 27.5	34.3	105.6	27 54.2	36.2	106.6	27 18.9	38.0	107.6	26 41.7	39.6	108.6
4	29 31.0	32.0	103.6	29 01.8	33.9	104.6	28 30.4	35.8	105.7	27 56.9	37.6	106.7	27 21.3	39.4	107.7
5	30 03.0	+31.5	102.6	29 35.7	+33.5	103.7	29 06.2	+35.4	104.8	28 34.5	+37.3	105.8	28 00.7	+39.0	106.9
6	30 34.5	31.1	101.6	30 09.2	33.1	102.7	29 41.6	35.1	103.9	29 11.8	36.9	105.0	28 39.7	38.8	106.0
7	31 05.6	30.6	100.6	30 42.3	32.7	101.8	30 16.7	34.6	102.9	29 48.7	36.5	104.0	29 18.5	38.3	105.1
8	31 36.2	30.2	99.6	31 15.0	32.2	100.8	30 51.3	34.2	102.0	30 25.2	36.2	103.1	29 56.8	38.0	104.3
9	32 06.4	29.6	98.6	31 47.2	31.8	99.8	31 25.5	33.8	101.0	31 01.4	35.7	102.2	30 34.8	37.7	103.4
10	32 36.0	+29.2	97.5	32 19.0	+31.2	98.8	31 59.3	+33.4	100.0	31 37.1	+35.4	101.3	31 12.5	+37.2	102.5
11	33 05.2	28.6	96.5	32 50.2	30.8	97.8	32 32.7	32.8	99.1	32 12.5	34.9	100.3	31 49.7	36.9	101.5
12	33 33.8	28.0	95.4	33 21.0	30.3	96.8	33 05.5	32.4	98.1	32 47.4	34.4	99.3	32 26.6	36.4	100.6
13	34 01.8	27.6	94.4	33 51.3	29.7	95.7	33 37.9	31.9	97.1	33 21.8	34.0	98.4	33 03.0	36.0	99.7
14	34 29.4	26.9	93.3	34 21.0	29.2	94.7	34 09.8	31.4	96.0	33 55.8	33.5	97.4	33 39.0	35.6	98.7
15	34 56.3	+26.4	92.2	34 50.2	+28.6	93.6	34 41.2	+30.8	95.0	34 29.3	+33.0	96.4	34 14.6	+35.0	97.7
16	35 22.7	25.7	91.1	35 18.8	28.1	92.5	35 12.0	30.3	94.0	35 02.3	32.5	95.4	34 49.6	34.6	96.7
17	35 48.4	25.2	90.0	35 46.9	27.4	91.5	35 42.3	29.8	92.9	35 34.8	31.9	94.3	35 24.2	34.1	95.7
18	36 13.6	24.5	88.9	36 14.3	26.9	90.4	36 12.1	29.1	91.8	36 06.7	31.4	93.3	35 58.3	33.6	94.7
19	36 38.1	23.8	87.8	36 41.2	26.2	89.2	36 41.2	28.6	90.7	36 38.1	30.9	92.2	36 31.9	33.1	93.7
20	37 01.9	+23.2	86.6	37 07.4	+25.6	88.1	37 09.8	+27.9	89.6	37 09.0	+30.2	91.1	37 05.0	+32.5	92.7
21	37 25.1	22.5	85.5	37 33.0	24.9	87.0	37 37.7	27.3	88.5	37 39.2	29.6	90.1	37 37.5	31.9	91.6
22	37 47.6	21.8	84.3	37 57.9	24.3	85.8	38 05.0	26.7	87.4	38 08.8	29.0	89.0	38 09.4	31.3	90.5
23	38 09.4	21.0	83.1	38 22.2	23.5	84.7	38 31.7	25.9	86.3	38 37.8	28.4	87.8	38 40.7	30.7	89.4
24	38 30.4	20.4	81.9	38 45.7	22.8	83.5	38 57.6	25.3	85.1	39 06.2	27.7	86.7	39 11.4	30.1	88.3
25	38 50.8	+19.6	80.7	39 08.5	+22.1	82.3	39 22.9	+24.6	83.9	39 33.9	+27.0	85.6	39 41.5	+29.4	87.2
26	39 10.4	18.8	79.5	39 30.6	21.4	81.1	39 47.5	23.8	82.7	40 00.9	26.3	84.4	40 10.9	28.7	86.1
27	39 29.2	18.0	78.3	39 52.0	20.5	79.9	40 11.3	23.1	81.5	40 27.2	25.6	83.2	40 39.6	28.1	84.9
28	39 47.2	17.3	77.0	40 12.5	19.8	78.7	40 34.4	22.3	80.3	40 52.8	24.9	82.0	41 07.7	27.3	83.8
29	40 04.5	16.4	75.8	40 32.3	19.0	77.4	40 56.7	21.6	79.1	41 17.7	24.0	80.8	41 35.0	26.6	82.6

20°			22°			24°			26°			28°			Dec.
Hc	d	Z	Hc	d	Z	Hc	d	Z	Hc	d	Z	Hc	d	Z	
29 51.9	-23.9	102.1	29 25.7	-26.1	103.2	28 57.2	-28.1	104.3	28 26.6	-30.1	105.3	27 53.8	-32.0	106.3	0
29 28.0	24.4	103.1	28 59.6	26.5	104.2	28 29.1	28.5	105.3	27 56.5	30.6	106.3	27 21.8	32.5	107.3	1
29 03.6	24.9	104.2	28 33.1	26.9	105.2	28 00.6	29.0	106.3	27 25.9	30.9	107.3	26 49.3	32.8	108.2	2
28 38.7	25.4	105.2	28 06.2	27.5	106.2	27 31.6	29.4	107.3	26 55.0	31.3	108.2	26 16.5	33.2	109.2	3
28 13.3	25.8	106.2	27 38.7	27.8	107.3	27 02.2	29.8	108.2	26 23.7	31.7	109.2	25 43.3	33.5	110.1	4
27 47.5	-26.3	107.3	27 10.9	-28.3	108.2	26 32.4	-30.2	109.2	25 52.0	-32.1	110.1	25 09.8	-33.9	111.0	5
27 21.2	26.7	108.3	26 42.6	28.6	109.2	26 02.2	30.6	110.2	25 19.9	32.4	111.1	24 35.9	34.2	111.9	6
26 54.5	27.1	109.3	26 14.0	29.1	110.2	25 31.6	31.0	111.1	24 47.5	32.8	112.0	24 01.7	34.5	112.8	7
26 27.4	27.6	110.3	25 44.9	29.5	111.2	25 00.6	31.3	112.1	24 14.7	33.1	112.9	23 27.2	34.8	113.7	8
25 59.8	27.9	111.3	25 15.4	29.8	112.2	24 29.3	31.6	113.0	23 41.6	33.4	113.8	22 52.4	35.1	114.6	9
25 31.9	-28.4	112.2	24 45.6	-30.2	113.1	23 57.7	-32.0	113.9	23 08.2	-33.7	114.7	22 17.3	-35.4	115.5	10
25 03.5	28.7	113.2	24 15.4	30.5	114.1	23 25.7	32.3	114.9	22 34.5	34.0	115.6	21 41.9	35.7	116.4	11
24 34.8	29.1	114.2	23 44.9	30.9	115.0	22 53.4	32.6	115.8	22 00.5	34.3	116.5	21 06.2	35.9	117.2	12
24 05.7	29.4	115.2	23 14.0	31.2	115.9	22 20.8	33.0	116.7	21 26.2	34.6	117.4	20 30.3	36.2	118.1	13
23 36.3	29.8	116.1	22 42.8	31.6	116.9	21 47.8	33.2	117.6	20 51.6	34.8	118.3	19 54.1	36.4	118.9	14
23 06.5	-30.1	117.0	22 11.2	-31.8	117.8	21 14.6	-33.5	118.5	20 16.8	-35.1	119.2	19 17.7	-36.6	119.8	15
22 36.4	30.5	118.0	21 39.4	32.1	118.7	20 41.1	33.7	119.4	19 41.7	35.4	120.0	18 41.1	36.9	120.6	16
22 05.9	30.7	118.9	21 07.3	32.5	119.6	20 07.4	34.1	120.3	19 06.3	35.5	120.9	18 04.2	37.0	121.5	17
21 35.2	31.1	119.8	20 34.8	32.7	120.5	19 33.3	34.2	121.1	18 30.8	35.8	121.7	17 27.2	37.3	122.3	18
21 04.1	31.4	120.8	20 02.1	32.9	121.4	18 59.1	34.6	122.0	17 55.0	36.1	122.6	16 49.9	37.5	123.1	19
20 32.7	-31.6	121.7	19 29.2	-33.3	122.3	18 24.5	-34.7	122.9	17 18.9	-36.2	123.4	16 12.4	-37.6	123.9	20
20 01.1	31.9	122.6	18 55.9	33.4	123.2	17 49.8	35.0	123.7	16 42.7	36.4	124.2	15 34.8	37.9	124.7	21
19 29.2	32.2	123.5	18 22.5	33.7	124.1	17 14.8	35.2	124.6	16 06.3	36.6	125.1	14 56.9	38.0	125.5	22
18 57.0	32.5	124.4	17 48.8	34.0	124.9	16 39.6	35.4	125.4	15 29.7	36.9	125.9	14 18.9	38.1	126.3	23
18 24.5	32.6	125.3	17 14.8	34.2	125.8	16 04.2	35.6	126.3	14 52.8	36.9	126.7	13 40.8	38.3	127.1	24
17 51.9	-33.0	126.1	16 40.6	-34.3	126.6	15 28.6	-35.8	127.1	14 15.9	-37.2	127.5	13 02.5	-38.5	127.9	25
17 18.9	33.1	127.0	16 06.3	34.6	127.5	14 52.8	35.9	127.9	13 38.7	37.3	128.3	12 24.0	38.6	128.7	26
16 45.8	33.4	127.9	15 31.7	34.8	128.3	14 16.9	36.1	128.8	13 01.4	37.4	129.1	11 45.4	38.7	129.5	27
16 12.4	33.6	128.8	14 56.9	34.9	129.2	13 40.8	36.3	129.6	12 24.0	37.6	129.9	11 06.7	38.8	130.3	28
15 38.8	33.8	129.6	14 22.0	35.2	130.0	13 04.5	36.5	130.4	11 46.4	37.7	130.7	10 27.9	39.0	131.0	29

30°			32°			34°			36°			38°			Dec.
Hc	d	Z	Hc	d	Z	Hc	d	Z	Hc	d	Z	Hc	d	Z	
27 19.1	-34.0	107.4	26 42.3	-35.8	108.3	26 03.6	-37.5	109.3	25 23.2	-39.2	110.2	24 40.9	-40.8	111.0	0
26 45.1	34.3	108.3	26 06.5	36.0	109.2	25 26.1	37.8	110.1	24 44.0	39.5	111.0	24 00.1	41.0	111.8	1
26 10.8	34.6	109.2	25 30.5	36.5	110.1	24 48.3	38.1	111.0	24 04.5	39.7	111.8	23 19.1	41.3	112.6	2
25 36.2	35.0	110.1	24 54.0	36.7	111.0	24 10.2	38.3	111.8	23 24.8	40.0	112.7	22 37.8	41.5	113.4	3
25 01.2	35.3	111.0	24 17.3	37.0	111.9	23 31.9	38.7	112.7	22 44.8	40.2	113.5	21 56.3	41.7	114.2	4
24 25.9	-35.6	111.9	23 40.3	-37.3	112.7	22 53.2	-38.9	113.5	22 04.6	-40.4	114.3	21 14.6	-41.9	115.0	5
23 50.3	36.0	112.8	23 03.0	37.5	113.6	22 14.3	39.1	114.3	21 24.2	40.7	115.1	20 32.7	42.1	115.8	6
23 14.3	36.2	113.6	22 25.5	37.9	114.4	21 35.2	39.4	115.1	20 43.5	40.9	115.8	19 50.6	42.4	116.5	7
22 38.1	36.4	114.5	21 47.6	38.0	115.3	20 55.8	39.6	116.0	20 02.6	41.1	116.6	19 08.2	42.5	117.3	8
22 01.7	36.8	115.4	21 09.6	38.3	116.1	20 16.2	39.9	116.8	19 21.5	41.2	117.4	18 25.7	42.6	118.0	9
21 24.9	-37.0	116.2	20 31.3	-38.6	116.9	19 36.3	-40.0	117.6	18 40.3	-41.5	118.2	17 43.1	-42.9	118.7	10
20 47.9	37.2	117.1	19 52.7	38.8	117.7	18 56.3	40.2	118.3	17 58.8	41.7	118.9	17 00.2	43.0	119.5	11
20 10.7	37.5	117.9	19 13.9	39.0	118.5	18 16.1	40.4	119.1	17 17.1	41.8	119.7	16 17.2	43.1	120.2	12
19 33.2	37.7	118.7	18 35.0	39.2	119.3	17 35.6	40.6	119.9	16 35.3	41.9	120.4	15 34.1	43.3	120.9	13
18 55.5	37.9	119.6	17 55.8	39.4	120.1	16 55.0	40.7	120.7	15 53.4	42.2	121.2	14 50.8	43.4	121.6	14
18 17.6	-38.1	120.4	17 16.4	-39.6	120.9	16 14.3	-41.0	121.4	15 11.2	-42.2	121.9	14 07.4	-43.5	122.4	15
17 39.5	38.4	121.2	16 36.8	39.7	121.7	15 33.3	41.1	122.2	14 29.0	42.4	122.7	13 23.9	43.7	123.1	16
17 01.1	38.5	122.0	15 57.1	39.9	122.5	14 52.2	41.2	123.0	13 46.6	42.6	123.4	12 40.2	43.8	123.8	17
16 22.6	38.7	122.8	15 17.2	40.1	123.3	14 11.0	41.4	123.7	13 04.0	42.6	124.1	11 56.4	43.8	124.5	18
15 43.9	38.9	123.6	14 37.1	40.2	124.0	13 29.6	41.5	124.5	12 21.4	42.8	124.8	11 12.6	44.0	125.2	19
15 05.0	-39.0	124.4	13 56.9	-40.3	124.8	12 48.1	-41.7	125.2	11 38.6	-42.8	125.5	10 28.6	-44.1	125.9	20
14 26.0	39.2	125.2	13 16.6	40.5	125.6	12 06.4	41.7	125.9	10 55.8	43.0	126.3	9 44.5	44.1	126.6	21
13 46.8	39.3	125.9	12 36.1	40.7	126.3	11 24.7	41.9	126.7	10 12.8	43.1	127.0	9 00.4	44.2	127.2	22
13 07.5	39.5	126.7	11 55.4	40.7	127.1	10 42.8	41.9	127.4	9 29.7	43.1	127.7	8 16.2	44.3	127.9	23
12 28.0	39.6	127.5	11 14.7	40.8	127.8	10 00.9	42.1	128.1	8 46.6	43.3	128.4	7 31.9	44.4	128.6	24
11 48.4	-39.7	128.3	10 33.9	-41.0	128.6	9 18.8	-42.1	128.8	8 03.3	-43.2	129.1	6 47.5	-44.4	129.3	25
11 08.7	39.8	129.0	9 52.9	41.1	129.3	8 36.7	42.3	129.6	7 20.1	43.4	129.8	6 03.1	44.4	130.0	26
10 28.9	40.0	129.8	9 11.8	41.1	130.1	7 54.4	42.3	130.3	6 36.7	43.4	130.5	5 18.7	44.5	130.6	27
9 48.9	40.0	130.5	8 30.7	41.2	130.8	7 12.1	42.3	131.0	5 53.3	43.5	131.2	4 34.2	44.6	131.3	28
9 08.9	40.2	131.3	7 49.5	41.3	131.5	6 29.8	42.4	131.7	5 09.8	43.5	131.9	3 49.6	44.5	132.0	29

Dec.	40° Hc	d	Z	42° Hc	d	Z	44° Hc	d	Z	46° Hc	d	Z	48° Hc	d	Z
0	23 57.0	+42.1	111.9	23 11.5	+43.6	112.7	22 24.5	+44.9	113.5	21 36.0	+46.3	114.2	20 46.1	+47.6	114.9
1	24 39.1	41.8	111.1	23 55.1	43.3	111.9	23 09.4	44.8	112.7	22 22.3	46.2	113.5	21 33.7	47.5	114.3
2	25 20.9	41.6	110.3	24 38.4	43.1	111.2	23 54.2	44.6	112.0	23 08.5	45.9	112.8	22 21.2	47.2	113.6
3	26 02.5	41.3	109.5	25 21.5	42.9	110.4	24 38.8	44.4	111.3	23 54.4	45.8	112.1	23 08.4	47.2	112.9
4	26 43.8	41.1	108.7	26 04.4	42.6	109.6	25 23.2	44.1	110.5	24 40.2	45.6	111.4	23 55.6	46.9	112.3
5	27 24.9	+40.7	107.9	26 47.0	+42.4	108.9	26 07.3	+43.9	109.8	25 25.8	+45.4	110.7	24 42.5	+46.8	111.6
6	28 05.6	40.4	107.1	27 29.4	42.1	108.1	26 51.2	43.7	109.0	26 11.2	45.1	110.0	25 29.3	46.5	110.9
7	28 46.0	40.2	106.2	28 11.5	41.8	107.3	27 34.9	43.4	108.3	26 56.3	44.9	109.2	26 15.8	46.4	110.2
8	29 26.2	39.7	105.4	28 53.3	41.5	106.4	28 18.3	43.1	107.5	27 41.2	44.7	108.5	27 02.2	46.1	109.5
9	30 05.9	39.5	104.5	29 34.8	41.2	105.6	29 01.4	42.8	106.7	28 25.9	44.4	107.7	27 48.3	45.9	108.7
10	30 45.4	+39.1	103.6	30 16.0	+40.8	104.8	29 44.2	+42.6	105.9	29 10.3	+44.2	107.0	28 34.2	+45.7	108.0
11	31 24.5	38.7	102.7	30 56.8	40.6	103.9	30 26.8	42.2	105.1	29 54.5	43.8	106.2	29 19.9	45.4	107.3
12	32 03.2	38.4	101.8	31 37.4	40.1	103.1	31 09.0	42.0	104.2	30 38.3	43.6	105.4	30 05.3	45.2	106.5
13	32 41.6	37.9	100.9	32 17.5	39.8	102.2	31 51.0	41.5	103.4	31 21.9	43.3	104.6	30 50.5	44.9	105.8
14	33 19.5	37.5	100.0	32 57.3	39.4	101.3	32 32.5	41.3	102.5	32 05.2	43.0	103.8	31 35.4	44.6	105.0
15	33 57.0	+37.1	99.1	33 36.7	+39.1	100.4	33 13.8	+40.8	101.7	32 48.2	+42.6	103.0	32 20.0	+44.3	104.2
16	34 34.1	36.7	98.1	34 15.8	38.6	99.5	33 54.6	40.5	100.8	33 30.8	42.3	102.1	33 04.3	44.0	103.4
17	35 10.8	36.1	97.2	34 54.4	38.1	98.5	34 35.1	40.1	99.9	34 13.1	41.9	101.3	33 48.3	43.7	102.6
18	35 46.9	35.7	96.2	35 32.5	37.8	97.6	35 15.2	39.7	99.0	34 55.0	41.5	100.4	34 32.0	43.3	101.7
19	36 22.6	35.2	95.2	36 10.3	37.2	96.6	35 54.9	39.2	98.1	35 36.5	41.2	99.5	35 15.3	42.9	100.9
20	36 57.8	+34.7	94.2	36 47.5	+36.8	95.7	36 34.1	+38.8	97.1	36 17.7	+40.7	98.6	35 58.2	+42.6	100.0
21	37 32.5	34.1	93.1	37 24.3	36.3	94.7	37 12.9	38.4	96.2	36 58.4	40.3	97.7	36 40.8	42.2	99.2
22	38 06.6	33.6	92.1	38 00.6	35.7	93.7	37 51.3	37.8	95.2	37 38.7	39.9	96.8	37 23.0	41.8	98.3
23	38 40.2	33.0	91.0	38 36.3	35.2	92.6	38 29.1	37.4	94.2	38 18.6	39.4	95.8	38 04.8	41.4	97.4
24	39 13.2	32.3	90.0	39 11.5	34.7	91.6	39 06.5	36.8	93.2	38 58.0	38.9	94.8	38 46.2	40.9	96.5
25	39 45.5	+31.8	88.9	39 46.2	+34.0	90.5	39 43.3	+36.2	92.2	39 36.9	+38.4	93.9	39 27.1	+40.5	95.5
26	40 17.3	31.1	87.8	40 20.2	33.4	89.5	40 19.5	35.7	91.2	40 15.3	37.9	92.9	40 07.6	39.9	94.5
27	40 48.4	30.5	86.6	40 53.6	32.9	88.4	40 55.2	35.1	90.1	40 53.2	37.3	91.8	40 47.5	39.5	93.6
28	41 18.9	29.8	85.5	41 26.5	32.1	87.3	41 30.3	34.5	89.0	41 30.5	36.8	90.8	41 27.0	38.9	92.6
29	41 48.7	29.0	84.3	41 58.6	31.5	86.1	42 04.8	33.9	87.9	42 07.3	36.1	89.7	42 05.9	38.4	91.5

Dec.	50° Hc	d	Z	52° Hc	d	Z	54° Hc	d	Z	56° Hc	d	Z	58° Hc	d	Z
0	19 54.9	+48.8	115.6	19 02.5	+49.9	116.2	18 08.9	+51.0	116.8	17 14.2	+52.1	117.4	16 18.5	+53.0	117.9
1	20 43.7	48.7	115.0	19 52.4	49.9	115.6	18 59.9	51.0	116.3	18 06.3	51.9	116.9	17 11.5	52.9	117.4
2	21 32.4	48.6	114.3	20 42.3	49.7	115.0	19 50.9	50.8	115.7	18 58.2	51.9	116.3	18 04.4	52.9	116.9
3	22 21.0	48.3	113.7	21 32.0	49.6	114.4	20 41.7	50.7	115.1	19 50.1	51.8	115.8	18 57.3	52.7	116.4
4	23 09.3	48.3	113.1	22 21.6	49.5	113.8	21 32.4	50.6	114.6	20 41.9	51.6	115.3	19 50.0	52.7	115.9
5	23 57.6	+48.1	112.4	23 11.1	+49.3	113.2	22 23.0	+50.5	114.0	21 33.5	+51.6	114.7	20 42.7	+52.5	115.4
6	24 45.7	47.9	111.8	24 00.4	49.1	112.6	23 13.5	50.3	113.4	22 25.1	51.4	114.2	21 35.2	52.5	114.9
7	25 33.6	47.7	111.1	24 49.5	49.0	112.0	24 03.8	50.2	112.8	23 16.5	51.4	113.6	22 27.7	52.4	114.4
8	26 21.3	47.5	110.4	25 38.5	48.7	111.3	24 54.0	50.1	112.2	24 07.9	51.2	113.0	23 20.1	52.3	113.9
9	27 08.8	47.3	109.7	26 27.3	48.7	110.7	25 44.1	49.9	111.6	24 59.1	51.0	112.5	24 12.4	52.1	113.3
10	27 56.1	+47.1	109.0	27 16.0	+48.5	110.0	26 34.0	+49.7	111.0	25 50.1	+50.9	111.9	25 04.5	+52.1	112.8
11	28 43.2	46.9	108.3	28 04.5	48.2	109.3	27 23.7	49.6	110.3	26 41.0	50.8	111.3	25 56.6	51.9	112.2
12	29 30.1	46.7	107.6	28 52.7	48.1	108.7	28 13.3	49.4	109.7	27 31.8	50.6	110.7	26 48.5	51.7	111.7
13	30 16.8	46.4	106.9	29 40.8	47.8	108.0	29 02.7	49.1	109.1	28 22.4	50.5	110.1	27 40.2	51.7	111.1
14	31 03.2	46.1	106.2	30 28.6	47.7	107.3	29 51.8	49.0	108.4	29 12.9	50.3	109.5	28 31.9	51.4	110.5
15	31 49.3	+45.9	105.4	31 16.3	+47.3	106.6	30 40.8	+48.8	107.7	30 03.2	+50.1	108.8	29 23.3	+51.3	109.9
16	32 35.2	45.6	104.6	32 03.6	47.2	105.9	31 29.6	48.6	107.1	30 53.3	49.9	108.2	30 14.7	51.1	109.3
17	33 20.8	45.3	103.9	32 50.8	46.9	105.1	32 18.2	48.3	106.4	31 43.2	49.7	107.6	31 05.8	51.0	108.7
18	34 06.1	45.1	103.1	33 37.7	46.6	104.4	33 06.5	48.1	105.7	32 32.9	49.5	106.9	31 56.8	50.8	108.1
19	34 51.2	44.6	102.3	34 24.3	46.3	103.6	33 54.6	47.9	104.9	33 22.4	49.3	106.2	32 47.6	50.6	107.5
20	35 35.8	+44.4	101.5	35 10.6	+46.0	102.9	34 42.5	+47.6	104.2	34 11.7	+49.0	105.5	33 38.2	+50.4	106.8
21	36 20.2	44.0	100.6	35 56.6	45.7	102.1	35 30.1	47.3	103.5	35 00.7	48.8	104.8	34 28.6	50.2	106.2
22	37 04.2	43.6	99.8	36 42.3	45.3	101.3	36 17.4	47.0	102.7	35 49.5	48.5	104.1	35 18.8	50.0	105.5
23	37 47.8	43.3	98.9	37 27.6	45.1	100.4	37 04.4	46.6	101.9	36 38.0	48.3	103.4	36 08.8	49.7	104.8
24	38 31.1	42.8	98.0	38 12.7	44.6	99.6	37 51.0	46.4	101.1	37 26.3	48.0	102.7	36 58.5	49.5	104.1
25	39 13.9	+42.4	97.1	38 57.3	+44.3	98.7	38 37.4	+46.0	100.3	38 14.3	+47.7	101.9	37 48.0	+49.2	103.4
26	39 56.3	42.0	96.2	39 41.6	43.8	97.9	39 23.4	45.7	99.5	39 02.0	47.3	101.1	38 37.2	48.9	102.7
27	40 38.3	41.5	95.3	40 25.4	43.5	97.0	40 09.1	45.3	98.7	39 49.3	47.0	100.3	39 26.1	48.7	101.9
28	41 19.8	41.0	94.3	41 08.9	43.0	96.1	40 54.4	44.9	97.8	40 36.3	46.7	99.5	40 14.8	48.3	101.2
29	42 00.8	40.5	93.3	41 51.9	42.6	95.1	41 39.3	44.5	96.9	41 23.0	46.3	98.7	41 03.1	48.1	100.4

40°			42°			44°			46°			48°			Dec.
Hc	d	Z	Hc	d	Z	Hc	d	Z	Hc	d	Z	Hc	d	Z	
° ′	′	°	° ′	′	°	° ′	′	°	° ′	′	°	° ′	′	°	°
23 57.0	-42.3	111.9	23 11.5	-43.8	112.7	22 24.5	-45.2	113.5	21 36.0	-46.5	114.2	20 46.1	-47.8	114.9	0
23 14.7	42.5	112.7	22 27.7	44.0	113.4	21 39.3	45.4	114.2	20 49.5	46.7	114.9	19 58.3	47.9	115.6	1
22 32.2	42.8	113.4	21 43.7	44.1	114.2	20 53.9	45.5	114.9	20 02.8	46.8	115.6	19 10.4	48.0	116.2	2
21 49.4	43.0	114.2	20 59.6	44.4	114.9	20 08.4	45.7	115.6	19 16.0	47.0	116.2	18 22.4	48.2	116.8	3
21 06.4	43.1	114.9	20 15.2	44.5	115.6	19 22.7	45.8	116.3	18 29.0	47.1	116.9	17 34.2	48.2	117.5	4
20 23.3	-43.4	115.7	19 30.7	-44.7	116.3	18 36.9	-46.0	116.9	17 41.9	-47.2	117.5	16 46.0	-48.4	118.1	5
19 39.9	43.5	116.4	18 46.0	44.9	117.0	17 50.9	46.1	117.6	16 54.7	47.3	118.2	15 57.6	48.5	118.7	6
18 56.4	43.7	117.1	18 01.1	45.0	117.7	17 04.8	46.3	118.3	16 07.4	47.5	118.8	15 09.1	48.6	119.3	7
18 12.7	43.8	117.9	17 16.1	45.1	118.4	16 18.5	46.4	119.0	15 19.9	47.5	119.4	14 20.5	48.7	119.9	8
17 28.9	44.0	118.6	16 31.0	45.3	119.1	15 32.1	46.5	119.6	14 32.4	47.7	120.1	13 31.8	48.7	120.5	9
16 44.9	-44.2	119.3	15 45.7	-45.4	119.8	14 45.6	-46.6	120.3	13 44.7	-47.7	120.7	12 43.1	-48.9	121.1	10
16 00.7	44.3	120.0	15 00.3	45.6	120.5	13 59.0	46.7	120.9	12 57.0	47.9	121.3	11 54.2	48.9	121.7	11
15 16.4	44.4	120.7	14 14.7	45.6	121.1	13 12.3	46.8	121.6	12 09.1	47.9	121.9	11 05.3	49.0	122.3	12
14 32.0	44.5	121.4	13 29.1	45.7	121.8	12 25.5	46.9	122.2	11 21.2	48.0	122.6	10 16.3	49.0	122.9	13
13 47.5	44.7	122.1	12 43.4	45.9	122.5	11 38.6	47.0	122.8	10 33.2	48.1	123.2	9 27.3	49.1	123.5	14
13 02.8	-44.8	122.8	11 57.5	-45.9	123.1	10 51.6	-47.0	123.5	9 45.1	-48.1	123.8	8 38.2	-49.2	124.1	15
12 18.0	44.8	123.5	11 11.6	46.0	123.8	10 04.6	47.2	124.1	8 57.0	48.2	124.4	7 49.0	49.2	124.6	16
11 33.2	45.0	124.1	10 25.6	46.1	124.5	9 17.4	47.2	124.7	8 08.8	48.2	125.0	6 59.8	49.2	125.2	17
10 48.2	45.0	124.8	9 39.5	46.2	125.1	8 30.2	47.2	125.4	7 20.6	48.3	125.6	6 10.6	49.3	125.8	18
10 03.2	45.2	125.5	8 53.3	46.3	125.7	7 43.0	47.3	126.0	6 32.3	48.3	126.2	5 21.3	49.3	126.4	19
9 18.0	-45.2	126.1	8 07.0	-46.3	126.4	6 55.7	-47.4	126.6	5 44.0	-48.4	126.8	4 32.0	-49.4	126.9	20
8 32.8	45.2	126.8	7 20.7	46.3	127.0	6 08.3	47.4	127.2	4 55.6	48.4	127.4	3 42.6	49.3	127.5	21
7 47.6	45.4	127.5	6 34.4	46.4	127.7	5 20.9	47.4	127.8	4 07.2	48.5	128.0	2 53.3	49.4	128.1	22
7 02.2	45.4	128.1	5 48.0	46.3	128.3	4 33.5	47.5	128.5	3 18.7	48.4	128.6	2 03.9	49.4	128.6	23
6 16.8	45.4	128.8	5 01.5	46.4	128.9	3 46.0	47.5	129.1	2 30.3	48.5	129.2	1 14.5	49.4	129.2	24
5 31.4	-45.5	129.5	4 15.1	-46.6	129.6	2 58.5	-47.5	129.7	1 41.8	-48.4	129.7	0 25.1	-49.4	129.8	25
4 45.9	45.5	130.1	3 28.5	46.5	130.3	2 11.0	47.5	130.3	0 53.4	48.5	130.3	0 24.3	+49.4	49.7	26
4 00.4	45.5	130.8	2 42.0	46.6	130.8	1 23.5	47.6	130.9	0 04.9	-48.5	130.9	1 13.7	49.4	49.1	27
3 14.9	45.6	131.4	1 55.4	46.5	131.5	0 35.9	-47.5	131.5	0 43.6	+48.5	48.5	2 03.1	49.4	48.5	28
2 29.3	45.6	132.1	1 08.9	46.6	132.1	0 11.6	+47.6	47.9	1 32.1	48.5	47.9	2 52.5	49.4	48.0	29

50°			52°			54°			56°			58°			Dec.
Hc	d	Z	Hc	d	Z	Hc	d	Z	Hc	d	Z	Hc	d	Z	
° ′	′	°	° ′	′	°	° ′	′	°	° ′	′	°	° ′	′	°	°
19 54.9	-48.9	115.6	19 02.5	-50.1	116.2	18 08.9	-51.1	116.8	17 14.2	-52.1	117.4	16 18.5	-53.0	117.9	0
19 06.0	49.1	116.2	18 12.4	50.2	116.8	17 17.8	51.2	117.4	16 22.1	52.2	117.9	15 25.5	53.1	118.4	1
18 16.9	49.2	116.8	17 22.2	50.2	117.4	16 26.6	51.3	117.9	15 29.9	52.3	118.4	14 32.4	53.2	118.9	2
17 27.7	49.3	117.4	16 32.0	50.4	117.9	15 35.3	51.4	118.5	14 37.6	52.3	118.9	13 39.2	53.2	119.4	3
16 38.4	49.4	118.0	15 41.6	50.3	118.5	14 43.9	51.5	119.0	13 45.3	52.4	119.4	12 46.0	53.3	119.8	4
15 49.0	-49.5	118.6	14 51.1	-50.5	119.1	13 52.4	-51.5	119.5	12 52.9	-52.4	119.9	11 52.7	-53.3	120.3	5
14 59.5	49.6	119.2	14 00.6	50.6	119.6	13 00.9	51.6	120.0	12 00.5	52.5	120.4	10 59.4	53.4	120.8	6
14 09.9	49.6	119.8	13 10.0	50.7	120.2	12 09.3	51.6	120.6	11 08.0	52.6	120.9	10 06.0	53.4	121.2	7
13 20.3	49.7	120.3	12 19.3	50.7	120.7	11 17.7	51.7	121.1	10 15.4	52.6	121.4	9 12.6	53.4	121.7	8
12 30.6	49.9	120.9	11 28.6	50.8	121.3	10 26.0	51.8	121.6	9 22.8	52.6	121.9	8 19.2	53.5	122.2	9
11 40.7	-49.8	121.5	10 37.8	-50.9	121.8	9 34.2	-51.8	122.1	8 30.2	-52.7	122.4	7 25.7	-53.5	122.6	10
10 50.9	50.0	122.0	9 46.9	50.9	122.4	8 42.4	51.8	122.6	7 37.5	52.7	122.9	6 32.2	53.5	123.1	11
10 00.9	50.0	122.6	8 56.0	51.0	122.9	7 50.6	51.9	123.1	6 44.8	52.7	123.4	5 38.7	53.6	123.5	12
9 10.9	50.0	123.2	8 05.0	51.0	123.4	6 58.7	51.9	123.6	5 52.1	52.8	123.8	4 45.1	53.5	124.0	13
8 20.9	50.1	123.7	7 14.0	51.0	124.0	6 06.8	51.9	124.2	4 59.3	52.7	124.3	3 51.6	53.6	124.4	14
7 30.8	-50.2	124.3	6 23.0	-51.1	124.5	5 14.9	-51.9	124.7	4 06.6	-52.8	124.8	2 58.0	-53.6	124.9	15
6 40.6	50.2	124.8	5 31.9	51.1	125.0	4 23.0	52.0	125.2	3 13.8	52.8	125.3	2 04.4	53.6	125.3	16
5 50.5	50.3	125.4	4 40.8	51.1	125.5	3 31.0	52.0	125.7	2 21.0	52.9	125.7	1 10.8	53.6	125.8	17
5 00.3	50.3	125.9	3 49.7	51.1	126.1	2 39.0	52.0	126.2	1 28.1	52.8	126.2	0 17.2	-53.6	126.2	18
4 10.0	50.2	126.5	2 58.6	51.2	126.6	1 47.0	52.0	126.7	0 35.3	-52.8	126.7	0 36.4	+53.6	53.3	19
3 19.8	-50.3	127.0	2 07.4	-51.1	127.1	0 55.0	-52.0	127.2	0 17.5	+52.8	52.8	1 30.0	+53.6	52.9	20
2 29.5	50.3	127.6	1 16.3	51.2	127.6	0 03.0	-52.0	127.7	1 10.3	52.8	52.4	2 23.6	53.6	52.4	21
1 39.2	50.3	128.1	0 25.1	-51.1	128.2	0 49.0	+52.1	51.8	2 03.1	52.9	51.9	3 17.2	53.5	52.0	22
0 48.9	-50.3	128.7	0 26.1	+51.1	51.3	1 41.1	52.0	51.3	2 56.0	52.8	51.4	4 10.7	53.5	51.5	23
0 01.4	+50.3	50.8	1 17.2	51.2	50.8	2 33.1	51.9	50.9	3 48.8	52.7	50.9	5 04.3	53.5	51.1	24
0 51.7	+50.3	50.3	2 08.4	51.2	50.3	3 25.0	+52.0	50.4	4 41.5	+52.8	50.0	5 57.8	+53.5	50.6	25
1 42.0	50.3	49.7	2 59.6	51.1	49.8	4 17.0	52.0	49.8	5 34.3	52.7	50.0	6 51.3	53.5	50.1	26
2 32.3	50.2	49.1	3 50.7	51.1	49.2	5 09.0	51.9	49.3	6 27.0	52.7	49.5	7 44.8	53.5	49.7	27
3 22.5	50.3	48.6	4 41.8	51.1	48.7	6 00.9	51.9	48.8	7 19.7	52.7	49.0	8 38.3	53.4	49.2	28
4 12.8	50.2	48.1	5 32.9	51.1	48.2	6 52.8	51.9	48.3	8 12.4	52.7	48.5	9 31.7	53.4	48.8	29

LATITUDE **SAME** NAME · · · · · · · L.H.A. 122°, 238°

Dec.	0° Hc	d	Z	2° Hc	d	Z	4° Hc	d	Z	6° Hc	d	Z	8° Hc	d	Z
0	30 00.0 -	0.3	90.0	29 58.8 +	2.1	91.2	29 55.2 +	4.5	92.3	29 49.1 +	7.0	93.5	29 40.7 +	9.3	94.6
1	29 59.7	0.9	88.8	30 00.9	1.5	90.0	29 59.7	3.9	91.2	29 56.1	6.3	92.3	29 50.0	8.8	93.5
2	29 58.8	1.5	87.7	30 02.4	0.9	88.8	30 03.6	3.3	90.0	30 02.4	5.7	91.2	29 58.8	8.1	92.3
3	29 57.3	2.1	86.5	30 03.3 +	0.3	87.7	30 06.9	2.8	88.8	30 08.1	5.2	90.0	30 06.9	7.6	91.2
4	29 55.2	2.7	85.4	30 03.6 -	0.3	86.5	30 09.7	2.1	87.7	30 13.3	4.5	88.9	30 14.5	6.9	90.0
5	29 52.5 -	3.4	84.2	30 03.3 -	0.9	85.4	30 11.8 +	1.5	86.5	30 17.8 +	3.9	87.7	30 21.4 +	6.3	88.9
6	29 49.1	3.9	83.1	30 02.4	1.5	84.2	30 13.3	0.9	85.4	30 21.7	3.3	86.5	30 27.7	5.8	87.7
7	29 45.2	4.5	81.9	30 00.9	2.1	83.1	30 14.2 +	0.3	84.2	30 25.0	2.7	85.4	30 33.5	5.1	86.6
8	29 40.7	5.1	80.8	29 58.8	2.8	81.9	30 14.5 -	0.4	83.1	30 27.7	2.1	84.2	30 38.6	4.5	85.4
9	29 35.6	5.7	79.6	29 56.0	3.3	80.8	30 14.1	0.9	81.9	30 29.8	1.5	83.1	30 43.1	3.8	84.2
10	29 29.9 -	6.3	78.5	29 52.7 -	3.9	79.6	30 13.2 -	1.6	80.8	30 31.3 +	0.8	81.9	30 46.9 +	3.3	83.1
11	29 23.6	6.8	77.3	29 48.8	4.5	78.5	30 11.6	2.1	79.6	30 32.1	0.3	80.7	30 50.2	2.6	81.9
12	29 16.8	7.5	76.2	29 44.3	5.1	77.3	30 09.5	2.8	78.4	30 32.4 -	0.4	79.6	30 52.8	2.0	80.8
13	29 09.3	8.0	75.1	29 39.2	5.8	76.2	30 06.7	3.4	77.3	30 32.0	1.0	78.4	30 54.8	1.4	79.6
14	29 01.3	8.6	73.9	29 33.4	6.3	75.0	30 03.3	3.9	76.1	30 31.0	1.7	77.3	30 56.2	0.8	78.4
15	28 52.7 -	9.1	72.8	29 27.1 -	6.8	73.9	29 59.4 -	4.6	75.0	30 29.3 -	2.2	76.1	30 57.0 +	0.1	77.3
16	28 43.6	9.7	71.7	29 20.3	7.5	72.7	29 54.8	5.2	73.8	30 27.1	2.9	74.9	30 57.1 -	0.5	76.1
17	28 33.9	10.3	70.6	29 12.8	8.0	71.6	29 49.6	5.8	72.7	30 24.2	3.4	73.8	30 56.6	1.1	74.9
18	28 23.6	10.8	69.4	29 04.8	8.6	70.5	29 43.8	6.3	71.5	30 20.8	4.1	72.6	30 55.5	1.8	73.8
19	28 12.8	11.3	68.3	28 56.2	9.2	69.3	29 37.5	7.0	70.4	30 16.7	4.7	71.5	30 53.7	2.4	72.6
20	28 01.5 -	11.9	67.2	28 47.0 -	9.7	68.2	29 30.5 -	7.5	69.2	30 12.0 -	5.3	70.3	30 51.3 -	3.0	71.4
21	27 49.6	12.5	66.1	28 37.3	10.3	67.1	29 23.0	8.1	68.1	30 06.7	5.9	69.2	30 48.3	3.6	70.3
22	27 37.1	12.9	65.0	28 27.0	10.9	66.0	29 14.9	8.7	67.0	30 00.8	6.5	68.0	30 44.7	4.3	69.1
23	27 24.2	13.5	63.9	28 16.1	11.4	64.8	29 06.2	9.3	65.8	29 54.3	7.0	66.9	30 40.4	4.8	68.0
24	27 10.7	13.9	62.8	28 04.7	11.9	63.7	28 56.9	9.8	64.7	29 47.3	7.7	65.7	30 35.6	5.5	66.8
25	26 56.8 -	14.5	61.7	27 52.8 -	12.4	62.6	28 47.1 -	10.4	63.6	29 39.6 -	8.3	64.6	30 30.1 -	6.1	65.6
26	26 42.3	15.0	60.6	27 40.4	13.0	61.5	28 36.7	10.9	62.5	29 31.3	8.8	63.4	30 24.0	6.7	64.5
27	26 27.3	15.4	59.5	27 27.4	13.5	60.4	28 25.8	11.5	61.3	29 22.5	9.4	62.3	30 17.3	7.3	63.3
28	26 11.9	16.0	58.5	27 13.9	14.0	59.3	28 14.3	12.0	60.2	29 13.1	10.0	61.2	30 10.0	7.9	62.2
29	25 55.9	16.4	57.4	26 59.9	14.5	58.2	28 02.3	12.6	59.1	29 03.1	10.6	60.0	30 02.1	8.5	61.0

Dec.	10° Hc	d	Z	12° Hc	d	Z	14° Hc	d	Z	16° Hc	d	Z	18° Hc	d	Z
0	29 29.9 +	11.7	95.7	29 16.8 +	14.0	96.8	29 01.3 +	16.4	98.0	28 43.6 +	18.6	99.0	28 23.6 +	20.9	100.1
1	29 41.6	11.1	94.6	29 30.8	13.5	95.7	29 17.7	15.7	96.8	29 02.2	18.1	98.0	28 44.5	20.3	99.0
2	29 52.7	10.5	93.5	29 44.3	12.9	94.6	29 33.4	15.3	95.7	29 20.3	17.5	96.9	29 04.8	19.8	98.0
3	30 03.2	10.0	92.3	29 57.2	12.3	93.5	29 48.7	14.6	94.6	29 37.8	17.0	95.8	29 24.6	19.2	96.9
4	30 13.2	9.3	91.2	30 09.5	11.7	92.4	30 03.3	14.1	93.5	29 54.8	16.4	94.7	29 43.8	18.8	95.8
5	30 22.5 +	8.8	90.0	30 21.2 +	11.2	91.2	30 17.4 +	13.6	92.4	30 11.2 +	15.9	93.5	30 02.6 +	18.2	94.7
6	30 31.3	8.1	88.9	30 32.4	10.5	90.1	30 31.0	12.9	91.3	30 27.1	15.3	92.4	30 20.8	17.6	93.6
7	30 39.4	7.5	87.7	30 42.9	9.9	88.9	30 43.9	12.3	90.1	30 42.4	14.7	91.3	30 38.4	17.1	92.5
8	30 46.9	7.0	86.6	30 52.8	9.4	87.8	30 56.2	11.8	89.0	30 57.1	14.1	90.2	30 55.5	16.5	91.4
9	30 53.9	6.3	85.4	31 02.2	8.7	86.6	31 08.0	11.1	87.8	31 11.2	13.5	89.0	31 12.0	15.8	90.3
10	31 00.2 +	5.6	84.3	31 10.9 +	8.1	85.5	31 19.1 +	10.5	86.7	31 24.7 +	12.9	87.9	31 27.8 +	15.3	89.1
11	31 05.8	5.1	83.1	31 19.0	7.4	84.3	31 29.6	9.9	85.5	31 37.6	12.3	86.8	31 43.1	14.7	88.0
12	31 10.9	4.4	81.9	31 26.4	6.9	83.2	31 39.5	9.2	84.4	31 49.9	11.7	85.6	31 57.8	14.1	86.9
13	31 15.3	3.8	80.8	31 33.3	6.2	82.0	31 48.7	8.6	83.2	32 01.6	11.1	84.5	32 11.9	13.5	85.7
14	31 19.1	3.1	79.6	31 39.5	5.5	80.8	31 57.3	8.0	82.0	32 12.7	10.4	83.3	32 25.4	12.8	84.6
15	31 22.2 +	2.5	78.4	31 45.0 +	4.9	79.7	32 05.3 +	7.4	80.9	32 23.1 +	9.7	82.1	32 38.2 +	12.2	83.4
16	31 24.7	1.9	77.3	31 49.9	4.3	78.5	32 12.7	6.6	79.7	32 32.8	9.1	81.0	32 50.4	11.5	82.2
17	31 26.6	1.2	76.1	31 54.2	3.6	77.3	32 19.3	6.1	78.5	32 41.9	8.5	79.8	33 01.9	10.8	81.1
18	31 27.8 +	0.6	74.9	31 57.8	3.0	76.1	32 25.4	5.3	77.4	32 50.4	7.7	78.6	33 12.7	10.3	79.9
19	31 28.4	0.0	73.8	32 00.8	2.3	75.0	32 30.7	4.7	76.2	32 58.1	7.1	77.4	33 23.0	9.5	78.7
20	31 28.4 -	0.7	72.6	32 03.1 +	1.7	73.8	32 35.4 +	4.1	75.0	33 05.2 +	6.5	76.2	33 32.5 +	8.8	77.5
21	31 27.7	1.3	71.4	32 04.8	1.0	72.6	32 39.5	3.3	73.8	33 11.7	5.7	75.1	33 41.3	8.2	76.3
22	31 26.4	2.0	70.2	32 05.8 +	0.3	71.4	32 42.8	2.7	72.6	33 17.4	5.1	73.9	33 49.5	7.5	75.1
23	31 24.4	2.6	69.1	32 06.1 -	0.3	70.2	32 45.5	2.1	71.4	33 22.5	4.4	72.7	33 57.0	6.8	73.9
24	31 21.8	3.2	67.9	32 05.8	0.9	69.1	32 47.6	1.3	70.2	33 26.9	3.7	71.5	34 03.8	6.1	72.7
25	31 18.6 -	3.9	66.7	32 04.9 -	1.7	67.9	32 48.9 +	0.7	69.1	33 30.6 +	3.0	70.3	34 09.9 +	5.4	71.5
26	31 14.7	4.5	65.6	32 03.2	2.2	66.7	32 49.6	0.0	67.9	33 33.6	2.4	69.1	34 15.3	4.6	70.3
27	31 10.2	5.2	64.4	32 01.0	3.0	65.5	32 49.6 -	0.7	66.7	33 36.0	1.6	67.9	34 19.9	4.0	69.1
28	31 05.0	5.7	63.2	31 58.0	3.5	64.3	32 48.9	1.3	65.5	33 37.6	0.9	66.7	34 23.9	3.2	67.9
29	30 59.3	6.4	62.1	31 54.5	4.3	63.2	32 47.6	2.0	64.3	33 38.5 +	0.2	65.5	34 27.1	2.6	66.7

LATITUDE **CONTRARY** NAME   L.H.A. 60°, 300°

0°			2°			4°			6°			8°			Dec.
Hc	d	Z	Hc	d	Z	Hc	d	Z	Hc	d	Z	Hc	d	Z	
30 00.0 - 0.3 90.0			29 58.8 - 2.7 91.2			29 55.2 - 5.2 92.3			29 49.1 - 7.5 93.5			29 40.7 - 9.9 94.6			0
29 59.7 0.9 91.2			29 56.1 3.3 92.3			29 50.0 5.7 93.5			29 41.6 8.1 94.6			29 30.8 10.5 95.7			1
29 58.8 1.5 92.3			29 52.8 4.0 93.5			29 44.3 6.3 94.6			29 33.5 8.7 95.7			29 20.3 11.0 96.9			2
29 57.3 2.1 93.5			29 48.8 4.5 94.6			29 38.0 6.9 95.7			29 24.8 9.3 96.9			29 09.3 11.6 98.0			3
29 55.2 2.7 94.6			29 44.3 5.1 95.8			29 31.1 7.5 96.9			29 15.5 9.8 98.0			28 57.7 12.2 99.1			4
29 52.5 - 3.4 95.8			29 39.2 - 5.7 96.9			29 23.6 - 8.1 98.0			29 05.7 - 10.4 99.1			28 45.5 - 12.7 100.2			5
29 49.1 3.9 96.9			29 33.5 6.3 98.1			29 15.5 8.6 99.2			28 55.3 11.0 100.3			28 32.8 13.3 101.3			6
29 45.2 4.5 98.1			29 27.2 6.9 99.2			29 06.9 9.2 100.3			28 44.3 11.5 101.4			28 19.5 13.8 102.4			7
29 40.7 5.1 99.2			29 20.3 7.4 100.3			28 57.7 9.8 101.4			28 32.8 12.1 102.5			28 05.7 14.3 103.6			8
29 35.6 5.7 100.4			29 12.9 8.0 101.5			28 47.9 10.3 102.6			28 20.7 12.6 103.6			27 51.4 14.8 104.7			9
29 29.9 - 6.3 101.5			29 04.9 - 8.6 102.6			28 37.6 - 10.9 103.7			28 08.1 - 13.1 104.7			27 36.6 - 15.4 105.7			10
29 23.6 6.8 102.7			28 56.3 9.2 103.7			28 26.7 11.5 104.8			27 55.0 13.7 105.8			27 21.2 15.8 106.8			11
29 16.8 7.5 103.8			28 47.1 9.7 104.9			28 15.2 11.9 105.9			27 41.3 14.2 106.9			27 05.4 16.4 107.9			12
29 09.3 8.0 104.9			28 37.4 10.3 106.0			28 03.3 12.6 107.0			27 27.1 14.7 108.0			26 49.0 16.8 109.0			13
29 01.3 8.6 106.1			28 27.1 10.9 107.1			27 50.7 13.0 108.1			27 12.4 15.2 109.1			26 32.2 17.4 110.1			14
28 52.7 - 9.1 107.2			28 16.2 - 11.3 108.2			27 37.7 - 13.6 109.2			26 57.2 - 15.7 110.2			26 14.8 - 17.8 111.1			15
28 43.6 9.8 108.3			28 04.9 12.0 109.3			27 24.1 14.1 110.3			26 41.5 16.2 111.3			25 57.0 18.2 112.2			16
28 33.9 10.3 109.4			27 52.9 12.4 110.5			27 10.0 14.5 111.4			26 25.3 16.7 112.4			25 38.8 18.8 113.3			17
28 23.6 10.8 110.6			27 40.5 13.0 111.6			26 55.5 15.1 112.5			26 08.6 17.1 113.4			25 20.0 19.1 114.3			18
28 12.8 11.3 111.7			27 27.5 13.5 112.7			26 40.4 15.6 113.6			25 51.5 17.7 114.5			25 00.9 19.6 115.4			19
28 01.5 - 11.9 112.8			27 14.0 - 14.0 113.8			26 24.8 - 16.1 114.7			25 33.8 - 18.0 115.6			24 41.3 - 20.1 116.4			20
27 49.6 12.5 113.9			27 00.0 14.5 114.9			26 08.7 16.5 115.8			25 15.8 18.5 116.6			24 21.2 20.4 117.4			21
27 37.1 12.9 115.0			26 45.5 15.0 115.9			25 52.2 17.0 116.8			24 57.3 19.0 117.7			24 00.8 20.9 118.5			22
27 24.2 13.5 116.1			26 30.5 15.5 117.0			25 35.2 17.5 117.9			24 38.3 19.4 118.7			23 39.9 21.2 119.5			23
27 10.7 13.9 117.2			26 15.0 15.9 118.1			25 17.7 17.9 118.9			24 18.9 19.8 119.8			23 18.7 21.7 120.5			24
26 56.8 - 14.5 118.3			25 59.1 - 16.5 119.2			24 59.8 - 18.3 120.0			23 59.1 - 20.2 120.8			22 57.0 - 22.0 121.5			25
26 42.3 15.0 119.4			25 42.6 16.9 120.2			24 41.5 18.8 121.1			23 38.9 20.7 121.8			22 35.0 22.5 122.5			26
26 27.3 15.4 120.5			25 25.7 17.3 121.3			24 22.7 19.3 122.1			23 18.2 21.0 122.8			22 12.5 22.8 123.5			27
26 11.9 16.0 121.5			25 08.4 17.9 122.4			24 03.4 19.6 123.1			22 57.2 21.4 123.9			21 49.7 23.1 124.5			28
25 55.9 16.4 122.6			24 50.5 18.2 123.4			23 43.8 20.1 124.2			22 35.8 21.8 124.9			21 26.6 23.5 125.5			29

10°			12°			14°			16°			18°			Dec.
Hc	d	Z	Hc	d	Z	Hc	d	Z	Hc	d	Z	Hc	d	Z	
29 29.9 - 12.2 95.7			29 16.8 - 14.6 96.8			29 01.3 - 16.8 98.0			28 43.6 - 19.1 99.0			28 23.6 - 21.3 100.1			0
29 17.7 12.8 96.8			29 02.2 15.3 98.0			28 44.5 17.4 99.0			28 24.5 19.6 100.1			28 02.3 21.8 101.2			1
29 04.9 13.4 98.0			28 47.1 15.7 99.1			28 27.1 17.9 100.1			28 04.9 20.2 101.2			27 40.5 22.3 102.2			2
28 51.5 13.9 99.1			28 31.4 16.2 100.2			28 09.2 18.5 101.2			27 44.7 20.6 102.3			27 18.2 22.7 103.3			3
28 37.6 14.5 100.2			28 15.2 16.7 101.3			27 50.7 18.9 102.3			27 24.1 21.1 103.3			26 55.5 23.2 104.3			4
28 23.1 - 15.0 101.3			27 58.5 - 17.2 102.3			27 31.8 - 19.4 103.4			27 03.0 - 21.5 104.4			26 32.3 - 23.7 105.3			5
28 08.1 15.5 102.4			27 41.3 17.7 103.4			27 12.4 19.9 104.4			26 41.5 22.0 105.4			26 08.6 24.1 106.4			6
27 52.6 16.0 103.5			27 23.6 18.2 104.5			26 52.5 20.3 105.5			26 19.5 22.5 106.5			25 44.5 24.5 107.4			7
27 36.6 16.6 104.6			27 05.4 18.7 105.6			26 32.2 20.9 106.5			25 57.0 22.9 107.5			25 20.0 24.9 108.4			8
27 20.0 17.0 105.7			26 46.7 19.2 106.6			26 11.3 21.2 107.6			25 34.1 23.3 108.5			24 55.1 25.3 109.4			9
27 03.0 - 17.5 106.7			26 27.5 - 19.7 107.7			25 50.1 - 21.8 108.6			25 10.8 - 23.7 109.5			24 29.8 - 25.7 110.4			10
26 45.5 18.0 107.8			26 07.8 20.1 108.8			25 28.3 22.1 109.7			24 47.1 24.2 110.6			24 04.1 26.1 111.4			11
26 27.5 18.5 108.9			25 47.7 20.5 109.8			25 06.2 22.6 110.7			24 22.9 24.5 111.6			23 38.0 26.4 112.4			12
26 09.0 18.9 109.9			25 27.2 21.0 110.8			24 43.6 23.0 111.7			23 58.4 24.9 112.6			23 11.6 26.8 113.4			13
25 50.1 19.4 111.0			25 06.2 21.4 111.9			24 20.6 23.4 112.7			23 33.5 25.3 113.6			22 44.8 27.2 114.3			14
25 30.7 - 19.9 112.0			24 44.8 - 21.9 112.9			23 57.2 - 23.7 113.7			23 08.2 - 25.7 114.5			22 17.6 - 27.5 115.3			15
25 10.8 20.3 113.1			24 22.9 22.2 113.9			23 33.5 24.2 114.7			22 42.5 26.0 115.5			21 50.1 27.9 116.3			16
24 50.5 20.7 114.1			24 00.7 22.7 115.0			23 09.3 24.5 115.7			22 16.5 26.4 116.5			21 22.2 28.1 117.2			17
24 29.8 21.1 115.2			23 38.0 23.0 116.0			22 44.8 24.9 116.7			21 50.1 26.7 117.5			20 54.1 28.5 118.2			18
24 08.7 21.6 116.2			23 15.0 23.4 117.0			22 19.9 25.3 117.7			21 23.4 27.1 118.4			20 25.6 28.7 119.1			19
23 47.1 - 21.9 117.2			22 51.6 - 23.8 118.0			21 54.6 - 25.6 118.7			20 56.3 - 27.3 119.4			19 56.9 - 29.1 120.0			20
23 25.2 22.3 118.2			22 27.8 24.2 119.0			21 29.0 26.0 119.7			20 29.0 27.7 120.3			19 27.8 29.3 121.0			21
23 02.9 22.7 119.2			22 03.6 24.5 120.0			21 03.0 26.2 120.6			20 01.3 28.0 121.3			18 58.5 29.7 121.9			22
22 40.2 23.1 120.2			21 39.1 24.9 120.9			20 36.8 26.6 121.6			19 33.3 28.2 122.2			18 28.8 29.8 122.8			23
22 17.1 23.5 121.2			21 14.2 25.2 121.9			20 10.2 26.9 122.6			19 05.1 28.6 123.2			17 59.0 30.2 123.7			24
21 53.6 - 23.8 122.2			20 49.0 - 25.5 122.9			19 43.3 - 27.2 123.5			18 36.5 - 28.8 124.1			17 28.8 - 30.4 124.6			25
21 29.8 24.2 123.2			20 23.5 25.8 123.9			19 16.1 27.5 124.5			18 07.7 29.0 125.0			16 58.4 30.6 125.5			26
21 05.6 24.4 124.2			19 57.7 26.2 124.8			18 48.6 27.7 125.4			17 38.7 29.4 125.9			16 27.8 30.8 126.4			27
20 41.2 24.9 125.2			19 31.5 26.5 125.8			18 20.9 28.1 126.3			17 09.3 29.5 126.8			15 57.0 31.1 127.3			28
20 16.3 25.1 126.2			19 05.0 26.7 126.7			17 52.8 28.3 127.3			16 39.8 29.8 127.8			15 25.9 31.3 128.2			29

Dec.	20° Hc	d	Z	22° Hc	d	Z	24° Hc	d	Z	26° Hc	d	Z	28° Hc	d	Z
0	28 01.5	+23.0	101.2	27 37.1	+25.2	102.2	27 10.7	+27.3	103.2	26 42.3	+29.2	104.2	26 11.9	+31.2	105.2
1	28 24.5	22.5	100.1	28 02.3	24.7	101.2	27 38.0	26.7	102.2	27 11.5	28.9	103.2	26 43.1	30.8	104.2
2	28 47.0	22.0	99.1	28 27.0	24.2	100.1	28 04.7	26.4	101.2	27 40.4	28.4	102.2	27 13.9	30.4	103.2
3	29 09.0	21.5	98.0	28 51.2	23.7	99.1	28 31.1	25.8	100.2	28 08.8	27.9	101.2	27 44.3	30.0	102.3
4	29 30.5	21.0	96.9	29 14.9	23.2	98.0	28 56.9	25.4	99.1	28 36.7	27.6	100.2	28 14.3	29.6	101.3
5	29 51.5	+20.5	95.9	29 38.1	+22.7	97.0	29 22.3	+25.0	98.1	29 04.3	+27.0	99.2	28 43.9	+29.2	100.3
6	30 12.0	19.9	94.8	30 00.8	22.2	95.9	29 47.3	24.4	97.1	29 31.3	26.6	98.2	29 13.1	28.7	99.3
7	30 31.9	19.4	93.7	30 23.0	21.7	94.8	30 11.7	23.9	96.0	29 57.9	26.1	97.2	29 41.8	28.2	98.3
8	30 51.3	18.8	92.6	30 44.7	21.1	93.8	30 35.6	23.4	94.9	30 24.0	25.6	96.1	30 10.0	27.8	97.3
9	31 10.1	18.3	91.5	31 05.8	20.6	92.7	30 59.0	22.8	93.9	30 49.6	25.1	95.1	30 37.8	27.2	96.3
10	31 28.4	+17.7	90.4	31 26.4	+20.0	91.6	31 21.8	+22.3	92.8	31 14.7	+24.5	94.0	31 05.0	+26.8	95.2
11	31 46.1	17.0	89.2	31 46.4	19.4	90.5	31 44.1	21.7	91.7	31 39.2	24.0	92.9	31 31.8	26.2	94.2
12	32 03.1	16.5	88.1	32 05.8	18.8	89.4	32 05.8	21.2	90.6	32 03.2	23.5	91.9	31 58.0	25.8	93.1
13	32 19.6	15.8	87.0	32 24.6	18.2	88.2	32 27.0	20.6	89.5	32 26.7	22.9	90.8	32 23.8	25.1	92.0
14	32 35.4	15.3	85.8	32 42.8	17.7	87.1	32 47.6	20.0	88.4	32 49.6	22.3	89.7	32 48.9	24.6	91.0
15	32 50.7	+14.5	84.7	33 00.5	+16.9	86.0	33 07.6	+19.3	87.3	33 11.9	+21.7	88.6	33 13.5	+24.1	89.9
16	33 05.2	14.0	83.5	33 17.4	16.4	84.8	33 26.9	18.8	86.1	33 33.6	21.2	87.5	33 37.6	23.4	88.8
17	33 19.2	13.3	82.4	33 33.8	15.7	83.7	33 45.7	18.1	85.0	33 54.8	20.5	86.3	34 01.0	22.9	87.7
18	33 32.5	12.6	81.2	33 49.5	15.1	82.5	34 03.8	17.5	83.8	34 15.3	19.8	85.2	34 23.9	22.2	86.6
19	33 45.1	12.0	80.0	34 04.6	14.4	81.3	34 21.3	16.8	82.7	34 35.1	19.2	84.0	34 46.1	21.6	85.4
20	33 57.1	+11.3	78.8	34 19.0	+13.7	80.2	34 38.1	+16.1	81.5	34 54.3	+18.6	82.9	35 07.7	+21.0	84.3
21	34 08.4	10.6	77.6	34 32.7	13.0	79.0	34 54.2	15.5	80.3	35 12.9	17.9	81.7	35 28.7	20.3	83.1
22	34 19.0	9.9	76.5	34 45.7	12.3	77.8	35 09.7	14.7	79.2	35 30.8	17.2	80.6	35 49.0	19.6	82.0
23	34 28.9	9.2	75.3	34 58.0	11.7	76.6	35 24.4	14.1	78.0	35 48.0	16.5	79.4	36 08.6	19.0	80.8
24	34 38.1	8.5	74.1	35 09.7	10.9	75.4	35 38.5	13.4	76.8	36 04.5	15.8	78.2	36 27.6	18.2	79.6
25	34 46.6	+7.7	72.9	35 20.6	+10.2	74.2	35 51.9	+12.6	75.6	36 20.3	+15.1	77.0	36 45.8	+17.6	78.4
26	34 54.3	7.1	71.6	35 30.8	9.5	73.0	36 04.5	11.9	74.4	36 35.4	14.4	75.8	37 03.4	16.8	77.3
27	35 01.4	6.3	70.4	35 40.3	8.7	71.8	36 16.4	11.2	73.2	36 49.8	13.6	74.6	37 20.2	16.0	76.0
28	35 07.7	5.6	69.2	35 49.0	8.0	70.6	36 27.6	10.4	71.9	37 03.4	12.8	73.4	37 36.2	15.4	74.8
29	35 13.3	4.9	68.0	35 57.0	7.3	69.3	36 38.0	9.7	70.7	37 16.2	12.1	72.1	37 51.6	14.5	73.6

Dec.	30° Hc	d	Z	32° Hc	d	Z	34° Hc	d	Z	36° Hc	d	Z	38° Hc	d	Z
0	25 39.5	+33.1	106.1	25 05.3	+35.0	107.0	24 29.3	+36.8	107.9	23 51.6	+38.4	108.7	23 12.2	+40.1	109.6
1	26 12.6	32.8	105.2	25 40.3	34.6	106.1	25 06.1	36.4	107.0	24 30.0	38.2	107.9	23 52.3	39.8	108.8
2	26 45.4	32.4	104.2	26 14.9	34.3	105.2	25 42.5	36.1	106.1	25 08.2	37.8	107.1	24 32.1	39.5	107.9
3	27 17.8	31.9	103.3	26 49.2	33.9	104.3	26 18.6	35.7	105.3	25 46.0	37.6	106.2	25 11.6	39.3	107.1
4	27 49.7	31.6	102.3	27 23.1	33.5	103.4	26 54.3	35.4	104.4	26 23.6	37.2	105.3	25 50.9	39.0	106.3
5	28 21.3	+31.2	101.4	27 56.6	+33.1	102.4	27 29.7	+35.1	103.4	27 00.8	+36.9	104.4	26 29.9	+38.6	105.4
6	28 52.5	30.8	100.4	28 29.7	32.8	101.5	28 04.8	34.7	102.5	27 37.7	36.5	103.6	27 08.5	38.4	104.6
7	29 23.3	30.3	99.4	29 02.5	32.3	100.5	28 39.5	34.3	101.6	28 14.2	36.2	102.7	27 46.9	38.0	103.7
8	29 53.6	29.8	98.4	29 34.8	32.0	99.6	29 13.8	33.9	100.7	28 50.4	35.9	101.8	28 24.9	37.7	102.8
9	30 23.5	29.4	97.4	30 06.8	31.4	98.6	29 47.7	33.5	99.7	29 26.3	35.4	100.8	29 02.6	37.3	101.9
10	30 52.9	+28.9	96.4	30 38.2	+31.1	97.6	30 21.2	+33.0	98.8	30 01.7	+35.1	99.9	29 39.9	+37.0	101.0
11	31 21.8	28.4	95.4	31 09.3	30.5	96.6	30 54.2	32.7	97.8	30 36.8	34.6	99.0	30 16.9	36.5	100.1
12	31 50.2	28.0	94.4	31 39.8	30.1	95.6	31 26.9	32.2	96.8	31 11.4	34.2	98.0	30 53.4	36.2	99.2
13	32 18.2	27.4	93.3	32 09.9	29.6	94.6	31 59.1	31.7	95.8	31 45.6	33.8	97.1	31 29.6	35.8	98.3
14	32 45.6	26.8	92.3	32 39.5	29.1	93.5	32 30.8	31.2	94.8	32 19.4	33.3	96.1	32 05.4	35.3	97.3
15	33 12.4	+26.3	91.2	33 08.6	+28.5	92.5	33 02.0	+30.7	93.8	32 52.7	+32.8	95.1	32 40.7	+34.9	96.4
16	33 38.7	25.8	90.1	33 37.1	28.0	91.4	33 32.7	30.2	92.8	33 25.5	32.4	94.1	33 15.6	34.5	95.4
17	34 04.5	25.2	89.0	34 05.1	27.5	90.4	34 02.9	29.7	91.7	33 57.9	31.8	93.1	33 50.1	33.9	94.4
18	34 29.7	24.6	87.9	34 32.6	26.9	89.3	34 32.6	29.1	90.7	34 29.7	31.4	92.1	34 24.0	33.5	93.4
19	34 54.3	23.9	86.8	34 59.5	26.2	88.2	35 01.7	28.6	89.6	35 01.1	30.8	91.0	34 57.5	33.0	92.4
20	35 18.2	+23.4	85.7	35 25.7	+25.7	87.1	35 30.3	+28.0	88.5	35 31.9	+30.2	90.0	35 30.5	+32.4	91.4
21	35 41.6	22.7	84.6	35 51.4	25.1	86.0	35 58.3	27.4	87.4	36 02.1	29.7	88.9	36 02.9	31.9	90.4
22	36 04.3	22.0	83.4	36 16.5	24.4	84.9	36 25.7	26.8	86.3	36 31.8	29.1	87.8	36 34.8	31.3	89.3
23	36 26.3	21.4	82.3	36 40.9	23.8	83.7	36 52.5	26.1	85.2	37 00.9	28.4	86.7	37 06.1	30.8	88.2
24	36 47.7	20.6	81.1	37 04.7	23.1	82.6	37 18.6	25.5	84.1	37 29.3	27.9	85.6	37 36.9	30.2	87.2
25	37 08.3	+20.0	79.9	37 27.8	+22.4	81.4	37 44.1	+24.8	83.0	37 57.2	+27.2	84.5	38 07.1	+29.5	86.1
26	37 28.3	19.3	78.7	37 50.2	21.7	80.3	38 08.9	24.1	81.8	38 24.4	26.5	83.4	38 36.6	28.9	85.0
27	37 47.6	18.5	77.5	38 11.9	21.0	79.1	38 33.0	23.5	80.6	38 50.9	25.9	82.2	39 05.5	28.3	83.8
28	38 06.1	17.8	76.3	38 32.9	20.2	77.9	38 56.5	22.7	79.5	39 16.8	25.1	81.1	39 33.8	27.5	82.7
29	38 23.9	17.0	75.1	38 53.1	19.5	76.7	39 19.2	22.0	78.3	39 41.9	24.5	79.9	40 01.3	26.9	81.5

20°			22°			24°			26°			28°			Dec.
Hc	d	Z	Hc	d	Z	Hc	d	Z	Hc	d	Z	Hc	d	Z	
28 01.5	-23.5	101.2	27 37.1	-25.5	102.2	27 10.7	-27.6	103.2	26 42.3	-29.6	104.2	26 11.9	-31.6	105.2	0
27 38.0	24.0	102.2	27 11.6	26.1	103.2	26 43.1	28.1	104.2	26 12.7	30.1	105.2	25 40.3	31.9	106.1	1
27 14.0	24.4	103.2	26 45.5	26.4	104.2	26 15.0	28.4	105.2	25 42.6	30.4	106.1	25 08.4	32.3	107.0	2
26 49.6	24.8	104.3	26 19.1	26.9	105.2	25 46.6	28.9	106.2	25 12.2	30.7	107.1	24 36.1	32.7	108.0	3
26 24.8	25.3	105.3	25 52.2	27.3	106.2	25 17.7	29.2	107.1	24 41.5	31.2	108.0	24 03.4	32.9	108.9	4
25 59.5	-25.7	106.3	25 24.9	-27.6	107.2	24 48.5	-29.6	108.1	24 10.3	-31.4	109.0	23 30.5	-33.3	109.8	5
25 33.8	26.0	107.3	24 57.3	28.1	108.2	24 18.9	29.9	109.1	23 38.9	31.8	109.9	22 57.2	33.6	110.7	6
25 07.8	26.5	108.3	24 29.2	28.4	109.2	23 49.0	30.3	110.0	23 07.1	32.1	110.8	22 23.6	33.9	111.6	7
24 41.3	26.9	109.3	24 00.8	28.8	110.1	23 18.7	30.7	111.0	22 35.0	32.5	111.7	21 49.7	34.1	112.5	8
24 14.4	27.3	110.3	23 32.0	29.1	111.1	22 48.0	30.9	111.9	22 02.5	32.7	112.7	21 15.6	34.4	113.4	9
23 47.1	-27.6	111.2	23 02.9	-29.5	112.1	22 17.1	-31.3	112.8	21 29.8	-33.0	113.6	20 41.2	-34.7	114.3	10
23 19.5	27.9	112.2	22 33.4	29.8	113.0	21 45.8	31.6	113.7	20 56.8	33.3	114.5	20 06.5	35.0	115.1	11
22 51.6	28.4	113.2	22 03.6	30.1	113.9	21 14.2	31.9	114.7	20 23.5	33.6	115.3	19 31.5	35.2	116.0	12
22 23.2	28.6	114.1	21 33.5	30.5	114.9	20 42.3	32.1	115.6	19 49.9	33.8	116.2	18 56.3	35.4	116.9	13
21 54.6	29.0	115.1	21 03.0	30.7	115.8	20 10.2	32.4	116.5	19 16.1	34.1	117.1	18 20.9	35.7	117.7	14
21 25.6	-29.3	116.0	20 32.3	-31.0	116.7	19 37.8	-32.7	117.4	18 42.0	-34.3	118.0	17 45.2	-35.9	118.6	15
20 56.3	29.6	117.0	20 01.3	31.3	117.6	19 05.1	33.0	118.2	18 07.7	34.5	118.8	17 09.3	36.0	119.4	16
20 26.7	29.8	117.9	19 30.0	31.5	118.5	18 32.1	33.1	119.1	17 33.2	34.8	119.7	16 33.3	36.3	120.2	17
19 56.9	30.2	118.8	18 58.5	31.9	119.4	17 59.0	33.5	120.0	16 58.4	34.9	120.6	15 57.0	36.5	121.1	18
19 26.7	30.5	119.7	18 26.6	32.0	120.3	17 25.5	33.6	120.9	16 23.5	35.2	121.4	15 20.5	36.6	121.9	19
18 56.2	-30.7	120.6	17 54.6	-32.4	121.2	16 51.9	-33.9	121.7	15 48.3	-35.4	122.2	14 43.9	-36.9	122.7	20
18 25.5	30.9	121.5	17 22.2	32.5	122.1	16 18.0	34.1	122.6	15 12.9	35.5	123.1	14 07.0	36.9	123.5	21
17 54.6	31.3	122.5	16 49.7	32.8	123.0	15 43.9	34.2	123.5	14 37.4	35.8	123.9	13 30.1	37.2	124.3	22
17 23.3	31.4	123.3	16 16.9	33.0	123.9	15 09.7	34.5	124.3	14 01.6	35.9	124.7	12 52.9	37.3	125.1	23
16 51.9	31.7	124.2	15 43.9	33.1	124.7	14 35.2	34.6	125.2	13 25.7	36.0	125.6	12 15.6	37.4	125.9	24
16 20.2	-31.9	125.1	15 10.8	-33.4	125.6	14 00.6	-34.9	126.0	12 49.7	-36.2	126.4	11 38.2	-37.6	126.7	25
15 48.3	32.1	126.0	14 37.4	33.6	126.4	13 25.7	34.9	126.8	12 13.5	36.4	127.2	11 00.6	37.6	127.5	26
15 16.2	32.3	126.9	14 03.8	33.7	127.3	12 50.8	35.2	127.7	11 37.1	36.5	128.0	10 23.0	37.8	128.3	27
14 43.9	32.6	127.8	13 30.1	34.0	128.2	12 15.6	35.3	128.5	11 00.6	36.6	128.8	9 45.2	37.9	129.1	28
14 11.3	32.7	128.6	12 56.1	34.1	129.0	11 40.3	35.4	129.3	10 24.0	36.7	129.6	9 07.3	38.1	129.9	29

30°			32°			34°			36°			38°			Dec.
Hc	d	Z	Hc	d	Z	Hc	d	Z	Hc	d	Z	Hc	d	Z	
25 39.5	-33.4	106.1	25 05.3	-35.2	107.0	24 29.3	-37.0	107.9	23 51.6	-38.7	108.7	23 12.2	-40.3	109.6	0
25 06.1	33.8	107.0	24 30.1	35.6	107.9	23 52.3	37.3	108.8	23 12.9	38.9	109.6	22 31.9	40.5	110.4	1
24 32.3	34.1	107.9	23 54.5	35.9	108.8	23 15.0	37.5	109.6	22 34.0	39.2	110.4	21 51.4	40.8	111.2	2
23 58.2	34.5	108.8	23 18.6	36.2	109.7	22 37.5	37.9	110.5	21 54.8	39.5	111.2	21 10.6	41.0	112.0	3
23 23.7	34.7	109.7	22 42.4	36.4	110.5	21 59.6	38.1	111.3	21 15.3	39.7	112.0	20 29.6	41.2	112.7	4
22 49.0	-35.0	110.6	22 06.0	-36.7	111.4	21 21.5	-38.3	112.1	20 35.6	-39.9	112.8	19 48.4	-41.4	113.5	5
22 14.0	35.3	111.5	21 29.3	37.0	112.2	20 43.2	38.6	113.0	19 55.7	40.1	113.6	19 07.0	41.6	114.3	6
21 38.7	35.6	112.4	20 52.3	37.2	113.1	20 04.6	38.8	113.8	19 15.6	40.3	114.4	18 25.4	41.8	115.0	7
21 03.1	35.8	113.2	20 15.1	37.4	113.9	19 25.8	39.0	114.6	18 35.3	40.5	115.2	17 43.6	41.9	115.8	8
20 27.3	36.1	114.1	19 37.7	37.7	114.8	18 46.8	39.2	115.4	17 54.8	40.7	116.0	17 01.7	42.1	116.5	9
19 51.2	-36.3	114.9	19 00.0	-37.9	115.6	18 07.6	-39.4	116.2	17 14.1	-40.8	116.8	16 19.6	-42.3	117.3	10
19 14.9	36.6	115.8	18 22.1	38.1	116.4	17 28.2	39.6	117.0	16 33.3	41.1	117.5	15 37.3	42.4	117.8	11
18 38.3	36.8	116.6	17 44.0	38.3	117.2	16 48.6	39.8	117.8	15 52.2	41.2	118.3	14 54.9	42.5	118.8	12
18 01.5	37.0	117.5	17 05.7	38.5	118.0	16 08.8	39.9	118.5	15 11.0	41.3	119.0	14 12.4	42.7	119.5	13
17 24.5	37.2	118.3	16 27.2	38.7	118.8	15 28.9	40.1	119.3	14 29.7	41.5	119.8	13 29.7	42.8	120.2	14
16 47.3	-37.3	119.1	15 48.5	-38.8	119.6	14 48.8	-40.3	120.1	13 48.2	-41.6	120.5	12 46.9	-42.9	120.9	15
16 10.0	37.6	119.9	15 09.7	39.1	120.4	14 08.5	40.4	120.9	13 06.6	41.7	121.3	12 04.0	43.1	121.6	16
15 32.4	37.8	120.7	14 30.6	39.1	121.2	13 28.1	40.5	121.6	12 24.9	41.9	122.0	11 20.9	43.1	122.4	17
14 54.6	37.9	121.5	13 51.5	39.3	122.0	12 47.6	40.7	122.4	11 43.0	42.0	122.7	10 37.8	43.2	123.1	18
14 16.7	38.1	122.3	13 12.2	39.5	122.7	12 06.9	40.8	123.1	11 01.0	42.0	123.5	9 54.6	43.3	123.8	19
13 38.6	-38.2	123.1	12 32.7	-39.6	123.5	11 26.1	-40.9	123.9	10 19.0	-42.2	124.2	9 11.3	-43.4	124.5	20
13 00.4	38.4	123.9	11 53.1	39.7	124.3	10 45.2	41.0	124.6	9 36.8	42.3	124.9	8 27.9	43.5	125.2	21
12 22.0	38.5	124.7	11 13.4	39.8	125.1	10 04.2	41.1	125.4	8 54.5	42.3	125.6	7 44.4	43.5	125.9	22
11 43.5	38.6	125.5	10 33.6	40.0	125.8	9 23.1	41.2	126.1	8 12.2	42.4	126.3	7 00.9	43.6	126.6	23
11 04.9	38.8	126.3	9 53.6	40.0	126.6	8 41.9	41.3	126.8	7 29.8	42.5	127.1	6 17.3	43.7	127.3	24
10 26.1	-38.8	127.1	9 13.6	-40.1	127.3	8 00.6	-41.3	127.6	6 47.3	-42.6	127.8	5 33.6	-43.7	127.9	25
9 47.3	39.0	127.8	8 33.5	40.2	128.1	7 19.3	41.5	128.3	6 04.7	42.6	128.5	4 49.9	43.7	128.6	26
9 08.3	39.1	128.6	7 53.3	40.3	128.8	6 37.8	41.4	129.0	5 22.1	42.6	129.2	4 06.2	43.8	129.3	27
8 29.2	39.1	129.4	7 13.0	40.4	129.6	5 56.4	41.6	129.8	4 39.5	42.7	129.9	3 22.4	43.8	130.0	28
7 50.1	39.3	130.1	6 32.6	40.5	130.3	5 14.8	41.6	130.5	3 56.8	42.7	130.6	2 38.6	43.8	130.7	29

Dec.	40° Hc	d	Z	42° Hc	d	Z	44° Hc	d	Z	46° Hc	d	Z	48° Hc	d	Z
°	° ′	′	°	° ′	′	°	° ′	′	°	° ′	′	°	° ′	′	°
0	22 31.3	+41.6	110.4	21 48.8	+43.1	111.1	21 04.8	+44.6	111.9	20 19.4	+46.0	112.6	19 32.8	+47.2	113.2
1	23 12.9	41.4	109.6	22 31.9	42.9	110.4	21 49.4	44.4	111.1	21 05.4	45.8	111.9	20 20.0	47.1	112.6
2	23 54.3	41.2	108.8	23 14.8	42.7	109.6	22 33.8	44.2	110.4	21 51.2	45.6	111.2	21 07.1	46.9	111.9
3	24 35.5	40.9	108.0	23 57.5	42.5	108.8	23 18.0	43.9	109.7	22 36.8	45.4	110.5	21 54.0	46.8	111.2
4	25 16.4	40.6	107.2	24 40.0	42.3	108.1	24 01.9	43.8	108.9	23 22.2	45.2	109.8	22 40.8	46.6	110.6
5	25 57.0	+40.4	106.4	25 22.3	+41.9	107.3	24 45.7	+43.5	108.2	24 07.4	+45.0	109.0	23 27.4	+46.4	109.9
6	26 37.4	40.0	105.5	26 04.2	41.8	106.5	25 29.2	43.3	107.4	24 52.4	44.8	108.3	24 13.8	46.3	109.2
7	27 17.4	39.8	104.7	26 46.0	41.4	105.7	26 12.5	43.1	106.7	25 37.2	44.6	107.6	25 00.1	46.0	108.5
8	27 57.2	39.5	103.9	27 27.4	41.2	104.9	26 55.6	42.8	105.9	26 21.8	44.3	106.8	25 46.1	45.8	107.8
9	28 36.7	39.1	103.0	28 08.6	40.8	104.1	27 38.4	42.5	105.1	27 06.1	44.1	106.1	26 31.9	45.6	107.0
10	29 15.8	+38.8	102.1	28 49.4	+40.6	103.2	28 20.9	+42.2	104.3	27 50.2	+43.9	105.3	27 17.5	+45.4	106.3
11	29 54.6	38.4	101.3	29 30.0	40.2	102.4	29 03.1	42.0	103.5	28 34.1	43.6	104.5	28 02.9	45.1	105.6
12	30 33.0	38.1	100.4	30 10.2	39.9	101.5	29 45.1	41.6	102.7	29 17.7	43.3	103.8	28 48.0	44.9	104.8
13	31 11.1	37.7	99.5	30 50.1	39.6	100.7	30 26.7	41.3	101.8	30 01.0	43.0	103.0	29 32.9	44.6	104.1
14	31 48.8	37.3	98.6	31 29.7	39.1	99.8	31 08.0	41.0	101.0	30 44.0	42.7	102.2	30 17.5	44.4	103.3
15	32 26.1	+36.9	97.6	32 08.8	+38.8	98.9	31 49.0	+40.6	100.1	31 26.7	+42.4	101.3	31 01.9	+44.0	102.5
16	33 03.0	36.4	96.7	32 47.6	38.4	98.0	32 29.6	40.3	99.3	32 09.1	42.0	100.5	31 45.9	43.8	101.7
17	33 39.4	36.0	95.7	33 26.0	38.0	97.1	33 09.9	39.9	98.4	32 51.1	41.7	99.7	32 29.7	43.4	100.9
18	34 15.4	35.6	94.8	34 04.0	37.6	96.1	33 49.8	39.5	97.5	33 32.8	41.3	98.8	33 13.1	43.1	100.1
19	34 51.0	35.1	93.8	34 41.6	37.1	95.2	34 29.3	39.1	96.6	34 14.1	41.0	97.9	33 56.2	42.8	99.3
20	35 26.1	+34.5	92.8	35 18.7	+36.6	94.2	35 08.4	+38.6	95.6	34 55.1	+40.6	97.0	34 39.0	+42.4	98.4
21	36 00.6	34.1	91.8	35 55.3	36.2	93.3	35 47.0	38.2	94.7	35 35.7	40.1	96.1	35 21.4	42.0	97.5
22	36 34.7	33.6	90.8	36 31.5	35.7	92.3	36 25.2	37.8	93.7	36 15.8	39.8	95.2	36 03.4	41.7	96.7
23	37 08.3	32.9	89.8	37 07.2	35.2	91.3	37 03.0	37.2	92.8	36 55.6	39.3	94.3	36 45.1	41.2	95.8
24	37 41.2	32.5	88.7	37 42.4	34.6	90.2	37 40.2	36.8	91.8	37 34.9	38.8	93.3	37 26.3	40.8	94.9
25	38 13.7	+31.8	87.6	38 17.0	+34.0	89.2	38 17.0	+36.2	90.8	38 13.7	+38.3	92.4	38 07.1	+40.3	93.9
26	38 45.5	31.2	86.5	38 51.0	33.5	88.2	38 53.2	35.7	89.8	38 52.0	37.9	91.4	38 47.4	39.9	93.0
27	39 16.7	30.6	85.4	39 24.5	32.9	87.1	39 28.9	35.2	88.7	39 29.9	37.3	90.4	39 27.3	39.4	92.0
28	39 47.3	30.0	84.3	39 57.4	32.3	86.0	40 04.1	34.5	87.7	40 07.2	36.7	89.4	40 06.7	38.9	91.0
29	40 17.3	29.2	83.2	40 29.7	31.7	84.9	40 38.6	34.0	86.6	40 43.9	36.2	88.3	40 45.6	38.4	90.0

Dec.	50° Hc	d	Z	52° Hc	d	Z	54° Hc	d	Z	56° Hc	d	Z	58° Hc	d	Z
°	° ′	′	°	° ′	′	°	° ′	′	°	° ′	′	°	° ′	′	°
0	18 44.8	+48.5	113.9	17 55.7	+49.7	114.5	17 05.5	+50.7	115.0	16 14.2	+51.7	115.6	15 21.9	+52.7	116.1
1	19 33.3	48.4	113.2	18 45.4	49.5	113.9	17 56.2	50.6	114.5	17 05.9	51.7	115.1	16 14.6	52.7	115.6
2	20 21.7	48.2	112.6	19 34.9	49.4	113.3	18 46.8	50.6	113.9	17 57.6	51.6	114.5	17 07.3	52.6	115.1
3	21 09.9	48.0	112.0	20 24.3	49.3	112.7	19 37.4	50.4	113.3	18 49.2	51.5	114.0	17 59.9	52.5	114.6
4	21 57.9	47.9	111.3	21 13.6	49.1	112.1	20 27.8	50.3	112.8	19 40.7	51.4	113.4	18 52.4	52.4	114.1
5	22 45.8	+47.8	110.7	22 02.7	+49.0	111.4	21 18.1	+50.2	112.2	20 32.1	+51.3	112.9	19 44.8	+52.3	113.6
6	23 33.6	47.6	110.0	22 51.7	48.9	110.8	22 08.3	50.1	111.6	21 23.4	51.2	112.3	20 37.1	52.3	113.0
7	24 21.2	47.4	109.3	23 40.6	48.7	110.2	22 58.4	49.9	111.0	22 14.6	51.1	111.8	21 29.4	52.1	112.5
8	25 08.6	47.2	108.7	24 29.3	48.5	109.5	23 48.3	49.8	110.4	23 05.7	50.9	111.2	22 21.5	52.1	112.0
9	25 55.8	47.0	108.0	25 17.8	48.4	108.9	24 38.1	49.6	109.8	23 56.6	50.9	110.6	23 13.6	51.9	111.4
10	26 42.8	+46.8	107.3	26 06.2	+48.2	108.2	25 27.7	+49.5	109.2	24 47.5	+50.6	110.0	24 05.5	+51.8	110.9
11	27 29.6	46.7	106.6	26 54.4	48.0	107.6	26 17.2	49.3	108.5	25 38.1	50.6	109.4	24 57.3	51.7	110.3
12	28 16.3	46.3	105.9	27 42.4	47.8	106.9	27 06.5	49.1	107.9	26 28.7	50.4	108.8	25 49.0	51.5	109.8
13	29 02.6	46.2	105.2	28 30.2	47.6	106.2	27 55.6	49.0	107.2	27 19.1	50.2	108.2	26 40.5	51.4	109.2
14	29 48.8	45.9	104.4	29 17.8	47.3	105.5	28 44.6	48.7	106.6	28 09.3	50.0	107.6	27 31.9	51.3	108.6
15	30 34.7	+45.6	103.7	30 05.1	+47.2	104.8	29 33.3	+48.6	105.9	28 59.3	+49.9	107.0	28 23.2	+51.1	108.0
16	31 20.3	45.4	102.9	30 52.3	46.9	104.1	30 21.9	48.3	105.2	29 49.2	49.7	106.4	29 14.3	51.0	107.4
17	32 05.7	45.1	102.2	31 39.2	46.6	103.4	31 10.2	48.1	104.6	30 38.9	49.5	105.7	30 05.3	50.8	106.8
18	32 50.8	44.8	101.4	32 25.8	46.4	102.6	31 58.3	47.9	103.9	31 28.4	49.5	105.1	30 56.1	50.5	106.2
19	33 35.6	44.4	100.6	33 12.2	46.1	101.9	32 46.2	47.6	103.1	32 17.7	49.0	104.4	31 46.6	50.5	105.6
20	34 20.0	+44.2	99.8	33 58.3	+45.8	101.1	33 33.8	+47.4	102.4	33 06.7	+48.9	103.7	32 37.1	+50.2	104.9
21	35 04.2	43.8	98.9	34 44.1	45.5	100.3	34 21.2	47.1	101.7	33 55.6	48.6	103.0	33 27.3	50.0	104.3
22	35 48.0	43.5	98.1	35 29.6	45.2	99.5	35 08.3	46.8	100.9	34 44.2	48.3	102.3	34 17.3	49.8	103.6
23	36 31.5	43.0	97.3	36 14.8	44.8	98.7	35 55.1	46.5	100.1	35 32.5	48.1	101.6	35 07.1	49.5	102.9
24	37 14.5	42.7	96.4	36 59.6	44.5	97.9	36 41.6	46.2	99.4	36 20.6	47.8	100.8	35 56.6	49.3	102.3
25	37 57.2	+42.3	95.5	37 44.1	+44.2	97.0	37 27.8	+45.9	98.6	37 08.4	+47.5	100.1	36 45.9	+49.1	101.5
26	38 39.5	41.9	94.6	38 28.3	43.7	96.2	38 13.7	45.5	97.7	37 55.9	47.2	99.3	37 35.0	48.7	100.8
27	39 21.4	41.4	93.7	39 12.0	43.3	95.3	38 59.2	45.2	96.9	38 43.1	46.9	98.5	38 23.7	48.5	100.1
28	40 02.8	40.9	92.7	39 55.3	42.9	94.4	39 44.4	44.8	96.1	39 30.0	46.5	97.7	39 12.2	48.2	99.3
29	40 43.7	40.5	91.8	40 38.2	42.5	93.5	40 29.2	44.3	95.2	40 16.5	46.2	96.9	40 00.4	47.9	98.6

40°			42°			44°			46°			48°			Dec.
Hc	d	Z	Hc	d	Z	Hc	d	Z	Hc	d	Z	Hc	d	Z	
22 31.3	−41.9	110.4	21 48.8	−43.4	111.1	21 04.8	−44.8	111.9	20 19.4	−46.1	112.6	19 32.8	−47.4	113.2	0
21 49.4	42.1	111.1	21 05.4	43.5	111.9	20 20.0	44.9	112.6	19 33.3	46.2	113.2	18 45.4	47.5	113.9	1
21 07.3	42.3	111.9	20 21.9	43.7	112.6	19 35.1	45.1	113.3	18 47.1	46.4	113.9	17 57.9	47.7	114.5	2
20 25.0	42.4	112.7	19 38.2	43.9	113.3	18 50.0	45.2	114.0	18 00.7	46.6	114.6	17 10.2	47.7	115.2	3
19 42.6	42.7	113.4	18 54.3	44.1	114.1	18 04.8	45.4	114.7	17 14.1	46.6	115.2	16 22.5	47.9	115.8	4
18 59.9	−42.8	114.2	18 10.2	−44.2	114.8	17 19.4	−45.6	115.3	16 27.5	−46.8	115.9	15 34.6	−48.0	116.4	5
18 17.1	43.2	114.9	17 26.0	44.4	115.5	16 33.8	45.6	116.0	15 40.7	46.9	116.5	14 46.6	48.1	117.0	6
17 34.1	43.2	115.6	16 41.6	44.5	116.2	15 48.2	45.8	116.7	14 53.8	47.0	117.2	13 58.5	48.1	117.7	7
16 50.9	43.3	116.4	15 57.1	44.6	116.9	15 02.4	45.9	117.4	14 06.8	47.1	117.8	13 10.4	48.3	118.3	8
16 07.6	43.5	117.1	15 12.5	44.8	117.6	14 16.5	46.0	118.0	13 19.7	47.2	118.5	12 22.1	48.3	118.9	9
15 24.1	−43.6	117.8	14 27.7	−44.9	118.3	13 30.5	−46.1	118.7	12 32.5	−47.3	119.1	11 33.8	−48.5	119.5	10
14 40.5	43.7	118.5	13 42.8	45.0	118.9	12 44.4	46.3	119.4	11 45.2	47.4	119.7	10 45.3	48.4	120.1	11
13 56.8	43.9	119.2	12 57.8	45.1	119.6	11 58.1	46.3	120.0	10 57.8	47.5	120.4	9 56.9	48.6	120.7	12
13 12.9	44.0	119.9	12 12.7	45.2	120.3	11 11.8	46.4	120.7	10 10.3	47.5	121.0	9 08.3	48.6	121.3	13
12 28.9	44.0	120.6	11 27.5	45.3	121.0	10 25.4	46.4	121.3	9 22.8	47.6	121.6	8 19.7	48.7	121.9	14
11 44.9	−44.2	121.3	10 42.2	−45.4	121.6	9 39.0	−45.6	121.9	8 35.2	−47.6	122.2	7 31.0	−48.7	122.5	15
11 00.7	44.3	122.0	9 56.8	45.4	122.3	8 52.4	46.6	122.6	7 47.6	47.7	122.8	6 42.3	48.7	123.0	16
10 16.4	44.3	122.7	9 11.4	45.6	123.0	8 05.8	46.6	123.2	6 59.9	47.8	123.4	5 53.6	48.8	123.6	17
9 32.1	44.5	123.4	8 25.8	45.6	123.6	7 19.2	46.7	123.9	6 12.1	47.7	124.1	5 04.8	48.8	124.2	18
8 47.6	44.5	124.0	7 40.2	45.6	124.3	6 32.5	46.8	124.5	5 24.4	47.9	124.7	4 15.9	48.9	124.8	19
8 03.1	−44.5	124.7	6 54.6	−45.7	124.9	5 45.7	−46.8	125.1	4 36.5	−47.8	125.3	3 27.1	−48.8	125.4	20
7 18.6	44.7	125.4	6 08.9	45.8	125.6	4 58.9	46.8	125.8	3 48.7	47.9	125.9	2 38.3	48.9	126.0	21
6 33.9	44.7	126.1	5 23.1	45.8	126.2	4 12.1	46.9	126.4	3 00.8	47.9	126.5	1 49.4	48.9	126.5	22
5 49.2	44.7	126.7	4 37.3	45.8	126.9	3 25.2	46.9	127.0	2 12.9	47.9	127.1	1 00.5	48.9	127.1	23
5 04.5	44.8	127.4	3 51.5	45.9	127.5	2 38.3	46.9	127.6	1 25.0	47.9	127.7	0 11.6	−48.9	127.7	24
4 19.7	−44.8	128.1	3 05.6	−45.9	128.2	1 51.4	−46.9	128.3	0 37.1	−48.0	128.3	0 37.3	+48.9	51.7	25
3 34.9	44.8	128.7	2 19.7	45.9	128.8	1 04.5	47.0	128.9	0 10.9	+47.9	51.1	1 26.2	48.9	51.1	26
2 50.1	44.9	129.4	1 33.8	45.9	129.5	0 17.5	−46.9	129.5	0 58.8	47.9	50.5	2 15.1	48.8	50.6	27
2 05.2	44.9	130.1	0 47.9	45.9	130.1	0 29.4	+46.9	49.9	1 46.7	47.9	49.9	3 03.9	48.9	50.0	28
1 20.3	44.8	130.7	0 02.0	−45.9	130.8	1 16.3	47.0	49.3	2 34.6	47.9	49.3	3 52.8	48.8	49.4	29

50°			52°			54°			56°			58°			Dec.
Hc	d	Z	Hc	d	Z	Hc	d	Z	Hc	d	Z	Hc	d	Z	
18 44.8	−48.6	113.9	17 55.7	−49.7	114.5	17 05.5	−50.9	115.0	16 14.2	−51.9	115.6	15 21.9	−52.8	116.1	0
17 56.2	48.7	114.5	17 06.0	49.9	115.0	16 14.6	50.9	115.6	15 22.3	51.9	116.1	14 29.1	52.9	116.6	1
17 07.5	48.8	115.1	16 16.1	49.9	115.6	15 23.7	51.0	116.1	14 30.4	52.0	116.6	13 36.2	52.9	117.1	2
16 18.7	48.9	115.7	15 26.2	50.0	116.2	14 32.7	51.0	116.7	13 38.4	52.0	117.1	12 43.3	53.0	117.6	3
15 29.8	49.1	116.3	14 36.2	50.2	116.8	13 41.7	51.2	117.2	12 46.4	52.1	117.6	11 50.3	53.0	118.0	4
14 40.7	−49.1	116.9	13 46.0	−50.1	117.3	12 50.5	−51.2	117.8	11 54.3	−52.2	118.2	10 57.3	−53.1	118.5	5
13 51.6	49.2	117.5	12 55.9	50.3	117.9	11 59.3	51.3	118.3	11 02.1	52.2	118.7	10 04.2	53.1	119.0	6
13 02.4	49.2	118.1	12 05.6	50.3	118.5	11 08.1	51.4	118.8	10 09.9	52.3	119.2	9 11.1	53.1	119.5	7
12 13.2	49.4	118.7	11 15.3	50.4	119.0	10 16.7	51.3	119.4	9 17.6	52.3	119.7	8 18.0	53.2	119.9	8
11 23.8	49.4	119.2	10 24.9	50.5	119.6	9 25.4	51.5	119.9	8 25.3	52.3	120.2	7 24.8	53.2	120.4	9
10 34.4	−49.5	119.8	9 34.4	−50.5	120.1	8 33.9	−51.4	120.4	7 33.0	−52.4	120.6	6 31.6	−53.2	120.9	10
9 44.9	49.5	120.4	8 43.9	50.5	120.7	7 42.5	51.5	120.9	6 40.6	52.4	121.1	5 38.4	53.3	121.3	11
8 55.4	49.6	121.0	7 53.4	50.6	121.2	6 51.0	51.5	121.4	5 48.2	52.4	121.6	4 45.1	53.2	121.8	12
8 05.8	49.7	121.5	7 02.8	50.6	121.8	5 59.5	51.6	122.0	4 55.8	52.4	122.1	3 51.9	53.3	122.2	13
7 16.1	49.7	122.1	6 12.2	50.7	122.3	5 07.9	51.6	122.5	4 03.4	52.5	122.6	2 58.6	53.3	122.7	14
6 26.4	−49.7	122.7	5 21.5	−50.7	122.8	4 16.3	−51.6	123.0	3 10.9	−52.5	123.1	2 05.3	−53.3	123.2	15
5 36.7	49.7	123.2	4 30.8	50.7	123.4	3 24.7	51.6	123.5	2 18.4	52.5	123.6	1 12.0	53.3	123.6	16
4 47.0	49.8	123.8	3 40.1	50.7	123.9	2 33.1	51.6	124.0	1 25.9	52.5	124.1	0 18.7	−53.3	124.1	17
3 57.2	49.8	124.4	2 49.4	50.7	124.4	1 41.5	51.7	124.5	0 33.4	−52.5	124.5	0 34.6	+53.3	55.5	18
3 07.4	49.8	124.9	1 58.7	50.8	125.0	0 49.8	−51.6	125.0	0 19.1	+52.5	55.0	1 27.9	53.3	55.0	19
2 17.6	−49.9	125.5	1 07.9	−50.8	125.5	0 01.8	+51.7	54.5	1 11.6	+52.4	54.5	2 21.2	+53.3	54.5	20
1 27.7	49.8	126.0	0 17.1	−50.7	126.0	0 53.5	51.6	54.0	2 04.0	52.5	54.0	3 14.5	53.3	54.1	21
0 37.9	+49.9	126.6	0 33.6	+50.8	53.4	1 45.1	51.6	53.5	2 56.5	52.5	53.5	4 07.8	53.3	53.6	22
0 11.9	+49.9	52.9	1 24.4	50.8	52.9	2 36.7	51.7	52.9	3 49.0	52.4	53.0	5 01.1	53.2	53.2	23
1 01.8	49.8	52.3	2 15.1	50.8	52.4	3 28.4	51.6	52.4	4 41.4	52.5	52.5	5 54.3	53.2	52.7	24
1 51.6	+49.8	51.7	3 05.9	+50.7	51.8	4 20.0	+51.5	51.9	5 33.9	+52.4	52.1	6 47.5	+53.2	52.2	25
2 41.4	49.9	51.2	3 56.6	50.7	51.3	5 11.5	51.6	51.4	6 26.3	52.4	51.6	7 40.7	53.2	51.8	26
3 31.3	49.7	50.6	4 47.3	50.7	50.7	6 03.1	51.5	50.9	7 18.7	52.3	51.1	8 33.9	53.1	51.3	27
4 21.0	49.8	50.1	5 38.0	50.6	50.2	6 54.6	51.5	50.4	8 11.0	52.3	50.6	9 27.0	53.1	50.8	28
5 10.8	49.7	49.5	6 28.6	50.6	49.7	7 46.1	51.5	49.9	9 03.3	52.3	50.1	10 20.1	53.0	50.3	29

LATITUDE **SAME** NAME L.H.A. 120°, 240°

Dec.	0° Hc	d	Z	2° Hc	d	Z	4° Hc	d	Z	6° Hc	d	Z	8° Hc	d	Z
°	° ′	′	°	° ′	′	°	° ′	′	°	° ′	′	°	° ′	′	°
0	28 00.0 − 0.3		90.0	27 58.9 + 2.1		91.1	27 55.5 + 4.5		92.1	27 50.0 + 6.8		93.2	27 42.2 + 9.2		94.2
1	27 59.7	0.8	88.9	28 01.0	1.5	89.9	28 00.0	3.9	91.0	27 56.8	6.3	92.1	27 51.4	8.6	93.1
2	27 58.9	1.4	87.7	28 02.5	1.0	88.8	28 03.9	3.4	89.9	28 03.1	5.7	90.9	28 00.0	8.1	92.0
3	27 57.5	2.0	86.6	28 03.5 + 0.4		87.7	28 07.3	2.8	88.7	28 08.8	5.2	89.8	28 08.1	7.5	90.9
4	27 55.5	2.5	85.5	28 03.9 − 0.1		86.5	28 10.1	2.2	87.6	28 14.0	4.6	88.7	28 15.6	7.0	89.7
5	27 53.0 − 3.0		84.3	28 03.8 − 0.7		85.4	28 12.3 + 1.7		86.5	28 18.6 + 4.0		87.5	28 22.6 + 6.4		88.6
6	27 50.0	3.6	83.2	28 03.1	1.3	84.3	28 14.0	1.1	85.3	28 22.6	3.5	86.4	28 29.0	5.9	87.5
7	27 46.4	4.2	82.1	28 01.8	1.8	83.1	28 15.1 + 0.5		84.2	28 26.1	2.9	85.3	28 34.9	5.2	86.4
8	27 42.2	4.7	81.0	28 00.0	2.3	82.0	28 15.6	0.0	83.1	28 29.0	2.3	84.1	28 40.1	4.7	85.2
9	27 37.5	5.2	79.8	27 57.7	3.0	80.9	28 15.6 − 0.6		81.9	28 31.3	1.8	83.0	28 44.8	4.2	84.1
10	27 32.3 − 5.8		78.7	27 54.7 − 3.4		79.7	28 15.0 − 1.1		80.8	28 33.1 + 1.2		81.9	28 49.0 + 3.6		82.9
11	27 26.5	6.3	77.6	27 51.3	4.1	78.6	28 13.9	1.7	79.7	28 34.3 + 0.7		80.7	28 52.6	3.0	81.8
12	27 20.2	6.9	76.5	27 47.2	4.5	77.5	28 12.2	2.3	78.5	28 35.0	0.0	79.6	28 55.6	2.4	80.7
13	27 13.3	7.4	75.3	27 42.7	5.2	76.4	28 09.9	2.8	77.4	28 35.0 − 0.5		78.4	28 58.0	1.8	79.5
14	27 05.9	7.9	74.2	27 37.5	5.6	75.2	28 07.1	3.4	76.3	28 34.5	1.0	77.3	28 59.8	1.3	78.4
15	26 58.0 − 8.4		73.1	27 31.9 − 6.2		74.1	28 03.7 − 3.9		75.1	28 33.5 − 1.7		76.2	29 01.1 + 0.6		77.2
16	26 49.6	9.0	72.0	27 25.7	6.8	73.0	27 59.8	4.5	74.0	28 31.8	2.2	75.0	29 01.7 + 0.1		76.1
17	26 40.6	9.5	70.9	27 18.9	7.3	71.9	27 55.3	5.1	72.9	28 29.6	2.8	73.9	29 01.8 − 0.4		74.9
18	26 31.1	9.9	69.8	27 11.6	7.8	70.8	27 50.2	5.6	71.7	28 26.8	3.3	72.8	29 01.4	1.1	73.8
19	26 21.2	10.5	68.7	27 03.8	8.3	69.6	27 44.6	6.1	70.6	28 23.5	3.9	71.6	29 00.3	1.7	72.7
20	26 10.7 − 11.0		67.6	26 55.5 − 8.8		68.5	27 38.5 − 6.7		69.5	28 19.6 − 4.5		70.5	28 58.6 − 2.2		71.5
21	25 59.7	11.5	66.5	26 46.7	9.4	67.4	27 31.8	7.2	68.4	28 15.1	5.0	69.4	28 56.4	2.8	70.4
22	25 48.2	12.0	65.4	26 37.3	9.9	66.3	27 24.6	7.7	67.2	28 10.1	5.6	68.2	28 53.6	3.4	69.2
23	25 36.2	12.4	64.3	26 27.4	10.4	65.2	27 16.9	8.3	66.1	28 04.5	6.1	67.1	28 50.2	3.9	68.1
24	25 23.8	12.9	63.2	26 17.0	10.9	64.1	27 08.6	8.8	65.0	27 58.4	6.7	66.0	28 46.3	4.5	67.0
25	25 10.9 − 13.4		62.2	26 06.1 − 11.3		63.0	26 59.8 − 9.4		63.9	27 51.7 − 7.3		64.8	28 41.8 − 5.1		65.8
26	24 57.5	13.9	61.1	25 54.8	11.9	61.9	26 50.4	9.8	62.8	27 44.4	7.7	63.7	28 36.7	5.7	64.7
27	24 43.6	14.3	60.0	25 42.9	12.4	60.8	26 40.6	10.4	61.7	27 36.7	8.4	62.6	28 31.0	6.2	63.6
28	24 29.3	14.7	58.9	25 30.5	12.8	59.7	26 30.2	10.8	60.6	27 28.3	8.8	61.5	28 24.8	6.8	62.4
29	24 14.6	15.2	57.9	25 17.7	13.3	58.7	26 19.4	11.4	59.5	27 19.5	9.4	60.4	28 18.0	7.4	61.3

Dec.	10° Hc	d	Z	12° Hc	d	Z	14° Hc	d	Z	16° Hc	d	Z	18° Hc	d	Z
°	° ′	′	°	° ′	′	°	° ′	′	°	° ′	′	°	° ′	′	°
0	27 32.3 + 11.5		95.3	27 20.2 + 13.8		96.3	27 05.9 + 16.1		97.3	26 49.6 + 18.3		98.3	26 31.1 + 20.5		99.3
1	27 43.8	10.9	94.2	27 34.0	13.2	95.2	27 22.0	15.5	96.2	27 07.9	17.8	97.3	26 51.6	20.0	98.3
2	27 54.7	10.4	93.1	27 47.2	12.8	94.1	27 37.5	15.1	95.2	27 25.7	17.3	96.2	27 11.6	19.6	97.2
3	28 05.1	9.9	91.9	28 00.0	12.2	93.0	27 52.6	14.5	94.1	27 43.0	16.8	95.1	27 31.2	19.0	96.2
4	28 15.0	9.0	90.8	28 12.2	11.6	91.9	28 07.1	14.0	93.0	27 59.8	16.3	94.0	27 50.2	18.6	95.1
5	28 24.4 + 8.7		89.7	28 23.8 + 11.0		90.8	28 21.1 + 13.4		91.9	28 16.1 + 15.7		92.9	28 08.8 + 18.0		94.0
6	28 33.1	8.2	88.6	28 35.0	10.5	89.7	28 34.5	13.0	90.8	28 31.8	15.3	91.8	28 26.8	17.6	92.9
7	28 41.3	7.7	87.4	28 45.5	10.1	88.5	28 47.5	12.3	89.6	28 47.1	14.6	90.7	28 44.4	17.0	91.8
8	28 49.0	7.1	86.3	28 55.6	9.4	87.4	28 59.8	11.8	88.5	29 01.7	14.2	89.6	29 01.4	16.4	90.7
9	28 56.1	6.5	85.2	29 05.0	8.9	86.3	29 11.6	11.3	87.4	29 15.9	13.6	88.5	29 17.8	15.9	89.6
10	29 02.6 + 5.9		84.0	29 13.9 + 8.3		85.2	29 22.9 + 10.6		86.3	29 29.5 + 13.0		87.4	29 33.7 + 15.4		88.5
11	29 08.5	5.4	82.9	29 22.2	7.7	84.0	29 33.5	10.1	85.1	29 42.5	12.5	86.3	29 49.1	14.8	87.4
12	29 13.9	4.8	81.8	29 29.9	7.2	82.9	29 43.6	9.5	84.0	29 55.0	11.8	85.2	30 03.9	14.2	86.3
13	29 18.7	4.2	80.6	29 37.1	6.5	81.7	29 53.1	9.0	82.9	30 06.8	11.3	84.0	30 18.1	13.7	85.2
14	29 22.9	3.6	79.5	29 43.6	6.0	80.6	30 02.1	8.3	81.7	30 18.1	10.7	82.9	30 31.8	13.1	84.0
15	29 26.5 + 3.0		78.3	29 49.6 + 5.4		79.4	30 10.4 + 7.7		80.6	30 28.8 + 10.1		81.7	30 44.9 + 12.4		82.9
16	29 29.5	2.4	77.2	29 55.0	4.7	78.3	30 18.1	7.2	79.4	30 38.9	9.5	80.6	30 57.3	11.9	81.8
17	29 31.9	1.8	76.0	29 59.7	4.2	77.1	30 25.3	6.5	78.3	30 48.4	8.9	79.4	31 09.2	11.3	80.6
18	29 33.7	1.3	74.9	30 03.9	3.6	76.0	30 31.8	5.9	77.1	30 57.3	8.3	78.3	31 20.5	10.6	79.5
19	29 35.0	0.6	73.7	30 07.5	2.9	74.8	30 37.7	5.3	76.0	31 05.6	7.7	77.1	31 31.1	10.0	78.3
20	29 35.6 + 0.1		72.6	30 10.4 + 2.4		73.7	30 43.0 + 4.7		74.8	31 13.3 + 7.0		76.0	31 41.1 + 9.4		77.2
21	29 35.7 − 0.6		71.4	30 12.8	1.7	72.5	30 47.7	4.1	73.7	31 20.3	6.4	74.8	31 50.5	8.8	76.0
22	29 35.1	1.1	70.3	30 14.5	1.2	71.4	30 51.8	3.4	72.5	31 26.7	5.8	73.7	31 59.3	8.1	74.8
23	29 34.0	1.7	69.1	30 15.7 + 0.5		70.2	30 55.2	2.8	71.3	31 32.5	5.1	72.5	32 07.4	7.5	73.7
24	29 32.3	2.4	68.0	30 16.2 − 0.1		69.1	30 58.0	2.2	70.2	31 37.6	4.5	71.3	32 14.9	6.8	72.5
25	29 29.9 − 2.9		66.8	30 16.1 − 0.7		67.9	31 00.2 + 1.6		69.0	31 42.1 + 3.8		70.1	32 21.7 + 6.1		71.3
26	29 27.0	3.5	65.7	30 15.4	1.3	66.7	31 01.8	0.9	67.8	31 45.9	3.2	69.0	32 27.8	5.5	70.1
27	29 23.5	4.1	64.5	30 14.1	1.9	65.6	31 02.7 + 0.3		66.7	31 49.1	2.6	67.8	32 33.3	4.9	69.0
28	29 19.4	4.7	63.4	30 12.2	2.5	64.4	31 03.0 − 0.4		65.5	31 51.7	1.9	66.6	32 38.2	4.2	67.8
29	29 14.7	5.2	62.3	30 09.7	3.2	63.3	31 02.6	0.9	64.3	31 53.6	1.2	65.4	32 42.4	3.5	66.6

0°			2°			4°			6°			8°			Dec.
Hc	d	Z	Hc	d	Z	Hc	d	Z	Hc	d	Z	Hc	d	Z	
28 00.0 − 0.3		90.0	27 58.9 − 2.7		91.1	27 55.5 − 5.0		92.1	27 50.0 − 7.4		93.2	27 42.2 − 9.7		94.2	0
27 59.7	0.8	91.1	27 56.2	3.2	92.2	27 50.5	5.5	93.3	27 42.6	7.9	94.3	27 32.5	10.2	95.3	1
27 58.9	1.4	92.3	27 53.0	3.7	93.3	27 45.0	6.1	94.4	27 34.7	8.4	95.4	27 22.3	10.7	96.5	2
27 57.5	2.0	93.4	27 49.3	4.3	94.5	27 38.9	6.7	95.5	27 26.3	9.0	96.5	27 11.6	11.3	97.6	3
27 55.5	2.5	94.5	27 45.0	4.9	95.6	27 32.2	7.2	96.6	27 17.3	9.5	97.7	27 00.3	11.8	98.7	4
27 53.0 − 3.0		95.7	27 40.1 − 5.4		96.7	27 25.0 − 7.7		97.7	27 07.8 −10.0		98.8	26 48.5 −12.3		99.8	5
27 50.0	3.6	96.8	27 34.7	5.9	97.8	27 17.3	8.2	98.9	26 57.8	10.6	99.9	26 36.2	12.8	100.9	6
27 46.4	4.2	97.9	27 28.8	6.5	99.0	27 09.1	8.8	100.0	26 47.2	11.0	101.0	26 23.4	13.3	102.0	7
27 42.2	4.7	99.0	27 22.3	7.0	100.1	27 00.3	9.3	101.1	26 36.2	11.6	102.1	26 10.1	13.8	103.0	8
27 37.5	5.2	100.2	27 15.3	7.6	101.2	26 51.0	9.8	102.2	26 24.6	12.0	103.2	25 56.3	14.2	104.1	9
27 32.3 − 5.8		101.3	27 07.7 − 8.0		102.3	26 41.2 −10.4		103.3	26 12.6 −12.6		104.3	25 42.1 −14.8		105.2	10
27 26.5	6.3	102.4	26 59.7	8.6	103.4	26 30.8	10.8	104.4	26 00.0	13.0	105.4	25 27.3	15.2	106.3	11
27 20.2	6.9	103.5	26 51.1	9.1	104.5	26 20.0	11.3	105.5	25 47.0	13.5	106.4	25 12.1	15.7	107.3	12
27 13.3	7.4	104.7	26 42.0	9.7	105.6	26 08.7	11.9	106.6	25 33.5	14.0	107.5	24 56.4	16.1	108.4	13
27 05.9	7.9	105.8	26 32.3	10.1	106.7	25 56.8	12.3	107.7	25 19.5	14.5	108.6	24 40.3	16.5	109.5	14
26 58.0 − 8.4		106.9	26 22.2 −10.6		107.8	25 44.5 −12.8		108.8	25 05.0 −14.9		109.7	24 23.8 −17.0		110.5	15
26 49.6	9.0	108.0	26 11.6	11.2	108.9	25 31.7	13.3	109.9	24 50.1	15.4	110.7	24 06.8	17.5	111.6	16
26 40.6	9.5	109.1	26 00.4	11.6	110.0	25 18.4	13.7	110.9	24 34.7	15.8	111.8	23 49.3	17.8	112.6	17
26 31.1	9.9	110.2	25 48.8	12.1	111.1	25 04.7	14.2	112.0	24 18.9	16.3	112.9	23 31.5	18.3	113.7	18
26 21.2	10.5	111.3	25 36.7	12.6	112.2	24 50.5	14.7	113.1	24 02.6	16.7	113.9	23 13.2	18.7	114.7	19
26 10.7 −11.0		112.4	25 24.1 −13.1		113.3	24 35.8 −15.1		114.1	23 45.9 −17.1		115.0	22 54.5 −19.0		115.7	20
25 59.7	11.3	113.5	25 11.0	13.5	114.4	24 20.7	15.6	115.2	23 28.8	17.5	116.0	22 35.5	19.5	116.8	21
25 48.2	12.0	114.6	24 57.5	14.0	115.4	24 05.1	16.0	116.3	23 11.3	18.0	117.1	22 16.0	19.9	117.8	22
25 36.2	12.4	115.7	24 43.5	14.5	116.5	23 49.1	16.4	117.3	22 53.3	18.3	118.1	21 56.1	20.2	118.8	23
25 23.8	12.9	116.8	24 29.0	14.9	117.6	23 32.7	16.9	118.4	22 35.0	18.8	119.1	21 35.9	20.6	119.8	24
25 10.9 −13.4		117.8	24 14.1 −15.4		118.7	23 15.8 −17.2		119.4	22 16.2 −19.1		120.1	21 15.3 −20.9		120.8	25
24 57.5	13.9	118.9	23 58.7	15.7	119.7	22 58.6	17.7	120.5	21 57.1	19.5	121.2	20 54.4	21.3	121.8	26
24 43.6	14.3	120.0	23 43.0	16.2	120.8	22 40.9	18.1	121.5	21 37.6	19.9	122.2	20 33.1	21.7	122.8	27
24 29.3	14.7	121.1	23 26.8	16.7	121.8	22 22.8	18.4	122.5	21 17.7	20.2	123.2	20 11.4	21.9	123.8	28
24 14.6	15.2	122.1	23 10.1	17.0	122.9	22 04.4	18.9	123.6	20 57.5	20.6	124.2	19 49.5	22.3	124.8	29

10°			12°			14°			16°			18°			Dec.
Hc	d	Z	Hc	d	Z	Hc	d	Z	Hc	d	Z	Hc	d	Z	
27 32.3 −12.0		95.3	27 20.2 −14.3		96.3	27 05.9 −16.5		97.3	26 49.6 −18.8		98.3	26 31.1 −20.9		99.3	0
27 20.3	12.6	96.4	27 05.9	14.8	97.4	26 49.4	17.1	98.4	26 30.8	19.2	99.4	26 10.2	21.4	100.4	1
27 07.7	13.0	97.5	26 51.1	15.3	98.5	26 32.3	17.5	99.5	26 11.6	19.7	100.5	25 48.8	21.9	101.4	2
26 54.7	13.5	98.6	26 35.8	15.8	99.6	26 14.8	18.0	100.5	25 51.9	20.2	101.5	25 26.9	22.2	102.4	3
26 41.2	14.1	99.7	26 20.0	16.3	100.6	25 56.8	18.4	101.6	25 31.7	20.6	102.6	25 04.7	22.7	103.5	4
26 27.1 −14.5		100.8	26 03.7 −16.7		101.7	25 38.4 −18.9		102.7	25 11.1 −21.0		103.6	24 42.0 −23.1		104.5	5
26 12.6	15.0	101.8	25 47.0	17.2	102.8	25 19.5	19.4	103.7	24 50.1	21.5	104.6	24 18.9	23.5	105.5	6
25 57.6	15.5	102.9	25 29.8	17.7	103.9	25 00.1	19.8	104.8	24 28.6	21.8	105.7	23 55.4	23.9	106.5	7
25 42.1	16.0	104.0	25 12.1	18.1	104.9	24 40.3	20.2	105.8	24 06.8	22.3	106.7	23 31.5	24.3	107.5	8
25 26.1	16.4	105.1	24 54.0	18.6	106.0	24 20.1	20.6	106.8	23 44.5	22.7	107.7	23 07.2	24.7	108.5	9
25 09.7 −16.9		106.1	24 35.4 −18.9		107.0	23 59.5 −21.1		107.9	23 21.8 −23.0		108.7	22 42.5 −25.0		109.5	10
24 52.8	17.4	107.2	24 16.5	19.5	108.1	23 38.4	21.4	108.9	22 58.8	23.5	109.7	22 17.5	25.3	110.5	11
24 35.4	17.7	108.2	23 57.0	19.8	109.1	23 17.0	21.9	109.9	22 35.3	23.8	110.7	21 52.2	25.8	111.5	12
24 17.7	18.2	109.3	23 37.2	20.2	110.1	22 55.1	22.2	110.9	22 11.5	24.1	111.7	21 26.4	26.0	112.4	13
23 59.5	18.6	110.3	23 17.0	20.6	111.1	22 32.9	22.6	111.9	21 47.4	24.5	112.7	21 00.4	26.4	113.4	14
23 40.9 −19.1		111.4	22 56.4 −21.1		112.2	22 10.3 −22.9		112.9	21 22.9 −24.9		113.7	20 34.0 −26.7		114.4	15
23 21.8	19.4	112.4	22 35.3	21.4	113.2	21 47.4	23.3	113.9	20 58.0	25.2	114.6	20 07.3	27.0	115.3	16
23 02.4	19.9	113.4	22 13.9	21.7	114.2	21 24.1	23.7	114.9	20 32.8	25.5	115.6	19 40.3	27.3	116.3	17
22 42.5	20.2	114.5	21 52.2	22.2	115.2	21 00.4	24.0	115.9	20 07.3	25.8	116.6	19 13.0	27.6	117.2	18
22 22.3	20.6	115.5	21 30.0	22.5	116.2	20 36.4	24.3	116.9	19 41.5	26.1	117.5	18 45.4	27.8	118.2	19
22 01.7 −21.0		116.5	21 07.5 −22.8		117.2	20 12.1 −24.7		117.9	19 15.4 −26.4		118.5	18 17.6 −28.2		119.1	20
21 40.7	21.3	117.5	20 44.7	23.2	118.2	19 47.4	25.0	118.8	18 49.0	26.7	119.4	17 49.4	28.3	120.0	21
21 19.4	21.7	118.5	20 21.5	23.5	119.2	19 22.4	25.3	119.8	18 22.3	27.0	120.4	17 21.1	28.7	120.9	22
20 57.7	22.1	119.5	19 58.0	23.8	120.1	18 57.2	25.6	120.8	17 55.3	27.3	121.3	16 52.4	28.9	121.9	23
20 35.6	22.4	120.5	19 34.2	24.2	121.1	18 31.6	25.9	121.7	17 28.0	27.5	122.3	16 23.5	29.1	122.8	24
20 13.2 −22.7		121.5	19 10.0 −24.4		122.1	18 05.7 −26.1		122.7	17 00.5 −27.8		123.2	15 54.4 −29.4		123.7	25
19 50.5	23.0	122.5	18 45.6	24.8	123.1	17 39.6	26.4	123.6	16 32.7	28.0	124.1	15 25.0	29.6	124.6	26
19 27.5	23.4	123.5	18 20.8	25.0	124.0	17 13.2	26.6	124.5	16 04.7	28.2	125.0	14 55.4	29.7	125.5	27
19 04.1	23.7	124.4	17 55.8	25.3	125.0	16 46.6	27.0	125.5	15 36.5	28.5	126.0	14 25.7	30.0	126.4	28
18 40.4	23.9	125.4	17 30.5	25.6	125.9	16 19.6	27.1	126.4	15 08.0	28.7	126.9	13 55.7	30.2	127.3	29

LATITUDE **SAME** NAME

Dec.	20° Hc	d	Z	22° Hc	d	Z	24° Hc	d	Z	26° Hc	d	Z	28° Hc	d	Z
°	° ′	′	°	° ′	′	°	° ′	′	°	° ′	′	°	° ′	′	°
0	26 10.7	+22.6	100.3	25 48.2	+24.8	101.3	25 23.8	+26.8	102.2	24 57.5	+28.8	103.1	24 29.3	+30.8	104.0
1	26 33.3	22.2	99.3	26 13.0	24.3	100.3	25 50.6	26.4	101.2	25 26.3	28.5	102.2	25 00.1	30.4	103.1
2	26 55.5	21.7	98.2	26 37.3	23.9	99.2	26 17.0	26.0	100.2	25 54.8	28.0	101.2	25 30.5	30.1	102.1
3	27 17.2	21.3	97.2	27 01.2	23.4	98.2	26 43.0	25.6	99.2	26 22.8	27.6	100.2	26 00.6	29.6	101.2
4	27 38.5	20.8	96.1	27 24.6	23.0	97.2	27 08.6	25.1	98.2	26 50.4	27.3	99.2	26 30.2	29.3	100.2
5	27 59.3	+20.3	95.1	27 47.6	+22.5	96.1	27 33.7	+24.7	97.2	27 17.7	+26.7	98.2	26 59.5	+28.8	99.2
6	28 19.6	19.8	94.0	28 10.1	22.0	95.1	27 58.4	24.2	96.1	27 44.4	26.4	97.2	27 28.3	28.5	98.2
7	28 39.4	19.2	92.9	28 32.1	21.5	94.0	28 22.6	23.7	95.1	28 10.8	25.9	96.2	27 56.8	28.0	97.2
8	28 58.6	18.8	91.8	28 53.6	21.0	93.0	28 46.3	23.2	94.1	28 36.7	25.4	95.1	28 24.8	27.5	96.2
9	29 17.4	18.2	90.8	29 14.6	20.5	91.9	29 09.5	22.8	93.0	29 02.1	24.9	94.1	28 52.3	27.1	95.2
10	29 35.6	+17.7	89.7	29 35.1	+20.0	90.8	29 32.3	+22.2	91.9	29 27.0	+24.5	93.1	29 19.4	+26.7	94.2
11	29 53.3	17.1	88.6	29 55.1	19.4	89.7	29 54.5	21.7	90.9	29 51.5	23.9	92.0	29 46.1	26.1	93.2
12	30 10.4	16.6	87.5	30 14.5	18.9	88.6	30 16.2	21.2	89.8	30 15.4	23.5	91.0	30 12.2	25.6	92.1
13	30 27.0	16.0	86.3	30 33.4	18.4	87.5	30 37.4	20.6	88.7	30 38.9	22.9	89.9	30 37.8	25.2	91.1
14	30 43.0	15.4	85.2	30 51.8	17.7	86.4	30 58.0	20.1	87.6	31 01.8	22.3	88.8	31 03.0	24.6	90.0
15	30 58.4	+14.9	84.1	31 09.5	+17.2	85.3	31 18.1	+19.5	86.5	31 24.1	+21.8	87.7	31 27.6	+24.1	89.0
16	31 13.3	14.2	83.0	31 26.7	16.6	84.2	31 37.6	18.9	85.4	31 45.9	21.3	86.6	31 51.7	23.5	87.9
17	31 27.5	13.6	81.8	31 43.3	16.0	83.1	31 56.5	18.4	84.3	32 07.2	20.6	85.5	32 15.2	23.0	86.8
18	31 41.1	13.0	80.7	31 59.3	15.4	81.9	32 14.9	17.7	83.2	32 27.8	20.1	84.4	32 38.2	22.4	85.7
19	31 54.1	12.4	79.5	32 14.7	14.7	80.8	32 32.6	17.1	82.0	32 47.9	19.5	83.3	33 00.6	21.8	84.6
20	32 06.5	+11.8	78.4	32 29.4	+14.2	79.6	32 49.7	+16.5	80.9	33 07.4	+18.9	82.2	33 22.4	+21.2	83.5
21	32 18.3	11.1	77.2	32 43.6	13.5	78.5	33 06.2	15.9	79.7	33 26.3	18.2	81.0	33 43.6	20.6	82.4
22	32 29.4	10.5	76.1	32 57.1	12.8	77.3	33 22.1	15.2	78.6	33 44.5	17.6	79.9	34 04.2	20.0	81.2
23	32 39.9	9.8	74.9	33 09.9	12.2	76.1	33 37.3	14.6	77.4	34 02.1	17.0	78.7	34 24.2	19.3	80.1
24	32 49.7	9.2	73.7	33 22.1	11.5	75.0	33 51.9	13.9	76.3	34 19.1	16.2	77.6	34 43.5	18.7	78.9
25	32 58.9	+8.5	72.5	33 33.6	+10.9	73.8	34 05.8	+13.3	75.1	34 35.3	+15.7	76.4	35 02.2	+18.0	77.8
26	33 07.4	7.8	71.4	33 44.5	10.2	72.6	34 19.1	12.5	73.9	34 51.0	14.9	75.2	35 20.2	17.3	76.6
27	33 15.2	7.2	70.2	33 54.7	9.5	71.4	34 31.6	11.9	72.7	35 05.9	14.3	74.1	35 37.5	16.6	75.4
28	33 22.4	6.5	69.0	34 04.2	8.8	70.2	34 43.5	11.1	71.5	35 20.2	13.5	72.9	35 54.1	16.0	74.2
29	33 28.9	5.8	67.8	34 13.0	8.1	69.0	34 54.6	10.5	70.3	35 33.7	12.8	71.7	36 10.1	15.2	73.1

Dec.	30° Hc	d	Z	32° Hc	d	Z	34° Hc	d	Z	36° Hc	d	Z	38° Hc	d	Z
°	° ′	′	°	° ′	′	°	° ′	′	°	° ′	′	°	° ′	′	°
0	23 59.4	+32.7	104.9	23 27.7	+34.5	105.7	22 54.3	+36.3	106.6	22 19.3	+38.0	107.4	21 42.7	+39.7	108.1
1	24 32.1	32.3	104.0	24 02.2	34.2	104.8	23 30.6	36.0	105.7	22 57.3	37.7	106.5	22 22.4	39.4	107.3
2	25 04.4	32.0	103.0	24 36.4	33.9	103.9	24 06.6	35.7	104.8	23 35.0	37.5	105.7	23 01.8	39.1	106.5
3	25 36.4	31.6	102.1	25 10.3	33.5	103.0	24 42.3	35.4	103.9	24 12.5	37.1	104.8	23 40.9	38.9	105.7
4	26 08.0	31.3	101.2	25 43.8	33.2	102.1	25 17.7	35.0	103.0	24 49.6	36.9	104.0	24 19.8	38.6	104.8
5	26 39.3	+30.8	100.2	26 17.0	+32.8	101.2	25 52.7	+34.7	102.1	25 26.5	+36.6	103.1	24 58.4	+38.3	104.0
6	27 10.1	30.5	99.2	26 49.8	32.4	100.2	26 27.4	34.4	101.1	26 03.1	36.2	102.2	25 36.7	38.0	103.1
7	27 40.6	30.0	98.3	27 22.2	32.1	99.3	27 01.8	34.0	100.3	26 39.3	35.9	101.3	26 14.7	37.7	102.3
8	28 10.6	29.7	97.3	27 54.3	31.7	98.4	27 35.8	33.6	99.4	27 15.2	35.5	100.4	26 52.4	37.4	101.4
9	28 40.3	29.2	96.3	28 26.0	31.2	97.4	28 09.4	33.3	98.5	27 50.7	35.2	99.5	27 29.8	37.1	100.5
10	29 09.5	+28.7	95.3	28 57.2	+30.9	96.4	28 42.7	+32.8	97.5	28 25.9	+34.8	98.6	28 06.9	+36.7	99.6
11	29 38.2	28.3	94.3	29 28.1	30.4	95.4	29 15.5	32.5	96.5	29 00.7	34.4	97.7	28 43.6	36.3	98.7
12	30 06.5	27.9	93.3	29 58.5	29.9	94.4	29 48.0	32.0	95.6	29 35.1	34.0	96.7	29 19.9	36.0	97.8
13	30 34.4	27.3	92.3	30 28.4	29.5	93.4	30 20.0	31.5	94.6	30 09.1	33.6	95.8	29 55.9	35.5	96.9
14	31 01.7	26.8	91.2	30 57.9	29.0	92.4	30 51.5	31.2	93.6	30 42.7	33.2	94.8	30 31.4	35.2	96.0
15	31 28.5	+26.3	90.2	31 26.9	+28.5	91.4	31 22.7	+30.6	92.6	31 15.9	+32.7	93.8	31 06.6	+34.8	95.0
16	31 54.8	25.8	89.1	31 55.4	28.0	90.4	31 53.3	30.2	91.6	31 48.6	32.3	92.9	31 41.4	34.3	94.1
17	32 20.6	25.3	88.1	32 23.4	27.4	89.3	32 23.5	29.6	90.6	32 20.9	31.8	91.9	32 15.7	33.9	93.1
18	32 45.9	24.6	87.0	32 50.8	27.0	88.3	32 53.1	29.2	89.6	32 52.7	31.3	90.8	32 49.6	33.4	92.1
19	33 10.5	24.2	85.9	33 17.8	26.4	87.2	33 22.3	28.6	88.5	33 24.0	30.8	89.8	33 23.0	32.9	91.1
20	33 34.7	+23.5	84.8	33 44.2	+25.8	86.1	33 50.9	+28.1	87.5	33 54.8	+30.3	88.8	33 55.9	+32.4	90.1
21	33 58.2	22.9	83.7	34 10.0	25.2	85.0	34 19.0	27.5	86.4	34 25.1	29.7	87.8	34 28.3	32.0	89.1
22	34 21.1	22.3	82.6	34 35.2	24.6	83.9	34 46.5	26.9	85.3	34 54.8	29.2	86.7	35 00.3	31.4	88.1
23	34 43.4	21.7	81.4	34 59.8	24.1	82.8	35 13.4	26.3	84.2	35 24.0	28.6	85.6	35 31.7	30.8	87.1
24	35 05.1	21.0	80.3	35 23.9	23.4	81.7	35 39.7	25.8	83.1	35 52.6	28.0	84.5	36 02.5	30.3	86.0
25	35 26.1	+20.4	79.2	35 47.3	+22.7	80.6	36 05.5	+25.1	82.0	36 20.6	+27.5	83.5	36 32.8	+29.7	84.9
26	35 46.5	19.8	78.0	36 10.0	22.1	79.4	36 30.6	24.4	80.9	36 48.1	26.8	82.3	37 02.5	29.1	83.8
27	36 06.3	19.0	76.8	36 32.1	21.4	78.3	36 55.0	23.8	79.7	37 14.9	26.1	81.2	37 31.6	28.5	82.7
28	36 25.3	18.3	75.7	36 53.5	20.8	77.1	37 18.8	23.1	78.6	37 41.0	25.5	80.1	38 00.1	27.8	81.6
29	36 43.6	17.6	74.5	37 14.3	20.0	75.9	37 41.9	22.5	77.4	38 06.5	24.8	78.9	38 27.9	27.2	80.5

20°			22°			24°			26°			28°			Dec.
Hc	d	Z	Hc	d	Z	Hc	d	Z	Hc	d	Z	Hc	d	Z	
26 10.7	−23.1	100.3	25 48.2	−25.2	101.3	25 23.8	−27.2	102.2	24 57.5	−29.2	103.1	24 29.3	−31.1	104.0	0
25 47.6	23.5	101.3	25 23.0	25.5	102.3	24 56.6	27.6	103.2	24 28.3	29.6	104.1	23 58.2	31.4	105.0	1
25 24.1	24.0	102.4	24 57.5	26.0	103.3	24 29.0	28.0	104.2	23 58.7	29.9	105.0	23 26.8	31.8	105.9	2
25 00.1	24.3	103.4	24 31.5	26.4	104.3	24 01.0	28.3	105.1	23 28.8	30.2	106.0	22 55.0	32.2	106.8	3
24 35.8	24.7	104.4	24 05.1	26.7	105.2	23 32.7	28.7	106.1	22 58.6	30.6	106.9	22 22.8	32.4	107.7	4
24 11.1	−25.2	105.4	23 38.4	−27.1	106.2	23 04.0	−29.0	107.1	22 28.0	−30.9	107.9	21 50.4	−32.9	108.6	5
23 45.9	25.5	106.4	23 11.3	27.5	107.2	22 35.0	29.4	108.0	21 57.1	31.2	108.8	21 17.7	33.0	109.5	6
23 20.4	25.9	107.4	22 43.8	27.8	108.2	22 05.6	29.7	108.9	21 25.9	31.5	109.7	20 44.7	33.3	110.4	7
22 54.5	26.2	108.3	22 16.0	28.2	109.1	21 35.9	30.0	109.9	20 54.4	31.8	110.6	20 11.4	33.5	111.3	8
22 28.3	26.6	109.3	21 47.8	28.4	110.1	21 05.9	30.3	110.8	20 22.6	32.1	111.5	19 37.9	33.8	112.2	9
22 01.7	−26.9	110.3	21 19.4	−28.8	111.0	20 35.6	−30.6	111.7	19 50.5	−32.3	112.4	19 04.1	−34.0	113.1	10
21 34.8	27.3	111.2	20 50.6	29.1	112.0	20 05.0	30.8	112.7	19 18.2	32.6	113.3	18 30.1	34.3	113.9	11
21 07.5	27.6	112.2	20 21.5	29.4	112.9	19 34.2	31.2	113.6	18 45.6	32.9	114.2	17 55.8	34.5	114.8	12
20 39.9	27.8	113.1	19 52.1	29.7	113.8	19 03.0	31.4	114.5	18 12.7	33.1	115.1	17 21.3	34.7	115.7	13
20 12.1	28.2	114.1	19 22.4	29.9	114.7	18 31.6	31.7	115.4	17 39.6	33.3	116.0	16 46.6	35.0	116.5	14
19 43.9	−28.5	115.0	18 52.5	−30.2	115.7	17 59.9	−31.9	116.3	17 06.3	−33.6	116.8	16 11.6	−35.1	117.4	15
19 15.4	28.8	116.0	18 22.3	30.5	116.6	17 28.0	32.1	117.2	16 32.7	33.7	117.7	15 36.5	35.3	118.2	16
18 46.6	29.0	116.9	17 51.8	30.7	117.5	16 55.9	32.4	118.0	15 59.0	34.0	118.6	15 01.2	35.5	119.0	17
18 17.6	29.3	117.8	17 21.1	31.0	118.4	16 23.5	32.6	118.9	15 25.0	34.1	119.4	14 25.7	35.7	119.9	18
17 48.3	29.6	118.7	16 50.1	31.2	119.3	15 50.9	32.8	119.8	14 50.9	34.4	120.3	13 50.0	35.9	120.7	19
17 18.7	−29.8	119.6	16 18.9	−31.4	120.2	15 18.1	−33.0	120.7	14 16.5	−34.5	121.1	13 14.1	−36.0	121.5	20
16 48.9	30.0	120.6	15 47.5	31.7	121.1	14 45.1	33.2	121.5	13 42.0	34.7	122.0	12 38.1	36.1	122.4	21
16 18.9	30.3	121.5	15 15.8	31.8	121.9	14 11.9	33.3	122.4	13 07.3	34.9	122.8	12 02.0	36.3	123.2	22
15 48.6	30.5	122.4	14 44.0	32.1	122.8	13 38.6	33.6	123.2	12 32.4	35.0	123.6	11 25.7	36.5	124.0	23
15 18.1	30.7	123.3	14 11.9	32.2	123.7	13 05.0	33.7	124.1	11 57.4	35.1	124.5	10 49.2	36.5	124.8	24
14 47.4	−30.9	124.1	13 39.7	−32.4	124.6	12 31.3	−33.9	124.9	11 22.3	−35.3	125.3	10 12.7	−36.7	125.6	25
14 16.5	31.1	125.0	13 07.3	32.6	125.4	11 57.4	34.0	125.8	10 47.0	35.5	126.1	9 36.0	36.8	126.4	26
13 45.4	31.3	125.9	12 34.7	32.7	126.3	11 23.4	34.2	126.6	10 11.5	35.5	126.9	8 59.2	36.9	127.2	27
13 14.1	31.4	126.8	12 02.0	32.9	127.1	10 49.2	34.3	127.5	9 36.0	35.7	127.8	8 22.3	37.0	128.0	28
12 42.7	31.7	127.7	11 29.1	33.1	128.0	10 14.9	34.4	128.3	9 00.3	35.8	128.6	7 45.3	37.1	128.8	29

30°			32°			34°			36°			38°			Dec.
Hc	d	Z	Hc	d	Z	Hc	d	Z	Hc	d	Z	Hc	d	Z	
23 59.4	−33.0	104.9	23 27.7	−34.8	105.7	22 54.3	−36.5	106.6	22 19.3	−38.2	107.4	21 42.7	−39.8	108.1	0
23 26.4	33.3	105.8	22 52.9	35.1	106.6	22 17.8	36.9	107.4	21 41.1	38.5	108.2	21 02.9	40.1	108.9	1
22 53.1	33.6	106.7	22 17.8	35.4	107.5	21 40.9	37.1	108.3	21 02.6	38.8	109.0	20 22.8	40.3	109.7	2
22 19.5	34.0	107.6	21 42.4	35.7	108.4	21 03.8	37.3	109.1	20 23.8	38.9	109.8	19 42.5	40.6	110.5	3
21 45.5	34.1	108.5	21 06.7	35.9	109.2	20 26.5	37.6	110.0	19 44.9	39.2	110.6	19 01.9	40.7	111.3	4
21 11.4	−34.5	109.4	20 30.8	−36.1	110.1	19 48.9	−37.8	110.8	19 05.7	−39.4	111.4	18 21.2	−40.9	112.1	5
20 36.9	34.7	110.3	19 54.7	36.4	110.9	19 11.1	38.0	111.6	18 26.3	39.6	112.2	17 40.3	41.1	112.8	6
20 02.2	35.0	111.1	19 18.3	36.5	111.8	18 33.1	38.2	112.4	17 46.7	39.7	113.0	16 59.2	41.2	113.6	7
19 27.2	35.3	112.0	18 41.6	36.8	112.6	17 54.9	38.5	113.2	17 07.0	40.0	113.8	16 18.0	41.4	114.4	8
18 51.9	35.4	112.8	18 04.8	37.1	113.5	17 16.4	38.6	114.0	16 27.0	40.1	114.6	15 36.6	41.6	115.1	9
18 16.5	−35.7	113.7	17 27.7	−37.3	114.3	16 37.8	−38.8	114.8	15 46.9	−40.3	115.4	14 55.0	−41.7	115.9	10
17 40.8	35.9	114.5	16 50.4	37.4	115.1	15 59.0	39.0	115.6	15 06.6	40.4	116.1	14 13.3	41.8	116.6	11
17 04.9	36.1	115.4	16 13.0	37.7	115.9	15 20.0	39.1	116.4	14 26.2	40.6	116.9	13 31.5	42.0	117.3	12
16 28.8	36.3	116.2	15 35.3	37.8	116.7	14 40.9	39.3	117.2	13 45.6	40.7	117.7	12 49.5	42.1	118.1	13
15 52.5	36.5	117.0	14 57.5	38.0	117.5	14 01.6	39.5	118.0	13 04.9	40.9	118.4	12 07.4	42.1	118.8	14
15 16.0	−36.7	117.9	14 19.5	−38.2	118.3	13 22.1	−39.6	118.8	12 24.0	−41.0	119.2	11 25.2	−42.3	119.5	15
14 39.3	36.8	118.7	13 41.3	38.3	119.1	12 42.5	39.7	119.5	11 43.0	41.1	119.9	10 42.9	42.4	120.3	16
14 02.5	37.0	119.5	13 03.0	38.4	119.9	12 02.8	39.8	120.3	11 01.9	41.2	120.7	10 00.5	42.5	121.0	17
13 25.5	37.2	120.3	12 24.6	38.6	120.7	11 23.0	40.0	121.1	10 20.7	41.3	121.4	9 18.0	42.6	121.7	18
12 48.3	37.3	121.1	11 46.0	38.7	121.5	10 43.0	40.1	121.8	9 39.4	41.4	122.1	8 35.4	42.7	122.4	19
12 11.0	−37.4	121.9	11 07.3	−38.9	122.3	10 02.9	−40.2	122.6	8 58.0	−41.4	122.9	7 52.7	−42.7	123.1	20
11 33.6	37.6	122.7	10 28.4	38.9	123.0	9 22.7	40.2	123.3	8 16.6	41.6	123.6	7 10.0	42.8	123.8	21
10 56.0	37.7	123.5	9 49.5	39.1	123.8	8 42.5	40.4	124.1	7 35.0	41.6	124.3	6 27.2	42.9	124.5	22
10 18.3	37.8	124.3	9 10.4	39.1	124.6	8 02.1	40.5	124.8	6 53.4	41.7	125.0	5 44.3	42.9	125.2	23
9 40.5	37.9	125.1	8 31.3	39.3	125.4	7 21.6	40.5	125.6	6 11.7	41.8	125.8	5 01.4	43.0	125.9	24
9 02.6	−38.1	125.9	7 52.0	−39.3	126.1	6 41.1	−40.6	126.3	5 29.9	−41.8	126.5	4 18.4	−43.0	126.6	25
8 24.5	38.1	126.7	7 12.7	39.4	126.9	6 00.5	40.6	127.1	4 48.1	41.9	127.2	3 35.4	43.0	127.3	26
7 46.4	38.2	127.4	6 33.3	39.4	127.6	5 19.9	40.7	127.8	4 06.2	41.9	127.9	2 52.4	43.1	128.0	27
7 08.2	38.2	128.2	5 53.9	39.6	128.4	4 39.2	40.7	128.5	3 24.3	41.9	128.7	2 09.3	43.1	128.7	28
6 30.0	38.4	129.0	5 14.3	39.6	129.2	3 58.5	40.8	129.3	2 42.4	41.9	129.4	1 26.2	43.0	129.4	29

Dec.	40° Hc	d	Z	42° Hc	d	Z	44° Hc	d	Z	46° Hc	d	Z	48° Hc	d	Z
0	21 04.7	+41.2	108.9	20 25.1	+42.8	109.6	19 44.2	+44.2	110.3	19 02.0	+45.6	110.9	18 18.5	+46.9	111.6
1	21 45.9	41.0	108.1	21 07.9	42.5	108.8	20 28.4	44.1	109.6	19 47.6	45.4	110.2	19 05.4	46.8	110.9
2	22 26.9	40.8	107.3	21 50.4	42.4	108.1	21 12.5	43.8	108.8	20 33.0	45.3	109.5	19 52.2	46.6	110.2
3	23 07.7	40.5	106.5	22 32.8	42.1	107.3	21 56.3	43.6	108.1	21 18.3	45.0	108.8	20 38.8	46.4	109.6
4	23 48.2	40.3	105.7	23 14.9	41.9	106.5	22 39.9	43.4	107.3	22 03.3	44.9	108.1	21 25.2	46.3	108.9
5	24 28.5	+40.0	104.9	23 56.8	+41.6	105.8	23 23.3	+43.2	106.5	22 48.2	+44.7	107.4	22 11.5	+46.1	108.2
6	25 08.5	39.7	104.1	24 38.4	41.4	105.0	24 06.5	43.0	105.8	23 32.9	44.5	106.7	22 57.6	46.0	107.5
7	25 48.2	39.5	103.2	25 19.8	41.1	104.2	24 49.5	42.7	105.1	24 17.4	44.3	106.0	23 43.6	45.7	106.8
8	26 27.7	39.1	102.4	26 00.9	40.9	103.4	25 32.2	42.5	104.3	25 01.7	44.0	105.2	24 29.3	45.5	106.1
9	27 06.8	38.9	101.6	26 41.8	40.6	102.5	26 14.7	42.3	103.5	25 45.7	43.8	104.5	25 14.8	45.4	105.4
10	27 45.7	+38.5	100.7	27 22.4	+40.2	101.7	26 57.0	+41.9	102.7	26 29.5	+43.6	103.7	26 00.2	+45.1	104.7
11	28 24.2	38.2	99.8	28 02.6	40.0	100.9	27 38.9	41.7	101.9	27 13.1	43.3	102.9	26 45.3	44.8	103.9
12	29 02.4	37.8	98.9	28 42.6	39.7	100.0	28 20.6	41.4	101.1	27 56.4	43.1	102.1	27 30.1	44.7	103.2
13	29 40.2	37.5	98.1	29 22.3	39.3	99.2	29 02.0	41.1	100.3	28 39.5	42.7	101.4	28 14.8	44.3	102.4
14	30 17.7	37.1	97.2	30 01.6	39.0	98.3	29 43.1	40.7	99.4	29 22.2	42.5	100.6	28 59.1	44.1	101.7
15	30 54.8	+36.7	96.2	30 40.6	+38.6	97.4	30 23.8	+40.5	98.6	30 04.7	+42.2	99.7	29 43.2	+43.9	100.9
16	31 31.5	36.4	95.3	31 19.2	38.2	96.5	31 04.3	40.0	97.7	30 46.9	41.8	98.9	30 27.1	43.5	100.1
17	32 07.9	35.8	94.4	31 57.4	37.8	95.6	31 44.3	39.8	96.9	31 28.7	41.6	98.1	31 10.6	43.3	99.3
18	32 43.7	35.5	93.4	32 35.2	37.5	94.7	32 24.1	39.3	96.0	32 10.3	41.1	97.2	31 53.9	42.9	98.5
19	33 19.2	35.0	92.5	33 12.7	37.0	93.8	33 03.4	39.0	95.1	32 51.4	40.9	96.4	32 36.8	42.6	97.6
20	33 54.2	+34.5	91.5	33 49.7	+36.6	92.8	33 42.4	+38.5	94.2	33 32.3	+40.4	95.5	33 19.4	+42.3	96.8
21	34 28.7	34.1	90.5	34 26.3	36.1	91.9	34 20.9	38.1	93.2	34 12.7	40.0	94.6	34 01.7	41.9	96.0
22	35 02.8	33.5	89.5	35 02.4	35.6	90.9	34 59.0	37.7	92.3	34 52.7	39.7	93.7	34 43.6	41.5	95.1
23	35 36.3	33.1	88.5	35 38.0	35.3	89.9	35 36.7	37.2	91.3	35 32.4	39.2	92.8	35 25.1	41.1	94.2
24	36 09.4	32.5	87.5	36 13.2	34.6	88.9	36 13.9	36.8	90.4	36 11.6	38.8	91.8	36 06.2	40.7	93.3
25	36 41.9	+31.9	86.4	36 47.8	+34.2	87.9	36 50.7	+36.2	89.4	36 50.4	+38.3	90.9	36 46.9	+40.3	92.4
26	37 13.8	31.4	85.3	37 22.0	33.5	86.9	37 26.9	35.8	88.4	37 28.7	37.8	89.9	37 27.2	39.9	91.5
27	37 45.2	30.7	84.3	37 55.5	33.1	85.8	38 02.7	35.2	87.4	38 06.5	37.3	88.9	38 07.1	39.4	90.5
28	38 15.9	30.2	83.2	38 28.6	32.4	84.8	38 37.9	34.6	86.3	38 43.8	36.8	87.9	38 46.5	38.9	89.6
29	38 46.1	29.5	82.1	39 01.0	31.8	83.7	39 12.5	34.1	85.3	39 20.6	36.3	86.9	39 25.4	38.4	88.6

Dec.	50° Hc	d	Z	52° Hc	d	Z	54° Hc	d	Z	56° Hc	d	Z	58° Hc	d	Z
0	17 33.8	+48.2	112.2	16 48.0	+49.4	112.7	16 01.1	+50.5	113.3	15 13.2	+51.5	113.8	14 24.3	+52.5	114.3
1	18 22.0	48.0	111.5	17 37.4	49.2	112.1	16 51.6	50.3	112.7	16 04.7	51.4	113.3	15 16.8	52.5	113.8
2	19 10.0	47.9	110.9	18 26.6	49.1	111.5	17 41.9	50.3	112.1	16 56.1	51.4	112.7	16 09.3	52.3	113.3
3	19 57.9	47.8	110.3	19 15.7	49.0	110.9	18 32.2	50.2	111.6	17 47.5	51.3	112.2	17 01.6	52.3	112.8
4	20 45.7	47.6	109.6	20 04.7	48.8	110.3	19 22.4	50.0	111.0	18 38.7	51.2	111.6	17 53.9	52.3	112.2
5	21 33.3	+47.4	109.0	20 53.5	+48.8	109.7	20 12.4	+49.9	110.4	19 29.9	+51.1	111.1	18 46.1	+52.1	111.7
6	22 20.7	47.3	108.3	21 42.3	48.6	109.1	21 02.3	49.8	109.8	20 21.0	50.9	110.5	19 38.2	52.1	111.2
7	23 08.0	47.1	107.6	22 30.9	48.4	108.4	21 52.1	49.7	109.2	21 11.9	50.9	110.0	20 30.3	51.9	110.7
8	23 55.1	47.0	107.0	23 19.3	48.3	107.8	22 41.8	49.6	108.6	22 02.8	50.7	109.4	21 22.2	51.8	110.1
9	24 42.1	46.7	106.3	24 07.6	48.1	107.1	23 31.4	49.3	108.0	22 53.5	50.6	108.8	22 14.0	51.7	109.6
10	25 28.8	+46.6	105.6	24 55.7	+47.9	106.5	24 20.7	+49.3	107.4	23 44.1	+50.4	108.2	23 05.7	+51.6	109.0
11	26 15.4	46.4	104.9	25 43.6	47.8	105.8	25 10.0	49.0	106.7	24 34.5	50.3	107.6	23 57.3	51.5	108.5
12	27 01.8	46.1	104.2	26 31.4	47.5	105.2	25 59.0	49.0	106.1	25 24.8	50.2	107.0	24 48.8	51.4	107.9
13	27 47.9	45.9	103.5	27 18.9	47.4	104.5	26 48.0	48.7	105.5	26 15.0	50.0	106.4	25 40.2	51.2	107.3
14	28 33.8	45.7	102.7	28 06.3	47.1	103.8	27 36.7	48.5	104.8	27 05.0	49.9	105.8	26 31.4	51.0	106.8
15	29 19.5	+45.4	102.0	28 53.4	+47.0	103.1	28 25.2	+48.4	104.1	27 54.9	+49.6	105.2	27 22.4	+51.0	106.2
16	30 04.9	45.1	101.2	29 40.4	46.6	102.4	29 13.6	48.1	103.5	28 44.5	49.5	104.5	28 13.4	50.7	105.6
17	30 50.0	44.9	100.5	30 27.0	46.5	101.6	30 01.7	47.9	102.8	29 34.0	49.3	103.9	29 04.1	50.6	105.0
18	31 34.9	44.6	99.7	31 13.5	46.2	100.9	30 49.6	47.7	102.1	30 23.3	49.1	103.2	29 54.7	50.4	104.4
19	32 19.5	44.3	98.9	31 59.7	45.9	100.1	31 37.3	47.4	101.4	31 12.4	48.9	102.6	30 45.1	50.3	103.7
20	33 03.8	+44.0	98.1	32 45.6	+45.6	99.4	32 24.7	+47.2	100.6	32 01.3	+48.7	101.9	31 35.4	+50.0	103.1
21	33 47.8	43.7	97.3	33 31.2	45.4	98.6	33 11.9	47.0	99.9	32 50.0	48.4	101.2	32 25.4	49.8	102.4
22	34 31.5	43.3	96.5	34 16.6	45.0	97.8	33 58.9	46.9	99.2	33 38.4	48.2	100.5	33 15.2	49.7	101.8
23	35 14.8	43.0	95.6	35 01.6	44.7	97.0	34 45.5	46.4	98.4	34 26.6	47.9	99.8	34 04.9	49.4	101.1
24	35 57.8	42.6	94.8	35 46.3	44.4	96.2	35 31.9	46.0	97.6	35 14.5	47.7	99.0	34 54.3	49.1	100.4
25	36 40.4	+42.2	93.9	36 30.7	+44.0	95.4	36 17.9	+45.8	96.8	36 02.2	+47.3	98.3	35 43.4	+48.9	99.7
26	37 22.6	41.7	93.0	37 14.7	43.6	94.5	37 03.7	45.4	96.0	36 49.5	47.1	97.5	36 32.3	48.7	99.0
27	38 04.3	41.4	92.1	37 58.3	43.3	93.6	37 49.1	45.0	95.2	37 36.6	46.8	96.7	37 21.0	48.3	98.3
28	38 45.7	40.9	91.2	38 41.6	42.8	92.8	38 34.1	44.7	94.4	38 23.4	46.4	95.9	38 09.3	48.1	97.5
29	39 26.6	40.5	90.2	39 24.4	42.5	91.9	39 18.8	44.3	93.5	39 09.8	46.1	95.1	38 57.4	47.8	96.7

40° Hc	d	Z	42° Hc	d	Z	44° Hc	d	Z	46° Hc	d	Z	48° Hc	d	Z	Dec.
21 04.7	−41.5	108.9	20 25.1	−42.9	109.6	19 44.2	−44.3	110.3	19 02.0	−45.7	110.9	18 18.5	−47.0	111.6	0
20 23.2	41.6	109.6	19 42.2	43.1	110.3	18 59.9	44.5	111.0	18 16.3	45.9	111.6	17 31.5	47.2	112.2	1
19 41.6	41.8	110.4	18 59.1	43.3	111.1	18 15.4	44.7	111.7	17 30.4	46.0	112.3	16 44.3	47.2	112.9	2
18 59.8	42.1	111.2	18 15.8	43.4	111.8	17 30.7	44.9	112.4	16 44.4	46.1	113.0	15 57.1	47.4	113.5	3
18 17.7	42.2	111.9	17 32.4	43.7	112.5	16 45.8	44.9	113.1	15 58.3	46.3	113.6	15 09.7	47.5	114.1	4
17 35.5	−42.3	112.7	16 48.7	−43.7	113.2	16 00.9	−45.1	113.8	15 12.0	−46.4	114.3	14 22.2	−47.6	114.8	5
16 53.2	42.5	113.4	16 05.0	43.9	114.0	15 15.8	45.3	114.5	14 25.6	46.5	114.9	13 34.6	47.7	115.4	6
16 10.7	42.7	114.1	15 21.1	44.0	114.7	14 30.5	45.3	115.1	13 39.1	46.6	115.6	12 46.9	47.8	116.0	7
15 28.0	42.8	114.9	14 37.1	44.2	115.4	13 45.2	45.6	115.8	12 52.5	46.6	116.2	11 59.1	47.9	116.6	8
14 45.2	43.0	115.6	13 52.9	44.3	116.1	12 59.8	45.6	116.5	12 05.9	46.8	116.9	11 11.2	47.9	117.3	9
14 02.2	−43.0	116.3	13 08.6	−44.4	116.8	12 14.2	−45.6	117.2	11 19.1	−46.9	117.5	10 23.3	−48.0	117.9	10
13 19.2	43.2	117.0	12 24.2	44.5	117.4	11 28.6	45.8	117.8	10 32.2	46.9	118.2	9 35.3	48.1	118.5	11
12 36.0	43.3	117.8	11 39.7	44.6	118.1	10 42.8	45.8	118.5	9 45.3	47.0	118.8	8 47.2	48.1	119.1	12
11 52.7	43.5	118.5	10 55.1	44.6	118.8	9 57.0	45.9	119.1	8 58.3	47.1	119.4	7 59.1	48.2	119.7	13
11 09.2	43.5	119.2	10 10.5	44.8	119.5	9 11.1	46.0	119.8	8 11.2	47.1	120.1	7 11.0	48.2	120.3	14
10 25.7	−43.6	119.9	9 25.7	−44.8	120.2	8 25.1	−46.0	120.4	7 24.1	−47.1	120.7	6 22.7	−48.3	120.9	15
9 42.1	43.7	120.6	8 40.9	45.0	120.8	7 39.1	46.1	121.1	6 37.0	47.3	121.3	5 34.4	48.3	121.5	16
8 58.4	43.7	121.3	7 55.9	44.9	121.5	6 53.0	46.1	121.7	5 49.7	47.2	121.9	4 46.1	48.3	122.1	17
8 14.7	43.8	122.0	7 11.0	45.1	122.2	6 06.9	46.2	122.4	5 02.5	47.3	122.5	3 57.8	48.4	122.7	18
7 30.9	43.9	122.6	6 25.9	45.0	122.8	5 20.7	46.2	123.0	4 15.2	47.3	123.2	3 09.4	48.3	123.3	19
6 47.0	−44.0	123.3	5 40.9	−45.2	123.5	4 34.5	−46.3	123.7	3 27.9	−47.4	123.8	2 21.1	−48.4	123.9	20
6 03.0	44.0	124.0	4 55.7	45.1	124.2	3 48.2	46.3	124.3	2 40.5	47.4	124.4	1 32.7	48.4	124.5	21
5 19.0	44.1	124.7	4 10.6	45.3	124.8	3 01.9	46.3	124.9	1 53.1	47.3	125.0	0 44.3	−48.4	125.0	22
4 34.9	44.1	125.4	3 25.4	45.3	125.5	2 15.6	46.3	125.6	1 05.8	47.4	125.6	0 04.1	+48.4	54.4	23
3 50.8	44.1	126.1	2 40.1	45.2	126.1	1 29.3	46.3	126.2	0 18.4	−47.4	126.2	0 52.5	48.5	53.8	24
3 06.7	−44.1	126.7	1 54.9	−45.3	126.8	0 43.0	−46.4	126.8	0 29.0	+47.4	53.2	1 41.0	+48.3	53.2	25
2 22.6	44.2	127.4	1 09.6	45.3	127.5	0 03.4	+46.3	52.5	1 16.4	47.4	52.5	2 29.3	48.4	52.6	26
1 38.4	44.2	128.1	0 24.3	−45.2	128.1	0 49.7	46.4	51.9	2 03.8	47.3	51.9	3 17.7	48.4	52.0	27
0 54.2	44.2	128.8	0 20.9	+45.3	51.2	1 36.1	46.3	51.3	2 51.1	47.4	51.3	4 06.1	48.3	51.4	28
0 10.0	−44.2	129.4	1 06.2	45.3	50.6	2 22.4	46.3	50.6	3 38.5	47.3	50.7	4 54.4	48.3	50.8	29

50° Hc	d	Z	52° Hc	d	Z	54° Hc	d	Z	56° Hc	d	Z	58° Hc	d	Z	Dec.
17 33.8	−48.2	112.2	16 48.0	−49.4	112.7	16 01.1	−50.5	113.3	15 13.2	−51.6	113.8	14 24.3	−52.5	114.3	0
16 45.6	48.4	112.8	15 58.6	49.6	113.3	15 10.6	50.7	113.8	14 21.6	51.6	114.3	13 31.8	52.7	114.8	1
15 57.2	48.5	113.4	15 09.0	49.6	113.9	14 19.9	50.7	114.4	13 30.0	51.8	114.8	12 39.1	52.6	115.3	2
15 08.7	48.6	114.0	14 19.4	49.7	114.5	13 29.2	50.7	114.9	12 38.2	51.7	115.4	11 46.5	52.9	115.8	3
14 20.1	48.6	114.6	13 29.7	49.8	115.1	12 38.5	50.9	115.5	11 46.5	51.9	115.9	10 53.7	52.7	116.2	4
13 31.5	−48.8	115.2	12 39.9	−49.8	115.6	11 47.6	−50.9	116.0	10 54.6	−51.9	116.4	10 01.0	−52.9	116.7	5
12 42.7	48.8	115.8	11 50.1	50.0	116.2	10 56.7	50.9	116.6	10 02.7	51.9	116.9	9 08.1	52.9	117.2	6
11 53.9	48.9	116.4	11 00.1	50.0	116.8	10 05.8	51.1	117.1	9 10.8	52.0	117.4	8 15.3	52.9	117.7	7
11 04.9	48.9	117.0	10 10.1	50.0	117.3	9 14.7	51.0	117.6	8 18.8	52.0	117.9	7 22.4	52.9	118.2	8
10 16.0	49.1	117.6	9 20.1	50.1	117.9	8 23.7	51.1	118.2	7 26.8	52.0	118.4	6 29.5	53.0	118.6	9
9 26.9	−49.1	118.2	8 30.0	−50.2	118.5	7 32.6	−51.2	118.7	6 34.8	−52.1	118.9	5 36.5	−52.9	119.1	10
8 37.8	49.1	118.8	7 39.8	50.1	119.0	6 41.4	51.1	119.2	5 42.7	52.1	119.4	4 43.6	53.0	119.6	11
7 48.7	49.2	119.3	6 49.7	50.3	119.6	5 50.3	51.2	119.8	4 50.6	52.2	119.9	3 50.6	53.0	120.0	12
6 59.5	49.3	119.9	5 59.4	50.2	120.1	4 59.1	51.3	120.3	3 58.4	52.1	120.4	2 57.6	53.0	120.5	13
6 10.2	49.3	120.5	5 09.2	50.3	120.7	4 07.8	51.2	120.8	3 06.3	52.2	120.9	2 04.6	53.0	121.0	14
5 20.9	−49.3	121.1	4 18.9	−50.3	121.2	3 16.6	−51.3	121.3	2 14.1	−52.1	121.4	1 11.6	−53.1	121.5	15
4 31.6	49.3	121.6	3 28.6	50.4	121.8	2 25.3	51.2	121.8	1 22.0	52.2	121.9	0 18.5	−53.0	121.9	16
3 42.3	49.4	122.2	2 38.2	50.3	122.3	1 34.1	51.3	122.4	0 29.8	−52.2	122.4	0 34.5	+53.0	57.6	17
2 52.9	49.4	122.8	1 47.9	50.4	122.8	0 42.8	−51.3	122.9	0 22.4	+52.2	57.1	1 27.5	53.0	57.1	18
2 03.5	49.3	123.3	0 57.5	50.3	123.4	0 08.5	+51.3	56.6	1 14.6	52.1	56.6	2 20.5	53.0	56.7	19
1 14.2	−49.4	123.9	0 07.2	−50.4	123.9	0 59.8	+51.3	56.1	2 06.7	+52.2	56.1	3 13.5	+53.0	56.2	20
0 24.8	−49.4	124.5	0 43.2	+50.3	55.5	1 51.1	51.3	55.6	2 58.9	52.1	55.6	4 06.5	53.0	55.7	21
0 24.6	+49.4	55.0	1 33.5	50.4	55.0	2 42.3	51.3	55.0	3 51.0	52.2	55.1	4 59.5	53.0	55.3	22
1 14.0	49.4	54.4	2 23.9	50.3	54.4	3 33.6	51.2	54.5	4 43.2	52.1	54.6	5 52.5	52.9	54.8	23
2 03.4	49.4	53.8	3 14.2	50.3	53.8	4 24.8	51.3	53.9	5 35.3	52.1	54.1	6 45.4	52.9	54.3	24
2 52.8	+49.4	53.2	4 04.5	+50.3	53.3	5 16.1	+51.2	53.5	6 27.4	+52.0	53.6	7 38.3	+52.9	53.8	25
3 42.2	49.3	52.7	4 54.8	50.3	52.8	6 07.3	51.1	53.0	7 19.4	52.0	53.1	8 31.2	52.8	53.4	26
4 31.5	49.3	52.1	5 45.1	50.2	52.3	6 58.4	51.2	52.4	8 11.4	52.0	52.6	9 24.0	52.8	52.9	27
5 20.8	49.3	51.5	6 35.3	50.2	51.7	7 49.6	51.0	51.9	9 03.4	51.9	52.1	10 16.8	52.8	52.4	28
6 10.1	49.2	51.0	7 25.5	50.2	51.1	8 40.6	51.1	51.4	9 55.3	51.9	51.6	11 09.6	52.7	51.9	29

Dec.	0° Hc	d	Z	2° Hc	d	Z	4° Hc	d	Z	6° Hc	d	Z	8° Hc	d	Z
°	° ′	′	°	° ′	′	°	° ′	′	°	° ′	′	°	° ′	′	°
0	26 00.0	− 0.3	90.0	25 59.0	+ 2.1	91.0	25 55.9	+ 4.4	91.9	25 50.8	+ 6.7	92.9	25 43.7	+ 9.0	93.9
1	25 59.7	0.7	88.9	26 01.1	1.5	89.9	26 00.3	3.9	90.8	25 57.5	6.3	91.8	25 52.7	8.5	92.8
2	25 59.0	1.3	87.8	26 02.6	1.1	88.8	26 04.2	3.4	89.7	26 03.8	5.7	90.7	26 01.2	8.1	91.7
3	25 57.7	1.8	86.7	26 03.7	+ 0.5	87.6	26 07.6	2.9	88.6	26 09.5	5.2	89.6	26 09.3	7.5	90.6
4	25 55.9	2.3	85.6	26 04.2	0.0	86.5	26 10.5	2.3	87.5	26 14.7	4.6	88.5	26 16.8	7.0	89.5
5	25 53.6	− 2.8	84.4	26 04.2	− 0.4	85.4	26 12.8	+ 1.9	86.4	26 19.3	+ 4.2	87.4	26 23.8	+ 6.5	88.4
6	25 50.8	3.3	83.3	26 03.8	1.0	84.3	26 14.7	1.3	85.3	26 23.5	3.7	86.3	26 30.3	6.0	87.3
7	25 47.5	3.8	82.2	26 02.8	1.6	83.2	26 16.0	0.8	84.2	26 27.2	3.1	85.1	26 36.3	5.4	86.1
8	25 43.7	4.3	81.1	26 01.2	2.0	82.1	26 16.8	+ 0.3	83.0	26 30.3	2.6	84.0	26 41.7	5.0	85.0
9	25 39.4	4.8	80.0	25 59.2	2.5	81.0	26 17.1	− 0.2	81.9	26 32.9	2.1	82.9	26 46.7	4.4	83.9
10	25 34.6	− 5.3	78.9	25 56.7	− 3.0	79.8	26 16.9	− 0.8	80.8	26 35.0	+ 1.6	81.8	26 51.1	+ 3.9	82.8
11	25 29.3	5.8	77.8	25 53.7	3.6	78.7	26 16.1	1.2	79.7	26 36.6	1.0	80.7	26 55.0	3.3	81.7
12	25 23.5	6.3	76.7	25 50.1	4.0	77.6	26 14.9	1.8	78.6	26 37.6	+ 0.5	79.6	26 58.3	2.8	80.6
13	25 17.2	6.8	75.6	25 46.1	4.6	76.5	26 13.1	2.3	77.5	26 38.1	0.0	78.4	27 01.1	2.3	79.4
14	25 10.4	7.3	74.5	25 41.5	5.0	75.4	26 10.8	2.8	76.4	26 38.1	− 0.5	77.3	27 03.4	1.8	78.3
15	25 03.1	− 7.8	73.4	25 36.5	− 5.6	74.3	26 08.0	− 3.3	75.2	26 37.6	− 1.1	76.2	27 05.2	+ 1.2	77.2
16	24 55.3	8.2	72.3	25 30.9	6.0	73.2	26 04.7	3.9	74.1	26 36.5	1.6	75.1	27 06.4	0.7	76.1
17	24 47.1	8.7	71.2	25 24.9	6.6	72.1	26 00.8	4.3	73.0	26 34.9	2.1	74.0	27 07.1	+ 0.1	74.9
18	24 38.4	9.2	70.1	25 18.3	7.0	71.0	25 56.5	4.8	71.9	26 32.8	2.6	72.9	27 07.2	− 0.4	73.8
19	24 29.2	9.6	69.0	25 11.3	7.5	69.9	25 51.7	5.4	70.8	26 30.2	3.2	71.7	27 06.8	0.9	72.7
20	24 19.6	− 10.1	68.0	25 03.8	− 8.0	68.8	25 46.3	− 5.8	69.7	26 27.0	− 3.6	70.6	27 05.9	− 1.4	71.6
21	24 09.5	10.6	66.9	24 55.8	8.5	67.7	25 40.5	6.4	68.6	26 23.4	4.2	69.5	27 04.5	2.0	70.5
22	23 58.9	11.0	65.8	24 47.3	8.9	66.6	25 34.1	6.8	67.5	26 19.2	4.7	68.4	27 02.5	2.6	69.3
23	23 47.9	11.4	64.7	24 38.4	9.4	65.5	25 27.3	7.4	66.4	26 14.5	5.2	67.3	26 59.9	3.0	68.2
24	23 36.5	11.9	63.6	24 29.0	9.9	64.5	25 19.9	7.8	65.3	26 09.3	5.8	66.2	26 56.9	3.6	67.1
25	23 24.6	− 12.4	62.6	24 19.1	− 10.3	63.4	25 12.1	− 8.3	64.2	26 03.5	− 6.2	65.1	26 53.3	− 4.1	66.0
26	23 12.2	12.7	61.5	24 08.8	10.8	62.3	25 03.8	8.8	63.1	25 57.3	6.7	64.0	26 49.2	4.7	64.9
27	22 59.5	13.2	60.5	23 58.0	11.3	61.2	24 55.0	9.2	62.0	25 50.6	7.3	62.9	26 44.5	5.2	63.7
28	22 46.3	13.6	59.4	23 46.7	11.7	60.1	24 45.8	9.8	60.9	25 43.3	7.7	61.7	26 39.3	5.6	62.6
29	22 32.7	14.0	58.3	23 35.0	12.1	59.1	24 36.0	10.2	59.8	25 35.6	8.2	60.6	26 33.7	6.3	61.5

Dec.	10° Hc	d	Z	12° Hc	d	Z	14° Hc	d	Z	16° Hc	d	Z	18° Hc	d	Z
°	° ′	′	°	° ′	′	°	° ′	′	°	° ′	′	°	° ′	′	°
0	25 34.6	+ 11.3	94.8	25 23.5	+ 13.5	95.8	25 10.4	+ 15.8	96.7	24 55.3	+ 18.1	97.7	24 38.4	+ 20.2	98.6
1	25 45.9	10.8	93.8	25 37.0	13.1	94.7	25 26.2	15.3	95.7	25 13.4	17.5	96.6	24 58.6	19.7	97.5
2	25 56.7	10.3	92.7	25 50.1	12.6	93.6	25 41.5	14.9	94.6	25 30.9	17.1	95.5	25 18.3	19.3	96.5
3	26 07.0	9.9	91.6	26 02.7	12.2	92.5	25 56.4	14.4	93.5	25 48.0	16.7	94.5	25 37.6	18.9	95.4
4	26 16.9	9.3	90.5	26 14.9	11.6	91.4	26 10.8	13.9	92.4	26 04.7	16.1	93.4	25 56.5	18.4	94.4
5	26 26.2	+ 8.8	89.4	26 26.5	+ 11.1	90.4	26 24.7	+ 13.4	91.3	26 20.8	+ 15.7	92.3	26 14.9	+ 17.9	93.3
6	26 35.0	8.3	88.3	26 37.6	10.6	89.3	26 38.1	12.9	90.3	26 36.5	15.2	91.3	26 32.8	17.5	92.3
7	26 43.3	7.8	87.1	26 48.2	10.1	88.2	26 51.0	12.4	89.2	26 51.7	14.7	90.2	26 50.3	16.9	91.2
8	26 51.1	7.2	86.0	26 58.3	9.6	87.0	27 03.4	11.9	88.1	27 06.4	14.2	89.1	27 07.2	16.5	90.1
9	26 58.3	6.8	84.9	27 07.9	9.1	85.9	27 15.3	11.4	87.0	27 20.6	13.7	88.0	27 23.7	16.0	89.0
10	27 05.1	+ 6.2	83.8	27 17.0	+ 8.5	84.8	27 26.7	+ 10.9	85.9	27 34.3	+ 13.1	86.9	27 39.7	+ 15.4	87.9
11	27 11.3	5.7	82.7	27 25.5	8.0	83.7	27 37.6	10.3	84.8	27 47.4	12.7	85.8	27 55.1	15.0	86.9
12	27 17.0	5.1	81.6	27 33.5	7.5	82.6	27 47.9	9.8	83.6	28 00.1	12.1	84.7	28 10.1	14.4	85.8
13	27 22.1	4.6	80.4	27 41.0	6.9	81.5	27 57.7	9.2	82.5	28 12.2	11.5	83.6	28 24.5	13.8	84.7
14	27 26.7	4.1	79.3	27 47.9	6.3	80.4	28 06.9	8.7	81.4	28 23.7	11.0	82.5	28 38.3	13.4	83.5
15	27 30.8	+ 3.5	78.2	27 54.2	+ 5.9	79.2	28 15.6	+ 8.1	80.3	28 34.7	+ 10.5	81.3	28 51.7	+ 12.8	82.4
16	27 34.3	2.9	77.1	28 00.1	5.2	78.1	28 23.7	7.6	79.2	28 45.2	9.9	80.2	29 04.5	12.2	81.3
17	27 37.2	2.5	75.9	28 05.3	4.8	77.0	28 31.3	7.0	78.0	28 55.1	9.4	79.1	29 16.7	11.6	80.2
18	27 39.7	1.8	74.8	28 10.1	4.1	75.8	28 38.3	6.5	76.9	29 04.5	8.7	78.0	29 28.3	11.1	79.1
19	27 41.5	1.4	73.7	28 14.2	3.6	74.7	28 44.8	5.9	75.8	29 13.2	8.2	76.8	29 39.4	10.5	77.9
20	27 42.9	+ 0.8	72.6	28 17.8	+ 3.1	73.5	28 50.7	+ 5.3	74.6	29 21.4	+ 7.6	75.7	29 49.9	+ 10.0	76.8
21	27 43.7	+ 0.2	71.4	28 20.9	2.4	72.4	28 56.0	4.8	73.5	29 29.0	7.1	74.6	29 59.9	9.3	75.7
22	27 43.9	− 0.3	70.3	28 23.3	1.9	71.3	29 00.8	4.1	72.4	29 36.1	6.4	73.4	30 09.2	8.8	74.5
23	27 43.6	0.9	69.2	28 25.2	1.4	70.2	29 04.9	3.6	71.2	29 42.5	5.9	72.3	30 18.0	8.1	73.4
24	27 42.7	1.4	68.0	28 26.6	0.8	69.0	29 08.5	3.0	70.1	29 48.4	5.2	71.1	30 26.1	7.5	72.2
25	27 41.3	− 2.0	66.9	28 27.4	+ 0.2	67.9	29 11.5	+ 2.4	68.9	29 53.6	+ 4.7	70.0	30 33.6	+ 7.0	71.1
26	27 39.3	2.5	65.8	28 27.6	− 0.4	66.8	29 13.9	1.9	67.8	29 58.3	4.1	68.8	30 40.6	6.3	69.9
27	27 36.8	3.1	64.7	28 27.2	0.9	65.6	29 15.8	1.2	66.6	30 02.4	3.4	67.7	30 46.9	5.7	68.8
28	27 33.7	3.6	63.5	28 26.3	1.5	64.5	29 17.0	0.7	65.5	30 05.8	2.9	66.5	30 52.6	5.1	67.6
29	27 30.1	4.2	62.4	28 24.8	2.1	63.4	29 17.7	+ 0.1	64.3	30 08.7	2.2	65.4	30 57.7	4.4	66.5

0° Hc	d	Z	2° Hc	d	Z	4° Hc	d	Z	6° Hc	d	Z	8° Hc	d	Z	Dec.
26 00.0	- 0.3	90.0	25 59.0	- 2.6	91.0	25 55.9	- 4.9	91.9	25 50.8	- 7.2	92.9	25 43.7	- 9.5	93.9	0
25 59.7	0.7	91.1	25 56.4	3.1	92.1	25 51.0	5.4	93.1	25 43.6	7.7	94.0	25 34.2	10.0	95.0	1
25 59.0	1.3	92.2	25 53.3	3.6	93.2	25 45.6	5.9	94.2	25 35.9	8.2	95.1	25 24.2	10.5	96.1	2
25 57.7	1.8	93.3	25 49.7	4.1	94.3	25 39.7	6.4	95.3	25 27.7	8.7	96.2	25 13.7	11.0	97.2	3
25 55.9	2.3	94.4	25 45.6	4.6	95.4	25 33.3	6.9	96.4	25 19.0	9.2	97.3	25 02.7	11.4	98.2	4
25 53.6	- 2.8	95.6	25 41.0	- 5.1	96.5	25 26.4	- 7.4	97.5	25 09.8	- 9.7	98.4	24 51.3	-11.9	99.3	5
25 50.8	3.3	96.7	25 35.9	5.6	97.6	25 19.0	7.9	98.6	25 00.1	10.1	99.5	24 39.4	12.4	100.4	6
25 47.5	3.8	97.8	25 30.3	6.1	98.7	25 11.1	8.4	99.7	24 50.0	10.6	100.6	24 27.0	12.8	101.5	7
25 43.7	4.3	98.9	25 24.2	6.6	99.8	25 02.7	8.8	100.8	24 39.4	11.1	101.7	24 14.2	13.3	102.6	8
25 39.4	4.8	100.0	25 17.6	7.1	100.9	24 53.9	9.3	101.8	24 28.3	11.5	102.7	24 00.9	13.7	103.6	9
25 34.6	- 5.3	101.1	25 10.5	- 7.6	102.0	24 44.6	- 9.8	102.9	24 16.8	-12.0	103.8	23 47.2	-14.1	104.7	10
25 29.3	5.8	102.2	25 02.9	8.0	103.1	24 34.8	10.3	104.0	24 04.8	12.4	104.9	23 33.1	14.6	105.8	11
25 23.5	6.3	103.3	24 54.9	8.5	104.2	24 24.5	10.7	105.1	23 52.4	12.9	106.0	23 18.5	15.0	106.8	12
25 17.2	6.8	104.5	24 46.4	9.0	105.3	24 13.8	11.2	106.2	23 39.5	13.3	107.0	23 03.5	15.4	107.9	13
25 10.4	7.3	105.5	24 37.4	9.5	106.4	24 02.6	11.6	107.3	23 26.2	13.8	108.1	22 48.1	15.8	108.9	14
25 03.1	- 7.8	106.6	24 27.9	- 9.9	107.5	23 51.0	-12.0	108.3	23 12.4	-14.1	109.2	22 32.3	-16.3	110.0	15
24 55.3	8.2	107.7	24 18.0	10.4	108.6	23 39.0	12.6	109.4	22 58.3	14.6	110.2	22 16.0	16.6	111.0	16
24 47.1	8.7	108.8	24 07.6	10.8	109.6	23 26.4	12.9	110.5	22 43.7	15.0	111.3	21 59.4	17.0	112.0	17
24 38.4	9.2	109.9	23 56.8	11.3	110.7	23 13.5	13.4	111.5	22 28.7	15.4	112.3	21 42.4	17.4	113.1	18
24 29.2	9.6	111.0	23 45.5	11.8	111.8	23 00.1	13.8	112.6	22 13.3	15.8	113.4	21 25.0	17.8	114.1	19
24 19.6	-10.1	112.0	23 33.7	-12.1	112.9	22 46.3	-14.2	113.7	21 57.5	-16.2	114.4	21 07.2	-18.1	115.1	20
24 09.5	10.6	113.1	23 21.6	12.6	113.9	22 32.1	14.6	114.7	21 41.3	16.6	115.4	20 49.1	18.5	116.1	21
23 58.9	11.0	114.2	23 09.0	13.1	115.0	22 17.5	15.0	115.8	21 24.7	17.0	116.5	20 30.6	18.9	117.2	22
23 47.9	11.4	115.3	22 55.9	13.4	116.1	22 02.5	15.4	116.8	21 07.7	17.3	117.5	20 11.7	19.2	118.2	23
23 36.5	11.9	116.4	22 42.5	13.9	117.1	21 47.1	15.8	117.8	20 50.4	17.7	118.5	19 52.5	19.6	119.2	24
23 24.6	-12.4	117.4	22 28.6	-14.3	118.2	21 31.3	-16.2	118.9	20 32.7	-18.0	119.6	19 32.9	-19.8	120.2	25
23 12.2	12.7	118.5	22 14.3	14.7	119.2	21 15.1	16.6	119.9	20 14.7	18.4	120.6	19 13.1	20.2	121.2	26
22 59.5	13.2	119.5	21 59.6	15.0	120.3	20 58.5	16.9	120.9	19 56.3	18.8	121.6	18 52.9	20.5	122.2	27
22 46.3	13.6	120.6	21 44.6	15.5	121.3	20 41.6	17.3	122.0	19 37.5	19.1	122.6	18 32.4	20.9	123.2	28
22 32.7	14.0	121.7	21 29.1	15.9	122.3	20 24.3	17.6	123.0	19 18.4	19.4	123.6	18 11.5	21.1	124.2	29

10° Hc	d	Z	12° Hc	d	Z	14° Hc	d	Z	16° Hc	d	Z	18° Hc	d	Z	Dec.
25 34.6	-11.8	94.8	25 23.5	-14.1	95.8	25 10.4	-16.3	96.7	24 55.3	-18.4	97.7	24 38.4	-20.6	98.6	0
25 22.8	12.3	95.9	25 09.4	14.5	96.9	24 54.1	16.7	97.8	24 36.9	18.9	98.7	24 17.8	21.0	99.6	1
25 10.5	12.7	97.0	24 54.9	15.0	97.9	24 37.4	17.2	98.8	24 18.0	19.3	99.7	23 56.8	21.5	100.6	2
24 57.8	13.2	98.1	24 39.9	15.4	99.0	24 20.2	17.6	99.9	23 58.7	19.7	100.8	23 35.3	21.8	101.6	3
24 44.6	13.7	99.2	24 24.5	15.8	100.1	24 02.6	18.0	101.0	23 39.0	20.2	101.8	23 13.5	22.2	102.7	4
24 30.9	-14.1	100.2	24 08.7	-16.3	101.1	23 44.6	-18.4	102.0	23 18.8	-20.5	102.8	22 51.3	-22.6	103.7	5
24 16.8	14.6	101.3	23 52.4	16.7	102.2	23 26.2	18.9	103.0	22 58.3	21.0	103.9	22 28.7	23.0	104.7	6
24 02.2	15.0	102.4	23 35.7	17.2	103.2	23 07.3	19.2	104.1	22 37.3	21.3	104.9	22 05.7	23.3	105.7	7
23 47.2	15.4	103.4	23 18.5	17.5	104.3	22 48.1	19.6	105.1	22 16.0	21.7	105.9	21 42.4	23.7	106.7	8
23 31.8	15.8	104.5	23 01.0	18.0	105.3	22 28.5	20.1	106.1	21 54.3	22.0	106.9	21 18.7	24.0	107.7	9
23 16.0	-16.3	105.5	22 43.0	-18.4	106.3	22 08.4	-20.4	107.1	21 32.3	-22.4	107.9	20 54.7	-24.4	108.6	10
22 59.7	16.7	106.6	22 24.6	18.7	107.4	21 48.0	20.8	108.2	21 09.9	22.8	108.9	20 30.3	24.7	109.6	11
22 43.0	17.1	107.6	22 05.9	19.1	108.4	21 27.2	21.1	109.2	20 47.1	23.1	109.9	20 05.6	25.0	110.6	12
22 25.9	17.5	108.7	21 46.8	19.6	109.4	21 06.1	21.5	110.2	20 24.0	23.4	110.9	19 40.6	25.3	111.6	13
22 08.4	17.8	109.7	21 27.2	19.8	110.4	20 44.6	21.8	111.2	20 00.6	23.7	111.9	19 15.3	25.6	112.5	14
21 50.6	-18.3	110.7	21 07.4	-20.3	111.5	20 22.8	-22.2	112.2	19 36.9	-24.1	112.8	18 49.7	-25.9	113.5	15
21 32.3	18.6	111.7	20 47.1	20.5	112.5	20 00.6	22.5	113.1	19 12.8	24.4	113.8	18 23.8	26.2	114.4	16
21 13.7	19.0	112.8	20 26.6	21.0	113.5	19 38.1	22.8	114.1	18 48.4	24.6	114.8	17 57.6	26.5	115.4	17
20 54.7	19.4	113.8	20 05.6	21.2	114.5	19 15.3	23.1	115.1	18 23.8	25.0	115.7	17 31.1	26.7	116.3	18
20 35.3	19.7	114.8	19 44.4	21.6	115.5	18 52.2	23.5	116.1	17 58.8	25.2	116.7	17 04.4	27.0	117.3	19
20 15.6	-20.0	115.8	19 22.8	-21.9	116.5	18 28.7	-23.7	117.1	17 33.6	-25.5	117.6	16 37.4	-27.2	118.2	20
19 55.6	20.4	116.8	19 00.9	22.3	117.4	18 05.0	24.0	118.0	17 08.1	25.8	118.6	16 10.2	27.5	119.1	21
19 35.2	20.7	117.8	18 38.6	22.5	118.4	17 41.0	24.3	119.0	16 42.3	26.0	119.5	15 42.7	27.7	120.0	22
19 14.5	21.1	118.8	18 16.1	22.8	119.4	17 16.7	24.6	120.0	16 16.3	26.3	120.5	15 15.0	27.9	121.0	23
18 53.4	21.3	119.8	17 53.3	23.1	120.4	16 52.1	24.8	120.9	15 50.0	26.5	121.4	14 47.1	28.2	121.9	24
18 32.1	-21.7	120.8	17 30.2	-23.4	121.3	16 27.3	-25.1	121.9	15 23.5	-26.7	122.3	14 18.9	-28.3	122.8	25
18 10.4	21.9	121.8	17 06.8	23.7	122.3	16 02.2	25.3	122.8	14 56.8	27.0	123.3	13 50.6	28.6	123.7	26
17 48.5	22.3	122.7	16 43.1	23.9	123.2	15 36.9	25.6	123.7	14 29.8	27.2	124.2	13 22.0	28.7	124.6	27
17 26.2	22.5	123.7	16 19.2	24.2	124.2	15 11.3	25.8	124.7	14 02.6	27.4	125.1	12 53.3	29.0	125.5	28
17 03.7	22.8	124.7	15 55.0	24.5	125.2	14 45.5	26.1	125.6	13 35.2	27.6	126.0	12 24.3	29.1	126.4	29

Dec.	20° Hc	d	Z	22° Hc	d	Z	24° Hc	d	Z	26° Hc	d	Z	28° Hc	d	Z
°	° ′	′	°	° ′	′	°	° ′	′	°	° ′	′	°	° ′	′	°
0	24 19.6	+22.3	99.5	23 58.9	+24.4	100.4	23 36.5	+26.4	101.2	23 12.2	+28.5	102.1	22 46.3	+30.4	102.9
1	24 41.9	21.9	98.5	24 23.3	24.0	99.4	24 02.9	26.1	100.2	23 40.7	28.1	101.1	23 16.7	30.0	102.0
2	25 03.8	21.5	97.4	24 47.3	23.6	98.3	24 29.0	25.7	99.3	24 08.8	27.7	100.1	23 46.7	29.7	101.0
3	25 25.3	21.0	96.4	25 10.9	23.2	97.3	24 54.7	25.2	98.3	24 36.5	27.3	99.2	24 16.4	29.4	100.1
4	25 46.3	20.6	95.4	25 34.1	22.8	96.3	25 19.9	24.9	97.3	25 03.8	27.0	98.2	24 45.8	29.0	99.1
5	26 06.9	+20.1	94.3	25 56.9	+22.3	95.3	25 44.8	+24.5	96.2	25 30.8	+26.5	97.2	25 14.8	+28.5	98.1
6	26 27.0	19.7	93.3	26 19.2	21.9	94.2	26 09.3	24.0	95.2	25 57.3	26.2	96.2	25 43.3	28.2	97.2
7	26 46.7	19.2	92.2	26 41.1	21.4	93.2	26 33.3	23.6	94.2	26 23.5	25.7	95.2	26 11.5	27.8	96.2
8	27 05.9	18.7	91.1	27 02.5	20.9	92.2	26 56.9	23.1	93.2	26 49.2	25.2	94.2	26 39.3	27.4	95.2
9	27 24.6	18.3	90.1	27 23.4	20.5	91.1	27 20.0	22.7	92.1	27 14.4	24.9	93.2	27 06.7	27.0	94.2
10	27 42.9	+17.7	89.0	27 43.9	+20.0	90.0	27 42.7	+22.2	91.1	27 39.3	+24.4	92.1	27 33.7	+26.5	93.2
11	28 00.6	17.2	87.9	28 03.9	19.4	89.0	28 04.9	21.7	90.0	28 03.7	23.9	91.1	28 00.2	26.1	92.2
12	28 17.8	16.7	86.8	28 23.3	19.0	87.9	28 26.6	21.2	89.0	28 27.6	23.4	90.1	28 26.3	25.6	91.2
13	28 34.5	16.2	85.7	28 42.3	18.5	86.8	28 47.8	20.7	87.9	28 51.0	22.9	89.0	28 51.9	25.1	90.1
14	28 50.7	15.6	84.6	29 00.8	17.9	85.7	29 08.5	20.2	86.8	29 13.9	22.5	88.0	29 17.0	24.7	89.1
15	29 06.3	+15.1	83.5	29 18.7	+17.4	84.6	29 28.7	+19.7	85.8	29 36.4	+21.9	86.9	29 41.7	+24.1	88.0
16	29 21.4	14.6	82.4	29 36.1	16.8	83.5	29 48.4	19.1	84.7	29 58.3	21.4	85.8	30 05.8	23.7	87.0
17	29 36.0	13.9	81.3	29 52.9	16.3	82.4	30 07.5	18.6	83.6	30 19.7	20.9	84.7	30 29.5	23.1	85.9
18	29 49.9	13.4	80.2	30 09.2	15.7	81.3	30 26.1	18.0	82.5	30 40.6	20.3	83.7	30 52.6	22.6	84.8
19	30 03.3	12.9	79.1	30 24.9	15.2	80.2	30 44.1	17.5	81.4	31 00.9	19.7	82.6	31 15.2	22.0	83.8
20	30 16.2	+12.2	77.9	30 40.1	+14.5	79.1	31 01.6	+16.9	80.3	31 20.6	+19.2	81.5	31 37.2	+21.5	82.7
21	30 28.4	11.7	76.8	30 54.6	14.0	78.0	31 18.5	16.3	79.1	31 39.8	18.6	80.3	31 58.7	20.9	81.6
22	30 40.1	11.0	75.7	31 08.6	13.4	76.8	31 34.8	15.6	78.0	31 58.4	18.0	79.2	32 19.6	20.3	80.5
23	30 51.1	10.5	74.5	31 22.0	12.8	75.7	31 50.4	15.1	76.9	32 16.4	17.4	78.1	32 39.9	19.7	79.4
24	31 01.6	9.8	73.4	31 34.8	12.1	74.5	32 05.5	14.5	75.7	32 33.8	16.8	77.0	32 59.6	19.1	78.2
25	31 11.4	+9.2	72.2	31 46.9	+11.5	73.4	32 20.0	+13.8	74.6	32 50.6	+16.2	75.8	33 18.7	+18.5	77.1
26	31 20.6	8.6	71.1	31 58.4	10.9	72.2	32 33.8	13.3	73.4	33 06.8	15.5	74.7	33 37.2	17.9	76.0
27	31 29.2	8.0	69.9	32 09.3	10.3	71.1	32 47.1	12.5	72.3	33 22.3	14.9	73.5	33 55.1	17.2	74.8
28	31 37.2	7.3	68.7	32 19.6	9.6	69.9	32 59.6	11.9	71.1	33 37.2	14.3	72.4	34 12.3	16.6	73.7
29	31 44.5	6.7	67.6	32 29.2	9.0	68.7	33 11.5	11.3	69.9	33 51.5	13.5	71.2	34 28.9	15.9	72.5

Dec.	30° Hc	d	Z	32° Hc	d	Z	34° Hc	d	Z	36° Hc	d	Z	38° Hc	d	Z
°	° ′	′	°	° ′	′	°	° ′	′	°	° ′	′	°	° ′	′	°
0	22 18.7	+32.3	103.7	21 49.5	+34.1	104.5	21 18.6	+35.9	105.3	20 46.3	+37.6	106.0	20 12.5	+39.3	106.7
1	22 51.0	31.9	102.8	22 23.6	33.8	103.6	21 54.5	35.6	104.4	21 23.9	37.4	105.2	20 51.8	39.0	105.9
2	23 22.9	31.7	101.9	22 57.4	33.5	102.7	22 30.1	35.4	103.5	22 01.3	37.0	104.3	21 30.8	38.8	105.1
3	23 54.6	31.2	100.9	23 30.9	33.2	101.8	23 05.5	35.0	102.6	22 38.3	36.9	103.5	22 09.6	38.5	104.3
4	24 25.8	31.0	100.0	24 04.1	32.8	100.9	23 40.5	34.7	101.8	23 15.2	36.5	102.6	22 48.1	38.3	103.4
5	24 56.8	+30.6	99.1	24 36.9	+32.6	100.0	24 15.2	+34.4	100.9	23 51.7	+36.2	101.7	23 26.4	+38.0	102.6
6	25 27.4	30.2	98.1	25 09.5	32.2	99.1	24 49.6	34.1	100.0	24 27.9	36.0	100.9	24 04.4	37.7	101.8
7	25 57.6	29.8	97.2	25 41.7	31.8	98.1	25 23.7	33.8	99.1	25 03.9	35.6	100.0	24 42.1	37.4	100.9
8	26 27.4	29.5	96.2	26 13.5	31.4	97.2	25 57.5	33.4	98.1	25 39.5	35.3	99.1	25 19.5	37.2	100.0
9	26 56.9	29.0	95.1	26 44.9	31.1	96.2	26 30.9	33.0	97.2	26 14.8	34.9	98.2	25 56.7	36.8	99.2
10	27 25.9	+28.6	94.2	27 16.0	+30.7	95.3	27 03.9	+32.7	96.3	26 49.7	+34.6	97.3	26 33.5	+36.5	98.3
11	27 54.5	28.2	93.2	27 46.7	30.2	94.3	27 36.6	32.3	95.3	27 24.3	34.3	96.4	27 10.0	36.1	97.4
12	28 22.7	27.8	92.2	28 16.9	29.9	93.3	28 08.9	31.8	94.4	27 58.6	33.8	95.4	27 46.1	35.8	96.5
13	28 50.5	27.3	91.2	28 46.8	29.4	92.3	28 40.7	31.5	93.4	28 32.4	33.5	94.5	28 21.9	35.4	95.6
14	29 17.8	26.8	90.2	29 16.2	28.9	91.3	29 12.2	31.0	92.4	29 05.9	33.1	93.6	28 57.3	35.0	94.7
15	29 44.6	+26.3	89.2	29 45.1	+28.5	90.3	29 43.2	+30.6	91.5	29 39.0	+32.6	92.6	29 32.3	+34.7	93.7
16	30 10.9	25.9	88.1	30 13.6	28.0	89.3	30 13.8	30.2	90.5	30 11.6	32.2	91.6	30 07.0	34.2	92.8
17	30 36.8	25.3	87.1	30 41.6	27.6	88.3	30 44.0	29.7	89.5	30 43.8	31.8	90.7	30 41.2	33.8	91.8
18	31 02.1	24.8	86.0	31 09.2	27.0	87.2	31 13.7	29.1	88.5	31 15.6	31.3	89.7	31 15.0	33.4	90.9
19	31 26.9	24.3	85.0	31 36.2	26.5	86.2	31 42.8	28.7	87.4	31 46.9	30.9	88.7	31 48.4	33.0	89.9
20	31 51.2	+23.8	83.9	32 02.7	+26.0	85.1	32 11.5	+28.2	86.4	32 17.8	+30.3	87.7	32 21.4	+32.4	88.9
21	32 15.0	23.2	82.8	32 28.7	25.4	84.1	32 39.7	27.7	85.4	32 48.1	29.9	86.6	32 53.8	32.0	87.9
22	32 38.2	22.6	81.7	32 54.1	24.9	83.0	33 07.4	27.1	84.3	33 18.0	29.3	85.6	33 25.8	31.5	86.9
23	33 00.8	22.0	80.6	33 19.0	24.3	81.9	33 34.5	26.6	83.2	33 47.3	28.8	84.6	33 57.3	31.0	85.9
24	33 22.8	21.4	79.5	33 43.3	23.7	80.8	34 01.1	26.0	82.1	34 16.1	28.2	83.5	34 28.3	30.4	84.9
25	33 44.2	+20.8	78.4	34 07.0	+23.1	79.7	34 27.1	+25.4	81.1	34 44.3	+27.7	82.4	34 58.7	+29.9	83.8
26	34 05.0	20.2	77.3	34 30.1	22.5	78.6	34 52.5	24.8	80.0	35 12.0	27.0	81.3	35 28.6	29.3	82.7
27	34 25.2	19.6	76.1	34 52.6	21.9	77.5	35 17.3	24.2	78.8	35 39.0	26.5	80.2	35 57.9	28.8	81.7
28	34 44.8	18.9	75.0	35 14.5	21.2	76.3	35 41.5	23.5	77.7	36 05.5	25.9	79.1	36 26.7	28.1	80.6
29	35 03.7	18.2	73.8	35 35.7	20.6	75.2	36 05.0	22.9	76.6	36 31.4	25.2	78.0	36 54.8	27.5	79.5

20°			22°			24°			26°			28°			Dec.
Hc	d	Z	Hc	d	Z	Hc	d	Z	Hc	d	Z	Hc	d	Z	°
24 19.6	-22.7	99.5	23 58.9	-24.8	100.4	23 36.5	-26.9	101.2	23 12.2	-28.8	102.1	22 46.3	-30.7	102.9	0
23 56.9	23.2	100.5	23 34.1	25.1	101.3	23 09.6	27.1	102.2	22 43.4	29.1	103.0	22 15.6	31.0	103.8	1
23 33.7	23.5	101.5	23 09.0	25.6	102.3	22 42.5	27.5	103.2	22 14.3	29.4	104.0	21 44.6	31.4	104.8	2
23 10.2	23.9	102.5	22 43.4	25.9	103.3	22 15.0	27.9	104.1	21 44.9	29.8	104.9	21 13.2	31.6	105.7	3
22 46.3	24.2	103.5	22 17.5	26.2	104.3	21 47.1	28.2	105.1	21 15.1	30.1	105.8	20 41.6	31.9	106.6	4
22 22.1	-24.6	104.5	21 51.3	-26.6	105.3	21 18.9	-28.5	106.0	20 45.0	-30.3	106.8	20 09.7	-32.2	107.5	5
21 57.5	25.0	105.5	21 24.7	26.9	106.2	20 50.4	28.8	107.0	20 14.7	30.7	107.7	19 37.5	32.4	108.4	6
21 32.5	25.3	106.4	20 57.8	27.2	107.2	20 21.6	29.1	107.9	19 44.0	30.9	108.6	19 05.1	32.7	109.3	7
21 07.2	25.6	107.4	20 30.6	27.6	108.1	19 52.5	29.4	108.8	19 13.1	31.2	109.5	18 32.4	33.0	110.2	8
20 41.6	26.0	108.4	20 03.0	27.8	109.1	19 23.1	29.7	109.8	18 41.9	31.5	110.4	17 59.4	33.2	111.0	9
20 15.6	-26.3	109.3	19 35.2	-28.2	110.0	18 53.4	-29.9	110.7	18 10.4	-31.7	111.3	17 26.2	-33.4	111.9	10
19 49.3	26.5	110.3	19 07.0	28.4	111.0	18 23.5	30.2	111.6	17 38.7	31.9	112.2	16 52.8	33.6	112.8	11
19 22.8	26.9	111.3	18 38.6	28.7	111.9	17 53.3	30.5	112.5	17 06.8	32.2	113.1	16 19.2	33.9	113.6	12
18 55.9	27.2	112.2	18 09.9	28.9	112.8	17 22.8	30.7	113.4	16 34.6	32.4	114.0	15 45.3	34.0	114.5	13
18 28.7	27.4	113.1	17 41.0	29.2	113.7	16 52.1	30.9	114.3	16 02.2	32.6	114.9	15 11.3	34.3	115.4	14
18 01.3	-27.7	114.1	17 11.8	-29.5	114.7	16 21.2	-31.2	115.2	15 29.6	-32.8	115.7	14 37.0	-34.4	116.2	15
17 33.6	28.0	115.0	16 42.3	29.7	115.6	15 50.0	31.4	116.1	14 56.8	33.0	116.6	14 02.6	34.6	117.1	16
17 05.6	28.2	115.9	16 12.6	29.9	116.5	15 18.6	31.5	117.0	14 23.8	33.2	117.5	13 28.0	34.7	117.9	17
16 37.4	28.4	116.9	15 42.7	30.1	117.4	14 47.1	31.8	117.9	13 50.6	33.4	118.3	12 53.3	35.0	118.7	18
16 09.0	28.7	117.8	15 12.6	30.4	118.3	14 15.3	32.0	118.7	13 17.2	33.6	119.2	12 18.3	35.0	119.6	19
15 40.3	-29.0	118.7	14 42.2	-30.6	119.2	13 43.3	-32.1	119.6	12 43.6	-33.7	120.0	11 43.3	-35.3	120.4	20
15 11.3	29.1	119.6	14 11.6	30.7	120.1	13 11.2	32.4	120.5	12 09.9	33.8	120.9	11 08.0	35.3	121.2	21
14 42.2	29.3	120.5	13 40.9	31.0	120.9	12 38.8	32.5	121.3	11 36.1	34.0	121.7	10 32.7	35.5	122.0	22
14 12.9	29.6	121.4	13 09.9	31.1	121.8	12 06.3	32.6	122.2	11 02.1	34.2	122.5	9 57.2	35.6	122.9	23
13 43.3	29.7	122.3	12 38.8	31.3	122.7	11 33.7	32.8	123.1	10 27.9	34.3	123.4	9 21.6	35.7	123.7	24
13 13.6	-30.0	123.2	12 07.5	-31.4	123.6	11 00.9	--33.0	123.9	9 53.6	-34.4	124.2	8 45.9	-35.8	124.5	25
12 43.6	30.1	124.1	11 36.1	31.6	124.4	10 27.9	33.1	124.8	9 19.2	34.5	125.1	8 10.1	35.9	125.3	26
12 13.5	30.2	125.0	11 04.5	31.8	125.3	9 54.8	33.2	125.6	8 44.7	34.5	125.9	7 34.2	36.0	126.1	27
11 43.3	30.5	125.9	10 32.7	31.9	126.2	9 21.6	33.3	126.5	8 10.1	34.7	126.7	6 58.2	36.1	126.9	28
11 12.8	30.6	126.7	10 00.8	32.0	127.0	8 48.3	33.4	127.3	7 35.4	34.8	127.5	6 22.1	36.1	127.7	29

30°			32°			34°			36°			38°			Dec.
Hc	d	Z	Hc	d	Z	Hc	d	Z	Hc	d	Z	Hc	d	Z	°
22 18.7	-32.6	103.7	21 49.5	-34.4	104.5	21 18.6	-36.1	105.3	20 46.3	-37.8	106.0	20 12.5	-39.4	106.7	0
21 46.1	32.9	104.6	21 15.1	34.7	105.4	20 42.5	36.4	106.1	20 08.5	38.1	106.8	19 33.1	39.7	107.5	1
21 13.2	33.1	105.5	20 40.4	34.9	106.2	20 06.1	36.6	107.0	19 30.4	38.3	107.6	18 53.4	39.9	108.3	2
20 40.1	33.4	106.4	20 05.5	35.2	107.1	19 29.5	36.9	107.8	18 52.1	38.5	108.5	18 13.5	40.1	109.1	3
20 06.7	33.7	107.3	19 30.3	35.4	108.0	18 52.6	37.1	108.6	18 13.6	38.7	109.3	17 33.4	40.2	109.9	4
19 33.0	-34.0	108.2	18 54.9	-35.7	108.8	18 15.5	-37.3	109.5	17 34.9	-38.9	110.1	16 53.2	-40.5	110.7	5
18 59.0	34.2	109.0	18 19.2	35.8	109.7	17 38.2	37.5	110.3	16 56.0	39.1	110.9	16 12.7	40.6	111.4	6
18 24.8	34.4	109.9	17 43.4	36.1	110.5	17 00.7	37.7	111.1	16 16.9	39.2	111.7	15 32.1	40.7	112.2	7
17 50.4	34.7	110.8	17 07.3	36.3	111.4	16 23.0	37.9	111.9	15 37.7	39.4	112.4	14 51.4	40.9	113.0	8
17 15.7	34.9	111.6	16 31.0	36.5	112.2	15 45.1	38.0	112.7	14 58.3	39.6	113.2	14 10.5	41.1	113.7	9
16 40.9	-35.1	112.5	15 54.5	-36.7	113.0	15 07.1	-38.3	113.5	14 18.7	-39.7	114.0	13 29.4	-41.1	114.5	10
16 05.8	35.3	113.3	15 17.8	36.9	113.8	14 28.8	38.4	114.3	13 39.0	39.9	114.8	12 48.3	41.3	115.2	11
15 30.5	35.4	114.2	14 40.9	37.0	114.7	13 50.4	38.5	115.1	12 59.1	40.0	115.5	12 07.0	41.5	115.9	12
14 55.1	35.7	115.0	14 03.9	37.2	115.5	13 11.9	38.7	115.9	12 19.1	40.2	116.3	11 25.5	41.6	116.7	13
14 19.4	35.8	115.8	13 26.7	37.3	116.3	12 33.2	38.8	116.7	11 38.9	40.2	117.1	10 44.0	41.6	117.4	14
13 43.6	-36.0	116.7	12 49.4	-37.5	117.1	11 54.4	-39.0	117.5	10 58.7	-40.4	117.8	10 02.4	-41.8	118.2	15
13 07.6	36.1	117.5	12 11.9	37.6	117.9	11 15.4	39.0	118.2	10 18.3	40.4	118.6	9 20.6	41.8	118.9	16
12 31.5	36.3	118.3	11 34.3	37.8	118.7	10 36.4	39.2	119.0	9 37.9	40.6	119.3	8 38.8	41.9	119.6	17
11 55.2	36.4	119.1	10 56.5	37.9	119.5	9 57.2	39.3	119.8	8 57.3	40.7	120.1	7 56.9	42.0	120.3	18
11 18.8	36.6	119.9	10 18.6	38.0	120.3	9 17.9	39.4	120.6	8 16.6	40.7	120.8	7 14.9	42.0	121.1	19
10 42.2	-36.6	120.7	9 40.6	-38.1	121.0	8 38.5	-39.5	121.3	7 35.9	-40.8	121.6	6 32.9	-42.1	121.8	20
10 05.6	36.8	121.5	9 02.5	38.2	121.8	7 59.0	39.5	122.1	6 55.1	40.9	122.3	5 50.8	42.2	122.5	21
9 28.8	36.9	122.3	8 24.3	38.3	122.6	7 19.5	39.7	122.8	6 14.2	40.9	123.0	5 08.6	42.2	123.2	22
8 51.9	37.0	123.1	7 46.0	38.3	123.4	6 39.8	39.7	123.6	5 33.3	41.0	123.8	4 26.4	42.2	123.9	23
8 14.9	37.1	123.9	7 07.7	38.5	124.2	6 00.1	39.8	124.3	4 52.3	41.1	124.5	3 44.2	42.3	124.6	24
7 37.8	-37.2	124.7	6 29.2	-38.5	124.9	5 20.3	-39.8	125.1	4 11.2	-41.1	125.2	3 01.9	-42.3	125.3	25
7 00.6	37.3	125.5	5 50.7	38.6	125.7	4 40.5	39.8	125.9	3 30.1	41.1	126.0	2 19.6	42.3	126.1	26
6 23.3	37.3	126.3	5 12.1	38.6	126.5	4 00.7	40.0	126.6	2 49.0	41.1	126.7	1 37.3	42.4	126.8	27
5 46.0	37.4	127.1	4 33.5	38.7	127.2	3 20.7	39.9	127.4	2 07.9	41.2	127.4	0 54.9	42.3	127.5	28
5 08.6	37.5	127.9	3 54.8	38.8	128.0	2 40.8	40.0	128.1	1 26.7	41.2	128.2	0 12.6	-42.4	128.2	29

Dec.	40° Hc	d	Z	42° Hc	d	Z	44° Hc	d	Z	46° Hc	d	Z	48° Hc	d	Z
0	19 37.3	+40.9	107.4	19 00.7	+42.4	108.1	18 22.9	+43.8	108.7	17 43.8	+45.2	109.3	17 03.4	+46.6	109.9
1	20 18.2	40.6	106.6	19 43.1	42.2	107.3	19 06.7	43.7	108.0	18 29.0	45.1	108.6	17 50.0	46.5	109.3
2	20 58.8	40.4	105.8	20 25.3	42.0	106.6	19 50.4	43.5	107.3	19 14.1	44.9	107.9	18 36.5	46.3	108.6
3	21 39.2	40.2	105.0	21 07.3	41.8	105.8	20 33.9	43.3	106.5	19 59.0	44.8	107.2	19 22.8	46.1	107.9
4	22 19.4	39.9	104.2	21 49.1	41.5	105.0	21 17.2	43.1	105.8	20 43.8	44.5	106.5	20 08.9	46.0	107.2
5	22 59.3	+39.7	103.4	22 30.6	+41.4	104.3	22 00.3	+42.9	105.0	21 28.3	+44.4	105.8	20 54.9	+45.8	106.6
6	23 39.0	39.5	102.6	23 12.0	41.1	103.5	22 43.2	42.7	104.3	22 12.7	44.2	105.1	21 40.7	45.7	105.9
7	24 18.5	39.2	101.8	23 53.1	40.8	102.7	23 25.9	42.4	103.5	22 56.9	44.0	104.4	22 26.4	45.7	105.2
8	24 57.7	38.9	101.0	24 33.9	40.6	101.9	24 08.3	42.2	102.8	23 40.9	43.8	103.6	23 11.8	45.3	104.5
9	25 36.6	38.6	100.1	25 14.5	40.3	101.1	24 50.5	42.0	102.0	24 24.7	43.6	102.9	23 57.1	45.1	103.7
10	26 15.2	+38.2	99.3	25 54.8	+40.1	100.2	25 32.5	+41.7	101.2	25 08.3	+43.3	102.1	24 42.2	+44.9	103.0
11	26 53.4	38.0	98.4	26 34.9	39.7	99.4	26 14.2	41.5	100.4	25 51.6	43.1	101.3	25 27.1	44.6	102.3
12	27 31.4	37.7	97.5	27 14.6	39.5	98.6	26 55.7	41.2	99.6	26 34.7	42.8	100.6	26 11.7	44.4	101.5
13	28 09.1	37.3	96.7	27 54.1	39.1	97.7	27 36.9	40.8	98.8	27 17.5	42.6	99.8	26 56.1	44.2	100.8
14	28 46.4	36.9	95.8	28 33.2	38.8	96.9	28 17.7	40.6	97.9	28 00.1	42.3	99.0	27 40.3	43.9	100.0
15	29 23.3	+36.6	94.9	29 12.0	+38.4	96.0	28 58.3	+40.3	97.1	28 42.4	+42.0	98.2	28 24.2	+43.6	99.3
16	29 59.9	36.2	94.0	29 50.4	38.1	95.1	29 38.6	39.9	96.2	29 24.4	41.7	97.4	29 07.8	43.4	98.5
17	30 36.1	35.8	93.0	30 28.5	37.8	94.2	30 18.5	39.6	95.4	30 06.1	41.3	96.5	29 51.2	43.1	97.7
18	31 11.9	35.4	92.1	31 06.3	37.3	93.3	30 58.1	39.2	94.5	30 47.4	41.1	95.7	30 34.3	42.8	96.9
19	31 47.3	35.0	91.1	31 43.6	37.0	92.4	31 37.3	38.9	93.6	31 28.5	40.7	94.8	31 17.1	42.4	96.1
20	32 22.3	+34.5	90.2	32 20.6	+36.5	91.5	32 16.2	+38.5	92.7	32 09.2	+40.3	94.0	31 59.5	+42.2	95.2
21	32 56.8	34.1	89.2	32 57.1	36.1	90.5	32 54.7	38.0	91.8	32 49.5	40.0	93.1	32 41.7	41.8	94.4
22	33 30.9	33.6	88.2	33 33.2	35.7	89.6	33 32.7	37.7	90.9	33 29.5	39.6	92.2	33 23.5	41.4	93.5
23	34 04.5	33.1	87.2	34 08.9	35.1	88.6	34 10.4	37.2	89.9	34 09.1	39.1	91.3	34 04.9	41.1	92.7
24	34 37.6	32.6	86.2	34 44.0	34.8	87.6	34 47.6	36.8	89.0	34 48.2	38.8	90.4	34 46.0	40.7	91.8
25	35 10.2	+32.1	85.2	35 18.8	+34.2	86.6	35 24.4	+36.3	88.0	35 27.0	+38.3	89.5	35 26.7	+40.2	90.9
26	35 42.3	31.5	84.2	35 53.0	33.7	85.6	36 00.7	35.8	87.0	36 05.3	37.9	88.5	36 06.9	39.9	90.0
27	36 13.8	31.0	83.1	36 26.7	33.1	84.6	36 36.5	35.3	86.1	36 43.2	37.4	87.5	36 46.8	39.4	89.0
28	36 44.8	30.4	82.0	36 59.8	32.7	83.5	37 11.8	34.8	85.0	37 20.6	36.9	86.6	37 26.2	38.9	88.1
29	37 15.2	29.8	81.0	37 32.5	32.0	82.5	37 46.6	34.2	84.0	37 57.5	36.3	85.6	38 05.1	38.5	87.1

Dec.	50° Hc	d	Z	52° Hc	d	Z	54° Hc	d	Z	56° Hc	d	Z	58° Hc	d	Z
0	16 22.0	+47.8	110.5	15 39.5	+49.0	111.0	14 55.9	+50.2	111.5	14 11.4	+51.3	112.0	13 26.0	+52.2	112.5
1	17 09.8	47.8	109.9	16 28.5	49.0	110.4	15 46.1	50.1	111.0	15 02.7	51.2	111.5	14 18.2	52.3	112.0
2	17 57.6	47.6	109.2	17 17.5	48.8	109.8	16 36.2	50.0	110.4	15 53.9	51.1	110.9	15 10.5	52.1	111.5
3	18 45.2	47.4	108.6	18 06.3	48.7	109.2	17 26.2	49.9	109.8	16 45.0	51.0	110.4	16 02.6	52.1	110.9
4	19 32.6	47.4	107.9	18 55.0	48.6	108.6	18 16.1	49.8	109.2	17 36.0	50.9	109.8	16 54.7	52.0	110.4
5	20 20.0	+47.2	107.3	19 43.6	+48.5	108.0	19 05.9	+49.7	108.6	18 26.9	+50.9	109.3	17 46.7	+51.9	109.9
6	21 07.2	47.0	106.6	20 32.1	48.3	107.3	19 55.6	49.6	108.0	19 17.8	50.7	108.7	18 38.6	51.8	109.4
7	21 54.2	46.8	106.0	21 20.4	48.2	106.7	20 45.2	49.4	107.4	20 08.5	50.6	108.2	19 30.4	51.7	108.8
8	22 41.0	46.7	105.3	22 08.6	48.1	106.1	21 34.6	49.3	106.8	20 59.1	50.5	107.6	20 22.1	51.7	108.3
9	23 27.7	46.6	104.6	22 56.7	47.8	105.4	22 23.9	49.2	106.2	21 49.6	50.4	107.0	21 13.8	51.5	107.8
10	24 14.3	+46.3	103.9	23 44.5	+47.8	104.8	23 13.1	+49.0	105.6	22 40.0	+50.3	106.4	22 05.3	+51.4	107.2
11	25 00.6	46.1	103.2	24 32.3	47.5	104.1	24 02.1	48.9	105.0	23 30.3	50.1	105.8	22 56.7	51.3	106.6
12	25 46.7	45.9	102.5	25 19.8	47.3	103.4	24 51.0	48.7	104.3	24 20.4	49.9	105.2	23 48.0	51.2	106.1
13	26 32.6	45.7	101.8	26 07.1	47.2	102.7	25 39.7	48.5	103.7	25 10.3	49.8	104.6	24 39.2	51.0	105.5
14	27 18.3	45.5	101.1	26 54.3	46.9	102.1	26 28.2	48.4	103.0	26 00.2	49.6	104.0	25 30.2	50.9	104.9
15	28 03.8	+45.2	100.3	27 41.2	+46.8	101.4	27 16.6	+48.1	102.4	26 49.8	+49.5	103.4	26 21.1	+50.7	104.3
16	28 49.0	45.0	99.6	28 28.0	46.5	100.6	28 04.7	48.0	101.7	27 39.3	49.3	102.7	27 11.8	50.6	103.7
17	29 34.0	44.7	98.8	29 14.5	46.2	99.9	28 52.7	47.7	101.0	28 28.6	49.2	102.1	28 02.4	50.5	103.1
18	30 18.7	44.5	98.0	30 00.7	46.1	99.2	29 40.4	47.5	100.3	29 17.8	48.9	101.4	28 52.9	50.2	102.5
19	31 03.2	44.1	97.3	30 46.8	45.7	98.4	30 27.9	47.3	99.6	30 06.7	48.7	100.8	29 43.1	50.1	101.9
20	31 47.3	+43.9	96.5	31 32.5	+45.5	97.7	31 15.2	+47.1	98.9	30 55.4	+48.5	100.1	30 33.2	+49.9	101.3
21	32 31.2	43.5	95.7	32 18.0	45.2	96.9	32 02.3	46.8	98.2	31 43.9	48.3	99.4	31 23.1	49.7	100.6
22	33 14.7	43.2	94.8	33 03.2	45.0	96.1	32 49.1	46.5	97.4	32 32.2	48.1	98.7	32 12.8	49.5	99.9
23	33 57.9	42.9	94.0	33 48.2	44.6	95.3	33 35.6	46.2	96.7	33 20.3	47.8	98.0	33 02.3	49.2	99.2
24	34 40.8	42.5	93.2	34 32.8	44.2	94.5	34 21.8	46.0	95.9	34 08.1	47.5	97.3	33 51.5	49.1	98.6
25	35 23.3	+42.2	92.3	35 17.0	+44.0	93.7	35 07.8	+45.6	95.1	34 55.6	+47.3	96.5	34 40.6	+48.8	97.9
26	36 05.5	41.7	91.4	36 01.0	43.6	92.9	35 53.4	45.4	94.3	35 42.9	47.0	95.8	35 29.4	48.5	97.2
27	36 47.2	41.4	90.5	36 44.6	43.2	92.0	36 38.8	44.9	93.5	36 29.9	46.6	95.0	36 17.9	48.3	96.5
28	37 28.6	40.9	89.6	37 27.8	42.8	91.2	37 23.7	44.7	92.7	37 16.5	46.4	94.2	37 06.2	47.9	95.7
29	38 09.5	40.5	88.7	38 10.6	42.4	90.3	38 08.4	44.2	91.8	38 02.9	46.0	93.4	37 54.1	47.7	95.0

40°			42°			44°			46°			48°			Dec.
Hc	d	Z	Hc	d	Z	Hc	d	Z	Hc	d	Z	Hc	d	Z	
° ′	′	°	° ′	′	°	° ′	′	°	° ′	′	°	° ′	′	°	°
19 37.3	−41.0	107.4	19 00.7	−42.5	108.1	18 22.9	−44.0	108.7	17 43.8	−45.4	109.3	17 03.4	−46.7	109.9	0
18 56.3	41.3	108.2	18 18.2	42.7	108.8	17 38.9	44.2	109.4	16 58.4	45.6	110.0	16 16.7	46.8	110.6	1
18 15.0	41.4	108.9	17 35.5	42.9	109.6	16 54.7	44.3	110.1	16 12.8	45.6	110.7	15 29.9	46.9	111.2	2
17 33.6	41.6	109.7	16 52.6	43.1	110.3	16 10.4	44.4	110.8	15 27.2	45.8	111.4	14 43.0	47.1	111.9	3
16 52.0	41.7	110.5	16 09.5	43.2	111.0	15 26.0	44.6	111.5	14 41.4	45.9	112.0	13 55.9	47.1	112.5	4
16 10.3	−41.9	111.2	15 26.3	−43.3	111.7	14 41.4	−44.7	112.2	13 55.5	−45.9	112.7	13 08.8	−47.2	113.2	5
15 28.4	42.1	112.0	14 43.0	43.4	112.5	13 56.7	44.8	112.9	13 09.6	46.1	113.4	12 21.6	47.4	113.8	6
14 46.3	42.2	112.7	13 59.6	43.6	113.2	13 11.9	44.9	113.6	12 23.5	46.2	114.0	11 34.2	47.4	114.4	7
14 04.1	42.3	113.4	13 16.0	43.7	113.9	12 27.0	45.0	114.3	11 37.3	46.3	114.7	10 46.8	47.4	115.0	8
13 21.8	42.5	114.2	12 32.3	43.8	114.6	11 42.0	45.1	115.0	10 51.0	46.4	115.3	9 59.4	47.6	115.7	9
12 39.3	−42.5	114.9	11 48.5	−43.9	115.3	10 56.9	−45.2	115.7	10 04.6	−46.4	116.0	9 11.8	−47.6	116.3	10
11 56.8	42.7	115.6	11 04.6	44.0	116.0	10 11.7	45.3	116.3	9 18.2	46.5	116.6	8 24.2	47.7	116.9	11
11 14.1	42.8	116.3	10 20.6	44.1	116.7	9 26.4	45.3	117.0	8 31.7	46.5	117.3	7 36.5	47.7	117.5	12
10 31.3	42.9	117.0	9 36.5	44.2	117.4	8 41.1	45.5	117.7	7 45.2	46.7	117.9	6 48.8	47.8	118.1	13
9 48.4	42.9	117.7	8 52.3	44.3	118.0	7 55.6	45.4	118.3	6 58.5	46.6	118.5	6 01.0	47.8	118.7	14
9 05.5	−43.1	118.5	8 08.0	−44.3	118.7	7 10.2	−45.6	119.0	6 11.9	−46.7	119.2	5 13.2	−47.8	119.3	15
8 22.4	43.1	119.2	7 23.7	44.4	119.4	6 24.6	45.6	119.6	5 25.2	46.8	119.8	4 25.4	47.9	119.9	16
7 39.3	43.2	119.9	6 39.3	44.4	120.1	5 39.0	45.6	120.3	4 38.4	146.8	120.4	3 37.5	47.9	120.5	17
6 56.1	43.3	120.6	5 54.9	44.5	120.8	4 53.4	45.7	120.9	3 51.6	46.8	121.0	2 49.6	47.9	121.1	18
6 12.8	43.3	121.3	5 10.4	44.5	121.4	4 07.7	45.7	121.6	3 04.8	46.8	121.7	2 01.7	47.9	121.7	19
5 29.5	−43.3	122.0	4 25.9	−44.6	122.1	3 22.0	−45.7	122.2	2 18.0	−46.9	122.3	1 13.8	−47.9	122.4	20
4 46.2	43.4	122.6	3 41.3	44.6	122.8	2 36.3	45.7	122.9	1 31.1	46.8	122.9	0 25.9	−48.0	123.0	21
4 02.8	43.4	123.3	2 56.7	44.6	123.4	1 50.6	45.8	123.5	0 44.3	−46.9	123.5	0 22.1	+47.9	56.4	22
3 19.4	43.5	124.0	2 12.1	44.6	124.1	1 04.8	45.8	124.2	0 02.6	+46.9	55.8	1 10.0	47.9	55.8	23
2 35.9	43.5	124.7	1 27.5	44.7	124.8	0 19.0	−45.8	124.8	0 49.5	46.8	55.2	1 57.9	47.9	55.2	24
1 52.4	−43.5	125.4	0 42.8	−44.6	125.4	0 26.8	+45.7	54.5	1 36.3	+46.9	54.6	2 45.8	+47.9	54.6	25
1 08.9	43.5	126.1	0 01.8	+44.7	53.9	1 12.5	45.7	53.9	2 23.2	46.8	54.0	3 33.7	47.9	54.0	26
0 25.4	−43.5	126.8	0 46.5	44.6	53.2	1 58.3	45.7	53.3	3 10.0	46.8	53.3	4 21.6	47.8	53.4	27
0 18.1	+43.5	52.5	1 31.1	44.6	52.5	2 44.0	45.8	52.6	3 56.8	46.8	52.7	5 09.4	47.9	52.8	28
1 01.6	43.5	51.8	2 15.7	44.6	51.9	3 29.8	45.6	52.0	4 43.6	46.8	52.1	5 57.3	47.7	52.2	29

50°			52°			54°			56°			58°			Dec.
Hc	d	Z	Hc	d	Z	Hc	d	Z	Hc	d	Z	Hc	d	Z	
° ′	′	°	° ′	′	°	° ′	′	°	° ′	′	°	° ′	′	°	°
16 22.0	−48.0	110.5	15 39.5	−49.2	111.0	14 55.9	−50.3	111.5	14 11.4	−51.4	112.0	13 26.0	−52.4	112.5	0
15 34.0	48.0	111.1	14 50.3	49.2	111.6	14 05.6	50.3	112.1	13 20.0	51.4	112.5	12 33.6	52.4	113.0	1
14 46.0	48.2	111.7	14 01.1	49.4	112.2	13 15.3	50.5	112.7	12 28.6	51.4	113.1	11 41.2	52.5	113.5	2
13 57.8	48.3	112.3	13 11.7	49.4	112.8	12 24.8	50.5	113.2	11 37.2	51.6	113.6	10 48.8	52.5	114.0	3
13 09.5	48.3	113.0	12 22.3	49.4	113.4	11 34.3	50.5	113.8	10 45.6	51.5	114.1	9 56.3	52.6	114.5	4
12 21.2	−48.4	113.6	11 32.9	−49.6	114.0	10 43.8	−50.6	114.3	9 54.1	−51.7	114.6	9 03.7	−52.6	114.9	5
11 32.8	48.5	114.2	10 43.3	49.6	114.5	9 53.2	50.7	114.9	9 02.4	51.6	115.2	8 11.1	52.6	115.4	6
10 44.3	48.6	114.8	9 53.7	49.7	115.1	9 02.5	50.7	115.4	8 10.8	51.7	115.7	7 18.5	52.6	115.9	7
9 55.7	48.6	115.4	9 04.0	49.7	115.7	8 11.8	50.8	115.9	7 19.1	51.8	116.2	6 25.9	52.7	116.4	8
9 07.1	48.7	116.0	8 14.3	49.8	116.2	7 21.0	50.8	116.5	6 27.3	51.8	116.7	5 33.2	52.7	116.9	9
8 18.4	−48.7	116.6	7 24.5	−49.8	116.8	6 30.2	−50.8	117.0	5 35.5	−51.8	117.2	4 40.5	−52.7	117.4	10
7 29.7	48.8	117.1	6 34.7	49.8	117.4	5 39.4	50.9	117.6	4 43.7	51.8	117.7	3 47.8	52.7	117.8	11
6 40.9	48.8	117.7	5 44.9	49.9	117.9	4 48.5	50.8	118.1	3 51.9	51.8	118.2	2 55.1	52.8	118.3	12
5 52.1	48.9	118.3	4 55.0	49.9	118.5	3 57.7	51.0	118.6	3 00.1	51.9	118.7	2 02.3	52.7	118.8	13
5 03.2	48.9	118.9	4 05.1	49.9	119.0	3 06.7	50.9	119.1	2 08.2	51.8	119.2	1 09.6	52.8	119.3	14
4 14.3	−48.9	119.5	3 15.2	−50.0	119.6	2 15.8	−50.9	119.7	1 16.4	−51.9	119.7	0 16.8	−52.7	119.8	15
3 25.4	48.9	120.1	2 25.2	50.0	120.1	1 24.9	50.9	120.2	0 24.5	−51.9	120.2	0 35.9	+52.8	59.8	16
2 36.5	49.0	120.6	1 35.2	49.9	120.7	0 34.0	−51.0	120.7	0 27.4	+51.8	59.3	1 28.7	52.7	59.3	17
1 47.5	49.0	121.2	0 45.3	−50.0	121.3	0 17.0	+50.9	58.7	1 19.2	51.9	58.8	2 21.4	52.8	58.8	18
0 58.5	48.9	121.8	0 04.7	+50.0	58.2	1 07.9	51.0	58.2	2 11.1	51.9	58.3	3 14.2	52.7	58.3	19
0 09.6	−49.0	122.4	0 54.7	+49.9	57.6	1 58.9	+50.9	57.7	3 03.0	+51.8	57.8	4 06.9	+52.7	57.9	20
0 39.4	+49.0	57.1	1 44.6	50.0	57.1	2 49.8	50.9	57.2	3 54.8	51.8	57.3	4 59.6	52.7	57.4	21
1 28.4	48.9	56.5	2 34.6	50.0	56.5	3 40.7	50.9	56.6	4 46.6	51.8	56.7	5 52.3	52.7	56.9	22
2 17.3	49.0	55.9	3 24.6	49.9	55.9	4 31.6	50.9	56.1	5 38.4	51.8	56.2	6 45.0	52.6	56.4	23
3 06.3	48.9	55.3	4 14.5	49.9	55.4	5 22.5	50.8	55.6	6 30.2	51.7	55.7	7 37.6	52.6	55.9	24
3 55.2	+48.9	54.7	5 04.4	+49.9	54.9	6 13.3	+50.8	55.0	7 21.9	+51.7	55.2	8 30.2	+52.6	55.5	25
4 44.1	48.9	54.2	5 54.3	49.8	54.3	7 04.1	50.8	54.5	8 13.6	51.7	54.7	9 22.8	52.5	55.0	26
5 33.0	48.8	53.6	6 44.1	49.8	53.7	7 54.9	50.7	53.9	9 05.3	51.6	54.2	10 15.3	52.5	54.5	27
6 21.8	48.8	53.0	7 33.9	49.8	53.2	8 45.6	50.7	53.4	9 56.9	51.6	53.7	11 07.8	52.4	54.0	28
7 10.6	48.8	52.4	8 23.7	49.7	52.6	9 36.3	50.6	52.9	10 48.5	51.5	53.2	12 00.2	52.4	53.5	29

Dec.	0° Hc	d	Z	2° Hc	d	Z	4° Hc	d	Z	6° Hc	d	Z	8° Hc	d	Z
0	24 00.0 −	0.2	90.0	23 59.1 +	2.0	90.9	23 56.3 +	4.3	91.8	23 51.6 +	6.6	92.7	23 45.1 +	8.9	93.5
1	23 59.8	0.7	88.9	24 01.1	1.6	89.8	24 00.6	3.9	90.7	23 58.2	6.2	91.6	23 54.0	8.5	92.5
2	23 59.1	1.2	87.8	24 02.7	1.1	88.7	24 04.5	3.4	89.6	24 04.4	5.7	90.5	24 02.5	7.9	91.4
3	23 57.9	1.6	86.7	24 03.8	0.7	87.6	24 07.9	3.0	88.5	24 10.1	5.3	89.4	24 10.4	7.6	90.3
4	23 56.3	2.1	85.6	24 04.5 +	0.2	86.5	24 10.9	2.5	87.4	24 15.4	4.7	88.3	24 18.0	7.0	89.2
5	23 54.2 −	2.6	84.5	24 04.7 −	0.3	85.4	24 13.4 +	2.0	86.3	24 20.1 +	4.3	87.2	24 25.0 +	6.6	88.1
6	23 51.6	3.0	83.4	24 04.4	0.7	84.3	24 15.4	1.5	85.2	24 24.4	3.9	86.1	24 31.6	6.1	87.0
7	23 48.6	3.5	82.3	24 03.7	1.2	83.2	24 16.9	1.1	84.1	24 28.3	3.3	85.0	24 37.7	5.7	85.9
8	23 45.1	3.9	81.3	24 02.5	1.7	82.1	24 18.0	0.6	83.0	24 31.6	2.9	83.9	24 43.4	5.1	84.8
9	23 41.2	4.4	80.2	24 00.8	2.2	81.0	24 18.6 +	0.1	81.9	24 34.5	2.4	82.8	24 48.5	4.7	83.7
10	23 36.8 −	4.9	79.1	23 58.6 −	2.6	79.9	24 18.7 −	0.4	80.8	24 36.9 +	1.9	81.7	24 53.2 +	4.2	82.6
11	23 31.9	5.3	78.0	23 56.0	3.1	78.8	24 18.3	0.8	79.7	24 38.8	1.4	80.6	24 57.4	3.7	81.5
12	23 26.6	5.7	76.9	23 52.9	3.5	77.8	24 17.5	1.3	78.6	24 40.2	1.0	79.5	25 01.1	3.2	80.4
13	23 20.9	6.2	75.8	23 49.4	4.0	76.7	24 16.2	1.8	77.5	24 41.2 +	0.5	78.4	25 04.3	2.8	79.3
14	23 14.7	6.7	74.7	23 45.4	4.5	75.6	24 14.4	2.2	76.4	24 41.7	0.0	77.3	25 07.1	2.2	78.2
15	23 08.0 −	7.1	73.7	23 41.0 −	5.0	74.5	24 12.2 −	2.7	75.3	24 41.7 −	0.5	76.2	25 09.3 +	1.8	77.1
16	23 00.9	7.5	72.6	23 36.0	5.3	73.4	24 09.5	3.2	74.2	24 41.2	1.0	75.1	25 11.1	1.2	76.0
17	22 53.4	8.0	71.5	23 30.7	5.8	72.3	24 06.3	3.6	73.2	24 40.2	1.4	74.0	25 12.3	0.8	74.9
18	22 45.4	8.4	70.4	23 24.9	6.3	71.2	24 02.7	4.2	72.1	24 38.8	2.0	72.9	25 13.1 +	0.3	73.8
19	22 37.0	8.8	69.3	23 18.6	6.7	70.1	23 58.5	4.5	71.0	24 36.8	2.4	71.8	25 13.4 −	0.2	72.7
20	22 28.2 −	9.2	68.3	23 11.9 −	7.2	69.1	23 54.0 −	5.1	69.9	24 34.4 −	2.9	70.7	25 13.2 −	0.7	71.6
21	22 19.0	9.7	67.2	23 04.7	7.6	68.0	23 48.9	5.5	68.8	24 31.5	3.3	69.6	25 12.5	1.2	70.5
22	22 09.3	10.1	66.1	22 57.1	8.0	66.9	23 43.4	5.9	67.7	24 28.2	3.9	68.5	25 11.3	1.7	69.4
23	21 59.2	10.4	65.1	22 49.1	8.5	65.8	23 37.5	6.4	66.6	24 24.3	4.3	67.4	25 09.6	2.2	68.3
24	21 48.8	10.9	64.0	22 40.6	8.9	64.8	23 31.1	6.9	65.5	24 20.0	4.8	66.3	25 07.4	2.7	67.2
25	21 37.9 −	11.3	63.0	22 31.7 −	9.3	63.7	23 24.2 −	7.3	64.4	24 15.2 −	5.2	65.2	25 04.7 −	3.2	66.1
26	21 26.6	11.7	61.9	22 22.4	9.7	62.6	23 16.9	7.7	63.4	24 10.0	5.7	64.2	25 01.5	3.6	65.0
27	21 14.9	12.1	60.8	22 12.7	10.2	61.5	23 09.2	8.2	62.3	24 04.3	6.2	63.1	24 57.9	4.1	63.9
28	21 02.8	12.5	59.8	22 02.5	10.5	60.5	23 01.0	8.6	61.2	23 58.1	6.6	62.0	24 53.8	4.7	62.8
29	20 50.3	12.8	58.8	21 52.0	11.0	59.4	22 52.4	9.1	60.1	23 51.5	7.1	60.9	24 49.1	5.1	61.7

Dec.	10° Hc	d	Z	12° Hc	d	Z	14° Hc	d	Z	16° Hc	d	Z	18° Hc	d	Z
0	23 36.8 +	11.1	94.4	23 26.6 +	13.4	95.3	23 14.7 +	15.6	96.1	23 00.9 +	17.8	97.0	22 45.4 +	20.0	97.8
1	23 47.9	10.7	93.3	23 40.0	12.9	94.2	23 30.3	15.1	95.1	23 18.7	17.3	96.0	23 05.4	19.5	96.8
2	23 58.6	10.3	92.3	23 52.9	12.6	93.2	23 45.4	14.7	94.0	23 36.0	17.0	94.9	23 24.9	19.1	95.8
3	24 08.9	9.8	91.2	24 05.5	12.0	92.1	24 00.1	14.3	93.0	23 53.0	16.5	93.9	23 44.0	18.7	94.8
4	24 18.7	9.3	90.1	24 17.5	11.6	91.0	24 14.4	13.9	91.9	24 09.5	16.1	92.8	24 02.7	18.2	93.7
5	24 28.0 +	8.9	89.0	24 29.1 +	11.1	89.9	24 28.3 +	13.4	90.8	24 25.6 +	15.6	91.8	24 20.9 +	17.9	92.7
6	24 36.9	8.4	87.9	24 40.2	10.7	88.9	24 41.7	12.9	89.8	24 41.2	15.2	90.7	24 38.8	17.4	91.6
7	24 45.3	7.9	86.8	24 50.9	10.2	87.8	24 54.6	12.5	88.7	24 56.4	14.7	89.6	24 56.2	16.9	90.6
8	24 53.2	7.5	85.8	25 01.1	9.7	86.7	25 07.1	12.0	87.6	25 11.1	14.2	88.6	25 13.1	16.5	89.5
9	25 00.7	6.9	84.7	25 10.8	9.3	85.6	25 19.1	11.5	86.5	25 25.3	13.8	87.5	25 29.6	16.0	88.4
10	25 07.6 +	6.5	83.6	25 20.1 +	8.8	84.5	25 30.6 +	11.0	85.5	25 39.1 +	13.3	86.4	25 45.6 +	15.6	87.4
11	25 14.1	6.0	82.5	25 28.9	8.2	83.4	25 41.6	10.6	84.4	25 52.4	12.9	85.3	26 01.2	15.1	86.3
12	25 20.1	5.5	81.4	25 37.1	7.8	82.3	25 52.2	10.1	83.3	26 05.3	12.3	84.2	26 16.3	14.6	85.2
13	25 25.6	5.0	80.3	25 44.9	7.3	81.2	26 02.3	9.5	82.2	26 17.6	11.8	83.1	26 30.9	14.1	84.1
14	25 30.6	4.5	79.2	25 52.2	6.8	80.1	26 11.8	9.1	81.1	26 29.4	11.4	82.1	26 45.0	13.6	83.0
15	25 35.1 +	4.0	78.1	25 59.0 +	6.3	79.0	26 20.9 +	8.5	80.0	26 40.8 +	10.8	81.0	26 58.6 +	13.1	82.0
16	25 39.1	3.5	76.9	26 05.3	5.7	77.9	26 29.4	8.1	78.9	26 51.6	10.3	79.9	27 11.7	12.6	80.9
17	25 42.6	3.0	75.8	26 11.0	5.3	76.8	26 37.5	7.5	77.8	27 01.9	9.8	78.7	27 24.3	12.1	79.8
18	25 45.6	2.5	74.7	26 16.3	4.7	75.7	26 45.0	7.0	76.6	27 11.7	9.3	77.6	27 36.4	11.5	78.7
19	25 48.1	2.0	73.6	26 21.0	4.3	74.6	26 52.0	6.5	75.5	27 21.0	8.7	76.5	27 47.9	11.0	77.5
20	25 50.1 +	1.5	72.5	26 25.3 +	3.7	73.5	26 58.5 +	5.9	74.4	27 29.7 +	8.2	75.4	27 58.9 +	10.5	76.4
21	25 51.6	1.0	71.4	26 29.0	3.2	72.3	27 04.4	5.5	73.3	27 37.9	7.7	74.3	28 09.4	9.9	75.3
22	25 52.6 +	0.5	70.3	26 32.2	2.6	71.2	27 09.9	4.8	72.2	27 45.6	7.1	73.2	28 19.3	9.4	74.2
23	25 53.1	0.0	69.2	26 34.8	2.2	70.1	27 14.7	4.4	71.1	27 52.7	6.6	72.1	28 28.7	8.8	73.1
24	25 53.1 −	0.6	68.1	26 37.0	1.6	69.0	27 19.1	3.8	69.9	27 59.3	6.0	70.9	28 37.5	8.3	71.9
25	25 52.5 −	1.0	67.0	26 38.6 +	1.1	67.9	27 22.9 +	3.3	68.8	28 05.3 +	5.5	69.8	28 45.8 +	7.7	70.8
26	25 51.5	1.6	65.8	26 39.7 +	0.6	66.7	27 26.2	2.7	67.7	28 10.8	4.9	68.7	28 53.5	7.1	69.7
27	25 49.9	2.0	64.7	26 40.3	0.0	65.6	27 28.9	2.2	66.6	28 15.7	4.4	67.5	29 00.6	6.5	68.6
28	25 47.9	2.6	63.6	26 40.3 −	0.4	64.5	27 31.1	1.7	65.4	28 20.1	3.8	66.4	29 07.1	6.0	67.4
29	25 45.3	3.1	62.5	26 39.9	1.0	63.4	27 32.8	1.1	64.3	28 23.9	3.2	65.3	29 13.1	5.4	66.3

0° Hc	d	Z	2° Hc	d	Z	4° Hc	d	Z	6° Hc	d	Z	8° Hc	d	Z	Dec.
24 00.0	- 0.2	90.0	23 59.1	- 2.6	90.9	23 56.3	- 4.8	91.8	23 51.6	- 7.1	92.7	23 45.1	- 9.3	93.5	0
23 59.8	0.7	91.1	23 56.5	2.9	92.0	23 51.5	5.3	92.9	23 44.5	7.5	93.7	23 35.8	9.8	94.6	1
23 59.1	1.2	92.2	23 53.6	3.5	93.1	23 46.2	5.7	94.0	23 37.0	8.0	94.8	23 26.0	10.3	95.7	2
23 57.9	1.6	93.3	23 50.1	3.9	94.2	23 40.5	6.2	95.0	23 29.0	8.4	95.9	23 15.7	10.6	96.8	3
23 56.3	2.1	94.4	23 46.2	4.4	95.3	23 34.3	6.6	96.1	23 20.6	8.9	97.0	23 05.1	11.1	97.8	4
23 54.2	- 2.6	95.5	23 41.8	- 4.8	96.3	23 27.7	- 7.1	97.2	23 11.7	- 9.3	98.1	22 54.0	- 11.6	98.9	5
23 51.6	3.0	96.6	23 37.0	5.3	97.4	23 20.6	7.6	98.3	23 02.4	9.8	99.1	22 42.4	11.9	100.0	6
23 48.6	3.5	97.7	23 31.7	5.7	98.5	23 13.0	7.9	99.4	22 52.6	10.2	100.2	22 30.5	12.4	101.0	7
23 45.1	4.0	98.7	23 26.0	6.0	99.6	23 05.1	8.4	100.5	22 42.4	10.6	101.3	22 18.1	12.8	102.1	8
23 41.2	4.4	99.8	23 19.8	6.6	100.7	22 56.7	8.9	101.5	22 31.8	11.0	102.4	22 05.3	13.1	103.2	9
23 36.8	- 4.9	100.9	23 13.2	- 7.1	101.8	22 47.8	- 9.2	102.6	22 20.8	- 11.4	103.4	21 52.2	- 13.6	104.2	10
23 31.9	5.3	102.0	23 06.1	7.5	102.9	22 38.6	9.7	103.7	22 09.4	11.9	104.5	21 38.6	14.0	105.3	11
23 26.6	5.7	103.1	22 58.6	8.0	103.9	22 28.9	10.2	104.7	21 57.5	12.2	105.5	21 24.6	14.4	106.3	12
23 20.9	6.2	104.2	22 50.6	8.4	105.0	22 18.7	10.5	105.8	21 45.3	12.7	106.6	21 10.2	14.7	107.3	13
23 14.7	6.7	105.3	22 42.2	8.8	106.1	22 08.2	10.9	106.9	21 32.6	13.1	107.6	20 55.5	15.1	108.4	14
23 08.0	- 7.1	106.3	22 33.4	- 9.2	107.2	21 57.3	- 11.4	107.9	21 19.5	- 13.4	108.7	20 40.4	- 15.5	109.4	15
23 00.9	7.5	107.4	22 24.2	9.7	108.2	21 45.9	11.8	109.0	21 06.1	13.8	109.7	20 24.9	15.9	110.4	16
22 53.4	8.0	108.5	22 14.5	10.0	109.3	21 34.1	12.1	110.0	20 52.3	14.2	110.8	20 09.0	16.2	111.5	17
22 45.4	8.4	109.6	22 04.5	10.5	110.4	21 22.0	12.6	111.1	20 38.1	14.6	111.8	19 52.8	16.5	112.5	18
22 37.0	8.8	110.7	21 54.0	10.9	111.4	21 09.4	12.9	112.1	20 23.5	14.9	112.8	19 36.3	16.9	113.5	19
22 28.2	- 9.2	111.7	21 43.1	- 11.3	112.5	20 56.5	- 13.3	113.2	20 08.6	- 15.3	113.9	19 19.4	- 17.3	114.5	20
22 19.0	9.7	112.8	21 31.8	11.7	113.5	20 43.2	13.7	114.2	19 53.3	15.7	114.9	19 02.1	17.6	115.6	21
22 09.3	10.1	113.9	21 20.1	12.1	114.6	20 29.5	14.1	115.3	19 37.6	16.0	115.9	18 44.5	17.9	116.6	22
21 59.2	10.4	114.9	21 08.0	12.5	115.6	20 15.4	14.4	116.3	19 21.6	16.3	117.0	18 26.6	18.2	117.6	23
21 48.8	10.9	116.0	20 55.5	12.8	116.7	20 01.0	14.8	117.3	19 05.3	16.7	118.0	18 08.4	18.5	118.6	24
21 37.9	- 11.3	117.0	20 42.7	- 13.3	117.7	19 46.2	- 15.1	118.4	18 48.6	- 17.0	119.0	17 49.9	- 18.8	119.6	25
21 26.6	11.7	118.1	20 29.4	13.6	118.8	19 31.1	15.5	119.4	18 31.6	17.3	120.0	17 31.1	19.1	120.6	26
21 14.9	12.1	119.2	20 15.8	14.0	119.8	19 15.6	15.8	120.4	18 14.3	17.7	121.0	17 12.0	19.5	121.6	27
21 02.8	12.5	120.2	20 01.8	14.3	120.8	18 59.8	16.2	121.5	17 56.6	17.9	122.0	16 52.5	19.7	122.6	28
20 50.3	12.8	121.2	19 47.5	14.7	121.9	18 43.6	16.5	122.5	17 38.7	18.3	123.0	16 32.8	19.9	123.5	29

10° Hc	d	Z	12° Hc	d	Z	14° Hc	d	Z	16° Hc	d	Z	18° Hc	d	Z	Dec.
23 36.8	- 11.6	94.4	23 26.6	- 13.8	95.3	23 14.7	- 16.0	96.1	23 00.9	- 18.1	97.0	22 45.4	- 20.3	97.8	0
23 25.2	12.0	95.5	23 12.8	14.2	96.3	22 58.7	16.5	97.2	22 42.8	18.6	98.0	22 25.1	20.6	98.9	1
23 13.2	12.5	96.6	22 58.6	14.7	97.4	22 42.2	16.8	98.2	22 24.2	19.0	99.1	22 04.5	21.1	99.9	2
23 00.7	12.9	97.6	22 43.9	15.0	98.5	22 25.4	17.2	99.3	22 05.2	19.3	100.1	21 43.4	21.4	100.9	3
22 47.8	13.3	98.7	22 28.9	15.5	99.5	22 08.2	17.6	100.3	21 45.9	19.7	101.1	21 22.0	21.8	101.9	4
22 34.5	- 13.7	99.7	22 13.4	- 15.9	100.6	21 50.6	- 18.0	101.3	21 26.2	- 20.1	102.1	21 00.2	- 22.1	102.9	5
22 20.8	14.1	100.8	21 57.5	16.2	101.6	21 32.6	18.4	102.4	21 06.1	20.4	103.1	20 38.1	22.5	103.9	6
22 06.7	14.5	101.8	21 41.3	16.7	102.6	21 14.2	18.7	103.4	20 45.7	20.8	104.1	20 15.6	22.8	104.9	7
21 52.2	15.0	102.9	21 24.6	17.0	103.7	20 55.5	19.1	104.4	20 24.9	21.1	105.1	19 52.8	23.1	105.8	8
21 37.2	15.3	103.9	21 07.6	17.4	104.7	20 36.4	19.4	105.4	20 03.8	21.5	106.1	19 29.7	23.4	106.8	9
21 21.9	- 15.7	105.0	20 50.2	- 17.8	105.7	20 17.0	- 19.8	106.4	19 42.3	- 21.8	107.1	19 06.3	- 23.8	107.8	10
21 06.2	16.0	106.0	20 32.4	18.1	106.7	19 57.2	20.2	107.4	19 20.5	22.1	108.1	18 42.5	24.0	108.8	11
20 50.2	16.5	107.0	20 14.3	18.5	107.8	19 37.0	20.4	108.4	18 58.4	22.4	109.1	18 18.5	24.3	109.7	12
20 33.7	16.7	108.1	19 55.8	18.8	108.8	19 16.6	20.8	109.4	18 36.0	22.7	110.1	17 54.2	24.6	110.7	13
20 17.0	17.2	109.1	19 37.0	19.1	109.8	18 55.8	21.1	110.4	18 13.3	23.1	111.1	17 29.6	24.9	111.7	14
19 59.8	- 17.5	110.1	19 17.9	- 19.5	110.8	18 34.7	- 21.4	111.4	17 50.2	- 23.3	112.0	17 04.7	- 25.2	112.6	15
19 42.3	17.8	111.1	18 58.4	19.8	111.8	18 13.3	21.7	112.4	17 26.9	23.5	113.0	16 39.5	25.4	113.6	16
19 24.5	18.2	112.1	18 38.6	20.1	112.8	17 51.6	22.0	113.4	17 03.4	23.9	114.0	16 14.1	25.7	114.5	17
19 06.3	18.5	113.2	18 18.5	20.4	113.8	17 29.6	22.3	114.4	16 39.5	24.1	114.9	15 48.4	25.9	115.4	18
18 47.8	18.9	114.2	17 58.1	20.7	114.8	17 07.3	22.6	115.3	16 15.4	24.4	115.9	15 22.5	26.1	116.4	19
18 28.9	- 19.1	115.2	17 37.4	- 21.1	115.7	16 44.7	- 22.8	116.3	15 51.0	- 24.6	116.8	14 56.4	- 26.3	117.3	20
18 09.8	19.6	116.2	17 16.3	21.3	116.7	16 21.9	23.1	117.3	15 26.4	24.8	117.8	14 30.1	26.6	118.2	21
17 50.3	19.7	117.2	16 55.0	21.5	117.7	15 58.8	23.4	118.2	15 01.6	25.1	118.7	14 03.5	26.8	119.2	22
17 30.6	20.1	118.1	16 33.5	21.9	118.7	15 35.4	23.6	119.2	14 36.5	25.4	119.7	13 36.7	27.0	120.1	23
17 10.5	20.3	119.1	16 11.6	22.1	119.7	15 11.8	23.8	120.1	14 11.1	25.5	120.6	13 09.7	27.2	121.0	24
16 50.2	- 20.6	120.1	15 49.5	- 22.3	120.6	14 48.0	- 24.1	121.1	13 45.6	- 25.7	121.5	12 42.5	- 27.4	121.9	25
16 29.6	20.9	121.1	15 27.2	22.7	121.6	14 23.9	24.3	122.0	13 19.9	26.0	122.5	12 15.1	27.5	122.8	26
16 08.7	21.2	122.1	15 04.5	22.8	122.5	13 59.6	24.5	123.0	12 53.9	26.1	123.4	11 47.6	27.7	123.7	27
15 47.5	21.4	123.0	14 41.7	23.1	123.5	13 35.1	24.7	123.9	12 27.8	26.3	124.3	11 19.9	27.9	124.6	28
15 26.1	21.7	124.0	14 18.6	23.3	124.5	13 10.4	25.0	124.9	12 01.5	26.5	125.2	10 52.0	28.1	125.6	29

LATITUDE **SAME** NAME

Dec.	20° Hc	d	Z	22° Hc	d	Z	24° Hc	d	Z	26° Hc	d	Z	28° Hc	d	Z
0	22 28.2	+22.0	98.7	22 09.3	+24.1	99.5	21 48.8	+26.1	100.3	21 26.6	+28.1	101.0	21 02.8	+30.0	101.8
1	22 50.2	21.7	97.7	22 33.4	23.7	98.5	22 14.9	25.7	99.3	21 54.7	27.7	100.1	21 32.8	29.7	100.9
2	23 11.9	21.2	96.6	22 57.1	23.4	97.5	22 40.6	25.4	98.3	22 22.4	27.5	99.1	22 02.5	29.4	99.9
3	23 33.1	20.9	95.6	23 20.5	22.9	96.5	23 06.0	25.1	97.3	22 49.9	27.0	98.2	22 31.9	29.1	99.0
4	23 54.0	20.4	94.6	23 43.4	22.6	95.5	23 31.1	24.7	96.3	23 16.9	26.8	97.2	23 01.0	28.7	98.1
5	24 14.4	+20.0	93.6	24 06.0	+22.2	94.5	23 55.8	+24.2	95.3	23 43.7	+26.3	96.2	23 29.7	+28.4	97.1
6	24 34.4	19.6	92.5	24 28.2	21.7	93.4	24 20.0	23.9	94.3	24 10.0	26.0	95.2	23 58.1	28.0	96.1
7	24 54.0	19.2	91.5	24 49.9	21.4	92.4	24 43.9	23.5	93.3	24 36.0	25.5	94.3	24 26.1	27.7	95.2
8	25 13.2	18.7	90.4	25 11.3	20.9	91.4	25 07.4	23.0	92.3	25 01.5	25.2	93.3	24 53.8	27.2	94.2
9	25 31.9	18.2	89.4	25 32.2	20.4	90.3	25 30.4	22.7	91.3	25 26.7	24.8	92.3	25 21.0	26.9	93.2
10	25 50.1	+17.8	88.3	25 52.6	+20.0	89.3	25 53.1	+22.2	90.3	25 51.5	+24.3	91.2	25 47.9	+26.4	92.2
11	26 07.9	17.4	87.3	26 12.6	19.6	88.3	26 15.3	21.7	89.2	26 15.8	23.9	90.2	26 14.3	26.0	91.2
12	26 25.3	16.8	86.2	26 32.2	19.1	87.2	26 37.0	21.3	88.2	26 39.7	23.5	89.2	26 40.3	25.6	90.2
13	26 42.1	16.4	85.1	26 51.3	18.6	86.1	26 58.3	20.8	87.2	27 03.2	23.0	88.2	27 05.9	25.2	89.2
14	26 58.5	15.8	84.1	27 09.9	18.1	85.1	27 19.1	20.3	86.1	27 26.2	22.5	87.1	27 31.1	24.7	88.2
15	27 14.3	+15.4	83.0	27 28.0	+17.6	84.0	27 39.4	+19.9	85.0	27 48.7	+22.1	86.1	27 55.8	+24.3	87.1
16	27 29.7	14.9	81.9	27 45.6	17.1	82.9	27 59.3	19.4	84.0	28 10.8	21.6	85.0	28 20.1	23.7	86.1
17	27 44.6	14.3	80.8	28 02.7	16.6	81.8	28 18.7	18.8	82.9	28 32.4	21.1	84.0	28 43.8	23.3	85.1
18	27 58.9	13.8	79.7	28 19.3	16.1	80.7	28 37.5	18.3	81.8	28 53.5	20.5	82.9	29 07.1	22.8	84.0
19	28 12.7	13.3	78.6	28 35.4	15.5	79.6	28 55.8	17.8	80.7	29 14.0	20.1	81.8	29 29.9	22.3	82.9
20	28 26.0	+12.7	77.5	28 50.9	+15.0	78.5	29 13.6	+17.3	79.6	29 34.1	+19.5	80.7	29 52.2	+21.8	81.9
21	28 38.7	12.2	76.4	29 05.9	14.5	77.4	29 30.9	16.7	78.5	29 53.6	19.0	79.7	30 14.0	21.2	80.8
22	28 50.9	11.7	75.2	29 20.4	13.9	76.3	29 47.6	16.2	77.4	30 12.6	18.4	78.6	30 35.2	20.7	79.7
23	29 02.6	11.0	74.1	29 34.3	13.3	75.2	30 03.8	15.6	76.3	30 31.0	17.9	77.5	30 55.9	20.1	78.6
24	29 13.6	10.5	73.0	29 47.6	12.8	74.1	30 19.4	15.1	75.2	30 48.9	17.3	76.3	31 16.0	19.6	77.5
25	29 24.1	+10.0	71.9	30 00.4	+12.2	73.0	30 34.5	+14.4	74.1	31 06.2	+16.7	75.2	31 35.6	+19.0	76.4
26	29 34.1	9.3	70.7	30 12.6	11.6	71.8	30 48.9	13.9	73.0	31 22.9	16.2	74.1	31 54.6	18.4	75.3
27	29 43.4	8.8	69.6	30 24.2	11.0	70.7	31 02.8	13.2	71.8	31 39.1	15.5	73.0	32 13.0	17.8	74.2
28	29 52.2	8.2	68.5	30 35.2	10.4	69.6	31 16.0	12.7	70.7	31 54.6	14.9	71.8	32 30.8	17.2	73.0
29	30 00.4	7.6	67.3	30 45.6	9.8	68.4	31 28.7	12.0	69.5	32 09.5	14.3	70.7	32 48.0	16.6	71.9

Dec.	30° Hc	d	Z	32° Hc	d	Z	34° Hc	d	Z	36° Hc	d	Z	38° Hc	d	Z
0	20 37.5	+31.9	102.6	20 10.7	+33.7	103.3	19 42.4	+35.5	104.0	19 12.7	+37.2	104.7	18 41.6	+38.9	105.3
1	21 09.4	31.6	101.6	20 44.4	33.5	102.4	20 17.9	35.3	103.1	19 49.9	37.0	103.8	19 20.5	38.7	104.5
2	21 41.0	31.3	100.7	21 17.9	33.2	101.5	20 53.2	35.0	102.3	20 26.9	36.8	103.0	19 59.2	38.5	103.7
3	22 12.3	31.0	99.8	21 51.1	32.9	100.6	21 28.2	34.7	101.4	21 03.7	36.5	102.1	20 37.7	38.2	102.9
4	22 43.3	30.7	98.9	22 24.0	32.5	99.7	22 02.9	34.4	100.5	21 40.2	36.2	101.3	21 15.9	38.0	102.1
5	23 14.0	+30.4	98.0	22 56.5	+32.3	98.8	22 37.3	+34.2	99.6	22 16.4	+36.0	100.4	21 53.9	+37.7	101.2
6	23 44.4	30.0	97.0	23 28.8	32.0	97.9	23 11.5	33.8	98.7	22 52.4	35.7	99.6	22 31.6	37.5	100.4
7	24 14.4	29.6	96.1	24 00.8	31.6	97.0	23 45.3	33.6	97.8	23 28.1	35.4	98.7	23 09.1	37.1	99.5
8	24 44.0	29.3	95.1	24 32.4	31.3	96.0	24 18.9	33.2	96.9	24 03.5	35.1	97.8	23 46.2	36.9	98.7
9	25 13.3	28.9	94.1	25 03.7	30.9	95.1	24 52.1	32.8	96.0	24 38.6	34.7	96.9	24 23.1	36.6	97.8
10	25 42.2	+28.5	93.2	25 34.6	+30.5	94.1	25 24.9	+32.5	95.1	25 13.3	+34.5	96.0	24 59.7	+36.3	97.0
11	26 10.7	28.2	92.2	26 05.1	30.2	93.2	25 57.4	32.2	94.2	25 47.8	34.0	95.1	25 36.0	36.0	96.1
12	26 38.9	27.7	91.2	26 35.3	29.7	92.2	26 29.6	31.8	93.2	26 21.8	33.8	94.2	26 12.0	35.7	95.2
13	27 06.6	27.3	90.2	27 05.0	29.4	91.2	27 01.4	31.4	92.3	26 55.6	33.4	93.3	26 47.7	35.3	94.3
14	27 33.9	26.8	89.2	27 34.4	29.0	90.3	27 32.8	31.0	91.3	27 29.0	33.0	92.3	27 23.0	34.9	93.4
15	28 00.7	+26.4	88.2	28 03.4	+28.5	89.3	28 03.8	+30.6	90.3	28 02.0	+32.6	91.4	27 57.9	+34.6	92.5
16	28 27.1	25.9	87.2	28 31.9	28.0	88.3	28 34.4	30.1	89.4	28 34.6	32.2	90.4	28 32.5	34.2	91.5
17	28 53.0	25.5	86.2	28 59.9	27.7	87.3	29 04.5	29.7	88.4	29 06.8	31.8	89.5	29 06.7	33.8	90.6
18	29 18.5	25.0	85.1	29 27.6	27.1	86.2	29 34.2	29.3	87.4	29 38.6	31.3	88.5	29 40.5	33.4	89.6
19	29 43.5	24.5	84.1	29 54.7	26.7	85.2	30 03.5	28.8	86.4	30 09.9	30.9	87.5	30 13.9	32.9	88.7
20	30 08.0	+24.0	83.0	30 21.4	+26.1	84.2	30 32.3	+28.3	85.4	30 40.8	+30.5	86.5	30 46.8	+32.6	87.7
21	30 32.0	23.4	82.0	30 47.5	25.7	83.1	31 00.6	27.9	84.3	31 11.3	29.9	85.5	31 19.4	32.0	86.7
22	30 55.4	23.0	80.9	31 13.2	25.1	82.1	31 28.5	27.3	83.3	31 41.2	29.5	84.5	31 51.4	31.6	85.7
23	31 18.4	22.3	79.8	31 38.3	24.7	81.0	31 55.8	26.8	82.2	32 10.7	29.0	83.5	32 23.0	31.2	84.7
24	31 40.7	21.9	78.7	32 03.0	24.0	79.9	32 22.6	26.3	81.2	32 39.7	28.5	82.4	32 54.2	30.6	83.7
25	32 02.6	+21.2	77.6	32 27.0	+23.5	78.9	32 48.9	+25.7	80.1	33 08.2	+27.9	81.4	33 24.8	+30.1	82.7
26	32 23.8	20.7	76.5	32 50.5	22.9	77.8	33 14.6	25.2	79.0	33 36.1	27.4	80.3	33 54.9	29.6	81.7
27	32 44.5	20.1	75.4	33 13.4	22.4	76.7	33 39.8	24.6	78.0	34 03.5	26.8	79.3	34 24.5	29.0	80.6
28	33 04.6	19.4	74.3	33 35.8	21.7	75.6	34 04.4	24.0	76.9	34 30.3	26.3	78.2	34 53.5	28.5	79.5
29	33 24.0	18.9	73.2	33 57.5	21.1	74.4	34 28.4	23.4	75.7	34 56.6	25.6	77.1	35 22.0	27.9	78.5

20°			22°			24°			26°			28°			Dec.
Hc	d	Z	Hc	d	Z	Hc	d	Z	Hc	d	Z	Hc	d	Z	
22 28.2	−24.4	98.7	22 09.3	−24.4	99.5	21 48.8	−26.5	100.3	21 26.6	−28.4	101.0	21 02.8	−30.3	101.8	0
22 05.8	22.7	99.7	21 44.9	24.8	100.5	21 22.3	26.8	101.2	20 58.2	28.8	102.0	20 32.5	30.7	102.7	1
21 43.1	23.1	100.7	21 20.1	25.1	101.4	20 55.5	27.1	102.2	20 29.4	29.0	102.9	20 01.8	30.9	103.6	2
21 20.0	23.5	101.7	20 55.0	25.5	102.4	20 28.4	27.4	103.1	20 00.4	29.3	103.9	19 30.9	31.1	104.6	3
20 56.5	23.8	102.6	20 29.5	25.8	103.4	20 01.0	27.7	104.1	19 31.1	29.6	104.8	18 59.8	31.5	105.5	4
20 32.7	−24.1	103.6	20 03.7	−26.1	104.3	19 33.3	−28.0	105.0	19 01.5	−29.9	105.7	18 28.3	−31.7	106.4	5
20 08.6	24.5	104.6	19 37.6	26.4	105.3	19 05.3	28.3	106.0	18 31.6	30.1	106.6	17 56.6	31.9	107.3	6
19 44.1	24.5	105.6	19 11.2	26.7	106.2	18 37.0	28.6	106.9	18 01.5	30.4	107.5	17 24.7	32.2	108.1	7
19 19.4	25.1	106.5	18 44.5	26.9	107.2	18 08.4	28.8	107.8	17 31.1	30.7	108.4	16 52.5	32.4	109.0	8
18 54.3	25.4	107.5	18 17.6	27.3	108.1	17 39.6	29.1	108.8	17 00.4	30.8	109.3	16 20.1	32.6	109.9	9
18 28.9	−25.6	108.5	17 50.3	−27.5	109.1	17 10.5	−29.3	109.7	16 29.6	−31.1	110.2	15 47.5	−32.8	110.8	10
18 03.3	25.9	109.4	17 22.8	27.8	110.0	16 41.2	29.6	110.6	15 58.5	31.3	111.1	15 14.7	33.0	111.6	11
17 37.4	26.2	110.4	16 55.0	28.0	110.9	16 11.6	29.8	111.5	15 27.2	31.6	112.0	14 41.7	33.2	112.5	12
17 11.2	26.5	111.3	16 27.0	28.2	111.9	15 41.8	30.0	112.4	14 55.6	31.7	112.9	14 08.5	33.4	113.4	13
16 44.7	26.7	112.2	15 58.8	28.5	112.8	15 11.8	30.2	113.3	14 23.9	31.9	113.8	13 35.1	33.6	114.2	14
16 18.0	−27.0	113.2	15 30.3	−28.7	113.7	14 41.6	−30.5	114.2	13 52.0	−32.1	114.6	13 01.5	−33.7	115.1	15
15 51.0	27.2	114.1	15 01.6	29.0	114.6	14 11.1	30.6	115.1	13 19.9	32.3	115.5	12 27.8	33.9	115.9	16
15 23.8	27.4	115.0	14 32.6	29.1	115.5	13 40.5	30.8	116.0	12 47.6	32.5	116.4	11 53.9	34.0	116.8	17
14 56.4	27.6	115.9	14 03.5	29.4	116.4	13 09.7	31.0	116.8	12 15.1	32.6	117.2	11 19.9	34.2	117.6	18
14 28.8	27.9	116.9	13 34.1	29.5	117.3	12 38.7	31.2	117.7	11 42.5	32.7	118.1	10 45.7	34.3	118.4	19
14 00.9	−28.0	117.8	13 04.6	−29.7	118.2	12 07.5	−31.3	118.6	11 09.8	−33.0	119.0	10 11.4	−34.5	119.3	20
13 32.9	28.3	118.7	12 34.9	29.9	119.1	11 36.2	31.5	119.5	10 36.8	33.0	119.8	9 36.9	34.5	120.1	21
13 04.6	28.4	119.6	12 05.0	30.1	120.0	11 04.7	31.6	120.3	10 03.8	33.2	120.7	9 02.4	34.7	120.9	22
12 36.2	28.7	120.5	11 34.9	30.2	120.9	10 33.1	31.8	121.2	9 30.6	33.3	121.5	8 27.7	34.8	121.8	23
12 07.5	28.8	121.4	11 04.7	30.4	121.7	10 01.3	31.9	122.1	8 57.3	33.4	122.3	7 52.9	34.9	122.6	24
11 38.7	−28.9	122.3	10 34.3	−30.5	122.6	9 29.4	−32.1	122.9	8 23.9	−33.5	123.2	7 18.0	−34.9	123.4	25
11 09.8	29.2	123.2	10 03.8	30.7	123.5	8 57.3	32.1	123.8	7 50.4	33.6	124.0	6 43.1	35.1	124.2	26
10 40.6	29.2	124.1	9 33.1	30.7	124.4	8 25.2	32.3	124.6	7 16.8	33.7	124.9	6 08.0	35.1	125.0	27
10 11.4	29.5	125.0	9 02.4	31.0	125.2	7 52.9	32.4	125.5	6 43.1	33.8	125.7	5 32.9	35.2	125.9	28
9 41.9	29.5	125.8	8 31.4	31.0	126.1	7 20.5	32.4	126.3	6 09.3	33.9	126.5	4 57.7	35.2	126.7	29

30°			32°			34°			36°			38°			Dec.
Hc	d	Z	Hc	d	Z	Hc	d	Z	Hc	d	Z	Hc	d	Z	
20 37.5	−32.2	102.6	20 10.7	−34.0	103.3	19 42.4	−35.8	104.0	19 12.7	−37.5	104.7	18 41.6	−39.1	105.3	0
20 05.3	32.5	103.5	19 36.7	34.3	104.2	19 06.6	36.0	104.8	18 35.2	37.6	105.5	18 02.5	39.3	106.1	1
19 32.8	32.7	104.3	19 02.4	34.5	105.0	18 30.6	36.2	105.7	17 57.6	37.9	106.3	17 23.2	39.4	106.9	2
19 00.1	33.0	105.2	18 27.9	34.7	105.9	17 54.4	36.4	106.5	17 19.7	38.1	107.1	16 43.8	39.7	107.7	3
18 27.1	33.2	106.1	17 53.2	35.0	106.7	17 18.0	36.6	107.4	16 41.6	38.2	107.9	16 04.1	39.8	108.5	4
17 53.9	−33.5	107.0	17 18.2	−35.2	107.6	16 41.4	−36.9	108.2	16 03.4	−38.5	108.7	15 24.3	−40.0	109.3	5
17 20.4	33.6	107.9	16 43.0	35.3	108.4	16 04.5	37.0	109.0	15 24.9	38.6	109.5	14 44.3	40.1	110.0	6
16 46.8	33.9	108.7	16 07.7	35.6	109.3	15 27.5	37.2	109.8	14 46.3	38.8	110.3	14 04.2	40.3	110.8	7
16 12.9	34.1	109.6	15 32.1	35.8	110.1	14 50.3	37.4	110.6	14 07.5	38.9	111.1	13 23.9	40.5	111.6	8
15 38.8	34.4	110.4	14 56.3	35.9	111.0	14 12.9	37.5	111.4	13 28.6	39.0	111.9	12 43.4	40.5	112.3	9
15 04.4	−34.4	111.3	14 20.4	−36.1	111.8	13 35.4	−37.7	112.2	12 49.6	−39.2	112.7	12 02.9	−40.7	113.1	10
14 30.0	34.7	112.1	13 44.3	36.3	112.6	12 57.7	37.8	113.0	12 10.4	39.2	113.5	11 22.2	40.8	113.8	11
13 55.3	34.9	113.0	13 08.0	36.4	113.4	12 19.9	38.0	113.8	11 31.0	39.4	114.2	10 41.4	40.9	114.6	12
13 20.4	35.0	113.8	12 31.6	36.6	114.2	11 41.9	38.1	114.6	10 51.6	39.6	115.0	10 00.5	40.9	115.3	13
12 45.4	35.1	114.7	11 55.0	36.7	115.1	11 03.8	38.2	115.4	10 12.0	39.7	115.8	9 19.6	41.1	116.1	14
12 10.3	−35.3	115.5	11 18.3	−36.9	115.9	10 25.6	−38.3	116.2	9 32.3	−39.7	116.5	8 38.5	−41.2	116.8	15
11 35.0	35.6	116.3	10 41.4	36.9	116.7	9 47.3	38.5	117.0	8 52.6	39.9	117.3	7 57.3	41.2	117.5	16
10 59.5	35.6	117.1	10 04.5	37.1	117.5	9 08.8	38.5	117.8	8 12.7	40.0	118.0	7 16.1	41.3	118.3	17
10 23.9	35.7	118.0	9 27.4	37.2	118.3	8 30.3	38.6	118.5	7 32.7	40.0	118.8	6 34.8	41.4	119.0	18
9 48.2	35.8	118.8	8 50.2	37.3	119.1	7 51.7	38.7	119.3	6 52.7	40.1	119.5	5 53.4	41.5	119.7	19
9 12.4	−36.0	119.6	8 12.9	−37.4	119.8	7 13.0	−38.8	120.1	6 12.6	−40.1	120.3	5 11.9	−41.4	120.5	20
8 36.4	36.0	120.4	7 35.5	37.5	120.6	6 34.2	38.9	120.9	5 32.5	40.3	121.0	4 30.5	41.6	121.2	21
8 00.4	36.1	121.2	6 58.0	37.5	121.4	5 55.3	38.9	121.6	4 52.2	40.2	121.8	3 48.9	41.5	121.9	22
7 24.3	36.2	122.0	6 20.5	37.6	122.2	5 16.4	39.0	122.4	4 12.0	40.3	122.5	3 07.4	41.6	122.6	23
6 48.1	36.3	122.8	5 42.9	37.7	123.0	4 37.4	39.0	123.1	3 31.7	40.4	123.3	2 25.8	41.6	123.4	24
6 11.8	−36.4	123.6	5 05.2	−37.7	123.8	3 58.4	−39.1	123.9	2 51.3	−40.3	124.0	1 44.2	−41.7	124.1	25
5 35.4	36.4	124.4	4 27.5	37.8	124.6	3 19.3	39.1	124.7	2 11.0	40.4	124.7	1 02.5	41.6	124.8	26
4 59.0	36.5	125.2	3 49.7	37.9	125.3	2 40.2	39.2	125.4	1 30.6	40.4	125.5	0 20.9	−41.7	125.5	27
4 22.5	36.6	126.0	3 11.8	37.8	126.1	2 01.0	39.1	126.2	0 50.2	40.5	126.2	0 20.8	+41.6	53.8	28
3 45.9	36.5	126.8	2 34.0	37.9	126.9	1 21.9	39.2	126.9	0 09.7	−40.4	127.0	1 02.4	41.6	53.0	29

Dec.	40° Hc	d	Z	42° Hc	d	Z	44° Hc	d	Z	46° Hc	d	Z	48° Hc	d	Z
0	18 09.3	+40.5	106.0	17 35.6	+42.1	106.6	17 00.8	+43.5	107.2	16 24.7	+44.9	107.8	15 47.6	+46.2	108.3
1	18 49.8	40.3	105.2	18 17.7	41.8	105.8	17 44.3	43.3	106.5	17 09.6	44.8	107.1	16 33.8	46.0	107.6
2	19 30.1	40.0	104.4	18 59.5	41.7	105.1	18 27.6	43.2	105.7	17 54.4	44.7	106.4	17 20.0	46.0	107.0
3	20 10.1	39.9	103.6	19 41.2	41.5	104.3	19 10.8	43.0	105.0	18 39.1	44.4	105.7	18 06.0	45.9	106.3
4	20 50.0	39.7	102.8	20 22.7	41.2	103.6	19 53.8	42.8	104.3	19 23.5	44.3	105.0	18 51.9	45.7	105.6
5	21 29.7	+39.4	102.0	21 03.9	+41.1	102.8	20 36.6	+42.7	103.5	20 07.8	+44.2	104.2	19 37.6	+45.6	104.9
6	22 09.1	39.2	101.2	21 45.0	40.8	102.0	21 19.3	42.4	102.8	20 52.0	43.9	103.5	20 23.2	45.4	104.2
7	22 48.3	38.9	100.4	22 25.8	40.6	101.2	22 01.7	42.2	102.0	21 35.9	43.8	102.8	21 08.6	45.2	103.5
8	23 27.2	38.7	99.6	23 06.4	40.4	100.4	22 43.9	42.0	101.2	22 19.7	43.5	102.0	21 53.8	45.1	102.8
9	24 05.9	38.4	98.7	23 46.8	40.1	99.6	23 25.9	41.7	100.5	23 03.2	43.4	101.3	22 38.9	44.8	102.1
10	24 44.3	+38.1	97.9	24 26.9	+39.8	98.8	24 07.6	+41.5	99.7	23 46.6	+43.1	100.5	23 23.7	+44.7	101.4
11	25 22.4	37.8	97.0	25 06.7	39.6	98.0	24 49.1	41.3	98.9	24 29.7	42.9	99.8	24 08.4	44.4	100.7
12	26 00.2	37.5	96.2	25 46.3	39.2	97.1	25 30.4	41.0	98.1	25 12.6	42.6	99.0	24 52.8	44.2	99.9
13	26 37.7	37.1	95.3	26 25.5	39.0	96.3	26 11.4	40.7	97.3	25 55.2	42.4	98.2	25 37.0	44.0	99.2
14	27 14.8	36.9	94.4	27 04.5	38.7	95.4	26 52.1	40.4	96.4	26 37.6	42.1	97.4	26 21.0	43.8	98.4
15	27 51.7	+36.4	93.5	27 43.2	+38.3	94.6	27 32.5	+40.2	95.6	27 19.7	+41.9	96.6	27 04.8	+43.5	97.7
16	28 28.1	36.2	92.6	28 21.5	38.0	93.7	28 12.7	39.8	94.8	28 01.6	41.5	95.8	27 48.3	43.2	96.9
17	29 04.3	35.7	91.7	28 59.5	37.7	92.8	28 52.5	39.5	93.9	28 43.1	41.3	95.0	28 31.5	43.0	96.1
18	29 40.0	35.4	90.8	29 37.2	37.3	91.9	29 32.0	39.1	93.1	29 24.4	40.9	94.2	29 14.5	42.6	95.3
19	30 15.4	35.0	89.9	30 14.5	36.9	91.0	30 11.1	38.8	92.2	30 05.3	40.7	93.3	29 57.1	42.4	94.5
20	30 50.4	+34.5	88.9	30 51.4	+36.5	90.1	30 49.9	+38.5	91.3	30 46.0	+40.2	92.5	30 39.5	+42.1	93.7
21	31 24.9	34.1	88.0	31 27.9	36.1	89.2	31 28.4	38.0	90.4	31 26.2	40.0	91.6	31 21.6	41.7	92.8
22	31 59.0	33.7	87.0	32 04.0	35.7	88.2	32 06.4	37.7	89.5	32 06.2	39.5	90.7	32 03.3	41.4	92.0
23	32 32.7	33.2	86.0	32 39.7	35.3	87.3	32 44.1	37.2	88.6	32 45.7	39.2	89.9	32 44.7	41.0	91.1
24	33 05.9	32.8	85.0	33 15.0	34.8	86.3	33 21.3	36.8	87.6	33 24.9	38.8	89.0	33 25.7	40.7	90.3
25	33 38.7	+32.2	84.0	33 49.8	+34.3	85.3	33 58.1	+36.4	86.7	34 03.7	+38.3	88.0	34 06.4	+40.2	89.4
26	34 10.9	31.8	83.0	34 24.1	33.9	84.4	34 34.5	35.9	85.7	34 42.0	38.0	87.1	34 46.6	39.9	88.5
27	34 42.7	31.2	82.0	34 58.0	33.3	83.4	35 10.4	35.5	84.7	35 20.0	37.4	86.2	35 26.5	39.5	87.6
28	35 13.9	30.6	80.9	35 31.3	32.9	82.3	35 45.9	34.9	83.8	35 57.4	37.0	85.2	36 06.0	39.0	86.6
29	35 44.5	30.2	79.9	36 04.2	32.3	81.3	36 20.8	34.5	82.8	36 34.4	36.6	84.2	36 45.0	38.5	85.7

Dec.	50° Hc	d	Z	52° Hc	d	Z	54° Hc	d	Z	56° Hc	d	Z	58° Hc	d	Z
0	15 09.4	+47.5	108.8	14 30.1	+48.8	109.3	13 49.9	+50.0	109.8	13 08.8	+51.0	110.3	12 26.8	+52.1	110.7
1	15 56.9	47.5	108.2	15 18.9	48.7	108.7	14 39.9	49.8	109.2	13 59.8	51.0	109.7	13 18.9	52.0	110.2
2	16 44.4	47.3	107.6	16 07.6	48.6	108.1	15 29.7	49.8	108.7	14 50.8	50.9	109.2	14 10.9	52.0	109.7
3	17 31.7	47.2	106.9	16 56.2	48.5	107.5	16 19.5	49.7	108.1	15 41.7	50.8	108.6	15 02.9	51.9	109.1
4	18 18.9	47.1	106.3	17 44.7	48.3	106.9	17 09.2	49.6	107.5	16 32.5	50.8	108.1	15 54.8	51.8	108.6
5	19 06.0	+46.9	105.6	18 33.0	+48.3	106.3	17 58.8	+49.4	106.9	17 23.3	+50.6	107.5	16 46.6	+51.7	108.1
6	19 52.9	46.8	105.0	19 21.3	48.1	105.6	18 48.2	49.4	106.3	18 13.9	50.5	106.9	17 38.3	51.6	107.6
7	20 39.7	46.7	104.3	20 09.4	47.9	105.0	19 37.6	49.2	105.7	19 04.4	50.4	106.4	18 29.9	51.6	107.0
8	21 26.4	46.4	103.6	20 57.3	47.9	104.4	20 26.8	49.1	105.1	19 54.8	50.4	105.8	19 21.5	51.4	106.5
9	22 12.8	46.3	102.9	21 45.2	47.6	103.7	21 15.9	49.0	104.5	20 45.2	50.2	105.2	20 12.9	51.4	105.9
10	22 59.1	+46.1	102.2	22 32.8	+47.5	103.1	22 04.9	+48.8	103.9	21 35.4	+50.0	104.6	21 04.3	+51.2	105.4
11	23 45.2	46.0	101.5	23 20.3	47.4	102.4	22 53.7	48.7	103.2	22 25.4	50.0	104.0	21 55.5	51.1	104.8
12	24 31.2	45.7	100.8	24 07.7	47.1	101.7	23 42.4	48.5	102.6	23 15.4	49.8	103.4	22 46.6	51.0	104.3
13	25 16.9	45.5	100.1	24 54.8	47.0	101.0	24 30.9	48.4	102.0	24 05.2	49.6	102.8	23 37.6	50.9	103.7
14	26 02.4	45.3	99.4	25 41.8	46.8	100.4	25 19.3	48.1	101.3	24 54.8	49.5	102.2	24 28.5	50.7	103.1
15	26 47.7	+45.1	98.7	26 28.6	+46.6	99.7	26 07.4	+48.0	100.6	25 44.3	+49.3	101.6	25 19.2	+50.6	102.5
16	27 32.8	44.8	97.9	27 15.2	46.3	99.0	26 55.4	47.8	100.0	26 33.6	49.2	101.0	26 09.8	50.5	101.9
17	28 17.6	44.6	97.2	28 01.5	46.2	98.2	27 43.2	47.6	99.3	27 22.8	49.0	100.3	27 00.3	50.3	101.3
18	29 02.2	44.3	96.4	28 47.7	45.8	97.5	28 30.8	47.4	98.6	28 11.8	48.8	99.7	27 50.6	50.1	100.7
19	29 46.5	44.1	95.6	29 33.5	45.7	96.8	29 18.2	47.2	97.9	29 00.6	48.6	99.0	28 40.7	50.0	100.1
20	30 30.6	+43.7	94.9	30 19.2	+45.4	96.0	30 05.4	+46.9	97.2	29 49.2	+48.4	98.3	29 30.7	+49.7	99.5
21	31 14.3	43.5	94.1	31 04.6	45.1	95.3	30 52.3	46.7	96.5	30 37.6	48.2	97.6	30 20.4	49.6	98.8
22	31 57.8	43.1	93.3	31 49.7	44.8	94.5	31 39.0	46.4	95.7	31 25.8	47.9	96.9	31 10.0	49.4	98.2
23	32 40.9	42.9	92.4	32 34.5	44.3	93.7	32 25.4	46.2	95.0	32 13.7	47.7	96.2	31 59.4	49.0	97.5
24	33 23.8	42.4	91.6	33 19.0	44.3	92.9	33 11.6	45.9	94.2	33 01.4	47.4	95.5	32 48.5	49.0	96.8
25	34 06.2	+42.2	90.7	34 03.3	+43.8	92.1	33 57.5	+45.5	93.4	33 48.8	+47.2	94.8	33 37.5	+48.7	96.1
26	34 48.4	41.7	89.9	34 47.1	43.6	91.3	34 43.0	45.3	92.7	34 36.0	46.9	94.0	34 26.2	48.4	95.4
27	35 30.1	41.4	89.0	35 30.7	43.2	90.4	35 28.3	45.0	91.9	35 22.9	46.7	93.3	35 14.6	48.2	94.7
28	36 11.5	40.9	88.1	36 13.9	42.8	89.6	36 13.3	44.6	91.0	36 09.6	46.3	92.5	36 02.8	47.9	94.0
29	36 52.4	40.5	87.2	36 56.7	42.4	88.7	36 57.9	44.2	90.2	36 55.9	45.9	91.7	36 50.7	47.6	93.2

40° Hc	d	Z	42° Hc	d	Z	44° Hc	d	Z	46° Hc	d	Z	48° Hc	d	Z	Dec.
18 09.3	-40.7	106.0	17 35.6	-42.2	106.6	17 00.8	-43.7	107.2	16 24.7	-45.0	107.8	15 47.6	-46.4	108.3	0
17 28.6	40.9	106.7	16 53.4	42.3	107.3	16 17.1	43.8	107.9	15 39.7	45.2	108.4	15 01.2	46.5	109.0	1
16 47.7	41.0	107.5	16 11.1	42.6	108.1	15 33.3	44.0	108.6	14 54.5	45.3	109.1	14 14.7	46.7	109.6	2
16 06.7	41.2	108.3	15 28.5	42.6	108.8	14 49.3	44.0	109.3	14 09.2	45.5	109.8	13 28.0	46.7	110.3	3
15 25.5	41.3	109.0	14 45.9	42.8	109.5	14 05.3	44.2	110.0	13 23.7	45.5	110.5	12 41.3	46.8	110.9	4
14 44.2	-41.5	109.8	14 03.1	-42.9	110.3	13 21.1	-44.3	110.7	12 38.2	-45.6	111.1	11 54.5	-46.9	111.6	5
14 02.7	41.6	110.5	13 20.2	43.1	111.0	12 36.8	44.4	111.4	11 52.6	45.7	111.8	11 07.6	46.9	112.2	6
13 21.1	41.8	111.3	12 37.1	43.1	111.7	11 52.4	44.5	112.1	11 06.9	45.8	112.5	10 20.7	47.1	112.8	7
12 39.3	41.8	112.0	11 54.0	43.3	112.4	11 07.9	44.6	112.8	10 21.1	45.9	113.1	9 33.6	47.1	113.5	8
11 57.5	42.0	112.7	11 10.7	43.3	113.1	10 23.3	44.7	113.5	9 35.2	46.0	113.8	8 46.5	47.2	114.1	9
11 15.5	-42.1	113.5	10 27.4	-43.5	113.8	9 38.6	-44.8	114.1	8 49.2	-46.0	114.4	7 59.3	-47.2	114.7	10
10 33.4	42.2	114.2	9 43.9	43.5	114.5	8 53.8	44.8	114.8	8 03.2	46.1	115.1	7 12.1	47.3	115.3	11
9 51.2	42.3	114.9	9 00.4	43.7	115.2	8 09.0	44.9	115.5	7 17.1	46.1	115.7	6 24.8	47.3	115.9	12
9 08.9	42.3	115.6	8 16.7	43.6	115.9	7 24.1	45.0	116.2	6 31.0	46.2	116.4	5 37.5	47.4	116.6	13
8 26.6	42.5	116.3	7 33.1	43.8	116.6	6 39.1	45.0	116.8	5 44.8	46.2	117.0	4 50.1	47.4	117.2	14
7 44.1	-42.5	117.1	6 49.3	-43.8	117.3	5 54.1	-45.1	117.5	4 58.6	-46.3	117.7	4 02.7	-47.4	117.8	15
7 01.6	42.6	117.8	6 05.5	43.9	118.0	5 09.0	45.1	118.1	4 12.3	46.3	118.3	3 15.3	47.5	118.4	16
6 19.0	42.6	118.5	5 21.6	43.9	118.7	4 23.9	45.1	118.8	3 26.0	46.3	119.0	2 27.8	47.4	119.0	17
5 36.4	42.7	119.2	4 37.7	44.0	119.3	3 38.8	45.2	119.5	2 39.7	46.4	119.6	1 40.4	47.5	119.6	18
4 53.7	42.7	119.9	3 53.8	44.0	120.0	2 53.6	45.2	120.1	1 53.3	46.3	120.2	0 52.9	47.5	120.2	19
4 11.0	-42.8	120.6	3 09.8	-44.0	120.7	2 08.4	-45.2	120.8	1 07.0	-46.4	120.8	0 05.4	-47.5	120.9	20
3 28.2	42.8	121.3	2 25.8	44.0	121.4	1 23.2	45.2	121.4	0 20.6	-46.4	121.5	0 42.1	+47.4	58.5	21
2 45.4	42.8	122.0	1 41.8	44.1	122.1	0 38.0	-45.2	122.1	0 25.8	+46.4	57.9	1 29.5	47.5	57.9	22
2 02.6	42.9	122.7	0 57.7	44.0	122.7	0 07.2	+45.2	57.2	1 12.2	46.3	57.3	2 17.0	47.5	57.3	23
1 19.7	42.8	123.4	0 13.7	-44.1	123.4	0 52.4	45.3	56.6	1 58.5	46.4	56.6	3 04.5	47.4	56.7	24
0 36.9	-42.9	124.1	0 30.4	+44.0	55.9	1 37.7	+45.2	55.9	2 44.9	+46.3	56.0	3 51.9	+47.4	56.1	25
0 06.0	+42.8	55.2	1 14.4	44.1	55.2	2 22.9	45.2	55.3	3 31.2	46.3	55.4	4 39.3	47.3	55.5	26
0 48.8	42.9	54.5	1 58.5	44.0	54.5	3 08.1	45.1	54.6	4 17.5	46.2	54.7	5 26.7	47.3	54.9	27
1 31.7	42.8	53.8	2 42.5	44.0	53.9	3 53.2	45.1	53.9	5 03.7	46.3	54.1	6 14.0	47.3	54.2	28
2 14.5	42.8	53.1	3 26.5	44.0	53.2	4 38.3	45.1	53.3	5 50.0	46.1	53.4	7 01.3	47.3	53.6	29

50° Hc	d	Z	52° Hc	d	Z	54° Hc	d	Z	56° Hc	d	Z	58° Hc	d	Z	Dec.
15 09.4	-47.7	108.8	14 30.1	-48.9	109.3	13 49.9	-50.0	109.8	13 08.8	-51.1	110.3	12 26.8	-52.1	110.7	0
14 21.7	47.8	109.5	13 41.2	48.9	109.9	12 59.9	50.1	110.4	12 17.7	51.2	110.8	11 34.7	52.2	111.2	1
13 33.9	47.9	110.1	12 52.3	49.1	110.5	12 09.8	50.2	110.9	11 26.5	51.2	111.3	10 42.5	52.2	111.7	2
12 46.0	47.9	110.7	12 03.2	49.1	111.1	11 19.6	50.2	111.5	10 35.3	51.3	111.9	9 50.3	52.3	112.2	3
11 58.1	48.0	111.3	11 14.1	49.2	111.7	10 29.4	50.3	112.1	9 44.0	51.3	112.4	8 58.0	52.3	112.7	4
11 10.1	-48.1	111.9	10 24.9	-49.2	112.3	9 39.1	-50.4	112.6	8 52.7	-51.4	112.9	8 05.7	-52.4	113.2	5
10 22.0	48.2	112.5	9 35.7	49.4	112.9	8 48.7	50.4	113.2	8 01.3	51.4	113.4	7 13.3	52.4	113.7	6
9 33.8	48.2	113.1	8 46.3	49.3	113.4	7 58.3	50.4	113.7	7 09.9	51.5	114.0	6 20.9	52.4	114.2	7
8 45.6	48.3	113.7	7 57.0	49.4	114.0	7 07.9	50.5	114.3	6 18.4	51.5	114.5	5 28.5	52.4	114.7	8
7 57.3	48.3	114.3	7 07.6	49.4	114.6	6 17.4	50.5	114.8	5 26.9	51.5	115.1	4 36.1	52.5	115.1	9
7 08.9	-48.3	114.9	6 18.1	-49.5	115.2	5 26.9	-50.5	115.3	4 35.4	-51.5	115.5	3 43.6	-52.5	115.6	10
6 20.6	48.5	115.5	5 28.6	49.5	115.7	4 36.4	50.6	115.9	3 43.9	51.6	116.0	2 51.1	52.5	116.1	11
5 32.1	48.4	116.1	4 39.1	49.4	116.3	3 45.8	50.5	116.4	2 52.3	51.5	116.5	1 58.7	52.5	116.6	12
4 43.7	48.5	116.7	3 49.6	49.6	116.9	2 55.3	50.6	117.0	2 00.8	51.6	117.0	1 06.2	52.5	117.1	13
3 55.2	48.5	117.3	3 00.0	49.6	117.4	2 04.7	50.7	117.5	1 09.2	51.6	117.6	0 13.7	-52.5	117.6	14
3 06.7	-48.6	117.9	2 10.4	-49.6	118.0	1 14.0	-50.6	118.0	0 17.6	-51.6	118.1	0 38.8	+52.5	61.9	15
2 18.1	48.5	118.5	1 20.8	49.6	118.6	0 23.4	-50.6	118.6	0 34.0	+51.5	61.4	1 31.3	52.5	61.5	16
1 29.6	48.6	119.1	0 31.2	-49.6	119.1	0 27.2	+50.6	60.9	1 25.5	51.6	60.9	2 23.8	52.5	61.0	17
0 41.0	-48.6	119.7	0 18.4	+49.6	60.3	1 17.8	50.6	60.3	2 17.1	51.6	60.4	3 16.3	52.5	60.5	18
0 07.7	+48.5	59.7	1 08.0	49.6	59.8	2 08.4	50.6	59.8	3 08.7	51.5	59.9	4 08.8	52.4	60.0	19
0 56.1	+48.6	59.2	1 57.6	+49.6	59.2	2 59.0	+50.6	59.3	4 00.2	+51.5	59.4	5 01.2	+52.5	59.5	20
1 44.7	48.5	58.6	2 47.2	49.6	58.6	3 49.6	50.6	58.7	4 51.7	51.5	58.9	5 53.7	52.4	59.0	21
2 33.2	48.6	58.0	3 36.8	49.5	58.1	4 40.1	50.6	58.2	5 43.2	51.5	58.3	6 46.1	52.3	58.5	22
3 21.8	48.5	57.4	4 26.3	49.6	57.5	5 30.7	50.5	57.7	6 34.7	51.5	57.8	7 38.4	52.4	58.0	23
4 10.3	48.5	56.8	5 15.9	49.5	56.9	6 21.2	50.4	57.1	7 26.2	51.4	57.3	8 30.8	52.3	57.6	24
4 58.8	+48.4	56.2	6 05.4	+49.4	56.4	7 11.6	+50.5	56.6	8 17.6	+51.3	56.8	9 23.1	+52.2	57.1	25
5 47.2	48.4	55.6	6 54.8	49.4	55.8	8 02.1	50.4	56.0	9 08.9	51.4	56.3	10 15.3	52.2	56.6	26
6 35.6	48.4	55.0	7 44.2	49.4	55.2	8 52.5	50.3	55.5	10 00.3	51.2	55.7	11 07.5	52.2	56.1	27
7 24.0	48.3	54.4	8 33.6	49.3	54.7	9 42.8	50.3	54.9	10 51.5	51.2	55.2	11 59.7	52.1	55.5	28
8 12.3	48.3	53.8	9 22.9	49.3	54.1	10 33.1	50.2	54.4	11 42.7	51.2	54.7	12 51.8	52.1	55.0	29

LATITUDE **SAME** NAME

Dec.	0° Hc	d	Z	2° Hc	d	Z	4° Hc	d	Z	6° Hc	d	Z	8° Hc	d	Z
°	° ′	′	°	° ′	′	°	° ′	′	°	° ′	′	°	° ′	′	°
0	22 00.0 − 0.2		90.0	21 59.2 + 2.0		90.8	21 56.6 + 4.3		91.6	21 52.4 + 6.5		92.4	21 46.5 + 8.8		93.2
1	21 59.8 0.6		88.9	22 01.2 1.6		89.7	22 00.9 3.9		90.5	21 58.9 6.2		91.3	21 55.3 8.4		92.2
2	21 59.2 1.1		87.8	22 02.8 1.2		88.7	22 04.8 3.5		89.5	22 05.1 5.7		90.3	22 03.7 7.9		91.1
3	21 58.1 1.5		86.8	22 04.0 0.8		87.6	22 08.3 3.0		88.4	22 10.8 5.3		89.2	22 11.6 7.5		90.0
4	21 56.6 1.9		85.7	22 04.8 + 0.4		86.5	22 11.3 2.6		87.3	22 16.1 4.8		88.1	22 19.1 7.2		88.9
5	21 54.7 − 2.3		84.6	22 05.2 − 0.1		85.4	22 13.9 + 2.2		86.2	22 20.9 + 4.5		87.0	22 26.3 + 6.7		87.9
6	21 52.4 2.7		83.5	22 05.1 0.5		84.3	22 16.1 1.7		85.1	22 25.4 4.0		86.0	22 33.0 6.2		86.8
7	21 49.7 3.2		82.5	22 04.6 0.9		83.3	22 17.8 1.3		84.1	22 29.4 3.6		84.9	22 39.2 5.8		85.7
8	21 46.5 3.6		81.4	22 03.7 1.4		82.2	22 19.1 0.9		83.0	22 33.0 3.1		83.8	22 45.0 5.4		84.6
9	21 42.9 4.0		80.3	22 02.3 1.8		81.1	22 20.0 + 0.5		81.9	22 36.1 2.7		82.7	22 50.4 5.0		83.6
10	21 38.9 − 4.4		79.2	22 00.5 − 2.2		80.0	22 20.5 0.0		80.8	22 38.8 + 2.3		81.6	22 55.4 + 4.5		82.5
11	21 34.5 4.8		78.2	21 58.3 2.6		78.9	22 20.5 − 0.4		79.7	22 41.1 1.8		80.6	22 59.9 4.1		81.4
12	21 29.7 5.2		77.1	21 55.7 3.0		77.9	22 20.1 0.8		78.7	22 42.9 1.4		79.5	23 04.0 3.6		80.3
13	21 24.5 5.7		76.0	21 52.7 3.5		76.8	22 19.3 1.3		77.6	22 44.3 0.9		78.4	23 07.6 3.2		79.2
14	21 18.8 6.0		74.9	21 49.2 3.8		75.7	22 18.0 1.6		76.5	22 45.2 + 0.6		77.3	23 10.8 2.7		78.1
15	21 12.8 − 6.4		73.9	21 45.4 − 4.3		74.6	22 16.4 − 2.2		75.4	22 45.8 0.0		76.2	23 13.5 + 2.3		77.0
16	21 06.4 6.9		72.8	21 41.1 4.7		73.6	22 14.2 2.5		74.3	22 45.8 − 0.3		75.1	23 15.8 1.8		76.0
17	20 59.5 7.2		71.8	21 36.4 5.1		72.5	22 11.7 3.0		73.3	22 45.5 0.8		74.1	23 17.6 1.4		74.9
18	20 52.3 7.6		70.7	21 31.3 5.6		71.4	22 08.7 3.4		72.2	22 44.7 1.3		73.0	23 19.0 0.9		73.8
19	20 44.7 8.1		69.6	21 25.7 5.9		70.4	22 05.3 3.8		71.1	22 43.4 1.7		71.9	23 19.9 + 0.5		72.7
20	20 36.6 − 8.4		68.6	21 19.8 − 6.3		69.3	22 01.5 − 4.2		70.0	22 41.7 − 2.1		70.8	23 20.4 0.0		71.6
21	20 28.2 8.8		67.5	21 13.5 6.8		68.2	21 57.3 4.7		69.0	22 39.6 2.5		69.7	23 20.4 − 0.4		70.5
22	20 19.4 9.1		66.5	21 06.7 7.1		67.1	21 52.6 5.1		67.9	22 37.1 3.0		68.6	23 20.0 0.9		69.4
23	20 10.3 9.6		65.4	20 59.6 7.6		66.1	21 47.5 5.5		66.8	22 34.1 3.4		67.6	23 19.1 1.3		68.3
24	20 00.7 9.9		64.3	20 52.0 7.9		65.0	21 42.0 5.9		65.7	22 30.7 3.9		66.5	23 17.8 1.8		67.3
25	19 50.8 − 10.3		63.3	20 44.1 − 8.3		64.0	21 36.1 − 6.3		64.7	22 26.8 − 4.3		65.4	23 16.0 − 2.2		66.2
26	19 40.5 10.6		62.3	20 35.8 8.7		62.9	21 29.8 6.7		63.6	22 22.5 4.7		64.3	23 13.8 2.7		65.1
27	19 29.9 11.0		61.2	20 27.1 9.1		61.8	21 23.1 7.1		62.5	22 17.8 5.1		63.2	23 11.1 3.1		64.0
28	19 18.9 11.4		60.2	20 18.0 9.4		60.8	21 16.0 7.6		61.5	22 12.7 5.6		62.2	23 08.0 3.6		62.9
29	19 07.5 11.7		59.1	20 08.6 9.9		59.7	21 08.4 7.9		60.4	22 07.1 6.0		61.1	23 04.4 4.0		61.8

Dec.	10° Hc	d	Z	12° Hc	d	Z	14° Hc	d	Z	16° Hc	d	Z	18° Hc	d	Z
°	° ′	′	°	° ′	′	°	° ′	′	°	° ′	′	°	° ′	′	°
0	21 38.9 + 11.0		94.0	21 29.7 + 13.2		94.8	21 18.8 + 15.4		95.6	21 06.4 + 17.5		96.4	20 52.3 + 19.6		97.1
1	21 49.9 10.6		93.0	21 42.9 12.8		93.8	21 34.2 15.0		94.5	21 23.9 17.2		95.3	21 11.9 19.4		96.1
2	22 00.5 10.2		91.9	21 55.7 12.4		92.7	21 49.2 14.6		93.5	21 41.1 16.8		94.3	21 31.3 18.9		95.1
3	22 10.7 9.8		90.8	22 08.1 12.0		91.6	22 03.8 14.2		92.5	21 57.9 16.3		93.3	21 50.2 18.5		94.1
4	22 20.5 9.4		89.8	22 20.1 11.6		90.6	22 18.0 13.9		91.4	22 14.2 16.0		92.2	22 08.7 18.2		93.0
5	22 29.9 + 8.9		88.7	22 31.7 + 11.2		89.5	22 31.9 + 13.3		90.4	22 30.2 + 15.6		91.2	22 26.9 + 17.8		92.0
6	22 38.8 8.5		87.6	22 42.9 10.7		88.5	22 45.2 13.0		89.3	22 45.8 15.2		90.1	22 44.7 17.3		91.0
7	22 47.3 7.8		86.6	22 53.6 10.4		87.4	22 58.2 12.6		88.2	23 01.0 14.8		89.1	23 02.0 17.0		89.9
8	22 55.4 7.6		85.5	23 04.0 9.8		86.3	23 10.8 12.1		87.2	23 15.8 14.3		88.0	23 19.0 16.5		88.9
9	23 03.0 7.2		84.4	23 13.8 9.5		85.3	23 22.9 11.7		86.1	23 30.1 13.9		87.0	23 35.5 16.2		87.8
10	23 10.2 + 6.8		83.3	23 23.3 + 9.0		84.2	23 34.6 + 11.2		85.0	23 44.0 + 13.5		85.9	23 51.7 + 15.7		86.8
11	23 17.0 6.3		82.2	23 32.3 8.5		83.1	23 45.8 10.8		84.0	23 57.5 13.0		84.8	24 07.4 15.2		85.7
12	23 23.3 5.9		81.2	23 40.8 8.2		82.0	23 56.6 10.4		82.9	24 10.5 12.6		83.8	24 22.6 14.8		84.7
13	23 29.2 5.4		80.1	23 49.0 7.6		80.9	24 07.0 9.8		81.8	24 23.1 12.1		82.7	24 37.4 14.4		83.6
14	23 34.6 4.9		79.0	23 56.6 7.2		79.8	24 16.8 9.5		80.7	24 35.2 11.7		81.6	24 51.8 13.9		82.5
15	23 39.5 + 4.5		77.9	24 03.8 + 6.7		78.8	24 26.3 + 8.9		79.6	24 46.9 + 11.2		80.6	25 05.7 + 13.4		81.5
16	23 44.0 4.1		76.8	24 10.5 6.3		77.7	24 35.2 8.5		78.6	24 58.1 10.7		79.5	25 19.1 13.0		80.4
17	23 48.1 3.6		75.7	24 16.8 5.8		76.6	24 43.7 8.1		77.5	25 08.8 10.3		78.4	25 32.1 12.4		79.3
18	23 51.7 3.1		74.6	24 22.6 5.3		75.5	24 51.8 7.5		76.4	25 19.1 9.8		77.3	25 44.5 12.0		78.2
19	23 54.8 2.6		73.5	24 27.9 4.9		74.4	24 59.3 7.1		75.3	25 28.9 9.3		76.2	25 56.5 11.6		77.1
20	23 57.4 + 2.2		72.4	24 32.8 + 4.4		73.3	25 06.4 + 6.6		74.2	25 38.2 + 8.8		75.1	26 08.1 + 11.0		76.0
21	23 59.6 1.8		71.3	24 37.2 3.9		72.2	25 13.0 6.1		73.1	25 47.0 8.3		74.0	26 19.1 10.5		74.9
22	24 01.4 1.2		70.3	24 41.1 3.4		71.1	25 19.1 5.6		72.0	25 55.3 7.8		72.9	26 29.6 10.0		73.9
23	24 02.6 0.8		69.2	24 44.5 3.0		70.0	25 24.7 5.1		70.9	26 03.1 7.2		71.8	26 39.6 9.5		72.7
24	24 03.4 + 0.4		68.1	24 47.5 2.4		68.9	25 29.8 4.6		69.8	26 10.3 6.8		70.7	26 49.1 9.0		71.6
25	24 03.8 − 0.2		67.0	24 49.9 + 2.0		67.8	25 34.4 + 4.1		68.7	26 17.1 + 6.3		69.6	26 58.1 + 8.4		70.5
26	24 03.6 0.6		65.9	24 51.9 1.5		66.7	25 38.5 3.6		67.6	26 23.4 5.8		68.5	27 06.5 7.9		69.4
27	24 03.0 1.0		64.8	24 53.4 1.0		65.6	25 42.1 3.1		66.5	26 29.2 5.2		67.4	27 14.4 7.4		68.3
28	24 02.0 1.6		63.7	24 54.4 + 0.5		64.5	25 45.2 2.7		65.4	26 34.4 4.7		66.3	27 21.8 6.9		67.2
29	24 00.4 2.0		62.6	24 54.9 0.0		63.4	25 47.9 2.1		64.3	26 39.1 4.3		65.1	27 28.7 6.3		66.1

0°			2°			4°			6°			8°			
Hc	d	Z	Hc	d	Z	Hc	d	Z	Hc	d	Z	Hc	d	Z	Dec.
° ′	′	°	° ′	′	°	° ′	′	°	° ′	′	°	° ′	′	°	°
22 00.0 − 0.2	90.0		21 59.2 − 2.5	90.8		21 56.6 − 4.7	91.6		21 52.4 − 7.0	92.4		21 46.5 − 9.2	93.2		0
21 59.8 0.6 91.1		21 56.7 2.9 91.9		21 51.9 5.1 92.7		21 45.4 7.3 93.5		21 37.3 9.6 94.3		1
21 59.2 1.1 92.2		21 53.8 3.3 93.0		21 46.8 5.6 93.8		21 38.1 7.8 94.6		21 27.7 10.0 95.3		2
21 58.1 1.5 93.2		21 50.5 3.7 94.0		21 41.2 6.0 94.8		21 30.3 8.2 95.6		21 17.7 10.4 96.4		3
21 56.6 1.9 94.3		21 46.8 4.2 95.1		21 35.2 6.3 95.9		21 22.1 8.6 96.7		21 07.3 10.8 97.5		4
21 54.7 − 2.3 95.4		21 42.6 − 4.5 96.2		21 28.9 − 6.8 97.0		21 13.5 − 9.0 97.7		20 56.5 −11.2 98.5		5
21 52.4 2.7 96.5		21 38.1 5.0 97.3		21 22.1 7.2 98.0		21 04.5 9.4 98.8		20 45.3 11.5 99.6		6
21 49.7 3.2 97.5		21 33.1 5.4 98.3		21 14.9 7.6 99.1		20 55.1 9.8 99.9		20 33.8 12.0 100.6		7
21 46.5 3.6 98.6		21 27.7 5.8 99.4		21 07.3 8.0 100.2		20 45.3 10.1 100.9		20 21.8 12.3 101.7		8
21 42.9 4.0 99.7		21 21.9 6.2 100.5		20 59.3 8.4 101.2		20 35.2 10.6 102.0		20 09.5 12.7 102.7		9
21 38.9 − 4.4 100.8		21 15.7 − 6.6 101.5		20 50.9 − 8.7 102.3		20 24.6 −10.9 103.0		19 56.8 −13.0 103.7		10
21 34.5 4.8 101.8		21 09.1 7.0 102.6		20 42.2 9.2 103.4		20 13.7 11.3 104.1		19 43.8 13.4 104.8		11
21 29.7 5.2 102.9		21 02.1 7.4 103.7		20 33.0 9.5 104.4		20 02.4 11.6 105.1		19 30.4 13.7 105.8		12
21 24.5 5.7 104.0		20 54.7 7.8 104.7		20 23.5 10.0 105.5		19 50.8 12.1 106.2		19 16.7 14.1 106.8		13
21 18.8 6.0 105.1		20 46.9 8.2 105.8		20 13.5 10.3 106.5		19 38.7 12.3 107.2		19 02.6 14.5 107.9		14
21 12.8 − 6.4 106.1		20 38.7 − 8.5 106.9		20 03.2 −10.6 107.6		19 26.4 −12.8 108.2		18 48.1 −14.7 108.9		15
21 06.4 6.9 107.2		20 30.2 9.0 107.9		19 52.6 11.1 108.6		19 13.6 13.1 109.3		18 33.4 15.2 109.9		16
20 59.5 7.2 108.2		20 21.2 9.3 109.0		19 41.5 11.3 109.7		19 00.5 13.4 110.3		18 18.2 15.4 110.9		17
20 52.3 7.6 109.3		20 11.9 9.7 110.0		19 30.2 11.8 110.7		18 47.1 13.8 111.3		18 02.8 15.7 112.0		18
20 44.7 8.1 110.4		20 02.2 10.1 111.1		19 18.4 12.1 111.7		18 33.3 14.1 112.4		17 47.1 16.1 113.0		19
20 36.6 − 8.4 111.4		19 52.1 −10.4 112.1		19 06.3 −12.5 112.8		18 19.2 −14.4 113.4		17 31.0 −16.3 114.0		20
20 28.2 8.8 112.5		19 41.7 10.8 113.2		18 53.8 12.7 113.8		18 04.8 14.7 114.4		17 14.7 16.7 115.0		21
20 19.4 9.1 113.5		19 30.9 11.2 114.2		18 41.1 13.4 114.8		17 50.1 15.1 115.4		16 58.0 17.0 116.0		22
20 10.3 9.6 114.6		19 19.7 11.5 115.3		18 27.9 13.4 115.9		17 35.0 15.4 116.5		16 41.0 17.2 117.0		23
20 00.7 9.9 115.7		19 08.2 11.9 116.3		18 14.5 13.8 116.9		17 19.6 15.6 117.5		16 23.8 17.5 118.0		24
19 50.8 −10.3 116.7		18 56.3 −12.2 117.3		18 00.7 −14.1 117.9		17 04.0 −16.0 118.5		16 06.3 −17.8 119.0		25
19 40.5 10.6 117.7		18 44.1 12.6 118.4		17 46.6 14.5 118.9		16 48.0 16.3 119.5		15 48.5 18.1 120.0		26
19 29.9 11.0 118.8		18 31.5 12.8 119.4		17 32.1 14.7 120.0		16 31.7 16.5 120.5		15 30.4 18.4 121.0		27
19 18.9 11.4 119.8		18 18.7 13.3 120.4		17 17.4 15.1 121.0		16 15.2 16.9 121.5		15 12.0 18.6 122.0		28
19 07.5 11.7 120.9		18 05.4 13.5 121.4		17 02.3 15.3 122.0		15 58.3 17.1 122.5		14 53.4 18.8 123.0		29

10°			12°			14°			16°			18°			
Hc	d	Z	Hc	d	Z	Hc	d	Z	Hc	d	Z	Hc	d	Z	Dec.
° ′	′	°	° ′	′	°	° ′	′	°	° ′	′	°	° ′	′	°	°
21 38.9 −11.4 94.0		21 29.7 −13.6 94.8		21 18.8 −15.7 95.6		21 06.4 −17.9 96.4		20 52.3 −20.0 97.1		0
21 27.5 11.8 95.1		21 16.1 14.0 95.8		21 03.1 16.2 96.6		20 48.5 18.3 97.4		20 32.3 20.4 98.1		1
21 15.7 12.2 96.1		21 02.1 14.4 96.9		20 46.9 16.5 97.6		20 30.2 18.6 98.4		20 11.9 20.7 99.1		2
21 03.5 12.6 97.2		20 47.7 14.7 97.9		20 30.4 16.9 98.7		20 11.6 19.0 99.4		19 51.2 21.0 100.1		3
20 50.9 12.9 98.2		20 33.0 15.1 99.0		20 13.5 17.2 99.7		19 52.6 19.3 100.4		19 30.2 21.4 101.1		4
20 38.0 −13.4 99.3		20 17.9 −15.5 100.0		19 56.3 −17.6 100.7		19 33.3 −19.7 101.4		19 08.8 −21.7 102.1		5
20 24.6 13.7 100.3		20 02.4 15.8 101.0		19 38.7 17.9 101.7		19 13.6 20.0 102.4		18 47.1 22.0 103.1		6
20 10.9 14.1 101.3		19 46.6 16.2 102.1		19 20.8 18.2 102.7		18 53.6 20.2 103.4		18 25.1 22.3 104.1		7
19 56.8 14.4 102.4		19 30.4 16.5 103.1		19 02.6 18.6 103.8		18 33.4 20.6 104.4		18 02.8 22.6 105.1		8
19 42.4 14.8 103.4		19 13.9 16.9 104.1		18 44.0 18.9 104.8		18 12.8 21.0 105.4		17 40.2 22.8 106.0		9
19 27.6 −15.1 104.4		18 57.0 −17.2 105.1		18 25.1 −19.2 105.8		17 51.8 −21.2 106.4		17 17.4 −23.2 107.0		10
19 12.5 15.5 105.5		18 39.8 17.5 106.1		18 05.9 19.6 106.8		17 30.6 21.4 107.4		16 54.2 23.4 108.0		11
18 57.0 15.8 106.5		18 22.3 17.8 107.1		17 46.3 19.8 107.8		17 09.2 21.8 108.4		16 30.8 23.7 108.9		12
18 41.2 16.1 107.5		18 04.5 18.2 108.1		17 26.5 20.1 108.7		16 47.4 22.1 109.3		16 07.1 23.9 109.9		13
18 25.1 16.5 108.5		17 46.3 18.4 109.1		17 06.4 20.4 109.7		16 25.3 22.3 110.3		15 43.2 24.2 110.8		14
18 08.6 −16.8 109.5		17 27.9 −18.7 110.1		16 46.0 −20.7 110.7		16 03.0 −22.5 111.3		15 19.0 −24.4 111.8		15
17 51.8 17.0 110.5		17 09.2 19.1 111.1		16 25.3 20.9 111.7		15 40.5 22.9 112.2		14 54.6 24.7 112.7		16
17 34.8 17.4 111.5		16 50.1 19.3 112.1		16 04.4 21.2 112.7		15 17.6 23.0 113.2		14 29.9 24.9 113.7		17
17 17.4 17.7 112.6		16 30.8 19.6 113.1		15 43.2 21.5 113.6		14 54.6 23.3 114.1		14 05.0 25.1 114.6		18
16 59.7 18.0 113.6		16 11.2 19.9 114.1		15 21.7 21.7 114.6		14 31.3 23.6 115.1		13 39.9 25.3 115.5		19
16 41.7 −18.3 114.5		15 51.3 −20.1 115.1		15 00.0 −21.9 115.6		14 07.7 −23.7 116.0		13 14.6 −25.5 116.5		20
16 23.4 18.5 115.5		15 31.2 20.4 116.1		14 38.0 22.2 116.5		13 44.0 24.0 117.0		12 49.1 25.7 117.4		21
16 04.9 18.8 116.5		15 10.8 20.6 117.0		14 15.8 22.4 117.5		13 20.0 24.2 117.9		12 23.4 25.9 118.3		22
15 46.1 19.1 117.5		14 50.2 20.9 118.0		13 53.4 22.7 118.5		12 55.8 24.4 118.9		11 57.5 26.0 119.3		23
15 27.0 19.4 118.5		14 29.3 21.1 119.0		13 30.7 22.8 119.4		12 31.4 24.5 119.8		11 31.5 26.3 120.2		24
15 07.6 −19.6 119.5		14 08.2 −21.4 119.9		13 07.9 −23.1 120.4		12 06.9 −24.8 120.7		11 05.2 −26.4 121.1		25
14 48.0 19.8 120.5		13 46.8 21.6 120.9		12 44.8 23.3 121.3		11 42.1 24.9 121.7		10 38.8 26.6 122.0		26
14 28.2 20.1 121.4		13 25.2 21.8 121.9		12 21.5 23.4 122.3		11 17.2 25.1 122.6		10 12.2 26.7 122.9		27
14 08.1 20.3 122.4		13 03.4 22.0 122.8		11 58.1 23.7 123.2		10 52.1 25.3 123.5		9 45.5 26.9 123.8		28
13 47.8 20.6 123.4		12 41.4 22.2 123.8		11 34.4 23.8 124.1		10 26.8 25.5 124.5		9 18.6 27.0 124.7		29

Dec.	20° Hc	d	Z	22° Hc	d	Z	24° Hc	d	Z	26° Hc	d	Z	28° Hc	d	Z
°	° ′	′	°	° ′	′	°	° ′	′	°	° ′	′	°	° ′	′	°
0	20 36.6	+21.8	97.9	20 19.4	+23.8	98.6	20 00.7	+25.8	99.3	19 40.5	+27.8	100.0	19 18.9	+29.7	100.7
1	20 58.4	21.4	96.9	20 43.2	23.5	97.6	20 26.5	25.5	98.4	20 08.3	27.5	99.1	19 48.6	29.4	99.8
2	21 19.8	21.0	95.9	21 06.7	23.1	96.6	20 52.0	25.2	97.4	20 35.8	27.2	98.2	20 18.0	29.1	98.9
3	21 40.8	20.7	94.9	21 29.8	22.8	95.7	21 17.2	24.8	96.4	21 03.0	26.8	97.2	20 47.1	28.9	98.0
4	22 01.5	20.3	93.9	21 52.6	22.4	94.7	21 42.0	24.5	95.5	21 29.8	26.5	96.2	21 16.0	28.5	97.0
5	22 21.8	+19.9	92.8	22 15.0	+22.1	93.7	22 06.5	+24.2	94.5	21 56.3	+26.2	95.3	21 44.5	+28.2	96.1
6	22 41.7	19.6	91.8	22 37.1	21.6	92.6	22 30.7	23.7	93.5	22 22.5	25.8	94.3	22 12.7	27.8	95.1
7	23 01.3	19.1	90.8	22 58.7	21.3	91.6	22 54.4	23.4	92.5	22 48.3	25.5	93.3	22 40.5	27.5	94.2
8	23 20.4	18.7	89.8	23 20.0	20.9	90.6	23 17.8	23.0	91.5	23 13.8	25.1	92.3	23 08.0	27.2	93.2
9	23 39.1	18.3	88.7	23 40.9	20.5	89.6	23 40.8	22.6	90.5	23 38.9	24.7	91.4	23 35.2	26.8	92.2
10	23 57.4	+17.9	87.7	24 01.4	+20.0	88.6	24 03.4	+22.3	89.5	24 03.6	+24.4	90.4	24 02.0	+26.4	91.2
11	24 15.3	17.5	86.6	24 21.4	19.7	87.5	24 25.7	21.8	88.4	24 28.0	23.9	89.4	24 28.4	26.0	90.3
12	24 32.8	17.0	85.6	24 41.1	19.2	86.5	24 47.5	21.3	87.4	24 51.9	23.5	88.3	24 54.4	25.6	89.3
13	24 49.8	16.6	84.5	25 00.3	18.8	85.5	25 08.8	21.0	86.4	25 15.4	23.1	87.3	25 20.0	25.2	88.3
14	25 06.4	16.1	83.5	25 19.1	18.3	84.4	25 29.8	20.5	85.4	25 38.5	22.7	86.3	25 45.2	24.8	87.3
15	25 22.5	+15.7	82.4	25 37.4	+17.9	83.3	25 50.3	+20.0	84.3	26 01.2	+22.2	85.3	26 10.0	+24.4	86.3
16	25 38.2	15.1	81.3	25 55.3	17.4	82.3	26 10.3	19.7	83.3	26 23.4	21.8	84.2	26 34.4	24.0	85.2
17	25 53.3	14.8	80.3	26 12.7	16.9	81.2	26 30.0	19.1	82.2	26 45.2	21.3	83.2	26 58.4	23.4	84.2
18	26 08.1	14.2	79.2	26 29.6	16.4	80.2	26 49.1	18.6	81.1	27 06.5	20.9	82.2	27 21.8	23.1	83.2
19	26 22.3	13.7	78.1	26 46.0	16.0	79.1	27 07.7	18.2	80.1	27 27.4	20.3	81.1	27 44.9	22.5	82.1
20	26 36.0	+13.3	77.0	27 02.0	+15.4	78.0	27 25.9	+17.7	79.0	27 47.7	+19.9	80.0	28 07.4	+22.1	81.1
21	26 49.3	12.7	75.9	27 17.4	15.0	76.9	27 43.6	17.2	77.9	28 07.6	19.4	79.0	28 29.5	21.6	80.0
22	27 02.0	12.2	74.8	27 32.4	14.4	75.8	28 00.8	16.6	76.8	28 27.0	18.9	77.9	28 51.1	21.1	79.0
23	27 14.2	11.7	73.7	27 46.8	14.0	74.7	28 17.4	16.2	75.8	28 45.9	18.3	76.8	29 12.2	20.5	77.9
24	27 25.9	11.2	72.6	28 00.8	13.4	73.6	28 33.6	15.6	74.7	29 04.2	17.9	75.7	29 32.7	20.1	76.8
25	27 37.1	+10.6	71.5	28 14.2	+12.8	72.5	28 49.2	+15.0	73.6	29 22.1	+17.2	74.6	29 52.8	+19.5	75.7
26	27 47.7	10.2	70.4	28 27.0	12.3	71.4	29 04.2	14.6	72.5	29 39.3	16.8	73.5	30 12.3	18.9	74.6
27	27 57.9	9.5	69.3	28 39.3	11.8	70.3	29 18.8	13.9	71.3	29 56.1	16.2	72.4	30 31.2	18.4	73.5
28	28 07.4	9.1	68.2	28 51.1	11.2	69.2	29 32.7	13.4	70.2	30 12.3	15.6	71.3	30 49.6	17.8	72.4
29	28 16.5	8.4	67.0	29 02.3	10.6	68.1	29 46.1	12.9	69.1	30 27.9	15.0	70.2	31 07.4	17.3	71.3

Dec.	30° Hc	d	Z	32° Hc	d	Z	34° Hc	d	Z	36° Hc	d	Z	38° Hc	d	Z
°	° ′	′	°	° ′	′	°	° ′	′	°	° ′	′	°	° ′	′	°
0	18 55.8	+31.6	101.4	18 31.4	+33.4	102.1	18 05.6	+35.2	102.7	17 38.5	+36.9	103.4	17 10.2	+38.5	104.0
1	19 27.4	31.3	100.5	19 04.8	33.1	101.2	18 40.8	34.9	101.9	18 15.4	36.7	102.5	17 48.7	38.4	103.2
2	19 58.7	31.1	99.6	19 37.9	32.9	100.3	19 15.7	34.7	101.0	18 52.1	36.5	101.7	18 27.1	38.1	102.4
3	20 29.8	30.7	98.7	20 10.8	32.7	99.4	19 50.4	34.5	100.2	19 28.6	36.2	100.9	19 05.2	38.0	101.5
4	21 00.5	30.5	97.8	20 43.5	32.3	98.5	20 24.9	34.2	99.3	20 04.8	36.0	100.0	19 43.2	37.7	100.7
5	21 31.0	+30.1	96.9	21 15.8	+32.1	97.6	20 59.1	+33.9	98.4	20 40.8	+35.7	99.2	20 20.9	+37.5	99.9
6	22 01.1	29.8	95.9	21 47.9	31.7	96.7	21 33.0	33.6	97.5	21 16.5	35.5	98.3	20 58.4	37.2	99.1
7	22 30.9	29.5	95.0	22 19.6	31.5	95.8	22 06.6	33.4	96.6	21 52.0	35.2	97.4	21 35.6	37.0	98.2
8	23 00.4	29.2	94.0	22 51.1	31.1	94.9	22 40.0	33.0	95.7	22 27.2	34.9	96.6	22 12.6	36.7	97.4
9	23 29.6	28.8	93.1	23 22.2	30.8	94.0	23 13.0	32.8	94.8	23 02.1	34.6	95.7	22 49.3	36.5	96.5
10	23 58.4	+28.5	92.1	23 53.0	+30.5	93.0	23 45.8	+32.4	93.9	23 36.7	+34.3	94.8	23 25.8	+36.1	95.6
11	24 26.9	28.0	91.2	24 23.5	30.1	92.1	24 18.2	32.0	93.0	24 11.0	34.0	93.9	24 01.9	35.9	94.8
12	24 54.9	27.7	90.2	24 53.6	29.7	91.1	24 50.2	31.7	92.1	24 45.0	33.6	93.0	24 37.8	35.5	93.9
13	25 22.6	27.4	89.2	25 23.3	29.3	90.2	25 21.9	31.4	91.1	25 18.6	33.3	92.1	25 13.3	35.2	93.0
14	25 50.0	26.9	88.2	25 52.6	29.0	89.2	25 53.3	31.0	90.2	25 51.9	33.0	91.1	25 48.5	34.9	92.1
15	26 16.9	+26.5	87.2	26 21.6	+28.6	88.2	26 24.3	+30.6	89.2	26 24.9	+32.6	90.2	26 23.4	+34.5	91.2
16	26 43.4	26.0	86.2	26 50.2	28.1	87.2	26 54.9	30.2	88.3	26 57.5	32.2	89.3	26 57.9	34.2	90.3
17	27 09.4	25.6	85.2	27 18.3	27.8	86.3	27 25.1	29.8	87.3	27 29.7	31.8	88.3	27 32.1	33.8	89.4
18	27 35.0	25.2	84.2	27 46.1	27.3	85.3	27 54.9	29.4	86.3	28 01.5	31.5	87.4	28 05.9	33.5	88.4
19	28 00.2	24.7	83.2	28 13.4	26.8	84.2	28 24.3	28.9	85.3	28 33.0	31.0	86.4	28 39.4	33.0	87.5
20	28 24.9	+24.3	82.1	28 40.2	+26.4	83.2	28 53.2	+28.5	84.3	29 04.0	+30.6	85.4	29 12.4	+32.6	86.5
21	28 49.2	23.7	81.1	29 06.6	25.9	82.2	29 21.7	28.1	83.3	29 34.6	30.1	84.4	29 45.0	32.2	85.6
22	29 12.9	23.3	80.1	29 32.5	25.5	81.2	29 49.8	27.6	82.3	30 04.7	29.7	83.4	30 17.2	31.8	84.6
23	29 36.2	22.8	79.0	29 58.0	24.9	80.1	30 17.4	27.1	81.3	30 34.4	29.2	82.4	30 49.0	31.3	83.6
24	29 59.0	22.2	77.9	30 22.9	24.4	79.1	30 44.5	26.6	80.2	31 03.6	28.7	81.4	31 20.3	30.8	82.6
25	30 21.2	+21.7	76.9	30 47.3	+23.9	78.0	31 11.1	+26.0	79.2	31 32.3	+28.3	80.4	31 51.1	+30.4	81.6
26	30 42.9	21.2	75.8	31 11.2	23.4	76.9	31 37.1	25.6	78.1	32 00.6	27.7	79.3	32 21.5	29.8	80.6
27	31 04.1	20.6	74.7	31 34.6	22.8	75.9	32 02.7	25.0	77.1	32 28.3	27.2	78.3	32 51.3	29.4	79.6
28	31 24.7	20.0	73.6	31 57.4	22.7	74.8	32 27.7	24.5	76.0	32 55.5	26.6	77.2	33 20.7	28.8	78.5
29	31 44.7	19.5	72.5	32 19.7	21.7	73.7	32 52.2	23.9	74.9	33 22.1	26.1	76.2	33 49.5	28.3	77.5

20°			22°			24°			26°			28°			Dec.
Hc	d	Z	Hc	d	Z	Hc	d	Z	Hc	d	Z	Hc	d	Z	
° ′	′	°	° ′	′	°	° ′	′	°	° ′	′	°	° ′	′	°	°
20 36.6	−22.1	97.9	20 19.4	−24.1	98.6	20 00.7	−26.1	99.3	19 40.5	−28.0	100.0	19 18.9	−30.0	100.7	0
20 14.5	22.4	98.9	19 55.3	24.4	99.6	19 34.6	26.4	100.3	19 12.5	28.4	101.0	18 48.9	30.2	101.7	1
19 52.1	22.7	99.8	19 30.9	24.8	100.6	19 08.2	26.7	101.2	18 44.1	28.6	101.9	18 18.7	30.6	102.6	2
19 29.4	23.1	100.8	19 06.1	25.0	101.5	18 41.5	27.0	102.2	18 15.5	28.9	102.8	17 48.1	30.7	103.5	3
19 06.3	23.4	101.8	18 41.1	25.4	102.5	18 14.5	27.3	103.1	17 46.6	29.2	103.8	17 17.4	31.0	104.4	4
18 42.9	−23.7	102.8	18 15.7	−25.6	103.4	17 47.2	−27.6	104.1	17 17.4	−29.4	104.7	16 46.4	−31.2	105.3	5
18 19.2	23.9	103.8	17 50.1	25.9	104.4	17 19.6	27.8	105.0	16 48.0	29.7	105.6	16 15.2	31.5	106.2	6
17 55.3	24.3	104.7	17 24.2	26.2	105.3	16 51.8	28.0	105.9	16 18.3	29.8	106.5	15 43.7	31.7	107.0	7
17 31.0	24.5	105.7	16 58.0	26.4	106.3	16 23.8	28.3	106.8	15 48.5	30.1	107.4	15 12.0	31.8	107.9	8
17 06.5	24.8	106.7	16 31.6	26.7	107.2	15 55.5	28.5	107.8	15 18.4	30.4	108.3	14 40.2	32.1	108.8	9
16 41.7	−25.1	107.6	16 04.9	−26.9	108.1	15 27.0	−28.8	108.7	14 48.0	−30.5	109.2	14 08.1	−32.2	109.7	10
16 16.6	25.3	108.5	15 38.0	27.2	109.1	14 58.2	28.9	109.6	14 17.5	30.7	110.1	13 35.9	32.5	110.5	11
15 51.3	25.5	109.5	15 10.8	27.4	110.0	14 29.3	29.2	110.5	13 46.8	30.9	111.0	13 03.4	32.6	111.4	12
15 25.8	25.8	110.4	14 43.4	27.6	110.9	14 00.1	29.4	111.4	13 15.9	31.1	111.8	12 30.8	32.7	112.3	13
15 00.0	26.0	111.3	14 15.8	27.8	111.8	13 30.7	29.5	112.3	12 44.8	31.3	112.7	11 58.1	33.0	113.1	14
14 34.0	−26.3	112.3	13 48.0	−28.0	112.7	13 01.2	−29.8	113.2	12 13.5	−31.4	113.6	11 25.1	−33.0	114.0	15
14 07.7	26.4	113.2	13 20.0	28.2	113.7	12 31.4	29.9	114.1	11 42.1	31.6	114.5	10 52.1	33.3	114.8	16
13 41.3	26.7	114.1	12 51.8	28.4	114.6	12 01.5	30.0	115.0	11 10.5	31.7	115.3	10 18.8	33.3	115.7	17
13 14.6	26.8	115.1	12 23.4	28.5	115.5	11 31.5	30.3	115.8	10 38.8	31.9	116.2	9 45.5	33.5	116.5	18
12 47.8	27.1	116.0	11 54.9	28.8	116.4	11 01.2	30.4	116.7	10 06.9	32.0	117.1	9 12.0	33.5	117.4	19
12 20.7	−27.2	116.9	11 26.1	−28.9	117.3	10 30.8	−30.5	117.6	9 34.9	−32.1	117.9	8 38.5	−33.7	118.2	20
11 53.5	27.4	117.8	10 57.2	29.0	118.2	10 00.3	30.7	118.5	9 02.8	32.3	118.8	8 04.8	33.8	119.0	21
11 26.1	27.6	118.7	10 28.2	29.2	119.0	9 29.6	30.8	119.4	8 30.5	32.3	119.6	7 31.0	33.9	119.9	22
10 58.5	27.7	119.6	9 59.0	29.4	119.9	8 58.8	30.9	120.2	7 58.2	32.5	120.5	6 57.1	34.0	120.7	23
10 30.8	27.9	120.5	9 29.6	29.5	120.8	8 27.9	31.1	121.1	7 25.7	32.6	121.3	6 23.1	34.0	121.5	24
10 02.9	−28.0	121.4	9 00.1	−29.6	121.7	7 56.8	−31.1	122.0	6 53.1	−32.6	122.2	5 49.1	−34.2	122.4	25
9 34.9	28.1	122.3	8 30.5	29.7	122.6	7 25.7	31.3	122.8	6 20.5	32.8	123.0	5 14.9	34.2	123.2	26
9 06.8	28.3	123.2	8 00.8	29.8	123.5	6 54.4	31.3	123.7	5 47.7	32.8	123.9	4 40.7	34.2	124.0	27
8 38.5	28.5	124.1	7 31.0	30.0	124.3	6 23.1	31.4	124.5	5 14.9	32.8	124.7	4 06.5	34.3	124.8	28
8 10.0	28.5	125.0	7 01.0	30.0	125.2	5 51.7	31.5	125.4	4 42.0	32.9	125.5	3 32.2	34.4	125.7	29

30°			32°			34°			36°			38°			Dec.
Hc	d	Z	Hc	d	Z	Hc	d	Z	Hc	d	Z	Hc	d	Z	
° ′	′	°	° ′	′	°	° ′	′	°	° ′	′	°	° ′	′	°	°
18 55.8	−31.8	101.4	18 31.4	−33.7	102.1	18 05.6	−35.4	102.7	17 38.5	−37.1	103.4	17 10.2	−38.8	104.0	0
18 24.0	32.1	102.3	17 57.7	33.9	103.0	17 30.2	35.6	103.6	17 01.4	37.3	104.2	16 31.4	38.9	104.8	1
17 51.9	32.3	103.2	17 23.8	34.1	103.8	16 54.6	35.9	104.4	16 24.1	37.5	105.0	15 52.5	39.1	105.6	2
17 19.6	32.6	104.1	16 49.7	34.3	104.7	16 18.7	36.0	105.3	15 46.6	37.7	105.8	15 13.4	39.3	106.3	3
16 47.0	33.0	105.0	16 15.4	34.5	105.5	15 42.7	36.2	106.1	15 08.9	37.8	106.6	14 34.1	39.4	107.1	4
16 14.2	−33.0	105.8	15 40.9	−34.7	106.4	15 06.5	−36.4	106.9	14 31.1	−38.0	107.4	13 54.7	−39.6	107.9	5
15 41.2	33.2	106.7	15 06.2	34.9	107.2	14 30.1	36.6	107.7	13 53.1	38.2	108.2	13 15.1	39.7	108.7	6
15 08.0	33.4	107.6	14 31.3	35.1	108.1	13 53.5	36.7	108.6	13 14.9	38.3	109.0	12 35.4	39.9	109.4	7
14 34.6	33.6	108.4	13 56.2	35.3	108.9	13 16.8	36.9	109.4	12 36.6	38.5	109.8	11 55.5	39.9	110.2	8
14 01.0	33.8	109.3	13 20.9	35.4	109.7	12 39.9	37.0	110.2	11 58.1	38.5	110.6	11 15.6	40.1	111.0	9
13 27.2	−33.9	110.1	12 45.5	−35.6	110.6	12 02.9	−37.1	111.0	11 19.6	−38.7	111.4	10 35.5	−40.2	111.7	10
12 53.3	34.1	111.0	12 09.9	35.7	111.4	11 25.8	37.3	111.8	10 40.9	38.9	112.2	9 55.3	40.3	112.5	11
12 19.2	34.2	111.8	11 34.2	35.9	112.2	10 48.5	37.5	112.6	10 02.0	38.9	112.9	9 15.0	40.4	113.2	12
11 45.0	34.4	112.7	10 58.3	35.9	113.0	10 11.0	37.5	113.4	9 23.1	39.0	113.7	8 34.6	40.5	114.0	13
11 10.6	34.6	113.5	10 22.4	36.2	113.9	9 33.5	37.6	114.2	8 44.1	39.1	114.5	7 54.1	40.5	114.7	14
10 36.0	−34.7	114.3	9 46.2	−36.3	114.7	8 55.9	−37.8	115.0	8 05.0	−39.2	115.2	7 13.6	−40.6	115.5	15
10 01.3	34.8	115.2	9 10.0	36.3	115.5	8 18.1	37.8	115.7	7 25.8	39.3	116.0	6 33.0	40.7	116.2	16
9 26.5	34.9	116.0	8 33.7	36.4	116.3	7 40.3	37.9	116.5	6 46.5	39.4	116.8	5 52.3	40.8	117.0	17
8 51.6	35.0	116.8	7 57.3	36.6	117.1	7 02.4	38.0	117.3	6 07.1	39.4	117.5	5 11.5	40.8	117.7	18
8 16.6	35.1	117.6	7 20.7	36.6	117.9	6 24.4	38.1	118.1	5 27.7	39.4	118.3	4 30.7	40.8	118.4	19
7 41.5	−35.2	118.5	6 44.1	−36.7	118.7	5 46.3	−38.1	118.9	4 48.3	−39.6	119.0	3 49.9	−40.9	119.2	20
7 06.3	35.3	119.3	6 07.4	36.7	119.5	5 08.2	38.2	119.6	4 08.7	39.5	119.8	3 09.0	40.9	119.9	21
6 31.0	35.4	120.1	5 30.7	36.8	120.3	4 30.0	38.2	120.4	3 29.2	39.6	120.5	2 28.1	40.9	120.6	22
5 55.6	35.4	120.9	4 53.9	36.9	121.1	3 51.8	38.3	121.2	2 49.6	39.7	121.3	1 47.2	41.0	121.4	23
5 20.2	35.5	121.7	4 17.0	36.9	121.9	3 13.5	38.3	122.0	2 09.9	39.6	122.0	1 06.2	40.9	122.1	24
4 44.7	−35.6	122.6	3 40.1	−37.0	122.6	2 35.2	−38.3	122.7	1 30.3	−39.7	122.7	0 25.3	−41.0	122.8	25
4 09.1	35.6	123.3	3 03.1	37.0	123.4	1 56.9	38.4	123.5	0 50.6	39.7	123.5	0 15.7	+41.0	56.4	26
3 33.5	35.7	124.1	2 26.1	37.0	124.2	1 18.5	38.3	124.3	0 10.9	−39.6	124.3	0 56.7	40.9	55.7	27
2 57.8	35.6	124.9	1 49.1	37.1	125.0	0 40.2	38.4	125.0	0 28.7	+39.7	55.0	1 37.6	41.0	55.0	28
2 22.2	35.8	125.7	1 12.0	37.1	125.8	0 01.8	−38.4	125.8	1 08.4	39.7	54.2	2 18.6	40.9	54.3	29

Dec.	40° Hc	d	Z	42° Hc	d	Z	44° Hc	d	Z	46° Hc	d	Z	48° Hc	d	Z
°	° ′	′	°	° ′	′	°	° ′	′	°	° ′	′	°	° ′	′	°
0	16 40.6	+ 40.2	104.6	16 09.8	+ 41.8	105.1	15 38.0	+ 43.2	105.7	15 05.0	+ 44.6	106.2	14 31.0	+ 46.0	106.7
1	17 20.8	39.9	103.8	16 51.6	41.5	104.4	16 21.2	43.0	105.0	15 49.6	44.5	105.5	15 17.0	45.9	106.0
2	18 00.7	39.8	103.0	17 33.1	41.4	103.6	17 04.2	42.9	104.2	16 34.1	44.4	104.8	16 02.9	45.7	105.4
3	18 40.5	39.7	102.2	18 14.5	41.2	102.9	17 47.1	42.8	103.5	17 18.5	44.2	104.1	16 48.6	45.7	104.7
4	19 20.2	39.3	101.4	18 55.7	41.0	102.1	18 29.9	42.5	102.8	18 02.7	44.1	103.4	17 34.3	45.5	104.0
5	19 59.5	+ 39.2	100.6	19 36.7	+ 40.8	101.3	19 12.4	+ 42.4	102.0	18 46.8	+ 43.9	102.7	18 19.8	+ 45.3	103.3
6	20 38.7	39.0	99.8	20 17.5	40.6	100.5	19 54.8	42.2	101.3	19 30.7	43.7	102.0	19 05.1	45.2	102.6
7	21 17.7	38.7	99.0	20 58.1	40.4	99.8	20 37.0	42.0	100.5	20 14.4	43.5	101.2	19 50.3	45.0	101.9
8	21 56.4	38.4	98.2	21 38.5	40.2	99.0	21 19.0	41.8	99.7	20 57.9	43.4	100.5	20 35.3	44.8	101.2
9	22 34.8	38.3	97.3	22 18.7	39.9	98.2	22 00.8	41.6	99.0	21 41.3	43.1	99.8	21 20.1	44.7	100.5
10	23 13.1	+ 37.9	96.5	22 58.6	+ 39.6	97.4	22 42.4	+ 41.3	98.2	22 24.4	+ 43.0	99.0	22 04.8	+ 44.5	99.8
11	23 51.0	37.7	95.7	23 38.2	39.5	96.5	23 23.7	41.1	97.4	23 07.4	42.7	98.3	22 49.3	44.2	99.1
12	24 28.7	37.3	94.8	24 17.7	39.1	95.7	24 04.8	40.8	96.6	23 50.1	42.5	97.5	23 33.5	44.1	98.4
13	25 06.0	37.1	93.9	24 56.8	38.9	94.9	24 45.6	40.6	95.8	24 32.6	42.2	96.7	24 17.6	43.8	97.6
14	25 43.1	36.7	93.1	25 35.7	38.5	94.0	25 26.2	40.3	95.0	25 14.8	42.0	95.9	25 01.4	43.7	96.9
15	26 19.8	+ 36.5	92.2	26 14.2	+ 38.3	93.2	26 06.5	+ 40.1	94.2	25 56.8	+ 41.7	95.1	25 45.1	+ 43.3	96.1
16	26 56.3	36.1	91.3	26 52.5	37.9	92.3	26 46.6	39.7	93.3	26 38.5	41.5	94.3	26 28.4	43.2	95.3
17	27 32.4	35.7	90.4	27 30.4	37.6	91.4	27 26.3	39.4	92.5	27 20.0	41.2	93.5	27 11.6	42.8	94.6
18	28 08.1	35.4	89.5	28 08.0	37.3	90.6	28 05.7	39.1	91.6	28 01.2	40.9	92.7	27 54.4	42.6	93.8
19	28 43.5	35.0	88.6	28 45.3	36.9	89.7	28 44.8	38.8	90.8	28 42.1	40.5	91.9	28 37.0	42.3	93.0
20	29 18.5	+ 34.6	87.7	29 22.2	+ 36.6	88.8	29 23.6	+ 38.4	89.9	29 22.6	+ 40.3	91.0	29 19.3	+ 42.0	92.2
21	29 53.1	34.2	86.7	29 58.8	36.1	87.9	30 02.0	38.1	89.0	30 02.9	39.9	90.2	30 01.3	41.7	91.3
22	30 27.3	33.8	85.8	30 34.9	35.8	86.9	30 40.1	37.7	88.1	30 42.8	39.6	89.3	30 43.0	41.4	90.5
23	31 01.1	33.3	84.8	31 10.7	35.4	86.0	31 17.8	37.3	87.2	31 22.4	39.2	88.4	31 24.4	41.0	89.7
24	31 34.4	33.0	83.8	31 46.1	34.9	85.1	31 55.1	36.9	86.3	32 01.6	38.8	87.5	32 05.4	40.7	88.8
25	32 07.4	+ 32.4	82.8	32 21.0	+ 34.5	84.1	32 32.0	+ 36.5	85.4	32 40.4	+ 38.4	86.6	32 46.1	+ 40.3	87.9
26	32 39.8	32.0	81.8	32 55.5	34.0	83.1	33 08.5	36.1	84.4	33 18.8	38.1	85.7	33 26.4	39.9	87.0
27	33 11.8	31.4	80.8	33 29.5	33.6	82.1	33 44.6	35.6	83.5	33 56.9	37.6	84.8	34 06.3	39.6	86.1
28	33 43.2	31.0	79.8	34 03.1	33.1	81.1	34 20.2	35.1	82.5	34 34.5	37.1	83.9	34 45.9	39.1	85.2
29	34 14.2	30.4	78.8	34 36.2	32.5	80.1	34 55.3	34.7	81.5	35 11.6	36.7	82.9	35 25.0	38.7	84.3

Dec.	50° Hc	d	Z	52° Hc	d	Z	54° Hc	d	Z	56° Hc	d	Z	58° Hc	d	Z
°	° ′	′	°	° ′	′	°	° ′	′	°	° ′	′	°	° ′	′	°
0	13 56.0	+ 47.3	107.2	13 20.1	+ 48.5	107.7	12 43.2	+ 49.7	108.1	12 05.5	+ 50.8	108.5	11 27.0	+ 51.9	108.9
1	14 43.3	47.2	106.6	14 08.6	48.5	107.1	13 32.9	49.7	107.5	12 56.3	50.8	108.0	12 18.9	51.8	108.4
2	15 30.5	47.1	105.9	14 57.1	48.3	106.4	14 22.6	49.5	106.9	13 47.1	50.7	107.4	13 10.7	51.8	107.9
3	16 17.6	47.0	105.3	15 45.4	48.3	105.8	15 12.1	49.5	106.4	14 37.8	50.6	106.9	14 02.5	51.7	107.4
4	17 04.6	46.8	104.6	16 33.7	48.1	105.2	16 01.6	49.4	105.8	15 28.4	50.6	106.3	14 54.2	51.6	106.8
5	17 51.4	+ 46.7	104.0	17 21.8	+ 48.0	104.6	16 51.0	+ 49.2	105.2	16 19.0	+ 50.4	105.8	15 45.8	+ 51.6	106.3
6	18 38.1	46.6	103.3	18 09.8	47.9	104.0	17 40.2	49.2	104.6	17 09.4	50.4	105.2	16 37.4	51.4	105.8
7	19 24.7	46.4	102.6	18 57.7	47.8	103.3	18 29.4	49.1	104.0	17 59.8	50.2	104.6	17 28.8	51.4	105.2
8	20 11.1	46.3	102.0	19 45.5	47.6	102.7	19 18.5	48.9	103.4	18 50.0	50.1	104.0	18 20.2	51.3	104.7
9	20 57.4	46.1	101.3	20 33.1	47.5	102.0	20 07.4	48.8	102.8	19 40.1	50.1	103.5	19 11.5	51.2	104.2
10	21 43.5	+ 46.0	100.6	21 20.6	+ 47.4	101.4	20 56.2	+ 48.6	102.1	20 30.2	+ 49.9	102.9	20 02.7	+ 51.1	103.6
11	22 29.5	45.7	99.9	22 08.0	47.1	100.7	21 44.8	48.5	101.5	21 20.1	49.8	102.3	20 53.8	51.0	103.0
12	23 15.2	45.6	99.2	22 55.1	47.0	100.1	22 33.3	48.4	100.9	22 09.9	49.6	101.7	21 44.8	50.8	102.5
13	24 00.8	45.3	98.5	23 42.1	46.9	99.4	23 21.7	48.2	100.2	22 59.5	49.5	101.1	22 35.6	50.8	101.9
14	24 46.1	45.2	97.8	24 29.0	46.6	98.7	24 09.9	48.0	99.6	23 49.0	49.4	100.5	23 26.4	50.6	101.3
15	25 31.3	+ 45.0	97.1	25 15.6	+ 46.4	98.0	24 57.9	+ 47.9	98.9	24 38.4	+ 49.2	99.8	24 17.0	+ 50.4	100.7
16	26 16.3	44.7	96.3	26 02.0	46.3	97.3	25 45.8	47.7	98.3	25 27.6	49.0	99.2	25 07.4	50.3	100.1
17	27 01.0	44.4	95.6	26 48.3	46.0	96.6	26 33.5	47.4	97.6	26 16.6	48.9	98.6	25 57.7	50.2	99.5
18	27 45.4	44.3	94.8	27 34.3	45.8	95.9	27 20.9	47.3	96.9	27 05.5	48.7	97.9	26 47.9	50.0	98.9
19	28 29.7	43.9	94.0	28 20.1	45.5	95.1	28 08.2	47.1	96.2	27 54.2	48.5	97.3	27 37.9	49.9	98.3
20	29 13.6	+ 43.7	93.3	29 05.6	+ 45.3	94.4	28 55.3	+ 46.8	95.5	28 42.7	+ 48.3	96.6	28 27.8	+ 49.6	97.7
21	29 57.3	43.4	92.5	29 50.9	45.1	93.6	29 42.1	46.6	94.8	29 31.0	48.0	95.9	29 17.4	49.5	97.0
22	30 40.7	43.1	91.7	30 36.0	44.7	92.9	30 28.7	46.4	94.0	30 19.0	47.9	95.2	30 06.9	49.3	96.4
23	31 23.8	42.8	90.9	31 20.7	44.5	92.1	31 15.1	46.1	93.3	31 06.9	47.6	94.5	30 56.2	49.1	95.7
24	32 06.6	42.5	90.0	32 05.2	44.2	91.3	32 01.2	45.8	92.6	31 54.5	47.4	93.8	31 45.3	48.8	95.0
25	32 49.1	+ 42.1	89.2	32 49.4	+ 43.9	90.5	32 47.0	+ 45.5	91.8	32 41.9	+ 47.1	93.1	32 34.1	+ 48.7	94.4
26	33 31.2	41.8	88.4	33 33.3	43.5	89.7	33 32.5	45.3	91.0	33 29.0	46.9	92.3	33 22.8	48.4	93.7
27	34 13.0	41.4	87.5	34 16.8	43.2	88.9	34 17.8	44.9	90.2	34 15.9	46.6	91.6	34 11.2	48.1	92.9
28	34 54.4	41.0	86.6	35 00.0	42.9	88.0	35 02.7	44.6	89.4	35 02.5	46.3	90.8	34 59.3	47.9	92.2
29	35 35.4	40.6	85.7	35 42.9	42.5	87.2	35 47.3	44.3	88.6	35 48.8	45.9	90.0	35 47.2	47.6	91.5

40° Hc	d	Z	42° Hc	d	Z	44° Hc	d	Z	46° Hc	d	Z	48° Hc	d	Z	Dec.
16 40.6	− 40.4	104.6	16 09.8	− 41.8	105.1	15 38.0	− 43.4	105.7	15 05.0	− 44.8	106.2	14 31.0	− 46.1	106.7	0
16 00.2	40.5	105.3	15 28.0	42.1	105.9	14 54.6	43.5	106.4	14 20.2	44.8	106.9	13 44.9	46.2	107.4	1
15 19.7	40.6	106.1	14 45.9	42.1	106.6	14 11.1	43.6	107.1	13 35.4	45.0	107.6	12 58.7	46.4	108.0	2
14 39.1	40.9	106.9	14 03.8	42.3	107.3	13 27.5	43.7	107.8	12 50.4	45.1	108.3	12 12.3	46.4	108.7	3
13 58.2	40.9	107.6	13 21.5	42.4	108.1	12 43.8	43.8	108.5	12 05.3	45.2	108.9	11 25.9	46.5	109.3	4
13 17.3	− 41.1	108.4	12 39.1	− 42.6	108.8	12 00.0	− 44.0	109.2	11 20.1	− 45.3	109.6	10 39.4	− 46.5	110.0	5
12 36.2	41.2	109.1	11 56.5	42.6	109.5	11 16.0	44.0	109.9	10 34.8	45.4	110.3	9 52.9	46.7	110.6	6
11 55.0	41.3	109.9	11 13.9	42.8	110.2	10 32.0	44.1	110.6	9 49.4	45.4	110.9	9 06.2	46.7	111.2	7
11 13.7	41.5	110.6	10 31.1	42.8	111.0	9 47.9	44.2	111.3	9 04.0	45.5	111.6	8 19.5	46.7	111.9	8
10 32.2	41.5	111.3	9 48.3	43.0	111.7	9 03.7	44.3	112.0	8 18.5	45.6	112.3	7 32.8	46.9	112.5	9
9 50.7	− 41.6	112.1	9 05.3	− 43.0	112.4	8 19.4	− 44.4	112.7	7 32.9	− 45.7	112.9	6 45.9	− 46.8	113.1	10
9 09.1	41.7	112.8	8 22.3	43.1	113.1	7 35.0	44.4	113.3	6 47.2	45.6	113.6	5 59.1	47.0	113.8	11
8 27.4	41.8	113.5	7 39.2	43.1	113.8	6 50.6	44.5	114.0	6 01.6	45.8	114.2	5 12.1	46.9	114.4	12
7 45.6	41.9	114.2	6 56.1	43.2	114.5	6 06.1	44.5	114.7	5 15.8	45.8	114.9	4 25.2	47.0	115.0	13
7 03.7	41.9	115.0	6 12.8	43.2	115.2	5 21.6	44.6	115.4	4 30.0	45.8	115.5	3 38.2	47.0	115.6	14
6 21.8	− 42.0	115.7	5 29.6	− 43.4	115.9	4 37.0	− 44.6	116.0	3 44.2	− 45.8	116.2	2 51.2	− 47.0	116.3	15
5 39.8	42.1	116.4	4 46.2	43.3	116.6	3 52.4	44.6	116.7	2 58.4	45.9	116.8	2 04.2	47.1	116.9	16
4 57.7	42.1	117.1	4 02.9	43.4	117.3	3 07.8	44.7	117.4	2 12.5	45.9	117.5	1 17.1	47.0	117.5	17
4 15.6	42.1	117.8	3 19.5	43.5	118.0	2 23.1	44.7	118.0	1 26.6	45.9	118.1	0 30.1	− 47.1	118.1	18
3 33.5	42.2	118.6	2 36.0	43.4	118.6	1 38.4	44.7	118.7	0 40.7	− 45.9	118.7	0 17.0	+ 47.0	61.2	19
2 51.3	− 42.2	119.3	1 52.6	− 43.5	119.3	0 53.7	− 44.7	119.4	0 05.2	+ 45.8	60.6	1 04.0	+ 47.1	60.6	20
2 09.1	42.2	120.0	1 09.1	43.5	120.0	0 09.0	− 44.7	120.0	0 51.0	45.9	60.0	1 51.1	47.0	60.0	21
1 26.9	42.2	120.7	0 25.6	− 43.5	120.7	0 35.7	+ 44.7	59.3	1 36.9	45.9	59.3	2 38.1	47.0	59.4	22
0 44.7	42.3	121.4	0 17.9	+ 43.4	58.6	1 20.4	44.7	58.6	2 22.8	45.8	58.7	3 25.1	47.0	58.8	23
0 02.4	− 42.2	122.1	1 01.3	43.5	57.9	2 05.1	44.6	58.0	3 08.7	45.8	58.0	4 12.1	47.0	58.1	24
0 39.8	+ 42.2	57.2	1 44.8	+ 43.5	57.2	2 49.7	+ 44.7	57.3	3 54.5	+ 45.8	57.4	4 59.1	+ 46.9	57.5	25
1 22.0	42.2	56.5	2 28.3	43.4	56.5	3 34.4	44.6	56.6	4 40.3	45.8	56.7	5 46.0	46.9	56.9	26
2 04.2	42.2	55.8	3 11.7	43.4	55.8	4 19.0	44.6	55.9	5 26.1	45.7	56.1	6 32.9	46.8	56.3	27
2 46.4	42.2	55.0	3 55.1	43.4	55.1	5 03.6	44.5	55.3	6 11.8	45.7	55.4	7 19.7	46.8	55.6	28
3 28.6	42.1	54.3	4 38.5	43.3	54.4	5 48.1	44.5	54.6	6 57.5	45.6	54.8	8 06.5	46.7	55.0	29

50° Hc	d	Z	52° Hc	d	Z	54° Hc	d	Z	56° Hc	d	Z	58° Hc	d	Z	Dec.
13 56.0	− 47.4	107.2	13 20.1	− 48.7	107.7	12 43.2	− 49.8	108.1	12 05.5	− 50.9	108.5	11 27.0	− 51.9	108.9	0
13 08.6	47.5	107.8	12 31.4	48.7	108.3	11 53.4	49.9	108.7	11 14.6	51.0	109.1	10 35.1	52.0	109.4	1
12 21.1	47.6	108.5	11 42.7	48.8	108.9	11 03.5	49.9	109.2	10 23.6	51.0	109.6	9 43.1	52.1	109.9	2
11 33.5	47.6	109.1	10 53.9	48.8	109.5	10 13.6	50.0	109.8	9 32.6	51.0	110.1	8 51.0	52.0	110.4	3
10 45.9	47.8	109.7	10 05.1	48.9	110.0	9 23.6	50.0	110.4	8 41.6	51.1	110.7	7 59.0	52.2	110.9	4
9 58.1	− 47.8	110.3	9 16.2	− 49.0	110.6	8 33.6	− 50.1	110.9	7 50.5	− 51.2	111.2	7 06.8	− 52.1	111.4	5
9 10.3	47.8	110.9	8 27.2	49.0	111.2	7 43.5	50.1	111.5	6 59.3	51.2	111.7	6 14.7	52.2	111.9	6
8 22.5	48.0	111.5	7 38.2	49.1	111.8	6 53.4	50.2	112.0	6 08.1	51.2	112.2	5 22.5	52.2	112.4	7
7 34.5	48.0	112.1	6 49.1	49.1	112.4	6 03.2	50.2	112.6	5 16.9	51.2	112.8	4 30.3	52.2	112.9	8
6 46.6	48.0	112.7	6 00.0	49.2	113.0	5 13.0	50.2	113.1	4 25.7	51.3	113.3	3 38.1	52.2	113.4	9
5 58.6	− 48.1	113.4	5 10.8	− 49.2	113.5	4 22.8	− 50.3	113.7	3 34.4	− 51.2	113.8	2 45.9	− 52.3	113.9	10
5 10.5	48.1	114.0	4 21.6	49.2	114.1	3 32.5	50.3	114.2	2 43.2	51.3	114.3	1 53.6	52.2	114.4	11
4 22.4	48.1	114.6	3 32.4	49.2	114.7	2 42.2	50.3	114.8	1 51.9	51.3	114.9	1 01.4	52.3	114.9	12
3 34.3	48.1	115.2	2 43.2	49.2	115.3	1 51.9	50.3	115.3	1 00.6	51.3	115.4	0 09.1	− 52.2	115.4	13
2 46.2	48.2	115.8	1 54.0	49.3	115.8	1 01.6	50.3	115.9	0 09.3	− 51.3	115.9	0 43.1	+ 52.3	64.1	14
1 58.0	− 48.2	116.3	1 04.7	− 49.3	116.4	0 11.3	− 50.3	116.4	0 42.0	+ 51.4	63.6	1 35.4	+ 52.3	63.6	15
1 09.8	48.1	116.9	0 15.4	− 49.2	117.0	0 39.0	+ 50.3	63.0	1 33.4	51.2	63.1	2 27.6	52.3	63.1	16
0 21.7	− 48.2	117.5	0 33.8	+ 49.3	62.5	1 29.3	50.3	62.5	2 24.6	51.3	62.6	3 19.9	52.2	62.6	17
0 26.5	+ 48.2	61.9	1 23.1	49.2	61.9	2 19.6	50.3	61.9	3 15.9	51.3	62.0	4 12.1	52.2	62.2	18
1 14.7	48.2	61.3	2 12.3	49.3	61.3	3 09.9	50.2	61.4	4 07.2	51.2	61.5	5 04.3	52.2	61.7	19
2 02.9	+ 48.1	60.7	3 01.6	+ 49.2	60.7	4 00.1	+ 50.3	60.9	4 58.4	+ 51.3	61.0	5 56.5	+ 52.1	61.2	20
2 51.0	48.2	60.1	3 50.8	49.2	60.2	4 50.4	50.2	60.3	5 49.7	51.2	60.5	6 48.6	52.2	60.7	21
3 39.2	48.1	59.5	4 40.0	49.2	59.6	5 40.6	50.2	59.8	6 40.9	51.1	59.9	7 40.8	52.0	60.2	22
4 27.3	48.1	58.9	5 29.2	49.1	59.0	6 30.8	50.1	59.2	7 32.0	51.1	59.4	8 32.8	52.1	59.7	23
5 15.4	48.0	58.3	6 18.3	49.1	58.4	7 20.9	50.1	58.7	8 23.1	51.1	58.9	9 24.9	52.0	59.2	24
6 03.4	+ 48.0	57.7	7 07.4	+ 49.1	57.9	8 11.0	+ 50.1	58.1	9 14.2	+ 51.0	58.4	10 16.9	+ 52.0	58.7	25
6 51.4	48.0	57.1	7 56.5	49.0	57.3	9 01.1	50.0	57.5	10 05.2	51.0	57.8	11 08.9	51.9	58.1	26
7 39.4	47.9	56.5	8 45.5	48.9	56.7	9 51.1	50.0	57.0	10 56.2	50.9	57.3	12 00.8	51.8	57.6	27
8 27.3	47.8	55.9	9 34.4	48.9	56.1	10 41.1	49.8	56.4	11 47.1	50.9	56.7	12 52.6	51.8	57.1	28
9 15.1	47.8	55.2	10 23.3	48.8	55.5	11 30.9	49.9	55.9	12 38.0	50.8	56.2	13 44.4	51.7	56.6	29

Dec.	0° Hc	d	Z	2° Hc	d	Z	4° Hc	d	Z	6° Hc	d	Z	8° Hc	d	Z
0	20 00.0 −	0.2	90.0	19 59.2 +	2.1	90.7	19 57.0 +	4.2	91.5	19 53.1 +	6.5	92.2	19 47.8 +	8.7	92.9
1	19 59.8	0.6	88.9	20 01.3	1.6	89.7	20 01.2	3.9	90.4	19 59.6	6.1	91.1	19 56.5	8.3	91.8
2	19 59.2	0.9	87.9	20 02.9	1.3	88.6	20 05.1	3.5	89.3	20 05.7	5.8	90.1	20 04.8	8.0	90.7
3	19 58.3	1.3	86.8	20 04.2	0.9	87.5	20 08.6	3.1	88.3	20 11.5	5.3	89.0	20 12.8	7.5	89.7
4	19 57.0	1.8	85.7	20 05.1	0.5	86.5	20 11.7	2.8	87.2	20 16.8	5.0	87.9	20 20.3	7.2	88.7
5	19 55.2 −	2.1	84.7	20 05.6 +	0.1	85.4	20 14.5 +	2.3	86.1	20 21.8 +	4.5	86.9	20 27.5 +	6.8	87.6
6	19 53.1	2.4	83.6	20 05.7 −	0.2	84.3	20 16.8	2.0	85.1	20 26.3	4.2	85.8	20 34.3	6.4	86.6
7	19 50.7	2.9	82.6	20 05.5	0.7	83.3	20 18.8	1.5	84.0	20 30.5	3.8	84.7	20 40.7	6.0	85.5
8	19 47.8	3.2	81.5	20 04.8	1.0	82.2	20 20.3	1.2	82.9	20 34.3	3.4	83.7	20 46.7	5.7	84.4
9	19 44.6	3.6	80.4	20 03.8	1.4	81.1	20 21.5	0.8	81.9	20 37.7	3.0	82.6	20 52.4	5.2	83.4
10	19 41.0 −	4.0	79.4	20 02.4 −	1.8	80.1	20 22.3 +	0.4	80.8	20 40.7 +	2.6	81.5	20 57.6 +	4.8	82.3
11	19 37.0	4.3	78.3	20 00.6	2.1	79.0	20 22.7 +	0.1	79.7	20 43.3	2.3	80.5	21 02.4	4.4	81.2
12	19 32.7	4.7	77.3	19 58.5	2.6	78.0	20 22.8 −	0.4	78.7	20 45.6	1.8	79.4	21 06.8	4.1	80.2
13	19 28.0	5.1	76.2	19 55.9	2.9	76.9	20 22.4	0.8	77.6	20 47.4	1.4	78.3	21 10.9	3.6	79.1
14	19 22.9	5.4	75.1	19 53.0	3.3	75.8	20 21.6	1.1	76.5	20 48.8	1.1	77.3	21 14.5	3.2	78.0
15	19 17.5 −	5.8	74.1	19 49.7 −	3.7	74.8	20 20.5 −	1.5	75.5	20 49.9 +	0.6	76.2	21 17.7 +	2.8	77.0
16	19 11.7	6.2	73.0	19 46.0	4.1	73.7	20 19.0	2.0	74.4	20 50.5 +	0.2	75.1	21 20.5	2.4	75.9
17	19 05.5	6.5	72.0	19 41.9	4.4	72.6	20 17.0	2.3	73.3	20 50.7 −	0.2	74.1	21 22.9	2.0	74.8
18	18 59.0	6.9	70.9	19 37.5	4.8	71.6	20 14.7	2.7	72.3	20 50.5	0.5	73.0	21 24.9	1.6	73.7
19	18 52.1	7.3	69.8	19 32.7	5.2	70.5	20 12.0	3.0	71.2	20 50.0	1.0	71.9	21 26.5	1.2	72.7
20	18 44.8 −	7.6	68.8	19 27.5 −	5.5	69.5	20 09.0 −	3.5	70.2	20 49.0 −	1.3	70.9	21 27.7 +	0.7	71.6
21	18 37.2	7.9	67.8	19 22.0	5.9	68.4	20 05.5	3.8	69.1	20 47.7	1.8	69.8	21 28.4 +	0.4	70.5
22	18 29.3	8.3	66.7	19 16.1	6.3	67.4	20 01.7	4.3	68.0	20 45.9	2.2	68.7	21 28.8 −	0.1	69.4
23	18 21.0	8.6	65.7	19 09.8	6.6	66.3	19 57.4	4.6	67.0	20 43.7	2.5	67.6	21 28.7	0.5	68.4
24	18 12.4	8.9	64.6	19 03.2	7.0	65.3	19 52.8	4.9	65.9	20 41.2	3.0	66.6	21 28.2	0.9	67.3
25	18 03.5 −	9.3	63.6	18 56.2 −	7.3	64.2	19 47.9 −	5.4	64.8	20 38.2 −	3.3	65.5	21 27.3 −	1.3	66.2
26	17 54.2	9.6	62.6	18 48.9	7.7	63.2	19 42.5	5.7	63.8	20 34.9	3.7	64.4	21 26.0	1.7	65.1
27	17 44.6	10.0	61.5	18 41.2	8.0	62.1	19 36.8	6.1	62.7	20 31.2	4.1	63.4	21 24.3	2.1	64.1
28	17 34.6	10.3	60.5	18 33.2	8.4	61.1	19 30.7	6.5	61.7	20 27.1	4.6	62.3	21 22.2	2.5	63.0
29	17 24.3	10.5	59.5	18 24.8	8.7	60.0	19 24.2	6.8	60.6	20 22.5	4.9	61.3	21 19.7	3.0	61.9

Dec.	10° Hc	d	Z	12° Hc	d	Z	14° Hc	d	Z	16° Hc	d	Z	18° Hc	d	Z
0	19 41.0 +	10.9	93.6	19 32.7 +	13.1	94.3	19 22.9 +	15.2	95.0	19 11.7 +	17.3	95.7	18 59.0 +	19.4	96.4
1	19 51.9	10.5	92.6	19 45.8	12.7	93.3	19 38.1	14.9	94.0	19 29.0	17.0	94.7	19 18.4	19.1	95.4
2	20 02.4	10.2	91.5	19 58.5	12.3	92.3	19 53.0	14.5	93.0	19 46.0	16.7	93.7	19 37.5	18.8	94.4
3	20 12.6	9.7	90.5	20 10.8	12.0	91.2	20 07.5	14.1	91.9	20 02.7	16.3	92.7	19 56.3	18.4	93.4
4	20 22.3	9.4	89.4	20 22.8	11.6	90.2	20 21.6	13.8	90.9	20 19.0	15.9	91.6	20 14.7	18.1	92.4
5	20 31.7 +	8.8	88.4	20 34.4 +	11.2	89.1	20 35.4 +	13.4	89.9	20 34.9 +	15.6	90.6	20 32.8 +	17.7	91.4
6	20 40.7	8.7	87.3	20 45.6	10.8	88.1	20 48.8	13.0	88.8	20 50.5	15.2	89.6	20 50.5	17.4	90.3
7	20 49.4	8.2	86.3	20 56.4	10.4	87.0	21 01.8	12.7	87.8	21 05.7	14.8	88.6	21 07.9	17.0	89.3
8	20 57.6	7.8	85.2	21 06.8	10.1	86.0	21 14.5	12.2	86.7	21 20.5	14.5	87.5	21 24.9	16.6	88.3
9	21 05.4	7.5	84.1	21 16.9	9.6	84.9	21 26.7	11.9	85.7	21 35.0	14.0	86.5	21 41.5	16.2	87.3
10	21 12.9 +	7.0	83.1	21 26.5 +	9.3	83.8	21 38.6 +	11.5	84.6	21 49.0 +	13.7	85.4	21 57.7 +	15.9	86.2
11	21 19.9	6.6	82.0	21 35.8	8.8	82.8	21 50.1	11.0	83.6	22 02.7	13.2	84.4	22 13.6	15.4	85.2
12	21 26.5	6.3	80.9	21 44.6	8.5	81.7	22 01.1	10.7	82.5	22 15.9	12.9	83.3	22 29.0	15.1	84.1
13	21 32.8	5.8	79.9	21 53.1	8.0	80.7	22 11.8	10.2	81.5	22 28.8	12.4	82.3	22 44.1	14.6	83.1
14	21 38.6	5.4	78.8	22 01.1	7.6	79.6	22 22.0	9.8	80.4	22 41.2	12.0	81.2	22 58.7	14.2	82.0
15	21 44.0 +	4.9	77.7	22 08.7 +	7.2	78.5	22 31.8 +	9.4	79.3	22 53.2 +	11.6	80.1	23 12.9 +	13.8	80.9
16	21 49.0	4.6	76.7	22 15.9	6.8	77.4	22 41.2	8.9	78.2	23 04.8	11.1	79.1	23 26.7	13.3	79.9
17	21 53.6	4.1	75.6	22 22.7	6.3	76.4	22 50.1	8.6	77.2	23 15.9	10.8	78.0	23 40.0	12.9	78.9
18	21 57.7	3.8	74.5	22 29.0	5.9	75.3	22 58.7	8.1	76.1	23 26.7	10.2	76.9	23 52.9	12.5	77.8
19	22 01.5	3.3	73.4	22 34.9	5.5	74.2	23 06.8	7.6	75.0	23 36.9	9.9	75.9	24 05.4	12.0	76.7
20	22 04.8 +	2.9	72.3	22 40.4 +	5.1	73.1	23 14.4 +	7.2	73.9	23 46.8 +	9.4	74.8	24 17.4 +	11.6	75.6
21	22 07.7	2.5	71.3	22 45.5	4.6	72.1	23 21.6	6.8	72.9	23 56.2	8.9	73.7	24 29.0	11.1	74.6
22	22 10.2	2.0	70.2	22 50.1	4.1	71.0	23 28.4	6.3	71.8	24 05.1	8.5	72.6	24 40.1	10.6	73.5
23	22 12.2	1.6	69.1	22 54.2	3.8	69.9	23 34.7	5.9	70.7	24 13.6	8.0	71.5	24 50.7	10.2	72.4
24	22 13.8	1.2	68.0	22 58.0	3.3	68.8	23 40.6	5.4	69.6	24 21.6	7.5	70.4	25 00.9	9.7	71.3
25	22 15.0 +	0.8	67.0	23 01.3 +	2.8	67.7	23 46.0 +	4.9	68.5	24 29.1 +	7.1	69.4	25 10.6 +	9.2	70.2
26	22 15.8 +	0.3	65.9	23 04.1	2.4	66.6	23 50.9	4.5	67.4	24 36.2	6.6	68.3	25 19.8	8.7	69.1
27	22 16.1 −	0.1	64.8	23 06.5	2.0	65.5	23 55.4	4.1	66.3	24 42.8	6.1	67.2	25 28.5	8.2	68.0
28	22 16.0	0.5	63.7	23 08.5	1.5	64.5	23 59.5	3.5	65.3	24 48.9	5.7	66.1	25 36.7	7.8	66.9
29	22 15.5	1.0	62.6	23 10.0	1.0	63.4	24 03.0	3.1	64.2	24 54.6	5.1	65.0	25 44.5	7.2	65.8

0°			2°			4°			6°			8°			
Hc	d	Z	Hc	d	Z	Hc	d	Z	Hc	d	Z	Hc	d	Z	Dec.
° ′	′	°	° ′	′	°	° ′	′	°	° ′	′	°	° ′	′	°	°
20 00.0 −	0.2	90.0	19 59.2 −	2.4	90.7	19 57.0 −	4.7	91.5	19 53.1 −	6.8	92.2	19 47.8 −	9.0	92.9	0
19 59.8	0.6	91.1	19 56.8	2.8	91.8	19 52.3	5.0	92.5	19 46.3	7.2	93.2	19 38.8	9.5	93.9	1
19 59.2	0.9	92.1	19 54.0	3.2	92.9	19 47.3	5.4	93.6	19 39.1	7.6	94.3	19 29.3	9.7	95.0	2
19 58.3	1.3	93.2	19 50.8	3.5	93.9	19 41.9	5.8	94.6	19 31.5	8.0	95.3	19 19.6	10.2	96.0	3
19 57.0	1.8	94.3	19 47.3	3.9	95.0	19 36.1	6.1	95.7	19 23.5	8.3	96.4	19 09.4	10.5	97.1	4
19 55.2 −	2.1	95.3	19 43.4 −	4.3	96.0	19 30.0 −	6.5	96.7	19 15.2 −	8.7	97.4	18 58.9 −	10.8	98.1	5
19 53.1	2.4	96.4	19 39.1	4.7	97.1	19 23.5	6.9	97.8	19 06.5	9.0	98.5	18 48.1	11.2	99.2	6
19 50.7	2.9	97.4	19 34.4	5.1	98.2	19 16.6	7.2	98.9	18 57.5	9.4	99.5	18 36.9	11.5	100.2	7
19 47.8	3.2	98.5	19 29.3	5.4	99.2	19 09.4	7.6	99.9	18 48.1	9.8	100.6	18 25.4	11.9	101.2	8
19 44.6	3.6	99.6	19 23.9	5.7	100.3	19 01.8	7.9	101.0	18 38.3	10.0	101.6	18 13.5	12.2	102.3	9
19 41.0 −	4.0	100.6	19 18.2 −	6.2	101.3	18 53.9 −	8.3	102.0	18 28.3 −	10.4	102.7	18 01.3 −	12.5	103.3	10
19 37.0	4.3	101.7	19 12.0	6.5	102.4	18 45.6	8.6	103.0	18 17.9	10.8	103.7	17 48.8	12.9	104.3	11
19 32.7	4.7	102.7	19 05.5	6.8	103.4	18 37.0	9.0	104.1	18 07.1	11.1	104.7	17 35.9	13.1	105.4	12
19 28.0	5.1	103.8	18 58.7	7.2	104.5	18 28.0	9.3	105.1	17 56.0	11.4	105.8	17 22.8	13.5	106.4	13
19 22.9	5.4	104.9	18 51.5	7.6	105.5	18 18.7	9.7	106.2	17 44.6	11.7	106.8	17 09.3	13.8	107.4	14
19 17.5 −	5.8	105.9	18 43.9 −	7.9	106.6	18 09.0 −	10.0	107.2	17 32.9 −	12.1	107.8	16 55.5 −	14.0	108.4	15
19 11.7	6.2	107.0	18 36.0	8.3	107.6	17 59.0	10.3	108.3	17 20.8	12.3	108.9	16 41.5	14.4	109.4	16
19 05.5	6.5	108.0	18 27.7	8.6	108.7	17 48.7	10.7	109.3	17 08.5	12.7	109.9	16 27.1	14.7	110.4	17
18 59.0	6.9	109.1	18 19.1	8.9	109.7	17 38.0	10.9	110.3	16 55.8	13.0	110.9	16 12.4	14.9	111.5	18
18 52.1	7.3	110.1	18 10.2	9.3	110.8	17 27.1	11.3	111.4	16 42.8	13.3	111.9	15 57.5	15.3	112.5	19
18 44.8 −	7.6	111.2	18 00.9 −	9.6	111.8	17 15.8 −	11.6	112.4	16 29.5 −	13.5	112.9	15 42.2 −	15.5	113.5	20
18 37.2	7.9	112.2	17 51.3	10.0	112.8	17 04.2	12.0	113.4	16 16.0	13.9	114.0	15 26.7	15.8	114.5	21
18 29.3	8.3	113.3	17 41.3	10.2	113.9	16 52.2	12.2	114.4	16 02.1	14.2	115.0	15 10.9	16.0	115.5	22
18 21.0	8.6	114.3	17 31.1	10.6	114.9	16 40.0	12.5	115.5	15 47.9	14.4	116.0	14 54.9	16.3	116.5	23
18 12.4	8.9	115.4	17 20.5	10.9	115.9	16 27.5	12.8	116.5	15 33.5	14.7	117.0	14 38.6	16.5	117.5	24
18 03.5 −	9.3	116.4	17 09.6 −	11.2	117.0	16 14.7 −	13.1	117.5	15 18.8 −	15.0	118.0	14 22.1 −	16.8	118.5	25
17 54.2	9.6	117.4	16 58.4	11.5	118.0	16 01.6	13.4	118.5	15 03.8	15.2	119.0	14 05.3	17.1	119.5	26
17 44.6	10.0	118.5	16 46.9	11.9	119.0	15 48.2	13.7	119.5	14 48.6	15.5	120.0	13 48.2	17.3	120.4	27
17 34.6	10.3	119.5	16 35.0	12.1	120.0	15 34.5	13.9	120.5	14 33.1	15.7	121.0	13 30.9	17.5	121.4	28
17 24.3	10.5	120.5	16 22.9	12.4	121.1	15 20.6	14.3	121.5	14 17.4	16.0	122.0	13 13.4	17.7	122.4	29

10°			12°			14°			16°			18°			
Hc	d	Z	Hc	d	Z	Hc	d	Z	Hc	d	Z	Hc	d	Z	Dec.
° ′	′	°	° ′	′	°	° ′	′	°	° ′	′	°	° ′	′	°	°
19 41.0 −	11.2	93.6	19 32.7 −	13.4	94.3	19 22.9 −	15.6	95.0	19 11.7 −	17.7	95.7	18 59.0 −	19.8	96.4	0
19 29.8	11.6	94.7	19 19.3	13.8	95.4	19 07.3	15.8	96.1	18 54.0	18.0	96.7	18 39.2	20.1	97.4	1
19 18.2	12.0	95.7	19 05.5	14.1	96.4	18 51.5	16.3	97.1	18 36.0	18.4	97.7	18 19.1	20.4	98.4	2
19 06.2	12.3	96.7	18 51.4	14.4	97.4	18 35.2	16.5	98.1	18 17.6	18.6	98.8	17 58.7	20.7	99.4	3
18 53.9	12.6	97.8	18 37.0	14.8	98.4	18 18.7	16.9	99.1	17 59.0	18.9	99.8	17 38.0	21.0	100.4	4
18 41.3 −	13.0	98.8	18 22.2 −	15.1	99.5	18 01.8 −	17.2	100.1	17 40.1 −	19.3	100.7	17 17.0 −	21.2	101.4	5
18 28.3	13.3	99.8	18 07.1	15.4	100.5	17 44.6	17.5	101.1	17 20.8	19.5	101.7	16 55.8	21.6	102.3	6
18 15.0	13.7	100.9	17 51.7	15.8	101.5	17 27.1	17.8	102.1	17 01.3	19.8	102.7	16 34.2	21.8	103.3	7
18 01.3	14.0	101.9	17 35.9	16.0	102.5	17 09.3	18.1	103.1	16 41.5	20.1	103.7	16 12.4	22.1	104.3	8
17 47.3	14.2	102.9	17 19.9	16.3	103.5	16 51.2	18.4	104.1	16 21.4	20.4	104.7	15 50.3	22.3	105.3	9
17 33.1 −	14.6	103.9	17 03.6 −	16.7	104.5	16 32.8 −	18.6	105.1	16 01.0 −	20.7	105.7	15 28.0 −	22.6	106.2	10
17 18.5	14.9	104.9	16 46.9	16.9	105.5	16 14.2	18.9	106.1	15 40.3	20.9	106.7	15 05.4	22.8	107.2	11
17 03.6	15.3	106.0	16 30.0	17.2	106.5	15 55.3	19.2	107.1	15 19.4	21.1	107.6	14 42.6	23.1	108.1	12
16 48.3	15.5	107.0	16 12.8	17.5	107.5	15 36.1	19.5	108.1	14 58.3	21.4	108.6	14 19.5	23.3	109.1	13
16 32.8	15.9	108.0	15 55.3	17.8	108.5	15 16.6	19.7	109.1	14 36.9	21.6	109.6	13 56.2	23.5	110.0	14
16 17.1 −	16.1	109.0	15 37.5 −	18.1	109.5	14 56.9 −	20.0	110.0	14 15.3 −	21.9	110.5	13 32.7 −	23.7	111.0	15
16 01.0	16.4	110.0	15 19.4	18.3	110.5	14 36.9	20.2	111.0	13 53.4	22.1	111.5	13 09.0	23.9	111.9	16
15 44.6	16.6	111.0	15 01.1	18.5	111.5	14 16.7	20.5	112.0	13 31.3	22.3	112.4	12 45.1	24.2	112.9	17
15 28.0	16.9	112.0	14 42.6	18.8	112.5	13 56.2	20.6	113.0	13 09.0	22.5	113.4	12 20.9	24.3	113.8	18
15 11.1	17.1	113.0	14 23.8	19.1	113.5	13 35.6	20.9	113.9	12 46.5	22.7	114.3	11 56.6	24.5	114.7	19
14 54.0 −	17.5	114.0	14 04.7 −	19.2	114.4	13 14.7 −	21.2	114.9	12 23.8 −	22.9	115.3	11 32.1 −	24.7	115.7	20
14 36.5	17.6	115.0	13 45.5	19.5	115.4	12 53.5	21.3	115.8	12 00.9	23.2	116.2	11 07.4	24.8	116.6	21
14 18.9	17.9	115.9	13 26.0	19.8	116.4	12 32.2	21.5	116.8	11 37.7	23.2	117.2	10 42.6	25.0	117.5	22
14 01.0	18.2	116.9	13 06.2	19.9	117.4	12 10.7	21.7	117.8	11 14.5	23.5	118.1	10 17.6	25.2	118.5	23
13 42.8	18.3	117.9	12 46.3	20.2	118.3	11 49.0	21.9	118.7	10 51.0	23.6	119.1	9 52.4	25.3	119.4	24
13 24.5 −	18.6	118.9	12 26.1 −	20.4	119.3	11 27.1 −	22.1	119.7	10 27.4 −	23.8	120.0	9 27.1 −	25.5	120.3	25
13 05.9	18.9	119.9	12 05.7	20.5	120.3	11 05.0	22.3	120.6	10 03.6	24.0	120.9	9 01.6	25.6	121.2	26
12 47.0	19.0	120.8	11 45.2	20.8	121.2	10 42.7	22.5	121.6	9 39.6	24.1	121.9	8 36.0	25.7	122.1	27
12 28.0	19.2	121.8	11 24.4	20.9	122.2	10 20.2	22.6	122.5	9 15.5	24.3	122.8	8 10.3	25.9	123.0	28
12 08.8	19.5	122.8	11 03.5	21.1	123.1	9 57.6	22.8	123.4	8 51.2	24.3	123.7	7 44.4	26.0	124.0	29

213

LATITUDE **SAME** NAME

Dec.	20° Hc	d	Z	22° Hc	d	Z	24° Hc	d	Z	26° Hc	d	Z	28° Hc	d	Z
°	° ′	′	°	° ′	′	°	° ′	′	°	° ′	′	°	° ′	′	°
0	18 44.8	+21.5	97.1	18 29.3	+23.6	97.8	18 12.4	+25.6	98.4	17 54.2	+27.5	99.1	17 34.6	+29.4	99.7
1	19 06.3	21.2	96.1	18 52.9	23.2	96.8	18 38.0	25.2	97.5	18 21.7	27.2	98.1	18 04.0	29.2	98.8
2	19 27.5	20.9	95.1	19 16.1	22.9	95.8	19 03.2	25.0	96.5	18 48.9	27.0	97.2	18 33.2	28.9	97.9
3	19 48.4	20.6	94.1	19 39.0	22.7	94.8	19 28.2	24.6	95.5	19 15.9	26.6	96.2	19 02.1	28.6	96.9
4	20 09.0	20.2	93.1	20 01.7	22.2	93.9	19 52.8	24.4	94.6	19 42.5	26.4	95.3	19 30.7	28.3	96.0
5	20 29.2	+19.8	92.1	20 23.9	+22.0	92.9	20 17.2	+24.0	93.6	20 08.9	+26.0	94.3	19 59.0	+28.1	95.1
6	20 49.0	19.5	91.1	20 45.9	21.6	91.9	20 41.2	23.7	92.6	20 34.9	25.7	93.4	20 27.1	27.7	94.1
7	21 08.5	19.2	90.1	21 07.5	21.3	90.9	21 04.9	23.3	91.6	21 00.6	25.4	92.4	20 54.8	27.4	93.2
8	21 27.7	18.7	89.1	21 28.8	20.8	89.9	21 28.2	23.0	90.7	21 26.0	25.1	91.4	21 22.2	27.1	92.2
9	21 46.4	18.4	88.1	21 49.6	20.6	88.9	21 51.2	22.6	89.7	21 51.1	24.7	90.5	21 49.3	26.7	91.3
10	22 04.8	+18.0	87.0	22 10.2	+20.1	87.8	22 13.8	+22.3	88.7	22 15.8	+24.3	89.5	22 16.0	+26.4	90.3
11	22 22.8	17.6	86.0	22 30.3	19.8	86.8	22 36.1	21.9	87.7	22 40.1	24.0	88.5	22 42.4	26.1	89.3
12	22 40.4	17.2	85.0	22 50.1	19.3	85.8	22 58.0	21.5	86.6	23 04.1	23.6	87.5	23 08.5	25.6	88.3
13	22 57.6	16.8	83.9	23 09.4	19.0	84.8	23 19.5	21.1	85.6	23 27.7	23.2	86.5	23 34.1	25.4	87.4
14	23 14.4	16.4	82.9	23 28.4	18.5	83.7	23 40.6	20.7	84.6	23 50.9	22.9	85.5	23 59.5	24.9	86.4
15	23 30.8	+16.0	81.8	23 46.9	+18.2	82.7	24 01.3	+20.3	83.6	24 13.8	+22.4	84.5	24 24.4	+24.5	85.4
16	23 46.8	15.5	80.8	24 05.1	17.7	81.7	24 21.6	19.8	82.6	24 36.2	22.0	83.5	24 48.9	24.1	84.4
17	24 02.3	15.1	79.7	24 22.8	17.3	80.6	24 41.4	19.5	81.5	24 58.2	21.6	82.4	25 13.0	23.7	83.4
18	24 17.4	14.6	78.7	24 40.1	16.8	79.6	25 00.9	19.0	80.5	25 19.8	21.1	81.4	25 36.7	23.3	82.3
19	24 32.0	14.2	77.6	24 56.9	16.4	78.5	25 19.9	18.5	79.4	25 40.9	20.7	80.4	26 00.0	22.9	81.3
20	24 46.2	+13.8	76.5	25 13.3	+15.9	77.4	25 38.4	+18.1	78.4	26 01.6	+20.3	79.3	26 22.9	+22.4	80.3
21	25 00.0	13.3	75.5	25 29.2	15.5	76.4	25 56.5	17.6	77.3	26 21.9	19.8	78.3	26 45.3	21.9	79.3
22	25 13.3	12.8	74.4	25 44.7	14.9	75.3	26 14.1	17.2	76.2	26 41.7	19.3	77.2	27 07.2	21.5	78.2
23	25 26.1	12.3	73.3	25 59.6	14.5	74.2	26 31.3	16.7	75.2	27 01.0	18.9	76.2	27 28.7	21.0	77.2
24	25 38.4	11.9	72.2	26 14.1	14.1	73.1	26 48.0	16.2	74.1	27 19.9	18.3	75.1	27 49.7	20.5	76.1
25	25 50.3	+11.3	71.1	26 28.2	+13.5	72.1	27 04.2	+15.7	73.0	27 38.2	+17.9	74.0	28 10.2	+20.1	75.0
26	26 01.6	10.9	70.0	26 41.7	13.0	71.0	27 19.9	15.1	71.9	27 56.1	17.3	72.9	28 30.3	19.5	74.0
27	26 12.5	10.4	68.9	26 54.7	12.5	69.9	27 35.0	14.7	70.8	28 13.4	16.9	71.9	28 49.8	19.0	72.9
28	26 22.9	9.8	67.8	27 07.2	12.0	68.8	27 49.7	14.2	69.8	28 30.3	16.3	70.8	29 08.8	18.4	71.8
29	26 32.7	9.4	66.7	27 19.2	11.5	67.7	28 03.9	13.6	68.7	28 46.6	15.7	69.7	29 27.2	18.0	70.7

Dec.	30° Hc	d	Z	32° Hc	d	Z	34° Hc	d	Z	36° Hc	d	Z	38° Hc	d	Z
°	° ′	′	°	° ′	′	°	° ′	′	°	° ′	′	°	° ′	′	°
0	17 13.8	+31.3	100.3	16 51.7	+33.1	100.9	16 28.3	+34.9	101.5	16 03.8	+36.6	102.1	15 38.1	+38.3	102.6
1	17 45.1	31.0	99.4	17 24.8	32.8	100.0	17 03.2	34.7	100.7	16 40.4	36.4	101.2	16 16.4	38.1	101.8
2	18 16.1	30.8	98.5	17 57.6	32.7	99.2	17 37.9	34.4	99.8	17 16.8	36.2	100.4	16 54.5	37.9	101.0
3	18 46.9	30.5	97.6	18 30.3	32.4	98.3	18 12.3	34.2	98.9	17 53.0	36.0	99.6	17 32.4	37.7	100.2
4	19 17.4	30.3	96.7	19 02.7	32.1	97.4	18 46.5	34.0	98.1	18 29.0	35.8	98.7	18 10.1	37.5	99.4
5	19 47.7	+29.9	95.8	19 34.8	+31.9	96.5	19 20.5	+33.7	97.2	19 04.8	+35.5	97.9	18 47.6	+37.2	98.6
6	20 17.6	29.7	94.9	20 06.7	31.6	95.6	19 54.2	33.5	96.3	19 40.3	35.3	97.0	19 24.8	37.1	97.7
7	20 47.3	29.4	93.9	20 38.3	31.3	94.7	20 27.7	33.2	95.4	20 15.6	35.0	96.2	20 01.9	36.8	96.9
8	21 16.7	29.1	93.0	21 09.6	31.0	93.8	21 00.9	32.9	·94.5	20 50.6	34.8	95.3	20 38.7	36.6	96.1
9	21 45.8	28.7	92.1	21 40.6	30.7	92.9	21 33.8	32.6	93.7	21 25.4	34.4	94.4	21 15.3	36.3	95.2
10	22 14.5	+28.4	91.1	22 11.3	+30.4	91.9	22 06.4	+32.4	92.7	21 59.8	+34.2	93.6	21 51.6	+36.0	94.4
11	22 42.9	28.1	90.2	22 41.7	30.1	91.0	22 38.8	32.0	91.8	22 34.0	34.0	92.7	22 27.6	35.8	93.5
12	23 11.0	27.8	89.2	23 11.8	29.7	90.1	23 10.8	31.7	90.9	23 08.0	33.6	91.8	23 03.4	35.4	92.6
13	23 38.8	27.3	88.2	23 41.5	29.4	89.1	23 42.5	31.3	90.0	23 41.6	33.2	90.9	23 38.8	35.2	91.7
14	24 06.1	27.0	87.3	24 10.9	29.0	88.2	24 13.8	31.0	89.1	24 14.8	33.0	90.0	24 14.0	34.9	90.9
15	24 33.1	+26.6	86.3	24 39.9	+28.7	87.2	24 44.8	+30.7	88.1	24 47.8	+32.6	89.0	24 48.9	+34.5	90.0
16	24 59.7	26.2	85.3	25 08.6	28.3	86.2	25 15.5	30.3	87.2	25 20.4	32.3	88.1	25 23.4	34.2	89.1
17	25 25.9	25.8	84.3	25 36.9	27.8	85.3	25 45.8	29.9	86.2	25 52.7	31.9	87.2	25 57.6	33.8	88.2
18	25 51.7	25.4	83.3	26 04.7	27.5	84.3	26 15.7	29.5	85.2	26 24.6	31.5	86.2	26 31.4	33.5	87.2
19	26 17.1	25.0	82.3	26 32.2	27.1	83.3	26 45.2	29.1	84.3	26 56.1	31.2	85.3	27 04.9	33.2	86.3
20	26 42.1	+24.5	81.3	26 59.3	+26.6	82.3	27 14.3	+28.7	83.3	27 27.3	+30.7	84.3	27 38.1	+32.7	85.4
21	27 06.6	24.1	80.3	27 25.9	26.2	81.3	27 43.0	28.3	82.3	27 58.0	30.4	83.4	28 10.8	32.4	84.4
22	27 30.7	23.6	79.2	27 52.1	25.7	80.3	28 11.3	27.9	81.3	28 28.4	29.9	82.4	28 43.2	31.9	83.5
23	27 54.3	23.2	78.2	28 17.8	25.3	79.2	28 39.2	27.4	80.3	28 58.3	29.4	81.4	29 15.1	31.5	82.5
24	28 17.5	22.7	77.1	28 43.1	24.8	78.2	29 06.6	26.9	79.3	29 27.7	29.1	80.4	29 46.6	31.1	81.5
25	28 40.2	+22.1	76.1	29 07.9	+24.4	77.2	29 33.5	+26.4	78.2	29 56.8	+28.5	79.4	30 17.7	+30.6	80.5
26	29 02.3	21.7	75.0	29 32.3	23.8	76.1	29 59.9	26.0	77.2	30 25.3	28.1	78.4	30 48.3	30.2	79.5
27	29 24.0	21.2	74.0	29 56.1	23.3	75.1	30 25.9	25.5	76.2	30 53.4	27.6	77.3	31 18.5	29.7	78.5
28	29 45.2	20.6	72.9	30 19.4	22.8	74.0	30 51.4	24.9	75.1	31 21.0	27.1	76.3	31 48.2	29.2	77.5
29	30 05.8	20.1	71.8	30 42.2	22.3	72.9	31 16.3	24.4	74.1	31 48.1	26.5	75.2	32 17.4	28.7	76.5

20°			22°			24°			26°			28°			Dec.
Hc	d	Z	Hc	d	Z	Hc	d	Z	Hc	d	Z	Hc	d	Z	
18 44.8	−21.8	97.1	18 29.3	−23.8	97.8	18 12.4	−25.8	98.4	17 54.2	−27.8	99.1	17 34.6	−29.7	99.7	0
18 23.0	22.1	98.1	18 05.5	24.2	98.7	17 46.6	26.1	99.4	17 26.4	28.0	100.0	17 04.9	29.9	100.6	1
18 00.9	22.4	99.1	17 41.3	24.4	99.7	17 20.5	26.4	100.3	16 58.4	28.3	100.9	16 35.0	30.1	101.5	2
17 38.5	22.7	100.0	17 16.9	24.7	100.7	16 54.1	26.6	101.3	16 30.1	28.5	101.8	16 04.9	30.4	102.4	3
17 15.8	23.0	101.0	16 52.2	24.9	101.6	16 27.5	26.9	102.2	16 01.6	28.8	102.8	15 34.5	30.6	103.3	4
16 52.8	−23.3	102.0	16 27.3	−25.2	102.6	16 00.6	−27.1	103.1	15 32.8	−29.0	103.7	15 03.9	−30.8	104.2	5
16 29.5	23.5	102.9	16 02.1	25.5	103.5	15 33.5	27.3	104.0	15 03.8	29.1	104.6	14 33.1	31.0	105.1	6
16 06.0	23.8	103.9	15 36.6	25.7	104.4	15 06.2	27.6	105.0	14 34.7	29.4	105.5	14 02.1	31.2	106.0	7
15 42.2	24.0	104.8	15 10.9	25.9	105.4	14 38.6	27.8	105.9	14 05.3	29.6	106.4	13 30.9	31.3	106.9	8
15 18.2	24.2	105.8	14 45.0	26.1	106.3	14 10.8	28.0	106.8	13 35.7	29.8	107.3	12 59.6	31.6	107.7	9
14 54.0	−24.5	106.7	14 18.9	−26.4	107.2	13 42.8	−28.1	107.7	13 05.9	−30.0	108.2	12 28.0	−31.7	108.6	10
14 29.5	24.8	107.7	13 52.5	26.5	108.2	13 14.7	28.4	108.6	12 35.9	30.2	109.1	11 56.3	31.9	109.5	11
14 04.7	24.9	108.6	13 26.0	26.8	109.1	12 46.3	28.6	109.5	12 05.7	30.3	109.9	11 24.4	32.0	110.3	12
13 39.8	25.1	109.6	12 59.2	27.0	110.0	12 17.7	28.7	110.4	11 35.4	30.4	110.8	10 52.4	32.2	111.2	13
13 14.7	25.4	110.5	12 32.2	27.1	110.9	11 49.0	28.9	111.3	11 05.0	30.7	111.7	10 20.2	32.3	112.1	14
12 49.3	−25.5	111.4	12 05.1	−27.4	111.8	11 20.1	−29.1	112.2	10 34.3	−30.7	112.6	9 47.9	−32.4	112.9	15
12 23.8	25.8	112.4	11 37.7	27.5	112.7	10 51.0	29.2	113.1	10 03.6	31.0	113.5	9 15.5	32.6	113.8	16
11 58.0	25.9	113.3	11 10.2	27.6	113.7	10 21.8	29.4	114.0	9 32.6	31.0	114.3	8 42.9	32.6	114.6	17
11 32.1	26.1	114.2	10 42.6	27.8	114.6	9 52.4	29.5	114.9	9 01.6	31.2	115.2	8 10.3	32.8	115.5	18
11 06.0	26.2	115.1	10 14.8	28.0	115.5	9 22.9	29.6	115.8	8 30.4	31.2	116.1	7 37.5	32.9	116.3	19
10 39.8	−26.4	116.0	9 46.8	−28.1	116.4	8 53.3	−29.8	116.7	7 59.2	−31.4	116.9	7 04.6	−32.9	117.2	20
10 13.4	26.6	116.9	9 18.7	28.2	117.3	8 23.5	29.9	117.5	7 27.8	31.5	117.8	6 31.7	33.1	118.0	21
9 46.8	26.7	117.9	8 50.5	28.4	118.1	7 53.6	30.0	118.4	6 56.3	31.6	118.6	5 58.6	33.1	118.8	22
9 20.1	26.8	118.8	8 22.1	28.5	119.0	7 23.6	30.1	119.3	6 24.7	31.6	119.5	5 25.5	33.2	119.7	23
8 53.3	27.0	119.7	7 53.6	28.6	119.9	6 53.5	30.1	120.2	5 53.1	31.8	120.3	4 52.3	33.2	120.5	24
8 26.3	−27.1	120.6	7 25.0	−28.7	120.8	6 23.4	−30.3	121.0	5 21.3	−31.8	121.2	4 19.1	−33.4	121.3	25
7 59.2	27.2	121.5	6 56.3	28.8	121.7	5 53.1	30.4	121.9	4 49.5	31.8	122.0	3 45.7	33.3	122.2	26
7 32.0	27.4	122.4	6 27.5	28.9	122.6	5 22.7	30.4	122.8	4 17.7	32.0	122.9	3 12.4	33.4	123.0	27
7 04.6	27.4	123.3	5 58.6	29.0	123.5	4 52.3	30.5	123.6	3 45.7	31.9	123.7	2 39.0	33.4	123.8	28
6 37.2	27.5	124.2	5 29.6	29.0	124.3	4 21.8	30.5	124.5	3 13.8	32.0	124.6	2 05.6	33.5	124.7	29

30°			32°			34°			36°			38°			Dec.
Hc	d	Z	Hc	d	Z	Hc	d	Z	Hc	d	Z	Hc	d	Z	
17 13.8	−31.6	100.3	16 51.7	−33.4	100.9	16 28.3	−35.1	101.5	16 03.8	−36.8	102.1	15 38.1	−38.4	102.6	0
16 42.2	31.7	101.2	16 18.3	33.5	101.8	15 53.2	35.2	102.3	15 27.0	37.0	102.9	14 59.7	38.6	103.4	1
16 10.5	32.0	102.1	15 44.8	33.8	102.6	15 18.0	35.5	103.2	14 50.0	37.1	103.7	14 21.1	38.8	104.2	2
15 38.5	32.2	103.0	15 11.0	33.9	103.5	14 42.5	35.7	104.0	14 12.9	37.3	104.5	13 42.3	38.9	105.0	3
15 06.3	32.3	103.8	14 37.1	34.1	104.4	14 06.8	35.8	104.9	13 35.6	37.5	105.3	13 03.4	39.1	105.8	4
14 34.0	−32.6	104.7	14 03.0	−34.3	105.2	13 31.0	−36.0	105.7	12 58.1	−37.6	106.1	12 24.3	−39.1	106.6	5
14 01.4	32.8	105.6	13 28.7	34.5	106.1	12 55.0	36.1	106.5	12 20.5	37.7	106.9	11 45.2	39.4	107.3	6
13 28.6	32.9	106.4	12 54.2	34.6	106.9	12 18.9	36.3	107.3	11 42.8	37.9	107.7	11 05.8	39.4	108.1	7
12 55.7	33.1	107.3	12 19.6	34.8	107.7	11 42.6	36.4	108.1	11 04.9	38.0	108.5	10 26.4	39.5	108.9	8
12 22.6	33.3	108.2	11 44.8	34.9	108.6	11 06.2	36.5	108.9	10 26.9	38.1	109.3	9 46.9	39.7	109.6	9
11 49.3	−33.4	109.0	11 09.9	−35.1	109.4	10 29.7	−36.7	109.8	9 48.8	−38.3	110.1	9 07.2	−39.7	110.4	10
11 15.9	33.5	109.9	10 34.8	35.2	110.2	9 53.0	36.8	110.6	9 10.5	38.3	110.9	8 27.5	39.8	111.2	11
10 42.4	33.7	110.7	9 59.6	35.3	111.0	9 16.2	36.9	111.4	8 32.2	38.4	111.6	7 47.7	39.9	111.9	12
10 08.7	33.9	111.5	9 24.3	35.4	111.9	8 39.3	37.0	112.2	7 53.8	38.5	112.4	7 07.8	40.0	112.7	13
9 34.8	33.9	112.4	8 48.9	35.6	112.7	8 02.3	37.1	113.0	7 15.3	38.6	113.2	6 27.8	40.0	113.4	14
9 00.9	−34.0	113.2	8 13.3	−35.6	113.5	7 25.2	−37.1	113.7	6 36.7	−38.6	114.0	5 47.8	−40.1	114.2	15
8 26.9	34.2	114.0	7 37.7	35.7	114.3	6 48.1	37.3	114.5	5 58.1	38.8	114.7	5 07.7	40.2	114.9	16
7 52.7	34.3	114.8	7 02.0	35.8	115.1	6 10.8	37.3	115.3	5 19.3	38.7	115.5	4 27.5	40.2	115.7	17
7 18.4	34.3	115.7	6 26.2	35.9	115.9	5 33.5	37.3	116.1	4 40.6	38.9	116.3	3 47.3	40.2	116.4	18
6 44.1	34.4	116.5	5 50.3	35.9	116.7	4 56.2	37.5	116.9	4 01.7	38.8	117.0	3 07.1	40.3	117.2	19
6 09.7	−34.5	117.4	5 14.4	−36.1	117.5	4 18.7	−37.4	117.7	3 22.9	−38.9	117.8	2 26.8	−40.3	117.9	20
5 35.2	34.6	118.2	4 38.3	36.0	118.2	3 41.3	37.6	118.5	2 44.0	39.0	118.6	1 46.5	40.3	118.6	21
5 00.6	34.6	119.0	4 02.3	36.1	119.1	3 03.7	37.5	119.2	2 05.0	38.9	119.3	1 06.2	40.3	119.4	22
4 26.0	34.7	119.8	3 26.2	36.2	119.9	2 26.2	37.6	120.0	1 26.1	39.0	120.1	0 25.9	−40.3	120.1	23
3 51.3	34.8	120.6	2 50.0	36.2	120.7	1 48.6	37.6	120.8	0 47.1	39.0	120.8	0 14.4	+40.4	59.1	24
3 16.5	−34.7	121.5	2 13.8	−36.2	121.5	1 11.0	−37.6	121.6	0 08.1	−38.9	121.6	0 54.8	40.3	58.4	25
2 41.8	34.9	122.3	1 37.6	36.2	122.3	0 33.4	−37.6	122.4	0 30.8	+39.0	57.6	1 35.1	40.3	57.7	26
2 06.9	34.8	123.1	1 01.4	36.2	123.1	0 04.2	+37.6	56.9	1 09.8	39.0	56.9	2 15.4	40.2	56.9	27
1 32.1	34.8	123.9	0 25.2	−36.2	123.9	0 41.8	37.6	56.1	1 48.8	38.9	56.1	2 55.6	40.3	56.2	28
0 57.3	34.9	124.7	0 11.1	+36.2	55.3	1 19.4	37.6	55.3	2 27.7	38.9	55.3	3 35.9	40.2	55.4	29

LATITUDE **SAME** NAME

Dec.	40° Hc	d	Z	42° Hc	d	Z	44° Hc	d	Z	46° Hc	d	Z	48° Hc	d	Z
°	° ′	′	°	° ′	′	°	° ′	′	°	° ′	′	°	° ′	′	°
0	15 11.3	+39.9	103.2	14 43.5	+41.4	103.7	14 14.6	+42.9	104.2	13 44.7	+44.3	104.7	13 13.8	+45.7	105.1
1	15 51.2	39.7	102.4	15 24.9	41.3	102.9	14 57.5	42.8	103.5	14 29.0	44.3	104.0	13 59.5	45.7	104.5
2	16 30.9	39.6	101.6	16 06.2	41.1	102.2	15 40.3	42.6	102.7	15 13.3	44.1	103.3	14 45.2	45.5	103.8
3	17 10.5	39.3	100.8	16 47.3	41.0	101.4	16 22.9	42.5	102.0	15 57.4	44.0	102.6	15 30.7	45.4	103.1
4	17 49.8	39.2	100.0	17 28.3	40.8	100.7	17 05.4	42.4	101.3	16 41.4	43.8	101.9	16 16.1	45.3	102.4
5	18 29.0	+39.0	99.2	18 09.1	+40.6	99.9	17 47.8	+42.2	100.5	17 25.2	+43.7	101.2	17 01.4	+45.1	101.8
6	19 08.0	38.7	98.4	18 49.7	40.4	99.1	18 30.0	41.9	99.8	18 08.9	43.5	100.4	17 46.5	45.0	101.1
7	19 46.7	38.5	97.6	19 30.1	40.2	98.3	19 11.9	41.9	99.0	18 52.4	43.4	99.7	18 31.5	44.8	100.4
8	20 25.2	38.3	96.8	20 10.3	39.9	97.5	19 53.8	41.6	98.3	19 35.8	43.1	99.0	19 16.3	44.7	99.7
9	21 03.5	38.1	96.0	20 50.2	39.8	96.7	20 35.4	41.4	97.5	20 18.9	43.0	98.2	20 01.0	44.5	99.0
10	21 41.6	+37.8	95.2	21 30.0	+39.5	95.9	21 16.8	+41.2	96.7	21 01.9	+42.8	97.5	20 45.5	+44.3	98.2
11	22 19.4	37.6	94.3	22 09.5	39.3	95.1	21 58.0	40.9	95.9	21 44.7	42.6	96.7	21 29.8	44.1	97.5
12	22 57.0	37.3	93.5	22 48.8	39.1	94.3	22 38.9	40.8	95.1	22 27.3	42.4	96.0	22 13.9	44.0	96.8
13	23 34.3	37.0	92.6	23 27.9	38.7	93.5	23 19.7	40.4	94.4	23 09.7	42.1	95.2	22 57.9	43.7	96.1
14	24 11.3	36.7	91.8	24 06.6	38.5	92.7	24 00.1	40.3	93.5	23 51.8	41.9	94.4	23 41.6	43.5	95.3
15	24 48.0	+36.4	90.9	24 45.1	+38.2	91.8	24 40.4	+39.9	92.7	24 33.7	+41.6	93.6	24 25.1	+43.3	94.6
16	25 24.4	36.0	90.0	25 23.3	38.0	91.0	25 20.3	39.7	91.9	25 15.3	41.4	92.9	25 08.4	43.0	93.8
17	26 00.4	35.8	89.1	26 01.3	37.6	90.1	26 00.0	39.4	91.1	25 56.7	41.2	92.1	25 51.4	42.8	93.0
18	26 36.2	35.4	88.2	26 38.9	37.2	89.2	26 39.4	39.1	90.2	26 37.9	40.8	91.2	26 34.2	42.6	92.2
19	27 11.6	35.1	87.3	27 16.1	37.0	88.4	27 18.5	38.8	89.4	27 18.7	40.6	90.4	27 16.8	42.2	91.4
20	27 46.7	+34.7	86.4	27 53.1	+36.6	87.5	27 57.3	+38.5	88.5	27 59.3	+40.2	89.6	27 59.0	+42.0	90.6
21	28 21.4	34.3	85.5	28 29.7	36.3	86.6	28 35.8	38.1	87.7	28 39.5	40.0	88.7	28 41.0	41.7	89.8
22	28 55.7	33.9	84.5	29 06.0	35.8	85.7	29 13.9	37.8	86.8	29 19.5	39.6	87.9	29 22.7	41.4	89.0
23	29 29.6	33.6	83.6	29 41.8	35.5	84.7	29 51.7	37.4	85.9	29 59.1	39.2	87.0	30 04.1	41.1	88.2
24	30 03.2	33.1	82.6	30 17.3	35.1	83.8	30 29.1	37.0	85.0	30 38.3	39.0	86.1	30 45.2	40.7	87.3
25	30 36.3	+32.6	81.7	30 52.4	+34.7	82.9	31 06.1	+36.6	84.1	31 17.3	+38.5	85.3	31 25.9	+40.4	86.5
26	31 08.9	32.3	80.7	31 27.1	34.2	81.9	31 42.7	36.2	83.1	31 55.8	38.1	84.4	32 06.3	40.0	85.6
27	31 41.2	31.7	79.7	32 01.3	33.8	80.9	32 18.9	35.8	82.2	32 33.9	37.8	83.4	32 46.3	39.6	84.7
28	32 12.9	31.3	78.7	32 35.1	33.4	80.0	32 54.7	35.4	81.2	33 11.7	37.3	82.5	33 25.9	39.3	83.8
29	32 44.2	30.8	77.7	33 08.5	32.8	79.0	33 30.1	34.9	80.3	33 49.0	36.9	81.6	34 05.2	38.8	82.9

Dec.	50° Hc	d	Z	52° Hc	d	Z	54° Hc	d	Z	56° Hc	d	Z	58° Hc	d	Z
°	° ′	′	°	° ′	′	°	° ′	′	°	° ′	′	°	° ′	′	°
0	12 42.0	+47.1	105.6	12 09.3	+48.4	106.0	11 35.8	+49.6	106.4	11 01.6	+50.6	106.8	10 26.5	+51.7	107.2
1	13 29.1	46.9	104.9	12 57.7	48.2	105.4	12 25.4	49.4	105.8	11 52.2	50.6	106.2	11 18.2	51.7	106.6
2	14 16.0	46.9	104.3	13 45.9	48.2	104.8	13 14.8	49.4	105.2	12 42.8	50.5	105.7	12 09.9	51.6	106.1
3	15 02.9	46.8	103.7	14 34.1	48.0	104.2	14 04.2	49.3	104.7	13 33.3	50.5	105.1	13 01.5	51.5	105.6
4	15 49.7	46.6	103.0	15 22.1	48.0	103.5	14 53.5	49.1	104.1	14 23.8	50.3	104.6	13 53.0	51.5	105.1
5	16 36.3	+46.5	102.4	16 10.1	+47.8	102.9	15 42.6	+49.1	103.5	15 14.1	+50.3	104.0	14 44.5	+51.4	104.5
6	17 22.8	46.4	101.7	16 57.9	47.7	102.3	16 31.7	49.0	102.9	16 04.4	50.2	103.5	15 35.9	51.3	104.0
7	18 09.2	46.3	101.0	17 45.6	47.6	101.7	17 20.7	48.9	102.3	16 54.6	50.1	102.9	16 27.2	51.3	103.5
8	18 55.5	46.1	100.4	18 33.2	47.5	101.0	18 09.6	48.8	101.7	17 44.7	50.0	102.3	17 18.5	51.1	102.9
9	19 41.6	45.9	99.7	19 20.7	47.3	100.4	18 58.4	48.6	101.1	18 34.7	49.8	101.7	18 09.6	51.1	102.4
10	20 27.5	+45.8	99.0	20 08.0	+47.2	99.7	19 47.0	+48.5	100.4	19 24.5	+49.8	101.1	19 00.7	+50.9	101.8
11	21 13.3	45.6	98.3	20 55.2	47.0	99.1	20 35.5	48.4	99.8	20 14.3	49.7	100.5	19 51.6	50.9	101.3
12	21 58.9	45.4	97.6	21 42.2	46.9	98.4	21 23.9	48.2	99.2	21 04.0	49.5	99.9	20 42.5	50.7	100.7
13	22 44.3	45.3	96.9	22 29.1	46.7	97.7	22 12.1	48.1	98.5	21 53.5	49.4	99.3	21 33.2	50.6	100.1
14	23 29.6	45.0	96.2	23 15.8	46.5	97.0	23 00.2	47.9	97.9	22 42.9	49.2	98.7	22 23.8	50.5	99.5
15	24 14.6	+44.9	95.5	24 02.3	+46.3	96.3	23 48.1	+47.8	97.2	23 32.1	+49.1	98.1	23 14.3	+50.4	99.0
16	24 59.5	44.6	94.7	24 48.6	46.2	95.7	24 35.9	47.5	96.6	24 21.2	48.9	97.5	24 04.7	50.2	98.4
17	25 44.1	44.4	94.0	25 34.8	45.9	94.9	25 23.4	47.4	95.9	25 10.1	48.8	96.8	24 54.9	50.1	97.8
18	26 28.5	44.2	93.2	26 20.7	45.7	94.2	26 10.8	47.2	95.2	25 58.9	48.6	96.2	25 45.0	49.9	97.1
19	27 12.7	43.9	92.5	27 06.4	45.5	93.5	26 58.0	47.0	94.5	26 47.5	48.4	95.5	26 34.9	49.7	96.5
20	27 56.6	+43.6	91.7	27 51.9	+45.2	92.8	27 45.0	+46.8	93.8	27 35.9	+48.2	94.9	27 24.6	+49.6	95.9
21	28 40.2	43.4	90.9	28 37.1	45.0	92.0	28 31.8	46.5	93.1	28 24.1	48.0	94.2	28 14.2	49.4	95.3
22	29 23.6	43.1	90.1	29 22.1	44.8	91.3	29 18.3	46.3	92.4	29 12.1	47.8	93.5	29 03.6	49.2	94.6
23	30 06.7	42.8	89.3	30 06.9	44.4	90.5	30 04.6	46.1	91.7	29 59.9	47.6	92.8	29 52.8	49.1	94.0
24	30 49.5	42.5	88.5	30 51.3	44.2	89.7	30 50.7	45.8	90.9	30 47.5	47.4	92.1	30 41.9	48.8	93.3
25	31 32.0	+42.2	87.7	31 35.5	+43.9	88.9	31 36.5	+45.5	90.2	31 34.9	+47.1	91.4	31 30.7	+48.6	92.6
26	32 14.2	41.8	86.9	32 19.4	43.6	88.1	32 22.0	45.3	89.4	32 22.0	46.8	90.7	32 19.3	48.3	91.9
27	32 56.0	41.5	86.0	33 03.0	43.2	87.3	33 07.3	44.9	88.6	33 08.8	46.6	89.9	33 07.6	48.1	91.2
28	33 37.5	41.1	85.1	33 46.2	43.0	86.5	33 52.2	44.7	87.8	33 55.4	46.3	89.2	33 55.7	47.9	90.5
29	34 18.6	40.7	84.3	34 29.2	42.5	85.6	34 36.9	44.3	87.0	34 41.7	46.0	88.4	34 43.6	47.6	89.8

40°			42°			44°			46°			48°			Dec.
Hc	d	Z	Hc	d	Z	Hc	d	Z	Hc	d	Z	Hc	d	Z	
15 11.3	-40.0	103.2	14 43.5	-41.6	103.7	14 14.6	-43.1	104.2	13 44.7	-44.5	104.7	13 13.8	-45.9	105.1	0
14 31.3	40.2	103.9	14 01.9	41.7	104.4	13 31.5	43.2	104.9	13 00.2	44.6	105.4	12 27.9	45.9	105.8	1
13 51.1	40.3	104.7	13 20.2	41.9	105.2	12 48.3	43.3	105.6	12 15.6	44.7	106.0	11 42.0	46.1	106.5	2
13 10.8	40.5	105.5	12 38.3	41.9	105.9	12 05.0	43.4	106.3	11 30.9	44.8	106.7	10 55.9	46.1	107.1	3
12 30.3	40.6	106.2	11 56.4	42.1	106.6	11 21.6	43.5	107.0	10 46.1	44.9	107.4	10 09.8	46.2	107.8	4
11 49.7	-40.7	107.0	11 14.3	-42.2	107.4	10 38.1	-43.6	107.7	10 01.2	-45.0	108.1	9 23.6	-46.3	108.4	5
11 09.0	40.8	107.7	10 32.1	42.3	108.1	9 54.5	43.7	108.4	9 16.2	45.0	108.8	8 37.3	46.3	109.1	6
10 28.2	41.0	108.5	9 49.8	42.4	108.8	9 10.8	43.8	109.1	8 31.2	45.1	109.4	7 51.0	46.4	109.7	7
9 47.2	41.0	109.2	9 07.4	42.4	109.5	8 27.0	43.8	109.8	7 46.1	45.2	110.1	7 04.6	46.4	110.3	8
9 06.2	41.1	110.0	8 25.0	42.6	110.2	7 43.2	43.9	110.5	7 00.9	45.2	110.8	6 18.2	46.5	111.0	9
8 25.1	-41.2	110.7	7 42.4	-42.6	111.0	6 59.3	-44.0	111.2	6 15.7	-45.3	111.4	5 31.7	-46.5	111.6	10
7 43.9	41.3	111.4	6 59.8	42.6	111.7	6 15.3	44.0	111.9	5 30.4	45.3	112.1	4 45.2	46.6	112.2	11
7 02.6	41.3	112.2	6 17.2	42.7	112.4	5 31.3	44.1	112.6	4 45.1	45.4	112.7	3 58.6	46.6	112.9	12
6 21.3	41.4	112.9	5 34.5	42.8	113.1	4 47.2	44.1	113.2	3 59.7	45.3	113.4	3 12.0	46.6	113.5	13
5 39.9	41.4	113.6	4 51.7	42.8	113.8	4 03.1	44.1	113.9	3 14.4	45.5	114.0	2 25.4	46.7	114.1	14
4 58.5	-41.5	114.3	4 08.9	-42.9	114.5	3 19.0	-44.2	114.6	2 28.9	-45.4	114.7	1 38.7	-46.6	114.8	15
4 17.0	41.6	115.1	3 26.0	42.9	115.2	2 34.8	44.2	115.3	1 43.5	45.4	115.4	0 52.1	46.7	115.4	16
3 35.4	41.6	115.8	2 43.1	42.9	115.9	1 50.6	44.2	116.0	0 58.1	45.5	116.0	0 05.4	-46.6	116.0	17
2 53.8	41.6	116.5	2 00.2	42.9	116.6	1 06.4	44.2	116.6	0 12.6	-45.4	116.7	0 41.2	+46.7	63.4	18
2 12.2	41.6	117.2	1 17.3	43.0	117.3	0 22.2	-44.2	117.3	0 32.8	+45.5	62.7	1 27.9	46.6	62.7	19
1 30.6	-41.6	118.0	0 34.3	-42.9	118.0	0 22.0	+44.2	62.0	1 18.3	+45.4	62.0	2 14.5	+46.6	62.1	20
0 49.0	41.7	118.7	0 08.6	+43.0	61.3	1 06.2	44.2	61.3	2 03.7	45.4	61.4	3 01.1	46.6	61.5	21
0 07.3	-41.6	119.4	0 51.6	42.9	60.6	1 50.4	44.2	60.7	2 49.1	45.4	60.7	3 47.7	46.6	60.8	22
0 34.3	+41.7	59.9	1 34.5	42.9	59.9	2 34.6	44.2	60.0	3 34.5	45.4	60.1	4 34.3	46.5	60.2	23
1 16.0	41.6	59.2	2 17.4	42.9	59.2	3 18.8	44.1	59.3	4 19.9	45.4	59.4	5 20.8	46.5	59.6	24
1 57.6	+41.6	58.4	3 00.3	+42.9	58.5	4 02.9	+44.1	58.6	5 05.3	+45.3	58.8	6 07.3	+46.5	58.9	25
2 39.2	41.6	57.7	3 43.2	42.8	57.8	4 47.0	44.1	57.9	5 50.6	45.2	58.1	6 53.8	46.4	58.3	26
3 20.8	41.5	57.0	4 26.0	42.8	57.1	5 31.1	44.0	57.3	6 35.8	45.2	57.4	7 40.2	46.4	57.7	27
4 02.3	41.6	56.3	5 08.8	42.8	56.4	6 15.1	44.0	56.6	7 21.0	45.2	56.8	8 26.6	46.2	57.0	28
4 43.9	41.4	55.6	5 51.6	42.7	55.7	6 59.1	43.9	55.9	8 06.2	45.0	56.1	9 12.8	46.3	56.4	29

50°			52°			54°			56°			58°			Dec.
Hc	d	Z	Hc	d	Z	Hc	d	Z	Hc	d	Z	Hc	d	Z	
12 42.0	-47.2	105.6	12 09.3	-48.4	106.0	11 35.8	-49.5	106.4	11 01.6	-50.7	106.8	10 26.5	-51.7	107.2	0
11 54.8	47.2	106.2	11 20.9	48.4	106.6	10 46.3	49.7	107.0	10 10.9	50.8	107.3	9 34.8	51.8	107.7	1
11 07.6	47.3	106.8	10 32.5	48.6	107.2	9 56.6	49.7	107.6	9 20.1	50.8	107.9	8 43.0	51.9	108.2	2
10 20.3	47.4	107.5	9 43.9	48.6	107.8	9 06.9	49.8	108.1	8 29.3	50.9	108.4	7 51.1	51.9	108.7	3
9 32.9	47.5	108.1	8 55.3	48.7	108.4	8 17.1	49.8	108.7	7 38.4	50.9	109.0	6 59.2	51.9	109.2	4
8 45.4	-47.5	108.7	8 06.6	-48.7	109.0	7 27.3	-49.8	109.2	6 47.5	-50.9	109.5	6 07.3	-51.9	109.7	5
7 57.9	47.6	109.3	7 17.9	48.7	109.6	6 37.5	49.9	109.8	5 56.6	50.9	110.0	5 15.4	52.0	110.2	6
7 10.3	47.6	109.9	6 29.2	48.8	110.2	5 47.6	49.9	110.4	5 05.7	51.0	110.5	4 23.4	52.0	110.7	7
6 22.7	47.7	110.6	5 40.4	48.9	110.8	4 57.7	50.0	110.9	4 14.7	51.0	111.1	3 31.4	52.0	111.2	8
5 35.0	47.7	111.2	4 51.5	48.8	111.3	4 07.7	49.9	111.5	3 23.7	51.1	111.6	2 39.4	52.0	111.7	9
4 47.3	-47.7	111.8	4 02.7	-48.9	111.9	3 17.8	-50.0	112.0	2 32.6	-51.0	112.1	1 47.4	-52.1	112.2	10
3 59.6	47.8	112.4	3 13.8	48.9	112.5	2 27.8	50.0	112.6	1 41.6	51.0	112.7	0 55.3	52.0	112.7	11
3 11.8	47.8	113.0	2 24.9	48.9	113.1	1 37.8	50.0	113.1	0 50.6	-51.1	113.2	0 03.3	-52.0	113.2	12
2 24.0	47.8	113.6	1 36.0	49.0	113.7	0 47.8	-50.1	113.7	0 00.5	+51.0	66.3	0 48.7	+52.0	66.3	13
1 36.2	47.8	114.2	0 47.0	-49.0	114.2	0 02.3	+50.0	65.8	0 51.5	51.1	65.8	1 40.7	52.1	65.8	14
0 48.4	-47.8	114.8	0 01.9	+49.0	65.2	0 52.3	+50.0	65.2	1 42.6	+51.0	65.2	2 32.8	+52.0	65.3	15
0 00.6	-47.8	115.4	0 50.9	48.9	64.6	1 42.3	50.0	64.6	2 33.6	51.0	64.7	3 24.8	52.0	64.8	16
0 47.2	+47.8	64.0	1 39.8	48.9	64.0	2 32.3	50.0	64.1	3 24.6	51.0	64.2	4 16.8	51.9	64.3	17
1 35.0	47.8	63.4	2 28.7	48.9	63.4	3 22.3	49.9	63.5	4 15.6	51.0	63.7	5 08.7	52.0	63.8	18
2 22.8	47.8	62.8	3 17.6	48.9	62.9	4 12.2	50.0	63.0	5 06.6	51.0	63.1	6 00.7	51.9	63.3	19
3 10.6	+47.8	62.2	4 06.5	+48.9	62.3	5 02.2	+49.9	62.4	5 57.6	+50.9	62.6	6 52.6	+51.9	62.8	20
3 58.4	47.7	61.6	4 55.4	48.8	61.7	5 52.1	49.9	61.9	6 48.5	50.9	62.1	7 44.5	51.9	62.3	21
4 46.1	47.7	61.0	5 44.2	48.8	61.1	6 42.0	49.8	61.3	7 39.4	50.8	61.5	8 36.4	51.8	61.8	22
5 33.8	47.7	60.4	6 33.0	48.8	60.5	7 31.8	49.8	60.8	8 30.2	50.9	61.0	9 28.2	51.7	61.3	23
6 21.5	47.6	59.7	7 21.8	48.7	60.0	8 21.6	49.8	60.2	9 21.1	50.7	60.5	10 19.9	51.8	60.8	24
7 09.1	+47.6	59.1	8 10.5	+48.6	59.4	9 11.4	+49.7	59.6	10 11.8	+50.7	59.9	11 11.7	+51.6	60.2	25
7 56.7	47.5	58.5	8 59.1	48.6	58.8	10 01.1	49.6	59.1	11 02.5	50.7	59.4	12 03.3	51.6	59.7	26
8 44.2	47.5	57.9	9 47.7	48.6	58.2	10 50.7	49.6	58.5	11 53.2	50.5	58.8	12 54.9	51.6	59.2	27
9 31.7	47.4	57.3	10 36.3	48.4	57.6	11 40.3	49.5	57.9	12 43.7	50.6	58.3	13 46.5	51.5	58.7	28
10 19.1	47.3	56.7	11 24.7	48.4	57.0	12 29.8	49.5	57.3	13 34.3	50.4	57.7	14 38.0	51.4	58.1	29

Dec.	0° Hc	d	Z	2° Hc	d	Z	4° Hc	d	Z	6° Hc	d	Z	8° Hc	d	Z
°	° ′	′	°	° ′	′	°	° ′	′	°	° ′	′	°	° ′	′	°
0	18 00.0 −	0.2	90.0	17 59.3 +	2.1	90.6	17 57.3 +	4.2	91.3	17 53.9 +	6.4	91.9	17 49.1 +	8.6	92.6
1	17 59.8	0.5	88.9	18 01.4	1.6	89.6	18 01.5	3.9	90.2	18 00.3	6.1	90.9	17 57.7	8.3	91.5
2	17 59.3	0.8	87.9	18 03.0	1.4	88.5	18 05.4	3.6	89.2	18 06.4	5.8	89.9	18 06.0	8.0	90.5
3	17 58.5	1.2	86.8	18 04.4	1.0	87.5	18 09.0	3.2	88.1	18 12.1	5.4	88.8	18 14.0	7.5	89.5
4	17 57.3	1.5	85.8	18 05.4	0.7	86.4	18 12.2	2.8	87.1	18 17.5	5.1	87.8	18 21.5	7.3	88.4
5	17 55.8 −	1.9	84.7	18 06.1 +	0.3	85.4	18 15.0 +	2.5	86.0	18 22.6 +	4.7	86.7	18 28.8 +	6.9	87.4
6	17 53.9	2.2	83.7	18 06.4	0.0	84.3	18 17.5	2.2	85.0	18 27.3	4.4	85.7	18 35.7	6.6	86.3
7	17 51.7	2.6	82.6	18 06.4 −	0.4	83.3	18 19.7	1.8	83.9	18 31.7	4.0	84.6	18 42.3	6.2	85.3
8	17 49.1	2.8	81.6	18 06.0	0.7	82.2	18 21.5	1.5	82.9	18 35.7	3.7	83.6	18 48.5	5.8	84.2
9	17 46.3	3.3	80.5	18 05.3	1.0	81.2	18 23.0	1.2	81.8	18 39.4	3.3	82.5	18 54.3	5.6	83.2
10	17 43.0 −	3.5	79.5	18 04.3 −	1.4	80.1	18 24.2 +	0.7	80.8	18 42.7 +	3.0	81.4	18 59.9 +	5.1	82.1
11	17 39.5	3.9	78.4	18 02.9	1.7	79.1	18 24.9	0.5	79.7	18 45.7	2.6	80.4	19 05.0	4.8	81.1
12	17 35.6	4.2	77.4	18 01.2	2.1	78.0	18 25.4 +	0.1	78.7	18 48.3	2.2	79.3	19 09.8	4.4	80.0
13	17 31.4	4.5	76.4	17 59.1	2.4	77.0	18 25.5 −	0.3	77.6	18 50.5	1.9	78.3	19 14.2	4.1	79.0
14	17 26.9	4.9	75.3	17 56.7	2.8	75.9	18 25.2	0.6	76.6	18 52.4	1.6	77.2	19 18.3	3.7	77.9
15	17 22.0 −	5.2	74.3	17 53.9 −	3.0	74.9	18 24.6 −	1.0	75.5	18 54.0 +	1.1	76.2	19 22.0 +	3.3	76.8
16	17 16.8	5.5	73.2	17 50.9	3.5	73.8	18 23.6	1.3	74.5	18 55.1	0.9	75.1	19 25.3	3.0	75.8
17	17 11.3	5.8	72.2	17 47.4	3.7	72.8	18 22.3	1.6	73.4	18 56.0	0.4	74.1	19 28.3	2.5	74.7
18	17 05.5	6.2	71.1	17 43.7	4.1	71.7	18 20.7	2.0	72.4	18 56.4 +	0.1	73.0	19 30.8	2.3	73.7
19	16 59.3	6.5	70.1	17 39.6	4.4	70.7	18 18.7	2.4	71.3	18 56.5 −	0.2	71.9	19 33.1	1.8	72.6
20	16 52.8 −	6.7	69.1	17 35.2 −	4.8	69.6	18 16.3 −	2.7	70.2	18 56.3 −	0.7	70.9	19 34.9 +	1.5	71.5
21	16 46.1	7.1	68.0	17 30.4	5.1	68.6	18 13.6	3.0	69.2	18 55.6	0.9	69.8	19 36.4	1.1	70.5
22	16 39.0	7.4	67.0	17 25.3	5.4	67.5	18 10.6	3.4	68.1	18 54.7	1.4	68.8	19 37.5	0.7	69.4
23	16 31.6	7.7	65.9	17 19.9	5.7	66.5	18 07.2	3.7	67.1	18 53.3	1.7	67.7	19 38.2 +	0.4	68.4
24	16 23.9	8.1	64.9	17 14.2	6.0	65.5	18 03.5	4.1	66.0	18 51.6	2.0	66.7	19 38.6	0.0	67.3
25	16 15.8 −	8.3	63.9	17 08.2 −	6.4	64.4	17 59.4 −	4.4	65.0	18 49.6 −	2.4	65.6	19 38.6 −	0.4	66.2
26	16 07.5	8.6	62.8	17 01.8	6.7	63.4	17 55.0	4.7	63.9	18 47.2	2.8	64.5	19 38.2	0.8	65.2
27	15 58.9	8.9	61.8	16 55.1	7.0	62.3	17 50.3	5.1	62.9	18 44.4	3.1	63.5	19 37.4	1.1	64.1
28	15 50.0	9.2	60.8	16 48.1	7.3	61.3	17 45.2	5.4	61.9	18 41.3	3.5	62.4	19 36.3	1.5	63.1
29	15 40.8	9.5	59.8	16 40.8	7.6	60.3	17 39.8	5.7	60.8	18 37.8	3.8	61.4	19 34.8	1.9	62.0

Dec.	10° Hc	d	Z	12° Hc	d	Z	14° Hc	d	Z	16° Hc	d	Z	18° Hc	d	Z
°	° ′	′	°	° ′	′	°	° ′	′	°	° ′	′	°	° ′	′	°
0	17 43.0 +	10.8	93.2	17 35.6 +	12.9	93.9	17 26.9 +	15.0	94.5	17 16.8 +	17.2	95.1	17 05.5 +	19.2	95.7
1	17 53.8	10.5	92.2	17 48.5	12.7	92.8	17 41.9	14.8	93.5	17 34.0	16.9	94.1	17 24.7	19.0	94.7
2	18 04.3	10.1	91.2	18 01.2	12.2	91.8	17 56.7	14.4	92.5	17 50.9	16.5	93.1	17 43.7	18.6	93.7
3	18 14.4	9.8	90.1	18 13.4	12.0	90.8	18 11.1	14.1	91.4	18 07.4	16.2	92.1	18 02.3	18.4	92.7
4	18 24.2	9.4	89.1	18 25.4	11.6	89.7	18 25.2	13.8	90.4	18 23.6	16.0	91.1	18 20.7	18.0	91.7
5	18 33.6 +	9.1	88.0	18 37.0 +	11.3	88.7	18 39.0 +	13.4	89.4	18 39.6 +	15.5	90.1	18 38.7 +	17.7	90.7
6	18 42.7	8.8	87.0	18 48.3	10.9	87.7	18 52.4	13.1	88.4	18 55.1	15.3	89.0	18 56.4	17.4	89.7
7	18 51.5	8.4	86.0	18 59.2	10.6	86.6	19 05.5	12.8	87.3	19 10.4	14.9	88.0	19 13.8	17.0	88.7
8	18 59.9	8.0	84.9	19 09.8	10.2	85.6	19 18.3	12.4	86.3	19 25.3	14.6	87.0	19 30.8	16.8	87.7
9	19 07.9	7.7	83.9	19 20.0	9.9	84.6	19 30.7	12.0	85.3	19 39.9	14.2	86.0	19 47.6	16.3	86.7
10	19 15.6 +	7.3	82.8	19 29.9 +	9.5	83.5	19 42.7 +	11.7	84.2	19 54.1 +	13.8	84.9	20 03.9 +	16.0	85.7
11	19 22.9	7.0	81.8	19 39.4	9.1	82.5	19 54.4	11.3	83.2	20 07.9	13.5	83.9	20 19.9	15.6	84.6
12	19 29.9	6.6	80.7	19 48.5	8.8	81.4	20 05.7	11.0	82.1	20 21.4	13.1	82.9	20 35.5	15.3	83.6
13	19 36.5	6.2	79.6	19 57.3	8.4	80.4	20 16.7	10.5	81.1	20 34.5	12.8	81.8	20 50.8	14.9	82.6
14	19 42.7	5.9	78.6	20 05.7	8.1	79.3	20 27.2	10.2	80.0	20 47.3	12.3	80.8	21 05.7	14.5	81.5
15	19 48.6 +	5.5	77.5	20 13.8 +	7.6	78.2	20 37.4 +	9.9	79.0	20 59.6 +	12.0	79.7	21 20.2 +	14.2	80.5
16	19 54.1	5.1	76.5	20 21.4	7.3	77.2	20 47.3	9.4	77.9	21 11.6	11.6	78.7	21 34.4	13.7	79.4
17	19 59.2	4.7	75.4	20 28.7	6.8	76.1	20 56.7	9.0	76.9	21 23.2	11.2	77.6	21 48.1	13.4	78.4
18	20 03.9	4.4	74.4	20 35.5	6.5	75.1	21 05.7	8.7	75.8	21 34.4	10.8	76.6	22 01.5	12.9	77.3
19	20 08.3	3.9	73.3	20 42.0	6.1	74.0	21 14.4	8.2	74.7	21 45.2	10.3	75.5	22 14.4	12.5	76.3
20	20 12.2 +	3.6	72.2	20 48.1 +	5.7	72.9	21 22.6 +	7.8	73.7	21 55.5 +	10.0	74.4	22 26.9 +	12.1	75.2
21	20 15.8	3.0	71.2	20 53.8	5.4	71.9	21 30.4	7.5	72.6	22 05.5	9.6	73.4	22 39.0	11.7	74.2
22	20 19.0	2.8	70.1	20 59.2	4.9	70.8	21 37.9	7.0	71.6	22 15.1	9.1	72.3	22 50.7	11.3	73.1
23	20 21.8	2.5	69.0	21 04.1	4.5	69.7	21 44.9	6.6	70.5	22 24.2	8.8	71.2	23 02.0	10.9	72.0
24	20 24.3	2.0	68.0	21 08.6	4.1	68.7	21 51.5	6.2	69.4	22 33.0	8.2	70.2	23 12.9	10.4	71.0
25	20 26.3 +	1.6	66.9	21 12.7 +	3.7	67.6	21 57.7 +	5.8	68.3	22 41.2 +	7.9	69.1	23 23.3 +	9.9	69.9
26	20 27.9	1.3	65.8	21 16.4	3.3	66.5	22 03.5	5.3	67.3	22 49.1	7.4	68.0	23 33.2	9.6	68.8
27	20 29.2	0.9	64.8	21 19.7	2.9	65.5	22 08.8	5.0	66.2	22 56.5	7.0	67.0	23 42.8	9.0	67.7
28	20 30.1	0.4	63.7	21 22.6	2.5	64.4	22 13.8	4.5	65.1	23 03.5	6.6	65.9	23 51.8	8.7	66.7
29	20 30.5 +	0.1	62.6	21 25.1	2.0	63.3	22 18.3	4.1	64.0	23 10.1	6.1	64.8	24 00.5	8.1	65.6

LATITUDE **CONTRARY** NAME   L.H.A. 72°, 288°

0° Hc	d	Z	2° Hc	d	Z	4° Hc	d	Z	6° Hc	d	Z	8° Hc	d	Z	Dec.
18 00.0	- 0.2	90.0	17 59.3	- 2.4	90.6	17 57.3	- 4.6	91.3	17 53.9	- 6.8	91.9	17 49.1	- 8.9	92.6	0
17 59.8	0.5	91.1	17 56.9	2.7	91.7	17 52.7	4.9	92.3	17 47.1	7.1	93.0	17 40.2	9.3	93.6	1
17 59.3	0.8	92.1	17 54.2	3.0	92.8	17 47.8	5.2	93.4	17 40.0	7.4	94.0	17 30.9	9.5	94.7	2
17 58.5	1.2	93.2	17 51.2	3.4	93.8	17 42.6	5.6	94.4	17 32.6	7.7	95.1	17 21.4	9.9	95.7	3
17 57.3	1.5	94.2	17 47.8	3.7	94.8	17 37.0	5.9	95.5	17 24.9	8.1	96.1	17 11.5	10.3	96.7	4
17 55.8	- 1.9	95.3	17 44.1	- 4.1	95.9	17 31.1	- 6.2	96.5	16 16.8	- 8.4	97.2	17 01.2	- 10.5	97.8	5
17 53.9	2.2	96.3	17 40.0	4.3	96.9	17 24.9	6.6	97.6	17 08.4	8.7	98.2	16 50.7	10.8	98.8	6
17 51.7	2.6	97.4	17 35.7	4.8	98.0	17 18.3	6.8	98.6	16 59.7	9.0	99.2	16 39.9	11.2	99.8	7
17 49.1	2.8	98.4	17 30.9	5.0	99.0	17 11.5	7.2	99.7	16 50.7	9.3	100.3	16 28.7	11.4	100.8	8
17 46.3	3.3	99.5	17 25.9	5.4	100.1	17 04.3	7.5	100.7	16 41.4	9.6	101.3	16 17.3	11.7	101.9	9
17 43.0	- 3.5	100.5	17 20.5	- 5.7	101.1	16 56.8	- 7.9	101.7	16 31.8	- 10.0	102.3	16 05.6	- 12.1	102.9	10
17 39.5	3.9	101.6	17 14.8	6.0	102.2	16 48.9	8.1	102.8	16 21.8	10.2	103.3	15 53.5	12.3	103.9	11
17 35.6	4.2	102.6	17 08.8	6.3	103.2	16 40.8	8.4	103.8	16 11.6	10.5	104.4	15 41.2	12.6	104.9	12
17 31.4	4.5	103.6	17 02.5	6.7	104.2	16 32.4	8.8	104.8	16 01.1	10.9	105.4	15 28.6	12.8	105.9	13
17 26.9	4.9	104.7	16 55.8	6.9	105.3	16 23.6	9.0	105.9	15 50.2	11.1	106.4	15 15.8	13.2	107.0	14
17 22.0	- 5.2	105.7	16 48.9	- 7.3	106.3	16 14.6	- 9.4	106.9	15 39.1	- 11.4	107.4	15 02.6	- 13.4	108.0	15
17 16.8	5.5	106.8	16 41.6	7.6	107.4	16 05.2	9.6	107.9	15 27.7	11.6	108.5	14 49.2	13.6	109.0	16
17 11.3	5.8	107.8	16 34.0	7.9	108.4	15 55.6	10.0	108.9	15 16.1	12.0	109.5	14 35.6	14.0	110.0	17
17 05.5	6.2	108.9	16 26.1	8.2	109.4	15 45.6	10.2	110.0	15 04.1	12.2	110.5	14 21.6	14.1	111.0	18
16 59.3	6.5	109.9	16 17.9	8.5	110.5	15 35.4	10.5	111.0	14 51.9	12.5	111.5	14 07.5	14.5	112.0	19
16 52.8	- 6.7	110.9	16 09.4	- 8.8	111.5	15 24.9	- 10.8	112.0	14 39.4	- 12.7	112.5	13 53.0	- 14.6	113.0	20
16 46.1	7.1	112.0	16 00.6	9.1	112.5	15 14.1	11.0	113.0	14 26.7	13.0	113.5	13 38.4	15.0	114.0	21
16 39.0	7.4	113.0	15 51.5	9.4	113.6	15 03.1	11.3	114.1	14 13.7	13.2	114.5	13 23.4	15.1	115.0	22
16 31.6	7.7	114.1	15 42.1	9.7	114.6	14 51.8	11.5	115.1	14 00.5	13.5	115.5	13 08.3	15.4	116.0	23
16 23.9	8.1	115.1	15 32.5	10.0	115.6	14 40.2	11.9	116.1	13 47.0	13.8	116.5	12 52.9	15.6	117.0	24
16 15.8	- 8.3	116.1	15 22.5	- 10.2	116.6	14 28.3	- 12.1	117.1	13 33.2	- 14.0	117.5	12 37.3	- 15.8	118.0	25
16 07.5	8.6	117.2	15 12.3	10.5	117.6	14 16.2	12.4	118.1	13 19.2	14.2	118.5	12 21.5	16.0	118.9	26
15 58.9	8.9	118.2	15 01.8	10.8	118.7	14 03.8	12.6	119.1	13 05.0	14.4	119.5	12 05.5	16.2	119.9	27
15 50.0	9.2	119.2	14 51.0	11.0	119.7	13 51.2	12.9	120.1	12 50.6	14.7	120.5	11 49.3	16.5	120.9	28
15 40.8	9.5	120.2	14 40.0	11.3	120.7	13 38.3	13.1	121.1	12 35.9	14.9	121.5	11 32.8	16.6	121.9	29

10° Hc	d	Z	12° Hc	d	Z	14° Hc	d	Z	16° Hc	d	Z	18° Hc	d	Z	Dec.
17 43.0	- 11.1	93.2	17 35.6	- 13.2	93.9	17 26.9	- 15.4	94.5	17 16.8	- 17.5	95.1	17 05.5	- 19.6	95.7	0
17 31.9	11.4	94.3	17 22.4	13.6	94.9	17 11.5	15.7	95.5	16 59.3	17.7	96.1	16 45.9	19.8	96.7	1
17 20.5	11.7	95.3	17 08.8	13.8	95.9	16 55.8	15.9	96.5	16 41.6	18.1	97.1	16 26.1	20.1	97.7	2
17 08.8	12.0	96.3	16 55.0	14.2	96.9	16 39.9	16.3	97.5	16 23.5	18.3	98.1	16 06.0	20.4	98.7	3
16 56.8	12.4	97.3	16 40.8	14.5	97.9	16 23.6	16.5	98.5	16 05.2	18.6	99.1	15 45.6	20.6	99.7	4
16 44.4	- 12.6	98.4	16 26.3	- 14.7	99.0	16 07.1	- 16.9	99.5	15 46.6	- 18.9	100.1	15 25.0	- 20.9	100.6	5
16 31.8	13.0	99.4	16 11.6	15.0	100.0	15 50.2	17.1	100.5	15 27.7	19.1	101.1	15 04.1	21.1	101.6	6
16 18.8	13.2	100.4	15 56.6	15.4	101.0	15 33.1	17.3	101.5	15 08.6	19.4	102.1	14 43.0	21.4	102.6	7
16 05.6	13.6	101.4	15 41.2	15.6	102.0	15 15.8	17.6	102.5	14 49.2	19.6	103.0	14 21.6	21.6	103.5	8
15 52.0	13.8	102.4	15 25.6	15.8	103.0	14 58.2	17.9	103.5	14 29.6	19.9	104.0	14 00.0	21.8	104.5	9
15 38.2	- 14.1	103.4	15 09.8	- 16.1	104.0	14 40.3	- 18.2	104.5	14 09.7	- 20.1	105.0	13 38.2	- 22.0	105.5	10
15 24.1	14.3	104.5	14 53.7	16.4	105.0	14 22.1	18.3	105.5	13 49.6	20.3	106.0	13 16.2	22.3	106.4	11
15 09.8	14.6	105.5	14 37.3	16.6	106.0	14 03.8	18.6	106.5	13 29.3	20.6	106.9	12 53.9	22.5	107.4	12
14 55.2	14.9	106.5	14 20.7	16.9	107.0	13 45.2	18.9	107.4	13 08.7	20.7	107.9	12 31.4	22.6	108.3	13
14 40.3	15.2	107.5	14 03.8	17.1	108.0	13 26.3	19.0	108.4	12 48.0	21.0	108.9	12 08.8	22.9	109.3	14
14 25.1	- 15.4	108.5	13 46.7	- 17.4	108.9	13 07.3	- 19.3	109.4	12 27.0	- 21.2	109.8	11 45.9	- 23.0	110.2	15
14 09.7	15.6	109.5	13 29.3	17.6	109.9	12 48.0	19.5	110.4	12 05.8	21.4	110.8	11 22.9	23.3	111.2	16
13 54.1	15.9	110.5	13 11.7	17.8	110.9	12 28.5	19.7	111.3	11 44.4	21.5	111.7	10 59.6	23.4	112.1	17
13 38.2	16.1	111.4	12 53.9	18.0	111.9	12 08.8	19.9	112.3	11 22.9	21.8	112.7	10 36.2	23.5	113.0	18
13 22.1	16.4	112.4	12 35.9	18.3	112.9	11 48.9	20.1	113.3	11 01.1	21.9	113.6	10 12.7	23.8	114.0	19
13 05.7	- 16.5	113.4	12 17.6	- 18.4	113.8	11 28.8	- 20.3	114.2	10 39.2	- 22.1	114.6	9 48.9	- 23.8	114.9	20
12 49.2	16.8	114.4	11 59.2	18.7	114.8	11 08.5	20.5	115.2	10 17.1	22.3	115.5	9 25.1	24.1	115.8	21
12 32.4	17.0	115.4	11 40.5	18.8	115.8	10 48.0	20.7	116.1	9 54.8	22.4	116.5	9 01.0	24.1	116.8	22
12 15.4	17.3	116.4	11 21.7	19.0	116.8	10 27.3	20.8	117.1	9 32.4	22.6	117.4	8 36.9	24.3	117.7	23
11 58.1	17.4	117.4	11 02.7	19.3	117.7	10 06.5	21.0	118.1	9 09.8	22.7	118.3	8 12.6	24.4	118.6	24
11 40.7	- 17.6	118.3	10 43.4	- 19.4	118.7	9 45.5	- 21.1	119.0	8 47.1	- 22.9	119.3	7 48.2	- 24.6	119.5	25
11 23.1	17.8	119.3	10 24.0	19.6	119.6	9 24.4	21.3	120.0	8 24.2	22.9	120.2	7 23.6	24.6	120.5	26
11 05.3	18.0	120.3	10 04.5	19.8	120.6	9 03.1	21.4	120.9	8 01.3	23.2	121.2	6 59.0	24.8	121.4	27
10 47.3	18.2	121.3	9 44.7	19.9	121.6	8 41.7	21.6	121.8	7 38.1	23.2	122.1	6 34.2	24.9	122.3	28
10 29.1	18.4	122.2	9 24.8	20.0	122.5	8 20.1	21.7	122.8	7 14.9	23.3	123.0	6 09.3	24.9	123.2	29

Dec.	20° Hc	d	Z	22° Hc	d	Z	24° Hc	d	Z	26° Hc	d	Z	28° Hc	d	Z
°	° ′	′	°	° ′	′	°	° ′	′	°	° ′	′	°	° ′	′	°
0	16 52.8 +21.4		96.3	16 39.0 +23.3		96.9	16 23.9 +25.3		97.5	16 07.5 +27.3		98.1	15 50.0 +29.2		98.7
1	17 14.2	21.0	95.4	17 02.3	23.0	96.0	16 49.2	25.0	96.6	16 34.8	27.0	97.2	16 19.2	28.9	97.8
2	17 35.2	20.7	94.4	17 25.3	22.8	95.0	17 14.2	24.8	95.6	17 01.8	26.8	96.2	16 48.1	28.7	96.8
3	17 55.9	20.4	93.4	17 48.1	22.5	94.0	17 39.0	24.5	94.7	17 28.6	26.4	95.3	17 16.8	28.4	95.9
4	18 16.3	20.2	92.4	18 10.6	22.2	93.1	18 03.5	24.2	93.7	17 55.0	26.3	94.4	17 45.2	28.2	95.0
5	18 36.5 +19.8		91.4	18 32.8 +21.9		92.1	18 27.7 +23.9		92.8	18 21.3 +25.9		93.4	18 13.4 +27.9		94.1
6	18 56.3	19.5	90.4	18 54.7	21.5	91.1	18 51.6	23.7	91.8	18 47.2	25.6	92.5	18 41.3	27.6	93.1
7	19 15.8	19.1	89.4	19 16.2	21.3	90.1	19 15.3	23.3	90.8	19 12.8	25.4	91.5	19 08.9	27.4	92.2
8	19 34.9	18.8	88.4	19 37.5	20.9	89.1	19 38.6	23.0	89.8	19 38.2	25.0	90.6	19 36.3	27.0	91.3
9	19 53.7	18.5	87.4	19 58.4	20.6	88.1	20 01.6	22.7	88.9	20 03.2	24.7	89.6	20 03.3	26.8	90.3
10	20 12.2 +18.2		86.4	20 19.0 +20.3		87.1	20 24.3 +22.3		87.9	20 27.9 +24.4		88.6	20 30.1 +26.4		89.4
11	20 30.4	17.7	85.4	20 39.3	19.9	86.1	20 46.6	22.0	86.9	20 52.3	24.1	87.6	20 56.5	26.1	88.4
12	20 48.1	17.5	84.4	20 59.2	19.5	85.1	21 08.6	21.6	85.9	21 16.4	23.7	86.7	21 22.6	25.7	87.4
13	21 05.6	17.0	83.3	21 18.7	19.2	84.1	21 30.2	21.3	84.9	21 40.1	23.4	85.7	21 48.3	25.5	86.5
14	21 22.6	16.7	82.3	21 37.9	18.8	83.1	21 51.5	20.9	83.9	22 03.5	23.0	84.7	22 13.8	25.0	85.5
15	21 39.3 +16.2		81.3	21 56.7 +18.4		82.1	22 12.4 +20.6		82.9	22 26.5 +22.6		83.7	22 38.8 +24.7		84.5
16	21 55.5	15.9	80.2	22 15.1	18.0	81.0	22 33.0	20.1	81.8	22 49.1	22.3	82.7	23 03.5	24.4	83.5
17	22 11.4	15.5	79.2	22 33.1	17.6	80.0	22 53.1	19.8	80.8	23 11.4	21.8	81.7	23 27.9	23.9	82.5
18	22 26.9	15.1	78.1	22 50.7	17.3	79.0	23 12.9	19.3	79.8	23 33.2	21.5	80.7	23 51.8	23.6	81.5
19	22 42.0	14.7	77.1	23 08.0	16.8	77.9	23 32.2	19.0	78.8	23 54.7	21.1	79.6	24 15.4	23.2	80.5
20	22 56.7 +14.3		76.0	23 24.8 +16.4		76.9	23 51.2 +18.5		77.7	24 15.8 +20.6		78.6	24 38.6 +22.7		79.5
21	23 11.0	13.8	75.0	23 41.2	16.0	75.8	24 09.7	18.1	76.7	24 36.4	20.3	77.6	25 01.3	22.4	78.5
22	23 24.8	13.4	73.9	23 57.2	15.5	74.8	24 27.8	17.7	75.6	24 56.7	19.7	76.5	25 23.7	21.9	77.5
23	23 38.2	13.0	72.9	24 12.7	15.1	73.7	24 45.5	17.2	74.6	25 16.4	19.4	75.5	25 45.6	21.4	76.4
24	23 51.2	12.5	71.8	24 27.8	14.7	72.7	25 02.7	16.8	73.5	25 35.8	18.9	74.4	26 07.0	21.0	75.4
25	24 03.7 +12.1		70.7	24 42.5 +14.2		71.6	25 19.5 +16.3		72.5	25 54.7 +18.4		73.4	26 28.0 +20.6		74.3
26	24 15.8	11.6	69.7	24 56.7	13.7	70.5	25 35.8	15.8	71.4	26 13.1	18.0	72.3	26 48.6	20.1	73.3
27	24 27.4	11.2	68.6	25 10.4	13.3	69.4	25 51.6	15.4	70.3	26 31.1	17.5	71.3	27 08.7	19.6	72.2
28	24 38.6	10.7	67.5	25 23.7	12.8	68.4	26 07.0	14.9	69.3	26 48.6	17.0	70.2	27 28.3	19.1	71.2
29	24 49.3	10.2	66.4	25 36.5	12.3	67.3	26 21.9	14.4	68.2	27 05.6	16.5	69.1	27 47.4	18.7	70.1

Dec.	30° Hc	d	Z	32° Hc	d	Z	34° Hc	d	Z	36° Hc	d	Z	38° Hc	d	Z
°	° ′	′	°	° ′	′	°	° ′	′	°	° ′	′	°	° ′	′	°
0	15 31.3 +31.1		99.2	15 11.5 +32.9		99.8	14 50.6 +34.7		100.3	14 28.7 +36.3		100.8	14 05.6 +38.0		101.3
1	16 02.4	30.8	98.3	15 44.4	32.6	98.9	15 25.3	34.4	99.5	15 05.0	36.1	100.0	14 43.6	37.9	100.5
2	16 33.2	30.6	97.4	16 17.0	32.5	98.0	15 59.7	34.2	98.6	15 41.1	36.0	99.2	15 21.5	37.6	99.7
3	17 03.8	30.3	96.5	16 49.5	32.1	97.2	16 33.9	34.0	97.7	16 17.1	35.8	98.3	15 59.1	37.5	98.9
4	17 34.1	30.1	95.6	17 21.6	32.0	96.3	17 07.9	33.8	96.9	16 52.9	35.6	97.5	16 36.6	37.3	98.1
5	18 04.2 +29.8		94.7	17 53.6 +31.7		95.4	17 41.7 +33.6		96.0	17 28.5 +35.3		96.6	17 13.9 +37.1		97.3
6	18 34.0	29.6	93.8	18 25.3	31.5	94.5	18 15.3	33.3	95.1	18 03.8	35.1	95.8	17 51.0	36.9	96.4
7	19 03.6	29.3	92.9	18 56.8	31.2	93.6	18 48.6	33.1	94.3	18 38.9	34.9	94.9	18 27.9	36.7	95.6
8	19 32.9	29.0	92.0	19 28.0	30.9	92.7	19 21.7	32.8	93.4	19 13.8	34.7	94.1	19 04.6	36.4	94.8
9	20 01.9	28.7	91.0	19 58.9	30.7	91.8	19 54.5	32.5	92.5	19 48.5	34.4	93.2	19 41.0	36.2	93.9
10	20 30.6 +28.4		90.1	20 29.6 +30.4		90.9	20 27.0 +32.3		91.6	20 22.9 +34.1		92.3	20 17.2 +36.0		93.1
11	20 59.0	28.1	89.2	21 00.0	30.0	89.9	20 59.3	32.0	90.7	20 57.0	33.9	91.5	20 53.2	35.7	92.2
12	21 27.1	27.8	88.2	21 30.0	29.8	89.0	21 31.3	31.7	89.8	21 30.9	33.6	90.6	21 28.9	35.4	91.4
13	21 54.9	27.5	87.3	21 59.8	29.4	88.1	22 03.0	31.4	88.9	22 04.5	33.3	89.7	22 04.3	35.1	90.5
14	22 22.4	27.1	86.3	22 29.2	29.1	87.1	22 34.4	31.0	88.0	22 37.8	33.0	88.8	22 39.4	34.9	89.6
15	22 49.5 +26.7		85.3	22 58.3 +28.8		86.2	23 05.4 +30.8		87.0	23 10.8 +32.6		87.9	23 14.3 +34.6		88.7
16	23 16.2	26.4	84.4	23 27.1	28.4	85.2	23 36.2	30.4	86.1	23 43.4	32.4	87.0	23 48.9	34.2	87.8
17	23 42.6	26.0	83.4	23 55.5	28.1	84.3	24 06.6	30.0	85.2	24 15.8	32.0	86.0	24 23.1	34.0	87.0
18	24 08.6	25.7	82.4	24 23.6	27.6	83.3	24 36.6	29.7	84.2	24 47.8	31.7	85.1	24 57.1	33.6	86.0
19	24 34.3	25.2	81.4	24 51.2	27.3	82.3	25 06.3	29.3	83.2	25 19.5	31.3	84.2	25 30.7	33.2	85.1
20	24 59.5 +24.8		80.4	25 18.5 +26.9		81.3	25 35.6 +29.0		82.3	25 50.8 +30.9		83.2	26 03.9 +32.9		84.2
21	25 24.3	24.5	79.4	25 45.4	26.5	80.3	26 04.6	28.5	81.3	26 21.7	30.6	82.3	26 36.8	32.5	83.3
22	25 48.8	24.0	78.4	26 11.9	26.1	79.3	26 33.1	28.2	80.3	26 52.3	30.1	81.3	27 09.3	32.2	82.3
23	26 12.8	23.5	77.4	26 38.0	25.7	78.3	27 01.3	27.7	79.3	27 22.4	29.8	80.3	27 41.5	31.7	81.4
24	26 36.3	23.2	76.3	27 03.7	25.2	77.3	27 29.0	27.3	78.3	27 52.2	29.3	79.4	28 13.2	31.4	80.4
25	26 59.5 +22.6		75.3	27 28.9 +24.8		76.3	27 56.3 +26.8		77.3	28 21.5 +28.9		78.4	28 44.6 +30.9		79.4
26	27 22.1	22.2	74.3	27 53.7	24.3	75.3	28 23.1	26.4	76.3	28 50.4	28.5	77.4	29 15.5	30.5	78.5
27	27 44.3	21.8	73.2	28 18.0	23.8	74.2	28 49.5	25.9	75.3	29 18.9	28.0	76.4	29 46.0	30.1	77.5
28	28 06.1	21.2	72.2	28 41.8	23.3	73.2	29 15.4	25.4	74.3	29 46.9	27.5	75.4	30 16.1	29.6	76.5
29	28 27.3	20.7	71.1	29 05.1	22.9	72.1	29 40.8	25.0	73.2	30 14.4	27.0	74.3	30 45.7	29.1	75.5

20° Hc	d	Z	22° Hc	d	Z	24° Hc	d	Z	26° Hc	d	Z	28° Hc	d	Z	Dec.
16 52.8	-21.5	96.3	16 39.0	-23.6	96.9	16 23.9	-25.6	97.5	16 07.5	-27.5	98.1	15 50.0	-29.4	98.7	0
16 31.3	21.9	97.3	16 15.4	23.9	97.9	15 58.3	25.8	98.5	15 40.0	27.7	99.0	15 20.6	29.6	99.6	1
16 09.4	22.1	98.3	15 51.5	24.1	98.9	15 32.5	26.1	99.4	15 12.3	27.9	100.0	14 51.0	29.8	100.5	2
15 47.3	22.4	99.3	15 27.4	24.3	99.8	15 06.4	26.2	100.3	14 44.4	28.2	100.9	14 21.2	30.0	101.4	3
15 24.9	22.6	100.2	15 03.1	24.6	100.8	14 40.2	26.5	101.3	14 16.2	28.4	101.8	13 51.2	30.2	102.3	4
15 02.3	-22.9	101.2	14 38.5	-24.8	101.7	14 13.7	-26.7	102.2	13 47.8	-28.6	102.7	13 21.0	-30.4	103.2	5
14 39.4	23.0	102.1	14 13.7	25.0	102.6	13 47.0	27.0	103.1	13 19.2	28.7	103.6	12 50.6	30.6	104.0	6
14 16.4	23.4	103.1	13 48.7	25.3	103.6	13 20.0	27.1	104.0	12 50.5	29.0	104.5	12 20.0	30.7	104.9	7
13 53.0	23.5	104.0	13 23.4	25.4	104.5	12 52.9	27.3	105.0	12 21.5	29.1	105.4	11 49.3	31.0	105.8	8
13 29.5	23.8	105.0	12 58.0	25.6	105.4	12 25.6	27.5	105.9	11 52.4	29.3	106.3	11 18.3	31.0	106.7	9
13 05.7	-23.9	105.9	12 32.4	-25.9	106.4	11 58.1	-27.6	106.8	11 23.1	-29.5	107.2	10 47.3	-31.2	107.5	10
12 41.8	24.2	106.9	12 06.5	26.0	107.3	11 30.5	27.8	107.7	10 53.6	29.6	108.1	10 16.1	31.4	108.4	11
12 17.6	24.3	107.8	11 40.5	26.2	108.2	11 02.7	28.0	108.6	10 24.0	29.7	108.9	9 44.7	31.4	109.3	12
11 53.3	24.5	108.7	11 14.3	26.3	109.1	10 34.7	28.2	109.5	9 54.3	29.9	109.8	9 13.3	31.6	110.1	13
11 28.8	24.8	109.7	10 48.0	26.5	110.0	10 06.5	28.3	110.4	9 24.4	30.0	110.7	8 41.7	31.7	111.0	14
11 04.0	-24.8	110.6	10 21.5	-26.7	111.0	9 38.2	-28.4	111.3	8 54.4	-30.2	111.6	8 10.0	-31.9	111.9	15
10 39.2	25.1	111.5	9 54.8	26.8	111.9	9 09.8	28.5	112.2	8 24.2	30.2	112.5	7 38.1	31.9	112.7	16
10 14.1	25.2	112.5	9 28.0	27.0	112.8	8 41.3	28.7	113.1	7 54.0	30.4	113.3	7 06.2	32.0	113.6	17
9 48.9	25.3	113.4	9 01.0	27.0	113.7	8 12.6	28.8	114.0	7 23.6	30.5	114.2	6 34.2	32.1	114.4	18
9 23.6	25.5	114.3	8 34.0	27.3	114.6	7 43.8	28.9	114.8	6 53.1	30.5	115.1	6 02.1	32.2	115.3	19
8 58.1	-25.6	115.2	8 06.7	-27.3	115.5	7 14.9	-29.0	115.7	6 22.6	-30.7	115.9	5 29.9	-32.2	116.1	20
8 32.5	25.8	116.1	7 39.4	27.4	116.4	6 45.9	29.1	116.6	5 51.9	30.7	116.8	4 57.7	32.3	117.0	21
8 06.7	25.8	117.0	7 12.0	27.6	117.3	6 16.8	29.2	117.5	5 21.2	30.8	117.7	4 25.4	32.4	117.8	22
7 40.9	26.0	117.9	6 44.4	27.6	118.2	5 47.6	29.3	118.4	4 50.4	30.8	118.5	3 53.0	32.4	118.7	23
7 14.9	26.1	118.9	6 16.8	27.8	119.1	5 18.3	29.3	119.2	4 19.6	31.0	119.4	3 20.6	32.5	119.5	24
6 48.8	-26.2	119.8	5 49.0	-27.8	120.0	4 49.0	-29.4	120.1	3 48.6	-30.9	120.2	2 48.1	-32.5	120.3	25
6 22.6	26.3	120.7	5 21.2	27.9	120.8	4 19.6	29.5	121.0	3 17.7	31.1	121.1	2 15.6	32.5	121.2	26
5 56.3	26.4	121.6	4 53.3	27.9	121.7	3 50.1	29.5	121.9	2 46.6	31.0	122.0	1 43.1	32.6	122.0	27
5 29.9	26.4	122.5	4 25.4	28.1	122.6	3 20.6	29.6	122.7	2 15.6	31.1	122.8	1 10.5	32.6	122.9	28
5 03.5	26.6	123.4	3 57.5	28.1	123.5	2 51.0	29.6	123.6	1 44.5	31.1	123.7	0 37.9	32.6	123.7	29

30° Hc	d	Z	32° Hc	d	Z	34° Hc	d	Z	36° Hc	d	Z	38° Hc	d	Z	Dec.
15 31.3	-31.2	99.2	15 11.5	-33.0	99.8	14 50.6	-34.8	100.3	14 28.7	-36.6	100.8	14 05.6	-38.1	101.3	0
15 00.1	31.4	100.1	14 38.5	33.2	100.6	14 15.8	34.9	101.1	13 52.1	36.6	101.6	13 27.5	38.4	102.1	1
14 28.7	31.7	101.0	14 05.3	33.5	101.5	13 40.9	35.2	102.0	13 15.5	36.9	102.4	12 49.1	38.4	102.9	2
13 57.0	31.8	101.9	13 31.8	33.5	102.3	13 05.7	35.3	102.8	12 38.6	36.9	103.3	12 10.7	38.6	103.7	3
13 25.2	32.0	102.7	12 58.3	33.8	103.2	12 30.4	35.4	103.6	12 01.7	37.1	104.1	11 32.1	38.7	104.5	4
12 53.2	-32.2	103.6	12 24.5	-33.9	104.0	11 55.0	-35.6	104.5	11 24.6	-37.3	104.9	10 53.4	-38.8	105.2	5
12 21.0	32.3	104.5	11 50.6	34.1	104.9	11 19.4	35.8	105.3	10 47.3	37.3	105.7	10 14.6	39.0	106.0	6
11 48.7	32.5	105.3	11 16.5	34.2	105.7	10 43.6	35.8	106.1	10 10.0	37.5	106.5	9 35.6	39.0	106.8	7
11 16.2	32.7	106.2	10 42.3	34.3	106.6	10 07.8	36.0	106.9	9 32.5	37.6	107.3	8 56.6	39.1	107.6	8
10 43.5	32.8	107.0	10 08.0	34.5	107.4	9 31.8	36.1	107.7	8 54.9	37.7	108.0	8 17.5	39.3	108.3	9
10 10.7	-32.9	107.9	9 33.5	-34.5	108.2	8 55.7	-36.2	108.5	8 17.2	-37.7	108.8	7 38.2	-39.3	109.1	10
9 37.8	33.0	108.8	8 59.0	34.7	109.1	8 19.5	36.3	109.3	7 39.5	37.9	109.6	6 58.9	39.3	109.8	11
9 04.8	33.2	109.6	8 24.3	34.8	109.9	7 43.2	36.4	110.2	7 01.6	37.9	110.4	6 19.6	39.5	110.6	12
8 31.6	33.2	110.4	7 49.5	34.9	110.7	7 06.8	36.5	111.0	6 23.7	38.1	111.2	5 40.1	39.5	111.4	13
7 58.4	33.4	111.3	7 14.6	35.0	111.5	6 30.3	36.5	111.8	5 45.6	38.0	112.0	5 00.6	39.5	112.1	14
7 25.0	-33.4	112.1	6 39.6	-35.1	112.3	5 53.8	-36.6	112.6	5 07.6	-38.1	112.7	4 21.1	-39.6	112.9	15
6 51.6	33.6	113.0	6 04.5	35.1	113.2	5 17.2	36.7	113.3	4 29.5	38.2	113.5	3 41.5	39.7	113.6	16
6 18.0	33.6	113.8	5 29.4	35.2	114.0	4 40.5	36.7	114.1	3 51.3	38.2	114.3	3 01.8	39.6	114.4	17
5 44.4	33.7	114.6	4 54.2	35.2	114.8	4 03.8	36.8	114.9	3 13.1	38.3	115.1	2 22.2	39.7	115.1	18
5 10.7	33.8	115.5	4 19.0	35.3	115.6	3 27.0	36.8	115.7	2 34.8	38.3	115.8	1 42.5	39.7	115.9	19
4 36.9	-33.8	116.3	3 43.7	-35.4	116.4	2 50.2	-36.9	116.5	1 56.5	-38.3	116.6	1 02.8	-39.8	116.6	20
4 03.1	33.9	117.1	3 08.3	35.4	117.2	2 13.3	36.8	117.3	1 18.2	38.3	117.4	0 23.0	-39.7	117.4	21
3 29.2	33.9	117.9	2 32.9	35.4	118.0	1 36.5	36.9	118.1	0 39.9	38.3	118.1	0 16.7	+39.7	61.9	22
2 55.3	33.9	118.8	1 57.5	35.4	118.8	0 59.6	36.9	118.9	0 01.6	-38.3	118.9	0 56.4	39.7	61.1	23
2 21.4	34.0	119.6	1 22.1	35.5	119.6	0 22.7	-36.9	119.7	0 36.7	+38.4	60.3	1 36.1	39.7	60.4	24
1 47.4	-34.0	120.4	0 46.6	-35.5	120.5	0 14.2	+36.9	59.5	1 15.1	+38.3	59.6	2 15.8	+39.7	59.6	25
1 13.4	34.0	121.2	0 11.1	-35.4	121.3	0 51.1	36.9	58.7	1 53.4	38.2	58.8	2 55.5	39.6	58.9	26
0 39.4	34.1	122.1	0 24.3	+35.5	57.9	1 28.0	36.9	58.0	2 31.6	38.3	58.0	3 35.1	39.6	58.1	27
0 05.3	-34.0	122.9	0 59.8	35.5	57.1	2 04.9	36.9	57.2	3 09.9	38.2	57.2	4 14.7	39.6	57.4	28
0 28.7	+34.0	56.3	1 35.3	35.4	56.3	2 41.8	36.8	56.4	3 48.1	38.2	56.5	4 53.3	39.5	56.6	29

LATITUDE **SAME** NAME L.H.A. 108°, 252°

Dec.	40° Hc	d	Z	42° Hc	d	Z	44° Hc	d	Z	46° Hc	d	Z	48° Hc	d	Z
°	° ′	′	°	° ′	′	°	° ′	′	°	° ′	′	°	° ′	′	°
0	13 41.6	+39.6	101.8	13 16.6	+41.2	102.3	12 50.6	+42.7	102.7	12 23.7	+44.2	103.2	11 56.0	+45.5	103.6
1	14 21.2	39.5	101.0	13 57.8	41.0	101.5	13 33.3	42.6	102.0	13 07.9	44.0	102.5	12 41.5	45.4	102.9
2	15 00.7	39.3	100.2	14 38.8	40.9	100.8	14 15.9	42.4	101.3	13 51.9	43.9	101.8	13 26.9	45.4	102.2
3	15 40.0	39.1	99.5	15 19.7	40.7	100.0	14 58.3	42.3	100.5	14 35.8	43.8	101.1	14 12.3	45.2	101.6
4	16 19.1	39.0	98.7	16 00.4	40.6	99.2	15 40.6	42.1	99.8	15 19.6	43.6	100.4	14 57.5	45.1	100.9
5	16 58.1	+38.8	97.9	16 41.0	+40.4	98.5	16 22.7	+42.0	99.1	16 03.2	+43.5	99.6	15 42.6	+44.9	100.2
6	17 36.9	38.6	97.1	17 21.4	40.3	97.7	17 04.7	41.8	98.3	16 46.7	43.4	98.9	16 27.5	44.8	99.5
7	18 15.5	38.3	96.3	18 01.7	40.0	96.9	17 46.5	41.7	97.6	17 30.1	43.2	98.2	17 12.3	44.7	98.8
8	18 53.8	38.2	95.5	18 41.7	39.9	96.1	18 28.2	41.4	96.8	18 13.3	43.0	97.5	17 57.0	44.5	98.1
9	19 32.0	38.0	94.6	19 21.6	39.6	95.4	19 09.6	41.3	96.0	18 56.3	42.8	96.7	18 41.5	44.4	97.4
10	20 10.0	+37.7	93.8	20 01.2	+39.4	94.6	19 50.9	+41.1	95.3	19 39.1	+42.7	96.0	19 25.9	+44.2	96.7
11	20 47.7	37.5	93.0	20 40.6	39.2	93.7	20 32.0	40.9	94.5	20 21.8	42.5	95.2	20 10.1	44.0	96.0
12	21 25.2	37.2	92.2	21 19.8	39.0	92.9	21 12.9	40.6	93.7	21 04.3	42.2	94.5	20 54.1	43.8	95.3
13	22 02.4	36.9	91.3	21 58.8	38.7	92.1	21 53.5	40.4	92.9	21 46.5	42.1	93.7	21 37.9	43.7	94.5
14	22 39.3	36.7	90.5	22 37.5	38.5	91.3	22 33.9	40.2	92.1	22 28.6	41.8	93.0	22 21.6	43.4	93.8
15	23 16.0	+36.4	89.6	23 16.0	+38.2	90.5	23 14.1	+39.9	91.3	23 10.4	+41.6	92.2	23 05.0	+43.2	93.0
16	23 52.4	36.2	88.7	23 54.2	37.9	89.6	23 54.0	39.7	90.5	23 52.0	41.4	91.4	23 48.2	43.0	92.3
17.	24 28.6	35.8	87.9	24 32.1	37.6	88.8	24 33.7	39.4	89.7	24 33.4	41.1	90.6	24 31.2	42.8	91.5
18	25 04.4	35.4	87.0	25 09.7	37.3	87.9	25 13.1	39.1	88.9	25 14.5	40.9	89.8	25 14.0	42.5	90.7
19	25 39.8	35.2	86.1	25 47.0	37.1	87.0	25 52.2	38.8	88.0	25 55.4	40.5	89.0	25 56.5	42.2	90.0
20	26 15.0	+34.8	85.2	26 24.1	+36.7	86.2	26 31.0	+38.6	87.2	26 35.9	+40.3	88.2	26 38.7	+42.0	89.2
21	26 49.8	34.5	84.3	27 00.8	36.3	85.3	27 09.6	38.2	86.3	27 16.2	40.0	87.3	27 20.7	41.8	88.4
22	27 24.3	34.1	83.4	27 37.1	36.0	84.4	27 47.8	37.8	85.4	27 56.2	39.7	86.5	28 02.5	41.4	87.5
23	27 58.4	33.7	82.4	28 13.1	35.7	83.5	28 25.6	37.6	84.6	28 35.9	39.3	85.6	28 43.9	41.1	86.7
24	28 32.1	33.4	81.5	28 48.8	35.2	82.6	29 03.2	37.1	83.7	29 15.2	39.1	84.8	29 25.0	40.8	85.9
25	29 05.5	+32.9	80.5	29 24.0	+34.9	81.6	29 40.3	+36.8	82.8	29 54.3	+38.6	83.9	30 05.8	+40.5	85.0
26	29 38.4	32.5	79.6	29 58.9	34.5	80.7	30 17.1	36.4	81.9	30 32.9	38.3	83.0	30 46.3	40.1	84.2
27	30 10.9	32.1	78.6	30 33.4	34.1	79.8	30 53.5	36.1	80.9	31 11.2	38.0	82.1	31 26.4	39.8	83.3
28	30 43.0	31.6	77.6	31 07.5	33.6	78.8	31 29.6	35.6	80.0	31 49.2	37.5	81.2	32 06.2	39.4	82.4
29	31 14.6	31.2	76.6	31 41.1	33.2	77.8	32 05.2	35.2	79.0	32 26.7	37.1	80.3	32 45.6	39.1	81.6

Dec.	50° Hc	d	Z	52° Hc	d	Z	54° Hc	d	Z	56° Hc	d	Z	58° Hc	d	Z
°	° ′	′	°	° ′	′	°	° ′	′	°	° ′	′	°	° ′	′	°
0	11 27.4	+46.9	104.0	10 58.0	+48.2	104.4	10 27.9	+49.3	104.7	9 57.0	+50.5	105.1	9 25.5	+51.5	105.4
1	12 14.3	46.7	103.3	11 46.2	48.0	103.8	11 17.2	49.3	104.1	10 47.5	50.4	104.5	10 17.0	51.6	104.9
2	13 01.0	46.7	102.7	12 34.2	48.0	103.1	12 06.5	49.2	103.6	11 37.9	50.4	104.0	11 08.6	51.4	104.4
3	13 47.7	46.6	102.1	13 22.2	47.8	102.5	12 55.7	49.1	103.0	12 28.3	50.3	103.4	12 00.0	51.4	103.8
4	14 34.3	46.4	101.4	14 10.0	47.8	101.9	13 44.8	49.0	102.4	13 18.6	50.2	102.9	12 51.4	51.3	103.3
5	15 20.7	+46.4	100.7	14 57.8	+47.7	101.3	14 33.8	+49.0	101.8	14 08.8	+50.1	102.3	13 42.7	+51.3	102.8
6	16 07.1	46.2	100.1	15 45.5	47.6	100.6	15 22.8	48.8	101.2	14 58.9	50.1	101.7	14 34.0	51.2	102.2
7	16 53.3	46.1	99.4	16 33.1	47.4	100.0	16 11.6	48.7	100.6	15 49.0	49.9	101.2	15 25.2	51.1	101.7
8	17 39.4	46.0	98.8	17 20.5	47.3	99.4	17 00.3	48.6	100.0	16 38.9	49.9	100.6	16 16.3	51.0	101.2
9	18 25.4	45.8	98.1	18 07.8	47.2	98.7	17 48.9	48.6	99.4	17 28.8	49.7	100.0	17 07.3	50.9	100.6
10	19 11.2	+45.6	97.4	18 55.0	+47.1	98.1	18 37.5	+48.3	98.7	18 18.5	+49.7	99.4	17 58.2	+50.9	100.1
11	19 56.8	45.5	96.7	19 42.1	46.9	97.4	19 25.8	48.3	98.1	19 08.2	49.5	98.8	18 49.1	50.7	99.5
12	20 42.3	45.3	96.0	20 29.0	46.7	96.8	20 14.1	48.1	97.5	19 57.7	49.4	98.2	19 39.8	50.6	98.9
13	21 27.6	45.2	95.3	21 15.7	46.6	96.1	21 02.2	48.0	96.9	20 47.1	49.3	97.6	20 30.4	50.6	98.4
14	22 12.8	45.0	94.6	22 02.3	46.5	95.4	21 50.2	47.8	96.2	21 36.4	49.1	97.0	21 21.0	50.3	97.8
15	22 57.8	+44.7	93.9	22 48.8	+46.2	94.7	22 38.0	+47.7	95.6	22 25.5	+49.0	96.4	22 11.3	+50.3	97.2
16	23 42.5	44.6	93.2	23 35.0	46.1	94.0	23 25.7	47.5	94.9	23 14.5	48.9	95.8	23 01.6	50.2	96.6
17	24 27.1	44.3	92.4	24 21.1	45.8	93.3	24 13.2	47.3	94.2	24 03.4	48.7	95.1	23 51.8	49.9	96.0
18	25 11.4	44.2	91.7	25 06.9	45.7	92.6	25 00.5	47.1	93.6	24 52.1	48.5	94.5	24 41.7	49.9	95.4
19	25 55.6	43.8	90.9	25 52.6	45.4	91.9	25 47.6	46.9	92.9	25 40.6	48.4	93.8	25 31.6	49.7	94.8
20	26 39.4	+43.7	90.2	26 38.0	+45.3	91.2	26 34.5	+46.8	92.2	26 29.0	+48.1	93.2	26 21.3	+49.5	94.2
21	27 23.1	43.4	89.4	27 23.3	45.0	90.4	27 21.3	46.5	91.5	27 17.1	48.0	92.5	27 10.8	49.3	93.5
22	28 06.5	43.1	88.6	28 08.3	44.7	89.7	28 07.8	46.3	90.8	28 05.1	47.8	91.8	28 00.2	49.1	92.9
23	28 49.6	42.8	87.8	28 53.0	44.5	88.9	28 54.1	46.0	90.0	28 52.9	47.5	91.1	28 49.3	49.0	92.2
24	29 32.4	42.6	87.0	29 37.5	44.2	88.2	29 40.1	45.9	89.3	29 40.4	47.4	90.4	29 38.3	48.8	91.6
25	30 15.0	+42.2	86.2	30 21.7	+43.9	87.4	30 26.0	+45.5	88.5	30 27.8	+47.1	89.7	30 27.1	+48.6	90.9
26	30 57.2	41.9	85.4	31 05.6	43.6	86.6	31 11.5	45.3	87.8	31 14.9	46.8	89.0	31 15.7	48.3	90.2
27	31 39.1	41.6	84.5	31 49.2	43.4	85.8	31 56.8	45.0	87.0	32 01.7	46.6	88.3	32 04.0	48.1	89.5
28	32 20.7	41.2	83.7	32 32.6	43.0	85.0	32 41.8	44.7	86.2	32 48.3	46.3	87.5	32 52.1	47.9	88.8
29	33 01.9	40.9	82.8	33 15.6	42.6	84.1	33 26.5	44.4	85.4	33 34.6	46.1	86.8	33 40.0	47.6	88.1

40° Hc	d	Z	42° Hc	d	Z	44° Hc	d	Z	46° Hc	d	Z	48° Hc	d	Z	Dec.
13 41.6	−39.8	101.8	13 16.6	−41.3	102.3	12 50.6	−42.8	102.7	12 23.7	−44.2	103.2	11 56.0	−45.6	103.6	0
13 01.8	39.9	102.6	12 35.3	41.5	103.0	12 07.8	42.9	103.4	11 39.5	44.3	103.8	11 10.4	45.7	104.2	1
12 21.9	40.0	103.3	11 53.8	41.5	103.8	11 24.9	43.0	104.2	10 55.2	44.5	104.5	10 24.7	45.8	104.9	2
11 41.9	40.2	104.1	11 12.3	41.7	104.5	10 41.9	43.2	104.9	10 10.7	44.5	105.2	9 38.9	45.9	105.6	3
11 01.7	40.2	104.9	10 30.6	41.8	105.2	9 58.7	43.2	105.6	9 26.2	44.6	105.9	8 53.0	45.9	106.2	4
10 21.5	−40.4	105.6	9 48.8	−41.8	105.9	9 15.5	−43.2	106.3	8 41.6	−44.7	106.6	8 07.1	−46.0	106.9	5
9 41.1	40.5	106.4	9 07.0	41.9	106.7	8 32.3	43.4	107.0	7 56.9	44.7	107.2	7 21.1	46.0	107.5	6
9 00.6	40.5	107.1	8 25.1	42.1	107.4	7 48.9	43.4	107.7	7 12.2	44.8	107.9	6 35.1	46.1	108.2	7
8 20.1	40.6	107.9	7 43.0	42.1	108.1	7 05.5	43.5	108.4	6 27.4	44.8	108.6	5 49.0	46.2	108.8	8
7 39.5	40.8	108.6	7 00.9	42.1	108.8	6 22.0	43.6	109.1	5 42.6	44.9	109.3	5 02.8	46.2	109.4	9
6 58.7	−40.7	109.3	6 18.8	−42.2	109.6	5 38.4	−43.6	109.8	4 57.7	−44.9	109.9	4 16.6	−46.2	110.1	10
6 18.0	40.9	110.1	5 36.6	42.3	110.3	4 54.8	43.6	110.4	4 12.8	45.0	110.6	3 30.4	46.2	110.7	11
5 37.1	40.9	110.8	4 54.3	42.3	111.0	4 11.2	43.7	111.1	3 27.8	45.0	111.3	2 44.2	46.3	111.4	12
4 56.2	40.9	111.5	4 12.0	42.4	111.7	3 27.5	43.7	111.8	2 42.8	45.0	111.9	1 57.9	46.2	112.0	13
4 15.3	41.0	112.3	3 29.6	42.3	112.4	2 43.8	43.7	112.5	1 57.8	45.0	112.6	1 11.7	46.3	112.6	14
3 34.3	−41.1	113.0	2 47.3	−42.4	113.1	2 00.1	−43.8	113.2	1 12.8	−45.1	113.2	0 25.4	−46.3	113.3	15
2 53.2	41.0	113.7	2 04.9	42.3	113.8	1 16.3	43.7	113.9	0 27.7	−45.0	113.9	0 20.9	+46.3	66.1	16
2 12.2	41.1	114.5	1 22.4	42.4	114.5	0 32.6	−43.8	114.6	0 17.3	+45.0	65.4	1 07.2	46.2	65.5	17
1 31.1	41.1	115.2	0 40.0	−42.5	115.2	0 11.2	+43.7	64.8	1 02.3	45.1	64.8	1 53.4	46.3	64.8	18
0 50.0	41.1	115.9	0 02.5	+42.4	64.1	0 54.9	43.8	64.1	1 47.4	45.0	64.1	2 39.7	46.2	64.2	19
0 08.9	−41.1	116.7	0 44.9	+42.4	63.4	1 38.7	+43.7	63.4	2 32.4	+45.0	63.5	3 25.9	+46.2	63.5	20
0 32.2	+41.1	62.6	1 27.3	42.5	62.6	2 22.4	43.7	62.7	3 17.4	45.0	62.8	4 12.1	46.2	62.9	21
1 13.3	41.0	61.9	2 09.8	42.4	61.9	3 06.1	43.7	62.0	4 02.4	44.9	62.1	4 58.3	46.2	62.3	22
1 54.3	41.1	61.2	2 52.2	42.3	61.2	3 49.8	43.7	61.3	4 47.3	44.9	61.5	5 44.5	46.1	61.6	23
2 35.4	41.0	60.4	3 34.5	42.4	60.5	4 33.5	43.6	60.6	5 32.2	44.8	60.8	6 30.6	46.0	61.0	24
3 16.4	+41.0	59.7	4 16.9	+42.3	59.8	5 17.1	+43.6	60.0	6 17.0	+44.8	60.1	7 16.6	+46.0	60.3	25
3 57.4	41.0	59.0	4 59.2	42.3	59.1	6 00.7	43.5	59.3	7 01.8	44.8	59.5	8 02.6	46.0	59.7	26
4 38.4	40.9	58.2	5 41.5	42.2	58.4	6 44.2	43.5	58.6	7 46.6	44.7	58.8	8 48.6	45.8	59.0	27
5 19.3	40.9	57.5	6 23.7	42.1	57.7	7 27.7	43.4	57.9	8 31.3	44.6	58.1	9 34.4	45.8	58.4	28
6 00.2	40.8	56.8	7 05.8	42.1	57.0	8 11.1	43.3	57.2	9 15.9	44.5	57.4	10 20.2	45.7	57.7	29

50° Hc	d	Z	52° Hc	d	Z	54° Hc	d	Z	56° Hc	d	Z	58° Hc	d	Z	Dec.
11 27.4	−46.9	104.0	10 58.0	−48.2	104.4	10 27.9	−49.4	104.7	9 57.0	−50.5	105.1	9 25.5	−51.6	105.4	0
10 40.5	47.0	104.6	10 09.8	48.2	105.0	9 38.5	49.4	105.3	9 06.5	50.6	105.6	8 33.9	51.7	105.9	1
9 53.5	47.1	105.2	9 21.6	48.3	105.6	8 49.1	49.5	105.9	8 15.9	50.6	106.2	7 42.2	51.6	106.4	2
9 06.4	47.2	105.9	8 33.3	48.4	106.2	7 59.6	49.6	106.4	7 25.3	50.6	106.7	6 50.6	51.7	106.9	3
8 19.2	47.2	106.5	7 44.9	48.4	106.8	7 10.0	49.6	107.0	6 34.7	50.7	107.2	5 58.9	51.8	107.5	4
7 32.0	−47.2	107.1	6 56.5	−48.5	107.4	6 20.4	−49.6	107.6	5 44.0	−50.8	107.8	5 07.1	−51.7	108.0	5
6 44.8	47.3	107.7	6 08.0	48.5	108.0	5 30.8	49.7	108.2	4 53.2	50.7	108.3	4 15.4	51.8	108.5	6
5 57.5	47.4	108.4	5 19.5	48.6	108.5	4 41.1	49.7	108.7	4 02.5	50.8	108.8	3 23.6	51.8	109.0	7
5 10.1	47.4	109.0	4 30.9	48.5	109.1	3 51.4	49.7	109.3	3 11.7	50.8	109.4	2 31.8	51.8	109.5	8
4 22.7	47.4	109.6	3 42.4	48.6	109.7	3 01.7	49.7	109.8	2 20.9	50.8	109.9	1 40.0	51.9	110.0	9
3 35.3	−47.4	110.2	2 53.8	−48.7	110.3	2 12.0	−49.7	110.4	1 30.1	−50.8	110.5	0 48.1	−51.8	110.5	10
2 47.9	47.5	110.8	2 05.1	48.6	110.9	1 22.3	49.8	111.0	0 39.3	−50.8	111.0	0 03.7	+51.8	69.0	11
2 00.4	47.4	111.4	1 16.5	48.6	111.5	0 32.5	−49.7	111.5	0 11.5	+50.8	68.5	0 55.5	51.8	68.5	12
1 13.0	47.5	112.0	0 27.9	−48.7	112.1	0 17.2	+49.8	67.9	1 02.3	50.8	67.9	1 47.3	51.8	68.0	13
0 25.5	−47.5	112.7	0 20.8	+48.6	67.3	1 07.0	49.7	67.3	1 53.1	50.8	67.4	2 39.1	51.8	67.5	14
0 22.0	+47.5	66.1	1 09.4	+48.6	66.8	1 56.7	+49.7	66.8	2 43.9	+50.8	66.9	3 30.9	+51.8	67.0	15
1 09.5	47.5	66.1	1 58.0	48.6	66.2	2 46.4	49.8	66.2	3 34.7	50.7	66.3	4 22.7	51.8	66.5	16
1 57.0	47.5	65.5	2 46.6	48.6	65.6	3 36.2	49.6	65.7	4 25.4	50.8	65.8	5 14.5	51.7	66.0	17
2 44.4	47.5	64.9	3 35.2	48.6	65.0	4 25.8	49.7	65.1	5 16.2	50.7	65.3	6 06.2	51.7	65.5	18
3 31.9	47.4	64.3	4 23.8	48.6	64.4	5 15.5	49.7	64.6	6 06.9	50.7	64.7	6 57.9	51.7	64.9	19
4 19.3	+47.4	63.7	5 12.4	+48.5	63.8	6 05.2	+49.6	64.0	6 57.6	+50.6	64.2	7 49.6	+51.6	64.4	20
5 06.7	47.3	63.1	6 00.9	48.5	63.2	6 54.8	49.5	63.4	7 48.2	50.6	63.6	8 41.2	51.6	63.9	21
5 54.0	47.3	62.4	6 49.4	48.4	62.6	7 44.3	49.5	62.9	8 38.8	50.6	63.1	9 32.8	51.6	63.4	22
6 41.3	47.3	61.8	7 37.8	48.4	62.0	8 33.8	49.5	62.3	9 29.4	50.5	62.6	10 24.4	51.5	62.9	23
7 28.6	47.2	61.2	8 26.2	48.3	61.4	9 23.3	49.4	61.7	10 19.9	50.4	62.0	11 15.9	51.4	62.4	24
8 15.8	+47.2	60.6	9 14.5	+48.3	60.8	10 12.7	+49.4	61.0	11 10.3	+50.4	61.5	12 07.3	+51.4	61.8	25
9 03.0	47.0	59.9	10 02.8	48.2	60.2	11 02.1	49.2	60.6	12 00.7	50.3	60.9	12 58.7	51.3	61.3	26
9 50.0	47.1	59.3	10 51.0	48.1	59.6	11 51.3	49.3	60.0	12 51.0	50.3	60.4	13 50.0	51.3	60.8	27
10 37.1	46.9	58.7	11 39.1	48.1	59.0	12 40.6	49.1	59.4	13 41.3	50.2	59.8	14 41.3	51.1	60.2	28
11 24.0	46.9	58.1	12 27.4	48.0	58.4	13 29.7	49.0	58.8	14 31.5	50.1	59.2	15 32.4	51.1	59.7	29

Dec.	0° Hc	d	Z	2° Hc	d	Z	4° Hc	d	Z	6° Hc	d	Z	8° Hc	d	Z
0	16 00.0	− 0.2	90.0	15 59.4	+ 2.0	90.6	15 57.6	+ 4.2	91.1	15 54.6	+ 6.4	91.7	15 50.4	+ 8.5	92.3
1	15 59.8	0.4	89.0	16 01.4	1.8	89.5	16 01.8	3.9	90.1	16 01.0	6.1	90.7	15 58.9	8.3	91.3
2	15 59.4	0.8	87.9	16 03.2	1.4	88.5	16 05.7	3.6	89.1	16 07.1	5.7	89.6	16 07.2	7.9	90.2
3	15 58.6	1.0	86.9	16 04.6	1.1	87.5	16 09.3	3.3	88.0	16 12.8	5.5	88.6	16 15.1	7.7	89.2
4	15 57.6	1.4	85.8	16 05.7	0.8	86.4	16 12.6	3.0	87.0	16 18.3	5.2	87.6	16 22.8	7.3	88.2
5	15 56.2	− 1.6	84.8	16 06.5	+ 0.6	85.4	16 15.6	+ 2.7	86.0	16 23.5	+ 4.8	86.5	16 30.1	+ 7.0	87.1
6	15 54.6	1.9	83.8	16 07.1	+ 0.2	84.3	16 18.3	2.4	84.9	16 28.3	4.6	85.5	16 37.1	6.8	86.1
7	15 52.7	2.3	82.7	16 07.3	− 0.1	83.3	16 20.7	2.1	83.9	16 32.9	4.2	84.5	16 43.9	6.4	85.1
8	15 50.4	2.5	81.7	16 07.2	0.4	82.2	16 22.8	1.7	82.8	16 37.1	4.0	83.4	16 50.3	6.1	84.0
9	15 47.9	2.9	80.6	16 06.8	0.7	81.2	16 24.5	1.5	81.8	16 41.1	3.6	82.4	16 56.4	5.8	83.0
10	15 45.0	− 3.1	79.6	16 06.1	− 1.0	80.2	16 26.0	+ 1.2	80.7	16 44.7	+ 3.3	81.3	17 02.2	+ 5.4	81.9
11	15 41.9	3.4	78.6	16 05.1	1.3	79.1	16 27.2	0.8	79.7	16 48.0	3.0	80.3	17 07.6	5.2	80.9
12	15 38.5	3.7	77.5	16 03.8	1.6	78.1	16 28.0	0.5	78.7	16 51.0	2.7	79.2	17 12.8	4.8	79.8
13	15 34.8	4.0	76.5	16 02.2	1.9	77.0	16 28.5	+ 0.3	77.6	16 53.7	2.3	78.2	17 17.6	4.5	78.8
14	15 30.8	4.3	75.5	16 00.3	2.2	76.0	16 28.8	− 0.1	76.6	16 56.0	2.1	77.2	17 22.1	4.2	77.8
15	15 26.5	− 4.5	74.4	15 58.1	− 2.5	75.0	16 28.7	− 0.4	75.5	16 58.1	+ 1.7	76.1	17 26.3	+ 3.8	76.7
16	15 21.9	4.9	73.4	15 55.6	2.8	73.9	16 28.3	0.7	74.5	16 59.8	1.4	75.1	17 30.1	3.6	75.7
17	15 17.0	5.2	72.4	15 52.8	3.0	72.9	16 27.6	1.0	73.4	17 01.2	1.1	74.0	17 33.7	3.1	74.6
18	15 11.8	5.4	71.3	15 49.8	3.4	71.9	16 26.6	1.3	72.4	17 02.3	0.8	73.0	17 36.8	2.9	73.6
19	15 06.4	5.7	70.3	15 46.4	3.7	70.8	16 25.3	1.7	71.4	17 03.1	0.4	71.9	17 39.7	2.5	72.5
20	15 00.7	− 6.0	69.3	15 42.7	− 4.0	69.8	16 23.6	− 1.9	70.3	17 03.5	+ 0.1	70.9	17 42.2	+ 2.2	71.5
21	14 54.7	6.3	68.2	15 38.7	4.3	68.7	16 21.7	2.2	69.3	17 03.6	− 0.2	69.8	17 44.4	1.9	70.4
22	14 48.4	6.5	67.2	15 34.4	4.5	67.7	16 19.5	2.6	68.2	17 03.4	0.5	68.8	17 46.3	1.5	69.4
23	14 41.9	6.8	66.2	15 29.9	4.9	66.7	16 16.9	2.8	67.2	17 02.9	0.8	67.7	17 47.8	1.2	68.3
24	14 35.1	7.1	65.1	15 25.0	5.1	65.6	16 14.1	3.2	66.2	17 02.1	1.2	66.7	17 49.0	0.8	67.3
25	14 28.0	− 7.4	64.1	15 19.9	− 5.4	64.6	16 10.9	− 3.5	65.1	17 00.9	− 1.5	65.7	17 49.8	+ 0.5	66.2
26	14 20.6	7.6	63.1	15 14.5	5.7	63.6	16 07.4	3.7	64.1	16 59.4	1.8	64.6	17 50.3	+ 0.2	65.2
27	14 13.0	7.9	62.1	15 08.8	6.0	62.5	16 03.7	4.1	63.0	16 57.6	2.1	63.6	17 50.5	− 0.2	64.1
28	14 05.1	8.1	61.1	15 02.8	6.2	61.5	15 59.6	4.3	62.0	16 55.5	2.5	62.5	17 50.3	0.5	63.1
29	13 57.0	8.4	60.0	14 56.6	6.6	60.5	15 55.3	4.7	61.0	16 53.0	2.7	61.5	17 49.8	0.8	62.0

Dec.	10° Hc	d	Z	12° Hc	d	Z	14° Hc	d	Z	16° Hc	d	Z	18° Hc	d	Z
0	15 45.0	+ 10.7	92.9	15 38.5	+ 12.8	93.4	15 30.8	+ 14.9	94.0	15 21.9	+ 17.0	94.5	15 11.8	+ 19.1	95.1
1	15 55.7	10.4	91.8	15 51.3	12.5	92.4	15 45.7	14.6	93.0	15 38.9	16.7	93.5	15 30.9	18.9	94.1
2	16 06.1	10.1	90.8	16 03.8	12.3	91.4	16 00.3	14.4	92.0	15 55.6	16.5	92.5	15 49.8	18.5	93.1
3	16 16.2	9.8	89.8	16 16.1	11.9	90.4	16 14.7	14.1	90.9	16 12.1	16.2	91.5	16 08.3	18.3	92.1
4	16 26.0	9.5	88.7	16 28.0	11.7	89.3	16 28.8	13.8	89.9	16 28.3	15.9	90.5	16 26.6	18.0	91.1
5	16 35.5	+ 9.2	87.7	16 39.7	+ 11.3	88.3	16 42.6	+ 13.4	88.9	16 44.2	+ 15.6	89.5	16 44.6	+ 17.7	90.1
6	16 44.7	8.9	86.7	16 51.0	11.1	87.3	16 56.0	13.2	87.9	16 59.8	15.3	88.5	17 02.3	17.4	89.1
7	16 53.6	8.6	85.7	17 02.1	10.7	86.3	17 09.2	12.9	86.9	17 15.1	15.0	87.5	17 19.7	17.1	88.1
8	17 02.2	8.2	84.6	17 12.8	10.4	85.2	17 22.1	12.6	85.9	17 30.1	14.7	86.5	17 36.8	16.9	87.1
9	17 10.4	8.0	83.6	17 23.2	10.1	84.2	17 34.7	12.2	84.8	17 44.8	14.4	85.5	17 53.7	16.5	86.1
10	17 18.4	+ 7.6	82.5	17 33.3	+ 9.8	83.2	17 46.9	+ 11.9	83.8	17 59.2	+ 14.1	84.4	18 10.2	+ 16.1	85.1
11	17 26.0	7.3	81.5	17 43.1	9.4	82.1	17 58.8	11.6	82.8	18 13.3	13.7	83.4	18 26.3	15.9	84.1
12	17 33.3	7.0	80.5	17 52.5	9.2	81.1	18 10.4	11.3	81.7	18 27.0	13.4	81.4	18 42.2	15.5	83.1
13	17 40.3	6.6	79.4	18 01.7	8.7	80.1	18 21.7	10.9	80.7	18 40.4	13.1	81.4	18 57.7	15.2	82.0
14	17 46.9	6.3	78.4	18 10.4	8.5	79.0	18 32.6	10.6	79.7	18 53.5	12.7	80.3	19 12.9	14.9	81.0
15	17 53.2	+ 6.0	77.3	18 18.9	+ 8.1	78.0	18 43.2	+ 10.3	78.6	19 06.2	+ 12.4	79.3	19 27.8	+ 14.5	80.0
16	17 59.2	5.7	76.3	18 27.0	7.8	76.9	18 53.5	9.9	77.6	19 18.6	12.0	78.3	19 42.3	14.1	79.0
17	18 04.9	5.3	75.2	18 34.8	7.4	75.9	19 03.4	9.5	76.5	19 30.6	11.7	77.2	19 56.4	13.8	77.9
18	18 10.2	4.9	74.2	18 42.2	7.1	74.8	19 12.9	9.2	75.5	19 42.3	11.3	76.2	20 10.2	13.4	76.9
19	18 15.1	4.6	73.1	18 49.3	6.7	73.8	19 22.1	8.8	74.5	19 53.6	10.9	75.1	20 23.6	13.1	75.9
20	18 19.7	+ 4.3	72.1	18 56.0	+ 6.4	72.7	19 30.9	+ 8.5	73.4	20 04.5	+ 10.6	74.1	20 36.7	+ 12.7	74.8
21	18 24.0	3.9	71.0	19 02.4	6.0	71.7	19 39.4	8.1	72.4	20 15.1	10.2	73.0	20 49.4	12.3	73.8
22	18 27.9	3.6	70.0	19 08.4	5.6	70.6	19 47.5	7.7	71.3	20 25.3	9.8	72.0	21 01.7	11.9	72.7
23	18 31.5	3.2	68.9	19 14.0	5.3	69.6	19 55.2	7.4	70.2	20 35.1	9.4	70.9	21 13.6	11.5	71.7
24	18 34.7	2.9	67.9	19 19.3	4.9	68.5	20 02.6	7.0	69.2	20 44.5	9.1	69.9	21 25.1	11.1	70.6
25	18 37.6	+ 2.5	66.8	19 24.2	+ 4.6	67.5	20 09.6	+ 6.6	68.1	20 53.6	+ 8.6	68.8	21 36.2	+ 10.7	69.6
26	18 40.1	2.2	65.8	19 28.8	4.2	66.4	20 16.2	6.2	67.1	21 02.2	8.3	67.8	21 46.9	10.4	68.5
27	18 42.3	1.8	64.7	19 33.0	3.8	65.4	20 22.4	5.8	66.0	21 10.5	7.9	66.7	21 57.3	9.9	67.4
28	18 44.1	1.5	63.7	19 36.8	3.4	64.3	20 28.2	5.5	65.0	21 18.4	7.4	65.6	22 07.2	9.5	66.4
29	18 45.6	1.1	62.6	19 40.2	3.1	63.2	20 33.7	5.0	63.9	21 25.8	7.1	64.6	22 16.7	9.0	65.3

0° Hc	d	Z	2° Hc	d	Z	4° Hc	d	Z	6° Hc	d	Z	8° Hc	d	Z	Dec.
16 00.0	- 0.2	90.0	15 59.4	- 2.3	90.6	15 57.6	- 4.5	91.1	15 54.6	- 6.7	91.7	15 50.4	- 8.8	92.3	0
15 59.8	0.4	91.0	15 57.1	2.7	91.6	15 53.1	4.8	92.2	15 47.9	6.9	92.7	15 41.6	9.1	93.3	1
15 59.4	0.8	92.1	15 54.4	2.9	92.7	15 48.3	5.1	93.2	15 41.0	7.3	93.8	15 32.5	9.4	94.3	2
15 58.6	1.0	93.1	15 51.5	3.2	93.7	15 43.2	5.4	94.3	15 33.7	7.5	94.8	15 23.1	9.7	95.4	3
15 57.6	1.4	94.2	15 48.3	3.5	94.7	15 37.8	5.7	95.3	15 26.2	7.8	95.8	15 13.4	10.0	96.4	4
15 56.2	- 1.6	95.2	15 44.8	- 3.8	95.8	15 32.1	- 5.9	96.3	15 18.4	- 8.1	96.9	15 03.4	- 10.2	97.4	5
15 54.6	1.9	96.2	15 41.0	4.1	96.8	15 26.2	6.3	97.4	15 10.3	8.4	97.9	14 53.2	10.5	98.4	6
15 52.7	2.3	97.3	15 36.9	4.4	97.8	15 19.9	6.5	98.4	15 01.9	8.7	98.9	14 42.7	10.7	99.5	7
15 50.4	2.5	98.3	15 32.5	4.7	98.9	15 13.4	6.8	99.4	14 53.2	8.9	99.9	14 32.0	11.1	100.5	8
15 47.9	2.9	99.4	15 27.8	5.0	99.9	15 06.6	7.1	100.4	14 44.3	9.2	101.0	14 20.9	11.3	101.5	9
15 45.0	- 3.1	100.4	15 22.8	- 5.2	100.9	14 59.5	- 7.4	101.5	14 35.1	- 9.5	102.0	14 09.6	- 11.5	102.5	10
15 41.9	3.4	101.4	15 17.6	5.6	102.0	14 52.1	7.6	102.5	14 25.6	9.7	103.0	13 58.1	11.8	103.5	11
15 38.5	3.7	102.5	15 12.0	5.8	103.0	14 44.5	7.9	103.5	14 15.9	10.0	104.0	13 46.3	12.0	104.5	12
15 34.8	4.0	103.5	15 06.2	6.1	104.0	14 36.6	8.2	104.6	14 05.9	10.2	105.0	13 34.3	12.3	105.5	13
15 30.8	4.3	104.5	15 00.1	6.4	105.1	14 28.4	8.5	105.6	13 55.7	10.5	106.1	13 22.0	12.5	106.5	14
15 26.5	- 4.6	105.6	14 53.7	- 6.6	106.1	14 19.9	- 8.7	106.6	13 45.2	- 10.8	107.1	13 09.5	- 12.8	107.5	15
15 21.9	4.9	106.6	14 47.1	7.0	107.1	14 11.2	9.0	107.6	13 34.4	11.0	108.1	12 56.7	13.0	108.5	16
15 17.0	5.2	107.6	14 40.1	7.2	108.2	14 02.2	9.2	108.6	13 23.4	11.2	109.1	12 43.7	13.2	109.5	17
15 11.8	5.4	108.7	14 32.9	7.4	109.2	13 53.0	9.5	109.7	13 12.2	11.5	110.1	12 30.5	13.4	110.5	18
15 06.4	5.7	109.7	14 25.5	7.8	110.2	13 43.5	9.7	110.7	13 00.7	11.7	111.1	12 17.1	13.6	111.5	19
15 00.7	- 6.0	110.7	14 17.7	- 8.0	111.2	13 33.8	- 10.0	111.7	12 49.0	- 11.9	112.1	12 03.5	- 13.9	112.5	20
14 54.7	6.3	111.8	14 09.7	8.2	112.2	13 23.8	10.2	112.7	12 37.1	12.1	113.1	11 49.6	14.1	113.5	21
14 48.4	6.5	112.8	14 01.5	8.5	113.3	13 13.6	10.4	113.7	12 25.0	12.4	114.1	11 35.5	14.2	114.5	22
14 41.9	6.8	113.8	13 53.0	8.8	114.3	13 03.2	10.7	114.7	12 12.6	12.6	115.1	11 21.3	14.5	115.5	23
14 35.1	7.1	114.9	13 44.2	9.0	115.3	12 52.5	10.9	115.7	12 00.0	12.8	116.1	11 06.8	14.7	116.5	24
14 28.0	- 7.4	115.9	13 35.2	- 9.3	116.3	12 41.6	- 11.2	116.7	11 47.2	- 13.0	117.1	10 52.1	- 14.8	117.5	25
14 20.6	7.6	116.9	13 25.9	9.5	117.3	12 30.4	11.4	117.8	11 34.2	13.2	118.1	10 37.3	15.0	118.5	26
14 13.0	7.9	117.9	13 16.4	9.7	118.4	12 19.0	11.5	118.8	11 21.0	13.4	119.1	10 22.3	15.3	119.5	27
14 05.1	8.1	118.9	13 06.7	10.0	119.4	12 07.5	11.9	119.8	11 07.6	13.7	120.1	10 07.0	15.3	120.4	28
13 57.0	8.4	120.0	12 56.7	10.2	120.4	11 55.6	12.0	120.8	10 53.9	13.8	121.1	9 51.7	15.6	121.4	29

10° Hc	d	Z	12° Hc	d	Z	14° Hc	d	Z	16° Hc	d	Z	18° Hc	d	Z	Dec.
15 45.0	- 10.9	92.9	15 38.5	- 13.1	93.4	15 30.8	- 15.2	94.0	15 21.9	- 17.3	94.5	15 11.8	- 19.3	95.1	0
15 34.1	11.3	93.9	15 25.4	13.4	94.4	15 15.6	15.5	95.0	15 04.6	17.5	95.5	14 52.5	19.6	96.0	1
15 22.8	11.5	94.9	15 12.0	13.6	95.4	15 00.1	15.7	96.0	14 47.1	17.8	96.5	14 32.9	19.8	97.0	2
15 11.3	11.8	95.9	14 58.4	13.9	96.4	14 44.4	16.0	97.0	14 29.3	18.1	97.5	14 13.1	20.1	98.0	3
14 59.5	12.1	96.9	14 44.5	14.2	97.5	14 28.4	16.3	98.0	14 11.2	18.3	98.5	13 53.0	20.3	99.0	4
14 47.4	- 12.3	97.9	14 30.3	- 14.4	98.5	14 12.1	- 16.4	99.0	13 52.9	- 18.5	99.5	13 32.7	- 20.5	99.9	5
14 35.1	12.6	98.9	14 15.9	14.7	99.5	13 55.7	16.8	100.0	13 34.4	18.7	100.4	13 12.2	20.7	100.9	6
14 22.5	12.9	100.0	14 01.2	14.9	100.5	13 38.9	16.9	100.9	13 15.7	19.0	101.4	12 51.5	21.0	101.9	7
14 09.6	13.1	101.0	13 46.3	15.2	101.5	13 22.0	17.2	101.9	12 56.7	19.2	102.4	12 30.5	21.1	102.8	8
13 56.5	13.3	102.0	13 31.1	15.3	102.5	13 04.8	17.4	102.9	12 37.5	19.4	103.4	12 09.4	21.4	103.8	9
13 43.2	- 13.6	103.0	13 15.8	- 15.7	103.4	12 47.4	- 17.6	103.9	12 18.1	- 19.6	104.3	11 48.0	- 21.5	104.7	10
13 29.6	13.8	104.0	13 00.1	15.8	104.4	12 29.8	17.9	104.9	11 58.5	19.8	105.3	11 26.5	21.7	105.7	11
13 15.8	14.1	105.0	12 44.3	16.1	105.4	12 11.9	18.0	105.9	11 38.7	19.9	106.3	11 04.8	21.9	106.6	12
13 01.7	14.3	106.0	12 28.2	16.3	106.4	11 53.9	18.2	106.8	11 18.8	20.2	107.2	10 42.9	22.1	107.6	13
12 47.4	14.5	107.0	12 11.9	16.5	107.4	11 35.7	18.5	107.8	10 58.6	20.4	108.2	10 20.8	22.2	108.5	14
12 32.9	- 14.8	108.0	11 55.4	- 16.7	108.4	11 17.2	- 18.6	108.8	10 38.2	- 20.5	109.1	9 58.6	- 22.4	109.5	15
12 18.1	14.9	109.0	11 38.7	16.8	109.4	10 58.6	18.8	109.7	10 17.7	20.7	110.1	9 36.2	22.6	110.4	16
12 03.2	15.2	110.0	11 21.9	17.1	110.3	10 39.8	19.0	110.7	9 57.0	20.8	111.0	9 13.6	22.7	111.4	17
11 48.0	15.3	110.9	11 04.8	17.3	111.3	10 20.8	19.2	111.7	9 36.2	21.1	112.0	8 50.9	22.8	112.3	18
11 32.7	15.6	111.9	10 47.5	17.5	112.3	10 01.6	19.3	112.6	9 15.1	21.1	112.9	8 28.1	23.0	113.2	19
11 17.1	- 15.8	112.9	10 30.0	- 17.6	113.3	9 42.3	- 19.5	113.6	8 54.0	- 21.3	113.9	8 05.1	- 23.1	114.2	20
11 01.3	15.9	113.9	10 12.4	17.8	114.2	9 22.8	19.6	114.6	8 32.7	21.5	114.8	7 42.0	23.2	115.1	21
10 45.4	16.1	114.9	9 54.6	18.0	115.2	9 03.2	19.8	115.5	8 11.2	21.5	115.8	7 18.8	23.3	116.0	22
10 29.3	16.4	115.9	9 36.6	18.1	116.2	8 43.4	19.9	116.5	7 49.7	21.7	116.7	6 55.5	23.5	117.0	23
10 12.9	16.5	116.8	9 18.5	18.3	117.1	8 23.5	20.1	117.4	7 28.0	21.8	117.7	6 32.0	23.5	117.9	24
9 56.4	- 16.6	117.8	9 00.2	- 18.5	118.1	8 03.4	- 20.2	118.4	7 06.2	- 22.0	118.6	6 08.5	- 23.6	118.8	25
9 39.8	16.8	118.8	8 41.7	18.6	119.1	7 43.2	20.3	119.3	6 44.2	22.0	119.5	5 44.9	23.7	119.7	26
9 23.0	17.0	119.8	8 23.1	18.7	120.0	7 22.9	20.5	120.3	6 22.2	22.2	120.5	5 21.2	23.9	120.7	27
9 06.0	17.2	120.7	8 04.4	18.8	121.0	7 02.4	20.5	121.2	6 00.0	22.2	121.4	4 57.3	23.8	121.6	28
8 48.8	17.2	121.7	7 45.6	19.0	122.0	6 41.9	20.7	122.2	5 37.8	22.3	122.3	4 33.5	24.0	122.5	29

225

Dec.	20° Hc	d	Z	22° Hc	d	Z	24° Hc	d	Z	26° Hc	d	Z	28° Hc	d	Z
°	° ′	′	°	° ′	′	°	° ′	′	°	° ′	′	°	° ′	′	°
0	15 00.7	+21.1	95.6	14 48.4	+23.2	96.1	14 35.1	+25.1	96.7	14 20.6	+27.1	97.2	14 05.1	+29.0	97.7
1	15 21.8	20.9	94.6	15 11.6	22.8	95.2	15 00.2	24.8	95.7	14 47.7	26.8	96.2	14 34.1	28.7	96.8
2	15 42.7	20.6	93.7	15 34.4	22.7	94.2	15 25.0	24.7	94.8	15 14.5	26.6	95.3	15 02.8	28.5	95.9
3	16 03.3	20.3	92.7	15 57.1	22.4	93.3	15 49.7	24.4	93.8	15 41.1	26.3	94.4	15 31.3	28.3	94.9
4	16 23.6	20.1	91.7	16 19.5	22.1	92.3	16 14.1	24.1	92.9	16 07.4	26.1	93.5	15 59.6	28.1	94.0
5	16 43.7	+19.8	90.7	16 41.6	+21.8	91.3	16 38.2	+23.9	91.9	16 33.5	+25.9	92.5	16 27.7	+27.8	93.1
6	17 03.5	19.5	89.7	17 03.4	21.6	90.3	17 02.1	23.6	91.0	16 59.4	25.6	91.6	16 55.5	27.5	92.2
7	17 23.0	19.2	88.7	17 25.0	21.3	89.4	17 25.7	23.3	90.0	17 25.0	25.3	90.6	17 23.0	27.3	91.3
8	17 42.2	18.9	87.7	17 46.3	20.9	88.4	17 49.0	23.0	89.0	17 50.3	25.1	89.7	17 50.3	27.1	90.3
9	18 01.1	18.6	86.8	18 07.2	20.7	87.4	18 12.0	22.7	88.1	18 15.4	24.7	88.7	18 17.4	26.7	89.4
10	18 19.7	+18.3	85.8	18 27.9	+20.4	86.4	18 34.7	+22.5	87.1	18 40.1	+24.5	87.8	18 44.1	+26.5	88.4
11	18 38.0	18.0	84.7	18 48.3	20.1	85.4	18 57.2	22.1	86.1	19 04.6	24.2	86.8	19 10.6	26.2	87.5
12	18 56.0	17.6	83.7	19 08.4	19.7	84.4	19 19.3	21.8	85.1	19 28.8	23.8	85.8	19 36.8	25.8	86.5
13	19 13.6	17.3	82.7	19 28.1	19.4	83.4	19 41.1	21.5	84.1	19 52.6	23.6	84.8	20 02.6	25.6	85.6
14	19 30.9	17.0	81.7	19 47.5	19.1	82.4	20 02.6	21.1	83.1	20 16.2	23.2	83.9	20 28.2	25.3	84.6
15	19 47.9	+16.6	80.7	20 06.6	+18.7	81.4	20 23.7	+20.8	82.1	20 39.4	+22.8	82.9	20 53.5	+24.9	83.6
16	20 04.5	16.3	79.7	20 25.3	18.4	80.4	20 44.5	20.5	81.1	21 02.2	22.6	81.9	21 18.4	24.5	82.7
17	20 20.8	15.9	78.6	20 43.7	18.0	79.4	21 05.0	20.1	80.1	21 24.8	22.1	80.9	21 42.9	24.3	81.7
18	20 36.7	15.5	77.6	21 01.7	17.6	78.4	21 25.1	19.7	79.1	21 46.9	21.8	79.9	22 07.2	23.8	80.7
19	20 52.2	15.2	76.6	21 19.3	17.3	77.3	21 44.8	19.4	78.1	22 08.7	21.5	78.9	22 31.0	23.5	79.7
20	21 07.4	+14.8	75.5	21 36.6	+16.8	76.3	22 04.2	+19.0	77.1	22 30.2	+21.0	77.9	22 54.5	+23.2	78.7
21	21 22.2	14.4	74.5	21 53.4	16.5	75.3	22 23.2	18.5	76.1	22 51.2	20.7	76.9	23 17.7	22.7	77.7
22	21 36.6	14.0	73.5	22 09.9	16.1	74.2	22 41.7	18.3	75.0	23 11.9	20.3	75.9	23 40.4	22.3	76.7
23	21 50.6	13.6	72.4	22 26.0	15.7	73.2	22 59.9	17.8	74.0	23 32.2	19.9	74.8	24 02.7	22.0	75.7
24	22 04.2	13.2	71.4	22 41.7	15.3	72.1	23 17.7	17.4	73.0	23 52.1	19.4	73.8	24 24.7	21.5	74.7
25	22 17.4	+12.8	70.3	22 57.0	+14.9	71.1	23 35.1	+17.0	71.9	24 11.5	+19.0	72.8	24 46.2	+21.1	73.6
26	22 30.2	12.4	69.3	23 11.9	14.5	70.0	23 52.1	16.5	70.9	24 30.5	18.6	71.7	25 07.3	20.7	72.6
27	22 42.6	11.9	68.2	23 26.4	14.0	69.0	24 08.6	16.1	69.8	24 49.1	18.2	70.7	25 28.0	20.2	71.6
28	22 54.5	11.6	67.1	23 40.4	13.6	67.9	24 24.7	15.6	68.8	25 07.3	17.7	69.6	25 48.2	19.8	70.5
29	23 06.1	11.1	66.1	23 54.0	13.1	66.9	24 40.3	15.2	67.7	25 25.0	17.3	68.6	26 08.0	19.3	69.5

Dec.	30° Hc	d	Z	32° Hc	d	Z	34° Hc	d	Z	36° Hc	d	Z	38° Hc	d	Z
°	° ′	′	°	° ′	′	°	° ′	′	°	° ′	′	°	° ′	′	°
0	13 48.6	+30.8	98.2	13 31.1	+32.6	98.6	13 12.6	+34.4	99.1	12 53.1	+36.1	99.6	12 32.7	+37.8	100.0
1	14 19.4	30.6	97.3	14 03.7	32.4	97.8	13 47.0	34.2	98.3	13 29.2	35.9	98.7	13 10.5	37.6	99.2
2	14 50.0	30.4	96.4	14 36.1	32.3	96.9	14 21.2	34.0	97.4	14 05.1	35.8	97.9	13 48.1	37.5	98.4
3	15 20.4	30.2	95.5	15 08.4	32.0	96.0	14 55.2	33.8	96.6	14 40.9	35.6	97.1	14 25.6	37.3	97.6
4	15 50.6	29.9	94.6	15 40.4	31.8	95.2	15 29.0	33.7	95.7	15 16.5	35.4	96.3	15 02.9	37.1	96.8
5	16 20.5	+29.8	93.7	16 12.2	+31.6	94.3	16 02.7	+33.4	94.9	15 51.9	+35.2	95.4	15 40.0	+36.9	96.0
6	16 50.3	29.5	92.8	16 43.8	31.4	93.4	16 36.1	33.2	94.0	16 27.1	35.0	94.6	16 16.9	36.8	95.2
7	17 19.8	29.2	91.9	17 15.2	31.1	92.5	17 09.3	33.0	93.1	17 02.1	34.8	93.7	16 53.7	36.5	94.3
8	17 49.0	29.0	91.0	17 46.3	30.9	91.6	17 42.3	32.7	92.2	17 36.9	34.6	92.9	17 30.2	36.4	93.5
9	18 18.0	28.7	90.0	18 17.2	30.6	90.7	18 15.0	32.6	91.4	18 11.5	34.4	92.0	18 06.6	36.1	92.7
10	18 46.7	+28.4	89.1	18 47.8	+30.4	89.8	18 47.6	+32.2	90.5	18 45.9	+34.1	91.2	18 42.7	+35.9	91.8
11	19 15.1	28.2	88.2	19 18.2	30.1	88.9	19 19.8	32.0	89.6	19 20.0	33.8	90.3	19 18.6	35.7	91.0
12	19 43.3	27.9	87.2	19 48.3	29.8	88.0	19 51.8	31.7	88.7	19 53.8	33.6	89.4	19 54.3	35.4	90.1
13	20 11.2	27.5	86.3	20 18.1	29.5	87.0	20 23.5	31.5	87.8	20 27.4	33.3	88.5	20 29.7	35.2	89.3
14	20 38.7	27.3	85.4	20 47.6	29.3	86.1	20 55.0	31.1	86.9	21 00.7	33.1	87.6	21 04.9	34.9	88.4
15	21 06.0	+26.9	84.4	21 16.9	+28.9	85.2	21 26.1	+30.9	86.0	21 33.8	+32.7	86.7	21 39.8	+34.6	87.5
16	21 32.9	26.6	83.4	21 45.8	28.5	84.2	21 57.0	30.5	85.0	22 06.5	32.5	85.8	22 14.4	34.3	86.7
17	21 59.5	26.2	82.5	22 14.3	28.3	83.3	22 27.5	30.3	84.1	22 39.0	32.2	84.9	22 48.7	34.1	85.8
18	22 25.7	25.9	81.5	22 42.6	27.9	82.3	22 57.8	29.8	83.2	23 11.2	31.8	84.0	23 22.8	33.7	84.9
19	22 51.6	25.6	80.5	23 10.5	27.6	81.4	23 27.6	29.6	82.2	23 43.0	31.5	83.1	23 56.5	33.4	84.0
20	23 17.2	+25.1	79.5	23 38.1	+27.2	80.4	23 57.2	+29.2	81.3	24 14.5	+31.1	82.2	24 29.9	+33.1	83.1
21	23 42.3	24.8	78.6	24 05.3	26.8	79.4	24 26.4	28.8	80.3	24 45.6	30.8	81.2	25 03.0	32.7	82.1
22	24 07.1	24.4	77.6	24 32.1	26.4	78.4	24 55.2	28.4	79.3	25 16.4	30.5	80.3	25 35.7	32.4	81.2
23	24 31.5	24.0	76.6	24 58.5	26.1	77.5	25 23.6	28.1	78.4	25 46.9	30.0	79.3	26 08.1	32.1	80.3
24	24 55.5	23.6	75.5	25 24.6	25.6	76.5	25 51.7	27.7	77.4	26 16.9	29.7	78.4	26 40.2	31.6	79.3
25	25 19.1	+23.2	74.5	25 50.2	+25.2	75.5	26 19.4	+27.2	76.4	26 46.6	+29.3	77.4	27 11.8	+31.2	78.4
26	25 42.3	22.7	73.5	26 15.4	24.8	74.4	26 46.6	26.9	75.4	27 15.9	28.8	76.4	27 43.0	30.9	77.4
27	26 05.0	22.3	72.5	26 40.2	24.4	73.4	27 13.5	26.4	74.4	27 44.7	28.4	75.4	28 13.9	30.4	76.4
28	26 27.3	21.9	71.4	27 04.6	23.9	72.4	27 39.9	25.9	73.4	28 13.1	28.0	74.4	28 44.3	30.0	75.5
29	26 49.2	21.4	70.4	27 28.5	23.4	71.4	28 05.8	25.5	72.4	28 41.1	27.6	73.4	29 14.3	29.6	74.5

20°			22°			24°			26°			28°			Dec.
Hc	d	Z	Hc	d	Z	Hc	d	Z	Hc	d	Z	Hc	d	Z	
15 00.7	−21.4	95.6	14 48.4	−23.3	96.1	14 35.1	−25.4	96.7	14 20.6	−27.2	97.2	14 05.1	−29.1	97.7	0
14 39.3	21.6	96.6	14 25.1	23.6	97.1	14 09.7	25.5	97.6	13 53.4	27.5	98.1	13 36.0	29.3	98.6	1
14 17.7	21.8	97.5	14 01.5	23.8	98.0	13 44.2	25.8	98.5	13 25.9	27.6	99.0	13 06.7	29.6	99.5	2
13 55.9	22.1	98.5	13 37.7	24.1	99.0	13 18.4	25.9	99.4	12 58.3	27.9	99.9	12 37.1	29.6	100.4	3
13 33.8	22.3	99.4	13 13.6	24.2	99.9	12 52.5	26.2	100.4	12 30.4	28.0	100.8	12 07.5	29.9	101.2	4
13 11.5	−22.5	100.4	12 49.4	−24.4	100.9	12 26.3	−26.3	101.3	12 02.4	−28.2	101.7	11 37.6	−30.0	102.1	5
12 49.0	22.7	101.4	12 25.0	24.7	101.8	12 00.0	26.5	102.2	11 34.2	28.4	102.6	11 07.6	30.2	103.0	6
12 26.3	22.8	102.3	12 00.3	24.8	102.7	11 33.5	26.7	103.1	11 05.8	28.5	103.5	10 37.4	30.4	103.9	7
12 03.5	23.1	103.2	11 35.5	25.0	103.7	11 06.8	26.9	104.0	10 37.3	28.7	104.4	10 07.0	30.4	104.8	8
11 40.4	23.3	104.2	11 10.5	25.1	104.6	10 39.9	27.0	105.0	10 08.6	28.8	105.3	9 36.6	30.6	105.6	9
11 17.1	−23.5	105.1	10 45.4	−25.3	105.5	10 12.9	−27.1	105.9	9 39.8	−29.0	106.2	9 06.0	−30.7	106.5	10
10 53.6	23.6	106.1	10 20.1	25.5	106.4	9 45.8	27.3	106.8	9 10.8	29.1	107.1	8 35.3	30.9	107.4	11
10 30.0	23.8	107.0	9 54.6	25.6	107.4	9 18.5	27.5	107.7	8 41.7	29.2	108.0	8 04.4	30.9	108.3	12
10 06.2	23.9	107.9	9 29.0	25.8	108.3	8 51.0	27.5	108.6	8 12.5	29.3	108.9	7 33.5	31.1	109.1	13
9 42.3	24.1	108.9	9 03.2	25.9	109.2	8 23.5	27.7	109.5	7 43.2	29.4	109.7	7 02.4	31.1	110.0	14
9 18.2	−24.2	109.8	8 37.3	−26.1	110.1	7 55.8	−27.8	110.4	7 13.8	−29.6	110.6	6 31.3	−31.3	110.8	15
8 54.0	24.4	110.7	8 11.2	26.1	111.0	7 28.0	27.9	111.3	6 44.2	29.6	111.5	6 00.0	31.3	111.7	16
8 29.6	24.5	111.7	7 45.1	26.3	111.9	7 00.1	28.1	112.2	6 14.6	29.7	112.4	5 28.7	31.4	112.6	17
8 05.1	24.6	112.6	7 18.8	26.4	112.8	6 32.0	28.1	113.0	5 44.9	29.8	113.2	4 57.3	31.4	113.4	18
7 40.5	24.7	113.5	6 52.4	26.5	113.7	6 03.9	28.2	113.9	5 15.1	29.9	114.1	4 25.9	31.5	114.3	19
7 15.8	−24.9	114.4	6 25.9	−26.5	114.6	5 35.7	−28.2	114.8	4 45.2	−29.9	115.0	3 54.4	−31.6	115.1	20
6 50.9	25.0	115.3	5 59.4	26.7	115.5	5 07.5	28.4	115.7	4 15.3	30.0	115.9	3 22.8	31.6	116.0	21
6 25.9	25.0	116.2	5 32.7	26.8	116.4	4 39.1	28.4	116.6	3 45.3	30.1	116.7	2 51.2	31.6	116.8	22
6 00.9	25.2	117.2	5 05.9	26.8	117.3	4 10.7	28.5	117.5	3 15.2	30.1	117.6	2 19.6	31.7	117.7	23
5 35.7	25.2	118.1	4 39.1	26.9	118.2	3 42.2	28.5	118.4	2 45.1	30.1	118.5	1 47.9	31.7	118.5	24
5 10.5	−25.3	119.0	4 12.2	−26.9	119.1	3 13.7	−28.6	119.2	2 15.0	−30.1	119.3	1 16.2	−31.7	119.4	25
4 45.2	25.4	119.9	3 45.3	27.0	120.0	2 45.1	28.6	120.1	1 44.9	30.2	120.2	0 44.5	31.7	120.2	26
4 19.8	25.4	120.8	3 18.3	27.1	120.9	2 16.5	28.6	121.0	1 14.7	30.2	121.1	0 12.8	−31.8	121.1	27
3 54.4	25.5	121.7	2 51.2	27.1	121.8	1 47.9	28.7	121.9	0 44.5	30.2	121.9	0 19.0	+31.7	58.1	28
3 28.9	25.6	122.6	2 24.1	27.1	122.7	1 19.2	28.7	122.8	0 14.3	−30.2	122.8	0 50.7	31.7	57.2	29

30°			32°			34°			36°			38°			Dec.
Hc	d	Z	Hc	d	Z	Hc	d	Z	Hc	d	Z	Hc	d	Z	
13 48.6	−31.0	98.2	13 31.1	−32.8	98.6	13 12.6	−34.6	99.1	12 53.1	−36.3	99.6	12 32.7	−37.9	100.0	0
13 17.6	31.1	99.0	12 58.3	33.0	99.5	12 38.0	34.7	99.9	12 16.8	36.3	100.4	11 54.8	38.1	100.8	1
12 46.5	31.4	99.9	12 25.3	33.1	100.4	12 03.3	34.8	100.8	11 40.5	36.6	101.2	11 16.7	38.1	101.6	2
12 15.1	31.5	100.8	11 52.2	33.2	101.2	11 28.5	35.0	101.6	11 03.9	36.6	102.0	10 38.6	38.3	102.4	3
11 43.6	31.6	101.7	11 19.0	33.5	102.1	10 53.5	35.1	102.4	10 27.3	36.8	102.8	10 00.3	38.4	103.2	4
11 12.0	−31.9	102.5	10 45.5	−33.5	102.9	10 18.4	−35.3	103.3	9 50.5	−36.9	103.6	9 21.9	−38.5	103.9	5
10 40.1	31.9	103.4	10 12.0	33.7	103.7	9 43.1	35.3	104.1	9 13.6	37.0	104.4	8 43.4	38.6	104.7	6
10 08.2	32.1	104.3	9 38.3	33.8	104.6	9 07.8	35.5	104.9	8 36.6	37.1	105.2	8 04.8	38.7	105.5	7
9 36.1	32.2	105.1	9 04.5	33.9	105.4	8 32.3	35.6	105.7	7 59.5	37.2	106.0	7 26.1	38.7	106.3	8
9 03.9	32.3	106.0	8 30.6	34.0	106.3	7 56.7	35.7	106.5	7 22.3	37.3	106.8	6 47.4	38.9	107.0	9
8 31.6	−32.5	106.8	7 56.6	−34.2	107.1	7 21.0	−35.7	107.3	6 45.0	−37.3	107.6	6 08.5	−38.9	107.8	10
7 59.1	32.5	107.7	7 22.4	34.2	107.9	6 45.3	35.9	108.2	6 07.7	37.5	108.4	5 29.6	38.9	108.6	11
7 26.6	32.7	108.5	6 48.2	34.3	108.8	6 09.4	35.9	109.0	5 30.2	37.4	109.2	4 50.7	39.0	109.3	12
6 53.9	32.7	109.4	6 13.9	34.4	109.6	5 33.5	36.0	109.8	4 52.8	37.6	109.9	4 11.7	39.1	110.1	13
6 21.2	32.8	110.2	5 39.6	34.5	110.4	4 57.5	36.0	110.6	4 15.2	37.6	110.7	3 32.6	39.1	110.9	14
5 48.4	−32.9	111.0	5 05.1	−34.5	111.2	4 21.5	−36.1	111.4	3 37.6	−37.6	111.5	2 53.5	−39.1	111.6	15
5 15.5	33.0	111.9	4 30.6	34.6	112.0	3 45.4	36.1	112.2	3 00.0	37.6	112.3	2 14.4	39.1	112.4	16
4 42.5	33.0	112.7	3 56.0	34.6	112.9	3 09.3	36.2	113.0	2 22.4	37.7	113.1	1 35.3	39.2	113.1	17
4 09.5	33.1	113.6	3 21.4	34.6	113.7	2 33.1	36.2	113.8	1 44.7	37.7	113.8	0 56.1	39.1	113.9	18
3 36.4	33.1	114.4	2 46.8	34.7	114.5	1 56.9	36.2	114.6	1 07.0	37.7	114.6	0 17.0	−39.2	114.6	19
3 03.3	−33.1	115.2	2 12.1	−34.7	115.3	1 20.7	−36.2	115.4	0 29.3	−37.8	115.4	0 22.2	+39.2	64.6	20
2 30.2	33.2	116.1	1 37.4	34.8	116.1	0 44.5	36.3	116.2	0 08.5	+37.7	63.8	1 01.4	39.1	63.8	21
1 57.0	33.2	116.9	1 02.6	34.7	116.9	0 08.2	−36.2	117.0	0 46.2	37.7	63.0	1 40.5	39.2	63.1	22
1 23.8	33.3	117.7	0 27.9	−34.8	117.8	0 28.0	+36.2	62.2	1 23.9	37.7	62.3	2 19.7	39.1	62.3	23
0 50.5	33.2	118.6	0 06.9	+34.7	61.4	1 04.2	36.3	61.4	2 01.6	37.6	61.5	2 58.8	39.1	61.6	24
0 17.3	−33.2	119.4	0 41.6	+34.7	60.6	1 40.5	+36.2	60.6	2 39.2	+37.7	60.7	3 37.9	+39.0	60.8	25
0 15.9	+33.3	59.8	1 16.3	34.8	59.8	2 16.7	36.2	59.8	3 16.9	37.6	59.9	4 16.9	39.0	60.0	26
0 49.2	33.2	58.9	1 51.1	34.7	59.0	2 52.9	36.1	59.0	3 54.5	37.6	59.1	4 55.9	39.0	59.3	27
1 22.4	33.2	58.1	2 25.8	34.7	58.2	3 29.0	36.1	58.2	4 32.1	37.5	58.4	5 34.9	38.9	58.5	28
1 55.6	33.2	57.3	3 00.4	34.7	57.3	4 05.1	36.1	57.4	5 09.6	37.4	57.6	6 13.8	38.8	57.8	29

Dec.	40° Hc	d	Z	42° Hc	d	Z	44° Hc	d	Z	46° Hc	d	Z	48° Hc	d	Z
°	° ′	′	°	° ′	′	°	° ′	′	°	° ′	′	°	° ′	′	°
0	12 11.4	+39.4	100.4	11 49.2	+41.0	100.9	11 26.2	+42.4	101.3	11 02.3	+44.0	101.7	10 37.7	+45.3	102.0
1	12 50.8	39.2	99.7	12 30.2	40.8	100.1	12 08.6	42.4	100.5	11 46.3	43.8	101.0	11 23.0	45.1	101.4
2	13 30.0	39.1	98.9	13 11.0	40.7	99.4	12 51.0	42.2	99.8	12 30.1	43.7	100.3	12 08.3	45.1	100.7
3	14 09.1	39.0	98.1	13 51.7	40.6	98.6	13 33.2	42.1	99.1	13 13.8	43.6	99.6	12 53.4	45.0	100.0
4	14 48.1	38.8	97.3	14 32.3	40.4	97.8	14 15.3	42.0	98.4	13 57.4	43.5	98.9	13 38.4	44.9	99.3
5	15 26.9	+38.6	96.5	15 12.7	+40.2	97.1	14 57.3	+41.9	97.6	14 40.9	+43.3	98.1	14 23.3	+44.8	98.7
6	16 05.5	38.5	95.7	15 52.9	40.1	96.3	15 39.2	41.6	96.9	15 24.2	43.2	97.4	15 08.1	44.7	98.0
7	16 44.0	38.2	94.9	16 33.0	39.9	95.5	16 20.8	41.5	96.1	16 07.4	43.1	96.7	15 52.8	44.6	97.3
8	17 22.2	38.1	94.1	17 12.9	39.8	94.8	17 02.3	41.4	95.4	16 50.5	42.9	96.0	16 37.4	44.4	96.6
9	18 00.3	37.9	93.3	17 52.7	39.5	94.0	17 43.7	41.2	94.6	17 33.4	42.7	95.2	17 21.8	44.2	95.9
10	18 38.2	+37.6	92.5	18 32.2	+39.4	93.2	18 24.9	+41.0	93.8	18 16.1	+42.6	94.5	18 06.0	+44.1	95.2
11	19 15.8	37.5	91.7	19 11.6	39.1	92.4	19 05.9	40.8	93.1	18 58.7	42.4	93.8	18 50.1	43.9	94.4
12	19 53.3	37.2	90.9	19 50.7	38.9	91.6	19 46.7	40.6	92.3	19 41.1	42.2	93.0	19 34.0	43.8	93.7
13	20 30.5	36.9	90.0	20 29.6	38.7	90.8	20 27.3	40.3	91.5	20 23.3	42.0	92.3	20 17.8	43.6	93.0
14	21 07.4	36.7	89.2	21 08.3	38.5	89.9	21 07.6	40.2	90.7	21 05.3	41.8	91.5	21 01.4	43.4	92.3
15	21 44.1	+36.5	88.3	21 46.8	+38.2	89.1	21 47.8	+39.9	89.9	21 47.1	+41.6	90.7	21 44.8	+43.1	91.5
16	22 20.6	36.1	87.5	22 25.0	38.0	88.3	22 27.7	39.7	89.1	22 28.7	41.4	89.9	22 27.9	43.0	90.8
17	22 56.7	35.9	86.6	23 03.0	37.6	87.5	23 07.4	39.4	88.3	23 10.1	41.1	89.2	23 10.9	42.8	90.0
18	23 32.6	35.6	85.7	23 40.6	37.4	86.6	23 46.8	39.2	87.5	23 51.2	40.9	88.4	23 53.7	42.5	89.3
19	24 08.2	35.3	84.9	24 18.0	37.2	85.7	24 26.0	38.9	86.7	24 32.1	40.6	87.6	24 36.2	42.3	88.5
20	24 43.5	+35.0	84.0	24 55.2	+36.8	84.9	25 04.9	+38.6	85.8	25 12.7	+40.3	86.8	25 18.5	+42.0	87.7
21	25 18.5	34.6	83.1	25 32.0	36.5	84.0	25 43.5	38.3	85.0	25 53.0	40.1	85.9	26 00.5	41.8	86.9
22	25 53.1	34.3	82.2	26 08.5	36.1	83.1	26 21.8	38.0	84.1	26 33.1	39.8	85.1	26 42.3	41.5	86.1
23	26 27.4	34.0	81.2	26 44.6	35.9	82.2	26 59.8	37.7	83.2	27 12.9	39.4	84.3	27 23.8	41.2	85.3
24	27 01.4	33.5	80.3	27 20.5	35.5	81.3	27 37.5	37.3	82.4	27 52.3	39.2	83.4	28 05.0	40.9	84.5
25	27 34.9	+33.2	79.4	27 56.0	+35.1	80.4	28 14.8	+37.0	81.5	28 31.5	+38.8	82.6	28 45.9	+40.6	83.6
26	28 08.1	32.9	78.4	28 31.1	34.7	79.5	28 51.8	36.7	80.6	29 10.3	38.5	81.7	29 26.5	40.3	82.8
27	28 41.0	32.4	77.5	29 05.8	34.4	78.6	29 28.5	36.2	79.7	29 48.8	38.1	80.8	30 06.8	40.0	81.9
28	29 13.4	32.0	76.5	29 40.2	33.9	77.6	30 04.7	35.9	78.8	30 26.9	37.8	79.9	30 46.8	39.6	81.1
29	29 45.4	31.5	75.6	30 14.1	33.6	76.7	30 40.6	35.5	77.8	31 04.7	37.4	79.0	31 26.4	39.2	80.2

Dec.	50° Hc	d	Z	52° Hc	d	Z	54° Hc	d	Z	56° Hc	d	Z	58° Hc	d	Z
°	° ′	′	°	° ′	′	°	° ′	′	°	° ′	′	°	° ′	′	°
0	10 12.3	+46.7	102.4	9 46.2	+48.0	102.7	9 19.4	+49.2	103.1	8 52.0	+50.3	103.4	8 23.9	+51.5	103.7
1	10 59.0	46.6	101.7	10 34.2	47.8	102.1	10 08.6	49.1	102.5	9 42.3	50.3	102.8	9 15.4	51.3	103.1
2	11 45.6	46.5	101.1	11 22.0	47.8	101.5	10 57.7	49.0	101.9	10 32.6	50.2	102.3	10 06.7	51.3	102.6
3	12 32.1	46.4	100.5	12 09.8	47.7	100.9	11 46.7	49.0	101.3	11 22.8	50.1	101.7	10 58.0	51.3	102.1
4	13 18.5	46.3	99.8	12 57.5	47.7	100.3	12 35.7	48.9	100.7	12 12.9	50.1	101.1	11 49.3	51.2	101.6
5	14 04.8	+46.2	99.2	13 45.2	+47.5	99.6	13 24.6	+48.8	100.1	13 03.0	+50.0	100.6	12 40.5	+51.1	101.0
6	14 51.0	46.0	98.5	14 32.7	47.4	99.0	14 13.4	48.7	99.5	13 53.0	49.9	100.0	13 31.6	51.1	100.5
7	15 37.0	46.0	97.8	15 20.1	47.3	98.4	15 02.1	48.6	98.9	14 42.9	49.9	99.4	14 22.7	51.0	100.0
8	16 23.0	45.8	97.2	16 07.4	47.2	97.7	15 50.7	48.5	98.3	15 32.8	49.7	98.9	15 13.7	50.9	99.4
9	17 08.8	45.7	96.5	16 54.6	47.1	97.1	16 39.2	48.4	97.7	16 22.5	49.7	98.3	16 04.6	50.9	98.9
10	17 54.5	+45.6	95.8	17 41.7	+47.0	96.4	17 27.6	+48.3	97.1	17 12.2	+49.5	97.7	16 55.5	+50.7	98.3
11	18 40.1	45.4	95.1	18 28.7	46.8	95.8	18 15.9	48.1	96.5	18 01.7	49.4	97.1	17 46.2	50.6	97.7
12	19 25.5	45.4	94.4	19 15.5	46.7	95.1	19 04.0	48.1	95.8	18 51.1	49.4	96.5	18 36.8	50.6	97.2
13	20 10.8	45.0	93.7	20 02.2	46.5	94.5	19 52.1	47.9	95.2	19 40.5	49.2	95.9	19 27.4	50.4	96.6
14	20 55.8	44.9	93.0	20 48.7	46.4	93.8	20 40.0	47.7	94.5	20 29.7	49.0	95.3	20 17.8	50.3	96.0
15	21 40.7	+44.8	92.3	21 35.1	+46.1	93.1	21 27.7	+47.6	93.9	21 18.7	+49.0	94.7	21 08.1	+50.2	95.5
16	22 25.5	44.5	91.6	22 21.2	46.1	92.4	22 15.3	47.5	93.2	22 07.7	48.8	94.1	21 58.3	50.1	94.9
17	23 10.0	44.3	90.9	23 07.3	45.8	91.7	23 02.8	47.2	92.6	22 56.5	48.6	93.4	22 48.4	50.0	94.3
18	23 54.3	44.1	90.1	23 53.1	45.6	91.0	23 50.0	47.1	91.9	23 45.1	48.5	92.8	23 38.4	49.8	93.7
19	24 38.4	43.9	89.4	24 38.7	45.5	90.3	24 37.1	46.9	91.2	24 33.6	48.3	92.1	24 28.2	49.6	93.1
20	25 22.3	+43.7	88.6	25 24.2	+45.2	89.6	25 24.0	+46.8	90.5	25 21.9	+48.2	91.5	25 17.8	+49.5	92.4
21	26 06.0	43.4	87.9	26 09.4	45.0	88.9	26 10.8	46.5	89.8	26 10.1	47.9	90.8	26 07.3	49.3	91.8
22	26 49.4	43.2	87.1	26 54.4	44.8	88.1	26 57.3	46.3	89.1	26 58.0	47.8	90.2	26 56.6	49.2	91.2
23	27 32.6	42.9	86.3	27 39.2	44.5	87.4	27 43.6	46.0	88.4	27 45.8	47.5	89.5	27 45.8	48.9	90.5
24	28 15.5	42.6	85.5	28 23.7	44.2	86.6	28 29.6	45.9	87.7	28 33.3	47.4	88.8	28 34.7	48.8	89.9
25	28 58.1	+42.3	84.7	29 07.9	+44.0	85.8	29 15.5	+45.6	87.0	29 20.7	+47.1	88.1	29 23.5	+48.6	89.2
26	29 40.4	42.0	83.9	29 51.9	43.7	85.1	30 01.1	45.3	86.2	30 07.8	46.9	87.4	30 12.1	48.4	88.5
27	30 22.4	41.8	83.1	30 35.6	43.5	84.3	30 46.4	45.1	85.5	30 54.7	46.6	86.6	31 00.5	48.1	87.8
28	31 04.2	41.3	82.3	31 19.1	43.1	83.5	31 31.5	44.7	84.7	31 41.3	46.4	85.9	31 48.6	47.9	87.1
29	31 45.5	41.1	81.4	32 02.2	42.8	82.6	32 16.2	44.5	83.9	32 27.7	46.1	85.2	32 36.5	47.7	86.4

	40°			42°			44°			46°			48°		Dec.
	Hc	d	Z	Hc	d	Z	Hc	d	Z	Hc	d	Z	Hc	d	Z	
	° ′	′	°	° ′	′	°	° ′	′	°	° ′	′	°	° ′	′	°	°
	12 11.4	− 39.5	100.4	11 49.2	− 41.1	100.9	11 26.2	− 42.6	101.3	11 02.3	− 44.0	101.7	10 37.7	− 45.4	102.0	0
	11 31.9	39.7	101.2	11 08.1	41.2	101.6	10 43.6	42.7	102.0	10 18.3	44.1	102.3	9 52.3	45.5	102.7	1
	11 52.2	39.7	102.0	10 26.9	41.2	102.3	10 00.9	42.7	102.7	9 34.2	44.2	103.0	9 06.8	45.6	103.4	2
	10 12.5	39.9	102.7	9 45.7	41.4	103.1	9 18.2	42.9	103.4	8 50.0	44.3	103.7	8 21.2	45.6	104.0	3
	9 32.6	39.9	103.5	9 04.3	41.5	103.8	8 35.3	42.9	104.1	8 05.7	44.3	104.4	7 35.6	45.7	104.7	4
	8 52.7	− 40.1	104.3	8 22.8	− 41.5	104.5	7 52.4	− 43.0	104.8	7 21.4	− 44.4	105.1	6 49.9	− 45.7	105.3	5
	8 12.6	40.1	105.0	7 41.3	41.7	105.3	7 09.4	43.1	105.5	6 37.0	44.4	105.8	6 04.2	45.8	106.0	6
	7 32.5	40.3	105.8	6 59.6	41.6	106.0	6 26.3	43.1	106.2	5 52.6	44.5	106.4	5 18.4	45.8	106.6	7
	6 52.3	40.3	106.5	6 18.0	41.8	106.7	5 43.2	43.2	106.9	5 08.1	44.6	107.1	4 32.6	45.8	107.3	8
	6 12.0	40.3	107.3	5 36.2	41.8	107.4	5 00.0	43.2	107.6	4 23.5	44.5	107.8	3 46.8	45.9	107.9	9
	5 31.7	− 40.4	108.0	4 54.4	− 41.8	108.2	4 16.8	− 43.2	108.3	3 39.0	− 44.6	108.5	3 00.9	− 45.9	108.6	10
	4 51.3	40.5	108.7	4 12.6	41.9	108.9	3 33.6	43.3	109.0	2 54.4	44.7	109.1	2 15.0	46.0	109.2	11
	4 10.8	40.5	109.5	3 30.7	42.0	109.6	2 50.3	43.3	109.7	2 09.7	44.6	109.8	1 29.0	45.9	109.9	12
	3 30.3	40.5	110.2	2 48.7	41.9	110.3	2 07.0	43.3	110.4	1 25.1	44.7	110.5	0 43.1	− 45.9	110.5	13
	2 49.8	40.5	111.0	2 06.8	42.0	111.0	1 23.7	43.4	111.1	0 40.4	− 44.6	111.1	0 02.8	+ 46.0	68.9	14
	2 09.3	− 40.6	111.7	1 24.8	− 41.9	111.8	0 40.3	− 43.3	111.8	0 04.2	+ 44.7	68.2	0 48.8	+ 45.9	68.2	15
	1 28.7	40.6	112.4	0 42.9	42.0	112.5	0 03.0	+ 43.4	67.5	0 48.9	44.6	67.5	1 34.7	45.9	67.6	16
	0 48.1	40.6	113.2	0 00.9	− 42.0	113.2	0 46.4	43.3	66.8	1 33.5	44.7	66.9	2 20.6	45.9	66.9	17
	0 07.5	− 40.6	113.9	0 41.1	+ 42.0	66.1	1 29.7	43.3	66.1	2 18.2	44.6	66.2	3 06.5	45.9	66.3	18
	0 33.1	+ 40.6	65.4	1 23.1	42.0	65.4	2 13.0	43.3	65.4	3 02.8	44.6	65.5	3 52.4	45.9	65.6	19
	1 13.7	+ 40.6	64.6	2 05.1	+ 41.9	64.7	2 56.3	+ 43.3	64.8	3 47.4	+ 44.6	64.9	4 38.3	+ 45.8	65.0	20
	1 54.3	40.5	63.9	2 47.0	41.9	64.0	3 39.6	43.2	64.1	4 32.0	44.5	64.2	5 24.1	45.8	64.3	21
	2 34.8	40.5	63.1	3 28.9	41.9	63.2	4 22.8	43.3	63.4	5 16.5	44.5	63.5	6 09.9	45.7	63.7	22
	3 15.3	40.5	62.4	4 10.8	41.9	62.5	5 06.1	43.1	62.7	6 01.0	44.4	62.8	6 55.6	45.7	63.0	23
	3 55.8	40.5	61.7	4 52.7	41.8	61.8	5 49.2	43.1	61.8	6 45.4	44.4	62.2	7 41.3	45.6	62.4	24
	4 36.3	+ 40.4	60.9	5 34.5	+ 41.7	61.1	6 32.3	+ 43.1	61.3	7 29.8	+ 44.3	61.5	8 26.9	+ 45.5	61.7	25
	5 16.7	40.4	60.2	6 16.2	41.7	60.4	7 15.4	43.0	60.6	8 14.1	44.3	60.8	9 12.4	45.5	61.1	26
	5 57.1	40.3	59.4	6 57.9	41.6	59.6	7 58.4	42.9	59.9	8 58.4	44.2	60.1	9 57.9	45.4	60.4	27
	6 37.4	40.2	58.7	7 39.5	41.6	58.9	8 41.3	42.8	59.2	9 42.6	44.0	59.4	10 43.3	45.3	59.7	28
	7 17.6	40.2	58.0	8 21.1	41.5	58.2	9 24.1	42.8	58.5	10 26.6	44.0	58.7	11 28.6	45.2	59.1	29

	50°			52°			54°			56°			58°		Dec.
	Hc	d	Z	Hc	d	Z	Hc	d	Z	Hc	d	Z	Hc	d	Z	
	° ′	′	°	° ′	′	°	° ′	′	°	° ′	′	°	° ′	′	°	°
	10 12.3	− 46.7	102.4	9 46.2	− 48.0	102.7	9 19.4	− 49.2	103.1	8 52.0	− 50.4	103.4	8 23.9	− 51.4	103.7	0
	9 25.6	46.8	103.0	8 58.2	48.1	103.3	8 30.2	49.3	103.6	8 01.6	50.4	103.9	7 32.5	51.5	104.2	1
	8 38.8	46.9	103.7	8 10.1	48.1	103.9	7 40.9	49.3	104.2	7 11.2	50.4	104.5	6 41.0	51.5	104.7	2
	7 51.9	46.9	104.3	7 22.0	48.1	104.5	6 51.6	49.3	104.8	6 20.8	50.5	105.0	5 49.5	51.6	105.2	3
	7 05.0	47.0	104.9	6 33.9	48.3	105.1	6 02.3	49.4	105.4	5 30.3	50.5	105.6	4 57.9	51.6	105.7	4
	6 18.0	− 47.0	105.5	5 45.6	− 48.2	105.7	5 12.9	− 49.4	105.9	4 39.8	− 50.6	106.1	4 06.3	− 51.5	106.2	5
	5 31.0	47.1	106.2	4 57.4	48.3	106.3	4 23.5	49.5	106.5	3 49.2	50.6	106.6	3 14.8	51.7	106.8	6
	4 43.9	47.1	106.8	4 09.1	48.3	106.9	3 34.0	49.5	107.1	2 58.7	50.6	107.2	2 23.1	51.6	107.3	7
	3 56.8	47.1	107.4	3 20.8	48.3	107.5	2 44.5	49.4	107.6	2 08.1	50.6	107.7	1 31.5	51.6	107.8	8
	3 09.7	47.1	108.0	2 32.5	48.4	108.1	1 55.1	49.5	108.2	1 17.5	50.6	108.3	0 39.9	− 51.6	108.3	9
	2 22.6	− 47.2	108.7	1 44.1	− 48.3	108.7	1 05.6	− 49.5	108.8	0 26.9	− 50.6	108.8	0 11.7	+ 51.7	71.2	10
	1 35.4	47.1	109.3	0 55.8	48.4	109.3	0 16.1	− 49.5	109.3	0 23.7	+ 50.6	70.7	1 03.4	51.6	70.7	11
	0 48.3	47.2	109.9	0 07.4	− 48.4	109.9	0 33.4	+ 49.5	70.1	1 14.3	50.6	70.1	1 55.0	51.6	70.2	12
	0 01.1	− 47.2	110.5	0 41.0	+ 48.3	69.5	1 22.9	49.5	69.5	2 04.8	50.6	69.6	2 46.6	51.6	69.7	13
	0 46.1	+ 47.2	68.9	1 29.3	48.4	68.9	2 12.4	49.5	69.0	2 55.4	50.6	69.1	3 38.2	51.6	69.2	14
	1 33.3	+ 47 1	68.3	2 17.7	+ 48.3	68.3	3 01.9	+ 49.5	68.4	3 46.0	+ 50.5	68.5	4 29.8	+ 51.6	68.7	15
	2 20.4	47.2	67.6	3 06.0	48.3	67.7	3 51.4	49.4	67.8	4 36.5	50.5	68.0	5 21.4	51.5	68.1	16
	3 07.6	47.1	67.0	3 54.3	48.3	67.1	4 40.8	49.4	67.3	5 27.0	50.5	67.4	6 12.9	51.5	67.6	17
	3 54.7	47.1	66.4	4 42.6	48.3	66.5	5 30.2	49.4	66.7	6 17.5	50.5	66.9	7 04.4	51.5	67.1	18
	4 41.8	47.0	65.7	5 30.9	48.2	65.9	6 19.6	49.4	66.1	7 08.0	50.4	66.3	7 55.9	51.4	66.6	19
	5 28.8	+ 47.0	65.2	6 19.1	+ 48.2	65.3	7 09.0	+ 49.3	65.6	7 58.4	+ 50.4	65.8	8 47.3	+ 51.4	66.1	20
	6 15.9	46.9	64.5	7 07.3	48.1	64.7	7 58.3	49.2	65.0	8 48.8	50.3	65.2	9 38.7	51.4	65.5	21
	7 02.8	47.0	63.9	7 55.4	48.1	64.1	8 47.5	49.2	64.4	9 39.1	50.2	64.7	10 30.1	51.3	65.0	22
	7 49.8	46.9	63.3	8 43.5	48.0	63.5	9 36.7	49.1	63.8	10 29.3	50.3	64.1	11 21.4	51.2	64.5	23
	8 36.6	46.9	62.6	9 31.5	48.0	62.9	10 25.8	49.1	63.2	11 19.6	50.1	63.6	12 12.6	51.2	64.0	24
	9 23.5	+ 46.7	62.0	10 19.5	+ 47.9	62.3	11 14.9	+ 49.0	62.7	12 09.7	+ 50.1	63.0	13 03.8	+ 51.1	63.4	25
	10 10.2	46.7	61.4	11 07.4	47.8	61.7	12 03.9	49.0	62.1	12 59.8	50.0	62.5	13 54.9	51.0	62.9	26
	10 56.9	46.6	60.7	11 55.2	47.7	61.1	12 52.9	48.8	61.5	13 49.8	49.9	61.9	14 45.9	51.0	62.3	27
	11 43.4	46.5	60.1	12 42.9	47.7	60.5	13 41.7	48.8	60.9	14 39.7	49.9	61.3	15 36.9	50.9	61.8	28
	12 29.9	46.5	59.4	13 30.6	47.6	59.8	14 30.5	48.7	60.3	15 29.6	49.7	60.7	16 27.8	50.7	61.2	29

Dec.	0° Hc	d	Z	2° Hc	d	Z	4° Hc	d	Z	6° Hc	d	Z	8° Hc	d	Z
°	° ′	′	°	° ′	′	°	° ′	′	°	° ′	′	°	° ′	′	°
0	14 00.0 −	0.1	90.0	13 59.5 +	2.0	90.5	13 57.9 +	4.2	91.0	13 55.3 +	6.3	91.5	13 51.7 +	8.4	92.0
1	13 59.9	0.4	89.0	14 01.5	1.8	89.5	14 02.1	3.9	90.0	14 01.6	6.1	90.5	14 00.1	8.3	91.0
2	13 59.5	0.7	87.9	14 03.3	1.5	88.4	14 06.0	3.7	88.9	14 07.7	5.8	89.4	14 08.4	7.9	89.9
3	13 58.8	0.9	86.9	14 04.8	1.2	87.4	14 09.7	3.4	87.9	14 13.5	5.6	88.4	14 16.3	7.7	88.9
4	13 57.9	1.2	85.9	14 06.0	1.0	86.4	14 13.1	3.1	86.9	14 19.1	5.3	87.4	14 24.0	7.4	87.9
5	13 56.7 −	1.4	84.8	14 07.0 +	0.7	85.3	14 16.2 +	2.9	85.9	14 24.4 +	5.0	86.4	14 31.4 +	7.2	86.9
6	13 55.3	1.7	83.8	14 07.7	0.5	84.3	14 19.1	2.6	84.8	14 29.4	4.7	85.3	14 38.6	6.9	85.8
7	13 53.6	1.9	82.8	14 08.2 +	0.2	83.3	14 21.7	2.3	83.8	14 34.1	4.5	84.3	14 45.5	6.6	84.8
8	13 51.7	2.2	81.8	14 08.4 −	0.1	82.3	14 24.0	2.1	82.8	14 38.6	4.2	83.3	14 52.1	6.4	83.8
9	13 49.5	2.5	80.7	14 08.3	0.4	81.2	14 26.1	1.8	81.7	14 42.8	3.9	82.2	14 58.5	6.0	82.8
10	13 47.0 −	2.7	79.7	14 07.9 −	0.6	80.2	14 27.9 +	1.5	80.7	14 46.7 +	3.7	81.2	15 04.5 +	5.8	81.7
11	13 44.3	3.0	78.7	14 07.3	0.8	79.2	14 29.4	1.2	79.7	14 50.4	3.4	80.2	15 10.3	5.5	80.7
12	13 41.3	3.3	77.6	14 06.5	1.2	78.1	14 30.6	1.0	78.6	14 53.8	3.1	79.1	15 15.8	5.3	79.7
13	13 38.0	3.4	76.6	14 05.3	1.4	77.1	14 31.6	0.7	77.6	14 56.9	2.8	78.1	15 21.1	4.9	78.6
14	13 34.6	3.8	75.6	14 03.9	1.6	76.1	14 32.3	0.5	76.6	14 59.7	2.6	77.1	15 26.0	4.7	77.6
15	13 30.8 −	4.0	74.6	14 02.3 −	1.9	75.0	14 32.8 +	0.2	75.5	15 02.3 +	2.2	76.0	15 30.7 +	4.3	76.6
16	13 26.8	4.2	73.5	14 00.4	2.2	74.0	14 33.0 −	0.2	74.5	15 04.5	2.0	75.0	15 35.0	4.1	75.5
17	13 22.6	4.5	72.5	13 58.2	2.4	73.0	14 32.8	0.3	73.5	15 06.5	1.7	74.0	15 39.1	3.8	74.5
18	13 18.1	4.7	71.5	13 55.8	2.7	71.9	14 32.5	0.7	72.4	15 08.2	1.4	72.9	15 42.9	3.5	73.5
19	13 13.4	5.0	70.5	13 53.1	3.0	70.9	14 31.8	0.9	71.4	15 09.6	1.1	71.9	15 46.4	3.2	72.4
20	13 08.4 −	5.2	69.4	13 50.1 −	3.2	69.9	14 30.9 −	1.2	70.4	15 10.7 +	0.9	70.9	15 49.6 +	2.9	71.4
21	13 03.2	5.5	68.4	13 46.9	3.5	68.9	14 29.7	1.4	69.3	15 11.6	0.6	69.8	15 52.5	2.6	70.4
22	12 57.7	5.7	67.4	13 43.4	3.7	67.8	14 28.3	1.8	68.3	15 12.2 +	0.2	68.8	15 55.1	2.3	69.3
23	12 52.0	5.9	66.4	13 39.7	4.0	66.8	14 26.5	2.0	67.3	15 12.4	0.0	67.8	15 57.4	2.0	68.3
24	12 46.1	6.2	65.4	13 35.7	4.2	65.8	14 24.5	2.2	66.2	15 12.4 −	0.3	66.7	15 59.4	1.7	67.2
25	12 39.9 −	6.4	64.3	13 31.5 −	4.5	64.8	14 22.3 −	2.6	65.2	15 12.1 −	0.5	65.7	16 01.1 +	1.4	66.2
26	12 33.5	6.6	63.3	13 27.0	4.7	63.7	14 19.7	2.8	64.2	15 11.6	0.9	64.6	16 02.5	1.1	65.2
27	12 26.9	6.9	62.3	13 22.3	5.0	62.7	14 16.9	3.0	63.1	15 10.7	1.1	63.6	16 03.6	0.8	64.1
28	12 20.0	7.1	61.3	13 17.3	5.2	61.7	14 13.9	3.4	62.1	15 09.6	1.5	62.6	16 04.4	0.5	63.1
29	12 12.9	7.3	60.3	13 12.1	5.5	60.7	14 10.5	3.6	61.1	15 08.1	1.7	61.5	16 04.9 +	0.2	62.0

Dec.	10° Hc	d	Z	12° Hc	d	Z	14° Hc	d	Z	16° Hc	d	Z	18° Hc	d	Z
°	° ′	′	°	° ′	′	°	° ′	′	°	° ′	′	°	° ′	′	°
0	13 47.0 +	10.6	92.5	13 41.3 +	12.7	93.0	13 34.6 +	14.8	93.5	13 26.8 +	16.9	93.9	13 18.1 +	19.0	94.4
1	13 57.6	10.3	91.5	13 54.0	12.5	92.0	13 49.4	14.5	92.5	13 43.7	16.7	92.9	13 37.1	18.7	93.4
2	14 07.9	10.1	90.4	14 06.5	12.2	91.0	14 03.9	14.4	91.5	14 00.4	16.4	92.0	13 55.8	18.4	92.5
3	14 18.0	9.9	89.4	14 18.7	11.9	89.9	14 18.3	14.0	90.5	14 16.8	16.2	91.0	14 14.2	18.3	91.5
4	14 27.9	9.5	88.4	14 30.6	11.7	88.9	14 32.3	13.9	89.4	14 33.0	15.9	90.0	14 32.5	18.0	90.5
5	14 37.4 +	9.3	87.4	14 42.3 +	11.5	87.9	14 46.2 +	13.5	88.4	14 48.9 +	15.6	89.0	14 50.5 +	17.7	89.5
6	14 46.7	9.1	86.4	14 53.8	11.1	86.9	14 59.7	13.3	87.4	15 04.5	15.4	88.0	15 08.2	17.5	88.5
7	14 55.8	8.7	85.4	15 04.9	10.9	85.9	15 13.0	13.0	86.4	15 19.9	15.1	87.0	15 25.7	17.2	87.5
8	15 04.5	8.5	84.3	15 15.8	10.7	84.9	15 26.0	12.8	85.4	15 35.0	14.9	86.0	15 42.9	16.9	86.5
9	15 13.0	8.2	83.3	15 26.5	10.3	83.8	15 38.8	12.4	84.4	15 49.9	14.5	85.0	15 59.8	16.7	85.5
10	15 21.2 +	8.0	82.3	15 36.8 +	10.1	82.8	15 51.2 +	12.2	83.4	16 04.4 +	14.3	84.0	16 16.5 +	16.4	84.5
11	15 29.2	7.6	81.2	15 46.9	9.7	81.8	16 03.4	11.9	82.4	16 18.7	14.0	82.9	16 32.9	16.1	83.5
12	15 36.8	7.4	80.2	15 56.6	9.5	80.8	16 15.3	11.6	81.3	16 32.7	13.7	81.9	16 49.0	15.8	82.5
13	15 44.2	7.0	79.2	16 06.1	9.2	79.7	16 26.9	11.3	80.3	16 46.4	13.4	80.9	17 04.8	15.5	81.5
14	15 51.2	6.8	78.2	16 15.3	8.9	78.7	16 38.2	10.9	79.3	16 59.8	13.1	79.9	17 20.3	15.2	80.5
15	15 58.0 +	6.4	77.1	16 24.2 +	8.5	77.7	16 49.1 +	10.7	78.3	17 12.9 +	12.8	78.9	17 35.5 +	14.8	79.5
16	16 04.4	6.2	76.1	16 32.7	8.3	76.7	16 59.8	10.4	77.2	17 25.7	12.5	77.8	17 50.3	14.6	78.5
17	16 10.6	5.9	75.1	16 41.0	8.0	75.6	17 10.2	10.1	76.2	17 38.2	12.1	76.8	18 04.9	14.3	77.4
18	16 16.5	5.6	74.0	16 49.0	7.6	74.6	17 20.3	9.7	75.2	17 50.3	11.9	75.8	18 19.2	13.9	76.4
19	16 22.1	5.2	73.0	16 56.6	7.4	73.5	17 30.0	9.4	74.1	18 02.2	11.5	74.8	18 33.1	13.6	75.4
20	16 27.3 +	5.0	71.9	17 04.0 +	7.0	72.5	17 39.4 +	9.1	73.1	18 13.7 +	11.2	73.7	18 46.7 +	13.2	74.4
21	16 32.3	4.6	70.9	17 11.0	6.7	71.5	17 48.5	8.8	72.1	18 24.9	10.8	72.7	18 59.9	12.9	73.3
22	16 36.9	4.4	69.9	17 17.7	6.4	70.4	17 57.3	8.4	71.0	18 35.7	10.5	71.7	19 12.8	12.6	72.3
23	16 41.3	4.0	68.8	17 24.1	6.0	69.4	18 05.7	8.1	70.0	18 46.2	10.1	70.6	19 25.4	12.2	71.3
24	16 45.3	3.7	67.8	17 30.1	5.8	68.3	18 13.8	7.8	68.9	18 56.3	9.8	69.6	19 37.6	11.8	70.2
25	16 49.0 +	3.4	66.7	17 35.9 +	5.4	67.3	18 21.6 +	7.4	67.9	19 06.1 +	9.5	68.5	19 49.4 +	11.5	69.2
26	16 52.4	3.1	65.7	17 41.3	5.0	66.3	18 29.0	7.1	66.9	19 15.6	9.1	67.5	20 00.9	11.1	68.1
27	16 55.5	2.7	64.6	17 46.3	4.8	65.2	18 36.1	6.7	65.8	19 24.7	8.7	66.4	20 12.0	10.7	67.1
28	16 58.2	2.5	63.6	17 51.1	4.4	64.2	18 42.8	6.4	64.8	19 33.4	8.3	65.4	20 22.7	10.4	66.1
29	17 00.7	2.1	62.6	17 55.5	4.0	63.1	18 49.2	6.0	63.7	19 41.7	8.0	64.3	20 33.1	10.0	65.0

0° Hc	d	Z	2° Hc	d	Z	4° Hc	d	Z	6° Hc	d	Z	8° Hc	d	Z	Dec.
14 00.0	0.1	90.0	13 59.5 –	2.3	90.5	13 57.9 –	4.4	91.0	13 55.3 –	6.6	91.5	13 51.7 –	8.8	92.0	0
13 59.9	0.4	91.0	13 57.2	2.6	91.5	13 53.5	4.7	92.0	13 48.7	6.8	92.5	13 42.9	8.9	93.0	1
13 59.5	0.7	92.1	13 54.6	2.8	92.6	13 48.8	5.0	93.1	13 41.9	7.1	93.5	13 34.0	9.3	94.0	2
13 58.8	0.9	93.1	13 51.8	3.0	93.6	13 43.8	5.2	94.1	13 34.8	7.4	94.6	13 24.7	9.4	95.0	3
13 57.9	1.2	94.1	13 48.8	3.4	94.6	13 38.6	5.5	95.1	13 27.4	7.6	95.6	13 15.3	9.7	96.1	4
13 56.7 –	1.4	95.2	13 45.4 –	3.5	95.6	13 33.1 –	5.7	96.1	13 19.8 –	7.8	96.6	13 05.6 –	10.0	97.1	5
13 55.3	1.7	96.2	13 41.9	3.9	96.7	13 27.4	5.9	97.2	13 12.0	8.1	97.6	12 55.6	10.2	98.1	6
13 53.6	1.9	97.2	13 38.0	4.0	97.7	13 21.5	6.2	98.2	13 03.9	8.3	98.6	12 45.4	10.4	99.1	7
13 51.7	2.2	98.2	13 34.0	4.4	98.7	13 15.3	6.5	99.2	12 55.6	8.5	99.7	12 35.0	10.6	100.1	8
13 49.5	2.5	99.3	13 29.6	4.6	99.8	13 08.8	6.7	100.2	12 47.1	8.8	100.7	12 24.4	10.9	101.1	9
13 47.0 –	2.7	100.3	13 25.0 –	4.8	100.8	13 02.1 –	6.9	101.2	12 38.3 –	9.0	101.7	12 13.5 –	11.0	102.1	10
13 44.3	3.0	101.3	13 20.2	5.1	101.8	12 55.2	7.2	102.3	12 29.3	9.3	102.7	12 02.5	11.3	103.1	11
13 41.3	3.3	102.4	13 15.1	5.3	102.8	12 48.0	7.4	103.3	12 20.0	9.4	103.7	11 51.2	11.5	104.1	12
13 38.0	3.4	103.4	13 09.8	5.6	103.8	12 40.6	7.6	104.3	12 10.6	9.7	104.7	11 39.7	11.8	105.1	13
13 34.6	3.8	104.4	13 04.2	5.8	104.9	12 33.0	7.9	105.3	12 00.9	9.9	105.7	11 27.9	11.9	106.1	14
13 30.8 –	4.0	105.4	12 58.4 –	6.0	105.9	12 25.1 –	8.1	106.3	11 51.0 –	10.1	106.7	11 16.0 –	12.1	107.1	15
13 26.8	4.2	106.5	12 52.4	6.3	106.9	12 17.0	8.3	107.3	11 40.9	10.4	107.7	11 03.9	12.3	108.1	16
13 22.6	4.5	107.5	12 46.1	6.5	107.9	12 08.7	8.5	108.4	11 30.5	10.5	108.7	10 51.6	12.5	109.1	17
13 18.1	4.7	108.5	12 39.6	6.8	109.0	12 00.2	8.8	109.4	11 20.0	10.7	109.8	10 39.1	12.7	110.1	18
13 13.4	5.0	109.5	12 32.8	7.0	110.0	11 51.4	8.9	110.4	11 09.3	11.0	110.8	10 26.4	12.9	111.1	19
13 08.4 –	5.2	110.6	12 25.8 –	7.2	111.0	11 42.5 –	9.2	111.4	10 58.3 –	11.1	111.8	10 13.5 –	13.0	112.1	20
13 03.2	5.5	111.6	12 18.6	7.4	112.0	11 33.3	9.4	112.4	10 47.2	11.3	112.8	10 00.5	13.3	113.1	21
12 57.7	5.7	112.6	12 11.2	7.7	113.0	11 23.9	9.6	113.4	10 35.9	11.5	113.8	9 47.2	13.4	114.1	22
12 52.0	5.9	113.6	12 03.5	7.8	114.0	11 14.3	9.8	114.4	10 24.4	11.7	114.8	9 33.8	13.6	115.1	23
12 46.1	6.2	114.6	11 55.7	8.1	115.0	11 04.5	10.0	115.4	10 12.7	11.9	115.8	9 20.2	13.7	116.1	24
12 39.9 –	6.4	115.7	11 47.6 –	8.3	116.1	10 54.5 –	10.2	116.4	10 00.8 –	12.0	116.7	9 06.5 –	13.9	117.0	25
12 33.5	6.6	116.7	11 39.3	8.6	117.1	10 44.3	10.4	117.4	9 48.8	12.3	117.7	8 52.6	14.0	118.0	26
12 26.9	6.9	117.7	11 30.7	8.7	118.1	10 33.9	10.5	118.4	9 36.5	12.4	118.7	8 38.6	14.2	119.0	27
12 20.0	7.1	118.7	11 22.0	8.9	119.1	10 23.4	10.8	119.4	9 24.1	12.5	119.7	8 24.4	14.4	120.0	28
12 12.9	7.3	119.7	11 13.1	9.2	120.1	10 12.6	10.9	120.4	9 11.6	12.8	120.7	8 10.0	14.5	121.0	29

10° Hc	d	Z	12° Hc	d	Z	14° Hc	d	Z	16° Hc	d	Z	18° Hc	d	Z	Dec.
13 47.0 –	10.9	92.5	13 41.3 –	13.0	93.0	13 34.6 –	15.1	93.5	13 26.8 –	17.1	93.9	13 18.1 –	19.2	94.4	0
13 36.1	11.1	93.5	13 28.3	13.2	94.0	13 19.5	15.3	94.4	13 09.7	17.3	94.9	12 58.9	19.3	95.4	1
13 25.0	11.3	94.5	13 15.1	13.4	95.0	13 04.2	15.5	95.4	12 52.4	17.6	95.9	12 39.6	19.6	96.3	2
13 13.7	11.6	95.5	13 01.7	13.7	96.0	12 48.7	15.7	96.4	12 34.8	17.8	96.9	12 20.0	19.8	97.3	3
13 02.1	11.8	96.5	12 48.0	13.9	97.0	12 33.0	16.0	97.4	12 17.0	17.9	97.9	12 00.2	20.0	98.3	4
12 50.3 –	12.0	97.5	12 34.1 –	14.1	98.0	12 17.0 –	16.1	98.4	11 59.1 –	18.2	98.8	11 40.2 –	20.2	99.2	5
12 38.3	12.3	98.5	12 20.0	14.3	99.0	12 00.9	16.4	99.4	11 40.9	18.4	99.8	11 20.0	20.4	100.2	6
12 26.0	12.5	99.5	12 05.7	14.5	100.0	11 44.5	16.6	100.4	11 22.5	18.6	100.8	10 59.6	20.5	101.2	7
12 13.5	12.7	100.5	11 51.2	14.8	101.0	11 27.9	16.7	101.4	11 03.9	18.7	101.7	10 39.1	20.7	102.1	8
12 00.8	12.9	101.5	11 36.4	14.9	101.9	11 11.2	17.0	102.3	10 45.2	19.0	102.7	10 18.4	20.9	103.1	9
11 47.9 –	13.1	102.5	11 21.5 –	15.2	102.9	10 54.2 –	17.1	103.3	10 26.2 –	19.1	103.7	9 57.5 –	21.1	104.0	10
11 34.8	13.3	103.5	11 06.3	15.3	103.9	10 37.1	17.3	104.3	10 07.1	19.3	104.6	9 36.4	21.2	105.0	11
11 21.5	13.6	104.5	10 51.0	15.5	104.9	10 19.8	17.5	105.3	9 47.8	19.4	105.6	9 15.2	21.3	105.9	12
11 07.9	13.7	105.5	10 35.5	15.7	105.9	10 02.3	17.7	106.2	9 28.4	19.6	106.6	8 53.9	21.5	106.9	13
10 54.2	13.9	106.5	10 19.8	15.9	106.9	9 44.6	17.8	107.2	9 08.8	19.8	107.5	8 32.4	21.7	107.8	14
10 40.3 –	14.1	107.5	10 03.9 –	16.1	107.8	9 26.8 –	18.0	108.2	8 49.0 –	19.8	108.5	8 10.7 –	21.7	108.8	15
10 26.2	14.3	108.5	9 47.8	16.2	108.8	9 08.8	18.1	109.1	8 29.2	20.1	109.4	7 49.0	21.9	109.7	16
10 11.9	14.4	109.5	9 31.6	16.4	109.8	8 50.7	18.3	110.1	8 09.1	20.1	110.4	7 27.1	22.0	110.6	17
9 57.5	14.7	110.5	9 15.2	16.5	110.8	8 32.4	18.5	111.1	7 49.0	20.3	111.3	7 05.1	22.2	111.6	18
9 42.8	14.8	111.4	8 58.7	16.7	111.7	8 13.9	18.5	112.0	7 28.7	20.4	112.3	6 42.9	22.2	112.5	19
9 28.0 –	14.9	112.4	8 42.0 –	16.9	112.7	7 55.4 –	18.7	113.0	7 08.3 –	20.6	113.2	6 20.7 –	22.3	113.5	20
9 13.1	15.1	113.4	8 25.1	17.0	113.7	7 36.7	18.9	113.9	6 47.7	20.6	114.2	5 58.4	22.5	114.4	21
8 58.0	15.3	114.4	8 08.1	17.1	114.7	7 17.8	18.9	114.9	6 27.1	20.8	115.1	5 35.9	22.5	115.3	22
8 42.7	15.4	115.4	7 51.0	17.2	115.6	6 58.9	19.1	115.9	6 06.3	20.8	116.1	5 13.4	22.6	116.1	23
8 27.3	15.6	116.3	7 33.8	17.4	116.6	6 39.8	19.1	116.8	5 45.5	20.9	117.0	4 50.8	22.6	117.2	24
8 11.7 –	15.7	117.3	7 16.4 –	17.5	117.6	6 20.7 –	19.3	117.8	5 24.6 –	21.1	118.0	4 28.2 –	22.8	118.1	25
7 56.0	15.9	118.3	6 58.9	17.7	118.5	6 01.4	19.4	118.7	5 03.5	21.1	118.9	4 05.4	22.8	119.0	26
7 40.1	16.0	119.3	6 41.2	17.8	119.5	5 42.0	19.5	119.7	4 42.4	21.1	119.9	3 42.6	22.8	120.0	27
7 24.1	16.1	120.2	6 23.5	17.8	120.4	5 22.5	19.5	120.6	4 21.3	21.3	120.8	3 19.8	23.0	120.9	28
7 08.0	16.2	121.2	6 05.7	18.0	121.4	5 03.0	19.7	121.6	4 00.0	21.3	121.7	2 56.8	22.9	121.8	29

Dec.	20° Hc	d	Z	22° Hc	d	Z	24° Hc	d	Z	26° Hc	d	Z	28° Hc	d	Z
°	° ′	′	°	° ′	′	°	° ′	′	°	° ′	′	°	° ′	′	°
0	13 08.4	+21.0	94.9	12 57.7	+23.0	95.3	12 46.1	+24.9	95.8	12 33.5	+26.9	96.2	12 20.0	+28.8	96.7
1	13 29.4	20.7	93.9	13 20.7	22.7	94.4	13 11.0	24.7	94.9	13 00.4	26.6	95.3	12 48.8	28.5	95.8
2	13 50.1	20.5	92.9	13 43.4	22.6	93.4	13 35.7	24.5	93.9	13 27.0	26.5	94.4	13 17.3	28.4	94.9
3	14 10.6	20.3	92.0	14 06.0	22.3	92.5	14 00.2	24.3	93.0	13 53.5	26.2	93.5	13 45.7	28.2	94.0
4	14 30.9	20.1	91.0	14 28.3	22.0	91.5	14 24.5	24.1	92.0	14 19.7	26.1	92.5	14 13.9	27.9	93.1
5	14 51.0	+19.7	90.0	14 50.3	+21.9	90.6	14 48.6	+23.8	91.1	14 45.8	+25.8	91.6	14 41.8	+27.8	92.1
6	15 10.7	19.6	89.1	15 12.2	21.5	89.6	15 12.4	23.6	90.1	15 11.6	25.5	90.7	15 09.6	27.5	91.2
7	15 30.3	19.3	88.1	15 33.7	21.4	88.6	15 36.0	23.4	89.2	15 37.1	25.4	89.7	15 37.1	27.3	90.3
8	15 49.6	19.0	87.1	15 55.1	21.0	87.7	15 59.4	23.1	88.2	16 02.5	25.1	88.8	16 04.4	27.0	89.4
9	16 08.6	18.7	86.1	16 16.1	20.8	86.7	16 22.5	22.8	87.3	16 27.6	24.8	87.9	16 31.4	26.8	88.4
10	16 27.3	+18.5	85.1	16 36.9	+20.6	85.7	16 45.3	+22.6	86.3	16 52.4	+24.6	86.9	16 58.2	+26.6	87.5
11	16 45.8	18.2	84.1	16 57.5	20.2	84.7	17 07.9	22.2	85.3	17 17.0	24.3	86.0	17 24.8	26.3	86.6
12	17 04.0	17.8	83.1	17 17.7	19.9	83.7	17 30.1	22.0	84.4	17 41.3	24.0	85.0	17 51.1	26.0	85.6
13	17 21.8	17.6	82.1	17 37.6	19.7	82.8	17 52.1	21.7	83.4	18 05.3	23.7	84.0	18 17.1	25.7	84.7
14	17 39.4	17.3	81.1	17 57.3	19.3	81.8	18 13.8	21.4	82.4	18 29.0	23.4	83.1	18 42.8	25.4	83.7
15	17 56.7	+17.0	80.1	18 16.6	+19.1	80.8	18 35.2	+21.1	81.4	18 52.4	+23.2	82.1	19 08.2	+25.2	82.8
16	18 13.7	16.6	79.1	18 35.7	18.7	79.8	18 56.3	20.8	80.4	19 15.6	22.8	81.1	19 33.4	24.8	81.8
17	18 30.3	16.4	78.1	18 54.4	18.4	78.8	19 17.1	20.5	79.4	19 38.4	22.5	80.1	19 58.2	24.5	80.8
18	18 46.7	16.0	77.1	19 12.8	18.1	77.8	19 37.6	20.1	78.4	20 00.9	22.1	79.1	20 22.7	24.2	79.9
19	19 02.7	15.6	76.1	19 30.9	17.7	76.7	19 57.7	19.8	77.4	20 23.0	21.9	78.2	20 46.9	23.9	78.9
20	19 18.3	+15.3	75.0	19 48.6	+17.4	75.7	20 17.5	+19.4	76.4	20 44.9	+21.5	77.2	21 10.8	+23.5	77.9
21	19 33.6	15.0	74.0	20 06.0	17.0	74.7	20 36.9	19.1	75.4	21 06.4	21.1	76.2	21 34.3	23.1	76.9
22	19 48.6	14.6	73.0	20 23.0	16.7	73.7	20 56.0	18.7	74.4	21 27.5	20.8	75.2	21 57.4	22.8	75.9
23	20 03.2	14.3	72.0	20 39.7	16.3	72.7	21 14.7	18.4	73.4	21 48.3	20.4	74.2	22 20.2	22.5	74.9
24	20 17.5	13.9	71.0	20 56.0	15.9	71.6	21 33.1	18.0	72.4	22 08.7	20.0	73.1	22 42.7	22.0	73.9
25	20 31.4	+13.5	69.9	21 11.9	+15.6	70.6	21 51.1	+17.6	71.3	22 28.7	+19.6	72.1	23 04.7	+21.7	72.9
26	20 44.9	13.1	68.8	21 27.5	15.2	69.6	22 08.7	17.2	70.3	22 48.3	19.3	71.1	23 26.4	21.3	71.9
27	20 58.0	12.8	67.8	21 42.7	14.7	68.5	22 25.9	16.8	69.3	23 07.6	18.8	70.1	23 47.7	20.8	70.9
28	21 10.8	12.3	66.7	21 57.4	14.4	67.5	22 42.7	16.4	68.2	23 26.4	18.4	69.0	24 08.5	20.5	69.9
29	21 23.1	12.0	65.7	22 11.8	14.0	66.4	22 59.1	16.0	67.2	23 44.8	18.0	68.0	24 29.0	20.0	68.8

Dec.	30° Hc	d	Z	32° Hc	d	Z	34° Hc	d	Z	36° Hc	d	Z	38° Hc	d	Z
°	° ′	′	°	° ′	′	°	° ′	′	°	° ′	′	°	° ′	′	°
0	12 05.6	+30.6	97.1	11 50.3	+32.4	97.5	11 34.2	+34.2	97.9	11 17.2	+35.9	98.3	10 59.4	+37.6	98.7
1	12 36.2	30.4	96.2	12 22.7	32.3	96.7	12 08.4	34.0	97.1	11 53.1	35.8	97.5	11 37.0	37.4	97.9
2	13 06.6	30.3	95.3	12 55.0	32.1	95.8	12 42.4	33.8	96.3	12 28.9	35.6	96.7	12 14.4	37.3	97.1
3	13 36.9	30.0	94.5	13 27.1	31.9	94.9	13 16.2	33.7	95.4	13 04.5	35.4	95.9	12 51.7	37.1	96.3
4	14 06.9	29.9	93.6	13 59.0	31.7	94.1	13 49.9	33.6	94.6	13 39.9	35.3	95.0	13 28.8	37.0	95.5
5	14 36.8	+29.6	92.7	14 30.7	+31.5	93.2	14 23.5	+33.3	93.7	14 15.2	+35.1	94.2	14 05.8	+36.9	94.7
6	15 06.4	29.5	91.8	15 02.2	31.3	92.3	14 56.8	33.1	92.8	14 50.3	34.9	93.4	14 42.7	36.6	93.9
7	15 35.9	29.2	90.9	15 33.5	31.1	91.4	15 29.9	33.0	92.0	15 25.2	34.7	92.5	15 19.3	36.5	93.1
8	16 05.1	29.0	90.0	16 04.6	30.8	90.5	16 02.9	32.7	91.1	15 59.9	34.6	91.7	15 55.8	36.3	92.3
9	16 34.1	28.7	89.0	16 35.4	30.7	89.6	16 35.6	32.5	90.2	16 34.5	34.3	90.8	16 32.1	36.1	91.4
10	17 02.8	+28.5	88.1	17 06.1	+30.4	88.7	17 08.1	+32.3	89.4	17 08.8	+34.1	90.0	17 08.2	+35.9	90.6
11	17 31.3	28.2	87.2	17 36.5	30.1	87.8	17 40.4	32.0	88.5	17 42.9	33.9	89.1	17 44.1	35.6	89.8
12	17 59.5	28.0	86.3	18 06.6	29.9	86.9	18 12.4	31.8	87.6	18 16.8	33.6	88.2	18 19.7	35.5	88.9
13	18 27.5	27.7	85.3	18 36.5	29.7	86.0	18 44.2	31.5	86.7	18 50.4	33.4	87.4	18 55.2	35.2	88.1
14	18 55.2	27.4	84.4	19 06.2	29.3	85.1	19 15.7	31.3	85.8	19 23.8	33.1	86.5	19 30.4	35.0	87.2
15	19 22.6	+27.1	83.5	19 35.5	+29.1	84.2	19 47.0	+31.0	84.9	19 56.9	+32.9	85.6	20 05.4	+34.7	86.3
16	19 49.7	26.9	82.5	20 04.6	28.8	83.2	20 18.0	30.7	84.0	20 29.8	32.6	84.7	20 40.1	34.4	85.5
17	20 16.6	26.5	81.6	20 33.4	28.5	82.3	20 48.7	30.4	83.1	21 02.4	32.3	83.8	21 14.5	34.2	84.6
18	20 43.1	26.2	80.6	21 01.9	28.1	81.4	21 19.1	30.1	82.1	21 34.7	32.0	82.9	21 48.7	33.9	83.7
19	21 09.3	25.8	79.6	21 30.0	27.9	80.4	21 49.2	29.8	81.2	22 06.7	31.7	82.0	22 22.6	33.6	82.8
20	21 35.1	+25.5	78.7	21 57.9	+27.5	79.5	22 19.0	+29.5	80.3	22 38.4	+31.4	81.1	22 56.2	+33.3	81.9
21	22 00.6	25.2	77.7	22 25.4	27.1	78.5	22 48.5	29.1	79.3	23 09.8	31.1	80.2	23 29.5	32.9	81.0
22	22 25.8	24.8	76.7	22 52.5	26.9	77.5	23 17.6	28.8	78.4	23 40.9	30.7	79.2	24 02.4	32.7	80.1
23	22 50.6	24.5	75.7	23 19.4	26.4	76.6	23 46.4	28.4	77.4	24 11.6	30.4	78.3	24 35.1	32.3	79.2
24	23 15.1	24.1	74.7	23 45.8	26.1	75.6	24 14.8	28.1	76.5	24 42.0	30.0	77.3	25 07.4	32.0	78.2
25	23 39.2	+23.6	73.7	24 11.9	+25.7	74.6	24 42.9	+27.7	75.5	25 12.0	+29.7	76.4	25 39.4	+31.5	77.3
26	24 02.8	23.3	72.7	24 37.6	25.3	73.6	25 10.6	27.2	74.5	25 41.7	29.3	75.4	26 10.9	31.3	76.4
27	24 26.1	22.9	71.7	25 02.9	24.9	72.6	25 37.8	26.9	73.5	26 11.0	28.8	74.4	26 42.2	30.8	75.4
28	24 49.0	22.5	70.7	25 27.8	24.5	71.6	26 04.7	26.5	72.5	26 39.8	28.5	73.5	27 13.0	30.4	74.4
29	25 11.5	22.0	69.7	25 52.3	24.0	70.6	26 31.2	26.1	71.5	27 08.3	28.1	72.5	27 43.4	30.1	73.5

20° Hc	d	Z	22° Hc	d	Z	24° Hc	d	Z	26° Hc	d	Z	28° Hc	d	Z	Dec.
13 08.4	−21.2	94.9	12 57.7	−23.1	95.3	12 46.1	−25.1	95.8	12 33.5	−27.0	96.2	12 20.0	−28.9	96.7	0
12 47.2	21.4	95.8	12 34.6	23.4	96.3	12 21.0	25.3	96.7	12 06.5	27.2	97.2	11 51.1	29.1	97.6	1
12 25.8	21.6	96.8	12 11.2	23.6	97.2	11 55.7	25.5	97.6	11 39.3	27.4	98.1	11 22.0	29.2	98.5	2
12 04.2	21.7	97.7	11 47.6	23.7	98.2	11 30.2	25.7	98.6	11 11.9	27.6	99.0	10 52.8	29.4	99.4	3
11 42.5	22.0	98.7	11 23.9	23.9	99.1	11 04.5	25.8	99.5	10 44.3	27.7	99.9	10 23.4	29.6	100.2	4
11 20.5	−22.2	99.6	11 00.0	−24.1	100.0	10 38.7	−26.0	100.4	10 16.6	−27.8	100.8	9 53.8	−29.7	101.1	5
10 58.3	22.3	100.6	10 35.9	24.3	101.0	10 12.7	26.2	101.3	9 48.8	28.0	101.7	9 24.1	29.8	102.0	6
10 36.0	22.5	101.5	10 11.6	24.4	101.9	9 46.5	26.3	102.2	9 20.8	28.2	102.6	8 54.3	29.9	102.9	7
10 13.5	22.6	102.5	9 47.2	24.5	102.8	9 20.2	26.4	103.2	8 52.6	28.2	103.5	8 24.4	30.1	103.8	8
9 50.9	22.9	103.4	9 22.7	24.7	103.8	8 53.8	26.5	104.1	8 24.4	28.4	104.4	7 54.3	30.2	104.6	9
9 28.0	−22.9	104.4	8 58.0	−24.9	104.7	8 27.3	−26.7	105.0	7 56.0	−28.5	105.3	7 24.1	−30.2	105.5	10
9 05.1	23.1	105.3	8 33.1	25.0	105.6	8 00.6	26.8	105.9	7 27.5	28.6	106.1	6 53.9	30.4	106.4	11
8 42.0	23.3	106.2	8 08.1	25.0	106.5	7 33.8	27.0	106.8	6 58.9	28.7	107.0	6 23.5	30.4	107.2	12
8 18.7	23.3	107.2	7 43.1	25.3	107.4	7 06.8	27.0	107.7	6 30.2	28.8	107.9	5 53.1	30.6	108.1	13
7 55.4	23.5	108.1	7 17.8	25.3	108.3	6 39.8	27.1	108.6	6 01.4	28.9	108.8	5 22.5	30.6	109.0	14
7 31.9	−23.6	109.0	6 52.5	−25.4	109.3	6 12.7	−27.2	109.5	5 32.5	−29.0	109.7	4 51.9	−30.6	109.8	15
7 08.3	23.8	109.9	6 27.1	25.5	110.2	5 45.5	27.3	110.4	5 03.5	29.0	110.6	4 21.3	30.8	110.7	16
6 44.5	23.8	110.9	6 01.6	25.7	111.1	5 18.2	27.4	111.3	4 34.5	29.1	111.4	3 50.5	30.7	111.6	17
6 20.7	23.9	111.8	5 35.9	25.7	112.0	4 50.8	27.4	112.2	4 05.4	29.1	112.3	3 19.8	30.9	112.4	18
5 56.8	24.0	112.7	5 10.2	25.7	112.9	4 23.4	27.5	113.1	3 36.3	29.2	113.2	2 48.9	30.8	113.3	19
5 32.8	−24.1	113.6	4 44.5	−25.9	113.8	3 55.9	−27.6	113.9	3 07.1	−29.3	114.1	2 18.1	−30.9	114.1	20
5 08.7	24.2	114.6	4 18.6	25.9	114.7	3 28.3	27.6	114.8	2 37.8	29.2	114.9	1 47.2	30.9	115.0	21
4 44.5	24.3	115.5	3 52.7	26.0	115.6	3 00.7	27.6	115.7	2 08.6	29.3	115.8	1 16.3	31.0	115.9	22
4 20.2	24.3	116.4	3 26.7	26.0	116.5	2 33.1	27.7	116.6	1 39.3	29.4	116.7	0 45.3	30.9	116.7	23
3 55.9	24.4	117.3	3 00.7	26.0	117.4	2 05.4	27.7	117.5	1 09.9	29.3	117.6	0 14.4	−31.0	117.6	24
3 31.5	−24.4	118.2	2 34.7	−26.1	118.3	1 37.7	−27.8	118.4	0 40.6	−29.4	118.4	0 16.6	+30.9	61.6	25
3 07.1	24.5	119.1	2 08.6	26.2	119.2	1 09.9	27.9	119.3	0 11.2	−29.3	119.3	0 47.5	30.9	60.7	26
2 42.6	24.5	120.1	1 42.4	26.1	120.1	0 42.2	27.8	120.2	0 18.1	+29.4	59.8	1 18.4	30.9	59.9	27
2 18.1	24.6	121.0	1 16.3	26.2	121.0	0 14.4	−27.8	121.0	0 47.5	29.3	59.0	1 49.3	30.9	59.0	28
1 53.5	24.6	121.9	0 50.1	26.2	121.9	0 13.4	+27.8	58.1	1 16.8	29.4	58.1	2 20.2	30.9	58.1	29

30° Hc	d	Z	32° Hc	d	Z	34° Hc	d	Z	36° Hc	d	Z	38° Hc	d	Z	Dec.
12 05.6	−30.7	97.1	11 50.3	−32.5	97.5	11 34.2	−34.3	97.9	11 17.2	−36.0	98.3	10 59.4	−37.7	98.7	0
11 34.9	31.0	98.0	11 17.8	32.7	98.4	10 59.9	34.5	98.8	10 41.2	36.2	99.2	10 21.7	37.8	99.5	1
11 03.9	31.0	98.9	10 45.1	32.9	99.2	10 25.4	34.6	99.6	10 05.0	36.3	100.0	9 43.9	37.9	100.3	2
10 32.9	31.2	99.7	10 12.2	33.0	100.1	9 50.8	34.7	100.4	9 28.7	36.3	100.8	9 06.0	38.0	101.1	3
10 01.7	31.4	100.6	9 39.2	33.1	100.9	9 16.1	34.8	101.3	8 52.4	36.5	101.6	8 28.0	38.1	101.9	4
9 30.3	−31.5	101.5	9 06.1	−33.2	101.8	8 41.3	−34.9	102.1	8 15.9	−36.6	102.4	7 49.9	−38.2	102.7	5
8 58.8	31.6	102.3	8 32.9	33.3	102.6	8 06.4	35.0	102.9	7 39.3	36.7	103.2	7 11.7	38.3	103.4	6
8 27.2	31.7	103.2	7 59.6	33.5	103.5	7 31.4	35.2	103.7	7 02.6	36.7	104.0	6 33.4	38.3	104.2	7
7 55.5	31.8	104.0	7 26.1	33.5	104.3	6 56.2	35.2	104.5	6 25.9	36.9	104.8	5 55.1	38.5	105.0	8
7 23.7	31.9	104.9	6 52.6	33.6	105.1	6 21.0	35.2	105.4	5 49.0	36.8	105.6	5 16.6	38.5	105.8	9
6 51.8	−32.0	105.8	6 19.0	−33.7	106.0	5 45.8	−35.4	106.2	5 12.2	−37.0	106.4	4 38.2	−38.5	106.5	10
6 19.8	32.1	106.6	5 45.3	33.8	106.8	5 10.4	35.4	107.0	4 35.2	37.0	107.2	3 59.7	38.6	107.3	11
5 47.7	32.1	107.5	5 11.5	33.8	107.6	4 35.0	35.4	107.8	3 58.2	37.0	107.9	3 21.1	38.6	108.1	12
5 15.6	32.3	108.3	4 37.7	33.9	108.5	3 59.6	35.5	108.6	3 21.2	37.1	108.8	2 42.5	38.6	108.8	13
4 43.3	32.3	109.1	4 03.8	33.9	109.3	3 24.1	35.6	109.4	2 44.1	37.1	109.5	2 03.9	38.6	109.6	14
4 11.0	−32.3	110.0	3 29.9	−34.0	110.1	2 48.5	−35.6	110.2	2 07.0	−37.2	110.3	1 25.3	−38.7	110.4	15
3 38.7	32.4	110.8	2 55.9	34.0	110.9	2 12.9	35.6	111.0	1 29.8	37.1	111.1	0 46.6	38.7	111.1	16
3 06.3	32.4	111.7	2 21.9	34.1	111.8	1 37.3	35.6	111.8	0 52.7	37.2	111.9	0 07.9	−38.6	111.9	17
2 33.9	32.5	112.5	1 47.8	34.0	112.6	1 01.7	35.6	112.6	0 15.5	−37.2	112.7	0 30.7	+38.7	67.3	18
2 01.4	32.5	113.4	1 13.8	34.1	113.4	0 26.1	−35.7	113.4	0 21.7	+37.2	66.6	1 09.4	38.7	66.6	19
1 28.9	−32.5	114.2	0 39.7	−34.1	114.2	0 09.6	+35.6	64.9	0 58.9	+37.1	65.8	1 48.1	+38.6	65.8	20
0 56.4	32.5	115.0	0 05.6	−34.1	115.1	0 45.2	35.7	64.9	1 36.0	37.1	65.0	2 26.7	38.6	65.0	21
0 23.9	−32.5	115.9	0 28.5	+34.1	64.1	1 20.9	35.6	64.1	2 13.1	37.2	64.2	3 05.3	38.6	64.3	22
0 08.6	+32.6	63.3	1 02.6	34.1	63.3	1 56.5	35.6	63.3	2 50.3	37.0	63.4	3 43.9	38.5	63.5	23
0 41.2	32.6	62.4	1 36.7	34.0	62.5	2 32.1	35.5	62.5	3 27.3	37.1	62.6	4 22.4	38.6	62.7	24
1 13.7	+32.5	61.6	2 10.7	+34.0	61.6	3 07.6	+35.6	61.7	4 04.4	+37.0	61.8	5 00.9	+38.4	62.0	25
1 46.2	32.4	60.8	2 44.7	34.0	60.8	3 43.2	35.4	60.9	4 41.4	36.9	61.0	5 39.3	38.4	61.2	26
2 18.6	32.5	59.9	3 18.7	34.0	60.0	4 18.6	35.5	60.1	5 18.3	36.9	60.3	6 17.7	38.3	60.4	27
2 51.1	32.4	59.1	3 52.7	33.9	59.2	4 54.1	35.3	59.3	5 55.2	36.8	59.5	6 56.0	38.2	59.7	28
3 23.5	32.4	58.2	4 26.6	33.8	58.3	5 29.4	35.4	58.5	6 32.0	36.7	58.7	7 34.2	38.2	58.9	29

LATITUDE **SAME** NAME

Dec.	40° Hc	d	Z	42° Hc	d	Z	44° Hc	d	Z	46° Hc	d	Z	48° Hc	d	Z
°	° ′	′	°	° ′	′	°	° ′	′	°	° ′	′	°	° ′	′	°
0	10 40.8	+39.2	99.1	10 21.4	+40.8	99.5	10 01.3	+42.3	99.8	9 40.5	+43.7	100.2	9 19.0	+45.1	100.5
1	11 20.0	39.1	98.3	11 02.2	40.6	98.7	10 43.6	42.2	99.1	10 24.2	43.7	99.5	10 04.1	45.1	99.8
2	11 59.1	38.9	97.6	11 42.8	40.6	98.0	11 25.8	42.0	98.4	11 07.9	43.5	98.8	10 49.2	44.9	99.2
3	12 38.0	38.8	96.8	12 23.4	40.4	97.2	12 07.8	42.0	97.7	11 51.4	43.5	98.1	11 34.1	44.9	98.5
4	13 16.8	38.7	96.0	13 03.8	40.2	96.5	12 49.8	41.8	96.9	12 34.9	43.3	97.4	12 19.0	44.8	97.8
5	13 55.5	+38.5	95.2	13 44.0	+40.2	95.7	13 31.6	+41.7	96.2	13 18.2	+43.2	96.7	13 03.8	+44.7	97.1
6	14 34.0	38.3	94.4	14 24.2	40.0	94.9	14 13.3	41.6	95.4	14 01.4	43.1	95.9	13 48.5	44.5	96.4
7	15 12.3	38.2	93.6	15 04.2	39.8	94.2	14 54.9	41.4	94.7	14 44.5	43.0	95.2	14 33.0	44.5	95.7
8	15 50.5	38.0	92.8	15 44.0	39.7	93.4	15 36.3	41.3	93.9	15 27.5	42.8	94.5	15 17.5	44.5	95.0
9	16 28.5	37.8	92.0	16 23.7	39.4	92.6	16 17.6	41.1	93.2	16 10.3	42.7	93.8	16 01.8	44.2	94.3
10	17 06.3	+37.6	91.2	17 03.1	+39.3	91.8	16 58.7	+40.9	92.4	16 53.0	+42.5	93.0	16 46.0	+44.0	93.6
11	17 43.9	37.4	90.4	17 42.4	39.2	91.0	17 39.6	40.8	91.7	17 35.5	42.3	92.3	17 30.0	43.9	92.9
12	18 21.3	37.2	89.6	18 21.6	38.9	90.2	18 20.4	40.5	90.9	18 17.8	42.2	91.6	18 13.9	43.7	92.2
13	18 58.5	37.0	88.7	19 00.5	38.7	89.4	19 00.9	40.4	90.1	19 00.0	42.0	90.8	18 57.6	43.5	91.5
14	19 35.5	36.8	87.9	19 39.2	38.5	88.6	19 41.3	40.2	89.3	19 42.0	41.8	90.0	19 41.1	43.4	90.8
15	20 12.3	+36.5	87.1	20 17.7	+38.2	87.8	20 21.5	+39.9	88.5	20 23.8	+41.5	89.3	20 24.5	+43.2	90.0
16	20 48.8	36.2	86.2	20 55.9	38.0	87.0	21 01.4	39.8	87.7	21 05.3	41.4	88.5	21 07.7	42.9	89.3
17	21 25.0	36.0	85.4	21 33.9	37.8	86.1	21 41.2	39.4	86.9	21 46.7	41.2	87.7	21 50.6	42.8	88.5
18	22 01.0	35.8	84.5	22 11.7	37.5	85.3	22 20.6	39.3	86.1	22 27.9	40.9	87.0	22 33.4	42.6	87.8
19	22 36.8	35.4	83.6	22 49.2	37.2	84.5	22 59.9	39.0	85.3	23 08.8	40.7	86.2	23 16.0	42.3	87.0
20	23 12.2	+35.1	82.8	23 26.4	+37.0	83.6	23 38.9	+38.7	84.5	23 49.5	+40.4	85.4	23 58.3	+42.1	86.2
21	23 47.3	34.9	81.9	24 03.4	36.7	82.8	24 17.6	38.4	83.6	24 29.9	40.2	84.5	24 40.4	41.9	85.5
22	24 22.2	34.5	81.0	24 40.1	36.3	81.9	24 56.0	38.2	82.8	25 10.1	39.9	83.7	25 22.3	41.6	84.7
23	24 56.7	34.2	80.1	25 16.4	36.1	81.0	25 34.2	37.9	81.9	25 50.0	39.6	82.9	26 03.9	41.3	83.9
24	25 30.9	33.9	79.2	25 52.5	35.7	80.1	26 12.1	37.5	81.1	26 29.6	39.4	82.1	26 45.2	41.0	83.1
25	26 04.8	+33.5	78.3	26 28.2	+35.4	79.2	26 49.6	+37.2	80.2	27 09.0	+39.0	81.2	27 26.2	+40.8	82.2
26	26 38.3	33.1	77.3	27 03.6	35.0	78.3	27 26.8	36.9	79.3	27 48.0	38.7	80.4	28 07.0	40.5	81.4
27	27 11.4	32.8	76.4	27 38.6	34.7	77.4	28 03.7	36.5	78.4	28 26.7	38.3	79.5	28 47.5	40.1	80.6
28	27 44.2	32.3	75.5	28 13.3	34.3	76.5	28 40.2	36.2	77.5	29 05.0	38.1	78.6	29 27.6	39.8	79.7
29	28 16.5	32.0	74.5	28 47.6	33.9	75.5	29 16.4	35.8	76.6	29 43.1	37.6	77.7	30 07.4	39.5	78.9

Dec.	50° Hc	d	Z	52° Hc	d	Z	54° Hc	d	Z	56° Hc	d	Z	58° Hc	d	Z
°	° ′	′	°	° ′	′	°	° ′	′	°	° ′	′	°	° ′	′	°
0	8 56.8	+46.5	100.8	8 33.9	+47.8	101.1	8 10.5	+49.0	101.4	7 46.5	+50.2	101.7	7 21.9	+51.3	101.9
1	9 43.3	46.4	100.2	9 21.7	47.7	100.5	8 59.5	49.0	100.8	8 36.7	50.1	101.1	8 13.2	51.3	101.4
2	10 29.7	46.3	99.5	10 09.4	47.7	99.9	9 48.5	48.9	100.2	9 26.8	50.1	100.6	9 04.5	51.2	100.9
3	11 16.0	46.3	98.9	10 57.1	47.6	99.3	10 37.4	48.8	99.6	10 16.9	50.0	100.0	9 55.7	51.1	100.4
4	12 02.3	46.2	98.2	11 44.7	47.5	98.6	11 26.2	48.8	99.1	11 06.9	50.0	99.4	10 46.8	51.1	99.8
5	12 48.5	+46.0	97.6	12 32.2	+47.4	98.0	12 15.0	+48.6	98.5	11 56.9	+49.9	98.9	11 37.9	+51.1	99.3
6	13 34.5	46.0	96.9	13 19.6	47.3	97.4	13 03.6	48.6	97.9	12 46.8	49.8	98.3	12 29.0	50.9	98.8
7	14 20.5	45.9	96.3	14 06.9	47.2	96.8	13 52.2	48.6	97.3	13 36.6	49.7	97.7	13 19.9	50.9	98.2
8	15 06.4	45.7	95.6	14 54.1	47.1	96.1	14 40.8	48.4	96.6	14 26.3	49.7	97.2	14 10.8	50.9	97.7
9	15 52.1	45.6	94.9	15 41.2	47.0	95.5	15 29.2	48.3	96.0	15 16.0	49.5	96.6	15 01.7	50.7	97.1
10	16 37.7	+45.5	94.2	16 28.2	+46.9	94.8	16 17.5	+48.2	95.4	16 05.5	+49.4	96.0	15 52.4	+50.7	96.6
11	17 23.2	45.3	93.6	17 15.1	46.7	94.2	17 05.7	48.1	94.8	16 55.0	49.4	95.4	16 43.1	50.5	96.0
12	18 08.5	45.2	92.9	18 01.8	46.6	93.5	17 53.8	47.9	94.2	17 44.4	49.2	94.8	17 33.6	50.5	95.4
13	18 53.7	45.1	92.2	18 48.4	46.5	92.9	18 41.7	47.9	93.5	18 33.6	49.2	94.2	18 24.1	50.4	94.9
14	19 38.8	44.8	91.5	19 34.9	46.3	92.2	19 29.6	47.7	92.9	19 22.8	49.0	93.6	19 14.5	50.3	94.3
15	20 23.6	+44.7	90.8	20 21.2	+46.2	91.5	20 17.3	+47.6	92.3	20 11.8	+48.9	93.0	20 04.8	+50.1	93.7
16	21 08.3	44.6	90.1	21 07.4	46.0	90.8	21 04.9	47.4	91.6	21 00.7	48.7	92.4	20 54.9	50.0	93.1
17	21 52.9	44.3	89.3	21 53.4	45.8	90.1	21 52.3	47.2	90.9	21 49.4	48.7	91.7	21 44.9	49.9	92.5
18	22 37.2	44.1	88.6	22 39.2	45.7	89.4	22 39.5	47.1	90.3	22 38.1	48.4	91.1	22 34.8	49.8	91.9
19	23 21.3	43.9	87.9	23 24.9	45.4	88.7	23 26.6	46.9	89.6	23 26.5	48.3	90.5	23 24.6	49.6	91.3
20	24 05.2	+43.7	87.1	24 10.3	+45.3	88.0	24 13.5	+46.7	88.9	24 14.8	+48.2	89.8	24 14.2	+49.5	90.7
21	24 48.9	43.5	86.4	24 55.6	45.0	87.3	25 00.2	46.6	88.2	25 03.0	47.9	89.2	25 03.7	49.3	90.1
22	25 32.4	43.3	85.6	25 40.6	44.8	86.6	25 46.8	46.3	87.5	25 50.9	47.8	88.5	25 53.0	49.2	89.5
23	26 15.7	42.9	84.8	26 25.4	44.6	85.8	26 33.1	46.1	86.8	26 38.7	47.6	87.8	26 42.2	49.0	88.8
24	26 58.6	42.8	84.1	27 10.0	44.3	85.1	27 19.2	45.9	86.1	27 26.3	47.3	87.1	27 31.2	48.8	88.2
25	27 41.4	+42.4	83.3	27 54.3	+44.1	84.3	28 05.1	+45.7	85.4	28 13.6	+47.2	86.5	28 20.0	+48.6	87.5
26	28 23.8	42.2	82.5	28 38.4	43.8	83.6	28 50.8	45.5	84.6	29 00.8	47.0	85.7	29 08.6	48.4	86.9
27	29 06.0	41.9	81.7	29 22.2	43.6	82.8	29 36.2	45.1	83.9	29 47.8	46.7	85.0	29 57.0	48.1	86.2
28	29 47.9	41.5	80.8	30 05.8	43.2	82.0	30 21.3	44.9	83.1	30 34.5	46.4	84.3	30 45.1	48.0	85.5
29	30 29.4	41.3	80.0	30 49.0	43.0	81.2	31 06.2	44.6	82.4	31 20.9	46.2	83.6	31 33.1	47.7	84.8

40°			42°			44°			46°			48°			Dec.
Hc	d	Z	Hc	d	Z	Hc	d	Z	Hc	d	Z	Hc	d	Z	
10 40.8	-39.3	99.1	10 21.4	-40.8	99.5	10 01.3	-42.4	99.8	9 40.5	-43.8	100.2	9 19.0	-45.3	100.5	0
10 01.5	39.4	99.9	9 40.6	41.0	100.2	9 18.9	42.4	100.5	8 56.7	43.9	100.9	8 33.7	45.3	101.2	1
9 22.1	39.5	100.6	8 59.6	41.0	101.0	8 36.5	42.6	101.3	8 12.8	44.0	101.5	7 48.4	45.3	101.8	2
8 42.6	39.6	101.4	8 18.6	41.2	101.7	7 53.9	42.6	102.0	7 28.8	44.1	102.2	7 03.1	45.4	102.5	3
8 03.0	39.7	102.2	7 37.4	41.2	102.4	7 11.3	42.6	102.7	6 44.7	44.0	102.9	6 17.7	45.5	103.1	4
7 23.3	-39.8	102.9	6 56.2	-41.2	103.2	6 28.7	-42.8	103.4	6 00.7	-44.2	103.6	5 32.2	-45.5	103.8	5
6 43.5	39.8	103.7	6 15.0	41.4	103.9	5 45.9	42.7	104.1	5 16.5	44.2	104.3	4 46.7	45.5	104.5	6
6 03.7	39.9	104.4	5 33.6	41.4	104.6	5 03.2	42.9	104.8	4 32.3	44.2	105.0	4 01.2	45.6	105.1	7
5 23.8	39.9	105.2	4 52.2	41.4	105.3	4 20.3	42.8	105.5	3 48.1	44.2	105.6	3 15.6	45.6	105.8	8
4 43.9	40.0	105.9	4 10.8	41.5	106.1	3 37.5	42.9	106.2	3 03.9	44.3	106.3	2 30.0	45.6	106.4	9
4 03.9	-40.0	106.7	3 29.3	-41.5	106.8	2 54.6	-43.0	106.9	2 19.6	-44.3	107.0	1 44.4	-45.6	107.1	10
3 23.9	40.1	107.4	2 47.8	41.5	107.5	2 11.6	42.9	107.6	1 35.3	44.3	107.7	0 58.8	45.6	107.7	11
2 43.8	40.1	108.2	2 06.3	41.5	108.2	1 28.7	43.0	108.3	0 51.0	44.4	108.3	0 13.2	-45.7	108.4	12
2 03.7	40.1	108.9	1 24.8	41.6	109.0	0 45.7	43.0	109.0	0 06.6	-44.3	109.0	0 32.5	+45.6	71.0	13
1 23.6	40.1	109.7	0 43.2	41.6	109.7	0 02.8	-43.0	109.7	0 37.7	+44.3	70.3	1 18.1	45.6	70.3	14
0 43.5	-40.2	110.4	0 01.6	-41.5	110.4	0 40.2	+43.0	69.6	1 22.0	+44.3	69.6	2 03.7	+45.6	69.7	15
0 03.3	-40.1	111.1	0 39.9	+41.6	68.9	1 23.2	42.9	68.9	2 06.3	44.3	69.0	2 49.3	45.6	69.0	16
0 36.8	+40.1	68.1	1 21.5	41.6	68.1	2 06.1	42.9	68.2	2 50.6	44.3	68.3	3 34.9	45.6	68.4	17
1 16.9	40.2	67.4	2 03.1	41.5	67.4	2 49.0	42.9	67.5	3 34.9	44.2	67.6	4 20.5	45.5	67.7	18
1 57.1	40.1	66.6	2 44.6	41.5	66.7	3 32.0	42.8	66.8	4 19.1	44.2	66.9	5 06.0	45.5	67.1	19
2 37.2	+40.0	65.9	3 26.1	+41.5	66.0	4 14.8	+42.9	66.1	5 03.3	+44.2	66.3	5 51.5	+45.4	66.4	20
3 17.2	40.1	65.1	4 07.6	41.4	65.3	4 57.7	42.8	65.4	5 47.5	44.1	65.6	6 36.9	45.4	65.8	21
3 57.3	40.0	64.4	4 49.0	41.4	64.5	5 40.5	42.7	64.7	6 31.6	44.0	64.9	7 22.3	45.3	65.1	22
4 37.3	39.9	63.6	5 30.4	41.3	63.8	6 23.2	42.7	64.0	7 15.6	44.0	64.2	8 07.6	45.3	64.5	23
5 17.2	39.9	62.9	6 11.7	41.3	63.1	7 05.9	42.6	63.3	7 59.6	43.9	63.5	8 52.9	45.1	63.8	24
5 57.1	+39.9	62.1	6 53.0	+41.2	62.3	7 48.5	+42.5	62.6	8 43.5	+43.9	62.8	9 38.0	+45.2	63.1	25
6 37.0	39.7	61.4	7 34.2	41.1	61.6	8 31.0	42.5	61.9	9 27.4	43.7	62.1	10 23.2	45.0	62.5	26
7 16.7	39.7	60.6	8 15.3	41.1	60.9	9 13.5	42.4	61.1	10 11.1	43.7	61.4	11 08.2	44.9	61.8	27
7 56.4	39.6	59.9	8 56.4	41.0	60.1	9 55.9	42.3	60.4	10 54.8	43.6	60.8	11 53.1	44.9	61.1	28
8 36.0	39.5	59.1	9 37.4	40.8	59.4	10 38.2	42.2	59.7	11 38.4	43.5	60.0	12 38.0	44.7	60.4	29

50°			52°			54°			56°			58°			Dec.
Hc	d	Z	Hc	d	Z	Hc	d	Z	Hc	d	Z	Hc	d	Z	
8 56.8	-46.6	100.8	8 33.9	-47.8	101.1	8 10.5	-49.1	101.4	7 46.5	-50.2	101.7	7 21.9	-51.3	101.9	0
8 10.2	46.6	101.5	7 46.1	47.9	101.7	7 21.4	49.1	102.0	6 56.3	50.3	102.2	6 30.6	51.3	102.5	1
7 23.6	46.7	102.1	6 58.2	47.9	102.3	6 32.3	49.1	102.6	6 06.0	50.3	102.8	5 39.3	51.4	103.0	2
6 36.9	46.7	102.7	6 10.3	48.0	102.9	5 43.2	49.2	103.1	5 15.7	50.3	103.3	4 47.9	51.4	103.5	3
5 50.2	46.8	103.4	5 22.3	48.0	103.5	4 54.0	49.2	103.7	4 25.4	50.4	103.9	3 56.5	51.5	104.0	4
5 03.4	-46.8	104.0	4 34.3	-48.1	104.1	4 04.8	-49.2	104.3	3 35.0	-50.3	104.4	3 05.0	-51.4	104.5	5
4 16.6	46.8	104.6	3 46.2	48.0	104.7	3 15.6	49.3	104.9	2 44.7	50.4	105.0	2 13.6	51.5	105.0	6
3 29.8	46.9	105.2	2 58.1	48.0	105.3	2 26.3	49.3	105.4	1 54.3	50.4	105.5	1 22.1	51.4	105.6	7
2 42.9	46.8	105.9	2 10.1	48.1	105.9	1 37.0	49.3	106.0	1 03.9	50.4	106.1	0 30.7	-51.5	106.1	8
1 56.1	46.9	106.5	1 22.0	48.2	106.5	0 47.7	-49.2	106.6	0 13.5	-50.4	106.6	0 20.8	+51.4	73.4	9
1 09.2	-46.9	107.1	0 33.8	-48.1	107.1	0 01.5	+49.3	72.9	0 36.9	+50.4	72.9	1 12.2	+51.5	72.9	10
0 22.3	-46.9	107.7	0 14.3	+48.1	72.3	0 50.8	49.3	72.3	1 27.3	50.4	72.3	2 03.7	51.4	72.4	11
0 24.6	+46.9	71.6	1 02.4	48.1	71.7	1 40.1	49.3	71.7	2 17.7	50.4	71.8	2 55.1	51.5	71.9	12
1 11.5	46.9	71.0	1 50.5	48.1	71.1	2 29.4	49.2	71.1	3 08.1	50.3	71.2	3 46.6	51.4	71.3	13
1 58.4	46.9	70.4	2 38.6	48.1	70.5	3 18.6	49.3	70.6	3 58.4	50.4	70.7	4 38.0	51.4	70.8	14
2 45.3	+46.8	69.8	3 26.7	+48.0	69.9	4 07.9	+49.2	70.0	4 48.8	+50.3	70.1	5 29.4	+51.3	70.3	15
3 32.1	46.9	69.1	4 14.7	48.1	69.3	4 57.1	49.1	69.4	5 39.1	50.3	69.6	6 20.7	51.4	69.8	16
4 19.0	46.8	68.5	5 02.8	48.0	68.7	5 46.2	49.2	68.8	6 29.4	50.2	69.0	7 12.1	51.2	69.3	17
5 05.8	46.7	67.9	5 50.8	47.9	68.1	6 35.4	49.1	68.3	7 19.6	50.2	68.5	8 03.3	51.3	68.7	18
5 52.5	46.8	67.3	6 38.7	47.9	67.5	7 24.5	49.1	67.7	8 09.8	50.2	67.9	8 54.6	51.2	68.2	19
6 39.3	+46.6	66.6	7 26.6	+47.9	66.9	8 13.6	+49.0	67.1	9 00.0	+50.1	67.4	9 45.8	+51.2	67.7	20
7 25.9	46.6	66.0	8 14.5	47.8	66.2	9 02.6	48.9	66.5	9 50.1	50.0	66.8	10 37.0	51.1	67.2	21
8 12.5	46.5	65.4	9 02.3	47.8	65.6	9 51.5	48.9	65.9	10 40.1	50.0	66.3	11 28.1	51.0	66.6	22
8 59.1	46.5	64.7	9 50.1	47.6	65.0	10 40.4	48.8	65.4	11 30.1	50.0	65.7	12 19.1	51.0	66.1	23
9 45.6	46.4	64.1	10 37.7	47.6	64.4	11 29.2	48.8	64.8	12 20.1	49.8	65.1	13 10.1	50.9	65.6	24
10 32.0	+46.3	63.4	11 25.3	+47.6	63.8	12 18.0	+48.7	64.2	13 09.9	+49.8	64.6	14 01.0	+50.9	65.0	25
11 18.3	46.3	62.8	12 12.9	47.4	63.2	13 06.7	48.6	63.6	13 59.7	49.7	64.0	14 51.9	50.7	64.5	26
12 04.6	46.2	62.1	13 00.3	47.4	62.5	13 55.3	48.5	63.0	14 49.4	49.6	63.4	15 42.6	50.7	63.9	27
12 50.8	46.0	61.5	13 47.7	47.2	61.9	14 43.8	48.4	62.4	15 39.0	49.5	62.8	16 33.3	50.6	63.4	28
13 36.8	46.0	60.8	14 34.9	47.2	61.3	15 32.2	48.3	61.7	16 28.5	49.5	62.2	17 23.9	50.5	62.8	29

LATITUDE **SAME** NAME   L.H.A. 104°, 256°

Dec.	0° Hc	d	Z	2° Hc	d	Z	4° Hc	d	Z	6° Hc	d	Z	8° Hc	d	Z
0	12 00.0−	0.1	90.0	11 59.6+	2.0	90.4	11 58.2+	4.2	90.8	11 56.0+	6.3	91.3	11 52.9+	8.4	91.7
1	11 59.9	0.3	89.0	12 01.6	1.8	89.4	12 02.4	3.9	89.8	12 02.3	6.1	90.3	12 01.3	8.2	90.7
2	11 59.6	0.6	88.0	12 03.4	1.6	88.4	12 06.3	3.8	88.8	12 08.4	5.8	89.2	12 09.5	8.0	89.7
3	11 59.0	0.8	86.9	12 05.0	1.3	87.4	12 10.1	3.5	87.8	12 14.2	5.7	88.2	12 17.5	7.8	88.7
4	11 58.2	1.0	85.9	12 06.3	1.2	86.3	12 13.6	3.2	86.8	12 19.9	5.4	87.2	12 25.3	7.5	87.6
5	11 57.2−	1.2	84.9	12 07.5+	0.9	85.3	12 16.8+	3.1	85.7	12 25.3+	5.1	86.2	12 32.8+	7.3	86.6
6	11 56.0	1.4	83.9	12 08.4	0.7	84.3	12 19.9	2.8	84.7	12 30.4	5.0	85.2	12 40.1	7.1	85.6
7	11 54.6	1.7	82.8	12 09.1	0.4	83.3	12 22.7	2.6	83.7	12 35.4	4.7	84.1	12 47.2	6.8	84.6
8	11 52.9	1.9	81.8	12 09.5+	0.3	82.2	12 25.3	2.3	82.7	12 40.1	4.5	83.1	12 54.0	6.6	83.6
9	11 51.0	2.1	80.8	12 09.8	0.0	81.2	12 27.6	2.1	81.7	12 44.6	4.2	82.1	13 00.6	6.4	82.5
10	11 48.9−	2.3	79.8	12 09.8−	0.3	80.2	12 29.7+	1.9	80.6	12 48.8+	4.0	81.1	13 07.0+	6.1	81.5
11	11 46.6	2.6	78.8	12 09.5	0.4	79.2	12 31.6	1.7	79.6	12 52.8	3.8	80.1	13 13.1	5.9	80.5
12	11 44.0	2.7	77.7	12 09.1	0.7	78.2	12 33.3	1.4	78.6	12 56.6	3.5	79.0	13 19.0	5.6	79.5
13	11 41.3	3.0	76.7	12 08.4	0.9	77.1	12 34.7	1.2	77.6	13 00.1	3.3	78.0	13 24.6	5.4	78.5
14	11 38.3	3.2	75.7	12 07.5	1.1	76.1	12 35.9	1.0	76.5	13 03.4	3.1	77.0	13 30.0	5.1	77.4
15	11 35.1−	3.4	74.7	12 06.4−	1.3	75.1	12 36.9+	0.7	75.5	13 06.5+	2.8	76.0	13 35.1+	4.9	76.4
16	11 31.7	3.6	73.7	12 05.1	1.6	74.1	12 37.6	0.5	74.5	13 09.3	2.5	74.9	13 40.0	4.6	75.4
17	11 28.1	3.8	72.6	12 03.5	1.8	73.0	12 38.1	0.2	73.5	13 11.8	2.3	73.9	13 44.6	4.4	74.4
18	11 24.3	4.1	71.6	12 01.7	2.0	72.0	12 38.3+	0.1	72.4	13 14.1	2.1	72.9	13 49.0	4.1	73.3
19	11 20.2	4.2	70.6	11 59.7	2.2	71.0	12 38.4−	0.2	71.4	13 16.2	1.8	71.8	13 53.1	3.9	72.3
20	11 16.0−	4.5	69.6	11 57.5−	2.5	70.0	12 38.2−	0.5	70.4	13 18.0+	1.6	70.8	13 57.0+	3.6	71.3
21	11 11.5	4.6	68.6	11 55.0	2.7	69.0	12 37.7	0.7	69.4	13 19.6	1.3	69.8	14 00.6	3.3	70.2
22	11 06.9	4.9	67.6	11 52.3	2.9	67.9	12 37.0	0.9	68.3	13 20.9	1.1	68.8	14 03.9	3.1	69.2
23	11 02.0	5.1	66.5	11 49.4	3.1	66.9	12 36.1	1.1	67.3	13 22.0	0.8	67.7	14 07.0	2.8	68.2
24	10 56.9	5.2	65.5	11 46.3	3.3	65.9	12 35.0	1.4	66.3	13 22.8	0.6	66.7	14 09.8	2.6	67.2
25	10 51.7−	5.5	64.5	11 43.0−	3.6	64.9	12 33.6−	1.6	65.3	13 23.4+	0.3	65.7	14 12.4+	2.3	66.1
26	10 46.2	5.7	63.5	11 39.4	3.7	63.9	12 32.0	1.9	64.2	13 23.7+	0.1	64.7	14 14.7	2.0	65.1
27	10 40.5	5.8	62.5	11 35.7	4.0	62.8	12 30.1	2.1	63.2	13 23.8−	0.2	63.6	14 16.7	1.8	64.1
28	10 34.7	6.1	61.5	11 31.7	4.2	61.8	12 28.0	2.3	62.2	13 23.6	0.4	62.6	14 18.5	1.4	63.0
29	10 28.6	6.2	60.5	11 27.5	4.4	60.8	12 25.7	2.5	61.2	13 23.2	0.7	61.6	14 19.9	1.3	62.0

Dec.	10° Hc	d	Z	12° Hc	d	Z	14° Hc	d	Z	16° Hc	d	Z	18° Hc	d	Z
0	11 48.9+	10.5	92.1	11 44.0+	12.7	92.5	11 38.3+	14.7	92.9	11 31.7+	16.8	93.4	11 24.3+	18.8	93.8
1	11 59.4	10.4	91.1	11 56.7	12.4	91.5	11 53.0	14.5	92.0	11 48.5	16.6	92.4	11 43.1	18.6	92.8
2	12 09.8	10.1	90.1	12 09.1	12.2	90.5	12 07.5	14.3	91.0	12 05.1	16.3	91.4	12 01.7	18.4	91.8
3	12 19.9	9.8	89.1	12 21.3	11.8	89.5	12 21.8	14.1	90.0	12 21.4	16.2	90.4	12 20.1	18.2	90.8
4	12 29.7	9.7	88.1	12 33.3	11.8	88.5	12 35.9	13.9	89.0	12 37.6	15.9	89.4	12 38.3	18.0	89.9
5	12 39.4+	9.4	87.1	12 45.1+	11.5	87.5	12 49.8+	13.6	88.0	12 53.5+	15.8	88.4	12 56.3+	17.8	88.9
6	12 48.8	9.2	86.1	12 56.6	11.3	86.5	13 03.4	13.4	87.0	13 09.3	15.4	87.4	13 14.1	17.6	87.9
7	12 58.0	9.0	85.0	13 07.9	11.1	85.5	13 16.8	13.2	86.0	13 24.7	15.3	86.4	13 31.7	17.3	86.9
8	13 07.0	8.7	84.0	13 19.0	10.8	84.5	13 30.0	12.9	85.0	13 40.0	15.0	85.5	13 49.0	17.1	85.9
9	13 15.7	8.5	83.0	13 29.8	10.6	83.5	13 42.9	12.7	84.0	13 55.0	14.8	84.5	14 06.1	16.8	85.0
10	13 24.2+	8.2	82.0	13 40.4+	10.3	82.5	13 55.6+	12.4	83.0	14 09.8+	14.5	83.5	14 22.9+	16.6	84.0
11	13 32.4	8.0	81.0	13 50.7	10.1	81.5	14 08.0	12.2	82.0	14 24.3	14.3	82.5	14 39.5	16.4	83.0
12	13 40.4	7.7	80.0	14 00.8	9.8	80.4	14 20.2	12.0	80.9	14 38.6	14.0	81.5	14 55.9	16.1	82.0
13	13 48.1	7.5	78.9	14 10.6	9.6	79.4	14 32.2	11.6	79.9	14 52.6	13.8	80.4	15 12.0	15.8	81.0
14	13 55.6	7.2	77.9	14 20.2	9.3	78.4	14 43.8	11.4	78.9	15 06.4	13.4	79.4	15 27.8	15.5	80.0
15	14 02.8+	7.0	76.9	14 29.5+	9.1	77.4	14 55.2+	11.2	77.9	15 19.8+	13.2	78.4	15 43.3+	15.3	79.0
16	14 09.8	6.7	75.9	14 38.6	8.8	76.4	15 06.4	10.8	76.9	15 33.0	13.0	77.4	15 58.6	15.0	78.0
17	14 16.5	6.4	74.8	14 47.4	8.5	75.3	15 17.2	10.6	75.9	15 46.0	12.6	76.4	16 13.6	14.7	77.0
18	14 22.9	6.2	73.8	14 55.9	8.2	74.3	15 27.8	10.3	74.8	15 58.6	12.4	75.4	16 28.3	14.4	76.0
19	14 29.1	5.9	72.8	15 04.1	8.0	73.3	15 38.1	10.0	73.8	16 11.0	12.1	74.4	16 42.7	14.2	74.9
20	14 35.0+	5.7	71.8	15 12.1+	7.7	72.3	15 48.1+	9.7	72.8	16 23.1+	11.7	73.3	16 56.9+	13.8	73.9
21	14 40.7	5.3	70.7	15 19.8	7.4	71.2	15 57.8	9.5	71.8	16 34.8	11.5	72.3	17 10.7	13.5	72.9
22	14 46.0	5.1	69.7	15 27.2	7.1	70.2	16 07.3	9.1	70.7	16 46.3	11.2	71.3	17 24.2	13.2	71.9
23	14 51.1	4.8	68.7	15 34.3	6.8	69.2	16 16.4	8.9	69.7	16 57.5	10.8	70.3	17 37.4	12.9	70.9
24	14 55.9	4.6	67.6	15 41.1	6.5	68.1	16 25.3	8.5	68.7	17 08.3	10.6	69.2	17 50.3	12.6	69.8
25	15 00.5+	4.2	66.6	15 47.6+	6.3	67.1	16 33.8+	8.2	67.7	17 18.9+	10.2	68.2	18 02.9+	12.2	68.8
26	15 04.7	4.0	65.6	15 53.9	5.9	66.1	16 42.0	8.0	66.6	17 29.1	9.9	67.2	18 15.1	11.9	67.8
27	15 08.7	3.7	64.5	15 59.8	5.7	65.0	16 50.0	7.6	65.6	17 39.0	9.6	66.1	18 27.0	11.6	66.7
28	15 12.4	3.4	63.5	16 05.5	5.3	64.0	16 57.6	7.3	64.5	17 48.6	9.3	65.1	18 38.6	11.2	65.7
29	15 15.8	3.2	62.5	16 10.8	5.1	63.0	17 04.9	7.0	63.5	17 57.9	8.9	64.1	18 49.8	10.9	64.7

0°			2°			4°			6°			8°			Dec.
Hc	d	Z	Hc	d	Z	Hc	d	Z	Hc	d	Z	Hc	d	Z	
12 00.0 − 0.1		90.0	11 59.6 − 2.3		90.4	11 58.2 − 4.4		90.8	11 56.0 − 6.5		91.3	11 52.9 − 8.7		91.7	0
11 59.9 − 0.3		91.0	11 57.3	2.5	91.4	11 53.8	4.6	91.9	11 49.5	6.8	92.3	11 44.2	8.8	92.7	1
11 59.6	0.6	92.0	11 54.8	2.7	92.5	11 49.2	4.8	92.9	11 42.7	6.9	93.3	11 35.4	9.1	93.7	2
11 59.0	0.8	93.1	11 52.1	2.9	93.5	11 44.4	5.0	93.9	11 35.8	7.2	94.3	11 26.3	9.2	94.7	3
11 58.2	1.0	94.1	11 49.2	3.1	94.5	11 39.4	5.3	94.9	11 28.6	7.3	95.3	11 17.1	9.5	95.7	4
11 57.2 − 1.2		95.1	11 46.1 − 3.4		95.5	11 34.1 − 5.5		95.9	11 21.3 − 7.6		96.3	11 07.6 − 9.7		96.7	5
11 56.0	1.4	96.1	11 42.7	3.5	96.5	11 28.6	5.6	97.0	11 13.7	7.8	97.4	10 57.9	9.9	97.7	6
11 54.6	1.7	97.2	11 39.2	3.8	97.6	11 23.0	5.9	98.0	11 05.9	8.0	98.4	10 48.0	10.0	98.7	7
11 52.9	1.9	98.2	11 35.4	4.0	98.6	11 17.1	6.1	99.0	10 57.9	8.2	99.4	10 38.0	10.3	99.8	8
11 51.0	2.1	99.2	11 31.4	4.2	99.6	11 11.0	6.3	100.0	10 49.7	8.4	100.4	10 27.7	10.4	100.8	9
11 48.9 − 2.3		100.2	11 27.2 − 4.4		100.6	11 04.7 − 6.5		101.0	10 41.3 − 8.5		101.4	10 17.3 − 10.7		101.8	10
11 46.6	2.6	101.2	11 22.8	4.7	101.6	10 58.2	6.7	102.0	10 32.8	8.8	102.4	10 06.6	10.8	102.8	11
11 44.0	2.7	102.3	11 18.1	4.8	102.7	10 51.5	6.9	103.0	10 24.0	8.9	103.4	9 55.8	11.0	103.8	12
11 41.3	3.0	103.3	11 13.3	5.0	103.7	10 44.6	7.1	104.1	10 15.1	9.2	104.4	9 44.8	11.1	104.8	13
11 38.3	3.4	104.3	11 08.3	5.3	104.7	10 37.5	7.3	105.1	10 05.9	9.3	105.4	9 33.7	11.4	105.7	14
11 35.1 − 3.4		105.3	11 03.0 − 5.4		105.7	10 30.2 − 7.5		106.1	9 56.6 − 9.5		106.4	9 22.3 − 11.4		106.7	15
11 31.7	3.6	106.3	10 57.6	5.7	106.7	10 22.7	7.7	107.1	9 47.1	9.7	107.4	9 10.9	11.7	107.7	16
11 28.1	3.8	107.4	10 51.9	5.8	107.7	10 15.0	7.8	108.1	9 37.4	9.8	108.4	8 59.2	11.8	108.7	17
11 24.3	4.1	108.4	10 46.1	6.1	108.7	10 07.2	8.1	109.1	9 27.6	10.0	109.4	8 47.4	12.0	109.7	18
11 20.2	4.2	109.4	10 40.0	6.2	109.8	9 59.1	8.2	110.1	9 17.6	10.2	110.4	8 35.4	12.1	110.7	19
11 16.0 − 4.5		110.4	10 33.8 − 6.5		110.8	9 50.9 − 8.4		111.1	9 07.4 − 10.4		111.4	8 23.3 − 12.3		111.7	20
11 11.5	4.6	111.4	10 27.3	6.6	111.8	9 42.5	8.6	112.1	8 57.0	10.5	112.4	8 11.0	12.4	112.7	21
11 06.9	4.9	112.4	10 20.7	6.8	112.8	9 33.9	8.7	113.1	8 46.5	10.6	113.4	7 58.6	12.6	113.7	22
11 02.0	5.1	113.5	10 13.9	7.0	113.8	9 25.2	8.9	114.1	8 35.9	10.9	114.4	7 46.0	12.7	114.7	23
10 56.9	5.2	114.5	10 06.9	7.2	114.8	9 16.3	9.1	115.1	8 25.0	10.9	115.4	7 33.3	12.8	115.7	24
10 51.7 − 5.5		115.5	9 59.7 − 7.3		115.8	9 07.2 − 9.3		116.1	8 14.1 − 11.1		116.4	7 20.5 − 13.0		116.6	25
10 46.2	5.7	116.5	9 52.4	7.6	116.8	8 57.9	9.4	117.1	8 03.0	11.3	117.4	7 07.5	13.1	117.6	26
10 40.5	5.8	117.5	9 44.8	7.7	117.8	8 48.5	9.6	118.1	7 51.7	11.4	118.4	6 54.4	13.2	118.6	27
10 34.7	6.1	118.5	9 37.1	7.9	118.8	8 38.9	9.7	119.1	7 40.3	11.5	119.4	6 41.2	13.3	119.6	28
10 28.6	6.2	119.5	9 29.2	8.1	119.8	8 29.2	9.9	120.1	7 28.8	11.7	120.4	6 27.9	13.4	120.6	29

10°			12°			14°			16°			18°			Dec.
Hc	d	Z	Hc	d	Z	Hc	d	Z	Hc	d	Z	Hc	d	Z	
11 48.9 − 10.7		92.1	11 44.0 − 12.8		92.5	11 38.3 − 14.9		92.9	11 31.7 − 17.0		93.4	11 24.3 − 19.0		93.8	0
11 38.2	11.0	93.1	11 31.2	13.1	93.5	11 23.4	15.1	93.9	11 14.7	17.1	94.3	11 05.3	19.2	94.7	1
11 27.2	11.2	94.1	11 18.1	13.2	94.5	11 08.3	15.3	94.9	10 57.6	17.4	95.3	10 46.1	19.4	95.7	2
11 16.0	11.3	95.1	11 04.9	13.4	95.5	10 53.0	15.5	95.9	10 40.2	17.5	96.3	10 26.7	19.5	96.7	3
11 04.7	11.6	96.1	10 51.5	13.7	96.5	10 37.5	15.7	96.9	10 22.7	17.7	97.3	10 07.2	19.8	97.6	4
10 53.1 − 11.8		97.1	10 37.8 − 13.8		97.5	10 21.8 − 15.9		97.9	10 05.0 − 17.9		98.2	9 47.4 − 19.8		98.6	5
10 41.3	11.9	98.1	10 24.0	14.0	98.5	10 05.9	16.0	98.8	9 47.1	18.0	99.2	9 27.6	20.1	99.5	6
10 29.4	12.1	99.1	10 10.0	14.2	99.5	9 49.9	16.2	99.8	9 29.1	18.2	100.2	9 07.5	20.1	100.5	7
10 17.3	12.3	100.1	9 55.8	14.3	100.5	9 33.7	16.4	100.8	9 10.9	18.4	101.1	8 47.4	20.4	101.4	8
10 05.0	12.5	101.1	9 41.5	14.5	101.5	9 17.3	16.5	101.8	8 52.5	18.5	102.1	8 27.0	20.4	102.4	9
9 52.5 − 12.7		102.1	9 27.0 − 14.7		102.4	9 00.8 − 16.7		102.8	8 34.0 − 18.7		103.1	8 06.6 − 20.6		103.3	10
9 39.8	12.8	103.1	9 12.3	14.9	103.4	8 44.1	16.8	103.7	8 15.3	18.7	104.0	7 46.0	20.7	104.3	11
9 27.0	13.0	104.1	8 57.4	15.0	104.4	8 27.3	17.0	104.7	7 56.6	19.0	105.0	7 25.3	20.8	105.2	12
9 14.0	13.2	105.1	8 42.4	15.1	105.4	8 10.3	17.1	105.7	7 37.6	19.0	105.9	7 04.5	21.0	106.2	13
9 00.8	13.3	106.1	8 27.3	15.3	106.4	7 53.2	17.2	106.6	7 18.6	19.2	106.9	6 43.5	21.1	107.1	14
8 47.5 − 13.5		107.0	8 12.0 − 15.4		107.3	7 36.0 − 17.4		107.6	6 59.4 − 19.2		107.8	6 22.4 − 21.1		108.1	15
8 34.0	13.6	108.0	7 56.6	15.6	108.3	7 18.6	17.5	108.6	6 40.2	19.4	108.8	6 01.3	21.3	109.0	16
8 20.4	13.8	109.0	7 41.0	15.7	109.3	7 01.1	17.6	109.5	6 20.8	19.5	109.8	5 40.0	21.3	109.9	17
8 06.6	13.9	110.0	7 25.3	15.8	110.3	6 43.5	17.7	110.5	6 01.3	19.6	110.7	5 18.7	21.5	110.9	18
7 52.7	14.1	111.0	7 09.5	16.0	111.2	6 25.8	17.9	111.5	5 41.7	19.7	111.7	4 57.2	21.5	111.8	19
7 38.6 − 14.2		112.0	6 53.5 − 16.1		112.2	6 07.9 − 17.9		112.4	5 22.0 − 19.8		112.6	4 35.7 − 21.6		112.8	20
7 24.4	14.3	112.9	6 37.4	16.1	113.2	5 50.0	18.0	113.4	5 02.2	19.8	113.5	4 14.1	21.6	113.7	21
7 10.1	14.4	113.9	6 21.3	16.3	114.1	5 32.0	18.1	114.3	4 42.4	19.9	114.5	3 52.5	21.7	114.6	22
6 55.7	14.6	114.9	6 05.0	16.4	115.1	5 13.9	18.2	115.3	4 22.5	20.1	115.4	3 30.8	21.8	115.6	23
6 41.1	14.6	115.9	5 48.6	16.5	116.1	4 55.7	18.3	116.2	4 02.4	20.0	116.4	3 09.0	21.8	116.5	24
6 26.5 − 14.8		116.9	5 32.1 − 16.6		117.0	4 37.4 − 18.4		117.2	3 42.4 − 20.1		117.3	2 47.2 − 21.9		117.4	25
6 11.7	14.9	117.8	5 15.5	16.7	118.0	4 19.0	18.4	118.2	3 22.3	20.2	118.3	2 25.3	21.9	118.4	26
5 56.8	15.0	118.8	4 58.8	16.7	119.0	4 00.6	18.6	119.1	3 02.1	20.3	119.2	2 03.4	21.9	119.3	27
5 41.8	15.1	119.8	4 42.1	16.9	119.9	3 42.0	18.5	120.1	2 41.8	20.2	120.2	1 41.5	22.0	120.2	28
5 26.7	15.2	120.8	4 25.2	16.9	120.9	3 23.5	18.6	121.0	2 21.6	20.3	121.1	1 19.5	22.0	121.2	29

Dec.	20° Hc	d	Z	22° Hc	d	Z	24° Hc	d	Z	26° Hc	d	Z	28° Hc	d	Z
0	11 16.0	+20.8	94.2	11 06.9	+22.8	94.6	10 56.9	+24.8	94.9	10 46.2	+26.7	95.3	10 34.7	+28.6	95.7
1	11 36.8	20.7	93.2	11 29.7	22.6	93.6	11 21.7	24.6	94.0	11 12.9	26.5	94.4	11 03.3	28.4	94.8
2	11 57.5	20.4	92.2	11 52.3	22.5	92.7	11 46.3	24.4	93.1	11 39.4	26.4	93.5	11 31.7	28.2	93.9
3	12 17.9	20.3	91.3	12 14.8	22.2	91.7	12 10.7	24.3	92.1	12 05.8	26.2	92.6	11 59.9	28.1	93.0
4	12 38.2	20.0	90.3	12 37.0	22.1	90.8	12 35.0	24.0	91.2	12 32.0	25.9	91.7	12 28.0	27.9	92.1
5	12 58.2	+19.8	89.3	12 59.1	+21.8	89.8	12 59.0	+23.8	90.3	12 57.9	+25.8	90.7	12 55.9	+27.7	91.2
6	13 18.0	19.6	88.4	13 20.9	21.6	88.9	13 22.8	23.6	89.3	13 23.7	25.6	89.8	13 23.6	27.5	90.3
7	13 37.6	19.4	87.4	13 42.5	21.4	87.9	13 46.4	23.4	88.4	13 49.3	25.4	88.9	13 51.1	27.3	89.4
8	13 57.0	19.1	86.4	14 03.9	21.2	86.9	14 09.8	23.2	87.4	14 14.7	25.1	87.9	14 18.5	27.0	88.4
9	14 16.1	18.9	85.5	14 25.1	20.9	86.0	14 33.0	22.9	86.5	14 39.8	24.9	87.0	14 45.5	26.9	87.5
10	14 35.0	+18.7	84.5	14 46.0	+20.7	85.0	14 55.9	+22.8	85.5	15 04.7	+24.7	86.1	15 12.4	+26.7	86.6
11	14 53.7	18.4	83.5	15 06.7	20.5	84.0	15 18.7	22.4	84.6	15 29.4	24.5	85.1	15 39.1	26.4	85.7
12	15 12.1	18.1	82.5	15 27.2	20.2	83.1	15 41.1	22.2	83.6	15 53.9	24.2	84.2	16 05.5	26.2	84.7
13	15 30.2	17.9	81.5	15 47.4	19.9	82.1	16 03.3	22.0	82.6	16 18.1	23.9	83.2	16 31.7	25.9	83.8
14	15 48.1	17.6	80.5	16 07.3	19.6	81.1	16 25.3	21.6	81.7	16 42.0	23.7	82.3	16 57.6	25.6	82.9
15	16 05.7	+17.4	79.5	16 26.9	+19.4	80.1	16 46.9	+21.4	80.7	17 05.7	+23.4	81.3	17 23.2	+25.4	81.9
16	16 23.1	17.0	78.5	16 46.3	19.1	79.1	17 08.3	21.2	79.7	17 29.1	23.1	80.3	17 48.6	25.1	81.0
17	16 40.1	16.8	77.5	17 05.4	18.8	78.1	17 29.5	20.8	78.7	17 52.2	22.9	79.4	18 13.7	24.9	80.0
18	16 56.9	16.4	76.5	17 24.2	18.5	77.1	17 50.3	20.5	77.8	18 15.1	22.5	78.4	18 38.6	24.5	79.0
19	17 13.3	16.2	75.5	17 42.7	18.2	76.1	18 10.8	20.3	76.8	18 37.6	22.3	77.4	19 03.1	24.2	78.1
20	17 29.5	+15.9	74.5	18 00.9	+17.9	75.1	18 31.1	+19.9	75.8	18 59.9	+21.9	76.4	19 27.3	+23.9	77.1
21	17 45.4	15.5	73.5	18 18.8	17.6	74.1	18 51.0	19.6	74.8	19 21.8	21.6	75.5	19 51.2	23.6	76.1
22	18 00.9	15.2	72.5	18 36.4	17.2	73.1	19 10.6	19.2	73.8	19 43.4	21.3	74.5	20 14.8	23.3	75.2
23	18 16.1	15.0	71.5	18 53.6	17.0	72.1	19 29.8	19.0	72.8	20 04.7	20.9	73.5	20 38.1	23.0	74.2
24	18 31.1	14.5	70.5	19 10.6	16.6	71.1	19 48.8	18.6	71.8	20 25.6	20.6	72.5	21 01.1	22.6	73.2
25	18 45.6	+14.3	69.4	19 27.2	+16.2	70.1	20 07.4	+18.2	70.8	20 46.2	+20.3	71.5	21 23.7	+22.2	72.2
26	18 59.9	13.9	68.4	19 43.4	15.9	69.1	20 25.6	17.9	69.7	21 06.5	19.9	70.5	21 45.9	21.9	71.2
27	19 13.8	13.5	67.4	19 59.3	15.5	68.0	20 43.5	17.6	68.7	21 26.4	19.5	69.4	22 07.8	21.5	70.2
28	19 27.3	13.2	66.3	20 14.8	15.2	67.0	21 01.1	17.1	67.7	21 45.9	19.1	68.4	22 29.3	21.1	69.2
29	19 40.5	12.9	65.3	20 30.0	14.8	66.0	21 18.2	16.8	66.7	22 05.0	18.8	67.4	22 50.4	20.8	68.2

Dec.	30° Hc	d	Z	32° Hc	d	Z	34° Hc	d	Z	36° Hc	d	Z	38° Hc	d	Z
0	10 22.4	+30.4	96.1	10 09.3	+32.3	96.4	9 55.5	+34.0	96.8	9 41.0	+35.7	97.1	9 25.8	+37.4	97.5
1	10 52.8	30.3	95.2	10 41.6	32.1	95.6	10 29.5	33.9	95.9	10 16.7	35.6	96.3	10 03.2	37.2	96.7
2	11 23.1	30.1	94.3	11 13.7	31.9	94.7	11 03.4	33.7	95.1	10 52.3	35.5	95.5	10 40.4	37.2	95.9
3	11 53.2	30.0	93.4	11 45.6	31.8	93.8	11 37.1	33.6	94.3	11 27.8	35.3	94.7	11 17.6	37.0	95.1
4	12 23.2	29.7	92.5	12 17.4	31.6	93.0	12 10.7	33.4	93.4	12 03.1	35.2	93.8	11 54.6	36.9	94.3
5	12 52.9	+29.6	91.7	12 49.0	+31.5	92.1	12 44.1	+33.3	92.6	12 38.3	+35.0	93.0	12 31.5	+36.8	93.5
6	13 22.5	29.5	90.8	13 20.5	31.2	91.2	13 17.4	33.1	91.7	13 13.3	34.9	92.2	13 08.3	36.6	92.6
7	13 52.0	29.2	89.9	13 51.7	31.1	90.4	13 50.5	32.9	90.8	13 48.2	34.7	91.3	13 44.9	36.4	91.8
8	14 21.2	29.0	89.0	14 22.8	30.9	89.5	14 23.4	32.7	90.0	14 22.9	34.5	90.5	14 21.3	36.2	91.0
9	14 50.2	28.8	88.1	14 53.7	30.7	88.6	14 56.1	32.5	89.1	14 57.4	34.3	89.7	14 57.5	36.1	90.2
10	15 19.0	+28.5	87.1	15 24.4	+30.4	87.7	15 28.6	+32.3	88.2	15 31.7	+34.1	88.8	15 33.6	+35.9	89.4
11	15 47.5	28.4	86.2	15 54.8	30.3	86.8	16 00.9	32.1	87.4	16 05.8	34.0	87.9	16 09.5	35.7	88.5
12	16 15.9	28.1	85.3	16 25.1	30.0	85.9	16 33.0	31.9	86.5	16 39.8	33.7	87.1	16 45.2	35.5	87.7
13	16 44.0	27.9	84.4	16 55.1	29.8	85.0	17 04.9	31.7	85.6	17 13.5	33.5	86.2	17 20.7	35.3	86.8
14	17 11.9	27.6	83.5	17 24.9	29.5	84.1	17 36.6	31.4	84.7	17 47.0	33.2	85.4	17 56.0	35.1	86.0
15	17 39.5	+27.3	82.5	17 54.4	+29.3	83.2	18 08.0	+31.1	83.8	18 20.2	+33.0	84.5	18 31.1	+34.8	85.1
16	18 06.8	27.1	81.6	18 23.7	29.0	82.3	18 39.1	30.9	82.9	18 53.2	32.8	83.6	19 05.9	34.6	84.3
17	18 33.9	26.8	80.7	18 52.7	28.7	81.3	19 10.0	30.7	82.0	19 26.0	32.5	82.7	19 40.5	34.3	83.4
18	19 00.7	26.5	79.7	19 21.4	28.4	80.4	19 40.7	30.3	81.1	19 58.5	32.2	81.8	20 14.8	34.1	82.5
19	19 27.2	26.2	78.8	19 49.8	28.2	79.5	20 11.0	30.1	80.2	20 30.7	32.0	80.9	20 48.9	33.8	81.7
20	19 53.4	+25.9	77.8	20 18.0	+27.8	78.5	20 41.1	+29.8	79.3	21 02.7	+31.6	80.0	21 22.7	+33.5	80.8
21	20 19.3	25.5	76.9	20 45.8	27.6	77.6	21 10.9	29.4	78.3	21 34.3	31.4	79.1	21 56.2	33.3	79.9
22	20 44.8	25.3	75.9	21 13.4	27.2	76.6	21 40.3	29.2	77.4	22 05.7	31.1	78.2	22 29.5	32.9	79.0
23	21 10.1	24.9	74.9	21 40.6	26.8	75.7	22 09.5	28.8	76.5	22 36.8	30.7	77.3	23 02.4	32.6	78.1
24	21 35.0	24.6	73.9	22 07.4	26.6	74.7	22 38.3	28.5	75.5	23 07.5	30.4	76.3	23 35.0	32.3	77.2
25	21 59.6	+24.2	73.0	22 34.0	+26.2	73.7	23 06.8	+28.1	74.6	23 37.9	+30.1	75.4	24 07.3	+32.0	76.2
26	22 23.8	23.9	72.0	23 00.2	25.8	72.8	23 34.9	27.8	73.6	24 08.0	29.7	74.4	24 39.3	31.6	75.3
27	22 47.7	23.5	71.0	23 26.0	25.4	71.8	24 02.7	27.4	72.6	24 37.7	29.3	73.5	25 10.9	31.2	74.4
28	23 11.2	23.1	70.0	23 51.4	25.1	70.8	24 30.1	27.0	71.6	25 07.0	29.0	72.5	25 42.1	30.9	73.4
29	23 34.3	22.7	69.0	24 16.5	24.7	69.8	24 57.1	26.7	70.7	25 36.0	28.6	71.6	26 13.0	30.5	72.5

20°			22°			24°			26°			28°			Dec.
Hc	d	Z	Hc	d	Z	Hc	d	Z	Hc	d	Z	Hc	d	Z	
11 16.0 -21.0		94.2	11 06.9 -23.0		94.6	10 56.9 -24.9		94.9	10 46.2 -26.8		95.3	10 34.7 -28.7		95.7	0
10 55.0 21.0		95.1	10 43.9 23.2		95.5	10 32.0 25.1		95.9	10 19.4 27.0		96.2	10 06.0 28.9		96.6	1
10 33.8 21.4		96.1	10 20.7 23.3		96.4	10 06.9 25.2		96.8	9 52.4 27.2		97.1	9 37.1 29.0		97.5	2
10 12.4 21.5		97.0	9 57.4 23.5		97.4	9 41.7 25.4		97.7	9 25.2 27.3		98.0	9 08.1 29.2		98.4	3
9 50.9 21.7		98.0	9 33.9 23.6		98.3	9 16.3 25.6		98.6	8 57.9 27.4		98.9	8 38.9 29.2		99.3	4
9 29.2 -21.8		98.9	9 10.3 -23.8		99.2	8 50.7 -25.7		99.5	8 30.5 -27.5		99.8	8 09.7 -29.4		100.1	5
9 07.4 22.0		99.9	8 46.5 23.9		100.2	8 25.0 25.8		100.5	8 03.0 27.7		100.7	7 40.3 29.5		101.0	6
8 45.4 22.1		100.8	8 22.6 24.0		101.1	7 59.2 25.9		101.4	7 35.3 27.8		101.6	7 10.8 29.6		101.9	7
8 23.3 22.3		101.7	7 58.6 24.2		102.0	7 33.3 26.0		102.3	7 07.5 27.8		102.5	6 41.2 29.6		102.8	8
8 01.0 22.4		102.7	7 34.4 24.3		102.9	7 07.3 26.2		103.2	6 39.7 28.0		103.4	6 11.6 29.8		103.6	9
7 38.6 -22.5		103.6	7 10.1 -24.4		103.9	6 41.1 -26.2		104.1	6 11.7 -28.1		104.3	5 41.8 -29.8		104.5	10
7 16.1 22.6		104.5	6 45.7 24.6		104.8	6 14.9 26.3		105.0	5 43.6 28.1		105.2	5 12.0 29.9		105.4	11
6 53.5 22.7		105.5	6 21.3 24.6		105.7	5 48.6 26.4		105.9	5 15.5 28.2		106.1	4 42.1 30.0		106.3	12
6 30.8 22.9		106.4	5 56.7 24.7		106.6	5 22.2 26.5		106.8	4 47.3 28.3		107.0	4 12.1 30.1		107.1	13
6 07.9 22.9		107.3	5 32.0 24.8		107.5	4 55.7 26.6		107.7	4 19.0 28.3		107.9	3 42.0 30.0		108.0	14
5 45.0 -23.0		108.3	5 07.2 -24.8		108.4	4 29.1 -26.7		108.6	3 50.7 -28.4		108.7	3 12.0 -30.2		108.9	15
5 22.0 23.1		109.2	4 42.4 24.9		109.4	4 02.4 26.6		109.5	3 22.3 28.5		109.6	2 41.8 30.1		109.7	16
4 58.9 23.2		110.1	4 17.5 25.0		110.3	3 35.8 26.8		110.4	2 53.8 28.5		110.5	2 11.7 30.2		110.6	17
4 35.7 23.2		111.0	3 52.5 25.0		111.2	3 09.0 26.8		111.3	2 25.3 28.5		111.4	1 41.5 30.2		111.5	18
4 12.5 23.3		112.0	3 27.5 25.1		112.1	2 42.2 26.8		112.2	1 56.8 28.5		112.3	1 11.3 30.3		112.3	19
3 49.2 -23.4		112.9	3 02.4 -25.2		113.0	2 15.4 -26.9		113.1	1 28.3 -28.6		113.2	0 41.0 -30.2		113.2	20
3 25.8 23.4		113.8	2 37.2 25.1		113.9	1 48.5 26.9		114.0	0 59.7 28.6		114.0	0 10.8 -30.3		114.1	21
3 02.4 23.5		114.7	2 12.1 25.2		114.8	1 21.6 26.9		114.9	0 31.1 28.6		114.9	0 19.5 +30.2		65.1	22
2 38.9 23.5		115.7	1 46.9 25.3		115.7	0 54.7 26.9		115.8	0 02.5 -28.6		115.8	0 49.7 30.2		64.2	23
2 15.4 23.6		116.6	1 21.6 25.2		116.6	0 27.8 27.0		116.7	0 26.1 +28.6		63.3	1 19.9 30.2		63.4	24
1 51.8 -23.5		117.5	0 56.4 -25.3		117.5	0 00.8 -27.0		117.6	0 54.7 +28.5		62.5	1 50.1 +30.2		62.6	25
1 28.3 23.7		118.4	0 31.1 25.3		118.5	0 26.1 +26.9		61.5	1 23.2 28.6		61.6	2 20.3 30.2		61.6	26
1 04.6 23.6		119.3	0 05.8 -25.3		119.4	0 53.0 26.9		60.6	1 51.8 28.5		60.7	2 50.5 30.1		60.8	27
0 41.0 23.6		120.3	0 19.5 +25.2		59.7	1 19.9 26.9		59.8	2 20.3 28.5		59.8	3 20.6 30.1		59.9	28
0 17.4 -23.6		121.2	0 44.7 25.3		58.8	1 46.8 26.9		58.9	2 48.8 28.5		58.9	3 50.7 30.0		59.0	29

30°			32°			34°			36°			38°			Dec.
Hc	d	Z	Hc	d	Z	Hc	d	Z	Hc	d	Z	Hc	d	Z	
10 22.4 -30.6		96.1	10 09.3 -32.3		96.4	9 55.5 -34.1		96.8	9 41.0 -35.8		97.1	9 25.8 -37.5		97.5	0
9 51.8 30.7		96.9	9 37.0 32.5		97.3	9 21.4 34.2		97.6	9 05.2 36.0		97.9	8 48.3 37.6		98.2	1
9 21.1 30.8		97.8	9 04.5 32.6		98.1	8 47.2 34.4		98.4	8 29.2 36.0		98.7	8 10.7 37.7		99.0	2
8 50.3 31.0		98.7	8 31.9 32.8		99.0	8 12.8 34.4		99.3	7 53.2 36.1		99.6	7 33.0 37.8		99.8	3
8 19.3 31.0		99.5	7 59.1 32.8		99.8	7 38.4 34.6		100.1	7 17.1 36.3		100.4	6 55.2 37.8		100.6	4
7 48.3 -31.2		100.4	7 26.3 -32.9		100.7	7 03.8 -34.6		100.9	6 40.8 -36.3		101.2	6 17.4 -37.9		101.4	5
7 17.1 31.3		101.3	6 53.4 33.0		101.5	6 29.2 34.7		101.7	6 04.5 36.3		102.0	5 39.5 38.0		102.2	6
6 45.8 31.3		102.1	6 20.4 33.1		102.4	5 54.5 34.8		102.6	5 28.2 36.5		102.8	5 01.5 38.1		102.9	7
6 14.5 31.5		103.0	5 47.3 33.2		103.2	5 19.7 34.8		103.4	4 51.7 36.4		103.6	4 23.4 38.0		103.7	8
5 43.0 31.5		103.8	5 14.1 33.2		104.0	4 44.9 34.9		104.2	4 15.3 36.6		104.4	3 45.4 38.2		104.5	9
5 11.5 -31.6		104.7	4 40.9 -33.4		104.9	4 10.0 -35.0		105.0	3 38.7 -36.6		105.2	3 07.2 -38.1		105.3	10
4 39.9 31.6		105.6	4 07.6 33.3		105.7	3 35.0 35.0		105.8	3 02.1 36.6		105.9	2 29.1 38.2		106.0	11
4 08.3 31.7		106.4	3 34.3 33.4		106.5	3 00.0 35.0		106.6	2 25.5 36.6		106.7	1 50.9 38.2		106.8	12
3 36.6 31.7		107.3	3 00.9 33.4		107.4	2 25.0 35.1		107.5	1 48.9 36.7		107.5	1 12.7 38.2		107.6	13
3 04.9 31.8		108.1	2 27.5 33.5		108.2	1 49.9 35.1		108.3	1 12.2 36.6		108.3	0 34.5 -38.3		108.4	14
2 33.1 31.8		109.0	1 54.0 -33.5		109.0	1 14.8 -35.1		109.1	0 35.6 -36.7		109.1	0 03.8 +38.2		70.9	15
2 01.3 31.9		109.8	1 20.5 33.5		109.9	0 39.7 35.1		109.9	0 01.1 +36.7		70.1	0 42.0 38.2		70.1	16
1 29.4 31.9		110.7	0 47.0 33.5		110.7	0 04.6 -35.1		110.7	0 37.8 36.7		69.3	1 20.2 38.2		69.3	17
0 57.5 31.8		111.5	0 13.5 -33.5		111.5	0 30.5 +35.1		68.5	1 14.5 36.6		68.5	1 58.4 38.2		68.6	18
0 25.7 -31.9		112.3	0 20.0 +33.5		67.6	1 05.6 35.1		67.7	1 51.1 36.7		67.7	2 36.6 38.1		67.8	19
0 06.2 +31.9		66.8	0 53.5 +33.5		66.8	1 40.7 +35.1		66.9	2 27.8 +36.6		66.9	3 14.7 +38.1		67.0	20
0 38.1 31.9		66.0	1 27.0 33.5		66.0	2 15.8 35.0		66.0	3 04.4 36.6		66.1	3 52.8 38.1		66.2	21
1 10.0 31.8		65.1	2 00.5 33.4		65.2	2 50.8 35.0		65.2	3 41.0 36.5		65.3	4 30.9 38.0		65.5	22
1 41.8 31.8		64.3	2 33.9 33.4		64.3	3 25.8 35.0		64.4	4 17.5 36.5		64.5	5 08.9 38.0		64.7	23
2 13.7 31.8		63.4	3 07.3 33.4		63.5	4 00.8 34.9		63.6	4 54.0 36.4		63.7	5 46.9 37.9		63.9	24
2 45.5 +31.8		62.6	3 40.7 +33.3		62.7	4 35.7 +34.8		62.8	5 30.4 +36.4		63.0	6 24.8 +37.8		63.1	25
3 17.3 31.7		61.7	4 14.0 33.3		61.8	5 10.5 34.8		62.0	6 06.8 36.3		62.2	7 02.6 37.8		62.4	26
3 49.0 31.7		60.9	4 47.3 33.2		61.0	5 45.3 34.8		61.2	6 43.1 36.2		61.3	7 40.4 37.7		61.6	27
4 20.7 31.6		60.0	5 20.5 33.2		60.2	6 20.1 34.6		60.3	7 19.3 36.1		60.5	8 18.1 37.5		60.8	28
4 52.3 31.6		59.2	5 53.7 33.0		59.3	6 54.7 34.6		59.5	7 55.4 36.0		59.7	8 55.6 37.5		60.0	29

Dec.	40° Hc	d	Z	42° Hc	d	Z	44° Hc	d	Z	46° Hc	d	Z	48° Hc	d	Z
0	9 09.9	+39.0	97.8	8 53.3	+40.6	98.1	8 36.1	+42.1	98.4	8 18.2	+43.6	98.7	7 59.8	+45.0	99.0
1	9 48.9	38.9	97.0	9 33.9	40.5	97.3	9 18.2	42.0	97.7	9 01.8	43.5	98.0	8 44.8	44.9	98.3
2	10 27.8	38.8	96.2	10 14.4	40.4	96.6	10 00.2	42.0	97.0	9 45.3	43.4	97.3	9 29.7	44.9	97.6
3	11 06.6	38.7	95.5	10 54.8	40.3	95.8	10 42.2	41.8	96.2	10 28.7	43.4	96.6	10 14.6	44.7	97.0
4	11 45.3	38.5	94.7	11 35.1	40.1	95.1	11 24.0	41.7	95.5	11 12.1	43.2	95.9	10 59.3	44.7	96.3
5	12 23.8	+38.4	93.9	12 15.2	+40.1	94.3	12 05.7	+41.6	94.8	11 55.3	+43.1	95.2	11 44.0	+44.6	95.6
6	13 02.2	38.3	93.1	12 55.3	39.9	93.6	12 47.3	41.5	94.0	12 38.4	43.0	94.5	12 28.6	44.5	94.9
7	13 40.5	38.1	92.3	13 35.2	39.7	92.8	13 28.8	41.3	93.3	13 21.4	42.9	93.8	13 13.1	44.3	94.2
8	14 18.6	38.0	91.5	14 14.9	39.6	92.0	14 10.1	41.2	92.5	14 04.3	42.8	93.0	13 57.4	44.3	93.5
9	14 56.6	37.8	90.7	14 54.5	39.5	91.3	14 51.3	41.1	91.8	14 47.1	42.6	92.3	14 41.7	44.1	92.8
10	15 34.4	+37.6	89.9	15 34.0	+39.3	90.5	15 32.4	+40.9	91.0	15 29.7	+42.4	91.6	15 25.8	+44.0	92.1
11	16 12.0	37.4	89.1	16 13.3	39.1	89.7	16 13.3	40.8	90.3	16 12.1	42.4	90.9	16 09.8	43.8	91.4
12	16 49.4	37.3	88.3	16 52.4	38.9	88.9	16 54.1	40.5	89.5	16 54.5	42.1	90.1	16 53.6	43.7	90.7
13	17 26.7	37.0	87.5	17 31.3	38.8	88.1	17 34.6	40.4	88.7	17 36.6	42.0	89.4	17 37.3	43.5	90.0
14	18 03.7	36.8	86.6	18 10.1	38.5	87.3	18 15.0	40.2	88.0	18 18.6	41.8	88.6	18 20.8	43.4	89.3
15	18 40.5	+36.6	85.8	18 48.6	+38.3	86.5	18 55.2	+40.0	87.2	19 00.4	+41.7	87.9	19 04.2	+43.2	88.5
16	19 17.1	36.4	85.0	19 26.9	38.1	85.7	19 35.2	39.8	86.4	19 42.1	41.4	87.1	19 47.4	43.0	87.8
17	19 53.5	36.1	84.1	20 05.0	37.9	84.9	20 15.0	39.6	85.6	20 23.5	41.2	86.3	20 30.4	42.8	87.1
18	20 29.6	35.9	83.3	20 42.9	37.6	84.0	20 54.6	39.3	84.8	21 04.7	41.0	85.5	21 13.2	42.6	86.3
19	21 05.5	35.6	82.4	21 20.5	37.4	83.2	21 33.9	39.2	84.0	21 45.7	40.8	84.8	21 55.8	42.5	85.6
20	21 41.1	+35.4	81.6	21 57.9	+37.2	82.4	22 13.1	+38.8	83.2	22 26.5	+40.6	84.0	22 38.3	+42.1	84.8
21	22 16.5	35.0	80.7	22 35.1	36.8	81.5	22 51.9	38.6	82.3	23 07.1	40.3	83.2	23 20.4	42.0	84.0
22	22 51.5	34.8	79.8	23 11.9	36.6	80.6	23 30.5	38.4	81.5	23 47.4	40.0	82.4	24 02.4	41.7	83.2
23	23 26.3	34.5	78.9	23 48.5	36.3	79.8	24 08.9	38.0	80.7	24 27.4	39.8	81.6	24 44.1	41.5	82.5
24	24 00.8	34.1	78.0	24 24.8	36.0	78.9	24 46.9	37.8	79.8	25 07.2	39.5	80.7	25 25.6	41.2	81.7
25	24 34.9	+33.9	77.1	25 00.8	+35.6	78.0	25 24.7	+37.5	79.0	25 46.7	+39.3	79.9	26 06.8	+41.0	80.9
26	25 08.8	33.5	76.2	25 36.4	35.4	77.1	26 02.2	37.1	78.1	26 26.0	38.9	79.0	26 47.8	40.6	80.0
27	25 42.3	33.1	75.3	26 11.8	35.0	76.2	26 39.3	36.9	77.2	27 04.9	38.6	78.2	27 28.4	40.4	79.2
28	26 15.4	32.8	74.4	26 46.8	34.6	75.3	27 16.2	36.5	76.3	27 43.5	38.3	77.3	28 08.8	40.0	78.4
29	26 48.2	32.4	73.4	27 21.4	34.3	74.4	27 52.7	36.1	75.4	28 21.8	38.0	76.5	28 48.8	39.7	77.5

Dec.	50° Hc	d	Z	52° Hc	d	Z	54° Hc	d	Z	56° Hc	d	Z	58° Hc	d	Z
0	7 40.8	+46.4	99.2	7 21.3	+47.6	99.5	7 01.2	+48.9	99.8	6 40.6	+50.1	100.0	6 19.5	+51.2	100.2
1	8 27.2	46.2	98.6	8 08.9	47.6	98.9	7 50.1	48.9	99.2	7 30.7	50.0	99.4	7 10.7	51.1	99.7
2	9 13.4	46.3	98.0	8 56.5	47.5	98.3	8 38.9	48.8	98.6	8 20.7	49.9	98.9	8 01.8	51.2	99.2
3	9 59.7	46.1	97.3	9 44.0	47.5	97.7	9 27.7	48.7	98.0	9 10.6	50.0	98.3	8 53.0	51.0	98.6
4	10 45.8	46.1	96.7	10 31.5	47.4	97.0	10 16.4	48.7	97.4	10 00.6	49.8	97.8	9 44.0	51.0	98.1
5	11 31.9	+45.9	96.0	11 18.9	+47.3	96.4	11 05.1	+48.5	96.8	10 50.4	+49.8	97.2	10 35.0	+51.0	97.6
6	12 17.8	45.9	95.4	12 06.2	47.2	95.8	11 53.6	48.6	96.2	11 40.2	49.8	96.6	11 26.0	50.9	97.0
7	13 03.7	45.8	94.7	12 53.4	47.1	95.2	12 42.2	48.4	95.6	12 30.0	49.6	96.1	12 16.9	50.8	96.5
8	13 49.5	45.7	94.0	13 40.5	47.1	94.5	13 30.6	48.3	95.0	13 19.6	49.6	95.5	13 07.7	50.7	95.9
9	14 35.2	45.5	93.4	14 27.6	46.9	93.9	14 18.9	48.3	94.4	14 09.2	49.5	94.9	13 58.4	50.7	95.4
10	15 20.7	+45.4	92.7	15 14.5	+46.8	93.2	15 07.2	+48.1	93.8	14 58.7	+49.4	94.3	14 49.1	+50.6	94.8
11	16 06.1	45.3	92.0	16 01.3	46.7	92.6	15 55.3	48.1	93.2	15 48.1	49.3	93.7	15 39.7	50.6	94.3
12	16 51.4	45.2	91.3	16 48.0	46.6	91.9	16 43.4	47.9	92.5	16 37.4	49.2	93.1	16 30.3	50.4	93.7
13	17 36.6	45.0	90.6	17 34.6	46.5	91.3	17 31.3	47.8	91.9	17 26.6	49.2	92.5	17 20.7	50.3	93.2
14	18 21.6	44.9	89.9	18 21.1	46.3	90.6	18 19.1	47.7	91.3	18 15.8	48.9	91.9	18 11.0	50.3	92.6
15	19 06.5	+44.7	89.2	19 07.4	+46.1	89.9	19 06.8	+47.5	90.6	19 04.7	+48.9	91.3	19 01.3	+50.1	92.0
16	19 51.2	44.5	88.5	19 53.5	46.0	89.3	19 54.3	47.4	90.0	19 53.6	48.7	90.7	19 51.4	50.0	91.4
17	20 35.7	44.4	87.8	20 39.5	45.9	88.6	20 41.7	47.3	89.3	20 42.3	48.7	90.1	20 41.4	49.9	90.8
18	21 20.1	44.2	87.1	21 25.4	45.6	87.9	21 29.0	47.1	88.7	21 31.0	48.4	89.5	21 31.3	49.7	90.2
19	22 04.3	44.0	86.4	22 11.0	45.5	87.2	22 16.1	46.9	88.0	22 19.4	48.3	88.8	22 21.0	49.7	89.6
20	22 48.3	+43.7	85.6	22 56.5	+45.3	86.5	23 03.0	+46.8	87.3	23 07.7	+48.2	88.2	23 10.7	+49.4	89.0
21	23 32.0	43.6	84.9	23 41.8	45.1	85.8	23 49.8	46.5	86.6	23 55.9	48.0	87.5	24 00.1	49.4	88.4
22	24 15.6	43.3	84.1	24 26.9	44.9	85.0	24 36.3	46.4	85.9	24 43.9	47.8	86.9	24 49.5	49.1	87.8
23	24 58.9	43.1	83.4	25 11.8	44.7	84.3	25 22.7	46.2	85.2	25 31.7	47.6	86.2	25 38.6	49.0	87.2
24	25 42.0	42.9	82.6	25 56.5	44.4	83.6	26 08.9	46.0	84.5	26 19.3	47.4	85.5	26 27.6	48.9	86.5
25	26 24.9	+42.6	81.8	26 40.9	+44.2	82.8	26 54.9	+45.7	83.8	27 06.7	+47.3	84.8	27 16.5	+48.6	85.9
26	27 07.5	42.3	81.0	27 25.1	44.0	82.1	27 40.6	45.5	83.1	27 54.0	47.0	84.1	28 05.1	48.5	85.2
27	27 49.8	42.1	80.2	28 09.1	43.7	81.3	28 26.1	45.3	82.4	28 41.0	46.8	83.4	28 53.6	48.2	84.5
28	28 31.9	41.7	79.4	28 52.8	43.4	80.5	29 11.4	45.0	81.6	29 27.8	46.6	82.7	29 41.8	48.1	83.8
29	29 13.6	41.5	78.6	29 36.2	43.1	79.7	29 56.4	44.8	80.8	30 14.4	46.3	82.0	30 29.9	47.8	83.2

40°			42°			44°			46°			48°			Dec.
Hc	d	Z	Hc	d	Z	Hc	d	Z	Hc	d	Z	Hc	d	Z	
9 09.9	-39.1	97.8	8 53.3	-40.7	98.1	8 36.1	-42.2	98.4	8 18.2	-43.6	98.7	7 59.8	-45.0	99.0	0
8 30.8	39.2	98.5	8 12.6	40.7	98.8	7 53.9	42.3	99.1	7 34.6	43.7	99.4	7 14.8	45.2	99.6	1
7 51.6	39.3	99.3	7 31.9	40.9	99.3	7 11.6	42.3	99.8	6 50.9	43.8	100.1	6 29.6	45.1	100.3	2
7 12.3	39.4	100.1	6 51.0	40.9	100.3	6 29.3	42.4	100.5	6 07.1	43.8	100.8	5 44.5	45.2	101.0	3
6 32.9	39.4	100.8	6 10.1	40.9	101.1	5 46.9	42.4	101.3	5 23.3	43.9	101.5	4 59.3	45.3	101.6	4
5 53.5	-39.5	101.6	5 29.2	-41.1	101.8	5 04.5	-42.5	102.0	4 39.4	-43.9	102.1	4 14.0	-45.3	102.3	5
5 14.0	39.6	102.3	4 48.1	41.0	102.5	4 22.0	42.5	102.7	3 55.5	44.0	102.8	3 28.7	45.3	102.9	6
4 34.4	39.6	103.1	4 07.1	41.1	103.3	3 39.4	42.5	103.4	3 11.5	43.9	103.5	2 43.4	45.3	103.6	7
3 54.8	39.6	103.9	3 26.0	41.2	104.0	2 56.9	42.6	104.1	2 27.6	44.0	104.2	1 58.1	45.4	104.3	8
3 15.2	39.7	104.7	2 44.8	41.1	104.7	2 14.3	42.6	104.8	1 43.6	44.1	104.9	1 12.7	45.3	104.9	9
2 35.5	-39.6	105.4	2 03.7	-41.2	105.4	1 31.7	-42.7	105.5	0 59.5	-44.0	105.5	0 27.4	-45.4	105.6	10
1 55.9	39.8	106.1	1 22.5	41.2	106.2	0 49.0	42.6	106.2	0 15.5	-44.0	106.2	0 18.0	+45.4	73.8	11
1 16.1	39.7	106.9	0 41.3	41.2	106.9	0 06.4	-42.6	106.9	0 28.5	+44.0	73.1	1 03.4	45.3	73.1	12
0 36.4	-39.7	107.6	0 00.1	-41.2	107.6	0 36.2	+42.7	72.4	1 12.5	44.0	72.4	1 48.7	45.3	72.5	13
0 03.3	+39.8	71.6	0 41.1	+41.2	71.7	1 18.9	42.6	71.7	1 56.5	44.0	71.7	2 34.0	45.4	71.8	14
0 43.1	+39.7	70.9	1 22.3	+41.2	70.9	2 01.5	+42.6	71.0	2 40.5	+44.0	71.1	3 19.4	+45.3	71.2	15
1 22.8	39.7	70.1	2 03.5	41.2	70.2	2 44.1	42.5	70.3	3 24.5	43.9	70.4	4 04.7	45.2	70.5	16
2 02.5	39.7	69.4	2 44.7	41.1	69.5	3 26.6	42.5	69.6	4 08.4	43.9	69.7	4 49.9	45.2	69.8	17
2 42.2	39.6	68.6	3 25.8	41.1	68.7	4 09.2	42.5	68.9	4 52.3	43.9	69.0	5 35.1	45.2	69.2	18
3 21.8	39.7	67.9	4 06.9	41.1	68.0	4 51.7	42.5	68.2	5 36.2	43.8	68.3	6 20.3	45.1	68.5	19
4 01.5	+39.6	67.1	4 48.0	+41.0	67.3	5 34.2	+42.4	67.4	6 20.0	+43.8	67.6	7 05.4	+45.1	67.9	20
4 41.1	39.5	66.4	5 29.0	40.9	66.5	6 16.6	42.3	66.7	7 03.8	43.7	66.9	7 50.5	45.0	67.2	21
5 20.6	39.5	65.6	6 09.9	40.9	65.8	6 58.9	42.3	66.0	7 47.5	43.6	66.3	8 35.5	45.0	66.5	22
6 00.1	39.4	64.9	6 50.8	40.9	65.1	7 41.2	42.2	65.3	8 31.1	43.5	65.6	9 20.5	44.8	65.9	23
6 39.5	39.3	64.1	7 31.7	40.7	64.3	8 23.4	42.1	64.6	9 14.6	43.5	64.9	10 05.3	44.8	65.2	24
7 18.8	+39.3	63.4	8 12.4	+40.7	63.6	9 05.5	+42.1	63.9	9 58.1	+43.4	64.2	10 50.1	+44.7	64.5	25
7 58.1	39.2	62.6	8 53.1	40.6	62.9	9 47.6	42.0	63.1	10 41.5	43.3	63.5	11 34.8	44.6	63.8	26
8 37.3	39.1	61.8	9 33.7	40.5	62.1	10 29.6	41.8	62.4	11 24.8	43.2	62.8	12 19.4	44.5	63.1	27
9 16.4	39.0	61.1	10 14.2	40.4	61.4	11 11.4	41.8	61.7	12 08.0	43.1	62.1	13 03.9	44.4	62.4	28
9 55.4	38.9	60.3	10 54.6	40.3	60.6	11 53.2	41.6	61.0	12 51.1	43.0	61.3	13 48.3	44.2	61.8	29

50°			52°			54°			56°			58°			Dec.
Hc	d	Z	Hc	d	Z	Hc	d	Z	Hc	d	Z	Hc	d	Z	
7 40.8	-46.4	99.2	7 21.3	-47.7	99.5	7 01.2	-49.0	99.8	6 40.6	-50.1	100.0	6 19.5	-51.2	100.2	0
6 54.4	46.5	99.9	6 33.6	47.8	100.1	6 12.2	48.9	100.3	5 50.5	50.1	100.5	5 28.3	51.2	100.7	1
6 07.9	46.5	100.5	5 45.8	47.8	100.7	5 23.3	49.0	100.9	5 00.4	50.2	101.1	4 37.1	51.3	101.3	2
5 21.4	46.5	101.2	4 58.0	47.8	101.3	4 34.3	49.1	101.5	4 10.2	50.2	101.6	3 45.8	51.3	101.8	3
4 34.9	46.6	101.8	4 10.2	47.8	101.9	3 45.2	49.0	102.1	3 20.0	50.2	102.2	2 54.5	51.2	102.3	4
3 48.3	-46.6	102.4	3 22.4	-47.9	102.5	2 56.2	-49.1	102.7	2 29.8	-50.2	102.7	2 03.3	-51.4	102.8	5
3 01.7	46.6	103.1	2 34.5	47.9	103.2	2 07.1	49.0	103.2	1 39.6	50.2	103.3	1 11.9	51.3	103.3	6
2 15.1	46.6	103.7	1 46.6	47.9	103.8	1 18.1	49.1	103.8	0 49.4	-50.3	103.8	0 20.6	-51.3	103.9	7
1 28.5	46.7	104.3	0 58.7	47.9	104.4	0 29.0	-49.1	104.4	0 00.9	+50.2	75.6	0 30.7	+51.3	75.6	8
0 41.8	-46.6	104.9	0 10.8	-47.9	105.0	0 20.1	+49.1	75.0	0 51.1	50.2	75.1	1 22.0	51.3	75.1	9
0 04.8	+46.7	74.4	0 37.1	+47.8	74.4	1 09.2	+49.1	74.5	1 41.3	+50.2	74.5	2 13.3	+51.3	74.6	10
0 51.5	46.7	73.8	1 24.9	47.9	73.8	1 58.3	49.1	73.9	2 31.5	50.2	74.0	3 04.6	51.2	74.1	11
1 38.2	46.6	73.2	2 12.8	47.9	73.2	2 47.4	49.0	73.3	3 21.7	50.2	73.4	3 55.8	51.3	73.5	12
2 24.8	46.6	72.5	3 00.7	47.9	72.6	3 36.4	49.1	72.7	4 11.9	50.2	72.9	4 47.1	51.2	73.0	13
3 11.4	46.6	71.9	3 48.6	47.8	72.0	4 25.5	49.0	72.2	5 02.1	50.1	72.3	5 38.3	51.2	72.5	14
3 58.0	+46.6	71.3	4 36.4	+47.8	71.4	5 14.5	+48.9	71.6	5 52.2	+50.1	71.8	6 29.5	+51.2	72.0	15
4 44.6	46.5	70.6	5 24.2	47.7	70.8	6 03.4	49.0	71.0	6 42.3	50.1	71.2	7 20.7	51.1	71.4	16
5 31.1	46.5	70.0	6 11.9	47.8	70.2	6 52.4	48.9	70.4	7 32.4	50.0	70.7	8 11.8	51.1	70.9	17
6 17.6	46.4	69.4	6 59.7	47.6	69.6	7 41.3	48.8	69.8	8 22.4	49.9	70.1	9 02.9	51.1	70.4	18
7 04.0	46.4	68.7	7 47.3	47.6	69.0	8 30.1	48.8	69.2	9 12.3	50.0	69.5	9 54.0	51.0	69.9	19
7 50.4	+46.4	68.1	8 34.9	+47.6	68.4	9 18.9	+48.7	68.7	10 02.3	+49.8	69.0	10 45.0	+50.9	69.3	20
8 36.8	46.3	67.5	9 22.5	47.5	67.8	10 07.6	48.7	68.1	10 52.1	49.8	68.4	11 35.9	50.9	68.8	21
9 23.1	46.2	66.8	10 10.0	47.4	67.1	10 56.3	48.6	67.5	11 41.9	49.8	67.8	12 26.8	50.8	68.2	22
10 09.3	46.1	66.2	10 57.4	47.4	66.5	11 44.9	48.5	66.9	12 31.7	49.6	67.3	13 17.6	50.8	67.7	23
10 55.4	46.0	65.5	11 44.8	47.2	65.9	12 33.4	48.5	66.3	13 21.3	49.6	66.7	14 08.4	50.6	67.1	24
11 41.4	+46.0	64.9	12 32.0	+47.2	65.3	13 21.9	+48.3	65.7	14 10.9	+49.5	66.1	14 59.0	+50.6	66.6	25
12 27.4	45.8	64.2	13 19.2	47.1	64.6	14 10.2	48.3	65.1	15 00.4	49.4	65.5	15 49.6	50.5	66.0	26
13 13.2	45.8	63.5	14 06.3	47.0	64.0	14 58.5	48.2	64.4	15 49.8	49.3	64.9	16 40.1	50.4	65.5	27
13 59.0	45.6	62.9	14 53.3	46.8	63.3	15 46.7	48.0	63.8	16 39.1	49.2	64.3	17 30.5	50.3	64.9	28
14 44.6	45.6	62.2	15 40.1	46.8	62.7	16 34.7	48.0	63.2	17 28.3	49.1	63.8	18 20.8	50.3	64.3	29

LATITUDE **SAME** NAME   L.H.A. 102°, 258°

Dec.	0° Hc	d	Z	2° Hc	d	Z	4° Hc	d	Z	6° Hc	d	Z	8° Hc	d	Z
0	10 00.0 − 0.1	90.0		9 59.6 + 2.1	90.4		9 58.5 + 4.2	90.7		9 56.7 + 6.3	91.1		9 54.1 + 8.4	91.4	
1	9 59.9 0.3	89.0		10 01.7 1.8	89.3		10 02.7 4.0	89.7		10 03.0 6.0	90.0		10 02.5 8.2	90.4	
2	9 59.6 0.4	88.0		10 03.5 1.7	88.3		10 06.7 3.7	88.7		10 09.0 6.0	89.0		10 10.7 8.0	89.4	
3	9 59.2 0.7	87.0		10 05.2 1.5	87.3		10 10.4 3.6	87.7		10 15.0 5.7	88.0		10 18.7 7.8	88.4	
4	9 58.5 0.8	85.9		10 06.7 1.2	86.3		10 14.0 3.5	86.7		10 20.7 5.5	87.0		10 26.5 7.7	87.4	
5	9 57.7 − 1.0	84.9		10 07.9 + 1.1	85.3		10 17.5 + 3.2	85.6		10 26.2 + 5.3	86.0		10 34.2 + 7.4	86.4	
6	9 56.7 1.2	83.9		10 09.0 1.0	84.3		10 20.7 3.0	84.6		10 31.5 5.0	85.0		10 41.6 7.3	85.4	
7	9 55.5 1.4	82.9		10 10.0 0.7	83.2		10 23.7 2.8	83.6		10 36.7 4.9	84.0		10 48.9 7.1	84.4	
8	9 54.1 1.6	81.9		10 10.7 0.5	82.2		10 26.5 2.7	82.6		10 41.6 4.8	83.0		10 56.0 6.8	83.3	
9	9 52.5 1.7	80.9		10 11.2 0.4	81.2		10 29.2 2.4	81.6		10 46.4 4.6	81.9		11 02.8 6.7	82.3	
10	9 50.8 − 1.9	79.8		10 11.6 + 0.1	80.2		10 31.6 + 2.3	80.6		10 51.0 + 4.3	80.9		11 09.5 + 6.4	81.3	
11	9 48.9 2.1	78.8		10 11.7 0.0	79.2		10 33.9 2.1	79.5		10 55.3 4.2	79.9		11 15.9 6.3	80.3	
12	9 46.8 2.3	77.8		10 11.7 − 0.2	78.2		10 36.0 1.8	78.5		10 59.5 3.9	78.9		11 22.2 6.0	79.3	
13	9 44.5 2.5	76.8		10 11.5 0.4	77.1		10 37.8 1.7	77.5		11 03.4 3.8	77.9		11 28.2 5.8	78.3	
14	9 42.0 2.6	75.8		10 11.1 0.6	76.1		10 39.5 1.5	76.5		11 07.2 3.5	76.9		11 34.0 5.7	77.3	
15	9 39.4 − 2.9	74.8		10 10.5 − 0.8	75.1		10 41.0 + 1.3	75.5		11 10.7 + 3.3	75.8		11 39.7 + 5.4	76.2	
16	9 36.5 3.0	73.8		10 09.7 0.9	74.1		10 42.3 1.0	74.5		11 14.0 3.2	74.8		11 45.1 5.1	75.2	
17	9 33.5 3.1	72.8		10 08.8 1.2	73.1		10 43.3 0.9	73.4		11 17.2 2.9	73.8		11 50.2 5.0	74.2	
18	9 30.4 3.4	71.7		10 07.6 1.3	72.1		10 44.2 0.7	72.4		11 20.1 2.7	72.8		11 55.2 4.8	73.2	
19	9 27.0 3.5	70.7		10 06.3 1.5	71.1		10 44.9 0.5	71.4		11 22.8 2.5	71.8		12 00.0 4.5	72.2	
20	9 23.5 − 3.7	69.7		10 04.8 − 1.7	70.0		10 45.4 + 0.3	70.4		11 25.3 + 2.3	70.8		12 04.5 + 4.3	71.1	
21	9 19.8 3.9	68.7		10 03.1 1.9	69.0		10 45.7 0.1	69.4		11 27.6 2.1	69.7		12 08.8 4.1	70.1	
22	9 15.9 4.0	67.7		10 01.2 2.1	68.0		10 45.8 − 0.1	68.3		11 29.7 1.9	68.7		12 12.9 3.8	69.1	
23	9 11.9 4.2	66.7		9 59.1 2.3	67.0		10 45.7 0.4	67.3		11 31.6 1.6	67.7		12 16.7 3.7	68.1	
24	9 07.7 4.4	65.7		9 56.8 2.4	66.0		10 45.3 0.5	66.3		11 33.2 1.4	66.7		12 20.4 3.3	67.1	
25	9 03.3 − 4.6	64.7		9 54.4 − 2.7	65.0		10 44.8 − 0.7	65.3		11 34.6 + 1.3	65.7		12 23.7 + 3.2	66.0	
26	8 58.7 4.7	63.7		9 51.7 2.8	64.0		10 44.1 0.9	64.3		11 35.9 1.0	64.6		12 26.9 3.0	65.0	
27	8 54.0 4.8	62.6		9 48.9 3.0	62.9		10 43.2 1.1	63.3		11 36.9 0.8	63.6		12 29.9 2.7	64.0	
28	8 49.2 5.1	61.6		9 45.9 3.2	61.9		10 42.1 1.3	62.2		11 37.7 0.6	62.6		12 32.6 2.4	63.0	
29	8 44.1 5.2	60.6		9 42.7 3.3	60.9		10 40.8 1.5	61.2		11 38.3 0.3	61.6		12 35.0 2.3	61.9	

Dec.	10° Hc	d	Z	12° Hc	d	Z	14° Hc	d	Z	16° Hc	d	Z	18° Hc	d	Z
0	9 50.8 + 10.5	91.8		9 46.8 + 12.5	92.1		9 42.0 + 14.6	92.4		9 36.5 + 16.7	92.8		9 30.4 + 18.7	93.1	
1	10 01.3 10.3	90.8		9 59.3 12.4	91.1		9 56.6 14.5	91.5		9 53.2 16.5	91.8		9 49.1 18.5	92.2	
2	10 11.6 10.1	89.8		10 11.7 12.1	90.1		10 11.1 14.3	90.5		10 09.7 16.4	90.8		10 07.6 18.4	91.2	
3	10 21.7 9.9	88.8		10 23.9 12.1	89.1		10 25.4 14.1	89.5		10 26.1 16.2	89.8		10 26.0 18.2	90.2	
4	10 31.6 9.8	87.7		10 36.0 11.8	88.1		10 39.5 13.9	88.5		10 42.3 16.0	88.9		10 44.2 18.1	89.3	
5	10 41.4 + 9.6	86.7		10 47.8 + 11.7	87.1		10 53.4 + 13.8	87.5		10 58.3 + 15.7	87.9		11 02.3 + 17.8	88.3	
6	10 51.0 9.3	85.7		10 59.5 11.4	86.1		11 07.2 13.5	86.5		11 14.0 15.7	86.9		11 20.1 17.7	87.3	
7	11 00.3 9.2	84.7		11 10.9 11.3	85.1		11 20.7 13.3	85.5		11 29.7 15.4	85.9		11 37.8 17.4	86.3	
8	11 09.5 8.9	83.7		11 22.2 11.0	84.1		11 34.0 13.2	84.5		11 45.1 15.2	84.9		11 55.2 17.3	85.4	
9	11 18.4 8.8	82.7		11 33.2 10.9	83.1		11 47.2 12.9	83.5		12 00.3 15.0	83.9		12 12.5 17.0	84.4	
10	11 27.2 + 8.5	81.7		11 44.1 + 10.6	82.1		12 00.1 + 12.7	82.5		12 15.3 + 14.7	83.0		12 29.5 + 16.8	83.4	
11	11 35.7 8.4	80.7		11 54.7 10.4	81.1		12 12.8 12.5	81.5		12 30.0 14.6	82.0		12 46.3 16.7	82.4	
12	11 44.1 8.1	79.7		12 05.1 10.2	80.1		12 25.3 12.3	80.5		12 44.6 14.3	81.0		13 03.0 16.3	81.4	
13	11 52.2 7.9	78.7		12 15.3 10.0	79.1		12 37.6 12.0	79.5		12 58.9 14.1	80.0		13 19.3 16.2	80.4	
14	12 00.1 7.7	77.7		12 25.3 9.8	78.1		12 49.6 11.9	78.5		13 13.0 13.9	79.0		13 35.5 15.9	79.4	
15	12 07.8 + 7.5	76.6		12 35.1 + 9.5	77.1		13 01.5 + 11.5	77.5		13 26.9 + 13.7	78.0		13 51.4 + 15.7	78.5	
16	12 15.3 7.2	75.6		12 44.6 9.3	76.1		13 13.0 11.1	76.5		13 40.6 13.4	77.0		14 07.1 15.4	77.5	
17	12 22.5 7.0	74.6		12 53.9 9.1	75.1		13 24.4 11.1	75.5		13 54.0 13.1	76.0		14 22.5 15.2	76.5	
18	12 29.5 6.8	73.6		13 03.0 8.8	74.0		13 35.5 10.9	74.5		14 07.1 12.9	75.0		14 37.7 15.0	75.5	
19	12 36.3 6.6	72.6		13 11.8 8.6	73.0		13 46.4 10.6	73.5		14 20.0 12.7	74.0		14 52.7 14.6	74.5	
20	12 42.9 + 6.3	71.6		13 20.4 + 8.3	72.0		13 57.0 + 10.4	72.5		14 32.7 + 12.3	73.0		15 07.3 + 14.4	73.5	
21	12 49.2 6.1	70.5		13 28.7 8.1	71.0		14 07.4 10.1	71.5		14 45.0 12.2	71.9		15 21.7 14.2	72.5	
22	12 55.3 5.8	69.5		13 36.8 7.9	70.0		14 17.5 9.8	70.4		14 57.2 11.8	70.9		15 35.9 13.8	71.4	
23	13 01.1 5.6	68.5		13 44.7 7.6	68.9		14 27.3 9.6	69.4		15 09.0 11.6	69.9		15 49.7 13.6	70.4	
24	13 06.7 5.4	67.5		13 52.3 7.3	67.9		14 36.9 9.3	68.4		15 20.6 11.3	68.9		16 03.3 13.3	69.4	
25	13 12.1 + 5.1	66.5		13 59.6 + 7.1	66.9		14 46.2 + 9.1	67.4		15 31.9 + 11.0	67.9		16 16.6 + 13.0	68.4	
26	13 17.2 4.9	65.4		14 06.7 6.8	65.9		14 55.3 8.7	66.4		15 42.9 10.8	66.9		16 29.6 12.7	67.4	
27	13 22.1 4.6	64.4		14 13.5 6.6	64.9		15 04.0 8.5	65.3		15 53.7 10.4	65.8		16 42.3 12.4	66.4	
28	13 26.7 4.4	63.4		14 20.1 6.3	63.8		15 12.5 8.3	64.3		16 04.1 10.2	64.8		16 54.7 12.1	65.3	
29	13 31.1 4.1	62.4		14 26.4 6.0	62.8		15 20.8 7.9	63.3		16 14.3 9.8	63.8		17 06.8 11.8	64.3	

0°			2°			4°			6°			8°			Dec.
Hc	d	Z	Hc	d	Z	Hc	d	Z	Hc	d	Z	Hc	d	Z	
10 00.0	- 0.1	90.0	9 59.6	- 2.2	90.4	9 58.5	- 4.3	90.7	9 56.7	- 6.5	91.1	9 54.1	- 8.6	91.4	0
9 59.9	0.3	91.0	9 57.4	2.4	91.4	9 54.2	4.5	91.7	9 50.2	6.6	92.1	9 45.5	8.7	92.4	1
9 59.6	0.4	92.0	9 55.0	2.6	92.4	9 49.7	4.7	92.7	9 43.6	6.8	93.1	9 36.8	8.9	93.4	2
9 59.2	0.7	93.0	9 52.4	2.7	93.4	9 45.0	4.9	93.7	9 36.8	7.0	94.1	9 27.9	9.1	94.4	3
9 58.5	0.8	94.1	9 49.7	3.0	94.4	9 40.1	5.1	94.8	9 29.8	7.2	95.1	9 18.8	9.3	95.4	4
9 57.7	- 1.0	95.1	9 46.7	- 3.1	95.4	9 35.0	- 5.2	95.8	9 22.6	- 7.3	96.1	9 09.5	- 9.4	96.4	5
9 56.7	1.2	96.1	9 43.6	3.3	96.4	9 29.8	5.4	96.8	9 15.3	7.5	97.1	9 00.1	9.6	97.4	6
9 55.5	1.4	97.1	9 40.3	3.5	97.4	9 24.4	5.6	97.8	9 07.8	7.7	98.1	8 50.5	9.7	98.4	7
9 54.1	1.6	98.1	9 36.8	3.7	98.5	9 18.8	5.8	98.8	9 00.1	7.8	99.1	8 40.8	9.9	99.4	8
9 52.5	1.7	99.1	9 33.1	3.8	99.5	9 13.0	5.9	99.8	8 52.3	8.0	100.1	8 30.9	10.0	100.4	9
9 50.8	- 1.9	100.2	9 29.3	- 4.0	100.5	9 07.1	- 6.1	100.8	8 44.3	- 8.1	101.1	8 20.9	- 10.2	101.4	10
9 48.9	2.1	101.2	9 25.3	4.2	101.5	9 01.0	6.2	101.8	8 36.2	8.4	102.1	8.10.7	10.4	102.4	11
9 46.8	2.3	102.2	9 21.1	4.4	102.5	8 54.8	6.4	102.8	8 27.8	8.4	103.1	8 00.3	10.5	103.4	12
9 44.5	2.5	103.2	9 16.7	4.5	103.5	8 48.4	6.6	103.8	8 19.4	8.6	104.1	7 49.8	10.6	104.4	13
9 42.0	2.6	104.2	9 12.2	4.7	104.5	8 41.8	6.7	104.8	8 10.8	8.8	105.1	7 39.2	10.8	105.4	14
9 39.4	- 2.9	105.2	9 07.5	- 4.8	105.5	8 35.1	- 6.9	105.8	8 02.0	- 8.9	106.1	7 28.4	- 10.8	106.4	15
9 36.5	3.0	106.2	9 02.7	5.1	106.5	8 28.2	7.1	106.8	7 53.1	9.0	107.1	7 17.6	11.1	107.4	16
9 33.5	3.1	107.2	8 57.6	5.2	107.6	8 21.1	7.1	107.8	7 44.1	9.2	108.1	7 06.5	11.1	108.4	17
9 30.4	3.4	108.3	8 52.4	5.3	108.6	8 14.0	7.4	108.9	7 34.9	9.3	109.1	6 55.4	11.3	109.4	18
9 27.0	3.5	109.3	8 47.1	5.5	109.6	8 06.6	7.5	109.9	7 25.6	9.4	110.1	6 44.1	11.4	110.3	19
9 23.5	- 3.7	110.3	8 41.6	- 5.7	110.6	7 59.1	- 7.6	110.9	7 16.2	- 9.6	111.1	6 32.7	- 11.5	111.3	20
9 19.8	3.9	111.3	8 35.9	5.8	111.6	7 51.5	7.8	111.9	7 06.6	9.7	112.1	6 21.2	11.6	112.3	21
9 15.9	4.0	112.3	8 30.1	6.0	112.6	7 43.7	7.9	112.9	6 56.9	9.9	113.1	6 09.6	11.7	113.3	22
9 11.9	4.2	113.3	8 24.1	6.1	113.6	7 35.8	8.1	113.9	6 47.0	9.9	114.1	5 57.9	11.9	114.3	23
9 07.7	4.4	114.3	8 18.0	6.3	114.6	7 27.7	8.1	114.9	6 37.1	10.1	115.1	5 46.0	11.9	115.3	24
9 03.3	- 4.6	115.3	8 11.7	- 6.5	115.6	7 19.6	- 8.4	115.9	6 27.0	- 10.2	116.1	5 34.1	- 12.0	116.3	25
8 58.7	4.7	116.3	8 05.2	6.6	116.6	7 11.2	8.4	116.9	6 16.8	10.3	117.1	5 22.1	12.2	117.2	26
8 54.0	4.8	117.4	7 58.6	6.7	117.6	7 02.8	8.6	117.9	6 06.5	10.4	118.1	5 09.9	12.2	118.2	27
8 49.2	5.1	118.4	7 51.9	6.9	118.6	6 54.2	8.7	118.9	5 56.1	10.5	119.0	4 57.7	12.3	119.2	28
8 44.1	5.2	119.4	7 45.0	7.0	119.6	6 45.5	8.8	119.8	5 45.6	10.6	120.0	4 45.4	12.4	120.2	29

10°			12°			14°			16°			18°			Dec.
Hc	d	Z	Hc	d	Z	Hc	d	Z	Hc	d	Z	Hc	d	Z	
9 50.8	- 10.7	91.8	9 46.8	- 12.8	92.1	9 42.0	- 14.8	92.4	9 36.5	- 16.8	92.8	9 30.4	- 18.9	93.1	0
9 40.1	10.8	92.8	9 34.0	12.9	93.1	9 27.2	15.0	93.4	9 19.7	17.0	93.8	9 11.5	19.1	94.1	1
9 29.3	11.0	93.7	9 21.1	13.1	94.1	9 12.2	15.1	94.4	9 02.7	17.2	94.7	8 52.4	19.1	95.0	2
9 18.3	11.2	94.7	9 08.0	13.2	95.1	8 57.1	15.3	95.4	8 45.5	17.3	95.7	8 33.3	19.3	96.0	3
9 07.1	11.3	95.7	8 54.8	13.4	96.1	8 41.8	15.4	96.4	8 28.2	17.5	96.7	8 14.0	19.5	97.0	4
8 55.8	- 11.5	96.7	8 41.4	- 13.6	97.0	8 26.4	- 15.6	97.3	8 10.7	- 17.6	97.6	7 54.5	- 19.6	97.9	5
8 44.3	11.6	97.7	8 27.8	13.6	98.0	8 10.8	15.7	98.3	7 53.1	17.7	98.6	7 34.9	19.7	98.9	6
8 32.7	11.8	98.7	8 14.2	13.9	99.0	7 55.1	15.9	99.3	7 35.4	17.8	99.6	7 15.2	19.8	99.8	7
8 20.9	12.0	99.7	8 00.3	14.0	100.0	7 39.2	16.0	100.3	7 17.6	18.0	100.5	6 55.4	20.0	100.8	8
8 08.9	12.1	100.7	7 46.3	14.1	101.0	7 23.2	16.1	101.2	6 59.6	18.1	101.5	6 35.4	20.0	101.7	9
7 56.8	- 12.2	101.7	7 32.2	- 14.2	102.0	7 07.1	- 16.2	102.2	6 41.5	- 18.2	102.4	6 15.4	- 20.2	102.7	10
7 44.6	12.4	102.7	7 18.0	14.3	102.9	6 50.9	16.4	103.2	6 23.3	18.3	103.4	5 55.2	20.2	103.6	11
7 32.2	12.5	103.7	7 03.6	14.5	103.9	6 34.5	16.4	104.1	6 05.0	18.4	104.4	5 35.0	20.3	104.6	12
7 19.7	12.6	104.7	6 49.1	14.6	104.9	6 18.1	16.6	105.1	5 46.6	18.6	105.3	5 14.7	20.5	105.5	13
7 07.1	12.7	105.6	6 34.5	14.7	105.9	6 01.5	16.7	106.1	5 28.0	18.6	106.3	4 54.2	20.5	106.5	14
6 54.4	- 12.9	106.6	6 19.8	- 14.8	106.8	5 44.8	- 16.8	107.0	5 09.4	- 18.6	107.2	4 33.7	- 20.5	107.4	15
6 41.5	13.0	107.6	6 05.0	15.0	107.8	5 28.0	16.8	108.0	4 50.8	18.8	108.2	4 13.2	20.7	108.3	16
6 28.5	13.1	108.6	5 50.0	15.0	108.8	5 11.2	17.0	109.0	4 32.0	18.8	109.1	3 52.5	20.7	109.3	17
6 15.4	13.2	109.6	5 35.0	15.1	109.8	4 54.2	17.0	109.9	4 13.2	18.9	110.1	3 31.8	20.8	110.2	18
6 02.2	13.3	110.6	5 19.9	15.3	110.7	4 37.2	17.1	110.9	3 54.3	19.0	111.0	3 11.0	20.8	111.2	19
5 48.9	- 13.5	111.5	5 04.6	- 15.3	111.7	4 20.1	- 17.2	111.9	3 35.3	- 19.1	112.0	2 50.2	- 20.8	112.1	20
5 35.4	13.5	112.5	4 49.3	15.4	112.7	4 02.9	17.2	112.8	3 16.2	19.0	112.9	2 29.4	20.9	113.0	21
5 21.9	13.6	113.5	4 33.9	15.4	113.7	3 45.7	17.3	113.8	2 57.2	19.2	113.9	2 08.5	21.0	114.0	22
5 08.3	13.7	114.5	4 18.5	15.6	114.6	3 28.4	17.4	114.7	2 38.0	19.2	114.8	1 47.5	20.9	114.9	23
4 54.6	13.8	115.4	4 02.9	15.6	115.6	3 11.0	17.4	115.7	2 18.8	19.2	115.8	1 26.6	21.0	115.8	24
4 40.8	- 13.8	116.4	3 47.3	- 15.7	116.6	2 53.6	- 17.5	116.7	1 59.6	- 19.2	116.7	1 05.6	- 21.0	116.8	25
4 27.0	14.0	117.4	3 31.6	15.7	117.5	2 36.1	17.5	117.6	1 40.4	19.3	117.7	0 44.6	21.0	117.7	26
4 13.0	14.0	118.4	3 15.9	15.8	118.5	2 18.6	17.6	118.6	1 21.1	19.3	118.6	0 23.6	21.0	118.7	27
3 59.0	14.1	119.4	3 00.1	15.9	119.5	2 01.0	17.6	119.5	1 01.8	19.3	119.6	0 02.6	- 21.1	119.6	28
3 44.9	14.1	120.3	2 44.2	15.8	120.4	1 43.4	17.6	120.5	0 42.5	19.3	120.5	0 18.5	+ 21.0	59.5	29

LATITUDE **SAME** NAME · L.H.A. 100°, 260°

Dec.	20° Hc	d	Z	22° Hc	d	Z	24° Hc	d	Z	26° Hc	d	Z	28° Hc	d	Z
0	9 23.5	+20.7	93.5	9 15.9	+22.7	93.8	9 07.7	+24.6	94.1	8 58.7	+26.6	94.4	8 49.2	+28.4	94.7
1	9 44.2	20.6	92.5	9 38.6	22.6	92.8	9 32.3	24.5	93.2	9 25.3	26.4	93.5	9 17.6	28.3	93.8
2	10 04.8	20.4	91.5	10 01.2	22.3	91.9	9 56.8	24.4	92.3	9 51.7	26.3	92.6	9 45.9	28.2	92.9
3	10 25.2	20.2	90.6	10 23.5	22.3	91.0	10 21.2	24.1	91.3	10 18.0	26.1	91.7	10 14.1	28.0	92.0
4	10 45.4	20.0	89.6	10 45.8	22.0	90.0	10 45.3	24.1	90.4	10 44.1	26.0	90.8	10 42.1	27.9	91.2
5	11 05.4	+19.9	88.7	11 07.8	+21.9	89.1	11 09.4	+23.8	89.5	11 10.1	+25.8	89.9	11 10.0	+27.7	90.2
6	11 25.3	19.7	87.7	11 29.7	21.7	88.1	11 33.2	23.7	88.5	11 35.9	25.6	88.9	11 37.7	27.5	89.3
7	11 45.0	19.5	86.7	11 51.4	21.5	87.2	11 56.9	23.5	87.6	12 01.5	25.4	88.0	12 05.2	27.4	88.4
8	12 04.5	19.3	85.8	12 12.9	21.3	86.2	12 20.4	23.2	86.6	12 26.9	25.3	87.1	12 32.6	27.1	87.5
9	12 23.8	19.1	84.8	12 34.2	21.1	85.3	12 43.6	23.1	85.7	12 52.2	25.0	86.2	12 59.7	27.0	86.6
10	12 42.9	+18.8	83.8	12 55.3	+20.8	84.3	13 06.7	+22.9	84.8	13 17.2	+24.8	85.2	13 26.7	+26.8	85.7
11	13 01.7	18.7	82.9	13 16.1	20.7	83.3	13 29.6	22.7	83.8	13 42.0	24.7	84.3	13 53.5	26.6	84.8
12	13 20.4	18.4	81.9	13 36.8	20.4	82.4	13 52.3	22.4	82.8	14 06.7	24.4	83.3	14 20.1	26.3	83.8
13	13 38.8	18.2	80.9	13 57.2	20.3	81.4	14 14.7	22.2	81.9	14 31.1	24.2	82.4	14 46.4	26.1	82.9
14	13 57.0	17.9	79.9	14 17.5	19.9	80.4	14 36.9	22.0	80.9	14 55.3	23.9	81.5	15 12.5	25.9	82.0
15	14 14.9	+17.8	78.9	14 37.4	+19.8	79.5	14 58.9	+21.7	80.0	15 19.2	+23.7	80.5	15 38.4	+25.7	81.1
16	14 32.7	17.4	78.0	14 57.2	19.4	78.5	15 20.6	21.5	79.0	15 42.9	23.5	79.6	16 04.1	25.4	80.1
17	14 50.1	17.2	77.0	15 16.6	19.3	77.5	15 42.1	21.2	78.0	16 06.4	23.2	78.6	16 29.5	25.2	79.2
18	15 07.3	17.0	76.0	15 35.9	18.9	76.5	16 03.3	21.0	77.1	16 29.6	22.9	77.6	16 54.7	24.9	78.2
19	15 24.3	16.7	75.0	15 54.8	18.7	75.5	16 24.3	20.6	76.1	16 52.5	22.7	76.7	17 19.6	24.6	77.3
20	15 41.0	+16.4	74.0	16 13.5	+18.4	74.5	16 44.9	+20.5	75.1	17 15.2	+22.4	75.7	17 44.2	+24.4	76.3
21	15 57.4	16.1	73.0	16 31.9	18.3	73.5	17 05.4	20.1	74.1	17 37.6	22.1	74.7	18 08.6	24.0	75.4
22	16 13.5	15.9	72.0	16 50.1	17.8	72.6	17 25.5	19.8	73.1	17 59.7	21.8	73.8	18 32.6	23.8	74.4
23	16 29.4	15.5	71.0	17 07.9	17.6	71.6	17 45.3	19.5	72.1	18 21.5	21.5	72.8	18 56.4	23.4	73.4
24	16 44.9	15.3	70.0	17 25.5	17.2	70.6	18 04.8	19.3	71.2	18 43.0	21.2	71.8	19 19.8	23.2	72.4
25	17 00.2	+15.0	69.0	17 42.7	+17.0	69.5	18 24.1	+18.9	70.2	19 04.2	+20.8	70.8	19 43.0	+22.8	71.5
26	17 15.2	14.7	67.9	17 59.7	16.6	68.5	18 43.0	18.6	69.2	19 25.0	20.6	69.8	20 05.8	22.5	70.5
27	17 29.9	14.3	66.9	18 16.3	16.3	67.5	19 01.6	18.2	68.2	19 45.6	20.2	68.8	20 28.3	22.2	69.5
28	17 44.2	14.0	65.9	18 32.6	16.0	66.5	19 19.8	18.0	67.1	20 05.8	19.9	67.8	20 50.5	21.8	68.5
29	17 58.2	13.8	64.9	18 48.6	15.6	65.5	19 37.8	17.6	66.1	20 25.7	19.5	66.8	21 12.3	21.5	67.5

Dec.	30° Hc	d	Z	32° Hc	d	Z	34° Hc	d	Z	36° Hc	d	Z	38° Hc	d	Z
0	8 38.9	+30.3	95.0	8 28.1	+32.1	95.3	8 16.4	+33.9	95.6	8 04.6	+35.5	95.9	7 51.9	+37.2	96.2
1	9 09.2	30.2	94.2	9 00.2	32.0	94.5	8 50.5	33.7	94.8	8 40.1	35.5	95.1	8 29.1	37.2	95.4
2	9 39.4	30.0	93.3	9 32.2	31.8	93.6	9 24.2	33.6	94.0	9 15.6	35.3	94.3	9 06.3	37.0	94.6
3	10 09.4	29.9	92.4	10 04.0	31.7	92.8	9 57.8	33.5	93.1	9 50.9	35.3	93.5	9 43.3	37.0	93.8
4	10 39.3	29.7	91.5	10 35.7	31.6	91.9	10 31.3	33.4	92.3	10 26.2	35.1	92.6	10 20.3	36.8	93.0
5	11 09.0	+29.6	90.6	11 07.3	+31.4	91.0	11 04.7	+33.2	91.4	11 01.3	+35.0	91.8	10 57.1	+36.7	92.2
6	11 38.6	29.4	89.8	11 38.7	31.3	90.2	11 37.9	33.1	90.6	11 36.3	34.8	91.0	11 33.8	36.5	91.4
7	12 08.0	29.3	88.9	12 10.0	31.1	89.3	12 11.0	32.9	89.7	12 11.1	34.7	90.2	12 10.3	36.4	90.6
8	12 37.3	29.0	88.0	12 41.1	30.9	88.4	12 43.9	32.7	88.9	12 45.8	34.5	89.3	12 46.7	36.3	89.8
9	13 06.3	28.9	87.1	13 12.0	30.7	87.5	13 16.6	32.6	88.0	13 20.3	34.4	88.5	13 23.0	36.1	89.0
10	13 35.2	+28.7	86.2	13 42.7	+30.6	86.7	13 49.2	+32.4	87.1	13 54.7	+34.2	87.6	13 59.1	+35.9	88.1
11	14 03.9	28.5	85.3	14 13.3	30.3	85.8	14 21.6	32.2	86.3	14 28.9	34.0	86.8	14 35.0	35.8	87.3
12	14 32.4	28.3	84.4	14 43.6	30.2	84.9	14 53.8	32.0	85.4	15 02.9	33.8	85.9	15 10.8	35.6	86.5
13	15 00.7	28.0	83.4	15 13.8	29.9	84.0	15 25.8	31.8	84.5	15 36.7	33.6	85.1	15 46.4	35.4	85.6
14	15 28.7	27.8	82.5	15 43.7	29.8	83.1	15 57.6	31.6	83.6	16 10.3	33.4	84.2	16 21.8	35.1	84.8
15	15 56.5	+27.6	81.6	16 13.5	+29.4	82.2	16 29.2	+31.3	82.8	16 43.7	+33.2	83.4	16 56.9	+35.0	84.0
16	16 24.1	27.4	80.7	16 42.9	29.3	81.3	17 00.5	31.1	81.9	17 16.9	32.9	82.5	17 31.9	34.8	83.1
17	16 51.5	27.1	79.8	17 12.2	29.0	80.4	17 31.6	30.9	81.0	17 49.8	32.7	81.6	18 06.7	34.5	82.3
18	17 18.6	26.8	78.8	17 41.2	28.7	79.4	18 02.5	30.6	80.1	18 22.5	32.5	80.7	18 41.2	34.3	81.4
19	17 45.4	26.6	77.9	18 09.9	28.5	78.5	18 33.1	30.4	79.2	18 55.0	32.2	79.8	19 15.5	34.0	80.5
20	18 12.0	+26.2	76.9	18 38.4	+28.2	77.6	19 03.5	+30.1	78.3	19 27.2	+32.0	78.9	19 49.5	+33.8	79.6
21	18 38.2	26.0	76.0	19 06.6	27.9	76.7	19 33.6	29.8	77.3	19 59.2	31.7	78.0	20 23.3	33.5	78.8
22	19 04.2	25.8	75.0	19 34.5	27.7	75.7	20 03.4	29.5	76.4	20 30.9	31.4	77.1	20 56.8	33.3	77.9
23	19 30.0	25.4	74.1	20 02.2	27.3	74.8	20 32.9	29.3	75.5	21 02.3	31.1	76.2	21 30.1	32.9	77.0
24	19 55.4	25.0	73.1	20 29.5	27.0	73.8	21 02.2	28.9	74.6	21 33.4	30.8	75.3	22 03.0	32.7	76.1
25	20 20.4	+24.8	72.2	20 56.5	+26.7	72.9	21 31.1	+28.6	73.6	22 04.2	+30.5	74.4	22 35.7	+32.3	75.2
26	20 45.2	24.5	71.2	21 23.2	26.4	71.9	21 59.7	28.3	72.7	22 34.7	30.1	73.5	23 08.0	32.0	74.3
27	21 09.7	24.1	70.2	21 49.6	26.0	70.9	22 28.0	27.9	71.7	23 04.8	29.8	72.5	23 40.0	31.7	73.3
28	21 33.8	23.7	69.2	22 15.6	25.7	70.0	22 55.9	27.6	70.8	23 34.6	29.5	71.6	24 11.7	31.4	72.4
29	21 57.5	23.4	68.2	22 41.3	25.3	69.0	23 23.5	27.2	69.8	24 04.1	29.2	70.6	24 43.1	31.0	71.5

20°			22°			24°			26°			28°			Dec.
Hc	d	Z	Hc	d	Z	Hc	d	Z	Hc	d	Z	Hc	d	Z	
° ′	′	°	° ′	′	°	° ′	′	°	° ′	′	°	° ′	′	°	°
9 23.5	-20.9	93.5	9 15.9	-22.8	93.8	9 07.7	-24.8	94.1	8 58.7	-26.6	94.4	8 49.2	-28.6	94.7	0
9 02.6	21.0	94.4	8 53.1	23.0	94.7	8 42.9	24.9	95.0	8 32.1	26.9	95.3	8 20.6	28.7	95.6	1
8 41.6	21.2	95.3	8 30.1	23.1	95.6	8 18.0	25.1	95.9	8 05.2	26.9	96.2	7 51.9	28.8	96.5	2
8 20.4	21.3	96.3	8 07.0	23.3	96.6	7 52.9	25.2	96.9	7 38.3	27.1	97.1	7 23.1	28.9	97.4	3
7 59.1	21.4	97.2	7 43.7	23.4	97.5	7 27.7	25.2	97.8	7 11.2	27.1	98.0	6 54.2	29.0	98.3	4
7 37.7	-21.5	98.2	7 20.3	-23.4	98.4	7 02.5	-25.4	98.7	6 44.1	-27.3	98.9	6 25.2	-29.1	99.2	5
7 16.2	21.7	99.1	6 56.9	23.5	99.4	6 37.1	25.5	99.6	6 16.8	27.3	99.8	5 56.1	29.1	100.0	6
6 54.5	21.8	100.1	6 33.3	23.7	100.3	6 11.6	25.6	100.5	5 49.5	27.4	100.7	5 27.0	29.3	100.9	7
6 32.7	21.9	101.0	6 09.6	23.8	101.2	5 46.0	25.6	101.4	5 22.1	27.6	101.6	4 57.7	29.3	101.8	8
6 10.8	21.9	101.9	5 45.8	23.9	102.1	5 20.4	25.8	102.3	4 54.5	27.5	102.5	4 28.4	29.4	102.7	9
5 48.9	-22.1	102.9	5 21.9	-23.9	103.1	4 54.6	-25.8	103.2	4 27.0	-27.7	103.4	3 59.0	-29.4	103.5	10
5 26.8	22.2	103.8	4 58.0	24.1	104.0	4 28.8	25.9	104.1	3 59.3	27.7	104.3	3 29.6	29.5	104.4	11
5 04.6	22.2	104.7	4 33.9	24.1	104.9	4 02.9	25.9	105.1	3 31.6	27.7	105.2	3 00.1	29.5	105.3	12
4 42.4	22.3	105.7	4 09.8	24.1	105.8	3 37.0	26.0	106.0	3 03.9	27.8	106.1	2 30.6	29.6	106.2	13
4 20.1	22.4	106.6	3 45.7	24.3	106.7	3 11.0	26.1	106.9	2 36.1	27.9	107.0	2 01.0	29.6	107.0	14
3 57.7	-22.4	107.5	3 21.4	-24.2	107.7	2 44.9	-26.1	107.8	2 08.2	-27.8	107.8	1 31.4	-29.6	107.9	15
3 35.3	22.5	108.5	2 57.2	24.4	108.6	2 18.8	26.1	108.7	1 40.4	27.9	108.7	1 01.8	29.6	108.8	16
3 12.8	22.6	109.4	2 32.8	24.3	109.5	1 52.7	26.1	109.6	1 12.5	27.9	109.6	0 32.2	29.6	109.6	17
2 50.2	22.6	110.3	2 08.5	24.4	110.4	1 26.6	26.2	110.5	0 44.6	27.9	110.5	0 02.6	-29.7	110.5	18
2 27.6	22.6	111.2	1 44.1	24.4	111.3	1 00.4	26.2	111.4	0 16.7	-27.9	111.4	0 27.1	+29.6	68.6	19
2 05.0	-22.6	112.2	1 19.7	-24.5	112.2	0 34.2	-26.2	112.3	0 11.2	+28.0	67.7	0 56.7	+29.6	67.8	20
1 42.4	22.7	113.1	0 55.2	24.4	113.1	0 08.0	-26.2	113.2	0 39.2	27.9	66.8	1 26.3	29.6	66.9	21
1 19.7	22.7	114.0	0 30.8	24.5	114.1	0 18.2	+26.1	65.9	1 07.1	27.9	66.0	1 55.9	29.6	66.0	22
0 57.0	22.8	115.0	0 06.3	-24.5	115.0	0 44.3	26.2	65.0	1 35.0	27.8	65.1	2 25.5	29.5	65.1	23
0 34.2	22.7	115.9	0 18.2	+24.4	64.1	1 10.5	26.2	64.1	2 02.8	27.9	64.2	2 55.0	29.5	64.3	24
0 11.5	-22.7	116.8	0 42.6	+24.5	63.2	1 36.7	+26.1	63.2	2 30.7	+27.8	63.3	3 24.5	+29.4	63.4	25
0 11.2	+22.8	62.3	1 07.1	24.4	62.3	2 02.8	26.1	62.3	2 58.5	27.7	62.4	3 53.9	29.4	62.5	26
0 34.0	22.7	61.3	1 31.5	24.4	61.4	2 28.9	26.1	61.4	3 26.2	27.7	61.5	4 23.3	29.4	61.6	27
0 56.7	22.7	60.4	1 55.9	24.4	60.5	2 55.0	26.0	60.5	3 53.9	27.7	60.6	4 52.7	29.2	60.8	28
1 19.4	22.7	59.5	2 20.3	24.3	59.5	3 21.0	26.0	59.6	4 21.6	27.6	59.7	5 21.9	29.2	59.9	29

30°			32°			34°			36°			38°			Dec.
Hc	d	Z	Hc	d	Z	Hc	d	Z	Hc	d	Z	Hc	d	Z	
° ′	′	°	° ′	′	°	° ′	′	°	° ′	′	°	° ′	′	°	°
8 38.9	-30.4	95.0	8 28.1	-32.2	95.3	8 16.6	-33.9	95.6	8 04.6	-35.7	95.9	7 51.9	-37.3	96.2	0
8 08.5	30.5	95.9	7 55.9	32.3	96.2	7 42.7	34.1	96.5	7 28.9	35.8	96.7	7 14.6	37.5	97.0	1
7 38.0	30.6	96.8	7 23.6	32.4	97.0	7 08.6	34.1	97.3	6 53.1	35.8	97.5	6 37.1	37.4	97.8	2
7 07.4	30.7	97.6	6 51.2	32.5	97.9	6 34.5	34.2	98.1	6 17.3	35.9	98.3	5 59.7	37.6	98.6	3
6 36.7	30.8	98.5	6 18.7	32.6	98.7	6 00.3	34.3	98.9	5 41.4	36.0	99.2	5 22.1	37.6	99.3	4
6 05.9	-30.9	99.4	5 46.1	-32.6	99.6	5 26.0	-34.4	99.8	5 05.4	-36.0	100.0	4 44.5	-37.7	100.1	5
5 35.0	31.0	100.2	5 13.5	32.7	100.4	4 51.6	34.4	100.6	4 29.4	36.1	100.8	4 06.8	37.7	100.9	6
5 04.0	31.0	101.1	4 40.8	32.8	101.3	4 17.2	34.5	101.4	3 53.3	36.2	101.6	3 29.1	37.8	101.7	7
4 33.0	31.1	102.0	4 08.0	32.8	102.1	3 42.7	34.5	102.2	3 17.1	36.1	102.4	2 51.3	37.7	102.5	8
4 01.9	31.1	102.8	3 35.2	32.9	102.9	3 08.2	34.6	103.1	2 41.0	36.2	103.2	2 13.6	37.8	103.2	9
3 30.8	-31.2	103.7	3 02.3	-32.9	103.8	2 33.6	-34.6	103.9	2 04.8	-36.3	104.0	1 35.8	-37.9	104.0	10
2 59.6	31.2	104.5	2 29.4	32.9	104.6	1 59.0	34.6	104.7	1 28.5	36.2	104.8	0 57.9	37.8	104.8	11
2 28.4	31.3	105.4	1 56.5	33.0	105.5	1 24.4	34.6	105.5	0 52.3	36.3	105.5	0 20.1	-37.9	105.6	12
1 57.1	31.3	106.2	1 23.5	33.0	106.3	0 49.8	34.7	106.3	0 16.0	-36.2	106.3	0 17.8	+37.7	73.7	13
1 25.8	31.3	107.1	0 50.5	33.0	107.1	0 15.1	-34.6	107.1	0 20.2	+36.3	72.9	0 55.6	37.8	72.9	14
0 54.5	-31.3	107.9	0 17.5	-33.0	108.0	0 19.5	+34.6	72.0	0 56.5	+36.2	72.1	1 33.4	+37.8	72.1	15
0 23.2	-31.4	108.8	0 15.5	+33.0	71.2	0 54.1	34.7	71.2	1 32.7	36.3	71.3	2 11.2	37.8	71.3	16
0 08.2	+31.3	70.4	0 48.5	33.0	70.4	1 28.8	34.6	70.4	2 09.0	36.2	70.5	2 49.0	37.8	70.5	17
0 39.5	31.3	69.5	1 21.5	32.9	69.6	2 03.4	34.6	69.6	2 45.2	36.1	69.7	3 26.8	37.7	69.8	18
1 10.8	31.3	68.6	1 54.4	33.0	68.7	2 38.0	34.5	68.8	3 21.3	36.2	68.9	4 04.5	37.7	69.0	19
1 42.1	+31.3	67.8	2 27.4	+32.9	67.9	3 12.5	+34.5	68.0	3 57.5	+36.1	68.1	4 42.2	+37.6	68.2	20
2 13.4	31.2	66.9	3 00.3	32.9	67.0	3 47.0	34.5	67.1	4 33.6	36.0	67.3	5 19.8	37.5	67.4	21
2 44.6	31.2	66.1	3 33.2	32.8	66.2	4 21.5	34.4	66.3	5 09.6	36.0	66.5	5 57.3	37.5	66.6	22
3 15.8	31.2	65.2	4 06.0	32.8	65.3	4 55.9	34.4	65.5	5 45.6	35.9	65.7	6 34.8	37.5	65.9	23
3 47.0	31.1	64.4	4 38.8	32.7	64.5	5 30.3	34.3	64.7	6 21.5	35.8	64.9	7 12.3	37.3	65.1	24
4 18.1	+31.1	63.5	5 11.5	+32.7	63.7	6 04.6	+34.2	63.8	6 57.3	+35.7	64.0	7 49.6	+37.2	64.3	25
4 49.2	31.0	62.7	5 44.2	32.5	62.8	6 38.8	34.1	63.0	7 33.0	35.7	63.2	8 26.8	37.2	63.5	26
5 20.2	30.9	61.8	6 16.7	32.5	62.0	7 12.9	34.1	62.2	8 08.7	35.6	62.4	9 04.0	37.0	62.7	27
5 51.1	30.8	60.9	6 49.2	32.4	61.1	7 47.0	33.9	61.4	8 44.3	35.4	61.6	9 41.0	37.0	61.9	28
6 21.9	30.8	60.1	7 21.6	32.3	60.3	8 20.9	33.8	60.5	9 19.7	35.3	60.8	10 18.0	36.8	61.1	29

LATITUDE **SAME** NAME

Dec.	40° Hc	d	Z	42° Hc	d	Z	44° Hc	d	Z	46° Hc	d	Z	48° Hc	d	Z
°	° ′	′	°	° ′	′	°	° ′	′	°	° ′	′	°	° ′	′	°
0	7 38.7	+38.8	96.5	7 24.9	+40.4	96.7	7 10.5	+42.0	97.0	6 55.7	+43.4	97.2	6 40.3	+44.9	97.5
1	8 17.5	38.8	95.7	8 05.3	40.4	96.0	7 52.5	41.9	96.3	7 39.1	43.4	96.5	7 25.2	44.8	96.8
2	8 56.3	38.7	94.9	8 45.7	40.3	95.2	8 34.4	41.8	95.5	8 22.5	43.3	95.8	8 10.0	44.8	96.1
3	9 35.0	38.6	94.2	9 26.0	40.1	94.5	9 16.2	41.8	94.8	9 05.8	43.3	95.1	8 54.8	44.6	95.5
4	10 13.6	38.5	93.4	10 06.1	40.1	93.7	9 58.0	41.6	94.1	9 49.1	43.1	94.4	9 39.4	44.6	94.8
5	10 52.1	+38.3	92.6	10 46.2	+40.0	93.0	10 39.6	+41.5	93.4	10 32.2	+43.0	93.7	10 24.0	+44.5	94.1
6	11 30.4	38.2	91.8	11 26.2	39.8	92.2	11 21.1	41.5	92.6	11 15.2	43.0	93.0	11 08.5	44.4	93.4
7	12 08.6	38.1	91.0	12 06.0	39.8	91.5	12 02.6	41.3	91.9	11 58.2	42.8	92.3	11 52.9	44.3	92.7
8	12 46.7	38.0	90.2	12 45.8	39.6	90.7	12 43.9	41.1	91.1	12 41.0	42.7	91.6	12 37.2	44.2	92.0
9	13 24.7	37.8	89.4	13 25.4	39.4	89.9	13 25.0	41.1	90.4	13 23.7	42.6	90.9	13 21.4	44.1	91.3
10	14 02.5	+37.6	88.6	14 04.8	+39.3	89.1	14 06.1	+40.9	89.6	14 06.3	+42.5	90.1	14 05.5	+44.0	90.6
11	14 40.1	37.5	87.8	14 44.1	39.2	88.4	14 47.0	40.8	88.9	14 48.8	42.3	89.4	14 49.5	43.8	89.9
12	15 17.6	37.3	87.0	15 23.3	38.9	87.6	15 27.8	40.6	88.1	15 31.1	42.2	88.7	15 33.3	43.7	89.2
13	15 54.9	37.1	86.2	16 02.2	38.8	86.8	16 08.4	40.4	87.4	16 13.3	42.0	87.9	16 17.0	43.6	88.5
14	16 32.0	36.9	85.4	16 41.0	38.6	86.0	16 48.8	40.3	86.6	16 55.3	41.9	87.2	17 00.6	43.4	87.8
15	17 08.9	+36.8	84.6	17 19.6	+38.5	85.2	17 29.1	+40.0	85.8	17 37.2	+41.7	86.4	17 44.0	+43.2	87.1
16	17 45.7	36.5	83.7	17 58.1	38.2	84.4	18 09.1	39.9	85.0	18 18.9	41.5	85.7	18 27.2	43.1	86.3
17	18 22.2	36.3	82.9	18 36.3	38.0	83.6	18 49.0	39.7	84.2	19 00.4	41.3	84.9	19 10.3	42.9	85.6
18	18 58.5	36.0	82.1	19 14.3	37.8	82.8	19 28.7	39.5	83.4	19 41.7	41.1	84.2	19 53.2	42.7	84.9
19	19 34.5	35.8	81.2	19 52.1	37.6	81.9	20 08.2	39.3	82.6	20 22.8	40.9	83.4	20 35.9	42.5	84.1
20	20 10.3	+35.6	80.4	20 29.7	+37.3	81.1	20 47.5	+39.0	81.8	21 03.7	+40.7	82.6	21 18.4	+42.3	83.4
21	20 45.9	35.3	79.5	21 07.0	37.1	80.3	21 26.5	38.8	81.0	21 44.4	40.5	81.8	22 00.7	42.1	82.6
22	21 21.2	35.1	78.6	21 44.1	36.8	79.4	22 05.3	38.6	80.2	22 24.9	40.2	81.0	22 42.8	41.9	81.8
23	21 56.3	34.8	77.8	22 20.9	36.6	78.6	22 43.9	38.3	79.4	23 05.1	40.0	80.2	23 24.7	41.6	81.1
24	22 31.1	34.4	76.9	22 57.5	36.2	77.7	23 22.2	38.0	78.5	23 45.1	39.8	79.4	24 06.3	41.4	80.3
25	23 05.5	+34.2	76.0	23 33.7	+36.0	76.8	24 00.2	+37.7	77.7	24 24.9	+39.4	78.6	24 47.7	+41.1	79.5
26	23 39.7	33.9	75.1	24 09.7	35.7	76.0	24 37.9	37.5	76.8	25 04.3	39.2	77.7	25 28.8	40.9	78.7
27	24 13.6	33.5	74.2	24 45.4	35.3	75.1	25 15.4	37.1	76.0	25 43.5	38.9	76.9	26 09.7	40.6	77.9
28	24 47.1	33.2	73.3	25 20.7	35.1	74.2	25 52.5	36.8	75.1	26 22.4	38.6	76.1	26 50.3	40.3	77.0
29	25 20.3	32.9	72.4	25 55.8	34.7	73.3	26 29.3	36.6	74.2	27 01.0	38.3	75.2	27 30.6	40.0	76.2

Dec.	50° Hc	d	Z	52° Hc	d	Z	54° Hc	d	Z	56° Hc	d	Z	58° Hc	d	Z
°	° ′	′	°	° ′	′	°	° ′	′	°	° ′	′	°	° ′	′	°
0	6 24.5	+46.2	97.7	6 08.2	+47.6	97.9	5 51.5	+48.8	98.1	5 34.3	+50.0	98.3	5 16.8	+51.1	98.5
1	7 10.7	46.2	97.1	6 55.8	47.4	97.3	6 40.3	48.7	97.5	6 24.3	49.9	97.8	6 07.9	51.0	98.0
2	7 56.9	46.1	96.4	7 43.2	47.5	96.7	7 29.0	48.7	96.9	7 14.2	49.9	97.2	6 58.9	51.0	97.4
3	8 43.0	46.1	95.8	8 30.7	47.3	96.1	8 17.7	48.6	96.4	8 04.1	49.9	96.6	7 49.9	51.0	96.9
4	9 29.1	46.0	95.1	9 18.0	47.4	95.4	9 06.3	48.6	95.8	8 54.0	49.7	96.1	8 40.9	51.0	96.4
5	10 15.1	+45.9	94.5	10 05.4	+47.2	94.8	9 54.9	+48.5	95.2	9 43.7	+49.8	95.5	9 31.9	+50.8	95.8
6	11 01.0	45.8	93.8	10 52.6	47.1	94.2	10 43.4	48.5	94.6	10 33.5	49.6	94.9	10 22.7	50.9	95.3
7	11 46.8	45.7	93.1	11 39.7	47.1	93.6	11 31.9	48.3	94.0	11 23.1	49.6	94.4	11 13.6	50.8	94.8
8	12 32.5	45.6	92.5	12 26.8	47.0	92.9	12 20.2	48.3	93.4	12 12.7	49.6	93.8	12 04.4	50.7	94.2
9	13 18.1	45.5	91.8	13 13.8	46.9	92.3	13 08.5	48.2	92.8	13 02.3	49.4	93.2	12 55.1	50.6	93.7
10	14 03.6	+45.4	91.1	14 00.7	+46.8	91.6	13 56.7	+48.2	92.1	13 51.7	+49.4	92.6	13 45.7	+50.6	93.1
11	14 49.0	45.3	90.5	14 47.5	46.7	91.0	14 44.9	48.0	91.5	14 41.1	49.3	92.1	14 36.3	50.5	92.6
12	15 34.3	45.2	89.8	15 34.2	46.5	90.3	15 32.9	47.9	90.9	15 30.4	49.2	91.5	15 26.8	50.4	92.0
13	16 19.5	45.0	89.1	16 20.7	46.5	89.7	16 20.8	47.8	90.3	16 19.6	49.1	90.9	16 17.2	50.3	91.4
14	17 04.5	44.9	88.4	17 07.2	46.3	89.0	17 08.6	47.6	89.6	17 08.7	48.9	90.3	17 07.5	50.2	90.9
15	17 49.4	+44.7	87.7	17 53.5	+46.2	88.4	17 56.2	+47.6	89.0	17 57.6	+48.9	89.7	17 57.7	+50.1	90.3
16	18 34.1	44.6	87.0	18 39.7	46.0	87.7	18 43.8	47.4	88.4	18 46.5	48.8	89.0	18 47.8	50.0	89.7
17	19 18.7	44.4	86.3	19 25.7	45.9	87.0	19 31.2	47.3	87.7	19 35.3	48.6	88.4	19 37.8	49.9	89.1
18	20 03.1	44.3	85.6	20 11.6	45.7	86.3	20 18.5	47.1	87.1	20 23.9	48.5	87.8	20 27.7	49.8	88.6
19	20 47.4	44.0	84.9	20 57.3	45.6	85.6	21 05.6	47.0	86.4	21 12.4	48.3	87.2	21 17.5	49.6	88.0
20	21 31.4	+43.9	84.1	21 42.9	+45.3	84.9	21 52.6	+46.8	85.7	22 00.7	+48.2	86.5	22 07.1	+49.5	87.3
21	22 15.3	43.7	83.4	22 28.2	45.2	84.2	22 39.4	46.7	85.1	22 48.9	48.0	85.9	22 56.6	49.4	86.7
22	22 59.0	43.4	82.7	23 13.4	45.0	83.5	23 26.1	46.4	84.4	23 36.9	47.9	85.2	23 46.0	49.2	86.1
23	23 42.4	43.3	81.9	23 58.4	44.8	82.8	24 12.5	46.3	83.7	24 24.8	47.7	84.6	24 35.2	49.0	85.5
24	24 25.7	43.0	81.2	24 43.2	44.5	82.1	24 58.8	46.1	83.0	25 12.5	47.5	83.9	25 24.2	48.9	84.9
25	25 08.7	+42.7	80.4	25 27.7	+44.4	81.3	25 44.9	+45.8	82.3	26 00.0	+47.3	83.2	26 13.1	+48.7	84.2
26	25 51.4	42.6	79.6	26 12.1	44.1	80.6	26 30.7	45.7	81.6	26 47.3	47.1	82.6	27 01.8	48.6	83.6
27	26 34.0	42.2	78.8	26 56.2	43.9	79.8	27 16.4	45.4	80.8	27 34.4	47.0	81.9	27 50.4	48.3	82.9
28	27 16.2	42.0	78.0	27 40.1	43.6	79.1	28 01.8	45.2	80.1	28 21.4	46.6	81.1	28 38.7	48.1	82.2
29	27 58.2	41.7	77.2	28 23.7	43.3	78.3	28 47.0	44.9	79.3	29 08.0	46.5	80.4	29 26.8	48.0	81.5

40°			42°			44°			46°			48°			Dec.
Hc	d	Z	Hc	d	Z	Hc	d	Z	Hc	d	Z	Hc	d	Z	
7 38.7	-39.0	96.5	7 24.9	-40.6	96.7	7 10.5	-42.0	97.0	6 55.7	-43.5	97.2	6 40.3	-44.9	97.5	0
6 59.7	39.0	97.2	6 44.3	40.5	97.5	6 28.5	42.1	97.7	6 12.2	43.6	97.9	5 55.4	44.9	98.1	1
6 20.7	39.1	98.0	6 03.8	40.7	98.2	5 46.4	42.2	98.4	5 28.6	43.6	98.6	5 10.5	45.0	98.8	2
5 41.6	39.2	98.8	5 23.1	40.7	99.0	5 04.2	42.2	99.1	4 45.0	43.6	99.3	4 25.5	45.1	99.5	3
5 02.5	39.2	99.5	4 42.4	40.7	99.7	4 22.0	42.2	99.8	4 01.4	43.7	100.0	3 40.4	45.1	100.1	4
4 23.2	-39.2	100.3	4 01.7	-40.8	100.4	3 39.8	-42.3	100.6	3 17.7	-43.7	100.7	2 55.3	-45.1	100.8	5
3 44.0	39.3	101.0	3 20.9	40.9	101.2	2 57.5	42.3	101.3	2 34.0	43.8	101.4	2 10.2	45.1	101.4	6
3 04.7	39.3	101.8	2 40.0	40.8	101.9	2 15.2	42.3	102.0	1 50.2	43.7	102.0	1 25.1	45.1	102.1	7
2 25.4	39.4	102.6	1 59.2	40.9	102.7	1 32.9	42.3	102.7	1 06.5	43.8	102.7	0 40.0	-45.1	102.8	8
1 46.0	39.4	103.3	1 18.3	40.9	103.4	0 50.6	42.4	103.4	0 22.7	-43.7	103.4	0 05.1	+45.2	76.6	9
1 06.6	-39.3	104.1	0 37.4	-40.8	104.1	0 08.2	-42.3	104.1	0 21.0	+43.8	75.9	0 50.3	+45.1	75.9	10
0 27.3	-39.4	104.8	0 03.4	+40.9	75.2	0 34.1	+42.4	75.2	1 04.8	43.7	75.2	1 35.4	45.1	75.3	11
0 12.1	+39.4	74.4	0 44.3	40.9	74.4	1 16.5	42.3	74.5	1 48.5	43.8	74.5	2 20.5	45.1	74.6	12
0 51.5	39.4	73.7	1 25.2	40.9	73.7	1 58.8	42.3	73.8	2 32.3	43.7	73.8	3 05.6	45.0	73.9	13
1 30.9	39.3	72.9	2 06.1	40.8	73.0	2 41.1	42.3	73.1	3 16.0	43.7	73.2	3 50.6	45.1	73.3	14
2 10.2	+39.4	72.2	2 46.9	+40.8	72.2	3 23.4	+42.3	72.3	3 59.7	+43.6	72.5	4 35.7	+45.0	72.6	15
2 49.6	39.3	71.4	3 27.7	40.8	71.5	4 05.7	42.2	71.6	4 43.3	43.6	71.8	5 20.7	44.9	72.0	16
3 28.9	39.2	70.7	4 08.5	40.8	70.8	4 47.9	42.2	70.9	5 26.9	43.6	71.1	6 05.6	44.9	71.3	17
4 08.1	39.3	69.9	4 49.3	40.7	70.0	5 30.1	42.1	70.2	6 10.5	43.5	70.4	6 50.5	44.9	70.6	18
4 47.4	39.1	69.1	5 30.0	40.6	69.3	6 12.2	42.0	69.5	6 54.0	43.5	69.7	7 35.4	44.8	69.9	19
5 26.5	+39.2	68.4	6 10.6	+40.6	68.6	6 54.2	+41.9	68.8	7 37.5	+43.3	69.0	8 20.2	+44.7	69.3	20
6 05.7	39.0	67.6	6 51.2	40.5	67.8	7 36.2	42.0	68.1	8 20.8	43.4	68.3	9 04.9	44.5	68.6	21
6 44.7	39.0	66.8	7 31.7	40.4	67.1	8 18.2	41.8	67.3	9 04.2	43.2	67.6	9 49.4	44.5	67.9	22
7 23.7	38.9	66.1	8 12.1	40.4	66.3	9 00.0	41.8	66.6	9 47.4	43.1	66.9	10 34.1	44.3	67.2	23
8 02.6	38.8	65.3	8 52.5	40.2	65.6	9 41.8	41.7	65.9	10 30.5	43.1	66.2	11 18.6	44.4	66.6	24
8 41.4	+38.7	64.5	9 32.7	+40.2	64.8	10 23.5	+41.5	65.2	11 13.6	+42.9	65.5	12 03.0	+44.3	65.9	25
9 20.1	38.7	63.8	10 12.9	40.1	64.1	11 05.0	41.5	64.4	11 56.5	42.9	64.8	12 47.3	44.1	65.2	26
9 58.8	38.5	63.0	10 53.0	39.9	63.3	11 46.5	41.4	63.7	12 39.4	42.7	64.1	13 31.4	44.1	64.5	27
10 37.3	38.4	62.2	11 32.9	39.8	62.6	12 27.9	41.2	62.9	13 22.1	42.6	63.3	14 15.5	43.9	63.8	28
11 15.7	38.3	61.4	12 12.7	39.7	61.8	13 09.1	41.1	62.2	14 04.7	42.4	62.6	14 59.4	43.8	63.1	29

50°			52°			54°			56°			58°			Dec.
Hc	d	Z	Hc	d	Z	Hc	d	Z	Hc	d	Z	Hc	d	Z	
6 24.5	-46.3	97.7	6 08.2	-47.5	97.9	5 51.5	-48.8	98.1	5 34.3	-50.0	98.3	5 16.8	-51.1	98.5	0
5 38.2	46.3	98.3	5 20.7	47.6	98.5	5 02.7	48.8	98.7	4 44.3	50.0	98.9	4 25.7	51.2	99.0	1
4 51.9	46.3	99.0	4 33.0	47.6	99.1	4 13.8	48.8	99.3	3 54.3	50.0	99.4	3 34.5	51.2	99.6	2
4 05.6	46.4	99.6	3 45.4	47.7	99.7	3 25.0	48.9	99.9	3 04.3	50.1	100.0	2 43.4	51.2	100.1	3
3 19.2	46.4	100.2	2 57.7	47.6	100.4	2 36.1	48.9	100.4	2 14.2	50.0	100.5	1 52.2	51.2	100.6	4
2 32.8	-46.4	100.9	2 10.1	-47.7	101.0	1 47.2	-49.0	101.0	1 24.2	-50.1	101.1	1 01.0	-51.1	101.1	5
1 46.4	46.5	101.5	1 22.4	47.8	101.6	0 58.2	48.9	101.6	0 34.1	-50.1	101.6	0 09.9	-51.2	101.6	6
0 59.9	46.4	102.1	0 34.6	-47.7	102.2	0 09.3	-48.9	102.2	0 16.0	+50.1	77.8	0 41.3	+51.2	77.8	7
0 13.5	-46.5	102.8	0 13.1	+47.7	77.2	0 39.6	+48.9	77.2	1 06.1	50.1	77.3	1 32.5	51.2	77.3	8
0 33.0	+46.4	76.6	1 00.8	47.7	76.6	1 28.5	48.9	76.7	1 56.2	50.0	76.7	2 23.7	51.1	76.8	9
1 19.4	+46.4	76.0	1 48.5	+47.7	76.0	2 17.4	+48.9	76.1	2 46.2	+50.1	76.2	3 14.8	+51.2	76.3	10
2 05.8	46.5	75.3	2 36.2	47.7	75.4	3 06.3	48.9	75.5	3 36.3	50.0	75.6	4 06.0	51.1	75.7	11
2 52.3	46.4	74.7	3 23.9	47.6	74.8	3 55.2	48.9	74.9	4 26.3	50.0	75.1	4 57.1	51.1	75.2	12
3 38.7	46.3	74.1	4 11.5	47.6	74.2	4 44.1	48.8	74.3	5 16.3	50.0	74.5	5 48.2	51.0	74.7	13
4 25.0	46.4	73.4	4 59.1	47.6	73.6	5 32.9	48.8	73.8	6 06.3	49.9	73.9	6 39.2	51.1	74.2	14
5 11.4	+46.3	72.8	5 46.7	+47.6	73.0	6 21.7	+48.7	73.2	6 56.2	+49.9	73.4	7 30.3	+51.0	73.6	15
5 57.7	46.2	72.1	6 34.3	47.5	72.3	7 10.4	48.7	72.6	7 46.1	49.9	72.8	8 21.3	50.9	73.1	16
6 43.9	46.2	71.5	7 21.8	47.4	71.7	7 59.1	48.7	72.0	8 36.0	49.8	72.3	9 12.2	50.9	72.6	17
7 30.1	46.2	70.9	8 09.2	47.4	71.1	8 47.8	48.6	71.4	9 25.8	49.7	71.7	10 03.1	50.9	72.0	18
8 16.3	46.1	70.2	8 56.6	47.4	70.5	9 36.4	48.5	70.8	10 15.5	49.7	71.1	10 54.0	50.8	71.5	19
9 02.4	+46.0	69.6	9 44.0	+47.2	69.9	10 24.9	+48.5	70.2	11 05.2	+49.7	70.6	11 44.8	+50.7	70.9	20
9 48.4	45.9	68.9	10 31.2	47.2	69.2	11 13.4	48.4	69.6	11 54.9	49.5	70.0	12 35.5	50.7	70.4	21
10 34.3	45.9	68.3	11 18.4	47.1	68.6	12 01.8	48.3	69.0	12 44.4	49.5	69.4	13 26.2	50.6	69.8	22
11 20.2	45.8	67.6	12 05.5	47.1	68.0	12 50.1	48.3	68.4	13 33.9	49.4	68.8	14 16.8	50.5	69.3	23
12 06.0	45.6	66.9	12 52.6	46.9	67.3	13 38.4	48.1	67.8	14 23.3	49.3	68.2	15 07.3	50.4	68.7	24
12 51.6	+45.6	66.3	13 39.5	+46.9	66.6	14 26.5	+48.1	67.2	15 12.6	+49.2	67.7	15 57.7	+50.4	68.2	25
13 37.2	45.5	65.6	14 26.4	46.7	66.1	15 14.6	47.9	66.6	16 01.8	49.0	67.1	16 48.1	50.2	67.6	26
14 22.7	45.4	64.9	15 13.1	46.6	65.4	16 02.5	47.9	65.9	16 51.0	49.0	66.5	17 38.3	50.2	67.0	27
15 08.1	45.2	64.3	15 59.7	46.5	64.8	16 50.4	47.7	65.3	17 40.0	48.9	65.9	18 28.5	50.0	66.5	28
15 53.3	45.1	63.6	16 46.2	46.4	64.1	17 38.1	47.6	64.7	18 28.9	48.8	65.3	19 18.5	50.0	65.9	29

Dec.	0° Hc	d	Z	2° Hc	d	Z	4° Hc	d	Z	6° Hc	d	Z	8° Hc	d	Z
0	8 00.0-	0.1	90.0	7 59.7+	2.0	90.3	7 58.8+	4.2	90.6	7 57.4+	6.2	90.8	7 55.3+	8.4	91.1
1	7 59.9	0.2	89.0	8 01.7	1.9	89.3	8 03.0	4.0	89.6	8 03.6	6.1	89.8	8 03.7	8.2	90.1
2	7 59.7	0.4	88.0	8 03.6	1.8	88.3	8 07.0	3.8	88.5	8 09.7	6.0	88.8	8 11.9	8.0	89.1
3	7 59.3	0.5	87.0	8 05.4	1.6	87.3	8 10.8	3.7	87.5	8 15.7	5.8	87.8	8 19.9	8.0	88.1
4	7 58.8	0.6	86.0	8 07.0	1.4	86.2	8 14.5	3.6	86.5	8 21.5	5.7	86.8	8 27.9	7.7	87.1
5	7 58.2-	0.8	85.0	8 08.4+	1.3	85.2	8 18.1+	3.4	85.5	8 27.2+	5.5	85.8	8 35.6+	7.6	86.1
6	7 57.4	1.0	83.9	8 09.7	1.2	84.2	8 21.5	3.3	84.5	8 32.7	5.3	84.8	8 43.2	7.5	85.1
7	7 56.4	1.1	82.9	8 10.9	1.0	83.2	8 24.8	3.1	83.5	8 38.0	5.2	83.8	8 50.7	7.3	84.1
8	7 55.3	1.2	81.9	8 11.9	0.8	82.2	8 27.9	2.9	82.5	8 43.2	5.1	82.8	8 58.0	7.1	83.1
9	7 54.1	1.4	80.9	8 12.7	0.7	81.2	8 30.8	2.8	81.5	8 48.3	4.8	81.8	9 05.1	6.9	82.1
10	7 52.7-	1.6	79.9	8 13.4+	0.6	80.2	8 33.6+	2.6	80.5	8 53.1+	4.7	80.8	9 12.0+	6.8	81.1
11	7 51.1	1.7	78.9	8 14.0	0.3	79.2	8 36.2	2.5	79.5	8 57.8	4.6	79.8	9 18.8	6.7	80.1
12	7 49.4	1.8	77.9	8 14.3	0.3	78.2	8 38.7	2.3	78.5	9 02.4	4.4	78.8	9 25.5	6.4	79.1
13	7 47.6	1.9	76.9	8 14.6+	0.1	77.2	8 41.0	2.1	77.4	9 06.8	4.2	77.7	9 31.9	6.3	78.1
14	7 45.7	2.2	75.9	8 14.7-	0.1	76.1	8 43.1	2.0	76.4	9 11.0	4.0	76.7	9 38.2	6.1	77.1
15	7 43.5-	2.2	74.9	8 14.6-	0.2	75.1	8 45.1+	1.8	75.4	9 15.0+	3.9	75.7	9 44.3+	5.9	76.1
16	7 41.3	2.4	73.9	8 14.4	0.4	74.1	8 46.9	1.7	74.4	9 18.9	3.7	74.7	9 50.2	5.7	75.0
17	7 38.9	2.5	72.8	8 14.0	0.5	73.1	8 48.6	1.5	73.4	9 22.6	3.5	73.7	9 55.9	5.6	74.0
18	7 36.4	2.7	71.8	8 13.5	0.7	72.1	8 50.1	1.4	72.4	9 26.1	3.4	72.7	10 01.5	5.4	73.0
19	7 33.7	2.8	70.8	8 12.8	0.8	71.1	8 51.5	1.1	71.4	9 29.5	3.2	71.7	10 06.9	5.2	72.0
20	7 30.9-	3.0	69.8	8 12.0-	0.9	70.1	8 52.6+	1.1	70.4	9 32.7+	3.0	70.7	10 12.1+	5.0	71.0
21	7 27.9	3.1	68.8	8 11.1	1.2	69.1	8 53.7	0.8	69.3	9 35.7	2.8	69.7	10 17.1	4.8	70.0
22	7 24.8	3.2	67.8	8 09.9	1.2	68.1	8 54.5	0.7	68.3	9 38.5	2.7	68.6	10 21.9	4.6	69.0
23	7 21.6	3.3	66.8	8 08.7	1.5	67.0	8 55.2	0.5	67.3	9 41.2	2.4	67.6	10 26.5	4.5	68.0
24	7 18.3	3.5	65.8	8 07.2	1.5	66.0	8 55.7	0.4	66.3	9 43.6	2.3	66.6	10 31.0	4.2	66.9
25	7 14.8-	3.6	64.8	8 05.7-	1.8	65.0	8 56.1+	0.2	65.3	9 45.9+	2.2	65.6	10 35.2+	4.0	65.9
26	7 11.2	3.8	63.8	8 03.9	1.8	64.0	8 56.3	0.0	64.3	9 48.1	1.9	64.6	10 39.2	3.9	64.9
27	7 07.4	3.9	62.8	8 02.1	2.0	63.0	8 56.3-	0.1	63.3	9 50.0	1.7	63.6	10 43.1	3.7	63.9
28	7 03.5	4.0	61.8	8 00.1	2.2	62.0	8 56.2	0.3	62.3	9 51.7	1.6	62.6	10 46.8	3.4	62.9
29	6 59.5	4.1	60.8	7 57.9	2.3	61.0	8 55.9	0.5	61.3	9 53.3	1.4	61.5	10 50.2	3.3	61.9

Dec.	10° Hc	d	Z	12° Hc	d	Z	14° Hc	d	Z	16° Hc	d	Z	18° Hc	d	Z
0	7 52.7+	10.4	91.4	7 49.4+	12.6	91.7	7 45.7+	14.5	91.9	7 41.3+	16.6	92.2	7 36.4+	18.6	92.5
1	8 03.1	10.3	90.4	8 02.0	12.3	90.7	8 00.2	14.5	91.0	7 57.9	16.5	91.2	7 55.0	18.5	91.5
2	8 13.4	10.2	89.4	8 14.3	12.3	89.7	8 14.7	14.3	90.0	8 14.4	16.3	90.3	8 13.5	18.4	90.6
3	8 23.6	10.0	88.4	8 26.6	12.1	88.7	8 29.0	14.1	89.0	8 30.7	16.2	89.3	8 31.9	18.2	89.6
4	8 33.6	9.8	87.4	8 38.7	11.9	87.7	8 43.1	14.0	88.0	8 46.9	16.1	88.3	8 50.1	18.1	88.6
5	8 43.4+	9.7	86.4	8 50.6+	11.8	86.7	8 57.1+	13.9	87.0	9 03.0+	15.9	87.4	9 08.2+	17.9	87.7
6	8 53.1	9.6	85.4	9 02.4	11.6	85.7	9 11.0	13.7	86.1	9 18.9	15.7	86.4	9 26.1	17.8	86.7
7	9 02.7	9.3	84.4	9 14.0	11.5	84.7	9 24.7	13.5	85.1	9 34.6	15.6	85.4	9 43.9	17.6	85.7
8	9 12.0	9.2	83.4	9 25.5	11.2	83.7	9 38.2	13.3	84.1	9 50.2	15.4	84.4	10 01.5	17.4	84.8
9	9 21.2	9.1	82.4	9 36.7	11.2	82.7	9 51.5	13.2	83.1	10 05.6	15.2	83.4	10 18.9	17.3	83.8
10	9 30.3+	8.9	81.4	9 47.9+	10.9	81.8	10 04.7+	13.0	82.1	10 20.8+	15.1	82.5	10 36.2+	17.1	82.8
11	9 39.2	8.7	80.4	9 58.8	10.8	80.8	10 17.7	12.8	81.1	10 35.9	14.8	81.5	10 53.3	16.9	81.8
12	9 47.9	8.5	79.4	10 09.6	10.5	79.8	10 30.5	12.7	80.1	10 50.7	14.7	80.5	11 10.2	16.7	80.9
13	9 56.4	8.3	78.4	10 20.1	10.4	78.8	10 43.2	12.4	79.1	11 05.4	14.5	79.5	11 26.9	16.5	79.9
14	10 04.7	8.2	77.4	10 30.5	10.2	77.8	10 55.6	12.3	78.1	11 19.9	14.3	78.5	11 43.4	16.3	78.9
15	10 12.9+	7.9	76.4	10 40.7+	10.0	76.8	11 07.9+	12.0	77.1	11 34.2+	14.1	77.5	11 59.7+	16.1	77.9
16	10 20.8	7.8	75.4	10 50.7	9.9	75.7	11 19.9	11.9	76.1	11 48.3	13.9	76.5	12 15.8	15.9	76.9
17	10 28.6	7.6	74.4	11 00.6	9.6	74.7	11 31.8	11.6	75.1	12 02.2	13.6	75.5	12 31.7	15.7	76.0
18	10 36.2	7.4	73.4	11 10.2	9.4	73.7	11 43.4	11.4	74.1	12 15.8	13.5	74.5	12 47.4	15.4	75.0
19	10 43.6	7.2	72.4	11 19.6	9.2	72.7	11 54.8	11.3	73.1	12 29.3	13.2	73.5	13 02.8	15.3	74.0
20	10 50.8+	7.0	71.3	11 28.8+	9.0	71.7	12 06.1+	11.0	72.1	12 42.5+	13.0	72.5	13 18.1+	15.0	73.0
21	10 57.8	6.8	70.3	11 37.8	8.8	70.7	12 17.1	10.8	71.1	12 55.5	12.8	71.5	13 33.1	14.7	72.0
22	11 04.6	6.6	69.3	11 46.6	8.6	69.7	12 27.9	10.5	70.1	13 08.3	12.5	70.5	13 47.8	14.5	71.0
23	11 11.2	6.4	68.3	11 55.2	8.4	68.7	12 38.4	10.4	69.1	13 20.8	12.3	69.5	14 02.3	14.3	70.0
24	11 17.6	6.2	67.3	12 03.6	8.1	67.7	12 48.8	10.1	68.1	13 33.1	12.1	68.5	14 16.6	14.0	69.0
25	11 23.8+	6.0	66.3	12 11.7+	7.9	66.7	12 58.9+	9.8	67.1	13 45.2+	11.8	67.5	14 30.6+	13.8	68.0
26	11 29.8	5.8	65.3	12 19.6	7.7	65.7	13 08.7	9.7	66.1	13 57.0	11.6	66.5	14 44.4	13.5	67.0
27	11 35.6	5.5	64.3	12 27.3	7.5	64.6	13 18.4	9.3	65.0	14 08.6	11.3	65.5	14 57.9	13.2	66.0
28	11 41.1	5.4	63.2	12 34.8	7.3	63.6	13 27.7	9.2	64.0	14 19.9	11.0	64.5	15 11.1	13.0	65.0
29	11 46.5	5.1	62.2	12 42.1	7.0	62.6	13 36.9	8.9	63.0	14 30.9	10.8	63.5	15 24.1	12.7	63.9

0°			2°			4°			6°			8°			Dec.
Hc	d	Z	Hc	d	Z	Hc	d	Z	Hc	d	Z	Hc	d	Z	
° ′	′	°	° ′	′	°	° ′	′	°	° ′	′	°	° ′	′	°	°
8 00.0 −	0.1	90.0	7 59.7 −	2.2	90.3	7 58.8 −	4.3	90.6	7 57.4 −	6.5	90.8	7 55.3 −	8.5	91.1	0
7 59.9	0.2	91.0	7 57.5	2.3	91.3	7 54.5	4.4	91.6	7 50.9	6.5	91.8	7 46.8	8.6	92.1	1
7 59.7	0.4	92.0	7 55.2	2.5	92.3	7 50.1	4.6	92.6	7 44.4	6.7	92.8	7 38.2	8.8	93.1	2
7 59.3	0.5	93.0	7 52.7	2.6	93.3	7 45.5	4.7	93.6	7 37.7	6.8	93.9	7 29.4	8.9	94.1	3
7 58.8	0.6	94.0	7 50.1	2.8	94.3	7 40.8	4.9	94.6	7 30.9	7.0	94.9	7 20.5	9.1	95.1	4
7 58.2 −	0.8	95.0	7 47.3 −	2.9	95.3	7 35.9 −	5.0	95.6	7 23.9 −	7.1	95.9	7 11.4 −	9.2	96.1	5
7 57.4	1.0	96.1	7 44.4	3.1	96.3	7 30.9	5.2	96.6	7 16.8	7.2	96.9	7 02.2	9.3	97.1	6
7 56.4	1.1	97.1	7 41.3	3.1	97.3	7 25.7	5.2	97.6	7 09.6	7.4	97.9	6 52.9	9.4	98.1	7
7 55.3	1.2	98.1	7 38.2	3.4	98.3	7 20.5	5.5	98.6	7 02.2	7.4	98.9	6 43.5	9.5	99.1	8
7 54.1	1.4	99.1	7 34.8	3.5	99.4	7 15.0	5.5	99.6	6 54.8	7.7	99.9	6 34.0	9.7	100.1	9
7 52.7 −	1.6	100.1	7 31.3 −	3.6	100.4	7 09.5 −	5.7	100.6	6 47.1 −	7.7	100.9	6 24.3 −	9.8	101.1	10
7 51.1	1.7	101.1	7 27.7	3.7	101.4	7 03.8	5.8	101.6	6 39.4	7.8	101.9	6 14.5	9.9	102.1	11
7 49.4	1.8	102.1	7 24.0	3.9	102.4	6 58.0	5.9	102.6	6 31.6	8.0	102.9	6 04.6	10.0	103.1	12
7 47.6	1.9	103.1	7 20.1	4.0	103.4	6 52.1	6.1	103.6	6 23.6	8.1	103.9	5 54.6	10.1	104.1	13
7 45.7	2.2	104.1	7 16.1	4.2	104.4	6 46.0	6.2	104.6	6 15.5	8.2	104.8	5 44.5	10.2	105.1	14
7 43.5 −	2.2	105.1	7 11.9 −	4.2	105.4	6 39.8 −	6.3	105.6	6 07.3 −	8.3	105.8	5 34.3 −	10.3	106.0	15
7 41.3	2.4	106.1	7 07.7	4.5	106.4	6 33.5	6.4	106.6	5 59.0	8.4	106.8	5 24.0	10.4	107.0	16
7 38.9	2.5	107.2	7 03.2	4.5	107.4	6 27.1	6.5	107.6	5 50.6	8.5	107.8	5 13.6	10.5	108.0	17
7 36.4	2.7	108.2	6 58.7	4.7	108.4	6 20.6	6.7	108.6	5 42.1	8.7	108.8	5 03.1	10.5	109.0	18
7 33.7	2.8	109.2	6 54.0	4.8	109.4	6 13.9	6.7	109.6	5 33.4	8.7	109.8	4 52.6	10.7	110.0	19
7 30.9 −	3.0	110.2	6 49.2 −	4.9	110.4	6 07.2 −	6.9	110.6	5 24.7 −	8.8	110.8	4 41.9 −	10.8	111.0	20
7 27.9	3.1	111.2	6 44.3	5.0	111.4	6 00.3	7.0	111.6	5 15.9	8.9	111.8	4 31.1	10.8	112.0	21
7 24.8	3.2	112.2	6 39.3	5.2	112.4	5 53.3	7.1	112.6	5 07.0	9.0	112.8	4 20.3	10.9	113.0	22
7 21.6	3.3	113.2	6 34.1	5.3	113.4	5 46.2	7.2	113.6	4 58.0	9.1	113.8	4 09.4	11.0	113.9	23
7 18.3	3.5	114.2	6 28.8	5.4	114.4	5 39.0	7.3	114.6	4 48.9	9.2	114.8	3 58.4	11.0	114.9	24
7 14.8 −	3.6	115.2	6 23.4 −	5.5	115.4	5 31.7 −	7.4	115.6	4 39.7 −	9.3	115.8	3 47.4 −	11.2	115.9	25
7 11.2	3.8	116.2	6 17.9	5.6	116.4	5 24.3	7.5	116.6	4 30.4	9.3	116.8	3 36.2	11.1	116.9	26
7 07.4	3.9	117.2	6 12.3	5.7	117.4	5 16.8	7.6	117.6	4 21.1	9.5	117.8	3 25.1	11.3	117.9	27
7 03.5	4.0	118.2	6 06.6	5.9	118.4	5 09.2	7.6	118.6	4 11.6	9.5	118.8	3 13.8	11.3	118.9	28
6 59.5	4.1	119.2	6 00.7	6.0	119.4	5 01.6	7.8	119.6	4 02.1	9.5	119.7	3 02.5	11.3	119.9	29

10°			12°			14°			16°			18°			Dec.
Hc	d	Z	Hc	d	Z	Hc	d	Z	Hc	d	Z	Hc	d	Z	
° ′	′	°	° ′	′	°	° ′	′	°	° ′	′	°	° ′	′	°	°
7 52.7 −	10.6	91.4	7 49.4 −	12.6	91.7	7 45.7 −	14.8	91.9	7 41.3 −	16.8	92.2	7 36.4 −	18.8	92.5	0
7 42.1	10.8	92.4	7 36.8	12.8	92.7	7 30.9	14.8	92.9	7 24.5	16.8	93.2	7 17.6	18.9	93.4	1
7 31.3	10.8	93.4	7 24.0	12.9	93.6	7 16.1	15.0	93.9	7 07.7	17.0	94.2	6 58.7	19.0	94.4	2
7 20.5	11.0	94.4	7 11.1	13.1	94.6	7 01.1	15.1	94.9	6 50.7	17.2	95.1	6 39.7	19.1	95.4	3
7 09.5	11.1	95.4	6 58.0	13.2	95.6	6 46.0	15.2	95.9	6 33.5	17.2	96.1	6 20.6	19.2	96.3	4
6 58.4 − 11.3		96.4	6 44.8 −	13.2	96.6	6 30.8 −	15.3	96.8	6 16.3 −	17.3	97.0	6 01.4 −	19.3	97.3	5
6 47.1	11.3	97.3	6 31.6	13.4	97.6	6 15.5	15.4	97.8	5 59.0	17.4	98.0	5 42.1	19.5	98.2	6
6 35.8	11.5	98.3	6 18.2	13.6	98.6	6 00.1	15.6	98.8	5 41.6	17.6	99.0	5 22.6	19.5	99.2	7
6 24.3	11.6	99.3	6 04.6	13.6	99.5	5 44.5	15.6	99.7	5 24.0	17.6	99.9	5 03.1	19.5	100.1	8
6 12.7	11.7	100.3	5 51.0	13.7	100.5	5 28.9	15.7	100.7	5 06.4	17.7	100.9	4 43.6	19.7	101.1	9
6 01.0 −	11.8	101.3	5 37.3 −	13.8	101.5	5 13.2 −	15.8	101.7	4 48.7 −	17.8	101.9	4 23.9 −	19.7	102.0	10
5 49.2	11.9	102.3	5 23.5	13.9	102.5	4 57.4	15.9	102.7	4 30.9	17.8	102.8	4 04.2	19.8	103.0	11
5 37.3	12.0	103.3	5 09.6	14.0	103.5	4 41.5	16.0	103.6	4 13.1	18.0	103.8	3 44.4	19.9	103.9	12
5 25.3	12.1	104.3	4 55.6	14.1	104.4	4 25.5	16.0	104.6	3 55.1	17.9	104.7	3 24.5	19.9	104.9	13
5 13.2	12.2	105.2	4 41.5	14.2	105.4	4 09.5	16.2	105.6	3 37.2	18.1	105.7	3 04.6	20.0	105.8	14
5 01.0 −	12.3	106.2	4 27.3 −	14.2	106.4	3 53.3 −	16.1	106.5	3 19.1 −	18.1	106.6	2 44.6 −	20.0	106.7	15
4 48.7	12.4	107.2	4 13.1	14.3	107.4	3 37.2	16.3	107.5	3 01.0	18.2	107.6	2 24.6	20.0	107.7	16
4 36.3	12.4	108.2	3 58.8	14.4	108.3	3 20.9	16.3	108.4	2 42.8	18.2	108.5	2 04.6	20.1	108.6	17
4 23.9	12.5	109.2	3 44.4	14.5	109.3	3 04.6	16.4	109.4	2 24.6	18.2	109.5	1 44.5	20.1	109.6	18
4 11.4	12.6	110.1	3 29.9	14.5	110.3	2 48.2	16.4	110.4	2 06.4	18.3	110.5	1 24.4	20.1	110.5	19
3 58.8 −	12.7	111.1	3 15.4 −	14.6	111.2	2 31.8 −	16.4	111.3	1 48.1 −	18.3	111.4	1 04.3 −	20.2	111.5	20
3 46.1	12.7	112.1	3 00.8	14.6	112.2	2 15.4	16.5	112.3	1 29.8	18.3	112.4	0 44.1	20.2	112.4	21
3 33.4	12.8	113.1	2 46.2	14.6	113.2	1 58.9	16.5	113.3	1 11.5	18.4	113.3	0 23.9	20.1	113.3	22
3 20.6	12.9	114.1	2 31.6	14.8	114.2	1 42.4	16.6	114.2	0 53.1	18.4	114.3	0 03.8 − 20.2		114.3	23
3 07.7	12.9	115.0	2 16.8	14.7	115.1	1 25.8	16.5	115.2	0 34.7	18.3	115.2	0 16.4 + 20.2		64.7	24
2 54.8 −	12.9	116.0	2 02.1 −	14.8	116.1	1 09.3 −	16.6	116.1	0 16.4 − 18.4		116.2	0 36.6 + 20.1		63.8	25
2 41.9	13.0	117.0	1 47.3	14.8	117.1	0 52.7	16.6	117.1	0 02.0 + 18.4		62.9	0 56.7	20.2	62.9	26
2 28.9	13.1	118.0	1 32.5	14.8	118.0	0 36.1	16.7	118.1	0 20.4	18.4	61.9	1 16.9	20.1	62.0	27
2 15.8	13.1	119.0	1 17.7	14.9	119.0	0 19.4	16.6	119.0	0 38.8	18.3	61.0	1 37.0	20.1	61.0	28
2 02.7	13.1	119.9	1 02.8	14.9	120.0	0 02.8 − 16.6		120.0	0 57.1	18.4	60.0	1 57.1	20.0	60.1	29

Dec.	20° Hc	d	Z	22° Hc	d	Z	24° Hc	d	Z	26° Hc	d	Z	28° Hc	d	Z
°	° ′	′	°	° ′	′	°	° ′	′	°	° ′	′	°	° ′	′	°
0	7 30.9	+20.6	92.8	7 24.8	+22.7	93.0	7 18.3	+24.5	93.3	7 11.2	+26.4	93.5	7 03.5	+28.3	93.8
1	7 51.5	20.5	91.8	7 47.5	22.4	92.1	7 42.8	24.4	92.4	7 37.6	26.3	92.6	7 31.8	28.3	92.9
2	8 12.0	20.4	90.9	8 09.9	22.4	91.1	8 07.2	24.3	91.4	8 03.9	26.3	91.7	8 00.1	28.1	92.0
3	8 32.4	20.2	89.9	8 32.3	22.2	90.2	8 31.5	24.2	90.5	8 30.2	26.1	90.8	8 28.2	28.0	91.1
4	8 52.6	20.1	89.0	8 54.5	22.1	89.3	8 55.7	24.1	89.6	8 56.3	25.9	89.9	8 56.2	27.8	90.2
5	9 12.7	+20.0	88.0	9 16.6	+21.9	88.3	9 19.8	+23.8	88.7	9 22.2	+25.9	89.0	9 24.0	+27.7	89.3
6	9 32.7	19.8	87.0	9 38.5	21.8	87.4	9 43.6	23.8	87.7	9 48.1	25.6	88.1	9 51.7	27.6	88.4
7	9 52.5	19.6	86.1	10 00.3	21.6	86.4	10 07.4	23.6	86.8	10 13.7	25.5	87.1	10 19.3	27.5	87.5
8	10 12.1	19.4	85.1	10 21.9	21.4	85.5	10 31.0	23.4	85.9	10 39.2	25.4	86.2	10 46.8	27.2	86.6
9	10 31.5	19.3	84.2	10 43.3	21.3	84.5	10 54.4	23.2	84.9	11 04.6	25.2	85.3	11 14.0	27.1	85.7
10	10 50.8	+19.1	83.2	11 04.6	+21.1	83.6	11 17.6	+23.1	84.0	11 29.8	+25.0	84.4	11 41.1	+27.0	84.8
11	11 09.9	18.9	82.2	11 25.7	20.9	82.6	11 40.7	22.9	83.0	11 54.8	24.8	83.5	12 08.1	26.7	83.9
12	11 28.8	18.7	81.3	11 46.6	20.7	81.7	12 03.6	22.7	82.1	12 19.6	24.7	82.5	12 34.8	26.6	83.0
13	11 47.5	18.6	80.3	12 07.3	20.6	80.7	12 26.3	22.5	81.1	12 44.3	24.4	81.6	13 01.4	26.3	82.0
14	12 06.1	18.3	79.3	12 27.9	20.3	79.8	12 48.8	22.2	80.2	13 08.7	24.3	80.6	13 27.7	26.2	81.1
15	12 24.4	+18.1	78.3	12 48.2	+20.1	78.8	13 11.0	+22.1	79.2	13 33.0	+24.0	79.7	13 53.9	+26.0	80.2
16	12 42.5	17.9	77.4	13 08.3	19.9	77.8	13 33.1	21.9	78.3	13 57.0	23.8	78.8	14 19.9	25.7	79.3
17	13 00.4	17.7	76.4	13 28.2	19.6	76.9	13 55.0	21.6	77.3	14 20.8	23.6	77.8	14 45.6	25.5	78.3
18	13 18.1	17.4	75.4	13 47.8	19.5	75.9	14 16.6	21.4	76.4	14 44.4	23.3	76.9	15 11.1	25.3	77.4
19	13 35.5	17.2	74.4	14 07.3	19.1	74.9	14 38.0	21.2	75.4	15 07.7	23.1	75.9	15 36.4	25.0	76.4
20	13 52.7	+17.0	73.4	14 26.4	+19.0	73.9	14 59.2	+20.9	74.4	15 30.8	+22.9	75.0	16 01.4	+24.8	75.5
21	14 09.7	16.7	72.5	14 45.4	18.7	72.9	15 20.1	20.6	73.5	15 53.7	22.6	74.0	16 26.2	24.6	74.6
22	14 26.4	16.5	71.5	15 04.1	18.5	72.0	15 40.7	20.4	72.5	16 16.3	22.4	73.0	16 50.8	24.2	73.6
23	14 42.9	16.3	70.5	15 22.6	18.1	71.0	16 01.1	20.2	71.5	16 38.7	22.0	72.1	17 15.0	24.0	72.6
24	14 59.2	15.9	69.5	15 40.7	18.0	70.0	16 21.3	19.8	70.5	17 00.7	21.8	71.1	17 39.0	23.7	71.7
25	15 15.1	+15.7	68.5	15 58.7	+17.6	69.0	16 41.1	+19.6	69.5	17 22.5	+21.5	70.1	18 02.7	+23.5	70.7
26	15 30.8	15.5	67.5	16 16.3	17.4	68.0	17 00.7	19.3	68.6	17 44.0	21.3	69.1	18 26.2	23.1	69.8
27	15 46.3	15.1	66.5	16 33.7	17.1	67.0	17 20.0	19.0	67.6	18 05.3	20.9	68.2	18 49.3	22.8	68.8
28	16 01.4	14.9	65.5	16 50.8	16.8	66.0	17 39.0	18.7	66.6	18 26.2	20.6	67.2	19 12.1	22.5	67.8
29	16 16.3	14.6	64.5	17 07.6	16.4	65.0	17 57.7	18.4	65.6	18 46.8	20.3	66.2	19 34.6	22.2	66.8

Dec.	30° Hc	d	Z	32° Hc	d	Z	34° Hc	d	Z	36° Hc	d	Z	38° Hc	d	Z
°	° ′	′	°	° ′	′	°	° ′	′	°	° ′	′	°	° ′	′	°
0	6 55.4	+30.1	94.0	6 46.7	+32.0	94.3	6 37.5	+33.8	94.5	6 27.9	+35.4	94.7	6 17.8	+37.1	94.9
1	7 25.5	30.1	93.1	7 18.7	31.8	93.4	7 11.3	33.6	93.7	7 03.3	35.4	93.9	6 54.9	37.1	94.2
2	7 55.6	30.0	92.3	7 50.5	31.8	92.6	7 44.9	33.6	92.8	7 38.7	35.3	93.1	7 32.0	36.9	93.4
3	8 25.6	29.8	91.4	8 22.3	31.7	91.7	8 18.5	33.4	92.0	8 14.0	35.2	92.3	8 08.9	36.9	92.6
4	8 55.4	29.7	90.5	8 54.0	31.5	90.8	8 51.9	33.3	91.1	8 49.2	35.0	91.5	8 45.8	36.6	91.8
5	9 25.1	+29.6	89.6	9 25.5	+31.4	90.0	9 25.2	+33.2	90.3	9 24.2	+35.0	90.6	9 22.6	+36.6	91.0
6	9 54.7	29.5	88.8	9 56.9	31.3	89.1	9 58.4	33.1	89.5	9 59.2	34.8	89.8	9 59.2	36.6	90.2
7	10 24.2	29.3	87.9	10 28.2	31.2	88.2	10 31.5	33.0	88.6	10 34.0	34.7	89.0	10 35.8	36.4	89.4
8	10 53.5	29.1	87.0	10 59.4	31.0	87.4	11 04.5	32.8	87.8	11 08.7	34.6	88.2	11 12.2	36.3	88.6
9	11 22.6	29.0	86.1	11 30.4	30.8	86.5	11 37.3	32.6	86.9	11 43.3	34.4	87.3	11 48.5	36.1	87.8
10	11 51.6	+28.8	85.2	12 01.2	+30.7	85.6	12 09.9	+32.5	86.1	12 17.7	+34.3	86.5	12 24.6	+36.0	86.9
11	12 20.4	28.7	84.3	12 31.9	30.5	84.7	12 42.4	32.3	85.2	12 52.0	34.1	85.6	13 00.6	35.9	86.1
12	12 49.1	28.4	83.4	13 02.4	30.3	83.9	13 14.7	32.2	84.3	13 26.1	33.9	84.8	13 36.5	35.7	85.3
13	13 17.5	28.3	82.5	13 32.7	30.1	83.0	13 46.9	31.9	83.5	14 00.0	33.8	83.9	14 12.2	35.5	84.4
14	13 45.8	28.1	81.6	14 02.8	30.0	82.1	14 18.8	31.8	82.6	14 33.8	33.6	83.1	14 47.7	35.3	83.6
15	14 13.9	+27.8	80.7	14 32.8	+29.7	81.2	14 50.6	+31.6	81.7	15 07.4	+33.3	82.2	15 23.0	+35.2	82.8
16	14 41.7	27.7	79.8	15 02.5	29.5	80.3	15 22.2	31.3	80.8	15 40.7	33.2	81.4	15 58.2	34.9	81.9
17	15 09.4	27.4	78.8	15 32.0	29.3	79.4	15 53.5	31.2	79.9	16 13.9	33.0	80.5	16 33.1	34.7	81.1
18	15 36.8	27.2	77.9	16 01.3	29.1	78.5	16 24.7	30.9	79.1	16 46.9	32.7	79.6	17 07.8	34.6	80.2
19	16 04.0	26.9	77.0	16 30.4	28.8	77.6	16 55.6	30.7	78.2	17 19.6	32.5	78.8	17 42.4	34.3	79.4
20	16 30.9	+26.7	76.1	16 59.2	+28.6	76.7	17 26.3	+30.4	77.3	17 52.1	+32.3	77.9	18 16.7	+34.0	78.5
21	16 57.6	26.4	75.1	17 27.8	28.3	75.7	17 56.7	30.2	76.4	18 24.4	32.0	77.0	18 50.7	33.9	77.7
22	17 24.0	26.2	74.2	17 56.1	28.1	74.8	18 26.9	30.0	75.4	18 56.4	31.8	76.1	19 24.6	33.5	76.8
23	17 50.2	25.9	73.3	18 24.2	27.8	73.9	18 56.9	29.6	74.5	19 28.2	31.5	75.2	19 58.1	33.3	75.9
24	18 16.1	25.6	72.3	18 52.0	27.5	72.9	19 26.5	29.4	73.6	19 59.7	31.2	74.3	20 31.4	33.1	75.0
25	18 41.7	+25.4	71.3	19 19.5	+27.2	72.0	19 55.9	+29.1	72.7	20 30.9	+30.9	73.4	21 04.5	+32.7	74.1
26	19 07.1	25.0	70.4	19 46.7	26.9	71.1	20 25.0	28.8	71.8	21 01.8	30.7	72.5	21 37.2	32.5	73.2
27	19 32.1	24.7	69.4	20 13.6	26.6	70.1	20 53.8	28.4	70.8	21 32.5	30.3	71.5	22 09.7	32.2	72.3
28	19 56.8	24.4	68.5	20 40.2	26.3	69.1	21 22.2	28.2	69.9	22 02.8	30.0	70.6	22 41.9	31.8	71.4
29	20 21.2	24.1	67.5	21 06.5	26.0	68.2	21 50.4	27.8	68.9	22 32.8	29.7	69.7	23 13.7	31.5	70.5

20°			22°			24°			26°			28°			Dec.
Hc	d	Z	Hc	d	Z	Hc	d	Z	Hc	d	Z	Hc	d	Z	
7 30.9	-20.8	92.8	7 24.8	-22.7	93.0	7 18.3	-24.7	93.3	7 11.2	-26.6	93.5	7 03.5	-28.4	93.8	0
7 10.1	20.9	93.7	7 02.1	22.8	93.9	6 53.6	24.8	94.2	6 44.6	26.7	94.4	6 35.1	28.5	94.7	1
6 49.2	20.9	94.6	6 39.3	23.0	94.9	6 28.8	24.8	95.1	6 17.9	26.7	95.3	6 06.6	28.7	95.5	2
6 28.3	21.1	95.6	6 16.3	23.0	95.8	6 04.0	25.0	96.0	5 51.2	26.9	96.2	5 37.9	28.7	96.4	3
6 07.2	21.2	96.5	5 53.3	23.1	96.7	5 39.0	25.0	96.9	5 24.3	26.9	97.1	5 09.2	28.7	97.3	4
5 46.0	-21.3	97.5	5 30.2	-23.2	97.7	5 14.0	-25.1	97.9	4 57.4	-27.0	98.0	4 40.5	-28.9	98.2	5
5 24.7	21.4	98.4	5 07.0	23.3	98.6	4 48.9	25.2	98.8	4 30.4	27.0	98.9	4 11.6	28.8	99.1	6
5 03.3	21.4	99.3	4 43.7	23.4	99.5	4 23.7	25.3	99.7	4 03.4	27.2	99.8	3 42.8	29.0	100.0	7
4 41.9	21.5	100.3	4 20.3	23.4	100.4	3 58.4	25.3	100.6	3 36.2	27.1	100.7	3 13.8	29.0	100.8	8
4 20.4	21.6	101.2	3 56.9	23.5	101.4	3 33.1	25.4	101.5	3 09.1	27.2	101.6	2 44.8	29.0	101.7	9
3 58.8	-21.7	102.2	3 33.4	-23.6	102.3	3 07.7	-25.4	102.4	2 41.9	-27.3	102.5	2 15.8	-29.1	102.6	10
3 37.1	21.7	103.1	3 09.8	23.6	103.2	2 42.3	25.5	103.3	2 14.6	27.3	103.4	1 46.7	29.0	103.5	11
3 15.4	21.8	104.0	2 46.2	23.6	104.1	2 16.8	25.4	104.2	1 47.3	27.3	104.3	1 17.7	29.1	104.3	12
2 53.6	21.8	105.0	2 22.6	23.7	105.0	1 51.4	25.6	105.1	1 20.0	27.3	105.2	0 48.6	29.2	105.2	13
2 31.8	21.9	105.9	1 58.9	23.7	106.0	1 25.8	25.5	106.0	0 52.7	27.4	106.1	0 19.4	-29.1	106.1	14
2 10.0	-21.9	106.8	1 35.2	-23.7	106.9	1 00.3	-25.6	106.9	0 25.3	-27.3	107.0	0 09.7	+29.1	73.0	15
1 48.1	21.9	107.8	1 11.5	23.8	107.8	0 34.7	25.5	107.8	0 02.0	+27.4	72.2	0 38.8	29.1	72.2	16
1 26.2	21.9	108.7	0 47.7	23.8	108.7	0 09.2	-25.6	108.7	0 29.4	27.3	71.3	1 07.9	29.1	71.3	17
1 04.3	22.0	109.6	0 23.9	23.7	109.6	0 16.4	+25.6	70.4	0 56.7	27.3	70.4	1 37.0	29.0	70.4	18
0 42.3	22.0	110.5	0 00.2	-23.8	110.6	0 42.0	25.5	69.5	1 24.0	27.4	69.5	2 06.0	29.1	69.5	19
0 20.3	-21.9	111.5	0 23.6	+23.8	68.5	1 07.5	+25.6	68.5	1 51.4	+27.2	68.6	2 35.1	+29.0	68.7	20
0 01.6	+22.0	67.6	0 47.6	23.7	67.6	1 33.1	25.5	67.6	2 18.6	27.3	67.7	3 04.1	28.9	67.8	21
0 23.6	22.0	66.7	1 11.1	23.8	66.7	1 58.6	25.5	66.7	2 45.9	27.4	66.8	3 33.0	29.0	66.9	22
0 45.6	21.9	65.7	1 34.9	23.7	65.8	2 24.1	25.4	65.8	3 13.1	27.2	65.9	4 02.0	28.8	66.0	23
1 07.5	22.0	64.8	1 58.6	23.6	64.8	2 49.5	25.4	64.9	3 40.3	27.1	65.0	4 30.8	28.8	65.2	24
1 29.5	+21.9	63.9	2 22.2	+23.7	63.9	3 14.9	+25.4	64.0	4 07.4	+27.0	64.1	4 59.6	+28.7	64.3	25
1 51.4	21.8	62.9	2 45.9	23.6	63.0	3 40.3	25.3	63.1	4 34.4	27.0	63.2	5 28.3	28.7	63.4	26
2 13.2	21.9	62.0	3 09.5	23.5	62.1	4 05.6	25.2	62.2	5 01.4	26.9	62.3	5 57.0	28.5	62.5	27
2 35.1	21.8	61.1	3 33.0	23.5	61.2	4 30.8	25.2	61.3	5 28.3	26.8	61.4	6 25.5	28.5	61.6	28
2 56.9	21.7	60.1	3 56.5	23.5	60.2	4 56.0	25.1	60.4	5 55.1	26.8	60.5	6 54.0	28.3	60.7	29

30°			32°			34°			36°			38°			Dec.
Hc	d	Z	Hc	d	Z	Hc	d	Z	Hc	d	Z	Hc	d	Z	
6 55.4	-30.3	94.0	6 46.7	-32.1	94.3	6 37.5	-33.8	94.5	6 27.9	-35.5	94.7	6 17.8	-37.2	94.9	0
6 25.1	30.4	94.9	6 14.6	32.1	95.1	6 03.7	33.9	95.3	5 52.4	35.6	95.5	5 40.6	37.3	95.7	1
5 54.7	30.4	95.8	5 42.5	32.2	96.0	5 29.8	33.9	96.2	5 16.8	35.7	96.3	5 03.3	37.3	96.5	2
5 24.3	30.5	96.6	5 10.3	32.3	96.8	4 55.9	34.1	97.0	4 41.1	35.7	97.1	4 26.0	37.4	97.3	3
4 53.8	30.6	97.5	4 38.0	32.4	97.7	4 21.8	34.0	97.8	4 05.4	35.8	98.0	3 48.6	37.4	98.1	4
4 23.2	-30.6	98.4	4 05.6	-32.4	98.5	3 47.8	-34.2	98.6	3 29.6	-35.8	98.8	3 11.2	-37.4	98.9	5
3 52.6	30.7	99.2	3 33.2	32.4	99.3	3 13.6	34.1	99.5	2 53.8	35.8	99.6	2 33.8	37.5	99.7	6
3 21.9	30.7	100.1	3 00.8	32.5	100.2	2 39.5	34.2	100.3	2 18.0	35.9	100.4	1 56.3	37.5	100.4	7
2 51.2	30.8	100.9	2 28.3	32.5	101.0	2 05.3	34.3	101.1	1 42.1	35.9	101.2	1 18.8	37.5	101.2	8
2 20.4	30.8	101.8	1 55.8	32.5	101.9	1 31.0	34.2	101.9	1 06.2	35.9	102.0	0 41.3	37.5	102.0	9
1 49.6	-30.8	102.7	1 23.2	-32.5	102.7	0 56.8	-34.2	102.7	0 30.3	-35.9	102.8	0 03.8	-37.6	102.8	10
1 18.8	30.9	103.5	0 50.7	32.6	103.5	0 22.6	-34.3	103.6	0 05.6	+35.9	76.4	0 33.8	+37.5	76.4	11
0 47.9	30.8	104.4	0 18.1	-32.6	104.4	0 11.7	+34.3	75.6	0 41.5	35.9	75.6	1 11.3	37.5	75.7	12
0 17.1	-30.9	105.2	0 14.5	+32.6	74.8	0 46.0	34.2	74.8	1 17.4	35.9	74.8	1 48.8	37.5	74.9	13
0 13.8	+30.9	73.9	0 47.0	32.6	73.9	1 20.2	34.2	74.0	1 53.3	35.9	74.0	2 26.3	37.4	74.1	14
0 44.7	+30.8	73.1	1 19.6	+32.5	73.1	1 54.4	+34.2	73.1	2 29.2	35.0	73.2	3 03.7	+37.4	73.3	15
1 15.5	30.8	72.2	1 52.1	32.6	72.3	2 28.6	34.2	72.3	3 05.0	35.8	72.4	3 41.1	37.4	72.5	16
1 46.3	30.8	71.3	2 24.7	32.4	71.4	3 02.8	34.2	71.5	3 40.8	35.7	71.6	4 18.5	37.3	71.7	17
2 17.1	30.8	70.5	2 57.1	32.5	70.6	3 37.0	34.0	70.7	4 16.5	35.7	70.8	4 55.8	37.3	71.0	18
2 47.9	30.7	69.6	3 29.6	32.4	69.7	4 11.0	34.1	69.9	4 52.2	35.7	70.0	5 33.1	37.2	70.2	19
3 18.6	+30.7	68.8	4 02.0	+32.3	68.9	4 45.1	+34.0	69.0	5 27.9	+35.6	69.2	6 10.3	+37.2	69.4	20
3 49.3	30.7	67.9	4 34.3	32.3	68.0	5 19.1	33.9	68.2	6 03.5	35.6	68.4	6 47.5	37.0	68.6	21
4 20.0	30.6	67.0	5 06.6	32.3	67.2	5 53.0	33.8	67.4	6 39.0	35.4	67.6	7 24.5	37.0	67.8	22
4 50.6	30.5	66.2	5 38.9	32.1	66.3	6 26.8	33.8	66.5	7 14.4	35.3	66.8	8 01.5	36.9	67.0	23
5 21.1	30.4	65.3	6 11.0	32.1	65.5	7 00.6	33.7	65.7	7 49.7	35.3	65.9	8 38.4	36.8	66.2	24
5 51.5	+30.4	64.4	6 43.1	+32.0	64.6	7 34.3	+33.5	64.9	8 25.0	+35.1	65.1	9 15.2	+36.7	65.4	25
6 21.9	30.3	63.6	7 15.1	31.9	63.8	8 07.8	33.5	64.0	9 00.1	35.1	64.3	9 51.9	36.5	64.6	26
6 52.2	30.1	62.7	7 47.0	31.7	62.9	8 41.3	33.4	63.2	9 35.2	34.9	63.5	10 28.4	36.5	63.8	27
7 22.3	30.1	61.8	8 18.7	31.7	62.1	9 14.7	33.2	62.4	10 10.1	34.8	62.7	11 04.9	36.3	63.0	28
7 52.4	30.0	61.0	8 50.4	31.6	61.2	9 47.9	33.1	61.5	10 44.9	34.6	61.8	11 41.2	36.2	62.2	29

Dec.	40° Hc	d	Z	42° Hc	d	Z	44° Hc	d	Z	46° Hc	d	Z	48° Hc	d	Z
0	6 07.2	+38.8	95.2	5 56.2	+40.3	95.4	5 44.7	+41.9	95.6	5 32.9	+43.3	95.8	5 20.6	+44.8	96.0
1	6 46.0	38.6	94.4	6 36.5	40.3	94.6	6 26.6	41.8	94.9	6 16.2	43.3	95.1	6 05.4	44.7	95.3
2	7 24.6	38.6	93.6	7 16.8	40.2	93.9	7 08.4	41.7	94.1	6 59.5	43.2	94.4	6 50.1	44.6	94.6
3	8 03.2	38.6	92.9	7 57.0	40.1	93.1	7 50.1	41.7	93.4	7 42.7	43.2	93.7	7 34.7	44.6	93.9
4	8 41.8	38.4	92.1	8 37.1	40.0	92.4	8 31.8	41.6	92.7	8 25.9	43.0	93.0	8 19.3	44.5	93.3
5	9 20.2	+38.3	91.3	9 17.1	+39.9	91.6	9 13.4	+41.5	92.0	9 08.9	+43.0	92.3	9 03.8	+44.5	92.6
6	9 58.5	38.2	90.5	9 57.0	39.9	90.9	9 54.9	41.4	91.2	9 51.9	43.0	91.6	9 48.3	44.4	91.9
7	10 36.7	38.1	89.7	10 36.9	39.7	90.1	10 36.3	41.2	90.5	10 34.9	42.8	90.9	10 32.7	44.2	91.2
8	11 14.8	38.0	88.9	11 16.6	39.6	89.3	11 17.5	41.2	89.7	11 17.7	42.7	90.1	11 16.9	44.2	90.5
9	11 52.8	37.8	88.2	11 56.2	39.5	88.6	11 58.7	41.1	89.0	12 00.4	42.6	89.4	12 01.1	44.1	89.9
10	12 30.6	+37.7	87.4	12 35.7	+39.3	87.8	12 39.8	+40.9	88.3	12 43.0	+42.4	88.7	12 45.2	+44.0	89.2
11	13 08.3	37.6	86.6	13 15.0	39.2	87.0	13 20.7	40.8	87.5	13 25.4	42.4	88.0	13 29.2	43.8	88.5
12	13 45.9	37.3	85.8	13 54.2	39.1	86.3	14 01.5	40.7	86.8	14 07.8	42.2	87.3	14 13.0	43.8	87.8
13	14 23.2	37.3	85.0	14 33.3	38.8	85.5	14 42.2	40.5	86.0	14 50.0	42.1	86.5	14 56.8	43.6	87.0
14	15 00.5	37.0	84.1	15 12.1	38.8	84.7	15 22.7	40.4	85.2	15 32.1	41.9	85.8	15 40.4	43.4	86.3
15	15 37.5	+36.9	83.3	15 50.9	+38.5	83.9	16 03.1	+40.1	84.5	16 14.0	+41.8	85.0	16 23.8	+43.3	85.6
16	16 14.4	36.7	82.5	16 29.4	38.4	83.1	16 43.2	40.1	83.7	16 55.8	41.6	84.3	17 07.1	43.2	84.9
17	16 51.1	36.5	81.7	17 07.8	38.2	82.3	17 23.3	39.8	82.9	17 37.4	41.5	83.5	17 50.3	43.0	84.2
18	17 27.6	36.2	80.9	17 46.0	38.0	81.5	18 03.1	39.6	82.1	18 18.9	41.2	82.8	18 33.3	42.8	83.4
19	18 03.8	36.1	80.0	18 24.0	37.7	80.7	18 42.7	39.5	81.3	19 00.1	41.1	82.0	19 16.1	42.7	82.7
20	18 39.9	+35.8	79.2	19 01.7	+37.6	79.8	19 22.2	+39.2	80.5	19 41.2	+40.9	81.2	19 58.8	+42.4	81.9
21	19 15.7	35.6	78.3	19 39.3	37.3	79.0	20 01.4	39.0	79.7	20 22.1	40.6	80.5	20 41.2	42.3	81.2
22	19 51.3	35.4	77.5	20 16.6	37.1	78.2	20 40.4	38.8	78.9	21 02.7	40.5	79.7	21 23.5	42.0	80.4
23	20 26.7	35.0	76.6	20 53.7	36.8	77.3	21 19.2	38.6	78.1	21 43.2	40.2	78.9	22 05.5	41.8	79.7
24	21 01.7	34.9	75.7	21 30.5	36.6	76.5	21 57.8	38.2	77.3	22 23.4	39.9	78.1	22 47.3	41.6	78.9
25	21 36.6	+34.5	74.7	22 07.1	+36.3	75.6	22 36.0	+38.1	76.4	23 03.3	+39.8	77.3	23 28.9	+41.4	78.1
26	22 11.1	34.3	74.0	22 43.4	36.0	74.8	23 14.1	37.7	75.6	23 43.1	39.4	76.4	24 10.3	41.1	77.3
27	22 45.4	33.9	73.1	23 19.4	35.8	73.9	23 51.8	37.5	74.8	24 22.5	39.2	75.6	24 51.4	40.9	76.5
28	23 19.3	33.7	72.2	23 55.2	35.4	73.0	24 29.3	37.2	73.9	25 01.7	38.9	74.8	25 32.3	40.6	75.7
29	23 53.0	33.3	71.3	24 30.6	35.2	72.2	25 06.5	36.9	73.0	25 40.6	38.6	73.9	26 12.9	40.3	74.9

Dec.	50° Hc	d	Z	52° Hc	d	Z	54° Hc	d	Z	56° Hc	d	Z	58° Hc	d	Z
0	5 07.9	+46.2	96.1	4 54.9	+47.5	96.3	4 41.5	+48.7	96.5	4 27.8	+49.9	96.6	4 13.8	+51.0	96.8
1	5 54.1	46.1	95.5	5 42.4	47.4	95.7	5 30.2	48.7	95.9	5 17.7	49.8	96.1	5 04.8	51.0	96.3
2	6 40.2	46.0	94.9	6 29.8	47.3	95.1	6 18.9	48.6	95.3	6 07.5	49.9	95.5	5 55.8	50.9	95.7
3	7 26.2	46.0	94.2	7 17.1	47.3	94.5	7 07.5	48.6	94.7	6 57.4	49.7	95.0	6 46.7	50.9	95.2
4	8 12.2	45.9	93.6	8 04.4	47.3	93.8	7 56.1	48.5	94.1	7 47.1	49.8	94.4	7 37.6	50.9	94.7
5	8 58.1	+45.8	92.9	8 51.7	+47.1	93.2	8 44.6	+48.4	93.5	8 36.9	+49.6	93.8	8 28.5	+50.9	94.1
6	9 43.9	45.8	92.3	9 38.8	47.2	92.6	9 33.0	48.4	92.9	9 26.5	49.7	93.3	9 19.4	50.7	93.6
7	10 29.7	45.7	91.6	10 26.0	47.0	92.0	10 21.4	48.4	92.3	10 16.2	49.5	92.7	10 10.1	50.8	93.1
8	11 15.4	45.6	90.9	11 13.0	47.0	91.3	11 09.8	48.2	91.7	11 05.7	49.5	92.1	11 00.9	50.6	92.5
9	12 01.0	45.5	90.3	12 00.0	46.8	90.7	11 58.0	48.2	91.1	11 55.2	49.5	91.6	11 51.5	50.7	92.0
10	12 46.5	+45.4	89.6	12 46.8	+46.8	90.1	12 46.2	+48.1	90.5	12 44.7	+49.3	91.0	12 42.2	+50.5	91.4
11	13 31.9	45.3	88.9	13 33.6	46.7	89.4	13 34.3	48.0	89.9	13 34.0	49.3	90.4	13 32.7	50.5	90.9
12	14 17.2	45.2	88.3	14 20.3	46.6	88.8	14 22.3	47.9	89.3	14 23.3	49.2	89.8	14 23.2	50.4	90.3
13	15 02.4	45.0	87.6	15 06.9	46.4	88.1	15 10.2	47.9	88.7	15 12.5	49.1	89.2	15 13.6	50.3	89.8
14	15 47.4	45.0	86.9	15 53.3	46.4	87.5	15 58.1	47.7	88.0	16 01.6	49.0	88.6	16 03.9	50.2	89.2
15	16 32.4	+44.8	86.2	16 39.7	+46.2	86.8	16 45.8	+47.5	87.4	16 50.6	+48.8	88.0	16 54.1	+50.1	88.6
16	17 17.2	44.6	85.5	17 25.9	46.1	86.1	17 33.3	47.5	86.8	17 39.4	48.8	87.4	17 44.2	50.0	88.0
17	18 01.8	44.5	84.8	18 12.0	45.9	85.5	18 20.8	47.3	86.1	18 28.2	48.7	86.8	18 34.2	49.9	87.5
18	18 46.3	44.3	84.1	18 57.9	45.8	84.8	19 08.1	47.2	85.5	19 16.9	48.5	86.2	19 24.1	49.8	86.9
19	19 30.6	44.2	83.4	19 43.7	45.7	84.1	19 55.3	47.1	84.8	20 05.4	48.4	85.5	20 13.9	49.7	86.3
20	20 14.8	+44.0	82.7	20 29.4	+45.4	83.4	20 42.4	+46.8	84.2	20 53.8	+48.2	84.9	21 03.6	+49.6	85.7
21	20 58.8	43.8	81.9	21 14.8	45.3	82.7	21 29.2	46.8	83.5	21 42.0	48.1	84.3	21 53.2	49.4	85.1
22	21 42.6	43.6	81.2	22 00.1	45.1	82.0	22 16.0	46.5	82.8	22 30.1	48.0	83.6	22 42.6	49.3	84.5
23	22 26.2	43.4	80.5	22 45.2	44.9	81.3	23 02.5	46.4	82.1	23 18.1	47.8	83.0	23 31.9	49.1	83.8
24	23 09.6	43.2	79.7	23 30.1	44.8	80.6	23 48.9	46.2	81.4	24 05.9	47.6	82.3	24 21.0	49.0	83.2
25	23 52.8	+43.0	79.0	24 14.9	+44.5	79.8	24 35.1	+46.0	80.7	24 53.5	+47.4	81.6	25 10.0	+48.8	82.6
26	24 35.8	42.7	78.2	24 59.4	44.3	79.1	25 21.1	45.8	80.0	25 40.9	47.3	81.0	25 58.8	48.6	81.9
27	25 18.5	42.5	77.4	25 43.7	44.0	78.4	26 06.9	45.6	79.3	26 28.2	47.0	80.3	26 47.4	48.4	81.3
28	26 01.0	42.2	76.6	26 27.7	43.8	77.6	26 52.5	45.3	78.6	27 15.2	46.8	79.6	27 35.8	48.3	80.6
29	26 43.2	41.9	75.8	27 11.5	43.6	76.8	27 37.8	45.1	77.8	28 02.0	46.6	78.9	28 24.1	48.0	79.9

40°			42°			44°			46°			48°			Dec.
Hc	d	Z	Hc	d	Z	Hc	d	Z	Hc	d	Z	Hc	d	Z	
° ′	′	°	° ′	′	°	° ′	′	°	° ′	′	°	° ′	′	°	°
6 07.2 – 38.8		95.2	5 56.2 – 40.4		95.4	5 44.7 – 41.9		95.6	5 32.9 – 43.4		95.8	5 20.6 – 44.8		96.0	0
5 28.4	38.9	95.9	5 15.8	40.5	96.1	5 02.8	41.9	96.3	4 49.5	43.4	96.5	4 35.8	44.8	96.6	1
4 49.5	38.9	96.7	4 35.3	40.4	96.9	4 20.9	42.0	97.0	4 06.1	43.5	97.2	3 51.0	44.9	97.3	2
4 10.6	39.0	97.5	3 54.9	40.6	97.6	3 38.9	42.1	97.7	3 22.6	43.5	97.8	3 06.1	44.9	98.0	3
3 31.6	39.0	98.2	3 14.3	40.5	98.3	2 56.8	42.0	98.4	2 39.1	43.5	98.5	2 21.2	44.9	98.6	4
2 52.6 – 39.0		99.0	2 33.8 – 40.6		99.1	2 14.8 – 42.1		99.2	1 55.6 – 43.6		99.2	1 36.3 – 45.0		99.3	5
2 13.6	39.1	99.7	1 53.2	40.6	99.9	1 32.7	42.1	99.9	1 12.0	43.5	99.9	0 51.3	44.9	100.0	6
1 34.5	39.1	100.5	1 12.6	40.6	100.5	0 50.6	42.1	100.6	0 28.5 – 43.5		100.6	0 06.4 – 44.9		100.6	7
0 55.4	39.1	101.3	0 32.0 – 40.7		101.3	0 08.5 – 42.2		101.3	0 15.0 + 43.6		78.7	0 38.5 + 45.0		78.7	8
0 16.3 – 39.1		102.0	0 08.7 + 40.6		78.0	0 33.7 + 42.1		78.0	0 58.6	43.5	78.0	1 23.5	44.9	78.1	9
0 22.8 + 39.1		77.2	0 49.3 + 40.6		77.2	1 15.8 + 42.0		77.3	1 42.1 + 43.5		77.3	2 08.4 + 44.9		77.4	10
1 01.9	39.0	76.5	1 29.4	40.6	76.5	1 57.8	42.1	76.6	2 25.6	43.6	76.6	2 53.3	44.9	76.7	11
1 40.9	39.1	75.7	2 10.5	40.6	75.8	2 39.9	42.1	75.9	3 09.2	43.4	76.0	3 38.2	44.8	76.1	12
2 20.0	39.0	74.9	2 51.1	40.5	75.0	3 22.0	42.0	75.1	3 52.6	43.5	75.3	4 23.0	44.8	75.4	13
2 59.0	39.0	74.2	3 31.6	40.6	74.3	4 04.0	42.0	74.4	4 36.1	43.4	74.6	5 07.8	44.8	74.7	14
3 38.0 + 39.0		73.4	4 12.2 + 40.4		73.6	4 46.0 + 41.9		73.7	5 19.5 + 43.3		73.9	5 52.6 + 44.7		74.1	15
4 17.0	38.9	72.7	4 52.6	40.4	72.8	5 27.9	41.9	73.0	6 02.8	43.3	73.2	6 37.3	44.7	73.4	16
4 55.9	38.9	71.9	5 33.0	40.4	72.1	6 09.8	41.8	72.3	6 46.1	43.3	72.5	7 22.0	44.6	72.7	17
5 34.8	38.8	71.1	6 13.4	40.3	71.3	6 51.6	41.8	71.5	7 29.4	43.1	71.8	8 06.6	44.6	72.0	18
6 13.6	38.8	70.4	6 53.7	40.3	70.6	7 33.4	41.7	70.8	8 12.5	43.1	71.1	8 51.2	44.4	71.4	19
6 52.4 + 38.6		69.6	7 34.0 + 40.1		69.8	8 15.1 + 41.6		70.1	8 55.6 + 43.1		70.4	9 35.6 + 44.4		70.7	20
7 31.0	38.6	68.8	8 14.1	40.1	69.1	8 56.7	41.5	69.4	9 38.7	42.9	69.7	10 20.0	44.3	70.0	21
8 09.6	38.5	68.1	8 54.2	40.0	68.3	9 38.2	41.4	68.6	10 21.6	42.8	69.0	11 04.3	44.3	69.3	22
8 48.1	38.4	67.3	9 34.2	39.9	67.6	10 19.6	41.4	67.9	11 04.4	42.8	68.3	11 48.5	44.1	68.6	23
9 26.5	38.3	66.5	10 14.1	39.7	66.8	11 01.0	41.2	67.2	11 47.2	42.6	67.5	12 32.6	44.0	67.9	24
10 04.8 + 38.2		65.7	10 53.8 + 39.7		66.1	11 42.2 + 41.1		66.4	12 29.8 + 42.5		66.8	13 16.6 + 43.9		67.2	25
10 43.0	38.1	64.9	11 33.5	39.6	65.3	12 23.3	41.0	65.7	13 12.3	42.4	66.1	14 00.5	43.8	66.5	26
11 21.1	37.9	64.2	12 13.1	39.4	64.5	13 04.3	40.8	64.9	13 54.7	42.3	65.4	14 44.3	43.6	65.8	27
11 59.0	37.8	63.4	12 52.5	39.3	63.8	13 45.1	40.8	64.2	14 37.0	42.1	64.6	15 27.9	43.5	65.1	28
12 36.8	37.7	62.6	13 31.8	39.1	63.0	14 25.9	40.5	63.4	15 19.1	42.0	63.9	16 11.4	43.4	64.4	29

50°			52°			54°			56°			58°			Dec.
Hc	d	Z	Hc	d	Z	Hc	d	Z	Hc	d	Z	Hc	d	Z	
° ′	′	°	° ′	′	°	° ′	′	°	° ′	′	°	° ′	′	°	°
5 07.9 – 46.1		96.1	4 54.9 – 47.5		96.3	4 41.5 – 48.7		96.5	4 27.8 – 49.9		96.6	4 13.8 – 51.1		96.8	0
4 21.8	46.2	96.8	4 07.4	47.5	96.9	3 52.8	48.7	97.1	3 37.9	49.9	97.2	3 22.7	51.0	97.3	1
3 35.6	46.2	97.4	3 19.9	47.5	97.5	3 04.1	48.8	97.7	2 48.0	50.0	97.8	2 31.7	51.1	97.9	2
2 49.4	46.3	98.1	2 32.4	47.5	98.2	2 15.3	48.8	98.2	1 58.0	49.9	98.3	1 40.6	51.0	98.4	3
2 03.1	46.2	98.7	1 44.9	47.6	98.8	1 26.5	48.7	98.8	1 08.1	50.0	98.9	0 49.6 – 51.1		98.9	4
1 16.9 – 46.3		99.3	0 57.3 – 47.5		99.4	0 37.8 – 48.8		99.4	0 18.1 – 49.9		99.4	0 01.5 + 51.1		80.6	5
0 30.6 – 46.3		100.0	0 09.8 – 47.6		100.0	0 11.0 + 48.8		80.0	0 31.8 + 50.0		80.0	0 52.6	51.1	80.0	6
0 15.7 + 46.3		79.4	0 37.8 + 47.5		79.4	0 59.8	48.8	79.4	1 21.8	49.9	79.5	1 43.7	51.0	79.5	7
1 02.0	46.2	78.8	1 25.3	47.6	78.8	1 48.6	48.8	78.8	2 11.7	50.0	78.9	2 34.7	51.1	79.0	8
1 48.2	46.3	78.1	2 12.9	47.5	78.2	2 37.4	48.7	78.3	3 01.7	49.9	78.4	3 25.8	51.0	78.5	9
2 34.5 + 46.2		77.5	3 00.4 + 47.5		77.6	3 26.1 + 48.8		77.7	3 51.6 + 49.9		77.8	4 16.8 + 51.0		77.9	10
3 20.7	46.2	76.8	3 47.9	47.5	77.0	4 14.9	48.7	77.1	4 41.5	49.9	77.2	5 07.8	51.0	77.4	11
4 06.9	46.2	76.2	4 35.4	47.5	76.3	5 03.6	48.6	76.5	5 31.4	49.8	76.7	5 58.8	50.9	76.9	12
4 53.1	46.1	75.6	5 22.9	47.4	75.7	5 52.2	48.7	75.9	6 21.2	49.8	76.1	6 49.7	51.0	76.4	13
5 39.2	46.1	74.9	6 10.3	47.3	75.1	6 40.9	48.6	75.3	7 11.0	49.8	75.6	7 40.7	50.8	75.8	14
6 25.3 + 46.1		74.3	6 57.6 + 47.4		74.5	7 29.5 + 48.5		74.7	8 00.8 + 49.7		75.0	8 31.5 + 50.9		75.3	15
7 11.4	46.0	73.6	7 45.0	47.2	73.9	8 18.0	48.5	74.2	8 50.5	49.7	74.4	9 22.4	50.8	74.8	16
7 57.4	45.9	73.0	8 32.2	47.2	73.3	9 06.5	48.4	73.6	9 40.2	49.6	73.9	10 13.2	50.7	74.2	17
8 43.3	45.9	72.3	9 19.4	47.2	72.6	9 54.9	48.4	73.0	10 29.8	49.5	73.3	11 03.9	50.7	73.7	18
9 29.2	45.8	71.7	10 06.6	47.1	72.0	10 43.3	48.3	72.4	11 19.3	49.5	72.7	11 54.6	50.6	73.1	19
10 15.0 + 45.7		71.0	10 53.7 + 47.0		71.4	11 31.6 + 48.2		71.8	12 08.8 + 49.4		72.1	12 45.2 + 50.5		72.6	20
11 00.7	45.6	70.4	11 40.7	46.9	70.7	12 19.8	48.2	71.1	12 58.2	49.3	71.6	13 35.7	50.5	72.0	21
11 46.3	45.6	69.7	12 27.6	46.8	70.1	13 08.0	48.1	70.5	13 47.5	49.3	71.0	14 26.2	50.4	71.5	22
12 31.9	45.4	69.0	13 14.4	46.7	69.5	13 56.1	47.9	69.9	14 36.8	49.2	70.4	15 16.6	50.3	70.9	23
13 17.3	45.3	68.4	14 01.1	46.6	68.8	14 44.0	47.9	69.3	15 26.0	49.0	69.8	16 06.9	50.2	70.3	24
14 02.6 + 45.3		67.7	14 47.7 + 46.5		68.2	15 31.9 + 47.7		68.7	16 15.0 + 49.0		69.2	16 57.1 + 50.1		69.8	25
14 47.9	45.1	67.0	15 34.2	46.4	67.5	16 19.6	47.7	68.0	17 04.0	48.8	68.6	17 47.2	50.0	69.2	26
15 33.0	44.9	66.3	16 20.6	46.3	66.9	17 07.3	47.5	67.4	17 52.8	48.8	68.0	18 37.2	49.9	68.6	27
16 17.9	44.9	65.6	17 06.9	46.2	66.2	17 54.8	47.4	66.8	18 41.6	48.6	67.4	19 27.1	49.8	68.0	28
17 02.8	44.7	64.9	17 53.1	46.0	65.5	18 42.2	47.3	66.1	19 30.2	48.5	66.8	20 16.9	49.7	67.4	29

Dec.	0° Hc	d	Z	2° Hc	d	Z	4° Hc	d	Z	6° Hc	d	Z	8° Hc	d	Z
0	6 00.0	- 0.1	90.0	5 59.8	+ 2.0	90.2	5 59.1	+ 4.2	90.4	5 58.0	+ 6.3	90.6	5 56.5	+ 8.3	90.8
1	5 59.9	0.1	89.0	6 01.8	2.0	89.2	6 03.3	4.0	89.4	6 04.3	6.1	89.6	6 04.8	8.3	89.8
2	5 59.8	0.3	88.0	6 03.8	1.8	88.2	6 07.3	3.9	88.4	6 10.4	6.0	88.6	6 13.1	8.1	88.8
3	5 59.5	0.4	87.0	6 05.6	1.7	87.2	6 11.2	3.9	87.4	6 16.4	6.0	87.6	6 21.2	8.0	87.8
4	5 59.1	0.5	86.0	6 07.3	1.6	86.2	6 15.1	3.7	86.4	6 22.4	5.8	86.6	6 29.2	7.9	86.9
5	5 58.6	- 0.6	85.0	6 08.9	+ 1.5	85.2	6 18.8	+ 3.6	85.4	6 28.2	+ 5.6	85.6	6 37.1	+ 7.7	85.9
6	5 58.0	0.7	84.0	6 10.4	1.4	84.2	6 22.4	3.4	84.4	6 33.8	5.6	84.6	6 44.8	7.7	84.9
7	5 57.3	0.8	83.0	6 11.8	1.3	83.2	6 25.8	3.4	83.4	6 39.4	5.4	83.6	6 52.5	7.5	83.9
8	5 56.5	0.9	82.0	6 13.1	1.1	82.2	6 29.2	3.2	82.4	6 44.8	5.4	82.6	7 00.0	7.4	82.9
9	5 55.6	1.1	81.0	6 14.2	1.0	81.2	6 32.4	3.1	81.4	6 50.2	5.2	81.6	7 07.4	7.3	81.9
10	5 54.5	- 1.1	79.9	6 15.2	+ 1.0	80.2	6 35.5	+ 3.0	80.4	6 55.4	+ 5.0	80.6	7 14.7	+ 7.1	80.9
11	5 53.4	1.3	78.9	6 16.2	0.8	79.2	6 38.5	2.9	79.4	7 00.4	5.0	79.6	7 21.8	7.0	79.9
12	5 52.1	1.4	77.9	6 17.0	0.7	78.1	6 41.4	2.8	78.4	7 05.4	4.8	78.6	7 28.8	6.9	78.9
13	5 50.7	1.4	76.9	6 17.7	0.5	77.1	6 44.2	2.6	77.4	7 10.2	4.6	77.6	7 35.7	6.7	77.9
14	5 49.3	1.6	75.9	6 18.2	0.5	76.1	6 46.8	2.5	76.4	7 14.8	4.6	76.6	7 42.4	6.6	76.8
15	5 47.7	- 1.7	74.9	6 18.7	+ 0.3	75.1	6 49.3	+ 2.4	75.3	7 19.4	+ 4.4	75.6	7 49.0	+ 6.5	75.8
16	5 46.0	1.8	73.9	6 19.0	0.3	74.1	6 51.7	2.2	74.3	7 23.8	4.3	74.6	7 55.5	6.3	74.8
17	5 44.2	1.9	72.9	6 19.3	+ 0.1	73.1	6 53.9	2.1	73.3	7 28.1	4.1	73.6	8 01.8	6.1	73.8
18	5 42.3	2.0	71.9	6 19.4	0.0	72.1	6 56.0	2.0	72.3	7 32.2	4.0	72.6	8 07.9	6.0	72.8
19	5 40.3	2.1	70.9	6 19.4	- 0.1	71.1	6 58.0	1.9	71.3	7 36.2	3.9	71.6	8 13.9	5.9	71.8
20	5 38.2	- 2.2	69.9	6 19.3	- 0.3	70.1	6 59.9	+ 1.8	70.3	7 40.1	+ 3.7	70.6	8 19.8	+ 5.7	70.8
21	5 36.0	2.3	68.9	6 19.0	0.3	69.1	7 01.7	1.6	69.3	7 43.8	3.6	69.6	8 25.5	5.5	69.8
22	5 33.7	2.4	67.9	6 18.7	0.5	68.1	7 03.3	1.4	68.3	7 47.4	3.4	68.5	8 31.0	5.4	68.8
23	5 31.3	2.5	66.9	6 18.2	0.6	67.1	7 04.7	1.4	67.3	7 50.8	3.3	67.5	8 36.4	5.3	67.8
24	5 28.8	2.6	65.9	6 17.6	0.7	66.1	7 06.1	1.2	66.3	7 54.1	3.2	66.5	8 41.7	5.1	66.8
25	5 26.2	- 2.7	64.9	6 16.9	- 0.8	65.1	7 07.3	+ 1.1	65.3	7 57.3	+ 3.0	65.5	8 46.8	+ 4.9	65.8
26	5 23.5	2.9	63.9	6 16.1	0.9	64.1	7 08.4	1.0	64.3	8 00.3	2.8	64.5	8 51.7	4.7	64.8
27	5 20.6	2.9	62.9	6 15.2	1.0	63.1	7 09.4	0.8	63.3	8 03.1	2.8	63.5	8 56.4	4.6	63.8
28	5 17.7	3.0	61.9	6 14.2	1.2	62.0	7 10.2	0.7	62.3	8 05.9	2.5	62.5	9 01.0	4.5	62.8
29	5 14.7	3.1	60.9	6 13.0	1.3	61.0	7 10.9	0.6	61.2	8 08.4	2.4	61.5	9 05.5	4.2	61.8

Dec.	10° Hc	d	Z	12° Hc	d	Z	14° Hc	d	Z	16° Hc	d	Z	18° Hc	d	Z
0	5 54.5	+ 10.4	91.0	5 52.1	+ 12.5	91.3	5 49.3	+ 14.5	91.5	5 46.0	+ 16.6	91.7	5 42.3	+ 18.6	91.9
1	6 04.9	10.3	90.1	6 04.6	12.4	90.3	6 03.8	14.4	90.5	6 02.6	16.4	90.7	6 00.9	18.5	90.9
2	6 15.2	10.2	89.1	6 17.0	12.2	89.3	6 18.2	14.4	89.5	6 19.0	16.4	89.7	6 19.4	18.4	89.9
3	6 25.4	10.1	88.1	6 29.2	12.2	88.3	6 32.6	14.2	88.5	6 35.4	16.3	88.8	6 37.8	18.2	89.0
4	6 35.5	10.0	87.1	6 41.4	12.0	87.3	6 46.8	14.1	87.5	6 51.7	16.1	87.8	6 56.0	18.2	88.0
5	6 45.5	+ 9.9	86.1	6 53.4	+ 12.0	86.3	7 00.9	+ 13.9	86.6	7 07.8	+ 16.0	86.8	7 14.2	+ 18.0	87.1
6	6 55.4	9.7	85.1	7 05.4	11.8	85.3	7 14.8	13.9	85.6	7 23.8	15.9	85.8	7 32.2	17.9	86.1
7	7 05.1	9.6	84.1	7 17.2	11.6	84.4	7 28.7	13.7	84.6	7 39.7	15.6	84.9	7 50.1	17.8	85.1
8	7 14.7	9.4	83.1	7 28.8	11.5	83.4	7 42.4	13.6	83.6	7 55.5	15.6	83.9	8 07.9	17.7	84.2
9	7 24.1	9.4	82.1	7 40.3	11.4	82.4	7 56.0	13.4	82.6	8 11.1	15.4	82.9	8 25.6	17.4	83.2
10	7 33.5	+ 9.2	81.1	7 51.7	+ 11.3	81.4	8 09.4	+ 13.3	81.7	8 26.5	+ 15.4	81.9	8 43.0	+ 17.4	82.2
11	7 42.7	9.0	80.1	8 03.0	11.1	80.4	8 22.7	13.2	80.7	8 41.9	15.2	81.0	9 00.4	17.2	81.3
12	7 51.7	9.0	79.1	8 14.1	11.0	79.4	8 35.9	13.0	79.7	8 57.1	15.0	80.0	9 17.6	17.0	80.3
13	8 00.7	8.7	78.1	8 25.1	10.8	78.4	8 48.9	12.8	78.7	9 12.1	14.9	79.0	9 34.6	16.9	79.3
14	8 09.4	8.7	77.1	8 35.9	10.7	77.4	9 01.7	12.7	77.7	9 27.0	14.7	78.0	9 51.5	16.7	78.4
15	8 18.1	+ 8.4	76.1	8 46.6	+ 10.5	76.4	9 14.4	+ 12.6	76.7	9 41.7	+ 14.5	77.0	10 08.2	+ 16.6	77.4
16	8 26.5	8.4	75.1	8 57.1	10.3	75.4	9 27.0	12.3	75.7	9 56.2	14.4	76.1	10 24.8	16.3	76.4
17	8 34.9	8.1	74.1	9 07.4	10.2	74.4	9 39.3	12.2	74.7	10 10.6	14.2	75.1	10 41.1	16.2	75.4
18	8 43.0	8.1	73.1	9 17.6	10.0	73.4	9 51.5	12.0	73.7	10 24.8	14.0	74.1	10 57.3	16.0	74.5
19	8 51.1	7.8	72.1	9 27.6	9.9	72.4	10 03.5	11.9	72.7	10 38.8	13.8	73.1	11 13.3	15.8	73.5
20	8 58.9	+ 7.7	71.1	9 37.5	+ 9.6	71.4	10 15.4	+ 11.6	71.8	10 52.6	+ 13.6	72.1	11 29.1	+ 15.6	72.5
21	9 06.6	7.5	70.1	9 47.1	9.5	70.4	10 27.0	11.5	70.8	11 06.2	13.5	71.1	11 44.7	15.4	71.5
22	9 14.1	7.4	69.1	9 56.6	9.4	69.4	10 38.5	11.3	69.8	11 19.7	13.2	70.1	12 00.1	15.2	70.5
23	9 21.5	7.2	68.1	10 06.0	9.1	68.4	10 49.8	11.1	68.8	11 32.9	13.0	69.1	12 15.3	14.9	69.5
24	9 28.7	7.0	67.1	10 15.1	8.9	67.4	11 00.9	10.8	67.8	11 45.9	12.8	68.1	12 30.2	14.8	68.5
25	9 35.7	+ 6.8	66.1	10 24.0	+ 8.8	66.4	11 11.7	+ 10.7	66.8	11 58.7	+ 12.7	67.1	12 45.0	+ 14.5	67.5
26	9 42.5	6.7	65.1	10 32.8	8.6	65.4	11 22.4	10.5	65.8	12 11.4	12.4	66.1	12 59.5	14.3	66.5
27	9 49.2	6.5	64.1	10 41.4	8.4	64.4	11 32.9	10.3	64.7	12 23.8	12.1	65.1	13 13.8	14.1	65.5
28	9 55.7	6.3	63.1	10 49.8	8.1	63.4	11 43.2	10.1	63.7	12 35.9	12.0	64.1	13 27.9	13.8	64.5
29	10 02.0	6.1	62.0	10 57.9	8.0	62.4	11 53.3	9.8	62.7	12 47.9	11.7	63.1	13 41.7	13.6	63.5

0° Hc	d	Z	2° Hc	d	Z	4° Hc	d	Z	6° Hc	d	Z	8° Hc	d	Z	Dec.
6 00.0	− 0.1	90.0	5 59.8	− 2.2	90.2	5 59.1	− 4.2	90.4	5 58.0	− 6.3	90.6	5 56.5	− 8.5	90.8	0
5 59.9	0.1	91.0	5 57.6	2.2	91.2	5 54.9	4.4	91.4	5 51.7	6.5	91.6	5 48.0	8.5	91.8	1
5 59.8	0.3	92.0	5 55.4	2.4	92.2	5 50.5	4.5	92.4	5 45.2	6.6	92.6	5 39.5	8.7	92.8	2
5 59.5	0.4	93.0	5 53.0	2.5	93.2	5 46.0	4.6	93.4	5 38.6	6.6	93.6	5 30.8	8.7	93.8	3
5 59.1	0.5	94.0	5 50.5	2.6	94.2	5 41.4	4.7	94.4	5 32.0	6.8	94.6	5 22.1	8.9	94.8	4
5 58.6	− 0.6	95.0	5 47.9	− 2.7	95.2	5 36.7	− 4.7	95.4	5 25.2	− 6.9	95.6	5 13.2	− 8.9	95.8	5
5 58.0	0.7	96.0	5 45.2	2.8	96.2	5 32.0	4.9	96.4	5 18.3	7.0	96.6	5 04.3	9.1	96.8	6
5 57.3	0.8	97.0	5 42.4	2.9	97.2	5 27.1	5.0	97.4	5 11.3	7.0	97.6	4 55.2	9.1	97.8	7
5 56.5	0.9	98.0	5 39.5	3.0	98.2	5 22.1	5.1	98.4	5 04.3	7.2	98.6	4 46.1	9.2	98.8	8
5 55.6	1.1	99.0	5 36.5	3.1	99.2	5 17.0	5.2	99.4	4 57.1	7.2	99.6	4 36.9	9.3	99.8	9
5 54.5	− 1.1	100.1	5 33.4	− 3.3	100.3	5 11.8	− 5.3	100.4	4 49.9	− 7.3	100.6	4 27.6	− 9.3	100.8	10
5 53.4	1.3	101.1	5 30.1	3.3	101.3	5 06.5	5.3	101.4	4 42.6	7.5	101.6	4 18.3	9.5	101.8	11
5 52.1	1.4	102.1	5 26.8	3.4	102.3	5 01.2	5.5	102.4	4 35.1	7.4	102.6	4 08.8	9.5	102.7	12
5 50.7	1.4	103.1	5 23.4	3.5	103.3	4 55.7	5.6	103.4	4 27.7	7.6	103.6	3 59.3	9.6	103.7	13
5 49.3	1.6	104.1	5 19.9	3.6	104.3	4 50.1	5.6	104.4	4 20.1	7.7	104.6	3 49.7	9.7	104.7	14
5 47.7	− 1.7	105.1	5 16.3	− 3.7	105.3	4 44.5	− 5.7	105.4	4 12.4	− 7.7	105.6	3 40.0	− 9.7	105.7	15
5 46.0	1.8	106.1	5 12.6	3.8	106.3	4 38.8	5.8	106.4	4 04.7	7.8	106.6	3 30.3	9.8	106.7	16
5 44.2	1.9	107.1	5 08.8	3.9	107.3	4 33.0	5.9	107.4	3 56.9	7.9	107.6	3 20.5	9.8	107.7	17
5 42.3	2.0	108.1	5 04.9	4.0	108.3	4 27.1	6.0	108.4	3 49.0	7.9	108.6	3 10.7	9.9	108.7	18
5 40.3	2.1	109.1	5 00.9	4.1	109.3	4 21.1	6.0	109.4	3 41.1	8.0	109.6	3 00.8	10.0	109.7	19
5 38.2	− 2.2	110.1	4 56.8	− 4.2	110.3	4 15.1	− 6.2	110.4	3 33.1	− 8.1	110.6	2 50.8	− 10.0	110.7	20
5 36.0	2.3	111.1	4 52.6	4.2	111.3	4 08.9	6.2	111.4	3 25.0	8.2	111.5	2 40.8	10.0	111.6	21
5 33.7	2.4	112.1	4 48.4	4.4	112.3	4 02.7	6.2	112.4	3 16.8	8.1	112.5	2 30.8	10.1	112.6	22
5 31.3	2.5	113.1	4 44.0	4.4	113.3	3 56.5	6.4	113.4	3 08.7	8.3	113.5	2 20.7	10.2	113.6	23
5 28.8	2.6	114.1	4 39.6	4.5	114.3	3 50.1	6.4	114.4	3 00.4	8.3	114.5	2 10.5	10.2	114.6	24
5 26.2	− 2.7	115.1	4 35.1	− 4.6	115.3	3 43.7	− 6.5	115.4	2 52.1	− 8.4	115.5	2 00.3	− 10.2	115.6	25
5 23.5	2.9	116.1	4 30.5	4.7	116.3	3 37.2	6.5	116.4	2 43.7	8.4	116.5	1 50.1	10.2	116.6	26
5 20.6	2.9	117.1	4 25.8	4.8	117.3	3 30.7	6.7	117.4	2 35.3	8.4	117.5	1 39.9	10.3	117.6	27
5 17.7	3.0	118.1	4 21.0	4.8	118.3	3 24.0	6.6	118.4	2 26.9	8.5	118.5	1 29.6	10.3	118.5	28
5 14.7	3.1	119.1	4 16.2	5.0	119.3	3 17.4	6.8	119.4	2 18.4	8.5	119.5	1 19.3	10.3	119.5	29

10° Hc	d	Z	12° Hc	d	Z	14° Hc	d	Z	16° Hc	d	Z	18° Hc	d	Z	Dec.
5 54.5	− 10.5	91.0	5 52.1	− 12.6	91.3	5 49.3	− 14.7	91.5	5 46.0	− 16.7	91.7	5 42.3	− 18.7	91.9	0
5 44.0	10.6	92.0	5 39.5	12.7	92.2	5 34.6	14.7	92.4	5 29.3	16.7	92.6	5 23.6	18.7	92.8	1
5 33.4	10.8	93.0	5 26.8	12.8	93.2	5 19.9	14.8	93.4	5 12.6	16.9	93.6	5 04.9	18.9	93.8	2
5 22.6	10.8	94.0	5 14.0	12.8	94.2	5 05.1	15.0	94.4	4 55.7	16.9	94.6	4 46.0	18.9	94.7	3
5 11.8	10.9	95.0	5 01.2	13.0	95.2	4 50.1	14.9	95.4	4 38.8	17.0	95.5	4 27.1	19.0	95.7	4
5 00.9	− 11.0	96.0	4 48.2	− 13.1	96.2	4 35.2	− 15.1	96.3	4 21.8	− 17.1	96.5	4 08.1	− 19.1	96.6	5
4 49.9	11.1	97.0	4 35.1	13.1	97.1	4 20.1	15.2	97.3	4 04.7	17.2	97.4	3 49.0	19.1	97.6	6
4 38.8	11.2	98.0	4 22.0	13.2	98.1	4 04.9	15.3	98.3	3 47.5	17.2	98.4	3 29.9	19.2	98.5	7
4 27.6	11.2	98.9	4 08.8	13.3	99.1	3 49.7	15.3	99.2	3 30.3	17.3	99.4	3 10.7	19.3	99.5	8
4 16.4	11.3	99.9	3 55.5	13.3	100.1	3 34.4	15.3	100.2	3 13.0	17.3	100.3	2 51.4	19.3	100.4	9
4 05.1	− 11.4	100.9	3 42.2	− 13.4	101.0	3 19.1	− 15.4	101.2	2 55.7	− 17.4	101.3	2 32.1	− 19.3	101.4	10
3 53.7	11.5	101.9	3 28.8	13.5	102.0	3 03.7	15.5	102.1	2 38.3	17.4	102.2	2 12.8	19.3	102.3	11
3 42.2	11.5	102.9	3 15.3	13.5	103.0	2 48.2	15.5	103.1	2 20.9	17.5	103.2	1 53.4	19.4	103.3	12
3 30.7	11.6	103.9	3 01.8	13.6	104.0	2 32.7	15.6	104.1	2 03.4	17.5	104.2	1 34.0	19.4	104.2	13
3 19.1	11.7	104.8	2 48.2	13.6	105.0	2 17.1	15.5	105.0	1 45.9	17.5	105.1	1 14.6	19.4	105.2	14
3 07.4	− 11.7	105.8	2 34.6	− 13.7	105.9	2 01.6	− 15.7	106.0	1 28.4	− 17.5	106.1	0 55.2	− 19.5	106.1	15
2 55.7	11.8	106.8	2 20.9	13.7	106.9	1 45.9	15.6	107.0	1 10.9	17.6	107.0	0 35.7	19.5	107.1	16
2 43.9	11.8	107.8	2 07.2	13.8	107.9	1 30.3	15.7	107.9	0 53.3	17.6	108.0	0 16.2	− 19.4	108.0	17
2 32.1	11.8	108.8	1 53.4	13.7	108.9	1 14.6	15.7	108.9	0 35.7	17.6	108.9	0 03.2	+ 19.5	71.1	18
2 20.3	11.9	109.8	1 39.7	13.9	109.8	0 58.9	15.7	109.9	0 18.1	17.6	109.9	0 22.7	19.5	70.1	19
2 08.4	− 11.9	110.7	1 25.8	− 13.8	110.8	0 43.2	− 15.7	110.8	0 00.5	− 17.6	110.8	0 42.2	+ 19.4	69.2	20
1 56.5	12.0	111.7	1 12.0	13.9	111.8	0 27.5	15.8	111.8	0 17.1	+ 17.6	68.2	1 01.6	19.5	68.2	21
1 44.5	12.0	112.7	0 58.1	13.8	112.7	0 11.7	− 15.7	112.8	0 34.7	17.6	67.2	1 21.1	19.4	67.3	22
1 32.5	12.0	113.7	0 44.3	13.9	113.7	0 04.0	+ 15.7	66.3	0 52.3	17.6	66.3	1 40.5	19.4	66.3	23
1 20.5	12.1	114.7	0 30.4	13.9	114.7	0 19.7	15.8	65.3	1 09.9	17.5	65.3	1 59.9	19.4	65.3	24
1 08.4	− 12.0	115.6	0 16.5	− 13.9	115.7	0 35.5	+ 15.7	64.3	1 27.4	+ 17.5	64.4	2 19.3	+ 19.3	64.4	25
0 56.4	12.1	116.6	0 02.6	− 13.9	116.6	0 51.2	15.7	63.4	1 44.9	17.5	63.4	2 38.6	19.3	63.5	26
0 44.3	12.1	117.6	0 11.3	+ 13.9	62.4	1 06.9	15.7	62.4	2 02.4	17.5	62.5	2 57.9	19.2	62.5	27
0 32.2	12.1	118.6	0 25.2	13.9	61.4	1 22.6	15.7	61.4	2 19.9	17.4	61.5	3 17.1	19.2	61.6	28
0 20.1	12.1	119.6	0 39.1	13.9	60.4	1 38.3	15.6	60.5	2 37.3	17.4	60.5	3 36.3	19.1	60.6	29

Dec.	20° Hc	d	Z	22° Hc	d	Z	24° Hc	d	Z	26° Hc	d	Z	28° Hc	d	Z
0	5 38.2	+20.6	92.1	5 33.7	+22.5	92.3	5 28.8	+24.4	92.4	5 23.5	+26.3	92.6	5 17.7	+28.3	92.8
1	5 58.8	20.5	91.1	5 56.2	22.5	91.3	5 53.2	24.4	91.5	5 49.8	26.3	91.7	5 46.0	28.2	91.9
2	6 19.3	20.3	90.2	6 18.7	22.3	90.4	6 17.6	24.3	90.6	6 16.1	26.2	90.8	6 14.2	28.0	91.1
3	6 39.6	20.3	89.2	6 41.0	22.3	89.5	6 41.9	24.2	89.7	6 42.3	26.1	89.9	6 42.2	28.0	90.2
4	6 59.9	20.2	88.3	7 03.3	22.1	88.5	7 06.1	24.1	88.8	7 08.4	26.0	89.0	7 10.2	27.9	89.3
5	7 20.1	+20.0	87.3	7 25.4	+22.0	87.6	7 30.2	+23.9	87.8	7 34.4	+25.9	88.1	7 38.1	+27.8	88.4
6	7 40.1	19.9	86.4	7 47.4	21.9	86.6	7 54.1	23.9	86.9	8 00.3	25.8	87.2	8 05.9	27.6	87.5
7	8 00.0	19.8	85.4	8 09.3	21.7	85.7	8 18.0	23.7	86.0	8 26.1	25.6	86.3	8 33.5	27.5	86.6
8	8 19.8	19.6	84.5	8 31.0	21.7	84.8	8 41.7	23.6	85.1	8 51.7	25.5	85.4	9 01.0	27.4	85.7
9	8 39.4	19.5	83.5	8 52.7	21.4	83.8	9 05.3	23.4	84.1	9 17.2	25.3	84.5	9 28.4	27.3	84.8
10	8 58.9	+19.4	82.6	9 14.1	+21.4	82.9	9 28.7	+23.3	83.2	9 42.5	+25.3	83.5	9 55.7	+27.1	83.9
11	9 18.3	19.2	81.6	9 35.5	21.1	81.9	9 52.0	23.1	82.3	10 07.8	25.0	82.6	10 22.8	27.0	83.0
12	9 37.5	19.0	80.6	9 56.6	21.0	81.0	10 15.1	23.0	81.3	10 32.8	24.9	81.7	10 49.8	26.8	82.1
13	9 56.5	18.9	79.7	10 17.6	20.9	80.0	10 38.1	22.8	80.4	10 57.7	24.7	80.8	11 16.6	26.6	81.2
14	10 15.4	18.7	78.7	10 38.5	20.7	79.1	11 00.9	22.6	79.4	11 22.4	24.6	79.8	11 43.2	26.4	80.2
15	10 34.1	+18.5	77.7	10 59.2	+20.5	78.1	11 23.5	+22.4	78.5	11 47.0	+24.4	78.9	12 09.6	+26.3	79.3
16	10 52.6	18.3	76.8	11 19.7	20.3	77.2	11 45.9	22.3	77.6	12 11.4	24.1	78.0	12 35.9	26.1	78.4
17	11 10.9	18.2	75.8	11 40.0	20.1	76.2	12 08.2	22.0	76.6	12 35.5	24.0	77.0	13 02.0	25.9	77.5
18	11 29.1	17.9	74.8	12 00.1	19.9	75.2	12 30.2	21.9	75.7	12 59.5	23.8	76.1	13 27.9	25.7	76.6
19	11 47.0	17.8	73.9	12 20.0	19.8	74.3	12 52.1	21.6	74.7	13 23.3	23.6	75.2	13 53.6	25.5	75.6
20	12 04.8	+17.6	72.9	12 39.7	+19.5	73.3	13 13.7	+21.5	73.7	13 46.9	+23.3	74.2	14 19.1	+25.2	74.7
21	12 22.4	17.3	71.9	12 59.2	19.3	72.3	13 35.2	21.2	72.8	14 10.2	23.2	73.3	14 44.3	25.0	73.8
22	12 39.7	17.1	70.9	13 18.5	19.1	71.4	13 56.4	21.0	71.8	14 33.4	22.9	72.3	15 09.3	24.8	72.8
23	12 56.8	16.9	69.9	13 37.6	18.8	70.4	14 17.4	20.7	70.9	14 56.3	22.6	71.3	15 34.1	24.6	71.9
24	13 13.7	16.7	69.0	13 56.4	18.6	69.4	14 38.1	20.5	69.9	15 18.9	22.4	70.4	15 58.7	24.3	70.9
25	13 30.4	+16.5	68.0	14 15.0	+18.4	68.4	14 58.6	+20.3	68.9	15 41.3	+22.2	69.4	16 23.0	+24.0	70.0
26	13 46.9	16.2	67.0	14 33.4	18.1	67.4	15 18.9	20.0	67.9	16 03.5	21.9	68.5	16 47.0	23.8	69.0
27	14 03.1	16.0	66.0	14 51.5	17.8	66.5	15 38.9	19.8	67.0	16 25.4	21.6	67.5	17 10.8	23.5	68.0
28	14 19.1	15.7	65.0	15 09.3	17.6	65.5	15 58.7	19.4	66.0	16 47.0	21.4	66.5	17 34.3	23.2	67.1
29	14 34.8	15.4	64.0	15 26.9	17.4	64.5	16 18.1	19.3	65.0	17 08.4	21.0	65.5	17 57.5	22.9	66.1

Dec.	30° Hc	d	Z	32° Hc	d	Z	34° Hc	d	Z	36° Hc	d	Z	38° Hc	d	Z
0	5 11.6	+30.1	93.0	5 05.1	+31.9	93.2	4 58.3	+33.6	93.4	4 51.1	+35.3	93.5	4 43.5	+37.0	93.7
1	5 41.7	30.0	92.1	5 37.0	31.8	92.3	5 31.9	33.6	92.5	5 26.4	35.3	92.7	5 20.5	37.0	92.9
2	6 11.7	29.9	91.3	6 08.8	31.8	91.5	6 05.5	33.5	91.7	6 01.7	35.3	91.9	5 57.5	36.9	92.1
3	6 41.6	29.9	90.4	6 40.6	31.6	90.6	6 39.0	33.4	90.9	6 37.0	35.1	91.1	6 34.4	36.8	91.3
4	7 11.5	29.7	89.5	7 12.2	31.6	89.8	7 12.4	33.3	90.0	7 12.1	35.1	90.3	7 11.2	36.8	90.5
5	7 41.2	+29.6	88.6	7 43.8	+31.4	88.9	7 45.7	+33.3	89.2	7 47.2	+34.9	89.5	7 48.0	+36.7	89.7
6	8 10.8	29.5	87.8	8 15.2	31.3	88.1	8 19.0	33.1	88.3	8 22.1	34.9	88.6	8 24.7	36.5	88.9
7	8 40.3	29.4	86.9	8 46.5	31.3	87.2	8 52.1	33.0	87.5	8 57.0	34.7	87.8	9 01.2	36.5	88.1
8	9 09.7	29.3	86.0	9 17.8	31.0	86.3	9 25.1	32.9	86.7	9 31.7	34.7	87.0	9 37.7	36.3	87.3
9	9 39.0	29.1	85.1	9 48.8	31.0	85.5	9 58.0	32.7	85.8	10 06.4	34.5	86.2	10 14.0	36.3	86.5
10	10 08.1	+29.0	84.2	10 19.8	+30.8	84.6	10 30.7	+32.6	85.0	10 40.9	+34.4	85.3	10 50.3	+36.1	85.7
11	10 37.1	28.8	83.3	10 50.6	30.7	83.7	11 03.3	32.5	84.1	11 15.3	34.2	84.5	11 26.4	35.9	84.9
12	11 05.9	28.7	82.4	11 21.3	30.5	82.8	11 35.8	32.3	83.2	11 49.5	34.1	83.7	12 02.3	35.8	84.1
13	11 34.6	28.5	81.6	11 51.8	30.4	82.0	12 08.1	32.2	82.4	12 23.6	33.9	82.8	12 38.1	35.7	83.3
14	12 03.1	28.3	80.7	12 22.2	30.1	81.1	12 40.3	32.0	81.5	12 57.5	33.8	82.0	13 13.8	35.5	82.4
15	12 31.4	+28.2	79.8	12 52.3	+30.0	80.2	13 12.3	+31.8	80.7	13 31.3	+33.6	81.1	13 49.3	+35.4	81.6
16	12 59.6	28.0	78.8	13 22.3	29.8	79.3	13 44.1	31.6	79.8	14 04.9	33.4	80.3	14 24.7	35.1	80.8
17	13 27.6	27.7	77.9	13 52.1	29.7	78.4	14 15.7	31.5	78.9	14 38.3	33.2	79.4	14 59.8	35.0	79.9
18	13 55.3	27.6	77.0	14 21.8	29.4	77.5	14 47.2	31.2	78.0	15 11.5	33.1	78.6	15 34.8	34.8	79.1
19	14 22.9	27.3	76.1	14 51.2	29.2	76.6	15 18.4	31.1	77.1	15 44.6	32.8	77.7	16 09.6	34.6	78.2
20	14 50.2	+27.2	75.2	15 20.4	+29.0	75.7	15 49.5	+30.8	76.3	16 17.4	+32.6	76.8	16 44.2	+34.4	77.4
21	15 17.4	26.9	74.3	15 49.4	28.7	74.8	16 20.3	30.5	75.4	16 50.0	32.4	75.9	17 18.6	34.1	76.5
22	15 44.3	26.6	73.3	16 18.1	28.5	73.9	16 50.8	30.4	74.5	17 22.4	32.1	75.1	17 52.7	33.9	75.7
23	16 10.9	26.5	72.4	16 46.6	28.3	73.0	17 21.2	30.1	73.6	17 54.5	32.0	74.2	18 26.6	33.7	74.8
24	16 37.4	26.1	71.5	17 14.9	28.0	72.0	17 51.3	29.9	72.7	18 26.5	31.6	73.3	19 00.3	33.5	73.9
25	17 03.5	+25.9	70.5	17 42.9	+27.8	71.1	18 21.2	+29.5	71.7	18 58.1	+31.4	72.4	19 33.8	+33.2	73.1
26	17 29.4	25.7	69.6	18 10.7	27.5	70.2	18 50.7	29.4	70.8	19 29.5	31.1	71.5	20 07.0	33.0	72.2
27	17 55.1	25.3	68.6	18 38.2	27.2	69.3	19 20.1	29.0	69.9	20 00.6	30.9	70.6	20 39.9	32.6	71.3
28	18 20.4	25.1	67.7	19 05.4	26.9	68.3	19 49.1	28.8	69.0	20 31.5	30.6	69.7	21 12.5	32.4	70.4
29	18 45.5	24.8	66.7	19 32.3	26.6	67.4	20 17.9	28.4	68.0	21 02.1	30.2	68.7	21 44.9	32.0	69.5

20°			22°			24°			26°			28°			Dec.
Hc	d	Z	Hc	d	Z	Hc	d	Z	Hc	d	Z	Hc	d	Z	
5 38.2	-20.6	92.1	5 33.7	-22.6	92.3	5 28.8	-24.6	92.4	5 23.5	-26.5	92.6	5 17.7	-28.3	92.8	0
5 17.6	20.8	93.0	5 11.1	22.7	93.2	5 04.2	24.6	93.4	4 57.0	26.5	93.5	4 49.4	28.4	93.7	1
4 56.8	20.8	93.9	4 48.4	22.8	94.1	4 39.6	24.7	94.3	4 30.5	26.6	94.4	4 21.0	28.4	94.6	2
4 36.0	20.9	94.9	4 25.6	22.9	95.0	4 14.9	24.8	95.2	4 03.9	26.7	95.3	3 52.6	28.6	95.5	3
4 15.1	21.0	95.8	4 02.7	22.9	96.0	3 50.1	24.8	96.1	3 37.2	26.7	96.2	3 24.0	28.5	96.4	4
3 54.1	-21.0	96.8	3 39.8	-23.0	96.9	3 25.3	-24.9	97.0	3 10.5	-26.8	97.1	2 55.5	-28.6	97.2	5
3 33.1	21.1	97.7	3 16.8	23.0	97.8	3 00.4	24.9	97.9	2 43.7	26.8	98.0	2 26.9	28.6	98.1	6
3 12.0	21.2	98.6	2 53.8	23.0	98.7	2 35.5	25.0	98.8	2 16.9	26.8	98.9	1 58.3	28.7	99.0	7
2 50.8	21.2	99.6	2 30.8	23.2	99.7	2 10.5	25.0	99.8	1 50.1	26.8	99.8	1 29.6	28.7	99.9	8
2 29.6	21.2	100.5	2 07.6	23.1	100.6	1 45.5	25.0	100.7	1 23.3	26.9	100.7	1 00.9	28.7	100.8	9
2 08.4	-21.3	101.5	1 44.5	-23.2	101.5	1 20.5	-25.1	101.6	0 56.4	-26.9	101.6	0 32.2	-28.7	101.6	10
1 47.1	21.3	102.4	1 21.3	23.2	102.4	0 55.4	25.0	102.5	0 29.5	26.9	102.5	0 03.5	-28.7	102.5	11
1 25.8	21.3	103.3	0 58.1	23.2	103.4	0 30.4	25.1	103.4	0 02.6	-26.9	103.4	0 25.2	+28.7	76.6	12
1 04.5	21.3	104.3	0 34.9	23.2	104.3	0 05.3	-25.0	104.3	0 24.3	+26.9	75.7	0 53.9	28.7	75.7	13
0 43.2	21.3	105.2	0 11.7	-23.2	105.2	0 19.7	+25.1	74.8	0 51.2	26.9	74.8	1 22.6	28.7	74.9	14
0 21.9	-21.4	106.1	0 11.5	+23.2	73.9	0 44.8	+25.1	73.9	1 18.1	+26.8	73.9	1 51.3	+28.6	74.0	15
0 00.5	-21.3	107.1	0 34.7	23.2	72.9	1 09.9	25.0	73.0	1 44.9	26.9	73.0	2 19.9	28.6	73.1	16
0 20.8	+21.4	72.0	0 57.9	23.2	72.0	1 34.9	25.0	72.1	2 11.8	26.8	72.1	2 48.5	28.6	72.2	17
0 42.2	21.3	71.1	1 21.1	23.2	71.1	1 59.9	25.0	71.2	2 38.6	26.7	71.2	3 17.1	28.5	71.3	18
1 03.5	21.3	70.1	1 44.3	23.1	70.2	2 24.9	24.9	70.2	3 05.3	26.8	70.3	3 45.6	28.5	70.5	19
1 24.8	+21.3	69.2	2 07.4	+23.1	69.3	2 49.8	+24.9	69.3	3 32.1	+26.6	69.4	4 14.1	+28.4	69.6	20
1 46.1	21.3	68.3	2 30.5	23.1	68.3	3 14.7	24.9	68.4	3 58.7	26.6	68.5	4 42.5	28.3	68.7	21
2 07.4	21.2	67.3	2 53.6	23.0	67.4	3 39.6	24.8	67.5	4 25.3	26.6	67.6	5 10.8	28.3	67.8	22
2 28.6	21.2	66.4	3 16.6	23.0	66.5	4 04.4	24.7	66.6	4 51.9	26.5	66.7	5 39.1	28.2	66.9	23
2 49.8	21.2	65.5	3 39.6	22.9	65.6	4 29.1	24.7	65.7	5 18.4	26.4	65.8	6 07.3	28.1	66.0	24
3 11.0	+21.1	64.5	4 02.5	+22.8	64.6	4 53.8	+24.6	64.8	5 44.8	+26.3	64.9	6 35.4	+28.0	65.1	25
3 32.1	21.0	63.6	4 25.3	22.8	63.7	5 18.4	24.5	63.9	6 11.1	26.2	64.0	7 03.4	27.9	64.2	26
3 53.1	21.0	62.6	4 48.1	22.7	62.8	5 42.9	24.4	62.9	6 37.3	26.1	63.1	7 31.3	27.8	63.4	27
4 14.1	20.9	61.7	5 10.8	22.7	61.8	6 07.3	24.3	62.0	7 03.4	26.0	62.2	7 59.1	27.7	62.5	28
4 35.0	20.8	60.8	5 33.5	22.5	60.9	6 31.6	24.2	61.1	7 29.4	25.9	61.3	8 26.8	27.5	61.6	29

30°			32°			34°			36°			38°			Dec.
Hc	d	Z	Hc	d	Z	Hc	d	Z	Hc	d	Z	Hc	d	Z	
5 11.6	-30.1	93.0	5 05.1	-31.9	93.2	4 58.3	-33.7	93.4	4 51.1	-35.5	93.5	4 43.5	-37.1	93.7	0
4 41.5	30.3	93.9	4 33.2	32.0	94.0	4 24.6	33.8	94.2	4 15.6	35.4	94.3	4 06.4	37.1	94.5	1
4 11.2	30.2	94.7	4 01.2	32.1	94.9	3 50.8	33.8	95.0	3 40.2	35.5	95.2	3 29.3	37.2	95.3	2
3 41.0	30.4	95.6	3 29.1	32.1	95.7	3 17.0	33.9	95.9	3 04.7	35.6	96.0	2 52.1	37.2	96.1	3
3 10.6	30.3	96.5	2 57.0	32.2	96.6	2 43.1	33.8	96.7	2 29.1	35.6	96.8	2 14.9	37.3	96.8	4
2 40.3	-30.4	97.3	2 24.8	-32.1	97.4	2 09.3	-34.0	97.5	1 53.5	-35.6	97.6	1 37.6	-37.2	97.6	5
2 09.9	30.5	98.2	1 52.7	32.2	98.3	1 35.3	33.9	98.3	1 17.9	35.6	98.4	1 00.4	37.3	98.4	6
1 39.4	30.4	99.1	1 20.5	32.3	99.1	1 01.4	33.9	99.2	0 42.3	35.6	99.2	0 23.1	-37.2	99.2	7
1 09.0	30.5	99.9	0 48.2	32.2	100.0	0 27.5	-34.0	100.0	0 06.7	-35.7	100.0	0 14.1	+37.3	80.0	8
0 38.5	30.5	100.8	0 16.0	-32.2	100.8	0 06.5	+33.9	79.2	0 29.0	+35.6	79.2	0 51.4	37.3	79.2	9
0 08.0	-30.5	101.6	0 16.2	+32.3	78.4	0 40.4	+34.0	78.4	1 04.6	+35.6	78.4	1 28.7	+37.2	78.4	10
0 22.5	+30.5	77.5	0 48.5	32.2	77.5	1 14.4	33.9	77.5	1 40.2	35.6	77.6	2 05.9	37.2	77.7	11
0 53.0	30.4	76.6	1 20.7	32.2	76.7	1 48.3	33.9	76.7	2 15.8	35.6	76.8	2 43.1	37.2	76.9	12
1 23.4	30.5	75.8	1 52.9	32.2	75.8	2 22.2	33.9	75.9	2 51.4	35.5	75.9	3 20.3	37.2	76.1	13
1 53.9	30.4	74.9	2 25.1	32.1	75.0	2 56.1	33.8	75.1	3 26.9	35.5	75.2	3 57.5	37.1	75.3	14
2 24.3	+30.4	74.0	2 57.2	+32.1	74.1	3 29.9	+33.8	74.2	4 02.4	+35.4	74.4	4 34.6	+37.0	74.5	15
2 54.7	30.4	73.2	3 29.3	32.1	73.3	4 03.7	33.8	73.4	4 37.8	35.4	73.6	5 11.6	37.0	73.7	16
3 25.1	30.4	72.3	4 01.4	32.0	72.4	4 37.5	33.6	72.6	5 13.2	35.3	72.8	5 48.6	36.9	72.9	17
3 55.4	30.2	71.5	4 33.4	32.0	71.6	5 11.1	33.7	71.8	5 48.5	35.3	71.9	6 25.5	36.9	72.1	18
4 25.6	30.2	70.6	5 05.4	31.8	70.7	5 44.8	33.5	70.9	6 23.8	35.2	71.1	7 02.4	36.8	71.3	19
4 55.8	+30.1	69.7	5 37.2	+31.9	69.9	6 18.3	+33.5	70.1	6 59.0	+35.1	70.3	7 39.2	+36.9	70.6	20
5 25.9	30.1	68.9	6 09.1	31.7	69.0	6 51.8	33.4	69.3	7 34.1	35.0	69.5	8 15.8	36.6	69.8	21
5 56.0	30.0	68.0	6 40.8	31.6	68.2	7 25.2	33.2	68.4	8 09.1	34.9	68.7	8 52.4	36.5	69.0	22
6 26.0	29.8	67.1	7 12.4	31.6	67.3	7 58.4	33.2	67.6	8 44.0	34.8	67.8	9 28.9	36.4	68.1	23
6 55.8	29.8	66.2	7 44.0	31.4	66.5	8 31.6	33.1	66.7	9 18.8	34.6	67.0	10 05.3	36.2	67.3	24
7 25.6	+29.7	65.4	8 15.4	+31.4	65.6	9 04.7	+33.0	65.9	9 53.4	+34.6	66.2	10 41.5	+36.2	66.5	25
7 55.3	29.6	64.5	8 46.8	31.2	64.8	9 37.7	32.8	65.0	10 28.0	34.4	65.4	11 17.7	36.0	65.7	26
8 24.9	29.4	63.6	9 18.0	31.1	63.9	10 10.5	32.7	64.2	11 02.4	34.3	64.5	11 53.7	35.8	64.9	27
8 54.3	29.4	62.7	9 49.1	30.9	63.0	10 43.2	32.6	63.3	11 36.7	34.2	63.7	12 29.5	35.7	64.1	28
9 23.7	29.2	61.8	10 20.0	30.8	62.1	11 15.8	32.4	62.5	12 10.9	34.0	62.9	13 05.2	35.6	63.3	29

Dec.	40° Hc	d	Z	42° Hc	d	Z	44° Hc	d	Z	46° Hc	d	Z	48° Hc	d	Z
0	4 35.6	+38.6	93.9	4 27.3	+40.3	94.0	4 18.7	+41.8	94.2	4 09.8	+43.3	94.3	4 00.6	+44.7	94.5
1	5 14.2	38.6	93.1	5 07.6	40.2	93.3	5 00.5	41.7	93.5	4 53.1	43.2	93.6	4 45.3	44.7	93.8
2	5 52.8	38.6	92.3	5 47.8	40.1	92.5	5 42.2	41.7	92.7	5 36.3	43.2	92.9	5 30.0	44.6	93.1
3	6 31.4	38.5	91.6	6 27.9	40.1	91.8	6 23.9	41.6	92.0	6 19.5	43.1	92.2	6 14.6	44.5	92.5
4	7 09.9	38.4	90.8	7 08.0	40.0	91.0	7 05.5	41.6	91.3	7 02.6	43.0	91.5	6 59.1	44.5	91.8
5	7 48.3	+38.3	90.0	7 48.0	+39.9	90.3	7 47.1	+41.4	90.6	7 45.6	+43.0	90.8	7 43.6	+44.4	91.1
6	8 26.6	38.2	89.2	8 27.9	39.8	89.5	8 28.5	41.4	89.8	8 28.6	42.9	90.1	8 28.0	44.4	90.4
7	9 04.8	38.1	88.5	9 07.7	39.7	88.8	9 09.9	41.3	89.1	9 11.5	42.8	89.4	9 12.4	44.2	89.7
8	9 42.9	38.0	87.7	9 47.4	39.7	88.0	9 51.2	41.2	88.4	9 54.3	42.7	88.7	9 56.6	44.2	89.1
9	10 20.9	37.9	86.9	10 27.1	39.5	87.3	10 32.4	41.1	87.6	10 37.0	42.7	88.0	10 40.8	44.1	88.4
10	10 58.8	+37.8	86.1	11 06.6	+39.4	86.5	11 13.5	+41.0	86.9	11 19.7	+42.5	87.3	11 24.9	+44.0	87.7
11	11 36.6	37.7	85.3	11 46.0	39.3	85.7	11 54.5	40.9	86.1	12 02.2	42.4	86.6	12 08.9	43.9	87.0
12	12 14.3	37.5	84.5	12 25.3	39.1	84.9	12 35.4	40.8	85.4	12 44.6	42.3	85.8	12 52.8	43.8	86.3
13	12 51.8	37.3	83.7	13 04.4	39.1	84.2	13 16.2	40.6	84.6	13 26.9	42.2	85.1	13 36.6	43.7	85.6
14	13 29.1	37.2	82.9	13 43.5	38.8	83.4	13 56.8	40.4	83.9	14 09.1	42.0	84.4	14 20.3	43.5	84.9
15	14 06.3	+37.1	82.1	14 22.3	+38.7	82.6	14 37.2	+40.4	83.1	14 51.1	+41.9	83.6	15 03.8	+43.5	84.2
16	14 43.4	36.9	81.3	15 01.0	38.6	81.8	15 17.6	40.1	82.3	15 33.0	41.7	82.9	15 47.3	43.2	83.5
17	15 20.3	36.7	80.5	15 39.6	38.3	81.0	15 57.7	40.0	81.6	16 14.7	41.6	82.1	16 30.5	43.1	82.7
18	15 57.0	36.5	79.6	16 17.9	38.2	80.2	16 37.7	39.9	80.8	16 56.3	41.4	81.4	17 13.6	43.0	82.0
19	16 33.5	36.3	78.8	16 56.1	38.0	79.4	17 17.6	39.6	80.0	17 37.7	41.3	80.6	17 56.6	42.8	81.3
20	17 09.8	+36.1	78.0	17 34.1	+37.8	78.6	17 57.2	+39.5	79.2	18 19.0	+41.0	79.9	18 39.4	+42.6	80.5
21	17 45.9	35.9	77.1	18 11.9	37.6	77.8	18 36.7	39.2	78.4	19 00.0	40.9	79.1	19 22.0	42.5	79.8
22	18 21.8	35.5	76.3	18 49.5	37.4	77.0	19 15.9	39.0	77.6	19 40.9	40.7	78.3	20 04.5	42.2	79.0
23	18 57.4	35.5	75.5	19 26.9	37.1	76.1	19 54.9	38.9	76.8	20 21.6	40.4	77.5	20 46.7	42.0	78.3
24	19 32.9	35.2	74.6	20 04.0	36.9	75.3	20 33.8	38.6	76.0	21 02.0	40.3	76.8	21 28.7	41.9	77.5
25	20 08.1	+34.9	73.7	20 40.9	+36.7	74.5	21 12.4	+38.3	75.2	21 42.3	+40.0	76.0	22 10.6	+41.6	76.7
26	20 43.0	34.7	72.9	21 17.6	36.3	73.6	21 50.7	38.1	74.4	22 23.3	39.7	75.2	22 52.2	41.4	76.0
27	21 17.7	34.4	72.0	21 54.0	36.2	72.8	22 28.8	37.9	73.5	23 02.0	39.5	74.3	23 33.6	41.1	75.2
28	21 52.1	34.1	71.1	22 30.2	35.8	71.9	23 06.7	37.5	72.7	23 41.5	39.3	73.5	24 14.7	40.9	74.4
29	22 26.2	33.8	70.2	23 06.0	35.6	71.0	23 44.2	37.3	71.8	24 20.8	39.0	72.7	24 55.6	40.6	73.6

Dec.	50° Hc	d	Z	52° Hc	d	Z	54° Hc	d	Z	56° Hc	d	Z	58° Hc	d	Z
0	3 51.2	+46.0	94.6	3 41.4	+47.4	94.7	3 31.3	+48.7	94.9	3 21.1	+49.8	95.0	3 10.5	+51.0	95.1
1	4 37.2	46.0	94.0	4 28.8	47.3	94.1	4 20.0	48.6	94.3	4 10.9	49.8	94.4	4 01.5	50.9	94.6
2	5 23.2	46.0	93.3	5 16.1	47.3	93.5	5 08.6	48.5	93.7	5 00.7	49.7	93.9	4 52.4	50.9	94.0
3	6 09.2	45.9	92.7	6 03.4	47.2	92.9	5 57.1	48.5	93.1	5 50.4	49.8	93.3	5 43.3	50.9	93.5
4	6 55.1	45.9	92.0	6 50.6	47.2	92.3	6 45.6	48.5	92.5	6 40.2	49.7	92.7	6 34.2	50.8	93.0
5	7 41.0	+45.8	91.4	7 37.8	+47.2	91.6	7 34.1	+48.5	91.9	7 29.9	+49.6	92.2	7 25.0	+50.8	92.4
6	8 26.8	45.8	90.7	8 25.0	47.1	91.0	8 22.6	48.3	91.3	8 19.5	49.6	91.6	8 15.8	50.8	91.9
7	9 12.6	45.7	90.1	9 12.1	47.0	90.4	9 10.9	48.4	90.7	9 09.1	49.6	91.0	9 06.6	50.7	91.4
8	9 58.3	45.6	89.4	9 59.1	47.0	89.8	9 59.3	48.2	90.1	9 58.7	49.4	90.5	9 57.3	50.7	90.8
9	10 43.9	45.5	88.7	10 46.1	46.9	89.1	10 47.5	48.2	89.5	10 48.1	49.5	89.9	10 48.0	50.6	90.3
10	11 29.4	+45.4	88.1	11 33.0	+46.8	88.5	11 35.7	+48.1	88.9	11 37.6	+49.3	89.3	11 38.6	+50.5	89.7
11	12 14.8	45.3	87.4	12 19.8	46.7	87.9	12 23.8	48.0	88.3	12 26.9	49.3	88.7	12 29.1	50.5	89.2
12	13 00.1	45.3	86.7	13 06.5	46.6	87.2	13 11.8	48.0	87.7	13 16.2	49.2	88.1	13 19.6	50.4	88.6
13	13 45.4	45.1	86.1	13 53.1	46.5	86.6	13 59.8	47.8	87.1	14 05.4	49.1	87.6	14 10.0	50.3	88.1
14	14 30.5	45.0	85.4	14 39.6	46.4	85.9	14 47.6	47.7	86.4	14 54.5	49.0	87.0	15 00.3	50.3	87.5
15	15 15.5	+44.9	84.7	15 26.0	+46.3	85.3	15 35.3	+47.7	85.8	15 43.5	+49.0	86.4	15 50.6	+50.1	86.9
16	16 00.4	44.7	84.0	16 12.3	46.1	84.6	16 23.0	47.5	85.2	16 32.5	48.8	85.8	16 40.7	50.1	86.4
17	16 45.1	44.6	83.3	16 58.4	46.1	83.9	17 10.5	47.4	84.5	17 21.3	48.7	85.2	17 30.8	49.9	85.8
18	17 29.7	44.4	82.6	17 44.5	45.8	83.3	17 57.9	47.3	83.9	18 10.0	48.6	84.5	18 20.7	49.9	85.2
19	18 14.1	44.3	81.9	18 30.3	45.8	82.6	18 45.2	47.1	83.2	18 58.6	48.4	83.9	19 10.6	49.7	84.6
20	18 58.4	+44.2	81.2	19 16.1	+45.6	81.9	19 32.3	+47.0	82.6	19 47.0	+48.4	83.3	20 00.3	+49.6	84.0
21	19 42.6	43.9	80.5	20 01.7	45.3	81.2	20 19.3	46.8	81.9	20 35.4	48.2	82.7	20 49.9	49.5	83.4
22	20 26.5	43.8	79.8	20 47.1	45.3	80.5	21 06.1	46.7	81.3	21 23.6	48.0	82.0	21 39.4	49.3	82.8
23	21 10.3	43.6	79.0	21 32.4	45.0	79.8	21 52.8	46.5	80.6	22 11.6	47.9	81.4	22 28.7	49.3	82.2
24	21 53.9	43.4	78.3	22 17.4	44.9	79.1	22 39.3	46.4	79.9	22 59.5	47.7	80.7	23 18.0	49.0	81.5
25	22 37.3	+43.2	77.5	23 02.3	+44.7	78.4	23 25.7	+46.1	79.2	23 47.2	+47.6	80.1	24 07.0	+48.9	80.9
26	23 20.5	42.9	76.8	23 47.0	44.5	77.6	24 11.8	46.0	78.5	24 34.8	47.4	79.4	24 55.9	48.8	80.3
27	24 03.4	42.7	76.0	24 31.5	44.3	76.9	24 57.8	45.7	77.8	25 22.2	47.2	78.7	25 44.7	48.5	79.7
28	24 46.1	42.5	75.3	25 15.8	44.0	76.2	25 43.5	45.6	77.1	26 09.4	47.0	78.0	26 33.2	48.4	79.0
29	25 28.6	42.3	74.5	25 59.8	43.8	75.4	26 29.1	45.3	76.4	26 56.4	46.8	77.3	27 21.6	48.2	78.3

40° Hc	d	Z	42° Hc	d	Z	44° Hc	d	Z	46° Hc	d	Z	48° Hc	d	Z	Dec.
4 35.6	-38.7	93.9	4 27.3	-40.3	94.0	4 18.7	-41.8	94.2	4 09.8	-43.3	94.3	4 00.6	-44.7	94.5	0
3 56.9	38.8	94.6	3 47.0	40.3	94.8	3 36.9	41.8	94.9	3 26.5	43.3	95.0	3 15.9	44.7	95.1	1
3 18.1	38.8	95.4	3 06.7	40.4	95.5	2 55.1	41.9	95.6	2 43.2	43.3	95.7	2 31.2	44.8	95.8	2
2 39.3	38.8	96.2	2 26.3	40.4	96.2	2 13.2	41.9	96.3	1 59.9	43.4	96.4	1 46.4	44.7	96.5	3
2 00.5	38.9	96.9	1 45.9	40.4	97.0	1 31.3	41.9	97.0	1 16.5	43.4	97.1	1 01.7	44.8	97.1	4
1 21.6	-38.8	97.7	1 05.5	-40.4	97.7	0 49.4	-41.9	97.8	0 33.1	-43.3	97.8	0 16.9	-44.8	97.8	5
0 42.8	38.9	98.4	0 25.1	-40.4	98.5	0 07.5	-42.0	98.5	0 10.2	+43.4	81.5	0 27.9	+44.8	81.5	6
0 03.9	-38.8	99.2	0 15.3	+40.4	80.8	0 34.5	+41.9	80.8	0 53.6	43.4	80.8	1 12.7	44.8	80.9	7
0 34.9	+38.9	80.0	0 55.7	40.4	80.1	1 16.4	41.9	80.1	1 37.0	43.3	80.1	1 57.5	44.7	80.2	8
1 13.8	38.8	79.3	1 36.1	40.4	79.3	1 58.3	41.9	79.4	2 20.3	43.4	79.5	2 42.2	44.7	79.5	9
1 52.6	+38.9	78.5	2 16.5	+40.4	78.6	2 40.2	+41.8	78.7	3 03.7	+43.3	78.8	3 27.0	+44.7	78.9	10
2 31.5	38.8	77.7	2 56.9	40.3	77.8	3 22.0	41.9	77.9	3 47.0	43.3	78.1	4 11.7	44.6	78.2	11
3 10.3	38.7	77.0	3 37.2	40.3	77.1	4 03.9	41.8	77.2	4 30.3	43.2	77.4	4 56.3	44.7	77.5	12
3 49.0	38.8	76.2	4 17.5	40.3	76.4	4 45.7	41.7	76.5	5 13.5	43.2	76.7	5 41.0	44.6	76.9	13
4 27.8	38.6	75.4	4 57.8	40.2	75.6	5 27.4	41.7	75.8	5 56.7	43.1	76.0	6 25.6	44.5	76.2	14
5 06.4	+38.7	74.7	5 38.0	+40.1	74.9	6 09.1	+41.6	75.1	6 39.8	+43.1	75.3	7 10.1	+44.5	75.5	15
5 45.1	38.5	73.9	6 18.1	40.1	74.1	6 50.7	41.6	74.3	7 22.9	43.0	74.6	7 54.6	44.4	74.8	16
6 23.6	38.5	73.1	6 58.2	40.0	73.4	7 32.3	41.5	73.6	8 05.9	43.0	73.9	8 39.0	44.3	74.2	17
7 02.1	38.4	72.4	7 38.2	40.0	72.6	8 13.8	41.4	72.9	8 48.9	42.8	73.2	9 23.3	44.3	73.5	18
7 40.5	38.4	71.6	8 18.2	39.8	71.9	8 55.2	41.4	72.1	9 31.7	42.8	72.5	10 07.6	44.1	72.8	19
8 18.9	+38.2	70.8	8 58.0	+39.8	71.1	9 36.6	+41.2	71.4	10 14.5	+42.7	71.7	10 51.7	+44.1	72.1	20
8 57.1	38.1	70.0	9 37.8	39.6	70.3	10 17.8	41.1	70.7	10 57.2	42.5	71.0	11 35.8	44.0	71.4	21
9 35.2	38.1	69.3	10 17.4	39.6	69.6	10 58.9	41.1	69.9	11 39.7	42.5	70.3	12 19.8	43.9	70.7	22
10 13.3	37.9	68.5	10 57.0	39.4	68.8	11 40.0	40.9	69.2	12 22.2	42.4	69.6	13 03.7	43.7	70.0	23
10 51.2	37.8	67.7	11 36.4	39.3	68.0	12 20.9	40.8	68.4	13 04.6	42.2	68.9	13 47.4	43.7	69.3	24
11 29.0	+37.7	66.9	12 15.7	+39.2	67.3	13 01.7	+40.6	67.7	13 46.8	+42.1	68.1	14 31.1	+43.5	68.6	25
12 06.7	37.5	66.1	12 54.9	39.1	66.5	13 42.3	40.6	66.9	14 28.9	42.0	67.4	15 14.6	43.3	67.9	26
12 44.2	37.5	65.3	13 34.0	38.9	65.7	14 22.9	40.4	66.2	15 10.9	41.8	66.7	15 57.9	43.3	67.2	27
13 21.6	37.2	64.5	14 12.9	38.7	64.9	15 03.3	40.2	65.4	15 52.7	41.7	65.9	16 41.2	43.0	66.4	28
13 58.8	37.1	63.7	14 51.6	38.6	64.1	15 43.5	40.0	64.6	16 34.4	41.5	65.2	17 24.2	43.0	65.7	29

50° Hc	d	Z	52° Hc	d	Z	54° Hc	d	Z	56° Hc	d	Z	58° Hc	d	Z	Dec.
3 51.2	-46.1	94.6	3 41.4	-47.4	94.7	3 31.3	-48.6	94.9	3 21.1	-49.9	95.0	3 10.5	-50.9	95.1	0
3 05.1	46.1	95.2	2 54.0	47.4	95.3	2 42.7	48.7	95.4	2 31.2	49.9	95.5	2 19.6	51.0	95.6	1
2 19.0	46.1	95.9	2 06.6	47.4	96.0	1 54.0	48.6	96.0	1 41.4	49.9	96.1	1 28.6	51.0	96.1	2
1 32.9	46.2	96.5	1 19.2	47.5	96.6	1 05.4	48.7	96.6	0 51.5	49.9	96.7	0 37.6	-51.0	96.7	3
0 46.7	46.1	97.2	0 31.7	-47.4	97.2	0 16.7	-48.7	97.2	0 01.6	-49.8	97.2	0 13.4	+51.0	82.8	4
0 00.6	-46.2	97.8	0 15.7	+47.4	82.2	0 32.0	+48.7	82.2	0 48.2	+49.9	82.2	1 04.4	+51.0	82.3	5
0 45.6	+46.1	81.6	1 03.1	47.5	81.6	1 20.7	48.6	81.6	1 38.1	49.8	81.7	1 55.4	51.0	81.7	6
1 31.7	46.1	80.9	1 50.6	47.4	81.0	2 09.3	48.7	81.0	2 27.9	49.9	81.1	2 46.4	50.9	81.2	7
2 17.8	46.1	80.3	2 38.0	47.4	80.4	2 58.0	48.6	80.5	3 17.8	49.8	80.6	3 37.3	51.0	80.7	8
3 03.9	46.1	79.6	3 25.4	47.4	79.7	3 46.6	48.6	79.9	4 07.6	49.8	80.0	4 28.3	50.9	80.2	9
3 50.0	+46.0	79.0	4 12.8	+47.3	79.1	4 35.2	+48.6	79.3	4 57.4	+49.7	79.4	5 19.2	+50.9	79.6	10
4 36.0	46.1	78.4	5 00.1	47.3	78.5	5 23.8	48.6	78.7	5 47.1	49.8	78.9	6 10.1	50.8	79.1	11
5 22.1	45.9	77.7	5 47.4	47.3	77.9	6 12.4	48.5	78.1	6 36.9	49.7	78.3	7 00.9	50.9	78.6	12
6 08.0	46.0	77.1	6 34.7	47.2	77.3	7 00.9	48.4	77.5	7 26.6	49.6	77.8	7 51.8	50.7	78.0	13
6 54.0	45.9	76.4	7 21.9	47.2	76.7	7 49.3	48.5	76.9	8 16.2	49.6	77.2	8 42.5	50.8	77.5	14
7 39.9	+45.8	75.8	8 09.1	+47.1	76.0	8 37.8	+48.3	76.3	9 05.8	+49.6	76.6	9 33.3	+50.7	76.9	15
8 25.7	45.7	75.1	8 56.2	47.1	75.4	9 26.1	48.3	75.7	9 55.4	49.5	76.1	10 24.0	50.6	76.4	16
9 11.4	45.7	74.5	9 43.3	46.9	74.8	10 14.4	48.3	75.1	10 44.9	49.4	75.5	11 14.6	50.6	75.9	17
9 57.1	45.6	73.8	10 30.2	46.9	74.1	11 02.7	48.1	74.5	11 34.3	49.4	74.9	12 05.2	50.5	75.3	18
10 42.7	45.5	73.1	11 17.1	46.9	73.5	11 50.8	48.1	73.9	12 23.7	49.3	74.3	12 55.7	50.4	74.8	19
11 28.2	+45.5	72.5	12 04.0	+46.7	72.9	12 38.9	+48.0	73.3	13 13.0	+49.2	73.7	13 46.1	+50.4	74.2	20
12 13.7	45.3	71.8	12 50.7	46.7	72.2	13 26.9	47.9	72.7	14 02.2	49.1	73.1	14 36.5	50.2	73.6	21
12 59.0	45.2	71.1	13 37.4	46.5	71.6	14 14.8	47.8	72.1	14 51.3	49.0	72.6	15 26.7	50.3	73.1	22
13 44.2	45.2	70.5	14 23.9	46.4	70.9	15 02.6	47.7	71.4	15 40.3	48.9	72.0	16 16.9	50.1	72.5	23
14 29.4	45.0	69.8	15 10.3	46.4	70.3	15 50.3	47.6	70.8	16 29.2	48.9	71.4	17 07.0	50.0	71.9	24
15 14.4	+44.8	69.1	15 56.7	+46.2	69.6	16 37.9	+47.5	70.2	17 18.1	+48.7	70.7	17 57.0	+49.9	71.3	25
15 59.2	44.8	68.4	16 42.9	46.0	69.0	17 25.4	47.4	69.5	18 06.8	48.6	70.1	18 46.9	49.8	70.8	26
16 44.0	44.6	67.7	17 28.9	46.0	68.3	18 12.8	47.2	68.9	18 55.4	48.4	69.5	19 36.7	49.7	70.2	27
17 28.6	44.4	67.0	18 14.9	45.8	67.6	19 00.0	47.1	68.2	19 43.8	48.4	68.9	20 26.4	49.5	69.6	28
18 13.0	44.3	66.3	19 00.7	45.6	66.9	19 47.1	46.9	67.6	20 32.2	48.2	68.3	21 15.9	49.5	69.0	29

Dec.	0° Hc	d	Z	2° Hc	d	Z	4° Hc	d	Z	6° Hc	d	Z	8° Hc	d	Z
°	° ′	′	°	° ′	′	°	° ′	′	°	° ′	′	°	° ′	′	°
0	4 00.0	0.0	90.0	3 59.9 +	2.0	90.1	3 59.4 +	4.2	90.3	3 58.7 +	6.2	90.4	3 57.7 +	8.3	90.6
1	4 00.0 –	0.1	89.0	4 01.9	2.0	89.1	4 03.6	4.1	89.3	4 04.9	6.2	89.4	4 06.0	8.3	89.6
2	3 59.9	0.2	88.0	4 03.9	1.9	88.1	4 07.7	4.0	88.3	4 11.1	6.1	88.4	4 14.3	8.1	88.6
3	3 59.7	0.3	87.0	4 05.8	1.9	87.1	4 11.7	3.9	87.3	4 17.2	6.0	87.4	4 22.4	8.1	87.6
4	3 59.4	0.3	86.0	4 07.7	1.7	86.1	4 15.6	3.9	86.3	4 23.2	6.0	86.4	4 30.5	8.1	86.6
5	3 59.1 –	0.4	85.0	4 09.4 +	1.7	85.1	4 19.5 +	3.7	85.3	4 29.2 +	5.8	85.4	4 38.6 +	7.9	85.6
6	3 58.7	0.5	84.0	4 11.1	1.6	84.1	4 23.2	3.7	84.3	4 35.0	5.8	84.4	4 46.5	7.9	84.6
7	3 58.2	0.5	83.0	4 12.7	1.6	83.1	4 26.9	3.6	83.3	4 40.8	5.7	83.4	4 54.4	7.7	83.6
8	3 57.7	0.7	82.0	4 14.3	1.4	82.1	4 30.5	3.6	82.3	4 46.5	5.6	82.4	5 02.1	7.7	82.6
9	3 57.0	0.7	81.0	4 15.7	1.4	81.1	4 34.1	3.4	81.3	4 52.1	5.5	81.4	5 09.8	7.6	81.6
10	3 56.3 –	0.7	80.0	4 17.1 +	1.3	80.1	4 37.5 +	3.4	80.3	4 57.6 +	5.5	80.4	5 17.4 +	7.5	80.6
11	3 55.6	0.9	79.0	4 18.4	1.2	79.1	4 40.9	3.3	79.3	5 03.1	5.3	79.4	5 24.9	7.4	79.6
12	3 54.7	0.9	78.0	4 19.6	1.2	78.1	4 44.2	3.2	78.3	5 08.4	5.2	78.4	5 32.3	7.3	78.6
13	3 53.8	0.9	77.0	4 20.8	1.0	77.1	4 47.4	3.1	77.3	5 13.6	5.2	77.4	5 39.6	7.2	77.6
14	3 52.9	1.1	76.0	4 21.8	1.0	76.1	4 50.5	3.0	76.3	5 18.8	5.0	76.4	5 46.8	7.0	76.6
15	3 51.8 –	1.1	75.0	4 22.8 +	0.9	75.1	4 53.5 +	2.9	75.3	5 23.8 +	5.0	75.4	5 53.8 +	7.0	75.6
16	3 50.7	1.2	74.0	4 23.7	0.8	74.1	4 56.4	2.9	74.3	5 28.8	4.9	74.4	6 00.8	6.9	74.6
17	3 49.5	1.3	73.0	4 24.5	0.8	73.1	4 59.3	2.7	73.3	5 33.7	4.7	73.4	6 07.7	6.7	73.6
18	3 48.2	1.3	72.0	4 25.3	0.6	72.1	5 02.0	2.7	72.3	5 38.4	4.7	72.4	6 14.4	6.7	72.6
19	3 46.9	1.4	71.0	4 25.9	0.6	71.1	5 04.7	2.5	71.3	5 43.1	4.5	71.4	6 21.1	6.5	71.6
20	3 45.5 –	1.5	70.0	4 26.5 +	0.5	70.1	5 07.2 +	2.5	70.2	5 47.6 +	4.4	70.4	6 27.6 +	6.4	70.6
21	3 44.0	1.5	69.0	4 27.0	0.4	69.1	5 09.7	2.4	69.2	5 52.0	4.4	69.4	6 34.0	6.3	69.6
22	3 42.5	1.6	68.0	4 27.4	0.4	68.1	5 12.1	2.2	68.2	5 56.4	4.2	68.4	6 40.3	6.2	68.6
23	3 40.9	1.7	66.9	4 27.8	0.2	67.1	5 14.3	2.2	67.2	6 00.6	4.1	67.4	6 46.5	6.0	67.6
24	3 39.2	1.7	65.9	4 28.0	0.2	66.1	5 16.5	2.1	66.2	6 04.7	4.0	66.4	6 52.5	6.0	66.6
25	3 37.5 –	1.8	64.9	4 28.2 +	0.1	65.1	5 18.6 +	2.0	65.2	6 08.7 +	3.9	65.4	6 58.5 +	5.7	65.6
26	3 35.7	1.9	63.9	4 28.3	0.0	64.1	5 20.6	1.9	64.2	6 12.6	3.8	64.4	7 04.2	5.7	64.6
27	3 33.8	1.9	62.9	4 28.3 –	0.1	63.1	5 22.5	1.8	63.2	6 16.4	3.7	63.4	7 09.9	5.6	63.6
28	3 31.9	2.0	61.9	4 28.2	0.2	62.1	5 24.3	1.7	62.2	6 20.1	3.5	62.4	7 15.5	5.4	62.6
29	3 29.9	2.1	60.9	4 28.0	0.2	61.1	5 26.0	1.6	61.2	6 23.6	3.4	61.4	7 20.9	5.2	61.6

Dec.	10° Hc	d	Z	12° Hc	d	Z	14° Hc	d	Z	16° Hc	d	Z	18° Hc	d	Z
°	° ′	′	°	° ′	′	°	° ′	′	°	° ′	′	°	° ′	′	°
0	3 56.3 +	10.5	90.7	3 54.7 +	12.5	90.8	3 52.9 +	14.5	91.0	3 50.7 +	16.5	91.1	3 48.2 +	18.6	91.2
1	4 06.8	10.3	89.7	4 07.2	12.4	89.9	4 07.4	14.4	90.0	4 07.2	16.5	90.1	4 06.8	18.5	90.3
2	4 17.1	10.3	88.7	4 19.6	12.3	88.9	4 21.8	14.4	89.0	4 23.7	16.4	89.2	4 25.3	18.4	89.3
3	4 27.4	10.1	87.7	4 31.9	12.3	87.9	4 36.2	14.3	88.0	4 40.1	16.3	88.2	4 43.7	18.3	88.4
4	4 37.5	10.1	86.7	4 44.2	12.1	86.9	4 50.5	14.2	87.1	4 56.4	16.3	87.2	5 02.0	18.3	87.4
5	4 47.6 +	10.0	85.8	4 56.3 +	12.1	85.9	5 04.7 +	14.1	86.1	5 12.7 +	16.1	86.3	5 20.3 +	18.1	86.5
6	4 57.6	10.0	84.8	5 08.4	12.0	84.9	5 18.8	14.0	85.1	5 28.8	16.1	85.3	5 38.4	18.1	85.5
7	5 07.6	9.8	83.8	5 20.4	11.9	84.0	5 32.8	14.0	84.1	5 44.9	15.9	84.3	5 56.5	17.9	84.5
8	5 17.4	9.7	82.8	5 32.3	11.8	83.0	5 46.8	13.8	83.2	6 00.8	15.9	83.4	6 14.4	17.9	83.5
9	5 27.1	9.7	81.8	5 44.1	11.7	82.0	6 00.6	13.7	82.2	6 16.7	15.7	82.4	6 32.3	17.7	82.6
10	5 36.8 +	9.5	80.8	5 55.8 +	11.5	81.0	6 14.3 +	13.6	81.2	6 32.4 +	15.6	81.4	6 50.0 +	17.7	81.7
11	5 46.3	9.5	79.8	6 07.3	11.5	80.0	6 27.9	13.5	80.2	6 48.0	15.6	80.5	7 07.7	17.5	80.7
12	5 55.8	9.3	78.8	6 18.8	11.4	79.0	6 41.4	13.4	79.3	7 03.6	15.4	79.5	7 25.2	17.4	79.7
13	6 05.1	9.2	77.8	6 30.2	11.2	78.0	6 54.8	13.3	78.3	7 19.0	15.2	78.5	7 42.6	17.2	78.8
14	6 14.3	9.1	76.8	6 41.4	11.2	77.1	7 08.1	13.1	77.3	7 34.2	15.2	77.5	7 59.8	17.2	77.8
15	6 23.4 +	9.0	75.8	6 52.6 +	11.0	76.1	7 21.2 +	13.0	76.3	7 49.4 +	15.0	76.6	8 17.0 +	17.0	76.8
16	6 32.4	8.9	74.8	7 03.6	10.8	75.1	7 34.2	12.9	75.3	8 04.4	14.8	75.6	8 34.0	16.8	75.9
17	6 41.3	8.7	73.8	7 14.4	10.8	74.1	7 47.1	12.7	74.3	8 19.2	14.8	74.6	8 50.8	16.7	74.9
18	6 50.0	8.7	72.8	7 25.2	10.6	73.1	7 59.8	12.7	73.3	8 34.0	14.5	73.6	9 07.5	16.5	73.9
19	6 58.7	8.5	71.9	7 35.8	10.5	72.1	8 12.5	12.4	72.4	8 48.5	14.5	72.6	9 24.0	16.4	73.0
20	7 07.2 +	8.4	70.9	7 46.3 +	10.4	71.1	8 24.9 +	12.3	71.4	9 03.0 +	14.2	71.7	9 40.4 +	16.2	72.0
21	7 15.6	8.2	69.9	7 56.7	10.2	70.1	8 37.2	12.2	70.4	9 17.2	14.1	70.7	9 56.6	16.1	71.0
22	7 23.8	8.1	68.9	8 06.9	10.0	69.1	8 49.4	12.0	69.4	9 31.3	14.0	69.7	10 12.7	15.8	69.9
23	7 31.9	8.0	67.9	8 16.9	9.9	68.1	9 01.4	11.8	68.4	9 45.3	13.7	68.7	10 28.5	15.7	69.0
24	7 39.9	7.9	66.9	8 26.8	9.8	67.1	9 13.2	11.7	67.4	9 59.0	13.6	67.7	10 44.2	15.5	68.1
25	7 47.8 +	7.7	65.9	8 36.6 +	9.6	66.1	9 24.9 +	11.5	66.4	10 12.6 +	13.4	66.7	10 59.7 +	15.3	67.1
26	7 55.5	7.5	64.9	8 46.2	9.5	65.1	9 36.4	11.3	65.4	10 26.0	13.3	65.7	11 15.0	15.1	66.1
27	8 03.0	7.4	63.9	8 55.7	9.2	64.1	9 47.7	11.2	64.4	10 39.3	13.0	64.7	11 30.1	14.9	65.1
28	8 10.4	7.3	62.9	9 04.9	9.2	63.1	9 58.9	11.0	63.4	10 52.3	12.8	63.8	11 45.0	14.7	64.1
29	8 17.7	7.1	61.8	9 14.1	8.9	62.1	10 09.9	10.8	62.4	11 05.1	12.7	62.8	11 59.7	14.5	63.1

0°			2°			4°			6°			8°			Dec.
Hc	d	Z	Hc	d	Z	Hc	d	Z	Hc	d	Z	Hc	d	Z	
4 00.0	0.0	90.0	3 59.9 −	2.2	90.1	3 59.4 −	4.2	90.3	3 58.7 −	6.3	90.4	3 57.7 −	8.4	90.6	0
4 00.0 −	0.1	91.0	3 57.7	2.2	91.1	3 55.2	4.3	91.3	3 52.4	6.4	91.4	3 49.3	8.5	91.6	1
3 59.9	0.2	92.0	3 55.5	2.3	92.1	3 50.9	4.4	92.3	3 46.0	6.5	92.4	3 40.8	8.6	92.5	2
3 59.7	0.3	93.0	3 53.2	2.3	93.1	3 46.5	4.4	93.3	3 39.5	6.5	93.4	3 32.2	8.6	93.5	3
3 59.4	0.3	94.0	3 50.9	2.4	94.1	3 42.1	4.5	94.3	3 33.0	6.6	94.4	3 23.6	8.6	94.5	4
3 59.1 −	0.4	95.0	3 48.5 −	2.5	95.1	3 37.6 −	4.6	95.3	3 26.4 −	6.7	95.4	3 15.0 −	8.7	95.5	5
3 58.7	0.5	96.0	3 46.0	2.6	96.1	3 33.0	4.7	96.3	3 19.7	6.7	96.4	3 06.3	8.8	96.5	6
3 58.2	0.5	97.0	3 43.4	2.6	97.2	3 28.3	4.7	97.3	3 13.0	6.7	97.4	2 57.5	8.9	97.5	7
3 57.7	0.7	98.0	3 40.8	2.7	98.2	3 23.6	4.7	98.3	3 06.3	6.9	98.4	2 48.6	8.8	98.5	8
3 57.0	0.7	99.0	3 38.1	2.8	99.2	3 18.9	4.9	99.3	2 59.4	6.9	99.4	2 39.8	9.0	99.5	9
3 56.3 −	0.7	100.0	3 35.3 −	2.8	100.2	3 14.0 −	4.8	100.3	2 52.5 −	6.9	100.4	2 30.8 −	8.9	100.5	10
3 55.6	0.9	101.0	3 32.5	2.9	101.2	3 09.2	5.0	101.3	2 45.6	7.0	101.4	2 21.9	9.1	101.5	11
3 54.7	0.9	102.0	3 29.6	2.9	102.2	3 04.2	5.0	102.3	2 38.6	7.0	102.4	2 12.8	9.0	102.4	12
3 53.8	0.9	103.0	3 26.7	3.1	103.2	2 59.2	5.0	103.3	2 31.6	7.1	103.3	2 03.8	9.1	103.4	13
3 52.9	1.1	104.0	3 23.6	3.0	104.2	2 54.2	5.1	104.3	2 24.5	7.1	104.4	1 54.7	9.1	104.4	14
3 51.8 −	1.1	105.0	3 20.6 −	3.2	105.2	2 49.1 −	5.2	105.3	2 17.4 −	7.2	105.3	1 45.6 −	9.2	105.4	15
3 50.7	1.2	106.0	3 17.4	3.2	106.2	2 43.9	5.2	106.3	2 10.2	7.2	106.3	1 36.4	9.2	106.4	16
3 49.5	1.3	107.0	3 14.2	3.2	107.2	2 38.7	5.2	107.3	2 03.0	7.2	107.3	1 27.2	9.2	107.4	17
3 48.2	1.3	108.0	3 11.0	3.4	108.2	2 33.5	5.3	108.3	1 55.8	7.3	108.3	1 18.0	9.2	108.4	18
3 46.9	1.4	109.0	3 07.6	3.3	109.2	2 28.2	5.4	109.2	1 48.5	7.3	109.3	1 08.8	9.3	109.4	19
3 45.5 −	1.5	110.0	3 04.3 −	3.5	110.2	2 22.8 −	5.4	110.2	1 41.2 −	7.3	110.3	0 59.5 −	9.3	110.4	20
3 44.0	1.5	111.0	3 00.8	3.5	111.2	2 17.4	5.4	111.2	1 33.9	7.4	111.3	0 50.2	9.2	111.3	21
3 42.5	1.6	112.0	2 57.3	3.5	112.2	2 12.0	5.5	112.2	1 26.5	7.4	112.3	0 41.0	9.3	112.3	22
3 40.9	1.7	113.1	2 53.8	3.6	113.2	2 06.5	5.5	113.2	1 19.1	7.4	113.3	0 31.7	9.4	113.3	23
3 39.2	1.7	114.1	2 50.2	3.6	114.2	2 01.0	5.5	114.2	1 11.7	7.4	114.3	0 22.3	9.3	114.3	24
3 37.5 −	1.8	115.1	2 46.6 −	3.7	115.2	1 55.5 −	5.6	115.2	1 04.3 −	7.5	115.3	0 13.0 −	9.3	115.3	25
3 35.7	1.9	116.1	2 42.9	3.8	116.2	1 49.9	5.6	116.2	0 56.8	7.4	116.3	0 03.7 −	9.3	116.3	26
3 33.8	1.9	117.1	2 39.1	3.8	117.2	1 44.3	5.6	117.2	0 49.4	7.5	117.3	0 05.6 +	9.3	62.7	27
3 31.9	2.0	118.1	2 35.3	3.8	118.2	1 38.7	5.7	118.2	0 41.9	7.5	118.3	0 14.9	9.4	61.7	28
3 29.9	2.1	119.1	2 31.5	3.9	119.2	1 33.0	5.7	119.2	0 34.4	7.5	119.2	0 24.3	9.3	60.8	29

10°			12°			14°			16°			18°			Dec.
Hc	d	Z	Hc	d	Z	Hc	d	Z	Hc	d	Z	Hc	d	Z	
3 56.3 −	10.4	90.7	3 54.7 −	12.5	90.8	3 52.9 −	14.6	91.0	3 50.7 −	16.6	91.1	3 48.2 −	18.6	91.2	0
3 45.9	10.6	91.7	3 42.2	12.6	91.8	3 38.3	14.7	91.9	3 34.1	16.7	92.1	3 29.6	18.6	92.2	1
3 35.3	10.6	92.7	3 29.6	12.7	92.8	3 23.6	14.7	92.9	3 17.4	16.7	93.0	3 11.0	18.8	93.1	2
3 24.7	10.7	93.7	3 16.9	12.7	93.8	3 08.9	14.7	93.9	3 00.7	16.8	94.0	2 52.2	18.7	94.1	3
3 14.0	10.7	94.6	3 04.2	12.8	94.8	2 54.2	14.8	94.9	2 43.9	16.8	95.0	2 33.5	18.9	95.0	4
3 03.3 −	10.8	95.6	2 51.4 −	12.8	95.7	2 39.4 −	14.9	95.8	2 27.1 −	16.9	95.9	2 14.6 −	18.8	96.0	5
2 52.5	10.8	96.6	2 38.6	12.8	96.7	2 24.5	14.9	96.8	2 10.2	16.9	96.9	1 55.8	18.9	96.9	6
2 41.7	10.9	97.6	2 25.8	13.0	97.7	2 09.6	14.9	97.8	1 53.3	16.9	97.8	1 36.9	18.9	97.9	7
2 30.8	10.9	98.6	2 12.8	12.9	98.7	1 54.7	15.0	98.7	1 36.4	16.9	98.8	1 18.0	18.9	98.8	8
2 19.9	11.0	99.6	1 59.9	13.0	99.6	1 39.7	15.0	99.7	1 19.5	17.0	99.8	0 59.1	19.0	99.8	9
2 08.9 −	11.0	100.6	1 46.9 −	13.0	100.6	1 24.7 −	15.0	100.7	1 02.5 −	17.0	100.7	0 40.1 −	18.9	100.7	10
1 57.9	11.0	101.5	1 33.9	13.1	101.6	1 09.7	15.0	101.6	0 45.5	17.0	101.7	0 21.2	19.0	101.7	11
1 46.9	11.1	102.5	1 20.8	13.0	102.6	0 54.7	15.1	102.6	0 28.5	17.0	102.6	0 02.2 −	18.9	102.6	12
1 35.8	11.1	103.5	1 07.8	13.1	103.5	0 39.6	15.0	103.6	0 11.5 −	17.1	103.6	0 16.7 +	19.0	76.4	13
1 24.7	11.1	104.5	0 54.7	13.1	104.5	0 24.6	15.1	104.5	0 05.6 +	17.0	75.5	0 35.7	19.0	75.5	14
1 13.6 −	11.1	105.5	0 41.6 −	13.1	105.5	0 09.5 −	15.1	105.5	0 22.6 +	17.0	74.5	0 54.7 +	18.9	74.5	15
1 02.5	11.2	106.4	0 28.5	13.2	106.5	0 05.6 +	15.0	73.5	0 39.6	17.0	73.5	1 13.6	18.9	73.6	16
0 51.3	11.2	107.4	0 15.3	13.1	107.4	0 20.6	15.1	72.6	0 56.6	17.0	72.6	1 32.5	18.9	72.6	17
0 40.1	11.2	108.4	0 02.2 −	13.1	108.4	0 35.7	15.1	71.6	1 13.6	17.0	71.6	1 51.4	18.8	71.7	18
0 28.9	11.2	109.4	0 10.9 +	13.1	70.6	0 50.8	15.0	70.6	1 30.6	16.9	70.7	2 10.2	18.9	70.7	19
0 17.7 −	11.2	110.4	0 24.0 +	13.2	69.6	1 05.8 +	15.0	69.6	1 47.5 +	16.9	69.7	2 29.1 +	18.7	69.8	20
0 06.5 −	11.2	111.4	0 37.2	13.1	68.6	1 20.8	15.0	68.7	2 04.4	16.9	68.8	2 47.8	18.8	68.8	21
0 04.7 +	11.2	67.7	0 50.3	13.1	67.7	1 35.8	15.0	67.7	2 21.3	16.8	67.8	3 06.6	18.7	67.9	22
0 15.9	11.2	66.7	1 03.4	13.0	66.7	1 50.8	14.9	66.7	2 38.1	16.8	66.8	3 25.3	18.6	66.9	23
0 27.1	11.2	65.7	1 16.4	13.1	65.7	2 05.7	14.9	65.8	2 54.9	16.7	65.8	3 43.9	18.6	66.0	24
0 38.3 +	11.1	64.7	1 29.5 +	13.0	64.7	2 20.6 +	14.9	64.8	3 11.6 +	16.7	64.9	4 02.5 +	18.5	65.0	25
0 49.4	11.2	63.7	1 42.5	13.0	63.8	2 35.5	14.8	63.8	3 28.3	16.7	63.9	4 21.0	18.4	64.1	26
1 00.6	11.1	62.7	1 55.5	13.0	62.8	2 50.3	14.8	62.9	3 45.0	16.5	63.0	4 39.4	18.3	63.1	27
1 11.7	11.2	61.8	2 08.5	12.9	61.8	3 05.1	14.7	61.9	4 01.5	16.5	62.0	4 57.7	18.3	62.1	28
1 22.9	11.1	60.8	2 21.4	12.9	60.8	3 19.8	14.7	60.9	4 18.0	16.4	61.0	5 16.0	18.2	61.2	29

Dec.	20° Hc	d	Z	22° Hc	d	Z	24° Hc	d	Z	26° Hc	d	Z	28° Hc	d	Z
°	° ′	′	°	° ′	′	°	° ′	′	°	° ′	′	°	° ′	′	°
0	3 45.5	+20.5	91.4	3 42.5	+22.5	91.5	3 39.2	+24.4	91.6	3 35.7	+26.3	91.8	3 31.9	+28.2	91.9
1	4 06.0	20.5	90.4	4 05.0	22.4	90.6	4 03.6	24.4	90.7	4 02.0	26.3	90.9	4 00.1	28.1	91.0
2	4 26.5	20.4	89.5	4 27.4	22.4	89.6	4 28.0	24.3	89.8	4 28.3	26.2	90.0	4 28.2	28.1	90.1
3	4 46.9	20.3	88.5	4 49.8	22.3	88.7	4 52.3	24.2	88.9	4 54.5	26.1	89.1	4 56.3	28.0	89.2
4	5 07.2	20.3	87.6	5 12.1	22.2	87.8	5 16.5	24.2	88.0	5 20.6	26.0	88.1	5 24.3	27.9	88.3
5	5 27.5	+20.1	86.7	5 34.3	+22.1	86.8	5 40.7	+24.0	87.0	5 46.6	+26.0	87.2	5 52.2	+27.9	87.4
6	5 47.6	20.1	85.7	5 56.4	22.0	85.9	6 04.7	24.0	86.1	6 12.6	25.9	86.3	6 20.1	27.7	86.6
7	6 07.7	19.9	84.8	6 18.4	21.9	85.0	6 28.7	23.8	85.2	6 38.5	25.7	85.4	6 47.8	27.7	85.7
8	6 27.6	19.9	83.8	6 40.3	21.8	84.0	6 52.5	23.8	84.3	7 04.2	25.7	84.5	7 15.5	27.5	84.8
9	6 47.5	19.7	82.9	7 02.1	21.7	83.1	7 16.3	23.6	83.3	7 29.9	25.6	83.6	7 43.0	27.4	83.9
10	7 07.2	+19.6	81.9	7 23.8	+21.6	82.2	7 39.9	+23.5	82.4	7 55.5	+25.4	82.7	8 10.4	+27.4	83.0
11	7 26.8	19.5	81.0	7 45.4	21.5	81.2	8 03.4	23.4	81.5	8 20.9	25.3	81.8	8 37.8	27.1	82.1
12	7 46.3	19.4	80.0	8 06.9	21.3	80.3	8 26.8	23.3	80.6	8 46.2	25.2	80.9	9 04.9	27.1	81.2
13	8 05.7	19.2	79.0	8 28.2	21.2	79.3	8 50.1	23.1	79.6	9 11.4	25.0	79.9	9 32.0	26.9	80.3
14	8 24.9	19.1	78.1	8 49.4	21.0	78.4	9 13.2	23.0	78.7	9 36.4	24.9	79.0	9 58.9	26.8	79.4
15	8 44.0	+19.0	77.1	9 10.4	+20.9	77.4	9 36.2	+22.8	77.8	10 01.3	+24.7	78.1	10 25.7	+26.6	78.5
16	9 03.0	18.8	76.2	9 31.3	20.8	76.5	9 59.0	22.7	76.8	10 26.0	24.6	77.2	10 52.3	26.5	77.5
17	9 21.8	18.6	75.2	9 52.1	20.6	75.5	10 21.7	22.5	75.9	10 50.6	24.4	76.2	11 18.8	26.2	76.6
18	9 40.4	18.5	74.2	10 12.7	20.4	74.6	10 44.2	22.3	74.9	11 15.0	24.2	75.3	11 45.0	26.1	75.7
19	9 58.9	18.3	73.3	10 33.1	20.2	73.6	11 06.5	22.2	74.0	11 39.2	24.1	74.4	12 11.1	26.0	74.8
20	10 17.2	+18.1	72.3	10 53.3	+20.1	72.7	11 28.7	+22.0	73.0	12 03.3	+23.9	73.4	12 37.1	+25.7	73.9
21	10 35.3	18.0	71.3	11 13.4	19.9	71.7	11 50.7	21.7	72.1	12 27.2	23.6	72.5	13 02.8	25.5	72.9
22	10 53.3	17.8	70.4	11 33.3	19.7	70.7	12 12.4	21.6	71.1	12 50.8	23.5	71.6	13 28.3	25.4	72.0
23	11 11.1	17.6	69.4	11 53.0	19.6	69.8	12 34.0	21.4	70.2	13 14.3	23.2	70.6	13 53.7	25.1	71.1
24	11 28.7	17.4	68.4	12 12.4	19.3	68.8	12 55.4	21.2	69.2	13 37.5	23.1	69.7	14 18.8	24.9	70.1
25	11 46.1	+17.2	67.4	12 31.7	+19.1	67.8	13 16.6	+20.9	68.3	14 00.6	+22.8	68.7	14 43.7	+24.6	69.2
26	12 03.3	17.0	66.5	12 50.8	18.9	66.9	13 37.5	20.8	67.3	14 23.4	22.6	67.8	15 08.3	24.5	68.3
27	12 20.3	16.8	65.5	13 09.7	18.6	65.9	13 58.3	20.5	66.3	14 46.0	22.3	66.8	15 32.8	24.2	67.3
28	12 37.1	16.5	64.5	13 28.3	18.5	64.9	14 18.8	20.2	65.4	15 08.3	22.1	65.8	15 57.0	23.9	66.4
29	12 53.6	16.4	63.5	13 46.8	18.1	63.9	14 39.0	20.1	64.4	15 30.4	21.9	64.9	16 20.9	23.7	65.4

Dec.	30° Hc	d	Z	32° Hc	d	Z	34° Hc	d	Z	36° Hc	d	Z	38° Hc	d	Z
°	° ′	′	°	° ′	′	°	° ′	′	°	° ′	′	°	° ′	′	°
0	3 27.8	+30.0	92.0	3 23.5	+31.8	92.1	3 18.9	+33.6	92.2	3 14.1	+35.3	92.4	3 09.1	+36.9	92.5
1	3 57.8	30.0	91.1	3 55.3	31.8	91.3	3 52.5	33.5	91.4	3 49.4	35.3	91.5	3 46.0	37.0	91.7
2	4 27.8	29.9	90.3	4 27.1	31.7	90.4	4 26.0	33.5	90.6	4 24.7	35.2	90.7	4 23.0	36.9	90.9
3	4 57.7	29.9	89.4	4 58.8	31.7	89.6	4 59.5	33.4	89.7	4 59.9	35.1	89.9	4 59.9	36.8	90.1
4	5 27.6	29.7	88.5	5 30.5	31.5	88.7	5 32.9	33.4	88.9	5 35.0	35.1	89.1	5 36.7	36.7	89.3
5	5 57.3	+29.7	87.7	6 02.0	+31.5	87.9	6 06.3	+33.3	88.1	6 10.1	+35.0	88.3	6 13.4	+36.7	88.5
6	6 27.0	29.6	86.8	6 33.5	31.4	87.0	6 39.6	33.1	87.2	6 45.1	34.9	87.5	6 50.1	36.7	87.7
7	6 56.6	29.5	85.9	7 04.9	31.4	86.1	7 12.7	33.1	86.4	7 20.0	34.8	86.7	7 26.8	36.5	86.9
8	7 26.1	29.4	85.0	7 36.3	31.2	85.3	7 45.8	33.0	85.6	7 54.8	34.8	85.8	8 03.3	36.4	86.1
9	7 55.5	29.3	84.1	8 07.5	31.1	84.4	8 18.8	32.9	84.7	8 29.6	34.6	85.0	8 39.7	36.3	85.3
10	8 24.8	+29.2	83.3	8 38.6	+31.0	83.6	8 51.7	+32.8	83.9	9 04.2	+34.5	84.2	9 16.0	+36.3	84.5
11	8 54.0	29.0	82.4	9 09.6	30.8	82.7	9 24.5	32.6	83.0	9 38.7	34.4	83.4	9 52.3	36.1	83.7
12	9 23.0	28.9	81.5	9 40.4	30.7	81.8	9 57.1	32.6	82.2	10 13.1	34.3	82.5	10 28.4	36.0	82.9
13	9 51.9	28.8	80.6	10 11.2	30.6	81.0	10 29.7	32.3	81.3	10 47.4	34.1	81.7	11 04.4	35.8	82.1
14	10 20.7	28.6	79.7	10 41.8	30.4	80.1	11 02.0	32.3	80.5	11 21.5	34.0	80.8	11 40.2	35.7	81.3
15	10 49.3	+28.5	78.8	11 12.2	+30.3	79.2	11 34.3	+32.1	79.6	11 55.5	+33.9	80.0	12 15.9	+35.6	80.4
16	11 17.8	28.3	77.9	11 42.5	30.1	78.3	12 06.4	31.9	78.7	12 29.4	33.7	79.2	12 51.5	35.4	79.6
17	11 46.1	28.1	77.0	12 12.6	30.0	77.4	12 38.3	31.8	77.9	13 03.1	33.5	78.3	13 26.9	35.2	78.8
18	12 14.2	28.0	76.1	12 42.6	29.8	76.5	13 10.1	31.5	77.0	13 36.6	33.3	77.5	14 02.1	35.1	77.9
19	12 42.2	27.8	75.2	13 12.4	29.6	75.7	13 41.6	31.4	76.1	14 09.9	33.2	76.6	14 37.2	34.9	77.1
20	13 10.0	+27.6	74.3	13 42.0	+29.4	74.8	14 13.0	+31.2	75.2	14 43.1	+33.0	75.7	15 12.1	+34.7	76.3
21	13 37.6	27.3	73.4	14 11.4	29.2	73.9	14 44.2	31.0	74.4	15 16.1	32.7	74.9	15 46.8	34.5	75.4
22	14 04.9	27.2	72.5	14 40.6	29.0	73.0	15 15.2	30.8	73.5	15 48.8	32.6	74.0	16 21.3	34.3	74.6
23	14 32.1	27.0	71.6	15 09.6	28.8	72.1	15 46.0	30.6	72.6	16 21.4	32.3	73.1	16 55.6	34.1	73.7
24	14 59.1	26.7	70.6	15 38.4	28.5	71.1	16 16.6	30.3	71.7	16 53.7	32.2	72.3	17 29.7	33.9	72.8
25	15 25.8	+26.5	69.7	16 06.9	+28.3	70.2	16 46.9	+30.2	70.8	17 25.9	+31.8	71.4	18 03.6	+33.6	72.0
26	15 52.3	26.3	68.8	16 35.2	28.1	69.3	17 17.1	29.9	69.9	17 57.7	31.7	70.5	18 37.2	33.4	71.1
27	16 18.6	26.0	67.8	17 03.3	27.8	68.4	17 46.9	29.6	69.0	18 29.4	31.4	69.6	19 10.6	33.1	70.2
28	16 44.6	25.7	66.9	17 31.1	27.6	67.5	18 16.5	29.4	68.1	19 00.8	31.1	68.7	19 43.7	32.9	69.3
29	17 10.3	25.5	66.0	17 58.7	27.3	66.5	18 45.9	29.1	67.1	19 31.9	30.8	67.8	20 16.6	32.6	68.5

20°			22°			24°			26°			28°			Dec.
Hc	d	Z	Hc	d	Z	Hc	d	Z	Hc	d	Z	Hc	d	Z	
3 45.5	-20.6	91.4	3 42.5	-22.6	91.5	3 39.2	-24.5	91.6	3 35.7	-26.4	91.8	3 31.9	-28.3	91.9	0
3 24.9	20.6	92.3	3 19.9	22.6	92.4	3 14.7	24.5	92.5	3 09.3	26.4	92.7	3 03.6	28.3	92.8	1
3 04.3	20.7	93.3	2 57.3	22.6	93.4	2 50.2	24.6	93.5	2 42.9	26.5	93.6	2 35.3	28.3	93.6	2
2 43.6	20.8	94.2	2 34.7	22.7	94.3	2 25.6	24.6	94.4	2 16.4	26.5	94.5	2 07.0	28.3	94.5	3
2 22.8	20.8	95.1	2 12.0	22.7	95.2	2 01.0	24.6	95.3	1 49.9	26.5	95.4	1 38.7	28.4	95.4	4
2 02.0	-20.8	96.1	1 49.3	-22.8	96.1	1 36.4	-24.7	96.2	1 23.4	-26.6	96.2	1 10.3	-28.4	96.3	5
1 41.2	20.8	97.0	1 26.5	22.8	97.1	1 11.7	24.7	97.1	0 56.8	26.5	97.1	0 41.9	28.4	97.2	6
1 20.4	20.9	97.9	1 03.7	22.7	98.0	0 47.0	24.7	98.0	0 30.3	26.6	98.0	0 13.5	-28.4	98.1	7
0 59.5	20.9	98.8	0 41.0	22.8	98.9	0 22.3	-24.7	98.9	0 03.7	-26.6	98.9	0 14.9	+28.4	81.1	8
0 38.6	20.9	99.8	0 18.1	-22.8	99.8	0 02.4	+24.7	80.2	0 22.9	+26.5	80.2	0 43.3	28.4	80.2	9
0 17.7	-20.8	100.8	0 04.7	+22.8	79.2	0 27.1	+24.7	79.2	0 49.4	+26.6	79.3	1 11.7	+28.4	79.3	10
0 03.1	+20.9	78.3	0 27.5	22.8	78.3	0 51.8	24.6	78.3	1 16.0	26.5	78.4	1 40.1	28.4	78.4	11
0 24.0	20.9	77.4	0 50.3	22.8	77.4	1 16.4	24.7	77.4	1 42.5	26.5	77.5	2 08.5	28.3	77.5	12
0 44.9	20.9	76.4	1 13.1	22.7	76.5	1 41.1	24.6	76.5	2 09.0	26.5	76.6	2 36.8	28.3	76.7	13
1 05.8	20.9	75.5	1 35.8	22.8	75.5	2 05.7	24.6	75.6	2 35.5	26.4	75.7	3 05.1	28.2	75.8	14
1 26.7	+20.8	74.6	1 58.6	+22.7	74.6	2 30.3	+24.5	74.7	3 01.9	+26.4	74.8	3 33.3	+28.2	74.9	15
1 47.5	20.8	73.6	2 21.3	22.7	73.7	2 54.9	24.5	73.8	3 28.3	26.4	73.9	4 01.5	28.2	74.0	16
2 08.3	20.8	72.7	2 44.0	22.6	72.8	3 19.4	24.5	72.9	3 54.7	26.3	73.0	4 29.7	28.0	73.1	17
2 29.1	20.7	71.7	3 06.6	22.6	71.8	3 43.9	24.4	71.9	4 21.0	26.2	72.1	4 57.7	28.0	72.2	18
2 49.8	20.7	70.8	3 29.2	22.5	70.9	4 08.3	24.4	71.0	4 47.2	26.1	71.2	5 25.7	28.0	71.3	19
3 10.5	+20.6	69.9	3 51.7	+22.5	70.0	4 32.7	+24.2	70.1	5 13.3	+26.1	70.3	5 53.7	+27.8	70.5	20
3 31.1	20.6	68.9	4 14.2	22.4	69.0	4 56.9	24.2	69.2	5 39.4	26.0	69.4	6 21.5	27.7	69.6	21
3 51.7	20.5	68.0	4 36.6	22.3	68.1	5 21.1	24.2	68.3	6 05.4	25.9	68.5	6 49.2	27.7	68.7	22
4 12.2	20.5	67.0	4 58.9	22.2	67.2	5 45.3	24.0	67.4	6 31.3	25.8	67.6	7 16.9	27.5	67.8	23
4 32.7	20.3	66.1	5 21.1	22.2	66.2	6 09.3	23.9	66.4	6 57.1	25.7	66.6	7 44.4	27.5	66.9	24
4 53.0	+20.3	65.1	5 43.3	+22.1	65.3	6 33.2	+23.9	65.5	7 22.8	+25.6	65.7	8 11.9	+27.3	66.0	25
5 13.3	20.2	64.2	6 05.4	22.0	64.4	6 57.1	23.7	64.6	7 48.4	25.4	64.8	8 39.2	27.1	65.1	26
5 33.5	20.2	63.3	6 27.4	21.8	63.4	7 20.8	23.6	63.7	8 13.8	25.4	63.9	9 06.3	27.1	64.2	27
5 53.7	20.0	62.3	6 49.2	21.8	62.5	7 44.4	23.5	62.7	8 39.2	25.2	63.0	9 33.4	26.9	63.3	28
6 13.7	19.9	61.4	7 11.0	21.7	61.6	8 07.9	23.4	61.8	9 04.4	25.0	62.1	10 00.3	26.8	62.4	29

30°			32°			34°			36°			38°			Dec.
Hc	d	Z	Hc	d	Z	Hc	d	Z	Hc	d	Z	Hc	d	Z	
3 27.8	-30.1	92.0	3 23.5	-31.9	92.1	3 18.9	-33.6	92.2	3 14.1	-35.3	92.4	3 09.1	-37.0	92.5	0
2 57.7	30.1	92.9	2 51.6	31.9	93.0	2 45.3	33.7	93.1	2 38.8	35.4	93.2	2 32.1	37.1	93.3	1
2 27.6	30.1	93.7	2 19.7	31.9	93.8	2 11.6	33.7	93.9	2 03.4	35.4	94.0	1 55.0	37.1	94.0	2
1 57.5	30.2	94.6	1 47.8	32.0	94.7	1 37.9	33.7	94.7	1 28.0	35.4	94.8	1 17.9	37.0	94.8	3
1 27.3	30.2	95.5	1 15.8	32.0	95.5	1 04.2	33.7	95.6	0 52.6	35.4	95.6	0 40.9	37.1	95.6	4
0 57.1	-30.2	96.3	0 43.8	-32.0	96.4	0 30.5	-33.7	96.4	0 17.2	-35.5	96.4	0 03.8	-37.1	96.4	5
0 26.9	-30.2	97.2	0 11.8	-32.0	97.2	0 03.2	+33.8	82.8	0 18.3	+35.4	82.8	0 33.3	+37.1	82.8	6
0 03.3	+30.3	81.9	0 20.2	+32.0	81.9	0 37.0	33.7	82.0	0 53.7	35.4	82.0	1 10.4	37.0	82.0	7
0 33.6	30.2	81.1	0 52.2	31.9	81.1	1 10.7	33.7	81.1	1 29.1	35.4	81.2	1 47.4	37.1	81.2	8
1 03.8	30.2	80.2	1 24.1	32.0	80.3	1 44.4	33.7	80.3	2 04.5	35.4	80.4	2 24.5	37.0	80.5	9
1 34.0	+30.1	79.4	1 56.1	+31.9	79.4	2 18.1	+33.6	79.5	2 39.9	+35.3	79.6	3 01.5	+37.0	79.7	10
2 04.1	30.2	78.5	2 28.0	31.9	78.6	2 51.7	33.6	78.7	3 15.2	35.3	78.8	3 38.5	36.9	78.9	11
2 34.3	30.1	77.6	2 59.9	31.9	77.7	3 25.3	33.6	77.8	3 50.5	35.3	77.9	4 15.4	36.9	78.1	12
3 04.4	30.1	76.8	3 31.8	31.8	76.9	3 58.9	33.5	77.0	4 25.8	35.2	77.1	4 52.3	36.9	77.3	13
3 34.5	30.0	75.9	4 03.6	31.8	76.0	4 32.4	33.5	76.2	5 01.0	35.1	76.3	5 29.2	36.7	76.5	14
4 04.5	+29.9	75.0	4 35.4	+31.7	75.2	5 05.9	+33.4	75.3	5 36.1	+35.1	75.5	6 05.9	+36.8	75.7	15
4 34.4	29.9	74.2	5 07.1	31.6	74.3	5 39.3	33.4	74.5	6 11.2	35.0	74.7	6 42.7	36.6	74.9	16
5 04.3	29.9	73.3	5 38.7	31.5	73.5	6 12.7	33.2	73.7	6 46.2	34.9	73.9	7 19.3	36.5	74.1	17
5 34.2	29.7	72.4	6 10.2	31.5	72.6	6 45.9	33.2	72.8	7 21.1	34.8	73.1	7 55.8	36.5	73.3	18
6 03.9	29.7	71.5	6 41.7	31.4	71.7	7 19.1	33.1	72.0	7 55.9	34.8	72.2	8 32.3	36.3	72.5	19
6 33.6	+29.6	70.7	7 13.1	+31.3	70.9	7 52.2	+32.9	71.1	8 30.7	+34.6	71.4	9 08.6	+36.3	71.7	20
7 03.2	29.5	69.8	7 44.4	31.2	70.0	8 25.1	32.9	70.3	9 05.3	34.5	70.6	9 44.9	36.1	70.9	21
7 32.7	29.3	68.9	8 15.6	31.1	69.2	8 58.0	32.7	69.5	9 39.8	34.4	69.8	10 21.0	36.0	70.1	22
8 02.0	29.3	68.0	8 46.7	30.9	68.3	9 30.7	32.7	68.6	10 14.2	34.3	68.9	10 57.0	35.9	69.3	23
8 31.3	29.1	67.1	9 17.6	30.9	67.4	10 03.4	32.5	67.7	10 48.5	34.1	68.1	11 32.9	35.7	68.5	24
9 00.4	+29.0	66.3	9 48.5	+30.7	66.6	10 35.9	+32.3	66.9	11 22.6	+34.0	67.3	12 08.6	+35.6	67.6	25
9 29.4	28.9	65.4	10 19.2	30.5	65.7	11 08.2	32.2	66.0	11 56.6	33.8	66.4	12 44.2	35.5	66.8	26
9 58.3	28.8	64.5	10 49.7	30.4	64.8	11 40.4	32.1	65.2	12 30.4	33.7	65.6	13 19.7	35.3	66.0	27
10 27.1	28.6	63.6	11 20.1	30.3	63.9	12 12.5	31.9	64.3	13 04.1	33.5	64.7	13 55.0	35.1	65.2	28
10 55.7	28.4	62.7	11 50.4	30.1	63.1	12 44.4	31.7	63.4	13 37.6	33.4	63.8	14 30.1	34.9	64.3	29

LATITUDE **SAME** NAME   L.H.A. 94°, 266°

LATITUDE **SAME** NAME

Dec.	40° Hc	d	Z	42° Hc	d	Z	44° Hc	d	Z	46° Hc	d	Z	48° Hc	d	Z
0	3 03.8	+38.6	92.6	2 58.3	+40.2	92.7	2 52.6	+41.7	92.8	2 46.6	+43.2	92.9	2 40.5	+44.6	93.0
1	3 42.4	38.6	91.8	3 38.5	40.1	91.9	3 34.3	41.7	92.1	3 29.8	43.2	92.2	3 25.1	44.6	92.3
2	4 21.0	38.5	91.0	4 18.6	40.1	91.2	4 16.0	41.6	91.3	4 13.0	43.1	91.5	4 09.7	44.6	91.6
3	4 59.5	38.4	90.3	4 58.7	40.1	90.4	4 57.6	41.6	90.6	4 56.1	43.1	90.8	4 54.3	44.5	91.0
4	5 37.9	38.4	89.5	5 38.8	40.0	89.7	5 39.2	41.6	89.9	5 39.2	43.1	90.1	5 38.8	44.5	90.3
5	6 16.3	+38.4	88.7	6 18.8	+39.9	88.9	6 20.8	+41.4	89.2	6 22.3	+42.9	89.4	6 23.3	+44.4	89.6
6	6 54.7	38.2	88.0	6 58.7	39.9	88.2	7 02.2	41.5	88.4	7 05.2	43.0	88.7	7 07.7	44.4	88.9
7	7 32.9	38.2	87.2	7 38.6	39.8	87.4	7 43.7	41.3	87.7	7 48.2	42.8	88.0	7 52.1	44.3	88.3
8	8 11.1	38.1	86.4	8 18.4	39.7	86.7	8 25.0	41.2	87.0	8 31.0	42.8	87.3	8 36.4	44.2	87.6
9	8 49.2	38.0	85.6	8 58.1	39.6	85.9	9 06.2	41.2	86.2	9 13.8	42.7	86.6	9 20.6	44.2	86.9
10	9 27.2	+37.9	84.8	9 37.7	+39.5	85.2	9 47.4	+41.1	85.5	9 56.5	+42.5	85.9	10 04.8	+44.0	86.2
11	10 05.1	37.8	84.0	10 17.2	39.4	84.4	10 28.5	41.0	84.8	10 39.0	42.5	85.1	10 48.8	44.0	85.5
12	10 42.9	37.6	83.3	10 56.6	39.2	83.6	11 09.5	40.8	84.0	11 21.5	42.4	84.4	11 32.8	43.9	84.8
13	11 20.5	37.5	82.5	11 35.8	39.2	82.9	11 50.3	40.8	83.3	12 03.9	42.3	83.7	12 16.7	43.7	84.1
14	11 58.0	37.3	81.7	12 15.0	39.0	82.1	12 31.1	40.6	82.5	12 46.2	42.2	83.0	13 00.4	43.7	83.4
15	12 35.4	+37.3	80.9	12 54.0	+38.9	81.3	13 11.7	+40.5	81.8	13 28.4	+42.0	82.2	13 44.1	+43.5	82.7
16	13 12.7	37.1	80.1	13 32.9	38.8	80.5	13 52.2	40.3	81.0	14 10.4	41.9	81.5	14 27.6	43.4	82.0
17	13 49.8	36.9	79.3	14 11.7	38.5	79.7	14 32.5	40.2	80.2	14 52.3	41.8	80.8	15 11.0	43.3	81.3
18	14 26.7	36.8	78.4	14 50.2	38.5	79.0	15 12.7	40.0	79.5	15 34.1	41.6	80.0	15 54.3	43.1	80.6
19	15 03.5	36.6	77.6	15 28.7	38.3	78.2	15 52.7	39.9	78.7	16 15.7	41.4	79.3	16 37.4	43.0	79.9
20	15 40.1	+36.4	76.8	16 06.9	+38.1	77.4	16 32.6	+39.7	77.9	16 57.1	+41.3	78.5	17 20.4	+42.8	79.1
21	16 16.5	36.2	76.0	16 45.0	37.9	76.5	17 12.3	39.5	77.1	17 38.4	41.1	77.8	18 03.2	42.6	78.4
22	16 52.7	36.0	75.1	17 22.9	37.6	75.7	17 51.8	39.3	76.4	18 19.5	40.9	77.0	18 45.8	42.5	77.6
23	17 28.7	35.8	74.3	18 00.5	37.5	74.9	18 31.1	39.1	75.6	19 00.4	40.7	76.2	19 28.3	42.3	76.9
24	18 04.5	35.6	73.5	18 38.0	37.3	74.1	19 10.2	38.9	74.8	19 41.1	40.5	75.4	20 10.6	42.0	76.1
25	18 40.1	+35.3	72.6	19 15.3	+37.0	73.3	19 49.1	+38.7	74.0	20 21.6	+40.3	74.7	20 52.6	+41.9	75.4
26	19 15.4	35.1	71.8	19 52.3	36.8	72.4	20 27.8	38.5	73.1	21 01.9	40.1	73.9	21 34.5	41.7	74.6
27	19 50.5	34.9	70.9	20 29.1	36.6	71.6	21 06.3	38.2	72.3	21 42.0	39.9	73.1	22 16.2	41.4	73.8
28	20 25.4	34.6	70.0	21 05.7	36.3	70.7	21 44.5	38.0	71.5	22 21.9	39.6	72.3	22 57.6	41.2	73.1
29	21 00.0	34.3	69.2	21 42.0	36.0	69.9	22 22.5	37.7	70.7	23 01.5	39.3	71.4	23 38.8	41.0	72.3

Dec.	50° Hc	d	Z	52° Hc	d	Z	54° Hc	d	Z	56° Hc	d	Z	58° Hc	d	Z
0	2 34.2	+46.0	93.1	2 27.7	+47.3	93.2	2 21.0	+48.6	93.2	2 14.1	+49.8	93.3	2 07.1	+50.9	93.4
1	3 20.2	46.0	92.4	3 15.0	47.3	92.5	3 09.6	48.5	92.7	3 03.9	49.8	92.8	2 58.0	50.9	92.9
2	4 06.2	45.9	91.8	4 02.3	47.3	91.9	3 58.1	48.5	92.1	3 53.7	49.7	92.2	3 48.9	50.9	92.3
3	4 52.1	45.9	91.1	4 49.6	47.2	91.3	4 46.6	48.5	91.5	4 43.4	49.7	91.6	4 39.8	50.8	91.8
4	5 38.0	45.9	90.5	5 36.8	47.2	90.7	5 35.1	48.5	90.9	5 33.1	49.7	91.1	5 30.6	50.9	91.3
5	6 23.9	+45.8	89.8	6 24.0	+47.1	90.1	6 23.6	+48.4	90.3	6 22.8	+49.6	90.5	6 21.5	+50.8	90.7
6	7 09.7	45.7	89.2	7 11.1	47.1	89.4	7 12.0	48.4	89.7	7 12.4	49.6	89.9	7 12.3	50.7	90.2
7	7 55.4	45.7	88.5	7 58.2	47.1	88.8	8 00.4	48.3	89.1	8 02.0	49.6	89.3	8 03.0	50.7	89.6
8	8 41.1	45.7	87.9	8 45.3	46.9	88.2	8 48.7	48.3	88.5	8 51.6	49.5	88.8	8 53.7	50.7	89.1
9	9 26.8	45.5	87.2	9 32.2	46.9	87.6	9 37.0	48.2	87.9	9 41.1	49.4	88.2	9 44.4	50.6	88.6
10	10 12.3	+45.4	86.6	10 19.1	+46.9	86.9	10 25.2	+48.1	87.3	10 30.5	+49.4	87.7	10 35.0	+50.6	88.0
11	10 57.8	45.4	85.9	11 06.0	46.7	86.3	11 13.3	48.1	86.7	11 19.9	49.3	87.1	11 25.6	50.5	87.5
12	11 43.2	45.3	85.2	11 52.7	46.7	85.6	12 01.4	48.0	86.1	12 09.2	49.2	86.5	12 16.1	50.4	86.9
13	12 28.5	45.2	84.6	12 39.4	46.6	85.0	12 49.4	47.9	85.5	12 58.4	49.2	85.9	13 06.5	50.3	86.4
14	13 13.7	45.1	83.9	13 26.0	46.5	84.4	13 37.3	47.8	84.8	13 47.6	49.1	85.3	13 56.8	50.3	85.8
15	13 58.8	+45.0	83.2	14 12.5	+46.3	83.7	14 25.1	+47.7	84.2	14 36.6	+49.0	84.7	14 47.1	+50.2	85.3
16	14 43.8	44.8	82.5	14 58.8	46.3	83.1	15 12.8	47.6	83.6	15 25.6	48.9	84.1	15 37.3	50.1	84.7
17	15 28.6	44.7	81.8	15 45.1	46.1	82.4	16 00.4	47.5	83.0	16 14.5	48.8	83.5	16 27.4	50.0	84.1
18	16 13.3	44.6	81.1	16 31.2	46.0	81.7	16 47.9	47.3	82.3	17 03.3	48.7	82.9	17 17.4	49.9	83.5
19	16 57.9	44.5	80.4	17 17.2	45.9	81.1	17 35.2	47.3	81.7	17 52.0	48.5	82.3	18 07.3	49.9	83.0
20	17 42.4	+44.3	79.7	18 03.1	+45.7	80.4	18 22.5	+47.1	81.0	18 40.5	+48.4	81.7	18 57.2	+49.7	82.4
21	18 26.7	44.1	79.0	18 48.8	45.5	79.7	19 09.6	47.0	80.4	19 28.9	48.3	81.1	19 46.9	49.5	81.8
22	19 10.8	44.0	78.3	19 34.4	45.4	79.0	19 56.6	46.8	79.7	20 17.2	48.2	80.4	20 36.4	49.5	81.2
23	19 54.8	43.8	77.6	20 19.8	45.3	78.3	20 43.4	46.6	79.0	21 05.4	48.0	79.8	21 25.9	49.3	80.6
24	20 38.6	43.6	76.8	21 05.1	45.1	77.6	21 30.0	46.6	78.4	21 53.4	47.9	79.1	22 15.2	49.2	80.0
25	21 22.2	+43.4	76.1	21 50.2	+44.9	76.9	22 16.5	+46.4	77.7	22 41.3	+47.7	78.5	23 04.4	+49.0	79.3
26	22 05.6	43.2	75.4	22 35.1	44.7	76.2	23 02.9	46.1	77.0	23 29.0	47.6	77.8	23 53.4	48.9	78.7
27	22 48.8	43.0	74.6	23 19.8	44.5	75.5	23 49.0	46.0	76.3	24 16.6	47.3	77.2	24 42.3	48.7	78.1
28	23 31.8	42.8	73.9	24 04.3	44.2	74.7	24 35.0	45.7	75.6	25 03.9	47.2	76.5	25 31.0	48.5	77.4
29	24 14.6	42.5	73.1	24 48.5	44.1	74.0	25 20.7	45.6	74.9	25 51.1	47.0	75.8	26 19.5	48.4	76.8

40° Hc	d	Z	42° Hc	d	Z	44° Hc	d	Z	46° Hc	d	Z	48° Hc	d	Z	Dec.
3 03.8	−38.6	92.6	2 58.3	−40.2	92.7	2 52.6	−41.8	92.8	2 46.6	−43.2	92.9	2 40.5	−44.6	93.0	0
2 25.2	38.7	93.3	2 18.1	40.3	93.4	2 10.8	41.7	93.5	2 03.4	43.2	93.6	1 55.9	44.7	93.6	1
1 46.5	38.7	94.1	1 37.8	40.2	94.2	1 29.1	41.8	94.2	1 20.2	43.3	94.3	1 11.2	44.7	94.3	2
1 07.8	38.7	94.9	0 57.6	40.3	94.9	0 47.3	41.8	94.9	0 36.9	−43.2	95.0	0 26.5	−44.6	95.0	3
0 29.1	−38.7	95.6	0 17.3	−40.3	95.6	0 05.5	−41.8	95.7	0 06.3	+43.3	84.3	0 18.1	+44.7	84.4	4
0 09.6	+38.7	83.6	0 23.0	+40.2	83.6	0 36.3	+41.8	83.6	0 49.6	+43.2	83.7	1 02.8	+44.7	83.7	5
0 48.3	38.7	82.8	1 03.2	40.3	82.9	1 18.1	41.7	82.9	1 32.8	43.3	83.0	1 47.5	44.6	83.0	6
1 27.0	38.7	82.1	1 43.5	40.2	82.1	1 59.8	41.6	82.2	2 16.1	43.2	82.3	2 32.1	44.7	82.3	7
2 05.7	38.6	81.3	2 23.7	40.2	81.4	2 41.6	41.7	81.5	2 59.3	43.2	81.6	3 16.8	44.6	81.7	8
2 44.3	38.6	80.5	3 03.9	40.2	80.6	3 23.3	41.7	80.8	3 42.5	43.1	80.9	4 01.4	44.5	81.0	9
3 22.9	+38.6	79.8	3 44.1	+40.1	79.9	4 05.0	+41.7	80.0	4 25.6	+43.1	80.2	4 45.9	+44.6	80.3	10
4 01.5	38.6	79.0	4 24.2	40.1	79.2	4 46.7	41.6	79.3	5 08.7	43.1	79.5	5 30.5	44.4	79.7	11
4 40.1	38.4	78.2	5 04.3	40.1	78.4	5 28.3	41.5	78.6	5 51.8	43.0	78.8	6 14.9	44.5	79.0	12
5 18.5	38.5	77.5	5 44.4	40.0	77.7	6 09.8	41.5	77.9	6 34.8	43.0	78.1	6 59.4	44.4	78.3	13
5 57.0	38.4	76.7	6 24.4	39.9	76.9	6 51.3	41.5	77.1	7 17.8	42.9	77.4	7 43.8	44.3	77.6	14
6 35.4	+38.3	75.9	7 04.3	+39.9	76.2	7 32.8	+41.3	76.4	8 00.7	+42.8	76.7	8 28.1	+44.2	77.0	15
7 13.7	38.2	75.2	7 44.2	39.7	75.4	8 14.1	41.3	75.7	8 43.5	42.8	76.0	9 12.3	44.2	76.3	16
7 51.9	38.1	74.4	8 23.9	39.7	74.6	8 55.4	41.2	74.9	9 26.3	42.6	75.3	9 56.5	44.1	75.6	17
8 30.0	38.0	73.6	9 03.6	39.6	73.9	9 36.6	41.1	74.2	10 08.9	42.6	74.5	10 40.6	43.9	74.9	18
9 08.0	38.0	72.8	9 43.2	39.5	73.1	10 17.7	41.0	73.4	10 51.5	42.5	73.8	11 24.5	43.9	74.2	19
9 46.0	+37.8	72.0	10 22.7	+39.4	72.4	10 58.7	+40.9	72.7	11 34.0	+42.3	73.1	12 08.4	+43.8	73.5	20
10 23.8	37.7	71.2	11 02.1	39.2	71.6	11 39.6	40.8	72.0	12 16.3	42.3	72.4	12 52.2	43.7	72.8	21
11 01.5	37.6	70.4	11 41.3	39.2	70.8	12 20.4	40.6	71.2	12 58.6	42.1	71.7	13 35.9	43.5	72.1	22
11 39.1	37.5	69.6	12 20.5	39.0	70.0	13 01.0	40.5	70.5	13 40.7	42.0	70.9	14 19.4	43.3	71.4	23
12 16.6	37.3	68.9	12 59.5	38.8	69.3	13 41.5	40.4	69.7	14 22.7	41.8	70.2	15 02.9	43.3	70.7	24
12 53.9	+37.2	68.0	13 38.3	+38.8	68.5	14 21.9	+40.2	69.0	15 04.5	+41.7	69.4	15 46.2	+43.1	70.0	25
13 31.1	37.0	67.2	14 17.1	38.6	67.7	15 02.1	40.1	68.2	15 46.2	41.6	68.7	16 29.3	43.0	69.2	26
14 08.1	36.9	66.4	14 55.6	38.4	66.9	15 42.2	39.9	67.4	16 27.8	41.4	67.9	17 12.3	42.8	68.5	27
14 45.0	36.6	65.6	15 34.0	38.3	66.1	16 22.1	39.8	66.6	17 09.2	41.2	67.2	17 55.1	42.7	67.8	28
15 21.6	36.5	64.8	16 12.3	38.0	65.3	17 01.9	39.5	65.9	17 50.4	41.1	66.4	18 37.8	42.5	67.0	29

50° Hc	d	Z	52° Hc	d	Z	54° Hc	d	Z	56° Hc	d	Z	58° Hc	d	Z	Dec.
2 34.2	−46.0	93.1	2 27.7	−47.3	93.2	2 21.0	−48.6	93.2	2 14.1	−49.8	93.3	2 07.1	−50.9	93.4	0
1 48.2	46.1	93.7	1 40.4	47.4	93.8	1 32.4	48.6	93.8	1 24.3	49.7	93.9	1 16.2	50.9	93.9	1
1 02.1	46.0	94.4	0 53.0	47.3	94.4	0 43.8	−48.6	94.4	0 34.6	−49.8	94.4	0 25.3	−51.0	94.5	2
0 16.1	−46.0	95.0	0 05.7	−47.4	95.0	0 04.8	+48.6	85.0	0 15.2	+49.8	85.0	0 25.7	+50.9	85.0	3
0 29.9	+46.1	84.4	0 41.7	+47.3	84.4	0 53.4	48.6	84.4	1 05.0	49.8	84.4	1 16.6	50.9	84.5	4
1 16.0	+46.0	83.7	1 29.0	+47.4	83.8	1 42.0	+48.6	83.8	1 54.8	+49.8	83.9	2 07.5	+50.9	84.0	5
2 02.0	46.0	83.1	2 16.4	47.3	83.2	2 30.6	48.6	83.2	2 44.6	49.8	83.3	2 58.4	50.9	83.4	6
2 48.0	46.0	82.4	3 03.7	47.3	82.5	3 19.2	48.5	82.7	3 34.4	49.7	82.8	3 49.3	50.9	82.9	7
3 34.0	46.0	81.8	3 51.0	47.3	81.9	4 07.7	48.5	82.1	4 24.1	49.7	82.2	4 40.2	50.9	82.4	8
4 20.0	45.9	81.2	4 38.3	47.2	81.3	4 56.2	48.5	81.5	5 13.8	49.7	81.7	5 31.1	50.8	81.8	9
5 05.9	+45.9	80.5	5 25.5	+47.2	80.7	5 44.7	+48.5	80.9	6 03.5	+49.7	81.1	6 21.9	+50.8	81.3	10
5 51.8	45.8	79.9	6 12.7	47.2	80.1	6 33.2	48.4	80.3	6 53.2	49.6	80.5	7 12.7	50.7	80.8	11
6 37.6	45.8	79.2	6 59.9	47.1	79.4	7 21.6	48.3	79.7	7 42.8	49.5	80.0	8 03.4	50.7	80.2	12
7 23.4	45.8	78.6	7 47.0	47.0	78.8	8 09.9	48.4	79.1	8 32.3	49.6	79.4	8 54.1	50.7	79.7	13
8 09.2	45.7	77.9	8 34.0	47.0	78.2	8 58.3	48.2	78.5	9 21.9	49.4	78.8	9 44.8	50.6	79.1	14
8 54.9	+45.6	77.3	9 21.0	+46.9	77.6	9 46.5	+48.2	77.9	10 11.3	+49.4	78.2	10 35.4	+50.6	78.5	15
9 40.5	45.5	76.6	10 07.9	46.9	76.9	10 34.7	48.1	77.3	11 00.7	49.4	77.7	11 26.0	50.5	78.1	16
10 26.0	45.4	75.9	10 54.8	46.7	76.3	11 22.8	48.1	76.7	11 50.1	49.2	77.1	12 16.5	50.4	77.5	17
11 11.4	45.4	75.3	11 41.6	46.7	75.7	12 10.9	47.9	76.1	12 39.3	49.2	76.5	13 06.9	50.4	76.9	18
11 56.8	45.3	74.6	12 28.3	46.6	75.0	12 58.8	47.9	75.5	13 28.5	49.1	75.9	13 57.3	50.2	76.4	19
12 42.1	+45.1	73.9	13 14.9	+46.5	74.4	13 46.7	+47.8	74.8	14 17.6	+49.0	75.3	14 47.5	+50.2	75.8	20
13 27.2	45.1	73.3	14 01.4	46.3	73.7	14 34.5	47.7	74.2	15 06.6	49.0	74.7	15 37.7	50.1	75.3	21
14 12.3	44.9	72.6	14 47.7	46.3	73.1	15 22.2	47.6	73.6	15 55.6	48.7	74.1	16 27.8	50.0	74.7	22
14 57.2	44.9	71.9	15 34.0	46.2	72.4	16 09.8	47.4	73.0	16 44.4	48.7	73.5	17 17.8	50.0	74.1	23
15 42.1	44.6	71.2	16 20.2	46.0	71.7	16 57.2	47.4	72.3	17 33.1	48.6	72.9	18 07.8	49.8	73.5	24
16 26.7	+44.6	70.5	17 06.2	+45.9	71.1	17 44.6	+47.2	71.7	18 21.7	+48.5	72.3	18 57.6	+49.7	72.9	25
17 11.3	44.4	69.8	17 52.1	45.8	70.4	18 31.8	47.1	71.0	19 10.2	48.3	71.7	19 47.3	49.5	72.3	26
17 55.7	44.2	69.1	18 37.9	45.6	69.7	19 18.9	46.9	70.4	19 58.5	48.3	71.0	20 36.8	49.5	71.7	27
18 39.9	44.1	68.4	19 23.5	45.5	69.0	20 05.8	46.8	69.7	20 46.8	48.0	70.4	21 26.3	49.3	71.1	28
19 24.0	43.9	67.7	20 09.0	45.3	68.3	20 52.6	46.6	69.0	21 34.8	48.0	69.8	22 15.6	49.2	70.5	29

LATITUDE **SAME** NAME   L.H.A. 94°, 266°

LATITUDE **SAME** NAME

Dec.	0° Hc	d	Z	2° Hc	d	Z	4° Hc	d	Z	6° Hc	d	Z	8° Hc	d	Z
°	° ′	′	°	° ′	′	°	° ′	′	°	° ′	′	°	° ′	′	°
0	2 00.0	0.0	90.0	1 59.9 +	2.1	90.1	1 59.7 +	4.2	90.1	1 59.3 +	6.3	90.2	1 58.8 +	8.4	90.3
1	2 00.0 −	0.1	89.0	2 02.0	2.0	89.1	2 03.9	4.1	89.1	2 05.6	6.2	89.2	2 07.2	8.3	89.3
2	1 59.9	0.1	88.0	2 04.0	2.0	88.1	2 08.0	4.1	88.1	2 11.8	6.2	88.2	2 15.5	8.2	88.3
3	1 59.8	0.1	87.0	2 06.0	2.0	87.1	2 12.1	4.1	87.1	2 18.0	6.1	87.2	2 23.7	8.2	87.3
4	1 59.7	0.2	86.0	2 08.0	1.9	86.1	2 16.2	4.0	86.1	2 24.1	6.1	86.2	2 31.9	8.2	86.3
5	1 59.5 −	0.2	85.0	2 09.9 +	1.9	85.1	2 20.2 +	3.9	85.1	2 30.2 +	6.1	85.2	2 40.1 +	8.1	85.3
6	1 59.3	0.2	84.0	2 11.8	1.9	84.1	2 24.1	4.0	84.1	2 36.3	6.0	84.2	2 48.2	8.1	84.3
7	1 59.1	0.3	83.0	2 13.7	1.8	83.1	2 28.1	3.8	83.2	2 42.3	5.9	83.2	2 56.3	8.0	83.3
8	1 58.8	0.3	82.0	2 15.5	1.7	82.1	2 31.9	3.9	82.2	2 48.2	5.9	82.2	3 04.3	8.0	82.3
9	1 58.5	0.3	81.0	2 17.2	1.8	81.1	2 35.8	3.8	81.2	2 54.1	5.9	81.2	3 12.3	7.9	81.4
10	1 58.2 −	0.4	80.0	2 19.0 +	1.6	80.1	2 39.6 +	3.7	80.2	3 00.0 +	5.8	80.3	3 20.2 +	7.8	80.4
11	1 57.8	0.4	79.0	2 20.6	1.7	79.1	2 43.3	3.7	79.2	3 05.8	5.7	79.3	3 28.0	7.8	79.4
12	1 57.4	0.5	78.0	2 22.3	1.6	78.1	2 47.0	3.6	78.2	3 11.5	5.7	78.3	3 35.8	7.7	78.4
13	1 56.9	0.5	77.0	2 23.9	1.5	77.1	2 50.6	3.6	77.2	3 17.2	5.6	77.3	3 43.5	7.7	77.4
14	1 56.4	0.5	76.0	2 25.4	1.5	76.1	2 54.2	3.6	76.2	3 22.8	5.6	76.3	3 51.2	7.6	76.4
15	1 55.9 −	0.6	75.0	2 26.9 +	1.5	75.1	2 57.8 +	3.4	75.2	3 28.4 +	5.5	75.3	3 58.8 +	7.5	75.4
16	1 55.3	0.5	74.0	2 28.4	1.4	74.1	3 01.2	3.5	74.2	3 33.9	5.4	74.3	4 06.3	7.4	74.4
17	1 54.8	0.7	73.0	2 29.8	1.4	73.1	3 04.7	3.3	73.2	3 39.3	5.4	73.3	4 13.7	7.4	73.4
18	1 54.1	0.6	72.0	2 31.2	1.3	72.1	3 08.0	3.3	72.2	3 44.7	5.3	72.3	4 21.1	7.3	72.4
19	1 53.5	0.7	71.0	2 32.5	1.3	71.1	3 11.3	3.3	71.2	3 50.0	5.2	71.3	4 28.4	7.2	71.4
20	1 52.8 −	0.8	70.0	2 33.8 +	1.2	70.1	3 14.6 +	3.2	70.2	3 55.2 +	5.2	70.3	4 35.6 +	7.1	70.4
21	1 52.0	0.7	69.0	2 35.0	1.2	69.1	3 17.8	3.1	69.2	4 00.4	5.1	69.3	4 42.7	7.0	69.4
22	1 51.3	0.8	68.0	2 36.2	1.1	68.1	3 20.9	3.1	68.2	4 05.5	5.0	68.3	4 49.7	7.0	68.4
23	1 50.5	0.9	67.0	2 37.3	1.1	67.1	3 24.0	3.0	67.2	4 10.5	4.9	67.3	4 56.7	6.8	67.4
24	1 49.6	0.8	66.0	2 38.4	1.0	66.1	3 27.0	2.9	66.2	4 15.4	4.9	66.3	5 03.5	6.8	66.4
25	1 48.8 −	0.9	65.0	2 39.4 +	1.0	65.1	3 29.9 +	2.9	65.2	4 20.3 +	4.7	65.3	5 10.3 +	6.7	65.4
26	1 47.9	1.0	64.0	2 40.4	1.0	64.1	3 32.8	2.8	64.2	4 25.0	4.7	64.3	5 17.0	6.6	64.4
27	1 46.9	1.0	63.0	2 41.4	0.9	63.1	3 35.6	2.8	63.2	4 29.7	4.6	63.3	5 23.5	6.5	63.4
28	1 45.9	1.0	62.0	2 42.3	0.8	62.1	3 38.4	2.7	62.2	4 34.3	4.6	62.3	5 30.0	6.4	62.4
29	1 44.9	1.0	61.0	2 43.1	0.8	61.1	3 41.1	2.6	61.2	4 38.9	4.4	61.3	5 36.4	6.3	61.4

Dec.	10° Hc	d	Z	12° Hc	d	Z	14° Hc	d	Z	16° Hc	d	Z	18° Hc	d	Z
°	° ′	′	°	° ′	′	°	° ′	′	°	° ′	′	°	° ′	′	°
0	1 58.2 +	10.4	90.3	1 57.4 +	12.4	90.4	1 56.4 +	14.5	90.5	1 55.3 +	16.6	90.6	1 54.1 +	18.6	90.6
1	2 08.6	10.4	89.4	2 09.8	12.5	89.4	2 10.9	14.5	89.5	2 11.9	16.5	89.6	2 12.7	18.5	89.7
2	2 19.0	10.3	88.4	2 22.3	12.4	88.5	2 25.4	14.4	88.5	2 28.4	16.4	88.6	2 31.2	18.4	88.7
3	2 29.3	10.3	87.4	2 34.7	12.3	87.5	2 39.8	14.4	87.6	2 44.8	16.4	87.7	2 49.6	18.4	87.8
4	2 39.6	10.2	86.4	2 47.0	12.3	86.5	2 54.2	14.3	86.6	3 01.2	16.4	86.7	3 08.0	18.4	86.8
5	2 49.8 +	10.2	85.4	2 59.3 +	12.2	85.5	3 08.5 +	14.3	85.6	3 17.6 +	16.3	85.7	3 26.4 +	18.3	85.9
6	3 00.0	10.1	84.4	3 11.5	12.2	84.5	3 22.8	14.2	84.7	3 33.9	16.2	84.8	3 44.7	18.2	84.9
7	3 10.1	10.1	83.4	3 23.7	12.1	83.6	3 37.0	14.2	83.7	3 50.1	16.2	83.8	4 02.9	18.2	83.9
8	3 20.2	10.0	82.5	3 35.8	12.1	82.6	3 51.2	14.1	82.7	4 06.3	16.1	82.8	4 21.1	18.1	83.0
9	3 30.2	10.0	81.5	3 47.9	12.0	81.6	4 05.3	14.0	81.7	4 22.4	16.0	81.9	4 39.2	18.0	82.0
10	3 40.2 +	9.9	80.5	3 59.9 +	11.9	80.6	4 19.3 +	14.0	80.8	4 38.4 +	16.0	80.9	4 57.2 +	17.9	81.1
11	3 50.1	9.8	79.5	4 11.8	11.9	79.6	4 33.3	13.8	79.8	4 54.4	15.8	79.9	5 15.1	17.9	80.1
12	3 59.9	9.7	78.5	4 23.7	11.7	78.6	4 47.1	13.8	78.8	5 10.2	15.8	79.0	5 33.0	17.8	79.2
13	4 09.6	9.7	77.5	4 35.4	11.7	77.7	5 00.9	13.7	77.8	5 26.0	15.7	78.0	5 50.8	17.6	78.2
14	4 19.3	9.6	76.5	4 47.1	11.6	76.7	5 14.6	13.6	76.9	5 41.7	15.6	77.0	6 08.4	17.6	77.2
15	4 28.9 +	9.5	75.5	4 58.7 +	11.5	75.7	5 28.2 +	13.5	75.9	5 57.3 +	15.5	76.0	6 26.0 +	17.4	76.3
16	4 38.4	9.5	74.5	5 10.2	11.5	74.7	5 41.7	13.4	74.9	6 12.8	15.4	75.1	6 43.4	17.4	75.3
17	4 47.9	9.3	73.6	5 21.7	11.3	73.7	5 55.1	13.3	73.9	6 28.2	15.2	74.1	7 00.8	17.2	74.3
18	4 57.2	9.3	72.6	5 33.0	11.2	72.7	6 08.4	13.2	72.9	6 43.4	15.2	73.1	7 18.0	17.1	73.4
19	5 06.5	9.1	71.6	5 44.2	11.2	71.8	6 21.6	13.1	72.0	6 58.6	15.0	72.2	7 35.1	16.9	72.4
20	5 15.6 +	9.1	70.6	5 55.4 +	11.0	70.8	6 34.7 +	13.0	71.0	7 13.6 +	14.9	71.2	7 52.0 +	16.9	71.4
21	5 24.7	9.0	69.6	6 06.4	10.9	69.8	6 47.7	12.8	70.0	7 28.5	14.8	70.2	8 08.9	16.7	70.5
22	5 33.7	8.9	68.6	6 17.3	10.8	68.8	7 00.5	12.8	69.0	7 43.3	14.6	69.2	8 25.6	16.5	69.5
23	5 42.6	8.8	67.6	6 28.1	10.7	67.8	7 13.3	12.6	68.0	7 57.9	14.6	68.3	8 42.1	16.4	68.5
24	5 51.4	8.6	66.6	6 38.8	10.6	66.8	7 25.9	12.4	67.0	8 12.5	14.3	67.3	8 58.5	16.3	67.6
25	6 00.0 +	8.6	65.6	6 49.4 +	10.4	65.8	7 38.3 +	12.4	66.0	8 26.8 +	14.2	66.3	9 14.8 +	16.1	66.6
26	6 08.6	8.4	64.6	6 59.8	10.4	64.8	7 50.7	12.2	65.1	8 41.0	14.1	65.3	9 30.9	15.9	65.6
27	6 17.0	8.4	63.6	7 10.2	10.2	63.8	8 02.9	12.0	64.1	8 55.1	13.9	64.3	9 46.8	15.8	64.6
28	6 25.4	8.2	62.6	7 20.4	10.0	62.8	8 14.9	12.0	63.1	9 09.0	13.8	63.4	10 02.6	15.5	63.7
29	6 33.6	8.1	61.6	7 30.4	10.0	61.8	8 26.9	11.7	62.1	9 22.8	13.6	62.4	10 18.1	15.5	62.7

0° Hc	d	Z	2° Hc	d	Z	4° Hc	d	Z	6° Hc	d	Z	8° Hc	d	Z	Dec.
2 00.0	0.0	90.0	1 59.9 −	2.1	90.1	1 59.7 −	4.2	90.1	1 59.3 −	6.3	90.2	1 58.8 −	8.3	90.3	0
2 00.0 −	0.1	91.0	1 57.8	2.1	91.1	1 55.5	4.2	91.1	1 53.0	6.3	91.2	1 50.5	8.4	91.3	1
1 59.9	0.1	92.0	1 55.7	2.2	92.1	1 51.3	4.3	92.1	1 46.7	6.3	92.2	1 42.1	8.5	92.3	2
1 59.8	0.1	93.0	1 53.5	2.2	93.1	1 47.0	4.3	93.1	1 40.4	6.4	93.2	1 33.6	8.4	93.3	3
1 59.7	0.2	94.0	1 51.3	2.3	94.1	1 42.7	4.4	94.1	1 34.0	6.4	94.2	1 25.2	8.5	94.2	4
1 59.5 −	0.2	95.0	1 49.0 −	2.3	95.1	1 38.3 −	4.3	95.1	1 27.6 −	6.5	95.2	1 16.7 −	8.5	95.2	5
1 59.3	0.2	96.0	1 46.7	2.3	96.1	1 34.0	4.4	96.1	1 21.1	6.5	96.2	1 08.2	8.6	96.2	6
1 59.1	0.3	97.0	1 44.4	2.3	97.1	1 29.6	4.4	97.1	1 14.6	6.4	97.2	0 59.6	8.5	97.2	7
1 58.8	0.3	98.0	1 42.1	2.4	98.1	1 25.2	4.5	98.1	1 08.2	6.6	98.2	0 51.1	8.6	98.2	8
1 58.5	0.3	99.0	1 39.7	2.4	99.1	1 20.7	4.5	99.1	1 01.6	6.5	99.2	0 42.5	8.6	99.2	9
1 58.2 −	0.4	100.0	1 37.3 −	2.5	100.1	1 16.2 −	4.5	100.1	0 55.1 −	6.5	100.2	0 33.9 −	8.6	100.2	10
1 57.8	0.4	101.0	1 34.8	2.5	101.1	1 11.7	4.5	101.1	0 48.6	6.6	101.1	0 25.3	8.6	101.2	11
1 57.4	0.5	102.0	1 32.3	2.4	102.1	1 07.2	4.5	102.1	0 42.0	6.6	102.1	0 16.7	8.6	102.2	12
1 56.9	0.5	103.0	1 29.9	2.6	103.1	1 02.7	4.6	103.1	0 35.4	6.6	103.1	0 08.1 −	8.6	103.1	13
1 56.4	0.5	104.0	1 27.3	2.5	104.1	0 58.1	4.6	104.1	0 28.8	6.6	104.1	0 00.5 +	8.6	75.9	14
1 55.9 −	0.6	105.0	1 24.8 −	2.6	105.1	0 53.5 −	4.6	105.1	0 22.2 −	6.6	105.1	0 09.1 +	8.6	74.9	15
1 55.3	0.6	106.0	1 22.2	2.6	106.1	0 48.9	4.6	106.1	0 15.6	6.6	106.1	0 17.7	8.6	73.9	16
1 54.8	0.7	107.0	1 19.6	2.6	107.1	0 44.3	4.6	107.1	0 09.0	6.6	107.1	0 26.3	8.6	72.9	17
1 54.1	0.6	108.0	1 17.0	2.7	108.1	0 39.7	4.6	108.1	0 02.4 −	6.6	108.1	0 34.9	8.5	71.9	18
1 53.5	0.7	109.0	1 14.3	2.7	109.1	0 35.1	4.7	109.1	0 04.2 +	6.6	70.9	0 43.4	8.6	70.9	19
1 52.8 −	0.8	110.0	1 11.6 −	2.7	110.1	0 30.4 −	4.6	110.1	0 10.8 +	6.6	69.9	0 52.0 +	8.5	69.9	20
1 52.0	0.7	111.0	1 08.9	2.7	111.1	0 25.8	4.7	111.1	0 17.4	6.6	68.9	1 00.5	8.6	68.9	21
1 51.3	0.8	112.0	1 06.2	2.7	112.1	0 21.1	4.6	112.1	0 24.0	6.6	67.9	1 09.1	8.5	67.9	22
1 50.5	0.9	113.0	1 03.5	2.8	113.1	0 16.5	4.7	113.1	0 30.6	6.6	66.9	1 17.6	8.5	67.0	23
1 49.6	0.8	114.0	1 00.7	2.7	114.1	0 11.8	4.7	114.1	0 37.2	6.5	65.9	1 26.1	8.4	66.0	24
1 48.8 −	0.9	115.0	0 58.0 −	2.8	115.1	0 07.1 −	4.7	115.1	0 43.7 +	6.6	64.9	1 34.5 +	8.5	65.0	25
1 47.9	1.0	116.0	0 55.2	2.8	116.1	0 02.4 −	4.6	116.1	0 50.3	6.5	63.9	1 43.0	8.4	64.0	26
1 46.9	1.0	117.0	0 52.4	2.9	117.1	0 02.2 +	4.7	62.9	0 56.8	6.5	62.9	1 51.4	8.3	63.0	27
1 45.9	1.0	118.0	0 49.5	2.8	118.1	0 06.9	4.7	61.9	1 03.4	6.5	62.0	1 59.7	8.4	62.0	28
1 44.9	1.0	119.0	0 46.7	2.8	119.1	0 11.6	4.7	60.9	1 09.9	6.4	61.0	2 08.1	8.3	61.0	29

10° Hc	d	Z	12° Hc	d	Z	14° Hc	d	Z	16° Hc	d	Z	18° Hc	d	Z	Dec.
1 58.2 −	10.5	90.3	1 57.4 −	12.5	90.4	1 56.4 −	14.5	90.5	1 55.3 −	16.5	90.6	1 54.1 −	18.5	90.6	0
1 47.7	10.4	91.3	1 44.9	12.4	91.4	1 41.9	14.6	91.5	1 38.8	16.6	91.5	1 35.6	18.6	91.6	1
1 37.3	10.5	92.3	1 32.3	12.5	92.4	1 27.3	14.6	92.4	1 22.2	16.6	92.5	1 17.0	18.6	92.5	2
1 26.8	10.6	93.3	1 19.8	12.6	93.4	1 12.7	14.6	93.4	1 05.6	16.6	93.4	0 58.4	18.7	93.5	3
1 16.2	10.6	94.3	1 07.2	12.6	94.3	0 58.1	14.6	94.4	0 48.9	16.6	94.4	0 39.7	18.6	94.4	4
1 05.7 −	10.6	95.3	0 54.6 −	12.6	95.3	0 43.5 −	14.7	95.3	0 32.3 −	16.7	95.4	0 21.1 −	18.7	95.4	5
0 55.1	10.6	96.3	0 42.0	12.6	96.3	0 28.8	14.6	96.3	0 15.6 −	16.6	96.3	0 02.4 −	18.6	96.3	6
0 44.5	10.6	97.2	0 29.4	12.7	97.3	0 14.2 −	14.7	97.3	0 01.0 +	16.7	82.7	0 16.2 +	18.7	82.7	7
0 33.9	10.6	98.2	0 16.7	12.6	98.2	0 00.5 +	14.7	81.8	0 17.7	16.6	81.8	0 34.9	18.6	81.8	8
0 23.3	10.6	99.2	0 04.1 −	12.6	99.2	0 15.1	14.7	80.8	0 34.3	16.7	80.8	0 53.5	18.6	80.8	9
0 12.7 −	10.6	100.2	0 08.5 +	12.7	79.8	0 29.8 +	14.6	79.8	0 51.0 +	16.6	79.8	1 12.1 +	18.6	79.9	10
0 02.1 −	10.6	101.2	0 21.2	12.6	78.8	0 44.4	14.6	78.8	1 07.6	16.6	78.9	1 30.7	18.6	78.9	11
0 08.5 +	10.7	77.8	0 33.8	12.6	77.8	0 59.0	14.7	77.9	1 24.2	16.6	77.9	1 49.3	18.5	78.0	12
0 19.2	10.6	76.9	0 46.4	12.6	76.9	1 13.7	14.6	76.9	1 40.8	16.6	77.0	2 07.8	18.5	77.0	13
0 29.8	10.6	75.9	0 59.0	12.6	75.9	1 28.3	14.5	75.9	1 57.4	16.5	76.0	2 26.3	18.5	76.1	14
0 40.4 +	10.6	74.9	1 11.6 +	12.6	74.9	1 42.8 +	14.6	75.0	2 13.9 +	16.5	75.0	2 44.8 +	18.4	75.1	15
0 51.0	10.5	73.9	1 24.2	12.6	73.9	1 57.4	14.5	74.0	2 30.4	16.4	74.1	3 03.2	18.4	74.2	16
1 01.5	10.6	72.9	1 36.8	12.5	73.0	2 11.9	14.4	73.0	2 46.8	16.4	73.1	3 21.6	18.3	73.2	17
1 12.1	10.5	71.9	1 49.3	12.5	72.0	2 26.3	14.5	72.1	3 03.2	16.4	72.1	3 39.9	18.3	72.3	18
1 22.6	10.6	70.9	2 01.8	12.4	71.0	2 40.8	14.3	71.1	3 19.6	16.3	71.2	3 58.2	18.2	71.3	19
1 33.2 +	10.4	70.0	2 14.2 +	12.4	70.0	2 55.1 +	14.4	70.1	3 35.9 +	16.2	70.2	4 16.4 +	18.1	70.3	20
1 43.6	10.5	69.0	2 26.6	12.4	69.0	3 09.5	14.2	69.1	3 52.1	16.2	69.3	4 34.5	18.0	69.4	21
1 54.1	10.4	68.0	2 39.0	12.3	68.1	3 23.7	14.2	68.2	4 08.3	16.0	68.3	4 52.5	18.0	68.4	22
2 04.5	10.4	67.0	2 51.3	12.3	67.1	3 37.9	14.2	67.2	4 24.3	16.1	67.3	5 10.5	17.8	67.5	23
2 14.9	10.3	66.0	3 03.6	12.2	66.1	3 52.1	14.1	66.2	4 40.4	15.9	66.4	5 28.3	17.8	66.5	24
2 25.2 +	10.3	65.0	3 15.8 +	12.2	65.1	4 06.2 +	14.0	65.2	4 56.3 +	15.9	65.4	5 46.1 +	17.7	65.6	25
2 35.5	10.3	64.0	3 28.0	12.1	64.1	4 20.2	13.9	64.3	5 12.2	15.7	64.4	6 03.8	17.6	64.6	26
2 45.8	10.2	63.1	3 40.1	12.0	63.2	4 34.1	13.9	63.3	5 27.9	15.7	63.4	6 21.4	17.5	63.6	27
2 56.0	10.2	62.1	3 52.1	12.0	62.2	4 48.0	13.8	62.3	5 43.6	15.6	62.5	6 38.9	17.3	62.7	28
3 06.2	10.1	61.1	4 04.1	11.9	61.2	5 01.8	13.7	61.3	5 59.2	15.4	61.5	6 56.2	17.3	61.7	29

Dec.	20° Hc	d	Z	22° Hc	d	Z	24° Hc	d	Z	26° Hc	d	Z	28° Hc	d	Z
°	° ′	′	°	° ′	′	°	° ′	′	°	° ′	′	°	° ′	′	°
0	1 52.8	+20.5	90.7	1 51.3	+22.4	90.7	1 49.6	+24.4	90.8	1 47.9	+26.3	90.9	1 45.9	+28.2	90.9
1	2 13.3	20.5	89.7	2 13.7	22.5	89.8	2 14.0	24.4	89.9	2 14.2	26.2	90.0	2 14.1	28.2	90.1
2	2 33.8	20.4	88.8	2 36.2	22.4	88.9	2 38.4	24.3	89.0	2 40.4	26.2	89.1	2 42.3	28.1	89.2
3	2 54.2	20.4	87.9	2 58.6	22.3	88.0	3 02.7	24.3	88.1	3 06.6	26.2	88.2	3 10.4	28.0	88.3
4	3 14.6	20.3	86.9	3 20.9	22.3	87.0	3 27.0	24.2	87.2	3 32.8	26.2	87.3	3 38.4	28.0	87.4
5	3 34.9	+20.3	86.0	3 43.2	+22.3	86.1	3 51.2	+24.2	86.2	3 59.0	+26.0	86.4	4 06.4	+27.9	86.5
6	3 55.2	20.2	85.0	4 05.5	22.1	85.2	4 15.4	24.1	85.3	4 25.0	26.0	85.5	4 34.3	27.9	85.6
7	4 15.4	20.2	84.1	4 27.6	22.1	84.2	4 39.5	24.0	84.4	4 51.0	26.0	84.6	5 02.2	27.8	84.7
8	4 35.6	20.0	83.1	4 49.7	22.1	83.3	5 03.5	24.0	83.5	5 17.0	25.8	83.7	5 30.0	27.7	83.8
9	4 55.6	20.0	82.2	5 11.8	21.9	82.4	5 27.5	23.9	82.6	5 42.8	25.8	82.8	5 57.7	27.7	83.0
10	5 15.6	+20.0	81.3	5 33.7	+21.9	81.4	5 51.4	+23.7	81.6	6 08.6	+25.7	81.8	6 25.4	+27.5	82.1
11	5 35.6	19.8	80.3	5 55.6	21.7	80.5	6 15.1	23.7	80.7	6 34.3	25.5	80.9	6 52.9	27.5	81.2
12	5 55.4	19.7	79.4	6 17.3	21.7	79.6	6 38.8	23.6	79.8	6 59.8	25.5	80.0	7 20.4	27.3	80.3
13	6 15.1	19.6	78.4	6 39.0	21.5	78.6	7 02.4	23.5	78.9	7 25.3	25.4	79.1	7 47.7	27.2	79.4
14	6 34.7	19.5	77.5	7 00.5	21.5	77.7	7 25.9	23.3	77.9	7 50.7	25.2	78.2	8 14.9	27.1	78.5
15	6 54.2	+19.4	76.5	7 22.0	+21.3	76.7	7 49.2	+23.3	77.0	8 15.9	+25.1	77.3	8 42.0	+27.0	77.6
16	7 13.6	19.3	75.6	7 43.3	21.2	75.8	8 12.5	23.1	76.1	8 41.0	25.0	76.4	9 09.0	26.9	76.7
17	7 32.9	19.1	74.6	8 04.5	21.1	74.9	8 35.6	22.9	75.1	9 06.0	24.9	75.4	9 35.9	26.7	75.8
18	7 52.0	19.1	73.6	8 25.6	20.9	73.9	8 58.5	22.9	74.2	9 30.9	24.7	74.5	10 02.6	26.5	74.9
19	8 11.1	18.8	72.7	8 46.5	20.8	73.0	9 21.4	22.6	73.3	9 55.6	24.5	73.6	10 29.1	26.4	73.9
20	8 29.9	+18.8	71.7	9 07.3	+20.6	72.0	9 44.0	+22.6	72.3	10 20.1	+24.4	72.7	10 55.5	+26.2	73.0
21	8 48.7	18.6	70.8	9 27.9	20.5	71.1	10 06.6	22.3	71.4	10 44.5	24.2	71.7	11 21.7	26.1	72.1
22	9 07.3	18.4	69.8	9 48.4	20.4	70.1	10 28.9	22.2	70.4	11 08.7	24.1	70.8	11 47.8	25.9	71.2
23	9 25.7	18.3	68.8	10 08.8	20.1	69.2	10 51.1	22.0	69.5	11 32.8	23.8	69.9	12 13.7	25.7	70.3
24	9 44.0	18.2	67.9	10 28.9	20.0	68.2	11 13.1	21.9	68.6	11 56.6	23.7	68.9	12 39.4	25.5	69.3
25	10 02.2	+17.9	66.9	10 48.9	+19.8	67.2	11 35.0	+21.6	67.6	12 20.3	+23.5	68.0	13 04.9	+25.3	68.4
26	10 20.1	17.8	65.9	11 08.7	19.7	66.3	11 56.6	21.5	66.7	12 43.8	23.3	67.1	13 30.2	25.1	67.5
27	10 37.9	17.6	65.0	11 28.4	19.4	65.3	12 18.1	21.3	65.7	13 07.1	23.1	66.1	13 55.3	24.9	66.6
28	10 55.5	17.4	64.0	11 47.8	19.2	64.3	12 39.4	21.0	64.7	13 30.2	22.9	65.2	14 20.2	24.6	65.6
29	11 12.9	17.3	63.0	12 07.0	19.1	63.4	13 00.4	20.9	63.8	13 53.1	22.6	64.2	14 44.8	24.5	64.7

Dec.	30° Hc	d	Z	32° Hc	d	Z	34° Hc	d	Z	36° Hc	d	Z	38° Hc	d	Z
°	° ′	′	°	° ′	′	°	° ′	′	°	° ′	′	°	° ′	′	°
0	1 43.9	+30.0	91.0	1 41.8	+31.8	91.1	1 39.5	+33.5	91.1	1 37.1	+35.2	91.2	1 34.6	+36.9	91.2
1	2 13.9	30.0	90.1	2 13.6	31.7	90.2	2 13.0	33.6	90.3	2 12.3	35.3	90.4	2 11.5	36.9	90.4
2	2 43.9	29.9	89.3	2 45.3	31.8	89.4	2 46.6	33.4	89.5	2 47.6	35.2	89.6	2 48.4	36.9	89.7
3	3 13.8	29.9	88.4	3 17.1	31.6	88.5	3 20.0	33.5	88.6	3 22.8	35.2	88.7	3 25.3	36.9	88.9
4	3 43.7	29.8	87.5	3 48.7	31.7	87.7	3 53.5	33.4	87.8	3 58.0	35.1	87.9	4 02.2	36.8	88.1
5	4 13.5	+29.8	86.7	4 20.4	+31.6	86.8	4 26.9	+33.3	87.0	4 33.1	+35.1	87.1	4 39.0	+36.7	87.3
6	4 43.3	29.7	85.8	4 52.0	31.5	86.0	5 00.2	33.3	86.1	5 08.2	35.0	86.3	5 15.7	36.7	86.5
7	5 13.0	29.7	84.9	5 23.5	31.4	85.1	5 33.5	33.2	85.3	5 43.2	34.9	85.5	5 52.4	36.6	85.7
8	5 42.7	29.5	84.0	5 54.9	31.4	84.2	6 06.7	33.2	84.5	6 18.1	34.9	84.7	6 29.0	36.6	84.9
9	6 12.2	29.5	83.2	6 26.3	31.3	83.4	6 39.9	33.0	83.6	6 53.0	34.7	83.9	7 05.6	36.4	84.1
10	6 41.7	+29.4	82.3	6 57.6	+31.2	82.5	7 12.9	+33.0	82.8	7 27.7	+34.7	83.0	7 42.0	+36.4	83.3
11	7 11.1	29.3	81.4	7 28.8	31.0	81.7	7 45.9	32.8	81.9	8 02.4	34.6	82.2	8 18.4	36.3	82.5
12	7 40.4	29.2	80.5	7 59.8	31.0	80.8	8 18.7	32.8	81.1	8 37.0	34.5	81.4	8 54.7	36.1	81.7
13	8 09.6	29.0	79.7	8 30.8	30.9	79.9	8 51.5	32.6	80.2	9 11.5	34.4	80.6	9 30.8	36.1	80.9
14	8 38.6	29.0	78.8	9 01.7	30.7	79.1	9 24.1	32.5	79.4	9 45.9	34.2	79.7	10 06.9	35.9	80.1
15	9 07.6	+28.8	77.9	9 32.4	+30.6	78.2	9 56.6	+32.4	78.5	10 20.1	+34.1	78.9	10 42.8	+35.9	79.3
16	9 36.4	28.6	77.0	10 03.0	30.5	77.3	10 29.0	32.2	77.7	10 54.2	34.0	78.1	11 18.7	35.6	78.4
17	10 05.0	28.6	76.1	10 33.5	30.3	76.5	11 01.2	32.1	76.8	11 28.2	33.8	77.2	11 54.3	35.6	77.6
18	10 33.6	28.3	75.2	11 03.8	30.2	75.6	11 33.3	32.0	76.0	12 02.0	33.7	76.4	12 29.9	35.4	76.8
19	11 01.9	28.3	74.3	11 34.0	30.0	74.7	12 05.3	31.8	75.1	12 35.7	33.5	75.5	13 05.3	35.2	76.0
20	11 30.2	+28.0	73.4	12 04.0	+29.9	73.8	12 37.1	+31.6	74.2	13 09.2	+33.4	74.7	13 40.5	+35.0	75.1
21	11 58.2	27.9	72.5	12 33.9	29.6	72.9	13 08.7	31.4	73.4	13 42.6	33.2	73.8	14 15.5	34.9	74.3
22	12 26.1	27.7	71.6	13 03.5	29.5	72.0	13 40.1	31.3	72.5	14 15.8	32.9	73.0	14 50.4	34.7	73.5
23	12 53.8	27.5	70.7	13 33.0	29.3	71.1	14 11.4	31.0	71.6	14 48.7	32.8	72.1	15 25.1	34.5	72.6
24	13 21.3	27.3	69.8	14 02.3	29.1	70.2	14 42.4	30.9	70.7	15 21.5	32.6	71.2	15 59.6	34.3	71.8
25	13 48.6	+27.1	68.9	14 31.4	+28.9	69.3	15 13.3	+30.6	69.8	15 54.1	+32.4	70.4	16 33.9	+34.1	70.9
26	14 15.7	26.9	67.9	15 00.3	28.7	68.4	15 43.9	30.5	68.9	16 26.5	32.2	69.5	17 08.0	33.9	70.0
27	14 42.6	26.7	67.0	15 29.0	28.4	67.5	16 14.4	30.2	68.0	16 58.7	31.9	68.6	17 41.9	33.7	69.2
28	15 09.3	26.4	66.1	15 57.4	28.2	66.6	16 44.6	29.9	67.1	17 30.6	31.7	67.7	18 15.6	33.4	68.3
29	15 35.7	26.2	65.2	16 25.6	28.0	65.7	17 14.5	29.7	66.2	18 02.3	31.5	66.8	18 49.0	33.1	67.4

20°			22°			24°			26°			28°			Dec.
Hc	d	Z	Hc	d	Z	Hc	d	Z	Hc	d	Z	Hc	d	Z	
° ′	′	°	° ′	′	°	° ′	′	°	° ′	′	°	° ′	′	°	°
1 52.8	−20.6	90.7	1 51.3	−22.5	90.7	1 49.6	−24.4	90.8	1 47.9	−26.4	90.9	1 45.9	−28.1	90.9	0
1 32.2	20.6	91.6	1 28.8	22.6	91.7	1 25.2	24.5	91.7	1 21.5	26.3	91.8	1 17.8	28.3	91.8	1
1 11.6	20.5	92.6	1 06.2	22.5	92.6	1 00.7	24.4	92.6	0 55.2	26.4	92.7	0 49.5	28.2	92.7	2
0 51.1	20.7	93.5	0 43.7	22.6	93.5	0 36.3	24.5	93.6	0 28.8	26.4	93.6	0 21.3	−28.2	93.6	3
0 30.4	20.6	94.4	0 21.1	−22.5	94.5	0 11.8	−24.5	94.5	0 02.4	−26.3	94.5	0 06.9	+28.2	85.5	4
0 09.8	−20.6	95.4	0 01.4	+22.6	84.6	0 12.7	+24.5	84.6	0 23.9	+26.4	84.6	0 35.1	+28.1	84.6	5
0 10.8	+20.6	83.7	0 24.0	22.5	83.7	0 37.2	24.4	83.7	0 50.3	26.3	83.7	1 03.4	28.2	83.8	6
0 31.4	20.6	82.7	0 46.5	22.6	82.8	1 01.6	24.5	82.8	1 16.6	26.4	82.8	1 31.6	28.1	82.9	7
0 52.0	20.6	81.8	1 09.1	22.5	81.8	1 26.1	24.4	81.9	1 43.0	26.3	81.9	1 59.7	28.2	82.0	8
1 12.6	20.6	80.9	1 31.6	22.5	80.9	1 50.5	24.4	81.0	2 09.3	26.2	81.0	2 27.9	28.1	81.1	9
1 33.2	+20.5	79.9	1 54.1	+22.5	80.0	2 14.9	+24.4	80.1	2 35.5	+26.3	80.1	2 56.0	+28.1	80.2	10
1 53.7	20.5	79.0	2 16.6	22.4	79.1	2 39.3	24.3	79.1	3 01.8	26.2	79.2	3 24.1	28.0	79.3	11
2 14.2	20.5	78.0	2 39.0	22.4	78.1	3 03.6	24.3	78.2	3 28.0	26.1	78.3	3 52.1	28.0	78.5	12
2 34.7	20.4	77.1	3 01.4	22.3	77.2	3 27.9	24.2	77.3	3 54.1	26.1	77.4	4 20.1	27.9	77.6	13
2 55.1	20.4	76.2	3 23.7	22.3	76.3	3 52.1	24.2	76.4	4 20.2	26.0	76.5	4 48.0	27.8	76.7	14
3 15.5	+20.4	75.2	3 46.0	+22.3	75.3	4 16.3	+24.1	75.5	4 46.2	+26.0	75.6	5 15.8	+27.8	75.8	15
3 35.9	20.2	74.3	4 08.3	22.1	74.4	4 40.4	24.0	74.6	5 12.2	25.8	74.7	5 43.6	27.7	74.9	16
3 56.1	20.3	73.3	4 30.4	22.1	73.5	5 04.4	23.9	73.6	5 38.0	25.8	73.8	6 11.3	27.6	74.0	17
4 16.4	20.1	72.4	4 52.5	22.0	72.5	5 28.3	23.9	72.7	6 03.8	25.7	72.9	6 38.9	27.5	73.1	18
4 36.5	20.1	71.4	5 14.5	22.0	71.6	5 52.2	23.8	71.8	6 29.5	25.6	72.0	7 06.4	27.4	72.2	19
4 56.6	+20.0	70.5	5 36.5	+21.8	70.7	6 16.0	+23.7	70.9	6 55.1	+25.5	71.1	7 33.8	+27.3	71.3	20
5 16.6	19.9	69.6	5 58.3	21.8	69.7	6 39.7	23.5	69.9	7 20.6	25.4	70.2	8 01.1	27.1	70.4	21
5 36.5	19.8	68.6	6 20.1	21.6	68.8	7 03.2	23.5	69.0	7 46.0	25.2	69.3	8 28.2	27.1	69.5	22
5 56.3	19.7	67.7	6 41.7	21.5	67.9	7 26.7	23.4	68.1	8 11.2	25.2	68.3	8 55.3	26.9	68.6	23
6 16.0	19.6	66.7	7 03.2	21.5	66.9	7 50.1	23.2	67.2	8 36.4	25.0	67.4	9 22.2	26.7	67.7	24
6 35.6	+19.5	65.8	7 24.7	+21.3	66.0	8 13.3	+23.1	66.2	9 01.4	+24.9	66.5	9 48.9	+26.7	66.8	25
6 55.1	19.4	64.8	7 46.0	21.2	65.0	8 36.4	22.9	65.3	9 26.3	24.7	65.6	10 15.6	26.4	65.9	26
7 14.5	19.3	63.8	8 07.2	21.0	64.1	8 59.3	22.9	64.4	9 51.0	24.6	64.7	10 42.0	26.4	65.0	27
7 33.8	19.1	62.9	8 28.2	20.9	63.1	9 22.2	22.6	63.4	10 15.6	24.4	63.7	11 08.4	26.1	64.1	28
7 52.9	19.0	61.9	8 49.1	20.8	62.2	9 44.8	22.6	62.5	10 40.0	24.2	62.8	11 34.5	26.0	63.2	29

30°			32°			34°			36°			38°			Dec.
Hc	d	Z	Hc	d	Z	Hc	d	Z	Hc	d	Z	Hc	d	Z	
° ′	′	°	° ′	′	°	° ′	′	°	° ′	′	°	° ′	′	°	°
1 43.9	−30.0	91.0	1 41.8	−31.9	91.1	1 39.5	−33.6	91.1	1 37.1	−35.3	91.2	1 34.6	−37.0	91.2	0
1 13.9	30.0	91.9	1 09.9	31.8	91.9	1 05.9	33.6	91.9	1 01.8	35.3	92.0	0 57.6	37.0	92.0	1
0 43.9	30.1	92.7	0 38.1	31.8	92.8	0 32.3	−33.6	92.8	0 26.5	−35.3	92.8	0 20.6	−37.0	92.8	2
0 13.8	−30.0	93.6	0 06.3	−31.9	93.6	0 01.3	+33.6	86.4	0 08.8	+35.3	86.4	0 16.4	+36.9	86.4	3
0 16.3	+30.0	85.5	0 25.6	+31.8	85.5	0 34.9	33.6	85.6	0 44.1	35.3	85.6	0 53.3	37.0	85.6	4
0 46.3	+30.0	84.7	0 57.4	+31.8	84.7	1 08.5	+33.5	84.7	1 19.4	+35.3	84.8	1 30.3	+36.9	84.8	5
1 16.3	30.1	83.8	1 29.2	31.9	83.9	1 42.0	33.6	83.9	1 54.7	35.3	84.0	2 07.2	37.0	84.0	6
1 46.4	30.0	82.9	2 01.1	31.9	83.0	2 15.6	33.5	83.1	2 30.0	35.2	83.2	2 44.2	36.9	83.3	7
2 16.4	29.9	82.1	2 32.8	31.8	82.2	2 49.1	33.5	82.2	3 05.2	35.2	82.4	3 21.1	36.8	82.5	8
2 46.3	30.0	81.2	3 04.6	31.7	81.3	3 22.6	33.4	81.4	3 40.4	35.1	81.5	3 57.9	36.8	81.7	9
3 16.3	+29.8	80.3	3 36.3	+31.6	80.5	3 56.0	+33.4	80.6	4 15.5	+35.1	80.7	4 34.7	+36.8	80.9	10
3 46.1	29.9	79.5	4 07.9	31.6	79.6	4 29.4	33.4	79.8	4 50.6	35.1	79.9	5 11.5	36.7	80.1	11
4 16.0	29.8	78.6	4 39.5	31.6	78.8	5 02.8	33.3	78.9	5 25.7	34.9	79.1	5 48.2	36.6	79.3	12
4 45.8	29.7	77.7	5 11.1	31.5	77.9	5 36.1	33.2	78.1	6 00.6	34.9	78.3	6 24.8	36.5	78.5	13
5 15.5	29.6	76.9	5 42.6	31.4	77.0	6 09.3	33.1	77.2	6 35.5	34.7	77.5	7 01.3	36.6	77.7	14
5 45.1	+29.5	76.0	6 14.0	+31.3	76.2	6 42.4	+33.0	76.4	7 10.4	+34.7	76.6	7 37.8	+36.4	76.9	15
6 14.6	29.5	75.1	6 45.3	31.2	75.3	7 15.4	33.0	75.6	7 45.1	34.6	75.8	8 14.2	36.3	76.1	16
6 44.1	29.4	74.2	7 16.5	31.1	74.5	7 48.4	32.8	74.7	8 19.7	34.6	75.0	8 50.5	36.2	75.3	17
7 13.5	29.3	73.4	7 47.6	31.0	73.6	8 21.2	32.8	73.9	8 54.3	34.4	74.2	9 26.7	36.1	74.5	18
7 42.8	29.1	72.5	8 18.6	31.0	72.7	8 54.0	32.6	73.0	9 28.7	34.3	73.3	10 02.8	35.9	73.7	19
8 11.9	+29.1	71.6	8 49.6	+30.7	71.9	9 26.6	+32.5	72.2	10 03.0	+34.2	72.5	10 38.7	+35.8	72.9	20
8 41.0	28.9	70.7	9 20.3	30.7	71.0	9 59.1	32.4	71.3	10 37.2	34.0	71.7	11 14.5	35.7	72.0	21
9 09.9	28.8	69.8	9 51.0	30.5	70.1	10 31.5	32.2	70.5	11 11.2	33.9	70.8	11 50.2	35.6	71.2	22
9 38.7	28.7	68.9	10 21.5	30.4	69.3	11 03.7	32.1	69.6	11 45.1	33.8	70.0	12 25.8	35.4	70.4	23
10 07.4	28.5	68.0	10 51.9	30.3	68.4	11 35.8	31.9	68.8	12 18.9	33.6	69.1	13 01.2	35.2	69.6	24
10 35.9	+28.3	67.1	11 22.2	+30.0	67.5	12 07.7	+31.8	67.9	12 52.5	+33.4	68.3	13 36.4	+35.1	68.7	25
11 04.2	28.2	66.2	11 52.2	29.9	66.6	12 39.5	31.6	67.0	13 25.9	33.3	67.4	14 11.5	34.9	67.9	26
11 32.4	28.1	65.3	12 22.1	29.8	65.7	13 11.1	31.4	66.1	13 59.2	33.1	66.6	14 46.4	34.7	67.1	27
12 00.5	27.8	64.4	12 51.9	29.5	64.8	13 42.5	31.2	65.3	14 32.3	32.9	65.7	15 21.1	34.6	66.2	28
12 28.3	27.7	63.5	13 21.4	29.4	63.9	14 13.7	31.1	64.4	15 05.2	32.7	64.9	15 55.7	34.3	65.4	29

Dec.	40° Hc	d	Z	42° Hc	d	Z	44° Hc	d	Z	46° Hc	d	Z	48° Hc	d	Z
°	° ′	′	°	° ′	′	°	° ′	′	°	° ′	′	°	° ′	′	°
0	1 31.9	+38.6	91.3	1 29.2	+40.1	91.3	1 26.3	+41.7	91.4	1 23.4	+43.1	91.4	1 20.3	+44.6	91.5
1	2 10.5	38.5	90.5	2 09.3	40.2	90.6	2 08.0	41.7	90.7	2 06.5	43.2	90.7	2 04.9	44.6	90.8
2	2 49.0	38.6	89.8	2 49.5	40.1	89.9	2 49.7	41.6	89.9	2 49.7	43.1	90.0	2 49.5	44.5	90.1
3	3 27.6	38.4	89.0	3 29.6	40.0	89.1	3 31.3	41.6	89.2	3 32.8	43.1	89.4	3 34.0	44.5	89.5
4	4 06.0	38.5	88.2	4 09.6	40.0	88.4	4 12.9	41.6	88.5	4 15.9	43.0	88.7	4 18.5	44.5	88.8
5	4 44.5	+38.4	87.4	4 49.6	+40.0	87.6	4 54.5	+41.5	87.8	4 58.9	+43.0	88.0	5 03.0	+44.4	88.1
6	5 22.9	38.3	86.7	5 29.6	39.9	86.9	5 36.0	41.4	87.1	5 41.9	43.0	87.3	5 47.5	44.4	87.5
7	6 01.2	38.2	85.9	6 09.5	39.9	86.1	6 17.4	41.5	86.3	6 24.9	42.9	86.6	6 31.9	44.3	86.8
8	6 39.4	38.2	85.1	6 49.4	39.8	85.4	6 58.9	41.3	85.6	7 07.8	42.8	85.8	7 16.2	44.3	86.1
9	7 17.6	38.1	84.3	7 29.2	39.7	84.6	7 40.2	41.3	84.9	7 50.6	42.8	85.1	8 00.5	44.2	85.4
10	7 55.7	+38.1	83.6	8 08.9	+39.6	83.9	8 21.5	+41.1	84.1	8 33.4	+42.7	84.4	8 44.7	+44.2	84.7
11	8 33.8	37.9	82.8	8 48.5	39.6	83.1	9 02.6	41.1	83.4	9 16.1	42.6	83.7	9 28.9	44.0	84.1
12	9 11.7	37.8	82.0	9 28.1	39.4	82.3	9 43.7	41.0	82.7	9 58.7	42.5	83.0	10 12.9	44.0	83.4
13	9 49.5	37.7	81.2	10 07.5	39.3	81.6	10 24.7	40.9	81.9	10 41.2	42.4	82.3	10 56.9	43.9	82.7
14	10 27.2	37.6	80.4	10 46.8	39.2	80.8	11 05.6	40.8	81.2	11 23.6	42.3	81.6	11 40.8	43.8	82.0
15	11 04.8	+37.5	79.6	11 26.0	+39.1	80.0	11 46.4	+40.7	80.4	12 05.9	+42.2	80.8	12 24.6	+43.6	81.3
16	11 42.3	37.3	78.8	12 05.1	39.0	79.2	12 27.1	40.5	79.7	12 48.1	42.1	80.1	13 08.2	43.6	80.6
17	12 19.6	37.3	78.0	12 44.1	38.8	78.5	13 07.6	40.4	78.9	13 30.2	41.9	79.4	13 51.8	43.4	79.9
18	12 56.9	37.0	77.2	13 22.9	38.7	77.7	13 48.0	40.3	78.2	14 12.1	41.8	78.7	14 35.2	43.3	79.2
19	13 33.9	36.9	76.4	14 01.6	38.5	76.9	14 28.3	40.1	77.4	14 53.9	41.7	77.9	15 18.5	43.2	78.4
20	14 10.8	+36.7	75.6	14 40.1	+38.4	76.1	15 08.4	+40.0	76.6	15 35.6	+41.5	77.2	16 01.7	+43.0	77.7
21	14 47.5	36.6	74.8	15 18.5	38.2	75.3	15 48.4	39.8	75.9	16 17.1	41.4	76.4	16 44.7	42.9	77.0
22	15 24.1	36.4	74.0	15 56.7	38.0	74.5	16 28.2	39.6	75.1	16 58.5	41.2	75.7	17 27.6	42.7	76.3
23	16 00.5	36.1	73.1	16 34.7	37.8	73.7	17 07.8	39.4	74.3	17 39.7	41.0	74.9	18 10.3	42.5	75.5
24	16 36.6	36.0	72.3	17 12.5	37.7	72.9	17 47.2	39.3	73.5	18 20.7	40.8	74.1	18 52.8	42.4	74.8
25	17 12.6	+35.8	71.5	17 50.2	+37.4	72.1	18 26.5	+39.0	72.7	19 01.5	+40.6	73.4	19 35.2	+42.2	74.0
26	17 48.4	35.6	70.6	18 27.6	37.2	71.3	19 05.5	38.8	71.9	19 42.1	40.4	72.6	20 17.4	41.9	73.3
27	18 24.0	35.3	69.8	19 04.8	37.0	70.4	19 44.3	38.7	71.1	20 22.5	40.3	71.8	20 59.3	41.8	72.5
28	18 59.3	35.1	68.9	19 41.8	36.7	69.6	20 23.0	38.3	70.3	21 02.8	39.9	71.0	21 41.1	41.6	71.7
29	19 34.4	34.8	68.1	20 18.5	36.6	68.8	21 01.3	38.2	69.5	21 42.7	39.8	70.2	22 22.7	41.3	71.0

Dec.	50° Hc	d	Z	52° Hc	d	Z	54° Hc	d	Z	56° Hc	d	Z	58° Hc	d	Z
°	° ′	′	°	° ′	′	°	° ′	′	°	° ′	′	°	° ′	′	°
0	1 17.1	+46.0	91.5	1 13.9	+47.3	91.6	1 10.5	+48.6	91.6	1 07.1	+49.7	91.7	1 03.6	+50.9	91.7
1	2 03.1	45.9	90.9	2 01.2	47.2	91.0	1 59.1	48.5	91.0	1 56.8	49.8	91.1	1 54.5	50.8	91.2
2	2 49.0	46.0	90.2	2 48.4	47.3	90.3	2 47.6	48.5	90.4	2 46.6	49.7	90.5	2 45.3	50.9	90.6
3	3 35.0	45.9	89.6	3 35.7	47.2	89.7	3 36.1	48.5	89.9	3 36.3	49.7	90.0	3 36.2	50.9	90.1
4	4 20.9	45.9	89.0	4 22.9	47.2	89.1	4 24.6	48.5	89.3	4 26.0	49.7	89.4	4 27.1	50.8	89.6
5	5 06.8	+45.8	88.3	5 10.1	+47.2	88.5	5 13.1	+48.4	88.7	5 15.7	+49.6	88.9	5 17.9	+50.8	89.0
6	5 52.6	45.8	87.7	5 57.3	47.1	87.9	6 01.5	48.4	88.1	6 05.3	49.6	88.3	6 08.7	50.7	88.5
7	6 38.4	45.7	87.0	6 44.4	47.1	87.2	6 49.9	48.4	87.5	6 54.9	49.6	87.7	6 59.4	50.8	88.0
8	7 24.1	45.7	86.4	7 31.5	47.0	86.6	7 38.3	48.3	86.9	7 44.5	49.5	87.2	7 50.2	50.7	87.4
9	8 09.8	45.6	85.7	8 18.5	46.9	86.0	8 26.6	48.2	86.3	8 34.0	49.5	86.6	8 40.9	50.6	86.9
10	8 55.4	+45.6	85.0	9 05.4	+46.9	85.4	9 14.8	+48.2	85.7	9 23.5	+49.4	86.0	9 31.5	+50.6	86.3
11	9 41.0	45.4	84.4	9 52.3	46.9	84.7	10 03.0	48.1	85.1	10 12.9	49.4	85.4	10 22.1	50.5	85.8
12	10 26.4	45.4	83.7	10 39.2	46.7	84.1	10 51.1	48.1	84.5	11 02.3	49.3	84.9	11 12.6	50.5	85.3
13	11 11.8	45.3	83.1	11 25.9	46.7	83.5	11 39.2	47.9	83.9	11 51.6	49.2	84.3	12 03.1	50.4	84.7
14	11 57.1	45.2	82.4	12 12.6	46.5	82.8	12 27.1	47.9	83.3	12 40.8	49.1	83.7	12 53.5	50.3	84.1
15	12 42.3	+45.1	81.7	12 59.1	+46.5	82.2	13 15.0	+47.8	82.6	13 29.9	+49.1	83.1	13 43.8	+50.3	83.6
16	13 27.4	45.0	81.0	13 45.6	46.4	81.5	14 02.8	47.7	82.0	14 19.0	48.9	82.5	14 34.1	50.2	83.0
17	14 12.4	44.9	80.4	14 32.0	46.3	80.9	14 50.5	47.6	81.4	15 07.9	48.9	81.9	15 24.3	50.1	82.5
18	14 57.3	44.7	79.7	15 18.3	46.1	80.2	15 38.1	47.5	80.8	15 56.8	48.8	81.3	16 14.4	50.0	81.9
19	15 42.0	44.7	79.0	16 04.4	46.0	79.5	16 25.6	47.4	80.1	16 45.6	48.7	80.7	17 04.4	49.9	81.3
20	16 26.7	+44.4	78.3	16 50.4	+45.9	78.9	17 13.0	+47.2	79.5	17 34.3	+48.5	80.1	17 54.3	+49.8	80.7
21	17 11.1	44.4	77.6	17 36.3	45.8	78.2	18 00.2	47.1	78.8	18 22.8	48.4	79.5	18 44.1	49.6	80.1
22	17 55.5	44.2	76.9	18 22.1	45.6	77.5	18 47.3	47.0	78.2	19 11.2	48.3	78.8	19 33.7	49.6	79.5
23	18 39.7	44.0	76.2	19 07.7	45.4	76.8	19 34.3	46.9	77.5	19 59.5	48.2	78.2	20 23.3	49.4	78.9
24	19 23.7	43.8	75.4	19 53.1	45.3	76.1	20 21.2	46.6	76.9	20 47.7	48.0	77.6	21 12.7	49.3	78.2
25	20 07.5	+43.7	74.7	20 38.4	+45.1	75.4	21 07.8	+46.6	76.2	21 35.7	+47.9	76.9	22 02.1	+49.1	77.7
26	20 51.2	43.5	74.0	21 23.5	45.0	74.7	21 54.4	46.3	75.5	22 23.6	47.7	76.3	22 51.2	49.1	77.1
27	21 34.7	43.3	73.3	22 08.5	44.7	74.0	22 40.7	46.2	74.8	23 11.3	47.6	75.6	23 40.3	48.8	76.5
28	22 18.0	43.0	72.5	22 53.2	44.6	73.3	23 26.9	46.0	74.1	23 58.9	47.4	75.0	24 29.1	48.7	75.8
29	23 01.0	42.9	71.7	23 37.8	44.3	72.6	24 12.9	45.8	73.4	24 46.3	47.2	74.3	25 17.8	48.6	75.2

40°			42°			44°			46°			48°			Dec.
Hc	d	Z	Hc	d	Z	Hc	d	Z	Hc	d	Z	Hc	d	Z	
° ′	′	°	° ′	′	°	° ′	′	°	° ′	′	°	° ′	′	°	°
1 31.9	−38.6	91.3	1 29.2	−40.2	91.3	1 26.3	−41.7	91.4	1 23.4	−43.2	91.4	1 20.3	−44.6	91.5	0
0 53.3	38.6	92.1	0 49.0	40.2	92.1	0 44.6	41.7	92.1	0 40.2	−43.2	92.1	0 35.7	−44.6	92.2	1
0 14.7	−38.6	92.8	0 08.8	−40.2	92.8	0 02.9	−41.7	92.8	0 03.0	+43.2	87.2	0 08.9	+44.6	87.2	2
0 23.9	+38.6	86.4	0 31.4	+40.1	86.4	0 38.8	+41.7	86.5	0 46.2	43.2	86.5	0 53.5	44.6	86.5	3
1 02.5	38.5	85.7	1 11.5	40.2	85.7	1 20.5	41.7	85.7	1 29.4	43.1	85.8	1 38.1	44.6	85.8	4
1 41.0	+38.6	84.9	1 51.7	+40.1	84.9	2 02.2	+41.7	85.0	2 12.5	+43.2	85.1	2 22.7	+44.6	85.2	5
2 19.6	38.6	84.1	2 31.8	40.1	84.2	2 43.9	41.6	84.3	2 55.7	43.1	84.4	3 07.3	44.6	84.5	6
2 58.2	38.5	83.4	3 11.9	40.1	83.5	3 25.5	41.6	83.6	3 38.8	43.1	83.7	3 51.8	44.6	83.8	7
3 36.7	38.4	82.6	3 52.0	40.1	82.7	4 07.1	41.6	82.9	4 21.9	43.0	83.0	4 36.4	44.4	83.2	8
4 15.1	38.5	81.8	4 32.1	40.0	82.0	4 48.7	41.5	82.1	5 04.9	43.0	82.3	5 20.8	44.5	82.5	9
4 53.6	+38.3	81.0	5 12.1	+39.9	81.2	5 30.2	+41.5	81.4	5 47.9	+43.0	81.6	6 05.3	+44.3	81.8	10
5 31.9	38.3	80.3	5 52.0	39.9	80.5	6 11.7	41.4	80.7	6 30.9	42.9	80.9	6 49.6	44.4	81.1	11
6 10.2	38.3	79.5	6 31.9	39.8	79.7	6 53.1	41.3	79.9	7 13.8	42.8	80.2	7 34.0	44.2	80.4	12
6 48.5	38.2	78.7	7 11.7	39.8	79.0	7 34.4	41.3	79.2	7 56.6	42.8	79.5	8 18.2	44.2	79.8	13
7 26.7	38.1	77.9	7 51.5	39.6	78.2	8 15.7	41.2	78.5	8 39.4	42.6	78.8	9 02.4	44.1	79.1	14
8 04.8	+38.0	77.2	8 31.1	+39.6	77.4	8 56.9	+41.1	77.7	9 22.0	+42.6	78.1	9 46.5	+44.0	78.4	15
8 42.8	37.9	76.4	9 10.7	39.5	76.7	9 38.0	41.0	77.0	10 04.6	42.5	77.4	10 30.5	44.0	77.7	16
9 20.7	37.8	75.6	9 50.2	39.3	75.9	10 19.0	40.9	76.3	10 47.1	42.4	76.6	11 14.5	43.8	77.0	17
9 58.5	37.6	74.8	10 29.5	39.3	75.2	10 59.9	40.8	75.5	11 29.5	42.3	75.9	11 58.3	43.8	76.3	18
10 36.1	37.6	74.0	11 08.8	39.2	74.4	11 40.7	40.7	74.8	12 11.8	42.2	75.2	12 42.1	43.6	75.6	19
11 13.7	+37.5	73.2	11 48.0	+39.0	73.6	12 21.4	+40.6	74.0	12 54.0	+42.0	74.5	13 25.7	+43.5	74.9	20
11 51.2	37.3	72.4	12 27.0	38.9	72.8	13 02.0	40.4	73.3	13 36.0	42.0	73.7	14 09.2	43.4	74.2	21
12 28.5	37.1	71.6	13 05.9	38.7	72.1	13 42.4	40.3	72.5	14 18.0	41.8	73.0	14 52.6	43.2	73.5	22
13 05.6	37.1	70.8	13 44.6	38.6	71.3	14 22.7	40.1	71.7	14 59.8	41.6	72.2	15 35.8	43.1	72.8	23
13 42.7	36.8	70.0	14 23.2	38.4	70.5	15 02.8	40.0	71.0	15 41.4	41.5	71.5	16 18.9	43.0	72.0	24
14 19.5	+36.7	69.2	15 01.6	+38.3	69.7	15 42.8	+39.8	70.2	16 22.9	+41.3	70.7	17 01.9	+42.8	71.3	25
14 56.2	36.5	68.4	15 39.9	38.1	69.0	16 22.6	39.7	69.4	17 04.2	41.2	70.0	17 44.7	42.7	70.6	26
15 32.7	36.3	67.6	16 18.0	37.9	68.1	17 02.3	39.4	68.6	17 45.4	41.0	69.2	18 27.4	42.4	69.8	27
16 09.0	36.2	66.7	16 55.9	37.7	67.3	17 41.7	39.3	67.9	18 26.4	40.8	68.5	19 09.8	42.3	69.1	28
16 45.2	35.9	65.9	17 33.6	37.6	66.5	18 21.0	39.1	67.1	19 07.2	40.6	67.7	19 52.1	42.1	68.3	29

50°			52°			54°			56°			58°			Dec.
Hc	d	Z	Hc	d	Z	Hc	d	Z	Hc	d	Z	Hc	d	Z	
° ′	′	°	° ′	′	°	° ′	′	°	° ′	′	°	° ′	′	°	°
1 17.1	−46.0	91.5	1 13.9	−47.3	91.6	1 10.5	−48.5	91.6	1 07.1	−49.8	91.7	1 03.6	−50.9	91.7	0
0 31.1	−45.9	92.2	0 26.6	−47.3	92.2	0 22.0	−48.6	92.2	0 17.3	−49.7	92.2	0 12.7	−50.9	92.2	1
0 14.8	+46.0	87.2	0 20.7	+47.3	87.2	0 26.6	+48.5	87.2	0 32.4	+49.8	87.2	0 38.2	+50.9	87.2	2
1 00.8	46.0	86.5	1 08.0	47.3	86.6	1 15.1	48.6	86.6	1 22.2	49.7	86.7	1 29.1	50.9	86.7	3
1 46.8	45.9	85.9	1 55.3	47.3	86.0	2 03.7	48.5	86.0	2 11.9	49.7	86.1	2 20.0	50.9	86.2	4
2 32.7	+46.0	85.3	2 42.6	+47.2	85.3	2 52.2	+48.5	85.4	3 01.6	+49.8	85.5	3 10.9	+50.8	85.7	5
3 18.7	45.9	84.6	3 29.8	47.3	84.7	3 40.7	48.5	84.9	3 51.4	49.7	85.0	4 01.7	50.8	85.1	6
4 04.6	45.9	84.0	4 17.1	47.2	84.1	4 29.2	48.5	84.3	4 41.1	49.6	84.4	4 52.5	50.9	84.6	7
4 50.5	45.8	83.3	5 04.3	47.1	83.5	5 17.7	48.4	83.7	5 30.7	49.7	83.9	5 43.4	50.7	84.1	8
5 36.3	45.8	82.7	5 51.4	47.2	82.9	6 06.1	48.4	83.1	6 20.4	49.6	83.3	6 34.1	50.8	83.5	9
6 22.1	+45.8	82.0	6 38.6	+47.0	82.2	6 54.5	+48.4	82.5	7 10.0	+49.5	82.7	7 24.9	+50.7	83.0	10
7 07.9	45.7	81.4	7 25.6	47.1	81.6	7 42.9	48.3	81.9	7 59.5	49.5	82.2	8 15.6	50.6	82.4	11
7 53.6	45.6	80.7	8 12.7	46.9	81.0	8 31.1	48.3	81.3	8 49.0	49.5	81.6	9 06.2	50.7	81.9	12
8 39.2	45.6	80.1	8 59.6	46.9	80.4	9 19.4	48.2	80.7	9 38.5	49.4	81.0	9 56.9	50.5	81.4	13
9 24.8	45.5	79.4	9 46.5	46.9	79.7	10 07.6	48.1	80.1	10 27.9	49.3	80.4	10 47.4	50.5	80.8	14
10 10.3	+45.4	78.7	10 33.4	+46.7	79.1	10 55.7	+48.0	79.5	11 17.2	+49.3	79.9	11 37.9	+50.5	80.3	15
10 55.7	45.4	78.1	11 20.1	46.7	78.5	11 43.7	48.0	78.9	12 06.5	49.2	79.3	12 28.4	50.3	79.7	16
11 41.1	45.2	77.4	12 06.8	46.6	77.8	12 31.7	47.9	78.2	12 55.7	49.1	78.7	13 18.7	50.3	79.1	17
12 26.3	45.1	76.7	12 53.4	46.5	77.2	13 19.6	47.7	77.6	13 44.8	49.0	78.1	14 09.0	50.3	78.6	18
13 11.4	45.1	76.1	13 39.9	46.4	76.5	14 07.3	47.7	77.0	14 33.8	49.0	77.5	14 59.3	50.1	78.0	19
13 56.5	+44.9	75.4	14 26.3	+46.2	75.9	14 55.0	+47.6	76.4	15 22.8	+48.8	76.9	15 49.4	+50.0	77.5	20
14 41.4	44.8	74.7	15 12.5	46.2	75.2	15 42.6	47.5	75.7	16 11.6	48.7	76.3	16 39.4	50.0	76.9	21
15 26.2	44.6	74.0	15 58.7	46.0	74.5	16 30.1	47.4	75.1	17 00.3	48.7	75.7	17 29.4	49.8	76.3	22
16 10.8	44.6	73.3	16 44.7	45.9	73.9	17 17.5	47.2	74.5	17 49.0	48.5	75.1	18 19.2	49.8	75.7	23
16 55.4	44.4	72.6	17 30.6	45.8	73.2	18 04.7	47.1	73.8	18 37.5	48.4	74.5	19 09.0	49.6	75.1	24
17 39.8	+44.2	71.9	18 16.4	+45.6	72.5	18 51.8	+47.0	73.2	19 25.9	+48.3	73.8	19 58.6	+49.5	74.5	25
18 24.0	44.1	71.2	19 02.0	45.5	71.8	19 38.8	46.8	72.5	20 14.2	48.1	73.2	20 48.1	49.4	73.9	26
19 08.1	43.9	70.5	19 47.5	45.3	71.1	20 25.6	46.7	71.8	21 02.3	48.0	72.6	21 37.5	49.2	73.3	27
19 52.0	43.7	69.8	20 32.8	45.2	70.5	21 12.3	46.5	71.2	21 50.3	47.8	71.9	22 26.7	49.1	72.7	28
20 35.7	43.6	69.0	21 18.0	44.9	69.7	21 58.8	46.3	70.5	22 38.1	47.7	71.3	23 15.8	49.0	72.1	29

Dec.	0° Hc	d	Z	2° Hc	d	Z	4° Hc	d	Z	6° Hc	d	Z	8° Hc	d	Z
0	0 00.0	0.0	90.0	0 00.0	+2.1	90.0	0 00.0	+4.2	90.0	0 00.0	+6.3	90.0	0 00.0	+8.4	90.0
1	0 00.0	0.0	89.0	0 02.1	2.1	89.0	0 04.2	4.2	89.0	0 06.3	6.2	89.0	0 08.4	8.3	89.0
2	0 00.0	0.0	88.0	0 04.2	2.1	88.0	0 08.4	4.2	88.0	0 12.5	6.3	88.0	0 16.7	8.3	88.0
3	0 00.0	0.0	87.0	0 06.3	2.1	87.0	0 12.6	4.1	87.0	0 18.8	6.3	87.0	0 25.0	8.4	87.0
4	0 00.0	0.0	86.0	0 08.4	2.1	86.0	0 16.7	4.2	86.0	0 25.1	6.2	86.0	0 33.4	8.3	86.0
5	0 00.0	0.0	85.0	0 10.5	+2.0	85.0	0 20.9	+4.2	85.0	0 31.3	+6.3	85.0	0 41.7	+8.3	85.0
6	0 00.0	0.0	84.0	0 12.5	2.1	84.0	0 25.1	4.1	84.0	0 37.6	6.2	84.0	0 50.0	8.3	84.1
7	0 00.0	0.0	83.0	0 14.6	2.1	83.0	0 29.2	4.1	83.0	0 43.8	6.2	83.0	0 58.3	8.3	83.1
8	0 00.0	0.0	82.0	0 16.7	2.1	82.0	0 33.4	4.1	82.0	0 50.0	6.2	82.0	1 06.6	8.3	82.1
9	0 00.0	0.0	81.0	0 18.8	2.0	81.0	0 37.5	4.1	81.0	0 56.2	6.2	81.0	1 14.9	8.2	81.1
10	0 00.0	0.0	80.0	0 20.8	+2.1	80.0	0 41.6	+4.2	80.0	1 02.4	+6.2	80.1	1 23.1	+8.2	80.1
11	0 00.0	0.0	79.0	0 22.9	2.0	79.0	0 45.8	4.1	79.0	1 08.6	6.1	79.1	1 31.3	8.2	79.1
12	0 00.0	0.0	78.0	0 24.9	2.0	78.0	0 49.9	4.0	78.0	1 14.7	6.1	78.1	1 39.5	8.1	78.1
13	0 00.0	0.0	77.0	0 27.0	2.0	77.0	0 53.9	4.1	77.0	1 20.8	6.1	77.1	1 47.6	8.2	77.1
14	0 00.0	0.0	76.0	0 29.0	2.1	76.0	0 58.0	4.1	76.0	1 26.9	6.1	76.1	1 55.8	8.1	76.1
15	0 00.0	0.0	75.0	0 31.1	+2.0	75.0	1 02.1	+4.0	75.1	1 33.0	+6.1	75.1	2 03.9	+8.0	75.1
16	0 00.0	0.0	74.0	0 33.1	2.0	74.0	1 06.1	4.0	74.0	1 39.1	6.0	74.1	2 11.9	8.0	74.1
17	0 00.0	0.0	73.0	0 35.1	2.0	73.0	1 10.1	4.0	73.0	1 45.1	6.0	73.1	2 19.9	8.0	73.2
18	0 00.0	0.0	72.0	0 37.1	2.0	72.0	1 14.1	4.0	72.0	1 51.1	5.9	72.1	2 27.9	7.9	72.2
19	0 00.0	0.0	71.0	0 39.1	1.9	71.0	1 18.1	3.9	71.0	1 57.0	5.9	71.1	2 35.8	7.9	71.2
20	0 00.0	0.0	70.0	0 41.0	+2.0	70.0	1 22.0	+3.9	70.0	2 02.9	+5.9	70.1	2 43.7	+7.8	70.2
21	0 00.0	0.0	69.0	0 43.0	1.9	69.0	1 25.9	3.9	69.0	2 08.8	5.8	69.1	2 51.5	7.8	69.2
22	0 00.0	0.0	68.0	0 44.9	2.0	68.0	1 29.8	3.9	68.0	2 14.6	5.8	68.1	2 59.3	7.7	68.2
23	0 00.0	0.0	67.0	0 46.9	1.9	67.0	1 33.7	3.9	67.1	2 20.4	5.8	67.1	3 07.0	7.7	67.2
24	0 00.0	0.0	66.0	0 48.8	1.9	66.0	1 37.6	3.8	66.1	2 26.2	5.7	66.1	3 14.7	7.6	66.2
25	0 00.0	0.0	65.0	0 50.7	+1.9	65.0	1 41.4	+3.7	65.1	2 31.9	+5.7	65.1	3 22.3	+7.6	65.2
26	0 00.0	0.0	64.0	0 52.6	1.9	64.0	1 45.1	3.8	64.1	2 37.6	5.6	64.1	3 29.9	7.5	64.2
27	0 00.0	0.0	63.0	0 54.5	1.8	63.0	1 48.9	3.7	63.1	2 43.2	5.6	63.1	3 37.4	7.4	63.2
28	0 00.0	0.0	62.0	0 56.3	1.9	62.0	1 52.6	3.7	62.1	2 48.8	5.5	62.1	3 44.8	7.3	62.2
29	0 00.0	0.0	61.0	0 58.2	1.8	61.0	1 56.3	3.6	61.1	2 54.3	5.5	61.1	3 52.1	7.3	61.2

Dec.	10° Hc	d	Z	12° Hc	d	Z	14° Hc	d	Z	16° Hc	d	Z	18° Hc	d	Z
0	0 00.0	+10.4	90.0	0 00.0	+12.5	90.0	0 00.0	+14.5	90.0	0 00.0	+16.5	90.0	0 00.0	+18.5	90.0
1	0 10.4	10.4	89.0	0 12.5	12.4	89.0	0 14.5	14.5	89.0	0 16.5	16.6	89.0	0 18.5	18.6	89.0
2	0 20.8	10.4	88.0	0 24.9	12.4	88.0	0 29.0	14.5	88.1	0 33.1	16.5	88.1	0 37.1	18.5	88.1
3	0 31.2	10.4	87.0	0 37.4	12.5	87.1	0 43.5	14.5	87.1	0 49.6	16.5	87.1	0 55.6	18.5	87.1
4	0 41.6	10.4	86.1	0 49.9	12.4	86.1	0 58.0	14.5	86.1	1 06.1	16.5	86.2	1 14.1	18.5	86.2
5	0 52.0	+10.4	85.1	1 02.3	+12.4	85.1	1 12.5	+14.4	85.1	1 22.6	+16.5	85.2	1 32.6	+18.5	85.2
6	1 02.4	10.4	84.1	1 14.7	12.4	84.1	1 26.9	14.5	84.2	1 39.1	16.4	84.2	1 51.1	18.4	84.3
7	1 12.8	10.3	83.1	1 27.1	12.4	83.2	1 41.4	14.4	83.2	1 55.5	16.4	83.3	2 09.5	18.4	83.3
8	1 23.1	10.3	82.1	1 39.5	12.3	82.2	1 55.8	14.3	82.2	2 11.9	16.4	82.3	2 27.9	18.3	82.4
9	1 33.4	10.3	81.1	1 51.8	12.3	81.2	2 10.1	14.4	81.3	2 28.3	16.3	81.3	2 46.2	18.4	81.4
10	1 43.7	+10.2	80.1	2 04.1	+12.3	80.2	2 24.5	+14.2	80.3	2 44.6	+16.3	80.4	3 04.6	+18.2	80.5
11	1 53.9	10.2	79.2	2 16.4	12.3	79.2	2 38.7	14.3	79.3	3 00.9	16.2	79.4	3 22.8	18.2	79.5
12	2 04.1	10.2	78.2	2 28.7	12.1	78.3	2 53.0	14.2	78.3	3 17.1	16.2	78.5	3 41.0	18.2	78.6
13	2 14.3	10.2	77.2	2 40.8	12.2	77.3	3 07.2	14.1	77.4	3 33.3	16.1	77.5	3 59.2	18.0	77.6
14	2 24.5	10.1	76.2	2 53.0	12.1	76.3	3 21.3	14.1	76.4	3 49.4	16.1	76.5	4 17.2	18.0	76.7
15	2 34.6	+10.0	75.2	3 05.1	+12.0	75.3	3 35.4	+14.0	75.4	4 05.5	+15.9	75.6	4 35.2	+18.0	75.7
16	2 44.6	10.0	74.2	3 17.1	12.0	74.3	3 49.4	14.0	74.5	4 21.4	15.9	74.6	4 53.2	17.8	74.7
17	2 54.6	10.0	73.2	3 29.1	11.9	73.4	4 03.4	13.8	73.5	4 37.3	15.9	73.6	5 11.0	17.8	73.8
18	3 04.6	9.9	72.3	3 41.0	11.9	72.4	4 17.2	13.8	72.5	4 53.0	15.7	72.7	5 28.8	17.6	72.8
19	3 14.5	9.8	71.3	3 52.9	11.8	71.4	4 31.0	13.8	71.5	5 08.9	15.7	71.7	5 46.4	17.6	71.9
20	3 24.3	+9.8	70.3	4 04.7	+11.7	70.4	4 44.8	+13.6	70.5	5 24.6	+15.5	70.7	6 04.0	+17.5	70.9
21	3 34.1	9.7	69.3	4 16.4	11.6	69.4	4 58.4	13.6	69.6	5 40.1	15.5	69.7	6 21.5	17.3	69.9
22	3 43.8	9.6	68.3	4 28.0	11.6	68.4	5 12.0	13.4	68.6	5 55.6	15.4	68.8	6 38.8	17.3	69.0
23	3 53.4	9.6	67.3	4 39.6	11.5	67.5	5 25.4	13.4	67.6	6 11.0	15.2	67.8	6 56.1	17.1	68.0
24	4 03.0	9.5	66.3	4 51.1	11.4	66.5	5 38.8	13.3	66.6	6 26.2	15.2	66.8	7 13.2	17.0	67.1
25	4 12.5	+9.4	65.3	5 02.5	+11.3	65.5	5 52.1	+13.2	65.7	6 41.4	+15.0	65.9	7 30.2	+16.9	66.1
26	4 21.9	9.4	64.3	5 13.8	11.2	64.5	6 05.3	13.0	64.7	6 56.4	14.9	64.9	7 47.1	16.8	65.1
27	4 31.3	9.3	63.4	5 25.0	11.1	63.5	6 18.3	13.0	63.7	7 11.3	14.8	63.9	8 03.9	16.6	64.1
28	4 40.6	9.2	62.4	5 36.1	11.0	62.5	6 31.3	12.8	62.7	7 26.1	14.7	62.9	8 20.5	16.5	63.2
29	4 49.8	9.1	61.4	5 47.1	10.9	61.5	6 44.1	12.8	61.7	7 40.8	14.5	61.9	8 37.0	16.3	62.2

0°			2°			4°			6°			8°			
Hc	d	Z	Hc	d	Z	Hc	d	Z	Hc	d	Z	Hc	d	Z	Dec.
° ′	′	°	° ′	′	°	° ′	′	°	° ′	′	°	° ′	′	°	°
0 00.0	0.0	90.0	0 00.0 +	2.1	90.0	0 00.0 +	4.2	90.0	0 00.0 +	6.3	90.0	0 00.0 +	8.4	90.0	0
0 00.0	0.0	89.0	0 02.1	2.1	89.0	0 04.2	4.2	89.0	0 06.3	6.2	89.0	0 08.4	8.3	89.0	1
0 00.0	0.0	88.0	0 04.2	2.1	88.0	0 08.4	4.2	88.0	0 12.5	6.3	88.0	0 16.7	8.3	88.0	2
0 00.0	0.0	87.0	0 06.3	2.1	87.0	0 12.6	4.1	87.0	0 18.8	6.3	87.0	0 25.0	8.4	87.0	3
0 00.0	0.0	86.0	0 08.4	2.1	86.0	0 16.7	4.2	86.0	0 25.1	6.2	86.0	0 33.4	8.3	86.0	4
0 00.0	0.0	85.0	0 10.5 +	2.0	85.0	0 20.9 +	4.2	85.0	0 31.3 +	6.3	85.0	0 41.7 +	8.3	85.0	5
0 00.0	0.0	84.0	0 12.5	2.1	84.0	0 25.1	4.1	84.0	0 37.6	6.2	84.0	0 50.0	8.3	84.1	6
0 00.0	0.0	83.0	0 14.6	2.1	83.0	0 29.2	4.2	83.0	0 43.8	6.2	83.0	0 58.3	8.3	83.1	7
0 00.0	0.0	82.0	0 16.7	2.1	82.0	0 33.4	4.1	82.0	0 50.0	6.2	82.0	1 06.6	8.3	82.1	8
0 00.0	0.0	81.0	0 18.8	2.0	81.0	0 37.5	4.1	81.0	0 56.2	6.2	81.0	1 14.9	8.2	81.1	9
0 00.0	0.0	80.0	0 20.8 +	2.1	80.0	0 41.6 +	4.2	80.0	1 02.4 +	6.2	80.1	1 23.1 +	8.2	80.1	10
0 00.0	0.0	79.0	0 22.9	2.0	79.0	0 45.8	4.1	79.0	1 08.6	6.1	79.1	1 31.3	8.2	79.1	11
0 00.0	0.0	78.0	0 24.9	2.1	78.0	0 49.9	4.0	78.0	1 14.7	6.1	78.1	1 39.5	8.1	78.1	12
0 00.0	0.0	77.0	0 27.0	2.0	77.0	0 53.9	4.1	77.0	1 20.8	6.1	77.1	1 47.6	8.2	77.1	13
0 00.0	0.0	76.0	0 29.0	2.1	76.0	0 58.0	4.1	76.0	1 26.9	6.1	76.1	1 55.8	8.1	76.1	14
0 00.0	0.0	75.0	0 31.1 +	2.0	75.0	1 02.1 +	4.0	75.0	1 33.0 +	6.1	75.1	2 03.9 +	8.0	75.1	15
0 00.0	0.0	74.0	0 33.1	2.0	74.0	1 06.1	4.0	74.0	1 39.1	6.0	74.1	2 11.9	8.0	74.1	16
0 00.0	0.0	73.0	0 35.1	2.0	73.0	1 10.1	4.0	73.0	1 45.1	6.0	73.1	2 19.9	8.0	73.2	17
0 00.0	0.0	72.0	0 37.1	2.0	72.0	1 14.1	4.0	72.0	1 51.1	5.9	72.1	2 27.9	7.9	72.2	18
0 00.0	0.0	71.0	0 39.1	1.9	71.0	1 18.1	3.9	71.0	1 57.0	5.9	71.1	2 35.8	7.9	71.2	19
0 00.0	0.0	70.0	0 41.0 +	2.0	70.0	1 22.0 +	3.9	70.0	2 02.9 +	5.9	70.1	2 43.7 +	7.8	70.2	20
0 00.0	0.0	69.0	0 43.0	1.9	69.0	1 25.9	3.9	69.0	2 08.8	5.8	69.1	2 51.5	7.8	69.2	21
0 00.0	0.0	68.0	0 44.9	2.0	68.0	1 29.8	3.9	68.0	2 14.6	5.8	68.1	2 59.3	7.7	68.2	22
0 00.0	0.0	67.0	0 46.9	1.9	67.0	1 33.7	3.9	67.1	2 20.4	5.8	67.1	3 07.0	7.7	67.2	23
0 00.0	0.0	66.0	0 48.8	1.9	66.0	1 37.6	3.8	66.1	2 26.2	5.7	66.1	3 14.7	7.6	66.2	24
0 00.0	0.0	65.0	0 50.7 +	1.9	65.0	1 41.4 +	3.7	65.1	2 31.9 +	5.7	65.1	3 22.3 +	7.6	65.2	25
0 00.0	0.0	64.0	0 52.6	1.9	64.0	1 45.1	3.8	64.1	2 37.6	5.6	64.1	3 29.9	7.5	64.2	26
0 00.0	0.0	63.0	0 54.5	1.8	63.0	1 48.9	3.7	63.1	2 43.2	5.6	63.1	3 37.4	7.4	63.2	27
0 00.0	0.0	62.0	0 56.3	1.9	62.0	1 52.6	3.7	62.1	2 48.8	5.5	62.1	3 44.8	7.3	62.2	28
0 00.0	0.0	61.0	0 58.2	1.8	61.0	1 56.3	3.6	61.1	2 54.3	5.5	61.1	3 52.1	7.3	61.2	29

10°			12°			14°			16°			18°			
Hc	d	Z	Hc	d	Z	Hc	d	Z	Hc	d	Z	Hc	d	Z	Dec.
° ′	′	°	° ′	′	°	° ′	′	°	° ′	′	°	° ′	′	°	°
0 00.0 +	10.4	90.0	0 00.0 +	12.5	90.0	0 00.0 +	14.5	90.0	0 00.0 +	16.5	90.0	0 00.0 +	18.5	90.0	0
0 10.4	10.4	89.0	0 12.5	12.4	89.0	0 14.5	14.5	89.0	0 16.5	16.6	89.0	0 18.5	18.6	89.0	1
0 20.8	10.4	88.0	0 24.9	12.5	88.0	0 29.0	14.5	88.1	0 33.1	16.5	88.1	0 37.1	18.5	88.1	2
0 31.2	10.4	87.0	0 37.4	12.5	87.1	0 43.5	14.5	87.1	0 49.6	16.5	87.1	0 55.6	18.5	87.1	3
0 41.6	10.4	86.1	0 49.9	12.4	86.1	0 58.0	14.5	86.1	1 06.1	16.5	86.2	1 14.1	18.5	86.2	4
0 52.0 +	10.4	85.1	1 02.3 +	12.4	85.1	1 12.5 +	14.4	85.1	1 22.6 +	16.5	85.2	1 32.6 +	18.5	85.2	5
1 02.4	10.4	84.1	1 14.7	12.4	84.1	1 26.9	14.5	84.2	1 39.1	16.4	84.2	1 51.1	18.4	84.3	6
1 12.8	10.3	83.1	1 27.1	12.4	83.2	1 41.4	14.4	83.2	1 55.5	16.4	83.3	2 09.5	18.4	83.3	7
1 23.1	10.3	82.1	1 39.5	12.3	82.2	1 55.8	14.3	82.2	2 11.9	16.4	82.3	2 27.9	18.3	82.4	8
1 33.4	10.3	81.1	1 51.8	12.3	81.2	2 10.1	14.4	81.3	2 28.3	16.3	81.3	2 46.2	18.4	81.4	9
1 43.7 +	10.2	80.1	2 04.1 +	12.3	80.2	2 24.5 +	14.2	80.3	2 44.6 +	16.3	80.4	3 04.6 +	18.2	80.5	10
1 53.9	10.2	79.2	2 16.4	12.3	79.3	2 38.7	14.3	79.3	3 00.9	16.2	79.4	3 22.8	18.2	79.5	11
2 04.1	10.2	78.2	2 28.7	12.1	78.3	2 53.0	14.2	78.3	3 17.1	16.2	78.5	3 41.0	18.2	78.6	12
2 14.3	10.2	77.2	2 40.8	12.2	77.3	3 07.2	14.1	77.4	3 33.3	16.1	77.5	3 59.2	18.0	77.6	13
2 24.5	10.1	76.2	2 53.0	12.1	76.3	3 21.3	14.1	76.4	3 49.4	16.1	76.5	4 17.2	18.0	76.7	14
2 34.6 +	10.0	75.2	3 05.1 +	12.0	75.3	3 35.4 +	14.0	75.4	4 05.5 +	15.9	75.6	4 35.2 +	18.0	75.7	15
2 44.6	10.0	74.2	3 17.1	12.0	74.3	3 49.4	14.0	74.5	4 21.4	15.9	74.6	4 53.2	17.8	74.7	16
2 54.6	10.0	73.2	3 29.1	11.9	73.4	4 03.4	13.8	73.5	4 37.3	15.9	73.6	5 11.0	17.8	73.8	17
3 04.6	9.9	72.3	3 41.0	11.9	72.4	4 17.2	13.8	72.5	4 53.2	15.7	72.7	5 28.8	17.6	72.8	18
3 14.5	9.8	71.3	3 52.9	11.8	71.4	4 31.0	13.8	71.5	5 08.9	15.7	71.7	5 46.4	17.6	71.9	19
3 24.3 +	9.8	70.3	4 04.7 +	11.7	70.4	4 44.8 +	13.6	70.5	5 24.6 +	15.5	70.7	6 04.0 +	17.5	70.9	20
3 34.1	9.7	69.3	4 16.4	11.6	69.4	4 58.4	13.6	69.6	5 40.1	15.5	69.7	6 21.5	17.3	69.9	21
3 43.8	9.6	68.3	4 28.0	11.6	68.4	5 12.0	13.4	68.6	5 55.6	15.4	68.8	6 38.8	17.3	69.0	22
3 53.4	9.6	67.3	4 39.6	11.5	67.5	5 25.4	13.4	67.6	6 11.0	15.2	67.8	6 56.1	17.1	68.0	23
4 03.0	9.5	66.3	4 51.1	11.4	66.5	5 38.8	13.3	66.6	6 26.2	15.2	66.8	7 13.2	17.0	67.1	24
4 12.5 +	9.4	65.3	5 02.5 +	11.3	65.5	5 52.1 +	13.2	65.7	6 41.4 +	15.0	65.9	7 30.2 +	16.9	66.1	25
4 21.9	9.4	64.3	5 13.8	11.2	64.5	6 05.3	13.0	64.7	6 56.4	14.9	64.9	7 47.1	16.8	65.1	26
4 31.3	9.3	63.4	5 25.0	11.1	63.5	6 18.3	13.0	63.7	7 11.3	14.8	63.9	8 03.9	16.6	64.1	27
4 40.6	9.2	62.4	5 36.1	11.0	62.5	6 31.3	12.8	62.7	7 26.1	14.7	62.9	8 20.5	16.5	63.2	28
4 49.8	9.1	61.4	5 47.1	10.9	61.5	6 44.1	12.8	61.7	7 40.8	14.5	61.9	8 37.0	16.3	62.2	29

Dec.	20° Hc	d	Z	22° Hc	d	Z	24° Hc	d	Z	26° Hc	d	Z	28° Hc	d	Z
0	0 00.0	+20.5	90.0	0 00.0	+22.5	90.0	0 00.0	+24.4	90.0	0 00.0	+26.3	90.0	0 00.0	+28.2	90.0
1	0 20.5	20.5	89.1	0 22.5	22.4	89.1	0 24.4	24.4	89.1	0 26.3	26.3	89.1	0 28.2	28.1	89.1
2	0 41.0	20.5	88.1	0 44.9	22.5	88.1	0 48.8	24.4	88.2	0 52.6	26.3	88.2	0 56.3	28.2	88.2
3	1 01.5	20.5	87.2	1 07.4	22.4	87.2	1 13.2	24.4	87.3	1 18.9	26.2	87.3	1 24.5	28.1	87.4
4	1 22.0	20.5	86.2	1 29.8	22.5	86.3	1 37.6	24.3	86.3	1 45.1	26.2	86.4	1 52.6	28.1	86.5
5	1 42.5	+20.4	85.3	1 52.3	+22.3	85.4	2 01.9	+24.3	85.4	2 11.4	+26.2	85.5	2 20.7	+28.1	85.6
6	2 02.9	20.4	84.4	2 14.6	22.4	84.4	2 26.2	24.3	84.5	2 37.6	26.1	84.6	2 48.8	28.0	84.7
7	2 23.3	20.4	83.4	2 37.0	22.3	83.5	2 50.5	24.2	83.6	3 03.7	26.2	83.7	3 16.8	28.0	83.8
8	2 43.7	20.3	82.5	2 59.3	22.3	82.6	3 14.7	24.2	82.7	3 29.9	26.0	82.8	3 44.8	27.9	82.9
9	3 04.0	20.3	81.5	3 21.6	22.2	81.6	3 38.9	24.1	81.8	3 55.9	26.0	81.9	4 12.7	27.9	82.0
10	3 24.3	+20.2	80.6	3 43.8	+22.1	80.7	4 03.0	+24.1	80.8	4 21.9	+26.0	81.0	4 40.6	+27.8	81.2
11	3 44.5	20.2	79.6	4 05.9	22.1	79.8	4 27.1	24.0	79.9	4 47.9	25.9	80.1	5 08.4	27.7	80.3
12	4 04.7	20.1	78.7	4 28.0	22.0	78.9	4 51.1	23.9	79.0	5 13.8	25.8	79.2	5 36.1	27.6	79.4
13	4 24.8	20.0	77.8	4 50.0	22.0	77.9	5 15.0	23.8	78.1	5 39.6	25.7	78.3	6 03.7	27.6	78.5
14	4 44.8	19.9	76.8	5 12.0	21.8	77.0	5 38.8	23.8	77.2	6 05.3	25.6	77.4	6 31.3	27.4	77.6
15	5 04.7	+19.9	75.9	5 33.8	+21.8	76.0	6 02.6	+23.6	76.2	6 30.9	+25.5	76.5	6 58.7	+27.4	76.7
16	5 24.6	19.7	74.9	5 55.6	21.7	75.1	6 26.2	23.6	75.3	6 56.4	25.4	75.5	7 26.1	27.3	75.8
17	5 44.3	19.7	74.0	6 17.3	21.5	74.2	6 49.8	23.4	74.4	7 21.8	25.3	74.6	7 53.4	27.1	74.9
18	6 04.0	19.6	73.0	6 38.8	21.5	73.2	7 13.2	23.4	73.5	7 47.1	25.2	73.7	8 20.5	27.0	74.0
19	6 23.6	19.5	72.1	7 00.3	21.4	72.3	7 36.6	23.2	72.5	8 12.3	25.1	72.8	8 47.5	26.9	73.1
20	6 43.1	+19.3	71.1	7 21.7	+21.2	71.4	7 59.8	+23.1	71.6	8 37.4	+24.9	71.9	9 14.4	+26.7	72.2
21	7 02.4	19.3	70.2	7 42.9	21.1	70.4	8 22.9	22.9	70.7	9 02.3	24.8	71.0	9 41.1	26.6	71.3
22	7 21.7	19.1	69.2	8 04.0	21.0	69.5	8 45.8	22.9	69.7	9 27.1	24.7	70.0	10 07.7	26.5	70.4
23	7 40.8	19.0	68.3	8 25.0	20.8	68.5	9 08.7	22.6	68.8	9 51.8	24.5	69.1	10 34.2	26.3	69.5
24	7 59.8	18.9	67.3	8 45.8	20.7	67.6	9 31.3	22.6	67.9	10 16.3	24.3	68.2	11 00.5	26.1	68.5
25	8 18.7	+18.7	66.3	9 06.5	+20.6	66.6	9 53.9	+22.4	66.9	10 40.6	+24.2	67.3	11 26.6	+26.0	67.6
26	8 37.4	18.6	65.4	9 27.1	20.4	65.7	10 16.3	22.2	66.0	11 04.8	24.0	66.3	11 52.6	25.8	66.7
27	8 56.0	18.4	64.4	9 47.5	20.2	64.7	10 38.5	22.0	65.0	11 28.8	23.8	65.4	12 18.4	25.6	65.8
28	9 14.4	18.3	63.5	10 07.7	20.1	63.8	11 00.5	21.9	64.1	11 52.6	23.6	64.5	12 44.0	25.4	64.9
29	9 32.7	18.1	62.5	10 27.8	19.9	62.8	11 22.4	21.6	63.1	12 16.2	23.5	63.5	13 09.4	25.2	63.9

Dec.	30° Hc	d	Z	32° Hc	d	Z	34° Hc	d	Z	36° Hc	d	Z	38° Hc	d	Z
0	0 00.0	+30.0	90.0	0 00.0	+31.8	90.0	0 00.0	+33.6	90.0	0 00.0	+35.3	90.0	0 00.0	+36.9	90.0
1	0 30.0	30.0	89.1	0 31.8	31.8	89.2	0 33.6	33.5	89.2	0 35.3	35.2	89.2	0 36.9	37.0	89.2
2	1 00.0	30.0	88.3	1 03.6	31.8	88.3	1 07.1	33.5	88.3	1 10.5	35.3	88.4	1 13.9	36.9	88.4
3	1 30.0	29.9	87.4	1 35.4	31.7	87.5	1 40.6	33.5	87.5	1 45.8	35.2	87.6	1 50.8	36.9	87.6
4	1 59.9	30.0	86.5	2 07.1	31.7	86.6	2 14.1	33.5	86.7	2 21.0	35.2	86.8	2 27.7	36.9	86.8
5	2 29.9	+29.9	85.7	2 38.8	+31.7	85.8	2 47.6	+33.5	85.9	2 56.2	+35.1	86.0	3 04.6	+36.8	86.1
6	2 59.8	29.8	84.8	3 10.5	31.7	84.9	3 21.1	33.4	85.0	3 31.3	35.2	85.1	3 41.4	36.8	85.3
7	3 29.6	29.8	83.9	3 42.2	31.6	84.1	3 54.5	33.3	84.2	4 06.5	35.0	84.3	4 18.2	36.7	84.5
8	3 59.4	29.8	83.1	4 13.8	31.5	83.2	4 27.8	33.3	83.4	4 41.5	35.0	83.5	4 54.9	36.7	83.7
9	4 29.2	29.7	82.2	4 45.3	31.5	82.3	5 01.1	33.2	82.5	5 16.5	35.0	82.7	5 31.6	36.6	82.9
10	4 58.9	+29.6	81.3	5 16.8	+31.4	81.5	5 34.3	+33.2	81.7	5 51.5	+34.9	81.9	6 08.2	+36.6	82.1
11	5 28.5	29.5	80.4	5 48.2	31.3	80.6	6 07.5	33.1	80.8	6 26.4	34.8	81.1	6 44.8	36.5	81.3
12	5 58.0	29.5	79.6	6 19.5	31.3	79.8	6 40.6	33.0	80.0	7 01.2	34.7	80.2	7 21.3	36.3	80.5
13	6 27.5	29.4	78.7	6 50.8	31.1	78.9	7 13.6	32.9	79.2	7 35.9	34.6	79.4	7 57.6	36.3	79.7
14	6 56.9	29.2	77.8	7 21.9	31.1	78.1	7 46.5	32.8	78.3	8 10.5	34.5	78.6	8 33.9	36.2	78.9
15	7 26.1	+29.2	76.9	7 53.0	+30.9	77.2	8 19.3	+32.7	77.5	8 45.0	+34.4	77.8	9 10.1	+36.1	78.1
16	7 55.3	29.1	76.1	8 23.9	30.9	76.3	8 52.0	32.6	76.6	9 19.4	34.3	76.9	9 46.2	36.0	77.3
17	8 24.9	28.9	75.2	8 54.8	30.7	75.5	9 24.6	32.4	75.8	9 53.7	34.2	76.1	10 22.2	35.8	76.5
18	8 53.3	28.8	74.3	9 25.5	30.6	74.6	9 57.0	32.4	74.9	10 27.9	34.0	75.3	10 58.0	35.8	75.6
19	9 22.1	28.7	73.4	9 56.1	30.4	73.7	10 29.4	32.2	74.1	11 01.9	33.9	74.4	11 33.8	35.5	74.8
20	9 50.8	+28.5	72.5	10 26.5	+30.3	72.8	11 01.6	+32.0	73.2	11 35.8	+33.8	73.6	12 09.3	+35.5	74.0
21	10 19.3	28.4	71.6	10 56.8	30.2	72.0	11 33.6	31.9	72.3	12 09.6	33.6	72.7	12 44.8	35.3	73.2
22	10 47.7	28.3	70.7	11 27.0	29.9	71.1	12 05.5	31.7	71.5	12 43.2	33.4	71.9	13 20.1	35.1	72.3
23	11 16.0	28.0	69.8	11 57.0	29.8	70.2	12 37.2	31.6	70.6	13 16.6	33.3	71.0	13 55.2	34.9	71.5
24	11 44.0	27.9	68.9	12 26.8	29.7	69.3	13 08.8	31.4	69.7	13 49.9	33.1	70.2	14 30.1	34.8	70.7
25	12 11.9	+27.5	68.0	12 56.5	+29.5	68.3	13 40.2	+31.2	68.8	14 23.0	+32.9	69.3	15 04.9	+34.6	69.8
26	12 39.7	27.5	67.1	13 26.0	29.2	67.5	14 11.4	31.0	68.0	14 55.9	32.7	68.5	15 39.5	34.3	69.0
27	13 07.2	27.4	66.2	13 55.2	29.1	66.6	14 42.4	30.8	67.1	15 28.6	32.5	67.6	16 13.8	34.2	68.1
28	13 34.6	27.1	65.3	14 24.3	28.9	65.7	15 13.2	30.6	66.2	16 01.1	32.3	66.7	16 48.0	34.0	67.3
29	14 01.7	27.0	64.4	14 53.2	28.7	64.8	15 43.8	30.4	65.3	16 33.4	32.1	65.8	17 22.0	33.7	66.4

20°			22°			24°			26°			28°			Dec.
Hc	d	Z	Hc	d	Z	Hc	d	Z	Hc	d	Z	Hc	d	Z	
° ′	′	°	° ′	′	°	° ′	′	°	° ′	′	°	° ′	′	°	°
0 00.0	+20.5	90.0	0 00.0	+22.5	90.0	0 00.0	+24.4	90.0	0 00.0	+26.3	90.0	0 00.0	+28.2	90.0	0
0 20.5	20.5	89.1	0 22.5	22.4	89.1	0 24.4	24.4	89.1	0 26.3	26.3	89.1	0 28.2	28.1	89.1	1
0 41.0	20.5	88.1	0 44.9	22.5	88.1	0 48.8	24.4	88.2	0 52.6	26.3	88.2	0 56.3	28.2	88.2	2
1 01.5	20.5	87.2	1 07.4	22.4	87.2	1 13.2	24.4	87.3	1 18.9	26.2	87.3	1 24.5	28.1	87.4	3
1 22.0	20.5	86.2	1 29.8	22.5	86.3	1 37.6	24.3	86.3	1 45.1	26.3	86.4	1 52.6	28.1	86.5	4
1 42.5	+20.4	85.3	1 52.3	+22.3	85.4	2 01.9	+24.3	85.4	2 11.4	+26.2	85.5	2 20.7	+28.1	85.6	5
2 02.9	20.4	84.4	2 14.6	22.4	84.4	2 26.2	24.3	84.5	2 37.6	26.1	84.6	2 48.8	28.0	84.7	6
2 23.3	20.4	83.4	2 37.0	22.3	83.5	2 50.5	24.2	83.6	3 03.7	26.2	83.7	3 16.8	28.0	83.8	7
2 43.7	20.3	82.5	2 59.3	22.3	82.6	3 14.7	24.2	82.7	3 29.9	26.0	82.8	3 44.8	27.9	82.9	8
3 04.0	20.3	81.5	3 21.6	22.2	81.6	3 38.9	24.1	81.8	3 55.9	26.0	81.9	4 12.7	27.9	82.0	9
3 24.3	+20.2	80.6	3 43.8	+22.1	80.7	4 03.0	+24.1	80.8	4 21.9	+26.0	81.0	4 40.6	+27.8	81.2	10
3 44.5	20.2	79.6	4 05.9	22.1	79.8	4 27.1	24.0	79.9	4 47.9	25.9	80.1	5 08.4	27.7	80.3	11
4 04.7	20.1	78.7	4 28.0	22.0	78.9	4 51.1	23.9	79.0	5 13.8	25.8	79.2	5 36.1	27.6	79.4	12
4 24.8	20.0	77.8	4 50.0	22.0	77.9	5 15.0	23.8	78.1	5 39.6	25.7	78.3	6 03.7	27.6	78.5	13
4 44.8	19.9	76.8	5 12.0	21.8	77.0	5 38.8	23.8	77.2	6 05.3	25.6	77.4	6 31.3	27.4	77.6	14
5 04.7	+19.9	75.9	5 33.8	+21.8	76.0	6 02.6	+23.6	76.2	6 30.9	+25.5	76.5	6 58.7	+27.4	76.7	15
5 24.6	19.7	74.9	5 55.6	21.7	75.1	6 26.2	23.6	75.3	6 56.4	25.4	75.5	7 26.1	27.3	75.8	16
5 44.3	19.7	74.0	6 17.3	21.5	74.2	6 49.8	23.4	74.4	7 21.8	25.3	74.6	7 53.4	27.1	74.9	17
6 04.0	19.6	73.0	6 38.8	21.5	73.2	7 13.2	23.4	73.5	7 47.1	25.2	73.7	8 20.5	27.0	74.0	18
6 23.6	19.5	72.1	7 00.3	21.4	72.3	7 36.6	23.2	72.5	8 12.3	25.1	72.8	8 47.5	26.9	73.1	19
6 43.1	+19.3	71.1	7 21.7	+21.2	71.4	7 59.8	+23.1	71.6	8 37.4	+24.9	71.9	9 14.4	+26.7	72.2	20
7 02.4	19.3	70.2	7 42.9	21.1	70.4	8 22.9	22.9	70.7	9 02.3	24.8	71.0	9 41.1	26.6	71.3	21
7 21.7	19.1	69.2	8 04.0	21.0	69.5	8 45.8	22.9	69.7	9 27.1	24.7	70.0	10 07.7	26.5	70.4	22
7 40.8	19.0	68.3	8 25.0	20.8	68.5	9 08.7	22.6	68.8	9 51.8	24.5	69.1	10 34.2	26.3	69.5	23
7 59.8	18.9	67.3	8 45.8	20.7	67.6	9 31.3	22.6	67.9	10 16.3	24.3	68.2	11 00.5	26.1	68.5	24
8 18.7	+18.7	66.3	9 06.5	+20.6	66.6	9 53.9	+22.4	66.9	10 40.6	+24.2	67.3	11 26.6	+26.0	67.6	25
8 37.4	18.6	65.4	9 27.1	20.4	65.7	10 16.3	22.2	66.0	11 04.8	24.0	66.3	11 52.6	25.8	66.7	26
8 56.0	18.4	64.4	9 47.5	20.2	64.7	10 38.5	22.0	65.0	11 28.8	23.8	65.4	12 18.4	25.6	65.8	27
9 14.4	18.3	63.5	10 07.7	20.1	63.8	11 00.5	21.9	64.1	11 52.6	23.6	64.5	12 44.0	25.4	64.9	28
9 32.7	18.1	62.5	10 27.8	19.9	62.8	11 22.4	21.6	63.1	12 16.2	23.5	63.5	13 09.4	25.2	63.9	29

30°			32°			34°			36°			38°			Dec.
Hc	d	Z	Hc	d	Z	Hc	d	Z	Hc	d	Z	Hc	d	Z	
° ′	′	°	° ′	′	°	° ′	′	°	° ′	′	°	° ′	′	°	°
0 00.0	+30.0	90.0	0 00.0	+31.8	90.0	0 00.0	+33.6	90.0	0 00.0	+35.3	90.0	0 00.0	+36.9	90.0	0
0 30.0	30.0	89.1	0 31.8	31.8	89.2	0 33.6	33.5	89.2	0 35.3	35.2	89.2	0 36.9	37.0	89.2	1
1 00.0	30.0	88.3	1 03.6	31.8	88.3	1 07.1	33.5	88.3	1 10.5	35.3	88.4	1 13.9	36.9	88.4	2
1 30.0	29.9	87.4	1 35.4	31.7	87.5	1 40.6	33.5	87.5	1 45.8	35.2	87.6	1 50.8	36.9	87.6	3
1 59.9	30.0	86.5	2 07.1	31.7	86.6	2 14.1	33.5	86.7	2 21.0	35.2	86.8	2 27.7	36.9	86.8	4
2 29.9	+29.9	85.7	2 38.8	+31.7	85.8	2 47.6	+33.5	85.9	2 56.2	+35.1	86.0	3 04.6	+36.8	86.1	5
2 59.9	29.8	84.8	3 10.5	31.7	84.9	3 21.1	33.4	85.0	3 31.3	35.2	85.1	3 41.4	36.8	85.3	6
3 29.6	29.8	83.9	3 42.2	31.6	84.1	3 54.5	33.3	84.2	4 06.5	35.0	84.3	4 18.2	36.7	84.5	7
3 59.4	29.8	83.1	4 13.8	31.5	83.2	4 27.8	33.3	83.4	4 41.5	35.0	83.5	4 54.9	36.7	83.7	8
4 29.2	29.7	82.2	4 45.3	31.5	82.3	5 01.1	33.2	82.5	5 16.5	35.0	82.7	5 31.6	36.6	82.9	9
4 58.9	+29.6	81.3	5 16.8	+31.4	81.5	5 34.3	+33.2	81.7	5 51.5	+34.9	81.9	6 08.2	+36.6	82.1	10
5 28.5	29.5	80.4	5 48.2	31.3	80.6	6 07.5	33.1	80.8	6 26.4	34.8	81.1	6 44.8	36.5	81.3	11
5 58.0	29.5	79.6	6 19.5	31.3	79.8	6 40.6	33.0	80.0	7 01.2	34.7	80.2	7 21.3	36.3	80.5	12
6 27.5	29.4	78.7	6 50.8	31.1	78.9	7 13.6	32.9	79.2	7 35.9	34.6	79.4	7 57.6	36.3	79.7	13
6 56.9	29.2	77.8	7 21.9	31.1	78.1	7 46.5	32.8	78.3	8 10.5	34.5	78.6	8 33.9	36.2	78.9	14
7 26.1	+29.2	76.9	7 53.0	+30.9	77.2	8 19.3	+32.7	77.5	8 45.0	+34.4	77.8	9 10.1	+36.1	78.1	15
7 55.3	29.1	76.1	8 23.9	30.9	76.3	8 52.0	32.6	76.6	9 19.4	34.3	76.9	9 46.2	36.0	77.3	16
8 24.4	28.9	75.2	8 54.8	30.7	75.5	9 24.6	32.4	75.8	9 53.7	34.2	76.1	10 22.2	35.8	76.5	17
8 53.3	28.8	74.3	9 25.5	30.6	74.6	9 57.0	32.4	74.9	10 27.9	34.0	75.3	10 58.0	35.8	75.6	18
9 22.1	28.7	73.4	9 56.1	30.4	73.7	10 29.4	32.2	74.1	11 01.9	33.9	74.4	11 33.8	35.5	74.8	19
9 50.8	+28.5	72.5	10 26.5	+30.3	72.8	11 01.6	+32.0	73.2	11 35.8	+33.8	73.6	12 09.3	+35.5	74.0	20
10 19.3	28.4	71.6	10 56.8	30.2	72.0	11 33.6	31.9	72.3	12 09.6	33.6	72.7	12 44.8	35.3	73.2	21
10 47.7	28.3	70.7	11 27.0	30.0	71.1	12 05.5	31.7	71.5	12 43.2	33.4	71.9	13 20.1	35.1	72.3	22
11 16.0	28.0	69.8	11 57.0	29.8	70.2	12 37.2	31.6	70.6	13 16.6	33.3	71.0	13 55.2	34.9	71.5	23
11 44.0	27.9	68.9	12 26.8	29.7	69.3	13 08.8	31.4	69.7	13 49.9	33.1	70.2	14 30.1	34.8	70.7	24
12 11.9	+27.8	68.0	12 56.5	+29.5	68.4	13 40.2	+31.2	68.9	14 23.0	+32.9	69.3	15 04.9	+34.6	69.8	25
12 39.7	27.5	67.1	13 26.0	29.2	67.5	14 11.4	31.0	68.0	14 55.9	32.7	68.5	15 39.5	34.3	69.0	26
13 07.2	27.4	66.2	13 55.2	29.1	66.6	14 42.4	30.8	67.1	15 28.6	32.5	67.6	16 13.8	34.2	68.1	27
13 34.6	27.1	65.3	14 24.3	28.9	65.7	15 13.2	30.6	66.2	16 01.1	32.3	66.7	16 48.0	34.0	67.3	28
14 01.7	27.0	64.4	14 53.2	28.7	64.8	15 43.8	30.4	65.3	16 33.4	32.1	65.8	17 22.0	33.7	66.4	29

Dec.	40° Hc	d	Z	42° Hc	d	Z	44° Hc	d	Z	46° Hc	d	Z	48° Hc	d	Z
0	0 00.0	+38.6	90.0	0 00.0	+40.1	90.0	0 00.0	+41.7	90.0	0 00.0	+43.2	90.0	0 00.0	+44.6	90.0
1	0 38.6	38.5	89.2	0 40.1	40.2	89.3	0 41.7	41.7	89.3	0 43.2	43.1	89.3	0 44.6	44.6	89.3
2	1 17.1	38.6	88.5	1 20.3	40.1	88.5	1 23.4	41.6	88.6	1 26.3	43.2	88.6	1 29.2	44.5	88.7
3	1 55.7	38.5	87.7	2 00.4	40.1	87.8	2 05.0	41.6	87.8	2 09.5	43.1	87.9	2 13.7	44.6	88.0
4	2 34.2	38.5	86.9	2 40.5	40.1	87.0	2 46.6	41.7	87.1	2 52.6	43.1	87.2	2 58.3	44.5	87.3
5	3 12.7	+38.5	86.2	3 20.6	+40.0	86.3	3 28.3	+41.5	86.4	3 35.7	+43.0	86.5	3 42.8	+44.5	86.6
6	3 51.2	38.4	85.4	4 00.6	40.0	85.5	4 09.8	41.5	85.7	4 18.7	43.1	85.8	4 27.3	44.5	86.0
7	4 29.6	38.3	84.6	4 40.6	40.0	84.8	4 51.4	41.5	85.0	5 01.8	42.9	85.1	5 11.8	44.4	85.3
8	5 07.9	38.4	83.9	5 20.6	39.9	84.0	5 32.9	41.4	84.2	5 44.7	43.0	84.4	5 56.2	44.4	84.6
9	5 46.3	38.2	83.1	6 00.5	39.8	83.3	6 14.3	41.4	83.5	6 27.7	42.8	83.7	6 40.6	44.3	84.0
10	6 24.5	+38.2	82.3	6 40.3	+39.8	82.5	6 55.7	+41.3	82.8	7 10.5	+42.8	83.0	7 24.9	+44.2	83.3
11	7 02.7	38.1	81.5	7 20.1	39.7	81.8	7 37.0	41.2	82.0	7 53.3	42.8	82.3	8 09.1	44.2	82.6
12	7 40.8	38.0	80.8	7 59.8	39.6	81.0	8 18.2	41.2	81.3	8 36.1	42.6	81.6	8 53.3	44.1	81.9
13	8 18.8	38.0	80.0	8 39.4	39.6	80.3	8 59.4	41.1	80.6	9 18.7	42.6	80.9	9 37.4	44.0	81.2
14	8 56.8	37.8	79.2	9 19.0	39.4	79.5	9 40.5	41.0	79.8	10 01.3	42.5	80.2	10 21.4	44.0	80.5
15	9 34.6	+37.7	78.4	9 58.4	+39.3	78.7	10 21.5	+40.8	79.1	10 43.8	+42.4	79.5	11 05.4	+43.8	79.8
16	10 12.3	37.6	77.6	10 37.7	39.2	78.0	11 02.3	40.8	78.3	11 26.2	42.2	78.7	11 49.2	43.7	79.1
17	10 49.9	37.5	76.8	11 16.9	39.1	77.2	11 43.1	40.6	77.6	12 08.4	42.2	78.0	12 32.9	43.7	78.4
18	11 27.4	37.4	76.0	11 56.0	39.0	76.4	12 23.7	40.6	76.8	12 50.6	42.0	77.3	13 16.6	43.5	77.7
19	12 04.8	37.2	75.2	12 35.0	38.8	75.6	13 04.3	40.4	76.1	13 32.6	42.0	76.5	14 00.1	43.4	77.0
20	12 42.0	+37.1	74.4	13 13.8	+38.7	74.9	13 44.7	+40.2	75.3	14 14.6	+41.7	75.8	14 43.5	+43.2	76.3
21	13 19.1	36.9	73.6	13 52.5	38.5	74.1	14 24.9	40.1	74.6	14 56.3	41.7	75.1	15 26.7	43.1	75.6
22	13 56.0	36.8	72.8	14 31.0	38.4	73.3	15 05.0	39.9	73.8	15 38.0	41.4	74.3	16 09.8	43.0	74.9
23	14 32.8	36.6	72.0	15 09.4	38.2	72.5	15 44.9	39.8	73.0	16 19.4	41.4	73.6	16 52.8	42.8	74.1
24	15 09.4	36.4	71.2	15 47.6	38.0	71.7	16 24.7	39.6	72.2	17 00.8	41.1	72.8	17 35.6	42.7	73.4
25	15 45.8	+36.2	70.3	16 25.6	+37.8	70.9	17 04.3	+39.5	71.5	17 41.9	+41.0	72.1	18 18.3	+42.4	72.7
26	16 22.0	36.0	69.5	17 03.4	37.7	70.1	17 43.8	39.2	70.7	18 22.9	40.8	71.3	19 00.7	42.3	71.9
27	16 58.0	35.8	68.7	17 41.1	37.4	69.3	18 23.0	39.0	69.9	19 03.7	40.5	70.5	19 43.0	42.1	71.2
28	17 33.8	35.6	67.8	18 18.5	37.3	68.4	19 02.0	38.8	69.1	19 44.2	40.4	69.7	20 25.1	42.0	70.4
29	18 09.4	35.4	67.0	18 55.8	37.0	67.6	19 40.8	38.6	68.3	20 24.6	40.2	68.9	21 07.1	41.7	69.6

Dec.	50° Hc	d	Z	52° Hc	d	Z	54° Hc	d	Z	56° Hc	d	Z	58° Hc	d	Z
0	0 00.0	+46.0	90.0	0 00.0	+47.3	90.0	0 00.0	+48.5	90.0	0 00.0	+49.7	90.0	0 00.0	+50.9	90.0
1	0 46.0	45.9	89.4	0 47.3	47.3	89.4	0 48.5	48.6	89.4	0 49.7	49.8	89.4	0 50.9	50.9	89.5
2	1 31.9	46.0	88.7	1 34.6	47.2	88.8	1 37.1	48.5	88.8	1 39.5	49.7	88.9	1 41.8	50.8	88.9
3	2 17.9	45.9	88.1	2 21.8	47.3	88.2	2 25.6	48.5	88.2	2 29.2	49.7	88.3	2 32.6	50.9	88.4
4	3 03.8	45.9	87.4	3 09.1	47.2	87.5	3 14.1	48.5	87.6	3 18.9	49.7	87.8	3 23.5	50.8	87.9
5	3 49.7	+45.9	86.8	3 56.3	+47.2	86.9	4 02.6	+48.5	87.1	4 08.6	+49.7	87.2	4 14.3	+50.8	87.3
6	4 35.6	45.8	86.1	4 43.5	47.2	86.3	4 51.1	48.4	86.5	4 58.3	49.6	86.6	5 05.1	50.8	86.8
7	5 21.4	45.8	85.5	5 30.7	47.1	85.7	5 39.5	48.3	85.9	5 47.9	49.6	86.1	5 55.9	50.8	86.3
8	6 07.2	45.8	84.8	6 17.8	47.1	85.1	6 27.9	48.3	85.3	6 37.5	49.6	85.5	6 46.7	50.7	85.7
9	6 53.0	45.7	84.2	7 04.9	47.0	84.4	7 16.2	48.4	84.7	7 27.1	49.5	84.9	7 37.4	50.7	85.2
10	7 38.7	+45.6	83.5	7 51.9	+47.0	83.8	8 04.6	+48.2	84.1	8 16.6	+49.5	84.4	8 28.1	+50.6	84.7
11	8 24.3	45.6	82.9	8 38.9	46.9	83.2	8 52.8	48.2	83.5	9 06.1	49.4	83.9	9 18.7	50.6	84.1
12	9 09.9	45.5	82.2	9 25.8	46.8	82.5	9 41.0	48.1	82.9	9 55.5	49.4	83.2	10 09.3	50.6	83.6
13	9 55.4	45.3	81.6	10 12.6	46.8	81.9	10 29.1	48.1	82.3	10 44.9	49.3	82.6	10 59.9	50.4	83.0
14	10 40.8	45.3	80.9	10 59.4	46.7	81.3	11 17.2	48.0	81.7	11 34.2	49.2	82.1	11 50.3	50.4	82.5
15	11 26.1	+45.3	80.2	11 46.1	+46.6	80.6	12 05.2	+47.9	81.0	12 23.4	+49.2	81.5	12 40.7	+50.4	81.9
16	12 11.4	45.1	79.6	12 32.7	46.5	80.0	12 53.1	47.8	80.4	13 12.6	49.0	80.9	13 31.1	50.3	81.4
17	12 56.5	45.1	78.9	13 19.2	46.4	79.3	13 40.9	47.8	79.8	14 01.6	49.0	80.3	14 21.4	50.1	80.8
18	13 41.6	44.9	78.2	14 05.6	46.3	78.7	14 28.7	47.6	79.2	14 50.6	48.9	79.7	15 11.5	50.1	80.2
19	14 26.5	44.8	77.5	14 51.9	46.2	78.0	15 16.3	47.5	78.6	15 39.5	48.8	79.1	16 01.6	50.1	79.7
20	15 11.3	+44.7	76.8	15 38.1	+46.1	77.4	16 03.8	+47.4	77.9	16 28.3	+48.7	78.5	16 51.7	+49.9	79.1
21	15 56.0	44.6	76.1	16 24.2	46.0	76.7	16 51.2	47.3	77.3	17 17.0	48.6	77.9	17 41.6	49.8	78.5
22	16 40.6	44.4	75.4	17 10.2	45.8	76.0	17 38.5	47.2	76.6	18 05.6	48.4	77.3	18 31.4	49.7	77.9
23	17 25.0	44.3	74.7	17 56.0	45.6	75.4	18 25.7	47.0	76.0	18 54.0	48.4	76.6	19 21.1	49.6	77.3
24	18 09.3	44.1	74.0	18 41.6	45.6	74.7	19 12.7	46.9	75.3	19 42.4	48.2	76.0	20 10.7	49.4	76.7
25	18 53.4	+43.9	73.3	19 27.2	+45.3	74.0	19 59.6	+46.7	74.7	20 30.6	+48.0	75.3	21 00.1	+49.4	76.1
26	19 37.3	43.8	72.6	20 12.5	45.2	73.3	20 46.3	46.6	74.0	21 18.6	48.0	74.7	21 49.5	49.1	75.5
27	20 21.1	43.6	71.9	20 57.7	45.0	72.6	21 32.9	46.4	73.3	22 06.6	47.7	74.1	22 38.6	49.1	74.9
28	21 04.7	43.4	71.1	21 42.7	44.9	71.9	22 19.3	46.3	72.6	22 54.3	47.6	73.4	23 27.7	48.9	74.3
29	21 48.1	43.2	70.4	22 27.6	44.6	71.2	23 05.6	46.0	72.0	23 41.9	47.4	72.8	24 16.6	48.7	73.6

40°			42°			44°			46°			48°			Dec.
Hc	d	Z	Hc	d	Z	Hc	d	Z	Hc	d	Z	Hc	d	Z	°
0 00.0	+38.6	90.0	0 00.0	+40.1	90.0	0 00.0	+41.7	90.0	0 00.0	+43.2	90.0	0 00.0	+44.6	90.0	0
0 38.6	38.5	89.2	0 40.1	40.2	89.3	0 41.7	41.7	89.3	0 43.2	43.1	89.3	0 44.6	44.6	89.3	1
1 17.1	38.6	88.5	1 20.3	40.1	88.5	1 23.4	41.6	88.6	1 26.3	43.2	88.6	1 29.2	44.5	88.7	2
1 55.7	38.5	87.7	2 00.4	40.1	87.8	2 05.0	41.6	87.8	2 09.5	43.1	87.9	2 13.7	44.6	88.0	3
2 34.2	38.5	87.0	2 40.5	40.1	87.0	2 46.6	41.7	87.1	2 52.6	43.1	87.2	2 58.3	44.5	87.3	4
3 12.7	+38.5	86.2	3 20.6	+40.0	86.3	3 28.3	+41.5	86.4	3 35.7	+43.0	86.5	3 42.8	+44.5	86.6	5
3 51.2	38.4	85.4	4 00.6	40.0	85.5	4 09.8	41.6	85.7	4 18.7	43.1	85.8	4 27.3	44.5	86.0	6
4 29.6	38.3	84.6	4 40.6	40.0	84.8	4 51.4	41.5	85.0	5 01.8	42.9	85.1	5 11.8	44.4	85.3	7
5 07.9	38.4	83.9	5 20.6	39.9	84.0	5 32.9	41.4	84.2	5 44.7	43.0	84.4	5 56.2	44.4	84.6	8
5 46.3	38.2	83.1	6 00.5	39.8	83.3	6 14.3	41.4	83.5	6 27.7	42.8	83.7	6 40.6	44.3	84.0	9
6 24.5	+38.2	82.3	6 40.3	+39.8	82.5	6 55.7	+41.3	82.8	7 10.5	+42.8	83.0	7 24.9	+44.2	83.3	10
7 02.7	38.1	81.5	7 20.1	39.7	81.8	7 37.0	41.2	82.0	7 53.3	42.8	82.3	8 09.1	44.2	82.6	11
7 40.8	38.0	80.8	7 59.8	39.6	81.0	8 18.2	41.2	81.3	8 36.1	42.6	81.6	8 53.3	44.1	81.9	12
8 18.8	38.0	80.0	8 39.4	39.6	80.3	8 59.4	41.1	80.6	9 18.7	42.6	80.9	9 37.4	44.0	81.2	13
8 56.8	37.8	79.2	9 19.0	39.4	79.5	9 40.5	41.0	79.8	10 01.3	42.5	80.2	10 21.4	44.0	80.5	14
9 34.6	+37.7	78.4	9 58.4	+39.3	78.7	10 21.5	+40.8	79.1	10 43.8	+42.4	79.5	11 05.4	+43.8	79.8	15
10 12.3	37.6	77.6	10 37.7	39.2	78.0	11 02.3	40.8	78.3	11 26.2	42.2	78.7	11 49.2	43.7	79.1	16
10 49.9	37.5	76.8	11 16.9	39.1	77.2	11 43.1	40.6	77.6	12 08.4	42.2	78.0	12 32.9	43.7	78.4	17
11 27.4	37.4	76.0	11 56.0	39.0	76.4	12 23.7	40.6	76.8	12 50.6	42.0	77.3	13 16.6	43.5	77.7	18
12 04.8	37.2	75.2	12 35.0	38.8	75.6	13 04.3	40.4	76.1	13 32.6	42.0	76.5	14 00.1	43.4	77.0	19
12 42.0	+37.1	74.4	13 13.8	+38.7	74.9	13 44.7	+40.2	75.3	14 14.6	+41.7	75.8	14 43.5	+43.2	76.3	20
13 19.1	36.9	73.6	13 52.5	38.5	74.1	14 24.9	40.1	74.6	14 56.3	41.7	75.1	15 26.7	43.1	75.6	21
13 56.0	36.8	72.8	14 31.0	38.4	73.3	15 05.0	39.9	73.8	15 38.0	41.4	74.3	16 09.8	43.0	74.9	22
14 32.8	36.6	72.0	15 09.4	38.2	72.5	15 44.9	39.8	73.0	16 19.4	41.4	73.6	16 52.8	42.8	74.1	23
15 09.4	36.4	71.2	15 47.6	38.0	71.7	16 24.7	39.6	72.2	17 00.8	41.1	72.8	17 35.6	42.7	73.4	24
15 45.8	+36.2	70.3	16 25.6	+37.8	70.9	17 04.3	+39.5	71.5	17 41.9	+41.0	72.1	18 18.3	+42.4	72.7	25
16 22.0	36.0	69.5	17 03.4	37.7	70.1	17 43.8	39.2	70.7	18 22.9	40.8	71.3	19 00.7	42.3	71.9	26
16 58.0	35.8	68.7	17 41.1	37.4	69.3	18 23.0	39.0	69.9	19 03.7	40.5	70.5	19 43.0	42.1	71.2	27
17 33.8	35.6	67.8	18 18.5	37.3	68.4	19 02.0	38.8	69.1	19 44.2	40.4	69.7	20 25.1	42.0	70.4	28
18 09.4	35.4	67.0	18 55.8	37.0	67.6	19 40.8	38.6	68.3	20 24.6	40.2	68.9	21 07.1	41.7	69.6	29

50°			52°			54°			56°			58°			Dec.
Hc	d	Z	Hc	d	Z	Hc	d	Z	Hc	d	Z	Hc	d	Z	°
0 00.0	+46.0	90.0	0 00.0	+47.3	90.0	0 00.0	+48.5	90.0	0 00.0	+49.7	90.0	0 00.0	+50.9	90.0	0
0 46.0	45.9	89.4	0 47.3	47.3	89.4	0 48.5	48.6	89.4	0 49.7	49.8	89.4	0 50.9	50.9	89.5	1
1 31.9	46.0	88.7	1 34.6	47.2	88.8	1 37.1	48.5	88.8	1 39.5	49.7	88.9	1 41.8	50.8	88.9	2
2 17.9	45.9	88.1	2 21.8	47.3	88.2	2 25.6	48.5	88.2	2 29.2	49.7	88.3	2 32.6	50.9	88.4	3
3 03.8	45.9	87.4	3 09.1	47.2	87.5	3 14.1	48.5	87.6	3 18.9	49.7	87.8	3 23.5	50.8	87.9	4
3 49.7	+45.9	86.8	3 56.3	+47.2	86.9	4 02.6	+48.5	87.1	4 08.6	+49.7	87.2	4 14.3	+50.8	87.3	5
4 35.6	45.8	86.1	4 43.5	47.2	86.3	4 51.1	48.4	86.5	4 58.3	49.6	86.6	5 05.1	50.8	86.8	6
5 21.4	45.8	85.5	5 30.7	47.1	85.7	5 39.5	48.3	85.9	5 47.9	49.6	86.1	5 55.9	50.8	86.3	7
6 07.2	45.8	84.8	6 17.8	47.1	85.1	6 27.9	48.3	85.3	6 37.5	49.6	85.5	6 46.7	50.7	85.7	8
6 53.0	45.7	84.2	7 04.9	47.0	84.4	7 16.2	48.4	84.7	7 27.1	49.5	84.9	7 37.4	50.7	85.2	9
7 38.7	+45.6	83.5	7 51.9	+47.0	83.8	8 04.6	+48.2	84.1	8 16.6	+49.5	84.4	8 28.1	+50.6	84.7	10
8 24.3	45.6	82.9	8 38.9	46.9	83.2	8 52.8	48.2	83.5	9 06.1	49.4	83.8	9 18.7	50.6	84.1	11
9 09.9	45.5	82.2	9 25.8	46.8	82.5	9 41.0	48.1	82.9	9 55.5	49.4	83.2	10 09.3	50.6	83.6	12
9 55.4	45.3	81.6	10 12.6	46.8	81.9	10 29.1	48.1	82.3	10 44.9	49.3	82.6	10 59.9	50.4	83.0	13
10 40.8	45.3	80.9	10 59.4	46.7	81.3	11 17.2	48.0	81.7	11 34.2	49.2	82.1	11 50.3	50.4	82.5	14
11 26.1	+45.3	80.2	11 46.1	+46.6	80.6	12 05.2	+47.9	81.0	12 23.4	+49.2	81.5	12 40.7	+50.4	81.9	15
12 11.4	45.1	79.6	12 32.7	46.5	80.0	12 53.1	47.8	80.4	13 12.6	49.0	80.9	13 31.1	50.3	81.4	16
12 56.5	45.1	78.9	13 19.2	46.4	79.3	13 40.9	47.8	79.8	14 01.6	49.0	80.3	14 21.4	50.1	80.8	17
13 41.6	44.9	78.2	14 05.6	46.3	78.7	14 28.7	47.6	79.2	14 50.6	48.9	79.7	15 11.5	50.2	80.2	18
14 26.5	44.8	77.5	14 51.9	46.2	78.0	15 16.3	47.5	78.6	15 39.5	48.8	79.1	16 01.6	50.1	79.7	19
15 11.3	+44.7	76.8	15 38.1	+46.1	77.4	16 03.8	+47.4	77.9	16 28.3	+48.7	78.5	16 51.7	+49.9	79.1	20
15 56.0	44.6	76.1	16 24.2	46.0	76.7	16 51.2	47.3	77.3	17 17.0	48.6	77.9	17 41.6	49.8	78.5	21
16 40.6	44.4	75.4	17 10.2	45.8	76.0	17 38.5	47.2	76.6	18 05.6	48.4	77.3	18 31.4	49.7	77.9	22
17 25.0	44.3	74.7	17 56.0	45.6	75.4	18 25.7	47.0	76.0	18 54.0	48.4	76.6	19 21.1	49.6	77.3	23
18 09.3	44.1	74.0	18 41.6	45.6	74.6	19 12.7	46.9	75.3	19 42.4	48.2	76.0	20 10.7	49.4	76.7	24
18 53.4	+43.9	73.3	19 27.2	+45.3	74.0	19 59.6	+46.7	74.7	20 30.6	+48.0	75.4	21 00.1	+49.4	76.1	25
19 37.3	43.8	72.6	20 12.5	45.2	73.3	20 46.3	46.6	74.0	21 18.6	48.0	74.7	21 49.5	49.1	75.5	26
20 21.1	43.6	71.9	20 57.7	45.0	72.6	21 32.9	46.4	73.3	22 06.6	47.7	74.1	22 38.6	49.1	74.9	27
21 04.7	43.4	71.1	21 42.7	44.9	71.9	22 19.3	46.3	72.6	22 54.3	47.6	73.4	23 27.7	48.9	74.3	28
21 48.1	43.2	70.4	22 27.6	44.6	71.2	23 05.6	46.0	72.0	23 41.9	47.4	72.8	24 16.6	48.7	73.6	29

LATITUDE **SAME** NAME L.H.A. 90°, 270°

d \ '	1	2	3	4	5	6	7	8	9	10	11	12	13	14	15	16	17	18	19	20	21	22	23	24	25	26	27	28	29	30
0	0	0	0	0	0	0	0	0	0	0	0	0	0	0	0	0	0	0	0	0	0	0	0	0	0	0	0	0	0	0
1	0	0	0	0	0	0	0	0	0	0	0	0	0	0	0	0	0	0	0	0	0	0	0	0	0	0	0	0	0	0
2	0	0	0	0	0	0	0	0	0	0	0	0	1	1	1	1	1	1	1	1	1	1	1	1	1	1	1	1	1	1
3	0	0	0	0	0	0	0	1	1	1	1	1	1	1	1	1	1	1	1	1	1	1	1	1	1	1	1	1	1	1
4	0	0	0	0	0	0	0	1	1	1	1	1	1	1	1	1	1	1	1	2	2	2	2	2	2	2	2	2	2	
5	0	0	0	0	0	0	1	1	1	1	1	1	1	1	1	1	1	2	2	2	2	2	2	2	2	2	2	2	2	
6	0	0	0	0	0	1	1	1	1	1	1	1	1	1	2	2	2	2	2	2	2	2	2	2	2	3	3	3	3	
7	0	0	0	0	1	1	1	1	1	1	1	1	2	2	2	2	2	2	2	2	2	2	2	3	3	3	3	3	3	
8	0	0	0	1	1	1	1	1	1	1	1	2	2	2	2	2	2	2	3	3	3	3	3	3	3	3	4	4	4	
9	0	0	0	1	1	1	1	1	1	2	2	2	2	2	2	2	3	3	3	3	3	3	3	4	4	4	4	4	4	
10	0	0	0	1	1	1	1	1	2	2	2	2	2	2	2	3	3	3	3	3	4	4	4	4	4	4	4	5	5	
11	0	0	1	1	1	1	1	1	2	2	2	2	2	3	3	3	3	3	3	4	4	4	4	4	5	5	5	5	5	
12	0	0	1	1	1	1	1	2	2	2	2	2	3	3	3	3	3	4	4	4	4	4	5	5	5	5	5	6	6	
13	0	0	1	1	1	1	2	2	2	2	2	3	3	3	3	3	4	4	4	4	5	5	5	5	5	6	6	6	6	
14	0	0	1	1	1	1	2	2	2	2	3	3	3	3	4	4	4	4	4	5	5	5	5	6	6	6	6	7	7	
15	0	0	1	1	1	2	2	2	2	2	3	3	3	4	4	4	4	4	5	5	5	6	6	6	6	6	7	7	7	
16	0	1	1	1	1	2	2	2	2	3	3	3	3	4	4	5	5	5	5	5	6	6	6	6	7	7	7	7	8	
17	0	1	1	1	1	2	2	2	3	3	3	3	4	4	4	5	5	5	5	6	6	6	7	7	7	7	8	8	9	
18	0	1	1	1	2	2	2	2	3	3	3	4	4	4	4	5	5	5	6	6	6	7	7	7	8	8	8	8	9	
19	0	1	1	1	2	2	2	3	3	3	3	4	4	4	5	5	5	6	6	6	7	7	7	8	8	8	9	9	9	1
20	0	1	1	1	2	2	2	3	3	3	4	4	4	5	5	5	6	6	6	7	7	7	8	8	8	9	9	9	10	1
21	0	1	1	1	2	2	2	3	3	4	4	4	5	5	5	6	6	6	7	7	7	8	8	8	9	9	9	10	10	1
22	0	1	1	1	2	2	3	3	3	4	4	4	5	5	6	6	6	7	7	7	8	8	8	9	9	10	10	10	11	1
23	0	1	1	2	2	2	3	3	3	4	4	5	5	5	6	6	7	7	7	8	8	8	9	9	10	10	10	11	11	1
24	0	1	1	2	2	2	3	3	4	4	4	5	5	6	6	6	7	7	8	8	8	9	9	10	10	10	11	11	12	1
25	0	1	1	2	2	2	3	3	4	4	5	5	5	6	6	7	7	8	8	8	9	9	10	10	10	11	11	12	12	1
26	0	1	1	2	2	3	3	3	4	4	5	5	6	6	6	7	7	8	8	9	9	10	10	10	11	11	12	12	13	1
27	0	1	1	2	2	3	3	4	4	4	5	5	6	6	7	7	8	8	9	9	9	10	10	11	11	12	12	13	13	1
28	0	1	1	2	2	3	3	4	4	5	5	5	6	7	7	7	8	8	9	9	10	10	11	11	12	12	13	13	14	1
29	0	1	1	2	2	3	3	4	4	5	5	6	6	7	7	8	8	9	9	10	10	11	11	12	12	13	13	14	14	1
30	0	1	2	2	2	3	4	4	4	5	6	6	6	7	8	8	8	9	10	10	10	11	12	12	12	13	14	14	14	1
31	1	1	2	2	3	3	4	4	5	5	6	6	7	7	8	8	9	9	10	10	11	11	12	12	13	13	14	14	15	1
32	1	1	2	2	3	3	4	4	5	5	6	6	7	7	8	9	9	10	10	11	11	12	12	13	13	14	14	15	15	1
33	1	1	2	2	3	3	4	4	5	6	6	6	7	8	8	9	9	10	10	11	11	12	13	13	14	14	15	16	16	1
34	1	1	2	2	3	3	4	5	5	6	6	7	7	8	8	9	10	10	11	11	12	12	13	14	14	15	15	16	16	1
35	1	1	2	2	3	4	4	5	5	6	6	7	8	8	9	9	10	10	11	12	12	13	13	14	15	15	16	16	17	1
36	1	1	2	2	3	4	4	5	5	6	7	7	8	8	9	10	10	11	11	12	13	13	14	14	15	16	16	17	17	1
37	1	1	2	2	3	4	4	5	6	6	7	7	8	9	9	10	10	11	12	12	13	14	14	15	15	16	17	17	18	1
38	1	1	2	3	3	4	4	5	6	6	7	8	8	9	10	10	11	11	12	13	13	14	15	15	16	16	17	18	18	1
39	1	1	2	3	3	4	5	5	6	6	7	8	8	9	10	10	11	12	12	13	14	14	15	16	16	17	18	18	19	2
40	1	1	2	3	3	4	5	5	6	7	7	8	9	9	10	11	11	12	13	13	14	15	15	16	17	17	18	19	19	2
41	1	1	2	3	3	4	5	5	6	7	8	8	9	10	10	11	12	12	13	14	14	15	16	16	17	18	18	19	20	2
42	1	1	2	3	4	4	5	6	6	7	8	8	9	10	10	11	12	13	13	14	15	15	16	17	18	18	19	20	20	2
43	1	1	2	3	4	4	5	6	6	7	8	9	9	10	11	11	12	13	14	14	15	16	16	17	18	19	19	20	21	2
44	1	1	2	3	4	4	5	6	7	7	8	9	10	10	11	12	12	13	14	15	15	16	17	18	18	19	20	21	21	2
45	1	2	2	3	4	4	5	6	7	8	8	9	10	10	11	12	13	14	14	15	16	16	17	18	19	20	20	21	22	2
46	1	2	2	3	4	5	5	6	7	8	8	9	10	11	12	12	13	14	15	15	16	17	18	18	19	20	21	21	22	2
47	1	2	2	3	4	5	5	6	7	8	9	9	10	11	12	13	13	14	15	16	16	17	18	19	20	20	21	22	23	2
48	1	2	2	3	4	5	6	6	7	8	9	10	10	11	12	13	14	14	15	16	17	18	18	19	20	21	22	22	23	2
49	1	2	2	3	4	5	6	7	7	8	9	10	11	11	12	13	14	15	16	16	17	18	19	20	20	21	22	23	24	2
50	1	2	2	3	4	5	6	7	8	8	9	10	11	12	12	13	14	15	16	17	18	18	19	20	21	22	22	23	24	2
51	1	2	3	3	4	5	6	7	8	8	9	10	11	12	13	14	14	15	16	17	18	19	20	20	21	22	23	24	25	2
52	1	2	3	3	4	5	6	7	8	9	10	10	11	12	13	14	15	16	16	17	18	19	20	21	22	23	23	24	25	2
53	1	2	3	4	4	5	6	7	8	9	10	11	11	12	13	14	15	16	17	18	19	19	20	21	22	23	24	25	26	2
54	1	2	3	4	4	5	6	7	8	9	10	11	12	13	14	14	15	16	17	18	19	20	21	22	22	23	24	25	26	2
55	1	2	3	4	5	6	6	7	8	9	10	11	12	13	14	15	16	17	18	19	20	20	21	22	23	24	25	26	27	2
56	1	2	3	4	5	6	7	7	8	9	10	11	12	13	14	15	16	17	18	19	20	21	22	23	23	24	25	27	28	2
57	1	2	3	4	5	6	7	8	9	10	10	11	12	13	14	15	16	17	18	19	20	21	22	23	24	25	26	27	28	2
58	1	2	3	4	5	6	7	8	9	10	11	12	13	14	14	15	16	17	18	19	20	21	22	23	24	25	26	27	28	2
59	1	2	3	4	5	6	7	8	9	10	11	12	13	14	15	16	17	18	19	20	21	22	23	24	25	26	27	28	29	3